# SYSTEMATIC THEOLOGY

# SYSTEMATIC THEOLOGY

## An Introduction to Biblical Doctrine

# WAYNE GRUDEM

## Inter-Varsity Press
*Leicester, England*

## ZondervanPublishingHouse
*Grand Rapids, Michigan*

*A Division of HarperCollinsPublishers*

SYSTEMATIC THEOLOGY
Copyright © 1994, Wayne Grudem

This book is published jointly by Inter-Varsity Press, 38 De Montfort Street, Leicester LE1 7GP, Great Britain, and by Zondervan Publishing House, 5300 Patterson Avenue S.E., Grand Rapids, Michigan, USA.

Unless otherwise noted, Scripture quotations are taken from the Revised Standard Version of the Bible, copyright © 1946, 1952, 1971, by the Division of Christian Education of the National Council of Churches of Christ in the USA, and are used by permission. However, the author has, with permission, modernized archaic personal pronouns and has changed the verbs accordingly. Scripture quotations marked NASB are from the New American Standard Bible, copyright © 1960, 1962, 1963, 1968, 1971, 1972 by the Lockman Foundation, La Habra, California. Used by permission. Those marked NIV are from the Holy Bible, New International Version, copyright © 1973, 1978, 1984, by the International Bible Society. Used by permission of Hodder and Stoughton Ltd. and Zondervan Publishing House. Use of italic in Scripture quotations indicates Wayne Grudem's emphasis.

*British Library Cataloguing in Publication Data*
A catalogue record for this book is available from the British Library.

   GB ISBN 0-85110-652-8

*Library of Congress Cataloging-in-Publication Data*
Grudem, Wayne.
   Systematic theology : an introduction to biblical doctrine / Wayne Grudem.
    p.   cm.
   Includes index.
   USA ISBN 0-310-28670-0
   1. Theology, Doctrinal. I. title.
BT75.2.G78    1994                      94–8300
230'.046—dc20                           CIP

*Inter-Varsity Press, England, is the book-publishing division of the Universities and Colleges Christian Fellowship (formerly the Inter-Varsity Fellowship), a student movement linking Christian Unions in universities and colleges throughout the United Kingdom and the Republic of Ireland, and a member of the International Fellowship of Evangelical Students. For information about local and national activities, write to UCCF, 38 De Montfort Street, Leicester LE1 7GP, England.*

*Printed in the United Kingdom by Creative Print and Design (Wales), Ebbw Vale*

   98 /IV/ 10 9 8 7 6 5

*This book is dedicated to eight people*
*whom God sovereignly brought into my life:*

*Arden and Jean Grudem, my parents,*
*who taught me to believe the Bible,*
*to trust in God,*
*and to speak and write clearly;*

*A. Kenneth Ham, my Baptist pastor,*
*who awakened in me a love for systematic theology*
*by teaching a class on Christian doctrine*
*when I was thirteen years old,*
*and who taught me by example to believe*
*every word of Scripture;*

*Edmund Clowney, John Frame, and Vern Poythress,*
*Westminster Seminary professors and friends,*
*who influenced my theological understanding*
*more than anyone else,*
*and who taught me Reformed theology in*
*humble submission to every word of Scripture;*

*and Harald Bredesen and John Wimber,*
*pastors and friends,*
*who, more than anyone else,*
*taught me about the power and work*
*of the Holy Spirit.*

# Short List of Chapters for Survey Course

The following list is provided as a suggestion for professors who might like to use this book but do not want to assign nearly 1,200 pages. The list covers essential Christian doctrines and are recommended for a course on the survey of Christian doctrine.

On this schedule, students would read about half the book. Specifically, the program would comprise 622 pages from thirty chapters. The students would have the other parts of the book as a resource.

# Contents

# PART 3:
# THE DOCTRINE OF MAN

# PART 4:
# THE DOCTRINES OF CHRIST
# AND THE HOLY SPIRIT

# PART 5:
# THE DOCTRINE OF THE APPLICATION
# OF REDEMPTION

# PART 7:
# THE DOCTRINE OF THE FUTURE

# APPENDICES

# Abbreviations

| | |
|---|---|
| BAGD | *A Greek-English Lexicon of the New Testament and Other Early Christian Literature.* Ed. Walter Bauer. Rev. and trans. Wm. Arndt, F. W. Gingrich, and F. Danker. Chicago: University of Chicago Press, 1979. |
| BDB | *A Hebrew and English Lexicon of the Old Testament.* F. Brown, S. R. Driver, and C. Briggs. Oxford: Clarendon Press, 1907; reprinted, with corrections, 1968. |
| BETS | *Bulletin of the Evangelical Theological Society* |
| BibSac | *Bibliotheca Sacra* |
| cf. | compare |
| CRSQ | *Creation Research Society Quarterly* |
| CT | *Christianity Today* |
| CThRev | *Criswell Theological Review* |
| DPCM | *Dictionary of Pentecostal and Charismatic Movements.* Stanley M. Burgess and Gary B. McGee, eds. Grand Rapids: Zondervan, 1988. |
| EBC | *Expositor's Bible Commentary.* Frank E. Gaebelein, ed. Grand Rapids: Zondervan, 1976. |
| ed. | edited by, edition |
| EDT | *Evangelical Dictionary of Theology.* Walter Elwell, ed. Grand Rapids: Baker, 1984. |
| et al. | and others |
| IBD | *The Illustrated Bible Dictionary.* Ed. J. D. Douglas, et al. 3 vols. Leicester: Inter-Varsity Press, and Wheaton: Tyndale House, 1980. |
| ISBE | *International Standard Bible Encyclopedia.* Revised edition. G. W. Bromiley, ed. Grand Rapids: Eerdmans, 1982. |
| JAMA | *Journal of the American Medical Association* |
| JBL | *Journal of Biblical Literature* |
| JETS | *Journal of the Evangelical Theological Society* |
| JSOT | *Journal for the Study of the Old Testament* |
| KJV | King James Version (Authorized Version) |
| LSJ | *A Greek-English Lexicon,* ninth edition. Henry Liddell, Robert Scott, H. S. Jones, R. McKenzie. Oxford: Clarendon Press, 1940. |
| LXX | Septuagint |
| mg. | margin or marginal notes |

| | |
|---|---|
| n. | note |
| N.d. | no date of publication given |
| N.p. | no place of publication given |
| NASB | New American Standard Bible |
| *NDT* | *New Dictionary of Theology.* S. B. Ferguson, D. F. Wright, J. I. Packer, eds. Leicester and Downers Grove, Ill.: InterVarsity Press, 1988. |
| *NIDCC* | *New International Dictionary of the Christian Church.* Ed. J. D. Douglas et al. Grand Rapids: Zondervan, 1974. |
| *NIDNTT* | *The New International Dictionary of New Testament Theology.* 3 vols. Colin Brown, gen. ed. Grand Rapids: Zondervan, 1975–78. |
| NIGTC | New International Greek Testament Commentaries |
| NIV | New International Version |
| NKJV | New King James Version |
| *NTS* | *New Testament Studies* |
| *ODCC* | *Oxford Dictionary of the Christian Church.* Ed. F. L. Cross. London and New York: Oxford University Press, 1977. |
| rev. | revised |
| RSV | Revised Standard Version |
| *TB* | *Tyndale Bulletin* |
| *TDNT* | *Theological Dictionary of the New Testament.* 10 vols. G. Kittel and G. Friedrich, eds.; trans. G. W. Bromiley. Grand Rapids: Eerdmans, 1964–76. |
| TNTC | Tyndale New Testament Commentaries |
| TOTC | Tyndale Old Testament Commentaries |
| trans. | translated by |
| *TrinJ* | *Trinity Journal* |
| vol. | volume |
| WBC | Word Biblical Commentary |
| *WTJ* | *Westminster Theological Journal* |

# Preface

I have not written this book for other teachers of theology (though I hope many of them will read it). I have written it for students—and not only for students, but also for every Christian who has a hunger to know the central doctrines of the Bible in greater depth.

This is why I have called the book "An Introduction to Biblical Doctrine." I have tried to make it understandable even for Christians who have never studied theology before. I have avoided using technical terms without first explaining them. And most of the chapters can be read on their own, so that someone can begin at any chapter and grasp it without having read the earlier material.

Introductory studies do not have to be shallow or simplistic. I am convinced that most Christians are able to understand the doctrinal teachings of the Bible in considerable depth, provided that they are presented clearly and without the use of highly technical language. Therefore I have not hesitated to treat theological disputes in some detail where it seemed necessary.

Yet this book, despite its size, is still an *introduction* to systematic theology. Entire books have been written about the topics covered in each chapter of this book, and entire articles have been written about many of the verses quoted in this book. Therefore each chapter is capable of opening out into additional study in more breadth or more depth for those who are interested. The bibliographies at the end of each chapter give some help in that direction.

The following six distinctive features of this book grow out of my convictions about what systematic theology is and how it should be taught:

**1. A Clear Biblical Basis for Doctrines.** Because I believe that theology should be explicitly based on the teachings of Scripture, in each chapter I have attempted to show where the Bible gives support for the doctrines under consideration. In fact, because I believe that the words of Scripture themselves have power and authority greater than any human words, I have not just given Bible references; I have frequently *quoted* Bible passages at length so that readers can easily examine for themselves the scriptural evidence and in that way be like the noble Bereans, who were "examining the scriptures daily to see if these things were so" (Acts 17:11). This conviction about the unique nature of the Bible as God's words has also led to the inclusion of a Scripture memory passage at the end of each chapter.

**2. Clarity in the Explanation of Doctrines.** I do not believe that God intended the study of theology to result in confusion and frustration. A student who comes out of a course in theology filled only with doctrinal uncertainty and a thousand unanswered questions is hardly "able to give instruction in sound doctrine and also to confute those who contradict it" (Titus 1:9). Therefore I have tried to state the doctrinal positions of this book clearly and to show where in Scripture I find convincing evidence for those positions. I do not expect that everyone reading this book will agree with me at every point of doctrine; I do think that every reader will understand the positions I am arguing for and where Scripture can be found to support those positions.

I think it is only fair to readers of this book to say at the beginning what my own convictions are regarding certain points that are disputed within evangelical Christianity. I hold to a conservative view of biblical inerrancy, very much in agreement with the "Chicago Statement" of the International Council on Biblical Inerrancy (chapter 5 and appendix 1, pp. 1203–6), and a traditional Reformed position with regard to questions of God's sovereignty and man's responsibility (chapter 16), the extent of the atonement (chapter 27), and the question of predestination (chapter 32). Consistent with the Reformed view, I hold that those who are truly born again will never lose their salvation (chapter 40). With regard to male-female relationships, I argue for a view that is neither traditional nor feminist, but "complementarian"—namely, that God created man and woman equal in value and personhood, and equal in bearing his image, but that both creation and redemption indicate some distinct roles for men and women in marriage (chapter 22) and in the church (chapter 47). On church government, I advocate a modified congregational form of government, with plural elders in governing positions (chapter 47). I argue for a baptistic view of baptism, namely, that those who give a believable profession of personal faith should be baptized (chapter 49). I hold that "baptism in the Holy Spirit" is a phrase best applied to conversion, and subsequent experiences are better called "being filled with the Holy Spirit" (chapter 39); moreover, that all the gifts of the Holy Spirit mentioned in the New Testament are still valid for today, but that "apostle" is an office, not a gift, and that office does not continue today (chapters 52, 53). I believe that Christ's second coming could occur any day, that it will be premillennial—that is, that it will mark the beginning of his thousand-year reign of perfect peace on the earth—but that it will be post-tribulational—that is, that many Christians will go through the great tribulation (chapters 54, 55).

This does not mean that I ignore other views. Where there are doctrinal differences within evangelical Christianity I have tried to represent other positions fairly, to explain why I disagree with them, and to give references to the best available defenses of the opposing positions. In fact, I have made it easy for students to find a conservative evangelical statement on each topic from within their own theological traditions, because each chapter contains an index to treatments of that chapter's subject in thirty-four other theology texts classified by denominational background. (If I have failed to represent an opposing view accurately I would appreciate a letter from anyone who holds that view, and I will attempt to make corrections if a subsequent edition of this book is published.)

**3. Application to Life.** I do not believe that God intended the study of theology to be dry and boring. Theology is the study of God and all his works! Theology is meant to be *lived* and *prayed* and *sung!* All of the great doctrinal writings of the

Bible (such as Paul's epistle to the Romans) are full of praise to God and personal application to life. For this reason I have incorporated notes on application from time to time in the text, and have added "Questions for Personal Application" at the end of each chapter, as well as a hymn related to the topic of the chapter. True theology is "teaching which accords with godliness" (1 Tim. 6:3), and theology when studied rightly will lead to growth in our Christian lives, and to worship.

**4. Focus on the Evangelical World.** I do not think that a true system of theology can be constructed from within what we may call the "liberal" theological tradition—that is, by people who deny the absolute truthfulness of the Bible, or who do not think the words of the Bible to be God's very words (see chapter 4, on the authority of Scripture). For this reason, the other writers I interact with in this book are mostly within what is today called the larger "conservative evangelical" tradition—from the great Reformers John Calvin and Martin Luther, down to the writings of evangelical scholars today. I write as an evangelical and for evangelicals. This does not mean that those in the liberal tradition have nothing valuable to say; it simply means that differences with them almost always boil down to differences over the nature of the Bible and its authority. The amount of doctrinal agreement that can be reached by people with widely divergent bases of authority is quite limited. I am thankful for my evangelical friends who write extensive critiques of liberal theology, but I do not think that everyone is called to do that, or that an extensive analysis of liberal views is the most helpful way to build a positive system of theology based on the total truthfulness of the whole Bible. In fact, somewhat like the boy in Hans Christian Andersen's tale who shouted, "The Emperor has no clothes!" I think someone needs to say that it is doubtful that liberal theologians have given us any significant insights into the doctrinal teachings of Scripture that are not already to be found in evangelical writers.

It is not always appreciated that the world of conservative evangelical scholarship is so rich and diverse that it affords ample opportunity for exploration of different viewpoints and insights into Scripture. I think that ultimately we will attain much more depth of understanding of Scripture when we are able to study it in the company of a great number of scholars who all begin with the conviction that the Bible is completely true and absolutely authoritative. The cross-references to thirty-four other evangelical systematic theologies that I have put at the end of each chapter reflect this conviction: though they are broken down into seven broad theological traditions (Anglican/Episcopalian, Arminian/Wesleyan/Methodist, Baptist, Dispensational, Lutheran, Reformed/Presbyterian, and Renewal/Charismatic/Pentecostal), they all would hold to the inerrancy of the Bible and would belong to what would be called a conservative evangelical position today. (In addition to these thirty-four conservative evangelical works, I have also added to each chapter a section of cross-references to two representative Roman Catholic theologies, because Roman Catholicism continues to exercise such a significant influence worldwide.)

**5. Hope for Progress in Doctrinal Unity in the Church.** I believe that there is still much hope for the church to attain deeper and purer doctrinal understanding, and to overcome old barriers, even those that have persisted for centuries. Jesus is at work perfecting his church "that he might present the church to himself in splendor, without spot or wrinkle or any such thing, that she might be holy and without blemish" (Eph. 5:27), and he has given gifts to equip the church "until we all attain to the unity of the faith and of the knowledge of the Son of God" (Eph. 4:13). Though the past history of the church may discourage us, these Scriptures remain true, and we should not abandon hope of greater agreement. In fact, in this century we have already seen much greater understanding and some greater doctrinal agreement between Covenant and Dispensational theologians, and between charismatics and noncharismatics; moreover, I think the church's understanding of biblical inerrancy and of spiritual gifts has also increased significantly in the last few decades. I believe that the current debate over appropriate roles for men and women in marriage and the church will eventually result in much greater understanding of the teaching of Scripture as well, painful though the controversy may be at the present time. Therefore, in this book I have not hesitated to raise again some of the old differences (over baptism, the Lord's Supper, church government, the millennium and the tribulation, and predestination, for example) in the hope that, in some cases at least, a fresh look at Scripture may provoke a new examination of these doctrines and may perhaps prompt some movement not just toward greater understanding and tolerance of other viewpoints, but even toward greater doctrinal consensus in the church.

**6. A Sense of the Urgent Need for Greater Doctrinal Understanding in the Whole Church.** I am convinced that there is an urgent need in the church today for much greater understanding of Christian doctrine, or systematic theology. Not only pastors and teachers need to understand theology in greater depth—the *whole church* does as well. One day by God's grace we may have churches full of Christians who can discuss, apply, and *live* the doctrinal teachings of the Bible as readily as they can discuss the details of their own jobs or hobbies—or the fortunes of their favorite sports team or television program. It is not that Christians lack the *ability* to understand doctrine; it is just that they must have access to it in an understandable form. Once that happens, I think that many Christians will find that understanding (and living) the doctrines of Scripture is one of their greatest joys.

Many people have helped me in the writing of this book. First I should mention my students, past and present, both at Bethel College in St. Paul, Minnesota (1977–81), and then at Trinity Evangelical Divinity School (1981–present). Their thoughtful, insightful contributions during classroom discussions have influenced every chapter of this book.

God has blessed me with help from some excellent typists. The typing of the manuscript was started by Sherry Kull several years ago. Later, Mary Morris, Ron Tilley, Kathryn Sheehan, Shelly Mills, Rebecca Heidenreich, Jenny Hart, and Carol Pederson typed several portions. Then the largest part of the manuscript was typed with great skill and care by Tammy Thomas, who also helped with some editing. Andi Ledesma and Joyce Leong cheerfully helped with photocopying many times. Finally, Kim Pennington faithfully and accurately typed in the many corrections and changes that came during the editorial process. I am grateful to all of them for their help.

John O. Stevenson did excellent work in compiling the bibliographies, and Don Rothwell completed a significant portion of the cross-references to other theology texts. H. Scott Baldwin, Tom Provenzola, and Mark Rapinchuk were a great help in proofreading and in library research. Mark Rapinchuk also compiled the indexes of authors and Scripture references. Beth Manley provided excellent help in proofreading. George Knight III, Robert Reymond, Harold Hoehner, Robert Saucy, Doug Moo, Tom Nettles, Tom McComiskey, Doug Halsne, Steve Nicholson, Doug Brandt, Steve Figard, Gregg Allison, Ellyn Clark, and Terry Mortenson provided detailed comments on different portions. Raymond Dillard kindly provided me with a computerized text of the Westminster Confession of Faith. Bruce Shauger solved my computer problems several times, and Tim McLaughlin repaired my computer at a crucial time. My long-time friend John Hughes gave me needed advice on computers and manuscript publication several times. My sons also helped me when deadlines approached: Elliot with library research, and Oliver and Alexander (and Alexander's friend Matt Tooley) with compiling and correcting the indexes.

One person has had greater influence on the final form of this book than any other: David Kingdon, Theological Books Editor at Inter-Varsity Press, England, has been helpful far beyond my expectations in his work as an astute, conscientious, and wise editor. He has worked through every chapter with great care, suggesting corrections, additions, and deletions, and interacting with my arguments in extensive memos. His wide-ranging knowledge of theology, biblical studies, and the history of doctrine has been of immense value to me, and the book is much better as a result of his work. Moreover, Frank Entwistle of Inter-Varsity Press and Stan Gundry, Jim Ruark, and Laura Weller of Zondervan have been gracious and patient with me about many details regarding publication of the book.

I could not have completed this work without the generous provision of sabbaticals from Trinity Evangelical Divinity School in the fall of 1983, the fall of 1985, the winter of 1989, and the fall of 1991, and I am grateful to Trinity's board of directors for allowing me this time to write. I am also very thankful for the support of my parents, Arden and Jean Grudem, who generously provided financial help that enabled me to write during these and other times, and who have also been a constant encouragement to me along the way, both in their prayers and in their unwavering belief that a book like this—written in nontechnical language so that they and thousands of Christians like them could understand it—would be valuable for the church.

I think that almost everyone who knew me was praying for this project at some time or other—especially my student advisees over several years at Trinity, and many friends in my church. I have frequently been aware of the Lord's help in response to those prayers, giving me health and strength, freedom from interruptions, and an unwavering desire to complete the book.

Most of all, I am thankful for the support of my wife, Margaret, and my sons, Elliot, Oliver, and Alexander. They have been patient and encouraging, have prayed for me and loved me, and continue to be a great source of joy in my life, for which I thank God.

I am sure that this book, like all merely human books, has mistakes and oversights, and probably some faulty arguments as well. If I knew where they were, I would try to correct them! Therefore I would be grateful if any interested readers would send me suggestions for changes and corrections. I do not guarantee that I can acknowledge every letter, but I will give consideration to the material in every letter and make corrections where I can.

*"O give thanks to the LORD, for he is good; for his steadfast love endures for ever!"* (Ps. 118:29).

*"Not to us, O LORD, not to us, but to your name give glory"* (Ps. 115:1).

Wayne Grudem
Trinity Evangelical Divinity School
2065 Half Day Road
Deerfield, Illinois 60015
USA

# Chapter 1

# Introduction to Systematic Theology

*What is systematic theology? Why should Christians study it? How should we study it?*

## EXPLANATION AND SCRIPTURAL BASIS

### A. Definition of Systematic Theology

What is systematic theology? Many different definitions have been given, but for the purposes of this book the following definition will be used: *Systematic theology is any study that answers the question, "What does the whole Bible teach us today?" about any given topic.*[1]

This definition indicates that systematic theology involves collecting and understanding all the relevant passages in the Bible on various topics and then summarizing their teachings clearly so that we know what to believe about each topic.

**1. Relationship to Other Disciplines.** The emphasis of this book will not therefore be on *historical theology* (a historical study of how Christians in different periods have understood various theological topics) or *philosophical theology* (studying theological topics largely without use of the Bible, but using the tools and methods of philosophical reasoning and what can be known about God from observing the universe) or *apologetics* (providing a defense of the truthfulness of the Christian faith for the purpose of convincing unbelievers). These three subjects, which are worthwhile subjects for Christians to pursue, are sometimes also included in a broader definition of the term *systematic theology*. In fact, some consideration of historical, philosophical, and apologetic matters will be found at points throughout this book. This is because historical study informs us of the insights gained and the mistakes made by others previously in understanding Scripture; philosophical study helps us understand right and wrong thought forms common in our culture and others; and apologetic study helps us bring the teachings of Scripture to bear on the objections raised by unbelievers. But these

---

[1]This definition of systematic theology is taken from Professor John Frame, now of Westminster Seminary in Escondido, California, under whom I was privileged to study in 1971–73 (at Westminster Seminary, Philadelphia). Though it is impossible to acknowledge my indebtedness to him at every point, it is appropriate to express gratitude to him at this point, and to say that he has probably influenced my theological thinking more than anyone else, especially in the crucial areas of the nature of systematic theology and the doctrine of the Word of God. Many of his former students will recognize echoes of his teaching in the following pages, especially in those two areas.

areas of study are not the focus of this volume, which rather interacts directly with the biblical text in order to understand what the Bible itself says to us about various theological subjects.

If someone prefers to use the term *systematic theology* in the broader sense just mentioned instead of the narrow sense which has been defined above, it will not make much difference.[2] Those who use the narrower definition will agree that these other areas of study definitely contribute in a positive way to our understanding of systematic theology, and those who use the broader definition will certainly agree that historical theology, philosophical theology, and apologetics can be distinguished from the process of collecting and synthesizing all the relevant Scripture passages for various topics. Moreover, even though historical and philosophical studies do contribute to our understanding of theological questions, only Scripture has the final authority to define what we are to believe,[3] and it is therefore appropriate to spend some time focusing on the process of analyzing the teaching of Scripture itself.

Systematic theology, as we have defined it, also differs from *Old Testament theology*, *New Testament theology*, and *biblical theology*. These three disciplines organize their topics historically and in the order the topics are presented in the Bible. Therefore, in Old Testament theology, one might ask, "What does Deuteronomy teach about prayer?" or "What do the Psalms teach about prayer?" or "What does Isaiah teach about prayer?" or even, "What does the whole Old Testament teach about prayer and how is that teaching developed over the history of the Old Testament?" In New Testament theology one might ask, "What does John's gospel teach about prayer?" or "What does Paul teach about prayer?" or even "What does the New Testament teach about prayer and what is the historical development of that teaching as it progresses through the New Testament?"

"Biblical theology" has a technical meaning in theological studies. It is the larger category that contains both Old Testament theology and New Testament theology as we have defined them above. Biblical theology gives special attention to the teachings of *individual authors and sections* of Scripture, and to the place of each teaching in the *historical development* of Scripture.[4] So one might ask, "What is the historical development of the teaching about prayer as it is seen throughout the history of the Old Testament and then of the New Testament?" Of course, this question comes very close to the question, "What does the whole Bible teach us today about prayer?" (which would be *systematic theology* by our definition). It then becomes evident that the boundary lines between these various disciplines often overlap at the edges, and parts of one study blend into the next. Yet there is

---

[2]Gordon Lewis and Bruce Demarest have coined a new phrase, "integrative theology," to refer to systematic theology in this broader sense: see their excellent three-volume work, *Integrative Theology* (Grand Rapids: Zondervan, 1987–94). For each doctrine, they analyze historical alternatives and relevant biblical passages, give a coherent summary of the doctrine, answer philosophical objections, and give practical application.

[3]Charles Hodge says, "The Scriptures contain all the Facts of Theology" (section heading in *Systematic Theology*, 1:15). He argues that ideas gained from intuition or observation or experience are valid in theology only if they are supported by the teaching of Scripture.

[4]The term "biblical theology" might seem to be a natural and appropriate one for the process I have called "systematic theology." However, its usage in theological studies to refer to tracing the historical development of doctrines throughout the Bible is too well established, so that starting now to use the term *biblical theology* to refer to what I have called *systematic theology* would only result in confusion.

still a difference, for biblical theology traces the historical development of a doctrine and the way in which one's place at some point in that historical development affects one's understanding and application of that particular doctrine. Biblical theology also focuses on the understanding of each doctrine that the biblical authors and their original hearers or readers possessed.

Systematic theology, on the other hand, makes use of the material of biblical theology and often builds on the results of biblical theology. At some points, especially where great detail and care is needed in the development of a doctrine, systematic theology will even use a biblical-theological method, analyzing the development of each doctrine through the historical development of Scripture. But the focus of systematic theology remains different: its focus is on the collection and then the summary of the teaching of all the biblical passages on a particular subject. Thus systematic theology asks, for example, "What does the whole Bible teach us today about prayer?" It attempts to summarize the teaching of Scripture in a brief, understandable, and very carefully formulated statement.

**2. Application to Life.** Furthermore, systematic theology focuses on summarizing each doctrine as it should be understood by present-day Christians. This will sometimes involve the use of terms and even concepts that were not themselves used by any individual biblical author, but that are the proper result of combining the teachings of two or more biblical authors on a particular subject. The terms *Trinity, incarnation,* and *deity of Christ,* for example, are not found in the Bible, but they usefully summarize biblical concepts.

Defining systematic theology to include "what the whole Bible *teaches us* today" implies that application to life is a necessary part of the proper pursuit of systematic theology. Thus a doctrine under consideration is seen in terms of its practical value for living the Christian life. Nowhere in Scripture do we find doctrine studied for its own sake or in isolation from life. The biblical writers consistently apply their teaching to life. Therefore, any Christian reading this book should find his or her Christian life enriched and deepened during this study; indeed, if personal spiritual growth does not occur, then the book has not been written properly by the author or the material has not been rightly studied by the reader.

**3. Systematic Theology and Disorganized Theology.** If we use this definition of systematic theology, it will be seen that most Christians actually do systematic theology (or at least make systematic-theological statements) many times a week. For example: "The Bible says that everyone who believes in Jesus Christ will be saved." "The Bible says that Jesus Christ is the only way to God." "The Bible says that Jesus is coming again." These are all summaries of what Scripture says and, as such, they are systematic-theological statements. In fact, every time a Christian says something about what the whole Bible says, he or she is in a sense doing "systematic theology"—according to our definition—by thinking about various topics and answering the question, "What does the whole Bible teach us today?"[5]

[5]Robert L. Reymond, "The Justification of Theology with a Special Application to Contemporary Christology," in Nigel M. Cameron, ed., *The Challenge of Evangelical Theology: Essays in Approach and Method* (Edinburgh: Rutherford House, 1987), pp. 82–104, cites several examples from the New

How then does this book differ from the "systematic theology" that most Christians do? First, it treats biblical topics in a *carefully organized way* to guarantee that all important topics will receive thorough consideration. This organization also provides one sort of check against inaccurate analysis of individual topics, for it means that all other doctrines that are treated can be compared with each topic for consistency in methodology and absence of contradictions in the relationships between the doctrines. This also helps to ensure balanced consideration of complementary doctrines: Christ's deity and humanity are studied together, for example, as are God's sovereignty and man's responsibility, so that wrong conclusions will not be drawn from an imbalanced emphasis on only one aspect of the full biblical presentation.

In fact, the adjective *systematic* in systematic theology should be understood to mean something like "carefully organized by topics," with the understanding that the topics studied will be seen to fit together in a consistent way, and will include all the major doctrinal topics of the Bible. Thus "systematic" should be thought of as the opposite of "randomly arranged" or "disorganized." In systematic theology topics are treated in an orderly or "systematic" way.

A second difference between this book and the way most Christians do systematic theology is that it treats topics in *much more detail* than most Christians do. For example, an ordinary Christian as a result of regular reading of the Bible may make the theological statement, "The Bible says that everyone who believes in Jesus Christ will be saved." That is a perfectly true summary of a major biblical teaching. However, in this book we devote several pages to elaborating more precisely what it means to "believe in Jesus Christ,"[6] and twelve chapters (chapters 32–43) will be devoted to explaining what it means to "be saved" in all of the many implications of that term.

Third, a formal study of systematic theology will make it possible to formulate summaries of biblical teachings with *much more accuracy* than Christians would normally arrive at without such a study. In systematic theology, summaries of biblical teachings must be worded precisely to guard against misunderstandings and to exclude false teachings.

Fourth, a good theological analysis must find and treat fairly *all the relevant Bible passages* for each particular topic, not just some or a few of the relevant passages. This often means that it must depend on the results of careful exegesis (or interpretation) of Scripture generally agreed upon by evangelical interpreters or, where there are significant differences of interpretation, systematic theology will include detailed exegesis at certain points.

Because of the large number of topics covered in a study of systematic theology and because of the great detail with which these topics are analyzed, it is inevitable that someone studying a systematic theology text or taking a course in systematic theology for the first time will have many of his or her own personal beliefs challenged or modified, refined or enriched. It is of utmost importance therefore that each person beginning such a course firmly resolve in his or her own mind to

---

Testament of this kind of searching through all of Scripture to demonstrate doctrinal conclusions: Jesus in Luke 24:25–27 (and elsewhere); Apollos in Acts 18:28; the Jerusalem Council in Acts 15; and Paul in Acts 17:2–3; 20:27; and all of Romans. To this list could be added Heb. 1 (on Christ's divine Sonship), Heb. 11 (on the nature of true faith), and many other passages from the Epistles.

[6]See chapter 35, pp. 709–21, on saving faith.

abandon as false any idea which is found to be clearly contradicted by the teaching of Scripture. But it is also very important for each person to resolve not to believe any individual doctrine simply because this textbook or some other textbook or teacher says that it is true, unless this book or the instructor in a course can convince the student from the text of Scripture itself. It is Scripture alone, not "conservative evangelical tradition" or any other human authority, that must function as the normative authority for the definition of what we should believe.

**4. What Are Doctrines?** In this book, the word *doctrine* will be understood in the following way: *A doctrine is what the whole Bible teaches us today about some particular topic.* This definition is directly related to our earlier definition of systematic theology, since it shows that a "doctrine" is simply the result of the process of doing systematic theology with regard to one particular topic. Understood in this way, doctrines can be very broad or very narrow. We can speak of "the doctrine of God" as a major doctrinal category, including a summary of all that the Bible teaches us today about God. Such a doctrine would be exceptionally large. On the other hand, we may also speak more narrowly of the doctrine of God's eternity, or the doctrine of the Trinity, or the doctrine of God's justice.[7]

The book is divided into seven major sections according to seven major "doctrines" or areas of study:

Part 1: The Doctrine of the Word of God
Part 2: The Doctrine of God
Part 3: The Doctrine of Man
Part 4: The Doctrines of Christ and the Holy Spirit
Part 5: The Doctrine of the Application of Redemption
Part 6: The Doctrine of the Church
Part 7: The Doctrine of the Future

Within each of these major doctrinal categories many more specific teachings have been selected as appropriate for inclusion. Generally these meet at least one of the following three criteria: (1) they are doctrines that are most emphasized in Scripture; (2) they are doctrines that have been most significant throughout the history of the church and have been important for all Christians at all times; (3) they are doctrines that have become important for Christians in the present situation in the history of the church (even though some of these doctrines may not have been of such great interest earlier in church history). Some examples of doctrines in the third category would be the doctrine of the inerrancy of Scripture, the doctrine of baptism in the Holy Spirit, the doctrine of Satan and demons with particular reference to spiritual warfare, the doctrine of spiritual gifts in the New Testament age, and the doctrine of the creation of man as male and female in relation to the understanding of roles appropriate to men and women today. Because of their relevance to the contemporary situation, doctrines such as these have received more emphasis in the present volume than in most traditional textbooks of systematic theology.

---

[7]The word *dogma* is an approximate synonym for *doctrine*, but I have not used it in this book. *Dogma* is a term more often used by Roman Catholic and Lutheran theologians, and the term frequently refers to doctrines that have official church endorsement. *Dogmatic theology* is another term for *systematic theology*.

Finally, what is the difference between systematic theology and *Christian ethics*? Although there is inevitably some overlap between the study of theology and the study of ethics, I have tried to maintain a distinction in emphasis. The emphasis of systematic theology is on what God wants us to *believe* and to *know*, while the emphasis in Christian ethics is on what God wants us to *do* and what *attitudes* he wants us to have. Such a distinction is reflected in the following definition: *Christian ethics is any study that answers the question, "What does God require us to do and what attitudes does he require us to have today?" with regard to any given situation.* Thus theology focuses on ideas while ethics focuses on situations in life. Theology tells us how we should think while ethics tells us how we should live. A textbook on ethics, for example, would discuss topics such as marriage and divorce, lying and telling the truth, stealing and ownership of property, abortion, birth control, homosexuality, the role of civil government, discipline of children, capital punishment, war, care for the poor, racial discrimination, and so forth. Of course there is some overlap: theology must be applied to life (therefore it is often ethical to some degree). And ethics must be based on proper ideas of God and his world (therefore it is theological to some degree).

This book will emphasize systematic theology, though it will not hesitate to apply theology to life where such application comes readily. Still, for a thorough treatment of Christian ethics, another textbook similar to this in scope would be necessary.

## B. Initial Assumptions of This Book

We begin with two assumptions or presuppositions: (1) that the Bible is true and that it is, in fact, our only absolute standard of truth; (2) that the God who is spoken of in the Bible exists, and that he is who the Bible says he is: the Creator of heaven and earth and all things in them. These two presuppositions, of course, are always open to later adjustment or modification or deeper confirmation, but at this point, these two assumptions form the point at which we begin.

## C. Why Should Christians Study Theology?

Why should Christians study systematic theology? That is, why should we engage in the process of collecting and summarizing the teachings of many individual Bible passages on particular topics? Why is it not sufficient simply to continue reading the Bible regularly every day of our lives?

**1. The Basic Reason.** Many answers have been given to this question, but too often they leave the impression that systematic theology somehow can "improve" on the Bible by doing a better job of organizing its teachings or explaining them more clearly than the Bible itself has done. Thus we may begin implicitly to deny the clarity of Scripture (see chapter 6) or the sufficiency of Scripture (see chapter 8).

However, Jesus commanded his disciples and now commands us also to *teach* believers to observe all that he commanded:

Go therefore and make disciples of all nations, baptizing them in the name of the Father and of the Son and of the Holy Spirit, *teaching them* to observe all that I have commanded you; and lo, I am with you always, to the close of the age. (Matt. 28:19–20)

Now to teach all that Jesus commanded, in a narrow sense, is simply to teach the content of the oral teaching of Jesus as it is recorded in the gospel narratives. However, in a broader sense, "all that Jesus commanded" includes the interpretation and application of his life and teachings, because in the book of Acts it is implied that it contains a narrative of what Jesus *continued* to do and teach through the apostles after his resurrection (note that 1:1 speaks of "all that Jesus *began* to do and teach"). "All that Jesus commanded" can also include the Epistles, since they were written under the supervision of the Holy Spirit and were also considered to be a "command of the Lord" (1 Cor. 14:37; see also John 14:26; 16:13; 1 Thess. 4:15; 2 Peter 3:2; and Rev. 1:1–3). Thus in a larger sense, "all that Jesus commanded" includes all of the New Testament.

Furthermore, when we consider that the New Testament writings endorse the absolute confidence Jesus had in the authority and reliability of the Old Testament Scriptures as God's words (see chapter 4), and when we realize that the New Testament epistles also endorse this view of the Old Testament as absolutely authoritative words of God, then it becomes evident that we cannot teach "all that Jesus commanded" without including all of the Old Testament (rightly understood in the various ways in which it applies to the new covenant age in the history of redemption) as well.

The task of fulfilling the Great Commission includes therefore not only evangelism but also *teaching*. And the task of teaching all that Jesus commanded us is, in a broad sense, the task of teaching what the whole Bible says to us today. To effectively teach ourselves and to teach others what the whole Bible says, it is necessary to *collect* and *summarize* all the Scripture passages on a particular subject.

For example, if someone asks me, "What does the Bible teach about Christ's return?" I could say, "Just keep reading your Bible and you'll find out." But if the questioner begins reading at Genesis 1:1 it will be a long time before he or she finds the answer to his question. By that time many other questions will have needed answers, and his list of unanswered questions will begin to grow very long indeed. What does the Bible teach about the work of the Holy Spirit? What does the Bible teach about prayer? What does the Bible teach about sin? There simply is not time in our lifetimes to read through the entire Bible looking for an answer for ourselves every time a doctrinal question arises. Therefore, for us to learn what the Bible says, it is very helpful to have the benefit of the work of others who have searched through Scripture and found answers to these various topics.

We can teach others most effectively if we can direct them to the most relevant passages and suggest an appropriate summary of the teachings of those passages. Then the person who questions us can inspect those passages quickly for himself or herself and learn much more rapidly what the teaching of the Bible is on a particular subject. Thus the necessity of systematic theology for teaching what the Bible says comes about primarily because we are finite in our memory and in the amount of time at our disposal.

The basic reason for studying systematic theology, then, is that it enables us to teach ourselves and others what the whole Bible says, thus fulfilling the second part of the Great Commission.

**2. The Benefits to Our Lives.** Although the basic reason for studying systematic theology is that it is a means of obedience to our Lord's command, there are some additional specific benefits that come from such study.

First, studying theology helps us *overcome our wrong ideas*. If there were no sin in our hearts, we could read the Bible from cover to cover and, although we would not immediately learn everything in the Bible, we would most likely learn only true things about God and his creation. Every time we read it we would learn more true things and we would not rebel or refuse to accept anything we found written there. But with sin in our hearts we retain some rebelliousness against God. At various points there are—for all of us—biblical teachings which for one reason or another we do not want to accept. The study of systematic theology is of help in overcoming those rebellious ideas.

For example, suppose there is someone who does not want to believe that Jesus is personally coming back to earth again. We could show this person one verse or perhaps two that speak of Jesus' return to earth, but the person might still find a way to evade the force of those verses or read a different meaning into them. But if we collect twenty-five or thirty verses that say that Jesus is coming back to earth personally and write them all out on paper, our friend who hesitated to believe in Christ's return is much more likely to be persuaded by the breadth and diversity of biblical evidence for this doctrine. Of course, we all have areas like that, areas where our understanding of the Bible's teaching is inadequate. In these areas, it is helpful for us to be confronted with the *total weight of the teaching of Scripture* on that subject, so that we will more readily be persuaded even against our initial wrongful inclinations.

Second, studying systematic theology helps us to be *able to make better decisions later* on new questions of doctrine that may arise. We cannot know what new doctrinal controversies will arise in the churches in which we will live and minister ten, twenty, or thirty years from now, if the Lord does not return before then. These new doctrinal controversies will sometimes include questions that no one has faced very carefully before. Christians will be asking, "What does the whole Bible say about this subject?" (The precise nature of biblical inerrancy and the appropriate understanding of biblical teaching on gifts of the Holy Spirit are two examples of questions that have arisen in our century with much more forcefulness than ever before in the history of the church.)

Whatever the new doctrinal controversies are in future years, those who have learned systematic theology well will be much better able to answer the new questions that arise. The reason for this is that everything that the Bible says is somehow related to everything else the Bible says (for it all fits together in a consistent way, at least within God's own understanding of reality, and in the nature of God and creation as they really are). Thus the new question will be related to much that has already been learned from Scripture. The more thoroughly that earlier material has been learned, the better able we will be to deal with those new questions.

This benefit extends even more broadly. We face problems of applying Scripture to life in many more contexts than formal doctrinal discussions. What does the Bible teach about husband-wife relationships? About raising children? About witnessing to a friend at work? What principles does Scripture give us for studying psychology, or economics, or the natural sciences? How does it guide us in spending money, or in saving, or in tithing? In every area of inquiry certain theological principles will come to bear, and those who have learned well the theological teachings of the Bible will be much better able to make decisions that are pleasing to God.

A helpful analogy at this point is that of a jigsaw puzzle. If the puzzle represents "what the whole Bible teaches us today about everything" then a course in systematic theology would be like filling in the border and some of the major items pictured in the puzzle. But we will never know everything that the Bible teaches about everything, so our jigsaw puzzle will have many gaps, many pieces that remain to be put in. Solving a new real-life problem is analogous to filling in another section of the jigsaw puzzle: the more pieces one has in place correctly to begin with, the easier it is to fit new pieces in, and the less apt one is to make mistakes. In this book the goal is to enable Christians to put into their "theological jigsaw puzzle" as many pieces with as much accuracy as possible, and to encourage Christians to go on putting in more and more correct pieces for the rest of their lives. The Christian doctrines studied here will act as guidelines to help in the filling in of all other areas, areas that pertain to all aspects of truth in all aspects of life.

Third, studying systematic theology will *help us grow as Christians*. The more we know about God, about his Word, about his relationships to the world and mankind, the better we will trust him, the more fully we will praise him, and the more readily we will obey him. Studying systematic theology rightly will make us more mature Christians. If it does not do this, we are not studying it in the way God intends.

In fact, the Bible often connects sound doctrine with maturity in Christian living: Paul speaks of "*the teaching which accords with godliness*" (1 Tim. 6:3) and says that his work as an apostle is "to further the faith of God's elect and their knowledge of *the truth which accords with godliness*" (Titus 1:1). By contrast, he indicates that all kinds of disobedience and immorality are "contrary to sound doctrine" (1 Tim. 1:10).

In connection with this idea it is appropriate to ask what the difference is between a "major doctrine" and a "minor doctrine." Christians often say they want to seek agreement in the church on major doctrines but also to allow for differences on minor doctrines. I have found the following guideline useful:

A major doctrine is one that has a significant impact on our thinking about other doctrines, or that has a significant impact on how we live the Christian life. A minor doctrine is one that has very little impact on how we think about other doctrines, and very little impact on how we live the Christian life.

By this standard doctrines such as the authority of the Bible (chapter 4), the Trinity (chapter 14), the deity of Christ (chapter 26), justification by faith (chapter 36), and many others would rightly be considered major doctrines. People who disagree with the historic evangelical understanding of any of these doctrines will have wide areas of difference with evangelical Christians who affirm these doctrines. By contrast, it seems to me that differences over forms of church government (chapter 47) or some details about the Lord's Supper (chapter 50) or the timing of the great tribulation (chapter 55) concern minor doctrines. Christians who differ over these things can agree on perhaps every other area of doctrine, can live Christian lives that differ in no important way, and can have genuine fellowship with one another.

Of course, we may find doctrines that fall somewhere between "major" and "minor" according to this standard. For example, Christians may differ over the degree of significance that should attach to the doctrine of baptism (chapter 49) or the millennium (chapter 55) or the extent of the atonement (chapter 27). That is only natural, because many doctrines have *some* influence on other doctrines or on life, but we may differ over whether we think it to be a "significant" influence. We could even recognize that there will be a range of significance here and just say that the more influence a doctrine has on other doctrines and on life, the more "major" it becomes. This amount of influence may even vary according to the historical circumstances and needs of the church at any given time. In such cases, Christians will need to ask God to give them mature wisdom and sound judgment as they try to determine to what extent a doctrine should be considered "major" in their particular circumstances.

### D. A Note on Two Objections to the Study of Systematic Theology

1. **"The Conclusions Are 'Too Neat' to be True."** Some scholars look with suspicion at systematic theology when—or even because—its teachings fit together in a noncontradictory way. They object that the results are "too neat" and that systematic theologians must therefore be squeezing the Bible's teachings into an artificial mold, distorting the true meaning of Scripture to get an orderly set of beliefs.

To this objection two responses can be made: (1) We must first ask the people making the objection to tell us at what specific points Scripture has been misinterpreted, and then we must deal with the understanding of those passages. Perhaps mistakes have been made, and in that case there should be corrections.

Yet it is also possible that the objector will have no specific passages in mind, or no clearly erroneous interpretations to point to in the works of the most responsible evangelical theologians. Of course, incompetent exegesis can be found in the writings of the less competent scholars in *any* field of biblical studies, not just in systematic theology, but those "bad examples" constitute an objection not against the scholar's field but against the incompetent scholar himself.

It is very important that the objector be specific at this point because this objection is sometimes made by those who—perhaps unconsciously—have adopted from our culture a skeptical view of the possibility of finding universally true conclusions about anything, even about God from his Word. This kind of skepticism regarding theological truth is especially common in the modern university world where "systematic theology"—if it is studied at all—is studied only from the perspectives of philosophical theology and historical theology (including perhaps a historical study of the various ideas that were believed by the early Christians who wrote the New Testament, and by other Christians at that time and throughout church history). In this kind of intellectual climate the study of "systematic theology" as defined in this chapter would be considered impossible, because the Bible would be assumed to be merely the work of many human authors who wrote out of diverse cultures and experiences over the course of more than one thousand years: trying to find "what the whole Bible teaches" about any subject would be thought nearly as hopeless as trying to find "what all philosophers teach" about some question, for the answer in both cases would be thought to be not one view but many diverse and often conflicting views. This skeptical viewpoint must be rejected by evangelicals who see Scripture as the product of human *and* divine authorship, and therefore as a collection of writings that teach noncontradictory truths about God and about the universe he created.

(2) Second, it must be answered that in God's own mind, and in the nature of reality itself, *true* facts and ideas are all consistent with one another. Therefore if we have accurately understood the teachings of God in Scripture we should expect our conclusions to "fit together" and be mutually consistent. Internal consistency, then, is an argument for, not against, any individual results of systematic theology.

**2. "The Choice of Topics Dictates the Conclusions."** Another general objection to systematic theology concerns the choice and arrangement of topics, and even the fact that such topically arranged study of Scripture, using categories sometimes different from those found in Scripture itself, is done at all. Why are *these* theological topics treated rather than just the topics emphasized by the biblical authors, and why are the topics *arranged in this way* rather than in some other way? Perhaps—this objection would say—our traditions and our cultures have determined the topics we treat and the arrangement of topics, so that the results of this systematic-theological study of Scripture, though acceptable in our own theological tradition, will in fact be untrue to Scripture itself.

A variant of this objection is the statement that our starting point often determines our conclusions on controversial topics: if we decide to start with an emphasis on the divine authorship of Scripture, for example, we will end up believing in biblical inerrancy, but if we start with an emphasis on the human authorship of Scripture, we will end up believing there are some errors in the Bible. Similarly, if we start with an emphasis on God's sovereignty, we will end up as Calvinists, but if we start with an emphasis on man's ability to make free choices, we will end up as Arminians,[8] and so forth. This objection makes it sound as if the most important theological questions could probably be decided by flipping a coin to decide where to start, since *different* and *equally valid* conclusions will inevitably be reached from the different starting points.

Those who make such an objection often suggest that the best way to avoid this problem is not to study or teach systematic theology at all, but to limit our topical studies to the field of biblical theology, treating only the topics and themes the biblical authors themselves emphasize and describing the historical development of these biblical themes through the Bible.

In response to this objection, much of the discussion in this chapter about the necessity to teach Scripture will be relevant. Our choice of topics need not be restricted to the main concerns of the biblical authors, for our goal is to find out what God requires of us in all areas of concern to us today.

---

[8] See chapter 16, pp. 315, 337–51, for a discussion of the terms *Calvinist* and *Arminian*.

For example, it was not the *main* concern of any New Testament author to explain such topics as "baptism in the Holy Spirit," or women's roles in the church, or the doctrine of the Trinity, but these are valid areas of concern for us today, and we must look at all the places in Scripture that have relevance for those topics (whether those specific terms are mentioned or not, and whether those themes are of primary concern to each passage we examine or not) if we are going to be able to understand and explain to others "what the whole Bible teaches" about them.

The only alternative—for we *will* think *something* about those subjects—is to form our opinions haphazardly from a general impression of what we feel to be a "biblical" position on each subject, or perhaps to buttress our positions with careful analysis of one or two relevant texts, yet with no guarantee that those texts present a balanced view of "the whole counsel of God" (Acts 20:27) on the subject being considered. In fact this approach—one all too common in evangelical circles today—could, I suppose, be called "unsystematic theology" or even "disorderly and random theology"! Such an alternative is too subjective and too subject to cultural pressures. It tends toward doctrinal fragmentation and widespread doctrinal uncertainty, leaving the church theologically immature, like "children, tossed to and fro and carried about with every wind of doctrine" (Eph. 4:14).

Concerning the objection about the choice and sequence of topics, there is nothing to prevent us from going to Scripture to look for answers to *any* doctrinal questions, considered in *any sequence*. The sequence of topics in this book is a very common one and has been adopted because it is orderly and lends itself well to learning and teaching. But the chapters could be read in any sequence one wanted and the conclusions should not be different, nor should the persuasiveness of the arguments—if they are rightly derived from Scripture—be significantly diminished. In fact, I suspect that most readers of this book will not read it through from chapter 1 to chapter 57, but will begin with the chapters of most interest to them, and read others later. That does not really matter, because I have tried to write the chapters so that they can be read as independent units, and I have added cross-references to sections in other chapters where relevant. Whether one reads the chapter on the new heavens and new earth (chapter 57) first or last or somewhere in between, the arguments will be the same, the Scripture passages quoted for support will be the same, and the conclusions should be the same.

## E. How Should Christians Study Systematic Theology?

How then should we study systematic theology? The Bible provides some guidelines for answering this question.

**1. We Should Study Systematic Theology With Prayer.** If studying systematic theology is simply a certain way of studying the Bible, then the passages in Scripture that talk about the way in which we should study God's Word give guidance to us in this task. Just as the psalmist prays in Psalm 119:18, "Open my eyes, that I may behold wondrous things out of your law," so we should pray and seek God's help in understanding his Word. Paul tells us in 1 Corinthians 2:14

that "the unspiritual man does not receive the gifts of the Spirit of God, for they are folly to him, and he is not able to understand them because they are spiritually discerned." Studying theology is therefore a spiritual activity in which we need the help of the Holy Spirit.

No matter how intelligent, if the student does not continue to pray for God to give him or her an understanding mind and a believing and humble heart, and the student does not maintain a personal walk with the Lord, then the teachings of Scripture will be misunderstood and disbelieved, doctrinal error will result, and the mind and heart of the student will not be changed for the better but for the worse. Students of systematic theology should resolve at the beginning to keep their lives free from any disobedience to God or any known sin that would disrupt their relationship with him. They should resolve to maintain with great regularity their own personal devotional lives. They should continually pray for wisdom and understanding of Scripture.

Since it is the Holy Spirit who gives us the ability rightly to understand Scripture, we need to realize that the proper thing to do, particularly when we are unable to understand some passage or some doctrine of Scripture, is to pray for God's help. Often what we need is not more data but more insight into the data we already have available. This insight is given only by the Holy Spirit (cf. 1 Cor. 2:14; Eph. 1:17–19).

**2. We Should Study Systematic Theology With Humility.** Peter tells us, "Clothe yourselves, all of you, with humility toward one another, for 'God opposes the proud, but gives grace to the humble'" (1 Peter 5:5). Those who study systematic theology will learn many things about the teachings of Scripture that are perhaps not known or not known well by other Christians in their churches or by relatives who are older in the Lord than they are. They may also find that they understand things about Scripture that some of their church officers do not understand, and that even their pastor has perhaps forgotten or never learned well.

In all of these situations it would be very easy to adopt an attitude of pride or superiority toward others who have not made such a study. But how ugly it would be if anyone were to use this knowledge of God's Word simply to win arguments or to put down a fellow Christian in conversation, or to make another believer feel insignificant in the Lord's work. James' counsel is good for us at this point: "Let every man be quick to hear, slow to speak, slow to anger, for the anger of man does not work the righteousness of God" (James 1:19–20). He tells us that one's understanding of Scripture is to be imparted in humility and love:

> Who is wise and understanding among you? By his good life let him show his works in the meekness of wisdom. . . . But the wisdom from above is first pure, then peaceable, gentle, open to reason, full of mercy and good fruits, without uncertainty or insincerity. And the harvest of righteousness is sown in peace by those who make peace. (James 3:13, 17–18)

Systematic theology rightly studied will not lead to the knowledge that "puffs up" (1 Cor. 8:1) but to humility and love for others.

**3. We Should Study Systematic Theology With Reason.** We find in the New Testament that Jesus and the New Testament authors will often quote a verse of Scripture and then draw logical conclusions from it. They *reason* from Scripture. It is therefore not wrong to use human understanding, human logic, and human reason to draw conclusions from the statements of Scripture. Nevertheless, when we reason and draw what we think to be correct logical deductions from Scripture, we sometimes make mistakes. The deductions we draw from the statements of Scripture are not equal to the statements of Scripture themselves in certainty or authority, for our ability to reason and draw conclusions is not the ultimate standard of truth—only Scripture is.

What then are the limits on our use of our reasoning abilities to draw deductions from the statements of Scripture? The fact that reasoning to conclusions that go beyond the mere statements of Scripture is appropriate and even necessary for studying Scripture, and the fact that Scripture itself is the ultimate standard of truth, combine to indicate to us that *we are free to use our reasoning abilities to draw deductions from any passage of Scripture so long as these deductions do not contradict the clear teaching of some other passage of Scripture.*[9]

This principle puts a safeguard on our use of what we think to be logical deductions from Scripture. Our supposedly logical deductions may be erroneous, but Scripture itself cannot be erroneous. Thus, for example, we may read Scripture and find that God the Father is called God (1 Cor. 1:3), that God the Son is called God (John 20:28; Titus 2:13), and that God the Holy Spirit is called God (Acts 5:3–4). We might deduce from this that there are three Gods. But then we find the Bible explicitly teaching us that God is one (Deut. 6:4; James 2:19). Thus we conclude that what we *thought* to be a valid logical deduction about three Gods was wrong and that Scripture teaches both (a) that there are three separate persons (the Father, the Son, and the Holy Spirit), each of whom is fully God, and (b) that there is one God.

We cannot understand exactly how these two statements can both be true, so together they constitute a *paradox* ("a seemingly contradictory statement that may nonetheless be true").[10] We can tolerate a paradox (such as "God is three persons

---

[9]This guideline is also adopted from Professor John Frame at Westminster Seminary (see p. 21).

[10]The *American Heritage Dictionary of the English Language,* ed. William Morris (Boston: Houghton-Mifflin, 1980), p. 950 (first definition). Essentially the same meaning is adopted by the *Oxford English Dictionary* (1913 ed., 7:450), the *Concise Oxford Dictionary* (1981 ed., p. 742), the *Random House College Dictionary* (1979 ed., p. 964), and the *Chambers Twentieth Century Dictionary* (p. 780), though all note that *paradox* can also mean "contradiction" (though less commonly); compare the *Encyclopedia of Philosophy,* ed. Paul Edwards (New York: Macmillan and The Free Press, 1967), 5:45, and the entire article "Logical Paradoxes" by John van Heijenoort on pp. 45–51 of the same volume, which proposes solutions to many of the classical paradoxes in the history of philosophy. (If *paradox* meant "contradiction," such solutions would be impossible.)

When I use the word *paradox* in the primary sense defined by these dictionaries today I realize that I am differing somewhat with the article "Paradox" by K. S. Kantzer in the *EDT,* ed. Walter Elwell, pp. 826–27 (which takes *paradox* to mean essentially "contradiction"). However, I am using *paradox* in an ordinary English sense and one also familiar in philosophy. There seems to me to be available no better word than *paradox* to refer to an apparent but not real contradiction.

There is, however, some lack of uniformity in the use of the term *paradox* and a related term, *antinomy,* in contemporary evangelical discussion. The word *antinomy* has sometimes been used to apply to what I here call *paradox,* that is, "seemingly contradictory statements that may nonetheless both be true" (see, for example, John Jefferson Davis, *Theology Primer* [Grand Rapids: Baker, 1981], p. 18). Such a sense for *antinomy* gained support in a widely read book, *Evangelism and the Sovereignty*

and one God") because we have confidence that ultimately God knows fully the truth about himself and about the nature of reality, and that in his understanding the different elements of a paradox are fully reconciled, even though at this point God's thoughts are higher than our thoughts (Isa. 55:8–9). But a true contradiction (such as, "God is three persons and God is not three persons") would imply ultimate contradiction in God's own understanding of himself or of reality, and this cannot be.

When the psalmist says, "The sum of your word is truth; and every one of your righteous ordinances endures for ever" (Ps. 119:160), he implies that God's words are not only true individually but also viewed together as a whole. Viewed collectively, their "sum" is also "truth." Ultimately, there is no internal contradiction either in Scripture or in God's own thoughts.

**4. We Should Study Systematic Theology With Help From Others.** We need to be thankful that God has put teachers in the church ("And God has appointed in the church first apostles, second prophets, third *teachers* . . ." [1 Cor. 12:28]. We should allow those with gifts of teaching to help us understand Scripture. This means that we should make use of systematic theologies and other books that have been written by some of the teachers that God has given to the church over the course of its history. It also means that our study of theology should include *talking with other Christians* about the things we study. Among those with whom we talk will often be some with gifts of teaching who can explain biblical teachings clearly and help us to understand more easily. In fact, some of the most effective learning in systematic theology courses in colleges and seminaries often occurs outside the classroom in informal conversations among students who are attempting to understand Bible doctrines for themselves.

**5. We Should Study Systematic Theology by Collecting and Understanding All the Relevant Passages of Scripture on Any Topic.** This point was mentioned in our definition of systematic theology at the beginning of the chapter, but the actual process needs to be described here. How does one go about making a doctrinal summary of what all the passages of Scripture teach on a certain topic? For topics covered in this book, many people will think that studying the chapters in this book and reading the Bible verses noted in the chapters is enough. But some people will want to do further study of Scripture on a particular topic or study some new topic not covered here. How could a student

---

*of God,* by J. I. Packer (London: Inter-Varsity Press, 1961). On pp. 18–22 Packer defines *antinomy* as "an appearance of contradiction" (but admits on p. 18 that his definition differs with the *Shorter Oxford Dictionary*). My problem with using *antinomy* in this sense is that the word is so unfamiliar in ordinary English that it just increases the stock of technical terms Christians have to learn in order to understand theologians, and moreover such a sense is unsupported by any of the dictionaries cited above, all of which define *antinomy* to mean "contradiction" (e.g., *Oxford English Dictionary,* 1:371). The problem is not serious, but it would help communication if evangelicals could agree on uniform senses for these terms.

A paradox is certainly acceptable in systematic theology, and paradoxes are in fact inevitable so long as we have finite understanding of any theological topic. However, it is important to recognize that Christian theology should never affirm a *contradiction* (a set of two statements, one of which denies the other). A contradiction would be, "God is three persons and God is not three persons" (where the term *persons* has the same sense in both halves of the sentence).

go about using the Bible to research its teachings on some new subject, perhaps one not discussed explicitly in any of his or her systematic theology textbooks?

The process would look like this: (1) Find all the relevant verses. The best help in this step is a good concordance, which enables one to look up key words and find the verses in which the subject is treated. For example, in studying what it means that man is created in the image and likeness of God, one needs to find all the verses in which "image" and "likeness" and "create" occur. (The words "man" and "God" occur too often to be useful for a concordance search.) In studying the doctrine of prayer, many words could be looked up (*pray, prayer, intercede, petition, supplication, confess, confession, praise, thanks, thanksgiving,* et al.)—and perhaps the list of verses would grow too long to be manageable, so that the student would have to skim the concordance entries without looking up the verses, or the search would probably have to be divided into sections or limited in some other way. Verses can also be found by thinking through the overall history of the Bible and then turning to sections where there would be information on the topic at hand—for example, a student studying prayer would want to read passages like the one about Hannah's prayer for a son (in 1 Sam. 1), Solomon's prayer at the dedication of the temple (in 1 Kings 8), Jesus' prayer in the Garden of Gethsemane (in Matt. 26 and parallels), and so forth. Then in addition to concordance work and reading other passages that one can find on the subject, checking the relevant sections in some systematic theology books will often bring to light other verses that had been missed, sometimes because none of the key words used for the concordance were in those verses.[11]

(2) The second step is to read, make notes on, and try to summarize the points made in the relevant verses. Sometimes a theme will be repeated often and the summary of the various verses will be relatively easy. At other times, there will be verses difficult to understand, and the student will need to take some time to study a verse in depth (just by reading the verse in context over and over, or by using specialized tools such as commentaries and dictionaries) until a satisfactory understanding is reached.

(3) Finally, the teachings of the various verses should be summarized into one or more points that the Bible affirms about that subject. The summary does not have to take the exact form of anyone else's conclusions on the subject, because we each may see things in Scripture that others have missed, or we may organize the subject differently or emphasize different things.

On the other hand, at this point it is also helpful to read related sections, if any can be found, in several systematic theology books. This provides a useful check against error and oversight, and often makes one aware of alternative perspectives and arguments that may cause us to modify or strengthen our position. If a student finds that others have argued for strongly differing conclusions, then these other views need to be stated fairly and then answered. Sometimes other theology books will alert us to historical or philosophical considerations that have been

---

[11]I have read a number of student papers telling me that John's gospel says nothing about how Christians should pray, for example, because they looked at a concordance and found that the word *prayer* was not in John, and the word *pray* only occurs four times in reference to Jesus praying in John 14, 16, and 17. They overlooked the fact that John contains several important verses where the word *ask* rather than the word *pray* is used (John 14:13–14; 15:7, 16; et al.).

raised before in the history of the church, and these will provide additional insight or warnings against error.

The process outlined above is possible for any Christian who can read his or her Bible and can look up words in a concordance. Of course people will become faster and more accurate in this process with time and experience and Christian maturity, but it would be a tremendous help to the church if Christians generally would give much more time to searching out topics in Scripture for themselves and drawing conclusions in the way outlined above. The joy of discovery of biblical themes would be richly rewarding. Especially pastors and those who lead Bible studies would find added freshness in their understanding of Scripture and in their teaching.

**6. We Should Study Systematic Theology With Rejoicing and Praise.** The study of theology is not merely a theoretical exercise of the intellect. It is a study of the living God, and of the wonders of all his works in creation and redemption. We cannot study this subject dispassionately! We must love all that God is, all that he says and all that he does. "You shall love the LORD your God with all your heart" (Deut. 6:5). Our response to the study of the theology of Scripture should be that of the psalmist who said, "How precious to me are your thoughts, O God!" (Ps. 139:17). In the study of the teachings of God's Word, it should not surprise us if we often find our hearts spontaneously breaking forth in expressions of praise and delight like those of the psalmist:

> The precepts of the LORD are right,
> rejoicing the heart. (Ps. 19:8)

> In the way of your testimonies I delight
> as much as in all riches. (Ps. 119:14)

> How sweet are your words to my taste,
> sweeter than honey to my mouth! (Ps. 119:103)

> Your testimonies are my heritage for ever;
> yea, they are the joy of my heart. (Ps. 119:111)

> I rejoice at your word
> like one who finds great spoil. (Ps. 119:162)

Often in the study of theology the response of the Christian should be similar to that of Paul in reflecting on the long theological argument that he has just completed at the end of Romans 11:32. He breaks forth into joyful praise at the richness of the doctrine which God has enabled him to express:

> O the depth of the riches and wisdom and knowledge of God! How unsearchable are his judgments and how inscrutable his ways!

> > "For who has known the mind of the Lord,
> > or who has been his counselor?"
> > "Or who has given a gift to him
> > that he might be repaid?"

> For from him and through him and to him are all things. To him be glory for ever. Amen. (Rom. 11:33–36).

## QUESTIONS FOR PERSONAL APPLICATION

These questions at the end of each chapter focus on application to life. Because I think doctrine is to be felt at the emotional level as well as understood at the intellectual level, in many chapters I have included some questions about how a reader *feels* regarding a point of doctrine. I think these questions will prove quite valuable for those who take the time to reflect on them.

1. In what ways (if any) has this chapter changed your understanding of what systematic theology is? What was your attitude toward the study of systematic theology before reading this chapter? What is your attitude now?

2. What is likely to happen to a church or denomination that gives up learning systematic theology for a generation or longer? Has that been true of your church?

3. Are there any doctrines listed in the Contents for which a fuller understanding would help to solve a personal difficulty in your life at the present time? What are the spiritual and emotional dangers that you personally need to be aware of in studying systematic theology?

4. Pray for God to make this study of basic Christian doctrines a time of spiritual growth and deeper fellowship with him, and a time in which you understand and apply the teachings of Scripture rightly.

## SPECIAL TERMS

| | |
|---|---|
| apologetics | minor doctrine |
| biblical theology | New Testament theology |
| Christian ethics | Old Testament theology |
| contradiction | paradox |
| doctrine | philosophical theology |
| dogmatic theology | presupposition |
| historical theology | systematic theology |
| major doctrine | |

## BIBLIOGRAPHY

In these bibliographies I have usually listed only works written from what would today be called a conservative evangelical position. This is because the purpose of this section is to give the student ready access to other treatments of each topic by theologians who share with this book the same general convictions about the nature of Scripture—that all of it is totally truthful and that it is God's unique and absolutely authoritative Word to us. Once we step outside of that conviction, the variety of theological positions becomes amazingly large, and sufficient bibliographies are easily found in the more recent works cited below. (However, I have also included two representative Roman Catholic works because of the great influence of the Roman Catholic Church in almost every society in the world.)

Writers are grouped according to broad denominational categories, and the writers within the groups are arranged chronologically. Of course, the categories below are not airtight, for there is often overlap—many Anglicans and many Baptists are theologically "Reformed" while others in those groups are theologically "Arminian"; many Dispensationalists are also Baptists, while others are Presbyterians, and so forth. Yet the categories are fairly representative of distinguishable theological traditions within evangelicalism.

Dates given are the dates of publication of the final edition of each author's systematic theology or major theological writing. Where no single major theological work was published, the dates represent the years during which the author was actively teaching and writing about systematic theology. Complete bibliographical data may be found on pp. 1223–29.

## Sections in Evangelical Systematic Theologies

1. Anglican (Episcopalian)
   - 1882–92     Litton, 1–8
   - 1930     Thomas, xvii–xxviii, 146–52
2. Arminian (Wesleyan or Methodist)
   - 1875–76     Pope, 1:3–32, 42–46
   - 1892–94     Miley, 1:2–54
   - 1940     Wiley, 1:13–123
   - 1960     Purkiser, 19–38
   - 1983     Carter, 1:19–101
   - 1987–90     Oden, 1:11–14, 375–406
3. Baptist
   - 1767     Gill, 1:vii–xxx
   - 1887     Boyce, 1–8
   - 1907     Strong, 1–51
   - 1917     Mullins, 1–136
   - 1976–83     Henry, 1:13–411; 6:7–34
   - 1983–85     Erickson, 9–149
   - 1987–94     Lewis/Demarest, 1:13–123
4. Dispensational
   - 1947     Chafer, 1:3–17
   - 1949     Thiessen, 1–20
   - 1986     Ryrie, 9–22
5. Lutheran
   - 1917–24     Pieper, 1:3–190
   - 1934     Mueller, 1–89
6. Reformed (or Presbyterian)[12]

---

[12]In the Reformed category I have cross-referenced eleven systematic theologies (those listed in this chapter plus Bavinck in some chapters). Two other very well-written Reformed works are *Foundations of the Christian Faith* by James Montgomery Boice (Downers Grove, Ill.: InterVarsity Press, 1986) and *Concise Theology* by J. I. Packer (Wheaton, Ill.: Tyndale House, 1993), but I have not cross-referenced them at the end of every chapter, because they are written for more popular audiences than the other

|           |                                               |
|-----------|-----------------------------------------------|
| 1559      | Calvin, 1:3–33, 35–43 (prefaces and 1.1–2)    |
| 1724–58   | Edwards, 2:157–63                             |
| 1861      | Heppe, 1–11, 42–47                           |
| 1871–73   | Hodge, 1:1–150                               |
| 1878      | Dabney, 133–44                              |
| 1887–1921 | Warfield, SSW, 2:207–320                     |
| 1889      | Shedd, 1:3–58; 3:1–26                        |
| 1937–66   | Murray, CW, 1:3–8, 169–73; CW, 4:1–21        |
| 1938      | Berkhof, Intro., 15–128, 170–86             |
| 1962      | Buswell, 1:13–26                            |

7. Renewal (or charismatic/Pentecostal)

|           |                        |
|-----------|------------------------|
| 1988–92   | Williams, 1:11–28      |

## Sections in Representative Roman Catholic Systematic Theologies

1. Roman Catholic: Traditional

|      |             |
|------|-------------|
| 1955 | Ott, 1–10   |

2. Roman Catholic: Post-Vatican II

|      |                          |
|------|--------------------------|
| 1980 | McBrien, 1:3–78, 183–200 |

## Other Works

Baker, D. L. "Biblical Theology." In *NDT,* p. 671.

Berkhof, Louis. *Introduction to Systematic Theology.* Grand Rapids: Eerdmans, 1982, pp. 15–75 (first published 1932).

Bray, Gerald L., ed. *Contours of Christian Theology.* Downers Grove, Ill.: InterVarsity Press, 1993.

———. "Systematic Theology, History of." In *NDT,* pp. 671–72.

Cameron, Nigel M., ed. *The Challenge of Evangelical Theology: Essays in Approach and Method.* Edinburgh: Rutherford House, 1987.

Carson, D. A. "Unity and Diversity in the New Testament: The Possibility of Systematic Theology." In *Scripture and Truth.* Ed. by D. A. Carson and John Woodbridge. Grand Rapids: Zondervan, 1983, pp. 65–95.

Davis, John Jefferson. *Foundations of Evangelical Theology.* Grand Rapids: Baker, 1984.

———. *The Necessity of Systematic Theology.* Grand Rapids: Baker, 1980.

———. *Theology Primer: Resources for the Theological Student.* Grand Rapids: Baker, 1981.

Demarest, Bruce. "Systematic Theology." In *EDT,* pp. 1064–66.

Erickson, Millard. *Concise Dictionary of Christian Theology.* Grand Rapids: Baker, 1986.

Frame, John. *Van Til the Theologian.* Phillipsburg, N.J.: Pilgrim, 1976.

Geehan, E. R., ed. *Jerusalem and Athens.* Nutley, N.J.: Craig Press, 1971.

---

Reformed works listed and because I thought that eleven Reformed theologies were already enough to give a sufficient sampling of Reformed thought.

Grenz, Stanley J. *Revisioning Evangelical Theology: A Fresh Agenda for the 21st Century*. Downers Grove, Ill.: InterVarsity Press, 1993.

House, H. Wayne. *Charts of Christian Theology and Doctrine*. Grand Rapids: Zondervan, 1992.

Kuyper, Abraham. *Principles of Sacred Theology*. Trans. by J. H. DeVries. Grand Rapids: Eerdmans, 1968 (reprint; first published as *Encyclopedia of Sacred Theology* in 1898).

Machen, J. Gresham. *Christianity and Liberalism*. Grand Rapids: Eerdmans, 1923. (This 180-page book is, in my opinion, one of the most significant theological studies ever written. It gives a clear overview of major biblical doctrines and shows the vital differences with Protestant liberal theology at every point, differences that still confront us today. It is required reading in all my introductory theology classes.)

Morrow, T. W. "Systematic Theology." In *NDT*, p. 671.

Poythress, Vern. *Symphonic Theology: The Validity of Multiple Perspectives in Theology*. Grand Rapids: Zondervan, 1987.

Preus, Robert D. *The Theology of Post-Reformation Lutheranism: A Study of Theological Prolegomena*. 2 vols. St. Louis: Concordia, 1970.

Van Til, Cornelius. *In Defense of the Faith*, vol. 5: *An Introduction to Systematic Theology*. n.p.: Presbyterian and Reformed, 1976, pp. 1–61, 253–62.

_____. *The Defense of the Faith*. Philadelphia: Presbyterian and Reformed, 1955.

Vos, Geerhardus. "The Idea of Biblical Theology as a Science and as a Theological Discipline." In *Redemptive History and Biblical Interpretation*, pp. 3–24. Ed. by Richard Gaffin. Phillipsburg, N.J.: Presbyterian and Reformed, 1980 (article first published 1894).

Warfield, B. B. "The Indispensableness of Systematic Theology to the Preacher." In *Selected Shorter Writings of Benjamin B. Warfield*, 2:280–88. Ed. by John E. Meeter. Nutley, N.J.: Presbyterian and Reformed, 1973 (article first published 1897).

_____. "The Right of Systematic Theology." In *Selected Shorter Writings of Benjamin B. Warfield*, 2:21–279. Ed. by John E. Meeter. Nutley, N.J.: Presbyterian and Reformed, 1973 (article first published 1896).

Wells, David. *No Place for Truth, or, Whatever Happened to Evangelical Theology?* Grand Rapids: Eerdmans, 1993.

Woodbridge, John D., and Thomas E. McComiskey, eds. *Doing Theology in Today's World: Essays in Honor of Kenneth S. Kantzer*. Grand Rapids: Zondervan, 1991.

## SCRIPTURE MEMORY PASSAGE

Students have repeatedly mentioned that one of the most valuable parts of any of their courses in college or seminary has been the Scripture passages they were required to memorize. "I have hidden your word in my heart that I might not sin against you" (Ps. 119:11 NIV). In each chapter, therefore, I have included an appropriate memory passage so that instructors may incorporate Scripture memory into the course requirements wherever possible. (Scripture memory passages at the end of each chapter are taken from the RSV. These same passages in the NIV and NASB may be found in appendix 2.)

**Matthew 28:18–20:** *And Jesus came and said to them, "All authority in heaven and on earth has been given to me. Go therefore and make disciples of all nations, baptizing them in the name of the Father and of the Son and of the Holy Spirit, teaching them to observe all that I have commanded you; and lo, I am with you always, to the close of the age."*

## HYMN

Systematic theology at its best will result in praise. It is appropriate therefore at the end of each chapter to include a hymn related to the subject of that chapter. In a classroom setting, the hymn can be sung together at the beginning or end of class. Alternatively, an individual reader can sing it privately or simply meditate quietly on the words.

For almost every chapter the words of the hymns were found in *Trinity Hymnal* (Philadelphia: Great Commission Publications, 1990),[13] the hymnal of the Presbyterian Church in America and the Orthodox Presbyterian Church, but most of them are found in many other common hymnals. Unless otherwise noted,[14] the words of these hymns are now in public domain and no longer subject to copyright restrictions: therefore they may be freely copied for overhead projector use or photocopied.

Why have I used so many old hymns? Although I personally like many of the more recent worship songs that have come into wide use, when I began to select hymns that would correspond to the great doctrines of the Christian faith, I realized that the great hymns of the church throughout history have a doctrinal richness and breadth that is still unequaled. For several of the chapters in this book, I know of no modern worship song that covers the same subject in an extended way—perhaps this can be a challenge to modern songwriters to study these chapters and then write songs reflecting the teaching of Scripture on the respective subjects.[15]

For this chapter, however, I found no hymn ancient or modern that thanked God for the privilege of studying systematic theology from the pages of Scripture. Therefore I have selected a hymn of general praise, which is always appropriate.

### "O for a Thousand Tongues to Sing"

This hymn by Charles Wesley (1707–88) begins by wishing for "a thousand tongues" to sing God's praise. Verse 2 is a prayer that God would "assist me" in singing his praise throughout the earth. The remaining verses give praise to Jesus (vv. 3–6) and to God the Father (v. 7).

> O for a thousand tongues to sing
> My great Redeemer's praise,
> The glories of my God and King,
> The triumphs of His grace.

---

[13]This hymn book is completely revised from a similar hymnal of the same title published by the Orthodox Presbyterian Church in 1961.

[14]Copyright restrictions still apply to the hymns in chapters 21, 37, and 51, and these may not be reproduced without permission from the owner of the copyright.

[15]In appendix 3 (pp. 1221–22) I have listed the first lines of contemporary worship songs that correspond to twenty-six of the fifty-seven chapters in this book.

My gracious Master and my God,
Assist me to proclaim,
To spread through all the earth abroad,
The honors of Thy name.

Jesus! the name that charms our fears,
That bids our sorrows cease;
'Tis music in the sinner's ears,
'Tis life and health and peace.

He breaks the pow'r of reigning sin,
He sets the prisoner free;
His blood can make the foulest clean;
His blood availed for me.

He speaks and, list'ning to His voice,
New life the dead receive;
The mournful, broken hearts rejoice;
The humble poor believe.

Hear him, ye deaf; his praise, ye dumb,
Your loosened tongues employ,
Ye blind, behold your Savior come;
And leap, ye lame, for joy.

Glory to God and praise and love
Be ever, ever giv'n
By saints below and saints above—
The church in earth and heav'n.

AUTHOR: CHARLES WESLEY, 1739, ALT.

# Part 1

# The Doctrine of the Word of God

# Chapter 2

# The Word of God

*What are the different forms*
*of the Word of God?*

## EXPLANATION AND SCRIPTURAL BASIS

What is meant by the phrase "the Word of God"? Actually, there are several different meanings taken by this phrase in the Bible. It is helpful to distinguish these different senses clearly at the beginning of this study.

### A. "The Word of God" as a Person: Jesus Christ

Sometimes the Bible refers to the Son of God as "the Word of God." In Revelation 19:13, John sees the risen Lord Jesus in heaven and says, "The name by which he is called is The Word of God." Similarly, in the beginning of John's gospel we read, "In the beginning was the Word, and the Word was with God, and the Word was God" (John 1:1). It is clear that John is speaking of the Son of God here, because in verse 14 he says, "And the Word became flesh and dwelt among us, full of grace and truth; we have beheld his glory, glory as of the only Son from the Father." These verses (and perhaps 1 John 1:1) are the only instances where the Bible refers to God the Son as "the Word" or "the Word of God," so this usage is not common. But it does indicate that among the members of the Trinity it is especially God the Son who in his person as well as in his words has the role of communicating the character of God to us and of expressing the will of God for us.

### B. "The Word of God" as Speech by God

**1. God's Decrees.** Sometimes God's words take the form of powerful decrees that cause events to happen or even cause things to come into being. "And God said, 'Let there be light'; and there was light" (Gen. 1:3). God even created the animal world by speaking his powerful word: "And God said, 'Let the earth bring forth living creatures according to their kinds: cattle and creeping things and beasts of the earth according to their kinds.' And it was so" (Gen. 1:24). Thus, the psalmist can say, *"By the word of the Lord* the heavens were made, and all their host by the breath of his mouth" (Ps. 33:6).

These powerful, creative words from God are often called God's decrees. A *decree* of God is a word of God that causes something to happen. These decrees of

God include not only the events of the original creation but also the continuing existence of all things, for Hebrews 1:3 tells us that Christ is continually "upholding the universe by his word of power."

**2. God's Words of Personal Address.** God sometimes communicates with people on earth by speaking directly to them. These can be called instances of God's Word of *personal address*. Examples are found throughout Scripture. At the very beginning of creation God speaks to Adam: "And the LORD God commanded the man, saying, 'You may freely eat of every tree of the garden; but of the tree of the knowledge of good and evil you shall not eat, for in the day that you eat of it you shall die'" (Gen. 2:16–17). After the sin of Adam and Eve, God still comes and speaks directly and personally to them in the words of the curse (Gen. 3:16–19). Another prominent example of God's direct personal address to people on earth is found in the giving of the Ten Commandments: "And *God spoke all these words,* saying, 'I am the LORD your God, who brought you out of the land of Egypt, out of the house of bondage. You shall have no other gods before me . . .'" (Ex. 20:1–3). In the New Testament, at Jesus' baptism, God the Father spoke with a voice from heaven, saying, "This is my beloved Son, with whom I am well pleased" (Matt. 3:17).

In these and several other instances where God spoke words of personal address to individual people it was clear to the hearers that these were the actual words of God: they were hearing God's very voice, and they were therefore hearing words that had absolute divine authority and that were absolutely trustworthy. To disbelieve or disobey any of these words would have been to disbelieve or disobey God and therefore would have been sin.

Though the words of God's personal address are always seen in Scripture to be the actual words of God, they are *also "human" words* in that they are spoken in ordinary human language that is immediately understandable. The fact that these words are spoken in human language does not limit their divine character or authority in any way: they are still entirely the words of God, spoken by the voice of God himself.

Some theologians have argued that since human language is always in some sense "imperfect," any message that God addresses to us in human language must also be limited in its authority or truthfulness. But these passages and many others that record instances of God's words of personal address to individuals give no indication of any limitation of the authority or truthfulness of God's words when they are spoken in human language. Quite the contrary is true, for the words always place an absolute obligation upon the hearers to believe them and to obey them fully. To disbelieve or disobey any part of them is to disbelieve or disobey God himself.

**3. God's Words as Speech Through Human Lips.** Frequently in Scripture God raises up prophets through whom he speaks. Once again, it is evident that although these are human words, spoken in ordinary human language by ordinary human beings, the authority and truthfulness of these words is in no way diminished: they are still completely God's words as well.

In Deuteronomy 18, God says to Moses:

I will raise up for them a prophet like you from among their brethren; and *I will put my words in his mouth,* and he shall speak to them all that I command him. And whoever will not give heed to my words which he shall speak in my name, I myself will require it of him. But the prophet who presumes to speak a word in my name which I have not commanded him to speak, or who speaks in the name of other gods, that same prophet shall die. (Deut. 18:18–20)

God made a similar statement to Jeremiah: "Then the LORD put forth his hand and touched my mouth; and the LORD said to me, 'Behold, *I have put my words in your mouth*'" (Jer. 1:9). God tells Jeremiah, "Whatever I command you you shall speak" (Jer. 1:7; see also Ex. 4:12; Num. 22:38; 1 Sam. 15:3, 18, 23; 1 Kings 20:36; 2 Chron. 20:20; 25:15–16; Isa. 30:12–14; Jer. 6:10–12; 36:29–31; et al.). Anyone who claimed to be speaking for the Lord but who had not received a message from him was severely punished (Ezek. 13:1–7; Deut. 18:20–22).

Thus God's words spoken through human lips were considered to be just as authoritative and just as true as God's words of personal address. There was no diminishing of the authority of these words when they were spoken through human lips. To disbelieve or disobey any of them was to disbelieve or disobey God himself.

**4. God's Words in Written Form (the Bible).** In addition to God's words of decree, God's words of personal address, and God's words spoken through the lips of human beings, we also find in Scripture several instances where God's words were put in *written form*. The first of these is found in the narrative of the giving of the two tablets of stone on which were written the Ten Commandments: "And he gave to Moses, when he had made an end of speaking with him upon Mount Sinai, the two tables of the testimony, tables of stone, *written with the finger of God*" (Ex. 31:18). "And the tables were the work of God, and *the writing was the writing of God, graven upon the tables*" (Ex. 32:16; 34:1, 28).

Further writing was done by Moses:

And Moses *wrote this law,* and gave it to the priests the sons of Levi, who carried the ark of the covenant of the LORD, and to all the elders of Israel. And Moses commanded them, "At the end of every seven years . . . you shall read this law before all Israel in their hearing . . . that they may hear and learn to fear the LORD your God, and be careful to do all the words of this law, and that their children, who have not known it, may hear and learn to fear the LORD your God. . . ." (Deut. 31:9–13)

This book which Moses wrote was then deposited by the side of the ark of the covenant: "When Moses had finished *writing the words of this law in a book,* to the very end, Moses commanded the Levites who carried the ark of the covenant of the LORD, 'Take this book of the law, and put it by the side of the ark of the covenant of the Lord your God, that it may be there for a witness against you'" (Deut. 31:24–26).

Further additions were made to this book of God's words. "And *Joshua wrote these words* in the book of the law of God" (Josh. 24:26). God commanded Isaiah, "And now, go, *write it before them on a tablet, and inscribe it in a book,* that it may be for the time to come as a witness for ever" (Isa. 30:8). Once again, God said to Jeremiah, "*Write in a book* all the words that I have spoken to you" (Jer. 30:2; cf.

Jer. 36:2–4, 27–31; 51:60). In the New Testament, Jesus promises his disciples that the Holy Spirit would bring to their remembrance the words which he, Jesus, had spoken (John 14:26; cf. 16:12–13). Paul can say that the very words he writes to the Corinthians are "a command of the Lord" (1 Cor. 14:37; cf. 2 Peter 3:2).

Once again it must be noted that these words are still considered to be God's own words, even though they are written down mostly by human beings and always in human language. Still, they are absolutely authoritative and absolutely true: to disobey them or disbelieve them is a serious sin and brings judgment from God (1 Cor. 14:37; Jer. 36:29–31).

Several benefits come from the writing down of God's words. First, there is a much *more accurate preservation* of God's words for subsequent generations. To depend on memory and the repeating of oral tradition is a less reliable method of preserving these words throughout history than is their recording in writing (cf. Deut. 31:12–13). Second, the *opportunity for repeated inspection* of words that are written down permits careful study and discussion, which leads to better understanding and more complete obedience. Third, God's words in writing are *accessible to many more people* than they are when preserved merely through memory and oral repetition. They can be inspected at any time by any person and are not limited in accessibility to those who have memorized them or those who are able to be present when they are recited orally. Thus, the reliability, permanence, and accessibility of the form in which God's words are preserved are all greatly enhanced when they are written down. Yet there is no indication that their authority or truthfulness is diminished.

## C. The Focus of Our Study

Of all the forms of the Word of God,[1] the focus of our study in systematic theology is God's Word in written form, that is, the Bible. This is the form of God's Word that is available for study, for public inspection, for repeated examination, and as a basis for mutual discussion. It tells us about and points us to the Word of God as a person, namely Jesus Christ, whom we do not now have present in bodily form on earth. Thus, we are no longer able to observe and imitate his life and teachings firsthand.

The other forms of the Word of God are not suitable as the primary basis for the study of theology. We do not hear God's words of decree and thus cannot study them directly but only through observation of their effects. God's words of personal address are uncommon, even in Scripture. Furthermore, even if we did hear some words of personal address from God to ourselves today, we would not have certainty that our understanding of it, our memory of it, and our subsequent report of it was wholly accurate. Nor would we be readily able to convey to others

---

[1]In addition to the forms of God's Word mentioned above, God communicates to people through different types of "general revelation"—that is, revelation that is given not just to certain people but to all people generally. General revelation includes both the revelation of God that comes through nature (see Ps. 19:1–6; Acts 14:17) and the revelation of God that comes through the inner sense of right and wrong in every person's heart (Rom. 2:15). These kinds of revelation are nonverbal in form, and I have not included them in the list of various forms of the Word of God discussed in this chapter. (See chapter 7, pp. 122–24, for further discussion of general revelation.)

the certainty that the communication was from God, even if it was. God's words as spoken through human lips ceased to be given when the New Testament canon was completed.[2] Thus, these other forms of God's words are inadequate as a primary basis for study in theology.

It is most profitable for us to study God's words as written in the Bible. It is God's written Word that he commands us to study. The man is "blessed" who "meditates" on God's law "day and night" (Ps. 1:1–2). God's words to Joshua are also applicable to us: "This book of the law shall not depart out of your mouth, but *you shall meditate on it day and night,* that you may be careful to do all that is written in it; for then you shall make your way prosperous, and then you shall have good success" (Josh. 1:8). It is the Word of God in the form of written Scripture that is "God-breathed" and "useful for teaching, rebuking, correcting, and training in righteousness" (2 Tim. 3:16 NIV).

## QUESTIONS FOR PERSONAL APPLICATION

1. Do you think you would pay more attention if God spoke to you from heaven or through the voice of a living prophet than if he spoke to you from the written words of Scripture? Would you believe or obey such words more readily than you do Scripture? Do you think your present level of response to the written words of Scripture is an appropriate one? What positive steps can you take to make your attitude toward Scripture more like the kind of attitude God wants you to have?

2. When you think about the many ways in which God speaks and the frequency with which God communicates with his creatures through these means, what conclusions might you draw concerning the nature of God and the things that bring delight to him?

## SPECIAL TERMS

decree                                        personal address
Word of God

## BIBLIOGRAPHY

(For an explanation of this bibliography see the note on the bibliography to chapter 1, p. 38. Complete bibliographical data may be found on pp. 1223–29.) The subject of this chapter has not been treated explicitly in many systematic theologies, but similar material is often covered in the section on the authority of the Word of God: see the bibliography at the end of chapter 4 for that subject.

### Sections in Evangelical Systematic Theologies

1. Anglican (Episcopalian)
       1882–92      Litton, 9–10

---

[2]See chapter 3, pp. 54–72, on the canon of Scripture, and, for a discussion of the nature of contemporary Christian prophecy, see chapter 53, pp. 1049–61.

2. Arminian (Wesleyan or Methodist)

      1940     Wiley, 1:124–65

3. Baptist

      1917     Mullins, 137–53

6. Reformed (or Presbyterian)

      1861     Heppe, 12–21

      1889     Shedd, 1:61–70

## Sections in Representative Roman Catholic Systematic Theologies

No explicit treatment.

## Other Works

Kline, Meredith. *The Structure of Biblical Authority*. Grand Rapids: Eerdmans, 1972.

Kuyper, Abraham. *Principles of Sacred Theology*. Trans. by J. H. de Vries. Grand Rapids: Eerdmans, 1968, pp. 405–12 (originally published as *Encyclopedia of Sacred Theology* in 1898).

McDonald, H. D. *Theories of Revelation: An Historical Study, 1860–1960*. Grand Rapids: Baker, 1979.

————. "Word, Word of God, Word of the Lord." In *EDT*, pp. 1185–88.

Packer, J. I. "Scripture." In *NDT*, pp. 585–87.

Pinnock, C. H. "Revelation." In *NDT*, pp. 585–87.

Vos, Geerhardus. *Biblical Theology: Old and New Testaments*. Grand Rapids: Eerdmans, 1948, pp. 28–55; 321–27.

## SCRIPTURE MEMORY PASSAGE

**Ps. 1:1–2:**    *Blessed is the man*
*who walks not in the counsel of the wicked,*
*nor stands in the way of sinners,*
*nor sits in the seat of scoffers;*
*but his delight is in the law of the LORD,*
*and on his law he meditates day and night.*

## HYMN

### "Break Thou the Bread of Life"

This hymn is a prayer asking the Lord to give us not physical bread but spiritual nourishment from the "bread of life," a metaphor referring both to the written Word of God ("the sacred page," v. 1) and to Christ himself, the "Living Word" (see vv. 1, 3).

Break thou the bread of life, dear Lord, to me,
As thou didst break the loaves beside the sea;
Throughout the sacred page I seek thee, Lord,
My spirit pants for thee, O Living Word.

Bless thou the truth, dear Lord, to me, to me,
As thou didst bless the bread by Galilee;
Then shall all bondage cease, all fetters fall;
And I shall find my peace, my all in all.

Thou art the bread of life, O Lord, to me,
Thy holy Word the truth that saveth me;
Give me to eat and live with thee above;
Teach me to love thy truth, for thou art love.

O send thy Spirit, Lord, now unto me,
That he may touch mine eyes, and make me see:
Show me the truth concealed within thy Word,
And in thy Book revealed I see the Lord.

AUTHOR: MARY A. LATHBURY, 1877

# Chapter 3

# The Canon of Scripture

*What belongs in the Bible and what does not belong?*

## EXPLANATION AND SCRIPTURAL BASIS

The previous chapter concluded that it is especially the written words of God in the Bible to which we are to give our attention. Before we can do this, however, we must know which writings belong in the Bible and which do not. This is the question of the canon of Scripture, which may be defined as follows: *The canon of Scripture is the list of all the books that belong in the Bible.*

We must not underestimate the importance of this question. The words of Scripture are the words by which we nourish our spiritual lives. Thus we can reaffirm the comment of Moses to the people of Israel in reference to the words of God's law: "For it is no trifle for you, but *it is your life,* and thereby you shall live long in the land which you are going over the Jordan to possess" (Deut. 32:47).

To add to or subtract from God's words would be to prevent God's people from obeying him fully, for commands that were subtracted would not be known to the people, and words that were added might require extra things of the people which God had not commanded. Thus Moses warned the people of Israel, "You shall not *add to the word* which I command you, *nor take from it;* that you may keep the commandments of the LORD your God which I command you" (Deut. 4:2).

The precise determination of the extent of the canon of Scripture is therefore of the utmost importance. If we are to trust and obey God absolutely we must have a collection of words that we are certain are God's own words to us. If there are any sections of Scripture about which we have doubts whether they are God's words or not, we will not consider them to have absolute divine authority and we will not trust them as much as we would trust God himself.

## A. The Old Testament Canon

Where did the idea of a canon begin—the idea that the people of Israel should preserve a collection of written words from God? Scripture itself bears witness to the historical development of the canon. The earliest collection of written words of God was the Ten Commandments. The Ten Commandments thus form the beginning of the biblical canon. God himself wrote on two tablets of stone the words which he commanded his people: "And he gave to Moses, when he had made an end of speaking with him upon Mount Sinai, the two tables of the testimony, tables of stone, *written with the finger of God*" (Ex. 31:18). Again we read, "And the tables were the work of God, and *the writing was the writing of God,* graven upon the tables" (Ex. 32:16; cf. Deut. 4:13; 10:4). The tablets were deposited in the ark of the covenant (Deut. 10:5) and constituted the terms of the covenant between God and his people.[1]

This collection of absolutely authoritative words from God grew in size throughout the time of Israel's history. Moses himself wrote additional words to be deposited beside the ark of the covenant (Deut. 31:24–26). The immediate reference is apparently to the book of Deuteronomy, but other references to writing by Moses indicate that the first four books of the Old Testament were written by him as well (see Ex. 17:14; 24:4; 34:27; Num. 33:2; Deut. 31:22). After the death of Moses, Joshua also added to the collection of written words of God: "Joshua wrote these words in the book of the law of God" (Josh. 24:26). This is especially surprising in light of the command not to add to or take away from the words which God gave the people through Moses: "You shall not add to the word which I command you, nor take from it . . ." (Deut. 4:2; cf. 12:32). In order to have disobeyed such a specific command, Joshua must have been convinced that he was not taking it upon himself to add to the written words of God, but that God himself had authorized such additional writing.

Later, others in Israel, usually those who fulfilled the office of prophet, wrote additional words from God:

> Samuel told the people the rights and duties of the kingship; and he wrote them in a book and laid it up before the LORD. (1 Sam. 10:25)

> The acts of King David, from first to last, are written in the Chronicles of Samuel the seer, and in the Chronicles of Nathan the prophet, and in the Chronicles of Gad the seer. (1 Chron. 29:29)

> Now the rest of the acts of Jehoshaphat, from first to last, are written in the chronicles of Jehu the son of Hanani, which are recorded in the Book of the Kings of Israel. (2 Chron. 20:34; cf. 1 Kings 16:7 where Jehu the son of Hanani is called a prophet)

> Now the rest of the acts of Uzziah, from first to last, Isaiah the prophet the son of Amoz wrote. (2 Chron. 26:22)

> Now the rest of the acts of Hezekiah, and his good deeds, behold, they are written in the vision of Isaiah the prophet the son of Amoz, in the Book of the Kings of Judah and Israel. (2 Chron. 32:32)

> Thus says the LORD, the God of Israel: Write in a book all the words that I have spoken to you.[2] (Jer. 30:2)

The content of the Old Testament canon continued to grow until the time of the end of the writing process. If we date Haggai to 520 B.C., Zechariah to 520–518 B.C. (with perhaps more material added after 480 B.C.), and Malachi around 435 B.C., we have an idea of the approximate dates of the last Old Testament prophets. Roughly coinciding with this period are the last books of Old

---

[1]See Meredith Kline, *The Structure of Biblical Authority* (Grand Rapids: Eerdmans, 1972), esp. pp. 48–53 and 113–30.

[2]For other passages that illustrate the growth in the collection of written words from God see 2 Chron. 9:29; 12:15; 13:22; Isa. 30:8; Jer. 29:1; 36:1–32; 45:1; 51:60; Ezek. 43:11; Dan. 7:1; Hab. 2:2. Additions to it were usually through the agency of a prophet.

Testament history—Ezra, Nehemiah, and Esther. Ezra went to Jerusalem in 458 B.C., and Nehemiah was in Jerusalem from 445–433 B.C.[3] Esther was written sometime after the death of Xerxes I (= Ahasuerus) in 465 B.C., and a date during the reign of Artaxerxes I (464–423 B.C.) is probable. Thus, after approximately 435 B.C. there were no further additions to the Old Testament canon. The subsequent history of the Jewish people was recorded in other writings, such as the books of the Maccabees, but these writings were not thought worthy to be included with the collections of God's words from earlier years.

When we turn to Jewish literature outside the Old Testament, we see that the belief that divinely authoritative words from God had ceased is clearly attested in several different strands of extrabiblical Jewish literature. In 1 Maccabees (about 100 B.C.) the author writes of the defiled altar, "So they tore down the altar and stored the stones in a convenient place on the temple hill until there should come a prophet to tell what to do with them" (1 Macc. 4:45–46). They apparently knew of no one who could speak with the authority of God as the Old Testament prophets had done. The memory of an authoritative prophet among the people was one that belonged to the distant past, for the author could speak of a great distress "such as had not been since the time that prophets ceased to appear among them" (1 Macc. 9:27; cf. 14:41).

Josephus (born c. A.D. 37/38) explained, "From Artaxerxes to our own times a complete history has been written, but has not been deemed worthy of equal credit with the earlier records, because of the failure of the exact succession of the prophets" (*Against Apion* 1.41). This statement by the greatest Jewish historian of the first century A.D. shows that he knew of the writings now considered part of the "Apocrypha," but that he (and many of his contemporaries) considered these other writings "not . . . worthy of equal credit" with what we now know as the Old Testament Scriptures. There had been, in Josephus's viewpoint, no more "words of God" added to Scripture after about 435 B.C.

Rabbinic literature reflects a similar conviction in its repeated statement that the Holy Spirit (in the Spirit's function of inspiring prophecy) departed from Israel. "After the latter prophets Haggai, Zechariah, and Malachi had died, the Holy Spirit departed from Israel, but they still availed themselves of the *bath qôl*" (*Babylonian Talmud*, Yomah 9b, repeated in Sota 48b, Sanhedrin 11a, and Midrash Rabbah on Song of Songs, 8.9.3).[4]

The Qumran community (the Jewish sect that left behind the Dead Sea Scrolls) also awaited a prophet whose words would have authority to supersede any existing regulations (see 1 QS 9.11), and other similar statements are found elsewhere in ancient Jewish literature (see 2 Baruch 85.3 and Prayer of Azariah 15). Thus, writings subsequent to about 435 B.C. were not accepted by the Jewish people generally as having equal authority with the rest of Scripture.

In the New Testament, we have no record of any dispute between Jesus and the Jews over the extent of the canon. Apparently there was full agreement between Jesus and his disciples, on the one hand, and the Jewish leaders or Jewish people, on the other hand, that additions to the Old Testament canon had ceased after the

---

[3]See "Chronology of the Old Testament," in *IBD*, 1:277.

[4]That "the Holy Spirit" is primarily a reference to divinely authoritative prophecy is clear both from the fact that the *bath qôl* (a voice from heaven) is seen as a substitute for it, and from the very frequent use of "the Holy Spirit" to refer to prophecy elsewhere in Rabbinic literature.

time of Ezra, Nehemiah, Esther, Haggai, Zechariah, and Malachi. This fact is confirmed by the quotations of Jesus and the New Testament authors from the Old Testament. According to one count, Jesus and the New Testament authors quote various parts of the Old Testament Scriptures as divinely authoritative over 295 times,[5] but not once do they cite any statement from the books of the Apocrypha or any other writings as having divine authority.[6] The absence of any such reference to other literature as divinely authoritative, and the extremely frequent reference to hundreds of places in the Old Testament as divinely authoritative, gives strong confirmation to the fact that the New Testament authors agreed that the established Old Testament canon, no more and no less, was to be taken as God's very words.

What then shall be said about the Apocrypha, the collection of books included in the canon by the Roman Catholic Church but excluded from the canon by Protestantism?[7] These books were never accepted by the Jews as Scripture, but throughout the early history of the church there was a divided opinion on whether they should be part of Scripture or not. In fact, the earliest Christian evidence is decidedly against viewing the Apocrypha as Scripture, but the use of the Apocrypha gradually increased in some parts of the church until the time of the Reformation.[8] The fact that these books were included by Jerome in his Latin Vulgate translation of the Bible (completed in A.D. 404) gave support to their inclusion, even though Jerome himself said they were not "books of the canon" but merely "books of the church" that were helpful and useful for believers. The wide use of the Latin Vulgate in subsequent centuries guaranteed their continued accessibility, but the fact that they had no Hebrew original behind them, and their

---

[5] See Roger Nicole, "New Testament Use of the Old Testament," in *Revelation and the Bible,* ed. Carl F. H. Henry (London: Tyndale Press, 1959), pp. 137–41.

[6] Jude 14–15 does cite 1 Enoch 60.8 and 1.9, and Paul at least twice quotes pagan Greek authors (see Acts 17:28; Titus 1:12), but these citations are more for purposes of illustration than proof. Never are the works introduced with a phrase like, "God says," or "Scripture says," or "it is written," phrases that imply the attribution of divine authority to the words cited. (It should be noted that neither 1 Enoch nor the authors cited by Paul are part of the Apocrypha.) No book of the Apocrypha is even mentioned in the New Testament.

[7] The Apocrypha includes the following writings: 1 and 2 Esdras, Tobit, Judith, the Rest of Esther, the Wisdom of Solomon, Ecclesiasticus, Baruch (including the Epistle of Jeremiah), the Song of the Three Holy Children, Susanna, Bel and the Dragon, the Prayer of Manasseh, and 1 and 2 Maccabees. These writings are not found in the Hebrew Bible, but they were included with the Septuagint (the translation of the Old Testament into Greek, which was used by many Greek-speaking Jews at the time of Christ). A good modern translation is *The Oxford Annotated Apocrypha (RSV),* ed. Bruce M. Metzger (New York: Oxford University Press, 1965). Metzger includes brief introductions and helpful annotations to the books.

The Greek word *apocrypha* means "things that are hidden," but Metzger notes (p. ix) that scholars are not sure why this word came to be applied to these writings.

[8] A detailed historical survey of the differing views of Christians regarding the Apocrypha is found in F. F. Bruce, *The Canon of Scripture* (Downers Grove, Ill.: InterVarsity Press, 1988), pp. 68–97. An even more detailed study is found in Roger Beckwith, *The Old Testament Canon of the New Testament Church and Its Background in Early Judaism* (London: SPCK, 1985, and Grand Rapids: Eerdmans, 1986), esp. pp. 338–433. Beckwith's book has now established itself as the definitive work on the Old Testament canon. At the conclusion of his study Beckwith says, "The inclusion of various Apocrypha and Pseudepigrapha in the canon of the early Christians was not done in any agreed way or at the earliest period, but occurred in Gentile Christianity, after the church's breach with the synagogue, among those whose knowledge of the primitive Christian canon was becoming blurred." He concludes, "On the question of the canonicity of the Apocrypha and Pseudepigrapha the truly primitive Christian evidence is negative" (pp. 436–37).

exclusion from the Jewish canon, as well as the lack of their citation in the New Testament, led many to view them with suspicion or to reject their authority. For instance, the earliest Christian list of Old Testament books that exists today is by Melito, bishop of Sardis, writing about A.D. 170:[9]

> When I came to the east and reached the place where these things were preached and done, and learnt accurately the books of the Old Testament, I set down the facts and sent them to you. These are their names: five books of Moses, Genesis, Exodus, Numbers, Leviticus, Deuteronomy, Joshua the son of Nun, Judges, Ruth, four books of Kingdoms,[10] two books of Chronicles, the Psalms of David, the Proverbs of Solomon and his Wisdom,[11] Ecclesiastes, the Song of Songs, Job, the prophets Isaiah, Jeremiah, the Twelve in a single book, Daniel, Ezekiel, Ezra.[12]

It is noteworthy here that Melito names none of the books of the Apocrypha, but he includes all of our present Old Testament books except Esther.[13] Eusebius also quotes Origen as affirming most of the books of our present Old Testament canon (including Esther), but no book of the Apocrypha is affirmed as canonical, and the books of Maccabees are explicitly said to be "outside of these [canonical books]."[14] Similarly, in A.D. 367, when the great church leader Athanasius, bishop of Alexandria, wrote his Paschal Letter, he listed all the books of our present New Testament canon and all the books of our present Old Testament canon except Esther. He also mentioned some books of the Apocrypha such as the Wisdom of Solomon, the Wisdom of Sirach, Judith, and Tobit, and said these are "not indeed included in the Canon, but appointed by the Fathers to be read by those who newly join us, and who wish for instruction in the word of godliness."[15] However, other early church leaders did quote several of these books as Scripture.[16]

[9]From Eusebius, *Ecclesiastical History* 4.26.14. Eusebius, writing in A.D. 325, was the first great church historian. This quotation is from the translation by Kirsopp Lake, *Eusebius: The Ecclesiastical History*, two vols. (London: Heinemann; and Cambridge, Mass.: Harvard, 1975), 1:393.

[10]That is, 1 Samuel, 2 Samuel, 1 Kings, and 2 Kings.

[11]This does not refer to the apocryphal book called the Wisdom of Solomon but is simply a fuller description of Proverbs. Eusebius notes in 4.22.9 that Proverbs was commonly called Wisdom by ancient writers.

[12]Ezra would include both Ezra and Nehemiah, according to a common Hebrew way of referring to the combined books.

[13]For some reason there was doubt about the canonicity of Esther in some parts of the early church (in the East but not in the West), but the doubts were eventually resolved, and Christian usage eventually became uniform with the Jewish view, which had always counted Esther as part of the canon, although it had been opposed by certain rabbis for their own reasons. (See the discussion of the Jewish view in Beckwith, *Canon*, pp. 288–97.)

[14]Eusebius, *Ecclesiastical History* 6.15.2. Origen died about A.D. 254. Origen names all the books of the present Old Testament canon except the twelve minor prophets (which would be counted as one book), but this leaves his list of "twenty-two books" incomplete at twenty-one, so apparently Eusebius's citation is incomplete, at least in the form we have it today.

Eusebius himself elsewhere repeats the statement of the Jewish historian Josephus that the Scriptures contain twenty-two books, but nothing since the time of Artaxerxes (3.10.1–5), and this would exclude all of the Apocrypha.

[15]Athanasius, *Letter 39*, in *Nicene and Post Nicene Fathers*, 2d ser., ed. Philip Schaff and Henry Wace (Grand Rapids: Eerdmans, 1978), vol. 4: *Athanasius*, pp. 551–52.

[16]See Metzger, *Apocrypha*, pp. xii–xiii. Metzger notes that none of the early Latin and Greek church fathers who quoted from the Apocrypha as Scripture knew any Hebrew. Beckwith, *Canon*, pp. 386–89, argues that the evidence of Christian writers quoting the Apocrypha as Scripture is considerably less extensive and less significant than scholars often claim it to be.

There are doctrinal and historical inconsistencies with a number of these books. E. J. Young notes:

> There are no marks in these books which would attest a divine origin. . . . both Judith and Tobit contain historical, chronological and geographical errors. The books justify falsehood and deception and make salvation to depend upon works of merit. . . . Ecclesiasticus and the Wisdom of Solomon inculcate a morality based upon expediency. Wisdom teaches the creation of the world out of pre-existent matter (11:17). Ecclesiasticus teaches that the giving of alms makes atonement for sin (3:30). In Baruch it is said that God hears the prayers of the dead (3:4), and in I Maccabees there are historical and geographical errors.[17]

It was not until 1546, at the Council of Trent, that the Roman Catholic Church officially declared the Apocrypha to be part of the canon (with the exception of 1 and 2 Esdras and the Prayer of Manasseh). It is significant that the Council of Trent was the response of the Roman Catholic Church to the teachings of Martin Luther and the rapidly spreading Protestant Reformation, and the books of the Apocrypha contain support for the Catholic teaching of prayers for the dead and justification by faith plus works, not by faith alone. In affirming the Apocrypha as within the canon, Roman Catholics would hold that the church has the authority to constitute a literary work as "Scripture," while Protestants have held that the church cannot make something to be Scripture, but can only recognize what God has already caused to be written as his own words.[18] (One analogy here would be to say that a police investigator can recognize counterfeit money as counterfeit and can recognize genuine money as genuine, but he cannot make counterfeit money to be genuine, nor can any declaration by any number of police make counterfeit money to be something it is not. Only the official treasury of a nation can make money that is real money; similarly, only God can make words to be his very words and worthy of inclusion in Scripture.)

Thus the writings of the Apocrypha should not be regarded as part of Scripture: (1) they do not claim for themselves the same kind of authority as the Old Testament writings; (2) they were not regarded as God's words by the Jewish people from whom they originated; (3) they were not considered to be Scripture by Jesus or the New Testament authors; and (4) they contain teachings inconsistent with the rest of the Bible. We must conclude that they are merely human words, not God-breathed words like the words of Scripture. They do have value for historical and linguistic research, and they contain a number of helpful stories about the courage and faith of many Jews during the period after the Old Testament ends, but they have never been part of the Old Testament canon, and they should not be thought of as part of the Bible. Therefore, they have no binding authority for the thought or life of Christians today.

In conclusion, with regard to the canon of the Old Testament, Christians today should have no worry that anything needed has been left out or that anything that is not God's words has been included.

---

[17]E. J. Young, "The Canon of the Old Testament," in *Revelation and the Bible*, pp. 167–68.

[18]It should be noted that Roman Catholics use the term *deuterocanonical* rather than *apocryphal* to refer to these books. They understand this to mean "later added to the canon" (the prefix *deutero-* means "second").

## B. The New Testament Canon

The development of the New Testament canon begins with the writings of the apostles. It should be remembered that the writing of Scripture primarily occurs in connection with God's great acts in redemptive history. The Old Testament records and interprets for us the calling of Abraham and the lives of his descendants, the exodus from Egypt and the wilderness wanderings, the establishment of God's people in the land of Canaan, the establishment of the monarchy, and the Exile and return from captivity. Each of these great acts of God in history is interpreted for us in God's own words in Scripture. The Old Testament closes with the expectation of the Messiah to come (Mal. 3:1–4; 4:1–6). The next stage in redemptive history is the coming of the Messiah, and it is not surprising that no further Scripture would be written until this next and greatest event in the history of redemption occurred.

This is why the New Testament consists of the writings of the apostles.[19] It is primarily the apostles who are given the ability from the Holy Spirit to recall accurately the words and deeds of Jesus and to interpret them rightly for subsequent generations.

Jesus promised this empowering to his disciples (who were called apostles after the resurrection) in John 14:26: "But the Counselor, the Holy Spirit, whom the Father will send in my name, he will teach you all things, and bring to your remembrance all that I have said to you." Similarly, Jesus promised further revelation of truth from the Holy Spirit when he told his disciples, "When the Spirit of truth comes, he will guide you into all the truth; for he will not speak on his own authority, but whatever he hears he will speak, and he will declare to you the things that are to come. He will glorify me, for he will take what is mine and declare it to you" (John 16:13–14). In these verses the disciples are promised amazing gifts to enable them to write Scripture: the Holy Spirit would teach them "all things," would cause them to remember "all" that Jesus had said, and would guide them into "all the truth."

Furthermore, those who have the office of apostle in the early church are seen to claim an authority equal to that of the Old Testament prophets, an authority to speak and write words that are God's very words. Peter encourages his readers to remember "the commandment of the Lord and Savior through your apostles" (2 Peter 3:2). To lie to the apostles (Acts 5:2) is equivalent to lying to the Holy Spirit (Acts 5:3) and lying to God (Acts 5:4).

This claim to be able to speak words that were the words of God himself is especially frequent in the writings of the apostle Paul. He claims not only that the Holy Spirit has revealed to him "what no eye has seen, nor ear heard, nor the heart of man conceived" (1 Cor. 2:9), but also that when he declares this revelation, he speaks it "in words not taught by human wisdom but taught by the Spirit, interpreting Spiritual things in Spiritual words" (1 Cor. 2:13, author's translation).[20]

---

[19]A few New Testament books (Mark, Luke, Acts, Hebrews, and Jude) were not written by apostles but by others closely associated with them and apparently authorized by them: see the discussion below, pp. 62–63.

[20]This is my own translation of the last phrase of 1 Cor. 2:13: see Wayne Grudem, "Scripture's Self-Attestation," in *Scripture and Truth*, ed. D. A. Carson and John Woodbridge (Grand Rapids:

Similarly, Paul tells the Corinthians, "If any one thinks that he is a prophet, or spiritual, he should acknowledge that what I am writing to you is a command of the Lord" (1 Cor. 14:37). The word translated "what" in this verse is a plural relative pronoun in Greek (*ha*) and more literally could be translated "*the things that I am writing to you.*" Thus, Paul claims that his directives to the church at Corinth are not merely his own but a command of the Lord. Later, in defending his apostolic office, Paul says that he will give the Corinthians "proof that Christ is speaking in me" (2 Cor. 13:3). Other similar verses could be mentioned (for example, Rom. 2:16; Gal. 1:8–9; 1 Thess. 2:13; 4:8, 15; 5:27; 2 Thess. 3:6, 14).

The apostles, then, have authority to write words that are God's own words, equal in truth status and authority to the words of the Old Testament Scriptures. They do this to record, interpret, and apply to the lives of believers the great truths about the life, death, and resurrection of Christ.

It would not be surprising therefore to find some of the New Testament writings being placed with the Old Testament Scriptures as part of the canon of Scripture. In fact, this is what we find in at least two instances. In 2 Peter 3:16, Peter shows not only an awareness of the existence of written epistles from Paul, but also a clear willingness to classify "all of his [Paul's] epistles" with "the other scriptures": Peter says, "So also our beloved brother Paul wrote to you according to the wisdom given him, speaking of this as he does in all his letters. There are some things in them hard to understand, which the ignorant and unstable twist to their own destruction, *as they do the other scriptures*" (2 Peter 3:15–16). The word translated "scriptures" here is *graphē*, a word that occurs fifty-one times in the New Testament and that refers to the Old Testament Scriptures in every one of those occurrences. Thus, the word *Scripture* was a technical term for the New Testament authors, and it was used only of those writings that were thought to be God's words and therefore part of the canon of Scripture. But in this verse, Peter classifies Paul's writings with the "other Scriptures" (meaning the Old Testament Scriptures). Paul's writings are therefore considered by Peter also to be worthy of the title "Scripture" and thus worthy of inclusion in the canon.

A second instance is found in 1 Timothy 5:17–18. Paul says, "Let the elders who rule well be considered worthy of double honor, especially those who labor in preaching and teaching; *for the scripture* says, 'You shall not muzzle an ox when it is treading out the grain,' and, 'The laborer deserves his wages.'" The first quotation from "Scripture" is found in Deuteronomy 25:4, but the second quotation, "The laborer deserves his wages," is found nowhere in the Old Testament. It does occur, however, in Luke 10:7 (with exactly the same words in the Greek text). So here we have Paul apparently quoting a portion of Luke's gospel[21] and calling it "Scripture," that is, something that is to be considered part

---

Zondervan, 1983), p. 365, n. 61. But this translation is not crucial to the main point: namely, that Paul speaks words taught by the Holy Spirit, a point that is affirmed in the first part of the verse, no matter how the second half is translated.

[21]Someone might object that Paul could be quoting an oral tradition of Jesus' words rather than Luke's gospel, but it is doubtful that Paul would call any oral tradition "Scripture," since the word (Gk. *graphē*, "writing") is always in New Testament usage applied to written texts, and since Paul's close association with Luke makes it very possible that he would quote Luke's written gospel.

of the canon.[22] In both of these passages (2 Peter 3:16 and 1 Tim. 5.17–18) we see evidence that very early in the history of the church the writings of the New Testament began to be accepted as part of the canon.

Because the apostles, by virtue of their apostolic office, had authority to write words of Scripture, the authentic written teachings of the apostles were accepted by the early church as part of the canon of Scripture. If we accept the arguments for the traditional views of authorship of the New Testament writings,[23] then we have most of the New Testament in the canon because of direct authorship by the apostles. This would include Matthew; John; Romans to Philemon (all of the Pauline epistles); James;[24] 1 and 2 Peter; 1, 2, and 3 John; and Revelation.

This leaves five books, Mark, Luke, Acts, Hebrews, and Jude, which were not written by apostles. The details of the historical process by which these books came to be counted as part of Scripture by the early church are scarce, but Mark, Luke, and Acts were commonly acknowledged very early, probably because of the close association of Mark with the apostle Peter, and of Luke (the author of Luke-Acts) with the apostle Paul. Similarly, Jude apparently was accepted by virtue of the author's connection with James (see Jude 1) and the fact that he was the brother of Jesus.[25]

The acceptance of Hebrews as canonical was urged by many in the church on the basis of an assumed Pauline authorship. But from very early times there were others who rejected Pauline authorship in favor of one or another of several different suggestions. Origen, who died about A.D. 254, mentions various theories of authorship and concludes, "But who actually wrote the epistle, only God knows."[26] Thus, the acceptance of Hebrews as canonical was not entirely due to a belief in Pauline authorship. Rather, the intrinsic qualities of the book itself must have finally convinced early readers, as they continue to convince believers today, that whoever its human author may have been, its ultimate author can only have been God himself. The majestic glory of Christ shines forth from the pages of the epistle to the Hebrews so brightly that no believer who reads it seriously should ever want to question its place in the canon.

This brings us to the heart of the question of canonicity. For a book to belong in the canon, it is absolutely necessary that the book have divine authorship. If the words of the book are God's words (through human authors), and if the early church, under the direction of the apostles, preserved the book as part of Scripture, then the book belongs in the canon. But if the words of the book are not God's words, it does not belong in the canon. The question of authorship by an apostle is important because it was primarily the apostles to whom Christ gave the ability to write words with absolute divine authority. If a writing can be shown to be by an apostle, then its absolute divine authority is automatically

[22]Luke himself was not an apostle, but his gospel is here accorded authority equal with that of the apostolic writings. Apparently this was due to his very close association with the apostles, especially Paul, and the endangerment of his gospel by an apostle.

[23]For a defense of traditional views of authorship of the New Testament writings, see Donald Guthrie, *New Testament Introduction* (Downers Grove, Ill.: InterVarsity Press, 1970).

[24]James seems to be considered an apostle in 1 Cor. 15:7 and Gal. 1:19. He also fulfills functions appropriate to an apostle in Acts 12:17; 15:13; 21:18; Gal. 2:9, 12: see p. 908 below.

[25]The acceptance of Jude in the canon was slow, primarily because of doubts concerning his quotation of the noncanonical book of 1 Enoch.

[26]Origen's statement is quoted in Eusebius, *Ecclesiastical History*, 6.25.14.

established.[27] Thus, the early church automatically accepted as part of the canon the written teachings of the apostles which the apostles wanted preserved as Scripture.

But the existence of some New Testament writings that were not authored directly by apostles shows that there were others in the early church to whom Christ also gave the ability, through the work of the Holy Spirit, to write words that were God's own words and also therefore intended to be part of the canon. In these cases, the early church had the task of recognizing which writings had the characteristic of being God's own words (through human authors).

For some books (at least Mark, Luke, and Acts, and perhaps Hebrews and Jude as well), the church had, at least in some areas, the personal testimony of some living apostles to affirm the absolute divine authority of these books. For example, Paul would have affirmed the authenticity of Luke and Acts, and Peter would have affirmed the authenticity of Mark as containing the gospel which he himself preached. In other cases, and in some geographical areas, the church simply had to decide whether it heard the voice of God himself speaking in the words of these writings. In these cases, the words of these books would have been *self-attesting*; that is, the words would have borne witness to their own divine authorship as Christians read them. This seems to have been the case with Hebrews.

It should not surprise us that the early church should have been able to recognize Hebrews and other writings, not written by apostles, as God's very words. Had not Jesus said "My sheep hear my voice" (John 10:27)? It should not be thought impossible or unlikely, therefore, that the early church would be able to use a combination of factors, including apostolic endorsement, consistency with the rest of Scripture, and the perception of a writing as "God-breathed" on the part of an overwhelming majority of believers, to decide that a writing was in fact God's words (through a human author) and therefore worthy of inclusion in the canon. Nor should it be thought unlikely that the church would be able to use this process over a period of time—as writings were circulated to various parts of the early church—and finally to come to a completely correct decision, without excluding any writings that were in fact "God-breathed" and without including any that were not.[28]

In A.D. 367 the Thirty-ninth Paschal Letter of Athanasius contained an exact list of the twenty-seven New Testament books we have today. This was the list of books accepted by the churches in the eastern part of the Mediterranean world.

---

[27]Of course, this does not mean that everything an apostle wrote, including even grocery lists and receipts for business transactions, would be considered Scripture. We are speaking here of writings done when acting in the role of an apostle and giving apostolic instructions to churches and to individual Christians (such as Timothy or Philemon).

It is also very likely that the living apostles themselves gave some guidance to the churches concerning which works they intended to be preserved and used as Scripture in the churches (see Col. 4:16; 2 Thess. 3:14; 2 Peter 3:16). There were apparently some writings that had absolute divine authority but that the apostles did not decide to preserve as "Scripture" for the churches (such as Paul's "previous letter" to the Corinthians: see 1 Cor. 5:9). Moreover, the apostles did much more oral teaching, which had divine authority (see 2 Thess. 2:15) but was not written down and preserved as Scripture. Thus, in addition to apostolic authorship, preservation by the church under the direction of the apostles was necessary for a work to be included in the canon.

[28]I am not discussing at this point the question of textual variants (that is, differences in individual words and phrases that are to be found among the many ancient copies of Scripture that still exist). This question is treated in chapter 5, pp. 96–97.

Thirty years later, in A.D. 397, the Council of Carthage, representing the churches in the western part of the Mediterranean world, agreed with the eastern churches on the same list. These are the earliest final lists of our present-day canon.

Should we expect any more writings to be added to the canon? The opening sentence in Hebrews puts this question in the proper historical perspective, the perspective of the history of redemption: "In many and various ways God spoke of old to our fathers by the prophets; but in these last days he has spoken to us by a Son, whom he appointed the heir of all things, through whom also he created the world" (Heb. 1:1-2).

The contrast between the former speaking "of old" by the prophets and the recent speaking "in these last days" suggests that God's speech to us by his Son is the culmination of his speaking to mankind and is his greatest and final revelation to mankind in this period of redemptive history. The exceptional greatness of the revelation that comes through the Son, far exceeding any revelation in the old covenant, is emphasized again and again throughout chapters 1 and 2 of Hebrews. These facts all indicate that there is a finality to the revelation of God in Christ and that once this revelation has been completed, no more is to be expected.

But where do we learn about this revelation through Christ? The New Testament writings contain the final, authoritative, and sufficient interpretation of Christ's work of redemption. The apostles and their close companions report Christ's words and deeds and interpret them with absolute divine authority. When they have finished their writing, there is no more to be added with the same absolute divine authority. Thus, once the writings of the New Testament apostles and their authorized companions are completed, we have in written form the final record of everything that God wants us to know about the life, death, and resurrection of Christ, and its meaning for the lives of believers for all time. Since this is God's greatest revelation for mankind, no more is to be expected once this is complete. In this way, then, Hebrews 1:1-2 shows us why no more writings can be added to the Bible after the time of the New Testament. The canon is now closed.

A similar kind of consideration may be drawn from Revelation 22:18-19:

> I warn every one who hears the words of the prophecy of this book: if any one adds to them, God will add to him the plagues described in this book, and if any one takes away from the words of the book of this prophecy, God will take away his share in the tree of life and in the holy city, which are described in this book.

The primary reference of these verses is clearly to the book of Revelation itself, for John refers to his writing as "the words of the prophecy of this book" in verses 7 and 10 of this chapter (and the entire book is called a prophecy in Rev. 1:3). Furthermore, the reference to "the tree of life and . . . the holy city, which are described in this book" indicates that the book of Revelation itself is intended.

It is, however, not accidental that this statement comes at the end of the last chapter of Revelation, and that Revelation is the last book in the New Testament. In fact, Revelation has to be placed last in the canon. For many books, their placement in the assembling of the canon is of little consequence. But just as Genesis must be placed first (for it tells us of creation), so Revelation must be placed last (for its focus is to tell us of the future and God's new creation). The events described in Revelation are historically subsequent to the events described in the rest of the New Testament and require that Revelation be placed where it is. Thus, it is not inappropriate for us to understand this exceptionally strong warning at the end of Revelation as applying in a secondary way to the whole of Scripture. Placed here, where it must be placed, the warning forms an appropriate conclusion to the entire canon of Scripture. Along with Hebrews 1:1–2 and the history-of-redemption perspective implicit in those verses, this broader application of Revelation 22:18–19 also suggests to us that we should expect no more Scripture to be added beyond what we already have.

How do we know, then, that we have the right books in the canon of Scripture we now possess? The question can be answered in two different ways. First, if we are asking upon what we should base our confidence, the answer must ultimately be that our confidence is based on the faithfulness of God. We know that God loves his people, and it is supremely important that God's people have his own words, for they are our life (Deut. 32:47; Matt. 4:4). They are more precious, more important to us than anything else in this world. We also know that God our Father is in control of all history, and he is not the kind of Father who will trick us or fail to be faithful to us or keep from us something we absolutely need.

The severity of the punishments in Revelation 22:18–19 that come to those who add to or take from God's words also confirms the importance for God's people of having a correct canon. There could be no greater punishments than these, for they are the punishments of eternal judgment. This shows that God himself places supreme value on our having a correct collection of God-breathed writings, no more and no less. In the light of this fact, could it be right for us to believe that God our Father, who controls all history, would allow all of his church for almost two thousand years to be deprived of something he himself values so highly and is so necessary for our spiritual lives?[29]

The preservation and correct assembling of the canon of Scripture should ultimately be seen by believers, then, not as part of church history subsequent to God's great central acts of redemption for his people, but as an integral part of the history of redemption itself. Just as God was at work in creation, in the calling of his people Israel, in the life, death, and resurrection of Christ, and in the early work and writings of the apostles, so God was at work in the preservation and assembling together of the books of Scripture for the benefit of his people for the entire church age. Ultimately, then, we base our confidence in the correctness of our present canon on the faithfulness of God.

The question of how we know that we have the right books can, secondly, be answered in a somewhat different way. We might wish to focus on the process by which we become persuaded that the books we have now in the canon are the right ones. In this process two factors are at work: the activity of the Holy Spirit

---

[29]This is of course not to affirm the impossible notion that God providentially preserves every word in every copy of every text, no matter how careless the copyist, or that he must miraculously provide every believer with a Bible instantly. Nevertheless, this consideration of God's faithful care of his children should certainly cause us to be thankful that in God's providence there is no significantly attested textual variant that would change any point of Christian doctrine or ethics, so faithfully has the text been transmitted and preserved. However, we must say clearly that there are a number of differing words in the different ancient manuscripts of the Bible that are preserved today. These are called "textual variants." The question of textual variants within the surviving manuscripts of the books that belong in the canon is discussed in chapter 5, pp. 96–97.

convincing us as we read Scripture for ourselves, and the historical data that we
have available for our consideration.

As we read Scripture the Holy Spirit works to convince us that the books we
have in Scripture are all from God and are his words to us. It has been the
testimony of Christians throughout the ages that as they read the books of the
Bible, the words of Scripture speak to their hearts as no other books do. Day after
day, year after year, Christians find that the words of the Bible are indeed the
words of God speaking to them with an authority, a power, and a persuasiveness
that no other writings possess. Truly the Word of God is "living and active,
sharper than any two-edged sword, piercing to the division of soul and spirit, of
joints and marrow, and discerning the thoughts and intentions of the heart" (Heb.
4:12).

Yet the process by which we become persuaded that the present canon is right is
also helped by historical data. Of course, if the assembling of the canon was one
part of God's central acts in the history of redemption (as was stated above), then
Christians today should not presume to take it upon themselves to attempt to add
to or subtract from the books of the canon: the process was completed long ago.
Nevertheless, a thorough investigation of the historical circumstances surrounding
the assembling of the canon is helpful in confirming our conviction that the
decisions made by the early church were correct decisions. Some of this historical
data has been mentioned in the preceding pages. Other, more detailed data is
available for those who wish to pursue more specialized investigations.[30]

Yet one further historical fact should be mentioned. Today there exist no strong
candidates for addition to the canon and no strong objections to any book
presently in the canon. Of those writings that some in the early church wanted to
include in the canon, it is safe to say that there are none that present-day
evangelicals would want to include. Some of the very early writers distinguished
themselves quite clearly from the apostles and their writings from the writings of
the apostles. Ignatius, for example, about A.D. 110, said, "I do not order you as
did Peter and Paul; *they were apostles,* I am a convict; they were free, I am even
until now a slave" (Ignatius, *To the Romans,* 4.3; compare the attitude toward the
apostles in 1 Clement 42:1, 2; 44:1–2 [A.D. 95]; Ignatius, *To the Magnesians,* 7:1;
13:1–2; et al.).

Even those writings that were for a time thought by some to be worthy of
inclusion in the canon contain doctrinal teaching that is contradictory to the rest
of Scripture. "The Shepherd" of Hermas, for example, teaches "the necessity of
penance" and "the possibility of the forgiveness of sins at least once after
baptism. . . . The author seems to identify the Holy Spirit with the Son of God
before the Incarnation, and to hold that the Trinity came into existence only after

---

[30]A very helpful recent survey of this field is David Dunbar, "The Biblical Canon," in *Hermeneutics,
Authority, and Canon,* ed. D. A. Carson and John Woodbridge (Grand Rapids: Zondervan, 1986), pp.
295–360. In addition, three recent books are of such excellent quality that they will define the
discussion of canon for many years to come: Roger Beckwith, *The Old Testament Canon of the New
Testament Church and Its Background in Early Judaism* (London: SPCK, 1985, and Grand Rapids:
Eerdmans, 1986); Bruce Metzger, *The Canon of the New Testament: Its Origin, Development, and
Significance* (Oxford: Clarendon; New York: Oxford University Press, 1987); and F. F. Bruce, *The
Canon of Scripture* (Downers Grove, Ill.: InterVarsity Press, 1988).

the humanity of Christ had been taken up into heaven" (*Oxford Dictionary of the Christian Church*, p. 641).

The *Gospel of Thomas*, which for a time was held by some to belong to the canon, ends with the following absurd statement (par. 114):

> Simon Peter said to them: "Let Mary go away from us, for women are not worthy of life." Jesus said: "Lo, I shall lead her, so that I may make her a male, that she too may become a living spirit, resembling you males. For every woman who makes herself a male will enter the kingdom of heaven."[31]

All other existing documents that had in the early church any possibility of inclusion in the canon are similar to these in that they either contain explicit disclaimers of canonical status or include some doctrinal aberrations that clearly make them unworthy of inclusion in the Bible.[32]

On the other hand, there are no strong objections to any book currently in the canon. In the case of several New Testament books that were slow to gain approval by the whole church (books such as 2 Peter or 2 and 3 John), much of the early hesitancy over their inclusion can be attributed to the fact that they were not initially circulated very widely, and that full knowledge of the contents of all the New Testament writings spread through the church rather slowly. (Martin Luther's hesitancies concerning James are quite understandable in view of the doctrinal controversy in which he was engaged, but such hesitancy was certainly not necessary. The apparent doctrinal conflict with Paul's teaching is easily resolved once it is recognized that James is using three key terms, *justification, faith*, and *works* in senses different from those with which Paul used them.)[33]

There is therefore historical confirmation for the correctness of the current canon. Yet it must be remembered in connection with any historical investigation that the work of the early church was not to bestow divine authority or even ecclesiastical authority upon some merely human writings, but rather to recognize

---

[31]This document was not written by Thomas the apostle. Current scholarly opinion attributes it to an unknown author in the second century A.D. who used Thomas's name.

[32]It is appropriate here to say a word about the writing called the *Didache*. Although this document was not considered for inclusion in the canon during the early history of the church, many scholars have thought it to be a very early document and some today quote it as if it were an authority on the teaching of the early church on the same level as the New Testament writings. It was first discovered in 1875 at a library in Constantinople but probably dates from the first or second century A.D. Yet it contradicts or adds to the commands of the New Testament at many points. For example, Christians are told to let alms sweat in their hands until they know to whom they are giving (1.6); food offered to idols is forbidden (6.3); people are required to fast before baptism, and baptism must be done in running water (7.1–4); fasting is required on Wednesdays and Fridays but prohibited on Mondays and Thursdays (8.1); Christians are required to pray the Lord's Prayer three times a day (8.3); unbaptized persons are excluded from the Lord's Supper, and prayers unknown in the New Testament are given as a pattern for celebrating the Lord's Supper (9.1–5); apostles are prohibited from staying in a city more than two days (11.5; but note that Paul stayed a year and a half in Corinth and three years in Ephesus!); prophets who speak in the Spirit cannot be tested or examined (11.7, in contradiction to 1 Cor. 14:29 and 1 Thess. 5:20–21); salvation requires perfection at the last time (16.2). Such a document, of unknown authorship, is hardly a reliable guide for the teachings and practices of the early church.

[33]See R. V. G. Tasker, *The General Epistle of James*, TNTC (London: Tyndale Press, 1956), pp. 67–71. Although Luther placed James near the end of his German translation of the New Testament, he did not exclude it from the canon, and he cited over half of the verses in James as authoritative in various parts of his writings (see Douglas Moo, *The Letter of James*, TNTC (Leicester and Downers Grove, Ill.: InterVarsity Press, 1985), p. 18; see also pp. 100–117 on faith and works in James.

the divinely authored characteristic of writings that already had such a quality. This is because the ultimate criterion of canonicity is divine authorship, not human or ecclesiastical approval.

At this point someone may ask a hypothetical question about what we should do if another one of Paul's epistles were discovered, for example. Would we add it to Scripture? This is a difficult question, because two conflicting considerations are involved. On the one hand, if a great majority of believers were convinced that this was indeed an authentic Pauline epistle, written in the course of Paul's fulfillment of his apostolic office, then the nature of Paul's apostolic authority would guarantee that the writing would be God's very words (as well as Paul's), and that its teachings would be consistent with the rest of Scripture. But the fact that it was not preserved as part of the canon would indicate that it was not among the writings the apostles wanted the church to preserve as part of Scripture. Moreover, it must immediately be said that such a hypothetical question is just that: hypothetical. It is exceptionally difficult to imagine what kind of historical data might be discovered that could convincingly demonstrate to the church as a whole that a letter lost for over 1,900 years was genuinely authored by Paul, and it is more difficult still to understand how our sovereign God could have faithfully cared for his people for over 1,900 years and still allowed them to be continually deprived of something he intended them to have as part of his final revelation of himself in Jesus Christ. These considerations make it so highly improbable that any such manuscript would be discovered at some time in the future, that such a hypothetical question really does not merit further serious consideration.

In conclusion, are there any books in our present canon that should not be there? No. We can rest our confidence in this fact in the faithfulness of God our Father, who would not lead all his people for nearly two thousand years to trust as his Word something that is not. And we find our confidence repeatedly confirmed both by historical investigation and by the work of the Holy Spirit in enabling us to hear God's voice in a unique way as we read from every one of the sixty-six books in our present canon of Scripture.

But are there any missing books, books that should have been included in Scripture but were not? The answer must be no. In all known literature there are no candidates that even come close to Scripture when consideration is given both to their doctrinal consistency with the rest of Scripture and to the type of authority they claim for themselves (as well as the way those claims of authority have been received by other believers). Once again, God's faithfulness to his people convinces us that there is nothing missing from Scripture that God thinks we need to know for obeying him and trusting him fully. The canon of Scripture today is exactly what God wanted it to be, and it will stay that way until Christ returns.

## QUESTIONS FOR PERSONAL APPLICATION

1. Why is it important to your Christian life to know which writings are God's words and which are not? How would your relationship with God be different if you had to look for his words that were scattered among all the writings of Christians throughout church history? How would your Christian life be different if God's words were contained not only in the Bible but also in the official declarations of the church throughout history?

2. Have you had doubts or questions about the canonicity of any of the books of the Bible? What caused those questions? What should one do to resolve them?

3. Mormons, Jehovah's Witnesses, and members of other cults have claimed present-day revelations from God that they count equal to the Bible in authority. What reasons can you give to indicate the falsity of those claims? In practice, do these people treat the Bible as an authority equal to these other "revelations"?

4. If you have never read any parts of the Old Testament Apocrypha, perhaps you would want to read some sections.[34] Do you feel you can trust these writings in the same way you trust Scripture? Compare the effect these writings have on you with the effect Scripture has on you. You might want to make a similar comparison with some writings from a collection of books called the New Testament Apocrypha,[35] or perhaps with the *Book of Mormon* or the *Qur'an*. Is the spiritual effect of these writings on your life positive or negative? How does it compare with the spiritual effect the Bible has on your life?

## SPECIAL TERMS

| | |
|---|---|
| Apocrypha | covenant |
| apostle | God-breathed |
| canon | history of redemption |
| canonical | self-attesting |

## BIBLIOGRAPHY

(For an explanation of this bibliography see the note on the bibliography to chapter 1, p. 38. Complete bibliographical data may be found on pp. 1223–29.)

In the "Other Works" section of this chapter's bibliography I have included some works written from a nonevangelical perspective because of their importance for investigating the historical data relevant to the question of canon.

### Sections in Evangelical Systematic Theologies

1. Anglican (Episcopalian)
    1882–92  Litton, 10–18
    1930   Thomas, 101–15

---

[34]A good recent translation is *The Oxford Annotated Apocrypha* (RSV), ed. Bruce M. Metzger (New York: Oxford University Press, 1965). There is also a collection of nonbiblical writings from the time of the New Testament called "New Testament apocrypha" (see next note), but these are much less commonly read. When people speak of "the Apocrypha" without further specification, they are referring only to the Old Testament Apocrypha.

[35]E. Hennecke, *New Testament Apocrypha*, ed. W. Schneemelcher; English trans. ed. R. McL. Wilson (2 vols.: SCM Press, 1965). It should also be noted that some other, more orthodox literature from the early church can be found conveniently in a collection of writings referred to as the "Apostolic Fathers." A good translation is found in Kirsopp Lake, trans., *The Apostolic Fathers,* Loeb Classical Library (2 vols.: Cambridge, Mass.: Harvard University Press, 1912, 1913), but other useful translations are also available.

2. Arminian (Wesleyan or Methodist)

|        |                              |
|--------|------------------------------|
| 1875–76 | Pope, 1:193–230             |
| 1940    | Wiley, 1:185–214            |
| 1983    | Carter, 1:291–94            |

3. Baptist

|        |                              |
|--------|------------------------------|
| 1907    | Strong, 145–72; 236–40      |
| 1976–83 | Henry, 2:69–76; 4:405–75    |
| 1987–94 | Lewis/Demarest, 1:147–48    |

4. Dispensational

|        |                              |
|--------|------------------------------|
| 1947    | Chafer, 1:95–102, 124–28    |
| 1949    | Thiessen, 50–61             |
| 1986    | Ryrie, 105–9                |

5. Lutheran

|        |                              |
|--------|------------------------------|
| 1917–24 | Pieper, 1:330–48            |

6. Reformed (or Presbyterian)

|        |                              |
|--------|------------------------------|
| 1861    | Heppe, 12–21, 28–31         |
| 1871–73 | Hodge, 1:152–53             |
| 1887–1921 | Warfield, IAB, 411–18     |
| 1889    | Shedd, 1:134–47             |
| 1938    | Berkhof, Intro., 116–43     |
| 1962    | Buswell, 1:193–98           |

## Sections in Representative Roman Catholic Systematic Theologies

1. Roman Catholic: Traditional

|        |                              |
|--------|------------------------------|
| 1955    | Ott (no explicit treatment) |

2. Roman Catholic: Post-Vatican II

|        |                              |
|--------|------------------------------|
| 1980    | McBrien, 1:50–62, 201–43; 2:817–42 |

## Other Works

Beckwith, R. T. "Canon of the Old Testament." In *IBD*, 1:235–38.

Beckwith, Roger. *The Old Testament Canon of the New Testament Church and Its Background in Early Judaism*. Grand Rapids: Eerdmans, 1985.

Birdsall, J. N. "Apocrypha." In *IBD*, 1:75–77.

———. "Canon of the New Testament." In *IBD*, 1:240–45.

Bruce, F. F. *The Canon of Scripture*. Downers Grove, Ill: InterVarsity Press, 1988.

Carson, D. A., and John D. Woodbridge, eds. *Hermeneutics, Authority, and Canon*. Grand Rapids: Zondervan, 1986.

Dunbar, David G. "The Biblical Canon." In *Hermeneutics, Authority, and Canon*. Ed. by D. A. Carson and John Woodbridge. Grand Rapids: Zondervan, 1986.

Green, William Henry. *General Introduction to the Old Testament: The Canon*. New York: Scribners, 1898.

Harris, R. Laird. "Chronicles and the Canon in New Testament Times." *JETS*. Vol. 33, no. 1 (March 1990): 75–84.

————. *Inspiration and Canonicity of the Bible: An Historical and Exegetical Study*. Grand Rapids: Zondervan, 1989.

Kline, Meredith G. *The Structure of Biblical Authority*. Grand Rapids: Eerdmans, 1972.

Leiman, S. Z. *The Canonization of Hebrew Scripture: The Talmudic and Midrashic Evidence*. Hamden, Conn.: Archon, 1976.

McRay, J. R. "Bible, Canon of." In *EDT*, pp. 140–41.

Metzger, Bruce M. *The Canon of the New Testament: Its Origin, Development, and Significance*. Oxford: Clarendon; and New York: Oxford University Press, 1987.

Packer, J. I. "Scripture." *NDT*, 627–31.

Ridderbos, Herman N. *Redemptive History and the New Testament Scriptures*. Formerly, *The Authority of the New Testament Scriptures*. 2d rev. ed. Trans. by H. D. Jongste. Rev. by Richard B. Gaffin, Jr. Phillipsburg, N.J.: Presbyterian and Reformed, 1988.

Westcott, Brooke Foss. *The Bible in the Church: A Popular Account of the Collection and Reception of the Holy Scriptures in the Christian Churches*. First ed. with alterations. London: Macmillan, 1901.

Zahn, Theodor. *Geschichte des Neutestamentlichen Kanons*. 2 vols. Erlangen: Deichert, 1888–90. Reprint ed., Hildesheim and New York: Olms, 1975.

## SCRIPTURE MEMORY PASSAGE

**Hebrews 1:1–2:** *In many and various ways God spoke of old to our fathers by the prophets; but in these last days he has spoken to us by a Son, whom he appointed the heir of all things, through whom also he created the world.*

## HYMN

### "O Word of God Incarnate"

O Word of God incarnate, O wisdom from on high,
O truth unchanged, unchanging, O light of our dark sky;
We praise thee for the radiance that from the hallowed page,
A lantern to our footsteps, shines on from age to age.

The church from her dear Master received the gift divine,
And still that light she lifteth o'er all the earth to shine.
It is the golden casket, where gems of truth are stored;
It is the heav'n-drawn picture of Christ, the Living Word.

It floateth like a banner before God's host unfurled;
It shineth like a beacon above the darkling world.
It is the chart and compass that o'er life's surging sea,
'Mid mists and rocks and quicksands, still guides, O Christ, to thee.

O make thy church, dear Savior, a lamp of purest gold,
To bear before the nations thy true light, as of old.
O teach thy wand'ring pilgrims by this their path to trace,
Till, clouds and darkness ended, they see thee face to face.

AUTHOR: WILLIAM WALSHAM HOW, 1867

# Chapter 4

# The Four Characteristics of Scripture: (1) Authority

*How do we know that the Bible is God's Word?*

In the previous chapter our goal was to determine which writings belong in the Bible and which writings do not. But once we have determined what the Bible is, our next step is to ask what it is like. What does the whole Bible teach us about itself?

The major teachings of the Bible about itself can be classified into four characteristics (sometimes termed attributes): (1) the authority of Scripture; (2) the clarity of Scripture; (3) the necessity of Scripture; and (4) the sufficiency of Scripture.

With regard to the first characteristic, most Christians would agree that the Bible is our authority in some sense. But in exactly what sense does the Bible claim to be our authority? And how do we become persuaded that the claims of Scripture to be God's Word are true? These are the questions addressed in this chapter.

## EXPLANATION AND SCRIPTURAL BASIS

*The authority of Scripture means that all the words in Scripture are God's words in such a way that to disbelieve or disobey any word of Scripture is to disbelieve or disobey God.*

This definition may now be examined in its various parts.

### A. All the Words in Scripture Are God's Words

**1. This Is What the Bible Claims for Itself.** There are frequent claims in the Bible that all the words of Scripture are God's words (as well as words that were written down by men).[1] In the Old Testament, this is frequently seen in the introductory phrase, "Thus says the LORD," which appears hundreds of times. In the world of the Old Testament, this phrase would have been recognized as identical in form to the phrase, "Thus says king . . . ," which was used to preface the edict of a king to his subjects, an edict that could not be challenged or

---

[1]Of course, I do not mean to say that every word in Scripture was audibly spoken by God himself, since the Bible records the words of hundreds of different people, such as King David and Peter and even Satan himself. But I do mean that even the quotations of other people are *God's* reports of what they said, and, rightly interpreted in their contexts, come to us with God's authority.

questioned but that simply had to be obeyed.[2] Thus, when the prophets say, "Thus says the Lord," they are claiming to be messengers from the sovereign King of Israel, namely, God himself, and they are claiming that their words are the absolutely authoritative words of God. When a prophet spoke in God's name in this way, every word he spoke had to come from God, or he would be a false prophet (cf. Num. 22:38; Deut. 18:18–20; Jer. 1:9; 14:14; 23:16–22; 29:31–32; Ezek. 2:7; 13:1–16).

Furthermore, God is often said to speak "through" the prophet (1 Kings 14:18; 16:12, 34; 2 Kings 9:36; 14:25; Jer. 37:2; Zech. 7:7, 12). Thus, what the prophet says in God's name, God says (1 Kings 13:26 with v. 21; 1 Kings 21:19 with 2 Kings 9:25–26; Hag. 1:12; cf. 1 Sam. 15:3, 18). In these and other instances in the Old Testament, words that the prophets spoke can equally be referred to as words that God himself spoke. Thus, to disbelieve or disobey anything a prophet says is to disbelieve or disobey God himself (Deut. 18:19; 1 Sam. 10:8; 13:13–14; 15:3, 19, 23; 1 Kings 20:35, 36).

These verses of course do not claim that *all* the words in the Old Testament are God's words, for these verses themselves are referring only to specific sections of spoken or written words in the Old Testament. But the cumulative force of these passages, including the hundreds of passages that begin "Thus says the Lord," is to demonstrate that within the Old Testament we have written records of words that are said to be God's own words. These words when written down constitute large sections of the Old Testament.

In the New Testament, a number of passages indicate that all of the Old Testament writings are thought of as God's words. Second Timothy 3:16 says, "All Scripture is God-breathed and is useful for teaching, rebuking, correcting and training in righteousness" (NIV).[3] Here "Scripture" (*graphē*) must refer to the Old Testament written Scripture, for that is what the word *graphē* refers to in every one of its fifty-one occurrences in the New Testament.[4] Furthermore, the "sacred writings" of the Old Testament are what Paul[5] has just referred to in verse 15.

Paul here affirms that all of the Old Testament writings are *theopneustos,* "breathed out by God." Since it is *writings* that are said to be "breathed out," this breathing must be understood as a metaphor for speaking the words of Scripture. This verse thus states in brief form what was evident in many passages in the Old Testament: the Old Testament writings are regarded as God's Word in written

[2]See Wayne Grudem, *The Gift of Prophecy in 1 Corinthians* (Lanham, Md.: University Press of America, 1982), pp. 12–13; also Wayne Grudem, "Scripture's Self-Attestation," in *Scripture and Truth,* ed. D. A. Carson and J. Woodbridge, pp. 21–22.

[3]Some have suggested an alternative translation, namely, "Every God-breathed Scripture is also profitable for teaching. . . ." However, this translation is highly unlikely because it makes the *kai* ("also") extremely awkward in the Greek sentence. In coherent speech, one must say that something that has one characteristic before saying that it "also" has another characteristic. The "also" must indicate an addition to something that has previously been predicated. Thus, *theopneustos* ("God-breathed") and *ōphelimos* ("profitable") are both best understood as predicate adjectives, and the best translation is, "All Scripture is God-breathed and is profitable for teaching. . . ."

[4]In at least two cases, 1 Tim. 5:18 and 2 Peter 3:16, *graphē* also includes some of the New Testament writings along with the Old Testament writings that it is referring to (see discussion below).

[5]I assume Pauline authorship of 1 and 2 Timothy and Titus throughout this book. For recent arguments defending Pauline authorship see George W. Knight III, *The Pastoral Epistles,* NIGTC (Grand Rapids: Eerdmans, and Carlisle: Paternoster, 1992), pp. 4–54.

form. For every word of the Old Testament, God is the one who spoke (and still speaks) it, although God used human agents to write these words down.[6]

A similar indication of the character of all Old Testament writings as God's words is found in 2 Peter 1:21. Speaking of the prophecies of Scripture (v. 20), which means at least the Old Testament Scriptures to which Peter encourages his readers to give careful attention (v. 19), Peter says that none of these prophecies ever came "by the impulse of man," but that "men moved by the Holy Spirit spoke from God." It is not Peter's intention to deny completely human volition or personality in the writing of Scripture (he says that the men "spoke"), but rather to say that the ultimate source of every prophecy was never a man's decision about what he wanted to write, but rather the Holy Spirit's action in the prophet's life, carried out in ways unspecified here (or, in fact, elsewhere in Scripture). This indicates a belief that all of the Old Testament prophecies (and, in light of vv. 19– 20, this probably includes all of the written Scripture of the Old Testament) are spoken "from God": that is, they are God's own words.

Many other New Testament passages speak in similar ways about sections of the Old Testament. In Matthew 1:22, Isaiah's words in Isaiah 7:14 are cited as "what *the Lord had spoken* by the prophet." In Matthew 4:4 Jesus says to the devil, "Man shall not live by bread alone, but by *every word that proceeds from the mouth of God.*" In the context of Jesus' repeated citations from Deuteronomy to answer every temptation, the words that proceed "from the mouth of God" are the written Scriptures of the Old Testament.

In Matthew 19:5, the words of the author in Genesis 2:24, not attributed to God in the Genesis narrative, are quoted by Jesus as words that God "said." In Mark 7:9–13, the same Old Testament passage can be called interchangeably "the commandment of God," or what "Moses said," or "the word of God." In Acts 1:16, the words of Psalms 69 and 109 are said to be words which "*the Holy Spirit spoke* beforehand by the mouth of David." Words of Scripture are thus said to be spoken by the Holy Spirit. In Acts 2:16–17, in quoting "what was spoken by the prophet Joel" in Joel 2:28–32, Peter inserts "*God declares,*" thus attributing to God words written by Joel, and claiming that God is presently saying them.

Many other passages could be cited (see Luke 1:70; 24:25; John 5:45–47; Acts 3:18, 21; 4:25; 13:47; 28:25; Rom. 1:2; 3:2; 9:17; 1 Cor. 9:8–10; Heb. 1:1– 2, 6–7), but the pattern of attributing to God the words of Old Testament Scripture should be very clear. Moreover, in several places it is *all* of the words of the prophets or the words of the Old Testament Scriptures that are said to compel belief or to be from God (see Luke 24:25, 27, 44; Acts 3:18; 24:14; Rom. 15:4).

But if Paul meant only the Old Testament writings when he spoke of "Scripture" in 2 Timothy 3:16, how can this verse apply to the New Testament writings as well? Does it say anything about the character of the New Testament

---

[6]Older systematic theologies used the words *inspired* and *inspiration* to speak of the fact that the words of Scripture are spoken by God. This terminology was based especially on an older translation of 2 Tim. 3:16, which said, "All scripture is given by inspiration of God. . ." (KJV). However, the word *inspiration* has such a weak sense in ordinary usage today (every poet or songwriter claims to be "inspired" to write, and even athletes are said to give "inspired" performances) that I have not used it in this text. I have preferred the NIV rendering of 2 Tim. 3:16, "God-breathed," and have used other expressions to say that the words of Scripture are God's very words. The older phrase "*plenary* inspiration" meant that all the words of Scripture are God's words (the word *plenary* means "full"), a fact that I affirm in this chapter without using the phrase.

writings? To answer that question, we must realize that the Greek word *graphē* ("scripture") was a technical term for the New Testament writers and had a very specialized meaning. Even though it is used fifty-one times in the New Testament, every one of those instances uses it to refer to the Old Testament writings, not to any other words or writings outside the canon of Scripture. Thus, everything that belonged in the category "scripture" had the character of being "God-breathed": its words were God's very words.

But at two places in the New Testament we see New Testament writings also being called "scripture" along with the Old Testament writings. As we noted in chapter 3, in 2 Peter 3:16, Peter shows not only an awareness of the existence of written epistles from Paul, but also a clear willingness to classify "all of his [Paul's] epistles" with "the other scriptures." This is an indication that very early in the history of the church all of Paul's epistles were considered to be God's written words in the same sense as the Old Testament texts were. Similarly, in 1 Timothy 5:18, Paul quotes Jesus' words as found in Luke 10:7 and calls them "scripture."[7]

These two passages taken together indicate that during the time of the writing of the New Testament documents there was an awareness that *additions* were being made to this special category of writings called "scripture," writings that had the character of being God's very words. Thus, once we establish that a New Testament writing belongs to the special category "scripture," then we are correct in applying 2 Timothy 3:16 to that writing as well, and saying that that writing also has the characteristic Paul attributes to "all scripture": it is "God-breathed," and all its words are the very words of God.

Is there further evidence that the New Testament writers thought of their own writings (not just the Old Testament) as being words of God? In some cases, there is. In 1 Corinthians 14:37, Paul says, "If any one thinks that he is a prophet, or spiritual, he should acknowledge that *what I am writing to you is a command of the Lord.*" Paul has here instituted a number of rules for church worship at Corinth and has claimed for them the status of "commands of the Lord," for the phrase translated "what I am writing to you" contains a plural relative pronoun in Greek (*ha*) and is more literally translated "*the things* I am writing to you are a command of the Lord."

One objection to seeing the words of New Testament writers as words of God is sometimes brought from 1 Corinthians 7:12, where Paul distinguishes his words from words of the Lord: "To the rest I say, not the Lord . . ." A proper understanding of this passage is gained from verses 25 and 40, however. In verse 25 Paul says he has no command of the Lord concerning the unmarried but will give his own opinion. This must mean that he had possession of *no earthly word that Jesus had spoken on this subject* and probably also that he had received no subsequent revelation about it from Jesus. This is unlike the situation in verse 10 where he could simply repeat the content of Jesus' earthly teaching, "that the wife should not separate from her husband" and "that the husband should not divorce his wife." Thus, verse 12 must mean that Paul has *no record of any earthly teaching of Jesus* on the subject of a believer who is married to an unbelieving spouse. Therefore, Paul gives his own instructions: "To the rest *I say, not the Lord,* that if

---

[7]See chapter 3, pp. 61–62, for discussion of 2 Peter 3:16 and 1 Tim. 5:17–18.

any brother has a wife who is an unbeliever, and she consents to live with him, he should not divorce her" (1 Cor. 7:12).

It is remarkable therefore that Paul can go on in verses 12–15 to give several specific ethical standards for the Corinthians. What gave him the right to make such moral commands? He said that he spoke as one "who by the Lord's mercy is trustworthy" (1 Cor. 7:25). He seems to imply here that his considered judgments were able to be placed on the same authoritative level as the words of Jesus. Thus, 1 Corinthians 7:12, "To the rest I say, not the Lord," is an amazingly strong affirmation of Paul's own authority: if he did not have any words of Jesus to apply to a situation, he would simply use his own words, for his own words had just as much authority as the words of Jesus!

Indications of a similar view of the New Testament writings are found in John 14:26 and 16:13, where Jesus promised that the Holy Spirit would bring all that he had said to the disciples' remembrance and would guide them into all the truth. This indicates a special superintending work of the Holy Spirit whereby the disciples would be able to remember and record without error all that Jesus had said. Similar indications are also found in 2 Peter 3:2; 1 Corinthians 2:13; 1 Thessalonians 4:15; and Revelation 22:18–19.

**2. We Are Convinced of the Bible's Claims to Be God's Words as We Read the Bible.** It is one thing to affirm that the Bible *claims* to be the words of God. It is another thing to be convinced that those claims are true. Our ultimate conviction that the words of the Bible are God's words comes only when the Holy Spirit speaks *in* and *through* the words of the Bible to our hearts and gives us an inner assurance that these are the words of our Creator speaking to us. Just after Paul has explained that his apostolic speech consists of words taught by the Holy Spirit (1 Cor. 2:13), he says, "The natural man does not receive the things[8] of the Spirit of God, for they are folly to him, and he is not able to understand them because they are spiritually discerned" (1 Cor. 2:14). Apart from the work of the Spirit of God, a person will not receive spiritual truths and in particular will not receive or accept the truth that the words of Scripture are in fact the words of God.

But for those in whom God's Spirit is working there is a recognition that the words of the Bible are the words of God. This process is closely analogous to that by which those who believed in Jesus knew that his words were true. He said, "My sheep hear my voice, and I know them, and they follow me" (John 10:27). Those who are Christ's sheep hear the words of their great Shepherd as they read the words of Scripture, and they are convinced that these words are in fact the words of their Lord.

It is important to remember that this conviction that the words of Scripture are the words of God does *not* come *apart from* the words of Scripture or *in addition to* the words of Scripture. It is not as if the Holy Spirit one day whispers in our ear, "Do you see that Bible sitting on your desk? I want you to know that the words of

---

[8]I have translated the verse "things of the Spirit of God" because the Greek text has only the neuter plural definite article (*ta*) used as a substantive, and no specific noun is given. Thus, the RSV translation "the *gifts* of the Spirit of God" is more restrictive in subject matter than the actual words would justify and is certainly not required by the context.

that Bible are God's words." It is rather as people read Scripture that they hear their Creator's voice speaking to them in the words of Scripture and realize that the book they are reading is unlike any other book, that it is indeed a book of God's own words speaking to their hearts.

**3. Other Evidence Is Useful but Not Finally Convincing.** The previous section is not meant to deny the validity of other kinds of arguments that may be used to support the claim that the Bible is God's words. It is helpful for us to learn that the Bible is historically accurate, that it is internally consistent, that it contains prophecies that have been fulfilled hundreds of years later, that it has influenced the course of human history more than any other book, that it has continued changing the lives of millions of individuals throughout its history, that through it people come to find salvation, that it has a majestic beauty and a profound depth of teaching unmatched by any other book, and that it claims hundreds of times over to be God's very words. All of these arguments and others are useful to us and remove obstacles that might otherwise come in the way of our believing Scripture. But all of these arguments taken individually or together cannot finally be convincing. As the Westminster Confession of Faith said in 1643–46,

> We may be moved and induced by the testimony of the Church to an high and reverent esteem of the Holy Scripture. And the heavenliness of the matter, the efficacy of the doctrine, the majesty of the style, the consent of all the parts, the scope of the whole (which is, to give all glory to God), the full discovery it makes of the only way of man's salvation, the many other incomparable excellencies, and the entire perfection thereof, are arguments whereby it doth abundantly evidence itself to be the Word of God: yet notwithstanding, our full persuasion and assurance of the infallible truth and divine authority thereof, is from the inward work of the Holy Spirit bearing witness by and with the Word in our hearts. (chap. 1, para. 5)

**4. The Words of Scripture Are Self-Attesting.** Thus, the words of Scripture are "self-attesting." They cannot be "proved" to be God's words by appeal to any higher authority. For if an appeal to some higher authority (say, historical accuracy or logical consistency) were used to prove that the Bible is God's Word, then the Bible itself would not be our highest or absolute authority: it would be subordinate in authority to the thing to which we appealed to prove it to be God's Word. If we ultimately appeal to human reason, or to logic, or to historical accuracy, or to scientific truth, as the authority by which Scripture is shown to be God's words, then we have assumed the thing to which we appealed to be a higher authority than God's words and one that is more true or more reliable.

**5. Objection: This Is a Circular Argument.** Someone may object that to say Scripture proves itself to be God's words is to use a circular argument: we believe that Scripture is God's Word because it claims to be that. And we believe its claims because Scripture is God's Word. And we believe that it is God's Word because it claims to be that, and so forth.

It should be admitted that this is a kind of circular argument. However, that does not make its use invalid, for all arguments for an absolute authority must ultimately appeal to that authority for proof: otherwise the authority would not be an absolute or highest authority. This problem is not unique to the Christian who is arguing for the authority of the Bible. Everyone either implicitly or explicitly uses some kind of circular argument when defending his or her ultimate authority for belief.

Although these circular arguments are not always made explicit and are sometimes hidden beneath lengthy discussions or are simply assumed without proof, arguments for an ultimate authority in their most basic form take on a similar circular appeal to that authority itself, as some of the following examples show:

"My reason is my ultimate authority because it seems reasonable to me to make it so."

"Logical consistency is my ultimate authority because it is logical to make it so."

"The findings of human sensory experiences are the ultimate authority for discovering what is real and what is not, because our human senses have never discovered anything else: thus, human sense experience tells me that my principle is true."

"I know there can be no ultimate authority because I do not know of any such ultimate authority."

In all of these arguments for an ultimate standard of truth, an absolute authority for what to believe, there is an element of circularity involved.[9]

How then does a Christian, or anyone else, choose among the various claims for absolute authorities? Ultimately the truthfulness of the Bible will commend itself as being far more persuasive than other religious books (such as the *Book of Mormon* or the *Qur'an*), or than any other intellectual constructions of the human mind (such as logic, human reason, sense experience, scientific methodology, etc.). It will be more persuasive because in the actual experience of life, all of these other candidates for ultimate authority are seen to be inconsistent or to have shortcomings that disqualify them, while the Bible will be seen to be fully in accord with all that we know about the world around us, about ourselves, and about God.

The Bible will commend itself as being persuasive in this way, that is, if we are thinking rightly about the nature of reality, our perception of it and of ourselves, and our perception of God. The trouble is that because of sin our perception and analysis of God and creation is faulty. Sin is ultimately irrational, and sin makes us think incorrectly about God and about creation. Thus, in a world free from sin, the Bible would commend itself convincingly to all people as God's Word. But because sin distorts people's perception of reality, they do not recognize Scripture for what it really is. Therefore it requires the work of the Holy Spirit, overcoming the effects of sin, to enable us to be persuaded that the Bible is indeed the Word of God and that the claims it makes for itself are true.

Thus, in another sense, the argument for the Bible as God's Word and our ultimate authority is *not* a typical circular argument. The process of persuasion is

---

[9]This point has been made well by John M. Frame, "God and Biblical Language: Transcendence and Immanence," in *God's Inerrant Word*, ed. John Warwick Montgomery (Minneapolis: Bethany Fellowship, 1974), pp. 159–77. See also J. P. Moreland, "The Rationality of Belief in Inerrancy," *TrinJ* 7:1 (1986), 75–86, for a helpful discussion of the way we reach convictions about issues of major significance in our lives.

perhaps better likened to a spiral in which increasing knowledge of Scripture and increasingly correct understanding of God and creation tend to supplement one another in a harmonious way, each tending to confirm the accuracy of the other. This is not to say that our knowledge of the world around us serves as a higher authority than Scripture, but rather that such knowledge, if it is correct knowledge, continues to give greater and greater assurance and deeper conviction that the Bible is the only truly ultimate authority and that other competing claims for ultimate authority are false.

**6. This Does Not Imply Dictation From God as the Sole Means of Communication.** The entire preceding part of this chapter has argued that all the words of the Bible are God's words. At this point a word of caution is necessary. The fact that all the words of Scripture are God's words should not lead us to think that God dictated every word of Scripture to the human authors.

When we say that all the words of the Bible are God's words, we are talking about the *result* of the process of bringing Scripture into existence. To raise the question of dictation is to ask about the *process* that led to that result or the manner by which God acted in order to ensure the result that he intended.[10] It must be emphasized that the Bible does not speak of only one type of process or one manner by which God communicated to the biblical authors what he wanted to be said. In fact, there is indication of *a wide variety of processes* God used to bring about the desired result.

A few scattered instances of dictation are explicitly mentioned in Scripture. When the apostle John saw the risen Lord in a vision on the island of Patmos, Jesus spoke to him as follows: "To the angel of the church in Ephesus *write* . . ." (Rev. 2:1); "And to the angel of the church in Smyrna *write* . . ." (Rev. 2:8); "And to the angel of the church in Pergamum *write* . . ." (Rev. 2:12). These are examples of dictation pure and simple. The risen Lord tells John what to write, and John writes the words he hears from Jesus.

Something akin to this process is probably also seen occasionally in the Old Testament prophets. We read in Isaiah, "Then the word of the Lord came to Isaiah: 'Go and say to Hezekiah, Thus says the Lord, the God of David your father: I have heard your prayer, I have seen your tears; behold, I will add fifteen years to your life. I will deliver you and this city out of the hand of the king of Assyria, and defend this city'" (Isa. 38:4–6). The picture given us in this narrative is that Isaiah heard (whether with his physical ear or with a very forceful impression made upon his mind is difficult to say) the words God wanted him to say to Hezekiah, and Isaiah, acting as God's messenger, then took those words and *spoke* them as he had been instructed.

But in many other sections of Scripture such direct dictation from God is certainly not the manner by which the words of Scripture were caused to come into being. The author of Hebrews says that God spoke to our fathers by the prophets "in many and various ways" (Heb. 1:1). On the opposite end of the

---

[10]In some systematic theologies, this process by which God used human authors to write his very words is called "the mode of inspiration." I have not used this terminology in this book, since it does not seem to be a readily understandable phrase today.

spectrum from dictation we have, for instance, Luke's ordinary historical research for writing his gospel. He says:

> Inasmuch as many have undertaken to compile a narrative of the things which have been accomplished among us, just as they were delivered to us by those who from the beginning were eyewitnesses and ministers of the word, it seemed good to me also, having followed all things closely for some time past, to write an orderly account for you, most excellent Theophilus. . . ." (Luke 1:1-3)

This is clearly not a process of dictation. Luke used ordinary processes of speaking to eyewitnesses and gathering historical data in order that he might write an accurate account of the life and teachings of Jesus. He did his historical research thoroughly, listening to the reports of many eyewitnesses and evaluating his evidence carefully. The gospel he wrote emphasizes what he thought important to emphasize and reflects his own characteristic style of writing.

In between these two extremes of dictation pure and simple on the one hand, and ordinary historical research on the other hand, we have many indications of various ways by which God communicated with the human authors of Scripture. In some cases Scripture gives us hints of these various processes: it speaks of dreams, of visions, of hearing the Lord's voice or standing in the council of the Lord; it also speaks of men who were with Jesus and observed his life and listened to his teaching, men whose memory of these words and deeds was made completely accurate by the working of the Holy Spirit as he brought things to their remembrance (John 14:26). Yet in many other cases the manner used by God to bring about the result that the words of Scripture were his words is simply not disclosed to us. Apparently many different methods were used, but it is not important that we discover precisely what these were in each case.

In cases where the ordinary human personality and writing style of the author were prominently involved, as seems the case with the major part of Scripture, all that we are able to say is that God's providential oversight and direction of the life of each author was such that their personalities, their backgrounds and training, their abilities to evaluate events in the world around them, their access to historical data, their judgment with regard to the accuracy of information, and their individual circumstances when they wrote,[11] were all exactly what God wanted them to be, so that when they actually came to the point of putting pen to paper, the words were fully their own words but also fully the words that God wanted them to write, words that God would also claim as his own.

### B. Therefore to Disbelieve or Disobey Any Word of Scripture Is to Disbelieve or Disobey God

The preceding section has argued that all the words in Scripture are God's words. Consequently, to disbelieve or disobey any word of Scripture is to disbelieve or disobey God himself. Thus, Jesus can rebuke his disciples for not believing the Old Testament Scriptures (Luke 24:25). Believers are to keep or obey the disciples' words (John 15:20: "If they kept my word, they will keep yours also"). Christians are encouraged to remember "the commandment of the

---

[11]This would also include even the influence of a secretary (technically called an amanuensis) on the wording of a book: see the greeting from Tertius in Rom. 16:22.

Lord and Savior through your apostles" (2 Peter 3:2). To disobey Paul's writings was to make oneself liable to church discipline, such as excommunication (2 Thess. 3:14) and spiritual punishment (2 Cor. 13:2–3), including punishment from God (this is the apparent sense of the passive verb "he is not recognized" in 1 Cor. 14:38). By contrast, God delights in everyone who "trembles" at his word (Isa. 66:2).

Throughout the history of the church the greatest preachers have been those who have recognized that they have no authority in themselves and have seen their task as being to explain the words of Scripture and apply them clearly to the lives of their hearers. Their preaching has drawn its power not from the proclamation of their own Christian experiences or the experiences of others, nor from their own opinions, creative ideas, or rhetorical skills, but from God's powerful words.[12] Essentially they stood in the pulpit, pointed to the biblical text, and said in effect to the congregation, "This is what this verse means. Do you see that meaning here as well? Then you must believe it and obey it with all your heart, for God himself, your Creator and your Lord, is saying this to you today!" Only the written words of Scripture can give this kind of authority to preaching.

## C. The Truthfulness of Scripture

**1. God Cannot Lie or Speak Falsely.** The essence of the authority of Scripture is its ability to compel us to believe and to obey it and to make such belief and obedience equivalent to believing and obeying God himself. Because this is so, it is needful to consider the truthfulness of Scripture, since to believe all the words of Scripture implies confidence in the complete truthfulness of the Scripture that we believe. Although this issue will be dealt with more fully when we consider the inerrancy of Scripture (see chapter 5), a brief treatment is given here.

Since the biblical writers repeatedly affirm that the words of the Bible, though human, are God's own words, it is appropriate to look at biblical texts that talk about *the character of God's words* and to apply these to the character of the words of Scripture. Specifically, there are a number of biblical passages that talk about the truthfulness of God's speech. Titus 1:2 speaks of "God, who never lies," or (more literally translated), "the unlying God." Because God is a God who cannot speak a "lie," his words can always be trusted. Since all of Scripture is spoken by God, all of Scripture must be "unlying," just as God himself is: there can be no untruthfulness in Scripture.[13]

Hebrews 6:18 mentions two unchangeable things (God's oath and his promise) "in which *it is impossible for God to lie* (author's translation)." Here the author says not merely that God does not lie, but that it is not possible for him to lie.

---

[12]I am not denying that good speaking ability or creativity or telling of personal experiences have a place in preaching, for good preaching will include all of these (see Prov. 16:21, 23). I am saying that the power to change lives must come from the Word itself, and it will be evident to the hearers when a preacher really believes this.

[13]Some scholars object that it is "too simplistic" to argue as follows: "The Bible is God's words. God never lies. Therefore the Bible never lies." Yet it is precisely that kind of argument that Paul uses in Titus 1:2. He refers to the promises of eternal life made "ages ago" in Scripture and says the promises were made by God "who never lies." He thus calls on the truthfulness of God's own speech to prove the truthfulness of the words of Scripture. A "simple" argument this may be, but it is scriptural, and it is true. We should therefore not hesitate to accept it and use it.

Although the immediate reference is only to oaths and promises, if it is impossible for God to lie in these utterances, then certainly it is impossible for him ever to lie (for Jesus harshly rebukes those who tell the truth only when under oath: Matt. 5:33–37; 23:16–22). Similarly, David says to God, "You are God, and *your words are true*" (2 Sam. 7:28).

**2. Therefore All the Words in Scripture Are Completely True and Without Error in Any Part.** Since the words of the Bible are God's words, and since God cannot lie or speak falsely, it is correct to conclude that there is no untruthfulness or error in any part of the words of Scripture. We find this affirmed several places in the Bible. "The words of the LORD are *words that are pure,* silver refined in a furnace on the ground, purified seven times" (Ps. 12:6, author's translation). Here the psalmist uses vivid imagery to speak of the undiluted purity of God's words: there is no imperfection in them. Also in Proverbs 30:5, we read, "*Every word of God proves true;* he is a shield to those who take refuge in him." It is not just some of the words of Scripture that are true, but every word. In fact, God's Word is fixed in heaven for all eternity: "For ever, O LORD, *your word is firmly fixed in the heavens*" (Ps. 119:89). Jesus can speak of the eternal nature of his own words: "Heaven and earth will pass away, but my words will not pass away" (Matt. 24:35). God's speech is placed in marked contrast to all human speech, for "God is not man, that he should lie, or a son of man, that he should repent" (Num. 23:19). These verses affirm explicitly what was implicit in the requirement that we believe all of the words of Scripture, namely, that there is no untruthfulness or falsehood affirmed in any of the statements of the Bible.

**3. God's Words Are the Ultimate Standard of Truth.** In John 17 Jesus prays to the Father, "Sanctify them in the truth; *your word is truth*" (John 17:17). This verse is interesting because Jesus does not use the adjectives *alēthinos* or *alēthēs* ("true"), which we might have expected, to say, "Your word is true." Rather, he uses a noun, *alētheia* ("truth"), to say that God's Word is not simply "true," but it is truth itself.

The difference is significant, for this statement encourages us to think of the Bible not simply as being "true" in the sense that it conforms to some higher standard of truth, but rather to think of the Bible as being itself the final standard of truth. The Bible is God's Word, and God's Word is the ultimate definition of what is true and what is not true: God's Word is itself *truth.* Thus we are to think of the Bible as the ultimate standard of truth, the reference point by which every other claim to truthfulness is to be measured. Those assertions that conform with Scripture are "true" while those that do not conform with Scripture are not true.

What then is truth? Truth is what God says, and we have what God says (accurately but not exhaustively) in the Bible.

**4. Might Some New Fact Ever Contradict the Bible?** Will any new scientific or historical fact ever be discovered that will contradict the Bible? Here we can say with confidence that this will never happen—it is in fact impossible. If any supposed "fact" is ever discovered that is said to contradict Scripture, then (if we have understood Scripture rightly) that "fact" must be false, because God, the author of Scripture, knows all true facts (past, present, and future). No fact will ever turn up that God did not know about ages ago and take into account when he caused Scripture to be written. Every true fact is something that God has known already from all eternity and is something that therefore cannot contradict God's speech in Scripture.

Nevertheless, it must be remembered that scientific or historical study (as well as other kinds of study of creation) can cause us to reexamine Scripture to see if it really teaches what we thought it taught. The Bible certainly does not teach that the earth was created in the year 4004 B.C., as some once thought (for the genealogical lists in Scripture have gaps in them).[14] Yet it was in part historical, archaeological, astronomical, and geological study that caused Christians to reexamine Scripture to see if it really taught such a recent origin for the earth. Careful analysis of the biblical text showed that it did not teach this.

Similarly, the Bible does not teach that the sun goes around the earth, for it only uses descriptions of phenomena as we see them from our vantage point and does not purport to be describing the workings of the universe from some arbitrary "fixed" point somewhere out in space. Yet until the study of astronomy advanced enough to demonstrate the rotation of the earth on its axis, people *assumed* that the Bible taught that the sun goes around the earth. Then the study of scientific data prompted a reexamination of the appropriate biblical texts. Thus, whenever confronted with some "fact" that is said to contradict Scripture, we must not only examine the data adduced to demonstrate the fact in question; we must also reexamine the appropriate biblical texts to see if the Bible really teaches what we thought it to teach.

We should never fear but always welcome any new facts that may be discovered in any legitimate area of human research or study. For example, discoveries by archaeologists working in Syria have brought to light the Ebla Tablets. These extensive written records from the period around 2000 B.C. will eventually throw great light on our understanding of the world of the patriarchs and the events connected with the lives of Abraham, Isaac, and Jacob. Should Christians entertain any lingering apprehension that the publication of such data will prove some fact in Genesis to be incorrect? Certainly not! We should eagerly anticipate the publication of all such data with the absolute confidence that if it is correctly understood it will all be consistent with Scripture and will all confirm the accuracy of Scripture. No true fact will ever contradict the words of the God who knows all facts and who never lies.

## D. Written Scripture Is Our Final Authority

It is important to realize that the final form in which Scripture remains authoritative is its *written* form. It was the words of God *written* on the tablets of stone that Moses deposited in the ark of the covenant. Later, God commanded Moses and subsequent prophets to write their words in a book. And it was *written* Scripture (*graphē*) that Paul said was "God-breathed" (2 Tim. 3:16). Similarly, it

---

[14]See chapter 15, pp. 289–309, for discussion of the age of the earth, and pp. 290–91 for discussion of gaps in the genealogies.

is Paul's *writings* that are "a command of the Lord" (1 Cor. 14:37) and that could be classified with "the other scriptures" (2 Peter 3:16).

This is important because people sometimes (intentionally or unintentionally) attempt to substitute some other final standard than the written words of Scripture. For example, people will sometimes refer to "what Jesus really said" and claim that when we translate the Greek words of the Gospels back into the Aramaic language Jesus spoke, we can gain a better understanding of Jesus' words than was given by the writers of the Gospels. In fact, it is sometimes said that this work of reconstructing Jesus' words in Aramaic enables us to correct the erroneous translations made by the gospel authors.

In other cases, people have claimed to know "what Paul really thought" even when that is different from the meaning of the words he wrote. Or they have spoken of "what Paul should have said if he had been consistent with the rest of his theology." Similarly, others have spoken of "the church situation to which Matthew was writing" and have attempted to give normative force either to that situation or to the solution they think Matthew was attempting to bring about in that situation.

In all of these instances we must admit that asking about the words or situations that lie "behind" the text of Scripture may at times be helpful to us in understanding what the text means. Nevertheless, our hypothetical reconstructions of these words or situations can never replace or compete with Scripture itself as the final authority, nor should we ever allow them to contradict or call into question the accuracy of any of the words of Scripture. We must continually remember that we have in the Bible God's very words, and we must not try to "improve" on them in some way, for this cannot be done. Rather, we should seek to understand them and then trust them and obey them with our whole heart.

## QUESTIONS FOR PERSONAL APPLICATION

1. If you want to persuade someone that the Bible is God's Word, what do you want that person to read more than any other piece of literature?

2. Who would try to make people want to disbelieve something in Scripture? To disobey something in Scripture? Is there anything in the Bible that you do not want to believe? To obey? If your answers to either of the preceding two questions were positive, what is the best way to approach and to deal with the desires you have in this area?

3. Do you know of any proven fact in all of history that has shown something in the Bible to be false? Can the same be said about other religious writings such as the *Book of Mormon* or the *Qur'an*? If you have read in other books such as these, can you describe the spiritual effect they had on you? Compare that with the spiritual effect that reading the Bible has on you. Can you say that when you read the Bible you hear the voice of your Creator speaking to you in a way that is true of no other book?

4. Do you ever find yourself believing something not because you have external evidence for it but simply because it is written in Scripture? Is that proper faith, according to Hebrews 11:1? If you do believe things simply because Scripture says them, what do you think Christ will say to you about this habit when you stand before his judgment seat? Do you think that trusting and obeying everything that Scripture affirms will ever lead you into sin or away from God's blessing in your life?

## SPECIAL TERMS

| | |
|---|---|
| absolute authority | inspiration |
| authority | plenary inspiration |
| circular argument | Scripture |
| dictation | self-attesting |
| God-breathed | |

## BIBLIOGRAPHY

(For an explanation of this bibliography see the note on the bibliography to chapter 1, p. 38. Complete bibliographical data may be found on pp. 1223–29.)

### Sections in Evangelical Systematic Theologies

1. Anglican (Episcopalian)
    1882–92    Litton, 18–40
    1930    Thomas, 115–20, 123–33, 141–45
2. Arminian (Wesleyan or Methodist)
    1875–76    Pope, 1:92–99, 156–92
    1892–94    Miley, 2:481–89
    1940    Wiley, 1:166–84
    1960    Purkiser, 60–80
    1983    Carter, 1:287–330
3. Baptist
    1767    Gill, 1:15–37
    1907    Strong, 111–242
    1917    Mullins, 142–44, 150–53
    1976–83    Henry, 2:247–334; 3:28–47, 203–488; 4:7–271, 470–93
    1983–85    Erickson, 175–259
    1987–94    Lewis/Demarest, 1:93–171
4. Dispensational
    1947    Chafer, 1:21–104, 120–23
    1949    Thiessen, 43–49, 62–74
    1986    Ryrie, 20–22, 63–76
5. Lutheran
    1917–24    Pieper, 1:193–317, 349–59

```
          1934      Mueller, 90–136
6. Reformed (or Presbyterian)
          1559      Calvin, 1:7–8, 74–93
          1861      Heppe, 21–28
       1871–73      Hodge, 1:153–82
    1887–1921       Warfield, IAB, 3–410, 419–42; SSW, 2:537–638
          1889      Shedd, 1:70–110; 3:27–88
       1937–66      Murray, CW, 3:256–62; CW, 4:30–57
          1938      Berkhof, Intro., 144–65, 182–86
          1962      Buswell, 1:183–93, 198–213
7. Renewal (or charismatic/Pentecostal)
       1988–92      Williams, 1:22–25
```

**Sections in Representative Roman Catholic Systematic Theologies**

```
1. Roman Catholic: Traditional
          1955      Ott (no explicit treatment)
2. Roman Catholic: Post-Vatican II
          1980      McBrien, 1:62–77, 201–44
```

**Other Works**

Carson, D. A., and John Woodbridge, eds. *Hermeneutics, Authority, and Canon.* Grand Rapids: Zondervan, 1986.

———. *Scripture and Truth.* Grand Rapids: Zondervan, 1983.

Geisler, Norman L., ed. *Inerrancy.* Grand Rapids: Zondervan, 1980.

Grudem, Wayne A. *The Gift of Prophecy in 1 Corinthians.* Washington, D.C.: University Press of America, 1982, pp. 1–54.

Helm, Paul. *The Divine Revelation: The Basic Issues.* Westchester, Ill.: Crossway, 1982.

Henry, Carl F. H. "Bible, Inspiration of." In *EDT,* pp. 145–49.

Kuyper, Abraham. *Principles of Sacred Theology.* Trans. by J. H. de Vries. Repr. ed.: Grand Rapids: Eerdmans, 1968, pp. 413–563 (first published as *Encyclopedia of Sacred Theology* in 1898).

Montgomery, John W., ed. *God's Inerrant Word.* Minneapolis: Bethany Fellowship, 1974.

Nash, Ronald H. *The Word of God and the Mind of Man.* Grand Rapids: Zondervan, 1982.

Packer, J. I. *"Fundamentalism" and the Word of God.* London: Inter-Varsity Press, 1958.

———. "Infallibility and Inerrancy of the Bible." In *NDT,* pp. 337–39.

———. "Scripture." In *NDT,* pp. 627–31.

Pinnock, Clark. *Biblical Revelation.* Chicago: Moody, 1971.

Radmacher, Earl D., and Robert D. Preus, eds. *Hermeneutics, Inerrancy, and the Bible.* Grand Rapids: Zondervan, 1984.

Van Til, Cornelius. *In Defense of the Faith,* vol. 1: *The Doctrine of Scripture.* Ripon, Calif.: den Dulk Christian Foundation, 1967.

————. *In Defense of the Faith,* vol. 5: *An Introduction to Systematic Theology.* Phillipsburg, N.J.: Presbyterian and Reformed, 1976, pp. 110–58.

Warfield, B. B. *Limited Inspiration.* Philadelphia: Presbyterian and Reformed, 1962.

Wells, Paul. *James Barr and the Bible: Critique of a New Liberalism.* Phillipsburg, N.J.: Presbyterian and Reformed, 1980.

Wenham, John W. *Christ and the Bible.* London: Tyndale Press, 1972.

Woodbridge, John. *Biblical Authority: A Critique of the Rogers/McKim Proposal.* Grand Rapids: Zondervan, 1982.

Westminster Seminary Faculty. *The Infallible Word.* 3d ed. Philadelphia: Presbyterian and Reformed, 1967.

Young, Edward J. *Thy Word Is Truth.* Grand Rapids: Eerdmans, 1957.

## Works From a Noninerrancy Perspective

Baillie, John. *The Idea of Revelation in Recent Thought.* New York: Columbia University Press, 1956.

Barr, James. *Fundamentalism.* London: SCM, 1977.

Beegle, Dewey M. *Scripture, Tradition, and Infallibility.* Grand Rapids: Eerdmans, 1973.

Berkouwer, G. C. *Holy Scripture.* Trans. by Jack B. Rogers. Grand Rapids: Eerdmans, 1975.

Burtchaell, James Tunstead. *Catholic Theories of Biblical Inspiration Since 1810: A Review and Critique.* Cambridge: University Press, 1969.

Davis, Stephen T. *The Debate About the Bible.* Philadelphia: Westminster, 1977.

McKim, Donald K., ed. *The Authoritative Word: Essays on the Nature of Scripture.* Grand Rapids: Eerdmans, 1983.

Pinnock, Clark. *The Scripture Principle.* San Francisco: Harper and Row, 1984.

Rogers, Jack, ed. *Biblical Authority.* Waco, Tex.: Word, 1977.

Rogers, Jack, and Donald K. McKim. *The Authority and Interpretation of the Bible: An Historical Approach.* San Francisco: Harper and Row: 1979.

Vawter, Bruce. *Biblical Inspiration.* Philadelphia: Westminster, 1972 (a recent Roman Catholic work).

## SCRIPTURE MEMORY PASSAGE

**2 Timothy 3:16:** *All scripture is inspired by God and profitable for teaching, for reproof, for correction, and for training in righteousness.*

# HYMN

## "Standing on the Promises"

This hymn speaks of the promises of God's Word as the eternally firm and unchanging foundation on which we can rest our faith. In the midst of doubt and fear these promises "cannot fail." By standing firm on them we will be able to sing "Glory in the highest!" for all eternity. Yet the hymn speaks not merely of the promises of God's Word, but of all the contents of Scripture: the Bible is "the living Word of God" by which we "prevail" in the midst of adversity (v. 2), and it is the "Spirit's sword" by which we may be "overcoming daily" (v. 3). There is no other sure foundation on which to rest our faith than on the very words and promises of God. "I am standing on the promises of God!" is the joyful exclamation of a heart filled with faith, and it shall be our song throughout eternity.

Standing on the promises of Christ my King,
Through eternal ages let his praises ring!
Glory in the highest I will shout and sing
Standing on the promises of God!

*Chorus:*
Standing, standing, standing on the promises of God my Savior;
Standing, standing, I'm standing on the promises of God.

Standing on the promises that cannot fail
When the howling storms of doubt and fear assail;
By the living Word of God I shall prevail
Standing on the promises of God!

Standing on the promises of Christ the Lord,
Bound to him eternally by love's strong cord,
Overcoming daily with the Spirit's sword
Standing on the promises of God!

Standing on the promises I cannot fall,
List'ning every moment to the Spirit's call,
Resting in my Savior as my all in all
Standing on the promises of God!

AUTHOR: R. KELSO CARTER, 1886

# Chapter 5

# The Inerrancy of Scripture
*Are there any errors in the Bible?*

Most books on systematic theology have not included a separate chapter on the inerrancy of the Bible. The subject has usually been dealt with under the heading of the authority of Scripture, and no further treatment has been considered necessary. However, this issue of inerrancy is of such concern in the evangelical world today that it warrants a separate chapter following our treatment of the authority of the Word of God.

## EXPLANATION AND SCRIPTURAL BASIS

### A. The Meaning of Inerrancy

We will not at this point repeat the arguments concerning the authority of Scripture that were given in chapter 4. There it was argued that all the words in the Bible are God's words, and that therefore to disbelieve or disobey any word in Scripture is to disbelieve or disobey God. It was argued further that the Bible clearly teaches that God cannot lie or speak falsely (2 Sam. 7:28; Titus 1:2; Heb. 6:18). Therefore, all the words in Scripture are claimed to be completely true and without error in any part (Num. 23:19; Pss. 12:6; 119:89, 96; Prov. 30:5; Matt. 24:35). God's words are, in fact, the ultimate standard of truth (John 17:17).

Especially relevant at this point are those Scripture texts that indicate the total truthfulness and reliability of God's words. *"The promises of the LORD are promises that are pure,* silver refined in a furnace on the ground, purified seven times" (Ps. 12:6), indicates the flawlessness or absolute reliability and purity of Scripture. Similarly, *"Every word of God proves true;* he is a shield to those who take refuge in him" (Prov. 30:5), indicates the truthfulness of every word that God has spoken. Though error and at least partial falsehood may characterize the speech of every human being, it is the characteristic of God's speech even when spoken through sinful human beings that it is never false and that it never affirms error: "God is not man, that he should lie, or a son of man, that he should repent" (Num. 23:19) was spoken by sinful Balaam specifically about the prophetic words that God had spoken through his own lips.

With evidence such as this we are now in a position to define biblical inerrancy: *The inerrancy of Scripture means that Scripture in the original manuscripts does not affirm anything that is contrary to fact.*

This definition focuses on the question of truthfulness and falsehood in the language of Scripture. The definition in simple terms just means that *the Bible always tells the truth,* and that it always tells the truth *concerning everything it talks about.* This definition does not mean that the Bible tells us every fact there is to know about any one subject, but it affirms that what it does say about any subject is *true.*

It is important to realize at the outset of this discussion that the focus of this controversy is on the question of truthfulness in speech. It must be recognized that absolute truthfulness in speech is consistent with some other types of statements, such as the following:

**1. The Bible Can Be Inerrant and Still Speak in the Ordinary Language of Everyday Speech.** This is especially true in "scientific" or "historical" descriptions of facts or events. The Bible can speak of the sun rising and the rain falling because from the perspective of the speaker this is exactly what happens. From the standpoint of an observer standing on the sun (were that possible) or on some hypothetical "fixed" point in space, the earth rotates and brings the sun into view, and rain does not fall downward but upward or sideways or whatever direction necessary for it to be drawn by gravity toward the surface of the earth. But such explanations are hopelessly pedantic and would make ordinary communication impossible. From the standpoint of the speaker, the sun *does* rise and the rain *does* fall, and these are perfectly true descriptions of the natural phenomena the speaker observes.

A similar consideration applies to numbers when used in measuring or in counting. A reporter can say that 8,000 men were killed in a certain battle without thereby implying that he has counted everyone and that there are not 7,999 or 8,001 dead soldiers. If roughly 8,000 died, it would of course be false to say that 16,000 died, but it would not be false in most contexts for a reporter to say that 8,000 men died when in fact 7,823 or 8,242 had died: the limits of truthfulness would depend on the degree of precision implied by the speaker and expected by his original hearers.

This is also true for measurements. Whether I say, "I don't live far from my office," or "I live a little over a mile from my office," or "I live one mile from my office," or "I live 1.287 miles from my office," all four statements are still approximations to some degree of accuracy. Further degrees of accuracy might be obtained with more precise scientific instruments, but these would still be approximations to a certain degree of accuracy. Thus, measurements also, in order to be true, should conform to the degree of precision implied by the speaker and expected by the hearers in the original context. It should not trouble us, then, to affirm both that the Bible is absolutely truthful in everything it says and that it uses ordinary language to describe natural phenomena or to give approximations or round numbers when those are appropriate in the context.

We should also note that language can make vague or imprecise statements without being untrue. "I live a little over a mile from my office" is a vague and imprecise statement, but it is also inerrant: there is nothing untrue about it. It does not affirm anything that is contrary to fact. In a similar way, biblical statements can be imprecise and still be totally true. Inerrancy has to do with *truthfulness*, not with the degree of precision with which events are reported.

**2. The Bible Can Be Inerrant and Still Include Loose or Free Quotations.** The method by which one person quotes the words of another person is a procedure that in large part varies from culture to culture. In contemporary American and British culture we are used to quoting a person's exact words when we enclose the statement in quotation marks (this is called direct quotation). But when we use indirect quotation (with no quotation marks) we only expect an accurate report of the substance of a statement. Consider this sentence: "Elliot said that he would return home for supper right away." The sentence does not quote Elliot directly, but it is an acceptable and truthful report of Elliot's actual statement to his father, "I will come to the house to eat in two minutes," even though the indirect quotation included none of the speaker's original words.

Written Greek at the time of the New Testament had no quotation marks or equivalent kinds of punctuation, and an accurate citation of another person needed to include only a correct representation of the *content* of what the person said (rather like our indirect quotations): it was not expected to cite each word exactly. Thus, inerrancy is consistent with loose or free quotations of the Old Testament or of the words of Jesus, for example, so long as the *content* is not false to what was originally stated. The original writer did not ordinarily imply that he was using the exact words of the speaker and only those, nor did the original hearers expect verbatim quotation in such reporting.

**3. It Is Consistent With Inerrancy to Have Unusual or Uncommon Grammatical Constructions in the Bible.** Some of the language of Scripture is elegant and stylistically excellent. Other scriptural writings contain the rough-hewn language of ordinary people. At times this includes a failure to follow the commonly accepted "rules" of grammatical expression (such as the use of a plural verb where grammatical rules would require a singular verb, or the use of a feminine adjective where a masculine one would be expected, or different spelling for a word than the one commonly used, etc.). These stylistically or grammatically irregular statements (which are especially found in the book of Revelation) should not trouble us, for they do not affect the truthfulness of the statements under consideration: a statement can be ungrammatical but still be entirely true. For example, an uneducated backwoodsman in some rural area may be the most trusted man in the county even though his grammar is poor, because he has earned a reputation for never telling a lie. Similarly, there are a few statements in Scripture (in the original languages) that are ungrammatical (according to current standards of proper grammar at that time) but still inerrant because they are completely true. The issue is *truthfulness* in speech.

## B. Some Current Challenges to Inerrancy

In this section we examine the major objections that are commonly made against the concept of inerrancy.

**1. The Bible Is Only Authoritative for "Faith and Practice."** One of the most frequent objections is raised by those who say that the purpose of Scripture is to teach us in areas that concern "faith and practice" only; that is, in areas that directly relate to our religious faith or to our ethical conduct. This position would allow for the possibility of false statements in Scripture, for example, in *other* areas such as in minor historical details or scientific facts—these areas, it is said, do not concern the purpose of the Bible, which is to instruct us in what we should believe and how we are to live.[1] Its advocates often prefer to say that the Bible is *"infallible,"* but they hesitate to use the word *inerrant.*[2]

The response to this objection can be stated as follows: the Bible repeatedly affirms that all of Scripture is profitable for us (2 Tim. 3:16) and that *all* of it is "God-breathed." Thus it is completely pure (Ps. 12:6), perfect (Ps. 119:96), and true (Prov. 30:5). The Bible itself does not make any restriction on the kinds of subjects to which it speaks truthfully.

The New Testament contains further affirmations of the reliability of all parts of Scripture: in Acts 24:14, Paul says that he worships God, *"believing everything* laid down by the law or written in the prophets." In Luke 24:25, Jesus says that the disciples are "foolish men" because they are "slow of heart to believe all that the prophets have spoken." In Romans 15:4, Paul says that *"whatever* was written" in the Old Testament was "written for our instruction." These texts give no indication that there is any part of Scripture that is not to be trusted or relied on completely. Similarly, in 1 Corinthians 10:11, Paul can refer even to minor historical details in the Old Testament (sitting down to eat and drink, rising up to dance) and can say both that they *"happened"* (thus implying historical reliability) and "were written down for our instruction."

If we begin to examine the way in which the New Testament authors trust the smallest historical details of the Old Testament narrative, we see no intention to separate out matters of "faith and practice," or to say that this is somehow a recognizable category of affirmations, or to imply that statements not in that category need not be trusted or thought to be inerrant. Rather, it seems that the New Testament authors are willing to cite and affirm as true *every detail* of the Old Testament.

In the following list are some examples of these historical details cited by New Testament authors. If all of these are matters of "faith and practice," then *every* historical detail of the Old Testament is a matter of "faith and practice," and this objection ceases to be an objection to inerrancy. On the other hand, if so many details can be affirmed, then it seems that all of the historical details in the Old Testament can be affirmed as true, and we should not speak of restricting the necessary truthfulness of Scripture to some category of "faith and practice" that would exclude certain minor details. There are no types of details left that could not be affirmed as true.

---

[1] A good defense of this position can be found in a collection of essays edited by Jack Rogers, *Biblical Authority* (Waco, Tex.: Word, 1977); and, more extensively, in Jack B. Rogers and Donald McKim, *The Authority and Interpretation of the Bible: An Historical Approach* (San Francisco: Harper and Row, 1979).

[2] Until about 1960 or 1965 the word *infallible* was used interchangeably with the word *inerrant.* But in recent years, at least in the United States, the word *infallible* has been used in a weaker sense to mean that the Bible will not lead us astray in matters of faith and practice.

The New Testament gives us the following data: David ate the bread of the Presence (Matt. 12:3–4); Jonah was in the whale (Matt. 12:40); the men of Nineveh repented (Matt. 12:41); the queen of the South came to hear Solomon (Matt. 12:42); Elijah was sent to the widow of Zarephath (Luke 4:25–26); Naaman the Syrian was cleansed of leprosy (Luke 4:27); on the day Lot left Sodom fire and brimstone rained from heaven (Luke 17:29; cf. v. 32 with its reference to Lot's wife who turned to salt); Moses lifted up the serpent in the wilderness (John 3:14); Jacob gave a field to Joseph (John 4:5); many details of the history of Israel occurred (Acts 13:17–23); Abraham believed and received the promise before he was circumcised (Rom. 4:10); Abraham was about one hundred years old (Rom. 4:19); God told Rebekah before her children were born that the elder child would serve the younger (Rom. 9:10–12); Elijah spoke with God (Rom. 11:2–4); the people of Israel passed through the sea, ate and drank spiritual food and drink, desired evil, sat down to drink, rose up to dance, indulged in immorality, grumbled, and were destroyed (1 Cor. 10:11); Abraham gave a tenth of everything to Melchizedek (Heb. 7:1–2); the Old Testament tabernacle had a specific and detailed design (Heb. 9:1–5); Moses sprinkled the people and the tabernacle vessels with blood and water, using scarlet wool and hyssop (Heb. 9:19–21); the world was created by the Word of God (Heb. 11:3);[3] many details of the lives of Abel, Enoch, Noah, Abraham, Moses, Rahab, and others actually happened (Heb. 11, passim); Esau sold his birthright for a single meal and later sought it back with tears (Heb. 12:16–17); Rahab received the spies and sent them out another way (James 2:25); eight persons were saved in the ark (1 Peter 3:20; 2 Peter 2:5); God turned Sodom and Gomorrah to ashes but saved Lot (2 Peter 2:6–7); Balaam's donkey spoke (2 Peter 2:16).

This list indicates that the New Testament writers were willing to rely on the truthfulness of any part of the historical narratives of the Old Testament. No detail was too insignificant to be used for the instruction of New Testament Christians. There is no indication that they thought of a certain category of scriptural statements that were unreliable and untrustworthy (such as "historical and scientific" statements as opposed to doctrinal and moral passages). It seems clear that the Bible itself does not support any restriction on the kinds of subjects to which it speaks with absolute authority and truth; indeed, many passages in Scripture actually exclude the validity of this kind of restriction.

A second response to those who limit the necessary truthfulness of Scripture to matters of "faith and practice" is to note that this position mistakes the *major* purpose of Scripture for the *total* purpose of Scripture. To say that the major purpose of Scripture is to teach us in matters of "faith and practice" is to make a useful and correct summary of God's purpose in giving us the Bible. But as a *summary* it includes only the most prominent purpose of God in giving us Scripture. It is not, however, legitimate to use this summary to deny that it is *part* of the purpose of Scripture to tell us about minor historical details or about some aspects of astronomy or geography, and so forth. A summary cannot properly be

---

[3]This is not a minor detail, but it is useful as an example of a "scientific" fact that is affirmed in the Old Testament and one about which the author says that we have knowledge "by faith"; thus, faith here is explicitly said to involve trust in the truthfulness of a scientific and historical fact recorded in the Old Testament.

used to deny one of the things it is summarizing! To use it this way would simply show that the summary is not detailed enough to specify the items in question.

It is better to say that the *whole purpose* of Scripture is to say everything it does say, on whatever subject. Every one of God's words in Scripture was deemed by him to be important for us. Thus, God issues severe warnings to anyone who would take away even one word from what he has said to us (Deut. 4:2; 12:32; Rev. 22:18–19): we cannot add to God's words or take from them, for all are part of his larger purpose in speaking to us. Everything stated in Scripture is there because God intended it to be there: God does not say anything unintentionally! Thus, this first objection to inerrancy makes a wrong use of a summary and thereby incorrectly attempts to impose artificial limits on the kinds of things about which God can speak to us.

**2. The Term *Inerrancy* Is a Poor Term.** People who make this second objection say that the term *inerrancy* is too precise and that in ordinary usage it denotes a kind of absolute scientific precision that we do not want to claim for Scripture. Furthermore, those who make this objection note that the term *inerrancy* is not used in the Bible itself. Therefore, it is probably an inappropriate term for us to insist upon.

The response to this objection may be stated as follows: first, the scholars who have used the term *inerrancy* have defined it clearly for over a hundred years, and they have always allowed for the "limitations" that attach to speech in ordinary language. In no case has the term been used to denote a kind of absolute scientific precision by any responsible representative of the inerrancy position. Therefore those who raise this objection to the term are not giving careful enough attention to the way in which it has been used in theological discussions for more than a century.

Second, it must be noted that we often use nonbiblical terms to summarize a biblical teaching. The word *Trinity* does not occur in Scripture, nor does the word *incarnation*. Yet both of these terms are very helpful because they allow us to summarize in one word a true biblical concept, and they are therefore helpful in enabling us to discuss a biblical teaching more easily.

It should also be noted that no other single word has been proposed which says as clearly what we want to affirm when we wish to talk about total truthfulness in language. The word *inerrancy* does this quite well, and there seems no reason not to continue to use it for that purpose.

Finally, in the church today we seem to be unable to carry on the discussion around this topic without the use of this term. People may object to this term if they wish, but, like it or not, this is the term about which the discussion has focused and almost certainly will continue to focus in the next several decades. When the International Council on Biblical Inerrancy (ICBI) in 1977 began a ten-year campaign to promote and defend the idea of biblical inerrancy, it became inevitable that this word would be the one about which discussion would proceed. The "Chicago Statement on Biblical Inerrancy," which was drafted and published in 1978 under ICBI sponsorship (see appendix 1), defined what most evangelicals mean by inerrancy, perhaps not perfectly, but quite well, and further objections to such a widely used and well-defined term seem to be unnecessary and unhelpful for the church.

**3. We Have No Inerrant Manuscripts; Therefore, Talk About an Inerrant Bible Is Misleading.** Those who make this objection point to the fact that inerrancy has always been claimed for the first or *original copies of the biblical documents*.[4] Yet none of these survive: we have only copies of copies of what Moses or Paul or Peter wrote. What is the use, then, of placing so great importance on a doctrine that applies only to manuscripts that no one has?

In reply to this objection, it may first be stated that for over 99 percent of the words of the Bible, we *know* what the original manuscript said. Even for many of the verses where there are textual variants (that is, different words in different ancient copies of the same verse), the correct decision is often quite clear, and there are really very few places where the textual variant is both difficult to evaluate and significant in determining the meaning. In the small percentage of cases where there is significant uncertainty about what the original text said, the general sense of the sentence is usually quite clear from the context. (One does not have to be a Hebrew or Greek scholar to know where these variants are, because all modern English translations indicate them in marginal notes with words such as "some ancient manuscripts read . . ." or "other ancient authorities add. . . .")

This is not to say that the study of textual variants is unimportant, but it is to say that the study of textual variants has not left us in confusion about what the original manuscripts said.[5] It has rather brought us extremely close to the content of those original manuscripts. For most practical purposes, then, the *current published scholarly texts* of the Hebrew Old Testament and Greek New Testament *are the same as the original manuscripts*. Thus, when we say that the original manuscripts were inerrant, we are also implying that over 99 percent of the words in our present manuscripts are also inerrant, for they are exact copies of the originals. Furthermore, we *know* where the uncertain readings are (for where there are no textual variants we have no reason to expect faulty copying of the original).[6] Thus, our present manuscripts are for most purposes the same as the original manuscripts, and the doctrine of inerrancy therefore directly concerns our present manuscripts as well.

Furthermore, it is extremely important to affirm the inerrancy of the original documents, for the subsequent copies were made by men with no claim or guarantee by God that these copies would be perfect. But the original manuscripts

---

[4]In theological terms, these original copies are called the "autographs," using the prefix *auto-*, meaning "self," and the root *graph*, meaning "writing," to refer to a copy written by the author himself.

[5]An excellent survey of the work of studying textual variants in the extant manuscripts of the New Testament is Bruce M. Metzger, *The Text of the New Testament: Its Transmission, Corruption, and Restoration*, 2d ed. (Oxford: Clarendon Press, 1968).

[6]Of course the theoretical possibility exists that there was a copying error in the very first copy made of one of Paul's epistles, for instance, and that this error has been reproduced in all remaining copies. But this must be thought unlikely because (1) it would require that only one copy was made of the original, or that only one copy was the basis for all other extant copies, and (2) our earlier argument about the faithfulness of God in preserving the canon (see chapter 3, p. 65) would seem to imply that if such a mistake did occur, it would not be one that would materially affect our understanding of Scripture. The existence of such a copying error cannot be either proven or disproven, but further speculation about it apart from hard evidence does not appear to be profitable.

are those to which the claims to be God's very words apply. Thus, if we have mistakes in the copies (as we do), then these are only the *mistakes of men*. But if we have mistakes in the *original manuscripts*, then we are forced to say not only that men made mistakes, but that *God himself* made a mistake and spoke falsely. This we cannot do.

**4. The Biblical Writers "Accommodated" Their Messages in Minor Details to the False Ideas Current in Their Day, and Affirmed or Taught Those Ideas in an Incidental Way.** This objection to inerrancy is slightly different from the one that would restrict the inerrancy of Scripture to matters of faith and practice, but it is related to it. Those who hold this position argue that it would have been very difficult for the biblical writers to communicate with the people of their time if they had tried to correct all the false historical and scientific information believed by their contemporaries. Those who hold this position would not argue that the points where the Bible affirms false information are numerous, or even that these places are the main points of any particular section of Scripture. Rather, they would say that when the biblical writers were attempting to make a larger point, they sometimes incidentally affirmed some falsehood believed by the people of their time.[7]

To this objection to inerrancy it can be replied, first, that God is Lord of human language who can use human language to communicate perfectly without having to affirm any false ideas that may have been held by people during the time of the writing of Scripture. This objection to inerrancy essentially denies God's effective lordship over human language.

Second, we must respond that such "accommodation" by God to our misunderstandings would imply that God had acted contrary to his character as an "unlying God" (Num. 23:19; Titus 1:2; Heb. 6:18). It is not helpful to divert attention from this difficulty by repeated emphasis on the gracious condescension of God to speak on our level. Yes, God does condescend to speak our language, the language of human beings. But no passage of Scripture teaches that he "condescends" so as to act contrary to his moral character. He is never said to be able to condescend so as to affirm—even incidentally—something that is false. If God were to "accommodate" himself in this way, he would cease to be the "unlying God." He would cease to be the God the Bible represents him to be. Such activity would not in any way show God's greatness, for God does not manifest his greatness by acting in a way that contradicts his character. This objection thus at root misunderstands the purity and unity of God as they affect all of his words and deeds.

Furthermore, such a process of accommodation, if it actually had occurred, would create a serious moral problem for us. We are to be imitators of God's moral character (Lev. 11:44; Luke 6:36; Eph. 5:1; 1 Peter 5:1, et al.). Paul says, since in our new natures we are becoming more like God (Eph. 4:24), we should "put away falsehood" and "speak the truth" with one another (v. 25). We are to imitate God's truthfulness in our speech. However, if the accommodation theory is correct, then God *intentionally* made incidental affirmations of falsehood in

[7]An explanation of this view can be found in Daniel P. Fuller, "Benjamin B. Warfield's View of Faith and History," *BETS* 11 (1968): 75–83.

order to enhance communication. Therefore, would it not also be right for us intentionally to make incidental affirmations of falsehood whenever it would enhance communication? Yet this would be tantamount to saying that a minor falsehood told for a good purpose (a "white lie") is not wrong. Such a position, contradicted by the Scripture passages cited above concerning God's total truthfulness in speech, cannot be held to be valid.

**5. Inerrancy Overemphasizes the Divine Aspect of Scripture and Neglects the Human Aspect.** This more general objection is made by those who claim that people who advocate inerrancy so emphasize the divine aspect of Scripture that they downplay its human aspect.

It is agreed that Scripture has both a human and a divine aspect, and that we must give adequate attention to both. However, those who make this objection almost invariably go on to insist that the truly "human" aspects of Scripture *must* include the presence of some errors in Scripture. We can respond that though the Bible is fully human in that it was written by human beings using their own language, the activity of God in overseeing the writing of Scripture and causing it to be also his words means that it is different from much other human writing in precisely this aspect: it does not include error. That is exactly the point made even by sinful, greedy, disobedient Balaam in Numbers 23:19: God's speech through sinful human beings is different from the ordinary speech of men because "God is not man that he should lie." Moreover, it is simply not true that all human speech and writing contains error, for we make dozens of statements each day that are completely true. For example: "My name is Wayne Grudem." "I have three children." "I ate breakfast this morning."

**6. There Are Some Clear Errors in the Bible.** This final objection, that there are clear errors in the Bible, is either stated or implied by most of those who deny inerrancy, and for many of them the conviction that there are some actual errors in Scripture is a major factor in persuading them to challenge the doctrine of inerrancy.

In every case, the first answer that should be made to this objection is to ask where such errors are. In which specific verse or verses do these errors occur? It is surprising how frequently one finds that this objection is made by people who have little or no idea where the specific errors are, but who believe there are errors because others have told them so.

In other cases, however, people will mention one or more specific passages where, they claim, there is a false statement in Scripture. In these cases, it is important that we look at the biblical text itself, and look at it very closely. If we believe that the Bible is indeed inerrant, we should be eager and certainly not afraid to inspect these texts in minute detail. In fact, our expectation will be that close inspection will show there to be no error at all. Once again it is surprising how often it turns out that a careful reading just of the English text of the passage in question will bring to light one or more possible solutions to the difficulty.

In a few passages, no solution to the difficulty may be immediately apparent from reading the English text. At that point it is helpful to consult some commentaries on the text. Both Augustine (A.D. 354–430) and John Calvin

(1509–64), along with many more recent commentators, have taken time to deal with most of the alleged "problem texts" and to suggest plausible solutions to them. Furthermore some writers have made collections of all the most difficult texts and have provided suggested answers for them.[8]

There are a few texts where a knowledge of Hebrew or Greek may be necessary to find a solution, and those who do not have firsthand access to these languages may have to find answers either from a more technical commentary or by asking someone who does have this training. Of course, our understanding of Scripture is never perfect, and this means that there may be cases where we will be unable to find a solution to a difficult passage at the present time. This may be because the linguistic, historical, or contextual evidence we need to understand the passage correctly is presently unknown to us. This should not trouble us in a small number of passages so long as the overall pattern of our investigation of these passages has shown that there is, in fact, no error where one has been alleged.[9]

But while we must allow the *possibility* of being unable to solve a particular problem, it should also be stated that there are many evangelical Bible scholars today who will say that they do not presently know of any problem texts for which there is no satisfactory solution. It is possible, of course, that some such texts could be called to their attention in the future, but during the past fifteen years or so of controversy over biblical inerrancy, no such "unsolved" text has been brought to their attention.[10]

Finally, a historical perspective on this question is helpful. There are no really "new" problems in Scripture. The Bible in its entirety is over 1,900 years old, and the alleged "problem texts" have been there all along. Yet throughout the history of the church there has been a firm belief in the inerrancy of Scripture in the sense in which it is defined in this chapter. Moreover, for these hundreds of years highly competent biblical scholars have read and studied those problem texts and still have found no difficulty in holding to inerrancy. This should give us confidence that the solutions to these problems are available and that belief in inerrancy is entirely consistent with a lifetime of detailed attention to the text of Scripture.[11]

## C. Problems With Denying Inerrancy

The problems that come with a denial of biblical inerrancy are not insignificant, and when we understand the magnitude of these problems it gives us further

---

[8]The interested reader may consult, for example, Gleason L. Archer, *Encyclopedia of Bible Difficulties* (Grand Rapids: Zondervan, 1982); William Arndt, *Does the Bible Contradict Itself?* (St. Louis: Concordia, 1955); idem., *Bible Difficulties* (St. Louis: Concordia, 1932); and John W. Haley, *Alleged Discrepancies of the Bible* (1874; reprinted Grand Rapids: Baker, 1977). Almost all of the difficult texts have also received helpful analysis in the extensive notes to *The NIV Study Bible*, ed. Kenneth Barker et al. (Grand Rapids: Zondervan, 1985).

[9]J. P. Moreland, "The Rationality of Belief in Inerrancy," in *TrinJ* 7:1 (1986): 75–86, argues convincingly that Christians should not abandon the doctrine of inerrancy simply because of a small number of "problem texts" for which they presently have no clear solution.

[10]The present writer, for example, has during the last twenty years examined dozens of these "problem texts" that have been brought to his attention in the context of the inerrancy debate. In every one of those cases, upon close inspection of the text a plausible solution has become evident.

[11]On the history of inerrancy in the church, see the essays by Philip Hughes, Geoffrey W. Bromiley, W. Robert Godfrey, and John D. Woodbridge and Randall H. Balmer in *Scripture and Truth*. See also the more extensive study by John D. Woodbridge, *Biblical Authority: A Critique of the Rogers and McKim Proposal* (Grand Rapids: Zondervan, 1982).

encouragement not only to affirm inerrancy but also to affirm its importance for the church. Some of the more serious problems are listed here.

**1. If We Deny Inerrancy, a Serious Moral Problem Confronts Us: May We Imitate God and Intentionally Lie in Small Matters Also?** This is similar to the point made in response to objection #4, above, but here it applies not only to those who espouse objection #4 but also more broadly to all who deny inerrancy. Ephesians 5:1 tells us to be imitators of God. But a denial of inerrancy that still claims that the words of Scripture are God-breathed words necessarily implies that God intentionally spoke falsely to us in some of the less central affirmations of Scripture. But if this is right for God to do, how can it be wrong for us? Such a line of reasoning would, if we believed it, exert strong pressure on us to begin to speak untruthfully in situations where that might seem to help us communicate better, and so forth. This position would be a slippery slope with ever-increasing negative results in our own lives.

**2. If Inerrancy Is Denied, We Begin to Wonder If We Can Really Trust God in Anything He Says.** Once we become convinced that God has spoken falsely to us in some minor matters in Scripture, then we realize that God is *capable* of speaking falsely to us. This will have a detrimental effect on our ability to take God at his word and trust him completely or obey him fully in the rest of Scripture. We will begin to disobey initially those sections of Scripture that we least wish to obey, and to distrust initially those sections that we are least inclined to trust. But such a procedure will eventually increase, to the great detriment of our spiritual lives. Of course, such a decline in trust and obedience to Scripture may not necessarily follow in the life of every individual who denies inerrancy, but this will certainly be the general pattern, and it will be the pattern exhibited over the course of a generation that is taught to deny inerrancy.

**3. If We Deny Inerrancy, We Essentially Make Our Own Human Minds a Higher Standard of Truth Than God's Word Itself.** We use our minds to pass judgment on some sections of God's Word and pronounce them to be in error. But this is in effect to say that we know truth more certainly and more accurately than God's Word does (or than God does), at least in these areas. Such a procedure, making our own minds to be a higher standard of truth than God's Word, is the root of all intellectual sin.[12]

**4. If We Deny Inerrancy, Then We Must Also Say That the Bible Is Wrong Not Only in Minor Details but in Some of Its Doctrines as Well.** A denial of inerrancy means that we say that the Bible's teaching about the *nature of Scripture* and about the *truthfulness and reliability of God's words* is also false. These are not minor details but are major doctrinal concerns in Scripture.[13]

---

[12]See chapter 4, p. 83, for a discussion of the Bible as our absolute standard of truth.

[13]Although the undesirable positions listed above are logically related to a denial of inerrancy, a word of caution is in order: Not all who deny inerrancy will also adopt the undesirable conclusions just listed. Some people (probably inconsistently) will deny inerrancy but not take these next logical steps. In debates over inerrancy, as in other theological discussions, it is important that we criticize people on

## QUESTIONS FOR PERSONAL APPLICATION

1. Why do you think the debate about inerrancy has become such a large issue in this century? Why do people on both sides of the question think it to be important?

2. If you thought there were some small errors affirmed by Scripture, how do you think that would affect the way you read Scripture? Would it affect your concern for truthfulness in everyday conversation?

3. Do you know of any Scripture texts that seem to contain errors? What are they? Have you tried to resolve the difficulties in those texts? If you have not found a solution to some text, what further steps might you try?

4. As Christians go through life learning to know their Bibles better and growing in Christian maturity, do they tend to trust the Bible more or less? In heaven, do you think you will believe the Bible is inerrant? If so, will you believe it more firmly or less firmly than you do now?

5. If you are convinced that the Bible teaches the doctrine of inerrancy, how do you feel about it? Are you glad that such a teaching is there, or do you feel it to be something of a burden which you would rather not have to defend?

6. Does belief in inerrancy guarantee sound doctrine and a sound Christian life? How can Jehovah's Witnesses say that the Bible is inerrant while they themselves have so many false teachings?

7. If you agree with inerrancy, do you think belief in inerrancy should be a requirement for church membership? For teaching a Sunday school class? For holding a church office such as elder or deacon? For being ordained as a pastor? For teaching at a theological seminary? Why or why not?

8. When there is a doctrinal controversy in the church, what are the personal dangers facing those whose position is more consistent with Scripture? In particular, how could pride in correct doctrine become a problem? What is the solution? Do you think inerrancy is an important issue for the future of the church? Why or why not? How do you think it will be resolved?

## SPECIAL TERMS

| | |
|---|---|
| autograph | inerrant |
| faith and practice | infallible |
| ICBI | textual variant |

## BIBLIOGRAPHY

(For an explanation of this bibliography see the note on the bibliography to chapter 1, p. 38. Complete bibliographical data may be found on pp. 1223–29.)

---

the basis of views they actually hold, and distinguish those views clearly from positions we think they would hold if they were consistent with their stated views.

### Sections in Evangelical Systematic Theologies

(In this section, when referring to some significant older works that do not include a specific discussion of inerrancy, I have listed instead the pages where they discuss biblical authority generally. In those cases the pages here duplicate the listings for chapter 4 on the authority of Scripture.)

1. Anglican (Episcopalian)
   - 1882–92      Litton, 18–40
   - 1930         Thomas, 500–501
2. Arminian (Wesleyan or Methodist)
   - 1875–76      Pope, 1:36–192
   - 1892–94      Miley, 2:41–49
   - 1940         Wiley, 1:166–84
   - 1960         Purkiser, 66–80
3. Baptist
   - 1767         Gill, 11–18
   - 1907         Strong, 222–42
   - 1917         Mullins, 142–44, 150–53
   - 1976–83      Henry, 3:248–487; 4:129–255, 353–404
   - 1983–85      Erickson, 221–40
   - 1987–94      Lewis/Demarest, 1:93–171
4. Dispensational
   - 1947         Chafer, 1:63–88
   - 1949         Thiessen, 105–15
   - 1986         Ryrie, 77–104
5. Lutheran
   - 1917–24      Pieper, 1:232–65, 338–49
   - 1934         Mueller, 101–37
6. Reformed (or Presbyterian)
   - 1559         Calvin, 1:74–92
   - 1871–73      Hodge, 1:163–82
   - 1878         Dabney, DET, 1:282–313, 466–81
   - 1887–1921    Warfield, IAB, passim
   - 1889         Shedd, 1:93–110
   - 1937–66      Murray, CW, 1:9–15; CW, 4:22–29
   - 1938         Berkhof, Intro, 144–65, 182–86
7. Renewal (or charismatic/Pentecostal)
   - 1988–92      Williams, 1:36–43

### Sections in Representative Roman Catholic Systematic Theologies

1. Roman Catholic: Traditional

        1955    Ott (no explicit treatment)
    2. Roman Catholic: Post-Vatican II

        1980    McBrien, 1:64

## Other Works

(See also the bibliography for chapter 4, "Authority," much of which is also relevant here, but only part of which has been listed again.)

Archer, Gleason. *Encyclopedia of Bible Difficulties*. Grand Rapids: Zondervan, 1982.

Arndt, W. *Bible Difficulties*. St. Louis: Concordia, 1932.

————. *Does the Bible Contradict Itself?* St. Louis: Concordia, 1955.

Boice, James, ed. *The Foundation of Biblical Authority*. Grand Rapids: Zondervan, 1978.

Carson, D. A., and John Woodbridge, eds. *Hermeneutics, Authority, and Canon*. Grand Rapids: Zondervan, 1986.

————. *Scripture and Truth*. Grand Rapids: Zondervan, 1983.

Feinberg, Paul. "Bible, Inerrancy and Infallibility of." In *EDT*, pp. 141–45.

Geisler, Norman, ed. *Biblical Errancy: An Analysis of Its Philosophical Roots*. Grand Rapids: Zondervan, 1981.

————. ed. *Inerrancy*. Grand Rapids: Zondervan, 1979 (papers from the October 1978 Chicago Conference of the ICBI).

Haley, John W. *Alleged Discrepancies of the Bible*. Repr. ed. Grand Rapids: Baker, 1977 (first published 1874).

Lindsell, Harold. *The Battle for the Bible*. Grand Rapids: Zondervan, 1976.

————. *The Bible in the Balance*. Grand Rapids: Zondervan, 1979.

Montgomery, John W., ed. *God's Inerrant Word*. Minneapolis: Bethany Fellowship, 1974.

Packer, J. I. "Scripture." In *NDT*, pp. 627–31.

————. "Infallibility and Inerrancy of the Bible." In *NDT*, 337–39.

Schaeffer, Francis. *No Final Conflict: The Bible Without Error in All That It Affirms*. Downers Grove, Ill.: InterVarsity Press, 1975.

Warfield, B. B. *Limited Inspiration*. Philadelphia: Presbyterian and Reformed, 1962.

Woodbridge, John. *Biblical Authority: A Critique of the Rogers/McKim Proposal*. Grand Rapids: Zondervan, 1982.

Young, Edward J. *Thy Word Is Truth*. Grand Rapids: Eerdmans, 1957.

## Works From a Noninerrancy Perspective
### (See also the bibliography for chapter 4.)

Barr, James. *Fundamentalism*. London: SCM, 1977.

Beegle, Dewey M. *Scripture, Tradition, and Infallibility*. Grand Rapids: Eerdmans, 1973.

Davis, Stephen T. *The Debate About the Bible*. Philadelphia: Westminster, 1977.

McKim, Donald K., ed. *The Authoritative Word: Essays on the Nature of Scripture*. Grand Rapids: Eerdmans, 1983.

Rogers, Jack, ed. *Biblical Authority*. Waco, Tex.: Word, 1977.

Rogers, Jack B., and Donald K. McKim. *The Authority and Interpretation of the Bible: An Historical Approach*. San Francisco: Harper and Row, 1979.

## SCRIPTURE MEMORY PASSAGE

**Psalm 12:6:** *The promises [literally, "words"] of the LORD are promises ["words"] that are pure, silver refined in a furnace on the ground, purified seven times.*

## HYMN

### "The Law of the Lord is Perfect"

This modern setting of Psalm 19:7–11 expresses the perfection of God's Word in several different ways and shows various aspects of its application to our lives.

The law of the Lord is perfect,
    converting the soul.
The testimony of the Lord is sure,
    making wise the simple.

Refrain:
More to be desired are they than gold,
    yea than much fine gold.
Sweeter also than honey
    and the honeycomb.

The statutes of the Lord are right,
    rejoicing the heart.
The commandments of the Lord are pure,
    enlight'ning the eyes.

The fear of the Lord is clean,
    enduring forever.
The judgments of the Lord are true,
    and righteous altogether.

AUTHOR: ANONYMOUS (FROM PS. 19:7–11)

# Chapter 6

# The Four Characteristics of Scripture: (2) Clarity

*Can only Bible scholars understand the Bible rightly?*

## EXPLANATION AND SCRIPTURAL BASIS

Anyone who has begun to read the Bible seriously will realize that some parts can be understood very easily while other parts seem puzzling. In fact, very early in the history of the church Peter reminded his readers that some parts of Paul's epistles were difficult to understand: "So also our beloved brother Paul wrote to you according to the wisdom given him, speaking of this as he does in all his letters. There are some things in them *hard to understand,* which the ignorant and unstable twist to their own destruction, as they do the other scriptures" (2 Peter 3:15–16). We must admit therefore that not all parts of Scripture are able to be understood easily.

But it would be a mistake to think that most of Scripture or Scripture in general is difficult to understand. In fact, the Old Testament and New Testament frequently affirm that Scripture is written in such a way that its teachings are able to be understood by ordinary believers. Even in Peter's statement just quoted, the context is an appeal to the teachings of Paul's letter, which Peter's readers had read and understood (2 Peter 3:15). In fact, Peter assigns some moral blame to those who twist these passages "to their own destruction." And he does not say that there are things impossible to understand, but only difficult to understand.

## A. The Bible Frequently Affirms Its Own Clarity

The Bible's clarity and the responsibility of believers generally to read it and understand it are often emphasized. In a very familiar passage, Moses tells the people of Israel:

> And these words which I command you this day shall be upon your heart; and *you shall teach them diligently to your children,* and shall *talk of them* when you sit in your house, and when you walk by the way, and when you lie down, and when you rise. (Deut. 6:6–7)

All the people of Israel were expected to be able to understand the words of Scripture well enough to be able to "teach them diligently" to their children. This teaching would not have consisted merely of rote memorization devoid of understanding, for the people of Israel were to *discuss* the words of Scripture during their activities of sitting in the house or walking or going to bed or getting up in the morning. God expected that *all* of his people would know and be able to talk about his Word, with proper application to ordinary situations in life. Similarly, Psalm 1 tells us that the "blessed man," whom all the righteous in Israel were to emulate, was one who meditated on God's law "day and night" (Ps. 1:2). This daily meditation assumes an ability to understand Scripture rightly on the part of those who meditate.

The character of Scripture is said to be such that even the "simple" can understand it rightly and be made wise by it. "The testimony of the LORD is sure, *making wise the simple*" (Ps. 19:7). Again we read, "The unfolding of your words gives light; *it imparts understanding to the simple*" (Ps. 119:130). Here the "simple" person (Heb. *peti*) is not merely one who lacks intellectual ability, but one who lacks sound judgment, who is prone to making mistakes, and who is easily led astray.[1] God's Word is so understandable, so clear, that even this kind of person is made wise by it. This should be a great encouragement to all believers: no believer should think himself or herself too foolish to read Scripture and understand it sufficiently to be made wise by it.

There is a similar emphasis in the New Testament. Jesus himself, in his teachings, his conversations, and his disputes, never responds to any questions with a hint of blaming the Old Testament Scriptures for being unclear. Even while speaking to first-century people who were removed from David by 1,000 years, from Moses by about 1,500 years, and from Abraham by about 2,000 years, Jesus still assumes that such people are able to read and rightly to understand the Old Testament Scriptures.

In a day when it is common for people to tell us how hard it is to interpret Scripture rightly, we would do well to remember that not once in the Gospels do we ever hear Jesus saying anything like this: "I see how your problem arose—the Scriptures are not very clear on that subject." Instead, whether he is speaking to scholars or untrained common people, his responses always assume that the blame for misunderstanding any teaching of Scripture is not to be placed on the Scriptures themselves, but on those who misunderstand or fail to accept what is written. Again and again he answers questions with statements like, "Have you not read . . ." (Matt. 12:3, 5; 19:14; 22:31), "Have you never read in the scriptures . . ." (Matt. 21:42), or even, "You are wrong because you know neither the Scriptures nor the power of God" (Matt. 22:29; cf. Matt. 9:13; 12:7; 15:3; 21:13; John 3:10; et al.).

Similarly, most of the New Testament epistles are written not to church leaders but to entire congregations. Paul writes, "To the church of God which is at Corinth" (1 Cor. 1:2), "To the churches of Galatia" (Gal. 1:2), "To all the saints in Christ Jesus who are at Philippi, with the bishops and deacons" (Phil. 1:1), and so forth. Paul *assumes* that his hearers will *understand* what he writes, and he encourages the sharing of his letters with other churches: "And when this letter has been read among you, have it read also in the church of the Laodiceans; and see that you read also the letter from Laodicea" (Col. 4:16; cf. John 20:30–31;

---

[1]Compare the use of this same word in Prov. 1:4; 7:7; 8:5; 9:6; 14:15, 18; 22:3; 27:12.

2 Cor. 1:13; Eph. 3:4; 1 Tim. 4:13; James 1:1, 22–25; 1 Peter 1:1; 2:2; 2 Peter 1:19; 1 John 5:13).[2]

Second Peter 1:20 may be urged against the view of the clarity of Scripture explained in this chapter. The verse says, "no prophecy of scripture is a matter of one's own interpretation," and someone may claim that this means that ordinary believers are unable to interpret Scripture rightly for themselves. It is unlikely, however, that this implication should be drawn from 2 Peter 1:20, for the verse is probably discussing the *origin* and not the interpretation of Scripture. Thus the NIV translates it, "no prophecy of Scripture *came about by* the prophet's own interpretation."[3] Furthermore, even if the verse were understood as speaking of interpreting Scripture, it would be saying that the interpretation of Scripture must be done within the fellowship of believers and not merely as a personal activity. It still would not be implying that authoritative interpreters are needed to ascertain the true meaning of Scripture, but simply that reading and understanding Scripture should not be carried out entirely in isolation from other Christians.

Lest we think that understanding the Bible was somehow easier for first-century Christians than for us, it is important to realize that in many instances the New Testament epistles were written to churches that had large proportions of Gentile Christians. They were relatively new Christians who had no previous background in any kind of Christian society, and who had little or no prior understanding of the history and culture of Israel. Nevertheless, the New Testament authors show no hesitancy in expecting even these Gentile Christians to be able to read a translation of the Old Testament in their own language and to understand it rightly (cf. Rom. 4:1–25; 15:4; 1 Cor. 10:1–11; 2 Tim. 3:16–17; et al.).

## B. The Moral and Spiritual Qualities Needed for Right Understanding

The New Testament writers frequently state that the ability to understand Scripture rightly is more a moral and spiritual than intellectual ability: "The unspiritual man does not receive the gifts (literally "things") of the Spirit of God, for they are folly to him, and he is not able to understand them because they are spiritually discerned" (1 Cor. 2:14; cf. 1:18–3:4; 2 Cor. 3:14–16; 4:3–4, 6; Heb. 5:14; James 1:5–6; 2 Peter 3:5; cf. Mark 4:11–12; John 7:17; 8:43). Thus, although the New Testament authors affirm that the Bible *in itself* is written clearly, they also affirm that it will not be understood rightly by those who are unwilling to receive its teachings. Scripture is able to be understood by all unbelievers who will read it sincerely seeking salvation, and by all believers who will read it while seeking God's help in understanding it. This is because in both cases the Holy Spirit is at work overcoming the effects of sin, which otherwise will

---

[2]Paul tells the Corinthians, "We write you nothing but what you can read and understand," and then he adds, "I hope you will understand fully, as you have understood in part" (2 Cor. 1:13–14). The addition to his first statement does not negate his affirmation of the clarity of what he has written to them, but does encourage the Corinthians to be diligent in listening carefully to Paul's words, in order that their partial understanding may be deepened and enriched. Indeed, the very expression of such a hope shows that Paul assumes his writings are able to be understood (*elpizō*, "I hope," in the New Testament expresses a much more confident expectation of a future event than does the English word *hope*).

[3]This interpretation is well defended by Michael Green, *The Second Epistle of Peter and the Epistle of Jude*, TNTC (Grand Rapids: Eerdmans, 1987), pp. 100–102.

make the truth appear to be foolish (1 Cor. 2:14; 1:18–25; James 1:5–6, 22–25).

## C. Definition of the Clarity of Scripture

In order to summarize this biblical material, we can affirm that the Bible is written in such a way that all things necessary for our salvation and for our Christian life and growth are very clearly set forth in Scripture. Although theologians have sometimes defined the clarity of Scripture more narrowly (by saying, for example, only that Scripture is clear in teaching the way of salvation), the many texts cited above apply to many different aspects of biblical teaching and do not seem to support any such limitation on the areas to which Scripture can be said to speak clearly. It seems more faithful to those biblical texts to define the clarity[4] of Scripture as follows: *The clarity of Scripture means that the Bible is written in such a way that its teachings are able to be understood by all who will read it seeking God's help and being willing to follow it.* Once we have stated this, however, we must also recognize that many people, even God's people, do in fact misunderstand Scripture.

## D. Why Do People Misunderstand Scripture?

During Jesus' lifetime, his own disciples at times failed to understand the Old Testament and Jesus' own teachings (see Matt. 15:16; Mark 4:10–13; 6:52; 8:14–21; 9:32; Luke 18:34; John 8:27; 10:6). Although sometimes this was due to the fact that they simply needed to wait for further events in the history of redemption, and especially in the life of Christ himself (see John 12:16; 13:7; cf. John 2:22), there were also times when this was due to their own lack of faith or hardness of heart (Luke 24:25). Furthermore, there were times in the early church when Christians did not understand or agree on the teachings of the Old Testament or about the letters written by the apostles: note the process of growth in understanding concerning the implications of Gentile inclusion in the church (culminating in "much debate" [Acts 15:7] in the Jerusalem Council of Acts 15), or Peter's misunderstanding of this issue in Galatians 2:11–15, or the frequent doctrinal and ethical issues that had to be corrected by the New Testament epistles. In fact, throughout the history of the church, doctrinal disagreements have been many, and progress in resolving doctrinal differences has often been slow.

In order to help people to avoid making mistakes in interpreting Scripture, many Bible teachers have developed "principles of interpretation," or guidelines to encourage growth in the skill of proper interpretation. The word *hermeneutics* (from the Greek word *hermēneuō,* "to interpret") is the more technical term for this field of study: *hermeneutics is the study of correct methods of interpretation* (especially interpretation of Scripture).

Another technical term often used in discussions of biblical interpretation is "exegesis," a term that refers more to the actual practice of interpreting Scripture,

---

[4]The old term for the clarity of Scripture was *perspicuity,* a term that simply means "clarity." That term itself is not very clear to people today, and I have not used it in this book.

not to theories and principles about how it should be done: *exegesis is the process of interpreting a text of Scripture.* Consequently, when one studies principles of interpretation, that is "hermeneutics," but when one applies those principles and begins actually explaining a biblical text, he or she is doing "exegesis."

The existence of many disagreements about the meaning of Scripture throughout history reminds us that the doctrine of the clarity of Scripture does not imply or suggest that all believers will agree on all the teachings of Scripture. Nevertheless, it does tell us something very important—that the problem always lies not with Scripture but with ourselves. The situation is in fact similar to that of the authority of Scripture. Whereas we affirm that the words of Scripture have all the authority of God himself, we also realize that many people do not acknowledge that authority or submit themselves to it. Similarly, we affirm that all the teachings of Scripture are clear and able to be understood, but we also recognize that people often (through their own shortcomings) misunderstand what is clearly written in Scripture.

## E. Practical Encouragement From This Doctrine

The doctrine of the clarity of Scripture therefore has a very important, and ultimately very encouraging, practical implication. It tells us that where there are areas of doctrinal or ethical disagreement (for example, over baptism or predestination or church government), there are only two possible causes for these disagreements: (1) On the one hand, it may be that we are *seeking to make affirmations where Scripture itself is silent.* In such cases we should be more ready to admit that God has not given us the answer to our quest, and to allow for differences of viewpoint within the church. (This will often be the case with very practical questions, such as methods of evangelism or styles of Bible teaching or appropriate church size.) (2) On the other hand, it is possible that we have made *mistakes in our interpretation* of Scripture. This could have happened because the data we used to decide a question of interpretation were inaccurate or incomplete. Or it could be because there is some personal inadequacy on our part, whether it be, for example, personal pride, or greed, or lack of faith, or selfishness, or even failure to devote enough time to prayerfully reading and studying Scripture.

But in no case are we free to say that the teaching of the Bible on any subject is confusing or incapable of being understood correctly. In no case should we think that persistent disagreements on some subject through the history of the church mean that we will be unable to come to a correct conclusion on that subject ourselves. Rather, if a genuine concern about some such subject arises in our lives, we should sincerely ask God's help and then go to Scripture, searching it with all our ability, believing that God will enable us to understand rightly.

This truth should give great encouragement to all Christians to read their Bibles daily and with great eagerness. We should never assume, for example, that only those who know Greek and Hebrew, or only pastors or Bible scholars, are able to understand the Bible rightly—remember that the Old Testament was written in Hebrew and that many of the Christians to whom the New Testament letters were written had no knowledge of Hebrew at all: they had to read the Old Testament in a Greek translation. Yet the New Testament authors assume that these people can read it and understand it rightly even without scholarly ability in the original language. Christians must never give up to the scholarly "experts" the task of interpreting Scripture: they must keep doing it every day for themselves.[5]

Furthermore, even though we admit that there have been many doctrinal disagreements in the history of the church, we must not forget that there has been an amazing amount of doctrinal agreement on the most central truths of Scripture throughout the history of the church. Indeed, those who have had opportunities for fellowship with Christians in other parts of the world have discovered the remarkable fact that wherever we find a group of vital Christians, almost immediately a vast amount of agreement on all the central doctrines of the Christian faith becomes apparent. Why is this true, no matter what the society, or culture, or denominational affiliation? It is because they all have been reading and believing the same Bible, and its primary teachings have been clear.

## F. The Role of Scholars

Is there any role then for Bible scholars or for those with specialized knowledge of Hebrew (for the Old Testament) and Greek (for the New Testament)? Certainly there is a role for them in at least four areas:

1. They can *teach* Scripture clearly, communicating its content to others and thus fulfilling the office of "teacher" mentioned in the New Testament (1 Cor. 12:28; Eph. 4:11).

2. They can *explore* new areas of understanding the teachings of Scripture. This exploration will seldom (if ever) involve denial of the main teachings the church has held throughout its centuries, but it will often involve the application of Scripture to new areas of life, the answering of difficult questions that have been raised by both believers and unbelievers at each new period in history, and the continual activity of refining and making more precise the church's understanding of detailed points of interpretation of individual verses or matters of doctrine or ethics. Though the Bible may not seem large in comparison with the vast amount of literature in the world, it is a rich treasure-house of wisdom from God that surpasses in value all the other books that have ever been written. The process of relating its various teachings to one another, synthesizing them, and applying them to each new generation, is a greatly rewarding task that will never be completed in this age. Every scholar who deeply loves God's Word will soon realize that there is much more in Scripture than can be learned in any one lifetime!

3. They can *defend* the teachings of the Bible against attacks by other scholars or those with specialized technical training. The role of teaching God's Word also at times involves correcting false teachings. One must be able not only "to give instruction in sound doctrine" but also "to confute those who contradict it" (Titus 1:9; cf. 2 Tim. 2:25, "correcting his opponents with gentleness"; and Titus 2:7–8). Sometimes those who attack biblical teachings have specialized training and technical knowledge in historical, linguistic, or philosophical study, and they use

---

[5]I do not mean to suggest that the activity of interpreting Scripture should be an individualistic one: God will often use the writings of others or the personal advice of others to enable us to understand his Word rightly. The main point is that by whatever means, and primarily through the means of reading Scripture for themselves, Christians should expect that they will be enabled by God to understand the teachings of Scripture rightly.

that training to mount rather sophisticated attacks against the teaching of Scripture. In such cases, believers with similar specialized skills can use their training to understand and respond to such attacks. Such training is also very useful in responding to the false teachings of cults and sects. This is not to say that believers without specialized training are incapable of responding to false teaching (for most false teaching can be clearly refuted by a believer who prays and has a good knowledge of the English Bible), but rather that technical points in arguments can only be answered by those with skills in the technical areas appealed to.

4. They can *supplement* the study of Scripture for the benefit of the church. Bible scholars often have training that will enable them to relate the teachings of Scripture to the rich history of the church, and to make the interpretation of Scripture more precise and its meaning more vivid with a greater knowledge of the languages and cultures in which the Bible was written.

These four functions benefit the church as a whole, and all believers should be thankful for those who perform them. However, these functions do *not* include the right to decide for the church as a whole what is true and false doctrine or what is proper conduct in a difficult situation. If such a right were the preserve of formally trained Bible scholars, then they would become a governing elite in the church, and the ordinary functioning of the government of the church as described in the New Testament would cease. The process of decision-making for the church must be left to the officers of the church, whether they are scholars or not (and, in a congregational form of church government, not only to the officers but also to the people of the church as a whole).[6]

## QUESTIONS FOR PERSONAL APPLICATION

1. If the doctrine of the clarity of Scripture is true, why does there seem to be so much disagreement among Christians about the teaching of the Bible? Observing the diversity of interpretations of Scripture, some conclude, "People can make the Bible say anything they want." How do you think Jesus would respond to this statement?

2. What would happen to the church if most believers gave up reading the Bible for themselves and only listened to Bible teachers or read books about the Bible? If you thought that only expert scholars could understand the Bible rightly, what would happen to your personal reading of Scripture? Has this already happened to some extent in your life or in the lives of those you know?

3. Do you think that there are right and wrong interpretations of most or all passages of Scripture? If you thought the Bible was generally unclear, how would your answer change? Will a conviction about the clarity of Scripture affect the care you use when studying a text of Scripture? Will it affect the way you approach Scripture when trying to gain a biblical answer to some difficult doctrinal or moral problem?

---

[6]See the discussion of various forms of church government in chapter 47, pp. 923–37.

4. If even seminary professors disagree about some Bible teaching, can other Christians ever hope to come to a correct decision on that teaching? (Give reasons for your answer.) Do you think ordinary people among the Jews at the time of Jesus had a hard time deciding whether to believe Jesus or the scholarly experts who disagreed with him? Did Jesus expect them to be able to decide?

5. How can a pastor preach biblically based sermons each Sunday without giving the impression that only people with seminary training (like himself) are able to interpret Scripture rightly? Do you think it should ever be necessary, in a doctrinal or ethical controversy, for a Bible scholar to speak in a church and base his main arguments on special meanings of Greek or Hebrew words that the church members themselves are unable to evaluate or take issue with personally? Is there an appropriate way for a scholar to use such technical knowledge in popular writing or speaking?

6. Church leaders at the time of Martin Luther said they wanted to keep the Bible in Latin to prevent the common people from reading it and then misinterpreting it. Evaluate this argument. Why do you think Martin Luther was so anxious to translate the Bible into German? Why do you think church leaders in previous centuries have persecuted and even killed men—like William Tyndale in England—who were translating the Bible into the language of the people? Why is the task of Bible translation into other languages so important a part of the work of missions?

7. Does the doctrine of the clarity of Scripture mean that the New Testament can be fully understood by people who do not have access to an Old Testament?

## SPECIAL TERMS

clarity of Scripture  
exegesis  
hermeneutics  
perspicuity

## BIBLIOGRAPHY

(For an explanation of this bibliography see the note on the bibliography to chapter 1, p. 38. Complete bibliographical data may be found on pp. 1223–29.)

### Sections in Evangelical Systematic Theologies

1. Anglican (Episcopalian)
   - 1882–92   Litton (no explicit treatment)
2. Arminian (Wesleyan or Methodist)
   - 1875–76   Pope, 1:223–30
   - 1983   Carter, 2:747–67
3. Baptist
   - 1767   Gill, 30–32
   - 1976–83   Henry, 4:272–367

        1983–85     Erickson, 253–56
4. Dispensational
        1947        Chafer, 1:105–19
        1986        Ryrie, 110–18
5. Lutheran
        1917–24     Pieper, 1:319–30, 359–70
        1934        Mueller, 138–41
6. Reformed (or Presbyterian)
        1861        Heppe, 33–41
        1871–73     Hodge, 1:183–90
        1938        Berkhof, *Intro.*, 167

## Sections in Representative Roman Catholic Systematic Theologies

(no explicit treatment)

## Other Works

In this section I have listed several works on developing greater skill in biblical interpretation, including three helpful works by nonevangelical authors (one by Barr and two by Hirsch).

Barr, James. *The Semantics of Biblical Language*. London: Oxford University Press, 1961.

Berkhof, Louis. *Principles of Biblical Interpretation*. Grand Rapids: Baker, 1950.

Carson, D. A. *Exegetical Fallacies*. Grand Rapids: Baker, 1984.

Dockery, David S. *Biblical Interpretation Then and Now: Contemporary Hermeneutics in the Light of the Early Church*. Grand Rapids: Baker, 1992.

Fee, Gordon D., and Douglas Stuart. *How to Read the Bible for All Its Worth*. Grand Rapids: Zondervan, 1982.

Hirsch, E. D., Jr. *The Aims of Interpretation*. Chicago: University of Chicago Press, 1976.

———. *Validity in Interpretation*. New Haven and London: Yale University Press, 1967.

Hubbard, Robert L., William W. Klein, and Craig L. Blomberg. *Introduction to Biblical Interpretation*. Waco, Tex.: Word Books, 1993.

Inch, Morris A., and C. Hassell Bullock, eds. *The Literature and Meaning of Scripture*. Grand Rapids: Baker, 1981.

Kaiser, Walter C., Jr. *Toward an Exegetical Theology*. Grand Rapids: Baker, 1982.

Marshall, I. Howard, ed. *New Testament Interpretation: Essays on Principles and Methods*. Grand Rapids: Eerdmans, 1977.

McCown, Wayne, and James Earl Massey, eds. *Interpreting God's Word for Today: An Inquiry Into Hermeneutics From a Biblical Theological Perspective*. Wesleyan Theological Perspectives, vol. 2. Anderson, Ind.: Warner Press, 1982.

McKnight, Scot, ed. *Introducing New Testament Interpretation*. Grand Rapids: Baker, 1990.

———. *Interpreting the Synoptic Gospels*. Grand Rapids: Baker, 1988.

Mickelsen, A. Berkeley. *Interpreting the Bible*. Grand Rapids: Eerdmans, 1963.

Osborne, Grant R. *The Hermeneutical Spiral: A Comprehensive Introduction to Biblical Interpretation*. Downers Grove, Ill.: InterVarsity Press, 1992.

Packer, J. I. "Infallible Scripture and the Role of Hermeneutics." In *Scripture and Truth*. Ed. by D. A. Carson and John Woodbridge. Grand Rapids: Zondervan, 1983, pp. 325–56.

———. "Scripture." In *NDT*, pp. 627–31.

Ramm, Bernard. *Protestant Biblical Interpretation*. 3d ed. Grand Rapids: Baker, 1970.

Schultz, Samuel J., and Morris A. Inch, eds. *Interpreting the Word of God. Festschrift in Honor of Steven Barabas*. Chicago: Moody, 1976.

Silva, Moises. *Biblical Words and Their Meanings*. Grand Rapids: Zondervan, 1983.

———. *Has the Church Misread the Bible? The History of Interpretation in the Light of Contemporary Issues*. Grand Rapids: Zondervan, 1987.

Sire, James. *Scripture Twisting: Twenty Ways the Cults Misread the Bible*. Downers Grove, Ill.: InterVarsity Press, 1980.

Sproul, R. C. *Knowing Scripture*. Downers Grove, Ill.: InterVarsity Press, 1977.

Thiselton, Anthony C. *New Horizons in Hermeneutics: The Theory and Practice of Transforming Biblical Reading*. Grand Rapids: Zondervan, 1992.

———. *The Two Horizons: New Testament Hermeneutics and Philosophical Description*. Grand Rapids: Eerdmans, 1980.

## SCRIPTURE MEMORY PASSAGE

**Deuteronomy 6:6–7:** *And these words which I command you this day shall be upon your heart; and you shall teach them diligently to your children, and shall talk of them when you sit in your house, and when you walk by the way, and when you lie down, and when you rise.*

## HYMN

### "Jehovah's Perfect Law"

This section of Psalm 19 set to music reminds us of many excellent qualities of Scripture, among them the fact that it is written clearly: "The testimony of the LORD is sure, making wise the simple" (v. 7).

(Use the tune of "We Come, O Christ, to You.")

Jehovah's perfect law restores the soul again;
His testimony sure gives wisdom unto men;
The precepts of the LORD are right,
And fill the heart with great delight.

The LORD's commands are pure; they light and joy restore;
Jehovah's fear is clean, enduring evermore;
His statutes, let the world confess,
Are wholly truth and righteousness.

They are to be desired above the finest gold;
Than honey from the comb more sweetness far they hold;
With warnings they your servant guard,
In keeping them is great reward.

His errors who can know? Cleanse me from hidden stain;
Keep me from willful sins, nor let them o'er me reign;
And then I upright shall appear
And be from great transgressions clear.

Whene'er you search my life, may all my thoughts within
And all the words I speak your full approval win.
O Lord, you are a rock to me,
And my Redeemer you shall be.

FROM: *THE PSALTER*, 1912 (TAKEN FROM PS. 19:7–14)

# Chapter 7

# The Four Characteristics of Scripture: (3) Necessity

*For what purposes is the Bible necessary? How much can people know about God without the Bible?*

Do we need to have a Bible or to have someone tell us what the Bible says in order to know that God exists? Or that we are sinners needing to be saved? Or to know how to find salvation? Or to know God's will for our lives? These are the kinds of questions which an investigation of the necessity of Scripture is intended to answer.

## EXPLANATION AND SCRIPTURAL BASIS

The necessity of Scripture may be defined as follows: *The necessity of Scripture means that the Bible is necessary for knowing the gospel, for maintaining spiritual life, and for knowing God's will, but is not necessary for knowing that God exists or for knowing something about God's character and moral laws.*

That definition may now be explained in its various parts.[1]

### A. The Bible Is Necessary for Knowledge of the Gospel

In Romans 10:13–17 Paul says:

> For, "everyone who calls upon the name of the Lord will be saved." But how are men to call upon him in whom they have not believed? And *how are they to believe in him of whom they have never heard?* And how are they to hear without a preacher? . . . So *faith comes from what is heard,* and what is heard comes by the preaching of Christ.

This statement indicates the following line of reasoning: (1) It first assumes that one must call upon the name of the Lord to be saved. (In Pauline usage generally as well as in this specific context [see v. 9], "the Lord" refers to the Lord Jesus Christ.) (2) People can only call upon the name of Christ if they believe in him (that is, that he is a Savior worthy of calling upon and one who will answer those who call). (3) People cannot believe in Christ unless they have heard of

---

[1]As the subsequent sections indicate, when this definition says that the Bible is necessary for certain things, I do not mean to imply that an actual printed copy of the Bible is necessary for every person, because sometimes people hear the Bible read aloud or hear others tell them some of the contents of the Bible. But even these oral communications of the contents of the Bible are based on the existence of written copies of the Bible to which other people have access.

116

him. (4) They cannot hear of Christ unless there is someone to tell them about
Christ (a "preacher"). (5) The conclusion is that saving faith comes by hearing
(that is, by hearing the gospel message), and this hearing of the gospel message
comes about through the preaching of Christ. The implication seems to be that
without hearing the preaching of the gospel of Christ, no one can be saved.[2]

This passage is one of several that show that eternal salvation comes only
through belief in Jesus Christ and no other way. Speaking of Christ, John 3:18
says, "He who believes in him is not condemned; *he who does not believe is
condemned already,* because he has not believed in the name of the only Son of
God." Similarly, in John 14:6 Jesus says, "I am the way, and the truth, and the
life; *no one comes to the Father, but by me.*"

Peter, on trial before the Sanhedrin, says, "*there is salvation in no one else,* for
there is *no other name* under heaven given among men by which we must be saved"
(Acts 4:12). Of course, the exclusiveness of salvation through Christ is because
Jesus is the only one who ever died for our sins or whoever could have done so.
Paul says, "For there is one God, and *there is one mediator between God and men, the
man Christ Jesus, who gave himself as a ransom for all* . . ." (1 Tim. 2:5–6). There
is no other way to be reconciled to God than through Christ, for there is no other
way of dealing with the guilt of our sin before a holy God.[3]

But if people can be saved only through faith in Christ, someone might ask how
believers under the old covenant could have been saved. The answer must be that
those who were saved under the old covenant were also saved through trusting in
Christ, even though their faith was a forward-looking faith based on God's word
of promise that a Messiah or a Redeemer would come. Speaking of Old Testament
believers such as Abel, Enoch, Noah, Abraham, and Sarah, the author of Hebrews
says, "*These all died in faith,* not having received what was promised, but *having
seen it and greeted it from afar* . . ." (Heb. 11:13). The same chapter goes on to say
that Moses "considered abuse suffered *for the Christ* (or the Messiah) greater
wealth than the treasures of Egypt, for he looked to the reward" (Heb. 11:26).
And Jesus can say of Abraham, "Your father Abraham rejoiced that he was to see
my day; *he saw it* and was glad" (John 8:56). This again apparently refers to
Abraham's joy in looking forward to the day of the promised Messiah. Thus, even
Old Testament believers had saving faith in Christ, to whom they looked forward,
not with exact knowledge of the historical details of Christ's life, but with great
faith in the absolute reliability of God's word of promise.

The Bible is necessary for salvation, then, in this sense: one must either read the
gospel message in the Bible for oneself, or hear it from another person. Even those
believers who came to salvation in the old covenant did so by trusting in the
words of God that promised a Savior to come.

In fact, these repeated instances of people trusting in God's *words* of promise,

---

[2]Someone might object that the following verse, Rom. 10:18, in its quotation of Ps. 19:4, "Their
voice has gone out to all the earth, and their words to the ends of the world," implies that all people
everywhere have already heard the gospel message or the message of Christ. But in the context of
Psalm 19, verse 4 only speaks of the fact that the natural creation, especially the heavens above,
proclaim God's glory and the greatness of his creative activity. There is no thought here of the
proclamation of salvation through Christ. The idea that all people everywhere have heard the gospel of
Christ through natural revelation would also be contrary to Paul's missionary activities.

[3]On the question of whether it is fair of God to condemn people who have never heard of Christ,
see the discussion in chapter 19, pp. 402–3, and chapter 32, pp. 682–83.

together with the verses above that affirm the necessity of hearing about and believing in Christ, seem to indicate that sinful people need more on which to rest their faith than just an intuitive guess that God might provide a means of salvation. It seems that the only foundation firm enough to rest one's faith on is the *word* of God itself (whether spoken or written). This in the earliest times came in very brief form, but from the very beginning we have evidence of *words* of God promising a salvation yet to come, words that were trusted by those people whom God called to himself.

For example, even in the lifetime of Adam and Eve there are some words of God that point toward a future salvation: in Genesis 3:15 the curse on the serpent includes a promise that the seed of the woman (one of her descendants) would bruise the head of the serpent but would himself be hurt in the process—a promise ultimately fulfilled in Christ. The fact that the first two children of Adam and Eve, Cain and Abel, offered sacrifices to the LORD (Gen. 4:3–4) indicates their consciousness of a need to make some kind of payment for the guilt of their sin, and of God's promise of acceptance of sacrifices offered in the right way. Genesis 4:7, "If you do well, will you not be accepted?" indicates again in the very briefest form a word from God that offered the provision of some kind of salvation through trusting in the promise of God offered in that word. As the history of the Old Testament progressed, God's words of promise became more and more specific, and the forward-looking faith of God's people accordingly became more and more definite. Yet it seems always to have been a faith resting specifically on the *words* of God himself.

Thus, although it will be argued below that people can know that God *exists* and can know something of his *laws* apart from Scripture, it seems that there is no possibility of coming to *saving faith* apart from specific knowledge of God's words of promise.

## B. The Bible Is Necessary for Maintaining Spiritual Life

Jesus says in Matthew 4:4 (quoting Deut. 8:3), "Man shall not live on bread alone, but on every word that proceeds out of the mouth of God" (NASB). Here Jesus indicates that our spiritual life is maintained by daily nourishment with the Word of God, just as our physical lives are maintained by daily nourishment with physical food. To neglect regular reading of God's Word is as detrimental to the health of our souls as the neglect of physical food is detrimental to the health of our bodies.

Similarly, Moses tells the people of Israel of the importance of God's words for their lives: "For it is no trifle for you, but *it is your life,* and thereby you shall live long in the land which you are going over the Jordan to possess" (Deut. 32:47). And Peter encourages the Christians to whom he writes, "Like newborn babes, long for the pure spiritual milk, that by it you may grow up to salvation" (1 Peter 2:2). The "pure spiritual milk" in this context must refer to the Word of God about which Peter has been speaking (see 1 Peter 1:23–25). The Bible, then, is necessary for maintaining spiritual life and for growth in the Christian life.

## C. The Bible Is Necessary for Certain Knowledge of God's Will

It will be argued below that all people ever born have *some* knowledge of God's will through their consciences. But this knowledge is often indistinct and cannot give certainty. In fact, if there were *no* written Word of God, we *could not* gain certainty about God's will through other means such as conscience, advice from others, an internal witness of the Holy Spirit, changed circumstances, and the use of sanctified reasoning and common sense. These all might give an approximation of God's will in more or less reliable ways, but from these means alone no certainty about God's will could ever be attained, at least in a fallen world where sin distorts our perception of right and wrong, brings faulty reasoning into our thinking processes, and causes us to suppress from time to time the testimony of our consciences (cf. Jer. 17:9; Rom. 2:14–15; 1 Cor. 8:10; Heb. 5:14; 10:22; also 1 Tim. 4:2; Titus 1:15).

In the Bible, however, we have clear and definite statements about God's will. God has not revealed all things to us, but he has revealed enough for us to know his will: "The secret things belong to the LORD our God; but *the things that are revealed belong to us and to our children for ever,* that we may do all the words of this law" (Deut. 29:29). As it was in the time of Moses, so it is now with us: God has revealed his words to us that we might obey his laws and thereby do his will. To be "blameless" in God's sight is to "walk in the law of the LORD" (Ps. 119:1). The "blessed" man is one who does not follow the will of wicked people (Ps. 1:1), but delights "*in the law of the LORD,*" and meditates on God's law "day and night" (Ps. 1:2). To love God (and thereby to act in a way that is pleasing to him) is to "keep his commandments" (1 John 5:3). If we are to have a certain knowledge of God's will, then, we must attain it through the study of Scripture.

In fact, in one sense it can be argued that the Bible is necessary for certain knowledge about anything. A philosopher might argue as follows: The fact that we do not know everything requires us to be uncertain about everything we do claim to know. This is because some fact unknown to us may yet turn out to prove that what we thought to be true was actually false. For example, we think we know our date of birth, our name, our age, and so forth. But we must admit that it is possible that some day we could find that our parents had given us false information and our "certain" knowledge would then turn out to be incorrect. Regarding events that we personally have experienced, we all realize how it is possible for us to "remember" words or events incorrectly and find ourselves later corrected by more accurate information. We can usually be more certain about the events of our present experience, so long as it remains present (but even that, someone might argue, could be a dream, and we will only discover this fact when we wake up!). At any rate, it is difficult to answer the philosopher's question: If we do not know *all* the facts in the universe, past, present, and future, how can we ever attain *certainty* that we have correct information about any one fact?

Ultimately, there are only two possible solutions to this problem: (1) We must learn all the facts of the universe in order to be sure that no subsequently discovered fact will prove our present ideas to be false; or (2) someone who *does* know all the facts in the universe, and who never lies, could tell us some true facts that we can then be sure will never be contradicted.

This second solution is in fact what we have when we have God's words in

Scripture. God knows all facts that ever have been or ever will be. And this God who is omniscient (all-knowing) has absolutely certain knowledge: there can never be any fact that he does not already know; thus, there can never be any fact that would prove that something God thinks is actually false. Now it is from this infinite storehouse of certain knowledge that God, who never lies, has spoken to us in Scripture, in which he has told us many true things about himself, about ourselves, and about the universe that he has made. No fact can ever turn up to contradict the truth spoken by this one who is omniscient.

Thus, it is appropriate for us to be *more certain* about the truths we read in Scripture than about any other knowledge we have. If we are to talk about degrees of certainty of knowledge we have, then the knowledge we attain from Scripture would have the highest degree of certainty: if the word "certain" can be applied to any kind of human knowledge, it can be applied to this knowledge.[4]

This concept of the certainty of knowledge that we attain from Scripture then gives us a reasonable basis for affirming the correctness of much of the other knowledge that we have. We read Scripture and find that its view of the world around us, of human nature, and of ourselves corresponds closely to the information we have gained from our own sense-experiences of the world around us. Thus we are encouraged to trust our sense-experiences of the world around us: our observations correspond with the absolute truth of Scripture; therefore, our observations are also true and, by and large, reliable. Such confidence in the general reliability of observations made with our eyes and ears is further confirmed by the fact that it is God who has made these faculties and who in Scripture frequently encourages us to use them (compare also Prov. 20:12: "The hearing ear and the seeing eye, the LORD has made them both").

In this way the Christian who takes the Bible as God's Word escapes from philosophical skepticism about the possibility of attaining certain knowledge with our finite minds. In this sense, then, it is correct to say that for people who are not omniscient, the Bible is necessary for certain knowledge about anything.

This fact is important for the following discussion, where we affirm that unbelievers *can* know something about God from the general revelation that is

---

[4]This statement assumes that we have become convinced that Scripture is indeed the very words of God, and that we have understood at least some portions of Scripture correctly. Yet at this point the doctrine of the clarity of Scripture discussed in the previous chapter assures us that we will be able to understand the teachings of Scripture correctly, and the overwhelming testimony of Scripture to its own divine authorship (discussed in the chapters above concerning different forms of the Word of God and concerning the authority of Scripture), made persuasive to us by the work of the Holy Spirit, convinces us of the divine authorship of Scripture. In this sense the argument becomes not so much circular as something like a spiral where each section of the doctrine of Scripture reinforces the other and deepens our persuasion of the truthfulness of other sections of the doctrine of Scripture. By this process, our persuasion that Scripture is God's Word, that it is truth, that it is clear, and that knowledge which we attain from it is certain, becomes stronger and stronger the more we study and reflect on it.

We can of course speak of degrees of certainty that we might have concerning the fact that the Bible is God's Word, and degrees of certainty that our interpretation of any one teaching in Scripture is correct. Then from the standpoint of individual personal experience, we could say that our certainty of the correctness of knowledge that we have from Scripture becomes greater in proportion to our certainty about the God-breathed character and clarity of Scripture.

Yet from a theological standpoint, if we begin with an agreement that Scripture is God-breathed and that we do understand its teachings (at least its major teachings) correctly, then it is appropriate to say that the knowledge we attain from Scripture is more certain than any other knowledge we have.

seen in the world around them. Although this is true, we must recognize that in a fallen world knowledge gained by observation of the world is always imperfect and always liable to error or misinterpretation. Therefore the knowledge of God and creation gained from Scripture must be used to interpret correctly the creation around us. Using the theological terms that we will define below, we can say that we need special revelation to interpret general revelation rightly.[5]

## D. But the Bible Is Not Necessary for Knowing That God Exists

What about people who do not read the Bible? Can they obtain any knowledge of God? Can they know anything about his laws? Yes, without the Bible some knowledge of God is possible, even if it is not absolutely certain knowledge.

People can obtain a knowledge *that God exists,* and a knowledge of *some of his attributes,* simply from observation of themselves and the world around them. David says, *"The heavens are telling the glory of God; and the firmament proclaims his handiwork"* (Ps. 19:1). To look at the sky is to see evidence of the infinite power, wisdom, and even beauty of God; it is to observe a majestic witness to the glory of God. Similarly, Barnabas and Paul tell the Greek inhabitants of Lystra about the living God who made the heavens and the earth: "In past generations he allowed all the nations to walk in their own ways; yet *he did not leave himself without witness,* for he did good and gave you from heaven rains and fruitful seasons, satisfying your hearts with food and gladness" (Acts 14:16–17). Rains and fruitful seasons, food produced from the earth, and gladness in people's hearts, all bear witness to the fact that their Creator is a God of mercy, of love, and even of joy. These evidences of God are all around us in creation to be seen by those who are willing to see them.

Even those who by their wickedness suppress the truth cannot avoid the evidences of God's existence and nature in the created order:

> For *what can be known about God is plain to them,* because God has shown it to them. Ever since the creation of the world *his invisible nature,* namely, his eternal power and deity, *has been clearly perceived in the things that have been made.* So they are without excuse; for although *they knew God* they did not honor him as God or give thanks to him, but they became futile in their thinking and their senseless minds were darkened. (Rom. 1:19–21)

Here Paul says not only that creation gives evidence of God's existence and character, but also that even wicked men recognize that evidence. What can be known about God is "plain to them" and in fact "they knew God" (apparently, they knew who he was), but "they did not honor him as God or give thanks to him." This passage allows us to say that all persons, even the most wicked, have some internal knowledge or perception that God exists and that he is a powerful Creator. This knowledge is seen "in the things that have been made," a phrase that refers to all creation. Yet it is probably in seeing mankind created in the image of God—that is, in seeing both themselves and other people—that even wicked persons see the greatest evidence of God's existence and nature.[6]

---

[5]See pp. 122–23 for definitions of general revelation and special revelation.

[6]The Swiss theologian Karl Barth (1886–1968) denied that natural man can know anything of God through the general revelation found in nature, but insisted that knowledge of God can only come

Thus, even without the Bible, all persons who have ever lived have had evidence in creation that God exists, that he is the Creator and they are creatures, and have also had some evidence of his character. As a result, they themselves have known something about God from this evidence (even though this is never said to be a knowledge that is able to bring them to salvation).

## E. Furthermore, the Bible Is Not Necessary for Knowing Something About God's Character and Moral Laws

Paul goes on in Romans 1 to show that even unbelievers who have no written record of God's laws still have in their consciences some understanding of God's moral demands. Speaking of a long list of sins ("envy, murder, strife, deceit . . ."), Paul says of wicked people who practice them, "Though *they know God's decree that those who do such things deserve to die*, they not only do them but approve those who practice them" (Rom. 1:32). Wicked people know that their sin is wrong, at least in large measure.

Paul then talks about the activity of conscience in Gentiles who do not have the written law:

> When Gentiles who have not the law do by nature what the law requires, they are a law to themselves, even though they do not have the law. They show that *what the law requires is written on their hearts*, while their conscience also bears witness and their conflicting thoughts accuse or perhaps excuse them. . . ." (Rom. 2:14–15)

The consciences of unbelievers bear witness to God's moral standards, but at times this evidence of God's law on the hearts of unbelievers is distorted or suppressed.[7] Sometimes their thoughts "accuse" them and sometimes their thoughts "excuse" them, Paul says. The knowledge of God's laws derived from such sources is never perfect, but it is enough to give an awareness of God's moral demands to all mankind. (And it is on this basis that Paul argues that all humanity is held guilty before God for sin, even those who do not have the written laws of God in Scripture.)

The knowledge of God's existence, character, and moral law, which comes through creation to all humanity, is often called *"general revelation"* (because it comes to all people generally).[8] General revelation comes through observing nature, through seeing God's directing influence in history, and through an inner

---

through a knowledge of God's grace in Christ. His radical rejection of natural revelation has not gained wide acceptance; it rests upon the unlikely view that Rom. 1:21 refers to a knowledge of God in theory but not in fact.

[7]The consciences of unbelievers will be suppressed or hardened in various areas of morality, depending on cultural influences and personal circumstances. A cannibalistic society, for example, will have many members whose consciences are hardened and insensitive with regard to the evil of murder, while modern American society, for example, exhibits very little sensitivity of conscience with regard to the evil of falsehood in speech, or disrespect for parental authority, or sexual immorality. Moreover, individuals who repeatedly commit a certain sin will often find the pangs of conscience diminishing after time: a thief may feel very guilty after his first or second robbery but feel little guilt after his twentieth. The witness of conscience is still there in each case, but it is suppressed through repeated wickedness.

[8]For an extensive discussion of the history of the doctrine of general revelation and its basis in Scripture, see Bruce Demarest, *General Revelation* (Grand Rapids: Zondervan, 1982); see also the excellent treatment of this doctrine in Gordon R. Lewis and Bruce A. Demarest, *Integrative Theology*, 1:59–91.

sense of God's existence and his laws that he has placed inside every person. General revelation is distinct from "*special revelation*," which refers to God's words addressed to specific people, such as the words of the Bible, the words of the Old Testament prophets and New Testament apostles, and the words of God spoken in personal address, such as at Mount Sinai or at the baptism of Jesus.[9]

Special revelation includes all the words of Scripture but is not limited to the words of Scripture, for it also includes, for example, many words of Jesus that were not recorded in Scripture, and probably there were many words spoken by Old Testament prophets and New Testament apostles that were not recorded in Scripture either.

The fact that all people know something of God's moral laws is a great blessing for society, for unless they did there would be no societal restraint on the evil that people would do and no restraint from their consciences. Because there is some common knowledge of right and wrong, Christians can often find much consensus with non-Christians in matters of civil law, community standards, basic ethics for business and professional activity, and acceptable patterns of conduct in ordinary life. Moreover, we can appeal to the sense of rightness within people's hearts (Rom. 2:14) when attempting to enact better laws or overturn bad laws, or to right some other injustices in society around us. The knowledge of God's existence and character also provides a basis of information that enables the gospel to make sense to a non-Christian's heart and mind: unbelievers know that God exists and that they have broken his standards, so the news that Christ died to pay for their sins should truly come as *good news* to them.

However, it must be emphasized that Scripture nowhere indicates that people can know the gospel, or know the way of salvation, through such general revelation. They may know that God exists, that he is their Creator, that they owe him obedience, and that they have sinned against him. The existence of systems of sacrifice in primitive religions throughout history attests to the fact that these things can be clearly known by people apart from the Bible. The repeated occurrences of the "rain and fruitful seasons" mentioned in Acts 14:17 may even lead some people to reason that God is not only holy and righteous but also loving and forgiving. But how the *holiness and justice* of God can ever be reconciled with his *willingness to forgive sins* is a mystery that has never been solved by any religion apart from the Bible. Nor does the Bible give us any hope that it ever can be discovered apart from specific revelation from God. It is the great wonder of our redemption that God himself has provided the way of salvation by sending his own Son, who is both God and man, to be our representative and bear the penalty for our sins, thus combining the justice and love of God in one infinitely wise and amazingly gracious act. This fact, which seems commonplace to the Christian ear, should not lose its wonder for us: it could never have been conceived by man alone apart from God's special, verbal revelation.

Furthermore, even if an adherent of a primitive religion could think that God somehow *must have* himself paid the penalty for our sins, such a thought would only be an extraordinary speculation. It could never be held with enough certainty

---

[9]See chapter 2, pp. 48–50, for a discussion of God's words of personal address, God's words spoken through the lips of human beings, and God's words in Scripture, all of which fall in the category of special revelation.

to be the ground on which to rest saving faith unless God himself confirmed such speculation with his own words, namely, the words of the gospel proclaiming either that this indeed was going to happen (if the revelation came in the time before Christ) or that it indeed has happened (if the revelation came in the time after Christ). The Bible never views human speculation apart from the Word of God as a sufficient basis on which *to rest saving faith:* such saving faith, according to Scripture, is always confidence or trust in God that rests on the truthfulness of God's own words.[10]

## QUESTIONS FOR PERSONAL APPLICATION

1. When you are witnessing to an unbeliever, what is the one thing above all others that you should want him or her to read? Do you know of anyone who ever became a Christian without either reading the Bible or hearing someone tell him or her what the Bible said? What then is the primary task of an evangelistic missionary? How should the necessity of Scripture affect our missionary orientation?

2. Do you nourish your soul on the spiritual food of the Word as carefully and diligently as you nourish your body on physical food? What makes us so spiritually insensitive that we feel physical hunger much more acutely than spiritual hunger? What is the remedy?

3. When we are actively seeking to know God's will, where should we spend most of our time and effort? In practice, where do you spend most of your time and effort when seeking to find God's will? Do God's principles in Scripture and the apparent guidance we receive from feelings, conscience, advice, circumstances, human reasoning, or society ever seem to conflict? How should we seek to resolve the conflict?

4. Is it a hopeless task to work for civil legislation based on standards that accord with God's moral principles in Scripture? Why is there good reason to hope that we will finally be able to persuade a great majority of our society to adopt laws consistent with scriptural norms? What would hinder this effort?

## SPECIAL TERMS

general revelation                              necessity of Scripture
natural revelation                              special revelation

## BIBLIOGRAPHY

(For an explanation of this bibliography see the note on the bibliography to chapter 1, p. 38. Complete bibliographical data may be found on pp. 1223–29.)

---

[10]In the New Testament, we should also note that it is specifically the Word of God that is said to be the agent that God uses in giving people spiritual life (James 1:18; 1 Peter 1:23).

## Sections in Evangelical Systematic Theologies

1. Anglican (Episcopalian)
   - 1882–92    Litton (no explicit treatment)
   - 1930      Thomas, 258–60
2. Arminian (Wesleyan or Methodist)
   - 1983      Carter, 1:288–89
3. Baptist
   - 1767      Gill, 1:32–36
   - 1976–83   Henry, 1:17–29; 2:91–123; 4:494–522; 6:360–69
   - 1983–85   Erickson, 153–74
   - 1987–94   Lewis/Demarest, 1:59–92
4. Dispensational
   - 1947      Chafer, 1:48–60
5. Lutheran
   - 1934      Mueller, 90–98
6. Reformed (or Presbyterian)
   - 1559      Calvin, 1:69–74, 838–49 (1.6; 3.19.6–16)
   - 1724–58   Edwards, 2:479–85
   - 1861      Heppe, 31–33
   - 1871–73   Hodge, 1:18–60, 364–65
   - 1878      Dabney, 64–78
   - 1938      Berkhof, *Intro.*, 128–33; 165–66
7. Renewal (or charismatic/Pentecostal)
   - 1988–92   Williams, 33–36, 239–41

## Sections in Representative Roman Catholic Systematic Theologies

1. Roman Catholic: Traditional
   - 1955      Ott (no explicit treatment)
2. Roman Catholic: Post-Vatican II
   - 1980      McBrien, 1:151–61; 245–81

## Other Works

Berkouwer, G. C. *General Revelation.* (No translator named.) Grand Rapids: Eerdmans, 1955.

Demarest, Bruce A. *General Revelation.* Grand Rapids: Zondervan, 1982.

———. "Revelation, General." In *EDT,* pp. 944–45.

Henry, Carl F. H. "Revelation, Special." In *EDT,* pp. 945–48.

Kuyper, Abraham. *Principles of Sacred Theology.* Trans. by J. H. de Vries. Grand Rapids: Eerdmans, 1968, pp. 341–405 (originally published as *Encyclopedia of Sacred Theology* in 1898).

Packer, J. I. "Scripture." In *NDT,* pp. 627–31.

Van Til, Cornelius. *Common Grace and the Gospel*. Nutley, N.J.: Presbyterian and Reformed, 1973.

_____. *In Defense of the Faith*, vol. 1: *The Doctrine of Scripture*. Ripon, Calif.: den Dulk Christian Foundation, 1967, pp. 1–15.

_____. *In Defense of the Faith*, vol. 5: *An Introduction to Systematic Theology*. Phillipsburg, N.J.: Presbyterian and Reformed, 1976, pp. 62–109.

## SCRIPTURE MEMORY PASSAGE

**Matthew 4:4:** *But he answered, "It is written, 'Man shall not live by bread alone, but by every word that proceeds from the mouth of God.'"*

## HYMN

"Teach Me, O Lord, Your Way of Truth"
(Use the familiar tune of "Jesus Shall Reign.")

Teach me, O Lord, your way of truth,
    And from it I will not depart;
That I may steadfastly obey,
    Give me an understanding heart.

In your commandments make me walk,
    For in your law my joy shall be;
Give me a heart that loves your will,
    From discontent and envy free.

Turn now my eyes from vanity,
    And cause me in your ways to tread;
O let your servant prove your Word
    and thus to godly fear be led.

Turn away my reproach and fear;
    Your righteous judgments I confess;
To know your precepts I desire;
    Revive me in your righteousness.

FROM: *THE PSALTER*, 1912 (TAKEN FROM PS. 119:33–40)

An alternative hymn for this chapter is a modern Scripture song, "Seek Ye First the Kingdom of God." The second verse of this song ("Man shall not live on bread alone. . .") is a quotation of Matthew 4:4 and expresses the necessity of Scripture for maintaining our spiritual life: we live on every word that proceeds from the mouth of God. The other verses of the song do not speak directly of the doctrine of the necessity of Scripture but do contain the words of gospel invitation (vv. 1, 4, 5). All verses in the song are direct quotations of Scripture, and, as such, will be spiritually nourishing for us to sing and meditate on.

# Chapter 8

# The Four Characteristics
# of Scripture: (4) Sufficiency

*Is the Bible enough for knowing what God wants us
to think or do?*

## EXPLANATION AND SCRIPTURAL BASIS

Are we to look for other words from God in addition to those we have in
Scripture? The doctrine of the sufficiency of Scripture addresses this question.

### A. Definiton of the Sufficiency of Scripture

We can define the sufficiency of Scripture as follows: *The sufficiency of Scripture
means that Scripture contained all the words of God he intended his people to have at
each stage of redemptive history, and that it now contains all the words of God we need
for salvation, for trusting him perfectly, and for obeying him perfectly.*

This definition emphasizes that it is in Scripture alone that we are to search for
God's words to us. It also reminds us that God considers what he has told us in
the Bible to be enough for us, and that we should rejoice in the great revelation
that he has given us and be content with it.

Significant scriptural support and explanation of this doctrine is found in Paul's
words to Timothy, "from childhood you have been acquainted with the sacred
writings which are *able to instruct you for salvation* through faith in Christ Jesus"
(2 Tim. 3:15). The context shows that "sacred writings" here means the written
words of Scripture (2 Tim. 3:16). This is an indication that the words of God
which we have in Scripture are all the words of God we need in order to be saved:
these words are able to make us wise "for salvation." This is confirmed by other
passages that talk about the words of Scripture as the means God uses to bring us
to salvation (James 1:18; 1 Peter 1:23).

Other passages indicate that the Bible is sufficient to equip us for living the
Christian life. Once again Paul writes to Timothy, "All scripture is inspired by
God and profitable for teaching, for reproof, for correction, and for training in
righteousness, *that the man of God may be complete, equipped for every good work*"
(2 Tim. 3:16–17).

Here Paul indicates that one purpose for which God caused Scripture to be
written is to train us that we might be "equipped for every good work." If there is
any "good work" that God wants a Christian to do, this passage indicates that
God has made provision in his Word for training the Christian in it. Thus, there is

no "good work" that God wants us to do other than those that are taught somewhere in Scripture: it can equip us for *every* good work.

A similar teaching is found in Psalm 119: "Blessed are those whose way is *blameless* who *walk in the law of the LORD!*" (v. 1). This verse shows an equivalence between being "blameless" and "walking in the law of the LORD": those who are blameless are those who walk in the law of the Lord. Here again is an indication that all that God requires of us is recorded in his written Word: simply to do all that the Bible commands us is to be blameless in God's sight.

To be morally perfect in God's sight, then, what must we do in addition to what God commands us in Scripture? Nothing! Nothing at all! If we simply keep the words of Scripture we will be "blameless" and we will be doing "every good work" that God expects of us.

## B. We Can Find All That God Has Said on Particular Topics, and We Can Find Answers to Our Questions

Of course, we realize that we will never perfectly obey all of Scripture in this life (see James 3:2; 1 John 1:8–10; and chapter 24, below). Thus, it may not at first seem very significant to say that all we have to do is what God commands us in the Bible, since we will never be able to obey it all in this life anyway. But the truth of the sufficiency of Scripture is of great significance for our Christian lives, for it enables us to *focus* our search for God's words to us on the Bible alone and saves us from the endless task of searching through all the writings of Christians throughout history, or through all the teachings of the church, or through all the subjective feelings and impressions that come to our minds from day to day,[1] in order to find what God requires of us. In a very practical sense, it means that we are able to come to clear conclusions on many teachings of Scripture. For example, though it requires some work, it is possible to find all the biblical passages that are directly relevant to the matters of marriage and divorce, or the responsibilities of parents to children, or the relationship between a Christian and civil government.

This doctrine means, moreover, that it is possible to collect all the passages that directly relate to doctrinal issues such as the atonement, or the person of Christ, or

---

[1]This is not meant to imply that subjective impressions of God's will are useless or that they should be ignored. That would suggest almost a deistic view of God's (non-)involvement in the lives of his children and a rather mechanical, impersonal view of guidance. God can and indeed does use subjective impressions of his will to remind and encourage us and often to prompt our thoughts in the right direction in many rapid decisions that we make throughout the day—and it is Scripture itself that tells us about these subjective factors in guidance (see Acts 16:6–7; Rom. 8:9, 14, 16; Gal. 5:16–18, 25). Yet these verses on the sufficiency of Scripture teach us that such subjective impressions can only *remind* us of moral commands that are already in Scripture, or bring to mind facts that we (in theory at least) could have known or did know otherwise; they can never add to the commands of Scripture, or replace Scripture in defining what God's will is, or equal Scripture in authority in our lives.

Because people from all kinds of Christian traditions have made serious mistakes when they felt confident that God was "leading them" to make a particular decision, it is important to remember that, except where an explicit text of Scripture applies directly to a situation, we can never have 100 percent certainty in this life that we know what God's will is in a situation. We can only have varying degrees of confidence in different situations. Though our ability to discern God's will should increase as we grow in Christian maturity, we will inevitably make some mistakes. In this regard, I have found helpful a sentence from Edmund Clowney: "The degree of certainty we have with regard to God's will in a situation is directly proportional to the degree of clarity we have as to how the Word of God applies to the situation" (from a personal conversation, November 1992).

the work of the Holy Spirit in the believer's life today. In these and hundreds of other moral and doctrinal questions, the biblical teaching about the sufficiency of Scripture gives us confidence that we *will be able to find* what God requires us to think or to do in these areas. In many of these areas we can attain confidence that we, together with the vast majority of the church throughout history, have found and correctly formulated what God wants us to think or to do. Simply stated, the doctrine of the sufficiency of Scripture tells us that it is possible to study systematic theology and ethics and find answers to our questions.

At this point we differ from Roman Catholic theologians, who would say that we have not found all that God says to us about any particular subject until we have also listened to the official teaching of the church throughout its history. We would respond that although the history of the church may help us to *understand* what God says to us in the Bible, never in church history has God *added* to the teachings or commands of Scripture: Nowhere in church history outside of Scripture has God *added* anything that he requires us to believe or to do. Scripture is sufficient to equip us for "every good work," and to walk in its ways is to be "blameless" in God's sight.

At this point we also differ from nonevangelical theologians who are not convinced that the Bible is God's Word in any unique or absolutely authoritative sense, and who would therefore search not only the Bible but also many other early Christian writings in an attempt to find not so much *what God said* to mankind but rather *what many early Christians experienced* in their relationship with God. They would not expect to arrive at a single, unified conclusion about what God wants us to think or do with regard to any particular question, but to discover a variety of opinions and viewpoints collected around some major unifying ideas. All of the viewpoints held by early Christians in any of the early churches would then be potentially valid viewpoints for Christians to hold today as well. To this we would reply that our search for answers to theological and ethical questions is not a search to find what various believers have thought in the history of the church, but is a quest to find and understand what God himself says to us in his own words, which are found in Scripture and only in Scripture.

## C. The Amount of Scripture Given Was Sufficient at Each Stage of Redemptive History

The doctrine of the sufficiency of Scripture does not imply that *God* cannot add any more words to those he has already spoken to his people. It rather implies that *man* cannot add on his own initiative any words to those that God has already spoken. Furthermore, it implies that in fact *God has not spoken* to mankind any more words which he requires us to believe or obey other than those which we have now in the Bible.

This point is important, for it helps us to understand how God could tell his people that his words to them were sufficient at many different points in the history of redemption, and how he could nevertheless add to those words later. For example, in Deuteronomy 29:29 Moses says, "The secret things belong to the LORD our God; but the things that are revealed belong to us and to our children for ever, that we may do all the words of this law."

This verse reminds us that God has always taken the initiative in revealing things to us. He has decided what to reveal and what not to reveal. At each stage in redemptive history, the things that God had revealed were for his people for that time, and they were to study, believe, and obey those things. With further progress in the history of redemption, more of God's words were added, recording and interpreting that history (see chapter 3 above regarding the development of the canon).

Thus, at the time of the death of Moses, the first five books of our Old Testament were sufficient for God's people at that time. But God directed later authors to add more so that Scripture would be sufficient for believers in subsequent times. For Christians today, the words from God that we have in the Old and New Testaments together are sufficient for us during the church age. After the death, resurrection, and ascension of Christ, and the founding of the early church as recorded in the New Testament, and the assembling of the books of the New Testament canon, no further central redemptive acts of God in history (acts that have direct relevance for all God's people for all subsequent time) have occurred, and thus no further words of God have been given to record and interpret those acts for us.

This means that we can cite Scripture texts from throughout the canon to show that the principle of the sufficiency of God's revelation to his people at each particular time has remained the same. In this sense, these verses that talk about the sufficiency of Scripture in earlier periods are directly applicable to us as well, even though the extent of the Bible to which they refer in our situation is greater than the extent of the Scripture to which they referred in their original setting. The following texts from Scripture thus apply to us also in that sense:

*You shall not add to the word which I command you*, nor take from it; that you may keep the commandments of the LORD your God which I command you. (Deut. 4:2)

Everything that I command you you shall be careful to do; *you shall not add to it or take from it*. (Deut. 12:32)

Every word of God proves true; he is a shield to those who take refuge in him. *Do not add to his words*, lest he rebuke you, and you be found a liar. (Prov. 30:5–6)

I warn everyone who hears the words of the prophecy of this book: *if anyone adds to them*, God will add to him the plagues described in this book, and if anyone takes away from the words of the book of this prophecy, God will take away his share in the tree of life and in the holy city, which are described in this book. (Rev. 22:18–19)[2]

## D. Practical Applications of the Sufficiency of Scripture

The doctrine of the sufficiency of Scripture has several practical applications to our Christian lives. The following list is intended to be helpful but not exhaustive.

1. The sufficiency of Scripture should encourage us as we try to discover what God would have us to *think* (about a particular doctrinal issue) or to *do* (in a particular situation). We should be encouraged that *everything* God wants to tell

---

[2]The primary reference of this verse is of course to the book of Revelation itself, but its placement here at the very end of the only book that could come last in the New Testament canon can hardly be accidental. Thus, a secondary application of this verse to the entire canon does not seem inappropriate (see the discussion in chapter 3, pp. 64–65).

us about that question is to be found in Scripture. This does not mean that the Bible answers all the questions that we might think up, for "The secret things belong to the LORD our God" (Deut. 29:29). But it does mean that when we are facing a problem of genuine importance to our Christian life, we can approach Scripture with the confidence that from it God will provide us with guidance for that problem.

There will of course be some times when the answer we find is that Scripture does not speak directly to our question. (This would be the case, for example, if we tried to find from Scripture what "order of worship" to follow on Sunday mornings, or whether it is better to kneel or perhaps to stand when we pray, or at what time we should eat our meals during the day, etc.) In those cases, we may conclude that God has not required us to think or to act in any certain way with regard to that question (except, perhaps, in terms of more general principles regarding our attitudes and goals). But in many other cases we will find direct and clear guidance from the Lord to equip us for "every good work" (2 Tim. 3:17).

As we go through life, frequent practice in searching Scripture for guidance will result in an increasing ability to find accurate, carefully formulated answers to our problems and questions. Lifelong growth in understanding Scripture will thus include growth in the skill of rightly understanding the Bible's teachings and applying them to specific questions.

2. The sufficiency of Scripture reminds us that *we are to add nothing to Scripture,* and that *we are to consider no other writings of equal value to Scripture.* This principle is violated by almost all cults and sects. Mormons, for example, claim to believe the Bible, but they also claim divine authority for the *Book of Mormon.* Christian Scientists similarly claim to believe the Bible, but in practice they hold the book *Science and Health With a Key to the Scriptures,* by Mary Baker Eddy, on a par with Scripture or above it in authority. Since these claims violate God's commands not to add to his words, we should not think that any additional words from God to us would be found in these writings. Even in Christian churches a similar error is sometimes made when people go beyond what Scripture says and assert with great confidence new ideas about God or heaven, basing their teachings not on Scripture but on their own speculation or even on claimed experiences of dying and coming back to life.

3. The sufficiency of Scripture also tells us that *God does not require us to believe anything about himself or his redemptive work that is not found in Scripture.* Among writings from the time of the early church are some collections of alleged sayings of Jesus that were not preserved in the Gospels. It is likely that at least some of the "sayings of Jesus" found in these writings are rather accurate records of things Jesus actually said (though it is now impossible for us to determine with any high degree of probability which sayings those are). But it does not really matter at all for our Christian lives if we never read any of those sayings, for God has caused to be recorded in Scripture everything that we need to know about Jesus' words and deeds in order to trust and obey him perfectly. Though these collections of sayings do have some limited value in linguistic research and perhaps in the study of the history of the church, they are of no direct value whatever for us in learning what we should believe about the life and teachings of Christ, or in formulating our doctrinal or ethical convictions.

4. The sufficiency of Scripture shows us that *no modern revelations from God are*

*to be placed on a level equal to Scripture in authority.* At various times throughout the history of the church, and particularly in the modern charismatic movement, people have claimed that God has given revelations through them for the benefit of the church. However we may evaluate such claims,[3] we must be careful never to allow (in theory or in practice) the placing of such revelations on a level equal to Scripture.[4] We must insist that God does not require us to believe anything about himself or his work in the world that is contained in these revelations but not in Scripture. And we must insist that God does not require us to obey any moral directives that come to us through such means but that are not confirmed by Scripture. The Bible contains everything we need God to tell us for trusting and obeying him perfectly.[5]

It should also be noted at this point that whenever challenges to the sufficiency of Scripture have come in the form of other documents to be placed alongside Scripture (whether from extrabiblical Christian literature of the first century or from the accumulated teachings of the Roman Catholic Church, or from the books of various cults such as the *Book of Mormon*), the result has always been (1) to deemphasize the teachings of the Bible itself and (2) to begin to teach some things that are contrary to Scripture. This is a danger of which the church must constantly be aware.

5. With regard to living the Christian life, the sufficiency of Scripture reminds us that *nothing is sin that is not forbidden by Scripture either explicitly or by implication.* To walk in the law of the Lord is to be "blameless" (Ps. 119:1). Therefore we are not to add prohibitions to those already stated in Scripture. From time to time there may be situations in which it would be wrong, for example, for an individual Christian to drink coffee or Coca-Cola, or to attend movie theaters, or to eat meat offered to idols (see 1 Cor. 8–10), but unless some specific teaching or some general principle of Scripture can be shown to prohibit these (or any other activities) for all believers for all time, we must insist that these activities are not in themselves sinful and they are not in all situations prohibited by God for his people.[6]

---

[3]See chapter 52, pp. 1039–42, on the possibility of some kinds of revelation from God continuing today when the canon is closed, and especially chapter 53, pp. 1049–61, on the gift of prophecy.

[4]In fact, the more responsible spokesmen for the modern charismatic movement seem generally to agree with this caution: see Wayne Grudem, *The Gift of Prophecy in the New Testament and Today* (Eastbourne, England: Kingsway, and Westchester, Ill.: Crossway, 1988), pp. 110–12; 245–50.

[5]I do not wish to imply at this point that I am adopting a "cessationist" view of spiritual gifts (that is, a view that holds that certain gifts, such as prophecy and speaking in tongues, ceased when the apostles died). I only wish at this point to state that there is a danger in explicitly or even implicitly giving these gifts a status that effectively challenges the authority or the sufficiency of Scripture in Christians' lives. More detailed discussion of these gifts is given in chapter 53 below, and in Wayne Grudem, *The Gift of Prophecy in the New Testament and Today* (see n. 4 above).

[6]Of course, human societies such as nations, churches, families, etc. can make rules for the conduct of their own affairs (such as "Children in this family may not watch television on weeknights"). No such rule can be found in Scripture, nor is it likely that such a rule could be demonstrated by implication from the principles of Scripture. Yet obedience to these rules is required by God because Scripture tells us to be subject to governing authorities (Rom. 13:1–7; 1 Peter 2:13–3:6; et al.). A denial of the sufficiency of Scripture would occur only if someone attempted to give the rule a generalized application outside of the situation in which it should appropriately function ("No member of our church should watch TV on weeknights" or "No Christian should watch TV on weeknights"). In such a case it has become not a rule for conduct in one specific situation but a moral command apparently intended to apply to all Christians no matter what their situation. We are not free to add such rules to Scripture and to attempt to impose them on all the believers over whom we have influence, nor can the

This also is an important principle because there is always the tendency among believers to begin to neglect the regular daily searching of Scripture for guidance and to begin to live by a set of written or unwritten rules (or denominational traditions) concerning what one does or does not do in the Christian life.

Furthermore, whenever we add to the list of sins that are prohibited by Scripture itself, there will be harm to the church and to the lives of individual believers. The Holy Spirit will not empower obedience to rules that do not have God's approval from Scripture, nor will believers generally find delight in obedience to commands that do not accord with the laws of God written on their hearts. In some cases, Christians may repeatedly and earnestly plead with God for "victory" over supposed sins that are in fact no sins at all, yet no "victory" will be given, for the attitude or action in question is in fact not a sin and is not displeasing to God. Great discouragement in prayer and frustration in the Christian life generally may be the outcome.

In other cases, continued or even increasing disobedience to these new "sins" will result, together with a false sense of guilt and a resulting alienation from God. Often there arises an increasingly uncompromising and legalistic insistence on these new rules on the part of those who *do* follow them, and genuine fellowship among believers in the church will fade away. Evangelism will often be stifled, for the silent proclamation of the gospel that comes from the lives of believers will at least *seem* (to outsiders) to include the additional requirement that one must fit this uniform pattern of life in order to become a member of the body of Christ.

One clear example of such an addition to the commands of Scripture is found in the opposition of the Roman Catholic Church to "artificial" methods of birth control, a policy that finds no valid support in Scripture. Widespread disobedience, alienation, and false guilt have been the result. Yet such is the propensity of human nature to make such rules that other examples can probably be found in the written or unwritten traditions of almost every denomination.

6. The sufficiency of Scripture also tells us that *nothing is required of us by God that is not commanded in Scripture either explicitly or by implication.* This reminds us that the focus of our search for God's will ought to be on Scripture, rather than on seeking guidance through prayer for changed circumstances or altered feelings or direct guidance from the Holy Spirit apart from Scripture. It also means that if someone *claims* to have a message from God telling us what we ought to do, we need never assume that it is sin to disobey such a message unless it can be confirmed by the application of Scripture itself to our situation.

The discovery of this great truth could bring tremendous joy and peace to the lives of thousands of Christians who, spending countless hours seeking God's will outside of Scripture, are often uncertain about whether they have found it. In fact, many Christians today have very little confidence in their ability to discover God's will with any degree of certainty. Thus, there is little striving to do God's will (for who can know it?) and little growth in holiness before God.

The opposite ought to be true. Christians who are convinced of the sufficiency of Scripture should begin eagerly to seek and find God's will in Scripture. They

---

church as a whole attempt to do this. (Here again, Roman Catholics would differ and would say that God gives to the church the authority to impose moral rules in addition to Scripture on all the members of the church.)

should be eagerly and regularly growing in obedience to God, knowing great freedom and peace in the Christian life. Then they would be able to say with the psalmist:

> I will keep your law continually,
>> for ever and ever;
> and *I shall walk at liberty,*
>> *for I have sought your precepts.* . . .
>
> *Great peace have those who love your law;*
>> nothing can make them stumble. (Ps. 119:44–45, 165)

7. The sufficiency of Scripture reminds us that in our doctrinal and ethical teaching we should *emphasize what Scripture emphasizes and be content with what God has told us in Scripture.* There are some subjects about which God has told us little or nothing in the Bible. We must remember that "The secret things belong to the LORD our God" (Deut. 29:29) and that God has revealed to us in Scripture exactly what he deemed right for us. We must accept this and not think that Scripture is something less than it should be, or begin to wish that God had given us much more information about subjects on which there are very few scriptural references. Of course, there will be some situations where we are confronted with a particular problem that requires a great deal of attention, far greater than the emphasis that it receives in the teaching of Scripture. But those situations should be relatively infrequent and should not be representative of the general course of our lives or ministries.

It is characteristic of many cults that they emphasize obscure portions or teachings of Scripture (one thinks of the Mormon emphasis on baptism for the dead, a subject that is mentioned in only one verse in the Bible [1 Cor. 15:29], in a phrase whose exact meaning is apparently impossible now to determine with certainty). But a similar error was made by an entire generation of liberal New Testament scholars in the earlier part of this century, who devoted most of their scholarly lives to a futile search for the sources "behind" our present gospel narratives or to a search for the "authentic" sayings of Jesus.

Unfortunately, a similar pattern has too often occurred among evangelicals within various denominations. The doctrinal matters that have divided evangelical Protestant denominations from one another have almost uniformly been matters on which the Bible places relatively little emphasis, and matters in which our conclusions must be drawn from skillful inference much more than from direct biblical statements. For example, abiding denominational differences have occurred or have been maintained over the "proper" form of church government, the exact nature of Christ's presence in the Lord's Supper, the exact sequence of the events surrounding Christ's return, the categories of persons who should be admitted to the Lord's Supper, the way in which God planned that the merits of Christ's death would be applied to believers and not applied to unbelievers, the proper subjects for baptism, the correct understanding of the "baptism in the Holy Spirit," and so forth.

We should not say that these issues are all unimportant, nor should we say that Scripture gives no solution to any of them (indeed, with respect to many of them a specific solution will be defended in subsequent chapters of this book). However, since all of these topics receive *relatively little direct emphasis in Scripture,* it is ironic and tragic that denominational leaders will so often give much of their lives to defending precisely the minor doctrinal points that make their denominations different from others. Is such effort really motivated by a desire to bring unity of understanding to the church, or might it stem in some measure from human pride, a desire to retain power over others, and an attempt at self-justification, which is displeasing to God and ultimately unedifying to the church?

## QUESTIONS FOR PERSONAL APPLICATION

1. In the process of growing in the Christian life and deepening your relationship with God, approximately how much emphasis have you placed on reading the Bible itself and how much on reading other Christian books? In seeking to know God's will for your daily life, what is the relative emphasis you have put on reading Scripture itself and on reading other Christian books? Do you think the doctrine of the sufficiency of Scripture will cause you to place more emphasis on reading Scripture itself?

2. What are some of the doctrinal or moral questions you are wondering about? Has this chapter increased your confidence in the ability of Scripture to provide a clear answer for some of those questions?

3. Have you ever wished that the Bible would say more than it does about a certain subject? Or less? What do you think motivated that wish? After reading this chapter, how would you approach someone who expressed such a wish today? How is God's wisdom shown in the fact that he chose not to make the Bible a great deal longer or a great deal shorter than it actually is?

4. If the Bible contains everything we need God to tell us for obeying him perfectly, what is the role of the following in helping us to find God's will for ourselves: advice from others; sermons or Bible classes; our consciences; our feelings; the leading of the Holy Spirit as we sense him prompting our inward desires and subjective impressions; changes in circumstances; the gift of prophecy (if you think it can function today)?

5. In the light of this chapter, how would you find God's "perfect" will for your life? Is it possible that there would be more than one "perfect" choice in many decisions we make? (Consider Ps. 1:3 and 1 Cor. 7:39 in seeking an answer.)

6. Have there been times when you have understood the principles of Scripture well enough with regard to a specific situation but have not known the facts of the situation well enough to know how to apply those scriptural principles correctly? In seeking to know God's will, can there be any other things we need to know except (a) the teaching of Scripture and (b) the facts of the situation in question, together with (c) skill in applying (a) to (b) correctly? What then is the role of prayer in seeking guidance? What should we pray for?

## SPECIAL TERMS

blameless
sufficiency of Scripture

## BIBLIOGRAPHY

(For an explanation of this bibliography see the note on the bibliography to chapter 1, p. 38. Complete bibliographical data may be found on pp. 1223–29.)

### Sections in Evangelical Systematic Theologies

1. Anglican (Episcopalian)
   - 1930       Thomas, 120–23
2. Arminian (Wesleyan or Methodist)
   - 1875–76    Pope, 1:206–9
   - 1983       Carter, 1:290–91
3. Baptist
   - 1767       Gill, 1:25–30
   - 1983–85    Erickson, 256–59
4. Dispensational
   - 1947       Chafer, 1:60
5. Lutheran
   - 1917–24    Pieper, 1:317–19
   - 1934       Mueller, 137–38
6. Reformed (or Presbyterian)
   - 1559       Calvin, 1:93–96 (1.9)
   - 1861       Heppe, 28–31
   - 1871–73    Hodge, 1:182–83
   - 1937–66    Murray, *CW,* 1:16–22; *PC,* 11–26
   - 1938       Berkhof, *Intro.,* 167–69
7. Renewal (or charismatic/Pentecostal)
   - 1988–92    Williams, 1:43–44

### Sections in Representative Roman Catholic Systematic Theologies

1. Roman Catholic: Traditional
   - 1955       Ott (no explicit treatment)
2. Roman Catholic: Post-Vatican II
   - 1980       McBrien, 1:62–77

### Other Works

Friesen, Garry, and J. Robin Maxson. *Decision Making and the Will of God.* Portland, Ore.: Multnomah, 1981.

Packer, J. I. "Scripture." In *NDT*, pp. 627–31.
Weeks, Noel. *The Sufficiency of Scripture*. Edinburgh and Carlisle, Pa.: Banner of
    Truth, 1988.

## SCRIPTURE MEMORY PASSAGE

**Psalm 119:1:** *Blessed are those whose way is blameless, who walk in the law of the
LORD!*

## HYMN

### "How Firm a Foundation"

Few if any hymns deal specifically with the sufficiency of Scripture, perhaps because Christians have
failed to realize the great comfort and peace that this doctrine brings to the Christian life. But the first
verse of the following hymn contains a statement of this doctrine. It begins by telling us that God has
laid a firm foundation for our faith in his Word. Then it says, "What more can he say than to you he
hath said . . .?" The rich and full promises of God throughout Scripture are sufficient for our every
need in every circumstance. This should be great cause for rejoicing! The subsequent verses contain
quotations, paraphrases, and allusions to promises of God that are scattered throughout Scripture,
many of them from Isaiah. Verses 2–6 are all written as sentences that are spoken by God to us, and
when we sing them we should think of ourselves singing the words of God's promises to others in the
congregation for their comfort and encouragement.

How firm a foundation, ye saints of the Lord,
    Is laid for your faith in his excellent Word!
What more can he say than to you he hath said,
    You who unto Jesus for refuge have fled?
    You who unto Jesus for refuge have fled?

"Fear not, I am with thee, O be not dismayed;
    I, I am thy God, and will still give thee aid;
I'll strengthen thee, help thee, and cause thee to stand,
    Upheld by my righteous, omnipotent hand,
    Upheld by my righteous, omnipotent hand.

"When through the deep waters I call thee to go,
    The rivers of woe shall not thee overflow;
For I will be with thee thy troubles to bless,
    And sanctify to thee thy deepest distress,
    And sanctify to thee thy deepest distress.

"When through fiery trials thy pathway shall lie,
    My grace, all sufficient, shall be thy supply;
The flame shall not hurt thee; I only design
    Thy dross to consume, and thy gold to refine,
    Thy dross to consume, and thy gold to refine.

"E'en down to old age all my people shall prove
    My sovereign, eternal, unchangeable love;
And when hoary hairs shall their temples adorn,

Like lambs they shall still in my bosom be borne,
Like lambs they shall still in my bosom be borne.

"The soul that on Jesus hath leaned for repose,
I will not, I will not desert to his foes;
That soul, though all hell should endeavor to shake,
I'll never, no, never, no, never forsake,
I'll never, no, never, no, never forsake."

FROM: RIPPON'S *SELECTION OF HYMNS*, 1787

# Part 2

# The Doctrine of God

# Chapter 9

# The Existence of God

*How do we know that God exists?*

## EXPLANATION AND SCRIPTURAL BASIS

How do we know that God exists? The answer can be given in two parts: First, all people have an inner sense of God. Second, we believe the evidence that is found in Scripture and in nature.

### A. Humanity's Inner Sense of God

All persons everywhere have a deep, inner sense that God exists, that they are his creatures, and that he is their Creator. Paul says that even Gentile unbelievers "knew God" but did not honor him as God or give thanks to him (Rom. 1:21). He says that wicked unbelievers have "exchanged the truth about God for a lie" (Rom. 1:25), implying that they actively or willfully rejected some truth about God's existence and character that they knew. Paul says that "what can be known about God is plain to them," and adds that this is "because God has shown it to them" (Rom. 1:19).

Yet Scripture also recognizes that some people deny this inner sense of God and even deny that God exists. It is "the *fool*" who says in his heart, "There is no God" (Ps. 14:1; 53:1). It is the wicked person who first "curses and renounces the LORD" and then in pride repeatedly thinks "there is no God" (Ps. 10:3–4). These passages indicate both that sin leads people to think irrationally and to deny God's existence, and that it is someone who is thinking irrationally or who has been deceived who will say, "There is no God."

Paul also recognizes that sin will cause people to *deny* their knowledge of God: he speaks of those who "by their wickedness *suppress the truth*" (Rom. 1:18) and says that those who do this are "without excuse" for this denial of God (Rom. 1:20). A series of active verbs indicates that this is a willful suppression of the truth (Rom. 1:23, 25, 28, 32).[1]

---

[1]Some people deny that they have an inner sense of God. But their awareness of God will often make itself evident in a time of personal crisis, when deep-seated convictions of the heart show themselves in outward words and deeds. Several years ago I was a passenger in a car with several friends, including a young woman who in conversation was firmly denying that she had any inner awareness of God's existence. Shortly thereafter the car hit a patch of ice and spun around in a complete circle at high speed. Before the car came to rest in a large snow bank (with no serious damage) this same woman

In the life of a Christian this inner awareness of God becomes stronger and more distinct. We begin to know God as our loving Father in heaven (Rom. 8:15), the Holy Spirit bears witness with our spirits that we are children of God (Rom. 8:16), and we come to know Jesus Christ living within our hearts (Eph. 3:17; Phil. 3:8, 10; Col. 1:27; John 14:23). The intensity of this awareness for a Christian is such that though we have not seen our Lord Jesus Christ, we indeed love him (1 Peter 1:8).

## B. Believing the Evidence in Scripture and Nature

In addition to people's inner awareness of God that bears clear witness to the fact that God exists, clear evidence of his existence is to be seen in Scripture and in nature.

The evidence that God exists is of course found throughout the Bible. In fact, the Bible everywhere assumes that God exists. The first verse of Genesis does not present evidence for the existence of God but begins immediately to tell us what he has done: "In the beginning God created the heavens and the earth." If we are convinced that the Bible is true, then we know from the Bible not only that God exists but also very much about his nature and his acts.

The world also gives abundant evidence of God's existence. Paul says that God's eternal nature and deity have been "clearly perceived in the things that have been made" (Rom. 1:20). This broad reference to "the things that have been made" suggests that in some sense every created thing gives evidence of God's character. Nevertheless, it is man himself, created in the image of God, who most abundantly bears witness to the existence of God: whenever we meet another human being, we should (if our minds are thinking correctly) realize that such an incredibly intricate, skillful, communicative living creature could only have been created by an infinite, all-wise Creator.

In addition to the evidence seen in the existence of living human beings, there is further excellent evidence in nature. The "rains and fruitful seasons" as well as the "food and gladness" that all people experience and benefit from are also said by Barnabas and Paul to be witnesses to God (Acts 14:17). David tells us of the witness of the heavens: "*The heavens are telling the glory of God;* and the firmament proclaims his handiwork. Day to day pours forth speech, and night to night declares knowledge" (Ps. 19:1–2). To look upward into the sky by day or by night is to see sun, moon, and stars, sky and clouds, all continually declaring by their existence and beauty and greatness that a powerful and wise Creator has made them and sustains them in their order.

This wide variety of testimonies to God's existence from various parts of the created world suggests to us that in one sense *everything that exists* gives evidence of God's existence. For those who have eyes to see and evaluate the evidence correctly, every leaf on every tree, every blade of grass, every star in the sky, and every other part of creation all cry out continuously, "God made me! God made me! God made me!" If our hearts and minds were not so blinded by sin, it would be impossible for us to look closely at a leaf from any tree and say, "No one

could be heard distinctly calling out, "Lord Jesus, please help us!" The rest of us looked at her in amazement when we realized that her agnosticism had been disproved by words from her own mouth.

created this: it just happened." The beauty of a snowflake, the majestic power of a thunderstorm, the skill of a honeybee, the refreshing taste of cold water, the incredible abilities of the human hand—all these and thousands of other aspects of creation simply could not have come into existence apart from the activity of an all-powerful and all-wise Creator.

Thus, for those who are correctly evaluating the evidence, *everything* in Scripture and *everything* in nature proves clearly that God exists and that he is the powerful and wise Creator that Scripture describes him to be. Therefore, when we believe that God exists, we are basing our belief *not* on some blind hope apart from any evidence, but on *an overwhelming amount of reliable evidence from God's words and God's works.* It is a characteristic of true faith that it is a confidence based on reliable evidence, and faith in the existence of God shares this characteristic.

Furthermore, these evidences can all be seen as valid proofs for the existence of God, even though some people reject them. This does not mean that the evidence is invalid in itself, only that those who reject the evidence are evaluating it wrongly.

## C. Traditional "Proofs" for the Existence of God

The traditional "proofs" for the existence of God that have been constructed by Christian (and some non-Christian) philosophers at various points in history are in fact attempts to analyze the evidence, especially the evidence from nature, in extremely careful and logically precise ways, in order to persuade people that it is not rational to reject the idea of God's existence. If it is true that sin causes people to think *irrationally,* then these proofs are attempts to cause people to think *rationally* or correctly about the evidence for God's existence, in spite of the irrational tendencies caused by sin.

Most of the traditional proofs for the existence of God can be classified in four major types of argument:

1. The *cosmological argument* considers the fact that every known thing in the universe has a cause. Therefore, it reasons, the universe itself must also have a cause, and the cause of such a great universe can only be God.

2. The *teleological argument* is really a subcategory of the cosmological argument. It focuses on the evidence of harmony, order, and design in the universe, and argues that its design gives evidence of an intelligent purpose (the Greek word *telos* means "end" or "goal" or "purpose"). Since the universe appears to be designed with a purpose, there must be an intelligent and purposeful God who created it to function this way.

3. The *ontological argument* begins with the idea of God, who is defined as a being "greater than which nothing can be imagined." It then argues that the characteristic of existence must belong to such a being, since it is greater to exist than not to exist.[2]

4. The *moral argument* begins from man's sense of right and wrong, and of the need for justice to be done, and argues that there must be a God who is the source of right and wrong and who will someday mete out justice to all people.

Because all of these arguments are based on facts about the creation that are

---

[2]The stem *ont-* in "ontological" is derived from a Greek word that means "being."

indeed true facts, we may say that all of these proofs (when carefully constructed) are, in an objective sense, valid proofs. They are valid in that they correctly evaluate the evidence and correctly reason to a true conclusion—in fact, the universe *does* have God as its cause, and it *does* show evidence of purposeful design, and God *does* exist as a being greater than which nothing can be imagined, and God *has* given us a sense of right and wrong and a sense that his judgment is coming someday. The *actual facts* referred to in these proofs, therefore, are *true*, and in that sense the proofs are valid, even though not all people are persuaded by them.

But in another sense, if "valid" means "able to compel agreement even from those who begin with false assumptions," then of course none of the proofs is valid because not one of them is able to *compel agreement* from *everyone who considers them*. Yet this is because many unbelievers either begin with invalid assumptions or do not reason correctly from the evidence. It is not because the proofs are invalid in themselves.

The value of these proofs, then, lies chiefly in overcoming some of the intellectual objections of unbelievers. They cannot bring unbelievers to saving faith, for that comes about through belief in the testimony of Scripture. But they can help overcome objections from unbelievers, and, for believers, they can provide further intellectual evidence for something they have already been persuaded of from their own inner sense of God and from the testimony of Scripture.

## D. Only God Can Overcome Our Sin and Enable Us to Be Persuaded of His Existence

Finally, it must be remembered that in this sinful world *God must enable us to be persuaded* or we would never believe in him. We read that "the god of this world has *blinded the minds of the unbelievers,* to keep them from seeing the light of the gospel of the glory of Christ" (2 Cor. 4:4). Furthermore, Paul says that "since, in the wisdom of God, the world did not know God through wisdom, it pleased God through the folly of what we preach to save those who believe" (1 Cor. 1:21). In this sinful world, human wisdom is inadequate for coming to know God. Thus, Paul's preaching came "in demonstration of the Spirit and of power, *that your faith might not rest in the wisdom of men but in the power of God*" (1 Cor. 2:5). We are dependent upon God to remove the blindness and irrationality caused by sin and to enable us to evaluate the evidence rightly, believe what Scripture says, and come to saving faith in Christ.

## QUESTIONS FOR PERSONAL APPLICATION

1. When the seraphim around God's throne cry out, "Holy, holy, holy is the LORD of hosts; *the whole earth is full of his glory*" (Isa. 6:3), do you think they are seeing the earth from a somewhat different perspective than ours? In what ways? How can we begin to see the world more from this perspective?

2. When is your inner sense of God's existence strongest? Weakest? Why? In which of these situations are you in a condition more like the one you will have in heaven? In which of these types of situations are your judgments more reliable?

3. Look at your hand. Is it more or less complex than a wristwatch? Is it logical to think that either one of them just came about by an accidental combination of elements?

4. Do most people today believe in the existence of God? Has this been true throughout history? If they believe that God exists, why have they not worshiped him rightly?

5. Why do some people deny the existence of God? Does Romans 1:18 suggest there is often a moral factor influencing their intellectual denial of God's existence (cf. Ps. 14:1–3)? What is the best way to approach someone who denies the existence of God?

## SPECIAL TERMS

cosmological argument
inner sense of God
moral argument

ontological argument
teleological argument

## BIBLIOGRAPHY

(For an explanation of this bibliography see the note on the bibliography to chapter 1, p. 38. Complete bibliographical data may be found on pp. 1223–29.)

### Sections in Evangelical Systematic Theologies

1. Anglican (Episcopalian)
   - 1882–92    Litton, 42–58
   - 1930    Thomas, 3–14
2. Arminian (Wesleyan or Methodist)
   - 1875–76    Pope, 1:233–48
   - 1892–94    Miley, 1:57–136
   - 1940    Wiley, 1:217–40
   - 1960    Purkiser, 39–59
   - 1983    Carter, 1:107–11
   - 1983–    Cottrell, 1:419–42
   - 1987–90    Oden, 1:131–80
3. Baptist
   - 1767    Gill, 1:1–15
   - 1887    Boyce, 8–46
   - 1907    Strong, 52–110
   - 1917    Mullins, 35–48
   - 1983–85    Erickson, 156–74

4. Dispensational
      1947     Chafer, 1:129–78
      1949     Thiessen, 21–42
      1986     Ryrie, 25–34
5. Lutheran
    1917–24    Pieper, 1:371–74
      1934     Mueller, 143–47
6. Reformed (or Presbyterian)
      1559     Calvin, 1:43–69 (1.3–5)
      1861     Heppe, 47–56
    1871–73    Hodge, 1:191–334
      1878     Dabney, 5–26
   1887–1921   Warfield, *SSW,* 1:34–40
      1889     Shedd, 1:195–248
      1909     Bavinck, *DG,* 41–80
      1938     Berkhof, 19–28
      1962     Buswell, 1:72–161

## Sections in Representative Roman Catholic Systematic Theologies

1. Roman Catholic: Traditional
      1955     Ott, 13–17
2. Roman Catholic: Post-Vatican II
      1980     McBrien (no explicit treatment)

## Other Works

Brown, Colin. *Philosophy and the Christian Faith.* Downers Grove, Ill.: InterVarsity Press, 1968.

Charnock, Stephen. *The Existence and Attributes of God.* Repr. ed. Evansville, Ind.: Sovereign Grace Book Club, n.d., pp. 11–67 (first published 1655–80).

Clark, Gordon H. *Religion, Reason, and Revelation.* Nutley, N.J.: Craig Press, 1961.

France, R. T. *The Living God.* Downers Grove, Ill.: InterVarsity Press, 1970.

Geisler, Norman. *Christian Apologetics.* Grand Rapids: Baker, 1976.

———, and Paul Feinberg. *Introduction to Philosophy: A Christian Perspective.* Grand Rapids: Baker, 1980.

Hackett, Stuart. *The Resurrection of Theism.* Chicago: Moody, 1957.

Hoover, A. J. "God, Arguments for the Existence of." In *EDT,* pp. 447–51.

Lewis, Gordon R. *Testing Christianity's Truth Claims.* Chicago: Moody, 1976.

Mavrodes, George I. *Belief in God.* New York: Random House, 1970.

McDowell, Josh. *Evidence That Demands a Verdict.* San Bernardino, Calif.: Here's Life, 1972, 1979.

Packer, J. I. "God." In *NDT,* pp. 274–77.

Sire, James. *The Universe Next Door: A Basic World View Catalog.* Downers Grove, Ill.: InterVarsity Press, 1976.

Van Til, Cornelius. *The Defense of the Faith.* Philadelphia: Presbyterian and Reformed, 1955.

Yandell, Keith. *Christianity and Philosophy. Studies in a Christian World View.* Grand Rapids: Eerdmans, and Leicester: Inter-Varsity Press, 1984.

## SCRIPTURE MEMORY PASSAGE

**Romans 1:18–20:** *For the wrath of God is revealed from heaven against all ungodliness and wickedness of men who by their wickedness suppress the truth. For what can be known about God is plain to them, because God has shown it to them. Ever since the creation of the world his invisible nature, namely, his eternal power and deity, has been clearly perceived in the things that have been made. So they are without excuse.*

## HYMN

### "The Spacious Firmament on High"

This hymn, based on Psalm 19:1–4, speaks of the testimony of the sun, moon, and stars to their Creator. The word *firmament* in the first verse refers to the expanse or open space that is visible to us as we look upward from earth; it is the place in which the sun, moon, and stars exist, and might be translated "sky" or "heavens." The third verse reminds us that though these heavenly bodies make no sounds that can be heard by our physical ears, they nonetheless proclaim, to all who think rightly about them, "The hand that made us is divine."

> The spacious firmament on high,
> With all the blue ethereal sky,
> And spangled heav'ns, a shining frame,
> Their great original proclaim.
> Th' unwearied sun, from day to day,
> Does his Creator's pow'r display,
> And publishes to every land
> The work of an Almighty hand.
>
> Soon as the evening shades prevail,
> The moon takes up the wondrous tale,
> And nightly to the list'ning earth
> Repeats the story of her birth;
> Whilst all the stars that round her burn,
> And all the planets in their turn,
> Confirm the tidings as they roll,
> And spread the truth from pole to pole.
>
> What though in solemn silence all
> Move round this dark terrestrial ball?
> What though nor real voice nor sound
> Amidst their radiant orbs be found?

In reason's ear they all rejoice,
　　And utter forth a glorious voice;
For ever singing, as they shine,
　　"The hand that made us is divine."

AUTHOR: JOSEPH ADDISON, 1712

Alternative hymns: "I Sing th' Almighty Power of God"; "This Is My Father's World"; or "Day Is Dying in the West"

# Chapter 10

# The Knowability of God

*Can we really know God? How much of God can we know?*

## EXPLANATION AND SCRIPTURAL BASIS

### A. The Necessity for God to Reveal Himself to Us

If we are to know God at all, it is necessary that he reveal himself to us. Even when discussing the revelation of God that comes through nature, Paul says that what can be known about God is plain to people "because *God has shown it to them*" (Rom. 1:19). The natural creation reveals God because he chose to have himself revealed in this way.

With regard to the personal knowledge of God that comes in salvation, this idea is even more explicit. Jesus says, "No one knows the Son except the Father, and no one knows the Father except the Son and *any one to whom the Son chooses to reveal him*" (Matt. 11:27). This kind of knowledge of God is not found through human effort or wisdom: "in the wisdom of God, *the world did not know God through wisdom*" (1 Cor. 1:21; cf. 1 Cor. 2:14; 2 Cor. 4:3–4; John 1:18).

The necessity for God to reveal himself to us also is seen in the fact that sinful people misinterpret the revelation about God found in nature. Those who "by their wickedness suppress the truth" are those who "became futile in their thinking and their senseless minds were darkened . . . they exchanged the truth about God for a lie" (Rom. 1:18, 21, 25). Therefore, we need Scripture if we are to interpret natural revelation rightly. Hundreds of false religions in the world are evidence of the way sinful people, without guidance from Scripture, will always misunderstand and distort the revelation about God found in nature. But the Bible alone tells us *how to understand the testimony about God from nature*. Therefore we depend on God's active communication to us in Scripture for our true knowledge of God.

### B. We Can Never Fully Understand God

Because God is infinite and we are finite or limited, we can never fully understand God. In this sense God is said to be *incomprehensible*, where the term *incomprehensible* is used with an older and less common sense, "unable to be *fully* understood." This sense must be clearly distinguished from the more common meaning, "unable to be understood." It is not true to say that God is unable to be understood, but it is true to say that he cannot be understood fully or exhaustively.

Psalm 145 says, "Great is the LORD, and greatly to be praised, and *his greatness is unsearchable*" (Ps. 145:3). God's greatness is beyond searching out or discovering: it is too great ever to be fully known. Regarding God's understanding, Psalm 147 says, "Great is our LORD, and abundant in power; *his understanding is beyond measure*" (Ps. 147:5). We will never be able to measure or fully know the understanding of God: it is far too great for us to equal or to understand. Similarly, when thinking of God's knowledge of all his ways, David says, "*Such knowledge is too wonderful for me*; it is high, I cannot attain it" (Ps. 139:6; cf. v. 17).

Paul implies this incomprehensibility of God when he says that "the Spirit searches everything, even the depths of God," and then goes on to say that "no one comprehends the things[1] of God except the Spirit of God" (1 Cor. 2:10–12). At the end of a long discussion on the history of God's great plan of redemption, Paul breaks forth into praise: "O the depth of the riches and wisdom and knowledge of God! How unsearchable are his judgments and how inscrutable his ways!" (Rom. 11:33).

These verses allow us to take our understanding of the incomprehensibility of God one step further. It is not only true that we can never fully understand God; it is also true that *we can never fully understand any single thing about God*. His greatness (Ps. 145:3), his understanding (Ps. 147:5), his knowledge (Ps. 139:6), his riches, wisdom, judgments, and ways (Rom. 11:33) are *all* beyond our ability to understand fully. Other verses also support this idea: as the heavens are higher than the earth, so are God's ways higher than our ways and his thoughts than our thoughts (Isa. 55:9). Job says that God's great acts in creating and sustaining the earth are "but the outskirts of his ways," and exclaims, "how small a whisper do we hear of him! But the thunder of his power who can understand?" (Job 26:14; cf. 11:7–9; 37:5).

Thus, we may know *something* about God's love, power, wisdom, and so forth. But we can never know his love completely or *exhaustively*. We can never know his power exhaustively. We can never know his wisdom exhaustively, and so forth. In order to know any single thing about God exhaustively we would have to know it as he himself knows it. That is, we would have to know it in its relationship to everything else about God and in its relationship to everything else about creation throughout all eternity! We can only exclaim with David, "Such knowledge is too wonderful for me; it is high, I cannot attain it" (Ps. 139:6).

This doctrine of God's incomprehensibility has much positive application for our own lives. It means that we will never be able to know "too much" about God, for we will never run out of things to learn about him, and we will thus never tire in delighting in the discovery of more and more of his excellence and of the greatness of his works.

Even in the age to come, when we are freed from the presence of sin, we will never be able fully to understand God or any one thing about him. This is seen from the fact that the passages cited above attribute God's incomprehensibility not

---

[1]So KJV, quite literally translating the Greek phrase *ta tou theou*. RSV, NIV, and NASB all supply the word *thoughts*, because the parallel expression in v. 11, *ta tou anthrōpou* ("the things of the man"), seems to require that we supply the word *thoughts* as necessary to the context. But Paul's mention of "the depths of God" in v. 10 suggests that not only God's thoughts but all of God's being is referred to in both v. 10 and v. 12.

to our sinfulness but to his infinite greatness. It is because we are finite and God is infinite that we will never be able to understand him fully.[2] For all eternity we will be able to go on increasing in our knowledge of God and delighting ourselves more and more in him, saying with David as we learn more and more of God's own thoughts, "How precious to me are your thoughts, O God! How vast is the sum of them! If I would count them, they are more than the sand" (Ps. 139:17–18).

But if this is so in eternity future, then it certainly must be so in this life. In fact, Paul tells us that if we are to lead a life "worthy of the Lord, fully pleasing to him," it must be one in which we are continually *"increasing in the knowledge of God"* (Col. 1:10). We should be growing in our knowledge of God through our entire lives.

If we ever wished to make ourselves equal to God in knowledge, or if we wished to derive satisfaction from the sin of intellectual pride, the fact that we will never stop growing in knowledge of God would be a discouraging thing for us—we might become frustrated that God is a subject of study that we will never master! But if we rather delight in the fact that God alone is God, that he is always infinitely greater than we are, that we are his creatures who owe him worship and adoration, then this will be a very encouraging idea. Even though we spend time in Bible study and fellowship with God every day of our lives, there will always be more to learn about God and his relationships to us and the world, and thus there will always be more that we can be thankful for and for which we can give him praise. When we realize this, the prospect of a lifelong habit of regular Bible study, and even the prospect of a lifetime of study of theology (if it is theology that is solidly grounded in God's Word), should be a very exciting prospect to us. To study and to teach God's Word in both formal and informal ways will always be a great privilege and joy.

## C. Yet We Can Know God Truly

Even though we cannot know God exhaustively, we can know *true* things about God. In fact, *all that Scripture tells us* about God is true. It is true to say that God is love (1 John 4:8), that God is light (1 John 1:5), that God is spirit (John 4:24), that God is just or righteous (Rom. 3:26), and so forth. To say this, does not imply or require that we know everything about God or about his love or his righteousness or any other attribute. When I say that I have three sons, that statement is entirely true, even though I do not know everything about my sons, nor even about myself. So it is in our knowledge of God: we have true knowledge of God from Scripture, even though we do not have exhaustive knowledge. We can know some of God's thoughts—even many of them—from Scripture, and when we know them, we, like David, find them to be "precious" (Ps. 139:17). Even more significantly, it is *God himself* whom we know, not simply facts about

---

[2]This is not contradicted by 1 Cor. 13:12, "Now I know in part; then I shall understand fully, even as I have been fully understood." The phrase "know fully" is simply an attempt to translate the word *epiginōskō*, which suggests deeper or more accurate knowledge (or perhaps, in contrast with present partial knowledge, knowledge free from error or falsehood). Paul never says anything like, "Then I shall know all things," which would have been very easy to say in Greek (*tote epignōsomai ta panta*) if he had wished to do so.

him or actions he does. We make a distinction between knowing *facts* and knowing *persons* in our ordinary use of English. It would be true for me to say that I know many facts about the president of the United States, but it would not be true for me to say that I know *him*. To say that I know him would imply that I had met him and talked with him, and that I had developed at least to some degree a personal relationship with him.

Now some people say that we cannot know God himself, but that we can only know facts about him or know what he does. Others have said that we cannot know God as he is in himself, but we can only know him as he relates to us (and there is an implication that these two are somehow different). But Scripture does not speak that way. Several passages speak of our *knowing God himself*. We read God's words in Jeremiah:

> Let not the wise man glory in his wisdom, let not the mighty man glory in his might, let not the rich man glory in his riches; but let him who glories glory in this, that he understands and *knows me*, that I am the LORD who practices steadfast love, justice, and righteousness in the earth; for in these things I delight, says the LORD. (Jer. 9:23–24)

Here God says that the source of our joy and sense of importance ought to come not from our own abilities or possessions, but from the fact that we know him. Similarly, in praying to his Father, Jesus could say, "And this is eternal life, that *they know you* the only true God, and Jesus Christ whom you have sent" (John 17:3). The promise of the new covenant is that all shall know God, "from the least of them to the greatest" (Heb. 8:11), and John's first epistle tells us that the Son of God has come and given us understanding "*to know him* who is true" (1 John 5:20; see also Gal. 4:9; Phil. 3:10; 1 John 2:3; 4:8). John can say, "I write to you, children, because *you know the Father*" (1 John 2:13).

The fact that we do know God himself is further demonstrated by the realization that the richness of the Christian life includes a personal relationship with God. As these passages imply, we have a far greater privilege than mere knowledge of facts about God. We speak to God in prayer, and he speaks to us through his Word. We commune with him in his presence, we sing his praise, and we are aware that he personally dwells among us and within us to bless us (John 14:23). Indeed, this personal relationship with God the Father, with God the Son, and with God the Holy Spirit may be said to be the greatest of all the blessings of the Christian life.

## QUESTIONS FOR PERSONAL APPLICATION

1. Sometimes people say that heaven sounds boring. How does the fact that God is incomprehensible yet knowable help to answer that objection?

2. How can we be sure that when we reach heaven God will not tell us that most of what we had learned about him was wrong, and that we would have to forget what we had learned and begin to learn different things about him?

3. Do you want to go on knowing God more and more deeply for all eternity? Why or why not? Would you like sometime to be able to know God exhaustively? Why or why not?

4. Why do you think God decided to reveal himself to us? Do you learn more about God from his revelation in nature or his revelation in Scripture? Why do you think it is that God's thoughts are "precious" to us (Ps. 139:17)? Would you call your present relationship to God a personal relationship? How is it similar to your relationships with other people, and how is it different? What would make your relationship with God better?

## SPECIAL TERMS

incomprehensible
knowable

## BIBLIOGRAPHY

(For an explanation of this bibliography see the note on the bibliography to chapter 1, p. 38. Complete bibliographical data may be found on pp. 1223–29.)

### Sections in Evangelical Systematic Theologies

1. Anglican (Episcopalian)
   1882–92     Litton (no explicit treatment)
2. Arminian (Wesleyan or Methodist)
   1875–76     Pope, 1:242–48
   1892–94     Miley, 1:137–58
   1983–       Cottrell, 1:1–47, 306–87
   1987–90     Oden, 1:317–74
3. Baptist
   1767        Gill, 2:352–64
   1887        Boyce, 8–54
   1917        Mullins, 35–48
   1976–83     Henry, 2:17–167, 247–334; 5:375–409
   1983–85     Erickson, 137–40, 177–81, 268–71
4. Dispensational
   1947        Chafer, 1:179–86
   1986        Ryrie, 25–34
5. Lutheran
   1917–24     Pieper, 1:375–81
6. Reformed (or Presbyterian)
   1559        Calvin, 1:33–43 (1.1–2)
   1871–73     Hodge, 1:191–202, 335–65
   1909        Bavinck, DG, 13–110
   1938        Berkhof, 29–40

1962      Buswell, 1:29–30
7. Renewal (or charismatic/Pentecostal)
    1988–92      Williams, 1:29–46

## Sections in Representative Roman Catholic Systematic Theologies

1. Roman Catholic: Traditional
    1955      Ott, 17–24
2. Roman Catholic: Post-Vatican II
    1980      McBrien (no explicit treatment)

## Other Works

Bray, Gerald L. *The Doctrine of God.* Downers Grove, Ill.: InterVarsity Press, 1993.

Charnock, Stephen. *The Knowledge of God. The Complete Works of Stephen Charnock.* Vol. 4. Edinburgh: James Nichol, 1865. Repr. ed.: Edinburgh: Banner of Truth, 1985, esp. pp. 3–164.

Frame, John M. *The Doctrine of the Knowledge of God.* Phillipsburg, N.J.: Presbyterian and Reformed, 1987.

France, R. T. *The Living God.* Downers Grove, Ill.: InterVarsity Press, 1970.

Packer, J. I. "God." In *NDT,* pp. 274–77.

————. *Knowing God.* London: Inter-Varsity Press, 1973, pp. 13–37.

Piper, John. *Desiring God.* Portland, Ore.: Multnomah, 1986.

Tozer, A. W. *The Knowledge of the Holy.* New York: Harper and Row, 1961.

Van Til, Cornelius. *In Defense of the Faith,* vol. 5: *An Introduction to Systematic Theology.* n.p.: Presbyterian and Reformed, 1976, pp. 159–99.

## SCRIPTURE MEMORY PASSAGE

(Verse 3 of this passage tells us that God can never be fully known, but the fact that David is praising God and speaking to him shows also that he does know true things about God and does have a personal relationship to him.)

**Psalm 145:1–3:**

> *I will extol you, my God and King,*
>     *and bless your name for ever and ever.*
> *Every day I will bless you,*
>     *and praise your name for ever and ever.*
> *Great is the LORD, and greatly to be praised,*
>     *and his greatness is unsearchable.*

## HYMN

### "I Will Thee Praise, My God, O King"

Throughout the history of the church Christians have enjoyed rearranging the words of the psalms to fit some poetic meter and then setting these psalms to music for personal or group worship. This is an old metrical arrangement of the words to Psalm 145, set to the familiar melody of the hymn, "Jesus Shall Reign Where'er the Sun." Stanza 2 speaks of God's incomprehensibility ("The Lord is great; he praise exceeds; his greatness fully search can none"), and many of the other stanzas speak of various attributes of God that we know from Scripture. It should give us joy to sing this song, knowing both that we are singing absolutely true things about God, and that his greatness far exceeds any praise we will ever be able to sing to him.

I will thee praise, my God, O King,
And I will ever bless thy name;
I will extol thee every day
And evermore thy praise proclaim.

The Lord is great; he praise exceeds;
His greatness fully search can none;
Race shall to race extol thy deeds
And tell thy mighty acts each one.

Upon thy glorious majesty
And wondrous works my mind shall dwell;
Men shall recount thy dreadful acts,
And of thy greatness I will tell.

They utter shall abundantly
The mem'ry of thy goodness great,
And shall sing praises cheerfully
While they thy righteousness relate.

Jehovah very gracious is;
In him compassions also flow;
In lovingkindness he is great,
And unto anger he is slow.

O'er all his works his mercies are;
The Lord is good to all that live.
Praise, Lord, to thee thy works afford;
Thy saints to thee shall praises give.

FROM: *THE BOOK OF PSALMS WITH MUSIC*
(PITTSBURGH: REFORMED PRESBYTERIAN CHURCH OF NORTH AMERICA, 1973),
PSALM 145 (PP. 350–51)

Alternative hymn: "O Worship the King" (see this hymn at the end of chapter 12)

# Chapter 11

# The Character of God: "Incommunicable" Attributes

*How is God different from us?*

## EXPLANATION AND SCRIPTURAL BASIS

### A. Introduction to the Study of God's Character

**1. Classifying God's Attributes.** When we come to talk about the character of God, we realize that we cannot say everything the Bible teaches us about God's character at once. We need some way to decide which aspect of God's character to discuss first, which aspect to discuss second, and so forth. In other words, we need some way to categorize the attributes of God. This question is not as unimportant as it may seem. There is the possibility that we would adopt a misleading order of attributes or that we would emphasize some attributes so much that others would not be presented properly.

Several different methods of classifying God's attributes have been used. In this chapter we will adopt probably the most commonly used classification: the *incommunicable attributes* of God (that is, those attributes that God does not share or "communicate" to others) and the *communicable attributes* of God (those God shares or "communicates" with us).

Examples of the incommunicable attributes would be God's eternity (God has existed for all eternity, but we have not), unchangeableness (God does not change, but we do), or omnipresence (God is everywhere present, but we are present only in one place at one time). Examples of the communicable attributes would be love (God is love, and we are able to love as well), knowledge (God has knowledge, and we are able to have knowledge as well), mercy (God is merciful, and we are able to be merciful too), or justice (God is just and we, too, are able to be just). This classification of God's attributes into two major categories is helpful, and most people have an initial sense of which specific attributes should be called incommunicable and which should be called communicable. Thus it makes sense to say that God's love is communicable but his omnipresence is not.

However, upon further reflection we realize that this distinction, although helpful, is not perfect. That is because there is no attribute of God that is *completely* communicable, and there is no attribute of God that is *completely* incommunicable! This will be evident if we think for a moment about some things we already know about God.

For example, God's *wisdom* would usually be called a communicable attribute,

156

because we also can be wise. But we will never be infinitely wise as God is. His wisdom is *to some extent* shared with us, but it is never *fully* shared with us. Similarly, we can share God's *knowledge* in part, yet we shall never share it fully, for God's thoughts are higher than ours "as the heavens are higher than the earth" (Isa. 55:9). We can imitate God's love and share in that attribute to some degree, but we will never be infinitely loving as God is. So it is with all the attributes that are normally called "communicable attributes": God does indeed share them with us *to some degree,* but none of these attributes is completely communicable. It is better to say that those attributes we call "communicable" are those that are *more shared* with us.

Those attributes we call "incommunicable" are better defined by saying that they are attributes of God that are *less shared* by us. Not one of the incommunicable attributes of God is completely without some likeness in the character of human beings. For example, God is unchangeable, while we change. But we do not change completely, for there are some aspects of our characters that remain largely unchanged: our individual identities, many of our personality traits, and some of our long-term purposes remain substantially unchanged over many years (and will remain largely unchanged once we are set free from sin and begin to live in God's presence forever).

Similarly, God is eternal, and we are subject to the limitations of time. However, we see *some* reflection of God's eternity in the fact that we will live with him forever and enjoy eternal life, as well as in the fact that we have the ability to remember the past and to have a strong sense of awareness of the future (unlike much of God's creation; cf. Eccl. 3:11). God's attributes of independence and omnipresence are perhaps those that are least easy to see reflected in our own natures, but even these can be seen to be faintly reflected in us when we compare ourselves with much of the rest of God's creation: as we grow to adulthood we attain some degree of independence from others for our existence; and, though we cannot be at more than one place at one time, we have the ability to act in ways that have effects in many different places at once (this again sets us apart from most of the rest of creation).

We will use the two categories of "incommunicable" and "communicable" attributes then, while realizing that they are not entirely precise classifications, and that there is in reality much overlap between the categories.

**2. The Names of God in Scripture.** In the Bible a person's name is a description of his or her character. Likewise, the names of God in Scripture are various descriptions of his character. In a broad sense, then, God's "name" is equal to all that the Bible and creation tell us about God. When we pray, "Hallowed be your *name*" as part of the Lord's Prayer (Matt. 6:9), we are praying that people would speak about God in a way that is honoring to him and that accurately reflects his character. This honoring of God's name can be done with actions as well as words, for our actions reflect the character of the Creator whom we serve (Matt. 5:16). To honor God's name is therefore to honor him. The command, "You shall not take the *name* of the LORD your God in vain" (Ex. 20:7) is a command that we not dishonor God's reputation either by words that speak of him in a foolish or misleading way, or by actions that do not reflect his true character.

Now the Bible does give many individual names to God, all of which reflect some true aspect of his character. Many of these names are taken from human experience or emotions in order to describe parts of God's character, while many other names are taken from the rest of the natural creation. In a sense, all of these expressions of God's character in terms of things found in the universe are "names" of God because they tell us something true about him.

Herman Bavinck, in *The Doctrine of God*,[1] gives a long list of such descriptions of God taken from creation: God is compared to a lion (Isa. 31:4), an eagle (Deut. 32:11), a lamb (Isa. 53:7), a hen (Matt. 23:37), the sun (Ps. 84:11), the morning star (Rev. 22:16), a light (Ps. 27:1), a torch (Rev. 21:23), a fire (Heb. 12:29), a fountain (Ps. 36:9), a rock (Deut. 32:4), a hiding place (Ps. 119:114), a tower (Prov. 18:10), a shadow (Ps. 91:1), a shield (Ps. 84:11), a temple (Rev. 21:22), and so forth.

Taken from human experience, Bavinck finds an even more extensive list, which is reproduced here only in part: God is called bridegroom (Isa. 61:10), husband (Isa. 54:5), father (Deut. 32:6), judge and king (Isa. 33:22), man of war (Ex. 15:3), builder and maker (Heb. 11:10), shepherd (Ps. 23:1), physician (Ex. 15:26), and so forth. Furthermore, God is spoken of in terms of human actions such as knowing (Gen. 18:21), remembering (Gen. 8:1; Ex. 2:24), seeing (Gen. 1:10), hearing (Ex. 2:24), smelling (Gen. 8:21), tasting (Ps. 11:5), sitting (Ps. 9:7), rising (Ps. 68:1), walking (Lev. 26:12), wiping away tears (Isa. 25:8), and so forth. Human emotions are attributed to God, such as joy (Isa. 62:5), grief (Ps. 78:40; Isa. 63:10), anger (Jer. 7:18–19), love (John 3:16), hatred (Deut. 16:22), wrath (Ps. 2:5), and so forth.

Even though God does not have a physical body,[2] Scripture uses various parts of the human body to describe God's activities in a metaphorical way. Scripture can speak of God's face or countenance (Ex. 33:20, 23; Isa. 63:9; Ps. 16:11; Rev. 22:4), eyes (Ps. 11:4; Heb. 4:13), eyelids (Ps. 11:4), ears (Ps. 55:1; Isa. 59:1), nose (Deut. 33:10), mouth (Deut. 8:3), lips (Job 11:5), tongue (Isa. 30:27), neck (Jer. 18:17), arms (Ex. 15:16), hand (Num. 11:23), finger (Ex. 8:19), heart (Gen. 6:6), foot (Isa. 66:1), and so forth. Even terms describing personal characteristics such as good, merciful, gracious, righteous, holy, just, and many more, are terms whose meaning is familiar to us through an experience of these qualities in other human beings. And even those terms that seem least related to creation, such as eternity or unchangeableness, are understood by us not intuitively but by negating concepts that we know from our experience (eternity is not being limited by time and unchangeableness is not changing).

The point of collecting all these passages is to show, first, that in one sense or another *all of creation reveals something about God to us,* and that the higher creation, especially man who is made in God's image, reveals him more fully.

The second reason for mentioning this long list is to show that all that we know about God from Scripture comes to us in terms that we understand because they

---

[1]Herman Bavinck, *The Doctrine of God*, trans. and ed. by William Hendriksen (Grand Rapids: Eerdmans, 1951), pp. 86–89.

[2]Although Jesus Christ now has a physical body as God-man, the Father and Holy Spirit do not, nor did the Son before he was conceived in Mary's womb. (In the Old Testament "theophanies," where God appeared in human form, these human bodies were only temporary appearances and did not belong to the person of God.)

describe events or things common to human experience. Using a more technical term, we can say that *all that Scripture says about God uses anthropomorphic language—that is, language that speaks of God in human terms.*[3] Sometimes people have been troubled by the fact that there is anthropomorphic language in Scripture. But this should not be troubling to us, for, if God is going to teach us about things we do not know by direct experience (such as his attributes), he has to teach us in terms of what we do know. This is why all that Scripture says about God is "anthropomorphic" in a broad sense (speaking of God either in human terms or in terms of the creation we know). This fact does not mean that Scripture gives us wrong or misleading ideas about God, for this is the way that God has chosen to reveal himself to us, and to reveal himself truly and accurately. Nonetheless, it should caution us not to take any one of these descriptions by itself and isolate it from its immediate context or from the rest of what Scripture says about God.[4] If we did that, we would run the risk of misunderstanding or of having an imbalanced or inadequate picture of who God is. Each description of one of God's attributes must be understood in the light of everything else that Scripture tells us about God. If we fail to remember this, we will inevitably understand God's character wrongly.

For example, we have an *idea* of love from human experience. That helps us to understand what Scripture means when it says that God is love, but our understanding of the meaning of "love" when applied to God is not identical with our experience of love in human relationships. So we must learn from observing how God acts in all of Scripture and from the other attributes of God that are given in Scripture, as well as from our own real-life experiences of God's love, if we are to refine our idea of God's love in an appropriate way and avoid misunderstanding. Thus, anthropomorphic language about God is *true* when it occurs in Scripture, but it can be understood rightly only by continual reading of Scripture throughout our lives in order that we may understand this language in the context of all of Scripture.

There is yet a third reason for pointing out the great diversity of descriptions about God taken from human experience and from the natural world. This language should remind us that *God made the universe so that it would show forth the excellence of his character,* that is, that it would show forth his glory. God is worthy to receive glory because he created all things (Rev. 4:11); therefore, all things should honor him.

Psalm 148 is an example of all creation being summoned to give praise to God:

> Praise him, sun and moon,
>     praise him, all you shining stars! . . .
>
> Praise the LORD from the earth,
>     you sea monsters and all deeps,

---

[3]"Anthropomorphic" comes from two Greek words, *anthrōpos,* "man," and *morphē,* "form." An anthropomorphic description of God describes God in human forms or human terms.

[4]This mistake would be made, for example, by people who argue that God has a human body, because Scripture talks about his eyes, ears, mouth, etc. By the same reasoning they should say that God also looks like a lion, a lamb, an eagle, a fire, a rock, a hen, a fountain, the sun, a shield, a shadow, and a temple—all at once! The mistake is to fail to recognize that these are all metaphors that tell us about God's character, but that God himself is "spirit" (John 4:24) and has no material body.

fire and hail, snow and frost,
 stormy wind fulfilling his command!

Mountains and all hills,
 fruit trees and all cedars! . . .

Kings of the earth and all peoples . . .

Let them praise the name of the Lord,
 for his name alone is exalted;
 his glory is above earth and heaven. (Ps. 148:3, 7–11, 13)

As we learn about God's character from Scripture, it should open our eyes and enable us to interpret creation rightly. As a result, we will be able to see reflections of the excellence of God's character everywhere in creation: "the whole earth is full of his glory" (Isa. 6:3).

It must be remembered that though all that Scripture tells us about God is true, it is not exhaustive. Scripture does not tell us everything about God's character. Thus, we will never know God's *full or complete "name"* in the sense that we will never understand God's character exhaustively. We will never know all there is to know about God. For this reason theologians have sometimes said, "God has many names, yet God has no name." God has many names in that we know many true descriptions of his character from Scripture, but God has no name in that we will never be able to describe or understand all of his character.

**3. Balanced Definitions of God's Incommunicable Attributes.** The incommunicable attributes of God are perhaps the most easily misunderstood, probably because they represent aspects of God's character that are least familiar to our experience. In this chapter, therefore, each of the incommunicable attributes of God is defined with a two-part sentence. The first part defines the attribute under discussion, and the second part guards against misunderstanding the attribute by stating a balancing or opposite aspect that relates to that attribute. For example, God's unchangeableness is defined as follows: "God is unchanging in his being, perfections, purposes, and promises, *yet* God does act, and he acts differently in response to different situations." The second half of the sentence guards against the idea that unchangeableness means inability to act at all. Some people do understand unchangeableness in this way, but such an understanding is inconsistent with the biblical presentation of God's unchangeableness.

## B. The Incommunicable Attributes of God

**1. Independence.** God's independence is defined as follows: *God does not need us or the rest of creation for anything, yet we and the rest of creation can glorify him and bring him joy.* This attribute of God is sometimes called his self-existence or his *aseity* (from the Latin words *a se*, which mean "from himself").

Scripture in several places teaches that God does not need any part of creation in order to exist or for any other reason. God is absolutely independent and self-sufficient. Paul proclaims to the men of Athens, "The God who made the world and everything in it, being Lord of heaven and earth, does not live in shrines made by man, *nor is he served by human hands, as though he needed anything,* since he himself gives to all men life and breath and everything" (Acts 17:24–25). The implication is that God does not need anything from mankind.

God asks Job, "Who has given to me, that I should repay him? *Whatever is under the whole heaven is mine*" (Job 41:11). No one has ever contributed to God anything that did not first come from God who created all things. Similarly, we read God's word in Psalm 50, "every beast of the forest is mine, the cattle on a thousand hills. I know all the birds of the air, and all that moves in the field is mine. If I were hungry, I would not tell you; for *the world and all that is in it is mine*" (Ps. 50:10–12).

People have sometimes thought that God created human beings because he was lonely and needed fellowship with other persons. If this were true, it would certainly mean that God is not completely independent of creation. It would mean that God would *need* to create persons in order to be completely happy or completely fulfilled in his personal existence.

Yet there are some specific indications in Jesus' words that show this idea to be inaccurate. In John 17:5, Jesus prays, "Father, glorify me in your own presence with *the glory which I had with you before the world was made.*" Here is an indication that there was a sharing of glory between the Father and the Son before creation. Then in John 17:24, Jesus speaks to the Father of "my glory which you have given me *in your love for me before the foundation of the world.*" There was love and communication between the Father and the Son before creation.

These passages indicate explicitly what we can learn elsewhere from the doctrine of the Trinity, namely, that among the persons of the Trinity there has been perfect love and fellowship and communication for all eternity. The fact that God is three persons yet one God means that there was no loneliness or lack of personal fellowship on God's part before creation. In fact, the love and interpersonal fellowship, and the sharing of glory, have always been and will always be far more perfect than any communion we as finite human beings will ever have with God. And as the second verse quoted above speaks of the glory the Father gave to the Son, we should also realize that there is a giving of glory by the members of the Trinity to one another that far surpasses any bestowal of glory that could ever be given to God by all creation.

With regard to God's existence, this doctrine also reminds us that only God exists by virtue of his very nature, and that he was never created and never came into being. He always was. This is seen from the fact that all things that exist were made by him ("For you created *all things,* and by your will they existed and were created" [Rev. 4:11]; this is also affirmed in John 1:3; Rom. 11:35–36; 1 Cor. 8:6). Moses tells us that God existed before there was any creation: "*Before* the mountains were brought forth, or ever you had formed the earth and the world, from everlasting to everlasting *you are God*" (Ps. 90:2). God's independence is also seen in his self-designation in Exodus 3:14: "God said to Moses, *'I AM WHO I AM.'*" It is also possible to translate this statement "I will be what I will be," but in both cases the implication is that God's existence and character are determined by himself alone and are not dependent on anyone or anything else. This means that God's being has always been and will always be exactly what it is. God is not dependent upon any part of creation for his existence or his nature. Without creation, God would still be infinitely loving, infinitely just, eternal, omniscient, trinitarian, and so forth.

God's being is also something totally unique. It is not just that God *does not* need the creation for anything; God *could not* need the creation for anything. The difference between the creature and the Creator is an immensely vast difference, for God exists in a fundamentally different order of being. It is not just that we exist and God has always existed; it is also that God *necessarily* exists in an infinitely better, stronger, more excellent way. The difference between God's being and ours is more than the difference between the sun and a candle, more than the difference between the ocean and a raindrop, more than the difference between the arctic ice cap and a snowflake, more than the difference between the universe and the room we are sitting in: God's being is *qualitatively different*. No limitation or imperfection in creation should be projected onto our thought of God. He is the Creator; all else is creaturely. All else can pass away in an instant; he *necessarily exists* forever.

The balancing consideration with respect to this doctrine is the fact that *we and the rest of creation can glorify God and bring him joy*. This must be stated in order to guard against any idea that God's independence makes us meaningless. Someone might wonder, if God does not need us for anything, then are we important at all? Is there any significance to our existence or to the existence of the rest of creation? In response it must be said that we are in fact very meaningful because God has created us and he has determined that we would be *meaningful to him*. That is the final definition of genuine significance.

God speaks of his sons and daughters from the ends of the earth as "every one who is called by my name, whom I created *for my glory,* whom I formed and made" (Isa. 43:7). Although God did not have to create us, he chose to do so in a totally free choice. He decided that he would create us to glorify him (cf. Eph. 1:11–12; Rev. 4:11).

It is also true that we are able to bring real joy and delight to God. It is one of the most amazing facts in Scripture that God actually delights in his people and rejoices over them. Isaiah prophesies about the restoration of God's people:

> You shall be a crown of beauty in the hand of the LORD,
>     and a royal diadem in the hand of your God.
> You shall no more be termed Forsaken
>     and your land shall no more be termed Desolate;
> but you shall be called My delight is in her,
>     and your land Married;
> for *the LORD delights in you*
>     and your land shall be married. . . .
> *as the bridegroom rejoices over the bride,*
>     *so shall your God rejoice over you.* (Isa. 62:3–5)

Similarly, Zephaniah prophesies that the LORD "will rejoice over you with gladness, he will renew you in his love; *he will exult over you with loud singing* as on a day of festival" (Zeph. 3:17–18). God does not need us for anything, yet it is the amazing fact of our existence that he chooses to delight in us and to allow us to bring joy to his heart. This is the basis for personal significance in the lives of all

God's people: to be significant to God is to be significant in the most ultimate sense. No greater personal significance can be imagined.

**2. Unchangeableness.** We can define the unchangeableness of God as follows: *God is unchanging in his being, perfections, purposes, and promises, yet God does act and feel emotions, and he acts and feels differently in response to different situations.*[5] This attribute of God is also called God's *immutability.*

**a. Evidence in Scripture:** In Psalm 102 we find a contrast between things that we may think to be permanent such as the earth or the heavens, on the one hand, and God, on the other hand. The psalmist says:

> Of old you laid the foundation of the earth,
>     and the heavens are the work of your hands.
> They will perish, but you endure;
>     they will all wear out like a garment.
> You change them like raiment, and they pass away;
>     but *you are the same, and your years have no end.*
>                         *(Ps. 102:25–27)*[6]

God existed before the heavens and earth were made, and he will exist long after they have been destroyed. God causes the universe to change, but in contrast to this change he is "the same."

Referring to his own qualities of patience, long-suffering, and mercy, God says, "For *I the* LORD *do not change;* therefore you, O sons of Jacob, are not consumed" (Mal. 3:6). Here God uses a general statement of his unchangeableness to refer to some specific ways in which he does not change.

James reminds his readers that all good gifts come ultimately from God *"with whom there is no variation or shadow due to change"* (James 1:17). His argument is that since good gifts have always come from God, we can be confident that only good gifts will come from him in the future, because his character never changes in the slightest degree.

The definition given above specifies that God is unchanging—not in every way that we might imagine, but only in ways that Scripture itself affirms. The Scripture passages already cited refer either to God's own being or to some attribute of his character. From these we can conclude that God is unchanging, at least with respect to his *"being,"* and with respect to his *"perfections"* (that is, his attributes or the various aspects of his character).

The great Dutch theologian Herman Bavinck notes that the fact that God is unchanging in his being is of the utmost importance for maintaining the Creator/creature distinction, and for our worship of God:

---

[5]The four key words (*being, perfections, purposes, promises*) used as a summary of the ways in which God is unchanging are taken from Louis Berkhof, *Systematic Theology* (Grand Rapids: Eerdmans, 1939, 1941), p. 58.

[6]It is significant that this passage is quoted in Heb. 1:11–12 and applied to Jesus Christ. Heb. 13:8 also applies the attribute of unchangeableness to Christ: "Jesus Christ is the same yesterday and today and for ever." Thus, God the Son shares fully in this divine attribute.

The doctrine of God's immutability is of the highest significance for religion. The contrast between being and becoming marks the difference between the Creator and the creature. Every creature is continually becoming. It is changeable, constantly striving, seeks rest and satisfaction, and finds this rest in God, in him alone, for only he is pure being and no becoming. Hence, in Scripture God is often called the Rock. . . .[7]

. The definition given above also affirms God's unchangeableness or immutability with respect to his *purposes*. "The counsel of the LORD stands for ever, the thoughts of his heart to all generations" (Ps. 33:11). This general statement about God's counsel is supported by several specific verses that talk about individual plans or purposes of God that he has had for all eternity (Matt. 13:35; 25:34; Eph. 1:4, 11; 3:9, 11; 2 Tim. 2:19; 1 Peter 1:20; Rev. 13:8). Once God has determined that he will assuredly bring something about, his purpose is unchanging, and it will be achieved. In fact, God claims through Isaiah that no one else is like him in this regard:

> I am God, and there is none like me,
> declaring the end from the beginning
> 　and from ancient times things not yet done,
> saying, "My counsel shall stand,
> 　and I will accomplish all my purpose" . . .
> I have spoken, and I will bring it to pass;
> 　*I have purposed, and I will do it.* (Isa. 46:9–11)

Furthermore, God is unchanging in his *promises*. Once he has promised something, he will not be unfaithful to that promise: "God is not a man, that he should lie, or a son of man, that he should repent. Has he said, and will he not do it? Or has he spoken, and will he not fulfil it?" (Num. 23:19; cf. 1 Sam. 15:29).

**b. Does God Sometimes Change His Mind?** Yet when we talk about God being unchanging in his purposes, we may wonder about places in Scripture where God said he would judge his people and then because of prayer or the people's repentance (or both) God relented and did not bring judgment as he had said he would. Examples of such withdrawing from threatened judgment include the successful intervention of Moses in prayer to prevent the destruction of the people of Israel (Ex. 32:9–14), the adding of another fifteen years to the life of Hezekiah (Isa. 38:1–6), or the failure to bring promised judgment upon Nineveh when the people repented (Jonah 3:4, 10). Are these not cases where God's purposes in fact did change? Then there are other passages where God is said to be sorry that he had carried out some previous action. One thinks of God being sorry that he had made man upon the earth (Gen. 6:6), or sorry that he had made Saul king (1 Sam. 15:10). Did not God's purposes change in these cases?

These instances should all be understood as true expressions of God's *present* attitude or intention *with respect to the situation as it exists at that moment*. If the situation changes, then of course God's attitude or expression of intention will also change. This is just saying that *God responds differently to different situations*.

---

[7]Herman Bavinck, *The Doctrine of God*, trans. by William Hendriksen (Edinburgh: Banner of Truth, 1977, reprint of 1951 ed.), p. 149.

The example of Jonah preaching to Nineveh is helpful here. God sees the wickedness of Nineveh and sends Jonah to proclaim, "Yet forty days, and Nineveh shall be overthrown!" (Jonah 3:4). The possibility that God would withhold judgment if the people repented is not explicitly mentioned in Jonah's proclamation as recorded in Scripture, but it is of course *implicit* in that warning: the *purpose* for proclaiming a warning is to bring about repentance. Once the people repented, the situation was different, and God responded differently to that changed situation: "*When God saw what they did,* how they turned from their evil way, *God repented of the evil which he had said he would do to them;* and he did not do it" (Jonah 3:10).

The situations with Hezekiah and with the intercession of Moses are similar: God had said that he would send judgment, and that was a true declaration, *provided that the situation remained the same.* But then the situation changed: someone started to pray earnestly (Moses in one case and Hezekiah in the other). Here prayer itself was part of the new situation and was in fact what changed the situation. God responded to that changed situation by answering the prayer and withholding judgment.

In the cases of God being sorry that he had made man, or that he had made Saul king, these too can be understood as *expressions of God's present displeasure* toward the sinfulness of man. In neither case is the language strong enough to require us to think that if God could start again and act differently, he would in fact not create man or not make Saul king. It can instead imply that God's previous action led to events that, in the short term, caused him sorrow, but that nonetheless in the long term would ultimately achieve his good purposes. This is somewhat analogous to a human father who allows his child to embark on a course he knows will bring much sorrow, both to the parent and to the child, but who allows it nonetheless, because he knows that greater long-term good will come from it.

**c. The Question of God's Impassibility:** Sometimes in a discussion of God's attributes theologians have spoken of another attribute, namely, the *impassibility* of God. This attribute, if true, would mean that God does not have passions or emotions, but is "impassible," not subject to passions. In fact, chapter 2 of the Westminster Confession of Faith says that God is "without . . . passions." This statement goes beyond what we have affirmed in our definition above about God's unchangeableness, and affirms *more* than that God does not change in his being, perfections, purposes, or promises—it also affirms that God does not even feel emotions or "passions."

The Scripture proof given by the Westminster Confession of Faith is Acts 14:15, which in the King James Version reports Barnabas and Paul as rejecting worship from the people at Lystra, protesting that they are not gods but "men of *like passions* with you." The implication of the KJV translation might be that someone who is truly God would not have "like passions" as men do, or it might simply show that the apostles were responding to the false view of passionless gods assumed by the men of Lystra (see vv. 10–11). But if the verse is rightly translated, it certainly does not prove that God has no passions or emotions at all, for the Greek term here (*homoiopathēs*) can simply mean having similar circum-

stances or experiences, or being of a similar nature to someone else.[8] Of course,
God does not have *sinful* passions or emotions. But the idea that God has no
passions or emotions *at all* clearly conflicts with much of the rest of Scripture, and
for that reason I have not affirmed God's impassibility in this book. Instead, quite
the opposite is true, for God, who is the origin of our emotions and who created
our emotions, certainly does feel emotions: God rejoices (Isa. 62:5). He is grieved
(Ps. 78:40; Eph. 4:30). His wrath burns hot against his enemies (Ex. 32:10). He
pities his children (Ps. 103:13). He loves with everlasting love (Isa. 54:8; Ps.
103:17). He is a God whose passions we are to imitate for all eternity as we like
our Creator hate sin and delight in righteousness.

**d. The Challenge From Process Theology:** God's unchangeableness has been
denied frequently in recent years by the advocates of *process theology,* a theological
position that says that process and change are essential aspects of genuine
existence, and that therefore God must be changing over time also, just like
everything else that exists. In fact, Charles Hartshorne, the father of process
theology, would say that God is continually adding to himself all the experiences
that happen anywhere in the universe, and thus God is continually changing.[9] The
real appeal of process theology comes from the fact that all people have a deep
longing to mean something, to feel significant in the universe. Process theologians
dislike the doctrine of God's immutability because they think it implies that
nothing we do can really matter to God. If God is really unchangeable, process
theologians will say, then nothing we do—in fact, nothing that happens in the
universe—has any real effect on God, because God can never change. So what
difference do we make? How can we have any ultimate meaning? In response to
this question process theologians reject the doctrine of God's immutability and tell
us that our actions are so significant that they have an influence on the very being
of God himself! As we act, and as the universe changes, God is *truly* affected by
these actions and the being of God changes—God *becomes* something other than
what he was.[10]

Advocates of process theology often mistakenly accuse evangelical Christians
(or the biblical writers themselves) of believing in a God who does not act in the
world, or who cannot respond differently to different situations (errors we have
discussed above). With regard to the idea that we must be able to influence the
very being of God in order to be significant, we must respond that this is an
*incorrect assumption* imported into the discussion, and that it is not consistent with

[8]See *BAGD*, p. 566.
[9]Charles Hartshorne (born 1897) taught at the University of Chicago, Emory University, and the
University of Texas. An introduction to process theology by two of its advocates is *Process Theology: An
Introductory Exposition* by John B. Cobb, Jr., and David R. Griffin (Philadelphia: Westminster, 1976).
Detailed evangelical analyses may be found in Carl F. H. Henry, "The Resurgence of Process
Philosophy," in *God, Revelation, and Authority,* 6:52–75, and Royce Gruenler, *The Inexhaustible God:
Biblical Faith and the Challenge of Process Theism* (Grand Rapids: Baker, 1983).
Two excellent recent articles from an evangelical perspective have been written by Bruce A. Ware:
"An Exposition and Critique of the Process Doctrines of Divine Mutability and Immutability," *WTJ*
47 (1985): 175–96 (a critique of process theology), and "An Evangelical Reformulation of the
Doctrine of the Immutability of God," *JETS* 29 (1986): 431–46 (a positive restatement of an
orthodox view of God's immutability).
[10]See Ware's revealing discussion of Hartshorne's idea that we contribute value to God that he
would otherwise lack: "Exposition and Critique," pp. 183–85.

Scripture. Scripture is clear that our ultimate significance comes not from being able to change the being of God, but from the fact that God has created us for his glory and that *he* counts us as significant.[11] God alone gives the ultimate definition of what is significant and what is not significant in the universe, and if he counts us significant, then we are!

The other fundamental error in process theology is in assuming that God must be changeable like the universe he created. This is what Scripture explicitly denies: "You, Lord, did found the earth in the beginning, and the heavens are the work of your hands; they will perish, but you remain; they will all grow old like a garment . . . *they will be changed. But you are the same,* and your years will never end" (Heb. 1:10–12, quoting Ps. 102:25–27).

**e. God Is Both Infinite and Personal:** Our discussion of process theology illustrates a common difference between biblical Christianity and all other systems of theology. In the teaching of the Bible, God is both *infinite* and *personal:* he is infinite in that he is not subject to any of the limitations of humanity, or of creation in general. He is far greater than everything he has made, far greater than anything else that exists. But he is also personal: he interacts with us as a person, and we can relate to him as persons. We can pray to him, worship him, obey him, and love him, and he can speak to us, rejoice in us, and love us.

Apart from the true religion found in the Bible, no system of religion has a God who is both infinite and personal.[12] For example, the gods of ancient Greek and Roman mythology were *personal* (they interacted frequently with people), but they were not infinite: they had weaknesses and frequent moral failures, even petty rivalries. On the other hand, deism portrays a God who is *infinite* but far too removed from the world to be personally involved in it. Similarly, pantheism holds that God is infinite (since the whole universe is thought to be God), but such a God can certainly not be personal or relate to us as persons.

The error of process theology fits this general pattern. Its advocates are convinced that a God who is unchanging in his being is so different from the rest of creation—so infinite, so unlimited by the change that characterizes all of our existence—that he *cannot* also be personal in a way that we make a difference to him. So in order to gain a God who is personal, they think they have to give up a God who is infinite for a God who is continually in process of change. This kind of reasoning is typical of many (perhaps all) objections to the kind of God presented in the Bible. People say that if God is infinite, he cannot be personal, or they say that if God is personal, he cannot be infinite. The Bible teaches that God is both infinite and personal. We must affirm both that God is infinite (or unlimited) with respect to change that occurs in the universe (nothing will change God's being, perfections, purposes, or promises), that God is *also* personal, and that he relates to us personally and counts us valuable.

---

[11]See chapter 21, pp. 440–42, on the reasons for the creation of man.

[12]Technically speaking we must recognize that Judaism, so far as it is based on what we call the Old Testament, also has a view of God that shows him to be both infinite and personal, although Judaism has never recognized the indications of God's trinitarian nature that are present even in the Old Testament (see chapter 14, pp. 226–30).

**f. The Importance of God's Unchangeableness:** At first it may not seem very important to us to affirm God's unchangeableness. The idea is so abstract that we may not immediately realize its significance. But if we stop for a moment to imagine what it would be like if God *could* change, the importance of this doctrine becomes more clear. For example, if God *could* change (in his being, perfections, purposes, or promises), then any change would be either for the better or for the worse. But if God changed for the better, then he was not the best possible being when we first trusted him. And how could we be sure that he is the best possible being now? But if God could change for the worse (in his very *being*), then what kind of God might he become? Might he become, for instance, a little bit evil rather than wholly good? And if he could become a little bit evil, then how do we know he could not change to become largely evil—or *wholly* evil? And there would be not one thing we could do about it, for he is so much more powerful than we are. Thus, the idea that God could change leads to the horrible possibility that thousands of years from now we might come to live forever in a universe dominated by a wholly evil, omnipotent God. It is hard to imagine any thought more terrifying. How could we ever trust such a God who could change? How could we ever commit our lives to him?

Moreover, if God could change with regard to his *purposes,* then even though when the Bible was written he promised that Jesus would come back to rule over a new heaven and new earth, he has perhaps abandoned that plan now, and thus our hope in Jesus' return is in vain. Or, if God could change in regard to his *promises,* then how could we trust him completely for eternal life? Or for anything else the Bible says? Maybe when the Bible was written he promised forgiveness of sins and eternal life to those who trust in Christ, but (if God can change) perhaps he has changed his mind on those promises now—how could we be sure? Or perhaps his omnipotence will change someday, so that even though he wants to keep his promises, he will no longer be able to do so.

A little reflection like this shows how absolutely important the doctrine of God's unchangeableness is. If God is not unchanging, then the whole basis of our faith begins to fall apart, and our understanding of the universe begins to unravel. This is because our faith and hope and knowledge all ultimately depend on a *person* who is *infinitely worthy of trust*—because he is *absolutely* and *eternally* unchanging in his being, perfections, purposes, and promises.

**3. Eternity.** God's eternity may be defined as follows: *God has no beginning, end, or succession of moments in his own being, and he sees all time equally vividly, yet God sees events in time and acts in time.*

Sometimes this doctrine is called the doctrine of God's infinity with respect to time. To be "infinite" is to be unlimited, and this doctrine teaches that time does not limit God.

This doctrine is also related to God's unchangeableness. If it is true that God does not change, then we must say that *time* does not change God: it has no effect on his being, perfections, purposes, or promises. But that means that time has no effect on God's knowledge, for instance. God never learns new things or forgets things, for that would mean a change in his perfect knowledge. This implies also that the passing of time does not add to or detract from God's knowledge: he knows all things past, present, and future, and knows them all equally vividly.

**a. God Is Timeless in His Own Being:** The fact that God has no beginning or end is seen in Psalm 90:2: "Before the mountains were brought forth, or ever you had formed the earth and the world, *from everlasting to everlasting you are God.*" Similarly, in Job 36:26, Elihu says of God, "the number of his years is unsearchable."

God's eternity is also suggested by passages that talk about the fact that God always is or always exists. " 'I am the Alpha and the Omega,' says the Lord God, who is and who was and who is to come, the Almighty" (Rev. 1:8; cf. 4:8).[13]

It is also indicated in Jesus' bold use of a present tense verb that implies continuing present existence when he replied to his Jewish adversaries, "Before Abraham was, *I am*" (John 8:58). This statement is itself an explicit claiming of the name of God, "*I AM* WHO I AM," from Exodus 3:14, a name that also suggests a continual present existence: God is the eternal "I AM," the one who eternally exists.

The fact that God never began to exist can also be concluded from the fact that God created all things, and that he himself is an immaterial spirit. Before God made the universe, there was no matter, but then he created all things (Gen. 1:1; John 1:3; 1 Cor. 8:6; Col. 1:16; Heb. 1:2). The study of physics tells us that matter and time and space must all occur together: if there is no matter, there can be no space or time either. Thus, before God created the universe, there was no "time," at least not in the sense of a succession of moments one after another. Therefore, when God created the universe, he also created time. When God began to create the universe, time began, and there began to be a succession of moments and events one after another.[14] But before there was a universe, and before there was time, God always existed, without beginning, and without being influenced by time. And time, therefore, does not have existence in itself, but, like the rest of creation, depends on God's eternal being and power to keep it existing.

The foregoing Scripture passages and the fact that God always existed before there was any time combine to indicate to us that God's own being does not have a succession of moments or any progress from one state of existence to another. To God himself, all of his existence is always somehow "present,"[15] though admittedly that idea is difficult for us to understand, for it is a kind of existence different from that which we experience.

---

[13]Alpha and omega are the first and last letters of the Greek alphabet, so when God says that he is the Alpha and the Omega he implies that he is before everything else and he is after everything else; he is the beginning of everything and will always be the end (or goal) of everything.

[14]In fact, the alternative to saying that time began when God created the universe is to say that time never began, but there has *always* been a succession of moments one after another, extending infinitely far back into the past, but never having a starting point. But to have time without a beginning seems to many people to be absurd and is probably impossible. Bavinck says, "Eternal time in the sense of time without beginning is inconceivable" (*The Doctrine of God*, p. 157).

[15]As we shall see below, this does not mean that all events of history look to God as if they were present, for God sees events *in time* and acts *in time*.

**b. God Sees All Time Equally Vividly:** It is somewhat easier for us to understand that God sees all time equally vividly. We read in Psalm 90:4, "For a *thousand years* in your sight are but as *yesterday* when it is past, or as a *watch* in the night." It is sometimes difficult for us to remember events that occurred several weeks ago, or several months ago, or several years ago. We remember recent events more vividly, and the clarity of our memory fades with the passing of time. Even if it were possible for us to live "a thousand years," we would remember very few events from hundreds of years earlier, and the clarity of that memory would be very low. But here Scripture tells us that God views a thousand years "as yesterday." He can remember all the detailed events of a thousand years at least as clearly as we can remember the events of "yesterday." In fact, to him a thousand years is "as a watch in the night," a three- or four-hour period during which a guard would stand watch. Such a short period of time would pass quickly and all the events would be easily recalled. Yet this is how a thousand years seems to God.

When we realize that the phrase "a thousand years" does not imply that God forgets things after 1,100 or 1,200 years, but rather expresses as long a time as one might imagine, it becomes evident that *all of past history* is viewed by God with great clarity and vividness: all of time since the creation is to God as if it just happened. And it will always remain just that clear in his consciousness, throughout millions of years of eternity future.

In the New Testament, Peter tells us, "with the Lord one day is as a thousand years, and a thousand years as one day" (2 Peter 3:8). The second half of this statement had already been made in Psalm 90, but the first half introduces an additional consideration, "One day is as a thousand years"; that is, any one day from God's perspective seems to last for "a thousand years": it is as if that day never ends, but is always being experienced. Again, since "a thousand years" is a figurative expression for "as long a time as we can imagine," or "all history," we can say from this verse that any one day seems to God to be present to his consciousness forever.

Taking these two considerations together, we can say the following: in God's perspective, any extremely long period of time is as if it just happened. And any very short period of time (such as one day) seems to God to last forever: it never ceases to be "present" in his consciousness. Thus, God sees and knows all events past, present, and future with equal vividness. This should never cause us to think that God does not see events *in time* and act *in time* (see below), but just the opposite: God is the eternal Lord and Sovereign over history, and he sees it more clearly and acts in it more decisively than any other. But, once we have said that, we still must affirm that these verses speak of God's relationship to time in a way that we do not and cannot experience: God's experience of time is not just a patient endurance through eons of endless duration, but he has a *qualitatively different* experience of time than we do. This is consistent with the idea that in his own being, God is timeless; he does not experience a succession of moments. This has been the dominant view of Christian orthodoxy throughout the history of the church, though it has been frequently challenged, and even today many theologians deny it.[16]

---

[16]Carl F. H. Henry argues for God's timeless eternity as the historic position of Christian orthodoxy in *God, Revelation and Authority* (Waco, Tex.: Word, 1982), 5:235–67, and gives a detailed analysis of

We can picture God's relationship to time as in figure 11.1. This diagram is meant to show that God created time and is Lord over time. Therefore he can see all events in time equally vividly, yet he also can see events in time and act in time.

The diagram also anticipates the following discussion, since it indicates that God knows events in the future, even the infinitely long eternal future. With regard to the future, God frequently claims through the Old Testament prophets that *he alone is the one who knows and can declare future events.* "Who told this long ago? Who declared it of old? Was it not I, the LORD? And there is no other god besides me, a righteous God and a Savior; there is none besides me" (Isa. 45:21). Similarly, we read:

> For I am God, and there is no other;
> I am God, and *there is none like me,*
> *declaring the end from the beginning*
>     *and from ancient times things not yet done,*
> saying, "My counsel shall stand,
>     and I will accomplish all my purpose." (Isa. 46:9–10)

Thus God somehow stands above time and is able to see it all as present in his consciousness. Although the analogy is not perfect, we might think of the moment we finish reading a long novel. Before putting it back on the shelf we might flip quickly through the pages once more, calling to mind the many events that had occurred in that novel. For a brief moment, things that transpired over a long period of time all seem to be "present" to our minds. Perhaps this is faintly analogous to God's experience of seeing all of history as equally present in his consciousness.

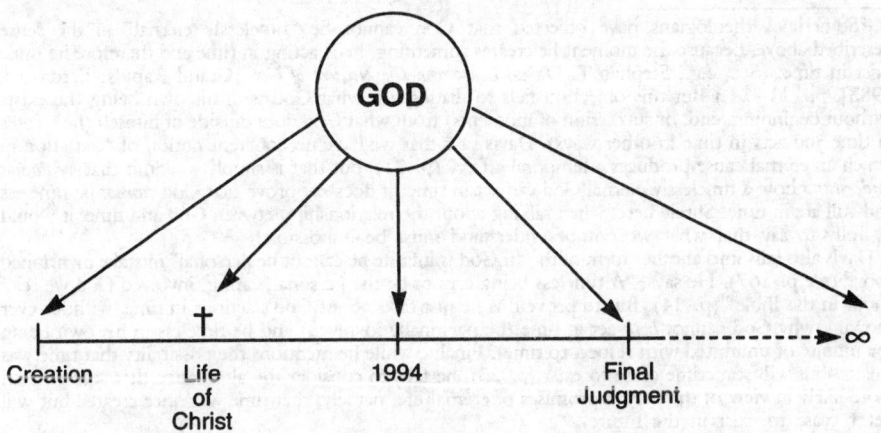

**THE RELATIONSHIP OF GOD TO TIME**
*Figure 11.1*

---

current challenges from both nonevangelical and evangelical theologians. A thorough recent philosophical defense of God's timeless eternity is Paul Helm, *Eternal God: A Study of God Without Time* (Oxford: Clarendon, 1988).

**c. God Sees Events in Time and Acts in Time:** Yet once all this has been said it is necessary to guard against misunderstanding by completing the definition of God's eternity: *"yet God sees events in time and acts in time."* Paul writes, *"when the time had fully come, God sent forth his Son,* born of woman, born under the law, to redeem those who were under the law" (Gal. 4:4–5). God observed clearly and knew exactly what was happening with events in his creation as they occurred over time. We might say that God watched the progress of time as various events occurred within his creation. Then at the right time, "when the time had fully come," God sent forth his Son into the world.

It is evident throughout Scripture that God acts within time and acts differently at different points in time. For example, Paul tells the men of Athens, "The times of ignorance God overlooked, but *now* he commands all men everywhere to repent, because *he has fixed a day on which he will judge the world* in righteousness by a man whom he has appointed . . ." (Acts 17:30–31). This statement includes a description of a previous way in which God acted, God's present way of acting, and a future activity that he will carry out, all in time.

Indeed, the repeated emphasis on God's ability to predict the future in the Old Testament prophets requires us to realize that God predicts his actions at one point in time and then carries out his actions at a later point in time. And on a larger scale, the entire Bible from Genesis to Revelation is God's own record of the way he has acted over time to bring redemption to his people.

We must therefore affirm both that God has no succession of moments in his own being and sees all history equally vividly, and that in his creation he sees the progress of events over time and acts differently at different points in time; in short, he is the Lord who created time and who rules over it and uses it for his own purposes. God can act in time *because* he is Lord of time.[17] He uses it to

---

[17]Sometimes theologians have objected that God cannot be "timelessly eternal" in the sense described above, because the moment he creates something, he is acting in time and therefore he must exist in time. (See, e.g., Stephen T. Davis, *Logic and the Nature of God* [Grand Rapids: Eerdmans, 1983], pp. 11–24.) But this objection fails to distinguish what God is in his own being (he exists without beginning, end, or succession of moments) from what God does outside of himself (he creates in time and acts in time in other ways). Davis says that we have no coherent notion of "causation in which an eternal cause produces a temporal effect" (p. 21), but that is simply to admit that *we do not understand* how a timelessly eternal God can act in time; it does *not* prove that God *cannot* be timeless and still act in time. Surely here, when talking about the relationship between God and time, it would be folly to say that what we cannot understand must be impossible!

Davis also falls into another form of the "if God is infinite he cannot be personal" mistake mentioned above (see p. 167). He says, "A timeless being cannot be the personal, caring, involved God we read about in the Bible" (p. 14). But to prove this he just talks about God's actions in time, without ever showing why God cannot *both* act in time (be personally involved) and be timeless in his own being (be infinite or unlimited with respect to time). Finally, while he mentions the possibility that time was created but will sometime cease to exist (p. 23), he fails to consider the alternative that seems much more likely in view of the Bible's promises of eternal life, namely, that time was once created but will never cease to exist in the future.

Those who, like Davis, deny that God is timelessly eternal, still say that God has eternally existed but that he has always existed in time and always experienced a succession of moments. But this position raises even more difficulties, because it requires that time never began, but stretches infinitely far into the past. However, that does not seem possible, because if the past is infinitely long, we could never have reached this moment. (This objection is one form of saying that an actual infinite cannot exist, a philosophical conception that is explained skillfully by William Lane Craig in *The Existence of God and the Beginning of the Universe* [San Bernardino, Calif.: Here's Life Publishers, 1979], pp. 35–53, and, with fuller reference to philosophical responses to this argument, by J. P. Moreland, *Scaling the Secular City: A Defense of Christianity* [Grand Rapids: Baker, 1987], pp. 15–34.)

display his glory. In fact, it is often God's good pleasure to fulfill his promises and carry out his works of redemption over a period of time so that we might more readily see and appreciate his great wisdom, his patience, his faithfulness, his lordship over all events, and even his unchangeableness and eternity.

**d. We Will Always Exist in Time:** Will we ever share in God's eternity? Specifically, in the new heaven and new earth which are yet to come, will time still exist? Some have thought that it would not. In fact, there is a hymn that begins, "When the trumpet of the Lord shall sound, and time shall be no more . . ." And we read in Scripture, "And the city has no need of sun or moon to shine upon it, for the glory of God is its light, and its lamp is the Lamb . . . and there shall be no night there" (Rev. 21:23, 25; cf. 22:5).

Nevertheless, it is not true to say that heaven will be "timeless," or without the presence of time or the passage of time. Rather, as long as we are finite creatures we will necessarily experience events one after another. Even the passage that talks about no night being in heaven also mentions the fact that the kings of the earth will bring into the heavenly city "the glory and the honor of the nations" (Rev. 21:26). We are told concerning the light of the heavenly city, "By its light shall the nations walk" (Rev. 21:24). These activities of bringing things into the heavenly city and walking by the light of the heavenly city imply that events are done one after another. Something is outside the heavenly city, and then at a later point in time this thing is part of the glory and honor of the nations that are brought into the heavenly city. To cast one's crown before the throne of God (Rev. 4:10) requires that at one moment the person has a crown and that at a later moment that crown is cast before the throne. To sing a new song of praise before God in heaven requires that one word be sung after another. In fact, the "tree of life" in the heavenly city is said to be *"yielding its fruit each month"* (Rev. 22:2), which implies a regular passage of time and the occurrence of events in time.[18]

Therefore, there will still be a succession of moments one after another and things happening one after another in heaven. We will experience eternal life not in an exact duplication of God's attribute of eternity, but rather in a duration of time that will never end: we, as God's people will experience fullness of joy in God's presence for all eternity—not in the sense that we will no longer experience time, but in the sense that our lives with him will go on forever: "And night shall be no more; they need no light of lamp or sun, for the Lord God will be their light, *and they shall reign for ever and ever*" (Rev. 22:5).

**4. Omnipresence.** Just as God is unlimited or infinite with respect to time, so God is unlimited with respect to space. This characteristic of God's nature is called God's omnipresence (the Latin prefix *omni-* means "all"). God's omnipresence may be defined as follows: *God does not have size or spatial dimensions and is present at every point of space with his whole being, yet God acts differently in different places.*

The fact that God is Lord of space and cannot be limited by space is evident first

---

[18]Rev. 10:6 in the KJV reads, "that there should be time no longer," but "delay" is a better translation for the Greek term *chronos* in this context (as in the RSV, NASB, NIV, and NKJV). In fact, the next verse assumes the continuation of time, for it talks of events to be fulfilled "in the days of the trumpet call to be sounded by the seventh angel" (Rev. 10:7).

from the fact that he created it, for the creation of the material world (Gen. 1:1) implies the creation of space as well. Moses reminded the people of God's lordship over space: "Behold, to the LORD your God belong heaven and the heaven of heavens, the earth with all that is in it" (Deut. 10:14).

**a. God Is Present Everywhere:** Yet there are also specific passages that speak of God's presence in every part of space. We read in Jeremiah, "Am I a God at hand, says the LORD, and not a God afar off? Can a man hide himself in secret places so that I cannot see him? says the LORD. *Do I not fill heaven and earth?* says the LORD" (Jer. 23:23–24). God is here rebuking the prophets who think their words or thoughts are hidden from God. He is everywhere and fills heaven and earth.

God's omnipresence is beautifully expressed by David:

> Whither shall I go from your Spirit?
> Or whither shall I flee from your presence?
> If I ascend to heaven, you are there!
> If I make my bed in Sheol, you are there!
> If I take the wings of the morning
>     and dwell in the uttermost parts of the sea,
> even there your hand shall lead me,
>     and your right hand shall hold me. (Ps. 139:7–10)

There is nowhere in the entire universe, on land or sea, in heaven or in hell, where one can flee from God's presence.

We should note also that there is no indication that simply a *part* of God is in one place and a part of him in another. It is *God himself* who is present wherever David might go. We cannot say that some of God or just part of God is present, for that would be to think of his being in spatial terms, as if he were limited somehow by space. It seems more appropriate to say that God is present *with his whole being* in every part of space (cf. also Acts 17:28 where Paul affirms the correctness of the words, "In him we live and move and have our being," and Col. 1:17, which says of Christ, "in him all things hold together").

**b. God Does Not Have Spatial Dimensions:** While it seems necessary for us to say that God's whole being is present in every part of space, or at every point in space, it is also necessary to say that *God cannot be contained by any space,* no matter how large. Solomon says in his prayer to God, "But will God indeed dwell on the earth? Behold, *heaven and the highest heaven cannot contain you;* how much less this house which I have built!" (1 Kings 8:27). Heaven and the highest heaven cannot contain God; indeed, he cannot be contained by the largest space imaginable (cf. Isa. 66:1–2; Acts 7:48). While the thought that God is everywhere present with his whole being ought to encourage us greatly in prayer no matter where we are, the fact that no one place can be said to contain God should also discourage us from thinking that there is some special place of worship that gives people special access to God: he cannot be contained in any one place.

We should guard against thinking that God extends infinitely far in all directions so that he himself exists in a sort of infinite, unending space. Nor should we think that God is somehow a "bigger space" or bigger area surrounding the space of the universe as we know it. All of these ideas continue to think of God's being in spatial terms, as if he were simply an extremely large being. Instead, we should try to avoid thinking of God in terms of size or spatial dimensions. God is a being who exists *without* size or dimensions in space. In fact, before God created the universe, there was no matter or material so there was no space either. Yet God still existed. Where was God? He was not in a place that we could call a "where," for there was no "where" or space. But God still was! This fact makes us realize that God relates to space in a far different way than we do or than any created thing does. He exists as a kind of being that is far different and far greater than we can imagine.

We must also be careful not to think that God himself is equivalent to any part of creation or to all of it. A pantheist believes that everything is God, or that God is everything that exists. The biblical perspective is rather that God is *present* everywhere in his creation, but that he is also distinct from his creation. How can this be? The analogy of a sponge filled with water is not perfect, but it is helpful. Water is present everywhere in the sponge, but the water is still completely distinct from the sponge. Now this analogy breaks down at very small points within the sponge, where we could say that there is sponge at one point and not water, or water and not sponge. Yet this is because the analogy is dealing with two materials that have spatial characteristics and dimensions, while God does not.

**c. God Can Be Present to Punish, to Sustain, or to Bless:** The idea of God's omnipresence has sometimes troubled people who wonder how God can be present, for example, in hell. In fact, isn't hell the opposite of God's presence, or the absence of God? This difficulty can be resolved by realizing that *God is present in different ways in different places,* or that God acts differently in different places in his creation. Sometimes God is *present to punish.* A terrifying passage in Amos vividly portrays this presence of God in judgment:

> Not one of them shall flee away,
> > not one of them shall escape.
> Though they dig into Sheol,
> > from there shall my hand take them;
> though they climb up to heaven,
> > from there I will bring them down.
> Though they hide themselves on the top of Carmel,
> > from there I will search out and take them;
> and though they hide from my sight at the bottom of the sea,
> > there I will command the serpent, and it shall bite them.
> And though they go into captivity before their enemies,
> > there I will command the sword, and it shall slay them;
> and I will set my eyes upon them for evil and not for good.
> > (Amos 9:1–4)

At other times God is present neither to punish nor to bless, but merely *present to sustain,* or to keep the universe existing and functioning in the way he intended it to function. In this sense the divine nature of Christ is everywhere present: "He is before all things, and in him all things hold together" (Col. 1:17). The author of

Hebrews says of God the Son that he is (continually) "upholding the universe by his word of power" (Heb. 1:3).[19]

Yet at other times or in other places God is *present to bless*. David says, "*in your presence* there is fulness of joy, in your right hand are pleasures for evermore" (Ps. 16:11). Here David is speaking not of God's presence to punish or merely to sustain, but of God's presence to bless.

. In fact, most of the time that the Bible talks about God's presence, it is referring to God's presence to bless. For example, it is in this way that we should understand God's presence above the ark of the covenant in the Old Testament. We read of "the ark of the covenant of the LORD of hosts, who is *enthroned on the cherubim*" (1 Sam. 4:4; cf. Ex. 25:22), a reference to the fact that God made his presence known and acted in a special way to bring blessing and protection to his people at the location he had designated as his throne, namely, the place above the two golden figures of heavenly beings ("cherubim") that were over the top of the ark of the covenant. It is not that God was not present elsewhere, but rather that here he especially made his presence known and here he especially manifested his character and brought blessing to his people.

In the new covenant, there is no one place on earth that God has chosen as his particular dwelling place, for we can worship him anywhere (see John 4:20). But now and for all eternity God has chosen the place the Bible calls "heaven" to be the focus of the manifestation of his character and the presence of his blessing and glory. So when the new Jerusalem comes down out of heaven from God, John in his vision hears a loud voice from God's throne saying, "Behold, the dwelling of God is with men. He will dwell with them, and they shall be his people, and God himself will be with them" (Rev. 21:3). We might find it misleading to say that God is "more present" in heaven than anywhere else, but it would not be misleading to say that God is present in a special way in heaven, present especially there to bless and to show forth his glory. We could also say that God manifests his presence more fully in heaven than elsewhere.

In this way also Paul's statement about Christ can be understood: "In him the whole fulness of deity dwells bodily" (Col. 2:9). In one sense of course we could say that God's whole being is present at every point in space and therefore at every point in every person, not only in Christ. But there are two difficulties with speaking this way: (1) The Bible never speaks about God's presence in unbelievers in a direct way, probably to avoid any connection between God and the responsibility or blame for evil deeds, and probably also to avoid any suggestion of God's presence to bless, since it is only a presence to sustain. (2) Furthermore, this sense of "present to sustain" is not the sense Paul has in mind in Colossians 2:9. In fact, there Paul does not even seem to mean simply "present to bless" in the same sense in which God is present to bless in the lives of all believers. Rather, Paul seems to mean that in Christ God's own nature is present to bless and to manifest his character in the fullest and most complete way possible.

Our difficulty in understanding how to express the way in which God is present

---

[19]The present participle *pherōn*, "carrying along," in Heb. 1:3 implies that Christ's activity of "carrying along all things" (that is, keeping all things in the universe existing and functioning regularly) is a continual activity, one that never ceases.

in unbelievers, for example, leads us to realize that although the Bible *can* speak of God as being present everywhere, when the Bible says that God is "present" it *usually* means "present to bless." That is, although there are a few references to God's presence to sustain or presence to punish, the vast majority of biblical references to God's presence are simply more brief ways of stating that he is *present to bless*. When we become more and more familiar with this biblical pattern of speech, it becomes more and more difficult to speak of God's presence in any other way. And perhaps it is even misleading to do so unless a clear explanation of our meaning can be given.

Some examples of the usual biblical means of expression are as follows: 2 Corinthians 3:17: "Where the Spirit of the Lord is, there is freedom"; Romans 8:9–10: "you are in the Spirit, if in fact the Spirit of God dwells in you. . . . if Christ is in you . . . your spirits are alive"; John 14:23: "If a man loves me, he will keep my word, and my Father will love him, and we will come to him and make our home with him," and so forth. All of these verses talk about God's presence and assume that we understand that they mean God's presence *to bless*.

In a parallel kind of expression, when the Bible talks about God being "far away" it usually means he is "not present to bless." For example, Isaiah 59:2 says, "Your iniquities have made a separation between you and your God," and Proverbs 15:29 declares: "The LORD is far from the wicked, but he hears the prayer of the righteous."

In summary, God is present in every part of space with his whole being, yet God acts differently in different places. Furthermore, when the Bible speaks of God's presence, it usually means his presence to bless, and it is only normal for our own speech to conform to this biblical usage.

Herman Bavinck, in *The Doctrine of God*, quotes a beautiful paragraph illustrating the practical application of the doctrine of God's omnipresence:

> When you wish to do something evil, you retire from the public into your house where no enemy may see you; from those places of your house which are open and visible to the eyes of men you remove yourself into your room; even in your room you fear some witness from another quarter; you retire into your heart, there you meditate: he is more inward than your heart. Wherever, therefore, you shall have fled, there he is. From yourself, whither will you flee? Will you not follow yourself wherever you shall flee? But since there is One more inward even than yourself, there is no place where you may flee from God angry but to God reconciled. There is no place at all whither you may flee. Will you flee from him? Flee unto him.[20]

**5. Unity.** The unity of God may be defined as follows: *God is not divided into parts, yet we see different attributes of God emphasized at different times*. This attribute of God has also been called *God's simplicity*, using *simple* in the less common sense of "not complex" or "not composed of parts." But since the word *simple* today has the more common sense of "easy to understand" and "unintelligent or foolish," it is more helpful now to speak of God's "unity" rather than his "simplicity."[21]

---

[20]Herman Bavinck, *The Doctrine of God*, p. 164. The citation is reproduced in the book with no indication of its source.

[21]Systematic theologians have often distinguished another aspect of God's unity at this point, namely the "unity" found in the fact that God is one God, not many gods. This fact has been called the "unity

When Scripture speaks about God's attributes it never singles out one attribute of God as more important than all the rest. There is an assumption that every attribute is completely true of God and is true of all of God's character. For example, John can say that "God is light" (1 John 1:5) and then a little later say also that "God is love" (1 John 4:8). There is no suggestion that part of God is light and part of God is love, or that God is partly light and partly love. Nor should we think that God is more light than love or more love than light. Rather it is *God himself* who is light, and it is *God himself* who is also love.

The same is true of other descriptions of God's character, such as that in Exodus 34:6–7:

> The LORD passed before him and proclaimed, "The LORD, the LORD, a God merciful and gracious, slow to anger, and abounding in steadfast love and faithfulness, keeping steadfast love for thousands, forgiving iniquity and transgression and sin, but who will by no means clear the guilty, visiting the iniquity of the fathers upon the children and the children's children, to the third and the fourth generation."

We would not want to say that these attributes are only characteristic of some part of God, but rather that they are characteristic of God himself and therefore characteristic of all of God.

These considerations indicate that we should not think of God as some kind of collection of various attributes added together as in figure 11:2.

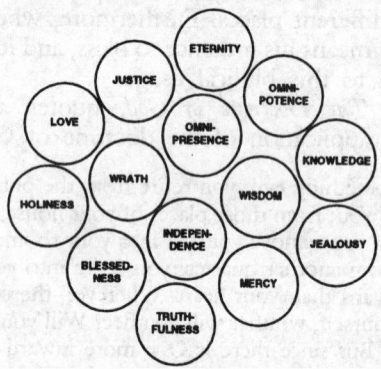

**GOD'S BEING IS NOT A COLLECTION OF ATTRIBUTES ADDED TOGETHER**
*Figure 11.2*

Nor should we think of the attributes of God as something external from God's real being or real self, something added on to who God really is, after the analogy of figure 11.3.

Rather, we must remember that God's *whole being* includes all of his attributes: he is *entirely* loving, *entirely* merciful, *entirely* just, and so forth. Every attribute of

---

of singularity," whereas what I have here called God's unity has then been called the "unity of simplicity."

While I agree that God is one God, it can be confusing to speak of two different kinds of unity in God. Therefore, I have not used the term "unity of singularity" or discussed the concept here, but have rather treated the question in chapter 14, on the Trinity.

God that we find in Scripture is true of *all* of God's being, and we therefore can say that *every attribute of God also qualifies every other attribute*.

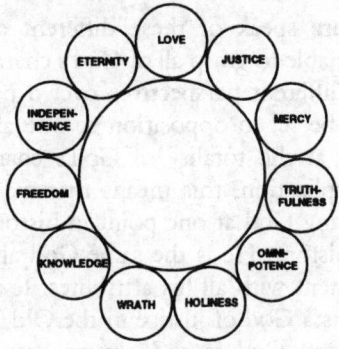

**GOD'S ATTRIBUTES ARE NOT ADDITIONS TO HIS REAL BEING**
*Figure 11.3*

Figure 11.4 may be helpful in understanding this doctrine of God's unity. In the diagram, let us assume that the horizontal lines represent the attribute of love, and that the vertical lines represent the aspect of God's justice.

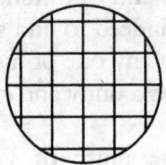

**GOD'S LOVE AND JUSTICE**
*Figure 11.4*

Furthermore, let us understand the diagonal lines going from upper left to lower right as representing God's holiness and the diagonal lines going from upper right to lower left as representing God's wisdom, as in figure 11.5.

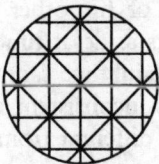

**GOD'S LOVE, JUSTICE, HOLINESS, AND WISDOM**
*Figure 11.5*

We could of course go on with different sorts of lines for each of the different attributes of God. But it should be clear that each attribute is simply a way of describing one aspect of God's total character or being. God himself is a *unity*, a unified and completely integrated whole person who is infinitely perfect in *all* of these attributes.

Why then does Scripture speak of these different attributes of God? It is probably because we are unable to grasp all of God's character at one time, and we need to learn of it from different perspectives over a period of time. Yet these perspectives should never be set in opposition to one another, for they are just different ways of looking at the totality of God's character.

In terms of practical application, this means that we should never think, for example, that God is a loving God at one point in history and a just or wrathful God at another point in history. He is the same God always, and everything he says or does is fully consistent with all his attributes. It is not accurate to say, as some have said, that God is a God of justice in the Old Testament and a God of love in the New Testament. God is and always has been infinitely just and infinitely loving as well, and everything he does in the Old Testament as well as the New Testament is completely consistent with both of those attributes.

Now it is true that some actions of God show certain of his attributes more prominently. Creation demonstrates his power and wisdom, the atonement demonstrates his love and justice, and the radiance of heaven demonstrates his glory and beauty. But all of these in some way or other *also* demonstrate his knowledge and holiness and mercy and truthfulness and patience and sovereignty, and so forth. It would be difficult indeed to find some attribute of God that is not reflected at least to some degree in any one of his acts of redemption. This is due to the fact mentioned above: God is a unity and everything he does is an act of the whole person of God.

Moreover, the doctrine of the unity of God should caution us against attempting to single out any one attribute of God as more important than all the others. At various times people have attempted to see God's holiness, or his love, or his self-existence, or his righteousness, or some other attribute as the most important attribute of his being. But all such attempts seem to misconceive of God as a combination of various parts, with some parts being somehow larger or more influential than others. Furthermore, it is hard to understand exactly what "most important" might mean. Does it mean that there are some actions of God that are not fully consistent with some of his other attributes? That there are some attributes that God somehow sets aside at times in order to act in ways slightly contrary to those attributes? Certainly we cannot maintain either of these views, for that would mean that God is inconsistent with his own character or that he changes and becomes something different from what he was previously. Rather, when we see all the attributes as merely various aspects of the total character of God, then such a question becomes quite unnecessary and we discover that there is no attribute that can be singled out as more important. It is *God himself in his whole being* who is supremely important, and it is God himself in his whole being whom we are to seek to know and to love.

## QUESTIONS FOR PERSONAL APPLICATION

1. As you think of God's independence, unchangeableness, eternity, omnipresence, and unity, can you see some faint reflections of these five incommunicable attributes in yourself as God created you to be? What would it mean to strive to become more like God in these areas? At what point would it be wrong to even want to be like God in each of these areas because it would be attempting to usurp his unique role as Creator and Lord?

2. Using each of these five incommunicable attributes, explain how we will be more like God in heaven than we are now, and also how we will for all eternity be unlike God in each of these five areas.

3. Explain how each aspect of the doctrine of God's independence makes you feel emotionally. Does this doctrine have a positive or negative effect on your spiritual life? Explain why.

4. Explain how the doctrine of God's immutability or unchangeableness helps to answer the following questions: Will we be able to do a good job of bringing up children in such an evil world as we have today? Is it possible to have the same close fellowship with God that people had during biblical times? What can we think or do to make Bible stories seem more real and less removed from our present life? Do you think that God is less willing to answer prayer today than he was in Bible times?

5. If you sin against God today, when would it start bringing sorrow to God's heart? When would it stop bringing sorrow to God's heart? Does this reflection help you understand why God's character requires that he punish sin? Why did God have to send his Son to bear the punishment for sin instead of simply forgetting about sin and welcoming sinners into heaven without having given the punishment for sin to anyone? Does God now think of your sins as forgiven or as unforgiven sins?

6. If you sing praise to God today, when will the sound of that praise cease being present in God's consciousness and bringing delight to his heart? Do songs of praise to God have any ultimate meaning? What about trusting in him hour by hour or obeying him throughout each day?

7. Is control over the use of your time a struggle in your own life? As we grow toward maturity in the Christian life and toward conformity to the image of Christ, will we become more like God in our mastery over time? In what ways?

8. Explain how each of the five incommunicable attributes of God discussed in this chapter can be a help in your own prayer life.

## SPECIAL TERMS

| | |
|---|---|
| anthropomorphic language | infinity with respect to space |
| aseity | infinity with respect to time |
| communicable attributes | names of God |
| eternity | omnipresence |

immutability                    self-existence
incommunicable attributes       simplicity
independence                    unchangeableness
infinite                        unity

## BIBLIOGRAPHY

(For an explanation of this bibliography see the note on the bibliography to chapter 1, p. 38. Complete bibliographical data may be found on pp. 1223–29.)

Note: For this chapter on God's incommunicable attributes, it should be noted that some systematic theologies classify and discuss God's attributes in categories other than communicable and incommunicable, so an exact cross-reference to parallel sections is not always possible. A fuller list of the sections in systematic theology texts that discuss the attributes of God in general will be found in the bibliography at the end of chapter 13.

### Sections in Evangelical Systematic Theologies

1. Anglican (Episcopalian)
   1882–92    Litton, 58–67
2. Arminian (Wesleyan or Methodist)
   1847       Finney, 49–65
   1875–76    Pope, 1:248–55, 287–325
   1892–94    Miley, 1:159–80, 214–22
   1940       Wiley, 1:241–393
   1960       Purkiser, 127–44
3. Baptist
   1767       Gill, 25–31, 33–50, 119–22
   1887       Boyce, 1:125–35, 183–90
   1907       Strong, 243–303
   1917       Mullins, 214–50
   1983–85    Erickson, 1:263–78
   1987–94    Lewis/Demarest, 1:175–248
4. Dispensational
   1947       Chafer, 1:179–191, 212–24, 260–71
   1949       Thiessen, 118–28
5. Lutheran
   1917–24    Pieper, 1:427–47
   1934       Mueller, 160–67
6. Reformed (or Presbyterian)
   1559       Calvin, 1:96–120
   1861       Heppe, 57–104
   1871–73    Hodge, 1:366–93
   1878       Dabney, ST, 38–45, 144–54

1887–1921    Warfield, *SSW*, 1:69–87; *ST*, 109–14
      1889    Shedd, 1:151–94, 334–92
      1909    Bavinck, *DG*, 113–72
      1938    Berkhof, 47–63
      1962    Buswell, 1:36–57
7. Renewal (or charismatic/Pentecostal)
   1988–92    Williams, 55–59, 77–79

## Sections in Representative Roman Catholic Systematic Theologies

1. Roman Catholic: Traditional
     1955    Ott, 24–38
2. Roman Catholic: Post-Vatican II
     1980    McBrien, 1:238–341

### Other Works

Bromiley, G. W. "God." In *ISBE*, 2:493–503.
Charnock, Stephen. *The Existence and Attributes of God*. Repr. ed. Evansville, Ind.: Sovereign Grace Book Club, n.d., pp. 69–180 (first published 1655–1680).
Diehl, D. W. "Process Theology." In *EDT*, pp. 880–85.
Helm, Paul. *Eternal God: A Study of God Without Time*. Oxford: Clarendon, 1988.
Kaiser, Christopher B. *The Doctrine of God*. Westchester, Ill.: Good News, 1982.
Lewis, Gordon R. "God, Attributes of." In *EDT*, pp. 451–59.
McComiskey, Thomas E. "God, Names of." In *EDT*, pp. 464–68.
Packer, J. I. *Knowing God*. London: Hodder and Stoughton, 1973, pp. 67–79.
Saucy, R. H. "God, Doctrine of." In *EDT*, pp. 459–64.
Tozer, A. W. *The Knowledge of the Holy*. New York: Harper and Row, 1961.

## SCRIPTURE MEMORY PASSAGE

**Psalm 102:25–27:**

> *Of old you laid the foundation of the earth,*
>     *and the heavens are the work of your hands.*
> *They will perish, but you endure;*
>     *they will all wear out like a garment.*
> *You change them like raiment, and they pass away;*
>     *but you are the same, and your years have no end.*

## HYMN

### "Immortal, Invisible, God Only Wise"

In several lines of this hymn the various attributes of God are mentioned in such rapid succession that it is impossible for us to reflect on each one individually as we sing. That is not entirely a disadvantage of the hymn, however, for it makes us realize that when we finally see God in all his glory in heaven, the wonder of beholding him and all his perfections at once will overwhelm us far more completely than does this hymn, and we will find ourselves lost in praise.

> Immortal, invisible, God only wise,
>     In light inaccessible hid from our eyes,

Most blessed, most glorious, the Ancient of Days,
  Almighty, victorious, thy great name we praise.

Unresting, unhasting, and silent as light,
  Nor wanting, nor wasting, thou rulest in might;
Thy justice like mountains high soaring above
  Thy clouds which are fountains of goodness and love.

Great Father of glory, pure Father of light,
  Thine angels adore thee, all veiling their sight;
All praise we would render; O help us to see
  'Tis only the splendor of light hideth thee!

AUTHOR: WALTER CHALMERS SMITH, 1867

Alternative hymn: "Have You Not Known, Have You Not Heard?"

# Chapter 12

# The Character of God: "Communicable" Attributes (Part 1)

*How is God like us in his being, and in mental and moral attributes?*

## EXPLANATION AND SCRIPTURAL BASIS

In this chapter we consider the attributes of God that are "communicable," or more shared with us than those mentioned in the previous chapter. It must be remembered that this division into "incommunicable" and "communicable" is not an absolute division and there is some room for difference of opinion concerning which attributes should fit into which categories.[1] The list of attributes here put in the category "communicable" is a common one, but understanding the definition of each attribute is more important than being able to categorize them in exactly the way presented in this book.

Furthermore, any list of God's attributes must be based on some understanding of how finely one wishes to make distinctions between various aspects of God's character. Are God's goodness and love two attributes or one? What about knowledge and wisdom, or spirituality and invisibility? In this chapter, each of these attributes is treated separately, and the result is a rather long list of various attributes. Yet in several cases it would not make much difference if someone were to treat these pairs as various aspects of the same attribute. If we remember that it is the entire and wholly integrated person of God about whom we are talking, it will be apparent that the division into various attributes is not a matter of great doctrinal significance but is something that must be based on one's judgment concerning the most effective way to present the biblical material.

This chapter divides God's "communicable" attributes into five major categories, with individual attributes listed under each category as follows:

A. Attributes Describing God's Being
    1. Spirituality
    2. Invisibility
B. Mental Attributes
    3. Knowledge (or Omniscience)
    4. Wisdom
    5. Truthfulness (and Faithfulness)
C. Moral Attributes

---

[1]See discussion of communicable and incommunicable attributes in chapter 11, pp. 156–57.

　　**6.** Goodness
　　**7.** Love
　　**8.** Mercy (Grace, Patience)
　　**9.** Holiness
　　**10.** Peace (or Order)
　　**11.** Righteousness (or Justice)
　　**12.** Jealousy
　　**13.** Wrath
　**D.** Attributes of Purpose
　　**14.** Will
　　**15.** Freedom
　　**16.** Omnipotence (or Power, and Sovereignty)
　**E.** "Summary" Attributes
　　**17.** Perfection
　　**18.** Blessedness
　　**19.** Beauty
　　**20.** Glory

Because God's communicable attributes are to be imitated in our lives,[2] each of these sections will include a short explanation of the way in which the attribute in question is to be imitated by us.

## A. Attributes Describing God's Being

**1. Spirituality.** People have often wondered, what is God made of? Is he made of flesh and blood like ourselves? Certainly not. What then is the material that forms his being? Is God made of matter at all? Or is God pure energy? Or is he in some sense pure thought?

The answer of Scripture is that God is none of these. Rather, we read that "God is *spirit*" (John 4:24). This statement is spoken by Jesus in the context of a discussion with the woman at the well in Samaria. The discussion is about the *location* where people should worship God, and Jesus is telling her that true worship of God does not require that one be *present* either in Jerusalem or in Samaria (John 4:21), for true worship has to do not with physical location but with one's inner spiritual condition. This is because "God is spirit" and this apparently signifies that God is in no way limited to a spatial location.

Thus, we should *not* think of God as having *size* or *dimensions,* even infinite ones (see the discussion on God's omnipresence in the previous chapter). We should not think of God's existence as spirit as meaning that God is infinitely large, for example, for it is not *part* of God but *all* of God that is in every point of space (see Ps. 139:7–10). Nor should we think that God's existence as spirit means that God is infinitely small, for no place in the universe can surround him or contain him

---

[2]Note that Eph. 5:1 tells us to "be imitators of God, as beloved children." See also the discussion of the fact that God created us to reflect his character in our lives, in chapter 21, pp. 440–50.

(see 1 Kings 8:27). Thus, God's being cannot be rightly thought of in terms of space, however we may understand his existence as "spirit."

We also find that God forbids his people to think of *his very being* as similar to *anything* else in the physical creation. We read in the Ten Commandments:

> You shall not make for yourself a graven image, or *any likeness of anything* that is in heaven above, or that is in the earth beneath, or that is in the water under the earth; you shall not bow down to them or serve them; *for I the* LORD *your God am a jealous God*, visiting the iniquity of the fathers upon the children to the third and the fourth generation of those who hate me, but showing steadfast love to thousands of those who love me and keep my commandments. (Ex. 20:4–6)

The creation language in this commandment ("heaven above, or . . . earth beneath, or . . . water under the earth") is a reminder that God's *being*, his essential mode of existence, is different from everything that he has created. To think of his being in terms of anything else in the created universe is to misrepresent him, to limit him, to think of him as less than he really is. To make a graven (or "carved" or "sculptured") image of God as a golden calf, for example, may have been an attempt to portray God as a God who is strong and full of life (like a calf), but to say that God was like a calf was a horribly false statement about God's knowledge, wisdom, love, mercy, omnipresence, eternity, independence, holiness, righteousness, justice, and so forth. Indeed, while we must say that God has made all creation so that each part of it reflects something of his own character, we must also now affirm that to picture God as *existing* in a form or *mode of being* that is like anything else in creation is to think of God in a horribly misleading and dishonoring way.

This is why God's jealousy is given as the reason for the prohibition against making images of him: "for I the LORD your God am a jealous God . . ." (Ex. 20:5). God is jealous to protect his own honor. He eagerly seeks for people to think of him as he is and to worship him for all his excellence, and he is angered when his glory is diminished or his character is falsely represented (cf. Deut. 4:23–24, where God's intense jealousy for his own honor is again given as the reason for a prohibition against making any images of him).

Thus, God does not have a physical body, nor is he made of any kind of matter like much of the rest of creation. Furthermore, God is not merely energy or thought or some other element of creation. He is also not like vapor or steam or air or space, all of which are created things: *God's being* is not like any of these. God's being is not even exactly like our own spirits, for these are created things that apparently are able to exist only in one place in one time.

Instead of all these ideas of God, we must say that God is *spirit*. Whatever this means, it is a kind of existence that is unlike anything else in creation. It is a kind of existence that is far superior to all our material existence. We might say that God is "pure being" or "the fullness or essence of being." Furthermore, this kind of existence is not less real or less desirable than our own existence. Rather, it is more real and more desirable than the material and immaterial existence of all creation. Before there was any creation, God existed as spirit. His own being is so very real that it was able to cause everything else to come into existence!

At this point we can define God's spirituality: *God's spirituality means that God exists as a being that is not made of any matter, has no parts or dimensions, is unable to be perceived by our bodily senses, and is more excellent than any other kind of existence.*

We may ask why God's being is this way. Why is God spirit? All that we can say is that this is the greatest, most excellent way to be! This is a form of existence far superior to anything we know. It is amazing to meditate on this fact.

These considerations make us wonder if God's spirituality should perhaps be called an "incommunicable" attribute. To do so would indeed be appropriate in some ways, since God's being is so different from ours. Nevertheless, the fact remains that God has given us spirits in which we worship him (John 4:24; 1 Cor. 14:14; Phil. 3:3), in which we are united with the Lord's spirit (1 Cor. 6:17), with which the Holy Spirit joins to bear witness to our adoption in God's family (Rom. 8:16), and in which we pass into the Lord's presence when we die (Luke 23:46; Eccl. 12:7; Heb. 12:23; cf. Phil. 1:23–24). Therefore there is clearly some communication from God to us of a spiritual nature that is something like his own nature, though certainly not in all respects. For this reason it also seems appropriate to think of God's spirituality as a communicable attribute.

**2. Invisibility.** Related to God's spirituality is the fact that God is invisible. Yet we also must speak of the visible ways in which God manifests himself. God's invisibility can be defined as follows: *God's invisibility means that God's total essence, all of his spiritual being, will never be able to be seen by us, yet God still shows himself to us through visible, created things.*

Many passages speak of the fact that God is not able to be seen. "No one has ever seen God" (John 1:18). Jesus says, "Not that any one has seen the Father except him who is from God; he has seen the Father" (John 6:46). Paul gives the following words of praise: "To the King of ages, immortal, *invisible,* the only God, be honor and glory for ever and ever. Amen" (1 Tim. 1:17). He speaks of God as one "who alone has immortality and dwells in unapproachable light, *whom no man has ever seen or can see*" (1 Tim. 6:16). John says, "No man has ever seen God" (1 John 4:12).

We must remember that these passages were all written after events in Scripture where people saw some outward manifestation of God. For example, very early in Scripture we read, "Thus the LORD used to speak to Moses face to face, as a man speaks to his friend" (Ex. 33:11). Yet God told Moses, "You cannot see my face; for man shall not see me and live" (Ex. 33:20). Nevertheless, God caused his glory to pass by Moses while he hid Moses in a cleft of the rock, and then God let Moses see his back after he had passed by, but said, "my face shall not be seen" (Ex. 33:21–23). This sequence of verses and others like it in the Old Testament indicate that there was a sense in which God could not be seen at all, but that there was also some outward form or manifestation of God which at least in part was able to be seen by man.

It is right, therefore, to say that although God's *total essence* will never be able to be seen by us, nevertheless, God still shows something of himself to us through visible, created things. This happens in a variety of ways.

If we are to *think* of God, we must think of him somehow. God understands this and gives us hundreds of different analogies taken from our human lives or from the creative world.[3] This huge diversity of analogies from all parts of creation reminds us that we should not focus overly much on any one of these analogies. Yet if we do not focus exclusively on any one of these analogies, all of them help to reveal God to us in a somewhat "visible" way (cf. Gen. 1:27; Ps. 19:1; Rom. 1:20).

The Old Testament also records a number of theophanies. A *theophany* is "an appearance of God." In these theophanies God took on various visible forms to show himself to people. God appeared to Abraham (Gen. 18:1–33), Jacob (Gen. 32:28–30), the people of Israel (as a pillar of cloud by day and fire by night: Ex. 13:21–22), the elders of Israel (Ex. 24:9–11), Manoah and his wife (Judg. 13:21–22), Isaiah (Isa. 6:1), and others.

A much greater visible manifestation of God than these Old Testament theophanies was found in the person of Jesus Christ himself. He could say, "He who has seen me has seen the Father" (John 14:9). And John contrasts the fact that no one has ever seen God with the fact that God's only Son has made him known to us: "No one has ever seen God; the only begotten God,[4] who is in the bosom of the Father, he has made him known" (John 1:18, author's translation). Furthermore, Jesus is "the image of the invisible God" (Col. 1:15), and is "the bright radiance of the glory of God" and is "the exact representation of his nature" (Heb. 1:3 author's translation). Thus, in the person of Jesus we have a unique visible manifestation of God in the New Testament that was not available to believers who saw theophanies in the Old Testament.

But how will we see God in heaven? We will never be able to see or know all of God, for "his greatness is unsearchable" (Ps. 145:3; cf. John 6:46; 1 Tim. 1:17; 6:16; 1 John 4:12, which were mentioned above). And we will not be able to see—at least with our physical eyes—the spiritual being of God. Nevertheless, Scripture says that we will see God himself. Jesus says, "Blessed are the pure in heart, for *they shall see God*" (Matt. 5:8). We will be able to see the human nature of Jesus, of course (Rev. 1:7). But it is not clear in exactly what sense we will be able to "see" the Father and the Holy Spirit, or the divine nature of God the Son (cf. Rev. 1:4; 4:2–3, 5; 5:6). Perhaps the nature of this "seeing" will not be known to us until we reach heaven.

Although what we see will not be an exhaustive vision of God, it will be a completely true and clear and real vision of God. We shall see "face to face" (1 Cor. 13:12) and "we shall see him as he is" (1 John 3:2). The most remarkable description of the open, close fellowship with God that we shall experience is seen in the fact that in the heavenly city "the throne of God and of the Lamb shall be in it, and his servants shall worship him; *they shall see his face,* and his name shall be on their foreheads" (Rev. 22:3–4).

When we realize that God is the perfection of all that we long for or desire, that he is the summation of everything beautiful or desirable, then we realize that the greatest joy of the life to come will be that we "shall see his face." This seeing of God "face to face" has been called the *beatific vision,* meaning "the vision that makes us blessed or happy" ("beatific" is from two Latin words, *beatus,* "blessed,"

---

[3]See the discussion of the names of God taken from creation in chapter 11, p. 158.

[4]There is a textual variant at this point, but "the only begotten God" (*monogenēs theos*) is better attested than "the only begotten Son," and this reading is not foreign to the context: see Leon Morris, *The Gospel According to John* (Grand Rapids: Eerdmans, 1971), pp. 113–14.

and *facere,* "to make"). To look at God changes us and makes us like him: "We shall be like him, for *we shall see him as he is*" (1 John 3:2; cf. 2 Cor. 3:18). This vision of God will be the consummation of our knowing God and will give us full delight and joy for all eternity: "in your presence there is fulness of joy, in your right hand are pleasures for evermore" (Ps. 16:11).

## B. Mental Attributes

**3. Knowledge (Omniscience).** God's knowledge may be defined as follows: *God fully knows himself and all things actual and possible in one simple and eternal act.*

Elihu says that God is the one "who is *perfect in knowledge*" (Job 37:16), and John says that God "*knows everything*" (1 John 3:20). The quality of knowing everything is called omniscience, and because God knows everything, he is said to be omniscient (that is, "all-knowing").

The definition given above explains omniscience in more detail. It says first that God fully knows himself. This is an amazing fact since God's own being is infinite or unlimited. Of course, only he who is infinite can fully know himself in every detail. This fact is implied by Paul when he says, "For the Spirit searches everything, even the depths of God. For what person knows a man's thoughts except the spirit of the man which is in him? So also no one comprehends the thoughts of God except the Spirit of God" (1 Cor. 2:10–11).

This idea is also suggested by John's statement that "God is light and in him is no darkness at all" (1 John 1:5). In this context "light" has a suggestion of both moral purity and full knowledge or awareness. If there is "no darkness at all" in God, but he is entirely "light," then God is himself both entirely holy and also entirely filled with self-knowledge.

The definition also says that God knows "all things *actual.*" This means all things that exist and all things that happen. This applies to creation, for God is the one before whom "no creature is hidden, but all are open and laid bare to the eyes of him with whom we have to do" (Heb. 4:13; cf. 2 Chron. 16:9; Job 28:24; Matt. 10:29–30). God also knows the future, for he is the one who can say, "I am God, and there is none like me, declaring the end from the beginning and from ancient times things not yet done" (Isa. 46:9–10; cf. 42:8–9 and frequent passages in the Old Testament prophets). He knows the tiny details of every one of our lives, for Jesus tells us, "Your Father knows what you need before you ask him" (Matt. 6:8), and, "Even the hairs of your head are all numbered" (Matt. 10:30).

In Psalm 139 David reflects on the amazing detail of God's knowledge of our lives. He knows our actions and thoughts: "O LORD, you have searched me and known me! You know when I sit down and when I rise up; you discern my thoughts from afar" (Ps. 139:1–2). He knows the words we will say before they are spoken: "Even before a word is on my tongue, lo, O LORD, you know it altogether" (Ps. 139:4). And he knows all the days of our lives even before we are born: "Your eyes beheld my unformed substance; in your book were written, every one of them, the days that were formed for me, when as yet there was none of them" (Ps. 139:16).

The definition of God's knowledge given above also specifies that God knows "all things *possible.*" This is because there are some instances in Scripture where

God gives information about events that might happen but that do not actually come to pass. For example, when David was fleeing from Saul he rescued the city of Keilah from the Philistines and then stayed for a time at Keilah. He decided to ask God whether Saul would come to Keilah to attack him and, if Saul came, whether the men of Keilah would surrender him into Saul's hand. David said:

> "Will Saul come down, as your servant has heard? O LORD, the God of Israel, I beseech you, tell your servant." And the LORD said, "He will come down." Then said David, "Will the men of Keilah surrender me and my men into the hand of Saul?" And the LORD said, "They will surrender you." Then David and his men, who were about six hundred, arose and departed from Keilah, and they went wherever they could go. When Saul was told that David had escaped from Keilah, he gave up the expedition. (1 Sam. 23:11–13)

Similarly, Jesus could state that Tyre and Sidon *would have* repented if Jesus' own miracles had been done there in former days: "Woe to you, Chorazin! woe to you, Bethsaida! for if the mighty works done in you had been done in Tyre and Sidon, they would have repented long ago in sackcloth and ashes" (Matt. 11:21). Similarly, he says, "And you, Capernaum, will you be exalted to heaven? You shall be brought down to Hades. For if the mighty works done in you had been done in Sodom, it would have remained until this day" (Matt. 11:23; cf. 2 Kings 13:19, where Elisha tells what would have happened if King Joash had struck the ground five or six times with the arrows).

The fact that God knows all things possible can also be deduced from God's full knowledge of himself. If God fully knows himself, he knows everything he is able to do, which includes all things that are possible. This fact is indeed amazing. God has made an incredibly complex and varied universe. But there are thousands upon thousands of other variations or kinds of things that God could have created but did not. God's infinite knowledge includes detailed knowledge of what each of those other possible creations would have been like and what would have happened in each of them! "Such knowledge is too wonderful for me; it is high, I cannot attain it" (Ps. 139:6). "For as the heavens are higher than the earth, so are my ways higher than your ways and my thoughts than your thoughts" (Isa. 55:9).

Our definition of God's knowledge speaks of God knowing everything in one "simple act." Here again the word *simple* is used in the sense "not divided into parts." This means that God is always fully aware of everything. If he should wish to tell us the number of grains of sand on the seashore or the number of stars in the sky, he would not have to count them all quickly like some kind of giant computer, nor would he have to call the number to mind because it was something he had not thought about for a time. Rather, he always knows all things at once. All of these facts and all other things that he knows are always fully present in his consciousness. He does not have to reason to conclusions or ponder carefully before he answers, for he knows the end from the beginning, and he never learns and never forgets anything (cf. Ps. 90:4; 2 Peter 3:8; and the verses cited above on God's perfect knowledge). Every bit of God's knowledge is always fully present in his consciousness; it never grows dim or fades into his nonconscious memory. Finally, the definition talks about God's knowledge as not only a simple act but also an "eternal act." This means that God's knowledge never changes or grows. If he were ever to learn something new, he would not have been omniscient beforehand. Thus, from all eternity God has known all things that would happen and all things that he would do.

Someone may object that God promises to forget our sins. For example, he says, "I will not remember your sins" (Isa. 43:25). Yet passages like this can certainly be understood to mean that God will never again let the knowledge of these sins play any part in the way he relates to us: he will "forget" them in his relationship to us. Another objection to the biblical teaching about God's omniscience has been brought from Jeremiah 7:31; 19:5; and 31:35, where God refers to the horrible practices of parents who burn to death their own children in the sacrificial fires of the pagan god Baal, and says, "which I did not command, *nor did it come into my mind*" (Jer. 7:31). Does this mean that before the time of Jeremiah God had never *thought* of the possibility that parents would sacrifice their own children? Certainly not, for that very practice had occurred a century earlier in the reigns of Ahaz (2 Kings 16:3) and Hoshea (2 Kings 17:17), and God himself had forbidden the practice eight hundred years earlier under Moses (Lev. 18:21). The verses in Jeremiah are probably better translated quite literally, "nor did it enter into my *heart*" (so KJV at Jer. 7:31, and the literal translation in the NASB mg.—the Hebrew word is *lēb*, most frequently translated "heart"), giving the sense, "nor did I wish for it, desire it, think of it in a positive way."[5]

Another difficulty that arises in this connection is the question of the relationship between God's knowledge of everything that will happen in the future and the reality and degree of freedom we have in our actions. If God knows everything that will happen, how can our choices be at all "free"? In fact, this difficulty has loomed so large that some theologians have concluded that God does not know all of the future. They have said that God does not know things that cannot (in their opinion) be known, such as the free acts of people that have not yet occurred (sometimes the phrase used is the "contingent acts of free moral agents," where "contingent" means "possible but not certain"). But such a position is unsatisfactory because it essentially denies God's knowledge of the future of human history at any point in time and thus is inconsistent with the passages cited above about God's knowledge of the future and with dozens of other Old Testament prophetic passages where God predicts the future far in advance and in great detail.[6]

How then are we to resolve this difficulty? Although this question will be treated in much more detail in chapter 16 on God's providence, it may be helpful at this point to note the suggestion of Augustine, who said that God has given us "reasonable self-determination." His statement does not involve the terms *free* or *freedom*, for these terms are exceptionally difficult to define in any way that satisfactorily accounts for God's complete knowledge of future events. But this statement does affirm what is important to us and what we sense to be true in our own experience, that our choices and decisions are "reasonable." That is, we think about what to do, consciously decide what we will do, and then we follow the course of action that we have chosen.

---

[5]The same phrase ("to have a thought enter into the heart") seems to have the sense "desire, wish for, long for" in all five of its occurrences in the Hebrew Old Testament: Isa. 65:17; Jer. 3:16 (where it cannot mean simply "have a factual knowledge of"); 7:31; 19:5; 32:35; as well as in the equivalent Greek phrase *anebē epi tēn kardian* in Acts 7:23.

[6]See additional discussion of this question in chapter 16, pp. 347–49.

Augustine's statement also says that we have "self-determination." This is simply affirming that our choices really do determine what will happen. It is not as if events occur *regardless* of what we decide or do, but rather that they occur *because of* what we decide and do. No attempt is made in this statement to define the sense in which we are "free" or "not free," but that is not the really important issue: for us, it is important that we think, choose, and act, and that these thoughts, choices, and actions are real and actually have eternal significance. If God knows all our thoughts, words, and actions long before they occur, then there must be some sense in which our choices are not absolutely free. But further definition of this issue is better left until it can be treated more fully in chapter 16.

**4. Wisdom.** *God's wisdom means that God always chooses the best goals and the best means to those goals.* This definition goes beyond the idea of God knowing all things and specifies that God's decisions about what he will do are always wise decisions: that is, they always will bring about the best results (from God's ultimate perspective), and they will bring about those results through the best possible means.

Scripture affirms God's wisdom in general in several places. He is called "the only wise God" (Rom. 16:27). Job says that God "is wise in heart" (Job 9:4), and "With him are wisdom and might; he has counsel and understanding" (Job 12:13). God's wisdom is seen specifically in creation. The psalmist exclaims, "O LORD, how manifold are your works! In wisdom you have made them all; the earth is full of your creatures" (Ps. 104:24). As God created the universe, it was perfectly suited to bring him glory, both in its day-by-day processes and in the goals for which he created it. Even now, while we still see the effects of sin and the curse on the natural world, we should be amazed at how harmonious and intricate God's creation is.

God's wisdom is also seen in his great plan of redemption. Christ is "the wisdom of God" to those who are called (1 Cor. 1:24, 30), even though the word of the cross is "foolishness" to those who reject it and think themselves to be wise in this world (1 Cor. 1:18–20). Yet even this is a reflection of God's wise plan: "For since, in the wisdom of God, the world did not know God through wisdom, it pleased God through the folly of what we preach to save those who believe. . . . God chose what is foolish in the world to shame the wise . . . so that no human being might boast in the presence of God" (1 Cor. 1:21, 27, 29).

Paul knows that what we now think of as the "simple" gospel message, understandable even to the very young, reflects an amazing plan of God, which in its depths of wisdom surpasses anything man could ever have imagined. At the end of eleven chapters of reflection on the wisdom of God's plan of redemption, Paul bursts forth into spontaneous praise: "O the depth of the riches and wisdom and knowledge of God! How unsearchable are his judgments and how inscrutable his ways!" (Rom. 11:33).

When Paul preaches the gospel both to Jews and to Gentiles, and they become unified in the one body of Christ (Eph. 3:6), the incredible "mystery" that was "hidden for ages in God who created all things" (Eph. 3:9) is plain for all to see, namely, that in Christ such totally diverse people become united. When groups so different racially and culturally become members of the one body of Christ, then

God's purpose is fulfilled, "that through the church the manifold *wisdom of God* might now be made known to the principalities and powers in the heavenly places" (Eph. 3:10).

Today this means that God's wisdom is shown even to angels and demons ("principalities and powers") when people from different racial and cultural backgrounds are united in Christ in the church. If the Christian church is faithful to God's wise plan, it will be always in the forefront in breaking down racial and social barriers in societies around the world, and will thus be a visible manifestation of God's amazingly wise plan to bring great unity out of great diversity and thereby to cause all creation to honor him.

God's wisdom is also shown in our individual lives. "We know that God works all things together for good for those who love him, who are called according to his purpose" (Rom. 8:28, author's translation). Here Paul affirms that God does work wisely in all the things that come into our lives, and that through all these things he advances us toward the goal of conformity to the image of Christ (Rom. 8:29). It should be our great confidence and a source of peace day by day to know that God causes all things to move us toward the ultimate goal he has for our lives, namely, that we might be like Christ and thereby bring glory to him. Such confidence enabled Paul to accept his "thorn in the flesh" (2 Cor. 12:7) as something that, though painful, God in his wisdom had chosen not to remove (2 Cor. 12:8–10).

Every day of our lives, we may quiet our discouragement with the comfort that comes from the knowledge of God's infinite wisdom: if we are his children, we can know that he is working wisely in our lives, even today, to bring us into greater conformity into the image of Christ.

God's wisdom is, of course, in part communicable to us. We can ask God confidently for wisdom when we need it, for he promises in his Word, "If any of you lacks wisdom, let him ask God, who gives to all men generously and without reproaching, and it will be given him" (James 1:5). This wisdom, or skill in living a life pleasing to God, comes primarily from reading and obeying his Word: "The testimony of the LORD is sure, making wise the simple" (Ps. 19:7; cf. Deut. 4:6–8).

"The fear of the LORD is the beginning of wisdom" (Ps. 111:10; Prov. 9:10; cf. Prov. 1:7), because if we fear dishonoring God or displeasing him, and if we fear his fatherly discipline, then we will have the motivation that makes us want to follow his ways and live according to his wise commands. Furthermore, the possession of wisdom from God will result not in pride but in humility (Prov. 11:2; James 3:13), not in arrogance but in a gentle and peaceful spirit (James 3:14–18). The person who is wise according to God's standards will continually walk in dependence on the Lord and with a desire to exalt him.

Yet we must also remember that God's wisdom is not entirely communicable: we can never fully share God's wisdom (Rom. 11:33). In practical terms, this means that there will frequently be times in this life when we will not be able to understand why God allowed something to happen. Then we have simply to trust him and go on obeying his wise commands for our lives: "Therefore let those who suffer according to God's will do right and entrust their souls to a faithful Creator" (1 Peter 4:19; cf. Deut. 29:29; Prov. 3:5–6). God is infinitely wise and we are not, and it pleases him when we have faith to trust his wisdom even when we do not understand what he is doing.

**5. Truthfulness (and Faithfulness).** *God's truthfulness means that he is the true God, and that all his knowledge and words are both true and the final standard of truth.* The term *veracity,* which means "truthfulness" or "reliability," has sometimes been used as a synonym for God's truthfulness.

The first part of this definition indicates that the God revealed in Scripture is the true or real God and that all other so-called gods are idols. "The LORD is the true God; he is the living God and the everlasting King. . . . The gods who did not make the heavens and the earth shall perish from the earth and from under the heavens" (Jer. 10:10–11). Jesus says to his Father, "And this is eternal life, that they know you *the only true God,* and Jesus Christ whom you have sent" (John 17:3; cf. 1 John 5:20).

We might ask what it means to be the true God as opposed to other beings who are not God. It must mean that God in his own being or character is the one who fully conforms to the idea of what God should be: namely, a being who is infinitely perfect in power, in wisdom, in goodness, in lordship over time and space, and so forth. But we may further ask, *whose* idea of God is this? What idea of God must one conform to in order to be the true God?

At this point our train of thought becomes somewhat circular, for we must not say that a being must conform to *our* idea of what God should be like in order to be the true God! We are mere creatures! We cannot define what the true God must be like! So we must say that it is *God himself* who has the only perfect idea of what the true God should be like. And he himself is the true God because in his being and character he perfectly conforms to his own idea of what the true God should be. In addition, he has implanted in our minds a reflection of his own idea of what the true God must be, and this enables us to recognize him as God.

The definition given above also affirms that all of God's *knowledge* is true and is the final standard of truth. Job tells us that God is "perfect in knowledge" (Job 37:16; see also the verses cited above under the discussion of God's omniscience). To say that God knows all things and that his knowledge is perfect is to say that he is never mistaken in his perception or understanding of the world: all that he knows and thinks is true and is a correct understanding of the nature of reality. In fact, since God knows all things infinitely well, we can say that the standard of true knowledge is conformity to God's knowledge. If we think the same thing God thinks about anything in the universe, we are thinking truthfully about it.

Our definition also affirms that God's words are both *true* and the *final standard of truth.* This means that God is reliable and faithful in his words. With respect to his promises, God always does what he promises to do, and we can depend on him never to be unfaithful to his promises. Thus, he is "a God of faithfulness" (Deut. 32:4). In fact, this specific aspect of God's truthfulness is sometimes viewed as a distinct attribute: *God's faithfulness means that God will always do what he has said and fulfill what he has promised* (Num. 23:19; cf. 2 Sam. 7:28; Ps. 141:6; et al.). He can be relied upon, and he will never prove unfaithful to those who trust what he has said. Indeed, the essence of true faith is taking God at his word and relying on him to do as he has promised.

In addition to the fact that God is faithful to his promises, we must also affirm that all of God's *words* about himself and about his creation completely correspond to reality. That is, God always speaks truth when he speaks. He is "the unlying God" (Titus 1:2, author's translation), the God for whom it is impossible to lie (Heb. 6:18), the God whose every word is perfectly "pure" (Ps. 12:6), the one of whom it can be said, "Every word of God proves true" (Prov. 30:5). God's words are not simply true in the sense that they conform to some standard of truthfulness outside of God. Rather, they are truth itself; they are the final standard and definition of truth. So Jesus can say to the Father, "Your word is *truth*" (John 17:17). What was said about the truthfulness of God's knowledge can also be said about God's words, for they are based on his perfect knowledge and accurately reflect that perfect knowledge: God's words are "truth" in the sense that they are the final standard by which truthfulness is to be judged: whatever conforms to God's own words is also true, and what fails to conform to his words is not true.

The truthfulness of God is also communicable in that we can in part imitate it by striving to have true knowledge about God and about his world. In fact, as we begin to think true thoughts about God and creation, thoughts that we learn from Scripture and from allowing Scripture to guide us in our observation and interpretation of the natural world, we begin to think God's own thoughts after him! We can exclaim with the psalmist, "How precious to me are your thoughts, O God! How vast is the sum of them!" (Ps. 139:17).

This realization should encourage us in the pursuit of knowledge in all areas of the natural and social sciences and the humanities. Whatever the area of our investigation, when we discover more truth about the nature of reality, we discover more of the truth that God already knows. In this sense we can affirm that "all truth is God's truth"[7] and rejoice whenever the learning or discovery of this truth is used in ways pleasing to God. Growth in knowledge is part of the process of becoming more like God or becoming creatures who are more fully in God's image. Paul tells us that we have put on the "new nature," which, he says, "is being *renewed in knowledge* after the image of its creator" (Col. 3:10).

In a society that is exceedingly careless with the truthfulness of spoken words, we as God's children are to imitate our Creator and take great care to be sure that our words are always truthful. "*Do not lie to one another,* seeing that you have put off the old nature with its practices and have put on the new nature" (Col. 3:9–10). Again Paul admonishes, "Therefore, putting away falsehood, let every one *speak the truth* with his neighbor" (Eph. 4:25). In his own ministry, Paul says that he sought to practice absolute truthfulness: "We have renounced disgraceful, underhanded ways; we refuse to practice cunning or to tamper with God's word, but by the open statement of the truth we would commend ourselves to every man's conscience in the sight of God" (2 Cor. 4:2). God is pleased when his people put "devious talk" far from them (Prov. 4:24) and speak with words that are acceptable not only in the sight of people but also in the sight of the Lord himself (Ps. 19:14).

Furthermore, we should imitate God's truthfulness in our own reaction to truth and falsehood. Like God, we should *love* truth and *hate* falsehood. The commandment not to bear false witness against our neighbor (Ex. 20:16), like the

---

[7]See *All Truth Is God's Truth* by Arthur Holmes (Grand Rapids: Eerdmans, 1977).

other commandments, requires not merely outward conformity but also conformity in heart attitude. One who is pleasing to God "speaks truth from his heart" (Ps. 15:2), and strives to be like the righteous man who "hates falsehood" (Prov. 13:5). God commands his people through Zechariah, "Do not devise evil in your hearts against one another, and love no false oath, for all these things I hate, says the LORD" (Zech. 8:17).

These commands are given because God himself loves truth and hates falsehood: "Lying lips are an abomination to the LORD, but those who act faithfully are his delight" (Prov. 12:22; cf. Isa. 59:3–4). Falsehood and lying come not from God but from Satan, who delights in falsehood: "When he lies, he speaks according to his own nature, for he is a liar and the father of lies" (John 8:44). It is appropriate then that with "the cowardly, the faithless, the polluted" and the "murderers, fornicators, sorcerers, [and] idolaters" who are found in "the lake that burns with fire and sulphur" far from the heavenly city, are found also "all *liars*" (Rev. 21:8).

Thus, Scripture teaches us that lying is wrong not only because of the great harm that comes from it (and much more harm comes from lying than we often realize), but also for an even deeper and more profound reason: when we lie we dishonor God and diminish his glory, for we, as those created in God's image and created for the purpose of reflecting God's glory in our lives, are acting in a way that is contrary to God's own character.

## C. Moral Attributes

**6. Goodness.** *The goodness of God means that God is the final standard of good, and that all that God is and does is worthy of approval.*

In this definition we find a situation similar to the one we faced in defining God as the true God. Here, "good" can be understood to mean "worthy of approval," but we have not answered the question, approval by whom? In one sense, we can say that anything that is truly good should be worthy of approval by us. But in a more ultimate sense, we are not free to decide by ourselves what is worthy of approval and what is not. Ultimately, therefore, God's being and actions are perfectly worthy of his own approval. He is therefore the final standard of good. Jesus implies this when he says, "No one is good but God alone" (Luke 18:19). The Psalms frequently affirm that "the LORD is good" (Ps. 100:5) or exclaim, "O give thanks to the LORD, for he is good" (Pss. 106:1; 107:1; et al.). David encourages us, "O taste and see that the LORD is good!" (Ps. 34:8).

But if God is himself good and therefore the ultimate standard of good, then we have a definition of the meaning of "good" that will greatly help us in the study of ethics and aesthetics. What is "good"? "Good" is what God approves. We may ask then, why is what God approves good? We must answer, "Because he approves it." That is to say, there is no higher standard of goodness than God's own character and his approval of whatever is consistent with that character. Nonetheless, God has given us some reflection of his own sense of goodness, so that when we evaluate things in the way God created us to evaluate them, we will also approve what God approves and delight in things in which he delights.

Our definition also states that all that God *does* is worthy of approval. We see evidence of this in the creation narrative: "And God saw everything that he had made, and behold, it was *very good*" (Gen. 1:31). The psalmist connects the goodness of God with the goodness of his actions: "You are good and you do *good;* teach me your statutes" (Ps. 119:68). Psalm 104 is an excellent example of praise to God for his goodness in creation, while many Psalms, such as Psalms 106 and 107, give thanks to God for his goodness in all his actions toward his people. And Paul encourages us to discover in practice how God's will for our lives is "*good* and acceptable and perfect" (Rom. 12:2).

Scripture also tells us that God is the source of all good in the world. "Every good endowment and every perfect gift is from above, coming down from the Father of lights with whom there is no variation or shadow due to change" (James 1:17; cf. Ps. 145:9; Acts 14:17). Moreover, God does only good things for his children. We read, "No good thing does the LORD withhold from those who walk uprightly" (Ps. 84:11). And in the same context in which Paul assures us that "in everything God works for good with those who love him" (Rom. 8:28), he also says, "He who did not spare his own Son but gave him up for us all, will he not also give us all things with him?" (Rom. 8:32). Much more than an earthly father, our heavenly Father will "give good things to those who ask him" (Matt. 7:11), and even his discipline is a manifestation of his love and is for our good (Heb. 12:10). This knowledge of God's great goodness should encourage us to "give thanks in all circumstances" (1 Thess. 5:18).

In imitation of this communicable attribute, we should ourselves do good (that is, we should do what God approves) and thereby imitate the goodness of our heavenly Father. Paul writes, "So then, as we have opportunity, let us do good to all men, and especially to those who are of the household of faith" (Gal. 6:10; cf. Luke 6:27, 33–35; 2 Tim. 3:17). Moreover, when we realize that God is the definition and source of all good, we will realize that God himself is the ultimate good that we seek. We will say with the psalmist, "Whom have I in heaven but you? And there is nothing upon earth that I desire besides you. My flesh and my heart may fail, but God is the strength of my heart and my portion for ever" (Ps. 73:25–26; cf. 16:11; 42:1–2).

God's goodness is closely related to several other characteristics of his nature, among them love, mercy, patience, and grace. Sometimes these are considered separate attributes and are treated individually. At other times these are considered part of God's goodness and are treated as various aspects of God's goodness. In this chapter we will treat love as a separate attribute since it is so prominent in Scripture. The other three characteristics (mercy, patience, and grace), while also prominent in Scripture, will be treated together as aspects of God's goodness to individuals in specific situations. Thus, God's *mercy* is *his goodness toward those in distress,* his *grace* is *his goodness toward those who deserve only punishment,* and his *patience* is *his goodness toward those who continue to sin over a period of time* (see below, section C.8, on mercy, patience, and grace).

### 7. Love. *God's love means that God eternally gives of himself to others.*

This definition understands love as self-giving for the benefit of others. This attribute of God shows that it is part of his nature to give of himself in order to bring about blessing or good for others.

John tells us that "God is love" (1 John 4:8). We see evidence that this attribute of God was active even before creation among the members of the Trinity. Jesus speaks to his Father of "my glory which you have given me in your *love* for me *before the foundation of the world*" (John 17:24), thus indicating that there was love and a giving of honor from the Father to the Son from all eternity. It continues at the present time, for we read, "The Father loves the Son, and has given all things into his hand" (John 3:35).

This love is also reciprocal, for Jesus says, "I do as the Father has commanded me, so that the world may know that I love the Father" (John 14:31). The love between the Father and the Son also presumably characterizes their relationship with the Holy Spirit, even though it is not explicitly mentioned. This eternal love of the Father for the Son, the Son for the Father, and of both for the Holy Spirit makes heaven a world of love and joy because each person of the Trinity seeks to bring joy and happiness to the other two.

The self-giving that characterizes the Trinity finds clear expression in God's relationship to mankind, and especially to sinful men. "In this is love, not that we loved God but that he loved us and sent his Son to be the propitiation for our sins" (1 John 4:10, author's translation). Paul writes, "God shows his love for us in that while we were yet sinners Christ died for us" (Rom. 5:8). John also writes, "For God so loved the world that he gave his only Son, that whoever believes in him should not perish but have eternal life" (John 3:16). Paul also speaks of "the Son of God, who *loved me* and gave himself for me" (Gal. 2:20), thus showing an awareness of the directly personal application of Christ's love to individual sinners. It should cause us great joy to know that it is the purpose of God the Father, Son, and Holy Spirit to give of themselves to us to bring us true joy and happiness. It is God's nature to act that way toward those upon whom he has set his love, and he will continue to act that way toward us for all eternity.

We imitate this communicable attribute of God, first by loving God in return, and second by loving others in imitation of the way God loves them. All our obligations to God can be summarized in this: "You shall love the Lord your God with all your heart, and with all your soul, and with all your mind. . . . You shall love your neighbor as yourself" (Matt. 22:37–38). If we love God, we will obey his commandments (1 John 5:3) and thus do what is pleasing to him. We will love God, not the world (1 John 2:15), and we will do all this because he first loved us (1 John 4:19).

It is one of the most amazing facts in all Scripture that just as God's love involves his giving of himself to make us happy, so we can in return give of ourselves and actually bring joy to God's heart. Isaiah promises God's people, "As the bridegroom rejoices over the bride, so *shall your God rejoice over you*" (Isa. 62:5), and Zephaniah tells God's people, "The LORD, your God, is in your midst . . . he will rejoice over you with gladness, he will renew you in his love; he will exult over you with loud singing as on a day of festival" (Zeph. 3:17–18).

Our imitation of God's love is also seen in our love for others. John makes this explicit: "Beloved, if God so loved us, we also ought to love one another" (1 John 4:11). In fact, our love for others within the fellowship of believers is so evidently an imitation of Christ that by it the world recognizes us as his: "By this all men will know that you are my disciples, if you have love for one another" (John 13:35; cf. 15:13; Rom. 13:10; 1 Cor. 13:4–7; Heb. 10:24). God himself gives us his love to enable us to love each other (John 17:26; Rom. 5:5). Moreover, our love for our enemies especially reflects God's love (Matt. 5:43–48).

**8. Mercy, Grace, Patience.** God's mercy, patience, and grace may be seen as three separate attributes, or as specific aspects of God's goodness. The definitions given here show these attributes as special examples of God's goodness when it is used for the benefit of specific classes of people.

God's *mercy* means God's goodness toward those in misery and distress.

God's *grace* means God's goodness toward those who deserve only punishment.

God's *patience* means God's goodness in withholding of punishment toward those who sin over a period of time.

These three characteristics of God's nature are often mentioned together, especially in the Old Testament. When God declared his name to Moses, he proclaimed, "The LORD, the LORD, a God merciful and gracious, slow to anger, and abounding in steadfast love and faithfulness" (Ex. 34:6). David says in Psalm 103:8, "The LORD is merciful and gracious, slow to anger and abounding in steadfast love."

Because these characteristics of God are often mentioned together, it may seem difficult to distinguish among them. Yet the characteristic of mercy is often emphasized where people are in misery or distress. David says, for example, "I am in great distress; let us fall into the hand of the LORD for his *mercy* is great . . ." (2 Sam. 24:14). The two blind men who wish Jesus to see their plight and heal them cry, "Have *mercy* on us, Son of David" (Matt. 9:27). When Paul speaks of the fact that God comforts us in affliction, he calls God the "Father of *mercies* and God of all comfort" (2 Cor. 1:3).[8] In time of need, we are to draw near to God's throne so that we might receive both mercy and grace (Heb. 4:16; cf. 2:17; James 5:11). We are to imitate God's mercy in our conduct toward others: "Blessed are the merciful, for they shall obtain mercy" (Matt. 5:7; cf. 2 Cor. 1:3–4).

With respect to the attribute of *grace,* we find that Scripture emphasizes that God's grace, or his favor toward those who deserve no favor but only punishment, is never obligated but is always freely given on God's part. God says, "I will be gracious to whom I will be gracious, and will show mercy on whom I will show mercy" (Ex. 33:19; quoted in Rom. 9:15). Yet God is regularly gracious toward his people: "Turn to me and be *gracious* to me, *After Thy manner* with those who love Thy name" (Ps. 119:132 NASB). In fact, Peter can call God "the God of all grace" (1 Peter 5:10).

Grace as God's goodness especially shown to those who do not deserve it is seen frequently in Paul's writings. He emphasizes that salvation by grace is the opposite of salvation by human effort, for grace is a freely given gift. "Since all have sinned and fall short of the glory of God, they are justified by his *grace* as a gift, through the redemption which is in Christ Jesus" (Rom. 3:23–24). The distinction between grace and a salvation earned by works that merit a reward is also seen in Romans 11:6: "But if it is by grace, it is no longer on the basis of works; otherwise grace would no longer be grace." Grace, then, is God's favor freely given to those who do not deserve this favor.

---

[8]This verse uses *oiktirmos,* "compassion, mercy," rather than *eleos,* "mercy," but the terms are closely related in meaning and both refer to compassion or goodness toward those in distress.

Paul also sees that if grace is unmerited, then there is only one human attitude appropriate as an instrument for receiving such grace, namely, faith: "That is why it depends on faith, in order that the promise may rest on grace . . ." (Rom. 4:16). Faith is the one human attitude that is the opposite of depending on oneself, for it involves trust in or dependence upon another. Thus, it is devoid of self-reliance or attempts to gain righteousness by human effort. If God's favor is to come to us apart from our own merit, then it must come when we depend not on our own merit but on the merits of another, and that is precisely when we have faith.

In the New Testament, and especially in Paul, not only the forgiveness of sins, but also *the entire living of the Christian life* can be seen to result from God's continuous bestowal of grace. Paul can say, "by the grace of God I am what I am" (1 Cor. 15:10). Luke speaks of Antioch as the place where Paul and Barnabas "had been commended to the grace of God for the work which they had fulfilled" (Acts 14:26), indicating that the church there, in sending out Paul and Barnabas, saw the success of their ministry as dependent upon God's continuing grace. Furthermore, the blessing of "grace" upon Paul's readers is the most frequent apostolic blessing in his letters (see, e.g., Rom. 1:7; 16:20; 1 Cor. 1:3; 16:23; 2 Cor. 1:2; 13:14; Gal. 1:3; 6:18).

God's *patience,* similarly, was mentioned in some of the verses cited above in connection with God's mercy. The Old Testament frequently speaks of God as "*slow to anger*" (Ex. 34:6; Num. 14:18; Pss. 86:15; 103:8; 145:8; Jonah 4:2; Nah. 1:3; et al.). In the New Testament, Paul speaks about God's "kindness and forbearance and patience" (Rom. 2:4), and says that Jesus Christ displayed his "perfect patience" toward Paul himself as an example for others (1 Tim. 1:16; cf. Rom. 9:22; 1 Peter 3:20).

We are also to imitate God's patience and be "slow to anger" (James 1:19), and be patient in suffering as Christ was (1 Peter 2:20). We are to lead a life "with patience" (Eph. 4:2), and "patience" is listed among the fruit of the Spirit in Galatians 5:22 (see also Rom. 8:25; 1 Cor. 13:4; Col. 1:11; 3:12; 2 Tim. 3:10; 4:2; James 5:7–8; Rev. 2:2–3; et al.). As with most of the attributes of God that we are to imitate in our lives, patience requires a moment-by-moment trust in God to fulfill his promises and purposes in our lives at his chosen time. Our confidence that the Lord will soon fulfill his purposes for our good and his glory will enable us to be patient. James makes this connection when he says, "You also be patient. Establish your hearts, for the coming of the Lord is at hand" (James 5:8).

**9. Holiness.** *God's holiness means that he is separated from sin and devoted to seeking his own honor.* This definition contains both a relational quality (separation from) and a moral quality (the separation is from sin or evil, and the devotion is to the good of God's own honor or glory). The idea of holiness as including both separation from evil and devotion to God's own glory is found in a number of Old Testament passages. The word *holy* is used to describe both parts of the tabernacle, for example. The tabernacle itself was a place separate from the evil and sin of the world, and the first room in it was called the "holy place." It was dedicated to God's service. But then God commanded that there be a veil, "and the veil shall separate for you the holy place from the most holy" (Ex. 26:33). The most holy place, where the ark of the covenant was kept, was the place most separated from evil and sin and most fully devoted to God's service.

The place where God himself dwelt was itself holy: "Who shall ascend the hill of the LORD? And who shall stand in his holy place?" (Ps. 24:3). The element of dedication to God's service is seen in the holiness of the sabbath day: "the LORD blessed the sabbath day and made it holy" (or "hallowed it"; the verb is a Piel form of *qādash* and means "to make holy") (Ex. 20:11; cf. Gen. 2:3). The sabbath day was made holy because it was set apart from the ordinary activities of the world and dedicated to God's service. In the same way the tabernacle and the altar, as well as Aaron and his sons, were to be "made holy" (Ex. 29:44), that is, set apart from ordinary tasks and from the evil and sin of the world and dedicated to God's service (cf. Ex. 30:25–33).

God himself is the Most Holy One. He is called the "Holy One of Israel" (Pss. 71:22; 78:41; 89:18; Isa. 1:4; 5:19, 24; et al.). The seraphim around God's throne cry, "Holy, holy, holy is the LORD of hosts; the whole earth is full of his glory" (Isa. 6:3). "The LORD our God is holy!" exclaims the psalmist (Ps. 99:9; cf. 99:3, 5; 22:3).

God's holiness provides the pattern for his people to imitate. He commands them, "You shall be holy; for I the LORD your God am holy" (Lev. 19:2; cf. 11:44–45; 20:26; 1 Peter 1:16). When God called his people out of Egypt and brought them to himself and commanded them to obey his voice, then he said, "You shall be to me a kingdom of priests and a *holy nation*" (Ex. 19:4–6). In this case the idea of separation from evil and sin (which here included in a very striking way separation from life in Egypt) and the idea of devotion to God (in serving him and in obeying his statutes) are both seen in the example of a "holy nation."

New covenant believers are also to "strive . . . for the *holiness* without which no one will see the Lord" (Heb. 12:14) and to know that God's discipline is given to us "that we may share his holiness" (Heb. 12:10). Paul encourages Christians to be separate from the dominating influence that comes from close association with unbelievers (2 Cor. 6:14–18) and then encourages them, "Let us cleanse ourselves from every defilement of body and spirit, and *make holiness perfect in the fear of God*" (2 Cor. 7:1; cf. Rom. 12:1). The church itself is intended by God to grow "into a holy temple in the Lord" (Eph. 2:21), and Christ's present work for the church is "that he might sanctify her . . . that he might present the church to himself in splendor . . . that she might be holy and without blemish" (Eph. 5:26–27). Not only individuals but also the church itself must grow in holiness!

Zechariah prophesies a day when everything on earth will be "holy to the LORD." He says:

> And on that day there shall be inscribed on the bells of the horses, "Holy to the LORD." And the pots in the house of the LORD shall be as the bowls before the altar; and every pot in Jerusalem and Judah shall be sacred to the LORD of hosts. (Zech. 14:20–21)

At that time, everything on earth will be separated from evil, purified from sin, and devoted to the service of God in true moral purity.

**10. Peace (or Order).** In 1 Corinthians 14:33 Paul says, "God is not a God of confusion but of *peace*." Although "peace" and "order" have not traditionally been classified as attributes of God, Paul here indicates another quality that we could think of as a distinct attribute of God. Paul says that God's actions are characterized by "peace" and not by "disorder" (Gk. *akatastasia,* a word meaning "disorder, confusion, unrest"). God himself is "the God of peace" (Rom. 15:33; 16:20; Phil. 4:9; 1 Thess. 5:23; Heb. 13:20; cf. Eph. 2:14; 2 Thess. 3:16). But those who walk in wickedness do not have peace: " 'There is no peace,' says the LORD, 'for the wicked' " (Isa. 48:22; 57:21; cf. 59:8).

However, when God looks with compassion upon the people whom he loves, he sees them as "afflicted . . . storm-tossed (LXX, *akatastatos,* "in disorder, in confusion"), and not comforted" (Isa. 54:11), and promises to establish their foundations with precious stones (Isa. 54:11–12) and lead them forth in "peace" (Isa. 55:12). The proclamation of God's plan of redemption contains the promise of peace to God's people (Pss. 29:11; 85:8; 119:165; Prov. 3:17; Isa. 9:6–7; 26:3; 57:19; John 14:27; Rom. 8:6; 2 Thess. 3:16; et al.). In fact, the third element that Paul lists as part of the fruit of the Spirit is "peace" (Gal. 5:22).

This peace certainly does not imply inactivity, for it was at a time of intense growth and activity that Luke could say that "the church throughout all Judea and Galilee and Samaria had peace and was built up" (Acts 9:31). Furthermore, although God is a God of peace, he is also the one who "will neither slumber nor sleep" (Ps. 121:4). He is the God who is continually working (John 5:17). And even though heaven is a place of peace, it is a place also of continual praise to God and service for him.

Thus, God's peace can be defined as follows: *God's peace means that in God's being and in his actions he is separate from all confusion and disorder, yet he is continually active in innumerable well-ordered, fully controlled, simultaneous actions.*

This definition indicates that God's peace does not have to do with inactivity, but with ordered and controlled activity. To engage in infinite activity of this sort, of course, requires God's infinite wisdom, knowledge, and power.

When we understand God's peace in this way we can see an imitation of this attribute of God not only in "peace" as part of the fruit of the Spirit in Galatians 5:22–23, but also in the last-mentioned element in the fruit of the Spirit, namely, "self-control" (Gal. 5:23). When we as God's people walk in his ways, we come to know more and more fully by experience that the kingdom of God is indeed "righteousness and *peace* and joy in the Holy Spirit" (Rom. 14:17), and we can say of the path of God's wisdom, "Her ways are ways of pleasantness, and all her paths are *peace*" (Prov. 3:17).

**11. Righteousness, Justice.** In English the terms *righteousness* and *justice* are different words, but in both the Hebrew Old Testament and the Greek New Testament there is only one word group behind these two English terms. (In the Old Testament the terms primarily translate forms of the *tsedek* word group, and the New Testament members of the *dikaios* word group.) Therefore, these two terms will be considered together as speaking of one attribute of God.

*God's righteousness means that God always acts in accordance with what is right and is himself the final standard of what is right.*

Speaking of God, Moses says, "All his ways are *justice.* A God of faithfulness and without iniquity, *just* and *right* is he" (Deut. 32:4). Abraham successfully appeals to God's own character of righteousness when he says, "Shall not the Judge of all the earth do right?" (Gen. 18:25). God also speaks and commands what is right: "The precepts of the LORD are *right,* rejoicing the heart" (Ps. 19:8). And God says of himself, "I the LORD speak the truth, I declare what is *right*" (Isa. 45:19). As a result of God's righteousness, it is necessary that he treat people according to what they deserve. Thus, it is necessary that God punish sin, for it does not deserve reward; it is wrong and deserves punishment.

When God does not punish sin, it seems to indicate that he is unrighteous, unless some other means of punishing sin can be seen. This is why Paul says that when God sent Christ as a sacrifice to bear the punishment for sin, it "was to show God's righteousness, because in his divine forbearance he had passed over former sins; it was to prove at the present time that he himself is righteous and that he justifies him who has faith in Jesus" (Rom. 3:25–26). When Christ died to pay the penalty for our sins it showed that God was truly righteous, because he did give appropriate punishment to sin, even though he did forgive his people their sins.

With respect to the definition of righteousness given above, we may ask, what is "right"? In other words, what *ought* to happen and what *ought* to be? Here we must respond that *whatever conforms to God's moral character is right.* But why is whatever conforms to God's moral character right? It is right because it conforms to his moral character! If indeed God is the final standard of righteousness, then there can be no standard outside of God by which we measure righteousness or justice. He himself is the final standard. (This is similar to the situation we encountered with respect to truth and God being the ultimate standard of truth.) Whenever Scripture confronts the question of whether God himself is righteous or not, the ultimate answer is always that we as God's creatures have no right to say that God is unrighteous or unjust. The creature cannot say that of the Creator. Paul responds to a very difficult question about God's righteousness by saying, "But who are you, a man, to answer back to God? Will what is molded say to its molder, 'Why have you made me thus?' Has the potter no right over the clay, to make out of the same lump one vessel for beauty and another for menial use?" (Rom. 9:20–21).

In answer to Job's questioning about whether God has been righteous in his dealings with him, God answers Job, "Shall a faultfinder contend with the Almighty? . . . Will you even put me in the wrong? Will you condemn me that you may be justified?" (Job 40:2, 8). Then God answers *not* in terms of an explanation that would allow Job to *understand* why God's actions were right, but rather in terms of a statement of God's own majesty and power! God does not need to explain the rightness of his actions to Job, for God is the Creator and Job is the creature. "Have you an arm like God, and can you thunder with a voice like his?" (Job 40:9). "Have you commanded the morning since your days began, and caused the dawn to know its place . . . ?" (Job 38:12). "Can you lift up your voice to the clouds, that a flood of waters may cover you? Can you send forth lightnings, that they may go and say to you, 'Here we are'?" (Job 38:34–35). "Do you give the horse his might?" (Job 39:19). "Is it by your wisdom that the hawk soars, and spreads his wings toward the south?" (Job 39:26). Job answers, "Behold, I am of small account; what shall I answer you? I lay my hand on my mouth" (Job 40:4).

Nevertheless, it should be a cause for thanksgiving and gratitude when we realize that righteousness and omnipotence are both possessed by God. If he were a God of perfect righteousness without power to carry out that righteousness, he would not be worthy of worship and we would have no guarantee that justice will ultimately prevail in the universe. But if he were a God of unlimited power, yet without righteousness in his character, how unthinkably horrible the universe would be! There would be unrighteousness at the center of all existence and there would be nothing anyone could do to change it. Existence would become meaningless, and we would be driven to the most utter despair. We ought therefore continually to thank and praise God for who he is, "for *all his ways are justice*. A God of faithfulness and without iniquity, just and right is he" (Deut. 32:4).

**12. Jealousy.** Although the word *jealous* is frequently used in a negative sense in English, it also takes a positive sense at times. For example, Paul says to the Corinthians, "I feel a divine jealousy for you" (2 Cor. 11:2). Here the sense is "earnestly protective or watchful." It has the meaning of being deeply committed to seeking the honor or welfare of someone, whether oneself or someone else.

Scripture represents God as being jealous in this way. He continually and earnestly seeks to protect his own honor. He commands his people not to bow down to idols or serve them, saying, "for I the LORD your God am a *jealous* God" (Ex. 20:5). He desires that worship be given to himself and not to false gods. Therefore, he commands the people of Israel to tear down the altars of pagan gods in the land of Canaan, giving the following reason: "For you shall worship no other god, for the LORD, whose name is Jealous, is a jealous God" (Ex. 34:14; cf. Deut. 4:24; 5:9).

Thus, God's jealousy may be defined as follows: *God's jealousy means that God continually seeks to protect his own honor.*

People sometimes have trouble thinking that jealousy is a desirable attribute in God. This is because jealousy for our own honor as human beings is almost always wrong. We are not to be proud, but humble. Yet we must realize that the reason pride is wrong is a theological reason: it is that we do not deserve the honor that belongs to God alone (cf. 1 Cor. 4:7; Rev. 4:11).

It is not wrong for God to seek his own honor, however, for he deserves it fully. God freely admits that his actions in creation and redemption are done for his own honor. Speaking of his decision to withhold judgment from his people, God says, "For my own sake, for my own sake, I do it. . . . *My glory I will not give to another*" (Isa. 48:11). It is healthy for us spiritually when we settle in our hearts the fact that God deserves all honor and glory from his creation, and that it is right for him to seek this honor. He alone is infinitely worthy of being praised. To realize this fact and to delight in it is to find the secret of true worship.

**13. Wrath.** It may surprise us to find how frequently the Bible talks about the wrath of God. Yet if God loves all that is right and good, and all that conforms to his moral character, then it should not be surprising that he would hate everything that is opposed to his moral character. God's wrath directed against sin is therefore closely related to God's holiness and justice. God's wrath may be defined as follows: *God's wrath means that he intensely hates all sin.*

Descriptions of God's wrath are found frequently in the narrative passages of Scripture, especially when God's people sin greatly against him. God sees the idolatry of the people of Israel and says to Moses, "I have seen this people . . . ; now therefore let me alone, that my *wrath* may burn hot against them and I may consume them" (Ex. 32:9–10). Later Moses tells the people, "Remember and do not forget how you provoked the LORD your God to *wrath* in the wilderness. . . . Even at Horeb you provoked the LORD to *wrath,* and the LORD was so angry with you that he was ready to destroy you" (Deut. 9:7–8; cf. 29:23; 2 Kings 22:13).

The doctrine of the wrath of God in Scripture is not limited to the Old Testament, however, as some have falsely imagined. We read in John 3:36, "He who believes in the Son has eternal life; he who does not obey the Son shall not see life, but *the wrath of God rests upon him.*" Paul says, "For the *wrath of God* is revealed from heaven against all ungodliness and wickedness of men" (Rom. 1:18; cf. 2:5, 8; 5:9; 9:22; Col. 3:6; 1 Thess. 1:10; 2:16; 5:9; Heb. 3:11; Rev. 6:16–17; 19:15). Many more New Testament verses also indicate God's wrath against sin.

As with the other attributes of God, this is an attribute for which we should thank and praise God. It may not immediately appear to us how this can be done, since wrath seems to be such a negative concept. Viewed alone, it would arouse only fear and dread. Yet it is helpful for us to ask what God would be like if he were a God that did not hate sin. He would then be a God who either delighted in sin or at least was not troubled by it. Such a God would not be worthy of our worship, for sin is hateful and it is *worthy* of being hated. Sin ought not to be. It is in fact a virtue to hate evil and sin (cf. Heb. 1:9; Zech. 8:17; et al.), and we rightly imitate this attribute of God when we feel hatred against great evil, injustice, and sin.[9]

Furthermore, we should feel no fear of God's wrath as Christians, for although "we were by nature children of wrath, like the rest of mankind" (Eph. 2:3), we now have trusted in Jesus, "who delivers us from the wrath to come" (1 Thess. 1:10; cf. Rom. 5:10). When we meditate on the wrath of God, we will be amazed to think that our Lord Jesus Christ bore the wrath of God that was due to our sin, in order that we might be saved (Rom. 3:25–26).[10]

Moreover, in thinking about God's wrath we must also bear in mind his patience. Both patience and wrath are mentioned together in Psalm 103: "The LORD is . . . *slow to anger* and abounding in steadfast love. He will not always chide, nor will he keep his anger for ever" (Ps. 103:8–9). In fact, the delay of the execution of God's wrath upon evil is for the purpose of leading people to repentance (see Rom. 2:4).

Thus, when we think of God's wrath to come, we should simultaneously be thankful for his patience in waiting to execute that wrath in order that yet more people may be saved: "The Lord is not slow about his promise as some count slowness, but is forbearing toward you, not wishing that any should perish, but

---

[9]It is appropriate for us in this regard to "hate the sin but love the sinner," as a popular slogan puts it.

[10]See the discussion of Christ's bearing of the wrath of God in chapter 27, pp. 574–77.

that all should reach repentance. But the day of the Lord will come like a thief, and then the heavens will pass away with a loud noise . . ." (2 Peter 3:9–10). God's wrath should motivate us to evangelism and should also cause us to be thankful that God finally will punish all wrongdoing and will reign over new heavens and a new earth in which there will be no unrighteousness.

## QUESTIONS FOR PERSONAL APPLICATION

### Spirituality

1. Why is God so strongly displeased at carved idols, even those that are intended to represent him? How then shall we picture God or think of God in our minds when we pray to him?

2. What is it about our culture or our way of thinking today that makes us think of the physical world as more real and more permanent than the spiritual world? What can we do to change our intuitive perspective on the reality of the spiritual world?

### Knowledge

3. When should we try to hide our thoughts and deeds from God? How is your answer to this question a blessing for your life?

4. With regard to the circumstances of your life, will God ever make a mistake, or fail to plan ahead, or fail to take into account all the eventualities that occur? How is the answer to this question a blessing in your life?

5. When did God learn that you would be at the location you are now in, reading this sentence, at this time on this day? How is the realization of your answer to this question a blessing to your life?

### Wisdom

6. Do you really believe that God is working wisely today in your life? In the world? If you find this difficult to believe at times, what might you do to change your attitude?

### Truthfulness

7. Why are people in our society, sometimes even Christians, quite careless with regard to truthfulness in speech? Why do we not very often realize that the greatest harm of all that comes from lying is the fact that God himself is dishonored? Do you need to ask God's help to more fully reflect his truthfulness in speech in any of the following areas: promising to pray for someone; saying that you will be some place at a certain time; exaggerating events to make a more exciting story; taking care to remember and then be faithful to what you have said in business commitments; reporting what other people have said or what you think someone else is thinking; fairly representing your opponent's viewpoint in an argument?

## Goodness

8. Remembering that every good and perfect gift is from God (James 1:17), see how many good gifts from God you can list on a piece of paper in five minutes. When you have finished, ask yourself how often you have an attitude of thankfulness to God for most of these gifts. Why do you think we tend to forget that these blessings come from God? What can we do to remember more frequently?

## Love

9. Is it appropriate to define love as "self-giving" with respect to our own interpersonal relationships? In what ways could you imitate God's love specifically today?

10. Is it possible to decide to love someone and then to act on that decision, or does love between human beings simply depend on spontaneous emotional feelings?

## Mercy

11. If you were to reflect God's mercy more fully, for whom among those you know would you show special care during the next week?

## Holiness

12. Are there activities or relationships in your present pattern of life that are hindering your growth in holiness because they make it difficult for you to be separated from sin and devoted to seeking God's honor?

## Peace

13. As you think about reflecting God's peace in your own life, think first about your own emotional, mental, and spiritual state. Can you say that by-and-large you have God's peace in the sense that your inner life is separate from confusion and disorder, and is frequently or continually active in well-ordered and well-controlled actions that further God's glory? Then ask the same questions concerning what may be called the "external circumstances" of your life, that is, your family relationships, your relationships with neighbors, your activities in studying or at your job, and your relationships in church activities. What about the overall picture of your life, viewed as a whole? Does it exhibit God's peace? What might you do to reflect God's peace more fully?

## Righteousness

14. Do you ever find yourself wishing that some of God's laws were different than they are? If so, does such a wish reflect a dislike for some aspect of God's moral character? What passages of Scripture might you read to convince yourself more fully that God's character and his laws are right in these areas?

## Jealousy

15. Do you reflect God's jealousy for his own honor instinctively when you hear him dishonored in conversation or on television or in other contexts? What can we do to deepen our jealousy for God's honor?

## Wrath

16. Should we love the fact that God is a God of wrath who hates sin? In what ways is it right for us to imitate this wrath, and in what ways is it wrong for us to do so?

## SPECIAL TERMS

| | | |
|---|---|---|
| attributes of being | jealousy | patience |
| beatific vision | justice | peace |
| communicable attributes | knowledge | reasonable self- |
| faithfulness | love | determination |
| good | mental attributes | righteousness |
| goodness | mercy | spirituality |
| grace | moral attributes | theophany |
| holiness | omniscience | truthfulness |
| impassible | one simple and eternal | veracity |
| invisibility | act | wisdom |
| | order | wrath |

## BIBLIOGRAPHY

Since chapters 12 and 13 are so closely related in subject matter, the bibliographic material for both is at the end of chapter 13.

## SCRIPTURE MEMORY PASSAGE

**Exodus 34:6–7:** *The LORD passed before him, and proclaimed, "The LORD, the LORD, a God merciful and gracious, slow to anger, and abounding in steadfast love and faithfulness, keeping steadfast love for thousands, forgiving iniquity and transgression and sin, but who will by no means clear the guilty, visiting the iniquity of the fathers upon the children and the children's children, to the third and the fourth generation."*

Note: The last section of this passage speaks of God "visiting the iniquity of the fathers upon the children and the children's children." Some might want to stop short of this part in memorizing the passage, but we should remember that this, too, is Scripture and is written for our edification. This statement shows the horrible nature of sin in the way it has effects far beyond the individual sinner, also harming those around the sinner and harming future generations as well. We see this in tragic ways in ordinary life, where the children of alcoholics often become alcoholics and the children of abusive parents often become abusive parents.

Christians who are forgiven by Christ should not think of these phrases as applying to them, however, for they are in the other category of people mentioned just before this section on "the guilty": they are among the "thousands" to whom God continually shows "steadfast love," and is continually "forgiving iniquity and transgression and sin" (v. 7). When someone comes to Christ the chain of sin is broken. Here it is important to remember Peter's words: "You know that *you were ransomed from the futile ways inherited from your fathers,* not with perishable things such as silver or gold, but with the precious blood of Christ" (1 Peter 1:18–19).

## HYMN

### "O Worship the King"

Almost the entire hymnbook could be used to sing of one aspect or another of God's character. Literally hundreds of hymns would be appropriate. Yet this hymn contains a listing of many of God's attributes and combines them in such a way that the hymn is worthy of being sung again and again. Verse 1 speaks of God's glory, power, love; verse 2 speaks of his might, grace, wrath; and so forth. In verse 6, "ineffable" means "incapable of being expressed fully." The hymn is written as an encouragement for Christians to sing to one another, exhorting each other to "worship the King, all glorious above." Yet in the process of such exhortation the song itself also contains much high praise.

O worship the King all glorious above,
O gratefully sing his pow'r and his love;
Our shield and defender, the Ancient of Days,
Pavilioned in splendor, and girded with praise.

O tell of his might, O sing of his grace,
Whose robe is the light, whose canopy space.
His chariots of wrath the deep thunder-clouds form,
And dark is his path on the wings of the storm.

The earth with its store of wonders untold,
Almighty, your power has founded of old;
Has 'stablished it fast by a changeless decree,
And round it has cast, like a mantle, the sea.

Your bountiful care what tongue can recite?
It breathes in the air; it shines in the light;
It streams from the hills; it descends to the plain;
And sweetly distills in the dew and the rain.

Frail children of dust, and feeble as frail,
In you do we trust, nor find you to fail;
Your mercies how tender, how firm to the end,
Our maker, defender, redeemer, and friend!

O measureless might! Ineffable love!
While angels delight to hymn you above,
The humbler creation, though feeble their ways,
With true adoration shall lisp to your praise.

AUTHOR: SIR ROBERT GRANT, 1833 (BASED ON PSALM 104)

Alternative hymn: "Round the Lord in Glory Seated"

# Chapter 13

# The Character of God: "Communicable" Attributes (Part 2)

*How is God like us in attributes of will and in attributes that summarize his excellence?*

In the previous chapter we discussed the attributes of God that described his *being* (spirituality, invisibility), his *mental* attributes (knowledge, wisdom, and truthfulness), and his *moral* attributes (goodness, love, mercy, grace, patience, holiness, peace, righteousness, jealousy, and wrath). In this chapter we will examine God's attributes of *purpose*, that is, attributes that have to do with making and carrying out decisions (will, freedom, and omnipotence) and his *summary* attributes (perfection, blessedness, beauty, and glory).

## D. Attributes of Purpose

In this category of attributes we will discuss first God's will in general, then the freedom of God's will, and finally the omnipotence (or infinite power) of God's will.

**14. Will.** *God's will is that attribute of God whereby he approves and determines to bring about every action necessary for the existence and activity of himself and all creation.*

This definition indicates that God's will has to do with deciding and approving the things that God is and does. It concerns God's choices of what to do and what not to do.

**a. God's Will in General:** Scripture frequently indicates God's will as the final or most ultimate reason for everything that happens. Paul refers to God as the one "who accomplishes all things *according to the counsel of his will*" (Eph. 1:11). The phrase here translated "all things" (*ta panta*) is used frequently by Paul to refer to everything that exists or everything in creation (see, for example, Eph. 1:10, 23; 3:9; 4:10; Col. 1:16 [twice], 17; Rom. 11:36; 1 Cor. 8:6 [twice]; 15:27–28 [twice]).[1] The word translated "accomplishes" (*energeō*, "works, works out, brings about, produces") is a present participle and suggests continual activity. The

---

[1]The phrase does not always carry that meaning (cf. Rom. 11:32; 1 Cor. 12:6; 2 Cor. 12:19), but in contexts where the scope of Paul's thought is cosmic or universal in nature (as in this passage), the phrase does seem quite clearly to refer to everything in all creation.

phrase might more explicitly be translated, "who continually brings about everything in the universe according to the counsel of his will."

More specifically, all things were created by God's will: "For you created all things, and *by your will they existed and were created*" (Rev. 4:11). Both Old and New Testaments speak of human government as coming about according to God's will: the voice from heaven tells Nebuchadnezzar that he is to learn "that the Most High rules the kingdom of men and gives it to whom he will" (Dan. 4:32), and Paul says that "there is no authority except from God, and those that exist have been instituted by God" (Rom. 13:1).

All the events connected with the death of Christ were according to God's will, the church at Jerusalem believed, for in their prayer they said, "truly in this city there were gathered together against your holy servant Jesus, whom you anointed, both Herod and Pontius Pilate, with all the Gentiles and the peoples of Israel, to do *whatever your hand and your plan had predestined to take place*" (Acts 4:27–28). The specific mention of the various parties involved at different stages of the crucifixion, together with the indefiniteness of the plural relative pronoun "whatever" (Gk. *hosa*, "the things which") implies that not simply the fact of Jesus' death but all the detailed events connected with it are comprehended in this statement: God's hand and will had predestined that all those things would come about.

Sometimes it is God's will that Christians suffer, as is seen in 1 Peter 3:17, for example: "For it is better to suffer for doing right, *if that should be God's will*, than for doing wrong." Then in the next chapter Peter says, "Therefore let those who suffer *according to God's will* do right and entrust their souls to a faithful Creator" (1 Peter 4:19). In this verse, the phrase "according to God's will" cannot refer to the manner in which Christians endure suffering, for then it would make the verse say essentially, "Let those who suffer *while doing right, do right* and entrust their souls. . . ." This would make the phrase "according to God's will" redundant. Rather, the phrase "according to God's will" must refer to the fact that these Christians are suffering, just as "God's will" referred to suffering in the previous chapter (1 Peter 3:17).

James encourages us to see all the events of our lives as subject to God's will. To those who say, "Today or tomorrow we will go into such and such a town and spend a year there and trade and get gain," James says, "You do not know about tomorrow. . . . Instead you ought to say, '*if the Lord wills,* we shall live and we shall do this or that'" (James 4:13–15). To attribute so many events, even evil events, to the will of God often causes misunderstanding and difficulty for Christians. Some of the difficulties connected with this subject will be treated here and others will be dealt with in chapter 16 on God's providence.

**b. Distinctions in Aspects of God's Will: (1) Necessary will and free will:** Some distinctions made in the past may help us understand various aspects of God's will. Just as we can will or choose something eagerly or reluctantly, happily or with regret, secretly or publicly, so also God in the infinite greatness of his personality is able to will different things in different ways.

One helpful distinction applied to aspects of God's will is the distinction between God's *necessary will* and God's *free will*. God's necessary will includes everything that he must will according to his own nature. What does God will necessarily? He wills himself. God eternally wills to be, or wants to be, who he is and what he is. He says, "I AM WHO I AM" or, "I WILL BE WHAT I WILL BE" (Ex. 3:14). God *cannot* choose to be different than he is or to cease to exist.

God's *free will* includes all things that God decided to will but had no necessity to will according to his nature. Here we must put God's decision to create the universe, and all the decisions relating to the details of that creation. Here we must also place all God's acts of redemption. There was nothing in God's own nature that required him to decide to create the universe or to redeem out of sinful mankind a people for himself (see the discussion above concerning God's independence). However, God did decide to create and to redeem, and these were totally free choices on his part. Though within the members of the Trinity love and fellowship and glory exist in infinite measure for all eternity (see John 17:5, 24), nonetheless God decided to create the universe and to redeem us for his own glory (cf. Isa. 43:7; 48:9–11; Rom. 11:36; 1 Cor. 8:6; Eph. 1:12; Rev. 4:11). It would be wrong for us ever to try to find a necessary cause for creation or redemption in the being of God himself, for that would rob God of his total independence. It would be to say that without us God could not truly be God. God's decisions to create and to redeem were totally free decisions.

**(2) Secret will and revealed will:** Another helpful distinction applied to different aspects of God's will is the distinction between God's *secret will* and his *revealed will*. Even in our own experience we know that we are able to will some things secretly and then only later make this will known to others. Sometimes we tell others before the thing that we have willed comes about, and at other times we do not reveal our secret will until the event we willed has happened.

Surely a distinction between aspects of God's will is evident in many passages of Scripture. According to Moses, "The *secret things* belong to the LORD our God; but the *things that are revealed* belong to us and to our children for ever, that we may do all the words of this law" (Deut. 29:29). Those things that God has revealed are given for the purpose of obeying God's will: "that we may *do* all the words of this law." There were many other aspects of his plan, however, that he had not revealed to them: many details about future events, specific details of hardship or of blessing in their lives, and so forth. With regard to these matters, they were simply to trust him.

Because God's revealed will usually contains his commands or "precepts" for our moral conduct, God's revealed will is sometimes also called God's *will of precept* or will of command. This revealed will of God is God's declared will concerning what we should do or what God commands us to do.

On the other hand, God's secret will usually includes his hidden decrees by which he governs the universe and determines everything that will happen. He does not ordinarily reveal these decrees to us (except in prophecies of the future), so these decrees really are God's "secret" will. We find out what God has decreed when events actually happen. Because this secret will of God has to do with his decreeing of events in the world, this aspect of God's will is sometimes also called God's *will of decree*.[2]

---

[2]See the discussion of God's decrees in chapter 16, pp. 332–33.

There are several instances where Scripture mentions God's revealed will. In the Lord's prayer the petition, "*Your will be done,* On earth as it is in heaven" (Matt. 6:10) is a prayer that people would obey God's *revealed* will, his commands, on earth just as they do in heaven (that is, fully and completely). This could not be a prayer that God's secret will (that is, his decrees for events that he has planned) would in fact be fulfilled, for what God has decreed in his secret will shall certainly come to pass. To ask God to bring about what he has already decreed to happen would simply be to pray, "May what is going to happen happen." That would be a hollow prayer indeed, for it would not be asking for anything at all. Furthermore, since we do not know God's secret will regarding the future, the person praying a prayer for God's secret will to be done would never know for what he or she was praying. It would be a prayer without understandable content and without effect. Rather, the prayer "*Your will* be done" must be understood as an appeal for the *revealed* will of God to be followed on earth.

If the phrase is understood in this way, it provides a pattern for us to pray on the basis of God's commands in Scripture. In this sense, Jesus provides us with a guide for an exceedingly broad range of prayer requests. We are encouraged by Christ here to pray that people would obey God's laws, that they would follow his principles for life, that they would obey his commands to repent of sin and trust in Christ as Savior. To pray these things is to pray that God's will would be done on earth as it is in heaven.

A little later, Jesus says, "Not every one who says to me, 'Lord, Lord,' shall enter the kingdom of heaven, but he who does the *will* of my Father who is in heaven" (Matt. 7:21). Once again, the reference cannot be to God's secret will or will of decree (for all mankind follows this, even if unknowingly), but to God's *revealed* will, namely, the moral law of God that Christ's followers are to obey (cf. Matt. 12:50; probably also 18:14). When Paul commands the Ephesians to "understand *what the will of the Lord is*" (Eph. 5:17; cf. Rom. 2:18), he again is speaking of God's revealed will. So also is John when he says, "If we ask anything *according to his will* he hears us" (1 John 5:14).

It is probably best to put 1 Timothy 2:4 and 2 Peter 3:9 in this category as well. Paul says that God "*desires* [or 'wills, wishes,' Gk. *theleō*] all men to be saved and to come to the knowledge of the truth" (1 Tim. 2:4). Peter says that the Lord "is not slow about his promise as some count slowness, but is forbearing toward you, not wishing that any should perish, but that all should reach repentance" (2 Peter 3:9). In neither of these verses can God's will be understood to be his secret will, his decree concerning what will certainly occur. This is because the New Testament is clear that there will be a final judgment and not all will be saved. It is best therefore to understand these references as speaking of God's *revealed will,* his commands for mankind to obey and his declaration to us of what is pleasing in his sight.

On the other hand, many passages speak of God's secret will. When James tells us to say, "*If the Lord wills,* we shall live and we shall do this or that" (James 4:15), he cannot be talking about God's revealed will or will of precept, for with regard to many of our actions we *know* that it is according to God's command that we do one or another activity that we have planned. Rather, to trust in the secret will of God overcomes pride and expresses humble dependence on God's sovereign control over the events of our lives.

Another instance is found in Genesis 50:20. Joseph says to his brothers, "As for you, you meant evil against me; but *God meant it for good,* to bring it about that many people should be kept alive, as they are today." Here God's *revealed* will to Joseph's brothers was that they should love him and not steal from him or sell him into slavery or make plans to murder him. But God's *secret* will was that in the disobedience of Joseph's brothers a greater good would be done when Joseph, having been sold into slavery into Egypt, gained authority over the land and was able to save his family.

When Paul says to the Corinthians, "I will come to you soon, *if the Lord wills*" (1 Cor. 4:19), he is not speaking of God's revealed will, for Paul has already determined, in obedience to God and in fulfillment of his apostolic office, to come to visit the Corinthians. He is speaking rather of God's secret will, his hidden plan for the future, which is unknown to Paul and which will be known only as it comes to pass (cf. Acts 21:14; Rom. 1:10; 15:32; Eph. 1:11; 1 Peter 3:17; 4:19).[3]

Both the revealing of the good news of the gospel to some and its hiding from others are said to be according to God's will. Jesus says, "I thank you, Father, Lord of heaven and earth, that you have hidden these things from the wise and understanding and revealed them to babes; yea, Father, *for such was your gracious will*" (Matt. 11:25–26). This again must refer to God's secret will, for his revealed will is that all come to salvation. Indeed, only two verses later, Jesus commands everyone, "Come to me, all who labor and are heavy laden, and I will give you rest" (Matt. 11:28). And both Paul and Peter tell us that God wills all people to be saved (see 1 Tim. 2:4; 2 Peter 3:9). Thus, the fact that some are not saved and some have the gospel hidden from them must be understood as happening according to God's secret will, unknown to us and inappropriate for us to seek to pry into. In the same way we must understand the mention of God's will in Romans 9:18 ("He has mercy upon whomever he wills, and he hardens the heart of whomever he wills") and Acts 4:28 ("to do whatever your hand and your plan had predestined to take place") as references to God's secret will.

There is danger in speaking about evil events as happening according to the will of God, even though we see Scripture speaking of them in this way. One danger is that we might begin to think that God takes pleasure in evil, which he does not do (see Ezek. 33:11), though he can use it for his good purposes (see chapter 16 for further discussion). Another danger is that we might begin to blame God for sin, rather than ourselves, or to think that we are not responsible for our evil actions. Scripture, however, does not hesitate to couple statements of God's sovereign will with statements of man's responsibility for evil. Peter could say in the same sentence that Jesus was "delivered up according to the definite plan and foreknowledge of God," and also that "this Jesus . . . *you crucified and killed* by the hands of *lawless men*" (Acts 2:23). Both God's hidden will of decree and the culpable wickedness of "lawless men" in carrying it out are affirmed in the same statement. However we may understand the secret workings of God's hidden will, we must never understand it to imply that we are freed from responsibility for evil,

---

[3]In Eph. 1:9–10 Paul says that God "has made known to us . . . the mystery of his will . . . to unite all things in him." Here he tells us that part of God's secret will has become God's revealed will because God made it known to the apostles and then to the church.

or that God is ever to be blamed for sin. Scripture never speaks that way, and we may not either, even though how this can be so may remain a mystery for us in this age.[4]

**15. Freedom.** *God's freedom is that attribute of God whereby he does whatever he pleases.* This definition implies that nothing in all creation can hinder God from doing his will. This attribute of God is therefore closely related to his will and his power. Yet this aspect of freedom focuses on the fact that God is not constrained by anything external to himself and that he is free to do whatever he wishes to do. There is no person or force that can ever dictate to God what he should do. He is under no authority or external restraint.

God's freedom is mentioned in Psalm 115, where his great power is contrasted with the weakness of idols: "Our God is in the heavens; *he does whatever he pleases*" (Ps. 115:3). Human rulers are not able to stand against God and effectively oppose his will, for "the king's heart is a stream of water in the hand of the LORD; he turns it wherever he will" (Prov. 21:1). Similarly, Nebuchadnezzar learns in his repentance that it is true to say of God, "*he does according to his will* in the host of heaven and among the inhabitants of the earth; and none can stay his hand or say to him, 'What are you doing?'" (Dan. 4:35).

Because God is free we should not try to seek any more ultimate answer for God's actions in creation than the fact that he willed to do something and that his will has perfect freedom (so long as the actions he takes are consistent with his own moral character). Sometimes people try to discover the reason why God had to do one or another action (such as create the world or save us). It is better simply to say that it was God's totally free will (working in a way consistent with his character) that was the final reason why he chose to create the world and to save sinners.

**16. Omnipotence (Power, Sovereignty).** *God's omnipotence means that God is able to do all his holy will.* The word *omnipotence* is derived from two Latin words, *omni,* "all," and *potens,* "powerful," and means "all-powerful." Whereas God's freedom referred to the fact that there are no external constraints on God's decisions, God's omnipotence has reference to his own power to do what he decides to do.

This power is frequently mentioned in Scripture. God is "The LORD, strong and mighty, the LORD, mighty in battle!" (Ps. 24:8). The rhetorical question, "Is anything too hard for the LORD?" (Gen. 18:14; Jer. 32:27) certainly implies (in the contexts in which it occurs) that nothing is too hard for the LORD. In fact, Jeremiah says to God, "*nothing* is too hard for you" (Jer. 32:17).

Paul says that God is "able to do far more abundantly than all that we ask or think" (Eph. 3:20), and God is called the "Almighty" (2 Cor. 6:18; Rev. 1:8), a term (Gk. *pantokratōr*) that suggests the possession of all power and authority. Furthermore, the angel Gabriel says to Mary, "With God nothing will be

---

[4]See chapter 16, pp. 322–30, 343 for further discussion of the relationship between the will of God and evil. See also the excellent essay by John Piper, "Are There Two Wills in God? Divine Election and God's Desire for All to Be Saved," in *The Grace of God, the Bondage of the Will,* vol. 2, ed. by Tom Schreiner and Bruce Ware (forthcoming: Grand Rapids: Baker, 1995).

impossible" (Luke 1:37), and Jesus says, "With God *all things are possible*" (Matt. 19:26).

These passages indicate that God's power is infinite, and that he is therefore not limited to doing only what he actually has done. In fact, God is able to do more than he actually does. For example, John the Baptist says in Matthew 3:9, "God is able from these stones to raise up children to Abraham." God is one who "does whatever he pleases" (Ps. 115:3); he could have destroyed Israel and raised up a great nation from Moses (cf. Ex. 32:10), but he did not do so.

However, there are some things that God cannot do. God cannot will or do anything that would deny his own character. This is why the definition of omnipotence is stated in terms of God's ability to do "all his holy will." It is not absolutely everything that God is able to do, but everything that is consistent with his character. For example, God cannot lie. In Titus 1:2 he is called (literally) "the unlying God" or the "God who never lies." The author of Hebrews says that in God's oath and promise "it is impossible for God to lie" (Heb. 6:18, author's translation). Second Timothy 2:13 says of Christ, "He cannot deny himself." Furthermore, James says, "God cannot be tempted with evil and he himself tempts no one" (James 1:13). Thus, God cannot lie, sin, deny himself, or be tempted with evil. He cannot cease to exist, or cease to be God, or act in a way inconsistent with any of his attributes.

This means that it is not entirely accurate to say that God can do anything. Even the Scripture passages quoted above that use phrases similar to this must be understood in their contexts to mean that God can do anything he wills to do or anything that is consistent with his character. Although God's power is infinite, his use of that power is qualified by his other attributes (just as all God's attributes qualify all his actions). This is therefore another instance where misunderstanding would result if one attribute were isolated from the rest of God's character and emphasized in a disproportionate way.

God's exercise of power over his creation is also called God's *sovereignty*. God's sovereignty is his exercise of rule (as "sovereign" or "king") over his creation. This subject will be discussed in more detail in chapter 16, on God's providence.

As we conclude our treatment of God's attributes of purpose, it is appropriate to realize that he has made us in such a way that we show in our lives some faint reflection of each of them. God has made us as creatures with a *will*. We exercise choice and make real decisions regarding the events of our lives. Although our will is not absolutely free in the way God's is, God has nonetheless given us *relative freedom* within our spheres of activity in the universe he has created.

In fact, we have an intuitive sense that it is our ability to exercise our wills and make choices, and to do so in a relatively free way, that is one of the most significant marks of God-likeness in our existence. Of course our desire to exercise our wills and our desire to be free from restraint can show themselves in sinful ways. People can become proud and can desire a kind of freedom that involves rebellion against God's authority and a refusal to obey his will. Nonetheless, when we use our will and our freedom to make choices that are pleasing to God, we reflect his character and bring glory to him. When human beings are deprived of their ability to make free choices by evil governments or by other circumstances, a significant part of their God-likeness is suppressed. It is not surprising that they will pay almost any price to regain their freedom. American revolutionary Patrick

Henry's cry, "Give me liberty or give me death!" finds an echo deep within every soul created in the image of God.

We do not of course have infinite power or omnipotence any more than we have infinite freedom or any of God's other attributes to an infinite degree. But even though we do not have omnipotence, God has given us *power* to bring about results, both physical power and other kinds of power: mental power, spiritual power, persuasive power, and power in various kinds of authority structures (family, church, civil government, and so forth). In all of these areas, the use of power in ways pleasing to God and consistent with his will is again something that brings him glory as it reflects his own character.

## E. "Summary" Attributes

**17. Perfection.** *God's perfection means that God completely possesses all excellent qualities and lacks no part of any qualities that would be desirable for him.*

It is difficult to decide whether this should be listed as a separate attribute or simply be included in the description of the other attributes. Some passages say that God is "perfect" or "complete." Jesus tells us, "You, therefore, must be perfect, *as your heavenly Father is perfect*" (Matt. 5:48). And David says of God, "His way is *perfect*" (Ps. 18:30; cf. Deut. 32:4). There is some scriptural precedent, therefore, for stating explicitly that God lacks nothing in his excellence: he fully possesses all of his attributes and lacks nothing from any one of those attributes. Furthermore, there is no quality of excellence that it would be desirable for God to have that he does not have: he is "complete" or "perfect" in every way.

This attribute is the first of those classified as a "summary" attribute because it does not fit well into the other categories that have been listed. Even though all the attributes of God modify all the others in some senses, those that fit in this category seem more directly to apply to all the attributes or to describe some aspect of all of the attributes that it is worthwhile to state explicitly.

**18. Blessedness.** To be "blessed" is to be happy in a very full and rich sense. Often Scripture talks about the blessedness of those people who walk in God's ways. Yet in 1 Timothy Paul calls God "the *blessed* and only Sovereign" (1 Tim. 6:15) and speaks of "the glorious gospel of the *blessed* God" (1 Tim. 1:11). In both instances the word is not *eulogētos* (which is often translated "blessed"), but *makarios* (which means "happy").

Thus, God's blessedness may be defined as follows: *God's blessedness means that God delights fully in himself and in all that reflects his character.* In this definition the idea of God's happiness or blessedness is connected directly to his own person as the focus of all that is worthy of joy or delight. This definition indicates that God is perfectly happy, that he has fullness of joy in himself.

The definition reflects the fact that God takes pleasure in everything in creation that mirrors his own excellence. When he finished his work of creation, he looked at everything that he had made and saw that it was "very good" (Gen. 1:31). This indicates God's delight in and approval of his creation. Then in Isaiah we read a promise of God's future rejoicing over his people: "As the bridegroom rejoices over the bride, so shall your God rejoice over you" (Isa. 62:5; cf. Prov. 8:30–31; Zeph. 3:17).

It may at first seem strange or even somewhat disappointing to us that when God rejoices in his creation, or even when he rejoices in us, it is really the reflection of his own excellent qualities in which he is rejoicing. But when we remember that the sum of everything that is desirable or excellent is found in infinite measure in God himself, then we realize that it could not be otherwise: *whatever* excellence there is in the universe, *whatever* is desirable, must ultimately have come from him, for he is the Creator of all and he is the source of all good. "*Every* good endowment and *every* perfect gift is from above, coming down from the Father of lights with whom there is no variation or shadow due to change" (James 1:17).

We ought therefore to say to ourselves, as Paul says to the Corinthians, "What have you that you did not receive? If then you received it, why do you boast as if it were not a gift?" (1 Cor. 4:7). "For from him and through him and to him are all things. To him be glory for ever" (Rom. 11:36).

We imitate God's blessedness when we find delight and happiness in all that is pleasing to God, both those aspects of our own lives that are pleasing to God and the deeds of others. In fact, when we are thankful for and delight in the specific abilities, preferences, and other characteristics with which God has created us as individuals, then we also imitate his attribute of blessedness. Furthermore, we imitate God's blessedness by rejoicing in the creation as it reflects various aspects of his excellent character. And we find our greatest blessedness, our greatest happiness, in delighting in the source of all good qualities, God himself.

**19. Beauty.** *God's beauty is that attribute of God whereby he is the sum of all desirable qualities.* This attribute of God has been implicit in a number of the preceding attributes, and is especially related to God's perfection. However, God's perfection was defined in such a way as to show that he does not *lack* anything that would be desirable for him. This attribute, beauty, is defined in a positive way to show that God actually does possess all desirable qualities: "perfection" means that God doesn't lack anything desirable; "beauty" means that God has everything desirable. They are two different ways of affirming the same truth.

Nevertheless, there is value in affirming this positive aspect of God's possession of everything that is desirable. It reminds us that all of our good and righteous desires, all of the desires that really ought to be in us or in any other creature, find their ultimate fulfillment in God and in no one else.

David speaks of the beauty of the LORD in Psalm 27:4: "One thing have I asked of the LORD, that will I seek after; that I may dwell in the house of the LORD all the days of my life, to behold *the beauty of the LORD,* and to inquire in his temple." A similar idea is expressed in another psalm: "Whom have I in heaven but you? And there is nothing upon earth that I desire besides you" (Ps. 73:25). In both cases, the psalmist recognizes that his desire for God, who is the sum of everything desirable, far surpasses all other desires. This desire culminates in a longing to be near God and to enjoy his presence forevermore. Thus, the greatest blessing of the heavenly city shall be this: "They shall see his face" (Rev. 22:4).

Anne R. Cousin certainly had a proper perspective on heaven, for in the last stanza of her hymn "The Sands of Time are Sinking" she wrote:

> The bride eyes not her garment,
>     But her dear bridegroom's face.
> I will not gaze at glory,
>     But on my King of grace;
> Not at the crown he giveth,
>     But on his pierced hand:
> The Lamb is all the glory
>     Of Emmanuel's land.

We reflect God's beauty in our own lives when we exhibit conduct that is pleasing to him. Thus, Peter tells wives in the churches to which he writes that their "adorning" (that is, their source of beauty) should be "the hidden person of the heart with the imperishable jewel of a gentle and quiet spirit, which in God's sight is very precious" (1 Peter 3:4). Similarly, Paul instructs servants that by their conduct they should "*adorn* the doctrine of God our Savior" (Titus 2:10).

The beauty of our lives is so important to Christ that his purpose now is to sanctify the entire church "that he might present the church to himself in splendor, without spot or wrinkle or any such thing, that she might be holy and without blemish" (Eph. 5:27). Thus, we individually and corporately reflect God's beauty in every way in which we exhibit his character. When we reflect his character, he delights in us and finds us beautiful in his sight.

But we also delight in God's excellence as we see it manifested in the lives of our brothers and sisters in the Lord. Therefore it is right that we feel joy and delight in the fellowship of one another, and that this joy deepens as our conformity to the life of Christ increases. It is right that we long to be in the fellowship of God's people in which God's character is manifested, for when we delight in the godliness of God's people, we are ultimately delighting in God himself as we see his character evidenced in the lives of his people.

**20. Glory.** In one sense of the word *glory* it simply means "honor" or "excellent reputation." This is the meaning of the term in Isaiah 43:7, where God speaks of his children, "whom I created for my *glory,*" or Romans 3:23, which says that all "have sinned and fall short of the *glory* of God." It also has that meaning in John 17:5, where Jesus speaks to the Father of "the *glory* which I had with you before the world was made," and in Hebrews 1:3, which says that the Son "is the radiance of God's *glory*" (author's translation). In this sense, the glory of God is not exactly an attribute of his being but rather describes the superlative honor that should be given to God by everything in the universe (including, in Heb. 1:3 and John 17:5, the honor that is shared among the members of the Trinity). But that is not the sense of the word *glory* that we are concerned with in this section.

In another sense, God's "glory" means the bright light that surrounds God's presence. Since God is spirit, and not energy or matter, this visible light is not part of God's being but is something that was created. We may define it as follows: *God's glory is the created brightness that surrounds God's revelation of himself.*

This "attribute" of God is really not an attribute of God in the sense that the others were, for here we are speaking not of God's own character but of the *created* light or brilliance that surrounds God as he manifests himself in his creation. Thus, God's glory in this sense is not actually an attribute of God in himself. Nevertheless, God's glory is something that belongs to him alone and is the appropriate outward expression of his own excellence. It seems right therefore to treat it here immediately after the attributes of God.

Scripture often speaks of God's glory. David asks, "Who is this King of glory? The LORD of hosts, *he is the King of glory!*" (Ps. 24:10). We read in Psalm 104:1–2, "O LORD my God, you are very great! You are clothed with honor and majesty, you who cover yourself with light as with a garment. . . ." This glory of God is frequently mentioned in the Old Testament.

It is mentioned again in the New Testament in connection with the annunciation of Jesus' birth to the shepherds: "And an angel of the Lord appeared to them, and *the glory of the Lord shone around them,* and they were filled with fear" (Luke 2:9). God's glory was also evident at the transfiguration of Christ (cf. Matt. 17:2), and we find in the heavenly city yet to come that "the city has no need of sun or moon to shine upon it, for *the glory of God is its light,* and its lamp is the Lamb" (Rev. 21:23).

It is very appropriate that God's revelation of himself should be accompanied by such splendor and brightness, for this glory of God is the visible manifestation of the excellence of God's character. The greatness of God's being, the perfection of all his attributes, is something that we can never fully comprehend, but before which we can only stand in awe and worship. Thus, it is appropriate indeed that the visible manifestation of God be such that we would be unable to gaze fully upon it, and that it would be so bright that it would call forth both great delight and deep awe from us when we behold it only in part.

Quite amazingly, God made us to reflect his glory. Paul tells us that even now in our Christian lives we all are being "changed into his likeness from one degree of glory to another" (2 Cor. 3:18; cf. Matt. 5:16; Phil. 2:15). Though we do not now find ourselves surrounded by a visible light, there is a brightness, a splendor, or a beauty about the manner of life of a person who deeply loves God, and it is often evident to those around such a person. In the life to come, such brightness will be intensified, so that as we reign with Christ, it seems that we also will receive an outward appearance that is appropriate to that reign and to our status as image bearers of God and servants of the Lord Jesus Christ (cf. Prov. 4:18; Dan. 12:3; Matt. 13:43; 1 Cor. 15:43).[5]

## QUESTIONS FOR PERSONAL APPLICATION

### Will, Freedom

1. As children grow toward adulthood, what are proper and improper ways for them to show in their own lives greater and greater exercise of individual will and freedom from parental control? Are these to be expected as evidence of our creation in the image of God?

---

[5]See the discussion of glorification in chapter 42, pp. 828–39.

## Power

2. If God's power is his ability to do what he wills to do, then is power for us the ability to obey God's will and bring about results in the world that are pleasing to him? Name several ways in which we can increase in such power in our lives.

## Perfection

3. How does God's attribute of perfection remind us that we can never be satisfied with the reflection of only some of God's character in our own lives? Can you describe some aspects of what it would mean to "be perfect" as our heavenly Father is perfect, with respect to your own life?

## Blessedness

4. Are you happy with the way God created you—with the physical, emotional, mental, and relational traits he gave you? With the sex he gave you (whether masculine or feminine)? With the spiritual gifts he has given you? In what ways is it right to be happy or pleased with our own personalities, physical characteristics, abilities, positions, etc.? In what ways is it wrong to be pleased or happy about these things? Will we ever be fully "blessed" or happy? When will that be and why?

5. Think about the qualities that you admire in other people, both Christians and non-Christians. Which of these are right to admire and which are not? How can you decide? How can we come to delight more frequently and more fully in God himself?

## Beauty

6. If we refuse to accept our society's definition of beauty, or even the definitions that we ourselves may have worked with previously, and decide that that which is truly beautiful is the character of God himself, then how will our understanding of beauty be different from the one we previously held? Will we still be able to rightly apply our new idea of beauty to some of the things we previously thought to be beautiful? Why or why not?

7. Can you understand why David's one desire above all others in life was "that I may dwell in the house of the LORD all the days of my life, to behold the beauty of the LORD, and to inquire in his temple" (Ps. 27:4)?

## Glory

8. When the shepherds near Bethlehem experienced the glory of the Lord shining around them, "they were filled with fear" (Luke 2:9). Yet when we come to live forever in the heavenly city, we will continually be surrounded by the light of the glory of the Lord (Rev. 21:23). Will we then continually feel this same fear the shepherds felt? Why or why not? Would you like to live in the presence of this glory? Can we experience any of it in this life?

## SPECIAL TERMS

| | |
|---|---|
| attributes of purpose | blessedness |
| beauty | freedom |
| free will | reasonable self-determination |
| glory | revealed will |
| necessary will | secret will |
| omnipotence | sovereignty |
| perfection | "summary attributes" |
| power | will |

## BIBLIOGRAPHY

(For an explanation of this bibliography see the note on the bibliography to chapter 1, p. 38. Complete bibliographical data may be found on pp. 1223–29.)

Because systematic theologies have different ways of classifying the attributes of God, some of the sections listed below discuss only the communicable attributes of God, and some discuss all the attributes of God.

### Sections in Evangelical Systematic Theologies

1. Anglican (Episcopalian)
    1882–92   Litton, 58–74
    1930   Thomas, 14–20, 495–500
2. Arminian (Wesleyan or Methodist)
    1847   Finney, 49–65, 135–80, 524–44
    1875–76   Pope, 1:248–55, 287–360
    1892–94   Miley, 1:159–222
    1940   Wiley, 1:241–393
    1960   Purkiser, 127–42
    1983   Carter, 1:111–27
    1983–   Cottrell, 1:192–305, 388–468; 3:175–400, 461–528
    1987–90   Oden, 1:15–130
3. Baptist
    1767   Gill, 1:37–187, 359–65
    1887   Boyce, 54–115
    1907   Strong, 243–303
    1917   Mullins, 214–50
    1976–83   Henry, 2:151–246; 5:9–164, 214–375; 6:35–89, 251–417
    1983–85   Erickson, 263–320
    1987–94   Lewis/Demarest, 1:175–248
4. Dispensational
    1947   Chafer, 1:179–224, 260–71
    1949   Thiessen, 75–88
    1986   Ryrie, 35–50
5. Lutheran
    1917–24   Pieper, 1:405–66

                    1934     Mueller, 160–75
6. Reformed (or Presbyterian)
                    1559     Calvin, 1:96–120 (1.10–12)
                    1861     Heppe, 57–104
                 1871–73     Hodge, 1:366–441
                    1878     Dabney, 38–54, 144–74
              1887–1921      Warfield, BTS, 505–22; SSW, 1:69–81; ST, 109–14
                    1889     Shedd, 1:151–94, 334–92; 3:89–248
                    1909     Bavinck, DG, 175–251 (this is an exceptionally valuable
                             discussion of the attributes of God)
                    1938     Berkhof, 41–81
                    1962     Buswell, 1:29–71
7. Renewal (or charismatic/Pentecostal)
                 1988–92     Williams, 1:47–82

### Sections in Representative Roman Catholic Systematic Theologies

1. Roman Catholic: Traditional
                    1955     Ott, 24–49
2. Roman Catholic: Post-Vatican II
                    1980     McBrien, 1:283–342

### Other Works

Bray, Gerald L. The Doctrine of God. Downers Grove, Ill.: InterVarsity Press, 1993.
Bromiley, G. W. "God." In ISBE, 2:493–503.
Charnock, Stephen. The Existence and Attributes of God. Repr. ed. Evansville, Ind.: Sovereign Grace Book Club, n.d., pp. 181–802 (first published 1655–1680).
Kaiser, Christopher B. The Doctrine of God. Westchester, Ill.: Good News, 1982.
Lewis, Gordon R. "God, Attributes of." In EDT, pp. 451–59.
———. "Impassibility of God." In EDT, pp. 553–54.
Packer, J. I. "God." In NDT, pp. 274–77.
———. Knowing God. London: Inter-Varsity Press, 1973, pp. 80–254.
Piper, John. Desiring God. Portland, Ore.: Multnomah, 1986.
———. The Pleasures of God. Portland, Ore.: Multnomah, 1991.
Saucy, R. L. "God, Doctrine of." In EDT, pp. 459–64.
Tozer, A. W. The Knowledge of the Holy. New York: Harper and Row, 1961.
Van Til, Cornelius. In Defense of the Faith, vol. 5: An Introduction to Systematic Theology. Phillipsburg, N.J.: Presbyterian and Reformed, 1976, pp. 200–252.
Wenham, John W. The Goodness of God. London: Inter-Varsity Press, 1974.

### SCRIPTURE MEMORY PASSAGE

**Psalm 73:25–26:** *Whom have I in heaven but you? And there is nothing upon earth that I desire besides you. My flesh and my heart may fail, but God is the strength of my heart and my portion for ever.*

## HYMN

### "If Thou but Suffer God to Guide Thee"

This is undoubtedly one of the most beautiful hymns ever written that expresses trust in God for his sovereignty.

If thou but suffer God to guide thee,
    And hope in him through all thy ways,
He'll give thee strength, whate'er betide thee,
    And bear thee through the evil days:
Who trusts in God's unchanging love
    Builds on the rock that naught can move.

What can these anxious cares avail thee,
    These never-ceasing moans and sighs?
What can it help, if thou bewail thee
    O'er each dark moment as it flies?
Our cross and trials do but press
    The heavier for our bitterness.

Only be still, and wait his leisure
    In cheerful hope, with heart content
To take whate'er thy Father's pleasure
    And all-deserving love hath sent;
Nor doubt our inmost wants are known
    To him who chose us for his own.

All are alike before the highest;
    'Tis easy to our God, we know,
To raise thee up though low thou liest,
    To make the rich man poor and low;
True wonders still by him are wrought
    Who setteth up and brings to naught.

Sing, pray, and keep his ways unswerving,
    So do thine own part faithfully,
And trust his Word, though undeserving,
    Thou yet shalt find it true for thee;
God never yet forsook at need
    The soul that trusted him indeed.

AUTHOR: GEORG NEUMARK, 1641

Alternative hymns: "God Moves in a Mysterious Way" (printed at the end of chapter 16); "Crown Him With Many Crowns"

# Chapter 14

# God in Three Persons: The Trinity

*How can God be three persons, yet one God?*

## EXPLANATION AND SCRIPTURAL BASIS

The preceding chapters have discussed many attributes of God. But if we understood only those attributes, we would not rightly understand God at all, for we would not understand that God, in his very being, has always existed as more than one person. In fact, God exists as three persons, yet he is one God.

It is important to remember the doctrine of the Trinity in connection with the study of God's attributes. When we think of God as eternal, omnipresent, omnipotent, and so forth, we may have a tendency to think only of God the Father in connection with these attributes. But the biblical teaching on the Trinity tells us that all of God's attributes are true of all three persons, for each is fully God. Thus, God the Son and God the Holy Spirit are also eternal, omnipresent, omnipotent, infinitely wise, infinitely holy, infinitely loving, omniscient, and so forth.

The doctrine of the Trinity is one of the most important doctrines of the Christian faith. To study the Bible's teachings on the Trinity gives us great insight into the question that is at the center of all of our seeking after God: What is God like in himself? Here we learn that in himself, in his very being, God exists in the persons of Father, Son, and Holy Spirit, yet he is one God.

## EXPLANATION AND SCRIPTURAL BASIS

We may define the doctrine of the Trinity as follows: *God eternally exists as three persons, Father, Son, and Holy Spirit, and each person is fully God, and there is one God.*

### A. The Doctrine of the Trinity Is Progressively Revealed in Scripture

**1. Partial Revelation in the Old Testament.** The word *trinity* is never found in the Bible, though the idea represented by the word is taught in many places. The word *trinity* means "tri-unity" or "three-in-oneness." It is used to summarize the teaching of Scripture that God is three persons yet one God.

Sometimes people think the doctrine of the Trinity is found only in the New Testament, not in the Old. If God has eternally existed as three persons, it would be surprising to find no indications of that in the Old Testament. Although the doctrine of the Trinity is not explicitly found in the Old Testament, several passages suggest or even imply that God exists as more than one person.

For instance, according to Genesis 1:26, God said, "Let *us* make man in *our* image, after *our* likeness." What do the plural verb ("let us") and the plural pronoun ("our") mean? Some have suggested they are plurals of majesty, a form of speech a king would use in saying, for example, "We are pleased to grant your request."[1] However, in Old Testament Hebrew there are no other examples of a monarch using plural verbs or plural pronouns of himself in such a "plural of majesty," so this suggestion has no evidence to support it.[2] Another suggestion is that God is here speaking to angels. But angels did not participate in the creation of man, nor was man created in the image and likeness of angels, so this suggestion is not convincing. The best explanation is that already in the first chapter of Genesis we have an indication of a plurality of persons in God himself.[3] We are not told how many persons, and we have nothing approaching a complete doctrine of the Trinity, but it is implied that more than one person is involved. The same can be said of Genesis 3:22 ("Behold, the man has become like one of *us,* knowing good and evil"), Genesis 11:7 ("Come, let *us* go down, and there confuse their language"), and Isaiah 6:8 ("Whom shall I send, and who will go for *us?*"). (Note the combination of singular and plural in the same sentence in the last passage.)

Moreover, there are passages where one person is called "God" or "the Lord" and is distinguished from another person who is also said to be God. In Psalm 45:6–7 (NIV), the psalmist says, "Your throne, O God, will last for ever and ever. . . . You love righteousness and hate wickedness; therefore God, your God, has set you above your companions by anointing you with the oil of joy." Here the psalm passes beyond describing anything that could be true of an earthly king and calls the king "God" (v. 6), whose throne will last "forever and ever." But then, still speaking to the person called "God," the author says that "God, your God, has set you above your companions" (v. 7). So two separate persons are called "God" (Heb. *'Elōhîm*). In the New Testament, the author of Hebrews quotes this passage and applies it to Christ: "Your throne, O God, is for ever and ever" (Heb. 1:8).[4]

---

[1]Both Alexander the Great (in 152 B.C.) and King Demetrius (about 145 B.C.) refer to themselves in this way, for example, in the Septuagint text of 1 Macc. 10:19 and 11:31, but this is in Greek, not Hebrew, and it is written long after Genesis 1.

[2]See E. Kautzsch, ed., *Gesenius' Hebrew Grammar,* 2d ed. (Oxford: Clarendon Press, 1910), Section 124g, n. 2, with reference to the suggestion of a plural of majesty: "The plural used by God in Genesis 1:26, 11:7, Isaiah 6:8 has been incorrectly explained in this way." They understand Gen. 1:26 as "a plural of self-deliberation." My own extensive search of subsequent Jewish interpretation in the Babylonian Talmud, the targumim and the midrashim showed only that later Rabbinic interpreters were unable to reach agreement on any satisfactory interpretation of this passage, although the "plural of majesty" and "God speaking to angels" interpretations were commonly suggested.

[3]"The plural 'We' was regarded by the fathers and earlier theologians almost unanimously as indicative of the Trinity" [Keil and Delitzsch, *Old Testament Commentaries* (Grand Rapids: Associated Publishers and Authors, n.d.], 1:48, with objections to other positions and an affirmation that Gen. 1:26 contains "the truth that lies at the foundation of the Trinitarian view").

[4]The RSV translates Ps. 45:6, "Your divine throne endures forever and ever," but this is a highly unlikely translation because it requires understanding the Hebrew noun for "throne" in construct state, something extremely unusual when a noun has a pronominal suffix, as this one does. The RSV translation would only be adopted because of a theological assumption (that an Old Testament psalmist could not predict a fully divine messianic king), but not on the grounds of language or grammar. The KJV, NIV, and NASB all take the verse in its plain, straightforward sense, as do the ancient translations and Heb. 1:8. Derek Kidner, *Psalms 1-72,* TOTC (London: Inter-Varsity Press, 1973), p. 172, says this verse is "an example of Old Testament language bursting its banks, to demand a more

Similarly, in Psalm 110:1, David says, "The LORD says to my lord: 'Sit at my right hand until I make your enemies a footstool for your feet'" (NIV). Jesus rightly understands that David is referring to two separate persons as "Lord" (Matt. 22:41–46), but who is David's "Lord" if not God himself? And who could be saying to God, "Sit at my right hand" except someone else who is also fully God? From a New Testament perspective, we can paraphrase this verse: "God the Father said to God the Son, 'Sit at my right hand.'" But even without the New Testament teaching on the Trinity, it seems clear that David was aware of a plurality of persons in one God. Jesus, of course, understood this, but when he asked the Pharisees for an explanation of this passage, "no one was able to answer him a word, nor from that day did any one dare to ask him any more questions" (Matt. 22:46). Unless they are willing to admit a plurality of persons in one God, Jewish interpreters of Scripture to this day will have no more satisfactory explanation of Psalm 110:1 (or of Gen. 1:26, or of the other passages just discussed) than they did in Jesus day.

Isaiah 63:10 says that God's people "rebelled and grieved his Holy Spirit" (NIV), apparently suggesting both that the Holy Spirit is distinct from God himself (it is "his Holy Spirit"), and that this Holy Spirit can be "grieved," thus suggesting emotional capabilities characteristic of a distinct person. (Isa. 61:1 also distinguishes "The Spirit of the Lord GOD" from "the LORD," even though no personal qualities are attributed to the Spirit of the Lord in that verse.)

Similar evidence is found in Malachi, when the Lord says, "The Lord whom you seek will suddenly come to his temple; the messenger of the covenant in whom you delight, behold, he is coming, says the LORD of hosts. But who can endure the day of his coming, and who can stand when he appears?" (Mal. 3:1–2). Here again the one speaking ("the LORD of hosts") distinguishes himself from "the Lord whom you seek," suggesting two separate persons, both of whom can be called "Lord."

In Hosea 1:7, the Lord is speaking, and says of the house of Judah, "I will deliver them by the LORD their God," once again suggesting that more than one person can be called "Lord" (Heb. *Yahweh*) and "God" (*'Elōhîm*).

And in Isaiah 48:16, the speaker (apparently the servant of the Lord) says, "And now the Lord GOD has sent me and his Spirit."[5] Here the Spirit of the Lord, like the servant of the Lord, has been "sent" by the Lord GOD on a particular mission. The parallel between the two objects of sending ("me" and "his Spirit") would be consistent with seeing them both as distinct persons: it seems to mean more than simply "the Lord has sent me and his power."[6] In fact, from a full New

---

than human fulfillment," and "this paradox is consistent with the Incarnation, but mystifying in any other context."

Though some ancient kings, such as the Egyptian pharaohs, were sometimes addressed as "gods," this was part of the falsehood connected with pagan idolatry, and it should not be confused with Ps. 45, which is part of Scripture and therefore true.

The suggested translation of Heb. 1:8 in the RSV margin, "God is your throne forever and ever," while possible grammatically, is completely inconsistent with the thinking of both Old and New Testaments: the mighty God who created everything and rules supreme over the universe would never be merely a "throne" for someone else. The thought itself is dishonoring to God, and it should certainly not be considered as a possibly appropriate translation.

[5]This RSV translation of Isa. 48:16 accurately reproduces both the literal sense of the Hebrew words and the word order in the Hebrew text.

[6]The NIV translation, "with his Spirit," is not required by the Hebrew text and tends to obscure the

Testament perspective (which recognizes Jesus the Messiah to be the true servant of the Lord predicted in Isaiah's prophecies), Isaiah 48:16 has trinitarian implications: "And now the Lord GOD has sent me and his Spirit," if spoken by Jesus the Son of God, refers to all three persons of the Trinity.

Furthermore, several Old Testament passages about "the angel of the LORD" suggest a plurality of persons in God. The word translated "angel" (Heb. *mal'ak*) means simply "messenger." If this angel of the LORD is a "messenger" of the LORD, he is then distinct from the LORD himself. Yet at some points the angel of the LORD is called "God" or "the LORD" (see Gen. 16:13; Ex. 3:2–6; 23:20–22 [note "my name is in him" in v. 21]; Num. 22:35 with 38; Judg. 2:1–2; 6:11 with 14). At other points in the Old Testament "the angel of the LORD" simply refers to a created angel, but at least at these texts the special angel (or "messenger") of the LORD seems to be a distinct person who is fully divine.

One of the most disputed Old Testament texts that could show distinct personality for more than one person is Proverbs 8:22–31. Although the earlier part of the chapter could be understood as merely a personification of "wisdom" for literary effect, showing wisdom calling to the simple and inviting them to learn, vv. 22–31, one could argue, say things about "wisdom" that seem to go far beyond mere personification. Speaking of the time when God created the earth, "wisdom" says, "Then I was the craftsman at his side. I was filled with delight day after day, rejoicing always in his presence, rejoicing in his whole world and delighting in mankind" (Prov. 8:30–31 NIV). To work as a "craftsman" at God's side in the creation suggests in itself the idea of distinct personhood, and the following phrases might seem even more convincing, for only real persons can be "filled with delight day after day" and can rejoice in the world and delight in mankind.[7]

But if we decide that "wisdom" here really refers to the Son of God before he became man, there is a difficulty. Verses 22–25 (RSV) seem to speak of the creation of this person who is called "wisdom":

> The LORD created me at the beginning of his work,
>     the first of his acts of old.
> Ages ago I was set up,
>     at the first, before the beginning of the earth.
> When there were no depths I was brought forth,
>     when there were no springs abounding with water.
> Before the mountains had been shaped,
>     before the hills, I was brought forth.

Does this not indicate that this "wisdom" was created?

In fact, it does not. The Hebrew word that commonly means "create" (*bārā'*) is not used in verse 22; rather the word is *qānāh*, which occurs eighty-four times in

---

parallel thoughts of the Lord sending "me" and "his Spirit." The word *with* in the NIV is the translators' interpretation of the Hebrew conjunction *w*, which most commonly means simply "and." The common Hebrew word for "with" (*'im*) is not in the text.

[7] In response to these arguments, one could argue that there are similarly detailed personifications of wisdom in Prov. 8:1–12 and 9:1–6, and of foolishness in Prov. 9:13–18, and no interpreter understands these to be actual persons. Therefore, Prov. 8:22–31 does not represent an actual person either. This argument seems convincing to me, but I have included the following paragraph because Prov. 8:22–31 has a long history of interpreters who think it refers to God the Son.

the Old Testament and almost always means "to get, acquire." The NASB is most clear here: "The Lord possessed me at the beginning of his way" (similarly KJV). (Note this sense of the word in Gen. 39:1; Ex. 21:2; Prov. 4:5, 7; 23:23; Eccl. 2:7; Isa. 1:3 ["owner"].) This is a legitimate sense and, if wisdom is understood as a real person, would mean only that God the Father began to direct and make use of the powerful creative work of God the Son at the time creation began[8]: the Father summoned the Son to work with him in the activity of creation. The expression "brought forth" in verses 24 and 25 is a different term but could carry a similar meaning: the Father began to direct and make use of the powerful creative work of the Son in the creation of the universe.

**2. More Complete Revelation of the Trinity in the New Testament.** When the New Testament opens, we enter into the history of the coming of the Son of God to earth. It is to be expected that this great event would be accompanied by more explicit teaching about the trinitarian nature of God, and that is in fact what we find. Before looking at this in detail, we can simply list several passages where all three persons of the Trinity are named together.

When Jesus was baptized, "the heavens were opened and he saw the Spirit of God descending like a dove, and alighting on him; and lo, a voice from heaven, saying, 'This is my beloved Son, with whom I am well pleased'" (Matt. 3:16–17). Here at one moment we have three members of the Trinity performing three distinct activities. God the Father is speaking from heaven; God the Son is being baptized and is then spoken to from heaven by God the Father; and God the Holy Spirit is descending from heaven to rest upon and empower Jesus for his ministry.

At the end of Jesus' earthly ministry, he tells the disciples that they should go "and make disciples of all nations, baptizing them in the name of the Father and of the Son and of the Holy Spirit" (Matt. 28:19). The very names "Father" and "Son," drawn as they are from the family, the most familiar of human institutions, indicate very strongly the distinct personhood of both the Father and the Son. When "the Holy Spirit" is put in the same expression and on the same level as the other two persons, it is hard to avoid the conclusion that the Holy Spirit is also viewed as a person and of equal standing with the Father and the Son.

When we realize that the New Testament authors generally use the name "God" (Gk. *theos*) to refer to God the Father and the name "Lord" (Gk. *kyrios*) to refer to God the Son, then it is clear that there is another trinitarian expression in 1 Corinthians 12:4–6: "Now there are varieties of gifts, but the same *Spirit;* and there are varieties of service, but the same *Lord;* and there are varieties of working, but it is the same *God* who inspires them all in every one."

Similarly, the last verse of 2 Corinthians is trinitarian in its expression: "The grace of the *Lord Jesus Christ* and the love of *God* and the fellowship of the *Holy Spirit* be with you all" (2 Cor. 13:14). We see the three persons mentioned

---

[8]The confusion surrounding the translation of the verse seems to have been caused by the unusual translation of the Septuagint, which used *ktizō* ("create") rather than the usual translation *ktaomai* ("acquire, take possession of") to translate the Hebrew term at this verse. *Qānāh* occurs eighty-four times in the Hebrew Old Testament and is translated more than seventy times by *ktaomai*, but only three times by *ktizō* (Gen. 14:19; Prov. 8:22; Jer. 39(32):15), all of which are questionable translations. The other Greek translations of the Old Testament by Aquila, Symmachus, and Theodotian all have *ktaomai* at Prov. 8:22.

separately in Ephesians 4:4–6 as well: "There is one body and one *Spirit*, just as you were called to the one hope that belongs to your call, one *Lord*, one faith, one baptism, one *God and Father* of us all, who is above all and through all and in all."

All three persons of the Trinity are mentioned together in the opening sentence of 1 Peter: "According to the foreknowledge of God the Father, by the sanctifying work of the Spirit, that you may obey Jesus Christ and be sprinkled with his blood" (1 Peter 1:2 NASB). And in Jude 20–21, we read: "But you, beloved, build yourselves up on your most holy faith; pray in the Holy Spirit; keep yourselves in the love of God; wait for the mercy of our Lord Jesus Christ unto eternal life."

However, the KJV translation of 1 John 5:7 should not be used in this connection. It reads, "For there are three that bear record in heaven, the Father, the Word, and the Holy Ghost: and these three are one."

The problem with this translation is that it is based on a very small number of unreliable Greek manuscripts, the earliest of which comes from the fourteenth century A.D. No modern translation includes this KJV reading, but all omit it, as do the vast majority of Greek manuscripts from all major text traditions, including several very reliable manuscripts from the fourth and fifth century A.D., and also including quotations by church fathers such as Irenaeus (d. ca. A.D. 202), Clement of Alexandria (d. ca. A.D. 212), Tertullian (died after A.D. 220), and the great defender of the Trinity, Athanasius (d. A.D. 373).

### B. Three Statements Summarize the Biblical Teaching

In one sense the doctrine of the Trinity is a mystery that we will never be able to understand fully. However, we can understand something of its truth by summarizing the teaching of Scripture in three statements:

1. God is three persons.
2. Each person is fully God.
3. There is one God.

The following section will develop each of these statements in more detail.

**1. God Is Three Persons.** The fact that God is three persons means that the Father is not the Son; they are distinct persons. It also means that the Father is not the Holy Spirit, but that they are distinct persons. And it means that the Son is not the Holy Spirit. These distinctions are seen in a number of the passages quoted in the earlier section as well as in many additional New Testament passages.

John 1:1–2 tells us: "In the beginning was the Word, and the Word was with God, and the Word was God. He was in the beginning with God." The fact that the "Word" (who is seen to be Christ in vv. 9–18) is "with" God shows distinction from God the Father. In John 17:24 (NIV), Jesus speaks to God the Father about "my glory, the glory you have given me because you loved me before the creation of the world," thus showing distinction of persons, sharing of glory, and a relationship of love between the Father and the Son before the world was created.

We are told that Jesus continues as our High Priest and Advocate before God the Father: "If any one does sin, we have an advocate with the Father, Jesus Christ the righteous" (1 John 2:1). Christ is the one who "is able for all time to save those who draw near to God through him, since he always lives to make intercession for them" (Heb. 7:25). Yet in order to intercede for us before God the Father, it is necessary that Christ be a person distinct from the Father.

Moreover, the Father is not the Holy Spirit, and the Son is not the Holy Spirit. They are distinguished in several verses. Jesus says, "But the Counselor, the Holy Spirit, whom the Father will send in my name, he will teach you all things, and bring to your remembrance all that I have said to you" (John 14:26). The Holy Spirit also prays or "intercedes" for us (Rom. 8:27), indicating a distinction between the Holy Spirit and God the Father to whom the intercession is made.

Finally, the fact that the Son is not the Holy Spirit is also indicated in the several trinitarian passages mentioned earlier, such as the Great Commission (Matt. 28:19), and in passages that indicate that Christ went back to heaven and then sent the Holy Spirit to the church. Jesus said, "It is to your advantage that I go away, for if I do not go away, the Counselor will not come to you; but if I go, I will send him to you" (John 16:7).

Some have questioned whether the Holy Spirit is indeed a distinct person, rather than just the "power" or "force" of God at work in the world. But the New Testament evidence is quite clear and strong.[9] First are the several verses mentioned earlier where the Holy Spirit is put in a coordinate relationship with the Father and the Son (Matt. 28:19; 1 Cor. 12:4–6; 2 Cor. 13:14; Eph. 4:4–6; 1 Peter 1:2): since the Father and Son are both persons, the coordinate expression strongly intimates that the Holy Spirit is a person also. Then there are places where the masculine pronoun *he* (Gk. *ekeinos*) is applied to the Holy Spirit (John 14:26; 15:26; 16:13–14), which one would not expect from the rules of Greek grammar, for the word "*spirit*" (Gk. *pneuma*) is neuter, not masculine, and would ordinarily be referred to with the neuter pronoun *ekeino*. Moreover, the name *counselor* or *comforter* (Gk. *paraklētos*) is a term commonly used to speak of a person who helps or gives comfort or counsel to another person or persons, but is used of the Holy Spirit in John's gospel (14:16, 26; 15:26; 16:7).

Other personal activities are ascribed to the Holy Spirit, such as teaching (John 14:26), bearing witness (John 15:26; Rom. 8:16), interceding or praying on behalf of others (Rom. 8:26–27), searching the depths of God (1 Cor. 2:10), knowing the thoughts of God (1 Cor. 2:11), willing to distribute some gifts to some and other gifts to others (1 Cor. 12:11), forbidding or not allowing certain activities (Acts 16:6–7), speaking (Acts 8:29; 13:2; and many times in both Old and New Testaments), evaluating and approving a wise course of action (Acts 15:28), and being grieved by sin in the lives of Christians (Eph. 4:30).

Finally, if the Holy Spirit is understood simply to be the power of God, rather than a distinct person, then a number of passages would simply not make sense, because in them the Holy Spirit and his power or the power of God are both mentioned. For example, Luke 4:14, "And Jesus returned in the power of the Spirit into Galilee," would have to mean, "Jesus returned in the power of the power of God into Galilee." In Acts 10:38, "God anointed Jesus of Nazareth with

---

[9]The following section on the distinct personality of the Holy Spirit follows quite closely the excellent material in Louis Berkhof, *Systematic Theology,* p. 96.

the Holy Spirit and with power," would mean, "God anointed Jesus with the power of God and with power" (see also Rom. 15:13; 1 Cor. 2:4).

Although so many passages clearly distinguish the Holy Spirit from the other members of the Trinity, one puzzling verse has been 2 Corinthians 3:17: "Now the Lord is the Spirit, and where the Spirit of the Lord is, there is freedom." Interpreters often assume that "the Lord" here must mean Christ, because Paul frequently uses "the Lord" to refer to Christ. But that is probably not the case here, for a good argument can be made from grammar and context to say that this verse is better translated with the Holy Spirit as subject, "Now the Spirit is the Lord. . . ."[10] In this case, Paul would be saying that the Holy Spirit is also "Yahweh" (or "Jehovah"), the Lord of the Old Testament (note the clear Old Testament background of this context, beginning at v. 7). Theologically this would be quite acceptable, for it could truly be said that just as God the Father is "Lord" and God the Son is "Lord" (in the full Old Testament sense of "Lord" as a name for God), so also the Holy Spirit is the one called "Lord" in the Old Testament—and it is the Holy Spirit who especially manifests the presence of the Lord to us in the new covenant age.[11]

**2. Each Person Is Fully God.** In addition to the fact that all three persons are distinct, the abundant testimony of Scripture is that each person is fully God as well.

First, *God the Father is clearly God.* This is evident from the first verse of the Bible, where God created the heaven and the earth. It is evident through the Old and New Testaments, where God the Father is clearly viewed as sovereign Lord over all and where Jesus prays to his Father in heaven.

Next, *the Son is fully God.* Although this point will be developed in greater detail in chapter 26, "The Person of Christ," we can briefly note several explicit passages at this point. John 1:1–4 clearly affirms the full deity of Christ:

> In the beginning was the Word, and the Word was with God, and the Word was God. He was in the beginning with God; all things were made through him, and without him was not anything made that was made. In him was life, and the life was the light of men.

Here Christ is referred to as "the Word," and John says both that he was "with God" and that he "was God." The Greek text echoes the opening words of Genesis 1:1 ("In the beginning . . .") and reminds us that John is talking about something that was true before the world was made. God the Son was always fully God.

---

[10]Grammatically both "the Spirit" (*to pneuma*) and "the Lord" (*ho kyrios*) are in the nominative case, which is the case taken both by the subject and by the predicate noun in a sentence with the verb "to be." And word order does not indicate the subject in Greek as it does in English. The definite article (*ho,* "the") before "Lord" here is probably anaphoric (that is, it refers back to the previous mention of "Lord" in v. 16 and says that the Spirit is "the Lord" who was just mentioned in the previous sentence). (See Murray Harris, "2 Corinthians," in *EBC* 10:338–39.)

[11]Another possible interpretation is to say that this is speaking of the function of Christ and the function of the Holy Spirit as so closely related in the New Testament age that they can be spoken of as one in purpose. The verse would then mean something like "The Lord Jesus is in this age seen and known through the activity of the Holy Spirit, for the Holy Spirit's function is to glorify Christ." But this is a less persuasive interpretation, since it seems unlikely that Paul would speak of an identity of function in such an obscure way, or even that Paul would want to say that the work of Christ and the work of the Spirit are identical.

The translation "the Word was God" has been challenged by the Jehovah's Witnesses, who translate it "the Word was *a god*," implying that the Word was simply a heavenly being but not fully divine. They justify this translation by pointing to the fact that the definite article (Gk. *ho*, "the") does not occur before the Greek word *theos* ("God"). They say therefore that *theos* should be translated "a god." However, their interpretation has been followed by no recognized Greek scholar anywhere, for it is commonly known that the sentence follows a regular rule of Greek grammar, and the absence of the definite article merely indicates that "God" is the predicate rather than the subject of the sentence.[12] (A recent publication by the Jehovah's Witnesses now acknowledges the relevant grammatical rule but continues to affirm their position on John 1:1 nonetheless.)[13]

The inconsistency of the Jehovah's Witnesses' position can further be seen in

---

[12]This rule (called "Colwell's rule") is covered as early as chapter 6 of a standard introductory Greek grammar: See John Wenham, *The Elements of New Testament Greek* (Cambridge: Cambridge University Press, 1965), p. 35; also, BDF, 273. The rule is simply that in sentences with the linking verb "to be" (such as Gk. *eimi*), a definite predicate noun will usually drop the definite article when it precedes the verb, but the subject of the sentence, if definite, will retain the definite article. So if John had wanted to say, "The Word was God," John 1:1 is exactly the way he would have said it. (Recent grammatical study has confirmed and even strengthened Colwell's original rule: see Lane C. McGaughy, *Toward a Descriptive Analysis of EINAI as a Linking Verb in the New Testament* [SBLDS 6; Missoula, Mont.: SBL, 1972], esp. pp. 49–53, 73–77; and the important review of this book by E. V. N. Goetchius in *JBL* 95 [1976]: 147–49.)

Of course, if John had wanted to say, "The Word was a god" (with an indefinite predicate, "a god"), it would also have been written this way, since there would have been no definite article to drop in the first place. But if that were the case, there would have to be some clues in the context that John was using the word *theos* to speak of a heavenly being that was not fully divine. So the question becomes, what kind of God (or "god") is John talking about in this context? Is he speaking of the one true God who created the heavens and the earth? In that case, *theos* was definite and dropped the definite article to show that it was the predicate. Or is he speaking about some other kind of heavenly being ("a god") who is not the one true God? In that case, *theos* was indefinite and never had a definite article in the first place.

The context decides this question clearly. From the other uses of the word *theos* to mean "God" in vv. 1, 2, 6, 12, 13, et al., and from the opening words that recall Gen. 1:1 ("In the beginning"), it is clear that John is speaking of the one true God who created the heavens and the earth. That means that *theos* in v. 2 must be understood to refer to that same God as well.

[13]The argument is found in a detailed, rather extensive attack on the doctrine of the Trinity: *Should You Believe in the Trinity?* (no author named; Brooklyn, N.Y.: Watchtower Bible and Tract Society, 1989). This group apparently deems this booklet a significant statement of their position, for page 2 states, "First printing in English: 5,000,000 copies." The booklet first advances the traditional argument that John 1:1 should be translated "a god" because of the absence on the definite article (p. 27). But then it later acknowledges that Colwell's rule is relevant for John 1:1 (p. 28) and there admits that the context, not the absence of the definite article, determines whether we should translate "the Word was God" (definite) or "the Word was a god" (indefinite). Then it argues as follows: ". . . when the context requires it, translators may insert an indefinite article in front of the noun in this type of sentence structure. Does the context require an indefinite article at John 1:1? Yes, for the testimony of the entire Bible is that Jesus is not Almighty God" (p. 28).

We should note carefully the weakness of this argument: They admit that context is decisive, but then they quote not one shred of evidence from the context of John 1:1. Rather, they simply assert again their conclusion about "the entire Bible." If they agree that this context is decisive, but they can find nothing in this context that supports their view, they have simply lost the argument. Therefore, having acknowledged Colwell's rule, they still hold their view on John 1:1, but with no supporting evidence. To hold a view with no evidence to support it is simply irrationality.

The booklet as a whole will give an appearance of scholarly work to laypersons, since it quotes dozens of theologians and academic reference works (always without adequate documentation). However, many quotations are taken out of context and made to say something the authors never intended, and others are from liberal Catholic or Protestant scholars who themselves are questioning both the doctrine of the Trinity and the truthfulness of the Bible.

their translation of the rest of the chapter. For various other grammatical reasons the word *theos* also lacks the definite article at other places in this chapter, such as verse 6 ("There was a man sent from God"), verse 12 ("power to become children of God"), verse 13 ("but of God"), and verse 18 ("No one has ever seen God"). If the Jehovah's Witnesses were consistent with their argument about the absence of the definite article, they would have to translate all of these with the phrase "a god," but they translate "God" in every case.

John 20:28 in its context is also a strong proof for the deity of Christ. Thomas had doubted the reports of the other disciples that they had seen Jesus raised from the dead, and he said he would not believe unless he could see the nail prints in Jesus' hands and place his hand in his wounded side (John 20:25). Then Jesus appeared to the disciples when Thomas was with them. He said to Thomas, "Put your finger here, and see my hands; and put out your hand, and place it in my side; do not be faithless, but believing" (John 20:27). In response to this, we read, "Thomas answered him, 'My Lord and my God!'" (John 20:28). Here Thomas calls Jesus "my God." The narrative shows that both John in writing his gospel and Jesus himself approve of what Thomas has said and encourage everyone who hears about Thomas to believe the same things that Thomas did. Jesus immediately responds to Thomas, "Have you believed because you have seen me? Blessed are those who have not seen and yet believe" (John 20:29). As far as John is concerned, this is the dramatic high point of the gospel, for he immediately tells the reader—in the very next verse—that this was the reason he wrote it:

> Now Jesus did many other signs in the presence of the disciples, which are not written in this book; but these are written that you may believe that Jesus is the Christ, the Son of God, and that believing you may have life in his name. (John 20:30–31)

Jesus speaks of those who will not see him and will yet believe, and John immediately tells the reader that he recorded the events written in his gospel in order that they may believe in just this way, imitating Thomas in his confession of faith. In other words, the entire gospel is written to persuade people to imitate Thomas, who sincerely called Jesus "My Lord and my God." Because this is set out by John as the purpose of his gospel, the sentence takes on added force.[14]

Other passages speaking of Jesus as fully divine include Hebrews 1, where the author says that Christ is the "exact representation" (Gk. *charaktēr*, "exact

---

[14]The Jehovah's Witnesses' booklet *Should You Believe in the Trinity?* offers two explanations for John 20:28: (1) "To Thomas, Jesus was like 'a god,' especially in the miraculous circumstances that prompted his exclamation" (p. 29). But this explanation is unconvincing, because Thomas did not say, "You are like a god," but rather called Jesus "my God." The Greek text has the definite article (it cannot be translated "a god") and is explicit: *ho theos mou* is not "a god of mine" but "my God."

(2) The second explanation offered is that "Thomas may simply have made an emotional exclamation of astonishment, spoken to Jesus but directed to God" (ibid.). The second part of this sentence, "spoken to Jesus but directed to God," is simply incoherent: it seems to mean, "spoken to Jesus but not spoken to Jesus," which is not only self-contradictory, but also impossible: if Thomas is speaking to Jesus he is also directing his words to Jesus. The first part of this sentence, the claim that Thomas is really not calling Jesus "God," but is merely swearing or uttering some involuntary words of exclamation, is without merit, for the verse makes it clear that Thomas was not speaking into the blue but was speaking directly to Jesus: "Thomas answered and said *to Him*, 'My Lord and my God!'" (John 20:28, NASB). And immediately both Jesus and John in his writing commend Thomas, certainly not for swearing but for believing in Jesus as his Lord and his God.

duplicate") of the nature or being (Gk. *hypostasis*) of God—meaning that God the Son exactly duplicates the being or nature of God the Father in every way: whatever attributes or power God the Father has, God the Son has them as well. The author goes on to refer to the Son as "God" in verse 8 ("But of the Son he says, 'Your throne, O God, is for ever and ever'"), and he attributes the creation of the heavens to Christ when he says of him, "You, Lord, did found the earth in the beginning, and the heavens are the work of your hands" (Heb. 1:10, quoting Ps. 102:25). Titus 2:13 refers to "our great *God* and Savior Jesus Christ," and 2 Peter 1:1 speaks of "the righteousness of our *God* and Savior Jesus Christ."[15] Romans 9:5, speaking of the Jewish people, says, "Theirs are the patriarchs, and from them is traced the human ancestry of Christ, who is God over all, forever praised! Amen" (NIV).[16]

In the Old Testament, Isaiah 9:6 predicts,

> "For to us a child is born,
>   to us a son is given;
> and the government will be upon his shoulder,
>   and his name will be called
> 'Wonderful Counselor, Mighty God.'"

As this prophecy is applied to Christ, it refers to him as "Mighty God." Note the similar application of the titles "LORD" and "God" in the prophecy of the coming of the Messiah in Isaiah 40:3, "In the wilderness prepare the way of the LORD,

---

[15]Both Titus 2:13 and 2 Peter 1:1 have marginal readings in the RSV whereby Jesus is referred to as a different person than "God" and therefore is not called God: "the great God and our Savior Jesus Christ" (Titus 2:13 mg.) and "our God and the Savior Jesus Christ" (2 Peter 1:1 mg.). These alternative translations are possible grammatically but are unlikely. Both verses have the same Greek construction, in which one definite article governs two nouns joined by the Greek word for *and* (*kai*). In all cases where this construction is found the two nouns are viewed as unified in some way, and often they are two separate names for the same person or thing. Especially significant is 2 Peter 1:1, for exactly the same construction is used by Peter three other times in this book to speak of "Our Lord and Savior Jesus Christ" (1 Peter 1:11; 2:20; 3:18). In these three other verses, the Greek wording is exactly the same in every detail except that the word *Lord* (*kyrios*) is used instead of the word *God* (*theos*). If these other three instances are all translated "Our *Lord* and Savior Jesus Christ," as they are in all major translations, then consistency in translation would seem to require the translation of 2 Peter 1:1 as "Our *God* and Savior Jesus Christ," again referring to Christ as God. In Titus 2:13 Paul is writing about the hope of Christ's second coming, which the New Testament writers consistently speak of in terms that emphasize the manifestation of Jesus Christ in his glory, not in terms that emphasize the glory of the Father.

[16]The marginal reading in the NIV is similar to the reading in the main text of the RSV, which is, "and of their race, according to the flesh, is the Christ. God who is over all be blessed for ever. Amen" (Rom. 9:5 RSV). But this translation is far less likely on grammatical and contextual grounds and is justified primarily by arguing that Paul would not have referred to Christ as "God." The NIV translation, which refers to Christ as "God over all," is preferable because (1) Paul's normal pattern is to declare a word of blessing concerning the person about whom he has just been speaking, who in this case is Christ; (2) the Greek participle *ōn*, "being," which makes the phrase say literally, "who, being God over all is blessed forever," would be redundant if Paul were starting a new sentence as the RSV has it; (3) when Paul elsewhere begins a new sentence with a word of blessing to God, the word "blessed" comes first in the Greek sentence (see 2 Cor. 1:3; Eph. 1:3; cf. Peter's pattern in 1 Peter 1:3), but here the expression does not follow that pattern, making the RSV translation unlikely. See Donald Guthrie, *New Testament Theology* (Leicester: Inter-Varsity Press, 1981), pp. 339–40. For a definitive treatment of all the New Testament texts that refer to Jesus as "God," see Murray Harris, *Jesus as God* (Grand Rapids: Baker, 1992).

make straight in the desert a highway for our God," quoted by John the Baptist in preparation for the coming of Christ in Matthew 3:3.

Many other passages will be discussed in chapter 26 below, but these should be sufficient to demonstrate that the New Testament clearly refers to Christ as fully God. As Paul says in Colossians 2:9, "In him the whole fulness of deity dwells bodily."

Next, *the Holy Spirit is also fully God.* Once we understand God the Father and God the Son to be fully God, then the trinitarian expressions in verses like Matthew 28:19 ("baptizing them in the name of the Father and of the Son and of the Holy Spirit") assume significance for the doctrine of the Holy Spirit, because they show that the Holy Spirit is classified on an equal level with the Father and the Son. This can be seen if we recognize how unthinkable it would have been for Jesus to say something like, "baptizing them in the name of the Father and of the Son and of the archangel Michael"—this would give to a created being a status entirely inappropriate even to an archangel. Believers throughout all ages can only be baptized into the name (and thus into a taking on of the character) of God himself.[17] (Note also the other trinitarian passages mentioned above: 1 Cor. 12:4–6; 2 Cor. 13:14; Eph. 4:4–6; 1 Peter 1:2; Jude 20–21.)

In Acts 5:3–4, Peter asks Ananias, "Why has Satan filled your heart to lie to the Holy Spirit . . . ? You have not lied to men but *to God.*" According to Peter's words, to lie to the Holy Spirit is to lie to God. Paul says in 1 Corinthians 3:16, "Do you not know that you are God's temple and that God's Spirit dwells in you?" God's temple is the place where God himself dwells, which Paul explains by the fact that "God's Spirit" dwells in it, thus apparently equating God's Spirit with God himself.

David asks in Psalm 139:7–8, "Whither shall I go from your Spirit? Or whither shall I flee from your presence? If I ascend to heaven, you are there!" This passage attributes the divine characteristic of omnipresence to the Holy Spirit, something that is not true of any of God's creatures. It seems that David is equating God's Spirit with God's presence. To go from God's Spirit is to go from his presence, but if there is nowhere that David can flee from God's Spirit, then he knows that wherever he goes he will have to say, "You are there."

Paul attributes the divine characteristic of omniscience to the Holy Spirit in 1 Corinthians 2:10–11: "For the Spirit searches everything, even the depths of God. For what person knows a man's thoughts except the spirit of the man which is in him? So also no one comprehends the thoughts of God [Gk., literally 'the things of God'] except the Spirit of God."

Moreover, the activity of giving new birth to everyone who is born again is the work of the Holy Spirit. Jesus said, "unless one is born of water and the Spirit, he cannot enter the kingdom of God. That which is born of the flesh is flesh, and that

---

[17]1 Tim. 5:21 should not be seen as a counter example to this claim, for there Paul is simply warning Timothy in the presence of a host of heavenly witnesses, both divine and angelic, who he knows are watching Timothy's conduct. This is similar to the mention of God and Christ and the angels of heaven and the "spirits of just men made perfect" in Heb. 12:22–24, where a great heavenly assembly is mentioned. 1 Tim. 5:21 should therefore be seen as significantly different from the trinitarian passages mentioned above, since those passages speak of uniquely divine activities, such as distributing gifts to every Christian (1 Cor. 12:4–6) or having the name into which all believers are baptized (Matt. 28:19).

which is born of the Spirit is spirit. Do not marvel that I said to you, 'You must be born anew'" (John 3:5–7). But the work of giving new spiritual life to people when they become Christians is something that only God can do (cf. 1 John 3:9, "born of God"). This passage therefore gives another indication that the Holy Spirit is fully God.

Up to this point we have two conclusions, both abundantly taught throughout Scripture:

1. God is three persons.
2. Each person is fully God.

If the Bible taught only these two facts, there would be no logical problem at all in fitting them together, for the obvious solution would be that there are three Gods. The Father is fully God, the Son is fully God, and the Holy Spirit is fully God. We would have a system where there are three equally divine beings. Such a system of belief would be called polytheism—or, more specifically, "tritheism," or belief in three Gods. But that is far from what the Bible teaches.

**3. There Is One God.** Scripture is abundantly clear that there is one and only one God. The three different persons of the Trinity are one not only in purpose and in agreement on what they think, but they are one in essence, one in their essential nature. In other words, God is only one being. There are not three Gods. There is only one God.

One of the most familiar passages of the Old Testament is Deuteronomy 6:4–5 (NIV): "Hear, O Israel: The LORD our God, *the LORD is one*. Love the LORD your God with all your heart and with all your soul and with all your strength."

When Moses sings,

> "Who is like you, O LORD, among the gods?
>  Who is like you, majestic in holiness,
>   terrible in glorious deeds, doing wonders?" (Ex. 15:11)

the answer obviously is "No one." God is unique, and there is no one like him and there can be no one like him. In fact, Solomon prays "that all the peoples of the earth may know that the LORD is God; there is no other" (1 Kings 8:60).

When God speaks, he repeatedly makes it clear that he is the only true God; the idea that there are three Gods to be worshiped rather than one would be unthinkable in the light of these extremely strong statements. God alone is the one true God and there is no one like him. When he speaks, he alone is speaking—he is not speaking as one God among three who are to be worshiped. He says:

> "I am the LORD, and there is no other,
>  besides me there is no God;
>  I gird you, though you do not know me,
>   that men may know, from the rising of the sun
>   and from the west, that there is none besides me;
>  I am the LORD, and there is no other." (Isa. 45:5–6)

Similarly, he calls everyone on earth to turn to him:

> "There is no other god besides me,
> a righteous God and a Savior;
> there is none besides me.
>
> "Turn to me and be saved,
> all the ends of the earth!
> For I am God, and there is no other."
> (Isa. 45:21–22; cf. 44:6–8)

The New Testament also affirms that there is one God. Paul writes, "For *there is one God,* and there is one mediator between God and men, the man Christ Jesus" (1 Tim. 2:5). Paul affirms that "God is one" (Rom. 3:30), and that "there is one God, the Father, from whom are all things and for whom we exist" (1 Cor. 8:6).[18] Finally, James acknowledges that even demons recognize that there is one God, even though their intellectual assent to that fact is not enough to save them: "You believe that God is one; you do well. Even the demons believe—and shudder" (James 2:19). But clearly James affirms that one "does well" to believe that "God is one."

**4. Simplistic Solutions Must All Deny One Strand of Biblical Teaching.** We now have three statements, all of which are taught in Scripture:

1. God is three persons.
2. Each person is fully God.
3. There is one God.

Throughout the history of the church there have been attempts to come up with a simple solution to the doctrine of the Trinity by denying one or another of these statements. If someone *denies the first statement,* then we are simply left with the fact that each of the persons named in Scripture (Father, Son, and Holy Spirit) is God, and there is one God. But if we do not have to say that they are distinct persons, then there is an easy solution: these are just different names for one person who acts differently at different times. Sometimes this person calls himself Father, sometimes he calls himself Son, and sometimes he calls himself Spirit.[19] We have no difficulty in understanding that, for in our own experience the same person can act at one time as a lawyer (for example), at another time as a father to his own children, and at another time as a son with respect to his parents: The same person is a lawyer, a father, and a son. But such a solution would deny the fact that the three persons are distinct individuals, that God the Father sends God

---

[18]1 Cor. 8:6 does not deny that God the Son and God the Holy Spirit are also "God," but here Paul says that God the Father is identified as this "one God." Elsewhere, as we have seen, he can speak of God the Son and God the Holy Spirit as also "God." Moreover, in this same verse, he goes on to speak of "one Lord, Jesus Christ, through whom are all things and through whom we exist." He is here using the word *Lord* in its full Old Testament sense of "Yahweh" as a name for God, and saying that this is the person through whom all things were created, thus affirming the full deity of Christ as well, but with a different name. Thus this verse affirms both the unity of God and the diversity of persons in God.

[19]The technical name for this view is modalism, a heresy condemned in the ancient church: see discussion below.

the Son into the world, that the Son prays to the Father, and that the Holy Spirit intercedes before the Father for us.

Another simple solution might be found by *denying the second statement*, that is, denying that some of the persons named in Scripture are really fully God. If we simply hold that God is three persons, and that there is one God, then we might be tempted to say that some of the "persons" in this one God are not fully God, but are only subordinate or created parts of God. This solution would be taken, for example, by those who deny the full deity of the Son (and of the Holy Spirit).[20] But, as we saw above, this solution would have to deny an entire category of biblical teaching.

Finally, as we noted above, a simple solution could come by *denying that there is one God*. But this would result in a belief in three Gods, something clearly contrary to Scripture.

Though the third error has not been common, as we shall see below, each of the first two errors has appeared at one time or another in the history of the church and they still persist today in some groups.

**5. All Analogies Have Shortcomings.** If we cannot adopt any of these simple solutions, then how can we put the three truths of Scripture together and maintain the doctrine of the Trinity? Sometimes people have used several analogies drawn from nature or human experience to attempt to explain this doctrine. Although these analogies are helpful at an elementary level of understanding, they all turn out to be inadequate or misleading on further reflection. To say, for example, that God is like a three-leaf clover, which has three parts yet remains one clover, fails because each leaf is only part of the clover, and any one leaf cannot be said to be the whole clover. But in the Trinity, each of the persons is not just a separate part of God, each person is fully God. Moreover, the leaf of a clover is impersonal and does not have distinct and complex personality in the way each person of the Trinity does.

Others have used the analogy of a tree with three parts: the roots, trunk, and branches all constitute one tree. But a similar problem arises, for these are only parts of a tree, and none of the parts can be said to be the whole tree. Moreover, in this analogy the parts have different properties, unlike the persons of the Trinity, all of whom possess all of the attributes of God in equal measure. And the lack of personality in each part is a deficiency as well.

The analogy of the three forms of water (steam, water, and ice) is also inadequate because (a) no quantity of water is ever all three of these at the same time,[21] (b) they have different properties or characteristics, (c) the analogy has nothing that corresponds to the fact that there is only one God (there is no such thing as "one water" or "all the water in the universe"), and (d) the element of intelligent personality is lacking.

Other analogies have been drawn from human experience. It might be said that the Trinity is something like a man who is both a farmer, the mayor of his town,

---

[20]The technical name for this view is Arianism, another heresy condemned in the ancient church: see discussion below.

[21]There is a certain atmospheric condition (called the "triple point" by chemists) at which steam, liquid water, and ice can all exist simultaneously, but even then the quantity of water that is steam is not ice or liquid, the quantity that is liquid is not steam or ice, etc.

and an elder in his church. He functions in different roles at different times, but he is one man. However, this analogy is very deficient because there is only one person doing these three activities at different times, and the analogy cannot deal with the personal interaction among the members of the Trinity. (In fact, this analogy simply teaches the heresy called modalism, discussed below.)

Another analogy taken from human life is the union of the intellect, the emotions, and the will in one human person. While these are parts of a personality, however, no one factor constitutes the entire person. And the parts are not identical in characteristics but have different abilities.

So what analogy shall we use to teach the Trinity? Although the Bible uses many analogies from nature and life to teach us various aspects of God's character (God is like a rock in his faithfulness, he is like a shepherd in his care, etc.), it is interesting that Scripture nowhere uses any analogies to teach the doctrine of the Trinity. The closest we come to an analogy is found in the titles "Father" and "Son" themselves, titles that clearly speak of distinct persons and of the close relationship that exists between them in a human family. But on the human level, of course, we have two entirely separate human beings, not one being comprised of three distinct persons. It is best to conclude that no analogy adequately teaches about the Trinity, and all are misleading in significant ways.

**6. God Eternally and Necessarily Exists as the Trinity.** When the universe was created God the Father spoke the powerful creative words that brought it into being, God the Son was the divine agent who carried out these words (John 1:3; 1 Cor. 8:6; Col. 1:16; Heb. 1:2), and God the Holy Spirit was active "moving over the face of the waters" (Gen. 1:2). So it is as we would expect: if all three members of the Trinity are equally and fully divine, then they have all three existed for all eternity, and God has eternally existed as a Trinity (cf. also John 17:5, 24). Moreover, God cannot be other than he is, for he is unchanging (see chapter 11 above). Therefore it seems right to conclude that God necessarily exists as a Trinity—he cannot be other than he is.

### C. Errors Have Come By Denying Any of the Three Statements Summarizing the Biblical Teaching

In the previous section we saw how the Bible requires that we affirm the following three statements:

1. God is three persons.
2. Each person is fully God.
3. There is one God.

Before we discuss further the differences between the Father, Son, and Holy Spirit, and the way they relate to one another, it is important that we recall some of the doctrinal errors about the Trinity that have been made in the history of the church. In this historical survey we will see some of the mistakes that we ourselves should avoid in any further thinking about this doctrine. In fact, the major trinitarian errors that have arisen have come through a denial of one or another of these three primary statements.[22]

**1. Modalism Claims That There Is One Person Who Appears to Us in Three Different Forms (or "Modes").** At various times people have taught that God is not really three distinct persons, but only one person who appears to people in different "modes" at different times. For example, in the Old Testament God appeared as "Father." Throughout the Gospels, this same divine person appeared as "the Son" as seen in the human life and ministry of Jesus. After Pentecost, this same person then revealed himself as the "Spirit" active in the church.

This teaching is also referred to by two other names. Sometimes it is called Sabellianism, after a teacher named Sabellius who lived in Rome in the early third century A.D. Another term for modalism is "modalistic monarchianism," because this teaching not only says that God revealed himself in different "modes" but it also says that there is only one supreme ruler ("monarch") in the universe and that is God himself, who consists of only one person.

Modalism gains its attractiveness from the desire to emphasize clearly the fact that there is only one God. It may claim support not only from the passages talking about one God, but also from passages such as John 10:30 ("I and the Father are one") and John 14:9 ("He who has seen me has seen the Father"). However, the last passage can simply mean that Jesus fully reveals the character of God the Father, and the former passage (John 10:30), in a context in which Jesus affirms that he will accomplish all that the Father has given him to do and save all whom the Father has given to him, seems to mean that Jesus and the Father are one in purpose.

The fatal shortcoming of modalism is the fact that it must deny the personal relationships within the Trinity that appear in so many places in Scripture (or it must affirm that these were simply an illusion and not real). Thus, it must deny three separate persons at the baptism of Jesus, where the Father speaks from heaven and the Spirit descends on Jesus like a dove. And it must say that all those instances where Jesus is praying to the Father are an illusion or a charade. The idea of the Son or the Holy Spirit interceding for us before God the Father is lost. Finally, modalism ultimately loses the heart of the doctrine of the atonement— that is, the idea that God sent his Son as a substitutionary sacrifice, and that the Son bore the wrath of God in our place, and that the Father, representing the interests of the Trinity, saw the suffering of Christ and was satisfied (Isa. 53:11).

Moreover, modalism denies the independence of God, for if God is only one person, then he has no ability to love and to communicate without other persons in his creation. Therefore it was necessary for God to create the world, and God would no longer be independent of creation (see chapter 12, above, on God's independence).

One present denomination within Protestantism (broadly defined), the United Pentecostal Church, is modalistic in its doctrinal position.[23]

---

[22]An excellent discussion of the history and theological implications of the trinitarian heresies discussed in this section is found in Harold O. J. Brown, *Heresies: The Image of Christ in the Mirror of Heresy and Orthodoxy from the Apostles to the Present* (Garden City, N.Y.: Doubleday, 1984), pp. 95–157.

[23]Some of the leaders who formed this group had earlier been forced out of the Assemblies of God

## 2. Arianism Denies the Full Deity of the Son and the Holy Spirit.

**a. The Arian Controversy:** The term *Arianism* is derived from Arius, a Bishop of Alexandria whose views were condemned at the Council of Nicea in A.D. 325, and who died in A.D. 336. Arius taught that God the Son was at one point created by God the Father, and that before that time the Son did not exist, nor did the Holy Spirit, but the Father only. Thus, though the Son is a heavenly being who existed before the rest of creation and who is far greater than all the rest of creation, he is still not equal to the Father in all his attributes—he may even be said to be "like the Father" or "similar to the Father" in his nature, but he cannot be said to be "of the same nature" as the Father.

The Arians depended heavily on texts that called Christ God's *"only begotten"* Son (John 1:14; 3:16, 18; 1 John 4:9). If Christ were "begotten" by God the Father, they reasoned, it must mean that he was brought into existence by God the Father (for the word "beget" in human experience refers to the father's role in conceiving a child). Further support for the Arian view was found in Colossians 1:15, "He is the image of the invisible God, *the first-born of all creation.*" Does not "first-born" here imply that the Son was at some point brought into existence by the Father?[24] And if this is true of the Son, it must necessarily be true of the Holy Spirit as well.

But these texts do not require us to believe the Arian position. Colossians 1:15, which calls Christ "the first-born of all creation," is better understood to mean that Christ has the rights or privileges of the "first-born"—that is, according to biblical usage and custom, the right of leadership or authority in the family for one's generation. (Note Heb. 12:16 where Esau is said to have sold his "first-born status" or "birthright"—the Greek word *prototokia* is cognate to the term *prototokos*, "first-born" in Col. 1:15.) So Colossians 1:15 means that Christ has the privileges of authority and rule, the privileges belonging to the "first-born," but

when the Assemblies decided to insist on a trinitarian statement of faith for its ministers in 1916. The United Pentecostal Church is sometimes identified with the slogan "Jesus only," and it insists that people should be baptized in the name of Jesus, not in the name of the Father, Son, and Holy Spirit. Because of its denial of the three distinct persons in God, the denomination should not be considered to be evangelical, and it is doubtful whether it should be considered genuinely Christian at all.

[24]Prov. 8:22 was also used by the Arians, who gained support from the fact that the Septuagint misleadingly translated it, "The Lord created me" (Gk. *ktizō*) rather than "The Lord acquired me or possessed me" (Gk. *ktaomai*). See discussion on this verse above, pp. 229–30.

The Jehovah's Witnesses, who are modern-day Arians, also point to Rev. 3:14, where Jesus calls himself "the beginning of God's creation," and take it to mean that "Jesus was created by God as the beginning of God's invisible creations" (no author named, *Should You Believe in the Trinity?* [Brooklyn, N.Y.: Watch Tower Bible and Tract Society, 1989], p. 14). But this verse does not mean that Jesus was the first being created, for the same word for "beginning" (Gk. *archē*) is used by Jesus when he says that he is "the Alpha and the Omega, the first and the last, the *beginning* and the end" (Rev. 22:13), and "beginning" here is a synonym for "Alpha" and "first." God the Father similarly says of himself, "I am the Alpha and the Omega" (Rev. 1:8). In both cases, to be "the Alpha" or "the beginning" means to be the one who was there before anything else existed. The word does not imply that the Son was created or that there was a time when he began to be, for both the Father and the Son have always been "the Alpha and the Omega" and "the beginning and the end," since they have existed eternally. (The Jewish historian Josephus uses this same word to call God the "beginning (*archē*)" of "all things," but certainly he does not think that God himself was created: see *Against Apion* 2.190.)

The NIV translates this verse differently: "the ruler of God's creation." This is an acceptable alternative sense for *archē*: see the same meaning in Luke 12:11; Titus 3:1.

with respect to the whole creation. The NIV translates it helpfully, "the firstborn *over all creation.*"

As for the texts that say that Christ was God's "only begotten Son," the early church felt so strongly the force of many other texts showing that Christ was fully and completely God, that it concluded that, whatever "only begotten" meant, it did not mean "created." Therefore the Nicene Creed in 325 affirmed that Christ was "begotten, not made":

> We believe in one God, the Father Almighty, Maker of all things visible and invisible.
>
> And in one Lord Jesus Christ, the Son of God, begotten of the Father, the only-begotten; that is, of the essence of the Father, God of God, Light of Light, very God of very God, begotten, not made, being of one substance (*homoousion*) with the Father. . . .[25]

This same phrase was reaffirmed at the Council of Constantinople in 381. In addition, the phrase "before all ages" was added after "begotten of the Father," to show that this "begetting" was eternal. It never began to happen, but is something that has been eternally true of the relationship between the Father and the Son. However, the nature of that "begetting" has never been defined very clearly, other than to say that it has to do with the relationship between the Father and the Son, and that in some sense the Father has eternally had a primacy in that relationship.

In further repudiation of the teaching of Arius, the Nicene Creed insisted that Christ was "of the same substance as the Father." The dispute with Arius concerned two words that have become famous in the history of Christian doctrine, *homoousios* ("of the same nature") and *homoiousios* ("of a similar nature").[26] The difference depends on the different meaning of two Greek prefixes, *homo-,* meaning "same," and *homoi-,* meaning "similar." Arius was happy to say that Christ was a supernatural heavenly being and that he was created by God before the creation of the rest of the universe, and even that he was "similar" to God in his nature. Thus, Arius would agree to the word *homoiousios.* But the Council of Nicea in 325 and the Council of Constantinople in 381 realized that this did not go far enough, for if Christ is not of exactly the same nature as the Father, then he is not fully God. So both councils insisted that orthodox Christians confess Jesus to be *homoousios,* of the *same* nature as God the Father. The difference between the two words was only one letter, the Greek letter iota, and some have criticized the church for allowing a doctrinal dispute over a single letter to consume so much attention for most of the fourth century A.D. Some have wondered, "Could anything be more foolish than arguing over a single letter in a word?" But the difference between the two words was profound, and the presence or absence of the iota really did mark the difference between biblical Christianity, with a true doctrine of the Trinity, and a heresy that did not accept the full deity of

---

[25]This is the original form of the Nicene Creed, but it was later modified at the Council of Constantinople in 381 and there took the form that is commonly called the "Nicene Creed" by churches today. This text is taken from Philip Schaff, *Creeds of Christendom,* 3 vols. (Grand Rapids: Baker, 1983 reprint of 1931 edition), 1:28–29.

[26]Older translations of *homoousios* sometimes use the term "consubstantial," an uncommon English word simply meaning "of the same substance or nature."

Christ and therefore was nontrinitarian and ultimately destructive to the whole Christian faith.

**b. Subordinationism:** In affirming that the Son was of the same nature as the Father, the early church also excluded a related false doctrine, subordinationism. While Arianism held that the Son was created and was not divine, subordinationism held that the Son was eternal (not created) and divine, but still not equal to the Father in being or attributes—the Son was inferior or "subordinate" in being to God the Father.[27] The early church father Origen (c. 185–c. A.D. 254) advocated a form of subordinationism by holding that the Son was inferior to the Father in being, and that the Son eternally derives his being from the Father. Origen was attempting to protect the distinction of persons and was writing before the doctrine of the Trinity was clearly formulated in the church. The rest of the church did not follow him but clearly rejected his teaching at the Council of Nicea.

Although many early church leaders contributed to the gradual formulation of a correct doctrine of the Trinity, the most influential by far was Athanasius. He was only twenty-nine years old when he came to the Council of Nicea in A.D. 325, not as an official member but as secretary to Alexander, the Bishop of Alexandria. Yet his keen mind and writing ability allowed him to have an important influence on the outcome of the Council, and he himself became Bishop of Alexandria in 328. Though the Arians had been condemned at Nicea, they refused to stop teaching their views and used their considerable political power throughout the church to prolong the controversy for most of the rest of the fourth century. Athanasius became the focal point of Arian attack, and he devoted his entire life to writing and teaching against the Arian heresy. "He was hounded through five exiles embracing seventeen years of flight and hiding," but, by his untiring efforts, "almost single-handedly Athanasius saved the Church from pagan intellectualism."[28] The "Athanasian Creed" which bears his name is not today thought to stem from Athanasius himself, but it is a very clear affirmation of trinitarian doctrine that gained increasing use in the church from about A.D. 400 onward and is still used in Protestant and Catholic churches today. (See appendix 1.)

**c. Adoptionism:** Before we leave the discussion of Arianism, one related false teaching needs to be mentioned. "Adoptionism" is the view that Jesus lived as an ordinary man until his baptism, but then God "adopted" Jesus as his "Son" and conferred on him supernatural powers. Adoptionists would not hold that Christ existed before he was born as a man; therefore, they would not think of Christ as eternal, nor would they think of him as the exalted, supernatural being created by God that the Arians held him to be. Even after Jesus' "adoption" as the "Son" of God, they would not think of him as divine in nature, but only as an exalted man whom God called his "Son" in a unique sense.

---

[27]The heresy of subordinationism, which holds that the Son is inferior in being to the Father, should be clearly distinguished from the orthodox doctrine that the Son is eternally subordinate to the Father in role or function: without this truth, we would lose the doctrine of the Trinity, for we would not have any eternal personal distinctions between the Father and the Son, and they would not eternally be Father and Son. (See section D. below on the differences between the Father, Son, and Holy Spirit.)

[28]S. J. Mikolaski, "Athanasius," *NIDCC*, 81.

Adoptionism never gained the force of a movement in the way Arianism did, but there were people who held adoptionist views from time to time in the early church, though their views were never accepted as orthodox. Many modern people who think of Jesus as a great man and someone especially empowered by God, but not really divine, would fall into the adoptionist category. We have placed it here in relation to Arianism because it, too, denies the deity of the Son (and, similarly, the deity of the Holy Spirit).

The controversy over Arianism was drawn to a close by the Council of Constantinople in A.D. 381. This council reaffirmed the Nicene statements and added a statement on the deity of the Holy Spirit, which had come under attack in the period since Nicea. After the phrase, "And in the Holy Spirit," Constantinople added, "the Lord and Giver of Life; who proceeds from the Father; who with the Father and the Son together is worshipped and glorified; who spake by the Prophets." The version of the creed that includes the additions at Constantinople is what is commonly known as the Nicene Creed today (See p. 1169 for the text of the Nicene Creed.)

**d. The Filioque Clause:** In connection with the Nicene Creed, one unfortunate chapter in the history of the church should be briefly noted, namely the controversy over the insertion of the filioque clause into the Nicene Creed, an insertion that eventually led to the split between western (Roman Catholic) Christianity and eastern Christianity (consisting today of various branches of eastern orthodox Christianity, such as the Greek Orthodox Church, the Russian Orthodox Church, etc.) in A.D. 1054.

The word *filioque* is a Latin term that means "and from the Son." It was not included in the Nicene Creed in either the first version of A.D. 325 or the second version of A.D. 381. Those versions simply said that the Holy Spirit "proceeds from the Father." But in A.D. 589, at a regional church council in Toledo (in what is now Spain), the phrase "and the Son" was added, so that the creed then said that the Holy Spirit "proceeds from the Father *and the Son (filioque)*." In the light of John 15:26 and 16:7, where Jesus said that he would send the Holy Spirit into the world, it seems there could be no objection to such a statement if it referred to the Holy Spirit proceeding from the Father and the Son at a point in time (particularly at Pentecost). But this was a statement about the nature of the Trinity, and the phrase was understood to speak of the *eternal* relationship between the Holy Spirit and the Son, something Scripture never explicitly discusses.[29] The form of the Nicene Creed that had this additional phrase gradually gained in general use and received an official endorsement in A.D. 1017. The entire controversy was complicated by ecclesiastical politics and struggles for power, and this apparently very insignificant doctrinal point was the main doctrinal issue in the split between eastern and western Christianity in A.D. 1054. (The underlying political issue, however, was the relation of the Eastern church to the authority of the Pope.) The doctrinal controversy and the split between the two branches of Christianity have not been resolved to this day.

---

[29]The word *proceeds* was not understood to refer to a creating of the Holy Spirit, or any deriving of his being from the Father and Son, but to indicate the way the Holy Spirit eternally relates to the Father and Son.

Is there a correct position on this question? The weight of evidence (slim though it is) seems clearly to favor the western church. In spite of the fact that John 15:26 says that the Spirit of truth "proceeds from the Father," this does not deny that he proceeds also from the Son (just as John 14:26 says that the Father will send the Holy Spirit, but John 16:7 says that the Son will send the Holy Spirit). In fact, in the same sentence in John 15:26 Jesus speaks of the Holy Spirit as one "whom I shall send to you from the Father." And if the Son together with the Father sends the Spirit into the world, by analogy it would seem appropriate to say that this reflects eternal ordering of their relationships. This is not something that we can clearly insist on based on any specific verse, but much of our understanding of the *eternal* relationships among the Father, Son, and Holy Spirit comes by analogy from what Scripture tells us about the way they relate to the creation *in time*. Moreover, the eastern formulation runs the danger of suggesting an unnatural distance between the Son and the Holy Spirit, leading to the possibility that even in personal worship an emphasis on more mystical, Spirit-inspired experience might be pursued to the neglect of an accompanying rationally understandable adoration of Christ as Lord. Nevertheless, the controversy was ultimately over such an obscure point of doctrine (essentially, the relationship between the Son and Spirit before creation) that it certainly did not warrant division in the church.

**e. The Importance of the Doctrine of the Trinity:** Why was the church so concerned about the doctrine of the Trinity? Is it really essential to hold to the full deity of the Son and the Holy Spirit? Yes it is, for this teaching has implications for the very heart of the Christian faith. First, the atonement is at stake. If Jesus is merely a created being, and not fully God, then it is hard to see how he, a creature, could bear the full wrath of God against all of our sins. Could any creature, no matter how great, really save us? Second, justification by faith alone is threatened if we deny the full deity of the Son. (This is seen today in the teaching of the Jehovah's Witnesses, who do not believe in justification by faith alone.) If Jesus is not fully God, we would rightly doubt whether we can really trust him to save us completely. Could we really depend on any creature fully for our salvation? Third, if Jesus is not infinite God, should we pray to him or worship him? Who but an infinite, omniscient God could hear and respond to all the prayers of all God's people? And who but God himself is worthy of worship? Indeed, if Jesus is merely a creature, no matter how great, it would be idolatry to worship him—yet the New Testament commands us to do so (Phil. 2:9–11; Rev. 5:12–14). Fourth, if someone teaches that Christ was a created being but nonetheless one who saved us, then this teaching wrongly begins to attribute credit for salvation to a creature and not to God himself. But this wrongfully exalts the creature rather than the Creator, something Scripture never allows us to do. Fifth, the independence and personal nature of God are at stake: If there is no Trinity, then there were no interpersonal relationships within the being of God before creation, and, without personal relationships, it is difficult to see how God could be genuinely personal or be without the need for a creation to relate to. Sixth, the unity of the universe is at stake: If there is not perfect plurality and perfect unity in God himself, then we have no basis for thinking there can be any ultimate unity among the diverse elements of the universe either. Clearly, in the doctrine of the Trinity, the heart of the Christian faith is at stake. Herman Bavinck says that "Athanasius understood better than any of his contemporaries that Christianity stands or falls with the confession of the deity of Christ and of the Trinity."[30] He adds, "In the confession of the Trinity throbs the heart of the Christian religion: every error results from, or upon deeper reflection may be traced to, a wrong view of this doctrine."[31]

**3. Tritheism Denies That There Is Only One God.** A final possible way to attempt an easy reconciliation of the biblical teaching about the Trinity would be to deny that there is only one God. The result is to say that God is three persons and each person is fully God. Therefore, there are three Gods. Technically this view would be called "tritheism."

Few persons have held this view in the history of the church. It has similarities to many ancient pagan religions that held to a multiplicity of gods. This view would result in confusion in the minds of believers. There would be no absolute worship or loyalty or devotion to one true God. We would wonder to which God we should give our ultimate allegiance. And, at a deeper level, this view would destroy any sense of ultimate unity in the universe: even in the very being of God there would be plurality but no unity.

Although no modern groups advocate tritheism, perhaps many evangelicals today unintentionally tend toward tritheistic views of the Trinity, recognizing the distinct personhood of the Father, the Son, and the Holy Spirit, but seldom being aware of the unity of God as one undivided being.

### D. What Are the Distinctions Between the Father, the Son, and the Holy Spirit?

After completing this survey of errors concerning the Trinity, we may now go on to ask if anything more can be said about the distinctions between the Father, Son, and Holy Spirit. If we say that each member of the Trinity is fully God, and that each person fully shares in all the attributes of God, then is there any difference at all among the persons? We cannot say, for example, that the Father is more powerful or wiser than the Son, or that the Father and Son are wiser than the Holy Spirit, or that the Father existed before the Son and Holy Spirit existed, for to say anything like that would be to deny the full deity of all three members of the Trinity. But what then are the distinctions between the persons?

**1. The Persons of the Trinity Have Different Primary Functions in Relating to the World.** When Scripture discusses the way in which God relates to the world, both in creation and in redemption, the persons of the Trinity are said to have different functions or primary activities. Sometimes this has been called the "economy of the Trinity," using *economy* in an old sense meaning "ordering of activities." (In this sense, people used to speak of the "economy of a household" or "home economics," meaning not just the financial affairs of a household, but all of the "ordering of activities" within the household.) The "economy of the Trinity"

---

[30]Bavinck, *The Doctrine of God*, p. 281.
[31]Ibid., p. 285.

means the different ways the three persons act as they relate to the world and (as we shall see in the next section) to each other for all eternity.

We see these different functions in the work of creation. God the Father spoke the creative words to bring the universe into being. But it was God the Son, the eternal Word of God, who carried out these creative decrees. "All things were made through him, and without him was not anything made that was made" (John 1:3). Moreover, "in him all things were created, in heaven and on earth, visible and invisible, whether thrones or dominions or principalities or authorities—all things were created through him and for him" (Col. 1:16; see also Ps. 33:6, 9; 1 Cor. 8:6; Heb. 1:2). The Holy Spirit was active as well in a different way, in "moving" or "hovering" over the face of the waters (Gen. 1:2), apparently sustaining and manifesting God's immediate presence in his creation (cf. Ps. 33:6, where "breath" should perhaps be translated "Spirit"; see also Ps. 139:7).

In the work of redemption there are also distinct functions. God the Father planned redemption and sent his Son into the world (John 3:16; Gal. 4:4; Eph. 1:9–10). The Son obeyed the Father and accomplished redemption for us (John 6:38; Heb. 10:5–7; et al.). God the Father did not come and die for our sins, nor did God the Holy Spirit. That was the particular work of the Son. Then, after Jesus ascended back into heaven, the Holy Spirit was sent by the Father and the Son to apply redemption to us. Jesus speaks of "the Holy Spirit, whom the Father will send in my name" (John 14:26), but also says that he himself will send the Holy Spirit, for he says, "If I go, I will send him to you" (John 16:7), and he speaks of a time "when the Counselor comes, whom I shall send to you from the Father, even the Spirit of truth" (John 15:26). It is especially the role of the Holy Spirit to give us regeneration or new spiritual life (John 3:5–8), to sanctify us (Rom. 8:13; 15:16; 1 Peter 1:2), and to empower us for service (Acts 1:8; 1 Cor. 12:7–11). In general, the work of the Holy Spirit seems to be to bring to completion the work that has been planned by God the Father and begun by God the Son. (See chapter 30, on the work of the Holy Spirit.)

So we may say that the role of the Father in creation and redemption has been to plan and direct and send the Son and Holy Spirit. This is not surprising, for it shows that the Father and the Son relate to one another as a father and son relate to one another in a human family: the father directs and has authority over the son, and the son obeys and is responsive to the directions of the father. The Holy Spirit is obedient to the directives of both the Father and the Son.

Thus, while the persons of the Trinity are equal in all their attributes, they nonetheless differ in their relationships to the creation. The Son and Holy Spirit are equal in deity to God the Father, but they are subordinate in their roles.

Moreover, these differences in role are not temporary but will last forever: Paul tells us that even after the final judgment, when the "last enemy," that is, death, is destroyed and when all things are put under Christ's feet, "then the Son himself will also be subjected to him who put all things under him, that God may be everything to every one" (1 Cor. 15:28).

**2. The Persons of the Trinity Eternally Existed as Father, Son, and Holy Spirit.** But why do the persons of the Trinity take these different roles in relating to creation? Was it accidental or arbitrary? Could God the Father have come instead of God the Son to die for our sins? Could the Holy Spirit have sent God the Father to die for our sins, and then sent God the Son to apply redemption to us?

No, it does not seem that these things could have happened, for the role of commanding, directing, and sending is appropriate to the position of the Father, after whom all human fatherhood is patterned (Eph. 3:14–15). And the role of obeying, going as the Father sends, and revealing God to us is appropriate to the role of the Son, who is also called the Word of God (cf. John 1:1–5, 14, 18; 17:4; Phil. 2:5–11). These roles could not have been reversed or the Father would have ceased to be the Father and the Son would have ceased to be the Son. And by analogy from that relationship, we may conclude that the role of the Holy Spirit is similarly one that was appropriate to the relationship he had with the Father and the Son before the world was created.

Second, before the Son came to earth, and even before the world was created, for all eternity the Father has been the Father, the Son has been the Son, and the Holy Spirit has been the Holy Spirit. These relationships are eternal, not something that occurred only in time. We may conclude this first from the unchangeableness of God (see chapter 11): if God now exists as Father, Son, and Holy Spirit, then he has always existed as Father, Son, and Holy Spirit. We may also conclude that the relationships are eternal from other verses in Scripture that speak of the relationships the members of the Trinity had to one another before the creation of the world. For instance, when Scripture speaks of God's work of election (see chapter 32) before the creation of the world, it speaks of the Father choosing us "in" the Son: "Blessed be the God and Father of our Lord Jesus Christ . . . *he chose us in him before the foundation of the world*, that we should be holy and blameless before him" (Eph. 1:3–4). The initiatory act of choosing is attributed to God the Father, who regards us as united to Christ or "in Christ" before we ever existed. Similarly, of God the Father, it is said that "those whom he foreknew he also predestined to be conformed to the image of his Son" (Rom. 8:29). We also read of the "foreknowledge of God the Father" in distinction from particular functions of the other two members of the Trinity (1 Peter 1:2 NASB; cf. 1:20).[32] Even the fact that the Father "gave his only Son" (John 3:16) and "sent the Son into the world" (John 3:17) indicate that there was a Father-Son relationship before Christ came into the world. The Son did not become the Son when the Father sent him into the world. Rather, the great love of God is shown in the fact that the one who was *always* Father gave the one who was *always* his only Son: "For God so loved the world that he gave his only Son . . ." (John 3:16). "But when the time had fully come, God sent forth his Son" (Gal. 4:4).

When Scripture speaks of creation, once again it speaks of the Father creating *through* the Son, indicating a relationship prior to when creation began (see John 1:3; 1 Cor. 8:6; Heb. 1:2; also Prov. 8:22–31). But nowhere does it say that the Son or Holy Spirit created through the Father. These passages again imply that there was a relationship of Father (as originator) and Son (as active agent) before

---

[32]Another passage that may suggest such a distinction in function is John 17:5: When Jesus asks the Father, "glorify me in your own presence with the glory which I had with you before the world was made" (John 17:5), he suggests that it is the Father's right to give glory to whom he will and that this glory had been given to the Son by the Father because the Father loved the Son before the foundation of the world.

creation, and that this relationship made it appropriate for the different persons of the Trinity to fulfill the roles they actually did fulfill.

Therefore, the different functions that we see the Father, Son, and Holy Spirit performing are simply outworkings of an eternal relationship between the three persons, one that has always existed and will exist for eternity. God has always existed as three distinct persons: Father, Son, and Holy Spirit. These distinctions are essential to the very nature of God himself, and they could not be otherwise.

Finally, it may be said that there are no differences in deity, attributes, or essential nature between the Father, Son, and Holy Spirit. Each person is fully God and has all the attributes of God. *The only distinctions between the members of the Trinity are in the ways they relate to each other and to the rest of creation.* In those relationships they carry out roles that are appropriate to each person.

This truth about the Trinity has sometimes been summarized in the phrase "ontological equality but economic subordination," where the word *ontological* means "being."[33] Another way of expressing this more simply would be to say "equal in being but subordinate in role." Both parts of this phrase are necessary to a true doctrine of the Trinity: If we do not have ontological equality, not all the persons are fully God. But if we do not have economic subordination,[34] then there is no inherent difference in the way the three persons relate to one another, and consequently we do not have the three distinct persons existing as Father, Son, and Holy Spirit for all eternity. For example, if the Son is not eternally subordinate to the Father in role, then the Father is not eternally "Father" and the Son is not eternally "Son." This would mean that the Trinity has not eternally existed.

This is why the idea of eternal equality in being but subordination in role has been essential to the church's doctrine of the Trinity since it was first affirmed in the Nicene Creed, which said that the Son was "begotten of the Father before all ages" and that the Holy Spirit "proceeds from the Father and the Son." Surprisingly, some recent evangelical writings have denied an eternal subordination in role among the members of the Trinity,[35] but it has clearly been part of the

---

[33]See section D.1, above, where *economy* was explained to refer to different activities or roles.

[34]Economic subordination should be carefully distinguished from the error of "subordinationism," which holds that the Son or Holy Spirit are inferior in being to the Father (see section C.2, above, p. 245.)

[35]See, for example, Richard and Catherine Kroeger, in the article "Subordinationism" in *EDT*: They define subordinationism as "a doctrine which assigns an inferiority of being, status, *or role* to the Son or the Holy Spirit within the Trinity. Condemned by numerous church councils, this doctrine has continued in one form or another throughout the history of the church" (p. 1058, emphasis mine). When the Kroegers speak of "inferiority of . . . role" they apparently mean to say that any affirmation of eternal subordination in role belongs to the heresy of subordinationism. But if this is what they are saying, then they are condemning all orthodox Christology from the Nicene Creed onward and thereby condemning a teaching that Charles Hodge says has been a teaching of "the Church universal."

Similarly, Millard Erickson, in his *Christian Theology* (Grand Rapids: Baker, 1983–85), pp. 338 and 698, is willing only to affirm that Christ had a temporary subordination in function for the period of ministry on earth, but nowhere affirms an eternal subordination in role of the Son to the Father or the Holy Spirit to the Father and the Son. (Similarly, his *Concise Dictionary of Christian Theology*, p. 161.)

Robert Letham, in "The Man-Woman Debate: Theological Comment," *WTJ* 52:1 (Spring 1990), pp. 65–78, sees this tendency in recent evangelical writings as the outworking of an evangelical feminist claim that a subordinate role necessarily implies lesser importance or lesser personhood. Of course, if this is not true among members of the Trinity, then it is not necessarily true between husband and wife either.

church's doctrine of the Trinity (in Catholic, Protestant, and Orthodox expressions), at least since Nicea (A.D. 325). So Charles Hodge says:

> The Nicene doctrine includes, (1) the principle of the subordination of the Son to the Father, and of the Spirit to the Father and the Son. But this subordination does not imply inferiority. . . . The subordination intended is only that which concerns the mode of subsistence and operation. . . .
>
> The creeds are nothing more than a well-ordered arrangement of the facts of Scripture which concern the doctrine of the Trinity. They assert the distinct personality of the Father, Son, and Spirit . . . and their consequent perfect equality; and the subordination of the Son to the Father, and of the Spirit to the Father and the Son, as to the mode of subsistence and operation. These are scriptural facts, to which the creeds in question add nothing; *and it is in this sense they have been accepted by the Church universal.*[36]

Similarly, A. H. Strong says:

> Father, Son, and Holy Spirit, while equal in essence and dignity, stand to each other in an order of personality, office, and operation. . . .
>
> The subordination of the *person* of the Son to the *person* of the Father, or in other words an order of personality, office, and operation which permits the Father to be officially first, the Son second, and the Spirit third, is perfectly consistent with equality. Priority is not necessarily superiority. . . . *We frankly recognize an eternal subordination of Christ to the Father,* but we maintain at the same time that this subordination is a subordination of order, office, and operation, not a subordination of essence.[37]

**3. What Is the Relationship Between the Three Persons and the Being of God?** After the preceding discussion, the question that remains unresolved is, What is the difference between "person" and "being" in this discussion? How can we say that God is one undivided being, yet that in this one being there are three persons?

First, it is important to affirm that each person is completely and fully God; that is, that each person has the whole fullness of God's being in himself. The Son is not partly God or just one-third of God, but the Son is wholly and fully God, and so is the Father and the Holy Spirit. Thus, it would not be right to think of the Trinity according to figure 14.1, with each person representing only one-third of God's being.

Rather, we must say that the person of the Father possesses the *whole being* of God in himself. Similarly, the Son possesses the *whole being* of God in himself, and the Holy Spirit possesses the *whole being* of God in himself. When we speak of the Father, Son, and Holy Spirit together we are not speaking of any greater being than when we speak of the Father alone, or the Son alone, or the Holy Spirit alone. The Father is *all* of God's being. The Son also is *all* of God's being. And the Holy Spirit is *all* of God's being.

[36]*Systematic Theology* (3 vols.; Grand Rapids: Eerdmans, 1970 [reprint; first published 1871–73]), 1:460–62 (italics mine).
[37]*Systematic Theology* (Valley Forge, Pa.: Judson, 1907), p. 342 (third italics mine).

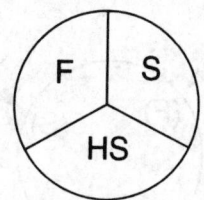

**GOD'S BEING IS NOT DIVIDED INTO THREE EQUAL PARTS
BELONGING TO THE THREE MEMBERS OF THE TRINITY**
*Figure 14.1*

This is what the Athanasian Creed affirmed in the following sentences:

And the Catholic Faith is this: That we worship one God in Trinity, and Trinity in Unity; Neither confounding the Persons: nor dividing the Substance [Essence]. For there is one Person of the Father: another of the Son: and another of the Holy Spirit. But the Godhead of the Father, of the Son, and of the Holy Spirit, is all one: the Glory equal, the Majesty coeternal. Such as the Father is: such is the Son: and such is the Holy Spirit. . . . For like as we are compelled by the Christian verity: to acknowledge every Person by himself to be God and Lord: So are we forbidden by the Catholic Religion: to say, There be [are] three Gods, or three Lords.

But if each person is fully God and has all of God's being, then we also should not think that the personal distinctions are any kind of additional attributes added on to the being of God, something after the pattern of figure 14.2.

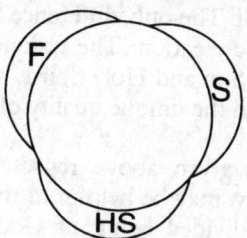

**THE PERSONAL DISTINCTIONS IN THE TRINITY ARE NOT
SOMETHING ADDED ONTO GOD'S REAL BEING**
*Figure 14.2*

Rather, each person of the Trinity has all of the attributes of God, and no one person has any attributes that are not possessed by the others.

On the other hand, we must say that the persons are real, that they are not just different ways of looking at the one being of God. (This would be modalism or Sabellianism, as discussed above.) So figure 14.3 would not be appropriate.

Rather, we need to think of the Trinity in such a way that the reality of the three persons is maintained, and each person is seen as relating to the others as an "I" (a first person) and a "you" (a second person) and a "he" (a third person).

The only way it seems possible to do this is to say that the distinction between

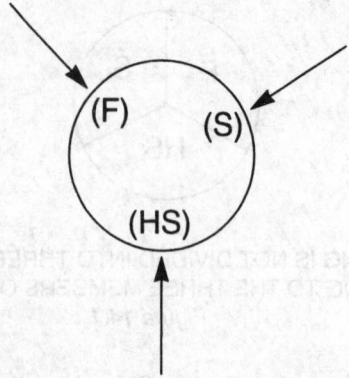

**THE PERSONS OF THE TRINITY ARE NOT JUST THREE DIFFERENT WAYS OF LOOKING AT THE ONE BEING OF GOD**
*Figure 14.3*

the persons is not a difference in "being" but a difference in "relationships." This is something far removed from our human experience, where every different human "person" is a different being as well. Somehow God's being is so much greater than ours that within his one undivided being there can be an unfolding into interpersonal relationships, so that there can be three distinct persons.

What then are the differences between Father, Son, and Holy Spirit? There is no difference in attributes at all. The only difference between them is the way they relate to each other and to the creation. The unique quality of the Father is the way he *relates as Father* to the Son and Holy Spirit. The unique quality of the Son is the way he *relates as Son*. And the unique quality of the Holy Spirit is the way he *relates as Spirit*.[38]

While the three diagrams given above represented erroneous ideas to be avoided, the following diagram may be helpful in thinking about the existence of three persons in the one undivided being of God.

In this diagram, the Father is represented as the section of the circle designated by F, and also the rest of the circle, moving around clockwise from the letter F; the Son is represented as the section of the circle designated by S, and also the rest of the circle, moving around clockwise from the letter S; and the Holy Spirit is represented as the section of the circle marked HS and also the rest of the circle, moving around clockwise from the HS. Thus, there are three distinct persons, but each person is fully and wholly God. Of course the representation is imperfect, for it cannot represent God's infinity, or personality, or indeed any of his attributes. It also requires looking at the circle in more than one way in order to understand it:

---

[38]Some systematic theologies give names to these different relationships: "paternity" (or "generation") for the Father, "begottenness" (or "filiation") for the Son, and "procession" (or "spiration") for the Holy Spirit, but the names do not mean anything more than "relating as a Father," and "relating as a Son," and "relating as Spirit." In an attempt to avoid the proliferation of technical terms that do not exist in contemporary English, or whose meaning differs from their ordinary English sense, I have not used these terms in this chapter.

the dotted lines must be understood to indicate personal relationship, not any division in the one being of God. Thus, the circle itself represents God's being while the dotted lines represent a form of personal existence other than a difference in being. But the diagram may nonetheless help guard against some misunderstanding.

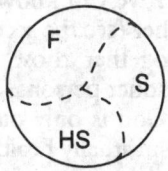

**THERE ARE THREE DISTINCT PERSONS, AND THE BEING OF EACH PERSON IS EQUAL TO THE WHOLE BEING OF GOD**
*Figure 14.4*

Our own human personalities provide another faint analogy that can provide some help in thinking about the Trinity. A man can think about different objects outside of himself, and when he does this he is the subject who does the thinking. He can also think about himself, and then he is the object who is being thought about: then he is both subject and object. Moreover, he can reflect on his ideas about himself as a third thing, neither subject nor object, but *thoughts* that he as a subject has about himself as an object. When this happens, the subject, object, and thoughts are three distinct things. Yet each thing in a way includes his whole being: All of the man is the subject, and all of the man is the object, and the thoughts (though in a lesser sense) are thoughts about all of himself as a person.[39]

But if the unfolding of human personality allows this kind of complexity, then the unfolding of God's personality must allow for far greater complexity than this. Within the one being of God the "unfolding" of personality must allow for the existence of three distinct persons, while each person still has the whole of God's being in himself. The difference in persons must be one of relationship, not one of being, and yet each person must really exist. This tri-personal form of being is far beyond our ability to comprehend. *It is a kind of existence far different from anything we have experienced,* and far different from anything else in the universe.

Because the existence of three persons in one God is something beyond our understanding, Christian theology has come to use the word *person* to speak of these differences in relationship, not because we fully understand what is meant by the word *person* when referring to the Trinity, but rather so that we might say something instead of saying nothing at all.

**4. Can We Understand the Doctrine of the Trinity?** We should be warned by the errors that have been made in the past. They have all come about through

---

[39]We said above that no analogy teaches the Trinity perfectly, and this one has several shortcomings as well: this man remains as one person; he is not three persons. And his "thoughts" do not equal all of him as a person. But the analogy is helpful in hinting at something of the complexity even of human personality and suggesting that the complexity of divine personality is something far greater than this.

attempts to simplify the doctrine of the Trinity and make it completely understandable, removing all mystery from it. This we can never do. However, it is not correct to say that we cannot understand the doctrine of the Trinity at all. Certainly we can understand and know that God is three persons, and that each person is fully God, and that there is one God. We can know these things because the Bible teaches them. Moreover, we can know some things about the way in which the persons relate to each other (see the section above). But what we cannot understand fully is how to fit together those distinct biblical teachings. We wonder how there can be three distinct persons, and each person have the whole being of God in himself, and yet God is only one undivided being. This we are unable to understand. In fact, it is spiritually healthy for us to acknowledge openly that God's very being is far greater than we can ever comprehend. This humbles us before God and draws us to worship him without reservation.

But it should also be said that Scripture does not ask us to believe in a contradiction. A contradiction would be "There is one God and there is not one God," or "God is three persons and God is not three persons," or even (which is similar to the previous statement) "God is three persons and God is one person." But to say that "God is three persons and there is one God" is not a contradiction. It is something we do not understand, and it is therefore a mystery or a paradox, but that should not trouble us as long as the different aspects of the mystery are clearly taught by Scripture, for as long as we are finite creatures and not omniscient deity, there will always (for all eternity) be things that we do not fully understand. Louis Berkhof wisely says:

> The Trinity is a mystery . . . man cannot comprehend it and make it intelligible. It is intelligible in some of its relations and modes of manifestation, but unintelligible in its essential nature. . . . The real difficulty lies in the relation in which the persons in the Godhead stand to the divine essence and to one another; and this is a difficulty which the Church cannot remove, but only try to reduce to its proper proportion by a proper definition of terms. It has never tried to explain the mystery of the Trinity but only sought to formulate the doctrine of the Trinity in such a manner that the errors which endangered it were warded off.[40]

Berkhof also says, "It is especially when we reflect on the relation of the three persons to the divine essence that all analogies fail us and we become deeply conscious of the fact that the Trinity is a mystery far beyond our comprehension. It is the incomprehensible glory of the Godhead."[41]

## E. Application

Because God in himself has both unity and diversity, it is not surprising that unity and diversity are also reflected in the human relationships he has established. We see this first in marriage. When God created man in his own image, he did not create merely isolated individuals, but Scripture tells us, "male and female he created them" (Gen. 1:27). And in the unity of marriage (see Gen. 2:24) we see, not a triunity as with God, but at least a remarkable unity of two persons, persons who remain distinct individuals yet also become one in body, mind, and spirit (cf.

---

[40]Berkhof, *Systematic Theology*, p. 89.
[41]Ibid., p. 88.

1 Cor. 6:16–20; Eph. 5:31). In fact, in the relationship between man and woman in marriage we see also a picture of the relationship between the Father and Son in the Trinity. Paul says, "But I want you to understand that the head of every man is Christ, the head of a woman is her husband, and the head of Christ is God" (1 Cor. 11:3). Here, just as the Father has authority over the Son in the Trinity, so the husband has authority over the wife in marriage. The husband's role is parallel to that of God the Father and the wife's role is parallel to that of God the Son. Moreover, just as Father and Son are equal in deity and importance and personhood, so the husband and wife are equal in humanity and importance and personhood. And, although it is not explicitly mentioned in Scripture, the gift of children within marriage, coming from both the father and the mother, and subject to the authority of both father and mother, is analogous to the relationship of the Holy Spirit to the Father and Son in the Trinity.

But the human family is not the only way in which God has ordained that there would be both diversity and unity in the world that reflect something of his own excellence. In the church we have "many members" yet "one body" (1 Cor. 12:12). Paul reflects on the great diversity among members of the human body (1 Cor. 12:14–26) and says that the church is like that: We have many different members in our churches with different gifts and interests, and we depend on and help each other, thereby demonstrating great diversity and great unity at the same time. When we see different people doing many different things in the life of a church we ought to thank God that this allows us to glorify him by reflecting something of the unity and diversity of the Trinity.

We should also notice that God's purpose in the history of the universe has frequently been to display unity in diversity, and thus to display his glory. We see this not only in the diversity of gifts in the church (1 Cor. 12:12–26), but also in the unity of Jews and Gentiles, so that all races, diverse as they are, are united in Christ (Eph. 2:16; 3:8–10; see also Rev. 7:9). Paul is amazed that God's plans for the history of redemption have been like a great symphony so that his wisdom is beyond finding out (Rom. 11:33–36). Even in the mysterious unity between Christ and the church, in which we are called the bride of Christ (Eph. 5:31–32), we see unity beyond what we ever would have imagined, unity with the Son of God himself. Yet in all this we never lose our individual identity but remain distinct persons always able to worship and serve God as unique individuals.

Eventually the entire universe will partake of this unity of purpose with every diverse part contributing to the worship of God the Father, Son, and Holy Spirit, for one day, at the name of Jesus every knee will bow "in heaven and on earth and under the earth, and every tongue confess that Jesus Christ is Lord, to the glory of God the Father" (Phil. 2:10–11).

On a more everyday level, there are many activities that we carry out as human beings (in the labor force, in social organizations, in musical performances, and in athletic teams, for example) in which many distinct individuals contribute to a unity of purpose or activity. As we see in these activities a reflection of the wisdom of God in allowing us both unity and diversity, we can see a faint reflection of the glory of God in his trinitarian existence. Though we will never fully comprehend the mystery of the Trinity, we can worship God for who he is both in our songs of praise, and in our words and actions as they reflect something of his excellent character.

## QUESTIONS FOR PERSONAL APPLICATION

1. Why is God pleased when people exhibit faithfulness, love, and harmony within a family? What are some ways in which members of your family reflect the diversity found in the members of the Trinity? How does your family reflect the unity found among members of the Trinity? What are some ways in which your family relationships could reflect the unity of the Trinity more fully? How might the diversity of persons in the Trinity encourage parents to allow their children to develop different interests from each other, and from their parents, without thinking that the unity of the family will be damaged?

2. Have you ever thought that if your church allows new or different kinds of ministries to develop, that it might hinder the unity of the church? Or have you thought that encouraging people to use other gifts for ministry than those that have been used in the past might be divisive in the church? How might the fact of unity and diversity in the Trinity help you to approach those questions?

3. Do you think that the trinitarian nature of God is more fully reflected in a church in which all the members have the same racial background, or one in which the members come from many different races (see Eph. 3:1–10)?

4. In addition to our relationships within our families, we all exist in other relationships to human authority in government, in employment, in voluntary societies, in educational institutions, and in athletics, for example. Sometimes we have authority over others, and sometimes we are subject to the authority of others. Whether in the family or one of these other areas, give one example of a way in which your use of authority or your response to authority might become more like the pattern of relationships in the Trinity.

5. If we see the trinitarian existence of God as the fundamental basis for all combinations of unity and diversity in the universe, then what are some other parts of creation that show both unity and diversity (for example: the interdependency of environmental systems on the earth, or the fascinating activity of bees in a hive, or the harmonious working of the various parts of the human body)? Do you think God has made us so that we take spontaneous delight in demonstrations of unity in diversity, such as a musical composition that manifests great unity and yet great diversity of various parts at the same time, or in the skillful execution of some planned strategy by members of an athletic team working together?

6. In the being of God we have infinite unity combined with the preservation of distinct personalities belonging to the members of the Trinity. How can this fact reassure us if we ever begin to fear that becoming more united to Christ as we grow in the Christian life (or becoming more united to one another in the church) might tend to obliterate our individual personalities? In heaven, do you think you will be exactly like everyone else, or will you have a personality that is distinctly your own? How do eastern religions (such as Buddhism) differ from Christianity in this regard?

## SPECIAL TERMS

adoptionism
Arianism
economic subordination
eternal begetting of the Son
eternal generation of the Son
*filioque*
*homoiousios*
*homoousios*

modalism
modalistic monarchianism
only-begotten
ontological equality
Sabellianism
subordinationism
Trinity
tritheism

## BIBLIOGRAPHY

(For an explanation of this bibliography see the note on the bibliography to chapter 1, p. 38. Complete bibliographical data may be found on pp. 1223–29.)

### Sections in Evangelical Systematic Theologies

1. Anglican (Episcopalian)
   - 1882–92   Litton, 91–108
   - 1930   Thomas, 20–31, 90–99
2. Arminian (Wesleyan or Methodist)
   - 1875–76   Pope, 1:253–87; 2:101–5
   - 1892–94   Miley, 1:223–75
   - 1940   Wiley, 1:394–439
   - 1960   Purkiser, 143–44, 199–203
   - 1983   Carter, 1:127–29, 375–414
   - 1983–   Cottrell, 3:117–74
   - 1987–90   Oden, 1:181–224
3. Baptist
   - 1767   Gill, 1:187–245
   - 1887   Boyce, 125–66
   - 1907   Strong, 304–52
   - 1917   Mullins, 203–13
   - 1976–83   Henry, 5:165–213
   - 1983–85   Erickson, 321–42
   - 1987–94   Lewis/Demarest, 1:251–88
4. Dispensational
   - 1947   Chafer, 1:272–347; 5:7–38; 6:7–46
   - 1949   Thiessen, 89–99
   - 1986   Ryrie, 51–59
5. Lutheran
   - 1917–24   Pieper, 1:381–404
   - 1934   Mueller, 147–60
6. Reformed (or Presbyterian)

|         |                                                       |
|---------|-------------------------------------------------------|
| 1559    | Calvin, 1:120–59 (1.13)                               |
| 1861    | Heppe, 105–32                                          |
| 1871–73 | Hodge, 1:442–534                                       |
| 1878    | Dabney, 174–211                                        |
| 1887–1921 | Warfield, *BTS*, 22–156; *SSW*, 1:88–92; *BD*, 133–74 |
| 1889    | Shedd, 1:249–332                                       |
| 1937–66 | Murray, *CW*, 4:58–81                                  |
| 1938    | Berkhof, 82–99                                         |
| 1962    | Buswell, 1:103–29                                      |

7. Renewal (or charismatic/Pentecostal)

|         |                     |
|---------|---------------------|
| 1988–92 | Williams, 1:83–94   |

## Sections in Representative Roman Catholic Systematic Theologies

1. Roman Catholic: Traditional

|      |              |
|------|--------------|
| 1955 | Ott, 50–75   |

2. Roman Catholic: Post-Vatican II

|      |                   |
|------|-------------------|
| 1980 | McBrien, 1:343–66 |

## Other Works

Augustine. *On the Trinity*. NPNF, First Series, 3:1–228. (This is considered the most thorough development of the orthodox doctrine of the Trinity in the history of the church.)

Bavinck, Herman. *The Doctrine of God*. Trans. by William Hendriksen (Edinburgh and Carlisle, Pa.: Banner of Truth, 1977 [reprint of 1951 edition]), pp. 255–334. (This is one of the most thorough modern discussions of the Trinity.)

Beisner, Calvin. *God in Three Persons*. Wheaton, Ill.: Tyndale Press, 1984.

Bickersteth, Edward H. *The Trinity*. Grand Rapids: Kregel, 1957 reprint.

Bloesch, Donald G. *The Battle for the Trinity: The Debate Over Inclusive God-Language*. Ann Arbor, Mich.: Servant, 1985.

Bowman, Robert M., Jr. *Why You Should Believe in the Trinity: An Answer to Jehovah's Witnesses*. Grand Rapids: Baker, 1989.

Bray, G. L. "Trinity." In *NDT*, pp. 691–94.

———. "Tritheism." In *NDT*, p. 694.

Brown, Harold O. J. *Heresies: The Image of Christ in the Mirror of Heresy and Orthodoxy From the Apostles to the Present*. Garden City, N.Y.: Doubleday, 1984, pp. 95–157.

Davis, Stephen T. *Logic and the Nature of God*. Grand Rapids: Eerdmans, 1983, pp. 132–44.

Gruenler, Royce Gordon. *The Trinity in the Gospel of John*. Grand Rapids: Baker, 1986.

Harris, Murray. *Jesus as God*. Grand Rapids: Baker, 1992.

Kaiser, Christopher B. *The Doctrine of God: An Historical Survey*. Westchester, Ill.: Crossway, 1982, pp. 23–71.

McGrath, Alister E. *Understanding the Trinity*. Grand Rapids: Zondervan, 1988.

Mikolaski, S. J. "The Triune God." In *Fundamentals of the Faith*. Ed. by C. F. H. Henry. Grand Rapids: Zondervan, 1969, pp. 59–76.

Packer, J. I. "God." *NDT,* 274–77.

———. *Knowing God*. Downers Grove, Ill.: InterVarsity Press, 1973, pp. 57–63.

Wright, D. F. "Augustine." In *NDT,* pp. 58–61.

## SCRIPTURE MEMORY PASSAGE

**Matthew 3:16–17:** *And when Jesus was baptized, he went up immediately from the water, and behold, the heavens were opened and he saw the Spirit of God descending like a dove, and alighting on him; and lo, a voice from heaven, saying, "This is my beloved Son, with whom I am well pleased."*

## HYMN

"Holy, Holy, Holy"

Holy, holy, holy, Lord God Almighty!
  Early in the morning our song shall rise to thee;
Holy, holy, holy! Merciful and mighty!
  God in three persons, blessed Trinity!

Holy, holy, holy! All the saints adore thee,
  Casting down their golden crowns around the glassy sea;
Cherubim and seraphim falling down before thee,
  Who wert, and art, and evermore shalt be.

Holy, holy, holy! Though the darkness hide thee,
  Though the eye of sinful man thy glory may not see,
Only thou art holy; there is none beside thee
  Perfect in pow'r, in love, and purity.

Holy, holy, holy! Lord God Almighty!
  All thy works shall praise thy name, in earth and sky and sea;
Holy, holy, holy! Merciful and mighty!
  God in three persons, blessed Trinity!

AUTHOR: REGINALD HEBER, 1826

# Chapter 15

# Creation

*Why, how, and when did God create the universe?*

## EXPLANATION AND SCRIPTURAL BASIS[1]

How did God create the world? Did he create every different kind of plant and animal directly, or did he use some kind of evolutionary process, guiding the development of living things from the simplest to the most complex? And how quickly did God bring about creation? Was it all completed within six twenty-four-hour days, or did he use thousands or perhaps millions of years? How old is the earth, and how old is the human race?

These questions face us when we deal with the doctrine of creation. Unlike most of the earlier material in this book, this chapter treats several questions on which evangelical Christians have differing viewpoints, sometimes very strongly held ones.

This chapter is organized to move from those aspects of creation that are most clearly taught in Scripture, and on which almost all evangelicals would agree (creation out of nothing, special creation of Adam and Eve, and the goodness of the universe), to other aspects of creation about which evangelicals have had disagreements (whether God used a process of evolution to bring about much of creation, and how old the earth and the human race are).

We may define the doctrine of creation as follows: *God created the entire universe out of nothing; it was originally very good; and he created it to glorify himself.*

## A. God Created the Universe Out of Nothing

**1. Biblical Evidence for Creation Out of Nothing.** The Bible clearly requires us to believe that God created the universe out of nothing. (Sometimes the Latin phrase *ex nihilo*, "out of nothing" is used; it is then said that the Bible teaches creation *ex nihilo*.) This means that before God began to create the universe, nothing else existed except God himself.[2]

---

[1] I am grateful for many helpful comments on this chapter made by friends with specialized knowledge about some aspects of it, especially Steve Figard, Doug Brandt, and Terry Mortenson.

[2] When we say that the universe was created "out of nothing," it is important to guard against a possible misunderstanding. The word *nothing* does not imply some kind of existence, as some philosophers have taken it to mean. We mean rather that God did not use any previously existing materials when he created the universe.

This is the implication of Genesis 1:1, which says, "In the beginning God created the heavens and the earth." The phrase "the heavens and the earth" includes the entire universe. Psalm 33 also tells us, "By the word of the LORD the heavens were made, and all their host by the breath of his mouth. . . . For he spoke, and it came to be; he commanded, and it stood forth" (Ps. 33:6, 9). In the New Testament, we find a universal statement at the beginning of John's gospel: "*All things* were made through him, and without him was not anything made that was made" (John 1:3). The phrase "all things" is best taken to refer to the entire universe (cf. Acts 17:24; Heb. 11:3). Paul is quite explicit in Colossians 1 when he specifies all the parts of the universe, both visible and invisible things: "For in him *all things* were created, in heaven and on earth, *visible and invisible,* whether thrones or dominions or principalities or authorities—all things were created through him and for him" (Col. 1:16). The song of the twenty-four elders in heaven likewise affirms this truth:

> "You are worthy, our Lord and God,
> to receive glory and honor and power,
> for you created *all things,*
> and by your will they existed and were created." (Rev. 4:11)

In the last phrase God's will is said to be the reason why things even "existed" at all and why they "were created."

That God created both the heavens and the earth and everything in them is affirmed several other times in the New Testament. For instance, Acts 4:24 speaks of God as the "Sovereign Lord, who made *the heaven and the earth and the sea and everything in them.*" One of the first ways of identifying God is to say that he is the one who created all things. Barnabas and Paul explain to the pagan audience at Lystra that they are messengers of "a living God who made the heaven and the earth and the sea and all that is in them" (Acts 14:15). Similarly, when Paul is speaking to pagan Greek philosophers in Athens, he identifies the true God as "The God who made the world and everything in it" and says that this God "gives to all men life and breath and everything" (Acts 17:24–25; cf. Isa. 45:18; Rev. 10:6).

Hebrews 11:3 says, "By faith we understand that the worlds were prepared by the word of God, so that what is seen was not made out of things which are visible" (NASB). This translation (as well as the NIV) most accurately reflects the Greek text.[3] Though the text does not quite teach the doctrine of creation out of nothing, it comes close to doing so, since it says that God did not create the universe out of anything that is visible. The somewhat strange idea that the universe might have been created out of something that was invisible is probably not in the author's mind. He is contradicting the idea of creation out of previously existing matter, and for that purpose the verse is quite clear.

Romans 4:17 also implies that God created out of nothing, even if it does not

---

[3]The RSV translation ("so that what is seen was made out of things which do not appear") apparently affirms that God made the universe out of invisible matter of some sort, but the word order of the Greek text (*mē ek phainomenōn*) shows that the word "not" negates the phrase "out of appearing things." The RSV translation reads as if the word "not" negated the participle "appearing," but it would need to appear immediately before it in order to do that. See discussion in Philip Hughes, *A Commentary on the Epistle to the Hebrews* (Grand Rapids: Eerdmans, 1977), pp. 443–52.

exactly state it. The Greek text literally speaks of God as one who "calls things not existing as existing." The RSV translation, "calls into existence the things that do not exist" (similarly NASB) is unusual but possible grammatically,[4] and it makes an explicit affirmation of creation out of nothing. Yet even if we translate it so that the Greek word *hos* takes its common sense "as," the verse says that God "calls the things which do not exist as existing" (NASB mg.). But if God speaks to or calls something that does not exist, as if in fact it did exist, then what is implied? If he calls things that do not exist as though they existed, it must mean that they will soon exist, irresistibly called into existence.

Because God created the entire universe out of nothing there is no matter in the universe that is eternal. All that we see—the mountains, the oceans, the stars, the earth itself—all came into existence when God created them. There was a time when they did not exist:

> "Before the mountains were brought forth,
> or ever you had formed the earth and the world,
> from everlasting to everlasting you are God." (Ps. 90:2)

This reminds us that God rules over all the universe and that nothing in creation is to be worshiped instead of God or in addition to him. However, were we to deny creation out of nothing, we would have to say that some matter has always existed and that it is eternal like God. This idea would challenge God's independence, his sovereignty, and the fact that worship is due to him alone: if matter existed apart from God, then what inherent right would God have to rule over it and use it for his glory? And what confidence could we have that every aspect of the universe will ultimately fulfill God's purposes, if some parts of it were not created by him?

The positive side of the fact that God created the universe out of nothing is that it has meaning and a purpose. God, in his wisdom, created it for something. We should try to understand that purpose and use creation in ways that fit that purpose, namely, to bring glory to God himself.[5] Moreover, whenever the creation brings us joy (cf. 1 Tim. 6:17), we should give thanks to the God who made it all.

**2. The Creation of the Spiritual Universe.** This creation of the entire universe includes the creation of an unseen, spiritual realm of existence: God created the angels and other kinds of heavenly beings as well as animals and man. He also created heaven as a place where his presence is especially evident. The creation of the spiritual realm is certainly implied in all the verses above that speak of God creating not only the earth but also "heaven and what is in it" (Rev. 10:6; cf. Acts 4:24), but it is also explicitly affirmed in a number of other verses. The prayer of Ezra says very clearly: "You are the LORD, you alone; you have made heaven, the heaven of heavens, with all their host, the earth and all that is on it, the seas and all that is in them; and you preserve all of them; and the host of heaven worships you" (Neh. 9:6). The "host of heaven" in this verse seems to refer to the angels and other heavenly creatures, since Ezra says that they engage in the activity of

---

[4] See C. E. B. Cranfield, *A Critical and Exegetical Commentary on the Epistle to the Romans,* ICC, vol. 1 (Edinburgh: T. & T. Clark, 1975), p. 244: Greek *hos* as expressing consequence.
[5] See section C below (pp. 271–72) on God's purpose for creation.

worshiping God (the same term *host* is used to speak of angels who worship God in Ps. 103:21 and 148:2).[6]

In the New Testament, Paul specifies that in Christ "all things were created, in heaven and on earth, visible *and invisible,* whether thrones or dominions or principalities or authorities—all things were created through him and for him" (Col. 1:16; cf. Ps. 148:2–5). Here the creation of invisible heavenly beings is also explicitly affirmed.

**3. The Direct Creation of Adam and Eve.** The Bible also teaches that God created Adam and Eve in a special, personal way. "The LORD God formed man of dust from the ground, and breathed into his nostrils the breath of life; and man became a living being" (Gen. 2:7). After that, God created Eve from Adam's body: "So the LORD God caused a deep sleep to fall upon the man, and while he slept took one of his ribs and closed up its place with flesh; and the rib which the LORD God had taken from the man he made into a woman and brought her to the man" (Gen. 2:21–22). God apparently let Adam know something of what had happened, for Adam said,

> "This at last is bone of my bones
>     and flesh of my flesh;
> she shall be called Woman,
>     because she was taken out of Man." (Gen. 2:23)

As we shall see below, Christians differ on the extent to which evolutionary developments may have occurred after creation, perhaps (according to some) leading to the development of more and more complex organisms. While there are sincerely held differences on that question among some Christians with respect to the plant and animal kingdoms, these texts are so explicit that it would be very difficult for someone to hold to the complete truthfulness of Scripture and still hold that human beings are the result of a long evolutionary process. This is because when Scripture says that the Lord "formed man of dust from the ground" (Gen. 2:7), it does not seem possible to understand that to mean that he did it over a process that took millions of years and employed the random development of thousands of increasingly complex organisms.[7] Even more impossible to reconcile with an evolutionary view is the fact that this narrative clearly portrays Eve as having no female parent: she was created directly from Adam's rib while Adam slept (Gen. 2:21). But on a purely evolutionary view, this would not be possible, for even the very first female "human being" would have been descended from some merely human creature that was still an animal. The New Testament reaffirms the historicity of this special creation of Eve from Adam when Paul says,

---

[6]The word translated "host" (Heb. *tsābā'*) is sometimes used to refer to the planets and stars (Deut. 4:19; Isa. 34:4; 40:26), but none of the examples cited in BDB, p. 839 (1.c) speak of the stars worshiping God, and most speak of the heavenly bodies as "the host of heaven" who are wrongly worshiped by pagans (Deut. 17:3; 2 Kings 17:16; 21:3; Jer. 8:2; et al.).

[7]In spite of this explicit statement in Gen. 2:7, Derek Kidner (who holds a view of the truthfulness of Scripture compatible with that advocated in this book), does advocate the possibility of evolutionary development of a long line of pre-Adamite creatures into one of whom God finally "breathed human life" (*Genesis: An Introduction and Commentary,* TOTC [London and Chicago: InterVarsity Press, 1967], p. 28). But he then affirms a special creation of Eve (p. 29).

"For man was not made from woman, but *woman from man*. Neither was man created for woman, but woman for man" (1 Cor. 11:8–9).

The special creation of Adam and Eve shows that, though we may be like animals in many respects in our physical bodies, nonetheless we are very different from animals. We are created "in God's image," the pinnacle of God's creation, more like God than any other creature, appointed to rule over the rest of creation. Even the brevity of the Genesis account of creation places a wonderful emphasis on the importance of man in distinction from the rest of the universe. It thus resists modern tendencies to see man as meaningless against the immensity of the universe. Derek Kidner notes that Scripture stands

> against every tendency to empty human history of meaning. . . . in presenting the tremendous acts of creation as a mere curtain-raiser to the drama that slowly unfolds throughout the length of the Bible. The prologue is over in a page; there are a thousand to follow.

By contrast, Kidner notes that the modern scientific account of the universe, true though it may be,

> overwhelms us with statistics that reduce our apparent significance to a vanishing-point. Not the prologue, but the human story itself, is now the single page in a thousand, and the whole terrestrial volume is lost among uncataloged millions.[8]

Scripture gives us the perspective on human significance that God intends us to have. (This fact will be discussed in more detail in chapter 21, below.)

**4. The Creation of Time.** One other aspect of God's creation is the creation of time (the succession of moments one after another). This idea was discussed with respect to God's attribute of eternity in chapter 11,[9] and we need only summarize it here. When we speak of God's existence "before" the creation of the world, we should not think of God as existing in an unending extension of time. Rather, God's eternity means that he has a different kind of existence, an existence without the passage of time, a kind of existence that is difficult for us even to imagine. (See Job 36:26; Ps. 90:2, 4; John 8:58; 2 Peter 3:8; Rev. 1:8). The fact that God created time reminds us of his lordship over it and our obligation to use it for his glory.

**5. The Work of the Son and of the Holy Spirit in Creation.** God the Father was the primary agent in initiating the act of creation. But the Son and the Holy Spirit were also active. The Son is often described as the one "through" whom creation came about. "All things were made *through* him, and without him was not anything made that was made" (John 1:3). Paul says there is "one Lord, Jesus Christ, *through* whom are all things and *through* whom we exist" (1 Cor. 8:6), and, "all things were created *through* him and for him" (Col. 1:16). We read also that the Son is the one "through whom" God "created the world" (Heb. 1:2). These passages give a consistent picture of the Son as the active agent carrying out the plans and directions of the Father.

---

[8]Kidner, *Genesis*, p. 57.
[9]See p. 169.

The Holy Spirit was also at work in creation. He is generally pictured as completing, filling, and giving life to God's creation. In Genesis 1:2, "the Spirit of God was moving over the face of the waters," indicating a preserving, sustaining, governing function. Job says, "The spirit of God has made me, and the breath of the Almighty gives me life" (Job 33:4). In a number of Old Testament passages, it is important to realize that the same Hebrew word (*rûach*) can mean, in different contexts, "spirit," or "breath," or "wind." But in many cases there is not much difference in meaning, for even if one decided to translate some phrases as the "breath of God" or even the "wind of God," it would still seem to be a figurative way of referring to the activity of the Holy Spirit in creation. So the psalmist, in speaking of the great variety of creatures on the earth and in the sea, says, "When you send forth your Spirit, they are created" (Ps. 104:30; note also, on the Holy Spirit's work, Job 26:13; Isa. 40:13; 1 Cor. 2:10). However, the testimony of Scripture to the specific activity of the Holy Spirit in creation is scarce. The work of the Holy Spirit is brought into much greater prominence in connection with the inspiring of the authors of Scripture and the applying of Christ's redemptive work to the people of God.[10]

## B. Creation Is Distinct From God Yet Always Dependent on God

The teaching of Scripture about the relationship between God and creation is unique among the religions of the world. The Bible teaches that God is distinct from his creation. He is not part of it, for he has made it and rules over it. The term often used to say that God is much greater than creation is the word *transcendent*. Very simply, this means that God is far "above" the creation in the sense that he is greater than the creation and he is independent of it.

God is also very much involved in creation, for it is continually dependent on him for its existence and its functioning. The technical term used to speak of God's involvement in creation is the word *immanent*, meaning "remaining in" creation. The God of the Bible is no abstract deity removed from, and uninterested in his creation. The Bible is the story of God's involvement with his creation, and particularly the people in it. Job affirms that even the animals and plants depend on God: "In his hand is the life of every living thing and the breath of all mankind" (Job 12:10). In the New Testament, Paul affirms that God "gives to all men life and breath and everything" and that "in him we live and move and have our being" (Acts 17:25, 28). Indeed, in Christ "all things hold together" (Col. 1:17), and he is continually "upholding the universe by his word of power" (Heb. 1:3). God's transcendence and immanence are both affirmed in a single verse when Paul speaks of "one God and Father of us all, who is above all and through all and in all" (Eph. 4:6).

The fact that creation is distinct from God yet always dependent on God, that God is far above creation yet always involved in it (in brief, that God is both transcendent and immanent), may be represented as in figure 15.1.

This is clearly distinct from *materialism*, which is the most common philosophy of unbelievers today, and which denies the existence of God altogether.

---

[10]See chapter 30, pp. 637–56, on the work of the Holy Spirit.

Materialism would say that the material universe is all there is. It may be
represented as in figure 15.2.

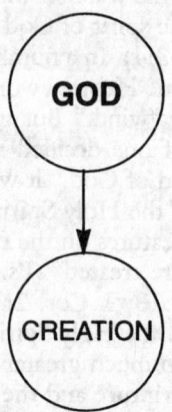

**CREATION IS DISTINCT FROM GOD YET ALWAYS DEPENDENT ON GOD
(GOD IS BOTH TRANSCENDENT AND IMMANENT)**
*Figure 15.1*

Christians today who focus almost the entire effort of their lives on earning
more money and acquiring more possessions become "practical" materialists in
their activity, since their lives would be not much different if they did not believe
in God at all.

**MATERIALISM**
*Figure 15.2*

The scriptural account of God's relation to his creation is also distinct from
pantheism. The Greek word *pan* means "all" or "every," and *pantheism* is the idea
that everything, the whole universe, is God, or is part of God. This can be
pictured as in figure 15.3.

Pantheism denies several essential aspects of God's character. If the whole
universe is God, then God has no distinct personality. God is no longer
unchanging, because as the universe changes, God also changes. Moreover, God is
no longer holy, because the evil in the universe is also part of God. Another
difficulty is that ultimately most pantheistic systems (such as Buddhism and many
other eastern religions) end up denying the importance of individual human

personalities: since everything is God, the goal of an individual should be to blend in with the universe and become more and more united with it, thus losing his or her individual distinctiveness. If God himself (or itself) has no distinct personal identity separate from the universe, then we should certainly not strive to have one either. Thus, pantheism destroys not only the personal identity of God, but also, ultimately, of human beings as well.

**PANTHEISM**
*Figure 15.3*

Any philosophy that sees creation as an "emanation" out of God (that is, something that comes out of God but is still part of God and not distinct from him) would be similar to pantheism in most or all of the ways in which aspects of God's character are denied.

The biblical account also rules out *dualism.* This is the idea that both God and the material universe have eternally existed side by side. Thus, there are two ultimate forces in the universe, God and matter. This may be represented as in figure 15.4.

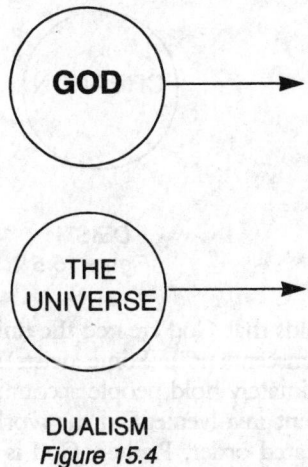

**DUALISM**
*Figure 15.4*

The problem with dualism is that it indicates an eternal conflict between God and the evil aspects of the material universe. Will God ultimately triumph over evil in the universe? We cannot be sure, because both God and evil have apparently always existed side by side. This philosophy would deny both God's ultimate lordship over creation and also that creation came about because of God's will, that it is to be used solely for his purposes, and that it is to glorify him. This viewpoint would also deny that all of the universe was created inherently good (Gen. 1:31) and would encourage people to view material reality as somewhat evil in itself, in contrast with a genuine biblical account of a creation that God made to be good and that he rules over for his purposes.

One recent example of dualism in modern culture is the series of *Star Wars* movies, which postulate the existence of a universal "Force" that has both a good and an evil side. There is no concept of one holy and transcendent God who rules over all and will certainly triumph over all. When non-Christians today begin to be aware of a spiritual aspect to the universe, they often become dualists, merely acknowledging that there are good and evil aspects to the supernatural or spiritual world. Most "New Age" religion is dualistic. Of course, Satan is delighted to have people think that there is an evil force in the universe that is perhaps equal to God himself.

The Christian view of creation is also distinct from the viewpoint of *deism*. Deism is the view that God is not now directly involved in the creation. It may be represented as in figure 15.5.

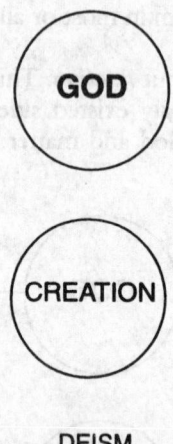

DEISM
*Figure 15.5*

Deism generally holds that God created the universe and is far greater than the universe (God is "transcendent"). Some deists also agree that God has moral standards and will ultimately hold people accountable on a day of judgment. But they deny God's present involvement in the world, thus leaving no place for his immanence in the created order. Rather, God is viewed as a divine clock maker who wound up the "clock" of creation at the beginning but then left it to run on its own.

While deism does affirm God's transcendence in some ways, it denies almost the entire history of the Bible, which is the history of God's active involvement in the world. Many "lukewarm" or nominal Christians today are, in effect, practical deists, since they live lives almost totally devoid of genuine prayer, worship, fear of God, or moment-by-moment trust in God to care for needs that arise.

## C. God Created the Universe to Show His Glory

It is clear that God created his people for his own glory, for he speaks of his sons and daughters as those "whom I created *for my glory,* whom I formed and made" (Isa. 43:7). But it is not only human beings that God created for this purpose. The entire creation is intended to show God's glory. Even the inanimate creation, the stars and sun and moon and sky, testify to God's greatness, "The heavens are telling the glory of God; and the firmament proclaims his handiwork. Day to day pours forth speech, and night to night declares knowledge" (Ps. 19:1–2). The song of heavenly worship in Revelation 4 connects God's creation of all things with the fact that he is worthy to receive glory from them:

> "You are worthy, our Lord and God,
>     to receive glory and honor and power,
> for you have created all things,
>     and by your will they existed and were created." (Rev. 4:11)

What does creation show about God? Primarily it shows his great power and wisdom, far above anything that could be imagined by any creature.[11] "It is he who made the earth by his power, who established the world by his wisdom, and by his understanding stretched out the heavens" (Jer. 10:12). In contrast to ignorant men and the "worthless" idols they make, Jeremiah says, "Not like these is he who is the portion of Jacob, for he is the one who formed all things . . . the LORD of hosts is his name" (Jer. 10:16). One glance at the sun or the stars convinces us of God's infinite power. And even a brief inspection of any leaf on a tree, or of the wonder of the human hand, or of any one living cell, convinces us of God's great wisdom. Who could make all of this? Who could make it out of nothing? Who could sustain it day after day for endless years? Such infinite power, such intricate skill, is completely beyond our comprehension. When we meditate on it, we give glory to God.

When we affirm that God created the universe to show his glory, it is important that we realize that he did not need to create it. We should not think that God needed more glory than he had within the Trinity for all eternity, or that he was somehow incomplete without the glory that he would receive from the created universe. This would be to deny God's independence and imply that God needed the universe in order to be fully God.[12] Rather, we must affirm that the creation of the universe was a *totally free act of God.* It was not a necessary act but something that God chose to do. "You created all things, and *by your will* they existed and were created" (Rev. 4:11). God desired to create the universe to demonstrate his excellence. The creation shows his great wisdom and power, and ultimately it shows all of his other attributes as well.[13] It seems that God created the universe,

---

[11]See chapter 7, pp. 119–23, for a discussion of the necessity of Scripture if we are to interpret creation rightly.

[12]See the discussion of God's independence in chapter 11, pp. 160–63.

[13]See the discussion in chapter 11, pp. 158–60, on the ways in which all of creation reveals various aspects of God's character.

then, to take delight in his creation, for as creation shows forth various aspects of God's character, to that extent he takes delight in it.

This explains why we take spontaneous delight in all sorts of creative activities ourselves. People with artistic or musical or literary skills enjoy creating things and seeing, hearing, or pondering their creative work. God has so made us to enjoy imitating, in a creaturely way, his creative activity. And one of the amazing aspects of humanity—in distinction from the rest of creation—is our ability to create new things. This also explains why we take delight in other kinds of "creative" activity: many people enjoy cooking, or decorating their home, or working with wood or other materials, or producing scientific inventions, or devising new solutions to problems in industrial production. Even children enjoy coloring pictures or building houses out of blocks. In all of these activities we reflect in small measure the creative activity of God, and we should delight in it and thank him for it.

## D. The Universe God Created Was "Very Good"

This point follows from the previous point. If God created the universe to show his glory, then we would expect that the universe would fulfill the purpose for which he created it. In fact, when God finished his work of creation, he did take delight in it. At the end of each stage of creation God saw that what he had done was "good" (Gen. 1:4, 10, 12, 18, 21, 25). Then at the end of the six days of creation, "God saw everything that he had made, and behold, it was very good" (Gen. 1:31). God delighted in the creation that he had made, just as he had purposed to do.

Even though there is now sin in the world, the material creation is still good in God's sight and should be seen as "good" by us as well. This knowledge will free of us from a false asceticism that sees the use and enjoyment of the material creation as wrong. Paul says that those who "forbid marriage," and "enjoin abstinence from foods which God created to be received with thanksgiving by those who believe and know the truth" (1 Tim. 4:1–3) are giving heed to "doctrines of demons." The apostle takes such a firm line because he understands that "everything created by God is good, and nothing is to be rejected if it is received with thanksgiving; for then it is consecrated by the word of God and prayer" (1 Tim. 4:4–5). Paul's mention of "the word of God" that consecrates or "sanctifies" the foods and other things we enjoy in the material creation is probably a reference to the blessing of God spoken in Genesis 1:31, "It was very good."

Though the created order can be used in sinful or selfish ways and can turn our affections away from God, nonetheless we must not let the danger of the abuse of God's creation keep us from a positive, thankful, joyful use of it for our own enjoyment and for the good of his kingdom. Shortly after Paul has warned against the desire to be rich and the "love of money" (1 Tim. 6:9–10), he affirms that it is God himself "who richly furnishes us with everything to enjoy" (1 Tim. 6:17). This fact gives warrant for Christians to encourage proper industrial and technological development (together with care for the environment), and joyful and thankful use of all the products of the abundant earth that God has created—both by ourselves and by those with whom we are to share generously of our possessions (note 1 Tim. 6:18). Yet in all of this we are to remember that material possessions are only temporary, not eternal. We are to set our hopes on God (see Ps. 62:10; 1 Tim. 6:17) and on receiving a kingdom that cannot be shaken (Col. 3:1–4; Heb. 12:28; 1 Peter 1:4).

## E. The Relationship Between Scripture and the Findings of Modern Science

At various times in history, Christians have found themselves dissenting from the accepted findings of contemporary science. In the vast majority of cases, sincere Christian faith and strong trust in the Bible have led scientists to the discovery of new facts about God's universe, and these discoveries have changed scientific opinion for all of subsequent history. The lives of Isaac Newton, Galileo Galilei, Johannes Kepler, Blaise Pascal, Robert Boyle, Michael Faraday, James Clerk Maxwell, and many others are examples of this.[14]

On the other hand, there have been times when accepted scientific opinion has been in conflict with people's understanding of what the Bible said. For example, when the Italian astronomer Galileo (1564–1642) began to teach that the earth was not the center of the universe but that the earth and other planets revolved around the sun (thus following the theories of the Polish astronomer Copernicus [1472–1543]), he was criticized, and eventually his writings were condemned by the Roman Catholic Church. This was because many people thought that the Bible taught that the sun revolved about the earth. In fact, the Bible does not teach that at all, but it was Copernican astronomy that made people look again at Scripture to see if it really taught what they thought it taught. In fact, descriptions of the sun rising and setting (Eccl. 1:5; et al.) merely portray events as they appear from the perspective of the human observer, and, from that perspective, they give an accurate description. But they imply nothing about the relative motion of the earth and the sun, and nowhere does the Bible explain what makes the sun go "down" in the viewpoint of a human observer. Scripture says nothing at all about whether the earth or the sun or some other body is the "center" of the universe or the solar system—that is not a question Scripture addresses. Yet the lesson of Galileo, who was forced to recant his teachings and who had to live under house arrest for the last few years of his life, should remind us that careful observation of the natural world can cause us to go back to Scripture and reexamine whether Scripture actually teaches what we think it teaches. Sometimes, on closer examination of the text, we may find that our previous interpretations were incorrect.

Scientific investigation has helped Christians reevaluate what earlier generations thought about the age of the earth, for example, so that no evangelical scholar today would hold that the world was created in 4004 B.C. Yet that date was once widely believed to be the date of the creation because of the writings of Irish Archbishop James Ussher (1581–1656), one of the great scholars of his day, who carefully added together the dates in the genealogies of the Bible to find when Adam was created. Today it is widely acknowledged that the Bible does not tell us the precise date of the creation of the earth or of the human race (see below).

[14]See August J. Kling, "Men of Science/ Men of Faith," *HIS*, May 1976, pp. 26–31, for a brief survey of the life and work of several of these scientists.

On the other hand, many people in the Christian community have steadfastly refused to agree with the dominant opinion of scientists today regarding evolution. On this matter, thousands of Christians have examined Scripture again and again in great detail, and many have concluded that Scripture is not silent on the process by which living organisms came into being. Moreover, careful observation of the facts of the created universe has produced widespread disagreement regarding theories of evolution (both from scientists who are Christians and from a number of non-Christian scientists as well).[15] So on both biblical and scientific grounds, theories of evolution have been challenged by Christians.

We should also remember that the question of the creation of the universe is unlike many other scientific questions because creation is not something that can be repeated in a laboratory experiment, nor were there any human observers of it. Therefore pronouncements by scientists about creation and the early history of the earth are at best educated speculation. If we are convinced, however, that the only observer of these events (God himself) has told us about them in the reliable words of the Bible, then we should pay careful attention to the biblical account.

In the following section, we have listed some principles by which the relationship between creation and the findings of modern science can be approached.

**1. When All the Facts Are Rightly Understood, There Will Be "No Final Conflict" Between Scripture and Natural Science.** The phrase "no final conflict" is taken from a very helpful book by Francis Schaeffer, *No Final Conflict*.[16] Regarding questions about the creation of the universe, Schaeffer lists several areas where, in his judgment, there is room for disagreement among Christians who believe in the total truthfulness of Scripture:

1. There is a possibility that God created a "grown-up" universe.
2. There is a possibility of a break between Genesis 1:1 and 1:2 or between 1:2 and 1:3.
3. There is a possibility of a long day in Genesis 1.
4. There is a possibility that the flood affected the geological data.
5. The use of the word "kinds" in Genesis 1 may be quite broad.
6. There is a possibility of the death of animals before the fall.
7. Where the Hebrew word *bārā'* is not used there is the possibility of sequence from previously existing things.[17]

Schaeffer makes clear that he is not saying that any of those positions is his own; only that they are theoretically possible. Schaeffer's major point is that in both our understanding of the natural world and our understanding of Scripture, our knowledge is not perfect. But we can approach both scientific and biblical study with the confidence that when all the facts are correctly understood, and when we

[15]For analysis of the increasingly large body of scientific evidence against evolution, see especially the books by Michael Denton and Philip E. Johnson cited in the bibliography to this chapter and discussed on pp. 280–84 below.
[16]Downers Grove, Ill.: InterVarsity Press, 1975.
[17]Ibid., pp. 25–33.

have understood Scripture rightly, our findings will never be in conflict with each other: there will be "no final conflict." This is because God, who speaks in Scripture, knows all facts, and he has not spoken in a way that would contradict any true fact in the universe.

This is a very helpful perspective with which the Christian should begin any study of creation and modern science. We should not fear to investigate scientifically the facts of the created world but should do so eagerly and with complete honesty, confident that when facts are rightly understood, they will always turn out to be consistent with God's inerrant words in Scripture. Similarly, we should approach the study of Scripture eagerly and with confidence that, when rightly understood, Scripture will never contradict facts in the natural world.[18]

Someone may object that this whole discussion is inappropriate, for the Bible is given to us to teach religious and ethical matters; it is not intended to teach "science." However, as we noted in chapter 5 above, Scripture itself places no such restriction on the subjects to which it can speak. Although the Bible is of course not a "textbook" of science in a formal sense, it does nonetheless contain many affirmations about the natural world—its origin, its purposes, its ultimate destiny—and many statements about how it functions from day to day. If we take seriously the idea that it is God himself (as well as the human authors) who speaks all the words of Scripture, then we must take these statements seriously and believe them as well. Indeed, Scripture says that our understanding of some "scientific" facts is a matter of our faith! Hebrews 11:3 tells us, *"By faith* we understand that the worlds were prepared by the word of God, so that what is seen was not made out of things which are visible" (NASB).

## 2. Some Theories About Creation Seem Clearly Inconsistent With the Teachings of Scripture.
In this section we will examine three types of explanation of the origin of the universe that seem clearly inconsistent with Scripture.

**a. Secular Theories:** For the sake of completeness we mention here only briefly that any purely secular theories of the origin of the universe would be unacceptable for those who believe in Scripture. A "secular" theory is any theory of the origin of the universe that does not see an infinite-personal God as responsible for creating the universe by intelligent design. Thus, the "big bang" theory (in a secular form in which God is excluded), or any theories that hold that matter has always existed, would be inconsistent with the teaching of Scripture that God created the universe out of nothing, and that he did so for his own glory. (When Darwinian evolution is thought of in a totally materialistic sense, as it most often is, it would belong in this category also.)[19]

**b. Theistic Evolution:** Ever since the publication of Charles Darwin's book *Origin of Species by Means of Natural Selection* (1859), some Christians have proposed that living organisms came about by the process of evolution that Darwin proposed, but that God guided that process so that the result was just

---

[18]See the discussion in chapter 4, pp. 83–84, on the relationship between Scripture and natural revelation.

[19]See pp. 279–87 below, for a discussion of Darwinian evolution.

what he wanted it to be. This view is called *theistic evolution* because it advocates belief in God (it is "theistic") and in evolution too. Many who hold to theistic evolution would propose that God intervened in the process at some crucial points, usually (1) the creation of matter at the beginning, (2) the creation of the simplest life form, and (3) the creation of man. But, with the possible exception of those points of intervention, theistic evolutionists hold that evolution proceeded in the ways now discovered by natural scientists, and that it was the process that God decided to use in allowing all of the other forms of life on earth to develop. They believe that the random mutation of living things led to the evolution of higher life forms through the fact that those that had an "adaptive advantage" (a mutation that allowed them to be better fitted to survive in their environment) lived when others did not.

Theistic evolutionists are quite prepared to change their views of the way evolution came about, because, according to their standpoint, the Bible does not specify how it happened. It is therefore up to us to discover this through ordinary scientific investigation. They would argue that as we learn more and more about the way in which evolution came about, we are simply learning more and more about the process that God used to bring about the development of life forms.

The objections to theistic evolution are as follows:

1. The clear teaching of Scripture that there is purposefulness in God's work of creation seems incompatible with the randomness demanded by evolutionary theory. When Scripture reports that God said, "Let the earth bring forth living creatures according to their kinds: cattle and creeping things and beasts of the earth according to their kinds" (Gen. 1:24), it pictures God as doing things intentionally and with a purpose for each thing he does. But this is the opposite of allowing mutations to proceed entirely *randomly,* with no purpose for the millions of mutations that would have to come about, under evolutionary theory, before a new species could emerge.

The fundamental difference between a biblical view of creation and theistic evolution lies here: the driving force that brings about change and the development of new species in all evolutionary schemes is *randomness.* Without the random mutation of organisms you do not have evolution in the modern scientific sense at all. Random mutation is the underlying force that brings about eventual development from the simplest to the most complex life forms. But the driving force in the development of new organisms according to Scripture is God's *intelligent design.* God created "the great creatures of the sea and every living and moving thing with which the water teems, according to their kinds, and every winged bird according to its kind" (Gen. 1:21 NIV). "God made the wild animals according to their kinds, the livestock according to their kinds, and all the creatures that move along the ground according to their kinds. And God saw that it was good" (Gen. 1:25 NIV). These statements seem inconsistent with the idea of God creating or directing or observing millions of random mutations, none of which were "very good" in the way he intended, none of which really were the kinds of plants or animals he wanted to have on the earth. Instead of the straightforward biblical account of God's creation, the theistic evolution view has to understand events to have occurred something like this:

And God said, "Let the earth bring forth living creatures according to their kinds." And after three hundred eighty-seven million four hundred ninety-two thousand eight hundred seventy-one attempts, God finally made a mouse that worked.

That may seem a strange explanation, but it is precisely what the theistic evolutionist must postulate for each of the hundreds of thousands of different kinds of plants and animals on the earth: they all developed through a process of random mutation over millions of years, gradually increasing in complexity as occasional mutations turned out to be advantageous to the creature.

A theistic evolutionist may object that God intervened in the process and guided it at many points in the direction he wanted it to go. But once this is allowed then there is purpose and intelligent design in the process—we no longer have evolution at all, because there is no longer random mutation (at the points of divine interaction). No secular evolutionist would accept such intervention by an intelligent, purposeful Creator. But once a Christian agrees to some active, purposeful design by God, then there is no longer any need for randomness or any development emerging from random mutation. Thus we may as well have God immediately creating each distinct creature without thousands of attempts that fail.

2. Scripture pictures God's creative word as bringing immediate response. When the Bible talks about God's creative word it emphasizes the power of his word and its ability to accomplish his purpose.

> By the word of the LORD the heavens were made,
>    and all their host by the breath of his mouth.
> ... For he spoke, and it came to be;
>    he commanded, and it stood forth. (Ps. 33:6, 9)

This kind of statement seems incompatible with the idea that God spoke and after millions of years and millions of random mutations in living things his power brought about the result that he had called for. Rather, as soon as God says, "Let the earth put forth vegetation," the very next sentence tells us, "And it was so" (Gen. 1:11).

3. When Scripture tells us that God made plants and animals to reproduce "*according to their kinds*" (Gen. 1:11, 24), it suggests that God created many different types of plants and animals and that, though there would be some differentiation among them (note many different sizes, races, and personal characteristics among human beings!), nonetheless there would be some narrow limits to the kind of change that could come about through genetic mutations.[20]

---

[20]We do not need to insist that the Hebrew word *min* ("kind") corresponds exactly with the biological category "species," for that is simply a modern means of classifying different living things. But the Hebrew word does seem to indicate a narrow specification of various types of living things. It is used, for example, to speak of several very specific types of animals that bear young and are distinguished according to their "kind." Scripture speaks of "the falcon according to its kind," "every raven according to its kind," "the hawk according to its kind," "the heron according to its kind," and "the locust according to its kind" (Lev. 11:14, 15, 16, 19, 22). Other animals that exist according to an individual "kind" are the cricket, grasshopper, great lizard, buzzard, kite, sea gull, and stork (Lev. 11:22, 29; Deut. 14:13, 14, 15, 18). These are very specific kinds of animals, and God created them so that they would reproduce only according to their own "kinds." It seems that this would allow only for diversification within each of these types of animals (larger or smaller hawks, hawks of different color and with different shapes of beaks, etc.), but certainly not any "macroevolutionary" change into

4. God's present active role in creating or forming every living thing that now comes into being is hard to reconcile with the distant "hands off" kind of oversight of evolution that is proposed by theistic evolution. David is able to confess, "You formed my inward parts, you knit me together in my mother's womb" (Ps. 139:13). And God said to Moses, "Who has made man's mouth? Who makes him dumb, or deaf, or seeing, or blind? Is it not I, the LORD?" (Ex. 4:11). God makes the grass grow (Ps. 104:14; Matt. 6:30) and feeds the birds (Matt. 6:26) and the other creatures of the forest (Ps. 104:21, 27–30). If God is so involved in causing the growth and development of every step of every living thing even now, does it seem consistent with Scripture to say that these life forms were originally brought about by an evolutionary process directed by random mutation rather than by God's direct, purposeful creation, and that only after they had been created did he begin his active involvement in directing them each moment?

5. The special creation of Adam, and Eve from him, is a strong reason to break with theistic evolution. Those theistic evolutionists who argue for a special creation of Adam and Eve because of the statements in Genesis 1–2 have really broken with evolutionary theory at the point that is of most concern to human beings anyway. But if, on the basis of Scripture, we insist upon God's special intervention at the point of the creation of Adam and Eve, then what is to prevent our allowing that God intervened, in a similar way, in the creation of living organisms?

We must realize that the special creation of Adam and Eve as recorded in Scripture shows them to be far different from the nearly animal, just barely human creatures that evolutionists would say were the first humans, creatures who descended from ancestors that were highly developed nonhuman apelike creatures. Scripture pictures the first man and woman, Adam and Eve, as possessing highly developed linguistic, moral, and spiritual abilities from the moment they were created. They can talk with each other. They can even talk with God. They are very different from the nearly animal first humans, descended from nonhuman apelike creatures, of evolutionary theory.

Some may object that Genesis 1–2 does not intend to portray Adam and Eve as literal individuals, but (a) the historical narrative in Genesis continues without a break into the obviously historical material about Abraham (Gen. 12), showing that the author intended the entire section to be historical,[21] and (b) in Romans 5:12–21 and 1 Corinthians 15:21–22, 45–49, Paul affirms the existence of the "one man" Adam through whom sin came into the world, and bases his discussion of Christ's representative work of earning salvation on the previous historical

---

entirely different kinds of birds. (Frair and Davis, *A Case for Creation*, p. 129, think that "kind" may correspond to family or order today, or else to no precise twentieth-century equivalent.)

[21]Note the phrase "These are the generations of" introducing successive sections in the Genesis narrative at Gen. 2:4 (heavens and the earth); 5:1 (Adam); 6:9 (Noah); 10:1 (the sons of Noah); 11:10 (Shem); 11:27 (Terah, the father of Abraham); 25:12 (Ishmael); 25:19 (Isaac); 36:1 (Esau); and 37:2 (Jacob). The translation of the phrase may differ in various English versions, but the Hebrew expression is the same and literally says, "These are the generations of. . . ." By this literary device the author has introduced various sections of his historical narrative, tying it all together in a unified whole, and indicating that it is to be understood as history-writing of the same sort throughout. If the author intends us to understand Abraham, Isaac, and Jacob as historical figures, then he also intends us to understand Adam and Eve as historical figures.

pattern of Adam being a representative for mankind as well. Moreover, the New Testament elsewhere clearly understands Adam and Eve to be historical figures (cf. Luke 3:38; Acts 17:26; 1 Cor. 11:8–9; 2 Cor. 11:3; 1 Tim. 2:13–14). The New Testament also assumes the historicity of the sons of Adam and Eve, Cain (Heb. 11:4; 1 John 3:12; Jude 11) and Abel (Matt. 23:35; Luke 11:51; Heb. 11:4; 12:24).

6. There are many scientific problems with evolutionary theory (see the following section). The increasing number of questions about the validity of the theory of evolution being raised even by non-Christians in various scientific disciplines indicates that anyone who claims to be forced to believe in evolution because the "scientific facts" leave no other option has simply not considered all the evidence on the other side. The scientific data do not force one to accept evolution, and if the scriptural record argues convincingly against it as well, it does not seem to be a valid theory for a Christian to adopt.

It seems most appropriate to conclude in the words of geologist Davis A. Young, "The position of theistic evolutionism as expressed by some of its proponents is not a consistently Christian position. It is not a truly biblical position, for it is based in part on principles that are imported into Christianity."[22] According to Louis Berkhof "theistic evolution is really a child of embarrassment, which calls God in at periodic intervals to help nature over the chasms that yawn at her feet. It is neither the biblical doctrine of creation, nor a consistent theory of evolution."[23]

c. Notes on the Darwinian Theory of Evolution: The word *evolution* can be used in different ways. Sometimes it is used to refer to "micro-evolution"—small developments within one species, so that we see flies or mosquitoes becoming immune to insecticides, or human beings growing taller, or different colors and varieties of roses being developed. Innumerable examples of such "micro-evolution" are evident today, and no one denies that they exist.[24] But that is not the sense in which the word *evolution* is usually used when discussing theories of creation and evolution.

The term *evolution* is more commonly used to refer to "macro-evolution"—that is, the "general theory of evolution" or the view that "nonliving substance gave rise to the first living material, which subsequently reproduced and diversified to

---

[22]Davis A. Young, *Creation and the Flood: An Alternative to Flood Geology and Theistic Evolution* (Grand Rapids: Baker, 1977), p. 38. Young includes a discussion of the views of Richard H. Bube, one of the leading proponents of theistic evolution today (pp. 33–35).

[23]Berkhof, *Systematic Theology,* pp. 139–40.

[24]Philip E. Johnson, *Darwin on Trial* (Downers Grove, Ill.: InterVarsity Press, 1991), points out that some studies frequently claimed as evidence of evolution are really just temporary population differences with no genetic change. For example, he mentions Kettlewell's observation of "industrial melanism" in the peppered moth, whereby the prevailing color of the moths changed from white to black and back to white again when leaves on trees were light colored, then covered with soot from pollution, then again light colored when the pollution ended. But at every stage, both black and white moths were present, even though in differing proportions (moths that did not match the leaf color were more easily seen and eaten by predators). No evolutionary change occurred at all, for both black and white moths were still industrial moths, just as black and white horses are both still horses. In fact, the moth functioned to preserve its genetic identity in differing circumstances, rather than evolving or becoming extinct (see pp. 26–28, 160–61).

produce all extinct and extant organisms."[25] In this chapter, when we use the word *evolution* it is used to refer to macro-evolution or the general theory of evolution.

## (1) Current Challenges to Evolution:

Since Charles Darwin first published his *Origin of Species by Means of Natural Selection* in 1859, there have been challenges to his theory by Christians and non-Christians alike. Current neo-Darwinian theory is still foundationally similar to Darwin's original position, but with refinements and modifications due to over a hundred years of research. In modern Darwinian evolutionary theory, the history of the development of life began when a mix of chemicals present on the earth spontaneously produced a very simple, probably one-celled life form. This living cell reproduced itself, and eventually there were some mutations or differences in the new cells produced. These mutations led to the development of more complex life forms. A hostile environment meant that many of them would perish, but those that were better suited to their environment would survive and multiply. Thus, nature exercised a process of "natural selection" in which the differing organisms most fitted to the environment survived. More and more mutations eventually developed into more and more varieties of living things, so that from the very simplest organism all the complex life forms on earth eventually developed through this process of mutation and natural selection.

The most recent, and perhaps most devastating, critique of current Darwinian theory comes from Philip E. Johnson, a law professor who specializes in analyzing the logic of arguments. In his book *Darwin on Trial*,[26] he quotes extensively from current evolutionary theorists to demonstrate that:

1. After more than one hundred years of experimental breeding of various kinds of animals and plants, the amount of variation that can be produced (even with intentional, not random, breeding) is extremely limited, due to the limited range of genetic variation in each type of living thing: dogs who are selectively bred for generations are still dogs, fruit flies are still fruit flies, etc. And when allowed to return to the wild state, "the most highly specialized breeds quickly perish and the survivors revert to the original wild type." He concludes that "natural selection," claimed by Darwinists to account for the survival of new organisms, is really a conservative force that works to preserve the genetic fitness of a population, not to change its characteristics.[27]

2. In current evolutionary arguments, the idea of "survival of the fittest" (or "natural selection") is popularly thought to mean that those animals whose different characteristics give them a comparative advantage will survive, and others will die out. But in actual practice almost any characteristic can be argued to be either an advantage or a disadvantage.[28] So how do Darwinists know which

---

[25]Wayne Frair and Percival Davis, *A Case for Creation* (Norcross, Ga.: CRS Books, 1983), p. 25.
[26]Downers Grove, Ill.: InterVarsity Press, 1991.
[27]Johnson, pp. 15–20 (quotation from p. 18). Johnson notes that in a few cases new "species" have been produced, in the sense of a part of a population that is incapable of interbreeding with another part: this has happened with fruit flies and with some plant hybrids (p. 19). But even though incapable of interbreeding with some other fruit flies, the new fruit flies still are fruit flies, not some other kind of creature: the amount of variation the fruit fly is capable of is inherently limited by the range of variability in its gene pool.
[28]Johnson notes (pp. 29–30) that Darwinists have even accounted for obviously disadvantageous characteristics by invoking pleiotropy, the idea that several genetic changes may occur all at once, so

characteristics have given an advantage in survival to certain animals? By observing which kinds survive. But this means that natural selection is often at bottom not a powerful new insight into what happens in nature but simply a tautology (a meaningless repetition of the same idea), since it boils down to saying that the "fittest" animals are those who have the most offspring. In this sense, natural selection means: animals who have the most offspring have the most offspring.[29] But this proves nothing about any supposed mutations to produce different, more fit offspring over the course of many generations.

3. The vast and complex mutations required to produce complex organs such as an eye or a bird's wing (or hundreds of other organs) could not have occurred in tiny mutations accumulating over thousands of generations, because the individual parts of the organ are useless (and give no "advantage") unless the entire organ is functioning. But the mathematical probability of such random mutations happening together in one generation is effectively zero. Darwinists are left saying that it must have happened because it happened.[30]

An amusing example of the need for all the parts of a complex organic system to be put in place at once is pointed out by Robert Kofahl and Kelly Segraves in their book, *The Creation Explanation: A Scientific Alternative to Evolution*.[31] They describe the "Bombardier beetle," which repels enemies by firing a hot charge of chemicals from two swivel tubes in its tail. The chemicals fired by this beetle will spontaneously explode when mixed together in a laboratory, but apparently the beetle has an inhibitor substance that blocks the explosive reaction until the beetle squirts some of the liquid into its "combustion chambers," where an enzyme is added to catalyze the reaction. An explosion takes place and the chemical repellent is fired at a temperature of 212°F at the beetle's enemies. Kofahl and Segraves rightly ask whether any evolutionary explanation can account for this amazing mechanism:

> Note that a rational evolutionary explanation for the development of this creature must assign some kind of adaptive advantage to each of the millions of hypothetical intermediate stages in the construction process. But would the stages of one-fourth, one-half, or two-thirds completion, for example, have conferred any advantage? After all, a rifle is useless without all of its parts functioning. . . . Before this defensive mechanism could afford any protection to the beetle, all of its parts, together with the proper explosive mixture of chemicals, plus the instinctive behavior required for its use, would have to be assembled in the insect. The partially developed set of organs would be useless. Therefore, according to the principles of evolutionary theory, there would be no selective pressure to cause the system to evolve from a partially completed stage toward the final completed system. . . . If a

---

that the negative ones come along with the positive ones. On this basis no existing characteristic in any animal could be cited to disprove the claim that the fittest survive, for it really becomes a claim that those that have survived have survived. But then how do we really know that survival of the fittest has been the mechanism that has led to current diversity of life forms?

[29]Johnson does not say that all evolutionists argue this way, but he quotes several who do (pp. 20–23).

[30]Johnson, pp. 32–44.

[31]Robert E. Kofahl and Kelly L. Segraves, *The Creation Explanation: A Scientific Alternative to Evolution* (Wheaton, Ill.: Harold Shaw, 1975). This book is a fascinating collection of scientific evidence favoring creation by intelligent design.

theory fails to explain the data in any science, that theory should be either revised or replaced with a theory that is in agreement with the data.[32]

In this case, of course, the amusing question is, What would happen if the explosive chemical mixture developed in the beetle without the chemical inhibitor?

4. The fossil record was Darwin's greatest problem in 1859, and it has simply become a greater problem since then. In Darwin's time, hundreds of fossils were available showing the existence of many distinct kinds of animals and plants in the distant past. But Darwin was unable to find any fossils from "intermediate types" to fill in the gaps between distinct kinds of animals—fossils showing some characteristics of one animal and a few characteristics of the next developmental type, for example. In fact, many ancient fossils exactly resembled present-day animals—showing that (according to the chronological assumptions of his view) numerous animals have persisted for millions of years essentially unchanged. Darwin realized that the absence of "transitional types" in the fossil record weakened his theory, but he thought it was due to the fact that not enough fossils had been discovered, and was confident that further discoveries would unearth many transitional types of animals. However, the subsequent 130 years of intensive archaeological activity has still failed to produce one convincing example of a needed transitional type.[33]

Johnson quotes noted evolutionist Stephen Jay Gould of Harvard as saying that there are two characteristics of the fossil record that are inconsistent with the idea of gradual change through generations:

1. Stasis. Most species exhibit no directional change during their tenure on earth. They appear in the fossil record looking pretty much the same as when they disappear; morphological change is usually limited and directionless.

2. Sudden appearance. In any local area, a species does not arise gradually by the steady transformation of its ancestors; it appears all at once and "fully formed."[34]

So difficult is this problem for Darwinian evolution that many evolutionary scientists today propose that evolution came about in sudden jumps to new life forms—so that each of the thirty-two known orders of mammals, for example, appeared quite suddenly in the history of Europe.[35]

But how could hundreds or thousands of genetic changes come about all at

---

[32]Kofahl and Segraves, *The Creation Explanation,* pp. 2–3. They give many other similar examples.

[33]Johnson, pp. 73–85, discusses the two examples sometimes claimed out of perhaps 100 million fossils that have been discovered, Archaeopteryx (a bird with some characteristics that resemble reptiles), and some ape-like examples thought to be prehuman hominids. Archaeopteryx is still very much a bird, not a near-reptile, and studies of the characteristics of the supposedly prehuman fossils include large amounts of subjective speculation, resulting in strong differences among experts who have examined them.

A helpful discussion of the gaps that remain in the fossil record is found in Frair and Davis, *A Case for Creation,* pp. 55–65. They note that the continued discovery and classification of fossils since Darwin's time has resulted in the fact that "on the whole, the discontinuities have been emphasized with increased collecting. There appears to be little question that the gaps are real, and it seems increasingly less likely that they will be filled" (p. 57).

[34]Johnson, p. 50, apparently quoting a paper by Gould and Niles Eldredge, "Punctuated Equilibria, an Alternative to Phyletic Gradualism," printed as a appendix to Eldredge's book, *Time Frames* (Johnson, p. 167).

[35]This view is called "punctuated equilibrium," meaning that the ordinary equilibrium of the natural world was occasionally interrupted (punctuated) by the sudden appearance of new life forms.

once? No explanation has been given other than to say that it must have happened, because it happened. (A glance at the dotted lines in any current biology textbook, showing the supposed transitions from one kind of animal to another, will indicate the nature of the gaps still unfilled after 130 years of investigation.) The significance of this problem is demonstrated forcefully in a recent book by a non-Christian writer, Michael Denton, *Evolution: A Theory in Crisis*.[36] Denton himself proposes no alternative explanation for the emergence of life in its present form upon the earth, but he notes that since Darwin's time,

> neither of the two fundamental axioms of Darwin's macroevolutionary theory—the concept of the continuity of nature, that is the idea of a functional continuum of all life forms linking all species together and ultimately leading back to a primeval cell, and the belief that all the adaptive design of life has resulted from a blind random process—have been validated by one single empirical discovery or scientific advance since 1859.[37]

5. The molecular structures of living organisms do show relationships, but Darwinists simply assume that relationships imply common ancestry, a claim that certainly has not been proven. Moreover, there are amazing molecular differences between living things, and no satisfactory explanation for the origin of those differences has been given.[38]

Of course, similarity of design at any level (including levels above the molecular level) has often been used as a argument for evolution. The assumption of evolutionists is that similarity of design between two species implies that the "lower" species evolved into the "higher" species, but the proof for that assumption has never been given. Gleason Archer illustrates this well by supposing that one visits a museum of science and industry and finds a display of how human beings evolved from earlier apelike creatures into progressively more human-looking beings and finally into modern man. But he rightly notes that

> a continuity of basic design furnishes no evidence whatever that any "lower" species phased into the next "higher" species by any sort of internal dynamic, as evolution demands. For if the museum visitor were to go to another part of that museum of science and industry, he would find a completely analogous series of automobiles, commencing with 1900 and extending up until the present decade. Stage by stage, phase by phase, he could trace the development of the Ford from its earliest Model-T prototype to the large and luxurious LTD of the 1970's.[39]

Of course, a much better explanation for the similarities in various models of Ford automobiles is the fact that an intelligent designer (or group of designers) used similar structures in successively more complex automobiles—if a steering mechanism works well in one model, there is no need to invent a different kind of steering mechanism for another model. In the same way, similarities in design among all living things can equally well be taken as evidence of the work of an intelligent master craftsman, the Creator himself.

---

[36]Bethesda, Md.: Adler and Adler, 1986.
[37]Denton, p. 345. An earlier analysis of evolution by a respected British biologist who is himself an evolutionist is G. A. Kerkut, *Implications of Evolution* (New York: Pergamon, 1960). This is a very technical study pointing out numerous remaining difficulties in the theory of evolution.
[38]Johnson, pp. 86–99.
[39]Gleason L. Archer, *Encyclopedia of Bible Difficulties*, p. 57.

6. Probably the greatest difficulty of all for evolutionary theory is explaining how any life could have begun in the first place. The spontaneous generation of even the simplest living organism capable of independent life (the prokaryote bacterial cell) from inorganic materials on the earth could not happen by random mixing of chemicals: it requires intelligent design and craftsmanship so complex that no advanced scientific laboratory in the world has been able to do it. Johnson quotes a now-famous metaphor: "That a living organism emerged by chance from a pre-biotic soup is about as likely as that 'a tornado sweeping through a junkyard might assemble a Boeing 747 from the materials therein.' Chance assembly is just a naturalistic way of saying 'miracle.'"[40]

At a common-sense level, a simple illustration will show this. If I were to take my digital watch, hand it to someone, and say that I found it near an iron mine in northern Minnesota, and that it was my belief that the watch had come together by itself simply through the operation of random movement and environmental forces (plus some energy from a few bolts of lightning, perhaps), I would quickly be written off as mad. Yet any one living cell on the leaf of any tree, or any one cell in the human body, is thousands of times more complex than my digital watch. Even given 4.5 billion years the "chance" of even one living cell arising spontaneously is, for all practical purposes, zero.

In fact, some attempts have been made to calculate the probability of life arising spontaneously in this way. Kofahl and Segraves give a statistical model in which they begin with a very generous assumption: that every square foot of the earth's surface was somehow covered with 95 pounds of protein molecules that could mix freely, and that are all replaced with fresh protein every year for one billion years. They then estimate the probability that even one enzyme molecule would develop in each one billion years of the earth's history. The probability is 1.2 times $10^{11}$ or one chance in 80 billion. They note, however, that even with the generous assumptions and starting with fresh protein every year for a billion years, finding one enzyme molecule—for all practical purposes an impossible task—would not solve the problem at all:

> The probability of finding two of the active molecules would be about $10^{22}$, and the probability that they would be identical would be $10^{70}$. And could life start with just a single enzyme molecule? Furthermore, what is the possibility that an active enzyme molecule, once formed, could find its way through thousands of miles and millions of years to that randomly formed RNA or DNA molecule which contains the code for that particular enzyme molecule's amino acid sequence, so that new copies of itself could be produced? Zero for all practical purposes.[41]

Kofahl and Segraves report a study by an evolutionary scientist who formulates a model to calculate the probability for the formation, not just of one enzyme molecule but the smallest likely living organism by random processes. He comes up with a probability of one chance in $10^{340,000,000}$—that is, one chance in 10

---

[40]Johnson, p. 104, quoting Fred Hoyle. In fact, one could argue that the 747 is more likely to occur accidentally, because intelligent human designers have been able to make a 747, but they have not been able to make one living cell.

[41]Kofahl and Segraves, *The Creation Explanation*, pp. 99–100.

with 340 million zeros after it! But Kofahl and Segraves note, "Yet Dr. Morowitz and his fellow evolutionary scientists still believe that it happened!"[42]

If someone were to ask me to entrust my life to ride on an airplane, and then explained that the airline company completed its flights safely once in every $10^{340,000,000}$ times—or even one in every 80 billion flights—I certainly would not get on board, nor would anyone else in his or her right mind. Yet it is tragic that the common opinion, perpetuated in many science textbooks today, that evolution is an established "fact," has continued to persuade many people that they should not consider the total truthfulness of the Bible to be an intellectually acceptable viewpoint for responsible, thinking individuals to hold today. The myth that "evolution has disproved the Bible" persists and keeps many from considering Christianity as a valid option.

But what if some day life were actually "created" in the laboratory by scientists? Here it is important to understand what is meant. First, this would not be "creation" in the pure sense of the word, since all laboratory experiments begin with some kinds of previously existing matter. It would not give an explanation of the origin of matter itself, nor would it be the kind of creating that the Bible says God did. Second, most contemporary attempts to "create life" are really just very small steps in the gigantic process of moving from nonliving materials to an independently living organism, even one consisting of only one cell. The construction of a protein molecule or an amino acid nowhere approaches the complexity of a single living cell. But most importantly, what would it demonstrate if the collective work of thousands of the most intelligent scientists in the world, with the most expensive and complex laboratory equipment available, working over the course of several decades, actually did produce a living organism? Would that "prove" that God did not create life? Quite the opposite: it would demonstrate that life simply does not come about by chance but must be intentionally created by an intelligent designer. In theory at least, it is not impossible that human beings, created in the image of God and using their God-given intelligence could someday create a living organism out of nonliving substances (though the complexity of the task far surpasses any technology that exists today). But that would only show that God made us to be "God-like"—that in biological research as in many other areas of life we in a very small way can imitate God's activity. All such scientific research in this direction really ought to be done out of reverence for God and with gratitude for the scientific capability with which he has endowed us.

Many unbelieving scientists have been so influenced by the cumulative force of the objections brought against evolution that they have openly advocated novel positions for one part or another of the proposed evolutionary development of living things. Francis Crick, who won the Nobel Prize for helping to discover the structure of DNA molecules, proposed in 1973 that life may have been sent here

[42]Ibid., p. 101, quoting Harold J. Morowitz, *Energy Flow in Biology* (New York: Academic Press, 1968), p. 99. The classic study of the mathematical improbability of evolution is P. S. Moorehead and M. M. Kaplan, eds., *Mathematical Challenges to the Neo-Darwinian Interpretation of Evolution* (Philadelphia: The Wistar Institute Symposium Monograph, no. 5, 1967). See also the article "Heresy in the Halls of Biology: Mathematicians Question Darwinism," *Scientific Research* (November 1987), pp. 59–66, and I. L. Cohen, *Darwin Was Wrong—A Study in Probabilities* (Greenvale, N.Y.: New Research Publications, 1984).

by a spaceship from a distant planet, a theory that Crick calls "Directed Panspermia."[43] To the present author, it seems ironic that brilliant scientists could advocate so fantastic a theory without one shred of evidence in its favor, all the while rejecting the straightforward explanation given by the one book in the history of the world that has never been proven wrong, that has changed the lives of millions of people, that has been believed completely by many of the most intelligent scholars of every generation, and that has been a greater force for good than any other book in the history of the world. Why will otherwise intelligent people commit themselves to beliefs that seem so irrational? It seems as though they will believe in anything, so long as it is not belief in the personal God of Scripture, who calls us to forsake our pride, humble ourselves before him, ask his forgiveness for failure to obey his moral standards, and submit ourselves to his moral commands for the rest of our lives. To refuse to do this is irrational, but, as we shall see in the chapter on sin, all sin is ultimately irrational at its root.

Other challenges to the theory of evolution have been published in the last twenty or thirty years, and no doubt many more will be forthcoming. One only hopes it will not be too long before the scientific community publicly acknowledges the implausibility of evolutionary theory, and textbooks written for high school and college students openly acknowledge that evolution simply is not a satisfactory explanation for the origin of life on the earth.

## (2) The Destructive Influences of Evolutionary Theory in Modern Thought:

It is important to understand the incredibly destructive influences that evolutionary theory has had on modern thinking. If in fact life was not created by God, and if human beings in particular are not created by God or responsible to him, but are simply the result of random occurrences in the universe, then of what significance is human life? We are merely the product of matter plus time plus chance, and so to think that we have any eternal importance, or really any importance at all in the face of an immense universe, is simply to delude ourselves. Honest reflection on this notion should lead people to a profound sense of despair.

Moreover, if all of life can be explained by evolutionary theory apart from God, and if there is no God who created us (or at least if we cannot know anything about him with certainty), then there is no supreme Judge to hold us morally accountable. Therefore there are no moral absolutes in human life, and people's moral ideas are only subjective preferences, good for them perhaps but not to be imposed on others. In fact, in such a case the only thing forbidden is to say that one knows that certain things are right and certain things are wrong.

There is another ominous consequence of evolutionary theory: If the inevitable processes of natural selection continue to bring about improvement in life forms on earth through the survival of the fittest, then why should we hinder this process by caring for those who are weak or less able to defend themselves? Should we not rather allow them to die without reproducing so that we might move toward a

---

[43]*Time*, September 10, 1973, p. 53, summarizing the article "Directed Panspermia," by F. H. C. Crick and L. E. Orgel in *Icarus 19* (1973): 341–46.

new, higher form of humanity, even a "master race"? In fact, Marx, Nietzsche, and Hitler all justified war on these grounds.[44]

Moreover, if human beings are continually evolving for the better, then the wisdom of earlier generations (and particularly of earlier religious beliefs) is not likely to be as valuable as modern thought. In addition, the effect of Darwinian evolution on the people's opinions of the trustworthiness of Scripture has been a very negative one.

Contemporary sociological and psychological theories that see human beings as simply higher forms of animals are another outcome of evolutionary thought. And the extremes of the modern "animal rights" movement that oppose all killing of animals (for food, or for leather coats, or for medical research, for example) also flow naturally out of evolutionary thought.

**d. The Theory of a "Gap" Between Genesis 1:1 and 1:2:** Some evangelicals have proposed that there is a gap of millions of years between Genesis 1:1 ("In the beginning God created the heavens and the earth") and Genesis 1:2 ("The earth was without form and void, and darkness was upon the face of the deep"). According to this theory, God made an earlier creation, but there was eventually a rebellion against God (probably in connection with Satan's own rebellion), and God judged the earth so that "it became without form and void" (an alternative, but doubtful, translation proposed for Gen. 1:2).[45] What we read of in Genesis 1:3–2:3 is really the *second* creation of God, in six literal twenty-four-hour days, which occurred only recently (perhaps 10,000 to 20,000 years ago). The ancient fossils found on the earth, many of which are said to be millions of years old, stem from the *first* creation (4,500,000,000 years ago), which is mentioned only in Genesis 1:1.

The primary biblical argument for this theory is that the words "without form and void" and "darkness" in Genesis 1:2 picture an earth that has suffered the effects of judgment by God: darkness elsewhere in the Old Testament is frequently a sign of God's judgment, and the Hebrew words *tohû* ("without form") and *bohû* ("void, empty") in verses such as Isaiah 34:11 and Jeremiah 34:23 refer to places such as deserts that have suffered the desolating consequences of God's judgment.

But these arguments do not seem strong enough to persuade us that Genesis 1:2 pictures the earth as desolate after God's judgment. If God first forms the

---

[44]See *NIDCC*, p. 283.

[45]This "gap theory" is given as one possible interpretation of Gen. 1:1–2 in *The New Scofield Reference Bible* (Oxford: Oxford University Press, 1967), in notes to Gen. 1:2 and Isa. 45:18. It also remains commonplace in much popular Bible teaching. An extensive defense of this theory is found in Arthur C. Custance, *Without Form and Void: A Study of the Meaning of Genesis 1:2* (Brockville, Ontario: Doorway Papers, 1970). An extensive critique is in Weston W. Fields, *Unformed and Unfilled* (Nutley, N.J.: Presbyterian and Reformed, 1976). A substantial critique of the lexical and grammatical arguments used in the gap theory is also found in Oswald T. Allis, *God Spake by Moses* (Philadelphia: Presbyterian and Reformed, 1951), pp. 153–59.

Some readers may wonder why I have classified this view along with secular views and theistic evolution as a theory that seems "clearly inconsistent with the teachings of Scripture." I should note here that I am doing this only because the arguments for this position seem to me to be based on highly unlikely interpretations of the biblical text, and I do not wish to imply that those who hold to the gap theory are unbelievers, or that they are like many theistic evolutionists who think the Bible cannot teach us about science. On the contrary, advocates of the gap theory have uniformly been believers in the total truthfulness of Scripture on whatever subject it speaks to.

earth (v. 1) and then later creates light (v. 3), there would have to be darkness over the earth in verse 2—this indicates that creation is in progress, not that any evil is present. In addition, each day there is an "evening," and there is "darkness" present during the six days of creation (vv. 5, 8, 13, 18–19, et al.), with no suggestion of evil or of God's disapproval (cf. Ps. 104:20). As far as the phrase "without form and void," the sense is just that it is not yet fit for habitation: God's preparatory work has not yet been done. Of course, when God curses a desert, it does become unfit for habitation, but we should not read the cause of that unfitness in one case (God's curse on a desert) into another case, the creation, where the cause of unfitness for habitation is simply that God's work is still in progress; the preparation for man is not yet complete.[46] (It is not proper to read the circumstances that surround a word in one place into the use of that word in another place when the meaning of the word and its use in the second context do not require those same circumstances.)

In addition to the fact that Genesis 1:2 does not give support to this view, there are some other arguments that weigh strongly against the gap theory:

1. There is no verse in Scripture that explicitly talks about an earlier creation. So this theory is lacking even one verse of Scripture to give it explicit support.

2. In Genesis 1:31, when God finished his work of creation, we read, "And God saw everything that he had made, and behold, it was very good." But according to the gap theory, God would be looking at an earth full of the results of rebellion, conflict, and terrible divine judgment. He would also be looking at all the demonic beings, the hosts of Satan who had rebelled against him, and yet be calling everything "very good." It is difficult to believe that there was so much evil and so many evidences of rebellion and judgment on the earth, and that God could still say that creation was very good.

Moreover, Genesis 2:1 says, in an apparent summary of all that has happened in Genesis 1, "Thus the heavens and the earth were finished, and all the host of them." Here it is not just God's work on the earth, but all that he made in the heavens, that is said to have been completed in the narrative in Genesis 1. This would not allow for large parts of heaven and earth to have been finished long before the six creation days.

3. In a later description of God's work of creation found in the Ten Commandments, we read, "for *in six days the* LORD *made heaven and earth,* the sea, *and all that is in them,* and rested the seventh day; therefore the LORD blessed the sabbath day and hallowed it" (Ex. 20:11). Here the creation of both the heaven and the earth, and the making of "all that is in them," is attributed to God's work in the six days of creation. Whether we take these to be twenty-four-hour days or

---

[46]The second word, *bohû,* "void," only occurs two other times in Scripture (Isa. 34:11; Jer. 34:23), both picturing desolate lands that have experienced God's judgment. But the first word, *tohû,* which can mean "formlessness, confusion, unreality, emptiness" (*BDB,* p. 1062), occurs nineteen other times, sometimes to refer to a desolate place resulting from judgment (Isa. 34:11 and Jer. 34:23, both with *bohû*), and sometimes just to refer to an empty place, with no sense of evil or judgment implied (Job 26:7, of "space" over which God stretches the north, parallel to the "nothingness" in which he hangs the earth; also Deut. 32:10; Job 12:24; Ps. 107:40). The sense "uninhabitable" is especially appropriate in Isa. 45:18, speaking of God's creation of the earth: "He did not create it to be empty [*tohû*], but formed it to be inhabited" (NIV). (The fact that God did not create the earth to be "empty" but "formed it to be inhabited" [Isa. 45:18] speaks of God's completed work of creation and does not deny that it was "without form and void" at the earliest stage of creation.)

longer periods of time, on either view the making of the entire heavens and earth and *everything in them* is put within these six days. But the proponents of the gap theory would have to say that there are many things in the earth (such as fossil remains of dead animals, and the earth itself) and in the heavens (such as the stars) that God did not make in the six days specified in Exodus 20:11, a view that seems exactly contrary to what is affirmed in the verse.

Moreover, while some passages of Scripture do speak of God's judgment on rebellious angels or his judgment on the earth at various times (see Isa. 24:1; Jer. 4:23–26; 2 Peter 2:4), none of the passages places this judgment at a time before the creation narrative in Genesis 1:2–31.

4. This theory must assume that all of the fossils of animals from millions of years ago that resemble very closely animals from today indicate that God's first creation of the animal and plant kingdom resulted in a failure. These animals and plants did not fulfill God's original purpose, so he destroyed them, but in the second creation he made others that were exactly like them. Moreover, since Adam and Eve were the first man and woman, this theory must assume that there was a prior creation of God that existed for millions of years but lacked the highest aspect of God's creative work, namely, man himself. But both the failure of God to accomplish his purposes with the original plant and animal kingdoms, and the failure of God to crown creation with his highest creature, man, seem inconsistent with the biblical picture of God as one who always accomplishes his purposes in whatever he does. So the gap theory does not seem an acceptable alternative for evangelical Christians today.

**3. The Age of the Earth: Some Preliminary Considerations.** Up to this point, the discussions in this chapter have advocated conclusions that we hope will find broad assent among evangelical Christians. But now at last we come to a perplexing question about which Bible-believing Christians have differed for many years, sometimes very sharply. The question is simply this: How old is the earth?

It is appropriate to treat this question after all the earlier matters, because it is really much less important than the doctrines considered above. These earlier matters may be summarized as follows: (1) God created the universe out of nothing; (2) creation is distinct from God, yet always dependent on God; (3) God created the universe to show his glory; (4) the universe God created was very good; (5) there will be no final conflict between Scripture and science; (6) secular theories that deny God as Creator, including Darwinian evolution, are clearly incompatible with belief in the Bible.

The question of the age of the earth is also less important than matters to be treated in subsequent chapters, that is (7) the creation of the angelic world and (8) the creation of man in the image of God (chapters 19, 21, and 22). It is important to keep these things in mind, because there is a danger that Christians will spend too much time arguing over the age of the earth and neglect to focus on much more important and much clearer aspects of the overall teaching of the Bible on creation.

The two options to choose from for a date of the earth are the "old earth" position, which agrees with the consensus of modern science that the earth is 4,500,000,000 years old, and the "young earth" position, which says that the earth is 10,000 to 20,000 years old, and that secular scientific dating schemes are incorrect. The difference between these two views is enormous: 4,499,980,000 years!

Before considering the specific arguments for both positions, we will examine some preliminary questions about the genealogies in the Bible, current estimates for the age of the human race, differing views on the date of dinosaurs, and the length of the six creation days in Genesis 1.

**a. There Are Gaps in the Genealogies of the Bible:** When one reads the list of names in Scripture together with their ages, it might seem as though we could add together the ages of all the people in the history of redemption from Adam to Christ and come up with an approximate date for the creation of the earth. Certainly this would give a very recent date for creation (such as Archbishop Ussher's date of 4004 B.C.). But closer inspection of the parallel lists of names in Scripture will show that Scripture itself indicates the fact that the genealogies list only those names the biblical writers thought it important to record for their purposes. In fact, some genealogies include names that are left out by other genealogies in Scripture itself.

For instance, Matthew 1:8–9 tells us that Asa was "the father of Jehoshaphat, and Jehoshaphat the father of Joram, and Joram the father of Uzziah, and Uzziah the father of Jotham, and Jotham the father of Ahaz." But from 1 Chronicles 3:10–12 (which uses the alternate name Ahaziah for Uzziah), we learn that three generations have been omitted by Matthew: Joash, Amaziah, and Azariah. So these texts can be compared in the following table:

### Example of gaps in genealogies

| 1 Chronicles 3:10–12 | Matthew 1:8–9 |
| --- | --- |
| Asa | Asa |
| Jehoshaphat | Jehoshaphat |
| Joram | Joram |
| Ahaziah (Uzziah) | Uzziah |
| Joash | |
| Amaziah | |
| Azariah | |
| Jotham | Jotham |
| Ahaz | Ahaz |
| Hezekiah | Hezekiah |
| (etc.) | (etc.) |

Therefore, when Matthew says that Uzziah was "the father of Jotham," it can mean that he was the father of someone who led to Jotham. Matthew has selected those names that he wants to emphasize for his own purposes.[47] A similar phenomenon is evident in Matthew 1:20 where the angel of the Lord speaks to Joseph and calls him, "Joseph, son of David." Now Joseph is not directly the son of David (for David lived around 1000 B.C.), but Joseph is the descendant of David and is therefore called his "son."

---

[47]See a fuller discussion of the gaps in genealogies in Francis Schaeffer, *No Final Conflict,* pp. 37–43.

Another example is found in 1 Chronicles 26:24 in a list of officers appointed by King David near the end of his life. We read that "Shebuel the son of Gershom, son of Moses, was chief officer in charge of the treasuries" (1 Chron. 26:24). Now we know from Exodus 2:22 that Gershom was the son born to Moses before the Exodus, sometime around 1480 B.C. (or, on a late date for the exodus, around 1330 B.C.). But these officials mentioned in 1 Chronicles 26 were appointed at the time that David made Solomon king over Israel, around 970 B.C. (see 1 Chron. 23:1). That means that in 1 Chronicles 26:24 Shebuel is said to be "the son of Gershom," who was born 510 (or at least 360) years earlier. Ten or more generations have been omitted in this designation "son of."[48]

It seems only fair to conclude that the genealogies of Scripture have some gaps in them, and that God only caused to be recorded those names that were important for his purposes. How many gaps there are and how many generations are missing from the Genesis narratives, we do not know. The life of Abraham may be placed at approximately 2000 B.C., because the kings and places listed in the stories of Abraham's life (Gen. 12ff.) can be correlated with archaeological data that can be dated quite reliably,[49] but prior to Abraham the setting of dates is very uncertain. In view of the exceptionally long life spans reported for people prior to the flood, it would not seem unreasonable to think that a few thousand years have been passed over in the narrative. This gives us some flexibility in our thinking about the date that man first appeared on the earth. (It would seem to be quite another thing, however, and quite foreign to the sense of continuity in the narrative, to think that *millions* of years have been omitted, but that names and details of the lives of key persons have been remembered and passed down over such a long period of time.)

**b. The Age of the Human Race:** While current scientific estimates say that man first appeared on the earth about 2.5 million years ago, it is important to recognize what kind of "man" this is claimed to be. The following table is a rough guide to current scientific opinion:[50]

| | |
|---|---|
| *homo habilis* ("skillful man") stone tools | 2–3.5 million years B.C. |
| *homo erectus* variety of stone tools, used fire by 500,000 B.C., hunted large animals | 1.5 million years B.C. |
| *homo sapiens* ("wise man" or "thinking man") | 40,000–150,000 B.C. (or perhaps 300,000 B.C.) |

[48]The NIV translates the verse, "Shubael, *a descendant* of Gershom," but this is simply an interpretation, for the Hebrew text simply has the word *ben*, "son." It should not be objected that Gershom may have lived over 500 years, for such long life spans are not found after the flood (note Gen. 6:3); in fact, Abraham was miraculously given a son when he was almost 100 (cf. Rom. 4:19; Heb. 11:12); and Moses, long before David or Solomon, counted man's life as 70 or 80 years: "The years of our life are threescore and ten, or even by reason of strength fourscore" (Ps. 90:10).
[49]See "Chronology of the Old Testament" in *IBD*, esp. pp. 268–70.
[50]This table was adapted from Frair and Davis, *A Case for Creation*, pp. 122–26, and Karl W. Butzer, "Prehistoric People," in *World Book Encyclopedia* (Chicago: World Book, 1974), 15:666–74.

buried their dead
(example: Neanderthal man)

*homo sapiens sapiens* ("wise, wise     90,000 B.C.
man")
(example: Cro-Magnon man)      18,000–35,000 B.C.
cave paintings

(example: Neolithic man)         19,000 B.C.
cattle raising, agriculture,
metalwork

Whether Christians hold to a young earth or old earth view, they will agree that man is certainly on the earth by the time of the cave paintings by Cro-Magnon man, paintings which date from about 10,000 B.C. There is some variation in the date of Cro-Magnon man, however, since the dating of a Cro-Magnon burial site in Siberia is approximately 20,000 to 35,000 B.C. according to the geological evidence found there, but the Carbon-14 dating method gives a date of only 9,000 B.C., or 11,000 years ago.[51] Earlier than the paintings by Cro-Magnon man, there is disagreement. Was Neanderthal man really a man, or just a human-like creature?[52] How human were earlier man-like creatures? (Higher forms of animals, such as chimpanzees, can use tools, and burial of one's dead is not necessarily a uniquely human trait.) Moreover, dating methods used for earlier periods are very approximate with results that often conflict.[53]

So how long ago did man first appear on the earth? Certainly by 10,000 B.C., if the Cro-Magnon cave paintings have been dated correctly. But before that it is difficult to say.

**c. Did Animals Die Before the Fall?** For young earth advocates, there is no need to ask whether animals died before the fall, because animals and man were both created on the sixth day, and there may have been only a short time before Adam and Eve sinned. This could have introduced death into the animal kingdom as well, as part of the curse of the fall (Gen. 3:17–19; Rom. 8:20–23).

But for old earth advocates, this is an important question. There are millions of apparently ancient fossils in the earth. Might they have come from animals who lived and died for long ages before Adam and Eve were created? Might God have created an animal kingdom that was subject to death from the moment of creation? This is quite possible. There was no doubt death in the plant world, if Adam and Eve were to eat plants; and if God had made an original creation in which animals would reproduce and also live forever, the earth would soon be overcrowded with no hope of relief. The warning to Adam in Genesis 2:17 was only that *he* would die if he ate of the forbidden fruit, not that animals would also begin to die. When Paul says, "Sin came into the world through one man and

---

[51]Kofahl and Segraves, *The Creation Explanation,* p. 207.

[52]Two helpful discussions of the various proposed human ancestors are found in Frair and Davis, *A Case for Creation,* pp. 122–26, and Davis A. Young, *Creation and the Flood,* pp. 146–55. Frair and Davis think that Neanderthal man was "entirely human" although "racially distinct" (p. 125).

[53]Philip Johnson notes that a recent theory that has received support from several molecular biologists is that all humans descended from a "mitochondrial Eve" who lived in Africa less than 200,000 years ago (*Darwin on Trial,* pp. 83, 177–78).

death through sin" (Rom. 5:12a), the following phrase makes clear that he is talking about death for human beings, not for plants and animals, for he immediately adds, "and so death spread to all men because all men sinned" (Rom. 5:12b).

From the information we have in Scripture, we cannot now know whether God created animals subject to aging and death from the beginning, but it remains a real possibility.

**d. What About Dinosaurs?** Current scientific opinion holds that dinosaurs became extinct about 65 million years ago, millions of years before human beings appeared on the earth. But those who hold to six twenty-four-hour days of creation and a young earth would say that dinosaurs were among the creatures created by God on the same day he created man (the sixth day). They would therefore say that dinosaurs and human beings lived on the earth at the same time and that dinosaurs subsequently became extinct (perhaps in the flood). Young earth advocates of course would differ with the methods used to arrive at such ancient dates for dinosaurs.

Among those who hold to an old earth view, some would want to say that dinosaurs were among the creatures that Adam named in Genesis 2:19–20, and that they subsequently perished (perhaps in the flood). They would admit that dinosaurs may have existed earlier, but would say that they did not become extinct until after the time of Adam and Eve. Others would say that the sixth day of creation was millions of years long, and that dinosaurs had already become extinct by the time Adam was created and named the animals. In this case, Adam did not name dinosaurs (the Bible does not say that he did), but he only named all the creatures that were living at the time God brought him all the animals to name (Gen. 2:19–20; see NIV). Of course, this view would require that there was death in the animal world before there was sin (see previous section).

**e. Are the Six Days of Creation Twenty-four-Hour Days?** Much of the dispute between "young earth" and "old earth" advocates hinges on the interpretation of the length of "days" in Genesis 1. Old earth supporters propose that the six "days" of Genesis 1 refer not to periods of twenty-four hours, but rather to long periods of time, millions of years, during which God carried out the creative activities described in Genesis 1. This proposal has led to a heated debate with other evangelicals, which is far from being settled decisively one way or another.

In favor of viewing the six days as long periods of time is the fact that the Hebrew word *yôm*, "day," is sometimes used to refer not to a twenty-four-hour literal day, but to a longer period of time. We see this when the word is used in Genesis 2:4, for example: "In the *day* that the LORD God made the earth and the heavens," a phrase that refers to the entire creative work of the six days of creation. Other examples of the word *day* to mean a period of time are Job 20:28 ("the *day* of God's wrath"); Psalm 20:1 ("The LORD answer you in the *day* of trouble!"); Proverbs 11:4 ("Riches do not profit in the *day* of wrath"); 21:31 ("The horse is made ready for the *day* of battle"); 24:10 ("If you faint in the *day* of adversity, your strength is small"); 25:13 ("the *time* [*yôm*] of harvest"); Ecclesiastes 7:14 ("In the *day* of prosperity be joyful, and in the *day* of adversity consider; God has made the one as well as the other"); many passages referring to "the *day* of the LORD" (such as Isa. 2:12; 13:6, 9; Joel 1:15; 2:1; Zeph. 1:14); and many other Old Testament passages predicting times of judgment or blessing. A concordance will show that this is a frequent sense for the word *day* in the Old Testament.

An additional argument for a long period of time in these "days" is the fact that the sixth day includes so many events that it must have been longer than twenty-four hours. The sixth day of creation (Gen. 1:24–31) includes the creation of animals and the creation of man and woman both ("male and female he created them," Gen. 1:27). It was also on the sixth day that God blessed Adam and Eve and said to them, "Be fruitful and multiply, and fill the earth and subdue it; and have dominion over the fish of the sea and over the birds of the air and over every living thing that moves upon the earth" (Gen. 1:28). But that means that the sixth day included God's creation of Adam, God's putting Adam in the Garden of Eden to till it and keep it, and giving Adam directions regarding the tree of the knowledge of good and evil (Gen. 2:15–17), his bringing all the animals to man for them to be named (Gen. 2:18–20), finding no helper fit for Adam (Gen. 2:20), and then causing a deep sleep to fall upon Adam and creating Eve from his rib (Gen. 2:21–25). The finite nature of man and the incredibly large number of animals created by God would by itself seem to require that a much longer period of time than part of one day would be needed to include so many events—at least that would be an "ordinary" understanding of the passage for an original reader, a consideration that is not unimportant in a debate that often emphasizes what an ordinary reading of the text by the original readers would lead them to conclude.[54] If the sixth day is shown by contextual considerations to be considerably longer than an ordinary twenty-four-hour day, then does not the context itself favor the sense of *day* as simply a "period of time" of unspecified length?

Related to this is one more consideration. The seventh day, it should be noted, is not concluded with the phrase "and there was evening and there was morning, a seventh day." The text just says that God "rested on the seventh day from all his work which he had done" and that "God blessed the seventh day and hallowed it" (Gen. 2:2–3). The possibility, if not the implication, suggested by this is that the seventh day is still continuing. It never ended but is also a "day" that is really a long period of time (cf. John 5:17; Heb. 4:4, 9–10).

Some have objected that whenever the word *day* refers to a period of time other than a twenty-four-hour day in the Old Testament the context makes it clear that this is the case, but since the context does not make this clear in Genesis 1 we must assume that normal days are meant. But to this we may answer that whenever the word *day* means a twenty-four-hour day, the context makes this clear as well. Otherwise, we could not know that a twenty-four-hour day is meant in that context. So this is not a persuasive objection. It simply affirms what everyone agrees to, namely, that the context enables us to determine which sense a word will take when it has various possible meanings.

Another objection is that the Bible could have used other words if a period longer than a twenty-four-hour day was intended. However, if (as is clearly the

---

[54]Advocates of a twenty-four-hour day can give scenarios whereby Adam only named representative types of animals or named them rapidly without any observation of their activities or abilities, but both suggestions are much less likely interpretations in view of the importance attached to naming in the Old Testament.

case) the original readers knew that the word *day* could mean a long period of time, then there was no need to use some other word, for the word *yôm* conveyed the intended meaning quite well. Furthermore, it was a very appropriate word to use when describing six successive periods of work plus a period of rest that would set the pattern for the seven days of the week in which people would live.

That brings us back to the original question, namely, what does the word *day* mean in the context of Genesis 1? The fact that the word must refer to a longer period of time just a few verses later in the same narrative (Gen. 2:4) should caution us against making dogmatic statements that the original readers would have certainly known that the author was talking about twenty-four-hour days. In fact, both senses were commonly known meanings in the minds of the original readers of this narrative.[55]

It is important to realize that those who advocate long periods of time for the six "days" of creation are not saying that the context *requires* that these be understood as periods of time. They are simply saying that the context does not clearly specify for us one meaning of *day* or another, and if convincing scientific data about the age of the earth, drawn from many different disciplines and giving similar answers, convinces us that the earth is billions of years old, then this possible interpretation of *day* as a long period of time may be the best interpretation to adopt. In this way, the situation is something like that faced by those who first held that the earth rotates on its axis and revolves about the sun. They would not say that the passages about the sun "rising" or "going down" *require* us, in their contexts, to believe in a heliocentric (sun-centered) solar system, but that this is a *possible* understanding of the texts, seeing them as only speaking from the standpoint of the observer. Observational evidence taken from science informs us that this is in fact the correct way to interpret those texts.

On the other side of this question are the arguments in favor of understanding "day" as a twenty-four-hour day in Genesis 1:

1. It is significant that each of the days of Genesis 1 ends with an expression such as, "And there was evening, and there was morning—the first day" (Gen. 1:5 NIV). The phrase "And there was evening, and there was morning" is repeated in verses 8, 13, 19, 23, and 31. This seems to imply the sequence of events marking a literal twenty-four-hour day and suggests that the readers should understand it in that way.

This is a strong argument from context, and many have found it persuasive. Yet those who hold to a long period of time for these "days" could respond (a) that even evening and morning do not constitute an entire day, but only the end of one day and the beginning of another, so the expression itself may be simply part of the author's way of telling us that the end of the first creative day (that is, long period of time) occurred, and the beginning of the next creative "day" had come;[56] and also (b) that the first three creative "days" could not have been marked by evening and morning as caused by the sun shining on the earth, for the sun was not created until the fourth day (Gen. 1:14–19); thus, the very context shows

---

[55]I am assuming here that Moses wrote both Genesis and Exodus, and that the original readers were the people of Israel in the wilderness around 1440 B.C.

[56]In fact, the expression "and there was evening and there was morning" is never elsewhere used in the Hebrew Old Testament, so it cannot be said to be a common expression used to designate a normal day.

that "evening and morning" in this chapter does not refer to the ordinary evening and morning of days as we know them now. So the argument from "evening and morning," though it may give some weight to the twenty-four-hour view, does not seem to tip the balance decisively in its favor.

2. The third day of creation cannot be very long, because the sun does not come into being until the fourth day, and plants cannot live long without light. In response to this, it might be said that the light that God created on the first day energized the plants for millions of years. But that would suppose God to have created a light that is almost exactly like sunlight in brightness and power, but still not sunlight—an unusual suggestion.

3. It is hard to avoid the conclusion that in the Ten Commandments the word *day* is used to mean a twenty-four-hour day:

> Remember the sabbath day, to keep it holy. Six *days* you shall labor, and do all your work; but the seventh *day* is a sabbath to the LORD your God; . . . for in six *days* the LORD made heaven and earth, the sea, and all that is in them, and rested the seventh day; therefore the LORD blessed the sabbath day and hallowed it." (Ex. 20:8–11)

Certainly in that text the sabbath "day" is a twenty-four-hour day. And must we not say that verse 11, which in the same sentence says that the Lord made heaven and earth in "six days," uses "day" in the same sense? This is again a weighty argument, and on balance it gives additional persuasiveness to the twenty-four-hour day position. But once again it is not quite conclusive in itself, for one could respond that the readers were aware (from a careful reading of Gen. 1–2) that the days there were unspecified periods of time, and that the sabbath commandment merely told God's people that, just as he followed a six-plus-one pattern in creation (six periods of work followed by a period of rest), so they were to follow a six-plus-one pattern in their lives (six days of work followed by a day of rest; also six years of work followed by a sabbath year of rest, as in Ex. 23:10–11). In fact, in the very next sentence of the Ten Commandments, "day" means "a period of time": "Honor your father and your mother, that your *days* may be long in the land which the LORD your God gives you" (Ex. 20:12). Certainly here the promise is not for "long" literal days (such as twenty-five- or twenty-six-hour days!), but rather that the period of one's life may be lengthened upon the earth.[57]

4. Those who argue for "day" as a twenty-four-hour day also ask whether anywhere else in the Hebrew Bible the word "days" in the plural, especially when a number is attached (such as "six days"), ever refers to anything but twenty-four-hour days. This argument is not compelling, however, because (a) a plural example of "days" to mean periods of time is found in Exodus 20:12, discussed in the previous paragraph and (b) if the word clearly takes the sense "period of time" in the singular (which it does, as all admit), then to speak of six such "periods" of time would certainly be understandable to the readers, even if the Old Testament did not elsewhere have examples of such a meaning. The fact that such an expression does not appear elsewhere may mean nothing more than that there was no occasion to use it elsewhere.

---

[57]The Hebrew text does not say "that your days may be *many* (Heb. *rab*)" which is a common Hebrew expression (Gen. 21:34; 37:34; Ex. 2:23; Num. 9:19; et al.), but "that your days may be *long*" (Heb. *'arak,* "be long," used also as physical length in 1 Kings 8:8; Ps. 129:3; Isa. 54:2 ["lengthen your cords"]; Ezek. 31:5).

5. When Jesus says, "But from the beginning of creation, 'God made them male and female'" (Mark 10:6), he implies that Adam and Eve were not created billions of years after the beginning of creation, but at the beginning of creation. This argument also has some force, but old earth advocates may respond that Jesus is just referring to the whole of Genesis 1–2 as the "beginning of creation," in contrast to the argument from the laws given by Moses that the Pharisees were depending on (v. 4).

I have given an answer to each of the five arguments for a twenty-four-hour day, but these answers may not persuade its advocates. They would respond to the "period of time" position as follows: (1) Of course, it is true that *day* may mean "period of time" in many places in the Old Testament, but that does not demonstrate that *day* must have that meaning in Genesis 1. (2) The sixth day of creation need not have been longer than twenty-four hours, especially if Adam only named major representative kinds of birds and of "every beast of the field" (Gen. 2:20). (3) Though there was no sun to mark the first three days of creation, nonetheless, the earth was still rotating on its axis at a fixed speed, and there was "light" and "darkness" that God created on the first day (Gen. 1:3–4), and he called the light "day" and the darkness "night" (Gen. 3:5). So God in some way caused an alternation between day and night from the very first day of creation, according to Genesis 1:3–5.

What shall we conclude about the length of days in Genesis 1? It does not seem at all easy to decide with the information we now have. It is not simply a question of "believing the Bible" or "not believing the Bible," nor is it a question of "giving in to modern science" or "rejecting the clear conclusions of modern science." Even for those who believe in the complete truthfulness of Scripture (such as the present author), and who retain some doubt about the exceptionally long periods of time scientists propose for the age of the earth (such as the present author), the question does not seem to be easy to decide. At present, considerations of the power of God's creative word and the immediacy with which it seems to bring response, the fact that "evening and morning" and the numbering of days still suggest twenty-four-hour days, and the fact that God would seem to have no purpose for delaying the creation of man for thousands or even millions of years, seem to me to be strong considerations in favor of the twenty-four-hour day position. But even here there are good arguments on the other side: To the one who lives forever, for whom "one day is as a thousand years, and a thousand years as one day" (2 Peter 3:8), who delights in gradually working out all his purposes over time, perhaps 15 billion years is just the right amount of time to take in preparing the universe for man's arrival and 4.5 billion years in preparing the earth. The evidence of incredible antiquity in the universe would then serve as a vivid reminder of the even more amazing nature of God's eternity, just as the incredible size of the universe causes us to wonder at God's even greater omnipresence and omnipotence.

Therefore, with respect to the length of days in Genesis 1, the possibility must be left open that God has chosen not to give us enough information to come to a clear decision on this question, and the real test of faithfulness to him may be the degree to which we can act charitably toward those who in good conscience and full belief in God's Word hold to a different position on this matter.

**4. Both "Old Earth" and "Young Earth" Theories Are Valid Options for Christians Who Believe the Bible Today.** After discussing several preliminary considerations regarding the age of the earth, we come finally to the specific arguments for old earth and young earth views.

**a. "Old Earth" Theories of Creation:** In this first category we list two viewpoints held by those who believe in an old earth with an age of about 4.5 billion years and a universe about 15 billion years old.

**(1) Day-Age View:**

Many who believe that the earth is many millions of years old maintain that the days of Genesis 1 are extremely long "ages" of time.[58] The arguments given above for long days in Genesis 1 will apply here, and, as we argued above, the words of the Hebrew text do allow for the days to be long periods of time. The evident advantage of this view is that, if the current scientific estimate for an earth 4.5 billion years old is correct, it explains how the Bible is consistent with this fact. Among evangelicals who hold to an old earth view, this is a common position. This view is sometimes called a "concordist" view because it seeks agreement or "concord" between the Bible and scientific conclusions about dating.

Many have been attracted to this position because of scientific evidence regarding the age of the earth. A very helpful survey of the views of theologians and scientists regarding the age of the earth, from ancient Greece to the twentieth century, is found in a book by a professional geologist who is also an evangelical Christian, Davis A. Young, *Christianity and the Age of the Earth.*[59] Young demonstrates that in the nineteenth and twentieth centuries, many Christian geologists, under the weight of apparently overwhelming evidence, have concluded that the earth is about 4.5 billion years old. Although some "young earth" proponents (see discussion below) have claimed that radiometric dating techniques are inaccurate because of changes that occurred on the earth at the time of the flood, Young notes that radiometric dating of rocks from the moon and of meteorites recently fallen to the earth, which could not have been affected by Noah's flood, coincide with many other radiometric evidences from various materials on the earth, and that the results of these tests are "remarkably consistent in pointing to about 4.5–4.7 billion years."[60]

Some of Young's most forceful arguments for an old earth, in addition to those from radiometric dating, include the time required for liquid magma to cool (about 1 million years for a large formation in southern California), the time and pressure required for the formation of many metamorphic rocks that contain small fossils (some apparently could only be formed by the pressure of being buried twelve to eighteen miles under ground and later brought to the surface—but

---

[58]One variation of this view would say that the six days were twenty-four-hour days, but there were millions of years between each day and the following one. This is certainly possible, but the difficulty with this view is that it seems to be importing "gaps" between all the days simply to account for scientific chronology, with no clear evidence in the text to support it. This view is defended by Robert C. Newman and Herman J. Eckelmann, Jr., *Genesis One and the Origin of the Earth* (Downers Grove, Ill.: InterVarsity Press, 1977).

[59]Grand Rapids: Zondervan, 1982, pp. 13–67.

[60]*Christianity and the Age of the Earth*, p. 63; see also the detailed discussion on pp. 93–116, and *Creation and the Flood*, pp. 185–93.

when could this have happened on a young earth view?), continental drift (fossil-bearing rock fields near the coasts of Africa and South America were apparently previously joined together, then separated by continental drift, something that could not have happened in 20,000 years at the present rate of two centimeters per year),[61] and coral reefs (some of which apparently would have required hundreds of thousands of years of gradual deposits to attain their present state).[62] Several other arguments, especially from astronomy, have been summarized by Robert C. Newman and Herman J. Eckelmann, Jr., in *Genesis One and the Origin of the Earth*.[63] These arguments favor an old earth view, and the day-age theory is an attractive position for old earth advocates.

The day-age view is certainly possible, but it has several difficulties: (1) The sequence of events in Genesis 1 does not exactly correspond to current scientific understanding of the development of life, which puts sea creatures (Day 5) before trees (Day 3), and insects and other land animals (Day 6), as well as fish (Day 5), before birds (Day 5).[64] (2) The greatest difficulty for this view is that it puts the sun, moon, and stars (Day 4) millions of years *after* the creation of plants and trees (Day 3). That makes no sense at all according to current scientific opinion, which sees the stars as formed long before the earth or any living creatures on the earth. It also makes no sense in terms of the way the earth now operates, for plants do not grow without sunlight, and there are many plants (Day 3) that do not pollinate without birds or flying insects (Day 5), and there are many birds (Day 5) that live off creeping insects (Day 6). Moreover, how would the waters on the earth keep from freezing for millions of years without the sun?

In response, those who hold the concordist view say that the sun, moon, and stars were created on Day 1 (the creation of light) or before Day 1, when "in the beginning God created the heavens and the earth" (Gen. 1:1), and that the sun, moon, and stars were only *made visible* or *revealed* on Day 4 (Gen. 1:14–19). But this argument is not very convincing, because all the other five days of creation involve not *revealing* something that was previously created but actually *creating* things for the first time. Moreover, the creative statements are similar to those of other days, "And God said, 'Let there be lights in the firmament of the heavens to

---

[61]See *Creation and the Flood*, pp. 171–210, for these examples. A continental drift of 2 cm. per year x 20,000 years = 40,000 cm. or 400 m. (about 437 yd. or ¼ mile). This hardly accounts for the present distance between South America and Africa.

[62]*Christianity and the Age of the Earth*, pp. 84–86. Coral reefs are not formed by the immense pressure of a flood, but by tiny sea creatures (called coral polyps) who attach themselves to each other and build colorful limestone formations by removing calcium carbonate from seawater and depositing it around the lower half of their body. When they die, their limestone "skeletons" remain behind, and, over tens of thousands of years, huge coral reefs are formed. This can only happen in water warmer than 65° F (18° C), and in water clear and shallow enough for photosynthesis to occur in algae, which the coral polyps need to produce their skeletons. (See Robert D. Barnes, "Coral," in *World Book Encyclopedia* [Chicago: World Book, 1983], 4:828.)

[63]Downers Grove, Ill.: InterVarsity Press, 1977, pp. 15–34, 89–103. They show that the length of time required for light to reach the earth is not the only astronomical evidence for a very old universe: measurements of star movements show the universe has apparently been expanding for over 15 billion years; background radiation in the universe gives a similar age; and the kind of light coming from certain stars shows that many stars have an age consistent with this estimate. Young earth proponents (see below) may say that God created the light rays in place so Adam and Eve could see stars, but it is much harder to explain why God would have created these other evidences so consistent with a universe about 15 billion years old.

[64]Of course, current scientific hypotheses of these sequences may be incorrect.

separate the day from the night . . . to give light upon the earth.' And it was so"
(Gen. 1:14–15). This is the form of language used in verses 3, 6, 11, 20, and 24
for creating things, not revealing them. Furthermore, the creation (not the
revealing) of the sun, moon, and stars is made explicit in the next sentence: "And
God made the two great lights, the greater light to rule the day, and the lesser
light to rule the night; he made the stars also" (Gen. 1:16). Here the word "made"
(Heb. *'āsāh*) is the same word used when God *made* the firmament, the beasts of
the earth, and man (Gen. 1:7, 25, 26)—in none of these cases is it used to speak
of revealing something previously made. The Hebrew *'āsāh* is also the word used
in the summary in verse 31: "And God saw everything that he had made, and
behold, it was very good." This frequent use throughout Genesis 1 makes it very
unlikely that Genesis 1:16 merely refers to the revealing of the sun, moon, and
stars.

But a modification of the day-age view in response to these objections seems
possible. The verbs in Genesis 1:16 can be taken as perfects, indicating something
that God had done before: "And God *had made* the two great lights, the greater
light to rule the day, and the lesser light to rule the night; he *had made*[65] the stars
also." Grammatically this is possible (this is how the NIV translates the same verb
form in 2:8 and 2:19, for example). This view would imply that God had made the
sun, moon, and stars earlier (in v. 1, the creation of heavens and earth, or in
v. 3, the creation of light) but only placed them near the earth on Day 4, or
allowed them to be seen from the earth on Day 4 (vv. 14–15, 17–18). This
allows the word *made* (*'āsāh*) to mean "created" and thus avoids the difficulty
mentioned above with the view that it means "revealed" in verse 16. This option
remains as a genuine possibility for the day-age view, and in fact this view is the
one that seems most persuasive to the present author, if an old earth position is to
be adopted. With regard to light needed for the plants and warmth needed for the
waters, there was light available from Day 1—even if we are not sure whether this
light was light from the sun and stars or the light of God's glory (which will
replace the sun in the New Jerusalem, Rev. 21:23).[66]

Another answer from the day-age view might be that the fourth day is not
exactly in sequence, though an overall outline of progressive work of God is given.
Yet once we begin changing the sequence of events that is so prominent in this
progression of six creative days, it is doubtful that we need to allow the text to tell
us anything other than the bare fact that God created things—but in that case, the
whole inquiry about the age of the earth is unnecessary. (Further discussion of
disruption in the sequence of days is given in the next section.)

**(2) Literary Framework View:**

Another way of interpreting the days of Genesis 1 has gained a significant
following among evangelicals. Since it argues that Genesis 1 gives us no

---

[65]The second verb is implied by the direct object marker but is not expressed in the Hebrew text; it
would take the same form as the first verb in the sentence.

[66]The question of pollination without birds and insects remains a difficulty for this view, though it
should be noted that even today many plants self-pollinate or are cross-pollinated by the wind, and we
cannot be sure that pollination by flying insects was required before the fall and before creation was
complete. Similarly, the need for some birds to live off creeping insects is a difficulty, but they possibly
ate only plants and seeds before the fall.

information about the age of the earth, it would be compatible with current scientific estimates of a very old earth. This view argues that the six days of Genesis 1 are not intended to indicate a chronological sequence of events, but are rather a literary "framework," which the author uses to teach us about God's creative activity. The framework is skillfully constructed so that the first three days and the second three days correspond to each other.[67]

| Days of forming | Days of filling |
|---|---|
| Day 1: Light and darkness separated | Day 4: Sun, moon, and stars (lights in the heaven) |
| Day 2: Sky and waters separated | Day 5: Fish and birds |
| Day 3: Dry land and seas separated, plants and trees | Day 6: Animals and man |

In this way a parallel construction is seen. On Day 1 God separates light and darkness, while on Day 4 he puts the sun, moon, and stars in the light and in the darkness. On Day 2 he separates the waters and the sky, while on Day 5 he puts the fish in the waters and the birds in the sky. On Day 3 he separates the dry land and the seas and makes plants to grow, while on Day 6 he puts the animals and man on the dry land and gives the plants to them for food.

According to the "framework" view, Genesis 1 should not be read as though the author wanted to inform us about the sequence of days or the order in which things were created, nor did he intend to tell us about the length of time the creation took. The arrangement of six "days" is a literary device the author uses to teach that God created everything. The six "days," which are neither twenty-four-hour days nor long periods of time, give us six different "pictures" of creation, telling us that God made all aspects of the creation, that the pinnacle of his creative activity was man, and that over all creation is God himself, who rested on the seventh day and who calls man therefore to worship him on the sabbath day as well.[68]

In the words of a recent advocate of this position, "Chronology has no place here."[69] The attractions in favor of this hypothesis are (1) the neat correspondence between the pairs of days as shown in the table above, (2) the fact that it avoids any conflict with modern science over the age of the earth and the age of living creatures (since no chronology at all is implied), (3) the way it avoids the conflict of sequence between Genesis 1 and 2 in which man (Gen. 2:7) seems to be formed before plants (Gen. 2:8) and animals (Gen. 2:19), a sequence different from Genesis 1, and (4) the fact that Genesis 2:5 shows that the "days" of creation were not literal twenty-four-hour days, for it says that there were no

---

[67]The following table is adapted from *The NIV Study Bible*, ed. by Kenneth Barker et al. (Grand Rapids: Zondervan, 1985), p. 6 (note to Gen. 1:11). A forceful defense of the "framework" view is found in Henri Blocher, *In the Beginning: The Opening Chapters of Genesis*, trans. by David G. Preston (Leicester: Inter-Varsity Press, 1984), pp. 49–59. Blocher mentions several other evangelical scholars who hold this position, which he calls the "literary interpretation": N. H. Ridderbos, Bernard Ramm, Meredith G. Kline, D. F. Payne, and J. A. Thompson. This "framework" view is called the "pictorial day" view in Millard Erickson, *Christian Theology*, p. 381.

[68]This framework view is also defended by Ronald Youngblood, *How It All Began* (Ventura, Calif.: Regal, 1980), pp. 25–33.

[69]Henri Blocher, *In the Beginning*, p. 52.

plants on the earth because it had not yet rained, something that would not make sense in a six day creation, since plants can certainly survive three or four days without rain.

Several points may be made against the framework theory.

1. First, the proposed correspondence between the days of creation is not nearly as exact as its advocates have supposed. The sun, moon, and stars created on the fourth day as "lights in the firmament of the heavens" (Gen. 1:14) are placed not in any space created on Day 1 but in the "firmament" (Heb. *raqia*) that was created on the second day. In fact, the correspondence in language is quite explicit: this "firmament" is not mentioned at all on Day 1 but five times on Day 2 (Gen. 1: 6–8) and three times on Day 4 (Gen. 1:14–19). Of course Day 4 also has correspondences with Day 1 (in terms of day and night, light and darkness), but if we say that the second three days show the creation of things to fill the forms or spaces created on the first three days, then Day 4 overlaps at least as much with Day 2 as it does with Day 1.

Moreover, the parallel between Days 2 and 5 is not exact, because in some ways the preparation of a space for the fish and birds of Day 5 does not come in Day 2 but in Day 3. It is not until Day 3 that God gathers the waters together and calls them "seas" (Gen. 1:10), and on Day 5 the fish are commanded to "fill the waters in the *seas*" (Gen. 1:22). Again in verses 26 and 28 the fish are called "fish of the *sea*," giving repeated emphasis to the fact that the sphere the fish inhabit was specifically formed on Day 3. Thus, the fish formed on Day 5 seem to belong much more to the place prepared for them on Day 3 than to the widely dispersed waters below the firmament on Day 2. Establishing a parallel between Day 2 and Day 5 faces further difficulties in that nothing is created on Day 5 to inhabit the "waters above the firmament," and the flying things created on this day (the Hebrew word would include flying insects as well as birds) not only fly in the sky created on Day 2, but also live and multiply on the "earth" or "dry land" created on Day 3. (Note God's command on Day 5: "Let birds multiply on the earth" [Gen. 1:22].) Finally, the parallel between Days 3 and 6 is not precise, for nothing is created on Day 6 to fill the seas that were gathered together on Day 3. With all of these points of imprecise correspondence and overlapping between places and things created to fill them, the supposed literary "framework," while having an initial appearance of neatness, turns out to be less and less convincing upon closer reading of the text.

2. Since all proposals for understanding Genesis 1 attempt to provide explanations for scientific data about the age of the earth, this is not a unique argument in favor of the framework theory. However, we must recognize that one aspect of the attractiveness of this theory is the fact that it relieves evangelicals of the burden of even trying to reconcile scientific findings with Genesis 1. Yet, in the words of one advocate of this theory, "So great is the advantage, and for some the relief, that it could constitute a temptation." He wisely adds, "We must not espouse the theory on grounds of its convenience but only if the text leads us in that direction."[70]

3. Those who have not adopted the framework theory have seen no conflict in sequence between Genesis 1 and 2, for it has been commonly understood that

---

[70]Ibid., p. 50.

Genesis 2 implies no description of sequence in the original creation of the animals or plants, but simply recapitulates some of the details of Genesis 1 as important for the specific account of the creation of Adam and Eve in Genesis 2. The NIV avoids the appearance of conflict by translating, "Now the LORD God *had planted* a garden in the East, in Eden" (Gen. 2:8) and "Now the LORD God *had formed out* of the ground all the beasts of the field and all the birds of the air" (Gen. 2:19).

4. Genesis 2:5 does not really say that plants were not on the earth because the earth was too dry to support them. If we adopt that reasoning we would also have to say there were no plants because "there was no man to till the ground" (Gen. 2:5), for that is the second half of the comment about no rain coming on the earth. Moreover, the remainder of the sentence says that the earth was the opposite of being too dry to support plants: "streams came up from the earth and watered the whole surface of the ground" (Gen. 2:6 NIV). The statement in Genesis 2:5 is simply to be understood as an explanation of the general time frame in which God created man. Genesis 2:4–6 sets the stage, telling us that "no plant of the field was yet in the earth and no herb of the field had yet sprung up—for the LORD God had not caused it to rain upon the earth, and there was no man to till the ground; but a mist went up from the earth and watered the whole face of the ground." The statements about lack of rain and no man to till the ground do not give the *physical reason* why there were no plants, but only explain that God's work of creation was not complete. This introduction puts us back into the first six days of creation as a general setting—into "the day that the LORD God made the earth and the heavens" (Gen. 2:4). Then in that setting it abruptly introduces the main point of chapter 2—the creation of man. The Hebrew text does not include the word "then" at the beginning of verse 7, but simply begins, "And the LORD God formed man" (Gen. 2:7 KJV).[71]

5. Finally, the strongest argument against the framework view, and the reason why comparatively few evangelicals have adopted it, is that the whole of Genesis 1 strongly suggests not just a literary framework but a chronological sequence of events. When the narrative proceeds from the less complex aspects of creation (light and darkness, waters, sky, and dry land) to the more complex aspects (fish and birds, animals and man) we see a progressive build-up and an ordered sequence of events that are entirely understandable chronologically. When a sequence of numbers (1-2-3-4-5-6) is attached to a set of days that correspond exactly to the ordinary week human beings experience (Day 1, Day 2, Day 3, Day 4, Day 5, Day 6, Day 7, with rest on Day 7), the implication of chronological sequence in the narrative is almost inescapable. The sequence of days seems more clearly intended than a literary framework which is nowhere made explicit in the text, and in which many details simply do not fit. As Derek Kidner observes:

> The march of the days is too majestic a progress to carry no implication of ordered sequence; it also seems over-subtle to adopt a view of the passage which discounts

---

[71]For further discussion on Gen. 2:5, see Meredith G. Kline, "Because It Had Not Rained," *WTJ* 20 (1957–58): 146–57; and, in response, Derek Kidner, "Genesis 2:5, 6: Wet or Dry?" *TB* 17 (1966): 109–14.

one of the primary impressions it makes on the ordinary reader. It is a story, not only a statement.[72]

6. A sequence of days is also implied in God's command to human beings to imitate his pattern of work plus rest: "Remember the sabbath day, to keep it holy. Six days you shall labor, and do all your work; but the seventh day is a sabbath to the LORD your God . . . for in six days the LORD made heaven and earth, the sea, and all that is in them, and rested the seventh day" (Ex. 20:8–11). But if God did not create the earth by working for six days and resting on the seventh, then the command to imitate him would be misleading or make no sense.

In conclusion, while the "framework" view does not deny the truthfulness of Scripture, it adopts an interpretation of Scripture which, upon closer inspection, seems very unlikely.

**b. "Young Earth" Theories of Creation:** Another group of evangelical interpreters rejects the dating systems that currently give an age of millions of years to the earth and argue instead that the earth is quite young, perhaps 10,000 to 20,000 years old. Young earth advocates have produced a number of scientific arguments for a recent creation of the earth.[73] Those who hold to a young earth generally advocate one or both of the following positions:

**(1) Creation With an Appearance of Age (Mature Creationism):**

Many who hold to a young earth point out that the original creation must have had an "appearance of age" even from the first day. (Another term for this view is "mature creationism," since it affirms that God created a mature creation.) The appearance of Adam and Eve as full-grown adults is an obvious example. They appeared as though they had lived for perhaps twenty or twenty-five years, growing up from infancy as human beings normally do, but in fact they were less than a day old. Similarly, they probably saw the stars the first night that they lived, but the light from most stars would take thousands or even millions of years to reach the earth. This suggests that God created the stars with light beams already in place. And full-grown trees would probably have had rings (Adam and Eve would not have had to wait years before God told them which trees of the garden they could eat from and which they could not, nor would they have had to wait weeks or months before edible plants grew large enough to provide them food). Following this line of reasoning, might we go further and suppose that many

---

[72]D. Kidner, *Genesis: An Introduction and Commentary*, TOTC (Chicago: InterVarsity Press, 1967), pp. 54–55.

[73]Several scientific arguments pointing to a young earth (about 10,000–20,000 years old) are given in Henry M. Morris, ed., *Scientific Creationism* (San Diego, Calif.: Creation-Life, 1974), esp. pp. 131–69; also Kofahl and Segraves, *The Creation Explanation*, pp. 181–213.

A response to most of these arguments, from an "old earth" perspective, is given by Davis A. Young in *Christianity and the Age of the Earth*, pp. 71–131, and, specifically in response to "flood geology," in *Creation and the Flood*, pp. 171–213. Another book, *Science Held Hostage: What's Wrong With Creation Science and Evolutionism*, by Howard J. Van Till, Davis A. Young, and Clarence Menninga (Downers Grove, Ill.: InterVarsity Press, 1988), raises serious objections against the evaluation and use of scientific research materials by some prominent young earth advocates (see pp. 45–125). A preliminary young earth response to Young's arguments is found in a thirty-four-page pamphlet by Henry M. Morris and John D. Morris, *Science, Scripture, and the Young Earth* (El Cajon, Calif.: Institute for Creation Research, 1989).

geological formations, when originally created, had a similar appearance to formations that would now take thousands or even millions of years to complete by present "slow" processes?

This suggestion has currently found many supporters, and, initially at least, it seems to be an attractive proposal. Those who hold this position often combine it with certain objections to current scientific dating processes. They question how we can be certain of the reliability of radiometric dating beyond a few thousand years, for example, and how scientists can know that the rates of decay of certain elements have been constant since creation. They also suggest that events such as the fall and the subsequent cursing of nature (which altered the productivity and ecological balance of the earth, and caused man himself to begin to age and decay, Gen. 3:17–19), or the flood in Noah's time (Gen. 6–9), may have brought about significant differences in the amount of radioactive material in living things. This would mean that estimates of the age of the earth using present methods of measurement would not be accurate.

A common objection to this "appearance of age" view is that it "makes God an apparent deceiver,"[74] something that is contrary to his nature. But is God a "deceiver" if he creates a mature man and woman in a day and then tells us explicitly that he did it? Or if he creates mature fish and animals and full-grown trees and tells us that he did it? Or if he allows Adam and Eve to see the stars, which he created in order that people might see them and give glory to him, on the first night that they lived? Rather than manifesting deception, it seems that these actions point to God's infinite wisdom and power. This is particularly so if God explicitly tells us that he created everything in "six days." According to this position, those who are deceived are those who refuse to hear God's own explanation of how the creation came about.

The real problem with the appearance of age view is that there are some things in the universe that it cannot easily account for. Everyone will agree that Adam and Eve were created as adults, not newborn infants, and therefore had an appearance of age. Most who hold to twenty-four-hour days in Genesis 1 would also say there was an appearance of age with plants and trees, and with all the animals when they were first created (the chicken came before the egg!), and probably with light from the stars. But the creation of fossils presents a real problem, for responsible Christians would not want to suggest that God scattered fossils throughout the earth to give an added appearance of age! This would not be creating something "in process" or in a state of maturity; it would be creating the remains of a dead animal, not so that the animal could serve Adam and Eve, but simply to make people think the earth was older than it really was. Furthermore, one would have to say that God created all these dead animals and called them "very good."[75]

While the creation of stars with light beams in place or trees that are mature would be for the purpose of enabling human beings to glorify God for the

---

[74]Millard Erickson, *Christian Theology*, p. 382.

[75]We should note that old earth advocates must also have God speaking in Gen. 1:31 and calling the old fossils "very good." This is not a decisive objection if the death of animals before the fall did not result from sin, but it is a difficulty. Only flood geology advocates (see below) will say that no fossils existed at Gen. 1:31, but that they were deposited suddenly by the flood in Gen. 6–9. This perhaps is a consideration in favor of the flood geology position.

excellence of his creation, the depositing of fossils in the earth could only be for the purpose of misleading or deceiving human beings regarding the earlier history of the world. More problematic is that Adam, the plants, the animals, and the stars all would have appeared to have different ages (because they were created with mature functions in place), whereas modern geological research gives approximately the same age estimates from radiometric dating, astronomical estimates, rock formations, samples of moon rocks and meteorites, etc. Why would God create so many different indications of an earth that is 4.5 billion years old if this were not true? Would it not be better to conclude that the earth is 4.5 billion years old, and that God left many indications there to show us this fact rather than in any way imply that he deceived us? So it seems the only credible explanations for the fossil record that Christians can adopt are: (a) current dating methods are incorrect by colossal proportions because of flawed assumptions or because of changes brought about by the fall or the flood; or (b) current dating methods are approximately correct and the earth is many millions or even billions of years old.

### (2) Flood Geology:

Another common view among evangelicals is what may be called "flood geology." This is the view that the tremendous natural forces unleashed by the flood at the time of Noah (Gen. 6–9) significantly altered the face of the earth, causing the creation of coal and diamonds, for example, within the space of a year rather than hundreds of millions of years, because of the extremely high pressure exerted by the water on the earth. This view also claims that the flood deposited fossils in layers of incredibly thick sediment all over the earth.[76] The flood geology view is also called "neo-catastrophism" because its advocates attribute most of the present geological status of the earth to the immense catastrophe of the flood.

The geological arguments put forth by advocates of this view are technical and difficult for the nonspecialist to evaluate. Personally, though I think the flood of Genesis 6–9 was world-wide, and that it did have a significant impact on the face of the earth, and that all living people and animals outside the ark perished in the flood, I am not persuaded that all of the earth's geological formations were caused by Noah's flood rather than by millions of years of sedimentation, volcanic eruptions, movement of glaciers, continental drift, and so forth. The controversy over flood geology is strikingly different from the other areas of dispute regarding creation, for its advocates have persuaded almost no professional geologists, even those who are Bible-believing evangelical Christians. By contrast, the books objecting to evolution that we mentioned above chronicle 130 years of cogent objections to Darwinian evolution that have been raised by a significant number of biologists, biochemists, zoologists, anthropologists, and paleontologists, both Christian and non-Christian, because evolution has so many problems in explaining facts evident from observation of the created world. If present geological formations could only be explained as the result of a universal flood,

---

[76]See Henry M. Morris and John C. Whitcomb, *The Genesis Flood* (Philadelphia: Presbyterian and Reformed, 1961); John C. Whitcomb, *The World That Perished* (Grand Rapids: Baker, 1988); Stephen A. Austin, *Catastrophes in Earth History* (El Cajon, Calif.: Institute for Creation Research, 1984). Other studies by flood geology advocates have been published in the *CRSQ*, though by no means all articles in that journal advocate the flood geology perspective, nor do all members of the Creation Research Society hold to flood geology.

then would this not be evident even to non-Christians who look at the evidence? Would not the hundreds of Christians who are professional geologists be prepared to acknowledge the evidence if it were there? It may be that the flood geologists are right, but if they are, we would expect to see more progress in persuading some professional geologists that their case is a plausible one.[77]

**5. Conclusions on the Age of the Earth.** How old is the earth then? Where does this discussion leave us? Young's arguments for an old earth based on many kinds of scientific data from different disciplines seem (to the present writer at least) to be very strong. This is particularly true of arguments based on fossil-bearing rocks, coral reefs, continental drift, and the similarity of results from different kinds of radiometric dating. Newman and Eckelmann's arguments from astronomy indicating a very old universe give significant added weight. It is understandable, on the one hand, that God may have created a universe in which stars appeared to have been shining for 15 billion years, Adam appeared to have been living for 25 years, some trees appeared to have been living for 50 years, and some animals appeared to have been living for 1 to 10 years. But, on the other hand, it is difficult to understand why God would have created dozens or perhaps hundreds of different kinds of rocks and minerals on the earth, all of which actually were only one day old, but all of which had an appearance of being exactly 4.5 billion years old—exactly the apparent age that he also gave the moon and the meteorites when they, too, were only one day old. And it is difficult to understand why the evidence of star life cycles and the expansion of the universe would make the universe appear to be 15 billion years old if it were not. It is possible, but it seems unlikely, almost as if God's only purpose in giving these uniform apparent ages was to mislead us rather than simply to have a mature, functioning universe in place. So the old earth advocates seem to me to have a greater weight of scientific evidence on their side, and it seems that the weight of evidence is increasing yearly.

On the other hand, the interpretations of Genesis 1 presented by old earth advocates, while possible, do not seem as natural to the sense of the text. Davis Young's own solution of "seven successive figurative days of indeterminate duration"[78] really does not solve the problem, for he is willing to spread God's creative activities around on the various days as needed in order to make the sequence scientifically possible. For example, he thinks that some birds were created before Day 5:

> We may also suggest that even though birds were created on the fifth day, nevertheless, the most primitive birds or original bird ancestors were miraculously formed on a day prior to the fifth day. Hence the data of Genesis 1 actually allow for some overlap of the events of the days. If such overlap exists, then all apparent discrepancies between Genesis 1 and science would fall away (p. 131).

But this procedure allows us to say that the events of creation occurred at almost any time, no matter whether Scripture says they occurred then or not. Once this

---

[77]The arguments against flood geology have been marshalled by an evangelical who is also a professional geologist; see Davis A. Young, *Creation and the Flood: An Alternative to Flood Geology and Theistic Evolution,* and *Christianity and the Age of the Earth.*

[78]*Creation and the Flood,* p. 89.

procedure is adopted, then ultimately we can know little if anything about the sequence of creation events from Genesis 1, because any of the events narrated there may have had precursors at previous periods of time. This can hardly be the impression the original readers were intended to get from the text. (Much more likely, however, is the modified day-age view presented on pp. 298–300 above.)

**6. The Need for Further Understanding.** Although our conclusions are tentative, at this point in our understanding, Scripture seems to be more easily understood to *suggest* (but not to require) a young earth view, while the observable facts of creation seem increasingly to favor an old earth view. Both views are possible, but neither one is certain. And we must say very clearly that the age of the earth is a matter that is not directly taught in Scripture, but is something we can think about only by drawing more or less probable inferences from Scripture. Given this situation, it would seem best (1) to admit that God may not allow us to find a clear solution to this question before Christ returns, and (2) to encourage evangelical scientists and theologians who fall in both the young earth and old earth camps to begin to work together with much less arrogance, much more humility, and a much greater sense of cooperation in a common purpose.

There are difficulties with both old earth and young earth viewpoints, difficulties that the proponents of each view often seem unable to see in their own positions. Progress will certainly be made if old earth and young earth scientists who are Christians will be more willing to talk to each other without hostility, *ad hominem* attacks, or highly emotional accusations, on the one hand, and without a spirit of condescension or academic pride on the other, for these attitudes are not becoming to the body of Christ, nor are they characteristic of the way of wisdom, which is "first pure, then peaceable, gentle, open to reason, full of mercy and good fruits, without uncertainty or insincerity," and full of the recognition that "the harvest of righteousness is sown in peace by those who make peace" (James 3:17–18).

As for evangelism and apologetics done in publications designed to be read outside the evangelical world, young earth and old earth proponents could cooperate much more in amassing the extremely strong arguments for creation by intelligent design, and in laying aside their differences over the age of the earth. Too often young earth proponents have failed to distinguish scientific arguments for creation by design from scientific arguments for a young earth, and have therefore prevented old earth advocates from joining them in a battle for the minds of an unbelieving scientific community. Moreover, young earth proponents have sometimes failed to recognize that scientific arguments for a young earth (which seem to them to be very persuasive) are not nearly as strong as the overwhelming scientific arguments for creation by intelligent design. As a result, young earth proponents have too often given the impression that the only true "creationists" are those who believe not only in creation by God but also in a young earth. The result has been unfortunate divisiveness and lack of community among scientists who are Christians—to the delight of Satan and the grieving of God's Holy Spirit.

Finally, we can view this controversy with some expectancy that there will be further progress in scientific understanding of the age of the earth. It is likely that scientific research in the next ten or twenty years will tip the weight of evidence decisively toward either a young earth or an old earth view, and the weight of Christian scholarly opinion (from both biblical scholars and scientists) will begin to shift decisively in one direction or another. This should not cause alarm to advocates of either position, because the truthfulness of Scripture is not threatened (our interpretations of Genesis 1 have enough uncertainty that either position is possible). Both sides need to grow in knowledge of the truth, even if this means abandoning a long-held position.

## F. Application

The doctrine of creation has many applications for Christians today. It makes us realize that the material universe is good in itself, for God created it good and wants us to use it in ways pleasing to him. Therefore we should seek to be like the early Christians, who "partook of food with glad and generous hearts" (Acts 2:46), always with thanksgiving to God and trust in his provisions. A healthy appreciation of creation will keep us from false asceticism that denies the goodness of creation and the blessings that come to us through it. It will also encourage some Christians to do scientific and technological research into the goodness of God's abundant creation, or to support such research.[79] The doctrine of creation will also enable us to recognize more clearly that scientific and technological study in itself glorifies God, for it enables us to discover how incredibly wise, powerful, and skillful God was in his work of creation. "Great are the works of the LORD, studied by all who have pleasure in them" (Ps. 111:2).

The doctrine of creation also reminds us that God is sovereign over the universe he created. He made it all, and he is Lord of all of it. We owe all that we are and have to him, and we may have complete confidence that he will ultimately defeat all his enemies and be manifested as Sovereign King to be worshiped forever. In addition, the incredible size of the universe and the amazing complexity of every created thing will, if our hearts are right, draw us continually to worship and praise him for his greatness.

Finally, as we indicated above, we can wholeheartedly enjoy creative activities (artistic, musical, athletic, domestic, literary, etc.) with an attitude of thanksgiving that our Creator God enables us to imitate him in our creativity.

## QUESTIONS FOR PERSONAL APPLICATION

1. Are there ways in which you could be more thankful to God for the excellence of his creation? Look around you and give some examples of the goodness of the creation that God has allowed you to enjoy. Are there ways in which you could be a better steward of parts of God's creation of which he has entrusted to your care?

---

[79]Frair and Davis, *A Case for Creation,* pp. 135–40, have many specific practical challenges to scientists who believe in creation to do specific kinds of greatly needed research.

2. Might the goodness of all that God created encourage you to try to enjoy different kinds of foods than those you normally prefer? Can children be taught to thank God for variety in the things God has given us to eat? Does the doctrine of creation provide an answer to some strict animal rights advocates who say we should not eat steak or chicken or other meat, or wear clothing made from animal skins, since we are simply another form of animal ourselves? (See Gen. 3:21.)

3. In order to understand something of the despair felt by contemporary non-Christians, just try to imagine for a moment that you believe that there is no God and that you are just a product of matter plus time plus chance, the spontaneous result of random variation in organisms over millions of years. How would you feel differently about yourself? About other people? About the future? About right and wrong?

4. Why do we feel joy when we are able to "subdue" even a part of the earth and make it useful for serving us—whether it be in growing vegetables, developing a better kind of plastic or metal, or using wool to knit a piece of clothing? Should we feel joy at the accomplishment of these and other tasks? What other attitudes of heart should we feel as we do them?

5. When you think about the immensity of the stars, and that God put them in place to show us his power and glory, how does it make you feel about your place in the universe? Is this different from the way a non-Christian would feel?

6. Before reading this chapter, what did you think about the theory of evolution? How has your view changed, if at all?

7. What are some things that Christians can learn about theological discussion in general from observing the current controversy over the age of the earth? What significance do you see in this controversy for your own Christian faith?

## SPECIAL TERMS

concordist theory
creation *ex nihilo*
Cro-Magnon man
day-age theory
deism
dualism
flood geology
gap theory
*homo sapiens*

ideal time theory
immanent
literary framework
 theory
macro-evolution
materialism
mature creationism
micro-evolution
neo-catastrophism

old-earth theory
pantheism
pictorial-day theory
progressive creationism
theistic evolution
transcendent
twenty-four-hour day
 theory
young earth theory

## BIBLIOGRAPHY

(For an explanation of this bibliography see the note on the bibliography to chapter 1, p. 38. Complete bibliographical data may be found on pp. 1223–29.)

## Sections in Evangelical Systematic Theologies

1. Anglican (Episcopalian)
   1882–92     Litton, 74–76
2. Arminian (Wesleyan or Methodist)
   1875–76     Pope, 1:361–420
   1892–94     Miley, 1:276–310
   1940     Wiley, 1:440–72
   1960     Purkiser, 145–48, 149–63
   1983     Carter, 1:130–32, 145–94, 203–8
   1983–     Cottrell, 1:48–191
   1987–90     Oden, 1:225–69
3. Baptist
   1767     Gill, 1:366–75
   1887     Boyce, 166–73
   1907     Strong, 371–410
   1917     Mullins, 251–64
   1976–83     Henry, 6:108–96
   1983–85     Erickson, 365–86
   1987–94     Lewis/Demarest, 2:17–70
4. Dispensational
   1947     Chafer, 7:99–101, 146
   1949     Thiessen, 111–18
   1986     Ryrie, 171–94
5. Lutheran
   1917–24     Pieper, 1:467–82
   1934     Mueller, 179–88
6. Reformed (or Presbyterian)
   1559     Calvin, 1:159–83 (1.14)
   1724–58     Edwards, 1:94–121
   1861     Heppe, 190–200
   1871–73     Hodge, 1:550–574; 2:3–41
   1878     Dabney, 26–38, 247–63
   1887–1921     Warfield, SSW, 2:132–41
   1889     Shedd, 1:463–526; 2a:3–94
   1937–66     Murray, CW, 1:325–29; CW, 2:3–13
   1938     Berkhof, 126–40, 150–64
   1962     Buswell, 1:134–62, 321–43
7. Renewal (or charismatic/Pentecostal)
   1988–92     Williams, 1:95–116

### Sections in Representative Roman Catholic Systematic Theologies

1. Roman Catholic: Traditional
   1955    Ott, 79–86, 92–94, 100
2. Roman Catholic: Post-Vatican II
   1980    McBrien, 1:224–28

### Other Works

Several of these titles have been taken from an extensive bibliography on creation and evolution prepared by a professional biologist, Dr. Wayne Frair of The King's College, Briarcliff Manor, New York.

Anderson, J. Kerby, and Harold G. Coffin. *Fossils in Focus*. Grand Rapids: Zondervan, 1977.

Austin, Stephen A. *Catastrophes in Earth History*. El Cajon, Calif.: Institute of Creation Research, 1984. (young earth view)

Barclay, D. R. "Creation." In *NDT*, pp. 177–79.

Blocher, Henri. *In the Beginning: The Opening Chapters of Genesis*. Trans. by David G. Preston. Leicester: Inter-Varsity Press, 1984.

Cameron, Nigel M. de S. *Evolution and the Authority of the Bible*. Exeter: Paternoster, 1983.

———, ed. *In the Beginning. . . .: A Symposium on the Bible and Creation*. Glasgow: The Biblical Creation Society, 1980.

Clotz, J. W. *Genes, Genesis and Evolution*. St. Louis, Mo.: Concordia Publishing House, 1970.

———. *Studies in Creation*. St. Louis, Mo.: Concordia Publishing House, 1985.

Custance, Arthur C. *Evolution or Creation*. Grand Rapids: Zondervan, 1976.

———. *Without Form and Void: A Study of the Meaning of Genesis 1:2*. Brockville, Ontario: Doorway Papers, 1970.

Davidheiser, Bolton. *Evolution and the Christian Faith*. Grand Rapids: Baker, 1969.

Denton, Michael. *Evolution: A Theory in Crisis*. Bethesda, Md.: Adler and Adler, 1986.

De Young, Donald B. *Astronomy and the Bible: Questions and Answers*. Grand Rapids: Baker, 1989. (young earth view)

Fields, Weston W. *Unformed and Unfilled*. Nutley, N.J.: Presbyterian and Reformed, 1976.

Frair, Wayne, and Percival Davis. *A Case for Creation*. Norcross, Ga.: CRS Books, 1983.

Gange, Robert. *Origins and Destiny: A Scientist Examines God's Handiwork*. Waco, Tex.: Word, 1986.

Geisler, Norman L. and J. Kerby Anderson. *Origin Science: A Proposal for the Creation-Evolution Controversy*. Foreword by Walter L. Bradley. Grand Rapids: Baker, 1987.

Gentry, R. V. *Creation's Tiny Mystery*. Knoxville, Tenn.: Earth Science Associates, 1986.

Gish, D. T. *Evolution: The Challenge of the Fossil Record.* El Cajon, Calif.: Master Books, 1985. (young earth view)

Houston, James. *I Believe in the Creator.* Grand Rapids: Eerdmans, 1980.

Hummel, Charles E. *Creation or Evolution? Resolving the Crucial Issues.* Downers Grove, Ill.: InterVarsity Press, 1989.

Johnson, Philip E. *Darwin on Trial.* Downers Grove, Ill.: InterVarsity Press, 1991.

Kaiser, Christopher B. *Creation and the History of Science.* Grand Rapids: Eerdmans, 1991.

Kerkut, G. A. *Implications of Evolution.* New York: Pergamon, 1960.

Kofahl, Robert E., and Kelly L. Segraves. *The Creation Explanation: A Scientific Alternative to Evolution.* Wheaton, Ill.: Harold Shaw, 1975. (young earth view)

Lester, L. P., and R. G. Bohlin. *The Natural Limits to Biological Change.* Grand Rapids: Zondervan, 1984.

Maatman, Russell. *The Bible, Natural Science and Evolution.* Grand Rapids: Reformed Fellowship, 1970.

Morris, Henry M., ed. *Scientific Creationism.* San Diego, Calif.: Creation-Life, 1974. (young earth view)

————, and John C. Whitcomb. *The Genesis Flood.* Philadelphia: Presbyterian and Reformed, 1961. (young earth view)

————, and John D. Morris. *Science, Scripture, and the Young Earth: An Answer to Current Arguments Against the Biblical Doctrine of Recent Creation.* El Cajon, Calif.: Institute for Creation Research, 1989. (young earth view)

Newman, Robert C., and Herman J. Eckelmann. *Genesis One and the Origin of the Earth.* Downers Grove, Ill.: InterVarsity Press, 1977. (argues against young earth view)

Pitman, M. *Adam and Evolution.* Grand Rapids: Baker, 1984.

Ramm, Bernard. *The Christian View of Science and Scripture.* Grand Rapids: Eerdmans, 1954.

Ross, Hugh. *Creation and Time: A Biblical and Scientific Perspective on the Creation-Date Controversy.* Colorado Springs: NavPress, 1994. (an articulate and highly trained scientist who argues against the young earth view on the basis of recent scientific evidence)

Rusch, W. H., Sr. *The Argument—Creationism vs. Evolutionism.* Norcross, Ga: CRS Books, 1984.

Schaeffer, Francis. *No Final Conflict.* Downers Grove, Ill.: InterVarsity Press, 1975.

Thaxton, C. B., W. L. Bradley, and R. L. Olsen. *The Mystery of Life's Origin: Reassessing Current Theories.* New York: Philosophical Library, 1984.

Van Till, Howard J., Davis A. Young, and Clarence Menninga. *Science Held Hostage: What's Wrong With Creation Science and Evolutionism?* Downers Grove, Ill.: InterVarsity Press, 1988. (argues against young earth view)

Whitcomb, John C. *The World That Perished.* Grand Rapids: Baker, 1988. (young earth view)

————. *The Early Earth.* Revised edition. Grand Rapids: Baker, 1986. (young earth view)

Wilder-Smith, A. E. *The Natural Sciences Know Nothing of Evolution*. El Cajon, Calif.: Master Books, 1981.

Young, Davis A. *Christianity and the Age of the Earth*. Grand Rapids: Zondervan, 1982. (argues against young earth view)

————. *Creation and the Flood: An Alternative to Flood Geology and Theistic Evolution*. Grand Rapids: Baker, 1977. (argues against young earth view)

Youngblood, Ronald. *How It All Began*. Ventura, Calif.: Regal, 1980.

## SCRIPTURE MEMORY PASSAGE

**Nehemiah 9:6:** *And Ezra said: "You are the LORD, you alone; you have made heaven, the heaven of heavens, with all their host, the earth and all that is on it, the seas and all that is in them; and you preserve all of them; and the host of heaven worships you.*

## HYMN

### "Hallelujah, Praise Jehovah!"

This hymn contains the entire content of Psalm 148 set to music. It summons all creation, including "things visible and things invisible," to worship God our Creator.

Hallelujah, praise Jehovah, from the heavens praise his name;
Praise Jehovah in the highest, all his angels, praise proclaim.
All his hosts, together praise him, sun and moon and stars on high;
Praise him, O ye heav'ns of heavens, and ye floods above the sky.

*Refrain:*
Let them praises give Jehovah, for his name alone is high,
And his glory is exalted, and his glory is exalted, and his glory
is exalted
Far above the earth and sky.

Let them praises give Jehovah, they were made at his command;
Them for ever he established, his decree shall ever stand.
From the earth, O praise Jehovah, all ye seas, ye monsters all,
Fire and hail and snow and vapors, stormy winds that hear his call.

All ye fruitful trees and cedars, all ye hills and mountains high,
Creeping things and beasts and cattle, birds that in the heavens fly,
Kings of earth, and all ye people, princes great, earth's judges all;
Praise his name, young men and maidens, aged men,
and children small.

AUTHOR: WILLIAM J. KIRKPATRICK, 1838–1921

# Chapter 16

# God's Providence

*If God controls all things, how can our actions have real meaning? What are the decrees of God?*

## EXPLANATION AND SCRIPTURAL BASIS

Once we understand that God is the all-powerful Creator (see chapter 15), it seems reasonable to conclude that he also preserves and governs everything in the universe as well. Though the term *providence* is not found in Scripture, it has been traditionally used to summarize God's ongoing relationship to his creation. When we accept the biblical doctrine of providence, we avoid four common errors in thinking about God's relationship to creation. The biblical doctrine is not *deism* (which teaches that God created the world and then essentially abandoned it), nor *pantheism* (which teaches that the creation does not have a real, distinct existence in itself, but is only part of God), but *providence*, which teaches that though God is actively related to and involved in the creation at each moment, creation is distinct from him. Moreover, the biblical doctrine does not teach that events in creation are determined by *chance* (or randomness), nor are they determined by impersonal *fate* (or determinism), but by God, who is the personal yet infinitely powerful Creator and Lord.

We may define God's providence as follows: *God is continually involved with all created things in such a way that he (1) keeps them existing and maintaining the properties with which he created them; (2) cooperates with created things in every action, directing their distinctive properties to cause them to act as they do; and (3) directs them to fulfill his purposes.*

Under the general category of providence we have three subtopics, according to the three elements in the definition above: (1) Preservation, (2) Concurrence, and (3) Government.

We shall examine each of these separately, then consider differing views and objections to the doctrine of providence. It should be noted that this is a doctrine on which there has been substantial disagreement among Christians since the early history of the church, particularly with respect to God's relationship to the willing choices of moral creatures. In this chapter we will first present a summary of the position favored in this textbook (what is commonly called the "Reformed" or "Calvinist" position),[1] then consider arguments that have been made from another position (what is commonly called the "Arminian" position).

---

[1]Though philosophers may use the term *determinism* (or *soft determinism*) to categorize the position I

## A. Preservation

*God keeps all created things existing and maintaining the properties with which he created them.*

Hebrews 1:3 tells us that Christ is "upholding the universe by his word of power." The Greek word translated "upholding" is *pherō*, "carry, bear." This is commonly used in the New Testament for carrying something from one place to another, such as bringing a paralyzed man on a bed to Jesus (Luke 5:18), bringing wine to the steward of the feast (John 2:8), or bringing a cloak and books to Paul (2 Tim. 4:13). It does not mean simply "sustain," but has the sense of active, purposeful control over the thing being carried from one place to another. In Hebrews 1:3, the use of the present participle indicates that Jesus is *"continually carrying along all things"* in the universe by his word of power. Christ is actively involved in the work of providence.

Similarly, in Colossians 1:17, Paul says of Christ that "in him all things hold together." The phrase "all things" refers to every created thing in the universe (see v. 16), and the verse affirms that Christ keeps all things existing—in him they continue to exist or "endure" (NASB mg.). Both verses indicate that if Christ were to cease his continuing activity of sustaining all things in the universe, then all except the triune God would instantly cease to exist. Such teaching is also affirmed by Paul when he says, "In him we live and move and *have our being*" (Acts 17:28), and by Ezra: "You are the LORD, you alone; you have made heaven, the heaven of heavens, with all their host, the earth and all that is on it, the seas and all that is in them; *and you preserve all of them*; and the host of heaven worships you" (Neh. 9:6). Peter also says that "the heavens and earth that now exist" are "being *kept* until the day of judgment" (2 Peter 3:7).

One aspect of God's providential preservation is the fact that he continues to give us breath each moment. Elihu in his wisdom says of God, "If he should take back his spirit to himself, and gather to himself his breath, all flesh would perish together, and man would return to dust" (Job 34:14–15; cf. Ps. 104:29).

God, in preserving all things he has made, also causes them to maintain the properties with which he created them. God preserves water in such a way that it continues to act like water. He causes grass to continue to act like grass, with all its distinctive characteristics. He causes the paper on which this sentence is written to continue to act like paper so that it does not spontaneously dissolve into water and float away or change into a living thing and begin to grow! Until it is acted on by some other part of creation and thereby its properties are changed (for instance,

---

advocate in this chapter, I do not use that term because it is too easily misunderstood in everyday English: (1) It suggests a system in which human choices are not real and make no difference in the outcome of events; and (2) it suggests a system in which the ultimate cause of events is a mechanistic universe rather than a wise and personal God. Moreover, (3) it too easily allows critics to group the biblical view with non-Christian deterministic systems and blur the distinctions between them.

The view advocated in this chapter is also sometimes called "compatibilism," because it holds that absolute divine sovereignty is compatible with human significance and real human choices. I have no objection to the nuances of this term, but I have decided not to use it because (1) I want to avoid the proliferation of technical terms in studying theology, and (2) it seems preferable simply to call my position a traditional Reformed view of God's providence, and thereby to place myself within a widely understood theological tradition represented by John Calvin and the other systematic theologians listed in the "Reformed" category at the end of this chapter.

until it is burned with fire and it becomes ash), this paper will continue to act like paper so long as God preserves the earth and the creation that he has made.

We should not, however, think of God's preservation as a continuous new creation: he does not continuously create new atoms and molecules for every existing thing every moment. Rather, he *preserves* what has already been created: he "carries along all things" by his word of power (Heb. 1:3, author's translation). We must also appreciate that created things are *real* and that their characteristics are *real*. I do not just imagine that the rock in my hand is hard—it is hard. If I bump it against my head, I do not just imagine that it hurts—it *does* hurt! Because God keeps this rock maintaining the properties with which he created it, the rock has been hard since the day it was formed, and (unless something else in creation interacts with it and changes it) it will be hard until the day God destroys the heavens and the earth (2 Peter 3:7, 10–12).

God's providence provides a basis for science: God has made and continues to sustain a universe that acts in predictable ways. If a scientific experiment gives a certain result today, then we can have confidence that (if all the factors are the same) it will give the same result tomorrow and a hundred years from tomorrow. The doctrine of providence also provides a foundation for technology: I can be confident that gasoline will make my car run today just as it did yesterday, not simply because "it has always worked that way," but because God's providence sustains a universe in which created things maintain the properties with which he created them. The *result* may be similar in the life of an unbeliever and the life of a Christian: we both put gasoline in our cars and drive away. But he will do so without knowing the ultimate reason why it works that way, and I will do so with knowledge of the actual final reason (God's providence) and with thanks to my Creator for the wonderful creation that he has made and preserves.

## B. Concurrence

*God cooperates with created things in every action, directing their distinctive properties to cause them to act as they do.*

This second aspect of providence, *concurrence,* is an expansion of the idea contained in the first aspect, *preservation.* In fact, some theologians (such as John Calvin) treat the fact of concurrence under the category of preservation, but it is helpful to treat it as a distinct category.

In Ephesians 1:11 Paul says that God "accomplishes all things according to the counsel of his will." The word translated "accomplishes" (*energeō*) indicates that God "works" or "brings about" *all things* according to his own will. No event in creation falls outside of his providence. Of course this fact is hidden from our eyes unless we read it in Scripture. Like preservation, God's work of concurrence is not clearly evident from observation of the natural world around us.

In giving scriptural proof for concurrence, we will begin with the inanimate creation, then move to animals, and finally to different kinds of events in the life of human beings.

**1. Inanimate Creation.** There are many things in creation that we think of as merely "natural" occurrences. Yet Scripture says that God causes them to happen.

318          16 : GOD'S PROVIDENCE

We read of "fire and hail, snow and frost, stormy wind fulfilling his command!" (Ps. 148:8). Similarly,

> To the *snow* he says, "Fall on the earth";
> and to the shower and the *rain,* "Be strong." . . .
> By the breath of God *ice* is given,
> and the broad waters are frozen fast.
> He loads the thick cloud with moisture;
> the clouds scatter his *lightning.*
> They turn round and round by his guidance,
> to accomplish all that he commands them
> on the face of the habitable world.
> Whether for correction, or for his land,
> or for love, he causes it to happen.
> (Job 37:6–13; cf. similar statements in 38:22–30)

Again, the psalmist declares that "Whatever the LORD pleases he does, in heaven and on earth, in the seas and all deeps" (Ps. 135:6), and then in the next sentence he illustrates God's doing of his will in the weather: "He it is who makes the clouds rise at the end of the earth, who makes lightnings for the rain and brings forth the wind from his storehouses" (Ps. 135:7; cf. 104:4).

God also causes the grass to grow: *"You cause the grass to grow* for the cattle, and plants for man to cultivate, that he may bring forth food from the earth" (Ps. 104:14). God directs the stars in the heavens, asking Job, "Can you bring forth the constellations in their seasons or lead out the Bear with its cubs?" (Job 38:32 NIV; "the Bear" or Ursa Major is commonly called the Big Dipper; v. 31 refers to the constellations Pleiades and Orion). Moreover, God continually directs the coming of the morning (Job 38:12), a fact Jesus affirmed when he said that God *"makes his sun rise* on the evil and on the good, and *sends rain* on the just and on the unjust" (Matt. 5:45).

**2. Animals.** Scripture affirms that God feeds the wild animals of the field, for, "These all look to you, to give them their food in due season. When you give to them, they gather it up; when you open your hand, they are filled with good things. When you hide your face, they are dismayed" (Ps. 104:27–29; cf. Job 38:39–41). Jesus also affirmed this when he said, "Look at the *birds* of the air . . . your heavenly Father *feeds them"* (Matt. 6:26). And he said that not one sparrow "will fall to the ground without your Father's will" (Matt. 10:29).

**3. Seemingly "Random" or "Chance" Events.** From a human perspective, the casting of lots (or its modern equivalent, the rolling of dice or flipping of a coin) is the most typical of random events that occur in the universe. But Scripture affirms that the outcome of such an event is from God: "The lot is cast into the lap, but the decision is wholly from the LORD" (Prov. 16:33).[2]

---

[2]It is true that Eccl. 9:11 says that "the race is not to the swift, nor the battle to the strong, nor bread to the wise, nor riches to the intelligent, nor favor to the men of skill; but time and *chance* happen to them all." But Michael Eaton correctly observes, "On the lips of an Israelite 'chance' means what is unexpected, not what is random" (*Ecclesiastes,* TOTC [Leicester and Downers Grove, Ill.: InterVarsity

**4. Events Fully Caused by God and Fully Caused by the Creature as Well.** For any of these foregoing events (rain and snow, grass growing, sun and stars, the feeding of animals, or casting of lots), we could (at least in theory) give a completely satisfactory "natural" explanation. A botanist can detail the factors that cause grass to grow, such as sun, moisture, temperature, nutrients in the soil, etc. Yet Scripture says that *God* causes the grass to grow. A meteorologist can give a complete explanation of factors that cause rain (humidity, temperature, atmospheric pressure, etc.), and can even produce rain in a weather laboratory. Yet Scripture says that *God* causes the rain. A physicist with accurate information on the force and direction a pair of dice was rolled could fully explain what caused the dice to give the result they did—yet Scripture says that *God* brings about the decision of the lot that is cast.

This shows us that it is incorrect for us to reason that if we know the "natural" cause of something in this world, then God did not cause it. Rather, if it rains we should thank him. If crops grow we should thank him. In all of these events, it is not as though the event was partly caused by God and partly by factors in the created world. If that were the case, then we would always be looking for some small feature of an event that we could not explain and attribute that (say 1 percent of the cause) to God. But surely this is not a correct view. Rather, these passages affirm that such events are entirely caused by God. Yet we know that (in another sense) they are entirely caused by factors in the creation as well.

The doctrine of concurrence affirms that God *directs*, and *works through*, the distinctive properties of each created thing, so that these things themselves bring about the results that we see. In this way it is possible to affirm that in one sense events are fully (100 percent) caused by God and fully (100 percent) caused by the creature as well. However, divine and creaturely causes work in different ways. The divine cause of each event works as an invisible, behind-the-scenes, directing cause and therefore could be called the "primary cause" that plans and initiates everything that happens. But the created thing brings about actions in ways consistent with the creature's own properties, ways that can often be described by us or by professional scientists who carefully observe the processes. These creaturely factors and properties can therefore be called the "secondary" causes of everything that happens, even though they are the causes that are evident to us by observation.

**5. The Affairs of Nations.** Scripture also speaks of God's providential control of human affairs. We read that God "makes nations great, and he destroys them: he enlarges nations, and leads them away" (Job 12:23). "Dominion belongs to the LORD, and he rules over the nations" (Ps. 22:28). He has determined the time of existence and the place of every nation on the earth, for Paul says, "he made from one every nation of men to live on all the face of the earth, having determined allotted periods and the boundaries of their habitation" (Acts 17:26; cf. 14:16). And when Nebuchadnezzar repented, he learned to praise God,

---

Press, 1983], p. 70). The rare word here translated "chance" (Heb., *pega'*) occurs only once more in the Bible (1 Kings 5:4[18], of an evil *event*).

> For his dominion is an everlasting dominion,
>         and his kingdom endures from generation to generation;
> all the inhabitants of the earth are accounted as nothing;
>         and *he does according to his will in the host of heaven*
>         *and among the inhabitants of the earth;*
> and none can stay his hand or say to him,
>         "What are you doing?" (Dan. 4:34–35)

**6. All Aspects of Our Lives.** It is amazing to see the extent to which Scripture affirms that God brings about various events in our lives. For example, our dependence on God to give us food each day is affirmed every time we pray, "Give us this day our daily bread" (Matt. 6:11), even though we work for our food and (as far as mere human observation can discern) obtain it through entirely "natural" causes. Similarly, Paul, looking at events with the eye of faith, affirms that "my God will supply every need" of his children (Phil 4:19), even though God may use "ordinary" means (such as other people) to do so.

God plans our days before we are born, for David affirms, "In your book were written, every one of them, the days that were formed for me, when as yet there was none of them" (Ps. 139:16). And Job says that man's "days are determined, and the number of his months is with you, and you have appointed his bounds that he cannot pass" (Job 14:5). This can be seen in the life of Paul, who says that God "had set me apart before I was born" (Gal. 1:15), and Jeremiah, to whom God said, "Before I formed you in the womb I knew you, and before you were born I consecrated you; I appointed you a prophet to the nations" (Jer. 1:5).

All our actions are under God's providential care, for "in him we live and *move*" (Acts 17:28). The individual steps we take each day are directed by the Lord. Jeremiah confesses, "I know, O LORD, that the way of man is not in himself, that it is not in man who walks to direct his steps" (Jer. 10:23). We read that "a man's steps are ordered by the LORD" (Prov. 20:24), and that "a man's mind plans his way, but the LORD directs his steps" (Prov. 16:9). Similarly, Proverbs 16:1 affirms, "The plans of the mind belong to man, but the answer of the tongue is from the LORD."[3]

Success and failure come from God, for we read, "For not from the east or from the west and not from the wilderness comes lifting up; but it is God who executes judgment, putting down one and lifting up another" (Ps. 75:6–7). So Mary can say, "He has put down the mighty from their thrones, and exalted those of low degree" (Luke 1:52). The LORD gives children, for children "are a heritage from the LORD, the fruit of the womb a reward" (Ps. 127:3).

All our talents and abilities are from the Lord, for Paul can ask the Corinthians,

---

[3]David J. A. Clines, "Predestination in the Old Testament," in *Grace Unlimited*, ed. by Clark H. Pinnock (Minneapolis: Bethany House, 1975), pp. 116–17, objects that these verses simply affirm that "when it comes to conflict between God and man, undoubtedly it cannot be man who wins the day." He says that these verses do not describe life in general, but describe unusual situations where God overcomes man's will in order to bring about his special purposes. Clines denies that these verses mean that God always acts this way or that these verses represent God's control of human conduct generally. Yet no such restriction is seen in these passages (see Prov. 16:1, 9). The verses do not say that God directs a man's steps in rare instances where God needs to intervene to fulfill his purposes; they simply make general statements about the way the world works—God directs man's steps in general, not simply when there is conflict between God and man.

"What have you that you did not receive? If then you received it, why do you boast as if it were not a gift?" (1 Cor. 4:7). David knew that to be true regarding his military skill, for, though he must have trained many hours in the use of a bow and arrow, he could say of God, "He trains my hands for war, so that my arms can bend a bow of bronze" (Ps. 18:34).

God influences rulers in their decisions, for "the king's heart is a stream of water in the hand of the LORD; he turns it wherever he will" (Prov. 21:1). An illustration of this was when the Lord "turned the heart of the king of Assyria" to his people, "so that he aided them in the work of the house of God, the God of Israel" (Ezr. 6:22), or when "the LORD stirred up the spirit of Cyrus king of Persia" (Ezr. 1:1) to help the people of Israel. But it is not just the heart of the king that God influences, for he looks down "on all the inhabitants of the earth" and "fashions the hearts of them all" (Ps. 33:14–15). When we realize that the heart in Scripture is the location of our inmost thoughts and desires, this is a significant passage. God especially guides the desires and inclinations of believers, working in us "both *to will* and to work for his good pleasure" (Phil. 2:13).

All of these passages, reporting both general statements about God's work in the lives of all people and specific examples of God's work in the lives of individuals, lead us to conclude that God's providential work of concurrence extends to all aspects of our lives. Our words, our steps, our movements, our hearts, and our abilities are all from the Lord.

But we must guard against misunderstanding. Here also, as with the lower creation, God's providential direction as an unseen, behind-the-scenes, "primary cause," should not lead us to deny the reality of our choices and actions. Again and again Scripture affirms that we really do *cause* events to happen. We are significant and we are responsible. We *do have choices,* and these are real choices that bring about real results. Scripture repeatedly affirms these truths as well. Just as a rock is *really hard* because God has made it with the property of hardness, just as water is *really wet* because God has made it with the property of wetness, just as plants are *really alive* because God has made them with the property of life, so our choices are *real choices* and do have significant effects, because God has made us in such a wonderful way that he has endowed us with the property of willing choice.

One approach to these passages about God's concurrence is to say that if our choices are real, they *cannot* be caused by God (see below for further discussion of this viewpoint). But the number of passages that affirm this providential control of God is so considerable, and the difficulties involved in giving them some other interpretation are so formidable, that it does not seem to me that this can be the right approach to them. It seems better to affirm that God causes all things that happen, but that he does so in such a way that he somehow upholds our ability to make *willing, responsible choices,* choices that have *real and eternal results,* and for which we are *held accountable.* Exactly how God combines his providential control with our willing and significant choices, Scripture does not explain to us. But rather than deny one aspect or the other (simply because we cannot explain how both can be true), we should accept both in an attempt to be faithful to the teaching of all of Scripture.

The analogy of an author writing a play may help us to grasp how both aspects can be true. In the Shakespearean play *Macbeth,* the character Macbeth murders King Duncan. Now (if we assume for a moment that this is a fictional account), the question may be asked, "Who killed King Duncan?" On one level, the correct answer is "Macbeth." Within the context of the play he carried out the murder and is rightly to blame for it. But on another level, a correct answer to the question, "Who killed King Duncan?" would be "William Shakespeare": he wrote the play, he created all the characters in it, and he wrote the part where Macbeth killed King Duncan.

It would not be correct to say that because Macbeth killed King Duncan, William Shakespeare did not kill him. Nor would it be correct to say that because William Shakespeare killed King Duncan, Macbeth did not kill him. Both are true. On the level of the characters in the play Macbeth fully (100 percent) caused King Duncan's death, but on the level of the creator of the play, William Shakespeare fully (100 percent) caused King Duncan's death. In similar fashion, we can understand that God fully causes things in one way (as Creator), and we fully cause things in another way (as creatures).

Of course, someone may object that the analogy does not really solve the problem because characters in a play are not real persons; they are only characters with no freedom of their own, no ability to make genuine choices, and so forth. But in response we may point out that God is infinitely greater and wiser than we are. While we as finite creatures can only create fictional characters in a play, not real persons, God, our infinite Creator, has made an actual world and in it has created us as real persons who make willing choices. To say that God *could not* make a world in which he *causes us to make willing choices* (as some would argue today; see discussion below), is simply to limit the power of God. It seems also to deny a large number of passages of Scripture.[4]

**7. What About Evil?** If God does indeed cause, through his providential activity, everything that comes about in the world, then the question arises, "What is the relationship between God and evil in the world?" Does God actually cause the evil actions that people do? If he does, then is God not responsible for sin?

In approaching this question, it is best first to read the passages of Scripture that most directly address it. We can begin by looking at several passages that affirm that God did, indeed, cause evil events to come about and evil deeds to be done. But we must remember that in all these passages it is very clear that Scripture

---

[4]I. Howard Marshall, "Predestination in the New Testament" in *Grace Unlimited*, by Clark H. Pinnock, pp. 132–33, 139, objects to the analogy of an author and a play because the actors "are bound by the characters assigned to them and the lines that they have learned" so that even if the dramatist "makes [the characters] say 'I love my creator' in his drama, this is not mutual love in the real sense."

But Marshall limits his analysis to what is possible with human beings acting on a human level. He does not give consideration to the possibility (in fact, the reality!) that God is able to do far more than human beings are able to do, and that he can wonderfully create genuine human beings rather than mere characters in a play. A better approach to the analogy of an author and a play would be if Marshall would apply to this question a very helpful statement that he made in another part of the essay: "The basic difficulty is that of attempting to explain the nature of *the relationship between an infinite God and finite creatures.* Our temptation is to think of divine causation in much the same way as human causation, and this produces difficulties as soon as we try to relate divine causation and human freedom. It is beyond our ability to explain how God can cause us to do certain things (or to cause the universe to come into being and to behave as it does)" (pp. 137–38). I can agree fully with everything in Marshall's statement at that point, and find that to be a very helpful way of approaching this problem.

nowhere shows God as *directly doing anything evil*, but rather as bringing about evil deeds through the willing actions of moral creatures. Moreover, *Scripture never blames God for evil or shows God as taking pleasure in evil*, and Scripture never excuses human beings for the wrong they do. However we understand God's relationship to evil, we must *never* come to the point where we think that we are not responsible for the evil that we do, or that God takes pleasure in evil or is to be blamed for it. Such a conclusion is clearly contrary to Scripture.

There are literally dozens of Scripture passages that say that God (indirectly) brought about some kind of evil. I have quoted such an extensive list (in the next few paragraphs) because Christians often are unaware of the extent of this forthright teaching in Scripture. Yet it must be remembered that in all of these examples, the evil is actually done not by God but by people or demons who choose to do it.

A very clear example is found in the story of Joseph. Scripture clearly says that Joseph's brothers were wrongly jealous of him (Gen. 37:11), hated him (Gen. 37:4, 5, 8), wanted to kill him (Gen. 37:20), and did wrong when they cast him into a pit (Gen. 37:24) and then sold him into slavery in Egypt (Gen. 37:28). Yet later Joseph could say to his brothers, "*God sent me before you* to preserve life" (Gen. 45:5), and "You meant evil against me; but *God meant it for good*, to bring it about that many people should be kept alive, as they are today" (Gen. 50:20).[5] Here we have a combination of evil deeds brought about by sinful men who are rightly held accountable for their sin and the overriding providential control of God whereby God's own purposes were accomplished. Both are clearly affirmed.

The story of the exodus from Egypt repeatedly affirms that God hardened the heart of Pharaoh: God says, "I will harden his heart" (Ex. 4:21), "I will harden Pharaoh's heart" (Ex. 7:3), "the LORD hardened the heart of Pharaoh" (Ex. 9:12), "the LORD hardened Pharaoh's heart" (Ex. 10:20, repeated in 10:27 and again in 11:10), "I will harden Pharaoh's heart" (Ex. 14:4), and "the LORD hardened the heart of Pharaoh king of Egypt" (Ex. 14:8). It is sometimes objected that Scripture also says that Pharaoh hardened his own heart (Ex. 8:15, 32; 9:34), and that God's act of hardening Pharaoh's heart was only in response to the initial rebellion and hardness of heart that Pharaoh himself exhibited of his own free will. But it should be noted that God's promises that he would harden Pharaoh's heart (Ex. 4:21; 7:3) are made long before Scripture tells us that Pharaoh hardened his own heart (we read of this for the first time in Ex. 8:15). Moreover, our analysis of concurrence given above, in which both divine and human agents can cause the same event, should show us that both factors can be true at the same time: even when Pharaoh hardens his own heart, that is not inconsistent with saying that God is causing Pharaoh to do this and thereby God is hardening the heart of Pharaoh. Finally, if someone would object that God is just intensifying the evil desires and choices that were already in Pharaoh's heart, then this kind of action could still in theory at least cover all the evil in the world today, since all people have evil desires in their hearts and all people do in fact make evil choices.

What was God's purpose in this? Paul reflects on Exodus 9:16 and says, "For the scripture says to Pharaoh, 'I have raised you up for the very purpose of showing my power in you, so that my name may be proclaimed in all the earth'"

---

[5]Ps. 105:17 says that God "had sent a man ahead of them, Joseph, who was sold as a slave."

(Rom. 9:17). Then Paul infers a general truth from this specific example: "So then he has mercy upon whomever he wills, and he hardens the heart of whomever he wills" (Rom. 9:18). In fact, God also hardened the hearts of the Egyptian people so that they pursued Israel into the Red Sea: "I will harden the hearts of the Egyptians so that they shall go in after them, and I will get glory over Pharaoh and all his host, his chariots, and his horsemen" (Ex. 14:17). This theme is repeated in Psalm 105:25: "He turned their hearts to hate his people."

Later in the Old Testament narrative similar examples are found of the Canaanites who were destroyed in the conquest of Palestine under Joshua. We read, "For it was the LORD's doing to harden their hearts that they should come against Israel in battle, in order that they should be utterly destroyed" (Josh. 11:20; see also Judg. 3:12; 9:23). And Samson's demand to marry an unbelieving Philistine woman "was from the LORD; for he was seeking an occasion against the Philistines. At that time the Philistines had dominion over Israel" (Judg. 14:4). We also read that the sons of Eli, when rebuked for their evil deeds, "would not listen to the voice of their father; for it was the will of the LORD to slay them" (1 Sam. 2:25). Later, "an evil spirit from the LORD" tormented King Saul (1 Sam. 16:14).

When David sinned, the LORD said to him through Nathan the prophet, "I will raise up evil against you out of your own house; and I will take your wives before your eyes, and give them to your neighbor, and he shall lie with your wives in the sight of this sun. For you did it secretly; but I will do this thing before all Israel, and before the sun" (2 Sam. 12:11–12; fulfilled in 16:22). In further punishment for David's sin, "the LORD struck the child that Uriah's wife bore to David, and it became sick" and eventually died (2 Sam. 12:15–18). David remained mindful of the fact that God could bring evil against him, because at a later time, when Shimei cursed David and threw stones at him and his servants (2 Sam. 16:5–8), David refused to take vengeance on Shimei but said to his soldiers, "Let him alone, and let him curse; for the LORD has bidden him" (2 Sam. 16:11).

Still later in David's life, the Lord "incited"[6] David to take a census of the people (2 Sam. 24:1), but afterward David recognized this as sin, saying, "I have sinned greatly in what I have done" (2 Sam. 24:10), and God sent punishment on the land because of this sin (2 Sam. 24:12–17). However, it is also clear that "the anger of the LORD was kindled against Israel" (2 Sam. 24:1), so God's inciting of David to sin was a means by which he brought about punishment on the people of Israel. Moreover, the means by which God incited David is made clear in 1 Chronicles 21:1: "Satan stood up against Israel, and *incited* David to number Israel." In this one incident the Bible gives us a remarkable insight into the three influences that contributed in different ways to one action: God, in order to bring about his purposes, worked through Satan to incite David to sin, but Scripture regards David as being responsible for that sin. Again, after Solomon turned away from the Lord because of his foreign wives, "the LORD raised up an adversary against Solomon, Hadad the Edomite" (1 Kings 11:14), and "God also raised up

---

[6]The Hebrew word used when 2 Sam. 24:1 says that the Lord *incited* David against Israel is *sûth,* "to incite, allure, instigate" (BDB, p. 694). It is the same word used in 2 Chron. 21:1 to say that Satan *incited* David to number Israel, in 1 Kings 21:25 to say that Jezebel *incited* Ahab to do evil, in Deut. 13:6(7) to warn against a loved one *enticing* a family member secretly to serve other gods, and in 2 Chron. 18:31 to say that God *moved* the Syrian army to withdraw from Jehoshaphat.

as an adversary to him, Rezon the son of Eliada" (1 Kings 11:23). These were evil kings raised up by God.

In the story of Job, though the LORD gave Satan permission to bring harm to Job's possessions and children, and though this harm came through the evil actions of the Sabeans and the Chaldeans, as well as a windstorm (Job 1:12, 15, 17, 19), yet Job looks beyond those secondary causes and, with the eyes of faith, sees it all as from the hand of the Lord: "the LORD gave, and the LORD has taken away; *blessed be the name of the LORD*" (Job 1:21). The Old Testament author follows Job's statement immediately with the sentence, "In all this Job did not sin or charge God with wrong" (Job 1:22). Job has just been told that evil marauding bands had destroyed his flocks and herds, yet with great faith and patience in adversity, he says, "*The LORD* has taken away." Though he says that the LORD had done this, yet he does not blame God for the evil or say that God had done wrong: he says, "Blessed be the name of the LORD." To *blame* God for evil that he had brought about through secondary agents would have been to sin. Job does not do this, Scripture never does this, and neither should we.

Elsewhere in the Old Testament we read that the Lord "put a lying spirit in the mouth" of Ahab's prophets (1 Kings 22:23) and sent the wicked Assyrians as "the rod of my anger" to punish Israel (Isa. 10:5). He also sent the evil Babylonians, including Nebuchadnezzar, against Israel, saying, "I will bring them against this land and its inhabitants" (Jer. 25:9). Then God promised that later he would punish the Babylonians also: "I will punish the king of Babylon and that nation, the land of the Chaldeans, for their iniquity, says the LORD, making the land an everlasting waste" (Jer. 25:12). If there is a deceiving prophet who gives a false message, then the Lord says, "if the prophet be deceived and speak a word, I, the LORD, have deceived that prophet, and I will stretch out my hand against him, and will destroy him from the midst of my people Israel" (Ezek. 14:9, in the context of bringing judgment on Israel for their idolatry). As the culmination of a series of rhetorical questions to which the implied answer is always "no," Amos asks, "Is a trumpet blown in a city, and the people are not afraid? Does evil befall a city, unless the LORD has done it?" (Amos 3:6). There follows a series of natural disasters in Amos 4:6–12, where the LORD reminds the people that he gave them hunger, drought, blight and mildew, locusts, pestilence, and death of men and horses, "yet you did not return to me" (Amos 4:6, 8, 9, 10, 11).

In many of the passages mentioned above, God brings evil and destruction on people in judgment upon their sins: They have been disobedient or have strayed into idolatry, and then the LORD uses evil human beings or demonic forces or "natural" disasters to bring judgment on them. (This is not always said to be the case—Joseph and Job come to mind—but it is often so.) Perhaps this idea of judgment on sin can help us to understand, at least in part, how God can righteously bring about evil events. All human beings are sinful, for Scripture tells us that "all have sinned and fall short of the glory of God" (Rom. 3:23). None of us deserves God's favor or his mercy, but only eternal condemnation. Therefore, when God brings evil on human beings, whether to discipline his children, or to lead unbelievers to repentance, or to bring a judgment of condemnation and destruction upon hardened sinners, none of us can charge God with doing wrong. Ultimately all will work in God's good purposes to bring glory to him and good to his people. Yet we must realize that in punishing evil in those who are not redeemed (such as Pharaoh, the Canaanites, and the Babylonians), God is also glorified through the demonstration of his justice, holiness, and power (see Ex. 9:16; Rom. 9:14–24).

Through the prophet Isaiah God says, "I form the light, and create darkness: I make peace, and *create evil:*[7] I the LORD do all these things" (Isa. 45:7 KJV; the Hebrew word for "create" here is *bārā'*, the same word used in Gen. 1:1). In Lamentations 3:38 we read, "Is it not from the mouth of the Most High that good and evil come?"[8] The people of Israel, in a time of heartfelt repentance, cry out to God and say, "O LORD, why do you make us err from your ways and harden our heart, so that we fear you not?" (Isa. 63:17).[9]

The life of Jonah is a remarkable illustration of God's concurrence in human activity. The men on board the ship sailing to Tarshish threw Jonah overboard, for Scripture says, "So *they* took up Jonah and threw him into the sea; and the sea ceased from its raging" (Jonah 1:15). Yet only five verses later Jonah acknowledges God's providential direction in their act, for he says to God, "*You* cast me into the deep, into the heart of the seas" (Jonah 2:3). Scripture simultaneously affirms that the men threw Jonah into the sea and that God threw him into the sea. The providential direction of God did not force the sailors to do something against their will, nor were they conscious of any divine influence on them— indeed, they cried to the Lord for forgiveness as they threw Jonah overboard (Jonah 1:14). What Scripture reveals to us, and what Jonah himself realized, was that God was bringing about his plan through the willing choices of real human beings who were morally accountable for their actions. In a way not understood by us and not revealed to us, God *caused* them to make a *willing choice* to do what they did.

The most evil deed of all history, the crucifixion of Christ, was ordained by God—not just the fact that it would occur, but also all the individual actions connected with it. The church at Jerusalem recognized this, for they prayed:

> For truly in this city there were gathered together against your holy servant Jesus, whom you anointed, both Herod and Pontius Pilate, with the Gentiles and the peoples of Israel, *to do whatever your hand and your plan had predestined to take place.* (Acts 4:27)

---

[7]Other translations render the Hebrew word *rā'*, "evil," as "disaster" (NIV) or "woe" (RSV) or "calamity" (NASB), and indeed the word can be used to apply to natural disasters such as these words imply. But there is no compelling reason to restrict it to natural disasters, for the word is an extremely common word used of evil generally: It is used of the tree of the knowledge of good and *evil* (Gen. 2:9), of the *evil* among mankind that brought the judgment of the flood (Gen. 6:5), and of the *evil* of the men of Sodom (Gen. 13:13). It is used to say, "Depart from *evil* and do good" (Ps. 34:14), and to speak of the wrong of those who call *evil* good and good *evil* (Isa. 5:20), and of the sin of those whose "feet run to *evil*" (Isa. 59:7; see also 47:10, 11; 56:2; 57:1; 59:15; 65:12; 66:4). Dozens of other times throughout the Old Testament it refers to moral evil or sin. The contrast with "peace" (*shālôm*) in the same phrase in Isa. 45:7 might argue that only "calamity" is in view, but not necessarily so, for moral evil and wickedness is certainly also the opposite of the wholeness of God's "shalom" or peace. (In Amos 3:6, *rā'āh* is a different but related word and has a similar range of meanings.) But Isa. 45:7 does not say that God *does evil* (see discussion below).

[8]The Hebrew for "evil" here is *rā'āh*, as in Amos 3:6.

[9]Another kind of evil is physical infirmity. With regard to this, the Lord says to Moses, "Who has made man's mouth? Who makes him dumb, or deaf, or seeing, or blind? Is it not I, the LORD?" (Ex. 4:11).

All the actions of all the participants in the crucifixion of Jesus had been "predestined" by God. Yet the apostles clearly attach no moral blame to God, for the actions resulted from the willing choices of sinful men. Peter makes this clear in his sermon at Pentecost: "this Jesus, delivered up according to the definite plan and foreknowledge of God, *you crucified and killed by the hands of lawless men*" (Acts 2:23). In one sentence he links God's plan and foreknowledge with the moral blame that attaches to the actions of "lawless men." They were not forced by God to act against their wills; rather, God brought about his plan *through their willing choices,* for which they were nevertheless responsible.

In an example similar to the Old Testament account of God sending a lying spirit into the mouth of Ahab's prophets, we read of those who refuse to love the truth, "Therefore God sends upon them a strong delusion, to make them believe what is false, so that all may be condemned who did not believe the truth but had pleasure in unrighteousness" (2 Thess. 2:11–12). And Peter tells his readers that those who oppose them and persecute them, who reject Christ as Messiah, "stumble because they disobey the word, as they were destined to do" (1 Peter 2:8).[10]

**8. Analysis of Verses Relating to God and Evil.** After looking at so many verses that speak of God's providential use of the evil actions of men and demons, what can we say by way of analysis?

**a. God Uses All Things to Fulfill His Purposes and Even Uses Evil for His Glory and for Our Good:** Thus, when evil comes into our lives to trouble us, we can have from the doctrine of providence a deeper assurance that "God causes all things to work together for good to those who love God, to those who are called according to his purpose" (Rom. 8:28 NASB). This kind of conviction enabled Joseph to say to his brothers, "You meant evil against me; but *God meant it for good*" (Gen. 50:20).

We can also realize that God is glorified even in the punishment of evil. Scripture tells us that "the LORD has made everything for its purpose, even the wicked for the day of trouble" (Prov. 16:4).[11] Similarly, the psalmist affirms, "Surely the wrath of men shall praise you" (Ps. 76:10). And the example of Pharaoh (Rom. 9:14–24) is a clear example of the way God uses evil for his own glory and for the good of his people.

---

[10]The "destining" in this verse is best taken to refer to both the stumbling and the disobedience. It is incorrect to say that God only destined the fact that those who disobey would stumble, because it is not a fact but persons ("they") who are said to be "destined" in this case. (See discussion in Wayne Grudem, *The First Epistle of Peter*, TNTC [Leicester: Inter-Varsity Press, and Grand Rapids: Eerdmans, 1988], pp. 106–10.)

[11]David J. A. Clines, "Predestination in the Old Testament," p. 116, retranslates this, "The Lord has made everything with its counterpart, so the wicked will have his day of doom." He does this in order to avoid the conclusion that the Lord has made some wicked people for the day of evil. But his translation is not convincing. The Hebrew word translated "purpose" in the RSV (*ma'aneh*) occurs only eight times in the Old Testament and usually refers to an "answer" to a question or a statement. So it means something like "appropriate response" or "corresponding purpose." But the preposition *le* is much more accurately translated "for" (not "with"), so in either case the sentence affirms that the Lord has made everything for its appropriate purpose or the response appropriate to it. Therefore, whether we translate "purpose" or "counterpart," the verse affirms that even the wicked have been made by the Lord "for [Heb. *le*] the day of evil."

**b. Nevertheless, God Never Does Evil, and Is Never to Be Blamed for Evil:** In a statement similar to those cited above from Acts 2:23 and 4:27–28, Jesus also combines God's predestination of the crucifixion with moral blame on those who carry it out: "For the Son of man goes *as it has been determined;* but woe to that man by whom he is betrayed!" (Luke 22:22; cf. Matt. 26:24; Mark 14:21). And in a more general statement about evil in the world, Jesus says, "Woe to the world for temptations to sin! For it is necessary that temptations come, but woe to the man by whom the temptation comes!" (Matt. 18:7).

James speaks similarly in warning us not to blame God for the evil we do when he says, "Let no one say when he is tempted, 'I am tempted by God'; for God cannot be tempted with evil and he himself tempts no one; but each person is tempted when he is lured and enticed by his own desire" (James 1:13–14). The verse does not say that God never causes evil; it affirms that we should never think of him as the personal agent who is tempting us or who is to be held accountable for the temptation. We can never blame God for temptation nor think that he will approve of us if we give in to it. We are to resist evil and always blame ourselves or others who tempt us, but we must never blame God. Even a verse such as Isaiah 45:7, which speaks of God "creating evil," does not say that God himself *does* evil, but should be understood to mean that God ordained that evil would come about through the willing choices of his creatures.

These verses all make it clear that "secondary causes" (human beings, and angels and demons) are *real,* and that human beings do cause evil and are responsible for it. Though God ordained that it would come about, both in general terms and in specific details, yet *God is removed from actually doing evil,* and his bringing it about through "secondary causes" does not impugn his holiness or render him blameworthy. John Calvin wisely says:

> Thieves and murderers and other evildoers are the instruments of divine providence, and the Lord himself uses these to carry out the judgments that he has determined with himself. Yet I deny that they can derive from this any excuse for their evil deeds. Why? Will they either involve God in the same iniquity with themselves, or will they cloak their own depravity with his justice? They can do neither.[12]

A little later, Calvin heads a chapter, "God So Uses the Works of the Ungodly, and So Bends Their Minds to Carry Out His Judgments, That He Remains Pure From Every Stain."[13]

We should notice that the alternatives to saying that God *uses evil for his purposes,* but that *he never does evil* and is *not to be blamed* for it, are not desirable ones. If we were to say that God himself does evil, we would have to conclude that he is not a good and righteous God, and therefore that he is not really God at all. On the other hand, if we maintain that God does not use evil to fulfill his purposes, then we would have to admit that there is evil in the universe that God did not intend, is not under his control, and might not fulfill his purposes. This would make it very difficult for us to affirm that "all things" work together for good for those who love God and are called according to his purpose (Rom. 8:28). If evil came

---

[12]John Calvin, *Institutes of the Christian Religion,* Library of Christian Classics, ed. by John T. McNeill and trans. by F. L. Battles, 2 vols. (Philadelphia: Westminster, 1960), 1:217 (1.16.5).

[13]John Calvin, *Institutes,* 1:228 (1.18.title).

into the world in spite of the fact that God did not intend it and did not want it to be there, then what guarantee do we have that there will not be more and more evil that he does not intend and that he does not want? And what guarantee do we have that he will be able to use it for his purposes, or even that he can triumph over it? Surely this is an undesirable alternative position.

**c. God Rightfully Blames and Judges Moral Creatures for the Evil They Do:** Many passages in Scripture affirm this. One is found in Isaiah: "These have *chosen* their own ways, and their soul *delights in* their abominations; I also will choose affliction for them, and bring their fears upon them; because, when I called, no one answered, when I spoke they did not listen; but they did what was evil in my eyes, and *chose* that in which I did not delight" (Isa. 66:3–4). Similarly, we read, "God made man upright, but they have sought out many devices" (Eccl. 7:29). *The blame for evil is always on the responsible creature*, whether man or demon, who does it, and *the creature who does evil is always worthy of punishment*. Scripture consistently affirms that God is righteous and just to punish us for our sins. And if we object that he should not find fault with us because we cannot resist his will, then we must ponder the apostle Paul's own response to that question: "You will say to me then, 'Why does he still find fault? For who can resist his will?' But who are you, a man, to answer back to God? Will what is molded say to its molder, 'Why have you made me thus?'" (Rom. 9:19–20). In every case where we do evil, we know that we *willingly* choose to do it, and we realize that we are rightly to be blamed for it.

**d. Evil Is Real, Not an Illusion, and We Should Never Do Evil, for It Will Always Harm Us and Others:** Scripture consistently teaches that we never have a right to do evil, and that we should persistently oppose it in ourselves and in the world. We are to pray, "Deliver us from evil" (Matt. 6:13), and if we see anyone wandering from the truth and doing wrong, we should attempt to bring him back. Scripture says, "If any one among you wanders from the truth and someone brings him back, let him know that whoever brings back a sinner from the error of his way will save his soul from death and will cover a multitude of sins" (James 5:19–20). We should never even *will* evil to be done, for entertaining sinful desires in our minds is to allow them to "wage war" against our souls (1 Peter 2:11) and thereby to do us spiritual harm. If we are ever tempted to say, "Why not do evil that good may come?" as some people were slanderously charging Paul with teaching, we should remember what Paul says about people who teach that false doctrine: "Their condemnation is just" (Rom. 3:8).

In thinking about God using evil to fulfill his purposes, we should remember that there are things that are *right* for God to do but *wrong* for us to do: He requires others to worship him, and he accepts worship from them. He seeks glory for himself. He will execute final judgment on wrongdoers. He also uses evil to bring about good purposes, but he does not allow us to do so. Calvin quotes a statement of Augustine with approval: "There is a great difference between what is fitting for man to will and what is fitting for God. . . . For through the bad wills of evil men God fulfills what he righteously wills."[14] And Herman Bavinck uses

---

[14]John Calvin, *Institutes*, 1:234 (1.18.3).

the analogy of a parent who will himself use a very sharp knife but will not allow his child to use it, to show that God himself uses evil to bring about good purposes but never allows his children to do so. Though we are to imitate God's moral character in many ways (cf. Eph. 5:1), this is one of the ways in which we are not to imitate him.

**e. In Spite of All of the Foregoing Statements, We Have to Come to the Point Where We Confess That We Do Not Understand How It Is That God Can Ordain That We Carry Out Evil Deeds and Yet Hold Us Accountable for Them and Not be Blamed Himself:** We can affirm that all of these things are true, because Scripture teaches them. But Scripture does *not* tell us exactly *how* God brings this situation about or how it can be that God holds us accountable for what he ordains to come to pass. Here Scripture is silent, and we have to agree with Berkhof that ultimately "the problem of God's relation to sin remains a mystery."[15]

**9. Are We "Free"? Do We Have "Free Will"?** If God exercises providential control over all events are we in any sense free? The answer depends on what is meant by the word *free*. In some senses of the word *free*, everyone agrees that we are free in our will and in our choices. Even prominent theologians in the Reformed or Calvinistic tradition concur. Both Louis Berkhof in his *Systematic Theology* (pp. 103, 173) and John Calvin in his *Institutes of the Christian Religion*[16] are willing to speak *in some sense* of the "free" acts and choices of man. However, Calvin explains that the term is so subject to misunderstanding that he himself tries to avoid using it. This is because "free will is not sufficient to enable man to do good works, unless he be helped by grace."[17] Therefore, Calvin concludes:

> Man will then be spoken of as having this sort of free decision, not because he has free choice equally of good and evil, but because he acts wickedly by will, not by compulsion. Well put, indeed, but what purpose is served by labeling with a proud name such a slight thing?

Calvin continues by explaining how this term is easily misunderstood:

> But how few men are there, I ask, who when they hear free will attributed to man do not immediately conceive him to be master of both his own mind and will, able of his own power to turn himself toward either good or evil. . . . If anyone, then, can use this word without understanding it in a bad sense, I shall not trouble him

---

[15]Louis Berkhof, *Systematic Theology*, p. 175.
[16]*Institutes*, 1:296 (2.3.5), quoting St. Bernard with approval: "Among all living beings man alone is free. . . . For what is voluntary is also free." Later in the same passage he quotes St. Bernard with approval again, where he admits that the will is in bondage to sin and therefore sins of necessity, but then says that "this necessity is as it were voluntary. . . . Thus the soul . . . is at the same time enslaved and free: enslaved because of necessity; free because of will." A little later Calvin himself says that "man, while he sins of necessity, yet sins no less voluntarily" (1:309 [2.4.1]). Calvin clearly says that Adam, before there was sin in the world, "by free will had the power, if he so willed, to attain eternal life. . . . Adam could have stood if he wished, seeing that he fell solely by his own will. . . . His choice of good and evil was free" (1:195 [1.15.8]). So Calvin can use the term *free will* if it means "voluntary, willing," and he can use it of Adam before the fall. Yet he carefully avoids applying the term *free will* to sinful human beings if by it people mean "able to do good in one's own strength" (see text above).
[17]*Institutes*, 1:262 (2.2.6).

on this account . . . I'd prefer not to use it myself, and I should like others, if they seek my advice, to avoid it.[18]

Thus, when we ask whether we have "free will," it is important to be clear as to what is meant by the phrase. Scripture nowhere says that we are "free" in the sense of being outside of God's control[19] or of being able to make decisions that are not caused by anything. (This is the sense in which many people seem to assume we must be free; see discussion below.) Nor does it say we are "free" in the sense of being able to do right on our own apart from God's power. But we are nonetheless free in the greatest sense that any creature of God could be free—we make *willing* choices, choices that have *real effects*.[20] We are aware of no restraints on our will from God when we make decisions.[21] We must insist that we have the power of *willing* choice; otherwise we will fall into the error of fatalism or determinism and thus conclude that our choices do not matter, or that we cannot really make willing choices. On the other hand, the kind of freedom that is demanded by those who deny God's providential control of all things, a freedom to be outside of God's sustaining and controlling activity, would be impossible if Jesus Christ is indeed "continually carrying along things by his word of power" (Heb. 1:3, author's translation). If this is true, then to be outside of that providential control would simply be not to exist! An absolute "freedom," totally free of God's control, is simply not possible in a world providentially sustained and directed by God himself.

## C. Government

**1. Scriptural Evidence.** We have discussed the first two aspects of providence, (1) preservation and (2) concurrence. This third aspect of God's providence indicates that *God has a purpose in all that he does in the world and he providentially governs or directs all things in order that they accomplish his purposes.* We read in the Psalms, "His kingdom rules over all" (Ps. 103:19). Moreover, "he does according to his will in the host of heaven and among the inhabitants of the earth; and none can stay his hand or say to him, 'What are you doing?'" (Dan. 4:35). Paul affirms that "from him and through him and to him are all things" (Rom. 11:36), and that "God has put all things in subjection under his feet" (1 Cor. 15:27). God is the one who "accomplishes *all things* according to the counsel of his will" (Eph. 1:11), so that ultimately "at the name of Jesus" every knee will bow "in heaven and on earth and under the earth, and every tongue confess that Jesus Christ is Lord, to the glory of God the Father" (Phil. 2:10–11). It is because Paul knows

---

[18]Ibid., 1:264, 266 (2.2.7–8).

[19]In fact, our ability to make willing choices at all is simply a created reflection of God's will and his ability to make willing choices. However, if we were to be *totally* free in our choices, we would be equal to God in our will, and that is something we many never expect either in this life or in the one to come.

[20]Arminian theologians dissent from this understanding of free will and argue for a freedom that means our decisions are not caused by anything outside ourselves (see discussion of Jack Cottrell's objection that freedom must mean more than willing choices on pp. 340–47, below).

[21]John Feinberg says, "If the act is according to the agent's *desires,* then even though the act is causally determined, it is free and the agent is morally responsible" ("God Ordains All Things," in *Predestination and Free Will: Four Views of Divine Sovereignty and Human Freedom,* ed. by David Basinger and Randall Basinger [Downers Grove, Ill.: InterVarsity Press, 1986], p. 37).

that God is sovereign over all and works his purposes in every event that happens that he can declare that "God causes all things to work together for good to those who love God, to those who are called according to his purpose" (Rom. 8:28 NASB).

**2. Distinctions Concerning the Will of God.** Though *in God* his will is unified, and not divided or contradictory, we cannot begin to understand the depths of God's will, and only in a small part is it revealed to us. For this reason, as we saw in chapter 13,[22] two aspects of God's will appear to us. On the one hand, there is God's *moral will* (sometimes called his "revealed" will). This includes the moral standards of Scripture, such as the Ten Commandments and the moral commands of the New Testament. God's moral commands are given as descriptions of how *we* should conduct ourselves if we would act rightly before him. On the other hand, another aspect of God's will is his *providential government* of all things (sometimes called his "secret will"). This includes all the events of history that God has ordained to come about, for example, the fact that Christ would be crucified by "lawless men" (Acts 2:23). It also includes all the other evil acts that were mentioned in the preceding section.

Some have objected to this distinction between two aspects of the will of God, arguing that it means there is a "self-contradiction" in God.[23] However, even in the realm of human experience, we know that we can will and carry out something that is painful and that we do not desire (such as punishing a disobedient child or getting an inoculation that temporarily makes us ill) in order to bring about a long-term result that we desire more than the avoidance of short-term pain (to bring about the obedience of the child, for example, or to prevent us from getting a more serious illness). And God is infinitely greater and wiser than we are. Certainly it is possible for him to will that his creatures do something that in the short term displeases him in order that in the long term he would receive the greater glory. To say that this is a "self-contradiction" in God is to fail to understand the distinctions that have been made so that this explanation is not contradictory.[24]

## D. The Decrees of God

The decrees of God are *the eternal plans of God whereby, before the creation of the world, he determined to bring about everything that happens*. This doctrine is similar to the doctrine of providence, but here we are thinking about God's decisions *before the world was created*, rather than his providential actions in time. His providential actions are the outworking of the eternal decrees that he made long ago. (See chapter 2, p. 47, for "decree" used in a somewhat different sense.)

---

[22]See pp. 213–16 for a further discussion of God's secret and revealed will.
[23]This is the objection of I. Howard Marshall, "Predestination in the New Testament," p. 173.
[24]John Calvin says of those who object to two senses of the will of God, "Let them tell me, I pray, whether he exercises his judgments willingly or unwillingly. . . . When we do not grasp how God wills to take place what he forbids to be done, let us recall our mental incapacity." He also quotes with approval the statement of Augustine: "There is a great difference between what is fitting for man to will and what is fitting for God . . . for through the bad wills of evil men God fulfills what he righteously wills" (*Institutes,* 1:233–34 [1.18.3]).

David confesses, "in your book were written, every one of them, the days that were formed for me, when as yet there was none of them" (Ps. 139:16; cf. Job 14:5: the days, months, and bounds of man are determined by God). There was also a "definite *plan* and foreknowledge of God" (Acts 2:23) by which Jesus was put to death, and the actions of those who condemned and crucified him were "predestined" (Acts 4:28) by God. Our salvation was determined long ago because God "chose us in him (Christ) *before the foundation of the world,* that we should be holy and blameless before him" (Eph. 1:4). Our good works as believers are those "which God *prepared beforehand,* that we should walk in them" (Eph. 2:10; cf. Jude 4).

These examples take in many diverse aspects of human activity. It seems appropriate to conclude from these examples that all that God does he has planned before the creation of the world—in fact, these things have been an *eternal plan* with him. The benefit of an emphasis on God's decrees is that it helps us to realize that God does not make up plans suddenly as he goes along. He knows the end from the beginning, and he will accomplish all his good purposes. This should greatly increase our trust in him, especially in difficult circumstances.

## E. The Importance of Our Human Actions

We may sometimes forget that God works *through human actions* in his providential management of the world. If we do, then we begin to think that our actions and our choices do not make much difference or do not have much effect on the course of events. To guard against any misunderstanding of God's providence we make the following points of emphasis.

**1. We Are Still Responsible for Our Actions.** God has made us *responsible* for our actions, which have *real and eternally significant results.* In all his providential acts God will preserve these characteristics of responsibility and significance.

Some analogies from the natural world might help us understand this. God has created a rock with the characteristic of being *hard,* and so it is. God has created water with the characteristic of being *wet,* and so it is. God has created plants and animals with the characteristic of being *alive,* and so they are. Similarly, God has created us with the characteristic of being *responsible for our actions,* and so we are! If we do right and obey God, he will reward us and things will go well with us both in this age and in eternity. If we do wrong and disobey God, he will discipline and perhaps punish us, and things will go ill with us. The realization of these facts will help us have pastoral wisdom in talking to others and in encouraging them to avoid laziness and disobedience.

The fact that we are responsible for our actions means that we should never begin to think, "God made me do evil, and therefore I am not responsible for it." Significantly, Adam began to make excuses for the very first sin in terms that sounded suspiciously like this: "The woman whom you gave to be with me, she gave me fruit of the tree, and I ate" (Gen. 3:12). Unlike Adam, Scripture *never* blames God for sin. If we ever begin to *think* that God is to blame for sin, we have thought *wrongly* about God's providence, for it is always the creature, not God who is to be blamed. Now we may object that it is not right for God to hold us responsible if he has in fact ordained all things that happen, but Paul corrects us: "You will say to me then, 'Why does he still find fault? For who can resist his will?' But who are you, a man, to answer back to God?" (Rom. 9:19–20). We must realize and settle in our hearts that it is *right* for God to rebuke and discipline and punish evil. And, when we are responsible to do so, it is right for us to rebuke and discipline evil in our families, in the church, and even, in some ways, in the society around us. We should never say about an evil event, "God willed it and therefore it is good," because we must recognize that some things that God's will of decree has planned are not in themselves good, and should not receive our approval, just as they do not receive God's approval.

**2. Our Actions Have Real Results and Do Change the Course of Events.** In the ordinary working of the world, if I neglect to take care of my health and have poor eating habits, or if I abuse my body through alcohol or tobacco, I am likely to die sooner. God has ordained that our *actions* do have effects. God has ordained that *events* will come about *by our causing them.* Of course, we do not know what God has planned even for the rest of this day, to say nothing of next week or next year. But we *do* know that if we trust God and obey him, we will discover that he has planned *good things* to come about through that obedience! We cannot simply disregard others whom we meet, for God brings many people across our paths and gives *us* the responsibility to act toward them in eternally significant ways— whether for good or ill.

Calvin wisely notes that to encourage us to use ordinary caution in life and to plan ahead, "God is pleased to hide all future events from us, in order that we should resist them as doubtful, and not cease to oppose them with ready remedies, until they are either overcome or pass beyond all care. . . . God's providence does not always meet us in its naked form, but God in a sense clothes it with the means employed."[25]

By contrast, if we anticipate that some dangers or evil events may come in the future, and if we do not use reasonable means to avoid them, then we may in fact discover that our lack of action was the means that God used to allow them to come about!

**3. Prayer Is One Specific Kind of Action That Has Definite Results and That Does Change the Course of Events.** God has also ordained that prayer is a very significant means of bringing about results in the world.[26] When we earnestly intercede for a specific person or situation, we will often find that God had ordained that our prayer would be a *means* he would use to bring about the changes in the world. Scripture reminds us of this when it tells us, "You do not have, because you do not ask" (James 4:2). Jesus says, "Hitherto you have asked nothing in my name; ask, and you will receive, that your joy may be full" (John 16:24).

**4. In Conclusion, We Must Act!** The doctrine of providence in no way encourages us to sit back in idleness to await the outcome of certain events. Of

---

[25]John Calvin, *Institutes,* 1:216 (1.17.4).
[26]See chapter 18 for a more extensive discussion of prayer.

course, God may impress on us the need to wait on him before we act and to trust in him rather than in our own abilities—that is certainly not wrong. But simply to say that we are trusting in God *instead of* acting responsibly is sheer laziness and is a distortion of the doctrine of providence.

In practical terms, if one of my sons has school work that must be done the next day, I am right to make him complete that work before he can go out to play. I realize that his grade is in God's hands, and that God has long ago determined what it would be, but I do not know what it will be, and neither does he. What I do know is that if he studies and does his school work faithfully, he will receive a good grade. If he doesn't, he will not. So Calvin can say:

> Now it is very clear what our duty is: Thus, if the Lord has committed to us the protection of our life, our duty is to protect it; if he offers helps to us, to use them; if he forewarns us of dangers, not to plunge headlong; if he makes remedies available, not to neglect them. But no danger will hurt us, say they, unless it is fatal, and in this case it is beyond remedies. But what if the dangers are not fatal, because the Lord has provided you with remedies for repulsing and overcoming them?[27]

One good example of vigorous activity combined with trust in God is found in 2 Samuel 10:12, where Joab says, "*Be strong* and let us show ourselves courageous for the sake of our people and for the cities of our God," but then adds immediately in the same sentence, "*and may the Lord do what is good in His sight*" (NASB). Joab will both fight and trust God to do what he thinks to be good.

Similar examples are found in the New Testament. When Paul was in Corinth, in order to keep him from being discouraged about the opposition he had received from the Jews, the Lord appeared to him one night in a vision and said to him, "Do not be afraid, but speak and do not be silent; for I am with you, and no man shall attack you to harm you; for *I have many people in this city*" (Acts 18:9–10). If Paul had been a fatalist with an improper understanding of God's providence, he would have listened to God's words, "I have many people in this city," and concluded that God had determined to save many of the Corinthians, and that therefore it did not matter whether Paul stayed there or not: God had already chosen many people to be saved! Paul would have thought that he may as well pack his bags and leave! But Paul does not make that mistake. He rather concludes that if God has chosen many people, then it will probably be through the *means* of Paul's preaching the gospel that those many people would be saved. Therefore Paul makes a wise decision: "*And he stayed a year and six months*, teaching the word of God among them" (Acts 18:11).

Paul put this kind of responsible action in the light of God's providence into a single sentence in 2 Timothy 2:10, where he said, "I endure everything *for the sake of the elect*, that they also may obtain salvation in Christ Jesus with its eternal glory." He did not argue from the fact that God had chosen some to be saved that nothing had to be done; rather, he concluded that *much* had to be done in order that God's purposes might come about by the *means* that God had also established. Indeed, Paul was willing to endure "everything," including all kinds of hardship and suffering, that God's eternal plans might come about. A hearty belief in God's providence is not a discouragement but a spur to action.

---

[27]John Calvin, *Institutes*, 1:216 (1.17.4).

A related example is found in the story of Paul's journey to Rome. God had clearly revealed to Paul that no one on the ship would die from the long storm they had endured. Indeed, Paul stood before the passengers and crew and told them to take heart,

> for there will be no loss of life among you, but only of the ship. For this very night there stood by me an angel of the God to whom I belong and whom I worship, and he said, "Do not be afraid, Paul; you must stand before Caesar; and lo, God has granted you all those who sail with you." So take heart, men, for I have faith in God that it will be exactly as I have been told. But we shall have to run on some island. (Acts 27:22–26)

But shortly after Paul had said this, he noticed that the sailors on board the ship were secretly trying to lower a lifeboat into the sea, "seeking to escape from the ship" (Acts 27:30). They were planning to leave the others helpless with no one who knew how to sail the ship. When Paul saw this, he did not adopt an erroneous, fatalistic attitude, thinking that God would miraculously get the ship to shore. Rather, he immediately went to the centurion who was in charge of the sailors and "Paul said to the centurion and the soldiers, 'Unless these men stay in the ship, you cannot be saved'" (Acts 27:31). Wisely, Paul knew that God's providential oversight and even his clear prediction of what would happen still involved the use of ordinary human *means* to bring it about. He was even so bold to say that those means were *necessary*: "Unless these men stay in the ship, *you cannot be saved*" (Acts 27:31). We would do well to imitate his example, combining complete trust in God's providence with a realization that the use of ordinary means is necessary for things to come out the way God has planned them to come out.

**5. What If We Cannot Understand This Doctrine Fully?** Every believer who meditates on God's providence will sooner or later come to a point where he or she will have to say, "I cannot understand this doctrine fully." In some ways that must be said about every doctrine, since our understanding is finite, and God is infinite (see chapter 1, pp. 34–35; cf. p. 150). But particularly is this so with the doctrine of providence: we should believe it because Scripture teaches it even when we do not understand fully how it fits in with other teachings of Scripture. Calvin has some wise advice:

> Let those for whom this seems harsh consider for a little while how bearable their squeamishness is in refusing a thing attested by clear Scriptural proofs because it exceeds their mental capacity, and find fault that things are put forth publicly, which if God had not judged useful for men to know, he would never have bidden his prophets and apostles to teach. For our wisdom ought to be nothing else than to embrace with humble teachableness, and at least without finding fault, whatever is taught in sacred Scripture.[28]

### F. Further Practical Application

Although we have already begun to speak of the practical application of this doctrine, three additional points should be made.

---

[28]*Institutes*, 1:237 (1.18.4).

**1. Do Not Be Afraid, but Trust in God.** Jesus emphasizes the fact that our sovereign Lord watches over us and cares for us as his children. He says, "Look at the birds of the air: they neither sow nor reap nor gather into barns, and yet your heavenly Father feeds them. Are you not of more value than they? . . . Therefore do not be anxious, saying, 'What shall we eat?' or 'What shall we drink?' or 'What shall we wear?'" (Matt. 6:26, 31). If God feeds the birds and clothes the grass of the field, he will take care of us. Similarly, Jesus says, "Are not two sparrows sold for a penny? And not one of them will fall to the ground without your Father's will. . . . Fear not, therefore; you are of more value than many sparrows" (Matt. 10:29–31).

David was able to sleep in the midst of his enemies, because he knew that God's providential control made him "dwell in safety," and he could say, "In peace I will both lie down and sleep" (Ps. 4:8). Many of the psalms encourage us to trust God and not to fear, because the LORD keeps and protects his people—for example, Psalm 91 ("He who dwells in the shelter of the Most High . . .") or Psalm 121 ("I lift up my eyes to the hills . . ."). Because of our confidence in God's providential care, we need not fear any evil or harm, even if it does come to us—it can only come by God's will and ultimately for our good. Thus Peter can say that "now for a little while you may have to suffer various trials, so that the genuineness of your faith, more precious than gold . . . may redound to praise and glory and honor at the revelation of Jesus Christ" (1 Peter 1:6–7). In all of this we need not worry about the future but trust in God's omnipotent care.

**2. Be Thankful for All Good Things That Happen.** If we genuinely believe that all good things are caused by God, then our hearts will indeed be full when we say, "Bless the LORD, O my soul, and forget not all his benefits" (Ps. 103:2). We will thank him for our daily food (cf. Matt. 6:11; 1 Tim. 4:4–5); indeed, we will "give thanks in all circumstances" (1 Thess. 5:18).

**3. There Is No Such Thing as "Luck" or "Chance."** All things come to pass by God's wise providence. This means that we should adopt a much more "personal" understanding of the universe and the events in it. The universe is not governed by impersonal fate or luck, but by a personal God. Nothing "just happens"—we should see God's hand in events throughout the day, causing all things to work together for good for those who love him.

This confidence in God's wise providence certainly does not equal superstition, for that is a belief in impersonal or demonic control of circumstances, or control by a capricious deity concerned for meaningless ritual rather than obedience and faith. A deepened appreciation for the doctrine of providence will not make us more superstitious; it will make us trust in God more and obey him more fully.

### G. Another Evangelical View: the Arminian Position

There is a major alternative position held by many evangelicals, which for convenience we shall call the "Arminian" view.[29] Among denominations in

---

[29]The term *Arminianism* was recently chosen in the title of a responsible series of essays representing this position: See Clark H. Pinnock, ed., *The Grace of God, The Will of Man: A Case for Arminianism*

contemporary evangelicalism, Methodists and Nazarenes tend to be thoroughly
Arminian, whereas Presbyterians and the Christian Reformed tend to be
thoroughly Reformed (at least by denominational statement of faith). Both views
are found among Baptists, Episcopalians (though the Thirty-Nine Articles have a
clearly Reformed emphasis), Dispensationalists, Evangelical Free Churches,
Lutherans (though Martin Luther was in the Reformed camp on this issue), the
Churches of Christ, and most charismatic and Pentecostal groups (though
Pentecostal denominations such as the Assemblies of God have been predominantly Arminian).

Those who hold an Arminian position maintain that in order to preserve the
*real human freedom* and *real human choices* that are necessary for genuine human
personhood, God cannot cause or plan our voluntary choices. Therefore they
conclude that God's providential involvement in or control of history must *not*
include *every specific detail* of every event that happens, but that God instead simply
*responds* to human choices and actions as they come about and does so in such a
way that his purposes are ultimately accomplished in the world.

Those who hold this position argue that God's purposes in the world are more
general and could be accomplished through many different kinds of specific
events. So God's purpose or plan for the world "is not a blueprint encompassing
all future contingencies" but "a dynamic program for the world, the outworking
of which depends in part on man."[30] Cottrell says, "God does not have a specific,
unconditional purpose for each discrete particle, object, person, and event within
the creation."[31] Arminians believe that God achieves his overall goal by
responding to and utilizing the free choices of human beings, whatever they may
be.[32] Pinnock says that "predestination does not apply to every individual activity,

---

(Grand Rapids: Zondervan, 1989). In the following section I quote extensively from this book and
from an earlier book edited by Pinnock, *Grace Unlimited*. These two books are excellent recent defenses
of the Arminian position.

Jacob Arminius (1560–1609) was a Dutch theologian who differed with the predominant
Calvinism of his day. Though he is not personally quoted or referred to very often by Arminians today,
his name has become attached to a range of positions that have in common the fact that they differ
from the Calvinist position on the question of man's free will, both with respect to God's providence in
general (the subject of this chapter) and with respect to predestination or election in specific (the
subject of chapter 32).

The term *Arminian* should be distinguished from the term *Armenian*, which refers to people who
live in or descend from inhabitants of the ancient country of Armenia in western Asia (now part of
Turkey, Iran, and the CIS).

[30]Clark Pinnock, "Responsible Freedom in the Flow of Biblical History," in *Grace Unlimited*, p. 18.
[31]Jack Cottrell, "The Nature of the Divine Sovereignty," in *The Grace of God, the Will of Man*,
p. 107. Cottrell's essay is, in my view, the most comprehensive and persuasive of the many excellent
Arminian essays in this book—the book as a whole is responsibly done and is probably the best recent
representation of Arminian thinking. Cottrell does not deny divine omniscience regarding future
events as do the essays by Clark Pinnock and Richard Rice in the same volume, and this places him
closer to the intuitive Arminianism that seems right to many evangelical laypersons today.
[32]I. Howard Marshall claims this at several points in "Predestination in the New Testament," *Grace
Unlimited*, pp. 127–43. Marshall uses the analogy of a jazz band where individual players can
improvise freely but the overall goal and unity of the piece are preserved nonetheless (p. 133). Thus,
"the Bible has the picture of a God deciding fresh measures in history and interacting with the wills of
men alongside the picture of a God planning things in eternity past, and both pictures are equally
valid" (Marshall, p. 141).

but is rather the comprehensive purpose of God which is *the structural context* in which history moves."[33]

Moreover, advocates of the Arminian position maintain that God's will cannot include evil. Pinnock says, "The fall of man is an eloquent refutation to the theory that God's will is always done."[34] He states that it "is not the case" that God's will "is also accomplished in the lostness of the lost."[35] And I. Howard Marshall quite clearly affirms, "It is not true that everything that happens is what God desires."[36] These statements make it clear that the differences between the Reformed and Arminian positions are not merely differences in terminology: there is a real disagreement in substance. Several arguments are advanced in defense of the Arminian position. I have attempted to summarize them in the four major points that follow.

**1. The Verses Cited as Examples of God's Providential Control Are Exceptions and Do Not Describe the Way That God Ordinarily Works in Human Activity.** In surveying the Old Testament passages referring to God's providential involvement in the world, David J. A. Clines says that God's predictions and statements of his purposes refer to limited or specific events:

> Almost all of the specific references to God's plans have in view a particular event or a limited series of events, for example, "his purposes against the land of the Chaldeans" (Jer. 50:45). Furthermore, it is not a matter of a *single* divine plan; various passages speak of various intentions, and some references are in fact to God's plans in the plural. . . . [The passages are] an assertion that within history God is working his purposes out.[37]

Jack Cottrell agrees that in some cases God intervenes in the world in an uncommon way, using "subtle manipulation of such [natural] laws and of mental states." But he calls these unusual events "special providence," and says, "It is natural that the Old Testament teems with accounts of special providence. But we have no reason to assume that God was working in Australia and South America in such ways at the same time."[38]

**2. The Calvinist View Wrongly Makes God Responsible for Sin.** Those who hold an Arminian position ask, "How can God be holy if he decrees that we sin?" They affirm that God is not the "author of sin," that "God cannot be tempted with evil and he himself tempts no one" (James 1:13), that "God is light and in him is no darkness at all" (1 John 1:5), and that "the LORD is upright . . . and there is no unrighteousness in him" (Ps. 92:15).

The view of God's providence advocated above, they would say, makes us into

---

[33]Pinnock, "Responsible Freedom," p. 102.
[34]Ibid., p. 102.
[35]Ibid., p. 106.
[36]Marshall, "Predestination in the New Testament," p. 139.
[37]David J. A. Clines, "Predestination in the Old Testament," p. 122; see also pp. 116–17. Similarly, James D. Strauss, "God's Promise and Universal History," *Grace Unlimited,* p. 196, says that the example of Jacob and Esau that Paul mentions in Rom. 9:9–13 refers to God's corporate plans for the descendants of Jacob and Esau and should not be taken as an illustration of how God works in people's lives or hearts generally.
[38]Jack Cottrell, "The Nature of the Divine Sovereignty," pp. 112–13.

puppets or robots who cannot do anything other than what God causes us to do. But this brings moral reproach on God, for Marshall says, "I am responsible for what my agent does."[39] Pinnock affirms that "it is simply blasphemous to maintain, as this theory does, that man's rebellion against God is *in any sense* the product of God's sovereign will or primary causation."[40]

**3. Choices Caused by God Cannot Be Real Choices.** When the Calvinist claims that God causes us to choose things voluntarily, those who hold an Arminian position would respond that any choices that are ultimately caused by God cannot be real choices, and that, if God really causes us to make the choices we make, then we are not real persons. Cottrell says that the Calvinist view of God as the primary cause and men as secondary causes really breaks down so there is only one cause, God. If a man uses a lever to move a rock, he argues, "the lever is not a true second cause but is only an instrument of the real cause of the movement. . . . In my judgment the concept of cause has no real significance when used in this sense. In such a system man contributes only what has been predetermined."[41]

Pinnock writes:

Personal fellowship of the kind envisioned in the Gospel only exists where consummated in a free decision. If we wish to understand God's grace as personal address to his creatures, we must comprehend it in dynamic, non-manipulative, non-coercive terms, as the Bible does.[42]

He also says:

If the world were a completely determined structure on which no decision of man's would have any effect, that basic intuition of man's that he is an *actor* and a *free agent* would be nonsensical: There would then be no point to his making plans or exerting efforts intended to transform the world. . . . Human freedom is the precondition of moral and intellectual responsibility.[43]

Why then, in the Arminian view, did the fall and sin come about? Pinnock answers that "they occur because God refuses to mechanize man or to force his will upon him."[44] And Marshall says, with respect to the "possibility of my predetermining a course of action involving myself and another subject," that "on the level of free agents it is impossible."[45] He objects that the analogy of God and world as being like an author and a play is unhelpful because if we ask whether the characters are indeed free, "this is an unreal question."[46]

However, it should be noted that Arminian theologians are certainly willing to allow some kinds of influence by God on human beings. Marshall says, "Prayer also influences men. . . . The wills of men can thus be affected by prayer or else we

---

[39]Marshall, "Predestination," p. 136.
[40]Pinnock, "Responsible Freedom," p. 102.
[41]Jack Cottrell, "The Nature of the Divine Sovereignty," pp. 104–5.
[42]Pinnock, *Grace Unlimited*, p. 15.
[43]Pinnock, "Responsible Freedom," p. 95.
[44]Ibid., p. 108.
[45]Marshall, "Predestination," p. 132. Similarly, he says, "When we try to think of a person foreordaining the course of a relationship between himself and another person . . . *this concept is logically self-contradictory*" (p. 135).
[46]Ibid., p. 133.

would not pray for them. *To believe in prayer is thus to believe in some kind of limitation of human freedom, and in some kind of incomprehensible influence upon the wills of men.*[47]

To drive home their point about the essential freedom of the human will, advocates of an Arminian position draw attention to the frequency of the free offer of the gospel in the New Testament. They would say that these invitations to people to repent and come to Christ for salvation, if *bona fide*, must imply the *ability* to respond to them. Thus, all people without exception have the ability to respond, not just those who have been sovereignly given that ability by God in a special way.

In further support of this point, Arminians would see 1 Corinthians 10:13 as clearly affirming our ability not to sin. Paul says to the Corinthians, "No temptation has overtaken you that is not common to man. God is faithful, and he will not let you be tempted beyond your strength, but with the temptation will also provide the way of escape, *that you may be able to endure it.*" But, it is said, this statement would be false if God sometimes ordains that we sin, for then we would not be "able" to escape from temptation without sinning.

### 4. The Arminian View Encourages Responsible Christian Living, While the Calvinistic View Encourages a Dangerous Fatalism.
Christians who hold an Arminian position argue that the Calvinist view, when thoroughly understood, destroys motives for responsible Christian behavior. Randall Basinger says that the Calvinist view "establishes that what is ought to be and rules out the consideration that things could and/or should have been different."[48] Basinger continues by saying that Christians

> who evoke and act on the basis of God's sovereignty are guilty of an arbitrary, unlivable, and dangerous fatalism. . . . In contrast to this, the Arminian believes that what actually occurs in the world is, to an extent, consequent on the human will; God's exhaustive control over the world is denied. This means that things can occur that God does not will or want; things not only *can* be different but often *should* be different. And from all this follows our responsibility to work with God to bring about a better world.[49]

However, Basinger goes on to make a further point: Calvinists, in practice, often avoid such fatalism and "live and talk like Arminians."[50] Thus, on the one hand, Basinger's challenge is a warning against the practical extremes to which he claims Calvinism should logically drive Christians. On the other hand, his objection claims that when Calvinists live the way they know they must live, in responsible obedience to God, they are either inconsistent with their view of divine sovereignty or else not allowing their view of God's sovereign control to affect their daily lives.

---

[47]Ibid., pp. 139–40 (emphasis in original text).
[48]Randall G. Basinger, "Exhaustive Divine Sovereignty: A Practical Critique," in *The Grace of God, the Will of Man: A Case for Arminianism*, ed. Clark H. Pinnock, p. 94.
[49]Ibid., p. 196.
[50]Ibid., p. 204.

## H. Response to the Arminian Position

Many within the evangelical world will find these four Arminian arguments convincing. They will feel that these arguments represent what they intuitively know about themselves, their own actions, and the way the world functions, and that these arguments best account for the repeated emphasis in Scripture on our responsibility and the real consequences of our choices. However, there are some answers that can be given to the Arminian position.

**1. Are These Scripture Passages Unusual Examples, or Do They Describe the Way God Works Ordinarily?** In response to the objection that the examples of God's providential control only refer to limited or specific events, it may be said first that the examples are so numerous (see above, pp. 317–27) that they seem to be designed to describe to us the ways in which God works all the time. God does not just cause *some* grass to grow; he causes all grass to grow. He does not just send *some* rain; he sends all the rain. He does not just keep *some* sparrows from falling to the ground without his will; he keeps all sparrows from falling to the ground without his will. He does not just know every word on David's tongue before he speaks it; he knows the words on all our tongues before we speak them. He has not just chosen Paul and the Christians in the Ephesian churches to be holy and blameless before him; he has chosen all Christians to be holy and blameless before him. This is why Cottrell's claim, that God was working differently in Australia and South America than in the Old Testament,[51] is so unconvincing: Scripture is given to tell us the ways of God, and when we have dozens of examples throughout Old and New Testaments where there is such clear teaching on this, it is appropriate for us to conclude that this is the way in which God *always* works with human beings. By contrast, there seems to be nothing in Scripture that would indicate that some things are outside God's providential control, or that these ways of God's acting are unusual or unrepresentative of the ways in which he acts generally.

Moreover, many of the verses that speak of God's providence are very general: Christ "continually carries along *all things* by his word of power" (Heb. 1:3, author's translation), and "in him all things hold together" (Col. 1:17). "In him we live and move and have our being" (Acts 17:28). He "accomplishes *all things* according to the counsel of his will" (Eph. 1:11).[52] He provides our food (Matt.

---

[51]Jack Cottrell, "The Nature of the Divine Sovereignty," p. 113.

[52]Jack Cottrell, "The Nature of the Divine Sovereignty," argues that the context of Eph. 1:11 shows that it does not include all things in the universe but is restricted to a specific focus: "This focus is 'the mystery of his will' (1:9), which is the uniting of Jews and Gentiles together into one body, the church (3:6)." Thus, he says, the verse only "refers to 'all things' required for uniting Jews and Gentiles under one Head in one body" (p. 116).

But this argument is not convincing. Cottrell must skip over to Eph. 3:6 to get the contextual restriction he seeks for the "all things" in 1:11. In doing this he ignores the clearly cosmic scope of the context as defined in the immediately preceding verse, a verse that is in the same sentence in the Greek text: "as a plan for the fulness of time, to unite *all things* [*ta panta*] in him, *things in heaven and things on earth*" (Eph. 1:10). All things in heaven and on earth includes the whole universe. Eph. 1:21–22 further explains that God has exalted Christ "far above all rule and authority and power and dominion . . . and he has put *all things* under his feet and has made him the head over *all things* for the church." Once again the scope is universal. The "mystery" of God's will mentioned in Eph. 1:9 is not limited to the uniting of Jews and Gentiles (as in 3:6) but is defined by 1:10 as a plan to unite all things in Christ.

6:11), supplies all our needs (Phil. 4:19), directs our steps (Prov. 20:24) and works in us to will and to do his good pleasure (Phil. 2:13). Such Scripture passages have in view more than exceptional examples of an unusual intervention by God in the affairs of human beings; they describe the way God always works in the world.

## 2. Does the Calvinistic Doctrine of God's Providence Make God Responsible for Sin?

Against the Calvinistic view of God's providence (which allows that he decrees to permit sin and evil) Arminians would say that God is not responsible for sin and evil *because he did not ordain them or cause them in any way*. This is indeed *one way* of absolving God from responsibility and blame for sin, but is it the biblical way?

The problem is whether the Arminian position can really account for many texts that clearly say that God ordains that some people sin or do evil (see Section B.7, above, pp. 322–27). The death of Christ is the prime example of this, but there are many others in Scripture (Joseph's brothers, Pharaoh, the Egyptians, the Canaanites, Eli's sons, David's census, and the Babylonians, to mention a few). The response could be made that these were unusual events, exceptions to God's ordinary way of acting. But it does not solve the problem, for, on the Arminian view, how can God be holy if he ordains even one sinful act?

The Calvinist position seems preferable: God himself never sins but always brings about his will *through secondary causes;* that is, through personal moral agents who voluntarily, willingly do what God has ordained. These personal moral agents (both human beings and evil angels) are to blame for the evil they do. While the Arminian position objects that, on a human level, people are also responsible for *what they cause others to do,* we can answer that Scripture is not willing to apply such reasoning to God. Rather, Scripture repeatedly gives examples where God in a mysterious, hidden way somehow ordains that people do wrong, but continually places the blame for that wrong on the individual human who does wrong and never on God himself. The Arminian position seems to have failed to show why God *cannot* work in this way in the world, preserving both his holiness and our individual human responsibility for sin.

## 3. Can Choices Ordained by God Be Real Choices?

In response to the claim that choices ordained by God cannot be real choices, it must be said that this is simply an assumption based once again on human experience and intuition, not on specific texts of Scripture.[53] Yet Scripture does not indicate that we can extrapolate from our human experience when dealing with God's providential

---

The term *mystery* (Gk. *mystērion*) in Paul means something previously hidden but now made known by revelation, and it can refer to different things in different contexts: in Eph. 5:32 it refers to marriage as a symbol of the union between Christ and the church; in 1 Cor. 15:51 it refers to the resurrection body; etc.

[53]This is the case with Cottrell's analogy of the man who uses a lever to move a rock. He says the lever "is not a true second cause, but only an instrument of the real cause" ("The Nature of the Divine Sovereignty," p. 104). But here Cottrell makes a common mistake, assuming that analogies from human experience, rather than the testimony of Scripture itself, can determine what is a real cause and what is not. The analogy of a man using a lever to move a rock does not fit, because God is far greater than any man, and we as real persons are far greater than any lever.

control of his creatures, especially human beings. Arminians have simply not answered the question, Where does Scripture say that a choice ordained by God is not a real choice?[54] When we read passages indicating that God works through our will, our power to choose, and our personal volition, on what basis can we say that a choice brought about by God through these means is not a real choice? It seems better to affirm that God *says* that our choices are real and to conclude that therefore they *are real*. Scripture repeatedly affirms that our choices are genuine choices, that they have *real* results, and that those results last for eternity. "Do this, and you will live" (Luke 10:28). "For God so loved the world that he gave his only Son, that *whoever believes in him* should not perish but have eternal life" (John 3:16).

This causes us to conclude that God has made us in such a way that (1) he ordains all that we do, and (2) we exercise our personal will and make real, voluntary choices. Because we cannot understand this should we therefore reject it? We cannot understand (in any final sense) how a plant can live, or how a bumblebee can fly, or how God can be omnipresent or eternal. Should we therefore reject those facts? Should we not rather simply accept them as true either because we see that plants in fact do live and bumblebees in fact do fly, or because Scripture itself teaches that God is omnipresent and eternal?

Calvin several times distinguishes between "necessity" and "compulsion" with regard to our will: unbelievers necessarily sin, but no compulsion forces them to sin against their will.[55] In response to the objection that an act cannot be willing or voluntary if it is a necessary act, Calvin points to both the good deeds of God (who *necessarily* does good) and the evil deeds of the Devil (who *necessarily* does evil):

> If the fact that he must do good does not hinder God's free will in doing good; if the Devil, who can only do evil, yet sins with his will—who shall say that man therefore sins less willingly because he is subject to the necessity of sinning?[56]

Who are we to say that choices somehow caused by God *cannot* be real? On what basis can we prove that? God in Scripture tells us that he ordains all that comes to pass. He also tells us that our choices and actions are significant *in his sight,* and that we are responsible *before him* for our actions. We need simply to believe these things and to take comfort in them. After all, *he alone* determines what is significant, what is real, and what is genuine personal responsibility in the universe.

But do our actions have any effect on God? At this point Arminians will object that while Calvinists may *say* that a choice caused by God is a real choice, it is not

---

[54]The lack of scriptural support for this fundamental Arminian idea is evident in Jack Cottrell's discussion of free will. After accurately explaining that Calvinists say we are free only in the sense of making voluntary, willing choices, Cottrell says, "*In my judgment,* however, the mere ability to act in accord with one's desires is not a sufficient criterion of freedom" ("The Nature of the Divine Sovereignty," p. 103, emphasis mine). He then gives no evidence from Scripture to show why this is his judgment (pp. 103–4). I would respond that Cottrell has simply imported into the discussion a nonbiblical *assumption* about the nature of human freedom and then has pronounced Calvinism incapable of meeting his (nonbiblical) criterion.

[55]See *Institutes,* 1:294–96 (2.3.5).

[56]Ibid., p. 295 (2.3.5).

real in any ultimate sense, because, on a Calvinist view, nothing that God does can ever be a response to what we do. Jack Cottrell says:

> Calvinism is still a theology of determinism as long as it declares that nothing God does can be conditioned by man or can be a reaction to something in the world. The idea that a sovereign God must always *act* and never *react* is a point on which almost all Calvinists seem to agree. . . . Reformed theologians agree that the eternal decree is unconditional or absolute. . . . "Decretal theology" decrees that "God cannot be affected by, nor respond to, anything external to him," says Daane.[57]

But here Cottrell has misunderstood Reformed theology for two reasons. First, he has quoted James Daane, who, though he belongs to the Christian Reformed Church, has written as an opponent, not a defender, of classical Reformed theology, and his statement does not represent a position Reformed theologians would endorse. Second, Cottrell has confused God's decrees before creation with God's actions in time. It is true that Calvinists would say that God's eternal decrees were not influenced by any of our actions and cannot be changed by us, since they were made *before creation*.[58] But to conclude from that that Calvinists think God does not react *in time* to anything we do, or is not influenced by anything we do, is simply false. No Calvinist theologian known to me has ever said that God is not influenced by what we do or does not react to what we do. He is grieved at our sin. He delights in our praise. He answers our prayers. To say that God does not react to our actions is to deny the whole history of the Bible from Genesis to Revelation.

Now a Calvinist would add that God has eternally decreed that he would respond to us as he does. In fact, he has decreed that we would act as we do and he would respond to our actions. But his responses are still genuine responses, his answers to prayers are still genuine answers to prayer, his delight in our praise is still genuine delight. Cottrell may of course object that a response that God has planned long ago is not a real response, but this is far different from saying that Calvinists believe God does not respond to what we do. Moreover, we return to the same unsupported assumption underlying this objection: on what scriptural basis can Cottrell say that a response God has planned long ago is not a real response?[59]

Here it is helpful for us to realize that there is no other reality in the universe except what God himself has made. Is a thunderstorm caused by God a *real* thunderstorm? Is a king that God establishes on a throne a *real* king? Is a word that God causes me to speak (Ps. 139:4; Prov. 16:1) a *real* word? Of course they are real! There *is* no other reality than that which God brings about! Then is a

---

[57]Jack Cottrell, "The Nature of the Divine Sovereignty," pp. 102–3. The quotation at the end is from James Daane, *The Freedom of God* (Grand Rapids: Eerdmans, 1973), p. 160.

[58]See above, pp. 332–33, on God's decrees.

[59]I am not sure if Cottrell would be able to object that a response planned by God long ago is not a real response, because he himself talks about God foreknowing our actions and then planning how he will respond to them. He says, "Even before the creation God foreknew every free-will act. . . . Nothing takes God by surprise. . . . God knew, even before creation, when and how he would have to intervene in his world to accomplish his purposes. . . . God's foreknowledge also enables him to plan his own responses to and uses of human choices even before they are made" ("The Nature of the Divine Sovereignty," p. 112). But if Cottrell is willing to say that God planned long ago how he would respond to human choices, it is hard to see how he can object to the Calvinist position that God decreed long ago how he would respond when we pray or act.

human choice that God somehow causes to happen a *real* choice? Yes, it is, in the same way that a thunderstorm or a king is real according to their own characteristics and properties. The choice that I make is not a "forced" or "involuntary" choice—we make choices all the time, and we have absolutely no sense of being forced or compelled to choose one thing rather than another.

Now some may object that this view makes us mere "puppets" or "robots." But we are not puppets or robots; we are *real persons*. Puppets and robots do not have the power of personal choice or even individual thought. We, by contrast, think, decide, and choose. Again the Arminian wrongly takes information from our situation as human beings and then uses that information to place limitations on what God *can* or *cannot* do. All of these analogies from human experience fail to recognize that God is far greater than our limited human abilities. Moreover, we are far more real and complex than any robot or puppet would ever be—we are real persons created by an infinitely powerful and infinitely wise God.

Much of our difficulty in understanding how God can cause us to choose something willingly comes from the finite nature of our creaturely existence. In a hypothetical world where all living things created by God were plants rooted in the ground, we might imagine one plant arguing to another that God *could not* make living creatures who could move about on the earth, for how could they carry their roots with them? And if their roots were not in the ground, how could they receive nourishment? An "Arminian" plant might even argue, "In order for God to create a world with living things, he *had to* create them with roots and with the characteristic of living all their lives in a single place. To say that God *could not* create living things that move about on the earth does not challenge God's omnipotence, for that is simply to say that he cannot do things that logically cannot be done. Therefore it is impossible that God could create a world where living things also have the capacity of moving about on the earth." The problem with this plant is that it has limited God's power by virtue of its own "plant-like" experience.

On a higher level, we could imagine a creation that had both plants and animals but no human beings. In that creation, we can imagine an argument between a "Calvinist" dog and a "Arminian" dog, where the "Calvinist" dog would argue that it *is* possible for God to create creatures that not only can communicate by barking to one another but also can record their barks in marks on paper and can send them silently to be understood by other creatures many days' journey distant, creatures who have never been seen by the sending creature who first marked his barks down on paper. The "Arminian" dog would reply that God *cannot* do such a thing, because *essential* to the idea of creaturely communication is *hearing* and *seeing* (and usually *smelling!*) the creature from whom one receives the communication. To say that there can be communication without ever hearing or seeing or smelling the other creature is an absurd idea! It is beyond the range of possible occurrences and is logically inconceivable. Therefore it is impossible to think that God could create a creature with such communicating abilities.

In both cases the "Arminian" plant and the "Arminian" dog are in the wrong, because they have incorrectly limited the kind of thing God could create by deriving what was possible for God (in their opinion) from their own finite creaturely existence. But this is very similar to the Arminian theologian who simply asserts (on the basis of his own perception of human experience) that God *cannot* create a creature who makes willing, voluntary, meaningful choices, and that those choices are nonetheless ordained by God. Similarly, the Arminian theologian who argues that God *cannot* ordain that evil come about and not yet himself be responsible for evil, is limiting God based merely on observation of finite human experience.

**4. Does a Calvinistic View of Providence Encourage Either a Dangerous Fatalism or a Tendency to "Live Like Arminians"?** The view of providence presented above emphasizes the need for responsible obedience, so it is not correct to say that it encourages the kind of fatalism that says that whatever is, should be. Those who accuse Reformed writers of believing this have simply not understood the Reformed doctrine of providence.

But do Calvinists "live like Arminians" anyway? Both Calvinists and Arminians believe that our actions have real results and that they are eternally significant. Both agree that we are responsible for our actions and that we make voluntary, willing choices. Both groups will agree that God answers prayer, that proclaiming the gospel results in people being saved, and that obedience to God results in blessing in life, while disobedience results in lack of God's blessing.

But the differences are very significant. Calvinists when true to their doctrine will live with a far more comprehensive trust in God in all circumstances and a far greater freedom from worry about the future, because they are convinced, not just that God will somehow cause his major purposes to work out right in the end, but that *all things* work together for good for those who love God and are called according to his purpose (Rom. 8:28). They will also be thankful to God for *all* the benefits that come to us from whatever quarter, for the one who believes in providence is assured that the ultimate reason for all things that happen is not some chance occurrence in the universe, nor is it the "free will" of another human being, but it is ultimately the goodness of God himself. They will also have great patience in adversity, knowing that it has not come about because God was unable to prevent it, but because it, too, is part of his wise plan. So the differences are immense. Calvin says:

> Gratitude of mind for the favorable outcome of things, patience in adversity, and also incredible freedom from worry about the future all necessarily follow upon this knowledge. . . . Ignorance of providence is the ultimate of all miseries; the highest blessedness lies in the knowledge of it.[60]

**5. Additional Objections to the Arminian Position.** In addition to responding to the four specific Arminian claims mentioned above some remaining objections to it need to be considered.

**a. On an Arminian View, How Can God Know the Future?:** According to the Arminian view, our human choices are not caused by God. They are totally free. But Scripture gives many examples of God predicting the future and of prophecies being fulfilled exactly. How can God predict the future in this way if it is not certain what will happen?

---

[60]Calvin, *Institutes*, 1:219–25 (1.17.7, 11).

In response to this question, Arminians give three different kinds of answer. Some say that God is not able to know details about the future; specifically, they deny that God is able to know what choices individual human beings will make in the future.[61] This seems to me to be the most consistent Arminian position, but the result is that, while God may be able to make some fairly accurate predictions based on complete knowledge of the present, these cannot be certain predictions. Ultimately it also means that God is ignorant of *all future human choices,* which means that he does not even know what the stock market will do tomorrow, or who will be elected as the next president of the United States, or who will be converted. On this view, what event of human history *could* God know with certainty in advance? No event. This is a radical revision of the idea of omniscience and seems to be clearly denied by the dozens of examples of unfailing predictive prophecy in Scripture, the fulfillment of which demonstrates that God is the true God in opposition to false gods.[62]

Other Arminians simply affirm that God *knows* everything that will happen, but this does not mean that he has *planned* or *caused* what will happen—it simply means that he has the ability to see into the future. (The phrase sometimes used to express this view is "Foreknowledge does not imply foreordination.") This is probably the most common Arminian view, and it is ably expressed by Jack Cottrell: "I affirm that God has a true foreknowledge of future free-will choices without himself being the agent that causes them or renders them certain."[63]

The problem with this position is that, even if God did not plan or cause things to happen, the fact that they are foreknown means that they will *certainly come about.* And this means that our decisions are predetermined *by something* (whether fate or the inevitable cause-and-effect mechanism of the universe), and they still are not free in the sense the Arminian wishes them to be free. If our future choices are known, then they are fixed. And if they are fixed, then they are not "free" in the Arminian sense (undetermined or uncaused).

A third Arminian response is called "middle knowledge." Those who take this view would say that the future choices of people are not determined by God, but that God knows them anyway, because he knows *all future possibilities,* and he

[61]Richard Rice, "Divine Foreknowledge and Free-Will Theism," in *The Grace of God, the Will of Man,* pp. 121–39, takes this position (see esp. pp. 129, 134–37). Rice says, "God knows a great deal about what will happen. . . . All that God does not know is the content of future free decisions, and this is because decisions are not there to know until they occur" (p. 134). In order to take this position and maintain God's omniscience, Rice redefines omniscience: "An omniscient being knows everything logically knowable" (p. 128), and then he defines "logically knowable" to exclude future human choices. On this basis, Rice argues that God does not know the results of future free decisions of human beings, since these are not logically knowable.

Clark Pinnock also explains how he came to this position: "I knew the Calvinist argument that exhaustive foreknowledge was tantamount to predestination because it implies the fixity of all things from 'eternity past,' and I could not shake off its logical force" ("From Augustine to Arminius: A Pilgrimage in Theology," in *The Grace of God, the Will of Man,* p. 25). He rejected exhaustive foreknowledge and decided that "*God knows everything that can be known,* but that free choices would not be something that can be known even by God because they are not yet settled in reality. Decisions not yet made do not exist anywhere to be known even by God. . . . God too moves into a future not wholly known because not yet fixed" (ibid., pp. 25–26, emphasis mine).

[62]See chapter 11, pp. 171–72, also p. 190, on God's knowledge of the future.
[63]Jack Cottrell, "The Nature of the Divine Sovereignty," p. 111.

knows how each free creature will respond in any set of circumstances that might occur.[64] William Craig says:

> God's insight into the will of a free creature is of such a surpassing quality that God knows exactly what the free creature would do were God to place him in a certain set of circumstances. . . . By knowing what every possible free creature would do in any possible situation, God can by bringing about that situation know what the creature will freely do. . . . Thus he foreknows with certainty everything that happens in the world.[65]

But Craig's view does not sustain a view of freedom in the sense Arminians usually maintain: that no cause or set of causes made a person choose the way he or she did. On Craig's view, the surrounding circumstances and the person's own disposition *guarantee* that a certain choice will be made—otherwise, God could not know what the choice would be from his exhaustive knowledge of the person and the circumstances. But if God knows what the choice will be, and if that choice is guaranteed, then it could not be otherwise. Moreover, if both the person and the circumstances have been created by God, then ultimately the outcome has been determined by God. This sounds very close to freedom in a Calvinist sense, but it is certainly not the kind of freedom that most Arminians would accept.

**b. On an Arminian View, How Can Evil Exist If God Did Not Want It?:** Arminians quite clearly say that the entrance of evil into the world was not according to the will of God. Pinnock says, "The fall of man is an eloquent refutation to the theory that God's will is always done."[66] But how can evil exist if God did not want it to exist? If evil happens in spite of the fact that God does not want it to happen, this seems to deny God's omnipotence: he wanted to prevent evil, but he was unable to do so. How then can we believe that this God is omnipotent?

The common Arminian response is to say that God was *able* to prevent evil but he chose to *allow for the possibility* of evil in order to guarantee that angels and humans would have the freedom necessary for meaningful choices. In other words, God *had to* allow for the possibility of sinful choices in order to allow genuine human choices. Cottrell says, "This God-given freedom includes human freedom to rebel and to sin against the Creator himself. By creating a world in which sin was possible, God thereby bound himself to *react* in certain specific ways should sin become a reality."[67]

But this is not a satisfactory response either, for it implies that God will have to allow for the possibility of sinful choices in heaven eternally. On the Arminian position, if any of our choices and actions in heaven are to be genuine and real, then they will *have to* include the possibility of sinful choices. But this implies that even in heaven, for all eternity, we will face the real possibility of choosing evil—and therefore the possibility of rebelling against God and losing our salvation and

[64]See William L. Craig, "Middle Knowledge, a Calvinist-Arminian Rapprochement?" in *The Grace of God, the Will of Man*, pp. 141–64. See also his book *The Only Wise God: The Compatibility of Divine Foreknowledge and Human Freedom* (Grand Rapids: Baker, 1987).
[65]Craig, "Middle Knowledge," pp. 150–51.
[66]Pinnock, "Responsible Freedom," p. 102.
[67]Cottrell, "The Nature of Divine Sovereignty," p. 109.

being cast out of heaven! This is a terrifying thought, but it seems a necessary implication of the Arminian view.

Yet there is an implication that is more troubling: If *real* choices have to allow for the possibility of choosing evil, then (1) God's choices are not real, since he cannot choose evil, or (2) God's choices are real, and there is the genuine possibility that God might someday choose to do evil—perhaps a little, and perhaps a great deal. If we ponder the second implication it becomes terrifying. But it is contrary to the abundant testimony of Scripture.[68] On the other hand, the first implication is clearly false: God is the definition of what is real, and it is clearly an error to say that his choices are not real. Both implications therefore provide good reason for rejecting the Arminian position that real choices must allow the possibility of choosing evil. But this puts us back to the earlier question for which there does not seem to be a satisfactory answer from the Arminian position: How can evil exist if God did not want it to exist?

**c. On an Arminian View, How Can We Know That God Will Triumph Over Evil?:** If we go back to the Arminian assertion that evil is *not* according to the will of God, another problem arises: if all the evil now in the world came into the world even though God did not want it, how can we be sure that God will triumph over it in the end? Of course, God *says* in Scripture that he will triumph over evil. But if he was unable to keep it out of his universe in the first place and it came in against his will, and if he is unable to predict the outcome of any future events that involve free choices by human, angelic, and demonic agents, how then can we be sure that God's declaration that he will triumph over all evil is in itself true? Perhaps this is just a hopeful prediction of something that (on the Arminian viewpoint) God simply cannot know. Far from the "incredible freedom from worry about the future" which the Calvinist has because he knows that an omnipotent God makes "all things work together for good" (Rom. 8:28 KJV), the Arminian position seems logically to drive us to a deep-seated anxiety about the ultimate outcome of history.

Both of these last two objections regarding evil make us realize that, while we may have difficulties in thinking about the Reformed view of evil as ordained by God and completely under the control of God, there are far more serious difficulties with the Arminian view of evil as not ordained or even willed by God, and therefore not assuredly under the control of God.

**d. The Difference in the Unanswered Questions:** Since we are finite in our understanding, we inevitably will have some unanswered questions about every biblical doctrine. Yet on this issue the questions that Calvinists and Arminians must leave unanswered are quite different. On the one hand, Calvinists must say that they do not know the answer to the following questions:

1. Exactly how God can ordain that we do evil willingly, and yet God not be blamed for evil.

2. Exactly how God can cause us to choose something willingly.

---

[68]See chapter 13, pp. 197–98, 201–2, 203–5, for scriptural testimony to God's goodness, holiness, and righteousness, and chapter 11, pp. 163–68, on God's unchangeableness.

To both, Calvinists would say that the answer is somehow to be found in an awareness of God's infinite greatness, in the knowledge of the fact that he can do far more than we could ever think possible. So the effect of these unanswered questions is to increase our appreciation of the greatness of God.

On the other hand, Arminians must leave unanswered questions regarding God's knowledge of the future, why he would allow evil when it is against his will, and whether he will certainly triumph over evil. Their failure to resolve these questions tends to diminish the greatness of God—his omniscience, his omnipotence, and the absolute reliability of his promises for the future. And these unanswered questions tend to exalt the greatness of man (his freedom to do what God does not want) and the power of evil (it comes and remains in the universe even though God does not want it). Moreover, by denying that God can make creatures who have real choices that are nevertheless caused by him, the Arminian position diminishes the wisdom and skill of God the Creator.

## QUESTIONS FOR PERSONAL APPLICATION

1. Has thinking about the doctrine of providence increased your trust in God? How has it changed the way you think about the future? Are there difficulties or hardships in your life at this time? Give an example of a specific difficulty that you are now facing and explain how the doctrine of providence will help you in the way you think about it.

2. Can you name five good things that have happened to you so far today? Were you thankful to God for any of them?

3. Do you sometimes think of luck or chance as causing events that happen in your life? If you ever feel that way, does it increase or decrease your anxiety about the future? Now think for a moment about some events that you might have attributed to luck in the past. Instead, begin to think about those events as under the control of your wise and loving heavenly Father. How does that make you feel differently about them and about the future generally?

4. Do you ever fall into a pattern of little "superstitious" actions or rituals that you think will bring good luck or prevent bad luck (such as not walking under a ladder, being afraid when a black cat walks across your path, not stepping on cracks on a sidewalk, carrying a certain item "just for good luck," etc.)? Do you think those actions tend to increase or decrease your trust in God during the day and your obedience to him?

5. Explain how a proper understanding of the doctrine of providence should lead a Christian to a more active prayer life.

6. What has been the overall effect of this chapter on how you think and feel about God and the events of your life?

## SPECIAL TERMS

| | |
|---|---|
| Arminian | preservation |
| Calvinist | primary cause |
| concurrence | providence |

| decrees of God | Reformed |
|---|---|
| free choices | secondary cause |
| free will | voluntary choices |
| government | willing choices |
| middle knowledge | |

## BIBLIOGRAPHY

(For an explanation of this bibliography see the note on the bibliography to chapter 1, p. 38. Complete bibliographical data may be found on pp. 1223–29.)

### Sections in Evangelical Systematic Theologies

1. Anglican (Episcopalian)

| 1882–92 | Litton, 76–90 |
|---|---|
| 1930 | Thomas, 176–83 |

2. Arminian (Wesleyan or Methodist)

| 1847 | Finney, 515–44 |
|---|---|
| 1875–76 | Pope, 1:437–56; 2:363–67, 386–90 |
| 1892–94 | Miley, 1:211–349; 2:271–308 |
| 1940 | Wiley, 1:478–88 |
| 1983 | Carter, 1:122–24, 130–33, 222–23 |
| 1983– | Cottrell, 2:9–228, 265–333, 379–418 |
| 1987–90 | Oden, 1:270–316 |

3. Baptist

| 1767 | Gill, 1:246–51, 397–434 |
|---|---|
| 1887 | Boyce, 115–25, 217–30 |
| 1907 | Strong, 353–70, 410–43 |
| 1917 | Mullins, 265–76 |
| 1976–83 | Henry, 5:307–33; 6:455–91 |
| 1983–85 | Erickson, 345–64, 387–432 |
| 1987–94 | Lewis/Demarest, 1:291–335; 2:71–122 |

4. Dispensational

| 1947 | Chafer, 1:225–59 |
|---|---|
| 1949 | Thiessen, 100–110, 119–32 |

5. Lutheran

| 1917–24 | Pieper, 1:483–97 |
|---|---|
| 1934 | Mueller, 176–78, 189–95, 236–41 |

6. Reformed (or Presbyterian)

| 1559 | Calvin, 1:197–237, 309–407 (1.16–18; 2.4–5) |
|---|---|
| 1724–58 | Edwards, 1:3–93; 2:107–110, 525–43 |
| 1861 | Heppe, 133–89, 251–80 |
| 1871–73 | Hodge, 1:535–49, 575–616; 2:280–312 |
| 1878 | Dabney, 120–32, 221–23, 276–91 |

| 1887–1921 | Warfield, *SSW*, 1:93–115; *SSW*, 2:411–47 |
| 1889 | Shedd, 1:393–462, 527–33 |
| 1937–66 | Murray, *CW*, 3:161–67, 185–89; *CW*, 2:60–66 |
| 1938 | Berkhof, 100–108, 165–78 |
| 1962 | Buswell, 1:163–76 |

7. Renewal (or charismatic/Pentecostal)

| 1988–92 | Williams, 1:117–40, 215–19 |

## Sections in Representative Roman Catholic Systematic Theologies

1. Roman Catholic: Traditional

| 1955 | Ott, 87–91 |

2. Roman Catholic: Post-Vatican II

| 1980 | McBrien (no explicit treatment) |

## Other Works

Basinger, David, and Randall Basinger, eds. *Predestination and Free Will: Four Views of Divine Sovereignty and Human Freedom.* Downers Grove, Ill.: InterVarsity Press, 1986.

Berkouwer, G. C. *The Providence of God.* Trans. by Lewis B. Smedes. Grand Rapids: Eerdmans, 1952.

Cameron, N. M. de S. "Providence." In *NDT*, pp. 177–79.

Carson, D. A. *Divine Sovereignty and Human Responsibility: Biblical Perspectives in Tension.* New Foundations Theological Library. Atlanta: John Knox, and London: Marshall, Morgan and Scott, 1981.

———. *How Long, O Lord? Reflections on Suffering and Evil.* Grand Rapids: Baker, and Leicester: Inter-Varsity Press, 1990.

Craig, William Lane. *The Only Wise God: The Compatibility of Divine Foreknowledge and Human Freedom.* Grand Rapids: Baker, 1987.

Feinberg, John. *The Many Faces of Evil: Theological Systems and the Problem of Evil.* Zondervan, 1994.

Flavel, John. *The Mystery of Providence.* Edinburgh and Carlisle, Pa.: Banner of Truth, 1976. Reprint of 1698 edition.

Helm, Paul. *The Providence of God.* Leicester and Downers Grove, Ill.: InterVarsity Press, 1994.

Parker, T. H. L. "Providence of God." In *EDT*, pp. 890–91.

Pink, Arthur W. *The Sovereignty of God.* Grand Rapids: Baker, 1930.

Warfield, B. B. *Calvin and Calvinism.* London and New York: Oxford University Press, 1931.

## SCRIPTURE MEMORY PASSAGE

**Romans 8:28:** *We know that in everything God works for good with those who love him, who are called according to his purpose.*

## HYMN

"God Moves in a Mysterious Way"

God moves in a mysterious way
    his wonders to perform;
He plants his footsteps in the sea,
    and rides upon the storm.

Deep in unfathomable mines
    of never-failing skill
He treasures up his bright designs,
    and works his sovereign will.

Ye fearful saints, fresh courage take;
    the clouds ye so much dread
Are big with mercy, and shall break
    in blessings on your head.

Judge not the Lord by feeble sense,
    but trust him for his grace;
Behind a frowning providence
    he hides a smiling face.

His purposes will ripen fast,
    unfolding every hour;
The bud may have a bitter taste,
    but sweet will be the flow'r.

Blind unbelief is sure to err,
    and scan his work in vain;
God is his own interpreter,
    and he will make it plain.

AUTHOR: WILLIAM COWPER, 1774

# Chapter 17

# Miracles

*What are miracles? Can they happen today?*

## EXPLANATION AND SCRIPTURAL BASIS

A consideration of the subject of miracles is closely connected with God's providence, which was considered in the previous chapter. There we argued that God exercises an extensive, ongoing, sovereign control over all aspects of his creation. This chapter will assume an understanding of that discussion of providence and will build on it in approaching the question of miracles.

### A. Definition

We may define a miracle as follows: *A miracle is a less common kind of God's activity in which he arouses people's awe and wonder and bears witness to himself.*[1] This definition takes into account our previous understanding of God's providence whereby God preserves, controls, and governs all things. If we understand providence in this way, we will naturally avoid some other common explanations or definitions of miracles.

For example, one definition of miracle is "a direct intervention of God in the world." But this definition assumes a deistic view of God's relationship to the world, in which the world continues on its own and God only intervenes in it occasionally. This is certainly not the biblical view, according to which God makes the rain to fall (Matt. 5:45), causes the grass to grow (Ps. 104:14), and continually carries along all things by his word of power (Heb. 1:3). Another definition of miracle is "a more direct activity of God in the world." But to talk about a "more direct" working of God suggests that his *ordinary* providential activity is somehow not "direct" and again hints at a sort of deistic removal of God from the world.

Another definition is "God working in the world without using means to bring about the results he wishes." Yet to speak of God working "without means" leaves us with very few if any miracles in the Bible, for it is hard to think of a miracle that came about with no means at all: in the healing of people, for example, some of the physical properties of the sick person's body were doubtless involved as part of

---

[1] I have adapted this definition from unpublished lectures given by John Frame, professor of systematic theology at Westminster Theological Seminary.

the healing. When Jesus multiplied the loaves and fishes, he at least used the original five loaves and two fishes that were there. When he changed water to wine, he used water and made it become wine. This definition seems to be inadequate.[2]

Yet another definition of miracle is "an exception to a natural law" or "God acting contrary to the laws of nature." But the phrase "laws of nature" in popular understanding implies that there are certain qualities inherent in the things that exist, "laws of nature" that operate independently of God, and that God must intervene or "break" these laws for a miracle to occur.[3] Once again this definition does not adequately account for the biblical teaching on providence.

Another definition of miracle is "an event impossible to explain by natural causes." This definition is inadequate because (1) it does not include God as the one who brings about the miracle; (2) it assumes that God does not use some natural causes when he works in an unusual or amazing way, and thus it assumes again that God only occasionally intervenes in the world; and (3) it will result in a significant minimizing of actual miracles and an increase in skepticism, since many times when God works in answer to prayer the result is amazing to those who prayed but it is not absolutely impossible to explain by natural causes, especially for a skeptic who simply refuses to see God's hand at work.

Therefore, the original definition given above, where a miracle is simply a *less common* way of God's working in the world, seems to be preferable and more consistent with the biblical doctrine of God's providence. This definition does not say that a miracle is a different kind of working by God, but only that it is a less common way of God's working and that it is done so as to arouse people's surprise, awe, or amazement in such a way that God bears witness to himself.

The biblical terminology for miracles frequently points to this idea of God's power at work to arouse people's wonder and amazement. Primarily three sets of terms are employed: (1) "sign" (Heb. *'ôth;* Gk. *sēmeion*), which means something that points to or indicates something else, especially (with reference to miracles) God's activity and power; (2) "wonder" (Heb. *môpēth;* Gk. *teras*), an event that causes people to be amazed or astonished;[4] and (3) "miracle" or "mighty work" (Heb. *gᵉbûrāh;* Gk. *dynamis*), an act displaying great power, especially (with reference to miracles) divine power.[5] Often "signs and wonders" is used as a stock expression to refer to miracles (Ex. 7:3; Deut. 6:22; Ps. 135:9; Acts 4:30; 5:12; Rom. 15:19; et al.), and sometimes all three terms are combined, "mighty works and wonders and signs" (Acts 2:22) or "signs and wonders and mighty works" (2 Cor. 12:12; Heb. 2:4).

---

[2]However, if someone defined a miracle as "a work of God apart from the *ordinary* use of means, to arouse people's awe and wonder," this would be similar in force to the definition I proposed above and would be consistent with the Bible's teaching on God's providence (see L. Berkhof, *Systematic Theology,* pp. 176–77).

[3]If the phrase "natural law" is understood by Christians simply to refer to the predictable patterns of behavior that God gives to and maintains in each created thing, then this definition is less objectionable because it consciously takes into account God's providence. But the phrase "natural law" is not generally understood that way in English today.

[4]The verb *thaumazō,* "to wonder, be amazed," is frequently used in the Gospels to describe people's reaction to miracles.

[5]See the extensive discussion of New Testament vocabulary for miracles in W. Mundle, O. Hofius, and C. Brown, "Miracle, Wonder, Sign," *NIDNTT* 2:620–35.

In addition to the meanings of the terms used for miracles, another reason supporting our definition is the fact that miracles in Scripture do arouse people's awe and amazement and indicate that God's power is at work. The Bible frequently tells us that God himself is the one who performs "miracles" or "wondrous things." Psalm 136:4 says that God is the one "who alone does great wonders" (cf. Ps. 72:18). The song of Moses declares:

> Who is like you, O LORD, among the gods?
> Who is like you, majestic in holiness,
>  terrible in glorious deeds, doing *wonders*? (Ex. 15:11)

Thus, the miraculous signs that Moses did when his staff turned into a snake and back again, or when his hand became leprous and then clean again (Ex. 4:2–8), were given that Moses might demonstrate to the people of Israel that God had sent him. Similarly, the miraculous signs God did by the hand of Moses and Aaron through the plagues, far surpassing the false miracles or imitation signs done by the magicians in Pharaoh's court (Ex. 7:12; 8:18–19; 9:11), showed that the people of Israel were those who worshiped the one true God. When Elijah confronted the priests of Baal on Mount Carmel (1 Kings 18:17–40), the fire from heaven demonstrated that the LORD was the one true God.

Now if we accept the definition that a miracle is "a less common kind of God's activity in which he arouses people's awe and wonder and bears witness to himself," then we may ask what kinds of things should be considered miracles. Of course, we are right to consider the incarnation of Jesus as God-man and Jesus' resurrection from the dead as the central and most important miracles in all history. The events of the exodus such as the parting of the Red Sea and the fall of Jericho were remarkable miracles. When Jesus healed people and cleansed lepers and cast out demons, those were certainly miracles as well (see Matt. 11:4–5; Luke 4:36–41; John 2:23; 4:54; 6:2; 20:30–31).

But can we consider unusual answers to prayer to be miracles? Apparently so, if they are remarkable enough to arouse people's awe and wonder and cause them to acknowledge God's power at work: the answer to Elijah's prayer that God would send fire from heaven was a miracle (1 Kings 18:24, 36–38), as were the answers to his prayers that the widow's dead son would come back to life (1 Kings 17:21), or that the rain would stop and later start again (1 Kings 17:1; 18:41–45 with James 5:17–18). In the New Testament, the release of Peter from prison in answer to the prayers of the church was certainly a miracle (Acts 12:5–17; note also Paul's prayer for Publius's father in Acts 28:8). But there must have been many miracles not nearly as dramatic as those, because Jesus healed many hundreds of people, "*any* that were sick with *various diseases*" (Luke 4:40). Paul healed "the rest of the people on the island who had diseases" (Acts 28:9).

On the other hand, Christians see answers to prayer every day, and we should not water down our definition of miracle so much that every answer to prayer is called a miracle. But when an answer to prayer is so remarkable that people involved with it are amazed and acknowledge God's power at work in an unusual way, then it seems appropriate to call it a miracle.[6] This is consistent with our

---

[6]Others may prefer to be more restrictive in their definition of miracles, reserving the term (for example) for events that absolutely could not have happened by ordinary means and that are

definition and seems supported by the biblical evidence that works of God that aroused people's awe and wonder were called miracles (Gk. *dynamis*).[7]

But whether we adopt a broad or narrow definition of miracle, all should agree that if God really does work in answer to our prayers, whether in common or uncommon ways, it is important that we recognize this and give thanks to him, and that we not ignore it or go to great lengths to devise possible "natural causes" to explain away what God has in fact done in answer to prayer. While we must be careful not to exaggerate in reporting details of answers to prayer, we must also avoid the opposite error of failing to glorify and thank God for what he has done.

## B. Miracles as Characteristic of the New Covenant Age

In the New Testament, Jesus' miraculous signs attested that he had come from God: Nicodemus recognized, "No one can do these signs that you do, unless God is with him" (John 3:2). Jesus' changing of water into wine was a "sign" that "manifested his glory; and his disciples believed in him" (John 2:11). According to Peter, Jesus was "a man attested to you by God with *mighty works and wonders and signs* which God did through him in your midst" (Acts 2:22).

Then in the early church, the apostles and others who preached the gospel performed miracles that amazed people and gave confirmation of the gospel that was being preached (Acts 2:43; 3:6–10; 4:30; 8:6–8, 13; 9:40–42; et al.). Even in churches where no apostles were present miracles occurred. For example, Paul, in writing to several churches in the region of Galatia (see Gal. 1:1), assumes this when he asks, "Does he who supplies the Spirit to you and works miracles among you do so by works of the law, or by hearing with faith?" (Gal. 3:5). Similarly, he mentions in the church at Corinth "workers of miracles" (1 Cor. 12:28) and names "the working of miracles" (1 Cor. 12:10) as a gift distributed by the Holy Spirit. These last two verses are especially significant because 1 Corinthians 12:4–31 is not discussing a specific situation at Corinth but the nature of the church in general as the "body of Christ" with many members yet one body.[8]

---

thoroughly witnessed and documented by several impartial observers. In that case, they will see far fewer miracles, especially in a skeptical, anti-supernatural society. But such a definition may not encompass all the kinds of things Paul had in mind when he talked about miracles in the churches of Corinth (1 Cor. 12:10, 28–29) and Galatia (Gal. 3:5), and may prevent people from recognizing a gift of miracles when it is given to Christians today. (Of course, Christians who hold such a restrictive definition will still readily thank God for many answers to prayer that they would not call miracles.)

[7]The appropriateness of such a definition is not lost simply because the same event might be called a miracle by some people and an ordinary event by others, for people's evaluation of an event will vary depending on their nearness to the event, the assumptions of their worldview, and whether they are Christians or not.

[8]Note, for example, that Paul says that God has appointed in the church, "first apostles . . ." (1 Cor. 12:28). But there were no apostles given specifically to the church at Corinth. Therefore this passage must be talking about the church in general.

B. B. Warfield, *Counterfeit Miracles* (Edinburgh: Banner of Truth, 1972; first published in 1918), notes that in the church at Corinth those who took part in the ordinary church worship service "might often have a miraculous gift to exercise." He says that "there is no reason to believe that the infant congregation at Corinth was singular in this. The Apostle does not write as if he were describing a marvelous state of affairs peculiar to that church. . . . The hints in the rest of his letters and in the Book of Acts require us, accordingly, to look upon this beautiful picture of Christian worship as one which would be true to life for any of the numerous congregations planted by the Apostles in the length and breadth of the world visited and preached to by them. . . . We are justified in considering it

In fact, it seems to be a characteristic of the New Testament church that miracles occur.[9] In the Old Testament, miracles seemed to occur primarily in connection with one prominent leader at a time, such as Moses or Elijah or Elisha. In the New Testament, there is a sudden and unprecedented increase in the miracles when Jesus begins his ministry (Luke 4:36–37, 40–41). However, contrary to the pattern of the Old Testament, the authority to work miracles and to cast out demons was not confined to Jesus himself, nor did miracles die out when Jesus returned to heaven. Even during his ministry, Jesus gave authority to heal the sick and to cast out demons not only to the Twelve, but also to seventy of his disciples (Luke 10:1, 9, 17–19; cf. Matt. 10:8; Luke 9:49–50). Moreover, the passages noted above from 1 Corinthians and Galatians indicate that performing miracles was not confined to the seventy disciples, but was characteristic of the churches of Galatia and the New Testament churches generally. This suggests that the occurrence of miracles is a characteristic of the New Testament church and may be seen as an indication of the powerful new work of the Holy Spirit that began with Pentecost and may be expected to continue through the church age.[10]

## C. The Purposes of Miracles

One purpose of miracles is certainly to authenticate the message of the gospel. This was evident in Jesus' own ministry, as people like Nicodemus acknowledged: "We know that you are a teacher come from God; for no one can do these *signs* that you do, unless God is with him" (John 3:2). It also was evident as the gospel was proclaimed by those who heard Jesus, for as they preached, "God also bore witness by *signs and wonders and various miracles* and by gifts of the Holy Spirit distributed according to his own will" (Heb. 2:4). Whether this purpose was valid only when the gospel was first preached (before the New Testament was written), or whether it holds good throughout the church age, depends on what we think the miracles are confirming: are they confirming only the absolute truthfulness of the words of Scripture (as the very words of God), or are miracles given to confirm the truthfulness of the gospel generally, whenever it is preached? In other words, do miracles confirm Scripture or the gospel? As we shall see below, miracles were not limited to those who wrote Scripture or spoke with absolute apostolic authority.[11] This suggests that miracles given in confirmation of the gospel might be expected to continue throughout the church age.

---

characteristic of the Apostolic churches that such miraculous gifts should be displayed in them. The exception would be, not a church with, but a church without, such gifts" (pp. 4–5).

[9]Warfield continues, "Everywhere, the Apostolic Church was marked out as itself a gift from God, by showing forth the possession of the Spirit in appropriate works of the Spirit—miracles of healing and miracles of power, miracles of knowledge whether in the form of prophecy or of the discerning of spirits, miracles of speech, whether of the gift of tongues or of their interpretation. The Apostolic Church was characteristically a miracle-working church" (*Counterfeit Miracles*, p. 5). While I would agree with Warfield's analysis of the New Testament evidence on this question, there is certainly room to disagree with his subsequent point, and the main contention of his book, that the church after the age of the apostles experienced the cessation of miraculous gifts, and that we should not expect such gifts today because God intended them only to confirm the early apostolic message during the time when the apostles were still alive.

[10]See further discussion of this question in chapter 52 below, on spiritual gifts and the question of the time of cessation of some gifts.

[11]See Section D below, pp. 361–68.

When miracles occur, they give evidence that God is truly at work and so serve to advance the gospel: the Samaritan woman proclaimed to her village, "Come, see a man who told me all that I ever did" (John 4:29), and many of the Samaritans believed in Christ. This was frequently true in Jesus' ministry, but it was also true in the early church: when Philip went to a city in Samaria,

> the multitudes with one accord *gave heed to what was said by Philip,* when they heard him and saw the *signs* which he did. For unclean spirits came out of many who were possessed, crying with a loud voice; and many who were paralyzed or lame were healed. So there was much joy in that city. (Acts 8:6–8)

When Aeneas the paralytic was healed, "all the residents of Lydda and Sharon saw him, and *they turned to the Lord*" (Acts 9:35). When Tabitha was raised from the dead, "it became known throughout all Joppa, and *many believed in the Lord*" (Acts 9:42).[12]

In the New Testament, a second purpose of miracles is to bear witness to the fact that the kingdom of God has come and has begun to expand its beneficial results into people's lives, for the results of Jesus's miracles show the characteristics of God's kingdom: Jesus said, "If it is by the Spirit of God that I cast out demons, then the kingdom of God has come upon you" (Matt. 12:28). His triumph over the destructive forces of Satan showed what God's kingdom was like. In this way, every miracle of healing or deliverance from demonic oppression advanced the kingdom and helped fulfill Jesus' ministry, for he came with the Spirit of the Lord on him "to preach good news to the poor. . . . to proclaim release to the captives and recovering of sight to the blind, to set at liberty those who are oppressed" (Luke 4:18).

Similarly, Jesus gave his disciples "power and authority over all demons and to cure diseases, and he sent them out to preach the kingdom of God and to heal" (Luke 9:1–2). He commanded them, "Preach as you go, saying, 'The kingdom of heaven is at hand.' Heal the sick, raise the dead, cleanse lepers, cast out demons" (Matt. 10:7–8; cf. Matt. 4:23; 9:35; Acts 8:6–7, 13).

A third purpose of miracles is to help those who are in need. The two blind men

---

[12]The verses just quoted show the positive value of miracles in bringing people to faith. Some may object that when we say that miracles have value in bearing witness to the gospel this means that we think the gospel message by itself is weak and unable to bring people to faith (see especially James M. Boice, "A Better Way: The Power of Word and Spirit," in Michael Scott Horton, ed., *Power Religion* [Chicago: Moody, 1992], pp. 119–36). But this is not a valid objection, for Jesus and Paul did not reason that way—both performed miracles in conjunction with their preaching of the gospel, and Jesus commanded his disciples to do this as well (Matt. 10:7–8). We must remember that it is God himself who "bore witness" to the gospel "by signs and wonders and various miracles and by gifts of the Holy Spirit distributed according to his own will" (Heb. 2:4), and we cannot say that he has an inappropriate view of the power of the gospel message.

John's gospel is especially instructive in showing the value of miracles in encouraging people to believe in Christ (see John 2:11, 23; 3:2; 4:53–54; 6:2, 14; 7:31; 9:16; 11:48; 12:11; and, in summary, 20:30–31). This positive emphasis in John stands in contrast to the view of D. A. Carson in "The Purpose of Signs and Wonders in the New Testament," in Horton, *Power Religion,* pp. 100–101, where he admits but minimizes the positive role of miracles in bringing people to faith in John's gospel. Surprisingly, he fails to discuss several of the positive passages mentioned above and sees a depreciation of miracles in passages where no such negative evaluation exists, such as John 2:23–25; 4:48; and 20:29–31. We should not think that when miracles accompany the gospel those who believe will have inferior faith (as Carson suggests, p. 101), for that would lead us to say that those who believed the preaching of Jesus, Peter, and Paul had inferior faith—a conclusion hardly advanced by the New Testament!

near Jericho cried out, "Have mercy on us," and Jesus "in pity" healed them (Matt. 20:30, 34). When Jesus saw a great crowd of people, "he had compassion on them, and healed their sick" (Matt. 14:14; see also Luke 7:13). Here miracles give evidence of the compassion of Christ toward those in need.

A fourth purpose of miracles, related to the second, is to remove hindrances to people's ministries. As soon as Jesus had healed Peter's mother-in-law, "she rose and served him" (Matt. 8:15). When God had mercy on Epaphroditus and restored his health (whether through miraculous means or not, Paul attributes it to God's mercy in Phil. 2:27), Epaphroditus was then able to minister to Paul and complete his function as a messenger returning to the Philippian church (Phil. 2:25–30). Although the text does not explicitly say that Tabitha (or Dorcas) resumed her "good works and acts of charity" (Acts 9:36) after the Lord through Peter raised her from the dead (Acts 9:40–41), by mentioning her good works and those who bore witness to her selfless care for the needs of others (Acts 9:39), it suggests that she would resume a similar ministry of mercy when she was raised from the dead. Related to this category would be the fact that Paul expects people to be edified when miraculous gifts are used in the church (1 Cor. 12:7; 14:4, 12, 26).

Finally, a fifth purpose for miracles (and one to which all the others contribute) is to bring glory to God. After Jesus healed a paralytic, the crowds "were afraid, and they glorified God, who had given such authority to men" (Matt. 9:8). Similarly, Jesus said that the man who had been blind from birth was blind "that the works of God might be made manifest in him" (John 9:3).

## D. Were Miracles Restricted to the Apostles?

**1. An Unusual Concentration of Miracles in the Apostles' Ministry.** Some have argued that miracles were restricted to the apostles or to the apostles and those closely connected with them. Before considering their arguments, it is important to note that there are some indications that a remarkable concentration of miracles was characteristic of the apostles as special representatives of Christ. For example, God was pleased to allow extraordinary miracles to be done through both Peter and Paul. In the very early days of the church,

> many signs and wonders were done among the people by the hands of the apostles. . . . And more than ever believers were added to the Lord, multitudes both of men and women, so that they even carried out the sick into the streets, and laid them on beds and pallets, that as Peter came by at least his shadow might fall on some of them. The people also gathered from the towns around Jerusalem, bringing the sick and those afflicted with unclean spirits, and they were all healed. (Acts 5:12–16)

Similarly, when Paul was in Ephesus, "God did *extraordinary miracles* by the hands of Paul, so that handkerchiefs or aprons were carried away from his body to the sick, and diseases left them and the evil spirits came out of them" (Acts 19:11–12).[13] Another example is found in the raising of Tabitha: when she had died, the

---

[13]In neither case should these events be thought of as some kind of "magic" that came automatically through Peter's shadow or handkerchiefs that Paul had touched, but rather as an indication of the fact that the Holy Spirit was pleased to give such a full and remarkable empowering to the ministry of these

disciples at Joppa sent for Peter to come and pray for her to be raised from the dead (Acts 9:36–42), apparently because they thought that God had given an unusual concentration of miraculous power to Peter (or to the apostles generally). And Paul's ministry generally was characterized by miraculous events, because he summarizes his ministry by telling the Romans of the things that Christ had worked through him to win obedience from the Gentiles "by the power of *signs and wonders,* by the power of the Holy Spirit" (Rom. 15:19).

Nevertheless, the unusual concentration of miracles in the ministries of the apostles does not prove that *no* miracles were performed by others! As we have clearly seen, the "working of miracles" (1 Cor. 12:10) and other miraculous gifts (1 Cor. 12:4–11 mentions several) were part of the ordinary functioning of the Corinthian church, and Paul knows that God "works miracles" in the churches of Galatia as well (Gal. 3:5).

**2. What Are the "Signs of an Apostle" in 2 Corinthians 12:12?** Why then have some argued that miracles were uniquely the signs that distinguished an apostle? Their case is largely based on 2 Corinthians 12:12, where Paul says, "The *signs of a true apostle* were performed among you in all patience, with signs and wonders and mighty works" (2 Cor. 12:12).[14] They say that this implies that others who were not the apostles (or their close companions) did not have that authority or could not work these miraculous signs.[15] They further maintain that the working of the miracles ceased when the apostles and their close associates died. Therefore, they conclude, no further miracles are to be expected today. (Those who hold this position are sometimes known as "*cessationists,*" since they hold to the ceasing or "cessation" of miracles early in the history of the church.)

In considering this question, it should be remembered that in the key passage used to establish this point, where Paul talks about "the signs of a true apostle" in 2 Corinthians 12:12, he is *not* attempting to prove that he is an apostle *in distinction from other Christians* who are not apostles. He is rather attempting to prove that he is a true representative of Christ in distinction from others who are "false apostles" (2 Cor. 11:13), false representatives of Christ, servants of Satan who are disguising themselves as "servants of righteousness" (2 Cor. 11:14–15). In short, the contrast is not between apostles who could work miracles and ordinary Christians who could not, but between genuine Christian apostles through whom the Holy Spirit worked and *non-Christian pretenders to the apostolic office,* through whom the Holy Spirit did not work at all. Therefore, even if we understand the "signs of an apostle" to be miracles, we should recognize that those who use this passage to argue that miracles cannot be done through *Christians* today are taking the phrase "signs of an apostle" out of its context and using it in a

men that on occasion he extended his work beyond their individual bodily presence even to things that they came near or touched.
[14]The word "true" is not actually in the Greek text, which simply says, "the signs of an apostle." The RSV (which is quoted here) and NASB have added "true" to give the sense: Paul is contrasting his ministry with that of the false apostles.
[15]See Walter J. Chantry, *Signs of the Apostles,* 2d ed. (Edinburgh: Banner of Truth, 1976), esp. pp. 17–21; B. B. Warfield, *Counterfeit Miracles;* Norman Geisler, *Signs and Wonders* (Wheaton: Tyndale House, 1988).

way that Paul never intended. Paul is distinguishing himself from non-Christians, whereas they use the passage to distinguish Paul from other Christians.

Moreover, a close examination of 2 Corinthians 12:12 shows it to be very doubtful that the phrase "signs of an apostle" in this passage means miraculous signs. In this very verse, Paul distinguishes the "signs of a true apostle" from miracles, which he calls "signs and wonders and mighty works," noting that the miracles were done along with the signs of an apostle: "The *signs of a true apostle* were performed among you in all patience, *with signs and wonders and mighty works.*"[16] The latter phrase, "with signs and wonders and mighty works," has a piling up of all three terms used for miracles and therefore must refer to miracles (note "signs and wonders" in Acts 4:30; 5:12; 14:3; 15:12; Rom. 15:19; Heb. 2:4; et al.). Therefore the former phrase, "signs of a true apostle," must refer to something different, something that was *accompanied by* (done "with") signs and wonders.

In fact, although the word *sign* in Greek (*sēmeion*) often refers to miracles, it has a much broader range of meaning than just *miracle: sēmeion* simply means "something which indicates or refers to something else."[17] In 2 Corinthians 12:12, the "signs" of an apostle are best understood as everything that characterized Paul's apostolic mission and showed him to be a true apostle.[18] We need not guess at what these signs were, for elsewhere in 2 Corinthians Paul tells what marked him as a true apostle:

1. Spiritual power in conflict with evil (10:3–4, 8–11; 13:2–4, 10)

---

[16]The grammar of the Greek text forces us to this distinction, since "the signs of an apostle" is in the nominative case, while "signs and wonders and mighty works" is in the dative, and cannot therefore be simply a restatement of "signs of an apostle" in apposition to it: nouns in apposition in Greek must be in the same case. (The NIV ignores the grammar here and translates the two phrases as if they were in apposition; the RSV and NASB are more precise.)

[17]Many nonmiraculous things are called "signs." For example, Paul's handwritten signature is his "sign" (2 Thess. 3:17; RSV "mark"); circumcision is a "sign" of Abraham's imputed righteousness (Rom. 4:11); Judas's kiss is a "sign" to the Jewish leaders (Matt. 26:48); the rainbow is a "sign" of the covenant (Gen. 9:12, LXX); eating unleavened bread during Passover every year is a "sign" of the Lord's deliverance (Ex. 13:9, LXX); Rahab's scarlet cord is a "sign" that the spies told her to hang in her window (1 Clem. 12:7).

[18]Among modern commentators on 2 Corinthians, I found only three who understand the "signs of a true apostle" in 2 Cor. 12:12 to be miracles: Colin Kruse, *The Second Epistle of Paul to the Corinthians*, TNTC (Leicester: Inter-Varsity Press, and Grand Rapids: Eerdmans, 1987), p. 209; Jean Héring, *The Second Epistle of Saint Paul to the Corinthians*, trans. A. W. Heathcote and P. J. Allcock (London: Epworth, 1967), pp. 95–96; and Murray Harris, "2 Corinthians," *EBC*, 10:398, take it that way, but none of them gives any argument to support this view, and Harris notes an alternative view where the "signs" are the changed lives of the Corinthians and the Christlike character of Paul.
The majority of commentators understand "signs of a true apostle" to have a much broader meaning, including the qualities of Paul's life and the character and results of his ministry: see Philip E. Hughes, *Paul's Second Epistle to the Corinthians*, NIC (Grand Rapids: Eerdmans, 1962), pp. 456–58 (following Chrysostom and Calvin); Ralph P. Martin, *II Corinthians*, WBC (Waco, Tex.: Word, 1986), pp. 434–38 (with extensive discussion); Alfred Plummer, *A Critical and Exegetical Commentary on the Second Epistle of St. Paul to the Corinthians*, ICC (Edinburgh: T. & T. Clark, 1915), p. 359; R. V. G. Tasker, *2 Corinthians*, TNTC (London: Tyndale Press, 1958), p. 180; Charles Hodge, *An Exposition of 1 and 2 Corinthians* (Wilmington, Del.: Sovereign Grace, 1972 [reprint]), pp. 359–60; John Calvin, *The Second Epistle of Paul the Apostle to the Corinthians. . .*, trans. T. A. Smail, ed. by D. W. Torrance and T. F. Torrance (Edinburgh: Oliver and Boyd, and Grand Rapids: Eerdmans, 1964), pp. 163–64; see also J. B. Lightfoot, *The Epistle of St. Paul to the Galatians* (Grand Rapids: Zondervan, 1957), p. 99. Some of these commentators understand the "signs of a true apostle" as accompanied by or including miracles, but none understand the phrase to refer primarily or exclusively to miracles.

2. Jealous care for the welfare of the churches (11:1–6)
3. True knowledge of Jesus and his gospel plan (11:6)
4. Self-support (selflessness) (11:7–11)
5. Not taking advantage of churches; not striking people physically (11:20–21)
6. Suffering and hardship endured for Christ (11:23–29)
7. Being caught up into heaven (12:1–6)
8. Contentment and faith to endure a thorn in the flesh (12:7–9)
9. Gaining strength out of weakness (12:10).

The first item may have included miracles, but that is certainly not the primary focus of his reference to the "signs of a true apostle."

Another evidence that the "signs of a true apostle" in 2 Corinthians 12:12 were all these things and not simply miracles is the fact that Paul says, "The signs of a true apostle were performed among you *in all patience*." Now it would make little sense to say that miracles were performed "in all patience," for many miracles happen quite quickly, but it would make much sense to say that Paul's Christlike endurance of hardship for the sake of the Corinthians was performed "in all patience."

We should note that nowhere in this list does Paul claim miracles to prove his genuine apostleship. In fact, most of the things he mentions would not distinguish him from other true Christians. But these things do distinguish him from servants of Satan, false apostles who are not Christians at all: their lives will not be marked by humility, but pride; not by selflessness, but selfishness; not by generosity, but greed; not by seeking the advantage of others, but by taking advantage of others; not by spiritual power in physical weakness, but by confidence in their natural strength; not by enduring suffering and hardship, but by seeking their own comfort and ease.[19] When Paul acted in a Christlike manner among them, his actions were "signs" that his claim to be an apostle was a true claim: thus, these things were "signs of a true apostle." In this context, the "signs" that mark a true apostle need not be things that showed an absolute difference between him and other Christians, but rather things that showed his ministry to be genuine, in distinction from false ministries. He is not here telling the Corinthians how to tell who an apostle was in distinction from other Christians (he did that in 1 Cor. 9:1–2; 15:7–11; Gal. 1:1, 11–24, mentioning seeing the risen Christ and being commissioned by him as an apostle), but here he is telling how to recognize what a genuine, Christ-approved ministry was.

Why then does he add that all these signs of a true apostle were done among the Corinthians "with signs and wonders and mighty works"? He is simply adding one additional factor to all the previous marks of his genuine apostleship. Miracles of course had a significant function in confirming the truth of Paul's message, and Paul here makes explicit what the Corinthians may or may not have assumed to be included in the phrase "signs of a true apostle": in addition to all these other signs of a true apostle, his ministry showed miraculous demonstrations of God's power as well.[20]

---

[19]Some interpreters assume that the false apostles were working miracles and claiming revelations from God, so that Paul would have to claim greater miracles and revelations. But nothing in 2 Corinthians says that the false apostles claimed miracles or revelations.

[20]The following verse also gives confirmation to this interpretation: Paul says, "For in what were you less favored than the rest of the churches . . . ?" (2 Cor. 12:13). The fact that they were not lacking in

There is yet another very significant reason why miracles did not prove someone to be an apostle. In the larger context of the New Testament it is clear that miracles were worked by others than apostles, such as Stephen (Acts 6:8), Philip (Acts 8:6–7), Christians in the several churches in Galatia (Gal. 3:5), and those with gifts of "miracles" in the body of Christ generally (1 Cor. 12:10, 28). Miracles as such cannot then be regarded as exclusively signs of an apostle. In fact, "workers of miracles" and "healers" are actually distinguished from "apostles" in 1 Corinthians 12:28: "And God has appointed in the church first *apostles,* second prophets, third teachers, then *workers of miracles,* then healers. . . ."

Similar evidence is seen in Mark 16:17–18: Though there are serious questions about the authenticity of this passage as part of Mark's gospel,[21] the text is nonetheless very early[22] and at least bears witness to one strand of tradition within the early church. This text reports Jesus as saying,

> And these signs will accompany those who believe: in my name they will cast out demons; they will speak in new tongues; they will pick up serpents, and if they drink any deadly thing, it will not hurt them; they will lay their hands on the sick, and they will recover.

Here also the power to work miracles is assumed to be the common possession of Christians. Those who wrote and passed on this early tradition, and who thought it represented the genuine teaching of Jesus, were certainly not aware of any idea that miracles were to be limited to the apostles and their close associates.[23]

The argument that many other Christians in the New Testament worked miracles is sometimes answered by the claim that it was only the apostles *and those closely associated with them* or those on whom the apostles laid their hands who could work miracles.[24] However, this really proves very little because the story of the New Testament church is the story of what was done through the apostles and those closely associated with them. A similar argument might be made about evangelism or the founding of churches: "In the New Testament, churches were only founded by the apostles or their close associates; therefore, we should not found churches today." Or, "In the New Testament, missionary work in other countries was only done by the apostles or their close associates; therefore, we should not do missionary work in other countries today." These analogies show the inadequacy of the argument: the New Testament primarily shows how the church *should* seek to act, not how it *should not* seek to act.

But if many other Christians throughout the first-century church were working miracles by the power of the Holy Spirit, then the power to work miracles could not be a sign to distinguish the apostles from other Christians.

---

any of Paul's care and attention would prove to them that the "signs of a true apostle" were performed among them only if these "signs" included all of Paul's ministry to them, but not if the "signs of a true apostle" were just miracles.

[21]The manuscript evidence and considerations of style suggest that these verses were not originally part of the gospel that Mark wrote. (See discussion of textual variants on pp. 96–97.)

[22]It is included in several manuscripts of Tatian's Diatessaron (A.D. 170) and is quoted by Irenaeus (d. A.D. 202) and Tertullian (d. A.D. 220).

[23]I am grateful to Professor Harold Hoehner of Dallas Theological Seminary for suggesting to me the arguments given here regarding 1 Cor. 12:28 and Mark 16:17–18 (though he may disagree with my conclusion in this section).

[24]So Chantry, *Signs,* pp. 19–21.

**3. Norman Geisler's Restrictive Definition of Miracles.** A more recent attempt to deny that miracles occur today has been made by Norman Geisler.[25] Geisler has a much more restrictive definition of *miracle* than that presented in this chapter, and he uses that definition to argue against the possibility of contemporary miracles. Geisler says that "miracles (1) are always successful, (2) are immediate, (3) have no relapses, and (4) give confirmation of God's messenger" (pp. 28–30). He finds support for this thesis largely in the ministry of Jesus, but when he passes beyond the life of Jesus and attempts to show that others who had the power to work miracles were never unsuccessful, his thesis is much less convincing. With regard to the demon-possessed boy whom the disciples could not set free from the demon (Matt. 17:14–21), Geisler says that "the disciples simply forgot for the moment to faithfully exercise the power that Jesus had already given them" (p. 150). But this is an unpersuasive argument: Geisler says that the power to work miracles was always successful, and when the Bible talks about some who were unsuccessful (and who contradict his thesis) he simply says they "forgot." Jesus, however, gives a different reason than Geisler: "Because of your little faith" (Matt. 17:20). Lesser faith resulted in lesser power to work miracles.

With regard to Paul's failure to heal Epaphroditus (Phil. 2:27), Geisler is forced to make the dubious claim that perhaps Paul never attempted to heal Epaphroditus (though he had come to him in prison and was so ill he almost died), or that "Paul no longer possessed the gift of healing at this time" (p. 150). He employs the same claim to explain the fact that Paul left Trophimus ill at Miletus (2 Tim. 4:20). In these instances Geisler goes well beyond the usual cessationist claim that miracles ended with the death of the apostles—he is claiming that miracles ceased in the life of the greatest apostle before his first Roman imprisonment. That is simply an unconvincing argument with respect to the apostle whose ministry was repeatedly characterized "by the power of signs and wonders, by the power of the Holy Spirit" (Rom. 15:19), and who could say with triumph in his last epistle, "I have fought the good fight, I have finished the race, I have kept the faith" (2 Tim. 4:7).

Geisler's description of miracles does not fit the case of the blind man upon whom Jesus laid his hands, for at first the man did not see clearly but said he saw men who "look like trees, walking." After Jesus laid his hands on him a second time, the man "saw everything clearly" (Mark 8:24–25). Geisler responds that it was Jesus' intention to heal in two stages, to teach the disciples by using an object lesson about the gradual growth of their spiritual lives (pp. 153–54). Though the text says nothing to this effect, it may have been true, but even so it disproves Geisler's thesis, for if it was Jesus' intention to heal in two stages then, it may also be his intention to heal people in two stages today—or in three or four or more stages. Once Geisler admits that it may be God's intention to work a miracle in stages, in order to accomplish his own purposes, then his entire claim that miracles must be immediate and complete is lost.[26]

---

[25]Norman Geisler, *Signs and Wonders*. His definition of miracles is found on pp. 28–32 and 149–55.

[26]Geisler also has much difficulty explaining Mark 5:8 (where Jesus more than once commanded some demons to leave) and Mark 6:5 (where the text says that Jesus was not able to do any miracles in Nazareth because of the unbelief of the people there)(see pp. 149, 152).

Instead of accepting Geisler's definition, it seems better to conclude that even those whom God gifts with the ability to perform miracles may not be able to perform them whenever they wish, for the Holy Spirit continually is distributing them to each person "as he wills" (1 Cor. 12:11; the word *distributes* is a present participle in Greek, indicating a continuing activity of the Holy Spirit). Moreover, there seems no reason to exclude (as Geisler apparently wants to do) unusual or remarkable answers to prayer from the category of "miracle," thus making the definition extremely restrictive. If God answers persistent prayer, for instance, for a physical healing for which there is no known medical explanation, and does so only after several months or years of prayer, yet does so in such a way that it seems quite clearly to be in response to prayer so that people are amazed and glorify God, there seems no reason to deny that a miracle has occurred simply because the earlier prayers were not answered immediately. Finally, Geisler fails to recognize that several New Testament texts indicate that spiritual gifts, whether miraculous or nonmiraculous in nature, may vary in strength or degree of intensity.[27]

**4. Hebrews 2:3–4.** Another passage that is sometimes used to support the idea that miracles were limited to the apostles and their close associates is Hebrews 2:3–4. There the author says that the message of salvation "was declared at first by the Lord, and it was attested to us by those who heard him, while God also bore witness[28] by signs and wonders and various miracles and by gifts of the Holy Spirit distributed according to his own will."

Since the miracles here are said to come through those who heard the Lord firsthand ("those who heard him"), it is argued that we should not expect them to be done through others who were not firsthand witnesses to the Lord's teaching and ministry.[29]

But this argument also attempts to draw more from the passage than is there. First, the phrase "those who heard him" (Heb. 2:3) is certainly not limited to the apostles, for many others heard Jesus as well. But more importantly, this position is claiming something that the text simply does not say: the fact that (1) the gospel message was confirmed by miracles when it was preached by those who heard Jesus says nothing at all about (2) whether it would be confirmed by miracles when preached by others who did not hear Jesus. Finally, this passage says the message was confirmed not only by "signs and wonders and various miracles" but also by *"gifts of the Holy Spirit."* If someone argues that this passage limits miracles to the apostles and their companions, then he or she must also argue that gifts of the Holy Spirit are likewise limited to the first-century church. But few would argue that there are no gifts of the Holy Spirit today.[30]

---

[27]See discussion in chapter 52, pp. 1022–25, below.

[28]The KJV translates, "God also bearing *them* witness, both with signs and wonders. . . ." This translation suggests that the miracles bore witness to the people who heard Jesus and first preached. But the word "them" is represented by no word in the Greek text, and this translation is not followed by modern versions.

[29]So Chantry, *Signs of the Apostles,* pp. 18–19: "New Testament miracles are viewed in Scripture itself as God's stamp of approval upon the message of the apostles, which was an inspired record of the things they had seen and heard while with Jesus. Recalling these wonders should deepen our respect for the authority of their words and prompt us to give the more careful heed."

[30]Another argument limiting miracles to the first century is based on the claim that some miracles,

**5. Conclusion: Were Miracles Restricted to the Apostles?** If ministry in the power and glory of the Holy Spirit is characteristic of the new covenant age (2 Cor. 3:1–4:18), then our expectation would be just the opposite: we would expect that second and third and fourth generation Christians, who also know Christ and the power of his resurrection (Phil. 3:10), who are continually being filled with the Holy Spirit (Eph. 5:17), who are participants in a war that is not a worldly war, but one that is carried on with weapons that have divine power to destroy strongholds (2 Cor. 10:3–4), who have not been given a spirit of timidity but a "spirit of power and love and self-control" (2 Tim. 1:7), who are strong in the Lord and in the strength of his might, and who have put on the whole armor of God in order to be able to stand against principalities and powers and spiritual hosts of wickedness in the heavenly places (Eph. 6:10–12), would *also* have the ability to minister the gospel not only in truth and love but also with accompanying miraculous demonstrations of God's power. It is difficult to see, from the pages of the New Testament, any reason why only the preaching of the apostles should come "not in plausible words of wisdom, but *in demonstration of the Spirit and of power,* that your faith might not rest in the wisdom of men but in the power of God" (1 Cor. 2:4–5).

Though there does seem to have been an unusual concentration of miraculous power in the ministry of the apostles, this is not a reason for thinking that there would be few or no miracles following their deaths. Rather, the apostles were the leaders in a new covenant church whose life and message were characterized by the power of the Holy Spirit at work in miraculous ways. Furthermore, they set a pattern that the church throughout its history may well seek to imitate in its own life, insofar as God the Holy Spirit is pleased to work miracles for the edification of the church.[31]

## E. False Miracles

Pharaoh's magicians were able to work some false miracles (Ex. 7:11, 22; 8:7), though they soon had to admit that God's power was greater (Ex. 8:19). Simon the sorcerer in the city of Samaria amazed people with his magic (Acts 8:9–11), even though the miracles done through Philip were much greater (Acts 8:13). In Philippi Paul encountered a slave girl "who had a spirit of divination and brought her owners much gain by soothsaying" (Acts 16:16), but Paul rebuked the spirit and it came out of her (Acts 16:18). Moreover, Paul says that when the man of sin comes it "will be with all power and with pretended signs and wonders, and with all wicked deception for those who are to perish" (2 Thess. 2:9–10), but those who follow them and are deceived do so "because they refused to love the truth and so be saved" (2 Thess. 2:10). This indicates that those who work false miracles in the end times by the power of Satan will not speak the truth but will

such as the gift of prophecy, always give new Scripture-quality revelation. That argument is considered in detail in chapters 52–53 below, pp. 1039–42, 1049–61.

[31]However, Christians should be very cautious and take extreme care to be accurate in their reporting of miracles if they do occur. Much harm can be done to the gospel if Christians exaggerate or distort, even in small ways, the facts of a situation where a miracle has occurred. The power of the Holy Spirit is great enough to work however he wills, and we should never "embellish" the actual facts of the situation simply to make it sound even more exciting than it actually was. God does exactly what he is pleased to do in each situation.

preach a false gospel. Finally, Revelation 13 indicates that a second beast will rise "out of the earth," one that has "all the authority of the first beast" and "works great signs, even making fire come down from heaven to earth in the sight of men; and by the signs which it is allowed to work in the presence of the beast, it deceives those who dwell on earth" (Rev. 13:11–14). But once again a false gospel accompanies these miracles: this power is exercised in connection with the first beast who utters "haughty and blasphemous words . . . it opened its mouth to utter blasphemies against God, blaspheming his name and his dwelling" (Rev. 13:5–6).

Two conclusions become clear from this brief survey of false miracles in Scripture: (1) *The power of God is greater than the power of Satan* to work miraculous signs, and God's people triumph in confrontations of power with those who work evil. In connection with this, John assures believers that "he who is in you is greater than he who is in the world" (1 John 4:4).[32] (2) The identity of these workers of false miracles *is always known through their denial of the gospel. There is no indication anywhere in Scripture that genuine Christians with the Holy Spirit in them will work false miracles.* In fact, in a city filled with idolatry and demon worship (see 1 Cor. 10:20), Paul could say to the Corinthian believers, many of whom had come out of that kind of pagan background, that "no one can say 'Jesus is Lord' except by the Holy Spirit" (1 Cor. 12:3). Here he gives them reassurance that those who make a genuine profession of faith in Jesus as Lord do in fact have the Holy Spirit in them. It is significant that he immediately goes on to a discussion of spiritual gifts possessed by "each" true believer (1 Cor. 12:7).

This should reassure us that if we see miracles being worked by those who make a genuine profession of faith (1 Cor. 12:3), who believe in the incarnation and deity of Christ (1 John 4:2), and who show the fruit of the Holy Spirit in their lives and bear fruit in their ministry (Matt. 7:20; cf. John 15:5; Gal. 5:22–23), we should not be suspicious that they are false miracles but should be thankful to God that the Holy Spirit is working, even in those who may not hold exactly the same convictions that we do on every point of doctrine.[33] Indeed, if God waited to work miracles only through those who were perfect in both doctrine and conduct of life, no miracles would be worked until Christ returns.

## F. Should Christians Seek Miracles Today?

It is one thing to say that miracles might occur today. It is quite another thing to ask God for miracles. Is it right then for Christians to ask God to perform miracles?

---

[32]Some may object that one exception to this may be the vision of the end times in Rev. 13:7, where the beast "was allowed to make war on the saints and to conquer them" (Rev. 13:7). But even here there is no indication that the miraculous powers of the beast are greater than the power of the Holy Spirit. This seems to be best understood not as a confrontation of miraculous power but simply as a persecution by military force, for we read later of "those who had been beheaded for their testimony to Jesus and for the word of God, and who had not worshiped the beast or its image and had not received its mark on their foreheads or their hands" (Rev. 20:4).

[33]The fact that people who name the name of Christ are able to prophesy and cast out demons and do "many mighty works" in his name (Matt. 7:21–23) does not contradict this, because these are non-Christians: Jesus says to them, "I never knew you; depart from me, you evildoers" (Matt. 7:23). Although it is possible that these are false miracles worked by demonic power, it seems more likely that they are operations of common grace (see chapter 31) that God worked through in non-Christians, similar to the effectiveness of the gospel that God sometimes allows when it is preached by those who have impure motives and do not know Christ in their hearts (cf. Phil. 1:15–18).

The answer depends on the purpose for which miracles are sought. Certainly it is wrong to seek miraculous power to advance one's own power or fame, as Simon the magician did: Peter said to him, "your heart is not right before God. Repent therefore of this wickedness of yours, and pray to the Lord that, if possible, the intent of your heart may be forgiven you" (Acts 8:21–22).

It is also wrong to seek miracles simply to be entertained, as Herod did: "When Herod saw Jesus, he was very glad, for he had long desired to see him, because he had heard about him, and he was hoping to see some sign done by him" (Luke 23:8). But Jesus would not even answer Herod's questions.

It is also wrong for skeptical unbelievers to seek miracles simply to find ground to criticize those who preach the gospel:

> And the Pharisees and Sadducees came, and *to test him* they asked him to show them a sign from heaven. He answered them, ". . . An evil and adulterous generation seeks for a sign, but no sign shall be given to it except the sign of Jonah." (Matt. 16:1–4)

This rebuke against seeking signs is repeated elsewhere in the Gospels, but it is important to note that rebukes against seeking signs are always directed against hostile unbelievers who are seeking a miracle only as an opportunity to criticize Jesus.[34] Never does Jesus rebuke anyone who comes in faith, or in need, seeking healing or deliverance or any other kind of miracle, whether for himself or herself, or for others.

What shall we say then about 1 Corinthians 1:22–24, where Paul says, "For *Jews demand signs* and Greeks seek wisdom, but we preach Christ crucified, a stumbling block to Jews and folly to Gentiles, but to those who are called, both Jews and Greeks, Christ the power of God and the wisdom of God"? Does Paul mean that he did not work miracles ("signs") at Corinth, or perhaps in his evangelistic work generally?

Here Paul cannot be denying that he performed miracles in connection with the proclamation of the gospel. In fact, in Romans 15:18–19, a passage he wrote while in Corinth, he said,

> For I will not venture to speak of anything except what Christ has wrought through me to win obedience from the Gentiles, by word and deed, *by the power of signs and wonders*, by the power of the Holy Spirit, so that from Jerusalem and as far round as Illyricum I have fully preached the gospel of Christ.

---

[34]The fact that Jesus only rebukes hostile unbelievers who seek miracles is surprisingly never mentioned by D. A. Carson, "The Purpose of Signs and Wonders in the New Testament," in M. Horton, ed., *Power Religion*, pp. 89–118, or by James M. Boice, "A Better Way: The Power of Word and Spirit," in *Power Religion*, pp. 119–36. Both articles use Jesus' rebukes as a means of discouraging believers from seeking miracles today, but to do this they must apply Jesus' statements in a way not justified by the New Testament contexts. (See esp. Boice, p. 126, who quotes with approval a statement from John Woodhouse, "A desire for further signs and wonders is sinful and unbelieving.")

The explicit statement of intent "to test him" is also found in Mark 8:11 and Luke 11:16, parallel contexts where Jesus rebukes an evil generation for seeking a sign from him. The only other context where this rebuke occurs, Matt. 12:38–42, does not include an explicit statement of the intent to test, but Jesus is clearly responding to the "scribes and Pharisees" (v. 38), and the incident follows just after Matt. 12:14, where the Pharisees "went out and took counsel against him, how to destroy him," and Matt. 12:24, where the Pharisees say, "It is only by Be-elzebul, the prince of demons, that this man casts out demons."

And 2 Corinthians 12:12 affirms clearly that Paul did work "signs and wonders and mighty works" among them.

So 1 Corinthians 1:22–24 cannot mean that Paul was denying the validity of *wisdom* or the validity of *signs,* for through Christ he worked signs and he taught wisdom. Rather, here he is saying that signs and wisdom do not themselves save people, but the gospel saves people. Signs and the wisdom that Jews and Greeks were seeking were not the signs and wisdom of Christ but simply signs to entertain or to fuel their hostility and skepticism and wisdom that was the wisdom of the world rather than the wisdom of God.

There is nothing inappropriate in seeking miracles for the proper purposes for which they are given by God: to confirm the truthfulness of the gospel message, to bring help to those in need, to remove hindrances to people's ministries, and to bring glory to God (see Section C above). In the Gospels many people came to Jesus seeking miracles, and he healed them for these purposes. Moreover, when he sent his disciples out preaching that the kingdom of heaven was at hand, he told them, "Heal the sick, raise the dead, cleanse lepers, cast out demons" (Matt. 10:7–8). How could they do this without seeking God for miracles everywhere they went? Jesus' command required them to seek for miracles to happen.

After Pentecost, the early church prayed both for boldness to preach the gospel and for God to grant miracles to accompany its preaching. They cried out to God,

> And now, Lord, look upon their threats, and grant to your servants to speak your word with all boldness, *while you stretch out your hand to heal,* and *signs and wonders* are performed through the name of your holy servant Jesus. (Acts 4:29–30)

Far from teaching that we should not ask God for miracles, this example of the early church gives us some encouragement to do so. Similarly, the disciples in Lydda sent for Peter to come and pray for Tabitha after she had died, thereby seeking a miraculous intervention by God (Acts 9:38). And James directs that the elders of the church should pray and seek healing for those who are ill (James 5:14). Of course, we should not assume that an obviously miraculous answer to prayer is somehow better than one that comes through ordinary means (such as medical help for sickness), and we must also realize that asking God for a particular need does not guarantee that the prayer will be answered. On the other hand, our faith that God will work in powerful and even miraculous ways may be far too small. We must beware of being infected by a secular worldview that assumes that God will answer prayer only very seldom, if ever. And we should certainly not be embarrassed to talk about miracles if they occur—or think that a nonmiraculous answer to prayer is better! Miracles are God's work, and he works them to bring glory to himself and to strengthen our faith. When we encounter serious needs in people's lives today, it is right for us to seek God for an answer, and where miraculous intervention seems to be needed, then to ask God if he would be pleased to work in that way.[35] This would seem to be especially

---

[35]John Walvoord, the former President of Dallas Theological Seminary, understands the gift of miracles to be "the power to perform miracles at will in the name of Christ." Therefore he holds that the gift of miracles has ceased. But he still argues that we can pray for miracles today: "A Christian can still appeal to God to do wonders, and God does answer prayer. God can still heal and even raise the dead if he chooses, but these miracles are sovereign and individual. . . . While therefore the gift of

appropriate when our motivation is a Christlike compassion for those in need and a burning desire to see Christ's kingdom advance and his name glorified.

## QUESTIONS FOR PERSONAL APPLICATION

1. When you first came to faith in Christ, did the stories of miracles in the Bible have any influence (negative or positive) on your believing the message of Scripture?

2. Before reading this chapter, have you thought of the church at the time of the New Testament as a church with frequent miracles? Have you thought of the contemporary church as one with frequent miracles? After reading this chapter, how has your position changed, if at all?

3. If you think that miracles should be characteristic of the church until Christ returns, then why have we not seen very many miracles at many points in the history of the church, and why do we not see many miracles in large sections of the Christian church today?

4. If you hold a "cessationist" position, what kinds of unusual answers to prayer might you still think possible today? (For example, prayer for physical healing, for deliverance from danger, victory over demonic attack through prayer and/or verbal rebuke of an evil spirit, or sudden and unusual insight into a passage of Scripture or a situation in someone's life.) How would you distinguish these things that you might think possible today from "miracles" according to the definition given in this chapter? (You may wish to argue for a different definition of "miracle" as well.)

5. Do miracles have to be large and "remarkable" (such as raising the dead or healing a man blind from birth) to accomplish useful purposes in the church today? What kinds of "small-scale" miracles might also accomplish some of the purposes for miracles listed in this chapter? Have you known of any answers to prayer in your own church (or your own life) that you would characterize as "miraculous" according to the definition given at the beginning of the chapter?

6. Would you like to see more miraculous power of the Holy Spirit (or more unusual answers to prayer) at work in your own church today, or not? If more miracles did occur, what might be the dangers? What might be the benefits?

## SPECIAL TERMS

cessationist                              sign
mighty work                              "signs of a true apostle"
miracle                                   wonder
natural law

---

miracles is not part of the present program of God, the power of God to perform miracles must be affirmed" (*The Holy Spirit* [Wheaton, Ill.: Van Kampen, 1954], pp. 179–80).

# BIBLIOGRAPHY

(For an explanation of this bibliography see the note on the bibliography to chapter 1, p. 38. Complete bibliographical data may be found on pp. 1223–29.)

## Sections in Evangelical Systematic Theologies

1. Anglican (Episcopalian)
     1882–92    Litton (no explicit treatment)
2. Arminian (Wesleyan or Methodist)
     1875–76    Pope, 1:63–76
       1940    Wiley, 1:149, 150, 153, 154
       1983–   Cottrell, 2:229–604
3. Baptist
       1907    Strong, 117–33
       1917    Mullins, 172, 193
     1983–85   Erickson, 406–10
     1987–94   Lewis/Demarest, 1:100–109, 115–18
4. Dispensational
       1947    Chafer, 7:239
       1949    Thiessen, 11–13
       1986    Ryrie, 350–51, 372–73
5. Lutheran
     1917–24   Pieper, 1:459–60
       1934    Mueller, 174
6. Reformed (or Presbyterian)
       1559    Calvin, 1:14–18, 85–88; 2:1453–1455, 1465–67 (PA, 3; 1.8.5–8; 4.19.6, 18)
       1861    Heppe, 263–65
     1871–73   Hodge, 1:617–36
    1887–1921  Warfield, SSW, 2:167–206
       1889    Shedd, 1:533–46
     1937–66   Murray, CW, 3:210–14
       1938    Berkhof, 176–78
       1962    Buswell, 1:176–83
7. Renewal (or charismatic/Pentecostal)
     1988–92   Williams, 1:141–68

## Sections in Representative Roman Catholic Systematic Theologies

1. Roman Catholic: Traditional
       1955    Ott (no explicit treatment)
2. Roman Catholic: Post-Vatican II
       1980    McBrien, 1:325–28

## Other Works

Berkouwer, G. C. "Providence and Miracles." In *The Providence of God*. Trans. by Lewis B. Smedes. Grand Rapids: Eerdmans, 1952, pp. 188–231.

Boice, James Montgomery. "A Better Way: The Power of Word and Spirit." In *Power Religion: The Selling Out of the Evangelical Church?* Michael Scott Horton, ed. Chicago: Moody Press, 1992.

Bridge, Donald. *Signs and Wonders Today*. Leicester: Inter-Varsity Press, 1985.

Brown, Colin. "Miracle." In *NDT,* pp. 433–34.

———. *That You May Believe: Miracles and Faith—Then and Now*. Grand Rapids: Eerdmans, 1985.

Carson, D. A. "The Purpose of Signs and Wonders in the New Testament," In *Power Religion: The Selling Out of the Evangelical Church?* Michael Scott Horton, ed. Chicago: Moody Press, 1992.

Deere, Jack. *Surprised by the Power of the Spirit: A Former Dallas Seminary Professor Discovers That God Still Speaks and Heals Today*. Grand Rapids: Zondervan, 1993.

Geisler, Norman. *Signs and Wonders*. Wheaton: Tyndale, 1988.

———. *Miracles and Modern Thought*. With a response by R. C. Sproul. Grand Rapids: Zondervan, and Dallas: Probe Ministries, 1982.

Greig, Gary S., and Kevin N. Springer, eds. *The Kingdom and the Power*. Ventura, Calif.: Regal, 1993.

Gross, Edward N. *Miracles, Demons, and Spiritual Warfare: An Urgent Call for Discernment*. Grand Rapids: Baker, 1990.

Grudem, Wayne. *Power and Truth: A Response to the Critiques of Vineyard Teaching and Practice by D. A. Carson, James Montgomery Boice, and John H. Armstrong in Power Religion*. Anaheim, Calif.: Association of Vineyard Churches, 1993.

———. "Should Christians Expect Miracles Today? Objections and Answers From the Bible." In *The Kingdom and the Power*. Gary Greig and Kevin Springer, eds. Ventura, Calif.: Regal, 1993, pp. 55–110.

Horton, Michael S., ed. *Power Religion: The Selling Out of the Evangelical Church?* Chicago: Moody, 1992.

Kirk, J. A. "Power." In *NDT,* pp. 524–25.

Lewis, C. S. *Miracles: A Preliminary Study*. New York: Macmillan, 1947.

Moule, C. F. D., ed. *Miracles*. London: Mowbray, 1965.

Spiceland, J. D. "Miracles." In *EDT,* pp. 723–24.

Wenham, David, and Craig Blomberg, eds. *Miracles of Jesus*. Sheffield, England: JSOT, 1986.

Williams, Don. *Signs, Wonders, and the Kingdom of God: A Biblical Guide for the Skeptic*. Ann Arbor, Mich.: Servant, 1989.

Wimber, John, with Kevin Springer. *Power Evangelism*. Revised edition. San Francisco: Harper and Row, and London: Hodder and Stoughton, 1992.

## SCRIPTURE MEMORY PASSAGE

**Hebrews 2:3–4:** *How shall we escape if we neglect such a great salvation? It was declared at first by the Lord, and it was attested to us by those who heard him, while God* *also bore witness by signs and wonders and various miracles and by gifts of the Holy Spirit distributed according to his own will.*

## HYMN

### "A Mighty Fortress Is Our God"

A mighty fortress is our God, a bulwark never failing;
Our helper he amid the flood of mortal ills prevailing.
For still our ancient foe doth seek to work us woe;
His craft and pow'r are great; and, armed with cruel hate,
On earth is not his equal.

Did we in our own strength confide, our striving would be losing;
Were not the right man on our side, the man of God's
    own choosing.
Dost ask who that may be? Christ Jesus, it is he,
Lord Sabaoth his name, from age to age the same,
And he must win the battle.

And though this world, with devils filled, should threaten to undo us,
We will not fear, for God hath willed his truth to triumph
    through us.
The prince of darkness grim, we tremble not for him;
His rage we can endure, for lo! his doom is sure;
One little word shall fell him.

That word above all earthly powers, no thanks to them, abideth;
The Spirit and the gifts are ours through him who with us sideth;
Let goods and kindred go, this mortal life also;
The body they may kill: God's truth abideth still;
His kingdom is forever.

AUTHOR: MARTIN LUTHER, 1529

# Chapter 18

# Prayer

*Why does God want us to pray?*
*How can we pray effectively?*

## EXPLANATION AND SCRIPTURAL BASIS

The character of God and his relationship to the world, as discussed in the previous chapters, lead naturally to a consideration of the doctrine of prayer. Prayer may be defined as follows: *Prayer is personal communication with God.*

This definition is very broad. What we call "prayer" includes prayers of request for ourselves or for others (sometimes called prayers of petition or intercession), confession of sin, adoration, praise and thanksgiving, and also God communicating to us indications of his response.

### A. Why Does God Want Us to Pray?

Prayer is not made so that God can find out what we need, because Jesus tells us, "Your Father knows what you need before you ask him" (Matt. 6:8). God wants us to pray because prayer expresses our trust in God and is a means whereby our trust in him can increase. In fact, perhaps the primary emphasis of the Bible's teaching on prayer is that we are to pray with faith, which means trust or dependence on God. God as our Creator delights in being trusted by us as his creatures, for an attitude of dependence is most appropriate to the Creator/creature relationship. Praying in humble dependence also indicates that we are genuinely convinced of God's wisdom, love, goodness, and power—indeed of all of the attributes that make up his excellent character. When we truly pray, we as persons, in the wholeness of our character, are relating to God as a person, in the wholeness of his character. Thus, all that we think or feel about God comes to expression in our prayer. It is only natural that God would delight in such activity and place much emphasis on it in his relationship with us.

The first words of the Lord's Prayer, "Our Father who art in heaven" (Matt. 6:9), acknowledge our dependence on God as a loving and wise Father and also recognize that he rules over all from his heavenly throne. Scripture many times emphasizes our need to trust God as we pray. For example, Jesus compares our praying to a son asking his father for a fish or an egg (Luke 11:9–12) and then concludes, "If you then, who are evil, know how to give good gifts to your children, how much more will the heavenly Father give the Holy Spirit to those who ask him!" (Luke 11:13). As children look to their fathers to provide for

376

them, so God expects us to look to him in prayer. Since God is our Father, we should ask in faith. Jesus says, "Whatever you ask in prayer, you will receive, if you have faith" (Matt. 21:22; cf. Mark 11:24; James 1:6–8; 5:14–15).

But God does not only want us to trust him. He also wants us to love him and have fellowship with him. This, then, is a second reason why God wants us to pray: Prayer brings us into deeper fellowship with God, and he loves us and delights in our fellowship with him.

A third reason God wants us to pray is that in prayer God allows us as creatures to be involved in activities that are eternally important. When we pray, the work of the kingdom is advanced. In this way, prayer gives us opportunity to be involved in a significant way in the work of the kingdom and thus gives expression to our greatness as creatures made in God's image.

## B. The Effectiveness of Prayer

How exactly does prayer work? Does prayer not only do us good but also affect God and the world?

**1. Prayer Changes the Way God Acts.** James tells us, "You do not have, because you do not ask" (James 4:2). He implies that failure to ask deprives us of what God would otherwise have given to us. We pray, and God responds. Jesus also says, "Ask, and it will be given you; seek, and you will find; knock, and it will be opened to you. For every one who asks receives, and he who seeks finds, and to him who knocks it will be opened" (Luke 11:9–10). He makes a clear connection between seeking things from God and receiving them. When we ask, God responds.

We see this happening many times in the Old Testament. The Lord declared to Moses that he would destroy the people of Israel for their sin (Ex. 32:9–10): "But Moses besought the LORD his God, and said, 'O Lord. . . . Turn from your fierce wrath, and repent of this evil against your people'" (Ex. 32:11–12). Then we read, "And the LORD repented of the evil which he thought to do to his people" (Ex. 32:14). When God threatens to punish his people for their sins he declares, "If my people who are called by my name humble themselves, *and pray and seek my face,* and turn from their wicked ways, *then I will hear* from heaven, and will forgive their sin and heal their land" (2 Chron. 7:14). If and when God's people pray (with humility and repentance), *then* he will hear and forgive them. The prayers of his people clearly affect how God acts. Similarly, "If we confess our sins, he is faithful and just, and will forgive our sins and cleanse us from all unrighteousness" (1 John 1:9). We confess, and then he forgives.[1]

If we were really convinced that prayer changes the way God acts, and that God does bring about remarkable changes in the world in response to prayer, as Scripture repeatedly teaches that he does, then we would pray much more than we do. If we pray little, it is probably because we do not really believe that prayer accomplishes much at all.

---

[1] Other examples of God answering prayer in Scripture are too numerous to comment on (Gen. 18:22–33; 32:26; Dan. 10:12; Amos 7:1–6; Acts 4:29–31; 10:31; 12:5–11; et al.).

**2. Effective Prayer Is Made Possible by Our Mediator, Jesus Christ.** Because we are sinful and God is holy, we have no right on our own to enter into his presence. We need a mediator to come between us and God and to bring us into God's presence. Scripture clearly teaches, "There is one God, and there is one mediator between God and men, the man Christ Jesus" (1 Tim. 2:5).

But if Jesus is the only mediator between God and man, will God hear the prayers of those who do not trust in Jesus? The answer depends on what we mean by "hear." Since God is omniscient, he always "hears" in the sense that he is aware of the prayers made by unbelievers who do not come to him through Christ. God may even, from time to time, answer their prayers out of his mercy and in a desire to bring them to salvation through Christ. However, God has nowhere promised to respond to the prayers of unbelievers. The only prayers that he has promised to "hear" in the sense of listening with a sympathetic ear and undertaking to answer when they are made according to his will, are the prayers of Christians offered through the one mediator, Jesus Christ (cf. John 14:6).

Then what about believers in the Old Testament? How could they come to God through Jesus the mediator? The answer is that the work of Jesus as our mediator was foreshadowed by the sacrificial system and the offerings made by the priests in the temple (Heb. 7:23–28; 8:1–6; 9:1–14; et al.). There was no saving merit inherent in that system of sacrifices (Heb. 10:1–4), however. Through the sacrificial system believers were accepted by God only on the basis of the future work of Christ foreshadowed by that system (Rom. 3:23–26).

Jesus' activity as a mediator is especially seen in his work as a priest: he is our "great high priest who has passed through the heavens," one who "in every respect has been tempted as we are, yet without sin" (Heb. 4:14–15).

As recipients of the new covenant, we do not need to stay "outside the temple," as all believers except the priests were required to do under the old covenant. Nor do we need to stay outside of the "Holy of Holies" (Heb. 9:3), the inner room of the temple where God himself was enthroned above the ark of the covenant and where only the high priest could go, and he but once a year. But now, since Christ has died as our mediational High Priest (Heb. 7:26–27), he has gained for us boldness and access to the very presence of God. Therefore "we have confidence to enter *into the holy places* by the blood of Jesus" (Heb. 10:19, author's literal translation), that is, into the holy place and into the holy of holies, the very presence of God himself! We enter "by the new and living way" (Heb. 10:20) that Christ opened for us. The author of Hebrews concludes that since these things are true, "and since we have a great priest over the house of God, let us draw near with a true heart in full assurance of faith" (Heb. 10:22). In this way, Christ's mediational work gives us confidence to approach God in prayer.

We do not just come into God's presence as strangers, or as visitors, or as laypersons, but as priests—as people who belong in the temple and have a right and even a duty to be in the most sacred places in the temple. Using imagery from the ceremony for ordination of priests (see Ex. 29:4, 21), the author of Hebrews pictures all believers as having been ordained as priests to God and thus able to enter into his presence, for he says that we draw near "with our hearts sprinkled clean from an evil conscience and our bodies washed with pure water" (Heb. 10:22; cf. 1 Peter 2:9). Does all this make sense to a modern Christian? No one today goes to Jerusalem to enter the temple and there "draw near" to God. Even if we did go to Jerusalem, we would find no temple standing, since it was destroyed in A.D. 70. What then does the author of Hebrews mean when he says we enter into the "holy places"? He is talking about a reality in the unseen spiritual realm: With Christ as our Mediator we enter not into the earthly temple in Jerusalem, but into the true sanctuary, into "heaven itself," where Christ has gone "to appear in the presence of God on our behalf" (Heb. 9:24).

**3. What Is Praying "in Jesus' Name"?** Jesus says, "Whatever you ask *in my name*, I will do it, that the Father may be glorified in the Son; if you ask anything in my name, I will do it" (John 14:13–14). He also says that he chose his disciples "so that whatever you ask the Father *in my name*, he may give it to you" (John 15:16). Similarly, he says, "Truly, truly, I say to you, if you ask anything of the Father, he will give it to you in my name. Hitherto you have asked nothing *in my name;* ask, and you will receive, that your joy may be full" (John 16:23–24; cf. Eph. 5:20). But what does this mean?

Clearly it does not simply mean adding the phrase "in Jesus' name" after every prayer, because Jesus did not say, "If you ask anything and add the words 'in Jesus' name' after your prayer, I will do it." Jesus is not merely speaking about adding certain words as if these were a kind of magical formula that would give power to our prayers. In fact, none of the prayers recorded in Scripture have the phrase "in Jesus' name" at the end of them (see Matt. 6:9–13; Acts 1:24–25; 4:24–30;[2] 7:59; 9:13–14; 10:14; Rev. 6:10; 22:20).

To come in the name of someone means that another person has authorized us to come on his authority, not on our own. When Peter commands the lame man, "in the name of Jesus Christ of Nazareth, walk" (Acts 3:6), he is speaking on the authority of Jesus, not on his own authority. When the Sanhedrin asks the disciples, "By what power or *by what name* did you do this?" (Acts 4:7), they are asking, "By whose authority did you do this?" When Paul rebukes an unclean spirit "in the name of Jesus Christ" (Acts 16:18), he makes it clear that he is doing so on Jesus' authority, not his own. When Paul pronounces judgment "in the name of the Lord Jesus" (1 Cor. 5:4) on a church member who is guilty of immorality, he is acting with the authority of the Lord Jesus. *Praying in Jesus' name is therefore prayer made on his authorization.*

In a broader sense the "name" of a person in the ancient world represented the person himself and therefore all of his character. To have a "good name" (Prov. 22:1; Eccl. 7:1) was to have a good reputation. Thus, the name of Jesus represents all that he is, his entire character. This means that praying "in Jesus' name" is not only praying in his authority, but *also praying in a way that is consistent with his character,* that truly represents him and reflects his manner of life and his own holy will.[3] In this sense, to pray in Jesus' name comes close to the idea of praying "according to his will" (1 John 5:14–15).[4]

---

[2]In Acts 4:30 the phrase, "through the name of your holy servant Jesus," which appears at the end of a prayer, modifies the main clause immediately preceding it, "and signs and wonders are performed." It is not a general statement about the way in which the whole prayer is made.

[3]In fact, Paul says that not just our prayers but everything we do is to be done in Jesus' name: "And whatever you do, in word or deed, *do everything in the name of the Lord Jesus,* giving thanks to God the Father through him" (Col. 3:17).

[4]Leon Morris says of John 14:13, "This does not mean simply using the name as a formula. It means

Does this mean that it is wrong to add "in Jesus' name" to the end of our prayers? It is certainly not wrong, as long as we understand what is meant by it, and that it is not necessary to do so. There may be some danger, however, if we add this phrase to every public or private prayer we make, for very soon it will become to people simply a formula to which they attach very little meaning and say without thinking about it. It may even begin to be viewed, at least by younger believers, as a sort of magic formula that makes prayer more effective. To prevent such misunderstanding, it would probably be wise to decide not to use the formula frequently and to express the same thought in other words, or simply in the overall attitude and approach we take toward prayer. For example, prayers could begin, "Father, we come to you in the authority of our Lord Jesus, your Son . . ." or, "Father, we do not come on our own merits but on the merits of Jesus Christ, who has invited us to come before you . . ." or, "Father, we thank you for forgiving our sins and giving us access to your throne by the work of Jesus your Son. . . ." At other times even these formal acknowledgments should not be thought necessary, so long as our hearts continually realize that it is our Savior who enables us to pray to the Father at all. Genuine prayer is conversation with a Person whom we know well, and who knows us. Such genuine conversation between persons who know each other never depends on the use of certain formulas or required words, but is a matter of sincerity in our speech and in our heart, a matter of right attitudes, and a matter of the condition of our spirit.

**4. Should We Pray to Jesus and to the Holy Spirit?** A survey of the prayers of the New Testament indicates that they are usually addressed neither to God the Son nor to the Holy Spirit, but to God the Father. Yet a mere count of such prayers may be misleading, for the majority of the prayers we have recorded in the New Testament are those of Jesus himself, who constantly prayed to God the Father, but of course did not pray to himself as God the Son. Moreover, in the Old Testament, the trinitarian nature of God was not so clearly revealed, and it is not surprising that we do not find much evidence of prayer addressed directly to God the Son or God the Holy Spirit before the time of Christ.

Though there is a clear pattern of prayer directly to God the Father through the Son (Matt. 6:9; John 16:23; Eph. 5:20) there are indications that prayer spoken directly to Jesus is also appropriate. The fact that it was Jesus himself who appointed all of the other apostles, suggests that the prayer in Acts 1:24 is addressed to him: "Lord, who knows the hearts of all men, show which one of these two you have chosen. . . ." The dying Stephen prays, "Lord Jesus, receive my spirit" (Acts 7:59). The conversation between Ananias and "the Lord" in Acts 9:10–16 is with Jesus, because in verse 17 Ananias tells Saul, "The Lord Jesus . . . has sent me that you may regain your sight." The prayer, "Our Lord, come!" (1 Cor. 16:22) is addressed to Jesus, as is the prayer in Revelation 22:20, "Come, Lord Jesus!" And Paul also prayed to "the Lord" in 2 Corinthians 12:8 concerning his thorn in the flesh.[5]

---

that prayer is to be in accordance with all that the name stands for. It is prayer proceeding from faith in Christ, prayer that gives expression to a unity with all that Christ stands for, prayer which seeks to set forward Christ himself. And the purpose of it all is the glory of God" (*The Gospel According to John,* p. 646).

[5]The name *Lord* (Gk. *kyrios*) is used in Acts and the Epistles primarily to refer to the Lord Jesus Christ.

Moreover, the fact that Jesus is "a merciful and faithful high priest" (Heb. 2:17) who is able to "sympathize with our weaknesses" (Heb. 4:15), is viewed as an encouragement to us to come boldly before the "throne of grace" in prayer "that we may receive mercy and find grace to help in time of need" (Heb. 4:16). These verses must give us encouragement to come directly to Jesus in prayer, expecting that he will sympathize with our weaknesses as we pray.

There is therefore clear enough scriptural warrant to encourage us to pray not only to God the Father (which seems to be the primary pattern, and certainly follows the example that Jesus taught us in the Lord's Prayer), but also to pray directly to God the Son, our Lord Jesus Christ. Both are correct, and we may pray either to the Father or to the Son.

But should we pray to the Holy Spirit? Though no prayers directly addressed to the Holy Spirit are recorded in the New Testament, there is nothing that would forbid such prayer, for the Holy Spirit, like the Father and the Son, is fully God and is worthy of prayer and is powerful to answer our prayers. (Note also Ezekiel's invitation to the "breath" or "spirit" in Ezek. 37:9.) To say that we cannot pray to the Holy Spirit is really saying that we cannot talk to him or relate to him personally, which hardly seems right. He also relates to us in a personal way since he is a "Comforter" or "Counselor" (John 14:16, 26), believers "know him" (John 14:17), and he teaches us (cf. John 14:26), bears witness to us that we are children of God (Rom. 8:16), and can be grieved by our sin (Eph. 4:30). Moreover, the Holy Spirit exercises personal volition in the distribution of spiritual gifts, for he "continually distributes to each one individually to each one as he wills" (1 Cor. 12:11, author's translation). Therefore, it does not seem wrong to pray directly to the Holy Spirit at times, particularly when we are asking him to do something that relates to his special areas of ministry or responsibility.[6] In fact, through the history of the church several well-used hymns have been prayers to the Holy Spirit (see two at the end of chapter 30, pp. 655–56; one at chapter 52, pp. 1047–48; and one at chapter 53, pp. 1087–88). But this is not the New Testament pattern, and it should not become the dominant emphasis in our prayer life.

## 5. The Role of the Holy Spirit in Our Praying. In Romans 8:26–27 Paul says:

Likewise the Spirit helps us in our weakness; for we do not know how to pray as we ought, but the Spirit himself intercedes for us with sighs too deep for words. And he who searches the hearts of men knows what is the mind of the Spirit, because the Spirit intercedes for the saints according to the will of God.

Interpreters differ on whether the "sighs too deep for words" are the sighs the Holy Spirit himself makes or our own sighs and groans in prayer, which the Holy Spirit makes into effective prayer before God. It seems more likely that the "sighs" or "groans" here are our groans. When Paul says, "The Spirit helps us in our weakness" (v. 26), the word translated "helps" (Gk. *sunantilambanomai*) is the same word used in Luke 10:40, where Martha wants Mary to come and *help* her.

---

[6]J. I. Packer says, "Is it proper to pray to the Spirit? There is no example of doing this anywhere in Scripture, but since the Spirit is God, it cannot be wrong to invoke and address him if there is good reason to do so" (*Keep in Step With the Spirit* [Old Tappan, N.J.: Revell, 1984], p. 261).

The word does not indicate that the Holy Spirit prays instead of us, but that the Holy Spirit takes part with us and makes our weak prayers effective.[7] Thus, such sighing or groaning in prayer is best understood to be sighs or groans which we utter, expressing the desires of our heart and spirit, which the Holy Spirit then makes into effective prayer.[8]

Related to this is the question of what it means to pray "in the Spirit." Paul says, "Pray at all times in the Spirit, with all prayer and supplication" (Eph. 6:18), and Jude says, "pray in the Holy Spirit" (Jude 20).[9] In order to understand this phrase, we should realize that the New Testament tells us that many different activities can be done "in the Holy Spirit." It is possible just to be "in the Spirit" as John was on the Lord's day (Rev. 1:10; cf. 4:2). And it is possible to rejoice in the Holy Spirit (Luke 10:21), to resolve or decide something in the Holy Spirit (Acts 19:21), to have one's conscience bear witness in the Holy Spirit (Rom. 9:1), to have access to God in the Holy Spirit (Eph. 2:18), and to love in the Holy Spirit (Col. 1:8). As we will explain more fully in chapter 30, below (see pp. 647, 651–52), these expressions seem to refer to dwelling consciously in the presence of the Holy Spirit himself, a presence characterized by the Godlike qualities of power, love, joy, truth, holiness, righteousness, and peace. To pray "in the Holy Spirit," then, is to pray with the conscious awareness of God's presence surrounding us and sanctifying both us and our prayers.

## C. Some Important Considerations in Effective Prayer

Scripture indicates a number of considerations that need to be taken into account if we would offer the kind of prayer that God desires from us.

**1. Praying According to God's Will.** John tells us, "This is the confidence which we have in him, that if we ask anything according to his will he hears us. And if we know that he hears us in whatever we ask, we know that we have obtained the requests made of him" (1 John 5:14–15). Jesus teaches us to pray, "Your will be done" (Matt. 6:10), and he himself gives us an example, by praying in the garden of Gethsemane, "Nevertheless, not as I will, but as you will" (Matt. 26:39).

But how do we know what God's will is when we pray? If the matter we are praying about is covered in a passage of Scripture in which God gives us a command or a direct declaration of his will, then the answer to this question is easy: His will is that his Word be obeyed and that his commands be kept. We are to seek for perfect obedience to God's moral will on earth so that God's will may

---

[7] Other reasons why these sighs or groans are best understood to be our "groanings" in prayer are (1) v. 23 says that "we ourselves . . . groan," using a verb (*stenazō*) that is cognate to the noun translated "sighs" (*stenagmos*) in v. 26; (2) such "groanings," which seem to imply a degree of distress or anguish, are appropriate for creatures (vv. 22, 23) but not for the Creator; and (3) v. 26b, which mentions "sighs too deep for words," explains the first clause in v. 26, which says that the Spirit "helps" us, not that the Spirit replaces our prayers. The phrase "too deep for words" does not necessarily mean "silent or noiseless," but can rather mean "not able to be put into words."

[8] For a further discussion of Rom. 8:26–27, see chapter 53, pp. 1078–80.

[9] Some have thought this refers to speaking in tongues, since Paul calls speaking in tongues praying "with the spirit" (1 Cor. 14:15). But that is not a correct understanding, since in 1 Cor. 14:15 "the spirit" refers not to the Holy Spirit but to Paul's own human spirit: note the contrast between "my spirit" and "my mind" in v. 14.

be done "on earth as it is in heaven" (Matt. 6:10). For this reason knowledge of Scripture is a tremendous help in prayer, enabling us to follow the pattern of the first Christians who quoted Scripture when they prayed (see Acts 4:25–26). The regular reading and memorization of Scripture, cultivated over many years of a Christian's life, will increase the depth, power, and wisdom of his or her prayers. Jesus encourages us to have his words within us as we pray, for he says, "If you abide in me, *and my words abide in you*, ask whatever you will, and it shall be done for you" (John 15:7).

This means, for example, that if we are seeking wisdom in the making of an important decision, we do not have to wonder whether it is God's will that we receive wisdom to act rightly. Scripture has already settled that question for us, because there is a promise of Scripture that applies:

> If any of you lacks wisdom, let him ask God, who gives to all men generously and without reproaching, and it will be given him. But let him ask in faith, with no doubting, for he who doubts is like a wave of the sea that is driven and tossed by the wind. For that person must not suppose that a double-minded man, unstable in all his ways, will receive anything from the Lord. (James 1:5–8)

We should have great confidence that God will answer our prayer when we ask him for something that accords with a specific promise or command of Scripture like this. In such cases, we know what God's will is, because he has told us, and we simply need to pray believing that he will answer.

However, there are many other situations in life where we do not know what God's will is. We may not be sure, because no promise or command of Scripture applies, whether it is God's will that we get the job we have applied for, or win an athletic contest in which we are participating (a common prayer among children, especially), or be chosen to hold office in the church, and so on. In all of these cases, we should bring to bear as much of Scripture as we understand, perhaps to give us some general principles within which our prayer can be made. But beyond this, we often must admit that we simply do not know what God's will is. In such cases, we should ask him for deeper understanding and then pray for what seems best to us, giving reasons to the Lord why, in our present understanding of the situation, what we are praying for seems to be best. But it is always right to add, either explicitly or at least in the attitude of our heart, "Nevertheless, if I am wrong in asking this, and if this is not pleasing to you, then do as seems best in your sight," or, more simply, "If it is your will." Sometimes God will grant what we have asked. Sometimes he will give us deeper understanding or change our hearts so that we are led to ask something differently. Sometimes he will not grant our request at all but will simply indicate to us that we must submit to his will (see 2 Cor. 12:9–10).

Some Christians object that to add the phrase "if it is your will" to our prayers "destroys our faith." What it actually does is express uncertainty about whether what we pray for is God's will or not. And it is appropriate when we do not really know what God's will is. But at other times this would not be appropriate: to ask God to give us wisdom to make a decision and then say, "If it is your will to give me wisdom here" would be inappropriate, for it would be saying that we do not believe God meant what he said in James 1:5–8 when he told us to ask in faith and he would grant this request.[10]

Even when a command or promise of Scripture applies, there may be nuances of application that we do not at first fully understand. Therefore it is important in our prayer that we not only talk to God but also listen to him. We should frequently bring a request to God and then wait silently before him. In those times of waiting on the Lord (Pss. 27:14; 38:15; 130:5–6), God may change the desires of our heart, give us additional insight into the situation we are praying about, grant us additional insight into his Word, bring a passage of Scripture to mind that would enable us to pray more effectively, impart a sense of assurance of what his will is, or greatly increase our faith so that we are able to pray with much more confidence.

**2. Praying With Faith.** Jesus says, "Therefore I tell you, whatever you ask in prayer, believe that you have received it, and it will be yours" (Mark 11:24). Some translations vary, but the Greek text actually says, "believe that you *have received it.*" Later scribes who copied the Greek manuscripts and some later commentators have taken it to mean "believe that you *will* receive it." However, if we accept the text as it is in the earliest and best manuscripts ("believe that you have received it"), Jesus is apparently saying that when we ask for something, the kind of faith that will bring results is a settled assurance that when we prayed for something (or perhaps after we had been praying over a period of time), God agreed to grant our specific request. In the personal communion with God that occurs in genuine prayer, this kind of faith on our part could only come *as God gives us a sense of assurance that he has agreed to grant our request.* Of course, we cannot "work up" this kind of genuine faith by any sort of frenzied prayer or great emotional effort to try to make ourselves believe, nor can we force it upon ourselves by saying words we don't think to be true. This is something that only God can give us, and that he may or may not give us each time we pray. This assured faith will often come when we ask God for something and then quietly wait before him for an answer.

In fact, Hebrews 11:1 tells us that "faith is the *assurance* of things hoped for, the conviction of things not seen." Biblical faith is never a kind of wishful thinking or a vague hope that does not have any secure foundation to rest upon. It is rather trust in a person, God himself, based on the fact that we take him at his word and believe what he has said. This trust or dependence on God, when it has an element of assurance or confidence, is genuine biblical faith.

Several other passages encourage us to exercise faith when we pray. "Whatever you ask in prayer, you will receive, if you have faith," Jesus teaches his disciples (Matt. 21:22). And James tells us we are to "ask in faith, with no doubting" (James 1:6). Prayer is never wishful thinking, for it springs from trust in a personal God who wants us to take him at his word.

---

[10]To add, "If it is your will" to a prayer is still very different from not asking at all. If my children come and ask if I will take them to get ice cream, but then (feeling in a cooperative mood) add, "but only if you think it's right, Dad," that is still far removed from not asking me at all. If they had not asked, I would not have considered going to get ice cream. Once they ask, even with the qualification, I will often decide to take them.

**3. Obedience.** Since prayer is a relationship with God as a person, anything in our lives that displeases him will be a hindrance to prayer. The psalmist says, "If I had cherished iniquity in my heart, the Lord would not have listened" (Ps. 66:18). Though "The sacrifice of the wicked is an abomination to the LORD," by contrast, "the prayer of the upright is his delight" (Prov. 15:8). Again we read that "the LORD . . . hears the prayer of the righteous" (Prov. 15:29). But God is not favorably disposed to those who reject his laws: "If one turns away his ear from hearing the law, even his prayer is an abomination" (Prov. 28:9).

The apostle Peter quotes Psalm 34 to affirm that "the eyes of the Lord are upon the righteous, and his ears are open to their prayer" (1 Peter 3:12). Since the previous verses encourage good conduct in everyday life, in speaking and turning away from evil and doing right, Peter is saying that God readily hears the prayers of those who live lives of obedience to him. Similarly, Peter warns husbands to "live considerately" with their wives, "in order that your prayers may not be hindered" (1 Peter 3:7). Likewise, John reminds us of the need for a clear conscience before God when we pray, for he says, "If our hearts do not condemn us, we have confidence before God; and we receive from him whatever we ask, because we keep his commandments and do what pleases him" (1 John 3:21–22).

Now this teaching must not be misunderstood. We do not need to be freed from sin completely before God can be expected to answer our prayers. If God only answered the prayers of sinless people, then no one in the whole Bible except Jesus would have had his or her prayers answered. When we come before God through his grace, we come cleansed by the blood of Christ (Rom. 3:25; 5:9; Eph. 2:13; Heb. 9:14; 1 Peter 1:2). Yet we must not neglect the biblical emphasis on personal holiness of life. Prayer and holy living go together. There is much grace in the Christian life, but growth in personal holiness is also a route to much greater blessing, and that is true with respect to prayer as well. The passages quoted teach that, all other things being equal, more exact obedience will lead to increased effectiveness in prayer (cf. Heb. 12:14; James 4:3–4).

**4. Confession of Sins.** Because our obedience to God is never perfect in this life, we continually depend on his forgiveness for our sins. Confession of sins is necessary in order for God to "forgive us" in the sense of restoring his day-by-day relationship with us (see Matt. 6:12; 1 John 1:9). It is good when we pray to confess all known sin to the Lord and to ask for his forgiveness. Sometimes when we wait on him, he will bring other sins to mind that we need to confess. With respect to those sins that we do not remember or are unaware of, it is appropriate to pray the general prayer of David, "Clear me from hidden faults" (Ps. 19:12).

Sometimes confessing our sins to other trusted Christians will bring an assurance of forgiveness and encouragement to overcome sin as well. James relates mutual confession to prayer, for in a passage discussing powerful prayer, James encourages us, "Therefore *confess your sins to one another,* and pray for one another, that you may be healed" (James 5:16).

**5. Forgiving Others.** Jesus says, "If you forgive men their trespasses, your heavenly Father also will forgive you; but if you do not forgive men their trespasses, neither will your Father forgive your trespasses" (Matt. 6:14–15). Similarly, Jesus says, "Whenever you stand praying, forgive, if you have anything against any one; so that your Father also who is in heaven may forgive you your trespasses" (Mark 11:25). Our Lord does not have in mind the initial experience of forgiveness we know when we are justified by faith, for that would not belong in a prayer that we pray every day (see Matt. 6:12 with vv. 14–15). He refers rather to the *day-by-day relationship with God* that we need to have restored when we have sinned and displeased him. In fact, Jesus commands us to build into our prayers a request that God forgive us in the same way that we have forgiven others who have harmed us (in the same "personal relationship" sense of "forgive"—that is, not holding a grudge or cherishing bitterness against another person or harboring any desire to harm them): "Forgive us our sins, *as we also have forgiven those who sin against us*" (Matt. 6:12, author's translation). If there are those whom we have not forgiven when we pray this prayer, then we are asking God not to restore a right relationship with us after we sin, in just the same way as we have refused to do so with others.

Since prayer presumes a relationship with God as a person, this is not surprising. If we have sinned against him and grieved the Holy Spirit (cf. Eph. 4:30), and the sin has not been forgiven, it interrupts our relationship with God (cf. Isa. 59:1–2). Until sin is forgiven and the relationship is restored prayer will, of course, be difficult. Moreover, if we have unforgiveness in our hearts against someone else, then we are not acting in a way that is pleasing to God or helpful to us. So God declares (Matt. 6:12, 14–15) that he will distance himself from us until we forgive others.

**6. Humility.** James tells us that "God opposes the proud, but gives grace to the humble" (James 4:6; also 1 Peter 5:5). Therefore he says, "Humble yourselves before the Lord and he will exalt you" (James 4:10). Humility is thus the right attitude to have in praying to God, whereas pride is altogether inappropriate.

Jesus' parable about the Pharisee and the tax collector illustrates this. When the Pharisee stood to pray, he was boastful: "God, I thank you that I am not like other men, extortioners, unjust, adulterers, or even like this tax collector. I fast twice a week, I give tithes of all that I get" (Luke 18:11–12). By contrast, the humble tax collector "would not even lift up his eyes to heaven, but beat his breast, saying, 'God, be merciful to me a sinner!'" (Luke 18:13). Jesus said that he "went down to his house justified," rather than the Pharisee, "for every one who exalts himself will be humbled, but he who humbles himself will be exalted" (Luke 18:14). This is why Jesus condemned those who "for a pretense make long prayers" (Luke 20:47) and those hypocrites who "love to stand and pray in the synagogues and at the street corners, that they may be seen by men" (Matt. 6:5).

God is rightly jealous for his own honor.[11] Therefore he is not pleased to answer the prayers of the proud who take honor to themselves rather than giving it to him. True humility before God, which will also be reflected in genuine humility before others, is necessary for effective prayer.

---

[11]See discussion of God's attribute of jealousy, p. 205 above.

**7. Continuing in Prayer Over Time.** Just as Moses twice stayed on the mountain forty days before God for the people of Israel (Deut. 9:25–26; 10:10–11), and just as Jacob said to God, "I will not let you go, unless you bless me" (Gen. 32:26), so we see in Jesus' life a pattern of much time given to prayer. When great multitudes were following him, "he himself was often withdrawing into the wilderness regions and praying" (Luke 5:16, author's translation).[12] At another time, *"all night* he continued in prayer to God" (Luke 6:12).

Sometimes, as in the case of Moses and Jacob, prayer over a long period of time may be prayer for one specific item (cf. Luke 18:1–8). When we are earnestly seeking God for an answer to a specific prayer, we may in fact repeat the same request several times. Paul asked the Lord "three times" (2 Cor. 12:8) that his thorn in the flesh would be taken from him. Jesus himself, when he was in the garden of Gethsemane, asked the Father, "Remove this cup from me; yet not what I will, but what you will" (Mark 14:36). Then after he came and found the disciples sleeping, Jesus prayed again, making the same request in the same words: "And again he went away and prayed, *saying the same words*" (Mark 14:39). These are instances of earnest repetition in prayer for a deeply felt need. They are not examples of what Jesus forbids—the heaping up of "empty phrases" in the mistaken belief that "many words" will earn a hearing (Matt. 6:7).

There is also an element of a continual fellowship with God in praying over time. Paul calls on us to "pray constantly" (1 Thess. 5:17), and he encourages the Colossians to "continue steadfastly in prayer, being watchful in it with thanksgiving" (Col. 4:2). Such continual devotion to prayer even while about daily duties should characterize the life of every believer. The apostles are a telling example. They freed themselves from other responsibilities in order to give more time to prayer: "But *we will devote ourselves to prayer* and to the ministry of the word" (Acts 6:4).

**8. Praying Earnestly.** Jesus himself, who is our model for prayer, prayed earnestly. "In the days of his flesh, Jesus offered up prayers and supplications, with loud cries and tears, to him who was able to save him from death, and he was heard for his godly fear" (Heb. 5:7). In some of the prayers of Scripture, we can almost hear the great intensity with which the saints pour out their hearts before God. Daniel cries out, "O LORD, hear! O LORD, forgive! O LORD, listen and take action! For Thine own sake, O my God, do not delay, because Thy city and Thy people are called by Thy name" (Dan. 9:19 NASB). When God shows Amos the judgment that he is going to bring on his people, Amos pleads, "O Lord GOD, forgive, I beseech you! How can Jacob stand? He is so small!" (Amos 7:2).

In personal relationships, if we attempt to fake emotional intensity and put on an outward show of emotion that is not consistent with the feelings of our hearts, others involved will usually sense our hypocrisy at once and be put off by it. How much more is this true of God, who fully knows our hearts. Therefore, intensity and depth of emotional involvement in prayer should never be faked: we cannot fool God. Yet, if we truly begin to see situations as God sees them, if we begin to

---

[12]The periphrastic imperfect tense here (Gk. *ēn hypochōrōn*) emphasizes, even more than a simple imperfect would, the repeated or habitual nature of the activity of withdrawing into the wilderness (see *BDF*, 353[1]).

see the needs of a hurting and dying world as they really are, then it will be natural to pray with intense emotional involvement and to expect God, as a merciful Father, to respond to heartfelt prayer. And where such intensely felt prayer finds expression in group prayer meetings, Christians should certainly accept and be thankful for it, for it often indicates a deep work of the Holy Spirit in the heart of the person praying.

**9. Waiting on the Lord.** After crying out to God for help in distress, David says, "Wait for the LORD; be strong, and let your heart take courage; yea, wait for the LORD!" (Ps. 27:14). Similarly, he says, "But for you, O LORD, do I wait; it is you, O LORD my God, who will answer" (Ps. 38:15). The psalmist likewise says,

> I wait for the LORD, my soul waits,
>     and in his word I hope;
> my soul waits for the LORD
>     more than watchmen for the morning,
>     more than watchmen for the morning. (Ps. 130:5–6)

An analogy from human experience may help us to appreciate the benefit of waiting before the Lord for a response to prayer. If I wish to invite someone home for dinner, there are various ways I can do so. First, I can issue a vague, general invitation: "It would be nice to have you come to dinner sometime." Almost no one will come to dinner based on that kind of invitation alone. This is rather like the vague, general prayer, "God bless all my aunts and uncles and all the missionaries. Amen." Second, I could make a specific but hurried and impersonal kind of invitation: "Fred, can you come to dinner Friday night at 6:00?"—but as soon as the words are out of my mouth, I rush away leaving Fred with a puzzled expression on his face because I didn't allow him time to respond. This is like many of our prayer requests. We simply speak words to God as if the very act of voicing them, without any heart involvement in what we are saying, will itself bring an answer from God. But this kind of request forgets that prayer is a relationship between two persons, myself and God.

There is a third kind of invitation, one that is heartfelt, personal, and specific. After waiting until I'm sure I have Fred's full attention, I can look him directly in the eye and say, "Fred, Margaret and I would really love to have you come to dinner at our home this Friday at 6:00 P.M. Could you come?"—and then, continuing to look him in the eye, I wait silently and patiently while he decides what to answer. He knows from my facial expression, my tone of voice, my timing, and the setting in which I chose to talk to him that I am putting my whole self into this request, and that I am relating to him as a person and as a friend. Waiting patiently for an answer shows my earnestness, my sense of expectancy, and my respect for him as a person. This third kind of request is like that of the earnest Christian who comes before God, gains a sense of being in his presence, earnestly pours out a request to him, and then waits quietly for some sense of assurance of God's answer.

This is not to say that all our requests must be of this nature, or even that the first two kinds of requests are wrong. Indeed, in some situations we pray quickly because we have little time before we need an answer (see Neh. 2:4). And sometimes we do pray generally because we do not have more specific information about a situation, or because it is far removed from us or because of shortness of time. But the material in Scripture on earnest prayer and on waiting for the Lord, and the fact that prayer is personal communication between ourselves and God, do indicate that prayers such as the third kind of request are much deeper and will undoubtedly bring many more answers from God.

**10. Praying in Private.** Daniel went to his upper chamber and "got down upon his knees three times a day and prayed and gave thanks before his God" (Dan. 6:10).[13] Jesus frequently went out into solitary places to be alone to pray (Luke 5:16 et al.). And he also teaches us, "When you pray, go into your room and shut the door and pray to your Father who is in secret; and your Father who sees in secret will reward you" (Matt. 6:6). This statement is in the context of avoiding the error of the hypocrites who loved to pray at the street corners "that they may be seen by men" (Matt. 6:5). There is wisdom in Jesus' encouragement to pray in secret, not only that we might avoid hypocrisy, but also that we might not be distracted by the presence of other people and therefore modify our prayers to suit what we think they will expect to hear. When we are truly alone with God, in the privacy of a room to which we have "shut the door" (Matt. 6:6), then we can pour out our hearts to him.[14]

The need to pray in private may also have implications for small-group or church prayer meetings: when believers come together to seek the Lord earnestly about a specific matter, it is often helpful if they can be in the privacy of a home where the door is shut and they can collectively cry out to God. Apparently this was the way the early Christians prayed when they were making earnest supplication to God for the release of Peter from prison (see Acts 12:5, 12–16).

**11. Praying With Others.** Believers find strength in praying together with others. In fact, Jesus teaches us, "Again, I say to you, if two of you agree on earth about anything they ask, it will be done for them by my Father in heaven. For where two or three are gathered in my name, there am I in the midst of them" (Matt. 18:19–20).[15]

There are many other examples in Scripture where groups of believers prayed together or where one person led the entire congregation in prayer (note Solomon's prayer "in the presence of all the assembly of Israel" at the dedication of the temple in 1 Kings 8:22–53 or the prayer of the early church in Jerusalem

---

[13]Though Daniel's enemies saw him praying, it was only because they "came by agreement" and apparently spied on him.

[14]At this point we may also mention that Paul discusses a use of the gift of speaking in tongues during private prayer: "If I pray in a tongue, my spirit prays but my mind is unfruitful. What am I to do? I will pray with the spirit and I will pray with the mind also; I will sing with the spirit and I will sing with the mind also" (1 Cor. 14:14–15). When Paul says "my spirit prays," he is not referring to the Holy Spirit but to his own human spirit, for the contrast is with "my mind." His own spirit is pouring out requests before God, and those requests are understood by God and result in personal edification: "He who speaks in a tongue edifies himself" (1 Cor. 14:4). This gift will be discussed more fully in chapter 53, below.

[15]Although the previous four verses (vv.15–18) have to do with church discipline, the word "again" at the beginning of v. 19 signals a slight change in subject, and it is not inappropriate to take vv. 19–20 as a broader statement about prayer in general in the context of the church.

when "they lifted their voices together to God" in Acts 4:24). Even the Lord's Prayer is put in the plural: It does not say, "Give me this day my daily bread" but "Give *us* this day *our* daily bread" and "Forgive *us* our sins" and "Lead *us* not into temptation but deliver *us* from evil" (Matt. 6:11–13, author's translation). Praying with others, then, is also right and often increases our faith and the effectiveness of our prayers.

**12. Fasting.** Prayer is often connected with fasting in Scripture. Sometimes these are occasions of intense supplication before God, as when Nehemiah, on hearing of the ruin of Jerusalem, "continued *fasting* and praying before the God of Heaven" (Neh. 1:4), or when the Jews learned of the decree of Ahasuerus that they would all be killed, and "there was great mourning among the Jews, with *fasting* and weeping and lamenting" (Esth. 4:3), or when Daniel sought the LORD "by prayer and supplications with *fasting* and sackcloth and ashes" (Dan. 9:3). At other times fasting is connected with repentance, for God says to the people who have sinned against him, " 'Yet even now,' says the LORD, 'return to me with all your heart, with fasting, with weeping, and with mourning' " (Joel 2:12).

In the New Testament, Anna was "worshiping with *fasting* and prayer night and day" (Luke 2:37) in the temple, and the church at Antioch was "worshiping the Lord and *fasting*" when the Holy Spirit said, "Set apart for me Barnabas and Saul for the work to which I have called them" (Acts 13:2). The church responded with further fasting and prayer before sending Barnabas and Saul on their first missionary journey: "Then after fasting and praying they laid their hands on them and sent them off" (Acts 13:3). In fact, fasting was a routine part of seeking the Lord's guidance with regard to church officers, for on Paul's first missionary journey, we read that he and Barnabas, as they traveled back through the churches they had founded, "appointed elders for them in every church, with prayer and fasting" (Acts 14:23).

So fasting appropriately accompanied prayer in many situations: in times of intensive intercession, repentance, worship, and seeking of guidance. In each of these situations, several benefits come from fasting, all of which affect our relationship to God: (1) Fasting increases our sense of humility and dependence on the Lord (for our hunger and physical weakness continually remind us how we are not really strong in ourselves but need the Lord). (2) Fasting allows us to give more attention to prayer (for we are not spending time on eating), and (3) it is a continual reminder that, just as we sacrifice some personal comfort to the Lord by not eating, so we must continually sacrifice all of ourselves to him.[16] Moreover, (4) fasting is a good exercise in self-discipline, for as we refrain from eating food, which we would ordinarily desire, it also strengthens our ability to refrain from sin, to which we might otherwise be tempted to yield. If we train ourselves to accept the small "suffering" of fasting willingly, we will be better able to accept other suffering for the sake of righteousness (cf. Heb. 5:8; 1 Peter 4:1–2). (5) Fasting also heightens spiritual and mental alertness and a sense of God's presence as we focus less on the material things of this world (such as food) and as

---

[16]Similar reasons (devoting more time to prayer and giving up some personal pleasure) probably explain Paul's permission to married couples to give up sexual relations "by mutual consent and for a time, so that you may devote yourselves to prayer" (1 Cor. 7:5 NIV).

the energies of our body are freed from digesting and processing food. This enables us to focus on eternal spiritual realities that are much more important.[17] Finally, (6) fasting expresses earnestness and urgency in our prayers: if we continued to fast, eventually we would die. Therefore, in a symbolic way, fasting says to God that we are prepared to lay down our lives that the situation be changed rather than that it continue. In this sense fasting is especially appropriate when the spiritual state of the church is low.

> "Yet even now," says the LORD,
>   "return to me with all your heart,
> with fasting, with weeping, and with mourning;
>   and rend your hearts and not your garments."
>                                 (Joel 2:12–13a)

Though the New Testament does not specifically require that we fast, or set special times when we must fast, Jesus certainly assumes that we will fast, for he says to his disciples, "And *when* you fast" (Matt. 6:16). Moreover, Jesus also says, "The days will come, when the bridegroom is taken away from them, and then they will fast" (Matt. 9:15). He is the Bridegroom, we are his disciples, and during this present church age he has been "taken" away from us until the day he returns. Most western Christians do not fast, but, if we were willing to fast more regularly—even for one or two meals—we might be surprised how much more spiritual power and strength we would have in our lives and in our churches.

**13. What About Unanswered Prayer?** We must begin by recognizing that as long as God is God and we are his creatures, there must be some unanswered prayers. This is because God keeps hidden his own wise plans for the future, and even though people pray, many events will not come about until the time that God has decreed. The Jews prayed for centuries for the Messiah to come, and rightly so, but it was not until "the time had fully come" that "God sent forth his Son" (Gal. 4:4). The souls of martyrs in heaven, free from sin, cry out for God to judge the earth (Rev. 6:10), but God does not immediately answer; rather he tells them to rest a little longer (Rev. 6:11). It is clear that there can be long periods of delay during which prayers go unanswered, because the people praying do not know God's wise timing.

Prayer will also be unanswered because we do not always know how to pray as we ought (Rom. 8:26), we do not always pray according to God's will (James 4:3), and we do not always ask in faith (James 1:6–8). And sometimes we think that one solution is best, but God has a better plan, even to fulfill his purpose through suffering and hardship. Joseph no doubt prayed earnestly to be rescued from the pit and from being carried off into slavery in Egypt (Gen. 37:23–36),

---

[17]In Mark 9:29, when the disciples asked why they could not drive out a certain demon, Jesus replied, "This kind cannot be driven out by anything but prayer." Many early and quite reliable Greek manuscripts and several early manuscripts in other languages read "by prayer *and fasting*." In either case, it cannot mean prayer that is spoken at the time the demon is being cast out, for Jesus simply cast out the demon with a word and did not engage in an extended time of prayer. It must mean rather that the disciples had not previously been spending enough time in prayer and that their spiritual strength was weak. Therefore the "fasting" that is mentioned in many ancient manuscripts fits the pattern of an activity that increases one's spiritual strength and power.

but many years later he found how in all of these events "God meant it for good" (Gen. 50:20).

When we face unanswered prayer, we join the company of Jesus, who prayed, "Father, if you are willing, remove this cup from me; nevertheless not my will, but yours, be done" (Luke 22:42). We join also the company of Paul, who asked the Lord "three times" that his thorn in the flesh be removed, but it was not; rather, the Lord told him, "My grace is sufficient for you, for my power is made perfect in weakness" (2 Cor. 12:8–9). We join the company of David, who prayed for his son's life to be saved, but it was not, so he "went into the house of the LORD, and worshiped" and said of his son, "I shall go to him, but he will not return to me" (2 Sam. 12:20, 23). We join the company of the martyrs throughout history who prayed for deliverance that did not come, for they "loved not their lives even unto death" (Rev. 12:11).

When prayer remains unanswered we must continue to trust God, who "causes all things to work together for good" (Rom. 8:28 NASB), and to cast our cares on him, knowing that he continually cares for us (1 Peter 5:7). We must keep remembering that he will give strength sufficient for each day (Deut. 33:25) and that he has promised, "I will never fail you nor forsake you" (Heb. 13:5; cf. Rom. 8:35–39).

We also must continue to pray. Sometimes an answer, long awaited, will suddenly be given, as it was when Hannah after many years bore a child (1 Sam. 1:19–20), or when Simeon saw with his own eyes the long-expected Messiah come to the temple (Luke 2:25–35).

But sometimes prayers will remain unanswered in this life. At times God will answer those prayers after the believer dies. At other times he will not, but even then the faith expressed in those prayers and their heartfelt expressions of love for God and the people he has made will still ascend as a pleasing incense before God's throne (Rev. 5:8; 8:3–4) and will result in "praise and glory and honor at the revelation of Jesus Christ" (1 Peter 1:7).

## D. Praise and Thanksgiving

Praise and thanksgiving to God, which will be treated more fully in chapter 51, are an essential element of prayer. The model prayer that Jesus left us begins with a word of praise: "Hallowed be your name" (Matt. 6:9). And Paul tells the Philippians, "in everything by prayer and supplication *with thanksgiving* let your requests be made known to God" (Phil. 4:6), and the Colossians, "Continue steadfastly in prayer, being watchful in it *with thanksgiving*" (Col. 4:2). Thanksgiving, like every other aspect of prayer, should not be a mechanical mouthing of a "thank you" to God, but the expression of words that reflect the thankfulness of our hearts. Moreover, we should never think that thanking God for the answer to something we ask for can somehow force God to give it to us, for that changes the prayer from a genuine, sincere request to a demand that assumes we can make God do what we want him to do. Such a spirit in our prayers really denies the essential nature of prayer as dependence on God.

By contrast, the kind of thanksgiving that appropriately accompanies prayer must express thankfulness to God for all circumstances, for every event of life that he allows to come to us. When we join our prayers with humble, childlike thanksgiving to God "in all circumstances" (1 Thess. 5:18), they will be acceptable to God.

## QUESTIONS FOR PERSONAL APPLICATION

1. Do you often have difficulty with prayer? What things in this chapter have been helpful to you in this regard?

2. When have you known the most effective times of prayer in your own life? What factors contributed to making those times more effective? Which other factors need most attention in your prayer life? What can you do to strengthen each of these areas?

3. How does it help and encourage you (if it does) when you pray together with other Christians?

4. Have you ever tried waiting quietly before the Lord after making an earnest prayer request? If so, what has been the result?

5. Do you have a regular time each day for private Bible reading and prayer? Are you sometimes easily distracted and turned aside to other activities? If so, how can distractions be overcome?

6. Do you enjoy praying? Why or why not?

## SPECIAL TERMS

faith
"in Jesus' name"

prayer
waiting for the Lord

## BIBLIOGRAPHY

(For an explanation of this bibliography see the note on the bibliography to chapter 1, p. 38. Complete bibliographical data may be found on pp. 1223–29.)

### Sections in Evangelical Systematic Theologies

1. Anglican (Episcopalian)
    1882–92     Litton, 431–32
2. Arminian (Wesleyan or Methodist)
    1940        Wiley, 3:40–44, 153
    1960        Purkiser, 421–24
    1983–       Cottrell, 2:353–708
3. Baptist
    1907        Strong, 433–39
    1917        Mullins, 119, 192, 224, 274, 348
    1983–85     Erickson, 405–6
4. Dispensational
    1947        Chafer, 5:220–31; 7:252–54
    1949        Thiessen, 298–301

             1986        Ryrie, 381–82
5. Lutheran
          1917–24        Pieper, 3:215–19
             1934        Mueller, 428–34, 467–69
6. Reformed (or Presbyterian)
             1559        Calvin, 2:850–920 (3.20)
          1724–58        Edwards, 2:74–88, 113–18
          1871–73        Hodge, 3:692–709
             1878        Dabney, 713–25
          1937–66        Murray, *CW*, 3:168–71
7. Renewal (or charismatic/Pentecostal)
          1988–92        Williams, 2:295–98, 3:95–98

## Sections in Representative Roman Catholic Systematic Theologies

1. Roman Catholic: Traditional
             1955        Ott, 91
2. Roman Catholic: Post-Vatican II
             1980        McBrien, 1:331–32; 2:1057–99

## Other Works

Bennett, Arthur, ed. *The Valley of Vision: A Collection of Puritan Prayer and Devotions*. Edinburgh and Carlisle, Pa.: Banner of Truth, 1975.

Bounds, E. M. *Power Through Prayer*. Grand Rapids: Baker, 1963.

Brother Lawrence. *The Practice of the Presence of God*. New York: Revell, 1895.

Carson, D. A., ed. *Teach Us To Pray: Prayer in the Bible and the World*. Grand Rapids: Baker, and Exeter: Paternoster, 1990.

Clowney, Edmund. *Christian Meditation*. Philadelphia: Presbyterian and Reformed, 1979.

———. "Prayer, Theology of." In *NDT*, pp. 526–27.

Forsyth, P. T. *The Soul of Prayer*. Grand Rapids: Eerdmans, 1967 (reprint).

Foster, Richard J. *Celebration of Discipline: The Path to Spiritual Growth*. San Francisco: Harper and Row, 1988.

Hallesby, O. *Prayer*. Trans. by Clarence J. Carlsen. Minneapolis: Augsburg, 1959 (reprint).

Houston, James. *The Transforming Friendship*. Oxford and Batavia, Ill.: Lion, 1989.

Hunter, W. Bingham. *The God Who Hears*. Downers Grove, Ill.: InterVarsity Press, 1986.

Kelly, Thomas R. *A Testament of Devotion*. New York: Harper, 1941.

Law, William. *A Serious Call to a Devout and Holy Life*. Philadelphia: Westminster, 1948 (reprint).

M'Intyre, D. M. *The Hidden Life of Prayer*. Minneapolis: Bethany Fellowship Press, 1962 (reprint). (The author's name is sometimes spelled MacIntyre in other editions of this book.)

Murray, Andrew. *The Ministry of Intercessory Prayer*. Minneapolis: Bethany House, 1981 (reprint; originally published in 1897 as *The Ministry of Intercession*).

Ortlund, Raymond C., Jr. *A Passion for God: Prayers and Meditations on the Book of Romans*. Wheaton, Ill.: Crossway, 1994.

Prince, Derek. *Shaping History Through Prayer and Fasting*. Old Tappan, N.J.: Fleming H. Revell, 1973.

Smith, David R. *Fasting: A Neglected Discipline*. Fort Washington, Pa.: Christian Literature Crusade, 1969.

Spear, Wayne. *The Theology of Prayer*. Grand Rapids: Baker, 1979.

Thomas à Kempis. *The Imitation of Christ*. Grand Rapids: Baker, 1973 (reprint).

Unknown Christian. *The Kneeling Christian*. Grand Rapids: Zondervan, 1945.

Wallis, Arthur. *God's Chosen Fast: A Spiritual and Practical Guide to Fasting*. Fort Washington, Pa.: Christian Literature Crusade, 1987.

White, John. *Daring to Draw Near*. Downers Grove, Ill.: InterVarsity Press, 1977.

Willard, Dallas. *The Spirit of the Disciplines*. San Francisco: Harper and Row, 1988.

## SCRIPTURE MEMORY PASSAGE

**Hebrews 4:14–16:** *Since then we have a great high priest who has passed through the heavens, Jesus, the Son of God, let us hold fast our confession. For we have not a high priest who is unable to sympathize with our weaknesses, but one who in every respect has been tempted as we are, yet without sin. Let us then with confidence draw near to the throne of grace, that we may receive mercy and find grace to help in time of need.*

## HYMN

"From Every Stormy Wind"

From ev'ry stormy wind that blows,
    from ev'ry swelling tide of woes,
There is a calm, a sure retreat;
    'tis found beneath the Mercy Seat.

There is a place where Jesus sheds
    the oil of gladness on our heads,
A place than all besides more sweet;
    it is the blood-stained Mercy Seat.

There is a spot where spirits blend,
    where friend holds fellowship with friend,
Tho' sundered far; by faith they meet
    around the common Mercy Seat.

Ah, whither could we flee for aid,
    when tempted, desolate, dismayed,
Or how the hosts of hell defeat,
    had suff'ring saints no Mercy Seat?

There, there on eagle wings we soar,
    and time and sense seem all no more,

And heav'n comes down our souls to greet,
and glory crowns the Mercy Seat.

O may my hand forget her skill,
my tongue be silent, cold, and still,
This bounding heart forget to beat,
if I forget the Mercy Seat.

AUTHOR: HUGH STOWELL, 1828, 1831

# Chapter 19

# Angels

*What are angels? Why did God create them?*

## EXPLANATION AND SCRIPTURAL BASIS

### A. What Are Angels?

We may define angels as follows: *Angels are created, spiritual beings with moral judgment and high intelligence, but without physical bodies.*

**1. Created Spiritual Beings.** Angels have not always existed; they are part of the universe that God created. In a passage that refers to angels as the "host" of heaven (or "armies of heaven"), Ezra says, "You are the LORD, you alone; you have made heaven, the heaven of heavens, *with all their host* . . . and the host of heaven worships you" (Neh. 9:6; cf. Ps. 148:2, 5). Paul tells us that God created all things "visible and invisible" through Christ and for him, and then specifically includes the angelic world with the phrase "whether thrones or dominions or principalities or authorities" (Col. 1:16).

That angels exercise moral judgement is seen in the fact that some of them sinned and fell from their positions (2 Peter 2:4; Jude 6; see chapter 20). Their high intelligence is seen throughout Scripture as they speak to people (Matt. 28:5; Acts 12:6–11; et al.) and sing praise to God (Rev. 4:11; 5:11).

Since angels are "spirits" (Heb. 1:14) or spiritual creatures, they do not ordinarily have physical bodies (Luke 24:39). Therefore they cannot usually be seen by us unless God gives us a special ability to see them (Num. 22:31; 2 Kings 6:17; Luke 2:13). In their ordinary activities of guarding and protecting us (Ps. 34:7; 91:11; Heb. 1:14), and joining with us in worship to God (Heb. 12:22), they are invisible. However, from time to time angels took on a bodily form to appear to various people in Scripture (Matt. 28:5; Heb. 13:2).

**2. Other Names for Angels.** Scripture sometimes uses other terms for angels, such as "sons of God" (Job 1:6; 2:1), "holy ones" (Ps. 89:5, 7), "spirits" (Heb. 1:14), "watchers" (Dan. 4:13, 17, 23), "thrones," "dominions," "principalities," "authorities" (Col. 1:16), and "powers" (Eph. 1:21).

**3. Other Kinds of Heavenly Beings.** There are three other specific types of heavenly beings named in Scripture. Whether we think of these as special types of "angels" (in a broad sense of the term), or whether we think of them as heavenly beings distinct from angels, they are nonetheless created spiritual beings who serve and worship God.

**a. The "Cherubim":**[1] The cherubim were given the task of guarding the entrance to the Garden of Eden (Gen. 3:24), and God himself is frequently said to be enthroned on the cherubim or to travel with the cherubim as his chariot (Ps. 18:10; Ezek. 10:1–22). Over the ark of the covenant in the Old Testament were two golden figures of cherubim with their wings stretched out above the ark, and it was there that God promised to come to dwell among his people: "There I will meet with you, and from above the mercy seat, from between the two cherubim that are upon the ark of testimony, I will speak with you of all that I will give you in commandment for the people of Israel" (Ex. 25:22; cf. vv. 18–21).

**b. The "Seraphim":**[2] Another group of heavenly beings, the seraphim, are mentioned only in Isaiah 6:2–7, where they continually worship the LORD and call to one another, "Holy, holy, holy is the LORD of hosts; the whole earth is full of his glory" (Isa. 6:3).

**c. The Living Creatures:** Both Ezekiel and Revelation tell us of yet other kinds of heavenly beings known as "living creatures" around God's throne (Ezek. 1:5–14; Rev. 4:6–8).[3] With their appearances like a lion, an ox, a man, and an eagle, they are the mightiest representatives of various parts of God's entire creation (wild beasts, domesticated animals, human beings, and birds), and they worship God continually: "Day and night they never cease to sing, 'Holy, holy, holy, is the Lord God Almighty, who was and is and is to come!'" (Rev. 4:8)

**4. Rank and Order Among the Angels.** Scripture indicates that there is rank and order among the angels. One angel, Michael, is called an "archangel" in Jude 9, a title that indicates rule or authority over other angels. He is called "one of the chief princes" in Daniel 10:13. Michael also appears to be a leader in the angelic army: "Now war arose in heaven, Michael and his angels fighting against the dragon; and the dragon and his angels fought, but they were defeated" (Rev. 12:7–8). And Paul tells us that the Lord will return from heaven "with the archangel's call" (1 Thess. 4:16). Whether this refers to Michael as the only archangel, or whether there are other archangels, Scripture does not tell us.

**5. Names of Specific Angels.** Only two angels are specifically named in Scripture.[4] Michael is mentioned in Jude 9 and Revelation 12:7–8 as well as in

---

[1] In Hebrew, the word *cherub* is singular, while the plural form is *cherubim*.

[2] The Hebrew word *seraph* is singular, while *seraphim* is the plural form.

[3] The descriptions differ somewhat between Ezekiel and Revelation but also have many similarities. It is difficult to tell whether these are different groups of creatures or whether those in Revelation have been transformed from the form they took in Ezekiel's vision.

[4] I have not counted Satan here, who is a fallen angel, and who is sometimes called by other names as well. (See chapter 20, on Satan and demons.)

Daniel 10:13, 21, where he is called "Michael, one of the chief princes" (v. 13). The angel Gabriel is mentioned in Daniel 8:16 and 9:21 as a messenger who comes from God to speak to Daniel. Gabriel is also identified as God's messenger to Zechariah and Mary in Luke 1: the angel answers Zechariah, "I am Gabriel, who stand in the presence of God" (Luke 1:19). Then we read, "In the sixth month the angel Gabriel was sent from God to a city of Galilee named Nazareth, to a virgin . . . and the virgin's name was Mary" (Luke 1:26–27).

**6. Only One Place at One Time.** Scripture frequently represents angels as traveling from one place to another, as in the verse mentioned above where Gabriel "was sent from God to a city of Galilee named Nazareth" (Luke 1:26). This is made explicit when an angel comes to Daniel and says:

> I have come because of your words. The prince of the kingdom of Persia withstood me twenty-one days; but Michael, one of the chief princes, came to help me, so I left him there with the prince of the kingdom of Persia and came to make you understand what is to befall your people in the latter days. (Dan. 10:12–14)

The idea that an angel can be in only one place at one time is consistent with the fact that angels are created beings. Unlike God, who is omnipresent, they are finite creatures and therefore limited to being in one place at one time, as is everything else that God has created.[5]

**7. How Many Angels Are There?** Though Scripture does not give us a figure for the number of angels God created, it is apparently a very great number. We read that God on Mount Sinai "came from the *ten thousands of holy ones,* with flaming fire at his right hand" (Deut. 33:2). We also learn that, "the chariots of God are tens of thousands and thousands of thousands" (Ps. 68:17 NIV). When we come to worship we come into the presence of "*innumerable* angels" (Heb. 12:22).[6] Their number is even more strikingly emphasized in Revelation 5:11, where John says, "I heard around the throne and the living creatures and the elders the voice of many angels, numbering *myriads of myriads* and thousands of thousands." This expression indicates an amazingly large number (from a human standpoint)—an innumerable assembly of angelic beings praising God.

**8. Do People Have Individual Guardian Angels?** Scripture clearly tells us that God sends angels for our protection: "He will give his angels charge of you to guard you in all your ways. On their hands they will bear you up, lest you dash your foot against a stone" (Ps. 91:11–12). But some people have gone beyond this idea of general protection and wondered if God gives a specific "guardian

---

[5]Nevertheless, it seems that a very large number of angels can be in one place at the same time, at least if the example of evil angels or demons is a good indication of this fact. When Jesus asked the demonic forces in the Gadarene demoniac, "What is your name?" he said, "Legion"; for "many demons had entered him" (Luke 8:30). Even if we do not understand this literally to mean a number equal to a legion of the Roman army (3,000–6,000 men), and even if we allow that since Satan is the father of lies, the demons in the man could be greatly exaggerating, Luke still says that "many demons had entered him."

[6]The Greek term *myrias* ("myriad") is an expression referring to "a very large number, not exactly defined" (BAGD, p. 529). (See also Jer. 33:22.)

angel" for each individual in the world, or at least for each Christian. Support for this idea has been found in Jesus' words about little children, "in heaven *their angels* always behold the face of my Father who is in heaven" (Matt. 18:10). However, our Lord may simply be saying that angels who are assigned the task of protecting little children have ready access to God's presence. (To use an athletic analogy, the angels may be playing "zone" rather than "man-on-man" defense.)[7] When the disciples in Acts 12:15 say that Peter's "angel" must be knocking at the door, this does not necessarily imply belief in an individual guardian angel. It could be that an angel was guarding or caring for Peter just at that time. There seems to be, therefore, no convincing support for the idea of individual "guardian angels" in the text of Scripture.

**9. Angels Do Not Marry.** Jesus taught that in the resurrection people "neither marry nor are given in marriage, but are like angels in heaven" (Matt. 22:30; cf. Luke 20:34–36). This would suggest that angels do not have the kind of family relationships that exist among human beings. Scripture is otherwise silent on this point, so it is wise not to attempt to engage in speculation.[8]

**10. The Power of Angels.** Angels apparently have very great power. They are called "you mighty ones who do his word" (Ps. 103:20) and "powers" (cf. Eph. 1:21) and "dominions" and "authorities" (Col. 1:16). Angels are seemingly "greater in might and power" than rebellious human beings (2 Peter 2:11; cf. Matt. 28:2). At least for the time of their earthly existence, human beings are

---

[7]Another possibility is that "angel" in Matt. 18:10 and in Acts 12:15 (where the disciples think that Peter's "angel" is knocking at the gate) means not an angelic being but the "spirit" of the person who has died: for a defense of this view see B. B. Warfield, "The Angels of Christ's 'Little Ones,'" in *Selected Shorter Writings,* ed. John E. Meeter (Nutley, N.J.: Presbyterian and Reformed, 1970), 1:253–66; also D. A. Carson, "Matthew," *EBC,* 8:400–401.

The problem with this interpretation is that not one clear example has been found where the word *angel* (Gk. *angelos*) means "spirit of a person who has died." Warfield (pp. 265–66), followed by Carson, quotes two supposed examples from extrabiblical Jewish literature, 1 Enoch 51:4 and 2 Baruch 51:5, 12. But these texts are not convincing: 1 Enoch 51:4 simply says, "And the faces of [all] the angels in heaven shall be lighted up with joy" (R. H. Charles, *The Apocrypha and Pseudepigrapha of the Old Testament,* 2 vols. [Oxford: Clarendon Press, 1913], 2:219), but does not say that people will become angels. 2 Baruch 51:5 states that the righteous will be transformed "into the splendor of angels" (Charles, 2:508), but this simply means that they will have brightness like the angels, not that they will become angels.

In two related passages, 2 Baruch 51:12 states that the righteous will have excellency "surpassing that in the angels," and 2 Baruch 51:10 says that "they shall be made like unto the angels" (Charles, 2:509), but these texts do not say that people will become angels, either. Moreover, since no extant Greek text is available for any of these three passages (1 Enoch is an Ethiopic text with some Greek fragments and 2 Baruch is a Syriac text), they are not useful for determining the meaning of the Greek word *angelos.*

Warfield also cites *Acts of Paul and Thecla,* ed. Tischendorf, p. 42, para. 5, ad finem, as saying, "Blessed are they that fear God, for they shall become angels of God," but the text dates from the late second century A.D. (*ODCC,* p. 1049) and is an unreliable source of information about what the early church believed or what the New Testament teaches.

[8]We should note that this statement of Jesus is given in answer to the Sadducees' question about a woman who had been married seven times, and that Jesus said that their question showed lack of knowledge both of Scripture and of "the power of God" (Matt. 22:29). Jesus' answer, therefore, should comfort us and not trouble us: we should contemplate heaven not with sorrow at the anticipation of diminished interpersonal relationships, but with joy at the prospect of enriched relationships. (See chapter 20, pp. 413–14, for a discussion of the "sons of God" in Gen. 6:2, 4.)

made "lower than the angels" (Heb. 2:7). Though the power of angels is great, it is certainly not infinite, but it is used to battle against the evil demonic powers under the control of Satan (Dan. 10:13; Rev. 12:7–8; 20:1–3).[9] Nonetheless, when the Lord returns, we will be raised to a position higher than that of angels (1 Cor. 6:3; see section C.1, below).

**11. Who Is the Angel of the Lord?** Several passages of Scripture, especially in the Old Testament, speak of the angel of the Lord in a way that suggests that he is God himself taking on a human form to appear briefly to various people in the Old Testament.

In some passages "*the* angel of the LORD" (not "*an* angel of the LORD") is spoken of as the Lord himself. So "the angel of the LORD" who found Hagar in the wilderness promises her, "I will so greatly multiply your descendants that they cannot be numbered for multitude" (Gen. 16:10), and Hagar responds by calling "the name of *the LORD who spoke to her,* 'You are a God of seeing'" (Gen. 16:13). Similarly, when Abraham is about to sacrifice his son Isaac, "the angel of the LORD" calls to him from heaven and says, "Now I know that you fear God, seeing you have not withheld your son, your only son, *from me*" (Gen. 22:12). When "the angel of God" appeared to Jacob in a dream, he said, "I am the God of Bethel, where you anointed a pillar and made a vow to me" (Gen. 31:11, 13). Again, when "the angel of the LORD" appeared to Moses in a flame of fire out of the midst of a bush, he then said, "*I am the God of your father,* the God of Abraham, the God of Isaac, and the God of Jacob" (Ex. 3:2, 6). These are clear instances of the angel of the Lord or the angel of God appearing as God himself, perhaps more specifically as God the Son taking on a human body for a short time in order to appear to human beings.

At other times the angel of the Lord seems to be distinguished from God (see 2 Sam. 24:16; Ps. 34:7; Zech. 1:11–13), and passages that mention "*an* angel of the Lord" (e.g., Luke 1:11) usually indicate an angel sent by God.

## B. When Were Angels Created?

All the angels must have been created before the seventh day of creation, for we read, "Thus the heavens and the earth were finished, and all the host of them" (Gen. 2:1, understanding "host" to be the heavenly creatures that inhabit God's universe). Even more explicit than this is the statement, "In six days the LORD made heaven and earth, the sea, *and all that is in them,* and rested the seventh day" (Ex. 20:11). Therefore all the angels were created at least by the sixth day of creation.

But can we be any more specific? There may be a hint at the creation of angelic beings on the first day of creation when we read that "in the beginning God created the heavens and the earth" (Gen. 1:1), and then immediately after we read that "the *earth* was without form and void" (Gen. 1:2), but with no mention of the heavens in this second verse. This may suggest that the uninhabitable state of

---

[9]Whether the angels who sinned lost some of their power when they rebelled against God and became demons, or whether their power is still the same as it was when they were angels, Scripture does not tell us.

the earth is contrasted with the heavens where, perhaps, God had already created angelic beings and assigned them various roles and orders. This idea is made more plausible when we read that "the morning stars sang together, and all the sons of God shouted for joy" at the time when God laid the "cornerstone" of the earth and sunk its "bases" in the process of forming or founding it (Job 38:6–7). If the angels ("the sons of God") shouted for joy when God was making the earth inhabitable, this could imply that God created the angelic beings early on the first day.

However, since we have only hints in Scripture, we must remain content with the fact that God has not given us much information about the time of the creation of the angels. Further speculation, apart from clear scriptural data, would seem to be useless. "The secret things belong to the LORD our God; but the things that are revealed belong to us and to our children for ever, that we may do all the words of this law" (Deut. 29:29).

Some time before Satan tempted Eve in the garden (Gen. 3:1), a number of angels sinned and rebelled against God (2 Peter 2:4; Jude 6). This event occurred apparently after the sixth day of creation when "God saw everything that he had made, and behold, it was very good" (Gen. 1:31), but beyond this, Scripture gives us no further information.

## C. The Place of Angels in God's Purpose

**1. Angels Show the Greatness of God's Love and Plan for Us.** Human beings and angels (using the term broadly) are the only moral, highly intelligent creatures that God has made. Therefore we can understand much about God's plan and love for us when we compare ourselves with angels.

The first distinction to be noted is that angels are never said to be made "in the image of God," while human beings are several times said to be in God's image (Gen. 1:26–27; 9:6). Since being in the image of God means to be like God,[10] it seems fair to conclude that we are more like God even than the angels are.

This is supported by the fact that God will someday give us authority over angels, to judge them: "Do you not know that *we are to judge angels?*" (1 Cor. 6:3). Though we are "for a little while lower than the angels" (Heb. 2:7), when our salvation is complete we will be exalted above angels and rule over them. In fact, even now, angels already serve us: "Are they not all ministering spirits sent forth *to serve,* for the sake of those who are to obtain salvation?" (Heb. 1:14).

The ability of human beings to bear children like themselves (Adam "became the father of a son in his own likeness, after his image," Gen. 5:3) is another element of our superiority to angels, who apparently cannot bear children (cf. Matt. 22:30; Luke 20:34–36).

Angels also demonstrate the greatness of God's love for us in that, though many angels sinned, none were saved. Peter tells us that "*God did not spare the angels when they sinned,* but cast them into hell and committed them to pits of nether gloom to be kept until the judgment" (2 Peter 2:4). Jude says that "the angels that did not keep their own position but left their proper dwelling have been kept by him in eternal chains in the nether gloom until the judgment of the great day"

---

[10]See chapter 21, pp. 442–44.

(Jude 6). And we read in Hebrews, "For surely it is not with angels that he is concerned but with the descendants of Abraham" (Heb. 2:16).

We see, therefore, that God created two groups of intelligent, moral creatures. Among the angels, many sinned, but God decided to redeem none of them. This was perfectly just for God to do, and no angel can ever complain that he has been treated unfairly by God.

Now among the other group of moral creatures, human beings, we also find that a large number (indeed, all) have sinned and turned away from God. As with the angels that sinned: God could have let all of us go on our self-chosen path toward eternal condemnation. Had God decided to save no one out of the entire sinful human race, he would be perfectly just to do so, and no one could complain of unfairness on his part.

But God decided to do much more than merely meet the demands of justice. He decided to save some sinful human beings. If he had decided to save only five human beings out of the entire human race, that would have been much more than justice: it would have been a great demonstration of mercy and grace. If he had decided to save only one hundred out of the whole human race, it would have been an amazing demonstration of mercy and love. But God in fact has chosen to do much more than that. He has decided to redeem out of sinful mankind a great multitude, whom no man can number, "from every tribe and tongue and people and nation" (Rev. 5:9). This is incalculable mercy and love, far beyond our comprehension. It is all undeserved favor: it is all of grace. The striking contrast with the fate of angels brings this truth home to us.

The fact that we have been saved from a life of rebellion against God means that we are able to sing songs that angels will never be able to sing for all eternity.

> Redeemed—how I love to proclaim it!
> Redeemed by the blood of the lamb;
> Redeemed through his infinite mercy—
> His child, and forever, I am.

This song, and all the great songs proclaiming our redemption in Christ, are ours alone to sing. Unfallen angels see us sing these songs and they rejoice (Luke 15:10), but they will never be able to make them their own.

**2. Angels Remind Us That the Unseen World Is Real.** Just as the Sadducees in Jesus' day said that "there is no resurrection, nor angel, nor spirit" (Acts 23:8), so many in our day deny the reality of anything they cannot see. But the biblical teaching on the existence of angels is a constant reminder to us that there is an unseen world that is very real. It was only when the Lord opened the eyes of Elisha's servant to the reality of this invisible world that the servant saw that "the mountain was full of horses and chariots of fire round about Elisha" (2 Kings 6:17; this was a great angelic army sent to Dothan to protect Elisha from the Syrians). The psalmist, too, shows an awareness of the unseen world when he encourages the angels, "Praise him, all his angels, praise him, all his host!" (Ps. 148:2). The author of Hebrews reminds us that when we worship we come into the heavenly Jerusalem to gather with "innumerable angels in festal gathering" (Heb. 12:22), whom we do not see, but whose presence should fill us with both awe and joy. An unbelieving world may dismiss talk of angels as mere superstition, but Scripture offers it as insight into the state of affairs as they really are.

**3. Angels Are Examples for Us.** In both their obedience and their worship angels provide helpful examples for us to imitate. Jesus teaches us to pray, "Your will be done, on earth as it is in heaven" (Matt. 6:10). In heaven God's will is done by angels, immediately, joyfully, and without question. We are to pray daily that our obedience and the obedience of others would be like that of the angels in heaven. Their delight is to be God's humble servants, each faithfully and joyfully performing their assigned tasks, whether great or small. Our desire and prayer should be that we ourselves and all others on earth would do the same.

Angels also serve as our examples in their worship of God. The seraphim before God's throne see God in his holiness and continue to cry out, "Holy, holy, holy is the LORD of hosts; the whole earth is full of his glory" (Isa. 6:3). And John sees around God's throne a great angelic army, "numbering myriads of myriads and thousands of thousands, saying with a loud voice, 'Worthy is the Lamb who was slain, to receive power and wealth and wisdom and might and honor and glory and blessing!'" (Rev. 5:11–12). As angels find it their highest joy to praise God continuously, should we not also delight each day to sing God's praise, counting this as the highest and most worthy use of our time and our greatest joy?

**4. Angels Carry Out Some of God's Plans.** Scripture sees angels as God's servants who carry out some of his plans in the earth. They bring God's messages to people (Luke 1:11–19; Acts 8:26; 10:3–8, 22; 27:23–24). They carry out some of God's judgments, bringing a plague upon Israel (2 Sam. 24:16–17), smiting the leaders of the Assyrian army (2 Chron. 32:21), striking King Herod dead because he did not give God glory (Acts 12:23), or pouring out bowls of God's wrath on the earth (Rev. 16:1). When Christ returns, angels will come with him as a great army accompanying their King and Lord (Matt. 16:27; Luke 9:26; 2 Thess. 1:7).

Angels also patrol the earth as God's representatives (Zech. 1:10–11) and carry out war against demonic forces (Dan. 10:13; Rev. 12:7–8). John in his vision saw an angel coming down from heaven, and he records that the angel "seized the dragon, that ancient serpent, who is the Devil and Satan, and bound him for a thousand years, and threw him into the pit . . ." (Rev. 20:1–3). When Christ returns, an archangel will proclaim his coming (1 Thess. 4:16; cf. Rev. 18:1–2, 21; 19:17–18; et al.).

**5. Angels Directly Glorify God.** Angels also serve another function: they minister directly to God by glorifying him. Thus, in addition to human beings, there are other intelligent, moral creatures who glorify God in the universe.

Angels glorify God for who he is in himself, for his excellence.

> Bless the LORD, O you his angels,
>> you mighty ones who do his word,
>> hearkening to the voice of his word!
>>> (Ps. 103:20; cf. 148:2)

The seraphim continually praise God for his holiness (Isa. 6:2–3), as do the four living creatures (Rev. 4:8).

Angels also glorify God for his great plan of salvation as they see it unfold. When Christ was born in Bethlehem, a multitude of angels praised God and said, "Glory to God in the highest, and on earth peace among men with whom he is pleased!" (Luke 2:14; cf. Heb. 1:6). Jesus tells us, "There is joy before the angels of God over one sinner who repents" (Luke 15:10), indicating that angels rejoice every time someone turns from his or her sins and trusts in Christ as Savior.

When Paul proclaims the gospel so that people from diverse racial backgrounds, both Jews and Greeks, are brought into the church, he sees God's wise plan for the church as being displayed before the angels (and demons), for he says that he was called to preach to the Gentiles "that through the church the manifold wisdom of God might now be *made known to the principalities and powers in the heavenly places*" (Eph. 3:10). And Peter tells us that "angels long to look" (1 Peter 1:12) into the glories of the plan of salvation as it works out in the lives of individual believers each day.[11] Paul also notes that Christ was "seen by angels" (1 Tim. 3:16), suggesting that they glorified God for Christ's life of obedience. Moreover, the fact that women were to have clothing that appropriately signaled that they were women, "because of the angels" (1 Cor. 11:10), when the church assembled for worship, indicates that angels witness the lives of Christians and glorify God for our worship and obedience. Indeed, Paul reminds Timothy, when he wants to emphasize the seriousness of a command, that our actions are carried out in the presence of angelic witnesses: "In the presence of God and of Christ Jesus *and of the elect angels* I charge you to keep these rules without favor, doing nothing from partiality" (1 Tim. 5:21; cf. 1 Cor. 4:9). If Timothy follows Paul's instructions, angels will witness his obedience and glorify God; if he neglects to obey, angels will also see and be grieved.

### D. Our Relationship to Angels

**1. We Should Be Aware of Angels in Our Daily Lives.** Scripture makes it clear that God wants us to be aware of the existence of angels and of the nature of their activity. We should not therefore assume that its teaching about angels has nothing whatsoever to do with our lives today. Rather, there are several ways in which our Christian lives will be enriched by an awareness of the existence and ministry of angels in the world even today.

When we come before God in worship, we are joining not only with the great company of believers who have died and come into God's presence in heaven, "the spirits of just men made perfect," but also with a great throng of angels, "innumerable angels in festal gathering" (Heb. 12:22–23). Though we do not ordinarily see or hear evidence of this heavenly worship, it certainly enriches our sense of reverence and joy in God's presence if we appreciate the fact that angels join us in the worship of God.

Moreover, we should be aware that angels are watching our obedience or

---

[11]The present tense verb *epithymousin*, "long," gives the sense "are continually longing, even at the present time" to look into these things. This longing includes a holy curiosity to watch and delight in the glories of Christ's kingdom as they find ever fuller realization in the lives of individual Christians throughout the history of the church. (See discussion in Wayne Grudem, *1 Peter*, p. 73.)

disobedience to God through the day. Even if we think our sins are done in secret and bring grief to no one else, we should be sobered by the thought that perhaps even hundreds of angels witness our disobedience and are grieved.[12] On the other hand, when we are discouraged and think that our faithful obedience to God is witnessed by no one and is an encouragement to no one, we can be comforted by the realization that perhaps hundreds of angels witness our lonely struggle, daily "longing to look" at the way Christ's great salvation finds expression in our lives.

As if to make the reality of angelic observation of our service to God more vivid, the author of Hebrews suggests that angels can sometimes take human form, apparently to make "inspection visits," something like the newspaper's restaurant critic who disguises himself and visits a new restaurant. We read, "Do not neglect to show hospitality to strangers, for thereby some have entertained angels unawares" (Heb. 13:2; cf. Gen. 18:2–5; 19:1–3). This should make us eager to minister to the needs of others whom we do not know, all the while wondering if someday we will reach heaven and meet the angel whom we helped when he appeared temporarily as a human being in distress here on earth.

When we are suddenly delivered from a danger or distress, we might suspect that angels have been sent by God to help us, and we should be thankful. An angel shut the mouths of the lions so they would not hurt Daniel (Dan. 6:22), delivered the apostles from prison (Acts 5:19–20), later delivered Peter from prison (Acts 12:7–11), and ministered to Jesus in the wilderness at a time of great weakness, immediately after his temptations had ended (Matt. 4:11).[13]

When a car suddenly swerves from hitting us, when we suddenly find footing to keep from being swept along in a raging river, when we walk unscathed in a dangerous neighborhood, should we not suspect that God has sent his angels to protect us? Does not Scripture promise, "For he will give his angels charge of you to guard you in all your ways. On their hands they will bear you up, lest you dash your foot against a stone" (Ps. 91:11–12)? Should we not therefore thank God for sending angels to protect us at such times? It seems right that we should do so.

## 2. Cautions Regarding Our Relationship to Angels.

**a. Beware of Receiving False Doctrine From Angels:** The Bible warns against receiving false doctrine from supposed angels: "But even if we, or an angel from heaven, should preach to you a gospel contrary to that which we preached to you, let him be accursed" (Gal. 1:8). Paul makes this warning because he knows that there is a possibility of deception. He says, "Even Satan disguises himself as an angel of light" (2 Cor. 11:14). Similarly, the lying prophet who deceived the man of God in 1 Kings 13 claimed, "*An angel spoke to me* by the word of the LORD, saying, 'Bring him back with you into your house that he may eat bread and drink water'" (1 Kings 13:18). Yet the text of Scripture immediately adds in the same verse, "But he lied to him."

---

[12]This is not to deny that the primary deterrent against sinning must be fear of displeasing God himself; it is just to say that as the presence of other human beings serves as an additional deterrent, so the knowledge of the presence of angels should also serve as a deterrent to us.

[13]Note also the report in Luke 22:43 that when Jesus was praying in the Garden of Gethsemane, "there appeared to him an angel from heaven, strengthening him." This text has substantial ancient attestation.

These are all instances of *false* doctrine or guidance being conveyed by angels. It is interesting that these examples show the clear possibility of satanic deception tempting us to disobey the clear teachings of Scripture or the clear commands of God (cf. 1 Kings 13:9). These warnings should keep any Christians from being fooled by the claims of Mormons, for example, that an angel (Moroni) spoke to Joseph Smith and revealed to him the basis of the Mormon religion. Such "revelation" is contrary to the teachings of Scripture at many points (with respect to such doctrines as the Trinity, the person of Christ, justification by faith alone, and many others), and Christians should be warned against accepting these claims.[14] The closing of the canon of Scripture (see chapter 3) should also warn us that no further revelation of doctrine is to be given by God today, and any claims to have received additional revelation of doctrine from angels today should be immediately rejected as false.

**b. Do Not Worship Angels, Pray to Them, or Seek Them:** "Worship of angels" (Col. 2:18) was one of the false doctrines being taught at Colossae. Moreover, an angel speaking to John in the book of Revelation warns John not to worship him: "You must not do that! I am a fellow servant with you and your brethren who hold the testimony of Jesus. Worship God" (Rev. 19:10).

Nor should we pray to angels. We are to pray only to God, who alone is omnipotent and thus able to answer prayer and who alone is omniscient and therefore able to hear the prayers of all his people at once. By virtue of omnipotence and omniscience, God the Son and God the Holy Spirit are also worthy of being prayed to, but this is not true of any other being. Paul warns us against thinking that any other "mediator" can come between us and God, "for there is one God, and there is *one mediator* between God and men, the man Christ Jesus" (1 Tim. 2:5). If we were to pray to angels, it would be implicitly attributing to them a status equal to God, which we must not do. There is no example in Scripture of anyone praying to any specific angel or asking angels for help.

Moreover, Scripture gives us no warrant to seek for appearances of angels to us. They manifest themselves unsought. To seek such appearances would seem to indicate an unhealthy curiosity or a desire for some kind of spectacular event rather than a love for God and devotion to him and his work. Though angels did appear to people at various times in Scripture, the people apparently never sought those appearances. Our role is rather to talk to the Lord, who is himself the commander of all angelic forces. However, it would not seem wrong to ask God to fulfill his promise in Psalm 91:11 to send angels to protect us in times of need.

**c. Do Angels Appear to People Today?** In the earliest period of the church's history angels were active. An angel told Philip to travel south on a road that goes from Jerusalem to Gaza (Acts 8:26), instructed Cornelius to send a messenger to get Peter to come from Joppa (Acts 10:3–6), urged Peter to get up and walk out of the prison (Acts 12:6–11), and promised Paul that no one on his ship would

---

[14]Of course, there were times in Scripture when doctrinal truth came through angels (Luke 1:13–20, 30–37; 2:10–14; Acts 1:11; Heb. 2:2). The warning passages mentioned above forbid receiving doctrine contrary to Scripture from angels.

be lost and that he himself would stand before Caesar (Acts 27:23–24). Moreover, the author of Hebrews encourages his readers, none of whom are apostles or even first-generation believers associated with the apostles (see Heb. 2:3), that *they* should continue to show hospitality to strangers, apparently with the expectation that they too might sometime entertain angels without realizing it (Heb. 13:2).

There seems, therefore, no compelling reason to rule out the possibility of angelic appearances today. Some would dispute this on the grounds that the sufficiency of Scripture (see chapter 8) and the closing of its canon (see chapter 3) rule out the possibility of angelic manifestations now.[15] They would say that we are not to expect God to communicate to us through angels. However, this conclusion does not follow. Though angels would not add to the doctrinal and moral content of Scripture, God *could* communicate information to us through angels as he also does through prophecy[16] or through ordinary communication from other persons, or through our observation of the world. If God can send another human being to warn us of danger or encourage us when we are downcast, there seems no inherent reason why he could not occasionally send an angel to do this as well.

However, we should use *extreme caution* in receiving guidance from an angel should such an unusual event happen. (It is perhaps noteworthy that very few instances of such events are recorded today, and many of these involve the communication of antiscriptural doctrine, indicating that they are actually demonic appearances.) The fact that demons can appear as angels of light (see 2 Cor. 11:14) should warn us that the appearance of any angel-like creature does not guarantee that this being speaks truthfully: *Scripture* is our guide, and no angelic creature can give authoritative teaching that is contrary to Scripture (see Gal. 1:8).

An angelic appearance today would be unusual. If one should (apparently) occur, we should evaluate it with caution. But there is no convincing reason for saying that such an event absolutely could not happen, particularly in a time of extreme danger or intense conflict with the forces of evil.

## QUESTIONS FOR PERSONAL APPLICATION

1. How might this chapter affect how you think about angels from now on? What difference would it make in your attitude in worship if you consciously thought about being in the presence of angels when you were singing praises to God?

2. Do you think there are angels watching you right now? What attitude or attitudes do you think they have as they watch you? Have you ever experienced a remarkably elevated sense of joy just after praying with someone to receive Christ as personal Savior? Do you think one aspect contributing to that joy might be that angels are also rejoicing with you because a sinner has repented (Luke 15:10)?

[15]See the discussion of the cessation of some spiritual gifts in chapter 52, below.
[16]See chapter 53, pp. 1049–61.

3. Have you had a remarkable rescue from physical or other kinds of danger and wondered if angels were involved in helping you at the time?

4. How can the example of angels who joyfully and faithfully perform their assigned tasks, whether great or small, be of help to you in the responsibilities that you face today, whether at work or at home or in the church?

5. How do you think you will feel when God asks you to judge angels (1 Cor. 6:3)? Explain what that fact tells you about the greatness of your humanity as created in the image of God.

## SPECIAL TERMS

| | |
|---|---|
| angel | Michael |
| angel of the Lord | principalities and powers |
| archangel | seraphim |
| cherubim | sons of God |
| living creature | watchers |

## BIBLIOGRAPHY

(For an explanation of this bibliography see the note on the bibliography to chapter 1, p. 38. Complete bibliographical data may be found on pp. 1223–29.)

### Sections in Evangelical Systematic Theologies

1. Anglican (Episcopalian)
    1882–92    Litton, 125–29
2. Arminian (Wesleyan or Methodist)
    1892–94    Miley, 2:490–96
    1940    Wiley, 1:472–76
    1983    Carter, 2:1047–69
3. Baptist
    1767    Gill, 1:375–84, 434–35
    1887    Boyce, 174–81
    1907    Strong, 443–64
    1917    Mullins, 276–80
    1976–83    Henry, 6:229–50
    1983–85    Erickson, 433–51
4. Dispensational
    1947    Chafer, 2:3–32
    1949    Thiessen, 133–50
    1986    Ryrie, 121–34
5. Lutheran
    1917–24    Pieper, 1:498–508
    1934    Mueller, 196–202

6. Reformed (or Presbyterian)
> 1559    Calvin, 1:163–72 (1.14.3–12)
> 1724–58  Edwards, 2:604–7, 612–17
> 1861    Heppe, 201–19
> 1871–73  Hodge, 1:637–43
> 1878    Dabney, 264–75
> 1938    Berkhof, 141–48
> 1962    Buswell, 1:130–34

7. Renewal (or charismatic/Pentecostal)
> 1988–92  Williams, 1:169–96

## Sections in Representative Roman Catholic Systematic Theologies

1. Roman Catholic: Traditional
> 1955    Ott, 114–21

2. Roman Catholic: Post-Vatican II
> 1980    McBrien (no explicit treatment)

### Other Works

Bromiley, G. W. "Angel." In *EDT*, pp. 46–47.

Dickason, C. Fred. *Angels, Elect and Evil*. Chicago: Moody, 1975.

Graham, Billy. *Angels: God's Secret Agents*. Revised and expanded edition. Waco, Tex.: Word, 1986.

Joppie, A. S. *The Ministry of Angels*. Grand Rapids: Baker, 1953.

McComiskey, T. E. "Angel of the Lord." In *EDT*, pp. 47–48.

### SCRIPTURE MEMORY PASSAGE

**Revelation 5:11–12:** *Then I looked, and I heard around the throne and the living creatures and the elders the voice of many angels, numbering myriads of myriads and thousands of thousands, saying with a loud voice, "Worthy is the Lamb who was slain, to receive power and wealth and wisdom and might and honor and glory and blessing!"*

### HYMN

"Angels From the Realms of Glory"

Angels, from the realms of glory,
> wing your flight o'er all the earth
Ye who sang creation's story,
> now proclaim Messiah's birth:
Come and worship, come and worship,
> worship Christ the newborn King.

Shepherds, in the fields abiding,
> watching o'er your flocks by night;

God with man is now residing,
    yonder shines the infant light:
Come and worship, come and worship,
    worship Christ the newborn King.

Sages, leave your contemplations,
    brighter visions beam afar;
Seek the great desire of nations;
    ye have seen his natal star:
Come and worship, come and worship,
    worship Christ the newborn King.

Saints, before the altar bending,
    watching long in hope and fear,
Suddenly the Lord, descending,
    in his temple shall appear:
Come and worship, come and worship,
    worship Christ the newborn King.

All creation, join in praising
    God the Father, Spirit, Son;
Evermore your voices raising
    to th' eternal Three in One:
Come and worship, come and worship,
    worship Christ the newborn King.

AUTHOR: JAMES MONTGOMERY, 1816

# Chapter 20

# Satan and Demons

*How should Christians think of Satan and demons today? Spiritual warfare.*

## EXPLANATION AND SCRIPTURAL BASIS

The previous chapter leads naturally to a consideration of Satan and demons, since they are evil angels who once were like the good angels but who sinned and lost their privilege of serving God. Like angels, they are also created, spiritual beings with moral judgment and high intelligence but without physical bodies. We may define demons as follows: *Demons are evil angels who sinned against God and who now continually work evil in the world.*

### A. The Origin of Demons

When God created the world, he "saw everything that he had made, and behold, it was very good" (Gen. 1:31). This means that even the angelic world that God had created did not have evil angels or demons in it at that time. But by the time of Genesis 3, we find that Satan, in the form of a serpent, was tempting Eve to sin (Gen. 3:1–5). Therefore, sometime between the events of Genesis 1:31 and Genesis 3:1, there must have been a rebellion in the angelic world with many angels turning against God and becoming evil.

The New Testament speaks of this in two places. Peter tells us, "God did not spare the angels when they sinned, but cast them into hell and committed them to pits of nether gloom to be kept until the judgment" (2 Peter 2:4).[1] Jude also says that "the angels that did not keep their own position but left their proper dwelling have been kept by him in eternal chains in the nether gloom until the judgment of the great day" (Jude 6). Once again the emphasis is on the fact that they are removed from the glory of God's presence and their activity is restricted (metaphorically, they are in "eternal chains"), but the text does not imply either that the influence of demons has been removed from the world or that some demons are kept in a place of punishment apart from the world while others are

---

[1] This does not mean that these sinful angels have no current influence on the world, for in v. 9 Peter says that the Lord also knows how "to keep the unrighteous under punishment until the day of judgment," here referring to sinful human beings who were obviously still having influence in the world and even troubling Peter's readers. 2 Peter 2:4 simply means that the wicked angels have been removed from the presence of God and are kept under some kind of restraining influence until the final judgment, but this does not rule out their continued activity in the world meanwhile.

able to influence it.[2] Rather, both 2 Peter and Jude tell us that some angels rebelled against God and became hostile opponents to his Word. Their sin seems to have been pride, a refusal to accept their assigned place, for they "did not keep their own position but left their proper dwelling" (Jude 6).

It is also possible that there is a reference to the fall of Satan, the prince of demons, in Isaiah 14. As Isaiah is describing the judgment of God on the king of Babylon (an earthly, human king), he then comes to a section where he begins to use language that seems too strong to refer to any merely human king:

> How you are fallen from heaven,
> O Day Star,[3] son of Dawn!
> How you are cut down to the ground,
>    you who laid the nations low!
> You said in your heart,
> *"I will ascend to heaven;*
> *above the stars of God*
> *I will set my throne on high;*
> I will sit on the mount of assembly
>    in the far north;
> I will ascend above the heights of the clouds,
> *I will make myself like the Most High."*
> But you are brought down to Sheol,
>    to the depths of the Pit. (Isa. 14:12–15)

This language of ascending to heaven and setting his throne on high and saying, "I will make myself like the Most High" strongly suggests a rebellion by an angelic creature of great power and dignity. It would not be uncommon for Hebrew prophetic speech to pass from descriptions of human events to descriptions of heavenly events that are parallel to them and that the earthly events picture in a limited way.[4] If this is so, then the sin of Satan is described as one of pride and attempting to be equal to God in status and authority.

However, it is unlikely that Genesis 6:2–4 refers to the fall of demons. In these verses, we are told that "the sons of God saw that the daughters of men were fair; and they took to wife such of them as they chose. . . . The Nephilim were on the earth in those days, and also afterward, when the sons of God came in to the daughters of men, and they bore children to them." Although some have thought that the "sons of God" in this passage are angels who sinned by marrying human women, this is not a likely interpretation, for the following reasons:[5]

---

[2] 2 Peter 2:4 does not say, "God did not spare some of the angels when they sinned," or, "God cast some of the sinning angels into hell," but it speaks generally of "the angels" when they sinned, implying all of them who sinned. Similarly, Jude 6 speaks of "the angels that did not keep their own position," implying all who sinned. Therefore, these verses must say something that is true of all demons. Their current home, their dwelling place, is "hell" and "pits of nether gloom," although they can range from there to influence people in the world.

[3] The kjv translates "Day Star" as "Lucifer," a name meaning "bearer of light." The name Lucifer does not appear elsewhere in the kjv and does not appear at all in more modern translations of the Bible.

[4] See, for example, Ps. 45, which moves from a description of an earthly king to a description of a divine Messiah.

[5] For a more detailed argument see W. Grudem, *The First Epistle of Peter*, pp. 211–13, which is summarized in the discussion here. Later Jewish interpreters of these verses were about equally divided

Angels are nonmaterial beings and according to Jesus do not marry (Matt. 22:30), facts that cast doubt on the idea that "the sons of God" are angels who married human wives. Moreover, nothing in the *context* of Genesis 6 itself indicates that the "sons of God" should be understood as angels (this makes this passage unlike Job 1–2, for example, where the context of a heavenly council makes it clear to the reader that angels are being referred to). It is far more likely that the phrase "sons of God" here (as in Deut. 14:1) refers to people belonging to God and, like God, walking in righteousness (note Gen. 4:26 as an introduction to Gen. 5, marking the beginning of Seth's line at the same time as "men began to call upon the name of the LORD"). In fact, there is an emphasis on sonship as including likeness to one's father in Genesis 5:3. Moreover, the text traces the descendants from God through Adam and Seth to many "sons" in all of chapter 5. The larger purpose of the narrative seems to be to trace the parallel development of the godly (ultimately messianic) line of Seth and the ungodly descendants of the rest of mankind. Therefore, the "sons of God" in Genesis 6:2 are men who are righteous in their imitation of the character of their heavenly Father, and the "daughters of men" are the ungodly wives whom they marry.

## B. Satan as Head of the Demons

"Satan" is the personal name of the head of the demons. This name is mentioned in Job 1:6, where "the sons of God came to present themselves before the LORD, and *Satan* also came among them" (see also Job 1:7–2:7). Here he appears as the enemy of the Lord who brings severe temptations against Job. Similarly, near the end of David's life, "Satan stood up against Israel, and incited David to number Israel" (1 Chron. 21:1). Moreover, Zechariah saw a vision of "Joshua the high priest standing before the angel of the LORD, and Satan standing at his right hand to accuse him" (Zech. 3:1). The name "Satan" is a Hebrew word (*sātān*) that means "adversary."[6] The New Testament also uses the name "Satan," simply taking it over from the Old Testament. So Jesus, in his temptation in the wilderness, speaks to Satan directly saying, "Begone, Satan!" (Matt. 4:10), or "I saw Satan fall like lightning from heaven" (Luke 10:18).

The Bible uses other names for Satan as well. He is called "the devil"[7] (only in the New Testament: Matt. 4:1; 13:39; 25:41; Rev. 12:9; 20:2; et al.), "the serpent" (Gen. 3:1, 14; 2 Cor. 11:3; Rev. 12:9; 20:2), "Be-elzebul" (Matt. 10:25; 12:24, 27; Luke 11:15), "the ruler of this world" (John 12:31; 14:30; 16:11),[8] "the prince of the power of the air" (Eph. 2:2), or "the evil one" (Matt. 13:19; 1 John 2:13). When Jesus says to Peter, "Get behind me, Satan! You are a

---

between those who thought the "sons of God" were angels and those who thought they were human beings.

[6]BDB, p. 966.

[7]The word *devil* is an English translation of Greek *diabolos*, which means "slanderer" (BAGD, p. 182). In fact, the English word *devil* is ultimately derived from this same Greek word, but the sound of the word changed considerably as the word passed from Greek to Latin to Old English to modern English.

[8]John frequently uses "the world" or "this world" to refer to the present evil world system in opposition to God: John 7:7; 8:23; 12:31; 14:17, 30; 15:18, 19; 16:11; 17:14. Scripture does not teach that Satan rules over the entire world, but that he is ruler over the system of sinful opposition to God. Compare Paul's phrase "the god of this world" (2 Cor. 4:4).

hindrance to me; for you are not on the side of God, but of men" (Matt. 16:23), he recognizes that Peter's attempt to keep him from suffering and dying on the cross is really an attempt to keep him from obedience to the Father's plan. Jesus realizes that opposition ultimately comes not from Peter, but from Satan himself.

## C. The Activity of Satan and Demons

**1. Satan Was the Originator of Sin.** Satan sinned before any human beings did so, as is evident from the fact that he (in the form of the serpent) tempted Eve (Gen. 3:1–6; 2 Cor. 11:3). The New Testament also informs us that Satan was a "murderer from the beginning" and is "a liar and the father of lies" (John 8:44). It also says that "the devil has sinned *from the beginning*" (1 John 3:8). In both of these texts, the phrase "from the beginning" does not imply that Satan was evil from the time God began to create the world ("from the beginning of the world") or from the beginning of his existence ("from the beginning of his life"), but rather from the "beginning" parts of the history of the world (Genesis 3 and even before). The devil's characteristic has been to originate sin and tempt others to sin.

**2. Demons Oppose and Try to Destroy Every Work of God.** Just as Satan tempted Eve to sin against God (Gen. 3:1–6), so he tried to get Jesus to sin and thus fail in his mission as Messiah (Matt. 4:1–11). The tactics of Satan and his demons are to use lies (John 8:44), deception (Rev. 12:9), murder (Ps. 106:37; John 8:44), and every other kind of destructive activity to attempt to cause people to turn away from God and destroy themselves.[9] Demons will try every tactic to blind people to the gospel (2 Cor. 4:4) and keep them in bondage to things that hinder them from coming to God (Gal. 4:8). They will also try to use temptation, doubt, guilt, fear, confusion, sickness, envy, pride, slander, or any other means possible to hinder a Christian's witness and usefulness.

**3. Yet Demons Are Limited by God's Control and Have Limited Power.** The story of Job makes it clear that Satan could only do what God gave him permission to do and nothing more (Job 1:12; 2:6). Demons are kept in "eternal chains" (Jude 6) and can be successfully resisted by Christians through the authority that Christ gives them (James 4:7).

Moreover, the power of demons is limited. After rebelling against God they do not have the power they had when they were angels, for sin is a weakening and destructive influence. The power of demons, though significant, is therefore probably less than the power of angels.

In the area of knowledge, *we should not think that demons can know the future or that they can read our minds or know our thoughts.* In many places in the Old Testament, the Lord shows himself to be the true God in distinction from the false (demonic) gods of the nations by the fact that *he alone can know the future:* "I am God, and there is none like me, declaring the end from the beginning and from ancient times things not yet done" (Isa. 46:9–10).[10]

Even angels do not know the time of Jesus' return (Mark 13:32), and there is

---

[9]Cf. John 10:10: "The thief comes only to steal and kill and destroy."

[10]See the discussion of God's knowledge of the future in chapter 11, pp. 171–72, 190.

no indication in Scripture that they or demons know anything else about the future either.

With respect to knowing our thoughts, the Bible tells us that Jesus knew people's thoughts (Matt. 9:4; 12:25; Mark 2:8; Luke 6:8; 11:17) and that God knows people's thoughts (Gen. 6:5; Ps. 139:2, 4, 23; Isa. 66:18), but there is no indication that angels or demons can know our thoughts. In fact, Daniel told King Nebuchadnezzar that no one speaking by any other power than the God of heaven could tell the king what he had dreamed:

> Daniel answered the king, "No wise men, enchanters, magicians, or astrologers can show to the king the mystery which the king has asked, but there is a God in heaven who reveals mysteries, and he has made known to King Nebuchadnezzar what will be in the latter days. Your dream and the visions of your head as you lay in bed are these. . . ." (Dan. 2:27–28)[11]

But if demons cannot read people's minds, how shall we understand contemporary reports of witch doctors, fortune-tellers, or other people evidently under demonic influence who are able to tell people accurate details of their lives which they thought no one knew, such as (for example) what food they had for breakfast, where they keep some hidden money in their house, etc.? Most of these things can be explained by realizing that demons can *observe* what goes on in the world and can probably draw some conclusions from those observations. A demon may know what I ate for breakfast simply because it saw me eat breakfast! It may know what I said in a private telephone conversation because it listened to the conversation. Christians should not be led astray if they encounter members of the occult or of other false religions who seem to demonstrate such unusual knowledge from time to time. These results of observation do not prove that demons can read our thoughts, however, and nothing in the Bible would lead us to think they have that power.

### 4. There Have Been Differing Stages of Demonic Activity in the History of Redemption.

**a. In the Old Testament:** Because in the Old Testament the word *demon* is not often used, it might at first seem that there is little indication of demonic activity. However, the people of Israel often sinned by serving false gods, and when we realize that these false "gods" were really demonic forces, we see that there is quite a bit of Old Testament material referring to demons. This identification of false gods as demons is made explicit, for example, when Moses says,

> "They stirred him [God] to jealousy with strange gods;
> with abominable practices they provoked him to anger.

---

[11]Paul also says, "For what person knows a man's thoughts except the spirit of the man which is in him?" (1 Cor. 2:11), suggesting that there is no other creature who can know a person's thoughts (although admittedly the inclusion of angelic or demonic creatures in Paul's idea is not made explicit in this context as it is in Dan. 2). See also 1 Cor. 14:24–25, where the disclosure of the "secrets" of a visitor's heart is clear evidence that God himself is present, working through the gift of prophecy. This is significant in Corinth, which was filled with demon worship in idol temples (1 Cor. 10:20)—it indicates that demons could not know the secret thoughts in a person's heart.

*They sacrificed to demons which were no gods,*
   to gods they had never known." (Deut. 32:16–17)

Moreover, in reflecting on the horrible practice of child sacrifice, which the
Israelites imitated from the pagan nations, the psalmist says,

"They mingled with the nations
   and learned to do as they did.
They served their idols,
   which became a snare to them.
They sacrificed their sons
   and their daughters *to the demons.*" (Ps. 106:35–37)

These references demonstrate that the worship offered to idols in all the nations
surrounding Israel was really worship of Satan and his demons. This is why Paul
can say of the false religions of the first-century Mediterranean world, "What
pagans sacrifice *they offer to demons* and not to God" (1 Cor. 10:20). It is thus fair
to conclude that all the nations around Israel that practiced idol worship were
engaging in the worship of demons. The battles the Israelites fought against pagan
nations were battles against nations who were controlled by demonic forces and
thus "in the power of the evil one" (cf. 1 John 5:19). They were as much spiritual
battles as physical battles: the people of Israel needed to depend on God's power
to help them in the spiritual realm as much as in the physical.

In light of this, it is significant that there is no clear instance of the casting out
of demons in the Old Testament. The nearest analogy is the case of David playing
the lyre for King Saul: "And whenever the evil spirit from God was upon Saul,
David took the lyre and played it with his hand; so Saul was refreshed, and was
well, and the evil spirit departed from him" (1 Sam. 16:23). However, Scripture
speaks of this as a recurring event ("whenever"), indicating that the evil spirit
returned after David left Saul. This was not the completely effective triumph over
evil spirits that we find in the New Testament.

Consistent with the purpose of Satan to destroy all the good works of God,
pagan worship of demonic idols was characterized by destructive practices such as
the sacrifice of children (Ps. 106:35–37), inflicting bodily harm on oneself
(1 Kings 18:28; cf. Deut. 14:1), and cult prostitution as a part of pagan worship
(Deut. 23:17; 1 Kings 14:24; Hos. 4:14).[12] Worship of demons will regularly
lead to immoral and self-destructive practices.

**b. During the Ministry of Jesus:** After hundreds of years of inability to have any
effective triumph over demonic forces,[13] it is understandable that when Jesus came

---

[12]Even today, one distinguishing mark of many non-Christian religions is that their most devoted
adherents engage in religious rituals that destroy one or several aspects of humanity, such as their
physical health, their mental or emotional stability, or their human sexuality as God intended it to
function. Such things clearly fulfill the goals of Satan to destroy everything that God has created good
(cf. 1 Tim. 4:1–3). Since Satan is "a liar and the father of lies" (John 8:44), distortion or denial of the
truth is always present in false religions as well, particularly when there is strong demonic influence.
[13]There were Jewish exorcists in the period between the Old and the New Testaments who
attempted to deal with demonic forces, but it is doubtful whether they were very effective: Acts 19:13
mentions some "itinerant Jewish exorcists" who attempted to use the name of the Lord Jesus as a new
magic formula, though they were not Christians and did not have any spiritual authority from Jesus

casting out demons with absolute authority, the people were amazed: "And they were all amazed, so that they questioned among themselves, saying, 'What is this? A new teaching! With authority he commands even the unclean spirits, and they obey him'" (Mark 1:27). Such power over demonic forces had never before been seen in the history of the world.

Jesus explains that his power over demons is a distinguishing mark on his ministry to inaugurate the reign of the kingdom of God among mankind in a new and powerful way:

> But if it is by the Spirit of God that I cast out demons, *then the kingdom of God has come upon you.* Or how can one enter a strong man's house and plunder his goods, unless he first binds the strong man? Then indeed he may plunder his house. (Matt. 12:28–29)

The "strong man" is Satan, and Jesus had bound him, probably at the time of his triumph over him in the temptation in the wilderness (Matt. 4:1–11). During his earthly ministry, Jesus had entered the strong man's "house" (the world of unbelievers who are under the bondage of Satan), and he was plundering his house, that is, freeing people from satanic bondage and bringing them into the joy of the kingdom of God. It was "by the Spirit of God" that Jesus did this; the new power of the Holy Spirit working to triumph over demons was evidence that in the ministry of Jesus "the kingdom of God has come upon you."

**c. During the New Covenant Age:** This authority over demonic powers was not limited to Jesus himself, for he gave similar authority first to the Twelve (Matt. 10:8; Mark 3:15), and then to seventy disciples. After a period of ministry, the seventy "returned with joy, saying, 'Lord, even the demons are subject to us in your name!'" (Luke 10:17). Then Jesus responded, "I saw Satan fall like lightning from heaven" (Luke 10:18), indicating again a distinctive triumph over Satan's power (once again, this was probably at the time of Jesus' victory in the temptation in the wilderness, but Scripture does not explicitly specify that time).[14]

---

himself. They met with disastrous results (vv. 15–16). Also when confronting the Pharisees, Jesus said, "If I cast out demons by Be-elzebul, by whom do your sons cast them out?" (Matt. 12:27). His statement does not mean that their sons were very successful but only that they were casting out demons, or were trying to, with some limited success. In fact, Jesus' argument works very well if they generally failed: "If my great success in casting out demons is due to Satan, then what is your sons' limited success due to? Presumably a power less than Satan; certainly not God!" The suggestion is that the Jewish exorcists' limited power was not from God but was from Satan.

Josephus does record an apparently effective example of exorcism by a Jew named Eleazar who used an incantation said to be derived from Solomon (*Antiquities* 8:45–48; cf. a rabbinic story in Numbers Rabbah 19:8; Tobit 8:2–3; and The Testament of Solomon, throughout). It is difficult to know exactly how widespread and how successful such practices were. On the one hand, God himself could have granted some degree of spiritual power over demons to the faithful remnant of Jewish believers in all ages: he certainly did protect the faithful people of Israel in general from the demonic forces of the nations around them. On the other hand, it is not impossible that Satan would work among unbelieving Jews, as well as among many other unbelieving cultures, to give some appearance of limited power to exorcists, witch doctors, etc., but always with the result of bringing people ultimately into greater spiritual bondage. What is certain is that Jesus came with much more spiritual power over demons than the people had ever seen before, and they were amazed. (An extensive discussion of Jewish exorcism is found in Emil Schürer, *The History of the Jewish People in the Age of Jesus Christ*, rev. English ed., ed. G. Vermes et al. [3 vols. in 4; Edinburgh: T. & T. Clark, 1973–87], vol. 3.1, pp. 342–61, 376, 440.)

[14]Another interpretation says that in the mission of the seventy Jesus saw the fall of Satan.

Authority over unclean spirits later extended beyond the seventy disciples to those in the early church who ministered in Jesus' name (Acts 8:7; 16:18; James 4:7; 1 Peter 5:8–9), a fact consistent with the idea that ministry in Jesus' name in the new covenant age is characterized by triumph over the powers of the devil (1 John 3:8).

**d. During the Millennium:** During the millennium, the future thousand-year reign of Christ on earth mentioned in Revelation 20,[15] the activity of Satan and demons will be further restricted. Using language that suggests a much greater restriction of Satan's activity than we see today, John describes his vision of the beginning of the millennium as follows:

> Then I saw an angel coming down from heaven, holding in his hand the key of the bottomless pit and a great chain. And he seized the dragon, that ancient serpent, who is the Devil and Satan, and *bound him for a thousand years, and threw him into the pit, and shut it and sealed it over him, that he should deceive the nations no more,* till the thousand years were ended. After that he must be loosed for a little while. (Rev. 20:1–3)

Here Satan is described as completely deprived of any ability to influence the earth. During the millennium, however, there will still be sin in the hearts of the unbelievers, which will grow until the end of the thousand years when there will be a large-scale rebellion against Christ, led by Satan who, having been "loosed from his prison" (Rev. 20:7), will come to lead that rebellion (Rev. 20:8–9). The fact that sin and rebelliousness persist in people's hearts apart from the activity of Satan, even during the thousand-year reign of Christ, shows that we cannot blame all sin in the world on Satan and his demons. Even when Satan is without influence in the world, sin will remain and be a problem in people's hearts.

**e. At the Final Judgment:** At the end of the millennium, when Satan is loosed and gathers the nations for battle, he will be decisively defeated and "thrown into the lake of fire and sulphur" and "tormented day and night for ever and ever" (Rev. 20:10). Then the judgment of Satan and his demons will be complete.

## D. Our Relationship to Demons

**1. Are Demons Active in the World Today?** Some people, influenced by a naturalistic worldview that only admits the reality of what can be seen or touched or heard, deny that demons exist today and maintain that belief in their reality reflects an obsolete worldview taught in the Bible and other ancient cultures. For example, the German New Testament scholar Rudolf Bultmann emphatically denied the existence of a supernatural world of angels and demons. He argued that these were ancient "myths" and that the New Testament message had to be "demythologized" by removing such mythological elements so that the gospel could be received by modern, scientific people. Others have thought that the contemporary equivalent to the (unacceptable) demonic activity mentioned in Scripture is the powerful and sometimes evil influence of organizations and

---

[15]See chapter 55 for a discussion of the millennium.

"structures" in our society today—evil governments and powerful corporations that control thousands of people are sometimes said to be "demonic," especially in the writings of more liberal theologians.

However, if Scripture gives us a true account of the world as it really is, then we must take seriously its portrayal of intense demonic involvement in human society. Our failure to perceive that involvement with our five senses simply tells us that we have some deficiencies in our ability to understand the world, not that demons do not exist. In fact, there is no reason to think that there is any less demonic activity in the world today than there was at the time of the New Testament. We are in the same time period in God's overall plan for history (the church age or the new covenant age), and the millennium has not yet come when Satan's influence will be removed from the earth. Much of our western secularized society is unwilling to admit the existence of demons—except perhaps in "primitive" societies—and relegates all talk of demonic activity to a category of superstition. But the unwillingness of modern society to recognize the presence of demonic activity today is, from a biblical perspective, simply due to people's blindness to the true nature of reality.

But what kind of activity do demons engage in today? Are there some distinguishing characteristics that will enable us to recognize demonic activity when it occurs?

## 2. Not All Evil and Sin Is From Satan and Demons, but Some Is.

If we think of the overall emphasis of the New Testament epistles, we realize that very little space is given to discussing demonic activity in the lives of believers or methods to resist and oppose such activity. The emphasis is on telling believers not to sin but to live lives of righteousness. For example, in 1 Corinthians, when there is a problem of "dissensions," Paul does not tell the church to rebuke a spirit of dissension, but simply urges them to "agree" and "be united in the same mind and the same judgment" (1 Cor. 1:10). When there is a problem of incest, he does not tell the Corinthians to rebuke a spirit of incest, but tells them that they ought to be outraged and that they should exercise church discipline until the offender repents (1 Cor. 5:1–5). When there is a problem of Christians going to court to sue other believers, Paul does not command them to cast out a spirit of litigation (or selfishness, or strife), but simply tells them to settle those cases within the church and to be willing to give up their own self-interest (1 Cor. 6:1–8). When there is disorder at the Lord's Supper, he does not command them to cast out a spirit of disorder or gluttony or selfishness, but simply tells them that they should "wait for one another" and that each person should "examine himself, and so eat of the bread and drink of the cup" (1 Cor. 11:33, 28). These examples could be duplicated many times in the other New Testament epistles.

With regard to preaching the gospel to unbelievers, the New Testament pattern is the same: although occasionally Jesus or Paul would cast out a demonic spirit that was causing significant hindrance to proclaiming the gospel in a certain area (see Mark 5:1–20 [Gerasene demoniac]; 16:16–18 [soothsaying girl at Philippi]), that is not the usual pattern of ministry presented, where the emphasis is simply on preaching the gospel (Matt. 9:35; Rom. 1:18–19; 1 Cor. 1:17–2:5). Even in the examples above, the opposition was encountered in the process of gospel proclamation. In marked contrast to the practice of those who today emphasize "strategic level spiritual warfare," in no instance does anyone in the New Testament (1) *summon a "territorial spirit"* upon entering an area to preach the gospel (in both examples above the demon was in a person and the demon-influenced person initiated the confrontation), or (2) *demand information from demons about a local demonic hierarchy,* (3) *say that we should believe or teach information derived from demons,* or (4) teach by word or example that certain *"demonic strongholds" over a city have to be broken* before the gospel can be proclaimed with effectiveness. Rather, Christians just preach the gospel, and it comes with power to change lives! (Of course, demonic opposition may arise, or God himself may reveal the nature of certain demonic opposition, which Christians would then pray and battle against, according to 1 Cor. 12:10; 2 Cor. 10:3–6; Eph. 6:12).

Therefore, though the New Testament clearly recognizes the influence of demonic activity in the world, and even, as we shall see, upon the lives of believers, its primary focus regarding evangelism and Christian growth is on the choices and actions taken by people themselves (see also Gal. 5:16–26; Eph. 4:1–6:9; Col. 3:1–4:6; et al.). Similarly, this should be the primary focus of our efforts today when we strive to grow in holiness and faith and to overcome the sinful desires and actions that remain in our lives (cf. Rom. 6:1–23) and to overcome the temptations that come against us from an unbelieving world (1 Cor. 10:13).[16] We need to accept our own responsibility to obey the Lord and not to shift blame for our own misdeeds onto some demonic force.

Nevertheless, a number of passages show that the New Testament authors were definitely aware of the presence of demonic influence in the world and in the lives of Christians themselves. Writing to the church at Corinth, which was filled with temples devoted to worship of idols, Paul said that "what pagans sacrifice they offer to demons and not to God" (1 Cor. 10:20), a situation true not only of Corinth but also of most other cities in the ancient Mediterranean world. Paul also warned that in the latter days some would "depart from the faith by giving heed to deceitful spirits and doctrines of demons" (1 Tim. 4:1), and that this would lead to claims for avoiding marriage and avoiding certain foods (v. 3), both of which God had created as "good" (v. 4). Thus he saw some false doctrine as being demonic in origin. In 2 Timothy, Paul implies that those who oppose sound doctrine have been captured by the devil to do his will: "And the Lord's servant must not be quarrelsome but kindly to every one, an apt teacher, forbearing, correcting his opponents with gentleness. God may perhaps grant that they will repent and come to know the truth, and they may *escape from the snare of the devil, after being captured by him to do his will*" (2 Tim. 2:24–26).

Jesus had similarly asserted that the Jews who obstinately opposed him were following their father the devil: "You are of your father the devil, and your will is to do your father's desires. He was a murderer from the beginning and has nothing to do with the truth, because there is no truth in him. When he lies, he speaks according to his own nature, for he is a liar and the father of lies" (John 8:44).

---

[16]A common way of summarizing the three sources of evil in our lives today is "the world, the flesh, and the devil" (where "flesh" refers to our own sinful desires).

Emphasis on the hostile deeds of unbelievers as having demonic influence or sometimes demonic origin is made more explicit in John's first epistle. He makes a general statement that "he who commits sin is *of the devil*" (1 John 3:8), and goes on to say, "By this it may be seen who are the children of God, and who are the children of the devil: whoever does not do right is not of God, nor he who does not love his brother" (1 John 3:10). Here John characterizes all those who are not born of God as children of the devil and subject to his influence and desires. So Cain, when he murdered Abel, "was *of the evil one* and murdered his brother" (1 John 3:12), even though there is no mention of influence by Satan in the text of Genesis (Gen. 4:1–16). John also says, "We know that we are of God, and *the whole world is in the power of the evil one*" (1 John 5:19). Then in Revelation Satan is called "the deceiver of the whole world" (Rev. 12:9). As we noted above, Satan is also called "the ruler of this world" (John 14:30), "the god of this world" (2 Cor. 4:4), and "the spirit that is now at work in the sons of disobedience" (Eph. 2:2).

When we combine all of these statements and see that Satan is thought of as the originator of lies, murder, deception, false teaching, and sin generally, then it seems reasonable to conclude that the New Testament wants us to understand that there is some degree of demonic influence in nearly all wrongdoing and sin that occurs today. Not all sin is caused by Satan or demons, nor is the major influence or cause of sin demonic activity, but demonic activity is probably a factor in almost all sin and almost all destructive activity that opposes the work of God in the world today.

In the lives of Christians, as we noted above, the emphasis of the New Testament is not on the influence of demons but on the sin that remains in the believer's life. Nevertheless, we should recognize that sinning (even by Christians) does give a foothold for some kind of demonic influence in our lives. Thus Paul could say, "Be angry but do not sin; do not let the sun go down on your anger, and *give no opportunity to the devil*" (Eph. 4:26). Wrongful anger apparently can give opportunity for the devil (or demons) to exert some kind of negative influence in our lives—perhaps by attacking us through our emotions and perhaps by increasing the wrongful anger that we already feel against others. Similarly, Paul mentions "the breastplate of righteousness" (Eph. 6:14) as part of the armor that we are to use standing against "the wiles of the devil" and in contending "against the principalities, against the powers, against the world rulers of this present darkness, against the spiritual hosts of wickedness in the heavenly places" (Eph. 6:11–12). If we have areas of continuing sin in our lives, then there are weaknesses and holes in our "breastplate of righteousness," and these are areas in which we are vulnerable to demonic attack. By contrast, Jesus, who was perfectly free from sin, could say of Satan, "He has no power over me" (John 14:30). We may also note the connection between not sinning and not being touched by the evil one in 1 John 5:18: "We know that any one born of God does not sin,[17] but He who was born of God keeps him, and the evil one does not touch him."

The preceding passages suggest, then, that where there is a pattern of persistent sin in the life of a Christian in one area or another, the primary responsibility for that sin rests with the individual Christian and his or her choices to continue that

---

[17]The present tense of the Greek verb here gives the sense "does not continue to sin."

wrongful pattern (see Rom. 6, esp. vv. 12–16; also Gal. 5:16–26). Nevertheless, there could possibly be some demonic influence contributing to and intensifying that sinful tendency. For a Christian who has prayed and struggled for years to overcome a bad temper, for example, there might be a spirit of anger that is one factor in that continued pattern of sin. A Christian who has struggled for some time to overcome a sense of depression may have been under attack by a spirit of depression or discouragement, and this could be one factor contributing to the overall situation.[18] A believer who has struggled in other areas, such as unwillingness to submit to rightful authority, or lack of self-control in eating, or laziness, or bitterness, or envy, etc., may consider whether a demonic attack or influence could be contributing to this situation and hindering his or her effectiveness for the Lord.

**3. Can a Christian Be Demon Possessed?** The term *demon possession* is an unfortunate term that has found its way into some English translations of the Bible but is not really reflected in the Greek text. The Greek New Testament can speak of people who "have a demon" (Matt. 11:18; Luke 7:33; 8:27; John 7:20; 8:48, 49, 52; 10:20), or it can speak of people who are suffering from demonic influence (Gk. *daimonizomai*),[19] but it never uses language that suggests that a demon actually "possesses" someone.

The problem with the terms *demon possession* and *demonized* is that they give the nuance of such strong demonic influence that they seem to imply that the person who is under demonic attack has no choice but to succumb to it. They suggest that the person is unable any longer to exercise his or her will and is completely under the domination of the evil spirit. While this may have been true in extreme cases such as that of the Gerasene demoniac (see Mark 5:1–20; note that after Jesus cast the demons out of him, he was then "in his right mind," v. 15), it is certainly not true with many cases of demonic attack or conflict with demons in many people's lives.

So what should we say to the question, "Can a Christian be demon possessed?" The answer depends on what someone means by "possessed." Since the term does not reflect any word found in the Greek New Testament, people can define it to mean various things without having clear warrant to anchor it to any verse of Scripture, and it becomes difficult to say that one person's definition is right and

---

[18]Not all depression is demonic in origin. Some may be caused by chemical factors that will respond to medical treatment. Other depression may be due to a variety of behavioral patterns or interpersonal relationships that are not being conducted according to biblical standards. But we should not rule out demonic influence as a possible factor.

[19]This word *diamonizomai*, which may be translated "under demonic influence" or "to be demonized" occurs thirteen times in the New Testament, all in the Gospels: Matt. 4:24; 8:16, 28, 33; 9:32; 12:22; 15:22 ("badly demonized"); Mark 1:32; 5:15, 16, 18; Luke 8:36; and John 10:21. All of these instances indicate quite severe demonic influence. In light of this, it is perhaps better to reserve the English word *demonized* for more extreme or severe cases such as those represented by the instances that are used in the Gospels. The word *demonized* in English seems to me to suggest very strong demonic influence or control. (Cf. other similar "-ized" words: pasteurized, homogenized, tyrannized, materialized, nationalized, etc. These words all speak of a total transformation of the object being spoken about, not simply of mild or moderate influence.) But it has become common in some Christian literature today to speak of people under any kind of demonic attack as being "demonized." It would be wiser to reserve the term for more severe cases of demonic influence.

another one's wrong. My own preference, for reasons explained above, is not to use the phrase *demon possessed* at all, for any kinds of cases.

But if people explain clearly what they mean by "demon possessed," then an answer can be given depending on the definition they give. If by "demon possessed" they mean that a person's will is completely dominated by a demon, so that a person has no power left to chose to do right and obey God, then the answer to whether a Christian could be demon possessed would certainly be no, for Scripture guarantees that sin shall have no dominion over us since we have been raised with Christ (Rom. 6:14, see also vv. 4, 11).

On the other hand, most Christians would agree that there can be differing degrees of demonic attack or influence in the lives of believers (see Luke 4:2; 2 Cor. 12:7; Eph. 6:12; James 4:7; 1 Peter 5:8). A believer may come under demonic attack from time to time in a mild or more strong sense.[20] (Note the "daughter of Abraham" whom "Satan bound for eighteen years" so that she "had a spirit of infirmity" and "was bent over and could not fully straighten herself" [Luke 13:16, 11].) Though Christians after Pentecost have a fuller power of the Holy Spirit working within them to enable them to triumph over demonic attacks,[21] they do not always call upon or even know about the power that is rightfully theirs. So how severe can demonic influence become in the life of a Christian after Pentecost who is indwelt by the Holy Spirit?

Before answering this question, we should note that it is similar to a question about sin: "How much can a genuine Christian let his or her life be dominated by sin, and still be a born-again Christian?" It is difficult to answer that question in the abstract, because we realize that when Christians are not living as they ought to live, and when they are not benefiting from regular fellowship with other Christians and from regular Bible study and teaching, they can stray into significant degrees of sin and still can be said to be born-again Christians. But the situation is abnormal; it is not what the Christian life should be and can be. Similarly, if we ask how much demonic influence can come into the life of a genuine Christian, it is hard to give an answer in the abstract. We are simply asking how abnormal a Christian's life can become, especially if that person does not know about or make use of the weapons of spiritual warfare that are available to Christians, persists in some kinds of sin that give entrance to demonic activity, and is outside the reach of any ministry that is accustomed to giving spiritual help against demonic attack. It would seem that in such cases the degree of demonic attack or influence in a Christian's life could be quite strong. It would not be correct to say there can be no such influence because the person is a Christian. Therefore when someone asks, "Can a Christian be demon possessed?" but really means, "Can a Christian come under quite strong influence or attack by demons?" then the answer would have to be a positive one but with the caution that the word *possessed* is here being used in a confusing way. Since the term *demon possessed*

---

[20]It does not seem very helpful to attempt to define categories or degrees of demonic influence, as has sometimes been done, with words such as "depressed," "oppressed," "obsessed," etc., for Scripture does not define a list of categories like this for us to use, and such categories only tend to make complicated what is a simple truth: that there can be varying degrees of demonic attack or influence in a person's life.

[21]See chapter 30, p. 640, and chapter 39, pp. 770–72, for a discussion of the greater power of the Holy Spirit at work in believers' lives after Pentecost.

is a misleading one to use in all cases, especially when referring to Christians, I would prefer to avoid it altogether. It seems better simply to recognize that there can be varying degrees of demonic attack or influence on people, even on Christians, and to leave it at that. In all cases the remedy will be the same anyway: rebuke the demon in the name of Jesus and command it to leave (see discussion below).

**4. How Can Demonic Influences Be Recognized?** In severe cases of demonic influence, as reported in the Gospels, the affected person would exhibit bizarre and often violent actions, especially opposition to the preaching of the gospel. When Jesus came into the synagogue in Capernaum, "immediately there was in their synagogue a man with an unclean spirit; and he cried out, 'What have you to do with us, Jesus of Nazareth? Have you come to destroy us? I know who you are, the Holy One of God'" (Mark 1:23–24). The man stood up and interrupted the service by shouting these things (or, more precisely, the demon within the man shouted them).

After Jesus came down from the Mount of Transfiguration, a man brought his son to Jesus saying, "He has a dumb spirit; and wherever it seizes him, it dashes him down; and he foams and grinds his teeth and becomes rigid." Then they brought the boy to Jesus, "and when the spirit saw him, immediately it convulsed the boy, and he fell on the ground and rolled about, foaming at the mouth." The father said, "It has often cast him into the fire and into the water, to destroy him" (Mark 9:17–18, 20, 22). Such violent actions, especially those tending toward destruction of the affected person, were clear indications of demonic activity. Similar actions are seen in the case of the Gerasene demoniac,

> a man with an unclean spirit, who lived among the tombs; and no one could bind him any more, even with a chain; for he had often been bound with fetters and chains, but the chains he wrenched apart, and the fetters he broke in pieces; and no one had the strength to subdue him. Night and day among the tombs and on the mountains he was always crying out, and bruising himself with stones. (Mark 5:2–5)

When Jesus cast out the demons so that they could not destroy the man in whom they had lived, they destroyed the herd of swine into which they immediately entered (Mark 5:13). Satanic or demonic activity always tends toward the ultimate destruction of parts of God's creation and especially of human beings who are made in the image of God (cf. Ps. 106:37, on child sacrifice).

In this regard, it is interesting to note that in one case when Jesus healed an epileptic he did it by casting out a demon (Matt. 17:14–18), but elsewhere epileptics are distinguished from those who are under demonic influence: "They brought him all the sick, those afflicted with various diseases and pains, *demoniacs, epileptics,* and paralytics, and he healed them" (Matt. 4:24). So it is with other cases of physical sickness: in some cases, Jesus simply prayed for the person or spoke a word and the person was healed. In other cases there are hints or implicit statements of demonic influence in the affliction: a woman who had had "a spirit of infirmity for eighteen years" (Luke 13:11) was healed by Jesus, and then he explicitly said that she was "a daughter of Abraham *whom Satan bound* for eighteen years" (Luke 13:16). In healing Peter's mother-in-law, Jesus "rebuked the fever, and it left her" (Luke 4:39), suggesting that there was some personal influence (probably therefore demonic) that was capable of receiving a rebuke from Jesus.

In other cases, the Epistles indicate that demonic influence will lead to blatantly false doctrinal statements, such as exclaiming, "Jesus be cursed" (1 Cor. 12:3), or a refusal to confess "that Jesus Christ has come in the flesh" (1 John 4:2–3). In both instances, the context deals with the testing of people who may be "false prophets" and who want to use spiritual gifts to speak in the assembly of the church (1 Cor. 12) or specifically to prophesy (1 John 4:1–6). These passages do not indicate that all false doctrine should be thought to be demonically inspired, but blatantly false doctrinal statements made by those who profess to be speaking by the power of the Holy Spirit would certainly fall into this category. When at Corinth there was active, entrenched opposition to Paul's apostolic authority by those who claimed to be apostles but were not, Paul saw them as servants of Satan disguised as servants of righteousness (2 Cor. 11:13–15).

In addition to these outwardly evident indications, demonic activity was sometimes recognized by a subjective sense of the presence of an evil spiritual influence. In 1 Corinthians 12:10, Paul mentions "the ability to distinguish between spirits" ("discerning of spirits," KJV) as one kind of spiritual gift. This gift would seem to be an ability to sense or discern the difference in the working of the Holy Spirit and the working of evil spirits in a person's life.[22] The gift would apparently include an awareness of demonic influence that would be registered both in terms of objective, observable facts, and also in terms of emotional and/or spiritual uneasiness or perception of the presence of evil.

But does this ability to perceive demonic influence have to be limited to those with this special gift? As with all spiritual gifts, it would seem that there are degrees of intensity or strength in the development of this gift as well.[23] So some may have this gift developed to a very high degree and others may find it functioning only occasionally. Moreover, in the lives of all believers, there may be something analogous to this gift, some kind of ability to sense in their spirits the presence of the Holy Spirit or to sense demonic influence from time to time in other people. In fact, Paul speaks of a *positive* kind of spiritual perception that believers have when they encounter him and his co-workers: "For we are the aroma of Christ to God among those who are being saved and among those who are perishing, to one a fragrance from death to death, to the other a fragrance from life to life" (2 Cor. 2:15–16). In the ordinary course of life today, sometimes Christians will have a subjective sense that someone else is a Christian before they have opportunity to find out that that is in fact the case. And it seems likely that an opposite spiritual perception could also occur from time to time, whereby the believer would sense the presence of demonic influence in a person's life before there were other, more objective indications of that fact.

Moreover, sometimes a person who is under spiritual attack from a demonic power will know it or sense it. A mature pastor or a Christian friend, in counseling someone about a difficult problem, may find it wise to ask, "Do you think that an attack by any evil spiritual force could be a factor in this situation?" The person

---

[22]For an extensive analysis of the meaning of the Greek phrase *diakriseis pneumatōn*, "distinguishing between spirits," in 1 Cor. 12:10, see W. Grudem, "A Response to Gerhard Dautzenberg on 1 Corinthians 12:10," in *Biblische Zeitschrift*, NF, 22:2 (1978), pp. 253–70.

[23]See chapter 52, pp. 1022–25, on the fact that spiritual gifts may vary in strength.

may simply say, "No," but in many instances the person being counseled will have thought of that possibility or even have been quite clearly aware of it, but afraid to say anything for fear of being thought strange. Such a person will be encouraged that another Christian would consider this as a possible factor.

In all of these attempts to recognize demonic influence, we must remember that no spiritual gift functions perfectly in this age, nor do we have a full knowledge of people's hearts. "We all make many mistakes," as James recognizes (James 3:2). There are many cases where we are somewhat unsure whether a person is a genuine Christian or not, or where we are somewhat unsure whether a person's motives are sincere. There are also times when we are unclear as to the direction God is leading us in our lives, or we may be uncertain about whether it is appropriate to speak or remain silent about a certain matter. So it should not surprise us that there may be some degree of uncertainty in our perception of the presence of demonic influence as well. This does not mean that we should ignore the possibility of demonic influence, however, and as we grow in spiritual maturity and sensitivity, and as we gain experience in ministering to the needs of others, our ability to recognize demonic influence in various situations will no doubt increase.

**5. Jesus Gives All Believers Authority to Rebuke Demons and Command Them to Leave.** When Jesus sent the twelve disciples ahead of him to preach the kingdom of God, he "gave them power and authority over all demons" (Luke 9:1). After the seventy had preached the kingdom of God in towns ›and villages, they returned with joy, saying, "Lord, *even the demons are subject to us in your name!*" (Luke 10:17), and Jesus told them, "I have given you authority . . . over all the power of the enemy" (Luke 10:19). When Philip, the evangelist, went down to Samaria to preach the gospel of Christ, "unclean spirits came out of many who had them" (Acts 8:7, author's translation), and Paul used spiritual authority over demons to say to a spirit of divination in a soothsaying girl, "I charge you in the name of Jesus Christ to come out of her" (Acts 16:18).

Paul was aware of the spiritual authority he had, both in face-to-face encounters such as he had in Acts 16, and in his prayer life as well. He said, "For though we live in the world we are not carrying on a worldly war, for the weapons of our warfare are not worldly but have divine power to destroy strongholds" (2 Cor. 10:3–4). Moreover, he spoke at some length of the struggle Christians have against "the wiles of the devil" in his description of conflict "against the spiritual hosts of wickedness in the heavenly places" (see Eph. 6:10–18). James tells all his readers (in many churches) to "*resist the devil* and he will flee from you" (James 4:7). Similarly, Peter tells his readers in many churches in Asia Minor, "Your adversary the devil prowls around like a roaring lion, seeking some one to devour. *Resist him,* firm in your faith" (1 Peter 5:8–9).[24]

Some may object that Jude 9 teaches that Christians should not command or rebuke evil spirits. It says: "But when the archangel Michael, contending with the

---

[24]Of course, our greatest example of dealing with demonic powers by speaking to them directly and commanding them to leave is the example of Jesus himself, who frequently did this in the Gospels, and by example and word he taught the disciples to imitate him.

devil, disputed about the body of Moses, he did not presume to pronounce a reviling judgment upon him, but said, 'The Lord rebuke you.' "

However, in context Jude is not talking about Christians in their encounters with demonic forces, but is pointing out the error of immoral and rebellious false teachers who "reject authority" in general and "slander celestial beings" (v. 8 NIV): on their own authority they foolishly speak blasphemous words against heavenly beings, whether angelic or demonic. The reference to Michael is simply to show that the greatest angelic creature, no matter how powerful, did not presume to go beyond the limits of the authority that God had given him. The false teachers, however, have far overstepped their bounds, and they show their foolishness when they "revile whatever they do not understand" (v. 10). The lesson of the verse is simply, "Don't try to go beyond the authority God has given you!" When Jude 9 is viewed in this way, the only question that arises for a Christian from this verse is, "What authority has God given us over demonic forces?" And the rest of the New Testament speaks clearly to that in several places. Not only Jesus, and not only his twelve disciples, but also the seventy disciples, and Paul, and Philip (who was not an apostle) are given authority over demons by the Lord Jesus (see verses above). Jude 9 therefore simply cannot mean that it is wrong for human beings to rebuke or command demons, or that it is wrong for any but the apostles to do so. In fact, both Peter and James encourage all Christians to "resist" the devil, and Paul encourages believers in general to put on spiritual armor and prepare for spiritual warfare.

Before we examine in more detail how that authority works out in practice, it is important, first, that we recognize that the work of Christ on the cross is the ultimate basis for our authority over demons.[25] Though Christ won a victory over Satan in the wilderness, the New Testament epistles point to the cross as the moment when Satan was decisively defeated. Jesus took on flesh and blood, "that through death He might render powerless him who had the power of death, that is, the devil" (Heb. 2:14 NASB). At the cross God "disarmed the principalities and powers and made a public example of them, triumphing over them in him" (Col. 2:15). Therefore Satan hates the cross of Christ, because there he was decisively defeated forever. Because the blood of Christ speaks clearly of his death, we read in Revelation of those who overcame Satan by Christ's blood during conflict in this world: "And they have conquered him by the blood of the Lamb and by the word of their testimony" (Rev. 12:11). Because of Christ's death on the cross, our sins are completely forgiven, and Satan has no rightful authority over us.

Second, our membership as children in God's family is the firm spiritual position from which we engage in spiritual warfare. Paul says to every Christian, "For in Christ Jesus you are all sons of God, through faith" (Gal. 3:26). When Satan comes to attack us, he is attacking one of God's own children, a member of God's own family: this truth gives us authority to successfully wage war against him and defeat him.[26]

If we as believers find it appropriate to speak a word of rebuke to a demon, it is important to remember that we need not fear demons. Although Satan and

---

[25]In this paragraph and the following one on adoption I am indebted to the fine work of Timothy M. Warner, *Spiritual Warfare* (Wheaton, Ill.: Crossway, 1991), pp. 55–63.
[26]See chapter 37, pp. 736–45, on adoption.

demons have much less power than the power of the Holy Spirit at work within us, one of Satan's tactics is to attempt to cause us to be afraid. Instead of giving in to such fear, Christians should remind themselves of the truths of Scripture, which tell us, "You are of God, and have overcome them; for *he who is in you is greater than he who is in the world*" (1 John 4:4), and "God did not give us a spirit of timidity but a spirit of power and love and self-control" (2 Tim. 1:7). What Paul says about the Philippians in their relationship to human opponents can also be applied when facing demonic opposition to the gospel—Paul tells them to stand firm and to be "*not frightened in anything by your opponents*. This is a clear omen to them of their destruction, but of your salvation, and that from God" (Phil. 1:28). He also tells the Ephesians that in their spiritual warfare they are to use the "shield of faith" with which they can "quench all the flaming darts of the evil one" (Eph. 6:16). This is very important, since the opposite of fear is faith in God. He also tells them to be bold in their spiritual conflict, so that, having taken the whole armor of God, they "may be able to withstand in the evil day, and having done all, to stand" (Eph. 6:13). In their conflict with hostile spiritual forces, Paul's readers should not run away in retreat or cower in fear, but should stand their ground boldly, knowing that their weapons and their armor "have divine power to destroy strongholds" (2 Cor. 10:4; cf. 1 John 5:18).

We may ask, however, why does God want Christians to speak directly to the demon who is troubling someone rather than just praying and asking God to drive away the demon for them? In a way, this is similar to asking why Christians should share the gospel with another person rather than simply praying and asking God to reveal the gospel to that person directly. Or why should we speak words of encouragement to a Christian who is discouraged rather than just praying and asking God himself to encourage that person directly? Why should we speak a word of rebuke or gentle admonition to a Christian whom we see involved in some kind of sin, rather than just praying and asking God to take care of the sin in that person's life? The answer to all these questions is that in the world that God has created, he has given us a very *active* role in carrying out his plans, especially his plans for the advancement of the kingdom and the building up of the church. In all of these cases, our *direct involvement* and *activity* is important in addition to our prayers. And so it seems to be in our dealing with demonic forces as well. Like a wise father who does not settle all of his children's disputes for them, but sometimes sends them back out to the playground to settle a dispute themselves, so our heavenly Father encourages us to enter directly into conflict with demonic forces in the name of Christ and in the power of the Holy Spirit. Thereby he enables us to gain the joy of participating in eternally significant ministry and the joy of triumphing over the destructive power of Satan and his demons in people's lives. It is not that God could not deal with demonic attacks every time we prayed and asked him to do so, for he certainly could and he no doubt sometimes does. But the New Testament pattern seems to be that God ordinarily expects Christians themselves to speak directly to the unclean spirits.

In actual practice, this authority to rebuke demons may result in briefly speaking a command to an evil spirit to leave when we suspect the presence of demonic influence in our personal lives or the lives of those around us.[27] We are to "resist

---

[27]Because Scripture gives no indication that demons can know our thoughts (see above, pp. 415–16), it would seem that the command should be spoken audibly.

the devil" (James 4:7), and he will flee from us.[28] Sometimes a very brief command in the name of Jesus will be enough. At other times it will be helpful to quote Scripture in the process of commanding an evil spirit to leave a situation. Paul speaks of "the sword of the Spirit, which is the word of God" (Eph. 6:17).[29] And Jesus, when he was tempted by Satan in the wilderness, repeatedly quoted Scripture in response to Satan's temptations (Matt. 4:1–11). Appropriate Scriptures may include general statements of the triumph of Jesus over Satan (Matt. 12:28–29; Luke 10:17–19; 2 Cor. 10:3–4; Col. 2:15; Heb. 2:14; James 4:7; 1 Peter 5:8–9; 1 John 3:8; 4:4; 5:18),[30] but also verses that speak directly to the particular temptation or difficulty at hand.

In our own personal lives, if we find sinful emotions that are unusually strong welling up in our minds or hearts (whether they be emotions of irrational fear, anger, hatred, bitterness, lust, greed, etc.), in addition to praying and asking Jesus for help in overcoming them, it would also be appropriate for us to say something like, "Spirit of fear, in Jesus' name, I command you, go away from here and don't return!" Even though we may be unsure whether there is a demonic factor in that particular situation, and even though a demon's presence may be only one factor contributing to the situation, nonetheless, such words of rebuke will sometimes be very effective. Though we do not have in the New Testament a complete record of the personal prayer life of the apostle Paul, he talks openly about wrestling "not . . . against flesh and blood, but . . . against the spiritual hosts of wickedness in the heavenly places" (Eph. 6:12) and about "not carrying on a worldly war" (2 Cor. 10:3). It is reasonable to think that his own extensive prayer life included this kind of verbal rebuke of demonic forces as one aspect of his spiritual warfare.

Moreover, such wrestling against "the spiritual hosts of wickedness" may mean that in our private times of intercessory prayer for others we will include an element of verbal rebuke to demonic forces that may be a component in situations for which we are praying. (This kind of spiritual warfare would not be in the presence of the person for whom we are concerned, who in many cases would be confused or frightened unnecessarily.) For example, parents may appropriately include a brief word of rebuke to a spirit of rebelliousness in one child, of laziness in another, or of anger in yet another, in addition to praying that the Lord would give victory in those areas, and in addition to teaching and disciplining their children.[31]

---

[28]For example, if we or one of our children wakes up with a frightening dream, in addition to praying to Jesus for comfort and protection, we might also say, "In the name of Jesus, I command any evil spirit causing this frightening dream, begone!" Children from a very young age can be taught to say, "In Jesus' name, go away!" to any images of witches, goblins, etc. that may appear in their dreams or in mental images that trouble them at night, and then to pray to Jesus for protection and happy thoughts of him. Such action by those little ones who trust in Christ will often be remarkably effective, for their faith in Jesus is very simple and genuine (see Matt. 18:1–4).

[29]The Greek word here translated "word" is *rhēma*, which usually refers to spoken words (whether by God or by others). It is sometimes used to speak of the words of Scripture when they are spoken by God or by people quoting Scripture (Matt. 4:4; John 15:7; 17:8; Rom. 10:17; Heb. 6:5; 1 Peter 1:25 [twice]), and that is the sense in which Paul seems to use it in Eph. 6:17: as we speak the words of Scripture they are accompanied by the work of the Holy Spirit and have the power of a spiritual sword.

[30]It would be good for Christians to memorize the verses in the list just mentioned so as to be able to speak them from memory when involved in any spiritual warfare.

[31]Since Scripture gives no indication that demons can read our minds, such rebukes against demons

**6. Appropriate Use of the Christian's Spiritual Authority in Ministry to Other People.** When we pass from the discussion of private spiritual warfare in our own personal lives and perhaps the lives of close family members, we move to the question of direct personal ministry to others who have come under spiritual attack. For example, we may at times be involved in counseling or prayer with another person when we suspect that demonic activity is a factor in their situation. In these cases, some additional considerations must be kept in mind.

First, it is important not to frighten people by talking very glibly about an area that may be familiar to us but quite unfamiliar and somewhat frightening to others. The Holy Spirit is a Spirit of gentleness and peace (see 1 Cor. 14:33). Because of this, it is often considerate simply to ask questions of the person we are helping. We might ask, "Do you think an evil spirit may be attacking you in this situation?" or "Would you mind if I spoke a word of rebuke to any evil spirit that may be a factor in this?" It would also be important to assure the person that if there is a demonic factor involved, it should not be thought of as a negative reflection on the person's spiritual condition but may simply indicate that Satan is trying to attack the person to keep him or her from more effective ministry for the Lord. Each Christian is a soldier in the Lord's spiritual army and therefore subject to attacks from the forces of the enemy.

If the other person gives permission to do so, a brief command should be spoken aloud, telling the evil spirit to leave.[32] Since the person under attack will often have had a sense of a demonic presence, it would be appropriate, after commanding the evil spirit to leave, to ask the person if he or she felt or sensed anything different when those words were spoken. If there really was a demonic influence in the situation, the person may express an immediate feeling of relief or freedom, often with a sense of joy and peace as well.

All of this does not have to be a highly dramatic or emotionally charged procedure. Some contemporary stories tell of long, drawn-out battles in which the Christian counselor argues with the demon and shouts at it repeatedly over a period of several hours. But there is no indication in the New Testament that demons are hard of hearing, nor are there examples of such long periods of conflict in order to get a demon to leave. Jesus simply "cast out the spirits with a word" (Matt. 8:16), even though in one case (with the Gerasene demoniac) the evil spirit showed some initial resistance (see Mark 5:8; Luke 8:29). Jesus then asked its name and then cast out many demons at once (Mark 5:9–13; Luke 8:30–33). The power to cast out demons comes not from our own strength or the power of our own voice, but from the Holy Spirit (Matt. 12:28; Luke 11:20). Thus, a quiet, confident, authoritative tone of voice should be sufficient.

Second, to avoid being drawn into a long conversation or battle with the demon itself the Christian counselor should focus not on the demon but on the person being ministered to and the truths of the Bible that need to be affirmed and

---

would probably have to be spoken audibly, even if softly. By contrast, God of course knows our thoughts, and prayer to him can be in our minds only, without being spoken aloud.

[32]The verb *exorcise* in English means "to drive out (an evil spirit) by a magic formula or a spoken command." An "exorcism" is defined as the action of driving out an evil spirit in this way. These words do not occur in the Bible (although Acts 19:13 mentions Jewish exorcists). Because these terms are used in pagan as well as Christian contexts throughout history, there is room for Christians to differ over whether it is wise to use them to refer to Christian practices today.

believed. The "belt of truth" (Eph. 6:14 NIV) is part of the armor that protects us against Satan, as is the "sword of the Spirit, which is the word of God" (Eph. 6:17). If the person who is receiving ministry will focus on and believe the truth of Scripture and will renounce sin and thereby put on the "breastplate of righteousness" (Eph. 6:14), then the evil spirit will have no foothold in that person's life. If the demon refuses to leave in spite of the command given in the name of Jesus, then it may be best to wait until another time after more prayer and personal spiritual preparation on the part of the person being ministered to and the persons who are engaging in this ministry (Matt. 17:19–20; Mark 9:29; see discussions below).[33]

Third, it is important for Christians not to become overly curious in this area of demonic conflict. Though it is a ministry that the Lord gives all Christians authority to engage in, Scripture nonetheless tells us that we are to be "babes in evil" (1 Cor. 14:20). That is, we are not to become overly fascinated with matters of evil and attempt to become "experts" in some kinds of evil just to satisfy our curiosity.[34]

Fourth, if the person being ministered to is not a Christian, it is important that he or she be urged to come to Christ as Savior immediately after the demon is cast out so that the Holy Spirit will reside in the person and protect him or her from future attacks. Otherwise there may be a worse result later.

> When the unclean spirit has gone out of a man, he passes through waterless places seeking rest, but he finds none. Then he says, "I will return to my house from which I came." And when he comes he finds it empty, swept, and put in order. Then he goes and brings with him seven other spirits more evil than himself, and they enter and dwell there; and the last state of that man becomes worse than the first. So shall it be also with this evil generation. (Matt. 12:43–45)

Fifth, effectiveness in difficult cases of demonic influence may be related to our own spiritual condition. When Jesus had cast a demon out of an epileptic boy, and "the boy was cured instantly," the disciples privately came to Jesus and asked, "Why could we not cast it out?" (Matt. 17:18–19). Jesus said to them, "Because of your little faith" (Matt. 17:20). Mark's gospel reports that Jesus also said in response to the disciples, "This kind cannot be driven out by anything but prayer" (Mark 9:29). The disciples apparently were at that time weak in faith; they had not spent enough time in prayer recently and they were not walking fully in the power of the Holy Spirit.[35]

Jesus issues a clear warning that we should not rejoice too much or become proud in our power over demons, but that we should rejoice rather in our great salvation. We must keep this in mind lest we become proud and the Holy Spirit

---

[33]It would often be wise, in difficult cases, to have help from someone with more maturity and experience in this area.

[34]Christians should therefore not be preoccupied with matters concerning the occult or the New Age movement. We should think about things that are "honorable" and "pure" and "worthy of praise" (Phil. 4:8).

[35]When Jesus said, "This kind cannot be driven out by anything but prayer" (Mark 9:29), he cannot have meant that it was necessary to pray for a long time about that specific situation before the demon would be cast out, for he did not pray at all but simply spoke a word and cast out the demon at once. He must have meant, rather, that a continual life of prayer and abiding in God will result in a spiritual preparedness and a possession of a spiritual power through the anointing of the Holy Spirit that will be effective in conflict even over very severe demonic attack or influence.

withdraw his power from us. When the seventy returned with joy saying, "Lord, even the demons are subject to us in your name!" (Luke 10:17) Jesus told them, "Do not rejoice in this, that the spirits are subject to you; but rejoice that your names are written in heaven" (Luke 10:20).[36]

**7. We Should Expect the Gospel to Come in Power to Triumph Over the Works of the Devil.** When Jesus came preaching the gospel in Galilee, "demons also came out of many" (Luke 4:41). When Philip went to Samaria to preach the gospel, "unclean spirits came out of many . . . crying with a loud voice" (Acts 8:7). Jesus commissioned Paul to preach among the Gentiles "that they may turn from darkness to light and from the power of Satan to God, that they may receive forgiveness of sins and a place among those who are sanctified by faith in me" (Acts 26:18). Paul's proclamation of the gospel, he said, was "not in plausible words of wisdom, but in demonstration of the Spirit and of power, that your faith might not rest in the wisdom of men but in the power of God" (1 Cor. 2:4–5; cf. 2 Cor. 10:3–4). If we really believe the scriptural testimony to the existence and activity of demons, and if we really believe that "the reason the Son of God appeared was *to destroy the works of the devil*" (1 John 3:8), then it would seem appropriate to expect that even today when the gospel is proclaimed to unbelievers, and when prayer is made for believers who have perhaps been unaware of this dimension of spiritual conflict, there will be a genuine and often immediately recognizable triumph over the power of the enemy. We should expect that this would happen, think of it as a normal part of the work of Christ in building up his kingdom, and rejoice in Christ's victory in it.

## QUESTIONS FOR PERSONAL APPLICATION

1. Before reading this chapter, did you think that most demonic activity was confined to the time of the New Testament or to other cultures than your own? After reading this chapter, are there areas in your own society where you think there might be some demonic influence today? Do you feel some fear at the prospect of encountering demonic activity in your own life or the lives of others around you? What does the Bible say that will specifically address that feeling of fear? Do you think that the Lord wants you to feel that fear, if you do?

2. Are there any areas of sin in your own life now that might give a foothold to some demonic activity? If so, what would the Lord have you do with respect to that sin?

---

[36]Jesus cannot mean that it is wrong to rejoice when the enemy is vanquished and people are set free from bondage, for that is certainly a good reason for rejoicing. He must rather be putting a relative contrast in absolute terms in telling the disciples that the greatness of their salvation is the primary thing that they should be rejoicing in.

3. Are there cases where you have had victory over some demonic force by speaking to it in the name of Jesus? How can the material in this chapter help you be more effective in this kind of spiritual conflict? What are the dangers of becoming too interested in or too deeply involved in this kind of ministry? How can you safeguard against that excessive emphasis? What do you think Paul's procedure was when he came to preach the gospel in city after city where it had never been heard before and where there was demon worship? How could the church today profit from Paul's example?

## SPECIAL TERMS

demonized
demon possession
demons

distinguishing between spirits
exorcism
Satan

## BIBLIOGRAPHY

(For an explanation of this bibliography see the note on the bibliography to chapter 1, p. 38. Complete bibliographical data may be found on pp. 1223–29.)

### Sections in Evangelical Systematic Theologies

1. Anglican (Episcopalian)
   1882–92    Litton, 129–36
2. Arminian (Wesleyan or Methodist)
   1892–94    Miley, 1:539–40; 2:497–504
   1940    Wiley, 1:476–77
   1983    Carter, 2:1069–97
3. Baptist
   1767    Gill, 1:435–440
   1887    Boyce, 181–89
   1907    Strong, 450–64
   1917    Mullins, 279–80
   1976–83    Henry, 6:229–50
   1983–85    Erickson, 445–51
   1987–94    Lewis/Demarest, 2:257–63
4. Dispensational
   1947    Chafer, 2:33–124
   1949    Thiessen, 133–50
   1986    Ryrie, 135–68
5. Lutheran
   1917–24    Pieper, 1:504–14
   1934    Mueller, 202–4
6. Reformed (or Presbyterian)
   1559    Calvin, 1:172–79 (1.14.13–19)

| 1724–58 | Edwards, 2:607–12 |
| 1861 | Heppe, 201–19 |
| 1871–73 | Hodge, 1:643–48 |
| 1937–66 | Murray, *CW*, 2:67–70 |
| 1938 | Berkhof, 148–49 |

7. Renewal (or charismatic/Pentecostal)

| 1988–92 | Williams, 1:173, 224–36 |

## Sections in Representative Roman Catholic Systematic Theologies

1. Roman Catholic: Traditional
   | 1955 | Ott, 119–24 |
2. Roman Catholic: Post-Vatican II
   | 1980 | McBrien, 1:329; 2:1105, 1153–54 |

## Other Works

Anderson, Neil. *The Bondage Breaker*. Eugene, Ore.: Harvest House, 1990.

————. *Victory Over the Darkness*. Ventura, Calif.: Regal, 1990.

Dickason, C. Fred. *Angels, Elect and Evil*. Chicago: Moody, 1975.

————. *Demon Possession and the Christian: A New Perspective*. Westchester, Ill.: Crossway, 1991.

Green, Michael. *I Believe in Satan's Downfall*. Grand Rapids: Eerdmans, 1981.

Lewis, C. S. *The Screwtape Letters*. New York: Macmillan, 1961.

MacMillan, John A. *The Authority of the Believer: A Compilation of "The Authority of the Believer" and "The Authority of the Intercessor."* Harrisburg, Pa.: Christian Publications, 1980.

McClelland, S. E. "Demon, Demon Possession." In *EDT*, pp. 306–8.

Mallone, George. *Arming for Spiritual Warfare*. Downers Grove, Ill.: InterVarsity Press, 1991.

Penn-Lewis, Jessie, with Evan Roberts. *War on the Saints*. Unabridged ed. New York: Thomas E. Lowe, 1973.

Pentecost, Dwight. *The Adversary, the Devil*. Grand Rapids: Zondervan, 1969.

Twelftree, G. H. "Devil and Demons." In *NDT*, pp. 196–98.

Unger, M. F. "Satan." In *EDT*, pp. 972–73.

————. *Demons in the World Today: A Study of Occultism in the Light of God's Word*. Wheaton, Ill.: Tyndale, 1971.

Warner, Timothy M. *Spiritual Warfare: Victory Over the Powers of This Dark World*. Wheaton, Ill.: Crossway, 1991.

Wright, Nigel. *The Satan Syndrome: Putting the Power of Darkness In Its Place*. Grand Rapids: Zondervan, 1990.

## SCRIPTURE MEMORY PASSAGE

**James 4:7–8:** *Submit yourselves therefore to God. Resist the devil and he will flee from you. Draw near to God and he will draw near to you. Cleanse your hands, you sinners, and purify your hearts, you men of double mind.*

# HYMN

## "Christian, Dost Thou See Them?"

Christian, dost thou see them on the holy ground,
  How the pow'rs of darkness rage thy steps around?
Christian, up and smite them, counting gain but loss,
  In the strength that cometh by the holy Cross.

Christian, dost thou feel them, how they work within,
  Striving, tempting, luring, goading into sin?
Christian, never tremble; never be downcast;
  Gird thee for the battle, watch and pray and fast.

Christian, dost thou hear them, how they speak thee fair?
  "Always fast and vigil? Always watch and prayer?"
Christian, answer boldly, "While I breathe I pray!"
  Peace shall follow battle, night shall end in day.

Hear the words of Jesus: "O my servant true;
  Thou art very weary, I was weary too;
But that toil shall make thee some day all mine own,
  And the end of sorrow shall be near my throne."

AUTHOR: JOHN MASON NEALE, 1862

Alternative hymns: "Soldiers of Christ Arise"; "Lead On, O King Eternal"
"Onward, Christian Soldiers."

# Part 3

# The Doctrine of Man

# Chapter 21

# The Creation of Man

*Why did God create us? How did God make us like himself? How can we please him in everyday living?*

## EXPLANATION AND SCRIPTURAL BASIS

The previous chapters have discussed the nature of God and his creation of the universe, the spiritual beings that he created, and his relationship to the world in terms of working miracles and answering prayer. In this next section, we focus on the pinnacle of God's creative activity, his creation of human beings, both male and female, to be more like him than anything else he has made. We will consider first God's purpose in creating man and the nature of man as God created him to be (chapters 21–23). Then we will look at the nature of sin and man's disobedience to God (chapter 24). Finally, we will examine the initiation of God's plan for saving man, discussing man's relationship to God in the covenants that God established (chapter 25).

## A. The Use of the Word *Man* to Refer to the Human Race

Before discussing the subject matter of this chapter, it is necessary to consider briefly whether it is appropriate to use the word *man* to refer to the entire human race (as in the title for this chapter). Some people today object to ever using the word "man" to refer to the human race in general (including both men and women), because it is claimed that such usage is insensitive to women. Those who make this objection would prefer that we *only* use "gender neutral" terms such as "humanity," "humankind," "human beings," or "persons" to refer to the human race.

After considering this suggestion, I decided to continue to use the word "man" (as well as several of these other terms) to refer to the human race in this book because such usage has divine warrant in Genesis 5, and because I think there is a theological issue at stake. In Genesis 5:1–2 we read, "When God created man, he made him in the likeness of God. Male and female he created them, and he blessed them *and named them Man* when they were created" (cf. Gen. 1:27). The Hebrew term translated "Man" is *'ādām*, the same term used for the name of Adam, and the same term that is sometimes used of man in distinction from woman (Gen. 2:22, 25; 3:12; Eccl. 7:28). Therefore the practice of using the same term to refer (1) to male human beings and (2) to the human race generally is a practice that originated with God himself, and we should not find it objectionable or insensitive.

Someone might object that this is just an accidental feature of the Hebrew language, but this argument is not persuasive because Genesis 5:2 specifically describes God's activity of choosing a name that would apply to the human race as a whole.

I am *not* here arguing that we must always duplicate biblical patterns of speech, *or* that it is wrong to use gender-neutral terms sometimes to refer to the human race (as I just did in this sentence), but rather that God's *naming* activity reported in Genesis 5:2 indicates that the use of "man" to refer to the entire race is a good and very appropriate choice, and one that we should not avoid.[1]

The theological issue is whether there is a suggestion of male leadership or headship in the family from the beginning of creation. The fact that God did not choose to call the human race "woman," but "man," probably has some significance for understanding God's original plan for men and women.[2] Of course, this question of the name we use to refer to the race is not the only factor in that discussion, but it is one factor, and our use of language in this regard does have some significance in the discussion of male-female roles today.[3]

## B. Why Was Man Created?

**1. God Did Not Need to Create Man, Yet He Created Us for His Own Glory.** In the discussion of God's independence in chapter 11 (see pp. 160–63), we noted several Scripture passages that teach that God does not need us or the rest of creation for anything, yet we and the rest of creation glorify him and bring him joy. Since there was perfect love and fellowship among members of the Trinity for all eternity (John 17:5, 24), God did not create us because he was lonely or because he needed fellowship with other persons—God did not need us for any reason.

Nevertheless, *God created us for his own glory.* In our treatment of his independence we noted that God speaks of his sons and daughters from the ends of the earth as those "whom I created *for my glory*" (Isa. 43:7; cf. Eph. 1:11–12). Therefore, we are to "do all to the glory of God" (1 Cor. 10:31).

This fact guarantees that our lives are significant. When we first realize that God did not need to create us and does not need us for anything, we could conclude that our lives have no importance at all. But Scripture tells us that we were created to glorify God, indicating that we are important *to God himself.* This is the final definition of genuine importance or significance to our lives: If we are truly

---

[1]However, the question of whether to use "man" to refer to a person indefinitely, as in, "If any *man* would come after me, let him deny himself and take up his cross daily and follow me (Luke 9:23)," is a different question, because the naming of the human race is not in view. In these cases, considerateness toward women as well as men, and present-day language patterns, would make it appropriate to use gender-neutral language such as, "If any *one* would come after me."

[2]See chapter 22, p. 463; also Raymond C. Ortlund, Jr., "Male-Female Equality and Male Headship: Genesis 1–3," in *Recovering Biblical Manhood and Womanhood: A Response to Evangelical Feminism,* ed. John Piper and Wayne Grudem (Wheaton, Ill.: Crossway, 1991, p. 98).

[3]This is probably also recognized by many of those who raise the most objection to the use of "man" to refer to the race (namely, feminists who oppose any unique male headship in the family).

important to God for all eternity, then what greater measure of importance or significance could we want?

**2. What Is Our Purpose in Life?** The fact that God created us for his own glory determines the correct answer to the question, "What is our purpose in life?" Our purpose must be to fulfill the reason that God created us: to glorify him. When we are speaking with respect to God himself, that is a good summary of our purpose. But when we think of our own interests, we make the happy discovery that we are to enjoy God and take delight in him and in our relationship to him. Jesus says, "I came that they may have life, and have it abundantly" (John 10:10). David tells God, "In your presence there is *fulness of joy*, in your right hand are pleasures for evermore" (Ps. 16:11). He longs to dwell in the house of the Lord forever, "to behold the beauty of the LORD" (Ps. 27:4), and Asaph cries out,

> Whom have I in heaven but you?
>     And there is nothing upon earth that I desire besides you.
> My flesh and my heart may fail,
>     but God is the strength of my heart
>     and my portion for ever. (Ps. 73:25–26)

Fullness of joy is found in knowing God and delighting in the excellence of his character. To be in his presence, to enjoy fellowship with him, is a greater blessing than anything that can be imagined.

> How lovely is your dwelling place,
>     O LORD of hosts!
> My soul longs, yea, faints
>     for the courts of the LORD;
> my heart and flesh sing for joy
>     to the living God. . . .
>
> For a day in your courts is better
>     than a thousand elsewhere. (Ps. 84:1–2, 10)

Therefore, the normal heart attitude of a Christian is rejoicing in the Lord and in the lessons of the life he gives us (Rom. 5:2–3; Phil. 4:4; 1 Thess. 5:16–18; James 1:2; 1 Peter 1:6, 8; et al.).[4]

As we glorify God and enjoy him, Scripture tells us that he rejoices in us. We read, "As the bridegroom rejoices over the bride, *so shall your God rejoice over you*" (Isa. 62:5), and Zephaniah prophesies that the Lord "will rejoice over you with gladness, he will renew you in his love; he will exult over you with loud singing as on a day of festival" (Zeph. 3:17–18).

This understanding of the doctrine of the creation of man has very practical results. When we realize that God created us to glorify him, and when we start to act in ways that fulfill that purpose, then we begin to experience an intensity of joy in the Lord that we have never before known. When we add to that the realization that God himself is rejoicing in our fellowship with him, our joy becomes

---

[4]The first question in the Westminster Larger Catechism is "What is the chief and highest end of man?" The answer is, "Man's chief and highest end is to glorify God, and fully to enjoy Him forever."

"inexpressible and filled with heavenly glory" (1 Peter 1:8, author's expanded paraphrase).[5]

Someone might object that it is wrong for God to seek glory for himself in creating man. Certainly it is wrong for human beings to seek glory for themselves, as we see in the dramatic example of the death of Herod Agrippa I. When he proudly accepted the shout of the crowd, "The voice of a god, and not of man!" (Acts 12:22), "immediately an angel of the Lord smote him, because he did not give God the glory; and he was eaten by worms and died" (Acts 12:23). Herod died because he robbed God of glory, glory that God deserved and he did not.

But when God takes glory to himself, from whom is he robbing glory? Is there anyone who deserves glory more than he does? Certainly not! He is the Creator, he made all things, and he *deserves* all glory. He is *worthy* of receiving glory. *Man* may not seek glory for himself, but in this case what is wrong for man is right for God, because he is the Creator. It is *right,* not wrong, that he be glorified—in fact, if he did not receive glory from all creatures in the universe, that would be horribly wrong! The twenty-four elders around God's throne continually sing,

> "You are *worthy,* our Lord and God,
> *to receive glory* and honor and power,
> for you created all things,
> and by your will they existed and were created."
>                                           (Rev. 4:11)

Paul exclaims, "For from him and through him and to him are all things. To him be glory for ever. Amen" (Rom. 11:36). When we begin to appreciate the nature of God as the infinitely perfect Creator who deserves all praise, then our hearts will not rest until we give him glory with all of our "heart . . . soul . . . mind, and . . . strength" (Mark 12:30).

## C. Man in the Image of God

**1. The Meaning of "Image of God."** Out of all the creatures God made, only one creature, man, is said to be made "in the image of God."[6] What does that mean? We may use the following definition: *The fact that man is in the image of God means that man is like God and represents God.*

When God says, "Let us make man in our image, after our likeness" (Gen. 1:26), the meaning is that God plans to make a creature similar to himself. Both the Hebrew word for "image" (*tselem*) and the Hebrew word for "likeness" (*demût*) refer to something that is *similar* but not identical to the thing it represents or is an "image" of. The word *image* can also be used of something that *represents* something else.[7]

---

[5]See W. Grudem, *1 Peter,* p. 66.

[6]The Latin phrase *imago Dei* means "image of God" and is sometimes used in theological discussions in place of the English phrase "image of God." I have not used it elsewhere in this book.

[7]The word *image* (*tselem*) means an object similar to something else and often representative of it. The word is used to speak of statues or replicas of tumors and of mice (1 Sam. 6:5, 11), of paintings of soldiers on the wall (Ezek. 23:14), and of pagan idols or statues representing deities (Num. 33:42; 2 Kings 11:18; Ezek. 7:27; 16:17; et al.).

The word *likeness* (*demût*) also means an object similar to something else, but it tends to be used more frequently in contexts where the idea of similarity is emphasized more than the idea of being a

Theologians have spent much time attempting to specify one characteristic of man, or a very few, in which the image of God is primarily seen.[8] Some have thought that the image of God consists in man's intellectual ability, others in his power to make moral decisions and willing choices. Others have thought that the image of God referred to man's original moral purity, or his creation as male and female (see Gen. 1:27), or his dominion over the earth.

In this discussion it would be best to focus attention primarily on the *meanings* of the words "image" and "likeness." As we have seen, these terms had quite clear meanings to the original readers. When we realize that the Hebrew words for "image" and "likeness" simply informed the original readers that man was *like* God, and would in many ways *represent* God, much of the controversy over the meaning of "image of God" is seen to be a search for too narrow and too specific a meaning. When Scripture reports that God said, "Let us make man in our image, after our likeness" (Gen. 1:26), it simply would have meant to the original readers, "Let us make man to be *like* us and to *represent* us."

Because "image" and "likeness" had these meanings, Scripture does not need to say something like,

> The fact that man is in the image of God means that man is like God in the following ways: intellectual ability, moral purity, spiritual nature, dominion over the earth, creativity, ability to make ethical choices, and immortality [or some similar statement].

Such an explanation is unnecessary, not only because the terms had clear meanings, but also because no such list could do justice to the subject: the text only needs to affirm that man is *like God*, and the rest of Scripture fills in more details to explain this. In fact, as we read the rest of Scripture, we realize that a full understanding of man's likeness to God would require a full understanding of *who God is* in his being and in his actions and a full understanding of *who man is* and what he does. The more we know about God and man the more similarities we will recognize, and the more fully we will understand what Scripture means when it says that man is in the image of God. The expression refers to every way in which man is like God.

This understanding of what it means that man is created in the image of God is reinforced by the similarity between Genesis 1:26, where God declares his

---

representative or substitute (of a god, for example). King Ahaz's model or drawing of the altar he saw in Damascus is called a "likeness" (2 Kings 16:10), as are the figures of bulls beneath the bronze altar (2 Chron. 4:3–4), and the wall paintings of Babylonian chariot officers (Ezek. 23:15). In Ps. 58:4 (Heb. v. 5) the venom of the wicked is a "likeness" of the venom of a snake: here the idea is that they are very similar in their characteristics, but there is no thought of actual representation or substitution.

All of this evidence indicates that the English words *image* and *likeness* are very accurate equivalents for the Hebrew terms they translate.

[8]A brief survey of various views is found in D. J. A. Clines, "The Image of God in Man," *TB* (1968), pp. 54–61. Millard Erickson, *Christian Theology*, pp. 498–510, also gives a helpful summary of three major views of the image of God in man that have been held throughout the history of the church: (1) the substantive view, which identifies some particular quality of man (such as reason or spirituality) as being the image of God in man (Luther, Calvin, many early church writers); (2) relational views, which held that the image of God had to do with our interpersonal relationships (Emil Brunner; also Karl Barth, who saw the image of God specifically in our being created as male and female); and (3) the functional view, which holds that the image of God has to do with a function we carry out, usually our exercise of dominion over the creation (a Socinian view that is also held by some modern writers such as Norman Snaith and Leonard Verduin).

intention to create man in his image and likeness, and Genesis 5:3: "When Adam had lived a hundred and thirty years, he became the father of a son in his own likeness [*demût*], after his *image* [*tselem*], and named him Seth." Seth was not identical to Adam, but he was like him in many ways, as a son is like his father. The text simply means that Seth was like Adam. It does not specify any specific number of ways that Seth was like Adam, and it would be overly restrictive for us to assert that one or another characteristic determined the way in which Seth was in Adam's image and likeness. Was it his brown eyes? Or his curly hair? Perhaps it was his athletic prowess, or his serious disposition or even his quick temper? Of course, such speculation would be useless. It is evident that *every* way in which Seth was like Adam would be a part of his likeness to Adam and thus part of his being "in the image" of Adam. Similarly, *every* way in which man is like God is part of his being in the image and likeness of God.

**2. The Fall: God's Image Is Distorted but Not Lost.** We might wonder whether man could still be thought to be *like God* after he sinned. This question is answered quite early in Genesis where God gives Noah the authority to establish the death penalty for murder among human beings just after the flood: God says "Whoever sheds the blood of man, by man shall his blood be shed; *for God made man in his own image*" (Gen. 9:6). Even though men are sinful, there is still enough likeness to God remaining in them that to murder another person (to "shed blood" is an Old Testament expression for taking a human life) is to attack the part of creation that most resembles God, and it betrays an attempt or desire (if one were able) to attack God himself.[9] Man is still in God's image. The New Testament gives confirmation to this when James 3:9 says that men generally, not just believers, "are made in the likeness of God."

However, since man has sinned, he is certainly not as fully like God as he was before. His moral purity has been lost and his sinful character certainly does not reflect God's holiness. His intellect is corrupted by falsehood and misunderstanding; his speech no longer continually glorifies God; his relationships are often governed by selfishness rather than love, and so forth. Though man is still in the image of God, in every aspect of life *some* parts of that image have been distorted or lost. In short, "God made man upright, but they have sought out many devices" (Eccl. 7:29). After the fall, then, we are still in God's image—we are still like God and we still represent God—but the image of God in us is distorted; we are less fully like God than we were before the entrance of sin.

Therefore it is important that we understand the full meaning of the image of God not simply from observation of human beings as they currently exist, but from the biblical indications of the nature of Adam and Eve when God created them and when all that God had made was "very good" (Gen. 1:31). The true nature of man in the image of God was also seen in the earthly life of Christ. The full measure of the excellence of our humanity will not be seen again in life on earth until Christ returns and we have obtained all the benefits of the salvation he earned for us.

---

[9]For a detailed analysis of this passage, see John Murray, *Principles of Conduct* (Grand Rapids: Eerdmans, 1957), pp. 109–13.

**3. Redemption in Christ: a Progressive Recovering of More of God's Image.**
Nonetheless, it is encouraging to turn to the New Testament and see that our
redemption in Christ means that we can, even in this life, progressively grow into
more and more likeness to God. For example, Paul says that as Christians we have
a new nature that is "being renewed in knowledge after the image of its creator"
(Col. 3:10). As we gain in true understanding of God, his Word, and his world,
we begin to think more and more of the thoughts that God himself thinks. In this
way we are "renewed in knowledge" and we become more like God in our
thinking. This is a description of the ordinary course of the Christian life. So Paul
also can say that we "are being changed into his likeness [lit. "image," Gk. *eikōn*]
from one degree of glory to another" (2 Cor. 3:18).[10] Throughout this life, as we
grow in Christian maturity we grow in greater likeness to God. More particularly,
we grow in likeness to Christ in our lives and in our character. In fact, the goal for
which God has redeemed us is that we might be "conformed to the image of his
Son" (Rom. 8:29) and thus be exactly like Christ in our moral character.

**4. At Christ's Return: Complete Restoration of God's Image.** The amazing
promise of the New Testament is that just as we have been like Adam (subject to
death and sin), we shall also be like Christ (morally pure, never subject to death
again): "Just as we have borne the image of the man of dust, we shall also bear the
image of the man of heaven" (1 Cor. 15:49).[11] The full measure of our creation in
the image of God is not seen in the life of Adam who sinned, nor is it seen in our
lives now, for we are imperfect. But the New Testament emphasizes that God's
purpose in creating man in his image was completely realized in the person of
Jesus Christ. He himself "is the image of God" (2 Cor. 4:4 NASB); "He is the
image of the invisible God" (Col. 1:15). In Jesus we see human likeness to God as
it was intended to be, and it should cause us to rejoice that God has predestined us
"to be *conformed to the image of his son*" (Rom. 8:29; cf. 1 Cor. 15:49): "When he
appears *we shall be like him*" (1 John 3:2).

**5. Specific Aspects of Our Likeness to God.** Though we have argued above that
it would be difficult to define all the ways in which we are like God, we can
nevertheless mention several aspects of our existence that show us to be more like
God than all the rest of creation.[12]

**a. Moral Aspects:** (1) We are creatures who are morally accountable before God
for our actions. Corresponding to that accountability, we have (2) an inner sense
of right and wrong that sets us apart from animals (who have little if any innate
sense of morality or justice but simply respond from fear of punishment or hope of

---

[10]In this verse Paul specifically says that we are being changed into the image of Christ, but then four
verses later he says that Christ is the image of God (2 Cor. 4:4; both verses use *eikōn*).

[11]The New Testament Greek word for "image" (*eikōn*) has a similar meaning to its Old Testament
counterpart (see above). It indicates something that is similar to or very much like the thing it
represents. One interesting usage is a reference to the picture of Caesar on a Roman coin. Jesus asked
the Pharisees, "Whose likeness [Gk. *eikōn*, "image"] and inscription is this?" They replied, "Caesar's"
(Matt. 22:20–21). The image both resembles Caesar and represents him. (The Greek word *homoioma*,
"likeness," is not used in the New Testament to refer to man in the likeness of God.)

[12]However, angels also share a significant degree of likeness to God in a number of these aspects.

reward). When we act according to God's moral standards, our likeness to God is reflected in (3) behavior that is holy and righteous before him, but, by contrast, our *un*likeness to God is reflected whenever we sin.

**b. Spiritual Aspects:** (4) We have not only physical bodies but also immaterial spirits, and we can therefore act in ways that are significant in the immaterial, spiritual realm of existence. This means that we have (5) a spiritual life that enables us to relate to God as persons, to pray and praise him, and to hear him speaking his words to us.[13] No animal will ever spend an hour in intercessory prayer for the salvation of a relative or a friend! Connected with this spiritual life is the fact that we have (6) immortality; we will not cease to exist but will live forever.

**c. Mental Aspects:** (7) We have an ability to reason and think logically and learn that sets us apart from the animal world. Animals sometimes exhibit remarkable behavior in solving mazes or working out problems in the physical world, but they certainly do not engage in abstract reasoning—there is no such thing as the "history of canine philosophy," for example, nor have any animals since creation developed at all in their understanding of ethical problems or use of philosophical concepts, etc. No group of chimpanzees will ever sit around the table arguing about the doctrine of the Trinity or the relative merits of Calvinism or Arminianism! In fact, even in developing physical and technical skills we are far different from animals: beavers still build the same kind of dams they have built for a thousand generations, birds still build the same kind of nests, and bees still build the same kinds of hives. But we continue to develop greater skill and complexity in technology, in agriculture, in science, and in nearly every field of endeavor.

(8) Our use of complex, abstract language sets us far apart from the animals. I could tell my son, when he was four years old, to go and get the big, red screwdriver from my workbench in the basement. Even if he had never seen it before, he could easily perform the task because he knew meanings of "go," "get," "big," "red," "screwdriver," "workbench," and "basement." He could have done the same for a small, brown hammer or a black bucket beside the workbench or any of dozens of other items that he perhaps had never seen before but could visualize when I described them in a few brief words. No chimpanzee in all history has been able to perform such a task—a task that has not been learned through repetition with reward, but is simply described in words that refer to an item that the hearer has never seen before. Yet four-year-old human beings can do this routinely, and we think nothing of it. Most eight-year-olds can write an understandable letter to their grandparents describing a trip to the zoo, or can move to a foreign country and learn any other language in the world, and we think it entirely normal. But no animal will ever write such a letter to its grandparents, or give the past, present, and future of even one French verb, or

---

[13]Although it is not a separate aspect of our likeness to God, the fact that we have been redeemed by Christ sets us apart in an absolute way from every other creature God has made. This is a consequence of our being in God's image, and of God's love for us, rather than one part of what it means to be in his image.

read a detective story and understand it, or understand the meaning of even one verse from the Bible. Human children do all these things quite readily, and in so doing they show themselves so far superior to the whole animal kingdom that we wonder why people have sometimes thought that we are merely another kind of animal.

(9) Another mental difference between humans and animals is that we have an awareness of the distant future, even an inward sense that we will live beyond the time of our physical death, a sense that gives many people a desire to attempt to be right with God before they die (God "has put eternity into man's mind," Eccl. 3:11).

(10) Our likeness to God is also seen in our human creativity in areas such as art, music, and literature, and in scientific and technological inventiveness. We should not think of such creativity as restricted to world-famous musicians or artists—it is also reflected in a delightful way in the play acting or skits put on by children, in the skill reflected in the cooking of a meal or the decorating of a home or the planting of a garden, and in the inventiveness shown by every human being who "fixes" something that just wasn't working correctly.

The foregoing aspects of likeness to God have been ways in which we differ from animals *absolutely*, not merely in degree. But there are other areas where we differ from animals in significant degree, and these also can show our likeness to God.

(11) In the area of emotions, our likeness to God is seen in a large difference in degree and complexity of emotions. Of course, animals do show some emotions (anyone who has owned a dog can remember evident expressions of joy, sadness, fear of punishment when it has done wrong, anger if another animal invades its "turf," contentment, and affection, for example). But in the complexity of emotions that we experience, once again we are far different than the rest of creation. After watching my son's baseball game, I can simultaneously feel sad that his team lost, happy that he played well, proud that he was a good sport, thankful to God for giving me a son and giving me the joy of watching him grow up, joyful because of the song of praise that has been echoing in my mind all afternoon, and anxious because we are going to be late for dinner! It is very doubtful that an animal experiences anything approaching this complexity of emotional feeling.

**d. Relational Aspects:** In addition to our unique ability to relate to God (discussed above), there are other relational aspects of being in God's image. (12) Although animals no doubt have some sense of community with each other, the depth of interpersonal harmony experienced in human marriage, in a human family when it functions according to God's principles, and in a church when a community of believers is walking in fellowship with the Lord and with each other, is much greater than the interpersonal harmony experienced by any animals. In our family relationships and in the church, we are also superior to angels, who do not marry or bear children or live in the company of God's redeemed sons and daughters.

(13) In marriage itself we reflect the nature of God in the fact that as men and women we have equality in importance but difference in roles from the time that God created us (see discussion in chapter 22).

(14) Man is like God also in his relationship to the rest of creation. Specifically, man has been given the right to rule over the creation and when Christ returns will even be given authority to sit in judgment over angels (1 Cor. 6:3; Gen. 1:26, 28; Ps. 8:6–8).

**e. Physical Aspects:** Is there any sense in which our human bodies are also a part of what it means to be made in the image of God? Certainly we should not think that our physical bodies imply that God himself has a body, for "God is spirit" (John 4:24), and it is sin to think of him or to portray him in any way that would imply that he has a material or a physical body (see Ex. 20:4; Ps. 115:3–8; Rom. 1:23).[14] But even though our physical bodies should in no way be taken to imply that God has a physical body, are there still some ways in which our bodies reflect something of God's own character and thereby constitute part of what it means to be created in the image of God? Certainly this is true in some respects. For example, our physical bodies give us the ability to see with our eyes. This is a Godlike quality because God himself sees, and sees far more than we will ever see, although he does not do it with physical eyes like we have. Our ears give us the ability to hear, and this is a Godlike ability, even though God does not have physical ears. Our mouths give us the ability to speak, reflecting the fact that God is a God who speaks. Our senses of taste and touch and smell give us the ability to understand and enjoy God's creation, reflecting the fact that God himself understands and enjoys his creation, though in a far greater sense than we do.

It is important that we recognize that it is *man himself* who is created in the image of God, not just his spirit or his mind. Certainly our physical bodies are a very important part of our existence and, as transformed when Christ returns, they will continue to be part of our existence for all eternity (see 1 Cor. 15:43–45, 51–55). Our bodies therefore have been created by God as suitable instruments to represent in a physical way our human nature, which has been made to be like God's own nature. In fact, almost everything we do is done by means of the use of our physical bodies—our thinking, our moral judgments, our prayer and praise, our demonstrations of love and concern for each other—all are done using the physical bodies God has given us. Therefore, if we are careful to point out that we are *not* saying that God has a physical body, we may say that (15) our physical bodies in various ways reflect something of God's own character as well. Moreover, much physical movement and demonstration of God-given skill comes about through the use of our body. And certainly (16) the God-given physical ability to bear and raise children who are like ourselves (see Gen. 5:3) is a reflection of God's own ability to create human beings who are like himself.

Especially in the last several points, these differences between human beings and the rest of creation are not *absolute differences* but often differences of very great degree. We mentioned that there is some kind of emotion experienced by animals. There is some experience of authority in relationships where animal communities have leaders whose authority is accepted by the others in the group. Moreover, there is *some* similarity even in those differences we think more absolute: animals are able to reason to some extent and can communicate with each other in various ways that in some primitive sense can be called "language." This should not be

---

[14]See also the discussion of God's spirituality in chapter 12, pp. 186–88.

surprising: if God made the entire creation so that it reflects his character in various ways, this is what we would expect. In fact, the more complex and highly developed animals are *more* like God than lower forms of animals. Therefore we should not say that *only* man reflects any likeness to God at all, for in one way or another all of creation reflects some likeness to God.[15] But it is still important to recognize that *only man*, out of all of creation, is so like God that he can be said to be "in the image of God." This scriptural affirmation, together with the scriptural commands that we are to imitate God in our lives (Eph. 5:1; 1 Peter 1:16), and the observable facts that we can recognize in looking at ourselves and the rest of creation, all indicate that we are *much more like God* than all the rest of creation. In some respects the differences are absolute, and in other respects they are relative, but they are all significant.

Finally, our appreciation of the ways in which we are like God can be enhanced by the realization that, unlike the rest of God's creation, we have an ability to grow to become *more like God* throughout our lives. Our moral sense can be more highly developed through study of Scripture and prayer. Our moral behavior can reflect more and more the holiness of God (2 Cor. 7:1; 1 Peter 1:16; et al.). Our spiritual life can be enriched and deepened. Our use of reason and language can become more accurate and truthful and more honoring to God. Our sense of the future can become intensified as we grow in our hope of living with God forever. Our future existence can be enriched as we lay up treasures in heaven and seek for increased heavenly reward (see Matt. 6:19–21; 1 Cor. 3:10–15; 2 Cor. 5:10). Our ability to rule over the creation can be extended by faithful use of the gifts God has given us; our faithfulness to the God-given purposes for our creation as men and women can be increased as we follow biblical principles in our families; our creativity can be employed in ways that are more and more pleasing to God; our emotions can be more and more conformed to the pattern of Scripture so that we become more like David, a man after God's own heart (1 Sam. 13:14). Our interpersonal harmony in our families and in the church can reflect more and more the unity that exists among the persons in the Trinity. As we consciously seek to grow into greater likeness to God in all these areas, we also demonstrate an ability that itself sets us apart from the rest of creation.

**6. Our Great Dignity as Bearers of God's Image.** It would be good for us to reflect on our likeness to God more often. It will probably amaze us to realize that when the Creator of the universe wanted to create something "in his image," something *more like himself* than all the rest of creation, he made us. This realization will give us a profound sense of dignity and significance as we reflect on the excellence of all the rest of God's creation: the starry universe, the abundant earth, the world of plants and animals, and the angelic kingdoms are remarkable, even magnificent. But we are more like our Creator than any of these things. We are the culmination of God's infinitely wise and skillful work of creation. Even though sin has greatly marred that likeness, we nonetheless now reflect much of it and shall even more as we grow in likeness to Christ.

Yet we must remember that even fallen, sinful man has the *status* of being in

---

[15]See discussion of the names of God and the way God's nature is reflected in all of creation in chapter 11, pp. 157–60.

God's image (see discussion of Gen. 9:6, above). Every single human being, no matter how much the image of God is marred by sin, or illness, or weakness, or age, or any other disability, still has the *status* of being in God's image and therefore must be treated with the dignity and respect that is due to God's image-bearer. This has profound implications for our conduct toward others. It means that people of every race deserve equal dignity and rights. It means that elderly people, those seriously ill, the mentally retarded, and children yet unborn, deserve full protection and honor as human beings. If we ever deny our unique status in creation as God's only image-bearers, we will soon begin to depreciate the value of human life, will tend to see humans as merely a higher form of animal, and will begin to treat others as such. We will also lose much of our sense of meaning in life.

## QUESTIONS FOR PERSONAL APPLICATION

1. According to Scripture, what should be the major purpose of your life? If you consider the major commitments or goals of your life at the present time (with respect to friendships, marriage, education, job, use of money, church relationships, etc.), are you acting as though your goal were the one that Scripture specifies? Or do you have some other goals that you have acted upon (perhaps without consciously deciding to do so)? As you think about the pattern of most of your days, do you think that God delights in you and rejoices over you?

2. How does it make you feel to think that you, as a human being, are more like God than any other creature in the universe? How does that knowledge make you want to act?

3. Do you think that there are any more intelligent, more Godlike creatures anywhere else in the universe? What does the fact that Jesus became a man rather than some other kind of creature say about the importance of human beings in God's sight?

4. Do you think that God has made us so that we become more happy or less happy when we grow to become more like him? As you look over the list of ways in which we can be more like God, can you name one or two areas in which growth in likeness to God has given you increasing joy in your life? In which areas would you now like to make more progress in likeness to God?

5. Is it only Christians or all people who are in the image of God? How does that make you feel about your relationships to non-Christians?

6. Do you think an understanding of the image of God might change the way you think and act toward people who are racially different, or elderly, or weak, or unattractive to the world?

## SPECIAL TERMS

image of God
*imago Dei*
likeness

# BIBLIOGRAPHY

(For an explanation of this bibliography see the note on the bibliography to chapter 1, p. 38. Complete bibliographical data may be found on pp. 1223–29.)

## Sections in Evangelical Systematic Theologies

1. Anglican (Episcopalian)
   1882–92    Litton, 109–22
2. Arminian (Wesleyan or Methodist)
   1875–76    Pope, 1:430–36
   1892–94    Miley, 1:355–422, 406–8
   1940       Wiley, 2:7–50
   1960       Purkiser, 204–22
   1983       Carter, 1:195–236
3. Baptist
   1767       Gill, 1:440–51
   1887       Boyce, 189–94, 213–17
   1907       Strong, 465–83, 514–32
   1917       Mullins, 255–62
   1976–83    Henry, 2:124–42; 4:494–521
   1983–85    Erickson, 455–518, 541–58
   1987–94    Lewis/Demarest, 2:123–82
4. Dispensational
   1947       Chafer, 2:125–43, 161–73
   1949       Thiessen, 151–57
   1986       Ryrie, 189–94
5. Lutheran
   1917–24    Pieper, 1:515–27
   1934       Mueller, 205–9
6. Reformed (or Presbyterian)
   1559       Calvin, 1:183–96 (1.15)
   1861       Heppe, 4:197–228, 220–50
   1871–73    Hodge, 2:92–116
   1878       Dabney, 293–94
   1887–1921  Warfield, BTS, 238–61
   1889       Shedd, 2a:3–115; 3:249–377
   1937–66    Murray, CW, 2:14–22, 34–46
   1938       Berkhof, 181–90, 202–10
   1962       Buswell, 1:231–61
7. Renewal (or charismatic/Pentecostal)
   1988–92    Williams, 1:197–220

## Sections in Representative Roman Catholic Systematic Theologies

1. Roman Catholic: Traditional
    1955    Ott, 94–96, 101–6
2. Roman Catholic: Post-Vatican II
    1980    McBrien, 1:101–78

### Other Works

Barclay, D. R. "Creation." In *NDT*, pp. 177–79.
Berkouwer, G. C. *Man: The Image of God*. Grand Rapids: Eerdmans, 1962.
Boston, Thomas. *Human Nature in Its Fourfold State*. London: Banner of Truth, 1964 (first published 1720).
Ferguson, S. B. "Image of God." In *NDT*, pp. 328–29.
Henry, C. F. H. "Image of God." In *EDT*, pp. 545–48.
Hoekema, Anthony A. *Created in God's Image*. Grand Rapids: Eerdmans, and Exeter: Paternoster, 1986, pp. 1–111.
Hughes, Philip Edgcumbe. *The True Image: The Origin and Destiny of Man in Christ*. Grand Rapids: Eerdmans, and Leicester: Inter-Varsity Press, 1989, pp. 1–70.
Kline, Meredith G. *Images of the Spirit*. Grand Rapids: Baker, 1980.
Laidlaw, John. *The Bible Doctrine of Man*. Edinburgh: T. & T. Clark, 1905.
Machen, J. Gresham. *The Christian View of Man*. London: Banner of Truth, 1965 (reprint of 1937 edition).
McDonald, H. D. "Man, Doctrine of." In *EDT*, pp. 676–80.
————. *The Christian View of Man*. Westchester, Ill.: Crossway, 1981.
Robinson, H. W. *The Christian Doctrine of Man*. 3d ed. Edinburgh: T. & T. Clark, 1926.

## SCRIPTURE MEMORY PASSAGE

**Genesis 1:26–27**: *Then God said, "Let us make man in our image, after our likeness; and let them have dominion over the fish of the sea, and over the birds of the air, and over the cattle, and over all the earth, and over every creeping thing that creeps upon the earth." So God created man in his own image, in the image of God he created him; male and female he created them.*

## HYMNS

### "Love Divine, All Love Excelling"

Love divine, all love excelling,
    Joy of heav'n, to earth come down!
Fix in us thy humble dwelling;
    All thy faithful mercies crown.
Jesus, thou art all compassion,
    Pure, unbounded love thou art;

Visit us with thy salvation,
  Enter ev'ry trembling heart.

Breathe, O breathe thy loving Spirit
  Into ev'ry troubled breast!
Let us all in thee inherit,
  Let us find the promised rest.
Take away the love of sinning;
  Alpha and Omega be;
End of faith, as its beginning,
  Set our hearts at liberty.

Come, Almighty to deliver,
  Let us all thy life receive;
Suddenly return, and never,
  Never more thy temples leave.
Thee we would be always blessing,
  Serve thee as thy hosts above,
Pray, and praise thee, without ceasing,
  Glory in thy perfect love.

Finish, then, thy new creation;
  Pure and spotless let us be;
Let us see thy great salvation
  Perfectly restored in thee:
Changed from glory into glory,
  Till in heav'n we take our place,
Till we cast our crowns before thee,
  Lost in wonder, love, and praise.

AUTHOR: CHARLES WESLEY, 1747

**Alternative hymn:**
"Thou Art Worthy"

Thou art worthy, thou art worthy,
  thou art worthy, O Lord.
To receive glory, glory and honor,
  glory and honor and power.
For thou hast created, hast all things created,
  thou hast created all things;
And for thy pleasure, they are created,
  thou art worthy, O Lord.

AUTHOR: PAULINE MICHAEL MILLS

# Chapter 22

# Man As Male and Female

*Why did God create two sexes? Can men and women be equal and yet have different roles?*

## EXPLANATION AND SCRIPTURAL BASIS

We noted in the previous chapter that one aspect of man's creation in the image of God is his creation as male and female: "So God created man in his own image, in the image of God he created him; *male and female he created them*" (Gen. 1:27). The same connection between creation in the image of God and creation as male and female is made in Genesis 5:1–2, "When God created man, he made him in the likeness of God. *Male and female* he created them, and he blessed them and named them Man when they were created."[1] Although the creation of man as male and female is not the only way in which we are in the image of God, it is a significant enough aspect of our creation in the image of God that Scripture mentions it in the very same verse in which it describes God's initial creation of man. We may summarize the ways in which our creation as male and female represents something of our creation in God's image as follows:

The creation of man as male and female shows God's image in (1) harmonious interpersonal relationships, (2) equality in personhood and importance, and (3) difference in role and authority.[2]

## A. Personal Relationships

God did not create human beings to be isolated persons, but, in making us in his image, he made us in such a way that we can attain interpersonal unity of various sorts in all forms of human society. Interpersonal unity can be especially deep in the human family and also in our spiritual family, the church. Between men and women, interpersonal unity comes to its fullest expression in this age in marriage, where husband and wife become, in a sense, two persons in one: "Therefore a man leaves his father and his mother and cleaves to his wife, and they become one flesh" (Gen. 2:24). This unity is not only a physical unity; it is also a

---

[1]On the question of whether to use the English word *man* to refer to human beings generally (both male and female), see chapter 21, pp. 439–40.

[2]For a more extensive discussion of the theological implications of male-female differentiation in Genesis 1–3, see Raymond C. Ortlund, Jr., "Male-Female Equality and Male Headship: Genesis 1–3," in *Recovering Biblical Manhood and Womanhood: A Response to Evangelical Feminism*, ed. by John Piper and Wayne Grudem, p. 98. I have depended on Dr. Ortlund's analysis at several points in this chapter.

spiritual and emotional unity of profound dimensions. A husband and wife joined together in marriage are people that "God has joined together" (Matt. 19:6). Sexual union with someone other than one's own wife or husband is a specially offensive kind of sin against one's own body (1 Cor. 6:16, 18–20), and, within marriage, husbands and wives no longer have exclusive rule over their own bodies, but share them with their spouses (1 Cor. 7:3–5). Husbands "should love their wives as their own bodies" (Eph. 5:28). The union between husband and wife is not temporary but lifelong (Mal. 2:14–16; Rom. 7:2), and it is not trivial but is a profound relationship created by God in order to picture the relationship between Christ and his church (Eph. 5:23–32).

The fact that God created two distinct persons as male and female, rather than just one man, is part of our being in the image of God because it can be seen to reflect to some degree the plurality of persons within the Trinity. In the verse prior to the one that tells of our creation as male and female, we see the first explicit indication of a plurality of persons within God: "Then God said, 'Let *us* make man in *our* image, after our likeness; and let them have dominion'" (Gen. 1:26). There is some similarity here: just as there was fellowship and communication and sharing of glory among the members of the Trinity before the world was made (see John 17:5, 24, and chapter 14 on the Trinity, above), so God made Adam and Eve in such a way that they would share love and communication and mutual giving of honor to one another in their interpersonal relationship. Of course such reflection of the Trinity would come to expression in various ways within human society, but it would certainly exist from the beginning in the close interpersonal unity of marriage.

Someone might object that such a representation of the plurality of persons in God is not really a complete one, for God is three persons in one while God created Adam and Eve as only two persons in one. If God intended us to reflect the plurality of persons in the Trinity, why did he not create three persons rather than two who could reflect the interpersonal unity among the members of the Trinity? First, we must agree that this fact shows the analogy between marriage and the Trinity to be an inexact one. Second, although we cannot be certain of the reasons why God did not do something when Scripture does not explicitly tell us those reasons, we can suggest two possible answers: (1) The fact that God is three in one while Adam and Eve were only two in one may be a reminder that God's own excellence is far greater than ours, that he possesses far greater plurality and far greater unity than we ourselves, as creatures, can possess. (2) Though the unity is not exactly the same, the unity in a family among husband, wife, and children, does also reflect to some degree the interpersonal unity yet diversity of persons among the members of the Trinity.

A second objection might be raised from the fact that Jesus himself was unmarried, that Paul was unmarried at the time he was an apostle (and perhaps earlier), and that Paul in 1 Corinthians 7:1, 7–9 seems to say that it is better for Christians not to marry. If marriage is such an important part of our reflection of the image of God, then why were Paul and Jesus not married, and why did Paul encourage others not to be married?

For Jesus, the situation is unique, for he is both God and man, and sovereign Lord over all creation. Rather than being married to any one individual human being, he has taken the entire church as his bride (see Eph. 5:23–32) and enjoys with each member of his church a spiritual and emotional unity that will last for eternity.

The situation with Paul and his advice to the Corinthian Christians is somewhat different. There Paul does not say that it is wrong to marry (see 1 Cor. 7:28, 36), but rather views marriage as something good, a right and a privilege that may be given up for the sake of the kingdom of God: "I think that in view of the present distress it is well for a person to remain as he is . . . the appointed time has grown very short. . . . For the form of this world is passing away" (1 Cor. 7:26, 29, 31). In this way Paul gives up one way in which he might reflect likeness to God (marriage) in order to further other ways in which he might reflect likeness to God and further God's purposes in the world (namely, in his work for the church). For example, his evangelism and discipleship are thought of as bearing "spiritual children" and nurturing them in the Lord (see 1 Cor. 4:14, where he calls the Corinthians "my beloved children"; also Gal. 4:19; 1 Tim. 1:2; Titus 1:4). Moreover, the entire building up of the church was a process of bringing thousands of people to glorify God as they reflected his character more fully in their lives. In addition, we must realize that marriage is not the only way in which the unity and diversity in the Trinity can be reflected in our lives. It is also reflected in the union of believers in the fellowship of the church—and in genuine church fellowship, single persons (like Paul and Jesus) as well as those who are married can have interpersonal relationships that reflect the nature of the Trinity. Therefore, building the church and increasing its unity and purity also promote the reflection of God's character in the world.

## B. Equality in Personhood and Importance

Just as the members of the Trinity are equal in their importance and in their full existence as distinct persons (see chapter 14, above), so men and women have been created by God to be equal in their importance and personhood. When God created man, he created both "male and female" in his image (Gen. 1:27; 5:1–2). Men and women are made *equally in God's image,* and both men and women reflect God's character in their lives. This means that we should see aspects of God's character reflected in each other's lives. If we lived in a society consisting of only Christian men or a society consisting of only Christian women, we would not gain as full a picture of the character of God as when we see both godly men and godly women in their complementary differences together reflecting the beauty of God's character.

But if we are equally in God's image, then certainly men and women are *equally important* to God and *equally valuable* to him. We have equal worth before him for all eternity. The fact that both men and women are said by Scripture to be "in the image of God" should exclude all feelings of pride or inferiority and any idea that one sex is "better" or "worse" than the other. In particular, in contrast to many non-Christian cultures and religions, no one should feel proud or superior because he is a man, and no one should feel disappointed or inferior because she is a woman.[3] If God thinks us to be equal in value, then that settles the question, for God's evaluation is the true standard of personal value for all eternity.

---

[3]In the past decade news agencies have reported a common practice in China whereby parents of a

When in 1 Corinthians 11:7 Paul says, "A man ought not to cover his head, since he is the image and glory of God; but woman is the glory of man," he is not denying that woman was created in the image of God. He is simply saying that there are abiding differences between men and women that should be reflected in the way they dress and act in the assembled congregation. One of those differences is that man in relationship to woman has a particular role of representing God or showing what he is like, and woman in that relationship shows the excellence of the man from whom she was created. Yet in both cases Paul goes on to emphasize their interdependence (see vv. 11–12).

Our equality as persons before God, reflecting the equality of persons in the Trinity, should lead naturally to men and women giving honor to one another. Proverbs 31 is a beautiful picture of the honor given to a godly woman:

> A good wife who can find?
>> She is far more precious than jewels. . . .
> Her children rise up and call her blessed;
>> her husband also, and he praises her:
> "Many women have done excellently,
>> but you surpass them all."
> Charm is deceitful, and beauty is vain,
>> but a woman who fears the LORD is to be praised.
>> (Prov. 31:10, 28–30)

Similarly, Peter tells husbands that they are to "bestow honor" on their wives (1 Peter 3:7), and Paul emphasizes, "In the Lord woman is not independent of man nor man of woman; for as woman was made from man, so man is now born of woman" (1 Cor. 11:11, 12). Both men and women are equally important; both depend upon each other; both are worthy of honor.

The equality in personhood with which men and women were created is emphasized in a new way in the new covenant church. At Pentecost we see the fulfillment of Joel's prophecy in which God promises:

> "I will pour out my Spirit upon all flesh,
> and your *sons* and your *daughters* shall prophesy
> . . . and on my *menservants* and my *maidservants* in those days
> I will pour out my Spirit; and they shall prophesy."
> (Acts 2:17–18; quoting Joel 2:28–29)

The Holy Spirit is poured out in new power on the church, and men and women *both* are given gifts to minister in remarkable ways. Spiritual gifts are distributed to all men and women, beginning at Pentecost and continuing throughout the history of the church. Paul regards every Christian as a valuable member of the body of Christ, for "to *each* is given the manifestation of the Spirit for the

---

newborn daughter will often leave her to die in order that they might try again to have a son under China's strict "one couple, one child" policy. In contrast to the biblical view of equality in importance for men and women, such a tragic practice not only results in much loss of innocent human life, but also proclaims loudly to every woman in that society that she is less valuable than a man. (In other societies parents who secretly think that it is better to have a baby boy than a baby girl also show that they have not fully understood the biblical teaching on the fact that women and men are fully equal in value in God's sight.)

common good" (1 Cor. 12:7). After mentioning several gifts he says, "All these are inspired by one and the same Spirit, who apportions *to each one* individually as he wills," (1 Cor. 12:11). Peter also, in writing to many churches throughout Asia Minor, says, "As *each* has received a gift, employ it for one another, as good stewards of God's varied grace" (1 Peter 4:10). These texts do not teach that all believers have the same gifts, but they do mean that both men and women will have valuable gifts for the ministry of the church, and that we should expect that these gifts will be widely and freely distributed to both men and women.

It seems, therefore, pointless to ask, "Who can pray more effectively, men or women?" or, "Who can sing praise to God better, men or women?" or, "Who will have more spiritual sensitivity and depth of relationship with God?" To all of these questions, we simply cannot give an answer. Men and women are equal in their ability to receive the new covenant empowerment of the Holy Spirit. There have been both great men and great women of God throughout the history of the church. Both men and women have been mighty warriors in prayer, prevailing over earthly powers and kingdoms and spiritual strongholds in the authority of our Lord Jesus Christ.[4]

Equality before God is further emphasized in the new covenant church in the ceremony of baptism. At Pentecost, both men and women who believed were baptized: "those who received his word were baptized, and there were added that day about three thousand souls" (Acts 2:41). This is significant because in the old covenant, the sign of membership of God's people was circumcision, which was given only to men. The new sign of membership of God's people, the sign of baptism, given to both men and women, is further evidence that both should be seen as fully and equally members of the people of God.

Equality in status among God's people is also emphasized by Paul in Galatians: "For as many of you as were baptized into Christ have put on Christ. There is neither Jew nor Greek, there is neither slave nor free, *there is neither male nor female;* for you are all one in Christ Jesus" (Gal. 3:27–28). Paul is here underlining the fact that no class of people, such as the Jewish people who had come from Abraham by physical descent, or the freedmen who had greater economic and legal power, could claim special status or privilege in the church. Slaves should not think themselves inferior to free men or women, nor should the free think themselves superior to slaves. Jews should not think themselves superior to Greeks, nor should Greeks think themselves inferior to Jews. Similarly, Paul wants to insure that men will not adopt some of the attitudes of the surrounding culture, or even some of the attitudes of first-century Judaism, and think that they have greater importance than women or are of superior value before God. Nor should women think themselves inferior or less important in the church. Both men and women, Jews and Greeks, slaves and free, are equal in importance and

---

[4]Perhaps the answer to the questions, "Who can pray better?" and "Who can praise God better?" should be "both together." Although there is much value in a men's prayer meeting or in a gathering of women for prayer, there is nothing richer and more complete than the whole fellowship of God's people, both men and women, and even their children who are old enough to understand and participate, gathered together before God's throne in prayer: "When the day of Pentecost had come, they *were all together in one place*" (Acts 2:1). "And when they heard it, they lifted their voices *together* to God" (Acts 4:24). Peter "went to the house of Mary, the mother of John whose other name was Mark, where *many were gathered together* and were praying" (Acts 12:12).

value to God and equal in membership in Christ's body, the church, for all eternity.

In practical terms, we must never think that there are any second-class citizens in the church. Whether someone is a man or woman, employer or employee, Jew or Gentile, black or white, rich or poor, healthy or ill, strong or weak, attractive or unattractive, extremely intelligent or slow to learn, all are equally valuable to God and should be equally valuable to one another as well. This equality is an amazing and wonderful element of the Christian faith and sets Christianity apart from almost all religions and societies and cultures. The true dignity of godly manhood and womanhood can be fully realized only in obedience to God's redeeming wisdom as found in Scripture.

## C. Differences in Roles

**1. The Relationship Between the Trinity and Male Headship in Marriage.** Between the members of the Trinity there has been equality in importance, personhood, and deity throughout all eternity. But there have also been differences in roles between the members of the Trinity.[5] God the Father has always been the Father and has always related to the Son as a Father relates to his Son. Though all three members of the Trinity are equal in power and in all other attributes, the Father has a greater authority. He has a leadership role among all the members of the Trinity that the Son and Holy Spirit do not have. In creation, the Father speaks and initiates, but the work of creation is carried out through the Son and sustained by the continuing presence of the Holy Spirit (Gen. 1:1–2; John 1:1–3; 1 Cor. 8:6; Heb. 1:2). In redemption, the Father sends the Son into the world, and the Son comes and is obedient to the Father and dies to pay for our sins (Luke 22:42; Phil. 2:6–8). After the Son has ascended into heaven, the Holy Spirit comes to equip and empower the church (John 16:7; Acts 1:8; 2:1–36). The Father did not come to die for our sins, nor did the Holy Spirit. The Father was not poured out on the church at Pentecost in new covenant power, nor was the Son. Each member of the Trinity has distinct roles or functions. Differences in roles and authority between the members of the Trinity are thus completely consistent with equal importance, personhood, and deity.

If human beings are to reflect the character of God, then we would expect some similar differences in roles among human beings, even with respect to the most basic of all differences among human beings, the difference between male and female. And this is certainly what we find in the biblical text.

Paul makes this parallel explicit when he says, "I want you to understand that the head of every man is Christ, *the head of a woman is her husband,* and *the head of Christ is God*" (1 Cor. 11:3). Here is a distinction in authority that may be represented as in figure 22.1.

Just as God the Father has authority over the Son, though the two are equal in deity, so in a marriage, the husband has authority over the wife, though they are equal in personhood.[6] In this case, the man's role is like that of God the Father,

[5]See chapter 14, pp. 248–52, on role differences among the members of the Trinity.

[6]Some have suggested that the word "head" in 1 Cor. 11:3 means "source" and has nothing to do with authority in marriage. For example, when referring to Paul's use of the word "head" to say that "the head of every man is Christ, the head of woman is her husband, and the head of Christ is God"

and the woman's role is parallel to that of God the Son. They are equal in importance, but they have different roles. In the context of 1 Corinthians 11:2–16, Paul sees this as a basis for telling the Corinthians to wear the different kinds of clothing appropriate for the men and women of that day, so that the distinctions between men and women might be outwardly evident in the Christian assembly.[7]

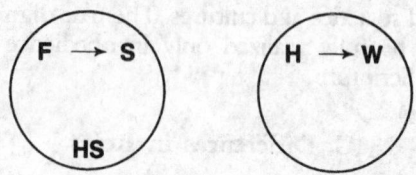

**EQUALITY AND DIFFERENCES IN THE TRINITY ARE REFLECTED IN EQUALITY AND DIFFERENCES IN MARRIAGE**
*Figure 22.1*

**2. Indications of Distinct Roles Before the Fall.** But were these distinctions between male and female roles part of God's original creation, or were they introduced as part of the punishment of the fall? When God told Eve, "Yet your desire shall be for your husband, and *he shall rule over you*" (Gen. 3:16), was that the time when Eve began to be subject to Adam's authority?

The idea that differences in authority were introduced only after there was sin in

---

(1 Cor. 11:3), Gordon Fee says that "Paul's understanding of the metaphor, therefore, and almost certainly the only one the Corinthians would have grasped, is 'head' as 'source,' especially 'source of life'" (*The First Epistle to the Corinthians,* NIC [Grand Rapids: Eerdmans, 1987], p. 503).

Similarly, the statement, "Men, Women and Biblical Equality," published as an advertisement in *CT,* April 9, 1990, pp. 36–37, says, "The husband's function as 'head' is to be understood as self-giving love and service within this relationship of mutual submission (Eph. 5:21–33; Col. 3:19; 1 Pet. 3:7)" (p. 1, para. 11). Thus they understand "head" to mean "source" (of love and service), not "authority over."

For a response to this interpretation and a discussion of reasons why the word "head" here must mean "authority over" not "source," see W. Grudem, "Does *Kephalē* ('Head') Mean 'Source' or 'Authority Over' in Greek Literature? A Survey of 2,336 Examples," *TrinJ* 6, n.s. (Spring 1985), pp. 38–59, and W. Grudem, "The Meaning of *Kephale* ('Head'): A Response to Recent Studies," *TrinJ* 11, n.s. (Spring 1990), pp. 3–72 (reprinted in *Recovering Biblical Manhood and Womanhood: A Response to Evangelical Feminism,* pp. 425–68). See also Joseph Fitzmyer, "Another Look at *Kephalē* in 1 Cor. 11:3," *NTS* 35 (1989), pp. 503–11. Even the few examples where people have claimed that "head" could mean "source" when applied to a person, the person is *always* one in authority. No counter-examples to this have ever been found in ancient Greek literature.

[7]The fact that head coverings were the kind of clothing that distinguished women from men in first-century Corinth meant that Paul directed the women to wear head coverings in church. But this does not mean that women should wear head coverings in societies where that is not a distinctive sign of being a woman. The contemporary application would be that women should dress to look like women and men should dress to look like men, in whatever form those clothing patterns are expressed in each society: Paul is not in favor of unisex clothing! For further discussion, see Thomas R. Schreiner, "Head Coverings, Prophecies and the Trinity: 1 Corinthians 11:2–16," in *Recovering Biblical Manhood and Womanhood,* pp. 124–39.

the world has been advocated by several writers such as Aida B. Spencer[8] and Gilbert Bilezikian.[9] Bilezikian says, "Because it resulted from the Fall, the rule of Adam over Eve is viewed as satanic in origin, no less than is death itself."[10]

However, if we examine the text of the creation narrative in Genesis, we see several indications of *differences in role* between Adam and Eve *even before there was sin in the world.*

**a. Adam Was Created First, Then Eve:** The fact that God first created Adam, then after a period of time created Eve (Gen. 2:7, 18–23), suggests that God saw Adam as having a leadership role in his family. No such two-stage procedure is mentioned for any of the animals God made, but here it seems to have a special purpose. The creation of Adam first is consistent with the Old Testament pattern of "primogeniture," the idea that the firstborn in any generation in a human family has leadership in the family for that generation. The right of primogeniture is assumed throughout the Old Testament text, even when at times because of God's special purposes the birthright is sold or otherwise transferred to a younger person (Gen. 25:27–34; 35:23; 38:27–30; 49:3–4; Deut. 21:15–17; 1 Chron. 5:1–2). The "birthright" belongs to the firstborn son and is his unless special circumstances intervene to change that fact.[11] The fact that we are correct in seeing a purpose of God in creating Adam first, and that this purpose reflects an abiding distinction in the roles God has given to men and women, is supported by 1 Timothy 2:13, where Paul uses the fact that "Adam was formed first, then Eve" as a reason for restricting some distinct governing and teaching roles in the church to men.

**b. Eve Was Created as a Helper for Adam:** Scripture specifies that God made Eve for Adam, not Adam for Eve. God said, "It is not good that the man should be alone; *I will make him a helper fit for him*" (Gen. 2:18). Paul sees this as significant enough to base a requirement for differences between men and women in worship on it. He says, "Neither was man created for woman, but *woman for man*" (1 Cor. 11:9). This should not be taken to imply lesser importance, but it does indicate that there was a difference in roles from the beginning.

Recently some writers have denied that the creation of Eve as a helper fit for Adam signals any difference in role or authority, because the word *helper* (Heb., *'ezer*) is often used in the Old Testament of someone who is greater or more powerful than the one who is being helped.[12] In fact, the word *helper* is used in the Old Testament of God himself who helps his people. But the point is that whenever someone "helps" someone else, whether in the Hebrew Old Testament

---

[8]*Beyond the Curse,* 2d ed. (Nashville: Thomas Nelson, 1985), pp. 20–42.

[9]*Beyond Sex Roles* (Grand Rapids: Baker, 1985), pp. 21–58.

[10]Ibid., p. 58.

[11]Some object that this would not be appropriate in the Genesis narrative, for animals were created before Adam, and this would give animals the authority to rule over humans (so Bilezikian, *Beyond Sex Roles,* p. 257, n. 13). But this objection fails to understand that the principle of primogeniture only occurs among human beings and is, in fact, limited to those in the same family. (Bilezikian raises other objections [pp. 255–57] but fails to deal with the New Testament endorsement of this understanding of Gen. 2 in 1 Tim. 2:13.)

[12]See Aida B. Spencer, *Beyond the Curse,* pp. 23–29.

or in our modern-day use of the word *help*, in the specific task in view the person who is helping is occupying a subordinate or inferior position with regard to the person being helped. That is true even when I "help" a young boy in my neighborhood to fix his bicycle—it is his responsibility, and his task, and I am only giving some assistance as needed; it is not my responsibility. David Clines concludes that this is the case throughout the Hebrew Old Testament:

> What I conclude, from viewing all of the occurrences in the Hebrew Bible, is that though superiors may help inferiors, strong may help weak, gods many help humans, in the act of helping they are being "inferior." That is to say, they are subjecting themselves to a secondary, subordinate position. Their help may be necessary or crucial, but they are assisting some task that is someone else's responsibility. They are not actually doing the task themselves, or even in cooperation, for there is different language for that. Being a helper is not a Hebrew way of being an equal.[13]

Another objection is that the Hebrew term translated "fit for" in Genesis 2:18 implies that Eve was actually superior to Adam, because the term really means "in front of."[14] But Raymond C. Ortlund correctly points out that the Hebrew term cannot mean "superior to" or Psalm 119:168 would have the psalmist saying to God, "All my ways are *superior* to you"! It simply means "corresponding to."[15]

**c. Adam Named Eve:** The fact that Adam gave names to all the animals (Gen. 2:19–20) indicated Adam's authority over the animal kingdom, because in Old Testament thought the right to name someone implied authority over that person (this is seen both when God gives names to people such as Abraham and Sarah, and when parents give names to their children). Since a Hebrew name designated the character or function of someone, Adam was specifying the characteristics or functions of the animals he named. Therefore when Adam named Eve by saying, "She shall be called Woman, because she was taken out of Man" (Gen. 2:23), it indicated a leadership role on his part as well.[16] This is true before the fall, where Adam names his wife "Woman," and it is true after the fall as well, when "the man called his wife's name Eve, because she was the mother of all living" (Gen. 3:20).[17] Some have objected that Adam doesn't really name Eve before the fall.[18] But certainly calling his wife "Woman" (Gen. 2:23), just as he called all the living creatures by their names (Gen. 2:19–20), is giving her a name. The fact that mothers sometimes give their children names in the Old Testament does not contradict the idea of name-giving as representing authority, since both mothers and fathers have parental authority over their children.

---

[13]David J. A. Clines, "What Does Eve Do to Help? and Other Irredeemably Androcentric Orientations in Genesis 1–3," paper read at Society of Biblical Literature annual meeting Dec. 7, 1987, in Boston, Massachusetts.

[14]So Aida Spencer, *Beyond the Curse*, pp. 23–26. She says, "The Hebrew text even signifies that the woman is 'in front of' the man or 'over' him!" (p. 26).

[15]Ortlund, "Male-Female Equality," pp. 103–4; cf. BDB, p. 617, 2a.

[16]See the discussion in Ortlund, "Male-Female Equality," pp. 102–3.

[17]Gerhard von Rad says, "Let us remind ourselves once more that name-giving in the ancient Orient was primarily an exercise of sovereignty, of command" (*Genesis: A Commentary*, rev. ed. [Philadelphia: Westminster, 1972], p. 83).

[18]See Bilezikian, *Beyond Sex Roles*, pp. 260–61.

**d. God Named the Human Race "Man," Not "Woman":** The fact that God named the human race "man," rather than "woman" or some gender-neutral term was explained in chapter 21.[19] Genesis 5:2 specifies that "in the day when they were created" (NASB) God *"named them Man."* The naming of the human race with a term that also referred to Adam in particular, or man in distinction from woman, suggests a leadership role belonging to the man. This is similar to the custom of a woman taking the last name of the man when she marries: it signifies his headship in the family.

**e. The Serpent Came to Eve First:** Satan, after he had sinned, was attempting to distort and undermine everything that God had planned and created as good. It is likely that Satan (in the form of a serpent), in approaching Eve first, was attempting to institute a role reversal by tempting Eve to take the leadership in disobeying God (Gen. 3:1). This stands in contrast to the way God approached them, for when God spoke to them, he spoke to Adam first (Gen. 2:15–17; 3:9). Paul seems to have this role reversal in mind when he says, "Adam was not deceived, but the woman was deceived and became a transgressor" (1 Tim. 2:14). This at least suggests that Satan was trying to undermine the pattern of male leadership that God had established in the marriage by going first to the woman.

**f. God Spoke to Adam First After the Fall:** Just as God spoke to Adam on his own even before Eve was created (Gen. 2:15–17), so, after the fall, even though Eve had sinned first, God *came first to Adam* and called *him* to account for his actions: "But the LORD God *called to the man,* and said to *him,* 'Where are you?'" (Gen. 3:9). God thought of Adam as the leader of his family, the one to be called to account first for what had happened in the family. It is significant that though this is after sin has occurred, it is before the statement to Eve, "He shall rule over you" in Genesis 3:16, where some writers today claim male headship in the family began.

**g. Adam, Not Eve, Represented the Human Race:** Even though Eve sinned first (Gen. 3:6), we are counted sinful because of Adam's sin, not because of Eve's sin. The New Testament tells us, *"In Adam* all die" (1 Cor 15:22; cf. v. 49), and, "Many died through *one man's* trespass" (Rom. 5:15; cf. vv. 12–21). This indicates that God had given Adam headship or leadership with respect to the human race, a role that was not given to Eve.

**h. The Curse Brought a Distortion of Previous Roles, Not the Introduction of New Roles:** In the punishments God gave to Adam and Eve, he did not introduce new roles or functions, but simply introduced pain and distortion into the functions they previously had. Thus, Adam would still have primary responsibility for tilling the ground and raising crops, but the ground would bring forth "thorns and thistles" and in the sweat of his face he would eat bread (Gen. 3:18, 19). Similarly, Eve would still have the responsibility of bearing children, but to do so would become painful: "In pain you shall bring forth children" (Gen.

---

[19]See pp. 439–40.

3:16). Then God also introduced conflict and pain into the previously harmonious relationship between Adam and Eve. God said to Eve, "Your *desire* shall be *for your husband,* and he shall rule over you" (Gen. 3:16). Susan Foh has effectively argued that the word translated "desire" (Heb. *teshûqāh*) means "desire to conquer," and that it indicates Eve would have a wrongful desire to usurp authority over her husband.[20] If this understanding of the word "desire" is correct, as it seems to be, then it would indicate that God is introducing *a conflict into the relationship* between Adam and Eve and a desire on Eve's part to rebel against Adam's authority.

Concerning Adam, God told Eve, "He shall *rule* over you" (Gen. 3:16). Here the word "rule" (Heb. *māshal*) is a strong term usually used of monarchical governments, not generally of authority within a family.[21] The word certainly does not imply any "participatory" government by those who are ruled, but rather has nuances of dictatorial or absolute, uncaring use of authority, rather than considerate, thoughtful rule. It suggests harshness rather than kindness. The sense here is that Adam will misuse his authority *by ruling harshly* over his wife, again introducing pain and conflict into a relationship that was previously harmonious. It is not that Adam had no authority before the fall; it is simply that he will misuse it after the fall.

So in both cases, the curse brought a *distortion* of Adam's humble, considerate leadership and Eve's intelligent, willing submission to that leadership which existed before the fall.

**i. Redemption in Christ Reaffirms the Creation Order:** If the previous argument about the distortion of roles introduced at the fall is correct, then what we would expect to find in the New Testament is an undoing of the painful aspects of the relationship that resulted from sin and the curse. We would expect that in Christ, redemption would encourage wives not to rebel against their husbands' authority and would encourage husbands not to use their authority harshly. In fact, that is indeed what we do find: "Wives, *be subject to your husbands,* as is fitting in the Lord. Husbands, *love your wives,* and do not be harsh with them" (Col. 3:18–19; cf. Eph. 5:22–33; Titus 2:5; 1 Peter 3:1–7). If it were a sinful pattern for wives to be subject to their husbands' authority, Peter and Paul would

---

[20]See Susan. T. Foh, "What is the Woman's Desire?" in *WTJ,* vol. 37 (1975), pp. 376–83. Foh notes that this same Hebrew word occurs in a closely parallel statement just a few verses later, when God says to Cain, "Sin is crouching at the door, and its *desire* is for you, but you must master it" (Gen. 4:7 NASB). The parallelism in the Hebrew text between the verses is quite remarkable: six words (counting conjunctions and prepositions) are exactly the same, and in the same order. Another four nouns and pronouns are in the same position and have the same function in the sentence, but they differ only because the parties involved are different. But in that sentence the "desire" that sin has for Cain is surely a *desire to overcome or conquer him,* as is evident from the image of an animal "crouching" at the door waiting for him. The only other example of this Hebrew word is found in Song of Sol. 7:10, where its meaning is unclear but where the sense "desire to have mastery over" is possible (note the progression in Song of Sol. 2:16; 6:3; 7:10). I have been unable to find any other occurrences of this word in ancient Hebrew literature, though Foh does point to some parallels in related Semitic languages to support her argument. (It is unlikely that the word means "sexual desire," for that did not begin with the fall, nor would it be part of God's curse.)

[21]See Deut. 15:6, "You shall rule over many nations, but they shall not rule over you"; Prov. 22:7, "The rich rules over the poor"; Jdg. 14:4; 15:11 (of the Philistines ruling over Israel); also Gen. 37:8; Prov. 12:24; et al.

not have commanded it to be maintained in Christian marriages! They do not say, for example, "Encourage thorns to grow in your garden," or "Make childbirth as painful as possible," or "Stay alienated from God, cut off from fellowship with him!" The redemption of Christ is aimed at *removing* the results of sin and of the fall in every way: "The reason the Son of God appeared was to destroy the works of the devil" (1 John 3:8). *New Testament commands concerning marriage do not perpetuate any elements of the curse or any sinful behavior patterns;* they rather reaffirm the order and distinction of roles that were there from the beginning of God's good creation.

In terms of practical application, as we grow in maturity in Christ, we will grow to delight in and rejoice in the God-ordained and wisely created differences in roles within the human family. When we understand this biblical teaching, both men and women should be able to say in their hearts, "This is what God has planned, and it is beautiful and right, and I rejoice in the way he has made me and the distinct role he has given me." There is eternal beauty and dignity and rightness in this differentiation in roles both within the Trinity and within the human family. With no sense of "better" or "worse," and with no sense of "more important" or "less important," both men and women should be able to rejoice fully in the way they have been made by God.

### 3. Ephesians 5:21–33 and the Question of Mutual Submission. In Ephesians 5 we read:

Wives, be subject to your husbands, as to the Lord. For the husband is the head of the wife as Christ is the head of the church, his body, and is himself its Savior. As the church is subject to Christ, so let wives also be subject in everything to their husbands. (Eph. 5:22–24)

While on the surface this would seem to confirm what we have argued above about the creation order for marriage, in recent years there has been some debate over the meaning of the verb "be subject to" (Gk. *hypotassō*) in this passage. Some people have understood it to mean "be thoughtful and considerate; act in love [toward one another]." If it is understood in this sense, then the text does not teach that a wife has any unique responsibility to submit to her husband's authority, because both husband and wife need to be considerate and loving toward one another, and because according to this view submission to an authority is not seen in this passage.[22]

However, this is not a legitimate meaning for the term *hypotassō*, which always implies a relationship of *submission to an authority*. It is used elsewhere in the New Testament of the submission of Jesus to the authority of his parents (Luke 2:51); of demons being subject to the disciples (Luke 10:17—clearly the meaning "act in love, be considerate" cannot fit here); of citizens being subject to government authorities (Rom. 13:1, 5; Titus 3:1; 1 Peter 2:13); of the universe being subject to Christ (1 Cor. 15:27; Eph. 1:22); of unseen spiritual powers being subject to Christ (1 Peter 3:22); of Christ being subject to God the Father (1 Cor. 15:28); of church members being subject to church leaders (1 Cor. 16:15–16 [see 1 Clem. 42:4]; 1 Peter 5:5); of wives being subject to their husbands (Col. 3:18;

22See, for example, Bilezikian, *Beyond Sex Roles*, p. 154.

Titus 2:5; 1 Peter 3:5; cf. Eph. 5:22, 24); of the church being subject to Christ (Eph. 5:24); of servants being subject to their masters (Titus 2:9; 1 Peter 2:18); and of Christians being subject to God (Heb. 12:9; James 4:7). *None of these relationships is ever reversed;* that is, husbands are never told to be subject (*hypotassō*) to wives, nor the government to citizens, nor masters to servants, nor the disciples to demons, etc. In fact, the term is used outside the New Testament to describe the submission and obedience of soldiers in an army to those of superior rank.[23]

The primary argument that has been used in favor of taking "be subject to" in the sense "be considerate of" is the use of *hypotassō* in Ephesians 5:21. There Paul tells Christians, "Be subject *to one another.*" Several writers have argued that this means that every Christian should be subject to every other Christian, and wives and husbands especially should be "subject to one another." The phrase "mutual submission" has often been used to describe this kind of relationship, and it has been understood to imply that there is no unique kind of submission that a wife owes to her husband.

However, the following context defines what Paul means by "be subject to one another" in Ephesians 5:21: he means "Be subject *to others in the church who are in positions of authority over you.*" This is explained by what follows: wives are to be subject to husbands (Eph. 5:22–24), but husbands are never told to be subject to wives. In fact, Paul tells wives to be subject "to *your own* husbands" (Eph. 5:22),[24] not to everyone in the church or to all husbands! Children are to be subject to their parents (to "obey" them, Eph. 6:1–3), but parents are never told to be subject to or to obey their children. Servants are to be subject to ("obey") their masters, but not masters to servants.[25] Therefore, the idea of mutual submission (in the sense, "everyone should be subject to everyone") is not affirmed in Ephesians 5:21.[26] Similarly, in Colossians 3:18–19 Paul says, "Wives, be subject to your husbands, as is fitting in the Lord. Husbands, love your wives, and do not be harsh with them" (see also Titus 2:4–5; 1 Peter 3:1–7).

---

[23]See Josephus, *War* 2.566, 578; 5.309; cf. the adverb in 1 Clem. 37:2; also *LSJ*, p. 1897, which defines *hypotassō* (passive) to mean "be obedient."

[24]Author's literal translation of Greek *idios,* "one's own."

[25]The misunderstanding of this verse has come about through an assumption that the term "one another" (*allēlous*) must be completely reciprocal (that it must mean "everyone to everyone"). Yet there are many cases where it does not take that sense, but rather means "some to others": for example, in Rev. 6:4, "so that men should slay *one another*" means "so that some would kill others"; in Gal. 6:2, "Bear *one another's* burdens" means not "Everyone should exchange burdens with everyone else," but "Some who are more able should help bear the burdens of others who are less able"; 1 Cor. 11:33, "When you come together to eat, wait for *one another*" means "those who are ready early should wait for others who are late"; etc. (cf. Luke 2:15; 21:1; 24:32). Similarly, both the following context and the meaning of *hypotassō* require that in Eph. 5:21 it means, "Those who are under authority should be subject to others among you who have authority over them." (Regarding the objection that submission in marriage is like submission in slavery, and both are wrong, see chapter 47, p. 943.)

[26]Certainly, all Christians are to love one another and to be considerate of one another. If that is what is meant by "mutual submission," then there should be no objection to it—even though that idea is not taught in Eph. 5:21, but elsewhere in the Bible, using words other than *hypotassō*. But usually the phrase "mutual submission" is used in a different sense than this, a sense that obliterates any unique authority for the husband in a marriage.

## D. Note on Application to Marriage

If our analysis is correct, then there are some practical applications, particularly within marriage, and also with regard to relationships between men and women generally.

When husbands begin to act in selfish, harsh, domineering, or even abusive and cruel ways, they should realize that this is a result of sin, a result of the fall, and is destructive and contrary to God's purposes for them. To act this way will bring great destructiveness in their lives, especially in their marriages. Husbands must rather fulfill the New Testament commands to love their wives, honor them, be considerate of them, and put them first in their interests.

Similarly, when wives feel rebellious, resentful of their husband's leadership in the family, or when they compete with their husbands for leadership in the family, they should realize that this is a result of sin, a result of the fall. They should not act that way, because to do so will bring destructive consequences to their marriages as well. A wife desiring to act in accordance with God's pattern should rather be submissive to her husband and agree that he is the leader in their home and rejoice in that.[27]

Once we have said this, we must realize that there are two other, nearly opposite, distortions of the biblical pattern that can occur. If tyranny by the husband and usurpation of authority by the wife are *errors of aggressiveness*, there are two other errors, *errors of passivity* or laziness. For a husband, the other extreme from being a domineering "tyrant" is to be entirely passive and to fail to take initiative in the family—in colloquial terms, to be a "wimp." In this distortion of the biblical pattern, a husband becomes so "considerate" of his wife that he allows her to make all the decisions and even agrees when she urges him to do wrong (note this behavior in Adam, Ahab, and Solomon, among others). Often such a husband is increasingly absent (either physically or emotionally) from the home and occupies his time almost exclusively with other concerns.

The corresponding error on the part of the wife, opposite of attempting to domineer or usurp authority over her husband, is becoming entirely passive, contributing nothing to the decision-making process of the family, and being unwilling to speak words of correction to her husband, even though he is doing wrong. Submission to authority does not mean being entirely passive and agreeing with everything that the person in authority says or suggests—it is certainly not that way when we are submissive to the authority of an employer or of government officials (we can certainly differ with our government and still be subject to it), or even of the authority of the officers in a church (we can be subject to them even though we may disagree with some of their decisions). A wife can certainly be subject to the authority of her husband and still participate fully in the decision-making process of the family.

Husbands, therefore, should aim for loving, considerate, thoughtful leadership in their families. Wives should aim for active, intelligent, joyful submission to their husbands' authority. In avoiding both kinds of mistakes and following a biblical pattern, husbands and wives will discover true biblical manhood and womanhood

---

[27]See the discussion of what submission means and what it does not mean in W. Grudem, "Wives Like Sarah, and the Husbands Who Honor Them: 1 Peter 3:1–7," in *Recovering Biblical Manhood and Womanhood: A Response to Evangelical Feminism*, pp. 194–205.

in all of their noble dignity and joyful complementarity, as God created them to be, and will thus reflect more fully the image of God in their lives.

## QUESTIONS FOR PERSONAL APPLICATION

1. If you are being honest about your feelings, do you think it is better to be a man or a woman? Are you happy with the gender God gave you or would you rather be a member of the opposite sex? How do you think God wants you to feel about that question?

2. Can you honestly say that you think members of the opposite sex are equally valuable in God's sight?

3. Before reading this chapter, have you thought of relationships in the family as reflecting something of the relationships between members of the Trinity? Do you think that is a helpful way of looking at the family? How does that make you feel about your own family relationships? Are there ways in which you might reflect God's character more fully in your own family?

4. How does the teaching of this chapter on differences in roles between men and women compare with some of the attitudes expressed in society today? If there are differences between what much of society is teaching and what Scripture teaches, do you think there will be times when it will be difficult to follow Scripture? What could your church do to help you in those situations?

5. Even apart from the questions of marriage or romantic involvement, do you think God intends us to enjoy times of fellowship with mixed groups of other Christian men and women? Why do you think God puts in our heart the desire to enjoy such fellowship? Does it also reflect something of the plurality of persons in the Trinity, together with the unity of God? Does this help you understand how it is important that unmarried people be included fully in the activities of the church? Do you think that in the past some religious groups have tended to neglect the importance of this or even wrongly to forbid such mixed fellowship among Christians? What are the dangers that should be guarded against in those situations, however?

6. If you are a husband, are you content with the role God has given you in your marriage? If you are a wife, are you content with the role God has given you in your marriage?

## SPECIAL TERMS

difference in role                    mutual submission
equality in personhood                primogeniture

## BIBLIOGRAPHY

(For an explanation of this bibliography see the note on the bibliography to chapter 1, p. 38. Complete bibliographical data may be found on pp. 1223–29.)

## Sections in Evangelical Systematic Theologies

The topic of this chapter has not commonly been treated as a distinct unit within systematic theologies. Therefore our usual arrangement of listings is abbreviated for this chapter.

2. Arminian (Wesleyan or Methodist)

    1983     Carter, 1:214–20

3. Baptist

    1983–85    Erickson, 545–49

4. Dispensational

    1947     Chafer, 7:233–34, 310–11

5. Lutheran

    1917–24    Pieper, 1:523–27

    1934     Mueller, 209

7. Renewal (or charismatic/Pentecostal)

    1988     Williams, 1:203–6

## Sections in Representative Roman Catholic Systematic Theologies

1. Roman Catholic: Traditional

    1955     Ott, 460–73 (on matrimony)

2. Roman Catholic: Post-Vatican II

    1980     McBrien, 2:848–54

## Other Works

[Works marked * agree in general with the viewpoint presented in this chapter, while those marked ** disagree.]

Bacchiocchi, Samuele. *Women in the Church*. Berrien Springs, Mich.: Biblical Perspectives, 1987.*

Bilezikian, Gilbert. *Beyond Sex Roles: What the Bible Says About a Woman's Place in Church and Family*. 2d ed. Grand Rapids: Baker, 1985.**

Clark, Stephen B. *Man and Woman in Christ: An Examination of the Roles of Men and Women in Light of Scripture and the Social Sciences*. Ann Arbor: Servant, 1980.*

Clouse, Bonnidell, and Robert G. Clouse, eds. *Women in Ministry: Four Views*. Downers Grove, Ill.: InterVarsity Press, 1989.

Colwell, J. E. "Anthropology." In *NDT*, pp. 28–30.

Conn, H. M. "Feminist Theology." In *NDT*, pp. 255–58.

Cottrell, Jack. *Feminism and the Bible; An Introduction to Feminism for Christians*. Joplin, Mo.: College Press, 1992.*

Evans, Mary J. *Women in the Bible: An Overview of All the Crucial Passages on Women's Roles*. Downers Grove, Ill.: InterVarsity Press, 1983.**

Foh, Susan. *Women and the Word of God: A Response to Biblical Feminism*. Phillipsburg, N.J.: Presbyterian and Reformed, 1980.*

Gundry, Patricia. *Heirs Together*. Grand Rapids: Zondervan, 1980.**

_____. *Woman Be Free! The Clear Message of Scripture*. Grand Rapids: Zondervan, 1988.**

House, H. Wayne. *The Role of Women in Ministry Today*. Nashville: Thomas Nelson, 1990.*

Hurley, James. *Man and Women in Biblical Perspective*. Leicester: Inter-Varsity Press, and Grand Rapids: Zondervan, 1981.*

Jepsen, Dee. *Women: Beyond Equal Rights*. Waco, Tex.: Word, 1984.*

Jewett, Paul K. *Man as Male and Female*. Grand Rapids: Eerdmans, 1975.**

Kassian, Mary A. *Women, Creation and the Fall*. Westchester, Ill.: Crossway, 1990.**

_____. *The Feminist Gospel: The Movement to Unite Feminism With the Church*. Wheaton, Ill.: Crossway, 1992.*

Knight, George W., III. *The Role Relationship of Man and Women: New Testament Teaching*. Chicago: Moody, 1985.*

Mickelsen, Alvera, ed. *Women, Authority, and the Bible*. Downers Grove, Ill.: InterVarsity Press, 1986.**

Neuer, Werner. *Man and Woman in Christian Perspective*. Trans. by Gordon Wenham. Westchester, Ill.: Crossway, 1991.*

Piper, John. *What's the Difference? Manhood and Womanhood Defined According to the Bible*. Westchester, Ill.: Crossway, 1990.*

_____, and Wayne Grudem, eds. *Recovering Biblical Manhood and Womanhood: A Response to Evangelical Feminism*. Westchester, Ill.: Crossway, 1991.*

Spencer, Aida Besancon. *Beyond the Curse: Women Called to Ministry*. Peabody, Mass.: Hendrickson, 1985.**

Tucker, Ruth A., and Walter Liefeld. *Daughters of the Church: Women in Ministry from New Testament Times to the Present*. Grand Rapids: Zondervan, 1987.**

Van Leeuwen, Mary Stewart. *Gender and Grace: Love, Work and Parenting in a Changing World*. Leicester and Downers Grove, Ill.: InterVarsity Press, 1990.**

## SCRIPTURE MEMORY PASSAGE

**Colossians 3:18–19:** *Wives, be subject to your husbands, as is fitting in the Lord. Husbands, love your wives, and do not be harsh with them.*

## HYMN

### "Blest the Man that Fears Jehovah"

This hymn is an older paraphrase of Psalm 128 set to music. It speaks about the blessings of a family that walks in God's ways. (Tune of "Jesus Calls Us.")

Blest the man that fears Jehovah,
    walking ever in his ways;
By thy toil thou shalt be prospered
    and be happy all thy days.

In thy wife thou shalt have gladness,
    she shall fill thy home with good,

Happy in her loving service
and the joys of motherhood.

Joyful children, sons and daughters,
shall about thy table meet,
Olive plants, in strength and beauty,
full of hope and promise sweet.

Lo, on him that fears Jehovah
shall this blessedness attend,
For Jehovah out of Zion
shall to thee his blessing send.

Thou shalt see God's kingdom prosper
all thy days, till life shall cease,
Thou shalt see thy children's children;
on thy people, Lord, be peace.

FROM *THE PSALTER*, 1912, FROM PSALM 128

# Chapter 23

# The Essential Nature of Man

*What does Scripture mean by "soul" and "spirit"?*
*Are they the same thing?*

## EXPLANATION AND SCRIPTURAL BASIS

### A. Introduction: Trichotomy, Dichotomy, and Monism

How many parts are there to man? Everyone agrees that we have physical bodies. Most people (both Christians and non-Christians) sense that they also have an immaterial part—a "soul" that will live on after their bodies die.

But here the agreement ends. Some people believe that in addition to "body" and "soul" we have a third part, a "spirit" that most directly relates to God. The view that man is made of three parts (*body, soul, and spirit*) is called *trichotomy*.[1] Though this has been a common view in popular evangelical Bible teaching, there are few scholarly defenses of it today. According to many trichotomists, man's *soul* includes his intellect, his emotions, and his will. They maintain that all people have such a soul, and that the different elements of the soul can either serve God or be yielded to sin. They argue that man's *spirit* is a higher faculty in man that comes alive when a person becomes a Christian (see Rom. 8:10: "If Christ is in you, although your bodies are dead because of sin, *your spirits are alive* because of righteousness"). The spirit of a person then would be that part of him or her that most directly worships and prays to God (see John 4:24; Phil. 3:3).

Others have said that "spirit" is not a separate part of man, but simply another term for "soul," and that both terms are used interchangeably in Scripture to talk about the immaterial part of man, the part that lives on after our bodies die. The view that man is made up of *two parts* (body and soul/spirit) is called *dichotomy*. Those who hold this view often agree that Scripture uses the word *spirit* (Heb. *rûach,* and Gk. *pneuma*) more frequently when referring to our relationship to God, but such usage (they say) is not uniform, and the word *soul* is also used in all the ways that *spirit* can be used.

Outside the realm of evangelical thought we find yet another view, the idea that man cannot exist at all apart from a physical body, and therefore there can be no separate existence for any "soul" after the body dies (although this view can allow for the resurrection of the whole person at some future time). The view that man

---

[1]For a defense of trichotomy, see Franz Delitzsch, *A System of Biblical Psychology,* trans. R. E. Wallis, 2d ed. (Grand Rapids: Baker, 1966).

472

is only one element, and that his body is the person, is called *monism*.[2] According to monism, the scriptural terms *soul* and *spirit* are just other expressions for the "person" himself, or for the person's "life." This view has not generally been adopted by evangelical theologians because so many scriptural texts seem clearly to affirm that our souls or spirits live on after our bodies die (see Gen. 35:18; Ps. 31:5; Luke 23:43, 46; Acts 7:59; Phil. 1:23–24; 2 Cor. 5:8; Heb. 12:23; Rev. 6:9; 20:4; and chapter 42, on the intermediate state, below).

But the other two views continue to be held in the Christian world today. Although dichotomy has been held more commonly through the history of the church and is far more common among evangelical scholars today, trichotomy has also had many supporters.[3]

This chapter will support the dichotomist view that man is two parts, body and soul (or spirit), but we shall also examine the arguments for trichotomy.

## B. Biblical Data

Before asking whether Scripture views "soul" and "spirit" as distinct parts of man, we must at the outset make it clear that the emphasis of Scripture is on the overall unity of man as created by God. When God made man he "breathed into his nostrils the breath of life; and man became a living being" (Gen. 2:7). Here Adam is a unified person with body and soul living and acting together. This original harmonious and unified state of man will occur again when Christ returns and we are fully redeemed in our bodies as well as our souls to live with him forever (see 1 Cor. 15:51–54). Moreover, we are to grow in holiness and love for God in every aspect of our lives, in our bodies as well as in our spirits or souls (cf. 1 Cor. 7:34). We are to "cleanse ourselves from every defilement *of body and spirit,* and make holiness perfect in the fear of God" (2 Cor. 7:1).

But once we have emphasized the fact that God created us to have a unity between body and soul, and that every action we take in this life is an act of our whole person, involving to some extent both body and soul, then we can go on to point out that Scripture quite clearly teaches that there is an immaterial part of man's nature. And we can investigate what that part is like.

**1. Scripture Uses "Soul" and "Spirit" Interchangeably.** When we look at the usage of the biblical words translated "soul" (Heb. *nephesh* and Gk. *psychē*) and "spirit" (Heb. *rûach* and Gk. *pneuma*),[4] it appears that they are sometimes used interchangeably. For example, in John 12:27, Jesus says, "Now is my *soul*

---

[2]For further information, see Millard Erickson, *Christian Theology,* pp. 524–27, and his notes regarding the view of J. A. T. Robinson.

[3]See Louis Berkhof, *Systematic Theology,* pp. 191–92, for a survey of views held in the history of the church.

[4]Throughout this chapter it is important to keep in mind that several recent Bible translations (especially the NIV) do not consistently translate the Hebrew and Greek terms noted above as "soul" and "spirit," but sometimes substitute other terms such as "life," "mind," "heart," or "person." The RSV, which I quote unless another version is specified, tends to be more literal in translating these words in most cases.

In certain contexts these terms can of course be used to refer to the person's life or to the whole person, but they are also used many times to refer to a distinct part of a person's nature (see BDB, pp. 659–61, 924–25; and BAGD, pp. 674–75, 893–94, for many examples).

troubled," whereas in a very similar context in the next chapter John says that Jesus was "troubled in *spirit*" (John 13:21). Similarly, we read Mary's words in Luke 1:46–47: "My *soul* magnifies the Lord, and my *spirit* rejoices in God my Savior." This seems to be quite an evident example of Hebrew parallelism, the poetic device in which the same idea is repeated using different but synonymous words. This interchangeability of terms also explains why people who have died and gone to heaven or hell can be called either "spirits" (Heb. 12:23, "the *spirits* of just men made perfect"; also 1 Peter 3:19, "*spirits* in prison") or "souls" (Rev. 6:9, "the *souls* of those who had been slain for the word of God and for the witness they had borne"; 20:4, "the souls of those who had been beheaded for their testimony to Jesus").

**2. At Death, Scripture Says Either That the "Soul" Departs or the "Spirit" Departs.** When Rachel died, Scripture says, "Her *soul* was departing (for she died)" (Gen. 35:18). Elijah prays that the dead child's "soul" would come into him again (1 Kings 17:21), and Isaiah predicts that the Servant of the Lord would "pour out his *soul* [Heb. *nephesh*] to death" (Isa. 53:12). In the New Testament God tells the rich fool, "This night your soul [Gk. *psychē*] is required of you" (Luke 12:20). On the other hand, sometimes death is viewed as the returning of the spirit to God. So David can pray, in words later quoted by Jesus on the cross, "Into your hand I commit my *spirit*" (Ps. 31:5; cf. Luke 23:46). At death, "the *spirit* returns to God who gave it" (Eccl. 12:7).[5] In the New Testament, when Jesus was dying, "he bowed his head and gave up his spirit" (John 19:30), and likewise Stephen before dying prayed, "Lord Jesus, receive my spirit" (Acts 7:59).

In response to these passages, a trichotomist might argue that they are talking about different things, for when a person dies both his soul and his spirit do in fact go to heaven. But it should be noted that Scripture nowhere says that a person's "soul and spirit" departed or went to heaven or were yielded up to God. If soul and spirit were separate and distinct things, we would expect that such language would be affirmed somewhere, if only to assure the reader that no essential part of the person is left behind. Yet we find no such language: the biblical authors do not seem to care whether they say that the soul departs or the spirit departs at death, for both seem to mean the same thing.

We should also note that these Old Testament verses quoted above indicate that it is not correct, as some have claimed, to say that the Old Testament so emphasizes the unity of man that it has no conception of the existence of the soul apart from the body. Certainly several of these Old Testament passages imply that the authors recognize that a person continues to exist after his or her body dies.

---

[5]George Ladd, *A Theology of the New Testament* (Grand Rapids: Eerdmans, 1974), says that in the Old Testament neither soul nor spirit "is conceived of as a part of man capable of surviving the death of *basar* [flesh]" (p. 459). This statement is not accurate in the light of the Old Testament verses just cited in this paragraph. Ladd's analysis in this section is heavily dependent on the work of W. D. Stacey, *The Pauline View of Man* (London: Macmillan, 1956), whom Ladd cites fourteen times on pp. 458–59. Yet Stacey himself thinks that death means extinction for human beings (Ladd, p. 463). Ladd also notes that Rudolf Bultmann vigorously denied that man has an invisible soul or spirit, but Ladd himself rejects Bultmann's view when dealing with the New Testament data (see p. 460, n. 17, and p. 464).

**3. Man Is Said to Be Either "Body and Soul" or "Body and Spirit."** Jesus tells us not to fear those who "kill the body but cannot kill the soul," but that we should rather "fear him who can destroy both soul and body in hell" (Matt. 10:28). Here the word "soul" clearly must refer to the part of a person that exists after death. It cannot mean "person" or "life," for it would not make sense to speak of those who "kill the body but cannot kill the person," or who "kill the body but cannot kill the life," unless there is some aspect of the person that lives on after the body is dead. Moreover, when Jesus talks about "soul and body" he seems quite clearly to be talking about the entire person even though he does not mention "spirit" as a separate component. The word "soul" seems to stand for the entire nonphysical part of man.

On the other hand, man is sometimes said to be "body and spirit." Paul wants the Corinthian church to deliver an erring brother to Satan "for the destruction of the flesh, that his spirit may be saved in the day of the Lord Jesus" (1 Cor. 5:5). It is not that Paul has forgotten the salvation of the man's soul as well; he simply uses the word "spirit" to refer to the whole of the person's immaterial existence. Similarly, James says that "the body apart from the spirit is dead" (James 2:26), but mentions nothing about a separate soul. Moreover, when Paul speaks of growth in personal holiness, he approves the woman who is concerned with "how to be holy in body and spirit" (1 Cor. 7:34), and he suggests that this covers the whole of the person's life. Even more explicit is 2 Corinthians 7:1, where he says, "let us cleanse ourselves from every defilement of body and spirit, and make holiness perfect in the fear of God."[6] Cleansing ourselves from defilement of the "soul" or of the "spirit" covers the whole immaterial side of our existence (see also Rom. 8:10; 1 Cor. 5:3; Col. 2:5).

**4. The "Soul" Can Sin or the "Spirit" Can Sin.** Those who hold to trichotomy will usually agree that the "soul" can sin since they think that the soul includes the intellect, the emotions, and the will. (We see the fact that our souls can sin implied in verses such as 1 Peter 1:22; Rev. 18:14.)

The trichotomist, however, generally thinks of the "spirit" as purer than the soul, and, when renewed, as free from sin and responsive to the prompting of the Holy Spirit. This understanding (which sometimes finds its way into popular Christian preaching and writing) is not really supported by the biblical text. When Paul encourages the Corinthians to cleanse themselves "from every defilement of body and *spirit*" (2 Cor. 7:1), he clearly implies that there can be defilement (or sin) in our spirits. Similarly, he speaks of the unmarried woman who is concerned with how to be holy "in body and *spirit*" (1 Cor. 7:34). Other verses speak in similar ways. For example, the Lord hardened the "spirit" of Sihon the king of Heshbon (Deut. 2:30). Psalm 78 speaks of the rebellious people of Israel "whose *spirit* was not faithful to God" (Ps. 78:8). A "haughty *spirit*" goes before a fall (Prov. 16:18), and it is possible for sinful people to be "proud in spirit" (Eccl. 7:8). Isaiah speaks of those "who err in spirit" (Isa. 29:24). Nebuchadnezzar's

---

[6]The verse is perhaps better translated, "making holiness perfect in the view of God," since the present participle *epitelountes* suggests actions simultaneous with the main verb "cleanse," and the verse thus gives the idea that the way in which we make holiness perfect is by cleansing ourselves from every defilement of body and spirit (grammatically this would then be a modal participle).

"spirit was hardened so that he dealt proudly" (Dan. 5:20). The fact that "All the ways of a man are pure in his own eyes, but the LORD weighs the spirit" (Prov. 16:2) implies that it is possible for our spirits to be wrong in God's sight. Other verses imply a possibility of sin in our spirits (see Ps. 32:2; 51:10). Finally, the fact that Scripture approves of one "who *rules his spirit*" (Prov. 16:32) implies that our spirits are not simply the spiritually pure parts of our lives that are to be followed in all cases, but that they can have sinful desires or directions as well.

**5. Everything That the Soul Is Said to Do, the Spirit Is Also Said to Do, and Everything That the Spirit Is Said to Do the Soul Is Also Said to Do.** Those who advocate trichotomy face a difficult problem defining clearly just what the difference is between the soul and the spirit (from their perspective). If Scripture gave clear support to the idea that our spirit is the part of us that directly relates to God in worship and prayer, while our soul includes our intellect (thinking), our emotions (feeling), and our will (deciding), then trichotomists would have a strong case. However, Scripture appears not to allow such a distinction to be made.

On the one hand, the activities of thinking, feeling, and deciding things are not said to be done by our souls only. Our spirits can also experience emotions, for example, as when Paul's "spirit was provoked within him" (Acts 17:16), or when Jesus was "troubled in spirit" (John 13:21). It is also possible to have a "downcast spirit," which is the opposite of a "cheerful heart" (Prov. 17:22).

Moreover, the functions of knowing, perceiving, and thinking are also said to be done by our spirits. For instance, Mark speaks of Jesus "perceiving [Gk. *epiginōskō*, 'knowing'] in his spirit" (Mark 2:8). When the Holy Spirit "bears witness with our spirit that we are children of God" (Rom. 8:16), our spirits receive and understand that witness, which is certainly a function of knowing something. In fact, our spirits seem to know our thoughts quite deeply, for Paul asks, "What person knows a man's thoughts except the spirit of the man which is in him?" (1 Cor. 2:11). (Cf. Isa. 29:24, speaking of those who now "err in spirit" but "will come to understanding.")

The point of these verses is not to say that it is the spirit rather than the soul that feels and thinks things, but rather that "soul" and "spirit" are both terms used of the immaterial side of people generally, and it is difficult to see any real distinction between the use of the terms.

In fact, we should not slip into the mistake of thinking that certain activities (such as thinking, feeling, or deciding things) are done by only one part of us. Rather, these activities are done by the whole person. When we think or feel things, certainly our physical bodies are involved at every point as well. Whenever we think we use the physical brain God has given us. Similarly, our brain and our entire nervous system are involved when we feel emotion, and sometimes those emotions are involved in physical sensations in other parts of our bodies. This is just to reemphasize what was said at the beginning of our discussion, that the overall focus of Scripture is primarily on man as a unity, with our physical bodies and the nonphysical part of our persons functioning together as a unity.

On the other hand, the trichotomist claim that our spirit is that element of us that relates most directly to God in worship and in prayer does not seem to be borne out by Scripture. We often read about our *soul* worshiping God and relating to him in other kinds of spiritual activity. "To you, O LORD, I lift up my *soul*" (Ps. 25:1). "For God alone my soul waits in silence" (Ps. 62:1). "Bless the LORD, O my *soul;* and all that is within me, bless his holy name!" (Ps. 103:1). "Praise the LORD, O my soul!" (Ps. 146:1). "My soul magnifies the Lord" (Luke 1:46).

These passages indicate that our souls can worship God, praise him, and give thanks to him. Our souls can pray to God, as Hannah implies when she says, "I have been pouring out my soul before the LORD" (1 Sam. 1:15). In fact, the great commandment is to "love the LORD your God with all your heart, and with all your soul, and with all your might" (Deut. 6:5; cf. Mark 12:30). Our souls can long for God and thirst for him (Ps. 42:1, 2), and can "hope in God" (Ps. 42:5). Our souls can rejoice and delight in God, for David says, "My soul shall rejoice in the LORD, exulting in his deliverance" (Ps. 35:9; cf. Isa. 61:10). The psalmist says, "My soul is consumed with longing for your ordinances at all times" (Ps. 119:20), and, "My soul keeps your testimonies; I love them exceedingly" (Ps. 119:167). There seems to be no area of life or relationship to God in which Scripture says our spirits are active rather than our souls. Both terms are used to speak of all of the aspects of our relationship to God.

However, it would be wrong, in the light of these passages, to suggest that only our souls (or spirits) worship God, for our bodies are involved in worship as well. We are a unity of body and soul/spirit. Our physical brains think about God when we worship and when we love him with all of our "minds" (Mark 12:30). David, longing to be in God's presence, can say, "My flesh faints for you, as in a dry and weary land where no water is" (Ps. 63:1). Again, we read, "My heart and flesh sing for joy to the living God" (Ps. 84:2). It is obvious that when we pray aloud or sing praise to God, our lips and our vocal cords are involved, and sometimes worship and prayer in Scripture involves clapping of hands (Ps. 47:1) or lifting of hands to God (Pss. 28:2; 63:4; 134:2; 143:6; 1 Tim. 2:8). Moreover, the playing of musical instruments in praise to God is an act that involves our physical bodies as well as the physical materials of which the musical instruments are made (see Ps. 150:3–5). We worship him as whole persons.

In conclusion, Scripture does not seem to support any distinction between soul and spirit. There does not seem to be a satisfactory answer to the questions that we may address to a trichotomist, "What can the spirit do that the soul cannot do? What can the soul do that the spirit cannot do?"

## C. Arguments for Trichotomy

Those who adopt the trichotomist position have appealed to a number of Scripture passages in support of it. We list here the ones that are most commonly used.

**1. 1 Thessalonians 5:23.** "May the God of peace himself sanctify you wholly; and may your *spirit and soul and body* be kept sound and blameless at the coming of our Lord Jesus Christ" (1 Thess. 5:23). Does not this verse clearly speak of three parts to man?

**2. Hebrews 4:12.** "The word of God is living and active, sharper than any two-edged sword, piercing to the *division of soul and spirit,* of joints and marrow, and discerning the thoughts and intentions of the heart" (Heb. 4:12). If the sword of Scripture divides soul and spirit, then are these not two separate parts of man?

**3. 1 Corinthians 2:14–3:4.** This passage speaks of different kinds of people, those who are "of the flesh" (Gk. *sarkinos,* 1 Cor. 3:1); those who are "unspiritual" (Gk. *psychikos,* lit. "soul-ish," 1 Cor. 2:14); and those who are "spiritual" (Gk. *pneumatikos,* 1 Cor. 2:15). Do not these categories suggest that there are different sorts of people, the non-Christians who are "of the flesh," "unspiritual" Christians who follow the desires of their souls, and more mature Christians who follow the desires of their spirits? Would this not suggest that soul and spirit are different elements of our nature?

**4. 1 Corinthians 14:14.** When Paul says, "If I pray in a tongue, my spirit prays but my mind is unfruitful" (1 Cor. 14:14), is he not implying that his mind does something different from his spirit, and would not this support the trichotomist's argument that our mind and our thinking are to be assigned to our souls, not to our spirit?

**5. The Argument From Personal Experience.** Many trichotomists say that they have a spiritual perception, a spiritual awareness of God's presence which affects them in a way that they know to be different from their ordinary thinking processes and different from their emotional experiences. They ask, "If I do not have a spirit that is distinct from my thoughts and my emotions, then what exactly is it that I feel that is different from my thoughts and my emotions, something that I can only describe as worshiping God in my spirit and sensing his presence in my spirit? Isn't there something in me that is more than just my intellect and my emotions and my will, and shouldn't this be called my spirit?"

**6. Our Spirit Is What Makes Us Different From Animals.** Some trichotomists argue that both humans and animals have souls, but maintain that it is the presence of a spirit that makes us different from animals.

**7. Our Spirit Is What Comes Alive at Regeneration.** Trichotomists also argue that when we become Christians our spirits come alive: "But if Christ is in you, although your bodies are dead because of sin, your spirits are alive because of righteousness" (Rom. 8:10).

Now we can consider the seven points given above:

## D. Responses to Arguments for Trichotomy

**1. 1 Thessalonians 5:23.** The phrase "your spirit and soul and body" is by itself inconclusive. Paul could be simply piling up synonyms for emphasis, as is sometimes done elsewhere in Scripture. For example, Jesus says, "You shall love the Lord your God with all your *heart,* and with all your *soul,* and with all your *mind*" (Matt. 22:37). Does this mean that the soul is different from the mind or from the heart?[7] The problem is even greater in Mark 12:30: "You shall love the Lord your God with all your *heart*, and with all your *soul*, and with all your *mind*, and with all your *strength*." If we go on the principle that such lists of terms tell us about more parts to man, then if we also add spirit to this list (and perhaps body as well), we would have five or six parts to man! But that is certainly a false conclusion. It is far better to understand Jesus as simply piling up roughly synonymous terms for emphasis to demonstrate that we must love God with all of our being.

Likewise, in 1 Thessalonians 5:23 Paul is not saying that soul and spirit are distinct entities, but simply that, whatever our immaterial part is called, he wants God to continue to sanctify us wholly to the day of Christ.

**2. Hebrews 4:12.** This verse, which talks about the Word of God "piercing to the division of soul and spirit, of joints and marrow," is best understood in a way similar to 1 Thessalonians 5:23. The author is not saying that the Word of God can divide "soul *from* spirit," but he is using a number of terms (soul, spirit, joints, marrow, thoughts and intentions of the heart) that speak of the deep inward parts of our being that are not hidden from the penetrating power of the Word of God. If we wish to call these our "soul," then Scripture pierces into the midst of it and divides it and discovers its inmost intentions. If we wish to call this inmost nonphysical side of our being our "spirit," then Scripture penetrates into the midst of it and divides it and knows its deepest intentions and thoughts. Or if we wish to think metaphorically of our inmost being as hidden in our joints and in the marrow, then we can think of Scripture being like a sword that divides our joints or that pierces deeply into our bones and even divides the marrow in the midst of the bones.[8] In all of these cases the Word of God is so powerful that it will search out and expose all disobedience and lack of submission to God. In any case, soul and spirit are not thought of as separate parts; they are simply additional terms for our inmost being.

**3. 1 Corinthians 2:14–3:4.** Paul certainly distinguishes a person who is "natural" (*psychikos*, "soul-ish") from one that is "spiritual" (*pneumatikos*, "spiritual") in 1 Corinthians 2:14–3:4. But in this context "spiritual" seems to mean "influenced by the Holy Spirit," since the entire passage is talking about the work of the Holy Spirit in revealing truth to believers. In this context, "spiritual" might almost be translated "Spiritual." But the passage does not imply that Christians have a spirit whereas non-Christians do not, or that the spirit of a Christian is alive while the spirit of a non-Christian is not. Paul is not talking about different parts of man at all, but about coming under the influence of the Holy Spirit.

---

[7]The "heart" in Scripture is an expression for the deepest, inmost thoughts and feelings of a person (see Gen. 6:5, 6; Lev. 19:17; Pss. 14:1; 15:2; 37:4; 119:10; Prov. 3:5; Acts 2:37; Rom. 2:5; 10:9; 1 Cor. 4:5; 14:25; Heb. 4:12; 1 Peter 3:4; Rev. 2:23; et al.).

[8]Note that we do not divide joints from marrow, for joints are the places where bones meet, not the places where joints meet marrow.

**4. 1 Corinthians 14:14.** When Paul says, "My *spirit* prays but my mind is unfruitful," he means he does not understand the content of what he is praying. He does imply that there is a nonphysical component to his being, a "spirit" within him that can pray to God. But nothing in this verse suggests that he regards his spirit as different from his soul. Such a misunderstanding results only if it is assumed that "mind" is part of the soul—a trichotomist claim that, as we noted above, is very difficult to substantiate from Scripture. Paul probably could equally have said, "My soul prays but my mind is unfruitful."[9] The point is simply that there is a nonphysical element to our existence that can at times function apart from our conscious awareness of how it is functioning.

**5. The Argument From Personal Experience.** Christians have a "spiritual perception," an inner awareness of the presence of God experienced in worship and in prayer. At this deep inward level we can also at times feel spiritually troubled, or depressed, or perhaps have a sense of the presence of hostile demonic forces. Often this perception is distinct from our conscious, rational thought processes. Paul realizes that at times his spirit prays but his mind does not understand (1 Cor. 14:14). But does inward spiritual perception occur in something other than what the Bible calls our "soul"? If we were using the vocabulary of Mary, we would be happy to say, "My soul magnifies the Lord" (Luke 1:46). David would say, "Bless the LORD, O my soul" (Ps. 103:1). Jesus would tell us to love God with all our soul (Mark 12:30). The apostle Paul uses the word *spirit,* but it is simply a difference in terminology and does not point to a different part of man. There is a "spirit" within us that can perceive things in the spiritual realm (note Rom. 8:16; also Acts 17:16), but we could just as well speak of it as our "soul" and mean the same thing, for Scripture uses both terms.

**6. What Makes Us Different From Animals?** It is true that we have spiritual abilities that make us different from animals:[10] we are able to relate to God in worship and prayer, and we enjoy spiritual life in fellowship with God who is spirit. But we should not assume that we have a distinct element called "spirit" that allows us to do this, for with our minds we can love God, read and understand his words, and believe his Word to be true. Our souls can worship God and rejoice in him (see above). Our bodies will also be resurrected and live with God forever. Therefore we do not have to say that we have a part distinct from our souls and bodies that makes us different from animals, for our souls and bodies (including our minds) relate to God in ways animals never can. Rather, what makes us different from animals is the spiritual abilities that God has given to both our bodies and souls (or spirits).

The question of whether an animal has a "soul" simply depends on how we define soul. If we define "soul" to mean "the intellect, emotions, and will," then

---

[9]However, it is much more characteristic of Paul's terminology to use the word "spirit" to talk about our relationship to God in worship and in prayer. Paul does not use the word "soul" (Gk. *psychē*) very frequently (14 times, compared with 101 occurrences in the New Testament as a whole), and when he does, he often uses it simply to refer a person's "life," or as a synonym or a person himself, as in Rom. 9:3; 13:1; 16:4; Phil. 2:30. Use of the word "soul" to refer to the non-physical side of man is more characteristic of the gospels, and of many passages in the Old Testament.

[10]See chapter 21, pp. 445–49, on the numerous differences between human beings and animals.

we will have to conclude that at least the higher animals have a soul. But if we define our "soul" as we have in this chapter, to mean the immaterial element of our nature that relates to God (Ps. 103:1; Luke 1:46; et al.) and lives forever (Rev. 6:9), then animals do not have a soul. The fact that the Hebrew word *nephesh*, "soul," is sometimes used of animals (Gen. 1:21; 9:4) shows that the word can sometimes simply mean "life"; it does not mean that animals have the same kind of soul as man.[11]

**7. Does Our Spirit Come Alive at Regeneration?** The human spirit is not something that is dead in an unbeliever but comes to life when someone trusts in Christ, because the Bible talks about unbelievers having a spirit that is obviously alive but is in rebellion against God—whether Sihon, King of Heshbon (Deut. 2:30: the Lord "hardened his spirit"), or Nebuchadnezzar (Dan. 5:20: "his spirit was hardened so that he dealt proudly"), or the unfaithful people of Israel (Ps. 78:8: their "spirit was not faithful to God"). When Paul says, "Your spirits are alive because of righteousness" (Rom. 8:10), he apparently means "alive to God," but he does not imply that our spirits were completely "dead" before, only that they were living out of fellowship with God and were dead in that sense.[12] In the same way, we as whole persons were "dead" in "trespasses and sins" (Eph. 2:1), but we were made alive to God, and we now must consider ourselves "dead to sin and alive to God" (Rom. 6:11). It is not just that one part of us (called the spirit) has been made alive; we as whole persons are a "new creation" in Christ (2 Cor. 5:17).

**8. Conclusion.** Although the arguments for trichotomy do have some force, none of them provides conclusive evidence that would overcome the wide testimony of Scripture showing that the terms *soul* and *spirit* are frequently interchangeable and are in many cases synonymous.

We might also note the observation of Louis Berkhof on the origin of trichotomy:

> The tripartite conception of man originated in Greek philosophy, which conceived of the relation of the body and the spirit of man to each other after the analogy of the mutual relation between the material universe and God. It was thought that, just as the latter could enter into communion with each other only by means of a third substance or an intermediate being, so the former could enter into mutual vital relationships only by means of a third or intermediate element, namely, the soul.[13]

---

[11]In fact, one passage even speculates about "the spirit of the beast" in contrast with "the spirit of man," (Eccl. 3:21), but the context (vv. 18–22) is one expressing a worldly, cynical perspective that shows the vanity of life and argues that man is but a beast (v. 18): in the overall context of the book it is not clear that this is something the author is encouraging his readers to believe.

[12]Another common view of Rom. 8:10 is that Paul is not referring to our human spirits at all but that *pneuma* here means the Holy Spirit, as in vv. 9 and 11, so that the phrase means, "The Spirit is life [for you] because of righteousness": see Douglas Moo, Romans 1–8, *Wycliffe Exegetical Commentary* (Chicago: Moody, 1991), p. 525; John Murray, *The Epistle to the Romans*, NIC, 2 vols. (Grand Rapids: Eerdmans, 1959, 1965), 1:289–91.

[13]Berkhof, *Systematic Theology*, p. 191.

Some trichotomists today have a tendency to adopt a related error that also was found in Greek philosophy—the idea that the material world, including our bodies, is essentially evil and something to be escaped from. The danger is to say that the realm of the "spirit" is the only thing that is really important, with a resultant depreciation of the value of our physical bodies as created by God and "very good" (Gen. 1:31), and therefore as something to be presented to God in service for him (Rom. 12:1).

Trichotomy can also have an anti-intellectual tendency. If we think of the spirit as that element of us that relates most directly to God, and if we think that the spirit is something distinct from our intellect, emotions, and will, we can easily fall into an anti-intellectual kind of Christianity that thinks that vigorous academic work is somehow "unspiritual"—a view that contradicts Jesus' command to love God with all our "mind" (Mark 12:30) and Paul's desire to "take every thought captive to obey Christ" (2 Cor. 10:5). Such a separation of the realm of the "spirit" from the realm of the intellect can too easily lead to a neglect of sound doctrine or of the need for extensive teaching and knowledge of the Word of God—in contradiction to Paul's goal that he would work among God's people to further both their "faith" and their "knowledge of the truth which accords with godliness" (Titus 1:1; cf. v. 9). Similarly, if we think of our spirits as a distinct part of us that relates most directly to God, we can easily begin to neglect the role of Bible study and mature wisdom in making decisions, and place too much reliance on "spiritual" discernment in the realm of guidance, an emphasis that has, through the history of the church, led many zealous Christians astray into false teaching and unwise practices. Finally, trichotomy can subtlely influence us to think that our emotions are not important or not really spiritual, since they are thought to be part of our soul, not part of out spirit.

By contrast, if we hold to a view of dichotomy that upholds the overall unity of man, it will be much easier to avoid the error of depreciating the value of our intellects, emotions, or physical bodies. We will not think of our bodies as inherently evil or unimportant. Such a view of dichotomy within unity will also help us to remember that, in this life, there is a continual interaction between our body and our spirit, and that they affect each other: "A cheerful heart is good medicine, but a downcast spirit dries up the bones" (Prov. 17:22).[14]

Moreover, a healthy emphasis on dichotomy within an overall unity reminds us that Christian growth must include all aspects of our lives. We are continually to "cleanse ourselves from every defilement of body and spirit, and make holiness perfect in the fear of God" (2 Cor. 7:1). We are to be "increasing in the knowledge of God" (Col. 1:10), and our emotions and desires are to conform increasingly to the "desires of the Spirit" (Gal. 5:17), including an increase in godly emotions such as peace, joy, love,[15] and so forth (Gal. 5:22).

---

[14]Although many passages of Scripture remind us that our bodies and our spirits do interact with each other and affect one another, Scripture does not tell us very much about how they interact. Berkhof wisely says, "Body and soul are distinct substances, which do interact, though their mode of interaction escapes human scrutiny and remains a mystery for us" (*Systematic Theology,* p. 195).

[15]Some people will object that love is not merely an emotion, because it shows itself in actions and often we can will to perform loving actions toward others even when we do not feel love toward them. I agree with this, but there certainly is an emotional component to love—we can feel love toward others—and we would lose much of the richness of our relationship to God and others if we tried to deny this.

## E. Scripture Does Speak of an Immaterial Part of Man That Can Exist Without His Body

A number of non-Christian philosophers have vigorously challenged the idea that man has any immaterial part at all such as a soul or spirit.[16] Perhaps partially in response to such criticism, some evangelical theologians have seemed hesitant to affirm dichotomy in human existence.[17] They have instead affirmed repeatedly that the Bible views man as a unity—a fact which is true but should not be used to deny that Scripture also views man's unified nature as made up of two distinct elements. Of course, philosophers who assume that there is no spiritual realm beyond the reach of our sense perception, and who then go from that assumption to argue on the basis of our sense perception that there is no God, or heaven, or angels, or demons, will use similar arguments to deny the existence of a distinct soul within human beings. The perception that we have a spirit or soul belongs to the invisible, spiritual realm, and is, even in Christians, generally only a faint, subjective perception. Therefore, our knowledge of the existence of the human soul must be primarily based on Scripture, in which God clearly testifies to the existence of this immaterial aspect of our beings. The fact that this truth about our existence cannot be clearly known apart from the testimony of Scripture should not cause us to shrink from affirming it.

Scripture is very clear that we do have a soul that is distinct from our physical bodies, which not only can function somewhat independently of our ordinary thought processes (1 Cor. 14:14; Rom. 8:16), but also, when we die, is able to go on consciously acting and relating to God apart from our physical bodies. Jesus told the dying thief, "Today you will be with me in Paradise" (Luke 23:43), even though, for both of them, their physical bodies were soon to die. When Stephen was dying, he knew he would immediately pass into the presence of the Lord, for he prayed, "Lord Jesus, receive my *spirit*" (Acts 7:59). Paul does not fear death, for he says, "My desire is to depart and be with Christ, for that is far better" (Phil. 1:23). He contrasts that with remaining in this life, which he calls "to remain in the flesh" (Phil. 1:24). In fact, he says, "We would rather be *away from the body* and at home with the Lord" (2 Cor. 5:8), indicating a confidence that if he were to die physically his spirit would go into the Lord's presence and there enjoy fellowship with the Lord at once. The book of Revelation reminds us that "the *souls* of those who had been slain for the word of God and for the witness they had borne" (Rev. 6:9) are in heaven and are able to cry out to God to bring justice on the earth (Rev. 6:10; cf. also 20:4).

Therefore, although we must agree that, in this life, Scripture views us as a unity in which body and spirit act together as one person, nonetheless, there will be a time between our death and the day Christ returns when our spirits will temporarily exist apart from our physical bodies.[18]

---

[16]See the discussion in Millard Erickson, *Christian Theology,* pp. 530–36, with notes to some literature.

[17]See, for example, G. C. Berkouwer, *Man, the Image of God,* pp. 194–233.

[18]See further discussion of "the intermediate state" between death and Christ's return in chapter 41, pp. 816–24.

## F. Where Do Our Souls Come From?

What is the origin of our individual souls? Two views have been common in the history of the church.

*Creationism* is the view that God creates a new soul for each person and sends it to that person's body sometime between conception and birth. *Traducianism,* on the other hand, holds that the soul as well as the body of a child are inherited from the baby's mother and father at the time of conception. Both views have had numerous defenders in the history of the church, with creationism eventually becoming the prevailing view in the Roman Catholic Church. Luther was in favor of traducianism, while Calvin favored creationism. On the other hand, there are some later Calvinist theologians such as Jonathan Edwards and A. H. Strong who favored traducianism (as do most Lutherans today). Creationism has had many modern evangelical advocates as well.[19]

There is one other popular view called *pre-existentianism,* namely, that the souls of people exist in heaven long before their bodies are conceived in the wombs of their mothers, and that God then brings the soul to earth to be joined with the baby's body as he or she grows in the womb. But this view is not held by either Roman Catholic or Protestant theologians and is dangerously akin to ideas of reincarnation found in Eastern religions. Moreover, there is no support for this view in Scripture. Before we were conceived in the wombs of our mothers, we simply did not exist. We were not. Of course, God looked forward into the future and knew that we would exist, but that is far removed from saying that we actually did exist at some previous time. Such an idea would tend to make us view this present life as transitional or unimportant and make us think of life in the body as less desirable and the bearing and raising of children as less important.

In favor of traducianism it may be argued that God created man in his own image (Gen. 1:27), and this includes a likeness to God in the amazing ability to "create" other human beings like ourselves. Therefore, just as the rest of the animal and plant world bears descendants "according to their kinds" (Gen. 1:24), so Adam and Eve also were able to bear children who were like themselves, with a spiritual nature as well as a physical body. This would imply that the spirits or souls of Adam and Eve's children were derived from Adam and Eve themselves. Moreover, Scripture sometimes can speak of descendants being somehow present in the body of someone in the previous generation, as when the author of Hebrews says that when Melchizedek met Abraham, "Levi . . . was still in the loins of his ancestor" (Heb. 7:10). Finally, traducianism could explain how the sins of the parents can be passed on to the children without making God directly responsible for the creation of a soul that is sinful or has a disposition that would tend toward sin.

However, the biblical arguments in favor of creationism seem to speak more directly to the issue and give quite strong support for this view. First, Psalm 127 says that "sons are a heritage from the LORD, the fruit of the womb a reward" (Ps. 127:3). This indicates that not only the soul, but also the entire person of the child, including his or her body, is a gift from God. From this standpoint, it seems strange to think of the mother and father as being responsible by themselves for

---

[19]See, for example, Berkhof, *Systematic Theology,* pp. 196–201.

any aspect of the child's existence. Was it not the Lord who, David says, "knit me together in my mother's womb" (Ps. 139:13)? Isaiah says that God gives breath to the people on the earth and "spirit to those who walk in it" (Isa. 42:5).[20] Zechariah talks of God as the one "who forms the spirit of man within him" (Zech. 12:1 NIV). The author of Hebrews speaks of God as "the Father of spirits" (Heb. 12:9). It is hard to escape the conclusion from these passages that God is the one who creates our spirits or souls.

Yet we must be cautious in drawing conclusions from this data. Our discussion of the doctrine of God's providence in chapter 16 demonstrated that God usually acts through secondary causes. God often brings about the results he seeks through the actions of human beings. Certainly this is so in the conception and bearing of children. Even if we say that God does create individual souls for human beings before they are born, and that he is the one who allows children to be conceived and born, we must also recognize that apart from the physical union of man and woman in the conception of a child, no children are born! So we must not make the mistake of saying that the father and mother have no role in the creation of the child. Even if we say that God is the "Father of spirits" and the Creator of every human soul, just as he is the Maker and Creator of each of us, we must still also affirm that God carries out this creative activity through the amazing process of human procreation. Whether God involves the human mother and father to some degree in the process of the creation of a soul as well as of a physical body, is impossible for us to say. It is something that occurs in the invisible realm of the spirit, which we do not have information about except from Scripture. And on this point Scripture simply does not give us enough information to decide.

However, the arguments listed above in favor of traducianism must be said not to be very compelling ones. The fact that Adam and Eve bear children in their own image (see Gen. 5:3) could suggest that children somehow inherit a soul from their parents, but it might also indicate that God gives an individually created soul to the child and that that soul is consistent with the hereditary traits and personality characteristics that God allowed the child to have through its descent from its parents. The idea that Levi was still in the body of Abraham (Heb. 7:10) is best understood in a representative, or figurative, sense, not in a literal sense. Moreover, it is not simply Levi's soul that is talked about in any case, but Levi himself, as a whole person, including body and soul—yet Levi's body was certainly not physically present in any meaningful sense in Abraham's body, for there was no distinct combination of genes at that time that could be said to be Levi and no one else. Finally, since God brings about events in the physical world that are consistent with the voluntary activities of human beings, there does not seem to be any real theological difficulty in saying that God gives each child a human soul that has tendencies to sin that are similar to the tendencies found in the parents. In fact, we read in the Ten Commandments of God "visiting the iniquity of the fathers upon the children to the third and the fourth generation of those who hate [him]" (Ex. 20:5), and, quite apart from the question of the human soul, we know from human experience that children do in fact tend to

---

[20]Instead of "spirit" the NIV translates "life," but the word is *rûach*, the common Hebrew word for "spirit."

imitate both the good and bad traits in their parents' lives, not only as a result of imitation but also because of hereditary disposition. For God to give each child a human soul that accords with the imitation of parents that we see in the lives of children would simply be an indication that God, in creating a human soul, acts consistently with the way he acts in relation to the human race in other matters as well.

In conclusion, it seems hard to avoid the testimony of Scripture to the effect that God actively creates each human soul, just as he is active in all the events of his creation. But the degree to which he allows the use of intermediate or secondary causes (that is, inheritance from parents) is simply not explained for us in Scripture. Therefore, it does not seem profitable for us to spend any more time speculating on this question.

## QUESTIONS FOR PERSONAL APPLICATION

1. In your own Christian experience, are you aware that you are more than just a physical body, that you have a nonphysical part that might be called a soul or spirit? At what times do you especially become aware of the existence of your spirit? Can you describe what it is like to know the witness of the Holy Spirit with your spirit that you are God's child (Rom. 8:16), or to have in your spirit a consciousness of God's presence (John 4:23; Phil. 3:3), or to be troubled in your spirit (John 12:27; 13:21; Acts 17:16; 2 Cor. 2:13), or to have your spirit worship God (Luke 1:47; Ps. 103:1), or to love God with all your soul (Mark 12:30)? By contrast, are there times when you feel spiritually dull or insensitive? Do you think that one aspect of Christian growth might include an increasing sensitivity to the state of your soul or spirit?

2. Before reading this chapter, did you hold to dichotomy or trichotomy? Now what is your view? If you have changed to an acceptance of dichotomy after reading this chapter, do you think you will have a higher appreciation for the activities of your body, your mind, and your emotions? If you hold to trichotomy, how can you guard against some of the dangers mentioned in this chapter?

3. When you are praying or singing praise to God, is it enough simply to sing or speak words, without being aware of what you are saying? Is it enough to be aware of what you are saying without really meaning it? If you really mean the words with your whole being, then what aspects of your person would be involved in genuine prayer and worship? Do you think you tend to neglect one or another aspect at times?

4. Since Scripture encourages us to grow in holiness in our bodies as well as our spirits (2 Cor. 7:1), what specifically would it mean for you to be more obedient to that command?

## SPECIAL TERMS

creationism
dichotomy
monism
soul

spirit
traducianism
trichotomy

## BIBLIOGRAPHY

(For an explanation of this bibliography see the note on the bibliography to chapter 1, p. 38. Complete bibliographical data may be found on pp. 1223–29.)

### Sections in Evangelical Systematic Theologies

1. Anglican (Episcopalian)
   - 1882–92    Litton, 113–16, 122–25
2. Arminian (Wesleyan or Methodist)
   - 1875–76    Pope, 1:435–36
   - 1892–94    Miley, 1:397–403
   - 1940    Wiley, 2:15–19
   - 1960    Purkiser, 215–20
3. Baptist
   - 1887    Boyce, 194–212
   - 1907    Strong, 483–513
   - 1917    Mullins, 256–57, 262–64
   - 1983–85    Erickson, 519–40
4. Dispensational
   - 1947    Chafer, 2:144–99
   - 1949    Thiessen, 158–67
   - 1986    Ryrie, 193–200
5. Lutheran
   - 1917–24    Pieper, 1:94, 476–77
   - 1934    Mueller, 58, 184
6. Reformed (or Presbyterian)
   - 1871–73    Hodge, 2:42–77, 78–91
   - 1878    Dabney, 317–21
   - 1937–66    Murray, *CW*, 2:23–33
   - 1938    Berkhof, 191–201
   - 1962    Buswell, 1:237–52
7. Renewal (or charismatic/Pentecostal)
   - 1988–92    Williams, 1:208–14

### Sections in Representative Roman Catholic Systematic Theologies

1. Roman Catholic: Traditional

1955        Ott, 96–101

2. Roman Catholic: Post-Vatican II

1980        McBrien (no explicit treatment)

### Other Works

Note: Several of the books listed in the bibliography for chapter 21, on the creation of man in the image of God, also have sections on the essential nature of man and the origin of the soul.

Colwell, J. E. "Anthropology." In *NDT*, pp. 28–30.

Cooper, John W. *Body, Soul, and Life Everlasting: Biblical Anthropology and the Monism-Dualism Debate.* Grand Rapids: Eerdmans, 1989.

Delitzsch, F. *A System of Biblical Psychology.* Trans. by R. E. Wallis. 2d ed. Grand Rapids: Baker, 1966.

Gundry, Robert H. *Sōma in Biblical Theology With Emphasis on Pauline Anthropology.* Grand Rapids: Zondervan, 1987.

Heard, J. B. *The Tripartite Nature of Man.* 5th ed. Edinburgh: T. & T. Clark, 1882.

Hoekema, Anthony A. "The Whole Person." In *Created in God's Image.* Grand Rapids: Eerdmans, and Exeter: Paternoster, 1986, pp. 203–26.

Ladd, George Eldon. "The Pauline Psychology." In *A Theology of the New Testament.* Grand Rapids: Eerdmans, 1974, pp. 457–78.

Laidlaw, John. *The Bible Doctrine of Man.* 2d ed. Edinburgh: T. & T. Clark, 1905.

McDonald, H. D. "Man, Doctrine of." In *EDT,* pp. 676–80.

## SCRIPTURE MEMORY PASSAGE

**2 Corinthians 7:1:** *Since we have these promises, beloved, let us cleanse ourselves from every defilement of body and spirit, and make holiness perfect in the fear of God.*

## HYMN

"Be Still, My Soul"

Be still, my soul: the Lord is on thy side;
    Bear patiently the cross of grief or pain;
Leave to thy God to order and provide;
    In ev'ry change he faithful will remain.
Be still, my soul: thy best, thy heav'nly friend
Through thorny ways leads to a joyful end.

Be still, my soul: thy God doth undertake
    To guide the future as he has the past.
Thy hope, thy confidence let nothing shake;
    All now mysterious shall be bright at last.
Be still, my soul: the waves and winds still know
His voice who ruled them while he dwelt below.

Be still, my soul: when dearest friends depart,
And all is darkened in the vale of tears,
Then shalt thou better know his love, his heart,
Who comes to soothe thy sorrow and thy fears.
Be still, my soul: thy Jesus can repay
From his own fullness all he takes away.

Be still, my soul: the hour is hast'ning on
When we shall be forever with the Lord,
When disappointment, grief, and fear are gone,
Sorrow forgot, love's purest joys restored.
Be still, my soul: when change and tears are past,
All safe and blessed we shall meet at last.

AUTHOR: KATHARINA VON SCHLEGEL, BORN 1697

# Chapter 24

# Sin

*What is sin? Where did it come from?*
*Do we inherit a sinful nature from Adam?*
*Do we inherit guilt from Adam?*

## EXPLANATION AND SCRIPTURAL BASIS

### A. The Definition of Sin

The history of the human race as presented in Scripture is primarily a history of man in a state of sin and rebellion against God and of God's plan of redemption to bring man back to himself. Therefore, it is appropriate now to consider the nature of the sin that separates man from God.

We may define sin as follows: *Sin is any failure to conform to the moral law of God in act, attitude, or nature.* Sin is here defined in relation to God and his moral law. Sin includes not only individual *acts* such as stealing or lying or committing murder, but also *attitudes* that are contrary to the attitudes God requires of us. We see this already in the Ten Commandments, which not only prohibit sinful actions but also wrong attitudes: "You shall not covet your neighbor's house. You shall not covet your neighbor's wife, or his manservant or maidservant, his ox or donkey, or anything that belongs to your neighbor" (Ex. 20:17 NIV). Here God specifies that a desire to steal or to commit adultery is also sin in his sight. The Sermon on the Mount also prohibits sinful attitudes such as anger (Matt. 5:22) or lust (Matt. 5:28). Paul lists attitudes such as jealousy, anger, and selfishness (Gal. 5:20) as things that are works of the flesh opposed to the desires of the Spirit (Gal. 5:20). Therefore a life that is pleasing to God is one that has moral purity not only in its actions, but also in its desires of heart. In fact, the greatest commandment of all requires that our heart be filled with an attitude of love for God: "You shall love the Lord your God with all your heart, and with all your soul, and with all your mind, and with all your strength" (Mark 12:30).

The definition of sin given above specifies that sin is a failure to conform to God's moral law not only in *action* and in *attitude,* but also in our *moral nature.* Our very nature, the internal character that is the essence of who we are as persons, can also be sinful. Before we were redeemed by Christ, not only did we do sinful acts and have sinful attitudes, we were also sinners by nature. So Paul can say that "while *we were yet sinners* Christ died for us" (Rom. 5:8), or that previously "we were *by nature* children of wrath, like the rest of mankind" (Eph. 2:3). Even while asleep, an unbeliever, though not committing sinful actions or

490

actively nurturing sinful attitudes, is still a "sinner" in God's sight; he or she still has a sinful nature that does not conform to God's moral law.

Other definitions of the essential character of sin have been suggested. Probably the most common definition is to say that the essence of sin is selfishness.[1] However, such a definition is unsatisfactory because (1) Scripture itself does not define sin this way. (2) Much self-interest is good and approved by Scripture, as when Jesus commands us to "lay up for yourselves treasures in heaven" (Matt. 6:20), or when we seek to grow in sanctification and Christian maturity (1 Thess. 4:3), or even when we come to God through Christ for salvation. God certainly appeals to the self-interest of sinful people when he says, "Turn back, turn back from your evil ways; for why will you die, O house of Israel?" (Ezek. 33:11). To define the essential character of sin as selfishness will lead many people to think that they should abandon all desire for their own personal benefit, which is certainly contrary to Scripture.[2] (3) Much sin is not selfishness in the ordinary sense of the term—people can show *selfless* devotion to a false religion or to secular and humanistic educational or political goals that are contrary to Scripture, yet these would not be due to "selfishness" in any ordinary sense of the word. Moreover, hatred of God, idolatry, and unbelief are not generally due to selfishness, but they are very serious sins. (4) Such a definition could suggest that there was wrongdoing or sinfulness even on God's part, since God's highest goal is to seek his own glory (Isa. 42:8; 43:7, 21; Eph. 1:12).[3] But such a conclusion is clearly wrong.

It is far better to define sin in the way Scripture does, in relationship to God's law and his moral character. John tells us that "sin is lawlessness" (1 John 3:4). When Paul seeks to demonstrate the universal sinfulness of mankind, he appeals to the law of God, whether the written law given to the Jew (Rom. 2:17–29) or the unwritten law that operates in the consciences of Gentiles who, by their behavior, "show that what the law requires is written on their hearts" (Rom. 2:15). In each case their sinfulness is demonstrated by their lack of conformity to the moral law of God.

---

[1]See, for example, A. H. Strong, *Systematic Theology*, pp. 567–73. However, Strong defines selfishness in a very specific way that is different from the ordinary sense of the term when used to mean simply self-interest or self-interest at the expense of other persons. Strong regards selfishness as "that choice of self as the supreme end which constitutes the antithesis of supreme love to God" (p. 567) and as "a fundamental and positive choice of preference of self instead of God, as the object of affection and the supreme end of being" (p. 572). By thus defining selfishness in relationship to God, and specifically as the opposite of love for God, and as the opposite of "love for that which is most characteristic and fundamental in God, namely, his holiness" (p. 567), Strong has actually made "selfishness" approximately equivalent to our definition (lack of conformity to the moral law of God), especially in the area of attitude (which, he explains, results in actions). When Strong defines "selfishness" in this unusual way, his definition is not really inconsistent with Scripture, for he is just saying that sin is the opposite of the great commandment to love God with all our heart. The problem with this definition, however, is that he uses the word *selfishness* in a way in which it is not commonly understood in English, and therefore his definition of sin is frequently open to misunderstanding. Our discussion in this section is not objecting to sin as selfishness in the unusual sense given by Strong, but rather in the way in which the term *selfishness* is ordinarily understood.

[2]Of course, selfishness that seeks our own good at the expense of others is wrong, and that is what is meant when Scripture tells us to "do nothing from selfishness or empty conceit, but with humility of mind let each of you regard one another as more important than himself" (Phil. 2:3 NASB). Yet the distinction between selfishness in the wrong sense and scripturally enlightened self-interest is unclear in the minds of many people.

[3]See discussion of God's jealousy, p. 205.

Finally, we should note that this definition emphasizes the seriousness of sin. We realize from experience that sin is harmful to our lives, that it brings pain and destructive consequences to us and to others affected by it. But to define sin as failure to conform to the moral law of God, is to say that sin is more than simply painful and destructive—it is also *wrong* in the deepest sense of the word. In a universe created by God, *sin ought not to be*. Sin is directly opposite to all that is good in the character of God, and just as God necessarily and eternally delights in himself and in all that he is, so God necessarily and eternally hates sin. It is, in essence, the contradiction of the excellence of his moral character. It contradicts his holiness, and he must hate it.

## B. The Origin of Sin

Where did sin come from? How did it come into the universe? First, we must clearly affirm that God himself did not sin, and God is not to be blamed for sin. It was man who sinned, and it was angels who sinned, and in both cases they did so by willful, voluntary choice. To blame God for sin would be blasphemy against the character of God. "His work is perfect; for all his ways are justice. A God of faithfulness and without iniquity, just and right is he" (Deut. 32:4). Abraham asks with truth and force in his words, "Shall not the Judge of all the earth do right?" (Gen. 18:25). And Elihu rightly says, "Far be it from God that he should do wickedness, and from the Almighty that he should do wrong" (Job 34:10). In fact, it is impossible for God even to desire to do wrong: "God cannot be tempted with evil and he himself tempts no one" (James 1:13).

Yet, on the other hand, we must guard against an opposite error: it would be wrong for us to say there is an eternally existing evil power in the universe similar to or equal to God himself in power. To say this would be to affirm what is called an ultimate "dualism" in the universe, the existence of two equally ultimate powers, one good and the other evil.[4] Also, we must never think that sin surprised God or challenged or overcame his omnipotence or his providential control over the universe. Therefore, even though we must never say that God himself sinned or he is to be blamed for. sin, yet we must also affirm that the God who "accomplishes all things according to the counsel of his will" (Eph. 1:11), the God who "does according to his will in the host of heaven and among the inhabitants of the earth; and none can stay his hand or say to him, 'What are you doing?'" (Dan. 4:35) did ordain that sin would come into the world, even though he does not delight in it and even though he ordained that it would come about through the voluntary choices of moral creatures.[5]

Even before the disobedience of Adam and Eve, sin was present in the angelic world with the fall of Satan and demons.[6] But with respect to the human race, the first sin was that of Adam and Eve in the Garden of Eden (Gen. 3:1–19). Their eating of the fruit of the tree of the knowledge of good and evil is in many ways

---

[4]See discussion of dualism in chapter 15, pp. 269–70.

[5]See chapter 16, pp. 322–30, for further discussion of God's providence in relationship to evil. God is "not a God who delights in wickedness" (Ps. 5:4) but one whose "soul hates him that loves violence" (Ps. 11:5), so that God certainly does not take pleasure in sin; nonetheless, for his own purposes, and in a way that still remains largely a mystery to us, God ordained that sin would come into the world.

[6]See discussion of the sin of angels in chapter 20, esp. pp. 412–14.

typical of sin generally. First, their sin struck at the basis for knowledge, for it gave a different answer to the question, "What is true?" Whereas God had said that Adam and Eve would die if they ate from the tree (Gen. 2:17), the serpent said, "You will not die" (Gen. 3:4). Eve decided to doubt the veracity of God's word and conduct an experiment to see whether God spoke truthfully.

Second, their sin struck at the basis for moral standards, for it gave a different answer to the question "What is right?" God had said that it was morally right for Adam and Eve not to eat from the fruit of that one tree (Gen. 2:17). But the serpent suggested that it would be right to eat of the fruit, and that in eating it Adam and Eve would become "like God" (Gen. 3:5). Eve trusted her own evaluation of what was right and what would be good for her, rather than allowing God's words to define right and wrong. She "saw that the tree was good for food, and that it was a delight to the eyes, and that the tree was to be desired to make one wise," and therefore she "took of its fruit and ate" (Gen. 3:6).

Third, their sin gave a different answer to the question, "Who am I?" The correct answer was that Adam and Eve were creatures of God, dependent on him and always to be subordinate to him as their Creator and Lord. But Eve, and then Adam, succumbed to the temptation to "be like God" (Gen. 3:5), thus attempting to put themselves in the place of God.

It is important to insist on the historical truthfulness of the narrative of the fall of Adam and Eve. Just as the account of the creation of Adam and Eve is tied in with the rest of the historical narrative in the book of Genesis,[7] so also this account of the fall of man, which follows the history of man's creation, is presented by the author as straightforward, narrative history. Moreover, the New Testament authors look back on this account and affirm that "sin came into the world through one man" (Rom. 5:12) and insist that "the judgment following one trespass brought condemnation" (Rom. 5:16) and that "the serpent deceived Eve by his cunning" (2 Cor. 11:3; cf. 1 Tim. 2:14). The serpent was no doubt, a real, physical serpent, but one that was talking because of the empowerment of Satan speaking through it (cf. Gen. 3:15 with Rom. 16:20; also Num. 22:28–30; Rev. 12:9; 20:2).

Finally, we should note that all sin is ultimately irrational. It really did not make sense for Satan to rebel against God in the expectation of being able to exalt himself above God. Nor did it make sense for Adam and Eve to think that there could be any gain in disobeying the words of their Creator. These were foolish choices. The persistence of Satan in rebelling against God even today is still a foolish choice, as is the decision on the part of any human being to continue in a state of rebellion against God. It is not the wise man but "the fool" who "says in his heart, 'There is no God'" (Ps. 14:1). It is the "fool" in the book of Proverbs who recklessly indulges in all kinds of sins (see Prov. 10:23; 12:15; 14:7, 16; 15:5; 18:2; et al.). Though people sometimes persuade themselves that they have good reasons for sinning, when examined in the cold light of truth on the last day, it will be seen in every case that sin ultimately just does not make sense.

---

[7]See also chapter 15, pp. 278–79, on the need to insist on the historicity of Adam and Eve as specific persons.

## C. The Doctrine of Inherited Sin[8]

How does the sin of Adam affect us? Scripture teaches that we inherit sin from Adam in two ways.

**1. Inherited Guilt: We Are Counted Guilty Because of Adam's Sin.** Paul explains the effects of Adam's sin in the following way: "Therefore . . . sin came into the world through one man and death through sin, and so death spread to all men because all men sinned" (Rom. 5:12). The context shows that Paul is not talking about actual sins that people commit every day of their lives, for the entire paragraph (Rom. 5:12–21) is taken up with the comparison between Adam and Christ. And when Paul says, "so [Gk. *houtōs,* "thus, in this way"; that is, through Adam's sin] death spread to all men because all men sinned," he is saying that through the sin of Adam "all men sinned."[9]

This idea, that "all men sinned" means that God thought of us all as having sinned when Adam disobeyed, is further indicated by the next two verses, where Paul says:

> Sin indeed was in the world before the law was given, but sin is not counted where there is no law. Yet death reigned from Adam to Moses, even over those whose sins were not like the transgression of Adam, who was a type of the one who was to come. (Rom. 5:13–14)

Here Paul points out that from the time of Adam to the time of Moses, people did not have God's written laws. Though their sins were "not counted" (as infractions of the law), they still died. The fact that they died is very good proof that God counted people guilty on the basis of Adam's sin.

The idea that God counted us guilty because of Adam's sin is further affirmed in Romans 5:18–19:

> Then as one man's trespass led to condemnation for all men, so one man's act of righteousness leads to acquittal and life for all men. For as *by one man's disobedience many were made sinners,* so by one man's obedience many will be made righteous.

Here Paul says explicitly that through the trespass of one man "many were made [Gk. *katestathēsan,* also an aorist indicative indicating completed past action] sinners." When Adam sinned, God thought of all who would descend from Adam

---

[8]I have used the phrase "inherited sin" rather than the more common designation "original sin" because the phrase "original sin" seems so easily to be misunderstood to refer to Adam's first sin, rather than to the sin that is ours as a result of Adam's fall (traditionally the technical meaning). The phrase "inherited sin" is much more immediately understandable and less subject to misunderstanding. Some may object that, technically speaking, we do not "inherit" guilt because it is directly imputed to us by God and does not come to us through inheritance from our parents as does the tendency toward sinful actions (traditionally called "original pollution," and here termed "inherited corruption"). But the fact that our legal guilt is inherited directly from Adam and not through a line of ancestors does not make it any less inherited: the guilt is ours because it belonged to our first father, Adam, and we inherit it from him.

[9]The aorist indicative verb *hēmarton* in the historical narrative indicates a completed past action. Here Paul is saying that something happened and was completed in the past, namely, that "all men sinned." But it was not true that all men had actually committed sinful actions at the time that Paul was writing, because some had not even been born yet, and many others had died in infancy before committing any conscious acts of sin. So Paul must be meaning that when Adam sinned, God considered it true that all men sinned in Adam.

as sinners. Though we did not yet exist, God, looking into the future and knowing that we would exist, began thinking of us as those who were guilty like Adam. This is also consistent with Paul's statement that "while we were yet sinners Christ died for us" (Rom. 5:8). Of course, some of us did not even exist when Christ died. But God nevertheless regarded us as sinners in need of salvation.

The conclusion to be drawn from these verses is that all members of the human race were represented by Adam in the time of testing in the Garden of Eden. As our representative, Adam sinned, and God counted us guilty as well as Adam. (A technical term that is sometimes used in this connection is *impute*, meaning "to think of as belonging to someone, and therefore to cause it to belong to that person.") God counted Adam's guilt as belonging to us, and since God is the ultimate judge of all things in the universe, and since his thoughts are always true, Adam's guilt does in fact belong to us. God rightly imputed Adam's guilt to us.

Sometimes the doctrine of inherited sin from Adam is termed the doctrine of "original sin." As explained above,[10] I have not used this expression. If this term is used, it should be remembered that the sin spoken of does not refer to Adam's first sin, but to the guilt and tendency to sin with which we are born. It is "original" in that it comes from Adam, and it is also original in that we have it from the beginning of our existence as persons, but it is still our sin, not Adam's sin, that is meant. Parallel to the phrase "original sin" is the phrase "original guilt." This is that aspect of inherited sin from Adam that we have been discussing above, namely, the idea that we inherit the guilt from Adam.

When we first confront the idea that we have been counted guilty because of Adam's sin, our tendency is to protest because it seems unfair. We did not actually decide to sin, did we? Then how can we be counted guilty? Is it just for God to act this way?

In response, three things may be said: (1) Everyone who protests that this is unfair has also voluntarily committed many actual sins for which God also holds us guilty. These will constitute the primary basis of our judgment on the last day, for God "will render to every man *according to his works*" (Rom. 2:6), and "the wrongdoer will be paid back *for the wrong he has done*" (Col. 3:25). (2) Moreover, some have argued, "If any one of us were in Adam's place, we also would have sinned as he did, and our subsequent rebellion against God demonstrates that." I think this is probably true, but it does not seem to be a conclusive argument, for it assumes too much about what would or would not happen. Such uncertainty may not help very much to lessen someone's sense of unfairness.

(3) The most persuasive answer to the objection is to point out that if we think it is unfair for us to be represented by Adam, then we should also think it is unfair for us to be represented by Christ and to have his righteousness imputed to us by God. For the procedure that God used was just the same, and that is exactly Paul's point in Romans 5:12–21: "As by one man's disobedience many were made sinners, so by one man's obedience many will be made righteous" (Rom. 5:19). Adam, our first representative sinned—and God counted us guilty. But Christ, the representative of all who believe in him, obeyed God perfectly—and God counted us righteous. That is simply the way in which God set up the human race to work. God regards the human race as an organic whole, a unity, represented by

[10]See note 8, above.

Adam as its head. And God also thinks of the new race of Christians, those who are redeemed by Christ, as an organic whole, a unity represented by Christ as head of his people.

Not all evangelical theologians, however, agree that we are counted guilty because of Adam's sin. Some, especially Arminian theologians, think this to be unfair of God and do not believe that it is taught in Romans 5.[11] However, evangelicals of all persuasions do agree that we receive a sinful disposition or a tendency to sin as an inheritance from Adam, a subject we shall now consider.

## 2. Inherited Corruption: We Have a Sinful Nature Because of Adam's Sin.

In addition to the legal guilt that God imputes to us because of Adam's sin, we also inherit a sinful nature because of Adam's sin. This inherited sinful nature is sometimes simply called "original sin" and sometimes more precisely called "original pollution." I have used instead the term "inherited corruption" because it seems to express more clearly the specific idea in view.

David says, "Behold, I was brought forth in iniquity, and in sin did my mother conceive me" (Ps. 51:5). Some have mistakenly thought that the sin of David's mother is in view here, but this is incorrect, for the entire context has nothing to do with David's mother. David is confessing his own personal sin throughout this section. He says:

> Have mercy on *me*, O God
> . . . blot out *my* transgressions.
> Wash *me* thoroughly from *my* iniquity
>
> . . . I know *my* transgressions.
> . . . Against you . . . have *I* sinned. (Ps. 51:1–4)

David is so overwhelmed with the consciousness of his own sin that as he looks back on his life he realizes that he was sinful from the beginning. As far back as he can think of himself, he realizes that he has had a sinful nature. In fact, when he was born or "brought forth" from his mother's womb, he was "*brought forth* in iniquity" (Ps. 51:5). Moreover, even before he was born, he had a sinful disposition: he affirms that at the moment of conception he had a sinful nature, for "in sin did my mother *conceive* me" (Ps. 51:5). Here is a strong statement of the inherent tendency to sin that attaches to our lives from the very beginning. A similar idea is affirmed in Psalm 58:3, "The wicked go astray from the womb, they err from their birth, speaking lies."

Therefore, our nature includes a disposition to sin so that Paul can affirm that before we were Christians "we were by nature children of wrath, like the rest of mankind" (Eph. 2:3). Anyone who has raised children can give experiential testimony to the fact that we are all born with a tendency to sin. Children do not have to be taught how to do wrong; they discover that by themselves. What we have to do as parents is to teach them how to do right, to "bring them up in the discipline and instruction of the Lord" (Eph. 6:4).

This inherited tendency to sin does not mean that human beings are all as bad as they could be. The constraints of civil law, the expectations of family and society,

---

[11]See, for example, the thorough discussion in H. Orton Wiley, *Christian Theology*, 3 vols. (Kansas City, Mo.: Beacon Hill Press, 1941–49), 3:109–40.

and the conviction of human conscience (Rom. 2:14–15) all provide restraining influences on the sinful tendencies in our hearts. Therefore, by God's "common grace" (that is, by his undeserved favor that is given to all human beings), people have been able to do much good in the areas of education, the development of civilization, scientific and technological progress, the development of beauty and skill in the arts, the development of just laws, and general acts of human benevolence and kindness to others.[12] In fact, the more Christian influence there is in a society in general, the more clearly the influence of "common grace" will be seen in the lives of unbelievers as well. But in spite of the ability to do good in many senses of that word, our inherited corruption, our tendency to sin, which we received from Adam, means that as far as God is concerned we are not able to do anything that pleases him. This may be seen in two ways:

**a. In Our Natures We Totally Lack Spiritual Good Before God:** It is not just that some parts of us are sinful and others are pure. Rather, every part of our being is affected by sin—our intellects, our emotions and desires, our hearts (the center of our desires and decision-making processes), our goals and motives, and even our physical bodies. Paul says, "I know that nothing good dwells within me, that is, in my flesh" (Rom. 7:18), and, "to the corrupt and unbelieving nothing is pure; their very minds and consciences are corrupted" (Titus 1:15). Moreover, Jeremiah tells us that "the heart is deceitful above all things, and desperately corrupt; who can understand it?" (Jer. 17:9). In these passages Scripture is not denying that unbelievers can do good in human society *in some senses*. But it is denying that they can do any *spiritual* good or be good *in terms of a relationship with God*. Apart from the work of Christ in our lives, we are like all other unbelievers who are "darkened in their understanding, alienated from the life of God because of the ignorance that is in them, due to their hardness of heart" (Eph. 4:18).[13]

**b. In Our Actions We Are Totally Unable to Do Spiritual Good Before God:** This idea is related to the previous one. Not only do we as sinners lack any spiritual good in ourselves, but we also lack the ability to do anything that will in itself please God and the ability to come to God in our own strength. Paul says that "those who are in the flesh *cannot please God*" (Rom. 8:8). Moreover, in terms of bearing fruit for God's kingdom and doing what pleases him, Jesus says, "Apart from me you can do nothing" (John 15:5). In fact, unbelievers are not pleasing to God, if for no other reason, simply because their actions do not proceed from faith in God or from love to him, and "without faith it is impossible to please him" (Heb. 11:6). When Paul's readers were unbelievers, he tells them, "You were dead through the trespasses and sins in which you once walked" (Eph. 2:1–2). Unbelievers are in a state of bondage or enslavement to sin, because "every one who commits sin is a slave to sin" (John 8:34). Though from a human standpoint

---

[12]See chapter 31, pp. 657–58, on common grace.
[13]This total lack of spiritual good and inability to do good before God has traditionally been called "total depravity," but I will not use the phrase here because it is easily subject to misunderstanding. It can give the impression that no good *in any sense* can be done by unbelievers, a meaning that is certainly not intended by that term or by this doctrine.

people might be able to do much good, Isaiah affirms that "all our righteous deeds are like a polluted garment" (Isa. 64:6; cf. Rom. 3:9–20). Unbelievers are not even able to understand the things of God correctly, for the "natural man does not receive the gifts [lit. 'things'] of the Spirit of God, for they are folly to him, and he is not able to understand them because they are spiritually discerned" (1 Cor. 2:14 RSV mg.). Nor can we come to God in our own power, for Jesus says, "No one can come to me unless the Father who sent me draws him" (John 6:44).

But if we have a total inability to do any spiritual good in God's sight, then do we still have any freedom of choice? Certainly, those who are outside of Christ do still make voluntary choices—that is, they decide what they want to do, then they do it. In this sense there is still a kind of "freedom" in the choices that people make.[14] Yet because of their inability to do good and to escape from their fundamental rebellion against God and their fundamental preference for sin, unbelievers do not have freedom in the most important sense of freedom—that is, the freedom to do right, and to do what is pleasing to God.

The application to our lives is quite evident: if God gives anyone a desire to repent and trust in Christ, he or she should not delay and should not harden his or her heart (cf. Heb. 3:7–8; 12:17). This ability to repent and desire to trust in God is not naturally ours but is given by the prompting of the Holy Spirit, and it will not last forever. "Today, when you hear his voice, do not harden your hearts" (Heb. 3:15).

## D. Actual Sins in Our Lives

**1. All People Are Sinful Before God.** Scripture in many places testifies to the universal sinfulness of mankind. "They have all gone astray, they are all alike corrupt; there is none that does good, no, not one" (Ps. 14:3). David says, "No man living is righteous before you" (Ps. 143:2). And Solomon says, "There is no man who does not sin" (1 Kings 8:46; cf. Prov. 20:9).

In the New Testament, Paul has an extensive argument in Romans 1:18–3:20 showing that all people, both Jews and Greeks, stand guilty before God. He says, "All men, both Jews and Greeks, are under the power of sin, as it is written: 'None is righteous, no, not one'" (Rom. 3:9–10). He is certain that "all have sinned and fall short of the glory of God" (Rom. 3:23). James, the Lord's brother, admits, "We all make many mistakes" (James 3:2), and if he, as a leader and an apostle[15] in the early church, could admit that he made many mistakes, then we also should be willing to admit that of ourselves. John, the beloved disciple, who was especially close to Jesus, said:

> If we say we have no sin, we deceive ourselves, and the truth is not in us. If we confess our sins, he is faithful and just, and will forgive our sins and cleanse us from all unrighteousness. If we say we have not sinned, we make him a liar, and his word is not in us. (1 John 1:8–10)[16]

---

[14]See discussion of the question of free will in chapter 16, pp. 330–31.

[15]See the note in chapter 3, p. 62, on whether James the Lord's brother was an apostle.

[16]Some popular explanations of this passage deny that v. 8 applies to all Christians. This position is taken in order to say that some Christians can be perfectly free from sin in this life, if they reach the state of perfect sanctification. According to this view, v. 8 ("If we say we have no sin, we deceive ourselves, and the truth is not in us") applies to Christians before they reach the stage of sinless

## 2. Does Our Ability Limit Our Responsibility?

Pelagius, a popular Christian teacher active in Rome about A.D. 383–410 and then later (until A.D. 424) in Palestine, taught that God holds man responsible only for those things that man is *able* to do. Since God warns us to do good, therefore, we must have the ability to do the good that God commands. The Pelagian position rejects the doctrine of "inherited sin" (or "original sin") and maintains that sin consists only in separate sinful acts.[17]

However, the idea that we are responsible before God only for what we are able to do is contrary to the testimony of Scripture, which affirms both that we "were *dead* through the trespasses and sins" in which we once walked (Eph. 2:1), and thus unable to do any spiritual good, and also that we are all guilty before God. Moreover, if our responsibility before God were limited by our ability, then extremely hardened sinners, who are in great bondage to sin, could be less guilty before God than mature Christians who were striving daily to obey him. And Satan himself, who is eternally able to do only evil, would have no guilt at all— surely an incorrect conclusion.

The true measure of our responsibility and guilt is not our own ability to obey God, but rather the absolute perfection of God's moral law and his own holiness (which is reflected in that law). "You, therefore, must be perfect, as your heavenly Father is perfect" (Matt. 5:48).

## 3. Are Infants Guilty Before They Commit Actual Sins?

Some maintain that Scripture teaches an "age of accountability" before which young children are not held responsible for sin and are not counted guilty before God.[18] However, the passages noted above in Section C about "inherited sin" indicate that even before birth children have a guilty standing before God and a sinful nature that not only gives them a tendency to sin but also causes God to view them as "sinners." "Behold, I was brought forth in iniquity, and in sin did my mother conceive me" (Ps. 51:5). The passages that speak of final judgment in terms of actual sinful deeds that have been done (e.g., Rom. 2:6–11) do not say anything about the

---

perfection. The next sentence, talking about our confession and God's cleansing us from "all unrighteousness," includes the process of dealing with that past sin and having it forgiven. Then the last sentence (v. 10) does include those who have obtained the state of sinless perfection—they do not any longer need to say that they have sin in the present in their lives, but simply have to admit that they had sinned in the past. For them it is true, "If we say we have not sinned, we make him a liar" (1 John 1:10).

But this explanation is not persuasive, because John writes the first sentence (v. 8) in the present tense, and it is something that is true of all Christians at all times. John does not write, "If we say while we are still immature Christians that we have no sin, we deceive ourselves." Nor does he say (as this view would hold), "If we say, before we have reached the state of sinless perfection, that we have no sin, we deceive ourselves." Rather, near the end of his life, writing a general letter to all Christians, including those who have grown in maturity in Christ for decades, John says in no uncertain terms something that he expects to be true of all Christians to whom he writes: "If we say we have no sin, we deceive ourselves, and the truth is not in us." This is a clear statement that applies to all Christians as long as they are in this life. If we say that it does not apply, "we deceive ourselves."

[17]Pelagianism was more fundamentally concerned with the question of salvation, holding that man can take the first and the most important steps toward salvation on his own, apart from God's intervening grace. Pelagianism was condemned as a heresy at the Council of Carthage on May 1, A.D. 418.

[18]This is the position of Millard Erickson, for example, in *Christian Theology*, p. 639. He uses the term "age of responsibility" rather than "age of accountability."

basis of judgment when there have been no individual actions of right or wrong, as with children dying in early infancy. In such cases we must accept the Scriptures that talk about ourselves as having a sinful nature from before the time of birth. Furthermore, we must realize that a child's sinful nature manifests itself very early, certainly within the first two years of a child's life, as anyone who has raised children can affirm. (David says, in another place, "The wicked go astray *from the womb*, they err *from their birth*," Ps. 58:3.)

But then what do we say about infants who die before they are old enough to understand and believe the gospel? Can they be saved?

Here we must say that if such infants are saved, it cannot be on their own merits, or on the basis of their own righteousness or innocence, but it must be entirely on the basis of Christ's redemptive work and regeneration by the work of the Holy Spirit within them. "There is one God, and there is one mediator between God and men, the man Christ Jesus" (1 Tim. 2:5). "Unless one is born anew, he cannot see the kingdom of God" (John 3:3).

Yet it certainly is possible for God to bring regeneration (that is, new spiritual life) to an infant even before he or she is born. This was true of John the Baptist, for the angel Gabriel, before John was born, said, "He will be filled with the Holy Spirit, *even from his mother's womb*" (Luke 1:15). We might say that John the Baptist was "born again" before he was born! There is a similar example in Psalm 22:10: David says, "Since my mother bore me you have been my God." It is clear, therefore, that God is able to save infants in an unusual way, apart from their hearing and understanding the gospel, by bringing regeneration to them very early, sometimes even before birth. This regeneration is probably also followed at once by a nascent, intuitive awareness of God and trust in him at an extremely early age, but this is something we simply cannot understand.[19]

We must, however, affirm very clearly that this is not the usual way for God to save people. Salvation usually occurs when someone hears and understands the gospel and then places trust in Christ. But in unusual cases like John the Baptist, God brought salvation before this understanding. And this leads us to conclude that it certainly is possible that God would also do this where he knows the infant will die before hearing the gospel.

How many infants does God save in this way? Scripture does not tell us, so we simply cannot know. Where Scripture is silent, it is unwise for us to make definitive pronouncements. However, we should recognize that it is God's frequent pattern throughout Scripture to save the children of those who believe in him (see Gen. 7:1; cf. Heb. 11:7; Josh. 2:18; Ps. 103:17; John 4:53; Acts 2:39; 11:14(?); 16:31; 18:8; 1 Cor. 1:16; 7:14; Titus 1:6). These passages do not show that God automatically saves the children of all believers (for we all know of children of godly parents who have grown up and rejected the Lord, and Scripture also gives such examples as Esau and Absalom), but they do indicate that God's ordinary pattern, the "normal" or expected way in which he acts, is to bring the children of believers to himself. With regard to believers' children who die very young, we have no reason to think that it would be otherwise.

---

[19]However, we all know that infants almost from the moment of birth show an instinctive trust in their mothers and awareness of themselves as persons distinct from their mothers. Thus we should not insist that it is impossible that they would also have an intuitive awareness of God, and if God gives it, an intuitive ability to trust in God as well.

Particularly relevant here is the case of the first child Bathsheba bore to King David. When the infant child had died, David said, "*I shall go to him*, but he will not return to me" (2 Sam. 12:23). David, who through his life had such great confidence that he would live forever in the Lord's presence (see Ps. 23:6, and many of David's psalms), also had confidence that he would see his infant son again when he died. This can only imply that he would be with his son in the presence of the Lord forever.[20] This passage, together with the others mentioned above, should be of similar assurance to all believers who have lost children in their infancy, that they will one day see them again in the glory of the heavenly kingdom.

Regarding the children of unbelievers who die at a very early age Scripture is silent. We simply must leave that matter in the hands of God and trust him to be both just and merciful. If they are saved, it will not be on the basis of any merit of their own or any innocence that we might presume that they have. If they are saved, it will be on the basis of Christ's redeeming work; and their regeneration, like that of John the Baptist before he was born, will be by God's mercy and grace. Salvation is always because of his mercy, not because of our merits (see Rom. 9:14–18). Scripture does not allow us to say more than that.

**4. Are There Degrees of Sin?** Are some sins worse than others? The question may be answered either yes or no, depending on the sense in which it is intended.

**a. Legal Guilt:** In terms of our legal standing before God, any one sin, even what may seem to be a very small one, makes us legally guilty before God and therefore worthy of eternal punishment. Adam and Eve learned this in the Garden of Eden, where God told them that one act of disobedience would result in the penalty of death (Gen. 2:17). And Paul affirms that "the judgment following one trespass brought condemnation" (Rom. 5:16). This one sin made Adam and Eve sinners before God, no longer able to stand in his holy presence.

This truth remains valid through the history of the human race. Paul (quoting Deut. 27:26) affirms it: "Cursed be every one who does not abide by *all things* written in the book of the law, and do them" (Gal. 3:10). And James declares:

> Whoever keeps the whole law but fails *in one point* has become guilty of all of it. For he who said, "Do not commit adultery," said also, "Do not kill." If you do not commit adultery but do kill, you have become a transgressor of the law. (James 2:10–11)[21]

---

[20]Someone might object that David is only saying that he would go to the state of death just as his son had. But this interpretation does not fit the language of the verse: David does not say, "I shall go *where he is*," but rather, "I shall go *to him*." This is the language of personal reunion, and it indicates David's expectation that he would one day see and be with his son.

[21]We may understand this principle more clearly when we realize that the various moral laws of God are simply different aspects of his perfect moral character, to which he expects us to conform. To violate any one part of it is to become unlike him. For example, if I were to steal, I would not only break the commandment against stealing (Commandment 8), but I would also dishonor God's name (Commandment 3; see Prov. 30:9), dishonor my parents and their good name (Commandment 5), covet something that does not belong to me (Commandment 10), put some material possession ahead of God himself (Commandment 1; see Eph. 5:5), and carry out an action that harms another human being and damages his or her life (Commandment 6; cf. Matt. 5:22). With a little reflection, we can see how almost any sin violates some of the principles embodied in each of the Ten Commandments. This

Therefore, in terms of legal guilt, all sins are equally bad because they make us legally guilty before God and constitute us as sinners.

**b. Results in Life and in Relationship With God:** On the other hand, some sins are worse than others in that they have more harmful consequences in our lives and in the lives of others, and, in terms of our personal relationship to God as Father, they arouse his displeasure more and bring more serious disruption to our fellowship with him.

Scripture sometimes speaks of degrees of seriousness of sin. When Jesus stood before Pontius Pilate, he said, "he who delivered me to you has the *greater sin*" (John 19:11). The reference is apparently to Judas, who had known Jesus intimately for three years and yet willfully betrayed him to death. Though Pilate had authority over Jesus by virtue of his governmental office and was wrong to allow an innocent man to be condemned to death, the sin of Judas was far "greater," probably because of the far greater knowledge and malice connected with it.

When God showed Ezekiel visions of sins in the temple of Jerusalem, he first showed Ezekiel certain things, then said, "But you will see *still greater* abominations" (Ezek. 8:6). Next he showed Ezekiel the secret sins of some of the elders of Israel and said, "You will see *still greater* abominations which they commit" (Ezek. 8:13). Then the Lord showed Ezekiel a picture of women weeping for a Babylonian deity and said, "Have you seen this, O son of man? You will see *still greater* abominations than these" (Ezek. 8:15). Finally, he showed Ezekiel twenty-five men in the temple, with their backs to the Lord and worshiping the sun instead. Here clearly we have degrees of increasing sin and hatefulness before God.

In the Sermon of the Mount, when Jesus says, "Whoever then relaxes one of *the least of these commandments* and teaches men so, shall be called least in the kingdom of heaven" (Matt. 5:19), he implies that there are lesser and greater commandments. Similarly, though he agrees that it is appropriate to give a tithe even on the household spices that people use, he pronounces woes on the Pharisees for neglecting "*the weightier matters of the law,* justice and mercy and faith" (Matt. 23:23). In both cases Jesus distinguishes between lesser and greater commandments, thus implying that some sins are worse than other sins in terms of God's own evaluation of their importance.

In general, we may say that some sins have more harmful consequences than others if they bring more dishonor to God or if they cause more harm to ourselves, to others, or to the church. Moreover, those sins that are done willfully, repeatedly, and knowingly, with a calloused heart, are more displeasing to God than those that are done out of ignorance and are not repeated, or are done with a mixture of good and impure motives and are followed by remorse and repentance. Thus the laws that God gave to Moses in Leviticus make provisions for cases where people sin "unwittingly" (Lev. 4:2, 13, 22). Unintentional sin is still sin: "If any one sins, doing any of the things which the LORD has commanded not to be done, though he does not know it, yet he is guilty and shall bear his iniquity"

---

is simply a reflection of the fact that God's laws are a unified whole and reflect the moral purity and perfection of God himself in the integrated oneness of his person.

(Lev. 5:17). Nonetheless, the penalties required and the degree of God's displeasure that results from the sin are less than in the case of intentional sin.

On the other hand, sins committed with "a high hand," that is, with arrogance and disdain for God's commandments, were viewed very seriously: "But the person who does anything with a high hand, whether he is native or a sojourner, reviles the LORD, and that person shall be cut off from among his people" (Num. 15:30; cf. vv. 27–29).

We can readily see how some sins have much more harmful consequences for ourselves and others and for our relationship with God. If I were to covet my neighbor's car, that would be sin before God. But if my coveting led me to actually steal the car, that would be more serious sin. If in the course of stealing the car I also fought with my neighbor and injured him or recklessly injured someone else as I drove the car, that would be even more serious sin.

Similarly, if a new Christian, who previously had a tendency to lose his temper and get into fights, begins witnessing to his unbelieving friends and, one day, is so provoked he loses his temper and actually strikes someone, that is certainly sin in God's sight. But if a mature pastor or other prominent Christian leader were to lose his temper publicly and strike someone, that would be even more serious in God's sight, both because of the harm that would come to the reputation of the gospel and because those in leadership positions are held to a higher standard of accountability by God: "We who teach shall be judged with greater strictness" (James 3:1; cf. Luke 12:48). Our conclusion, then, is that in terms of *results* and in terms of the *degree of God's displeasure,* some sins are certainly worse than others.

However, the distinction between degrees of seriousness of sin does not imply an endorsement of the Roman Catholic teaching that sins can be put into the two categories of "venial" and "mortal."[22] In Roman Catholic teaching, a venial sin can be forgiven, but often after punishments in this life or in Purgatory (after death, but before entrance into heaven). A mortal sin is a sin that causes spiritual death and cannot be forgiven; it excludes people from the kingdom of God.

According to Scripture, however, all sins are "mortal" in that even the smallest sin makes us legally guilty before God and worthy of eternal punishment. Yet even the most serious of sins are forgiven when one comes to Christ for salvation (note the combination of a list of sins that exclude from the kingdom of God and the affirmation that the Corinthians who had committed them have been saved by Christ in 1 Cor. 6:9–11). Thus, in that sense, all sins are "venial."[23] The Roman Catholic separation of sins into the category of "mortal" and "venial," calling some sins (such as suicide) "mortal," while calling others (such as dishonesty, anger, or

---

[22]The distinction between mortal and venial sins may seem to be supported by 1 John 5:16–17: "If any one sees his brother committing *what is not a mortal sin,* he will ask, and God will give him life for those whose sin is not mortal. There is sin which is mortal; I do not say that one is to pray for that. All wrongdoing is sin, but there is sin which is not mortal." The Greek phrase here translated "mortal" is more literally "toward death" or "unto death" (Gk. *pros thanaton*). In the light of John's concern in this epistle to combat a heresy that did not confess Jesus as God who came in the flesh (see 1 John 4:2–3), it is likely that this sin "unto death" is the serious heresy of denying Christ and subsequently failing to obtain salvation through Christ. In this case, John would simply be saying that we should not pray that God would forgive the sin of rejecting Christ and teaching seriously heretical doctrine about him. But the fact that John says there is one sin that is "unto death" (rejecting Christ), does not justify establishing a whole category of sins that cannot be forgiven.

[23]On "the unpardonable sin," which is the one exception to this statement, see pp. 507–9, below.

lust) "venial" sins can very easily lead either to carelessness with respect to some sins that greatly hinder sanctification and effectiveness in the Lord's work, or, with respect to other sins, to excessive fear, despair, and inability ever to have assurance of forgiveness. And we should realize that the same exact action (such as losing one's temper and striking someone in the example above) can be more or less serious, depending on the person and circumstances involved. It is much better simply to recognize that sins can vary in terms of their results and in terms of the degree to which they disrupt our relationship with God and incur his displeasure, and leave it at that. Then we do not go beyond the general teaching of Scripture on this subject.

The distinction that Scripture makes in degrees of sin does have positive value. First, it helps us to know where we should put more effort in our own attempts to grow in personal holiness. Second, it helps us to decide when we should simply overlook a minor fault in a friend or family member and when it would be appropriate to talk with an individual about some evident sin (see James 5:19–20). Third, it may help us decide when church discipline is appropriate, and it provides an answer to the objection that is sometimes raised against exercising church discipline, in which it is said that "we are all guilty of sin, so we have no business meddling in anyone else's life." Though we are all indeed guilty of sin, nonetheless, there are some sins that so evidently harm the church and relationships within the church that they must be dealt with directly. Fourth, this distinction may also help us realize that there is some basis for civil governments to have laws and penalties prohibiting certain kinds of wrongdoing (such as murder or stealing), but not other kinds of wrongdoing (such as anger, jealousy, greed, or selfish use of one's possessions). It is not inconsistent to say that some kinds of wrongdoing require civil punishment but not all kinds of wrongdoing require it.

## 5. What Happens When a Christian Sins?

### a. Our Legal Standing Before God Is Unchanged:
Though this subject could be treated later in relation to adoption or sanctification within the Christian life, it is quite appropriate to treat it at this point.

When a Christian sins, his or her legal standing before God is unchanged. He or she is still forgiven, for "there is therefore now no condemnation for those who are in Christ Jesus" (Rom. 8:1). Salvation is not based on our merits but is a free gift of God (Rom. 6:23), and Christ's death certainly paid for all our sins—past, present, and future—Christ died "for our sins" (1 Cor. 15:3), without distinction. In theological terms, we still keep our "justification."[24]

Moreover, we are still children of God and we still retain our membership in God's family. In the same epistle in which John says, "If we say we have no sin, we deceive ourselves, and the truth in not in us" (1 John 1:8), he also reminds his readers, "Beloved, we are God's children now" (1 John 3:2). The fact that we have sin remaining in our lives does not mean that we lose our status as God's children. In theological terms, we keep our "adoption."[25]

[24]See chapter 36, pp. 722–35, on justification.
[25]See chapter 37, pp. 736–45, on adoption.

**b. Our Fellowship With God Is Disrupted and Our Christian Life Is Damaged:** When we sin, even though God does not cease to love us, he is displeased with us. (Even among human beings, it is possible to love someone and be displeased with that person at the same time, as any parent will attest, or any wife, or any husband.) Paul tells us that it is possible for Christians to "grieve the Holy Spirit of God" (Eph. 4:30); when we sin, we cause him sorrow and he is displeased with us. The author of Hebrews reminds us that "the Lord disciplines him whom he loves" (Heb. 12:6, quoting Prov. 3:11–12), and that "the Father of spirits . . . disciplines us for our good, that we may share his holiness" (Heb. 12:9–10). When we disobey, God the Father is grieved, much as an earthly father is grieved with his children's disobedience, and he disciplines us. A similar theme is found in Revelation 3, where the risen Christ speaks from heaven to the church of Laodicea, saying, "Those whom I *love,* I *reprove* and *chasten;* so be zealous and repent" (Rev. 3:19). Here again love and reproof of sin are connected in the same statement. Thus, the New Testament attests to the displeasure of all three members of the Trinity when Christians sin. (See also Isa. 59:1–2; 1 John 3:21.)

The Westminster Confession of Faith wisely says, concerning Christians,

> Although they never can fall from the state of justification, yet they may, by their sins, fall under God's *fatherly displeasure,* and not have the light of His countenance restored unto them, until they humble themselves, confess their sins, beg pardon, and renew their faith and repentance. (chap. 11, sec. 5)

Hebrews 12, together with many historical examples in Scripture, shows that God's *fatherly displeasure* often leads to discipline in our Christian lives: "He disciplines us for our good, that we may share his holiness" (Heb. 12:10). Regarding the need for regular confession and repentance of sin, Jesus reminds us that we are to pray each day, "Forgive us our sins, as we also have forgiven those who sin against us" (Matt. 6:12, author's translation; cf. 1 John 1:9).

When we sin as Christians, it is not only our personal relationship with God that is disrupted. Our Christian life and fruitfulness in ministry are also damaged. Jesus warns us, "As the branch cannot bear fruit by itself, unless it abides in the vine, neither can you, unless you abide in me" (John 15:4). When we stray from fellowship with Christ because of sin in our lives, we diminish the degree to which we are abiding in Christ.

The New Testament writers frequently speak of the destructive consequences of sin in the lives of believers. In fact, many sections of the epistles are taken up with rebuking and discouraging Christians from sin that they are committing. Paul says that if Christians yield themselves to sin, they increasingly become "slaves" of sin (Rom. 6:16), whereas God wants Christians to progress upward on a path of ever-increasing righteousness in life. If our goal is to grow in increasing fullness of life until the day we die and pass into the presence of God in heaven, to sin is to do an about-face and begin to walk downhill away from the goal of likeness to God; it is to go in a direction that "leads to death" (Rom. 6:16) and eternal separation from God, the direction from which we were rescued when we became Christians.[26]

---

[26]Paul is not saying in Romans 6:16 that true Christians will ever actually regress to a point at which they fall under eternal condemnation, but he does seem to be saying that when we yield to sin we are (in a spiritual/moral sense) traveling in that direction.

Peter says that sinful desires that remain in our hearts *"wage war* against your soul" (1 Peter 2:11)—the military language correctly translates Peter's expression and conveys the imagery that sinful desires within us are like soldiers in a battle and their target is our spiritual well-being. To give in to such sinful desires, to nurture and cherish them in our hearts, is to give food, shelter, and welcome to the enemy's troops. If we yield to the desires that "wage war" against our souls, we will inevitably feel some loss of spiritual strength, some diminution of spiritual power, some loss of effectiveness in the work of God's kingdom.

Moreover, when we sin as Christians we suffer a loss of heavenly reward. A person who has built on the work of the church not with gold, silver, and precious stones, but with "wood, hay, stubble" (1 Cor. 3:12) will have his work "burned up" on the day of judgment and "he will suffer loss, though he himself will be saved, but only as through fire" (1 Cor. 3:15). Paul realizes that "we must all appear before the judgment seat of Christ, so that each one may receive good or evil, according to what he has done in the body" (2 Cor. 5:10). Paul implies that there are degrees of reward in heaven,[27] and that sin has negative consequences in terms of loss of heavenly reward.

**c. The Danger of "Unconverted Evangelicals":** While a genuine Christian who sins does not lose his or her justification or adoption before God (see above), there needs to be a clear warning that mere association with an evangelical church and outward conformity to accepted "Christian" patterns of behavior does not guarantee salvation. Particularly in societies and cultures where it is easy (or even expected) for people to profess to be Christians, there is a real possibility that some will associate with the church who are not genuinely born again. If such people then become more and more disobedient to Christ in their pattern of life, they should not be lulled into complacency by assurances that they still have justification or adoption in God's family. A consistent pattern of disobedience to Christ coupled with a lack of the elements of the fruit of the Holy Spirit such as love, joy, peace, and so forth (see Gal. 5:22–23) is a warning signal that the person is probably not a true Christian inwardly, that there probably has been no genuine heart-faith from the beginning and no regenerating work of the Holy Spirit. Jesus warns that he will say to some who have prophesied, cast out demons, and done many mighty works in his name, "I never knew you; depart from me, you evildoers" (Matt. 7:23). And John tells us that "he who says 'I know him' but disobeys his commandments is a liar, and the truth is not in him" (1 John 2:4; here John speaks of a persistent pattern of life). A long-term pattern of increasing disobedience to Christ should be taken as evidence to doubt that the person in question is really a Christian at all.

**6. What Is the Unpardonable Sin?** Several passages of Scripture speak about a sin that will not be forgiven. Jesus says:

> Therefore I tell you, every sin and blasphemy will be forgiven men, but the blasphemy against the Spirit will not be forgiven. And whoever says a word against

---

[27]See chapter 56, pp. 1140–57, on degrees of reward in heaven.

the Son of man will be forgiven; but whoever speaks against the Holy Spirit will
not be forgiven, either in this age or in the age to come. (Matt. 12:31–32)

A similar statement occurs in Mark 3:29–30, where Jesus says that "whoever
blasphemes against the Holy Spirit never has forgiveness" (Mark 3:29; cf. Luke
12:10). Similarly, Hebrews 6 says:

> For it is impossible to restore again to repentance those who have once been
> enlightened, who have tasted the heavenly gift, and have become partakers of the
> Holy Spirit, and have tasted the goodness of the word of God and the powers of
> the age to come, if they then commit apostasy, since they crucify the son of God on
> their own account and hold him up to contempt. (Heb. 6:4–6; cf. 10:26–27; also
> the discussion of the sin "that leads to death" [NIV] in 1 John 5:16–17)

These passages could be talking about the same or different sins; a decision
about this will have to be made from an examination of the passages in context.
Several different views of this sin have been taken.[28]

1. Some have thought that it was a sin that could only be committed while
Christ was on earth. But Jesus' statement that "every sin and blasphemy will be
forgiven men" (Matt. 12:31) is so general that it seems unwarranted to say it is
only referring to something that could only happen during his lifetime—the texts
in question do not specify such a restriction. Moreover, Hebrews 6:4–6 is
speaking of apostasy that has occurred a number of years after Jesus returned to
heaven.

2. Some have held that the sin is unbelief that continues until the time of death;
therefore, everyone who dies in unbelief (or at least everyone who has heard of
Christ and then dies in unbelief) has committed this sin. It is true, of course, that
those who persist in unbelief until death will not be forgiven, but the question is
whether that fact is what is being discussed in these verses. On close reading of the
verses, that explanation does not seem to fit the language of the texts cited, for
they do not talk of unbelief in general but specifically of someone who "speaks
against the Holy Spirit" (Matt. 12:32), "blasphemes against the Holy Spirit"
(Mark 3:29) or commits "apostasy" (Heb. 6:6). They have in view a specific sin—
willful rejection of the work of the Holy Spirit and speaking evil about it, or
willful rejection of the truth of Christ and holding Christ up to "contempt" (Heb.
6:6). Moreover, the idea that this sin is unbelief that persists until death does not
fit well with the context of a rebuke to the Pharisees for what they were saying in
both Matthew and Mark (see discussion of context below).

3. Some hold that this sin is serious apostasy by genuine believers, and that only
those who are truly born again could commit this sin. They base their view on
their understanding of the nature of the "apostasy" that is mentioned in Hebrews
6:4–6 (that it is a rejection of Christ and loss of salvation by a true Christian). But
that does not seem to be the best understanding of Hebrews 4–6.[29] Moreover,
though this view could perhaps be sustained with respect to Hebrews 6, it does
not explain blasphemy against the Holy Spirit in the gospel passages, in which
Jesus is responding to the Pharisees' hard-hearted denial of the work of the Holy
Spirit through him.

---

[28]See Berkhof, *Systematic Theology*, pp. 252–53, for representatives of each position.
[29]See the extended discussion of Hebrews 6:4–6 in chapter 40, pp. 796–801.

4. A fourth possibility is that this sin consists of unusually malicious, willful rejection and slander against the Holy Spirit's work attesting to Christ, and attributing that work to Satan. A closer look at the context of Jesus' statement in Matthew and Mark shows that Jesus was speaking in response to the accusation of the Pharisees that "it is only by Beelzebul, the prince of demons, that this man casts out demons" (Matt. 12:24). The Pharisees had seen Jesus' works repeatedly. He had just healed a blind and dumb demoniac so that he could see and speak (Matt. 12:22). The people were amazed and were following Jesus in large numbers, and the Pharisees themselves had repeatedly seen clear demonstrations of the amazing power of the Holy Spirit working through Jesus to bring life and health to many people. But the Pharisees, in spite of clear demonstrations of the work of the Holy Spirit in front of their eyes, willfully rejected Jesus' authority and his teaching and attributed it to the devil. Jesus then told them clearly that "no city or house divided against itself will stand; and if Satan casts out Satan, he is divided against himself; how then will his kingdom stand?" (Matt. 12:25–26). So it was irrational and foolish for the Pharisees to attribute Jesus' exorcisms to the power of Satan—it was a classic, willful, malicious lie.

After explaining, "If it is *by the Spirit of God* that I cast out demons, then the kingdom of God has come upon you" (Matt. 12:28), Jesus declares this warning: "He who is not with me is against me, and he who does not gather with me scatters" (Matt. 12:30). He warns that there is no neutrality, and certainly those who, like the Pharisees, oppose his message are against him. Then he immediately adds, "Therefore I tell you, every sin and blasphemy will be forgiven men, but the blasphemy against the Spirit will not be forgiven" (Matt. 12:31). The willful, malicious slander of the work of the Holy Spirit through Jesus, in which the Pharisees attributed it to Satan, would not be forgiven.

The context indicates that Jesus is speaking about a sin that is not simply unbelief or rejection of Christ, but one that includes (1) a clear knowledge of who Christ is and of the power of the Holy Spirit working through him, (2) a willful rejection of the facts about Christ that his opponents knew to be true, and (3) slanderously attributing the work of the Holy Spirit in Christ to the power of Satan. In such a case the hardness of heart would be so great that any ordinary means of bringing a sinner to repentance would already have been rejected. Persuasion of the truth will not work, for these people have already known the truth and have willfully rejected it. Demonstration of the power of the Holy Spirit to heal and bring life will not work, for they have seen it and rejected it. In this case it is not that the sin itself is so horrible that it could not be covered by Christ's redemptive work, but rather that the sinner's hardened heart puts him or her beyond the reach of God's ordinary means of bringing forgiveness through repentance and trusting Christ for salvation. The sin is unpardonable because it cuts off the sinner from repentance and saving faith through belief in the truth.

Berkhof wisely defines this sin in the following way:

> This sin consists in the conscious, malicious, and wilful rejection and slander, against evidence and conviction, of the testimony of the Holy Spirit respecting the grace of God in Christ, attributing it out of hatred and enmity to the Prince of Darkness. . . . in committing that sin man wilfully, maliciously, and intentionally

attributes what is clearly recognized as the work of God to the influence and operation of Satan.[30]

Berkhof explains that the sin itself consists "not in doubting the truth, nor in a sinful denial of it but in a contradiction of it that goes contrary to the conviction of the mind, to the illumination of the conscience, and even to the verdict of the heart."[31]

The fact that the unpardonable sin involves such extreme hardness of heart and lack of repentance indicates that those who fear they have committed it, yet still have sorrow for sin in their heart and desire to seek after God, certainly do not fall in the category of those who are guilty of it. Berkhof says that "we may be reasonably sure that those who fear that they have committed it and worry about this, and desire the prayers of others for them, have not committed it."[32]

This understanding of the unpardonable sin also fits well with Hebrews 6:4–6. There the persons who "commit apostasy" have had all sorts of knowledge and conviction of the truth: they have "been enlightened" and have "tasted the heavenly gift"; they have participated in some ways in the work of the Holy Spirit and "have tasted the goodness of the word of God and the powers of the age to come," yet they then willfully turn away from Christ and "hold him up to contempt" (Heb. 6:6). They too have put themselves beyond the reach of God's ordinary means of bringing people to repentance and faith. Knowing and being convinced of the truth, they willfully reject it.

First John 5:16–17, however, seems to fall in another category. That passage does not speak of a sin that can never be forgiven, but rather about a sin that, if persisted in, will lead to death. This sin seems to involve the teaching of serious doctrinal error about Christ. In the context of asking in faith according to God's will (1 John 5:14–15) John simply tells us that he does not say that we can pray in faith for God simply to forgive that sin unless the person repents—but he certainly does not prohibit praying that the heretical teachers would turn from their heresy and repent and thereby find forgiveness. Many people who teach serious doctrinal error have still not gone so far as to commit the unpardonable sin and bring on themselves the impossibility of repentance and faith by their own hardness of heart.

## E. The Punishment of Sin

Although God's punishment of sin does serve as a *deterrent* against further sinning and as a *warning* to those who observe it, this is not the primary reason why God punishes sin. The primary reason is that *God's righteousness demands it,* so that he might be glorified in the universe that he has created. He is the Lord who practices "steadfast love, justice, and righteousness in the earth; for in these things I delight, says the LORD" (Jer. 9:24).

Paul speaks of Christ Jesus "whom God put forward as a propitiation by his blood, through faith" (Rom. 3:25, author's translation). Paul then explains why God put forward Jesus as a "propitiation" (that is, a sacrifice that bears the wrath

---

[30]Berkhof, *Systematic Theology,* p. 253.
[31]Ibid.
[32]Ibid., p. 254.

of God against sin and thereby turns God's wrath into favor): "This was *to show God's righteousness,* because in his divine forbearance he had passed over former sins" (Rom. 3:25). Paul realizes that if Christ had not come to pay the penalty for sins, God could not be shown to be righteous. Because he had passed over sins and not punished them in the past, people could rightly accuse God of unrighteousness, the assumption being that a God who does not punish sins is not a righteous God. Therefore, when God sent Christ to die and pay the penalty for our sins, he showed how he could still be righteous—he had stored up the punishment due to previous sins (those of Old Testament saints) and then, in perfect righteousness, he gave that penalty to Jesus on the cross. The propitiation of Calvary thereby clearly demonstrated that God is perfectly righteous: "it was to prove at the present time *that he himself is righteous* and that he justifies him who has faith in Jesus" (Rom. 3:26).

Therefore in the cross we have a clear demonstration of the reason God punishes sin: if he did not punish sin he would not be a righteous God, and there would be no ultimate justice in the universe. But when sin is punished, God is showing himself to be a righteous judge over all, and justice is being done in his universe.

## QUESTIONS FOR PERSONAL APPLICATION

1. Has reading this chapter increased your awareness of the sin remaining in your own life? Are you able to mention any specific ways in which this was true? Did the chapter increase in you any sense of the hatefulness of sin? Why do you not feel more often a deeper sense of the hatefulness of sin? What do you think the overall effect of this chapter will be on your personal relationship with God?

2. Would it ultimately be more comforting to you to think that sin came into the world because God ordained that it would come through secondary agents, or because he could not prevent it, even though it was against his will? How would you feel about the universe and your place in it if you thought that evil had always existed and there was an ultimate "dualism" in the universe?

3. Can you name some parallels between the temptation faced by Eve and temptations that you face even now in your Christian life?

4. Do you feel a sense of unfairness that you are counted guilty because of Adam's sin (if you agree that Rom. 5:12–21 teaches this)? How can you deal with this sense of unfairness to keep it from becoming a hindrance in your relationship with God? At a level of deep conviction, do you really think that, before being a Christian, you were totally unable to do any spiritual good before God? Similarly, are you deeply convinced that this is true of all unbelievers, or do you think that this is just a doctrine that may or may not be true, or at least one that you do not find deeply convincing as you look at the lives of the unbelievers whom you know?

5. What kind of freedom of choice do the unbelievers whom you know actually have? Apart from the work of the Holy Spirit, are you convinced that they will not change their fundamental rebellion against God?

6. How can the biblical teaching of degrees of seriousness of sin help your Christian life at this point? Have you known a sense of God's "fatherly displeasure" when you have sinned? What is your response to that sense?

7. Do you think that Christians today have lost sight of the hatefulness of sin to a large extent? Have unbelievers also lost sight of this? Do you think that we as Christians have lost sight of the thoroughgoing pervasiveness of sin in unbelievers, of the truth that the greatest problem of the human race, and of all societies and civilizations, is not lack of education or lack of communication or lack of material well-being, but sin against God?

## SPECIAL TERMS

| | | |
|---|---|---|
| age of accountability | mortal sin | sin |
| dualism | original guilt | total depravity |
| impute | original pollution | total inability |
| inherited corruption | original sin | unpardonable sin |
| inherited guilt | Pelagius | venial sin |
| inherited sin | propitiation | |

## BIBLIOGRAPHY

(For an explanation of this bibliography see the note on the bibliography to chapter 1, p. 38. Complete bibliographical data may be found on pp. 1223–29.)

### Sections in Evangelical Systematic Theologies

1. Anglican (Episcopalian)
    1882–92    Litton, 136–77
    1930    Thomas, 155–75, 210–14, 234–35, 501–6
2. Arminian (Wesleyan or Methodist)
    1847    Finney, 180–214, 228–58
    1875–76    Pope, 2:1–86
    1892–94    Miley, 1:423–533; 2:505–24
    1940    Wiley, 2:51–140
    1960    Purkiser, 223–42
    1983    Carter, 1:27–86
3. Baptist
    1767    Gill, 1:451–90
    1887    Boyce, 230–47
    1907    Strong, 533–664
    1917    Mullins, 281–302
    1976–83    Henry, 6:229–50, 269–304
    1983–85    Erickson, 561–658
    1987–94    Lewis/Demarest, 2:183–245
4. Dispensational

## Sections in Representative Roman Catholic Systematic Theologies

## Other Works

Berkouwer, G. C. *Sin*. Trans. by Philip C. Holtrop. Grand Rapids: Eerdmans, 1971.

Bloesch, D. G. "Sin." In *EDT,* pp. 1012–16.

Carson, D. A. *How Long, O Lord? Reflections on Suffering and Evil.* Grand Rapids: Baker, 1990.

Colwell, J. E. "Anthropology." In *NDT,* pp. 28–30.

———. "Fall." In *NDT,* pp. 249–51.

———. "Sin." In *NDT,* pp. 641–43.

Demarest, B. A. "Fall of Man." In *EDT,* pp. 403–5.

Feinberg, J. S. *The Many Faces of Evil: Theological Systems and the Problem of Evil.* Grand Rapids: Zondervan, 1994.

———. *Theologies and Evil.* Washington, D.C.: University Press of America, 1979.

Geisler, Norman. *The Roots of Evil.* Grand Rapids: Zondervan, 1978.

Hoekema, Anthony A. *Created in God's Image.* Grand Rapids: Eerdmans, and Exeter: Paternoster, 1986, pp. 112–86.

Hughes, Philip Edgcumbe. *The True Image: The Origin and Destiny of Man in Christ.* Grand Rapids: Eerdmans, and Leicester: Inter-Varsity Press, 1989, pp. 71–210.

Johnson, R. K. "Imputation." In *EDT,* pp. 554–55.

Lewis, C. S. *The Problem of Pain.* New York: Macmillan, 1962.

Murray, John. *The Imputation of Adam's Sin.* Grand Rapids: Eerdmans, 1959.

Peterson, Michael L. *Evil and the Christian God.* Grand Rapids: Baker, 1982.

Pink, Arthur Walkington. *Gleanings From the Scriptures: Man's Total Depravity.* Chicago: Moody, 1970.

Plantinga, Alvin. *God, Freedom and Evil.* New York: Harper and Row, 1974.

Ramm, Bernard. *Offense to Reason: The Theology of Sin.* San Francisco: Harper and Row, 1985.

Ryrie, C. C. "Depravity, Total." In *EDT,* pp. 312–13.

Thomas, R. L. "Sin, Conviction of." In *EDT,* p. 1016.

Wenham, J. W. *The Enigma of Evil.* Formerly published as *The Goodness of God.* Grand Rapids: Zondervan, 1985.

## SCRIPTURE MEMORY PASSAGE

**Psalm 51:1–4:**

> *Have mercy on me, O God, according to your steadfast love;*
>  *according to your abundant mercy blot out my transgressions.*
> *Wash me thoroughly from my iniquity,*
>  *and cleanse me from my sin!*
> *For I know my transgressions,*
>  *and my sin is ever before me.*
> *Against you, you only, have I sinned,*
>  *and done that which is evil in your sight,*
> *so that you are justified in your sentence*
>  *and blameless in your judgment.*

## HYMN

### "God, Be Merciful to Me"

This is an excellent example of the words of a psalm set to music. The psalm was originally King David's heartfelt confession of great sin before God, but even today it is an excellent pattern of confession that we ourselves might speak to God.

> God, be merciful to me;
>  on thy grace I rest my plea;
> Plenteous in compassion thou,
>  blot out my transgressions now;
> Wash me, make me pure within,
>  cleanse, O cleanse me from my sin.
>
> My transgressions I confess,
>  grief and guilt my soul oppress;
> I have sinned against thy grace

and provoked thee to thy face;
I confess thy judgment just,
   speechless, I thy mercy trust.

I am evil, born in sin;
   thou desirest truth within.
Thou alone my Savior art,
   teach thy wisdom to my heart;
Make me pure, thy grace bestow,
   wash me whiter than the snow.

Broken, humbled to the dust
   by thy wrath and judgment just,
Let my contrite heart rejoice
   and in gladness hear thy voice;
From my sins O hide thy face,
   blot them out in boundless grace.

Gracious God, my heart renew,
   make my spirit right and true;
Cast me not away from thee,
   let thy Spirit dwell in me;
Thy salvation's joy impart,
   steadfast make my willing heart.

Sinners then shall learn from me
   and return, O God, to thee;
Savior, all my guilt remove,
   and my tongue shall sing thy love;
Touch my silent lips, O Lord,
   and my mouth shall praise accord.

FROM *THE PSALTER*, 1912, FROM PSALM 51:1–15

Alternate tune: "Rock of Ages"

# Chapter 25

# The Covenants Between God and Man

*What principles determine the way God relates to us?*

## EXPLANATION AND SCRIPTURAL BASIS

How does God relate to man? Since the creation of the world, God's relationship to man has been defined by specific requirements and promises. God tells people how he wants them to act and also makes promises about how he will act toward them in various circumstances. The Bible contains several summaries of the provisions that define the different relationships between God and man that occur in Scripture, and it often calls these summaries "covenants." With respect to covenants between God and man in Scripture, we may give the following definition: *A covenant is an unchangeable, divinely imposed legal agreement between God and man that stipulates the conditions of their relationship.*

Although this definition includes the word *agreement* in order to show that there are two parties, God and man, who must enter into the provisions of the relationship, the phrase "divinely imposed" is also included to show that man can never negotiate with God or change the terms of the covenant: he can only accept the covenant obligations or reject them. Probably for this reason the Greek translators of the Old Testament (known as the Septuagint), and, following them, the New Testament authors, did not use the ordinary Greek word for contracts or agreements in which both parties were equal (*synthēkē*), but rather chose a less common word, *diathēkē*, which emphasized that the provisions of the covenant were laid down by one of the parties only. (In fact, the word *diathēkē* was often used to refer to a "testament" or "will" that a person would leave to assign the distribution of his or her goods after death.)

This definition also notes that covenants are "unchangeable." They may be superseded or replaced by a different covenant, but they may not be changed once they are established. Although there have been many additional details specified in the covenants God has made with man throughout the history of Scripture, the essential element at the heart of all of them is the promise, "I will be their God, and they shall be my people" (Jer. 31:33; 2 Cor. 6:16; et al.).

Since the covenant relationship between God and man occurs in various forms throughout Scripture from Genesis to Revelation, a treatment of this subject might be put at several different points in the study of systematic theology. I have put it here at the end of the treatment of man as *created* (in the image of God) and man as *fallen* into sin, but before the discussion of the person and work of Christ.

## A. The Covenant of Works

Some have questioned whether it is appropriate to speak of a covenant of works that God had with Adam and Eve in the Garden of Eden. The actual word *covenant* is not used in the Genesis narratives. However, the essential parts of the covenant are all there—a clear definition of the parties involved, a legally binding set of provisions that stipulates the conditions of their relationship, the promise of blessings for obedience, and the condition for obtaining those blessings. Moreover, Hosea 6:7, in referring to the sins of Israel, says, "But *like Adam* they transgressed *the covenant*" (RSV mg.; SO NIV, NASB).[1] This passage views Adam as existing in a covenant relationship that he then transgressed in the Garden of Eden. In addition, in Romans 5:12–21 Paul sees both Adam and Christ as heads of a people whom they represent, something that would be entirely consistent with the idea of Adam being in a covenant before the fall.

In the Garden of Eden, it seems quite clear that there was a legally binding set of provisions that defined the conditions of the relationship between God and man. The two parties are evident as God speaks to Adam and gives commands to him. The requirements of the relationship are clearly defined in the commands that God gave to Adam and Eve (Gen. 1:28–30; cf. 2:15) and in the direct command to Adam, "You may freely eat of every tree of the garden; but of the tree of the knowledge of good and evil you shall not eat, for in the day that you eat of it you shall die" (Gen. 2:16–17).

In this statement to Adam about the tree of the knowledge of good and evil there is a promise of punishment for disobedience—death, most fully understood to mean death in an extensive sense, physical, spiritual, and eternal death and separation from God.[2] In the promise of punishment for disobedience there is implicit a promise of blessing for obedience. This blessing would consist of not receiving death, and the implication is that the blessing would be the opposite of "death." It would involve physical life that would not end and spiritual life in terms of a relationship with God that would go on forever. The presence of the "tree of life . . . in the midst of the garden" (Gen. 2:9) also signified the promise of eternal life with God if Adam and Eve had met the conditions of a covenant relationship by obeying God completely until he decided that their time of testing was finished. After the fall, God removed Adam and Eve from the garden, partly so that they would not be able to take from the tree of life "and eat, and live for ever" (Gen. 3:22).

---

[1]The RSV text translates, "But *at Adam* they transgressed the covenant," but the marginal note admits that this is a conjectural emendation and that the Hebrew text actually reads "like Adam" (Heb. *ke'ādām*). The Hebrew preposition *ke* means "like," not "at." The word translated "Adam" (Heb. *'ādām*) can also be translated "man," but the statement would make little sense: there is no single well-known transgression of a covenant by *man* to which it could refer. Moreover, it would do little good to compare the Israelites to what they already are (that is, men) and say that they "like man" broke the covenant. Such a sentence would almost imply that the Israelites were not men, but some other kind of creature. For these reasons, the translation "like Adam" is to be preferred. (The identical Hebrew expression is translated "like Adam" in Job 31:33 in the NASB, RSV margin, and NIV margin.)

[2]The punishment of death began to be carried out on the day that Adam and Eve sinned, but it was carried out slowly over time, as their bodies grew old and they eventually died. The promise of spiritual death was put into effect immediately, since they were cut off from fellowship with God. The death of eternal condemnation was rightfully theirs, but the hints of redemption in the text (see Gen. 3:15, 21) suggest that this penalty was ultimately overcome by the redemption that Christ purchased.

Another evidence that the covenant relationship with God in the garden included a promise of eternal life if Adam and Eve had perfectly obeyed is the fact that even in the New Testament Paul speaks as though perfect obedience, if it were possible, would actually lead to life. He speaks of a "commandment which promised life" (Rom. 7:10; lit., "the commandment unto life") and, in order to demonstrate that the law does not rest on faith, he quotes Leviticus 18:5 to say, about the provisions of the law, "He who does them shall live by them" (Gal. 3:12; cf. Rom. 10:5).

Other covenants in Scripture generally have an outward "sign" associated with them (such as circumcision, or baptism and the Lord's Supper). No "sign" for the covenant of works is clearly designated as such in Genesis, but if we were to name one, it would probably be the tree of life in the midst of the garden. By partaking of that tree Adam and Eve would be partaking of the promise of eternal life that God would give. The fruit itself did not have magical properties but would be a sign by which God outwardly guaranteed that the inward reality would occur.

Why is it important to speak of the relationship between God and man in the garden as a *covenant* relationship? To do so reminds us of the fact that this relationship, including the commands of obedience and promise of blessing for obedience, was not something that automatically occurred in the relationship between Creator and creature. God did not make any such covenant with the animals that he created, for example.[3] Nor did the nature of man as God created him demand that God have any fellowship with man or that God make any promises concerning his relationship with men or give man any clear directions concerning what he should do. All this was an expression of God's fatherly love for the man and woman he had created. Moreover, when we specify this relationship as a "covenant," it helps us to see the clear parallels between this and the subsequent covenant relationships that God had with his people. If all the elements of a covenant are present (clear stipulation of the parties involved, statement of the conditions of the covenant, and a promise of blessing for obedience and punishment for disobedience), then there seems no reason why we should not refer to it as a covenant, for that is indeed what it was.

Although the covenant that existed before the fall has been referred to by various terms (such as the Adamic Covenant, or the Covenant of Nature), the most helpful designation seems to be "covenant of works," since participation in the blessings of the covenant clearly depended on obedience or "works" on the part of Adam and Eve.

As in all covenants that God makes with man, there is here no negotiating over the provisions. God sovereignly imposes this covenant on Adam and Eve, and they have no opportunity to change the details—their only choice is to keep it or to break it.

Is the covenant of works still in force? In several important senses it is. First of all, Paul implies that perfect obedience to God's laws, if it were possible, would lead to life (see Rom. 7:10; 10:5; Gal. 3:12). We should also notice that the punishment for this covenant is still in effect, for "the wages of sin is death" (Rom. 6:23). This implies that the covenant of works is still in force for every

---

[3]However, animals were included with human beings in the covenant that God spoke to Noah, promising that he would never again destroy the earth with a flood (Gen. 9:8–17).

human being apart from Christ, even though no sinful human being can fulfill its provisions and gain blessing by it. Finally, we should note that Christ perfectly obeyed the covenant of works for us since he committed no sin (1 Peter 2:22) but completely obeyed God on our behalf (Rom. 5:18–19).

On the other hand, in certain senses, the covenant of works does not remain in force: (1) We no longer are faced with the specific command not to eat of the tree of the knowledge of good and evil. (2) Since we all have a sinful nature (both Christians and non-Christians), we are not able to fulfill the provisions of the covenant of works on our own and receive its benefits—as this covenant applies to people directly, it only brings punishments. (3) For Christians, Christ has fulfilled the provisions of this covenant successfully once for all, and we gain the benefits of it not by actual obedience on our part but by trusting in the merits of Christ's work. In fact, for Christians today to think of themselves as obligated to try to earn God's favor by obedience would be to cut themselves off from the hope of salvation. "All who rely on works of the law are under a curse. . . . Now it is evident that no man is justified before God by the law (Gal. 3:10–11). Christians have been freed from the covenant of works by virtue of Christ's work and their inclusion in the new covenant, the covenant of grace (see below).

## B. The Covenant of Redemption

Theologians speak of another kind of covenant, a covenant that is not between God and man, but is among the members of the Trinity. This covenant they call the "covenant of redemption." It is an agreement among the Father, Son, and Holy Spirit, in which the Son agreed to become a man, be our representative, obey the demands of the covenant of works on our behalf, and pay the penalty for sin, which we deserved. Does Scripture teach its existence? Yes, for it speaks about a specific plan and purpose of God that was agreed upon by the Father, Son, and Holy Spirit in order to gain our redemption.

On the part of the Father, this "covenant of redemption" included an agreement to give to the Son a people whom he would redeem for his own possession (John 17:2, 6), to send the Son to be their representative (John 3:16; Rom. 5:18–19), to prepare a body for the Son to dwell in as a man (Col. 2:9; Heb. 10:5), to accept him as representative of his people whom he had redeemed (Heb. 9:24), and to give him all authority in heaven and on earth (Matt. 28:18), including the authority to pour out the Holy Spirit in power to apply redemption to his people (Acts 1:4; 2:33).

On the part of the Son, there was an agreement that he would come into the world as a man and live as a man under the Mosaic law (Gal. 4:4; Heb. 2:14–18), and that he would be perfectly obedient to all the commands of the Father (Heb. 10:7–9), becoming obedient unto death, even death on a cross (Phil. 2:8). The Son also agreed that he would gather for himself a people in order that none whom the Father had given him would be lost (John 17:12).

The role of the Holy Spirit in the covenant of redemption is sometimes overlooked in discussions of this subject, but certainly it was a unique and essential one. He agreed to do the will of the Father and fill and empower Christ to carry out his ministry on earth (Matt. 3:16; Luke 4:1, 14, 18; John 3:34), and to apply the benefits of Christ's redemptive work to his people after Christ returned to heaven (John 14:16–17, 26; Acts 1:8; 2:17–18, 33).

To refer to the agreement among the members of the Trinity as a "covenant," reminds us that it was something voluntarily undertaken by God, not something that he had to enter into by virtue of his nature. However, this covenant is also different from the covenants between God and man because the parties enter into it as equals, whereas in covenants with man God is the sovereign Creator who imposes the provisions of the covenant by his own decree. On the other hand, it is like the covenants God makes with man in that it has the elements (specifying the parties, conditions, and promised blessings) that make up a covenant.

## C. The Covenant of Grace

**1. Essential Elements.** When man failed to obtain the blessing offered in the covenant of works, it was necessary for God to establish another means, one by which man could be saved. The rest of Scripture after the story of the fall in Genesis 3 is the story of God working out in history the amazing plan of redemption whereby sinful people could come into fellowship with himself. Once again, God clearly defines the provisions of a covenant that would specify the relationship between himself and those whom he would redeem. In these specifications we find some variation in detail throughout the Old and New Testaments, but the essential elements of a covenant are all there, and the nature of those essential elements remains the same throughout the Old Testament and the New Testament.

The *parties* to this covenant of grace are God and the people whom he will redeem. But in this case Christ fulfills a special role as "mediator" (Heb. 8:6; 9:15; 12:24) in which he fulfills the conditions of the covenant for us and thereby reconciles us to God. (There was no mediator between God and man in the covenant of works.)

The *condition* (or requirement) of participation in the covenant is *faith* in the work of Christ the redeemer (Rom. 1:17; 5:1; et al.). This requirement of faith in the redemptive work of the Messiah was also the condition of obtaining the blessings of the covenant in the Old Testament, as Paul clearly demonstrates through the examples of Abraham and David (Rom. 4:1–15). They, like other Old Testament believers, were saved by looking forward to the work of the Messiah who was to come and putting faith in him.[4]

But while the condition of *beginning* the covenant of grace is always faith in Christ's work alone, the condition of *continuing* in that covenant is said to be obedience to God's commands. Though this obedience did not in the Old Testament and does not in the New Testament earn us any merit with God, nonetheless, if our faith in Christ is genuine, it will produce obedience (see James 2:17), and obedience to Christ is in the New Testament seen as necessary evidence that we are truly believers and members of the new covenant (see 1 John 2:4–6).

The *promise* of blessings in the covenant was a promise of eternal life with God. This promise was repeated frequently throughout the Old and the New

---

[4]See chapter 7, pp. 117–18, for a discussion of the fact that Old Testament believers were saved only by trusting in the Messiah who was to come.

Testaments. God promised that he would be their God and that they would be his people. "And I will establish my covenant between me and you and your descendants after you throughout their generations for an everlasting covenant, *to be God to you* and to your descendants after you" (Gen. 17:7). "I will be their God, and they shall be my people" (Jer. 31:33). "And they shall be my people, and I will be their God . . . I will make with them an everlasting covenant" (Jer. 32:38–40; cf. Ezek. 34:30–31; 36:28; 37:26–27). That theme is picked up in the New Testament as well: "*I will be their God, and they shall be my people*" (2 Cor. 6:16; cf. a similar theme in vv. 17–18; also 1 Peter 2:9–10). In speaking of the new covenant, the author of Hebrews quotes Jeremiah 31: "I will be their God, and they shall be my people" (Heb. 8:10). This blessing finds fulfillment in the church, which is the people of God, but it finds its greatest fulfillment in the new heaven and new earth, as John sees in his vision of the age to come: "Behold, the dwelling of God is with men. He will dwell with them, and *they shall be his people, and God himself will be with them*" (Rev. 21:3).

The *sign* of this covenant (the outward, physical symbol of inclusion in the covenant) varies between the Old Testament and the New Testament. In the Old Testament the outward sign of beginning the covenant relationship was circumcision. The sign of continuing the covenant relationship was continuing to observe all the festivals and ceremonial laws that God gave the people at various times. In the new covenant, the sign of beginning a covenant relationship is baptism, while the sign of continuing in that relationship is participation in the Lord's Supper.

The reason this covenant is called a "covenant of grace" is that it is entirely based on God's "grace" or unmerited favor toward those whom he redeems.

## 2. Various Forms of the Covenant.

Although the essential elements of the covenant of grace remain the same throughout the history of God's people, the specific provisions of the covenant vary from time to time. At the time of Adam and Eve, there was only the bare hint of the possibility of a relationship with God found in the promise about the seed of the woman in Genesis 3:15 and in God's gracious provision of clothing for Adam and Eve (Gen. 3:21). The covenant that God made with Noah after the flood (Gen. 9:8–17) was not a covenant that promised all the blessings of eternal life or spiritual fellowship with God, but simply one in which God promised all mankind and the animal creation that the earth would no longer be destroyed by a flood. In this sense the covenant with Noah, although it certainly does depend on God's grace or unmerited favor, appears to be quite different in the parties involved (God and all mankind, not just the redeemed), the condition named (no faith or obedience is required of man), and the blessing that is promised (that the earth will not be destroyed again by flood, certainly a different promise from the that of eternal life). The sign of the covenant (the rainbow) is also different in that it requires no active or voluntary participation on man's part.

But beginning with the covenant with Abraham (Gen. 15:1–21; 17:1–27), the essential elements of the covenant of grace are all there. In fact, Paul can say that "the scripture . . . preached the gospel beforehand to Abraham" (Gal. 3:8). Moreover, Luke tells us that Zechariah, the father of John the Baptist, prophesied that the coming of John the Baptist to prepare the way for Christ was the beginning of God's working to fulfill the ancient covenant promises to Abraham ("to perform the mercy promised to our fathers, and *to remember his holy covenant,* the oath which he swore to our father Abraham," Luke 1:72–73). So the covenant promises to Abraham remained in force even as they found fulfillment in Christ (see Rom. 4:1–25; Gal. 3:6–18, 29; Heb. 2:16; 6:13–20).[5]

What then is the "old covenant" in contrast with the "new covenant" in Christ? *It is not the whole of the Old Testament,* because the covenants with Abraham and David are never called "old" in the New Testament. Rather, *only the covenant under Moses,* the covenant made at Mount Sinai (Ex. 19–24) is called the "old covenant" (2 Cor. 3:14; cf. Heb. 8:6, 13), to be replaced by the "new covenant" in Christ (Luke 22:20; 1 Cor. 11:25; 2 Cor. 3:6; Heb. 8:8, 13; 9:15; 12:24). The Mosaic covenant was an administration[6] of detailed written laws given for a time to restrain the sins of the people and to be a custodian to point people to Christ. Paul says, "Why then the law? It was added because of transgressions, till the offspring should come to whom the promise had been made" (Gal. 3:19), and, "The law was our custodian until Christ came" (Gal. 3:24).

We should not assume that there was no grace available to people from Moses until Christ, because the promise of salvation by faith that God had made to Abraham remained in force:

> Now the promises were made to Abraham and to his offspring . . . *the law,* which came four hundred and thirty years afterward, *does not annul a covenant previously ratified by God,* so as to make the promise void. For if the inheritance is by the law, it is no longer by promise; but God gave it to Abraham by a promise. (Gal. 3:16–18)

Moreover, although the sacrificial system of the Mosaic covenant did not really take away sins (Heb. 10:1–4), it foreshadowed the bearing of sin by Christ, the perfect high priest who was also the perfect sacrifice (Heb. 9:11–28). Nevertheless, the Mosaic covenant itself, with all its detailed laws, could not save people. It is not that the laws were wrong in themselves, for they were given by a holy God, but they had no power to give people new life, and the people were not able to obey them perfectly: "Is the law then against the promises of God? Certainly not; for if a law had been given which could make alive, then righteousness would indeed be by the law" (Gal. 3:21). Paul realizes that the Holy Spirit working within us can empower us to obey God in a way that the Mosaic law never could, for he says that God "has made us competent to be ministers of a new covenant, not in a written code but in the Spirit; for the written code kills, but the Spirit gives life" (2 Cor. 3:6).

The new covenant in Christ, then, is far better because it fulfills the promises made in Jeremiah 31:31–34, as quoted in Hebrews 8:

---

[5]The covenant promises to Abraham were renewed and further assurances given when God spoke with David (see esp. 2 Sam. 7:5–16; cf. Jer. 33:19–22), giving to David the promise that a Davidic king would reign over the people of God forever. For an excellent discussion of the continuity of God's promises as seen in the covenants made with Abraham and David, and in the new covenant, see Thomas E. McComiskey, *The Covenants of Promise: A Theology of the Old Testament Covenants* (Grand Rapids: Baker, 1985), esp. pp. 59–93.

[6]For an excellent discussion of the difference between the overarching covenant of promise and the various "administrative covenants" that God used at different times, see McComiskey, *Covenants of Promise,* esp. pp. 139–77 and 193–211.

But as it is, Christ has obtained a ministry which is as much more excellent than the old as the covenant he mediates is better, since it is enacted on better promises. For if that first covenant had been faultless, there would have been no occasion for a second.

For he finds fault with them when he says:

> "The days will come, says the Lord,
> when I will establish a new covenant with the house of Israel
> and with the house of Judah;
> not like the covenant that I made with their fathers
> on the day when I took them by the hand
> to lead them out of the land of Egypt;
> for they did not continue in my covenant,
> and so I paid no heed to them, says the Lord.
> This is the covenant that I will make with the house of Israel
> after those days, says the Lord:
> I will put my laws into their minds,
> and write them on their hearts,
> and I will be their God,
> and they shall be my people.
> And they shall not teach every one his fellow
> or every one his brother, saying, 'Know the Lord,'
> for all shall know me,
> from the least of them to the greatest.
> For I will be merciful toward their iniquities,
> and I will remember their sins no more."

In speaking of a new covenant he treats the first as obsolete. And what is becoming obsolete and growing old is ready to vanish away. (Heb. 8:6–13)

In this new covenant, there are far greater blessings, for Jesus the Messiah has come; he has lived, died, and risen among us, atoning once for all for our sins (Heb. 9:24–28); he has revealed God most fully to us (John 1:14; Heb. 1:1–3); he has poured out the Holy Spirit on all his people in new covenant power (Acts 1:8; 1 Cor. 12:13; 2 Cor. 3:4–18); he has written his laws on our hearts (Heb. 8:10). This new covenant is the "eternal covenant" (Heb. 13:20) in Christ, through which we shall forever have fellowship with God, and he shall be our God, and we shall be his people.

## QUESTIONS FOR PERSONAL APPLICATION

1. Before reading this chapter, had you thought of your relationship to God in terms of a "covenant"? Does it give you any added degree of certainty or sense of security in your relationship to God to know that he governs that relationship by a set of promises that he will never change?

2. If you were to think of the relationship between God and yourself personally in terms of a covenant, whereby you and God are the only two parties involved, then what would be the conditions of this covenant between you and God? Are you now fulfilling those conditions? What role does Christ play in the covenant relationship between you and God? What are the blessings God promises to you if you fulfill those conditions? What are the signs of participation in this covenant? Does this understanding of the covenant increase your appreciation of baptism and the Lord's Supper?

## SPECIAL TERMS

covenant

covenant of grace

covenant of redemption

covenant of works

new covenant

old covenant

## BIBLIOGRAPHY

(For an explanation of this bibliography see the note on the bibliography to chapter 1, p. 38. Complete bibliographical data may be found on pp. 1223–29.)

### Sections in Evangelical Systematic Theologies

1. Anglican (Episcopalian)

    1882–92        Litton (no explicit treatment)

    1930           Thomas, 134–41

2. Arminian (Wesleyan or Methodist)

    1983           Carter, 1:476–83

3. Baptist

    1767           Gill, 1:300–359, 491–530

    1887           Boyce, 247–58

4. Dispensational

    1947           Chafer, 7:96–99

    1949           Thiessen, 199–205

    1986           Ryrie, 453–60

5. Lutheran

    1934           Mueller (no explicit treatment)

6. Reformed (or Presbyterian)

    1861           Heppe, 281–319, 371–409

    1871–73        Hodge, 2:117–22, 354–77

    1878           Dabney, 292–305, 429–63

    1889           Shedd, 2a:148–67

    1937–66        Murray, CW, 2:47–59, 123–31

    1938           Berkhof, 211–18, 262–301

    1962           Buswell, 1:307–20

7. Renewal (or charismatic/Pentecostal)

    1988–92        Williams, 1:275–304

### Sections in Representative Roman Catholic Systematic Theologies

1. Roman Catholic: Traditional

    1955           Ott (no explicit treatment)

2. Roman Catholic: Post-Vatican II

    1980           McBrien (no explicit treatment)

## Other Works

Archer, G. L. "Covenant." In *EDT*, pp. 276–78.

Collins, G. N. M. "Federal Theology." In *EDT*, pp. 413–14.

Dumbrell, W. J. *Covenant and Creation*. Nashville: Thomas Nelson, 1984.

Fuller, Daniel P. *Gospel and Law: Contrast or Continuum? The Hermeneutics of Dispensationalism and Covenant Theology*. Grand Rapids: Eerdmans, 1980.

Jocz, Jakob. *The Covenant: A Theology of Human Destiny*. Grand Rapids: Eerdmans, 1968.

Kaiser, Walter C., Jr. *Toward An Old Testament Theology*. Grand Rapids: Zondervan, 1978.

Martens, Elmer. *God's Design: A Focus on Old Testament Theology*. Grand Rapids: Baker, 1981.

McComiskey, Thomas E. *The Covenants of Promise: A Theology of the Old Testament Covenants*. Grand Rapids: Baker, 1985.

Murray, John. *Covenant of Grace*. London: Tyndale, 1954.

Osterhaven, M. E. "Covenant Theology." In *EDT*, pp. 279–80.

Pentecost, J. Dwight. *Thy Kingdom Come*. Wheaton, Ill.: Scripture Press, 1990.

Peters, G. N. H. *The Theocratic Kingdom*. 3 vols. New York: Funk and Wagnalls, 1952 (first published 1884).

Rayburn, R. S. "Covenant, The New." In *EDT*, pp. 278–79.

Robertson, O. Palmer. *The Christ of the Covenants*. Grand Rapids: Baker, 1980.

Ryrie, C. C. *Dispensationalism Today*. Chicago: Moody, 1965.

VanGemeren, Willem. *The Progress of Redemption*. Grand Rapids: Zondervan, 1988.

## SCRIPTURE MEMORY PASSAGE

**Hebrews 8:10:**

*"This is the covenant that I will make with the house of Israel after those days," says the Lord:*
*"I will put my laws into their minds,*
*and write them on their hearts,*
*and I will be their God,*
*and they shall be my people."*

## HYMN

### "Trust and Obey"

This hymn reminds us that the enjoyment of God's blessings depends on our continuing to fulfill the conditions of faith and obedience as stipulated in the New Testament, which is the written record of the provisions of the new covenant that God has made with us.

When we walk with the Lord in the light of his Word,
   What a glory he sheds on our way!
While we do his good will, he abides with us still,
   And with all who will trust and obey.

*Chorus:*
Trust and obey, for there's no other way
    To be happy in Jesus, but to trust and obey.

Not a shadow can rise, not a cloud in the skies,
But his smile quickly drives it away;
    Not a doubt or a fear, not a sigh nor a tear,
Can abide while we trust and obey.

Not a burden we bear, not a sorrow we share,
But our toil he doth richly repay;
    Not a grief nor a loss, not a frown or a cross,
But is blest if we trust and obey.

But we never can prove the delights of his love
Until all on the altar we lay;
    For the favor he shows, and the joy he bestows,
Are for them who will trust and obey.

Then in fellowship sweet we will sit at his feet,
Or we'll walk by his side in the way;
    What he says we will do, where he sends we will go,
Never fear, only trust and obey.

AUTHOR: JAMES H. SAMMIS, D. 1919

# Part 4

# The Doctrines of Christ and the Holy Spirit

# Chapter 26

# The Person of Christ

*How is Jesus fully God and fully man,*
*yet one person?*

## EXPLANATION AND SCRIPTURAL BASIS

We may summarize the biblical teaching about the person of Christ as follows: *Jesus Christ was fully God and fully man in one person, and will be so forever.*

The scriptural material supporting this definition is extensive. We will discuss first the humanity of Christ, then his deity, and then attempt to show how Jesus' deity and humanity are united in the one person of Christ.

### A. The Humanity of Christ

**1. Virgin Birth.** When we speak of the humanity of Christ it is appropriate to begin with a consideration of the virgin birth of Christ. Scripture clearly asserts that Jesus was conceived in the womb of his mother Mary by a miraculous work of the Holy Spirit and without a human father.

"Now the birth of Jesus Christ took place in this way. When his mother Mary had been betrothed to Joseph, *before they came together* she was found to be with child *of the Holy Spirit*" (Matt. 1:18). Shortly after that an angel of the Lord said to Joseph, who was engaged to Mary, "Joseph, son of David, do not fear to take Mary your wife, for *that which is conceived in her is of the Holy Spirit*" (Matt. 1:20). Then we read that Joseph "did as the angel of the Lord commanded him; he took his wife, but knew her not until she had borne a son; and he called his name Jesus" (Matt. 1:24–25).

The same fact is affirmed in Luke's gospel, where we read about the appearance of the angel Gabriel to Mary. After the angel had told her that she would bear a son, Mary said, "How shall this be, since I have no husband?" The angel answered,

> "The Holy Spirit will come upon you,
> and the power of the Most High will overshadow you;
> *therefore the child to be born will be called holy,*
> the Son of God." (Luke 1:35; cf. 3:23)

The doctrinal importance of the virgin birth is seen in at least three areas.

1. It shows that salvation ultimately must come from the Lord. Just as God had promised that the "seed" of the woman (Gen. 3:15) would ultimately destroy the

serpent, so God brought it about by his own power, not through mere human effort. The virgin birth of Christ is an unmistakable reminder that salvation can never come through human effort, but must be the work of God himself. Our salvation only comes about through the supernatural work of God, and that was evident at the very beginning of Jesus' life when "God sent forth his Son, born of woman, born under the law, to redeem those who were under the law, so that we might receive adoption as sons" (Gal. 4:4–5).

2. The virgin birth made possible the uniting of full deity and full humanity in one person. This was the means God used to send his Son (John 3:16; Gal. 4:4) into the world as a man. If we think for a moment of other possible ways in which Christ might have come to the earth, none of them would so clearly unite humanity and deity in one person. It probably would have been possible for God to create Jesus as a complete human being in heaven and send him to descend from heaven to earth without the benefit of any human parent. But then it would have been very hard for us to see how Jesus could be fully human as we are, nor would he be a part of the human race that physically descended from Adam. On the other hand, it probably would have been possible for God to have Jesus come into the world with two human parents, both a father and a mother, and with his full divine nature miraculously united to his human nature at some point early in his life. But then it would have been hard for us to understand how Jesus was fully God, since his origin was like ours in every way. When we think of these two other possibilities, it helps us to understand how God, in his wisdom, ordained a combination of human and divine influence in the birth of Christ, so that his full humanity would be evident to us from the fact of his ordinary human birth from a human mother, and his full deity would be evident from the fact of his conception in Mary's womb by the powerful work of the Holy Spirit.[1]

3. The virgin birth also makes possible Christ's true humanity without inherited sin. As we noted in chapter 24, all human beings have inherited legal guilt and a corrupt moral nature from their first father, Adam (this is sometimes called "inherited sin" or "original sin"). But the fact that Jesus did not have a human father means that the line of descent from Adam is partially interrupted. Jesus did not descend from Adam in exactly the same way in which every other human being has descended from Adam. And this helps us to understand why the legal guilt and moral corruption that belongs to all other human beings did not belong to Christ.

This idea seems to be indicated in the statement of the angel Gabriel to Mary, where he says to her,

> "The Holy Spirit will come upon you,
>     and the power of the Most High will overshadow you;
> *therefore the child to be born will be called holy,*
>     the Son of God." (Luke 1:35)

---

[1]This is not to say that it would have been *impossible* for God to bring Christ into the world in any other way, but only to say that God, in his wisdom, decided that this would be the best way to bring it about, and part of that is evident in the fact that the virgin birth does help us understand how Jesus can be fully God and fully man. Whether any other means of bringing Christ into the world would have been "possible" in some absolute sense of "possible," Scripture does not tell us.

*Because* the Spirit brought about the conception of Jesus in the womb of Mary, the child was to be called "*holy.*"[2] Such a conclusion should not be taken to mean that the transmission of sin comes only through the father, for Scripture nowhere makes such an assertion. It is enough for us merely to say that *in this case* the unbroken line of descent from Adam was interrupted, and Jesus was conceived by the power of the Holy Spirit. Luke 1:35 connects this conception by the Holy Spirit with the holiness or moral purity of Christ, and reflection on that fact allows us to understand that through the absence of a human father, Jesus was not fully descended from Adam, and that this break in the line of descent was the method God used to bring it about that Jesus was fully human yet did not share inherited sin from Adam.

But why did Jesus not inherit a sinful nature from Mary? The Roman Catholic Church answers this question by saying that Mary herself was free from sin, but Scripture nowhere teaches this, and it would not really solve the problem anyway (for why then did Mary not inherit sin from her mother?).[3] A better solution is to say that the work of the Holy Spirit in Mary must have prevented not only the transmission of sin from Joseph (for Jesus had no human father) but also, in a miraculous way, the transmission of sin from Mary: "The Holy Spirit will come upon you . . . *therefore* the child to be born will be called *holy*" (Luke 1:35).

---

[2]I have quoted here the translation of the rsv, which I think to be correct (so niv margin). But it is also grammatically possible to translate the words as "so the holy one to be born will be called the Son of God" (niv; similarly, nasb). The Greek phrase is *dio kai to gennōmenon hagion klēthēsetai, huios theou.* The decision on which translation is correct depends on whether we take *to gennōmenon* as the subject, meaning "the child to be born," or whether we think that the subject is *to hagion,* "the holy one," with the participle *gennōmenon* then functioning as an adjective, giving the sense "the being-born holy one" (this is the way the niv and nasb understand it).

Recently, more extensive lexical research seems to indicate that the expression *to gennōmenon* was a fairly common expression that was readily understood to mean "the child to be born." Examples of this use can be seen in Plotinus, *Nead,* 3.6.20–24; Plato, *Menexenus,* 237E; *Laws,* 6,775C; Philo, *On the Creation,* 100; *On the Change of Names,* 267; Plutarch, *Moralia,* "Advice to Bride and Groom," 140F; "On Affection for Offspring," 495E. More examples could probably be found with a more extensive computer search, but these should be sufficient to demonstrate that the mere grammatical possibility of translating Luke 1:35 the way the niv and nasb do is not a strong argument in favor of their translations, because Greek-speaking readers in the first century would ordinarily have understood the words *to gennōmenon* as a unit meaning "the child to be born." Because of this fact, the rsv represents the sense that first-century readers would have understood from the sentence: "therefore *the child to be born* will be called holy." (I discovered these examples of *to gennōmenon* by searching the Thesaurus Linguae Graecae data base on the Ibycus computer at Trinity Evangelical Divinity School.)

[3]The Roman Catholic Church teaches the doctrine of the *immaculate conception.* This doctrine does not refer to the conception of Jesus in Mary's womb, but to the conception of *Mary* in her mother's womb, and teaches that Mary was free from inherited sin. On December 8, 1854, Pope Pius IX proclaimed, "The Most Holy Virgin Mary was, in the first moment of her conception . . . in view of the merits of Jesus Christ . . . preserved free from all stain of original sin" (Ludwig Ott, *Fundamentals of Catholic Dogma,* trans. Patrick Lynch [Rockford: Tan, 1960⁴], p. 190). (The Catholic Church also teaches that "in consequence of a Special Privilege of Grace from God, Mary was free from every personal sin during her whole life," p. 203.)

In response, we must say that the New Testament does highly honor Mary as one who has "found favor with God" (Luke 1:30) and one who is "Blessed . . . among women" (Luke 1:42), but nowhere does the Bible indicate that Mary was free from inherited sin. The expression, "Hail, O *favored one,* the Lord is with you!" (Luke 1:28) simply means that Mary has found much blessing from God; the same word translated "*favored*" in Luke 1:28 (Gk. *charitoō*) is used to refer to all Christians in Eph. 1:6: "his glorious grace which he *freely bestowed* on us in the Beloved." In fact, Ott says, "The doctrine of the Immaculate Conception of Mary is not explicitly revealed in Scripture" (p. 200), though he thinks it is implicit in Gen. 3:15 and Luke 1:28, 41.

It has been common, at least in previous generations, for those who do not accept the complete truthfulness of Scripture to deny the doctrine of the virgin birth of Christ. But if our beliefs are to be governed by the statements of Scripture, then we will certainly not deny this teaching. Whether or not we could discern any aspects of doctrinal importance for this teaching, we should believe it first of all simply because Scripture affirms it. Certainly such a miracle is not too hard for the God who created the universe and everything in it—anyone who affirms that a virgin birth is "impossible" is just confessing his or her own unbelief in the God of the Bible. Yet in addition to the fact that Scripture teaches the virgin birth, we can see that it is doctrinally important, and if we are to understand the biblical teaching on the person of Christ correctly, it is important that we begin with an affirmation of this doctrine.

## 2. Human Weaknesses and Limitations.

a. Jesus Had a Human Body: The fact that Jesus had a human body just like our human bodies is seen in many passages of Scripture. He was born just as all human babies are born (Luke 2:7). He grew through childhood to adulthood just as other children grow: "And the child grew and became strong, filled with wisdom; and the favor of God was upon him" (Luke 2:40). Moreover, Luke tells us that "Jesus increased in wisdom *and in stature,* and in favor with God and man" (Luke 2:52).

Jesus became tired just as we do, for we read that "Jesus, *wearied* as he was with his journey, sat down beside the well" in Samaria (John 4:6). He became thirsty, for when he was on the cross he said, "*I thirst*" (John 19:28). After he had fasted for forty days in the wilderness, we read that "he was *hungry*" (Matt. 4:2). He was at times physically weak, for during his temptation in the wilderness he fasted for forty days (the point at which a human being's physical strength is almost entirely gone and beyond which irreparable physical harm will occur if the fast continues). At that time "angels came and ministered to him" (Matt. 4:11), apparently to care for him and provide nourishment until he regained enough strength to come out of the wilderness. When Jesus was on his way to be crucified, the soldiers forced Simon of Cyrene to carry his cross (Luke 23:26), most likely because Jesus was so weak following the beating he had received that he did not have strength enough to carry it himself. The culmination of Jesus' limitations in terms of his human body is seen when he died on the cross (Luke 23:46). His human body ceased to have life in it and ceased to function, just as ours does when we die.

Jesus also rose from the dead in a physical, human body, though one that was made perfect and was no longer subject to weakness, disease, or death. He demonstrates repeatedly to his disciples that he does have a real physical body: he says, "See my hands and my feet, that it is I myself; handle me, and see; for *a spirit has not flesh and bones as you see that I have*" (Luke 24:39). He is showing them and teaching them that he has "flesh and bones" and is not merely a "spirit" without a body. Another evidence of this fact is that "they gave him a piece of broiled fish, and he took it and ate before them" (Luke 24:42; cf. v. 30; John 20:17, 20, 27; 21:9, 13).

In this same human body (though a resurrection body that was made perfect),

Jesus also ascended into heaven. He said before he left, "I am leaving the world and going to the Father" (John 16:28; cf. 17:11). The way in which Jesus ascended up to heaven was calculated to demonstrate the continuity between his existence in a physical body here on earth and his continuing existence in that body in heaven. Just a few verses after Jesus had told them, "A spirit has not flesh and bones as you see that I have" (Luke 24:39), we read in Luke's gospel that Jesus "led them out as far as Bethany, and lifting up his hands he blessed them. While he blessed them, he parted from them, and was carried up into heaven" (Luke 24:50–51). Similarly, we read in Acts, "As they were looking on, he was lifted up, and a cloud took him out of their sight" (Acts 1:9).

All of these verses taken together show that, as far as Jesus' human body is concerned, it was like ours in every respect before his resurrection, and after his resurrection it was still a human body with "flesh and bones," but made perfect, the kind of body that we will have when Christ returns and we are raised from the dead as well.[4] Jesus continues to exist in that human body in heaven, as the ascension is designed to teach.

**b. Jesus Had A Human Mind:** The fact that Jesus *"increased in wisdom"* (Luke 2:52) says that he went through a learning process just as all other children do— he learned how to eat, how to talk, how to read and write, and how to be obedient to his parents (see Heb. 5:8). This ordinary learning process was part of the genuine humanity of Christ.

We also see that Jesus had a human mind like ours when he speaks of the day on which he will return to earth: "But of that day or that hour no one knows, not even the angels in heaven, nor the Son, but only the Father" (Mark 13:32).[5]

**c. Jesus Had a Human Soul and Human Emotions:** We see several indications that Jesus had a human soul (or spirit). Just before his crucifixion, Jesus said, "Now is my soul *troubled*" (John 12:27). John writes just a little later, "When Jesus had thus spoken, he was *troubled* in spirit" (John 13:21). In both verses the word *troubled* represents the Greek term *tarassō*, a word that is often used of people when they are anxious or suddenly very surprised by danger.[6]

Moreover, before Jesus' crucifixion, as he realized the suffering he would face, he said, "My soul is very sorrowful, even to death" (Matt. 26:38). So great was the sorrow he felt that it seemed as though, if it were to become any stronger, it would take his very life.

Jesus had a full range of human emotions. He "marveled" at the faith of the centurion (Matt. 8:10). He wept with sorrow at the death of Lazarus (John

---

[4]See chapter 28, pp. 608–13, and chapter 42, pp. 831–35, on the nature of the resurrection body.
[5]See further discussion of this verse below, pp. 560–63.
[6]The word *tarassō*, "troubled," is used, for example, to speak of the fact that Herod was "troubled" when he heard that the wise men had come looking for the new king of the Jews (Matt. 2:3); the disciples "were troubled" when they suddenly saw Jesus walking on the sea and thought he was a ghost (Matt. 14:26); Zechariah was "troubled" when he suddenly saw an angel appear in the temple in Jerusalem (Luke 1:12); and the disciples were "troubled" when Jesus suddenly appeared among them after his resurrection (Luke 24:38). But the word is also used in John 14:1, 27, when Jesus says, "Let not your hearts be *troubled*." When Jesus was troubled in his spirit, therefore, we must not think that there was any lack of faith or any sin involved, but it was definitely a strong human emotion that accompanied a time of extreme danger.

11:35). And he prayed with a heart full of emotion, for "in the days of his flesh, Jesus offered up prayers and supplications, *with loud cries and tears*, to him who was able to save him from death, and he was heard for his godly fear" (Heb. 5:7).

Moreover, the author tells us, "Although he was a Son, *he learned obedience* through what he suffered; and being made perfect he became the source of eternal salvation to all who obey him" (Heb. 5:8–9). Yet if Jesus never sinned, how could he "learn obedience"? Apparently as Jesus grew toward maturity he, like all other human children, was able to take on more and more responsibility. The older he became the more demands his father and mother could place on him in terms of obedience, and the more difficult the tasks that his heavenly Father could assign to him to carry out in the strength of his human nature. With each increasingly difficult task, even when it involved some suffering (as Heb. 5:8 specifies), Jesus' human moral ability, his ability to obey under more and more difficult circumstances, increased. We might say that his "moral backbone" was strengthened by more and more difficult exercise. Yet in all this he never once sinned.

The complete absence of sin in the life of Jesus is all the more remarkable because of the severe temptations he faced, not only in the wilderness, but throughout his life. The author of Hebrews affirms that Jesus "*in every respect* has been tempted as we are, yet without sin" (Heb. 4:15). The fact that he faced temptation means that he had a genuine human nature that could be tempted, for Scripture clearly tells us that "God cannot be tempted with evil" (James 1:13).

**d. People Near Jesus Saw Him As Only a Man:** Matthew reports an amazing incident in the middle of Jesus' ministry. Even though Jesus had taught throughout all Galilee, "healing every disease and every infirmity among the people," so that "great crowds followed him" (Matt. 4:23–25), when he came to his own village of Nazareth, the people who had known him for many years did not receive him:

> And when Jesus had finished these parables, he went away from there, and coming to his own country he taught them in their synagogue, so that they were astonished, and said, "*Where did this man get this wisdom and these mighty works?* Is not this the carpenter's son? Is not his mother called Mary? And are not his brothers James and Joseph and Simon and Judas? And are not all his sisters with us? Where then did this man get all this?" And *they took offense at him.* . . . And he did not do many mighty works there, *because of their unbelief.* (Matt. 13:53–58)

This passage indicates that those people who knew Jesus best, the neighbors with whom he had lived and worked for thirty years, saw him as no more than an ordinary man—a good man, no doubt, fair and kind and truthful, but certainly not a prophet of God who could work miracles and certainly not God himself in the flesh. Although in the following sections we will see how Jesus was fully divine in every way—was truly God and man in one person—we must still recognize the full force of a passage like this. For the first thirty years of his life Jesus lived a human life that was so ordinary that the people of Nazareth who knew him best were amazed that he could teach with authority and work miracles. They knew him. He was one of them. He was "the carpenter's son" (Matt. 13:55), and he was himself "the carpenter" (Mark 6:3), so ordinary that they could ask, "Where then did this man get all this?" (Matt. 13:56). And John tells us, "*Even his brothers* did not believe in him" (John 7:5).

Was Jesus fully human? He was so fully human that even those who lived and worked with him for thirty years, even those brothers who grew up in his own household, did not realize that he was anything more than another very good human being. They apparently had no idea that he was God come in the flesh.

**3. Sinlessness.** Though the New Testament clearly affirms that Jesus was fully human just as we are, it also affirms that Jesus was different in one important respect: he was without sin, and he never committed sin during his lifetime. Some have objected that if Jesus did not sin, then he was not *truly* human, for all humans sin. But those making that objection simply fail to realize that human beings are now in an *abnormal* situation. God did not create us sinful, but holy and righteous. Adam and Eve in the Garden of Eden before they sinned were *truly* human, and we now, though human, do not match the pattern that God intends for us when our full, sinless humanity is restored.

The sinlessness of Jesus is taught frequently in the New Testament. We see suggestions of this early in his life when he was "filled with wisdom" and "the favor of God was upon him" (Luke 2:40). Then we see that Satan was unable to tempt Jesus successfully, but failed, after forty days, to persuade him to sin: "And when the devil had ended every temptation, he departed from him until an opportune time" (Luke 4:13). We also see in the synoptic gospels (Matthew, Mark, and Luke) no evidence of wrongdoing on Jesus' part. To the Jews who opposed him, Jesus asked, "Which of you convicts me of sin?" (John 8:46), and received no answer.

The statements about Jesus' sinlessness are more explicit in John's gospel. Jesus made the amazing proclamation, "I am the light of the world" (John 8:12). If we understand light to represent both truthfulness and moral purity, then Jesus is here claiming to be the source of truth and the source of moral purity and holiness in the world—an astounding claim, and one that could only be made by someone who was free from sin. Moreover, with regard to obedience to his Father in heaven, he said, "I always do what is pleasing to him" (John 8:29; the present tense gives the sense of continual activity, "I *am always doing* what is pleasing to him"). At the end of his life, Jesus could say, "I have kept my Father's commandments and abide in his love" (John 15:10). It is significant that when Jesus was put on trial before Pilate, in spite of the accusations of the Jews, Pilate could only conclude, "I find no crime in him" (John 18:38).

In the book of Acts Jesus is several times called the "Holy One" or the "Righteous One," or is referred to with some similar expression (see Acts 2:27; 3:14; 4:30; 7:52; 13:35). When Paul speaks of Jesus coming to live as a man he is careful not to say that he took on "sinful flesh," but rather says that God sent his own Son "*in the likeness of* sinful flesh and for sin" (Rom. 8:3). And he refers to Jesus as "him . . . who knew no sin" (2 Cor. 5:21).

The author of Hebrews affirms that Jesus was tempted but simultaneously insists that he did not sin: Jesus is "one who in every respect has been tempted as we are, *yet without sin*" (Heb. 4:15). He is a high priest who is "holy, blameless, unstained, separated from sinners, exalted above the heavens" (Heb. 7:26). Peter

speaks of Jesus as "a lamb without blemish or spot" (1 Peter 1:19), using Old
Testament imagery to affirm his freedom from any moral defilement. Peter directly
states, *"He committed no sin;* no guile was found on his lips" (1 Peter 2:22). When
Jesus died, it was "the righteous for the unrighteous, that he might bring us to
God" (1 Peter 3:18). And John, in his first epistle, calls him "Jesus Christ the
righteous" (1 John 2:1) and says, "In him there is no sin" (1 John 3:5). It is hard
to deny, then, that the sinlessness of Christ is taught clearly in all the major
sections of the New Testament. He was truly man yet without sin.

In connection with Jesus' sinlessness, we should notice in more detail the nature
of his temptations in the wilderness (Matt. 4:1–11; Mark 1:12–13; Luke 4:1–
13). The essence of these temptations was an attempt to persuade Jesus to escape
from the hard path of obedience and suffering that was appointed for him as the
Messiah. Jesus was "led by the Spirit for forty days in the wilderness, tempted by
the devil" (Luke 4:1–2). In many respects this temptation was parallel to the
testing that Adam and Eve faced in the Garden of Eden, but it was much more
difficult. Adam and Eve had fellowship with God and with each other and had an
abundance of all kinds of food, for they were only told not to eat from one tree.
By contrast, Jesus had no human fellowship and no food to eat, and after he had
fasted for forty days he was near the point of physical death. In both cases the kind
of obedience required was not obedience to an eternal moral principle rooted in
the character of God, but was a test of pure obedience to God's specific directive.
With Adam and Eve, God told them not to eat of the tree of the knowledge of
good and evil, and the question was whether they would obey simply because God
told them. In the case of Jesus, "led by the Spirit" for forty days in the wilderness,
he apparently realized that it was the Father's will that he eat nothing during those
days but simply remain there until the Father, through the leading of the Holy
Spirit, told him that the temptations were over and he could leave.

We can understand, then, the force of the temptation, "If you are the Son of
God, command this stone to become bread" (Luke 4:3). Of course Jesus was the
Son of God, and of course he had the power to make any stone into bread
instantly. He was the one who would soon change water into wine and multiply
the loaves and the fishes. The temptation was intensified by the fact that it seemed
as though, if he did not eat soon, his very life would be taken from him. Yet he
had come to obey God perfectly in our place, and to do so *as a man.* This meant
that he had to obey in his human strength alone. If he had called upon his divine
powers to make the temptation easier for himself, then he would not have obeyed
God fully *as a man.* The temptation was to use his divine power to "cheat" a bit on
the requirements and make obedience somewhat easier. But Jesus, unlike Adam
and Eve, refused to eat what appeared to be good and necessary for him, choosing
rather to obey the command of his heavenly Father.

The temptation to bow down and worship Satan for a moment and then receive
authority over "all the kingdoms of the world" (Luke 4:5) was a temptation to
receive power not through the path of lifelong obedience to his heavenly Father,
but through wrongful submission to the Prince of Darkness. Again, Jesus rejected
the apparently easy path and chose the path of obedience that led to the cross.

Similarly, the temptation to throw himself down from the pinnacle of the
temple (Luke 4:9–11) was a temptation to "force" God to perform a miracle and
rescue him in a spectacular way, thus attracting a large following from the people

without pursuing the hard path ahead, the path that included three years of ministering to people's needs, teaching with authority, and exemplifying absolute holiness of life in the midst of harsh opposition. But Jesus again resisted this "easy route" to the fulfillment of his goals as the Messiah (again, a route that would not actually have fulfilled those goals in any case).

These temptations were really the culmination of a lifelong process of moral strengthening and maturing that occurred throughout Jesus' childhood and early adulthood, as he "increased in wisdom . . . and in favor with God" (Luke 2:52) and as he *learned obedience* through what he suffered" (Heb. 5:8). In these temptations in the wilderness and in the various temptations that faced him through the thirty-three years of his life, Christ obeyed God in our place and as our representative, thus succeeding where Adam had failed, where the people of Israel in the wilderness had failed, and where we had failed (see Rom. 5:18–19).

As difficult as it may be for us to comprehend, Scripture affirms that in these temptations Jesus gained an ability to understand and help us in our temptations."*Because he himself has suffered and been tempted,* he is able to help those who are tempted" (Heb. 2:18). The author goes on to connect Jesus' ability to sympathize with our weaknesses to the fact the he was tempted as we are:

> For we have not a high priest who is unable to sympathize with our weaknesses, but one who in every respect has been tempted as we are, yet without sin. Let us then [lit., 'therefore'] with confidence draw near to the throne of grace, that we may receive mercy and find grace to help in time of need. (Heb. 4:15–16)

This has practical application for us: in every situation in which we are struggling with temptation, we should reflect on the life of Christ and ask if there were not similar situations that he faced. Usually, after reflecting for a moment or two, we will be able to think of some instances in the life of Christ where he faced temptations that, though they were not the same in every detail, were very similar to the situations that we face every day.[7]

**4. Could Jesus Have Sinned?** The question is sometimes raised, "Was it possible for Christ to have sinned?" Some people argue for the *impeccability* of Christ, in which the word *impeccable* means "not able to sin."[8] Others object that if Jesus were not able to sin, his temptations could not have been real, for how can a temptation be real if the person being tempted is not able to sin anyway?

In order to answer this question we must distinguish what Scripture clearly affirms, on the one hand, and, on the other hand, what is more in the nature of

---

[7]Particularly with respect to family life, it is helpful to remember that Joseph is nowhere mentioned in the Gospels after the incident in the temple when Jesus was twelve years old. It is especially interesting that Joseph is omitted from the verses that list Jesus' mother and other family members, even naming his brothers and sisters (see Matt. 13:55–56; Mark 6:3; cf. Matt. 12:48). It would seem very strange, for example, that "the mother of Jesus" was at the wedding at Cana in Galilee (John 2:1) but not his father, if his father were still living (cf. John 2:12). This suggests that sometime after Jesus was twelve Joseph had died, and that for a period in his life Jesus grew up in a "single-parent home." This would mean that, as he became older, he assumed more and more of the responsibility of male leadership in that family, earning a living as a "carpenter" (Mark 6:3) and no doubt helping care for his younger brothers and sisters as well. Therefore, although Jesus was never married, he no doubt experienced a wide range of family situations and conflicts similar to those experienced by families today.

[8]The Latin word *peccare* means "to sin."

possible inference on our part. (1) Scripture clearly affirms that Christ never actually sinned (see above). There should be no question in our minds at all on this fact. (2) It also clearly affirms that Jesus was tempted, and that these were real temptations (Luke 4:2). If we believe Scripture, then we must insist that Christ *"in every respect has been tempted as we are,* yet without sin" (Heb. 4:15). If our speculation on the question of whether Christ could have sinned ever leads us to say that he was not truly tempted, then we have reached a wrong conclusion, one that contradicts the clear statements of Scripture.

(3) We also must affirm with Scripture that "God cannot be tempted with evil" (James 1:13). But here the question becomes difficult: if Jesus was fully God as well as fully man (and we shall argue below that Scripture clearly and repeatedly teaches this), then must we not also affirm that (in some sense) Jesus also "could not be tempted with evil"?

This is as far as we can go in terms of clear and explicit affirmations of Scripture. At this point we are faced with a dilemma similar to a number of other doctrinal dilemmas where Scripture seems to be teaching things that are, if not directly contradictory, at least very difficult to combine together in our understanding. For example, with respect to the doctrine of the Trinity, we affirmed that God exists in three persons, and each is fully God, and there is one God. Although those statements are not contradictory, they are, nonetheless, difficult to understand in connection with each other, and although we can make some progress in understanding how they fit together, in this life, at least, we have to admit that there can be no final understanding on our part. Here the situation is somewhat similar. We do not have an actual contradiction. Scripture does not tell us that "Jesus was tempted" and that "Jesus was not tempted" (a contradiction if "Jesus" and "tempted" are used exactly in the same sense in both sentences). The Bible tells us that "Jesus was tempted" and "Jesus was fully man" and "Jesus was fully God" and "God cannot be tempted." This combination of teachings from Scripture leaves open the possibility that as we understand the way in which Jesus' human nature and divine nature work together, we might understand more of the way in which he could be tempted in one sense and yet, in another sense, not be tempted. (This possibility will be discussed further below.)

At this point, then, we pass beyond the clear affirmations of Scripture and attempt to suggest a solution to the problem of whether Christ could have sinned. But it is important to recognize that the following solution is more in the nature of a suggested means of combining various biblical teachings and is not directly supported by explicit statements of Scripture. With this in mind, it is appropriate for us to say:[9] (1) If Jesus' human nature had existed by itself, independent of his divine nature, then it would have been a human nature just like that which God gave Adam and Eve. It would have been free from sin but nonetheless *able to sin.* Therefore, if Jesus' human nature had existed by itself, there was the abstract or theoretical possibility that Jesus could have sinned, just as Adam and Eve's human natures were able to sin. (2) But Jesus' human nature never existed apart from union with his divine nature. From the moment of his conception, he existed as truly God and truly man as well. Both his human nature and his divine nature

---

[9]In this discussion I am largely following the conclusions of Geerhardus Vos, *Biblical Theology* (Grand Rapids: Eerdmans, 1948), pp. 339–42.

existed united in one person. (3) Although there were some things (such as being hungry or thirsty or weak) that Jesus experienced in his human nature alone and were not experienced in his divine nature (see below), nonetheless, an act of sin would have been a moral act that would apparently have involved the whole person of Christ. Therefore, if he had sinned, it would have involved both his human and divine natures. (4) But if Jesus as a person had sinned, involving both his human and divine natures in sin, then God himself would have sinned, and he would have ceased to be God. Yet that is clearly impossible because of the infinite holiness of God's nature. (5) Therefore, if we are asking if it was *actually* possible for Jesus to have sinned, it seems that we must conclude that it was not possible. The union of his human and divine natures in one person prevented it.

But the question remains, "How then could Jesus' temptations be real?" The example of the temptation to change the stones into bread is helpful in this regard. Jesus had the ability, by virtue of his divine nature, to perform this miracle, but if he had done it, he would no longer have been obeying in the strength of his human nature alone, he would have failed the test that Adam also failed, and he would not have earned our salvation for us. Therefore, Jesus refused to rely on his divine nature to make obedience easier for him. In like manner, it seems appropriate to conclude that Jesus met every temptation to sin, not by his divine power, but on the strength of his human nature alone (though, of course, it was not "alone" because Jesus, in exercising the kind of faith that humans should exercise, was perfectly depending on God the Father and the Holy Spirit at every moment). The moral strength of his divine nature was there as a sort of "backstop" that would have prevented him from sinning in any case (and therefore we can say that it was not possible for him to sin), but he did not rely on the strength of his divine nature to make it easier for him to face temptations, and his refusal to turn the stones into bread at the beginning of his ministry is a clear indication of this.

Were the temptations real then? Many theologians have pointed out that only he who successfully resists a temptation to the end most fully feels the force of that temptation. Just as a champion weightlifter who successfully lifts and holds over head the heaviest weight in the contest feels the force of it more fully than one who attempts to lift it and drops it, so any Christian who has successfully faced a temptation to the end knows that that is far more difficult than giving in to it at once. So it was with Jesus: every temptation he faced, he faced to the end, and triumphed over it. The temptations were real, even though he did not give in to them. In fact, they were most real *because* he did not give in to them.

What then do we say about the fact that "God cannot be tempted with evil" (James 1:13)? It seems that this is one of a number of things that we must affirm to be true of Jesus' divine nature but not of his human nature. His divine nature could not be tempted with evil, but his human nature could be tempted and was clearly tempted. How these two natures united in one person in facing temptations, Scripture does not clearly explain to us. But this distinction between what is true of one nature and what is true of another nature is an example of a number of similar statements that Scripture requires us to make (see more on this distinction, below, when we discuss how Jesus could be God and man in one person).

**5. Why Was Jesus' Full Humanity Necessary?** When John wrote his first epistle, a heretical teaching was circulating in the church to the effect that Jesus was not a man. This heresy became known as *docetism*.[10] So serious was this denial of truth about Christ, that John could say it was a doctrine of the antichrist: "By this you know the Spirit of God: every spirit which confesses *that Jesus Christ has come in the flesh* is of God, and every spirit which does not confess Jesus is not of God. This is the spirit of antichrist" (1 John 4:2–3). The apostle John understood that to deny Jesus' true humanity was to deny something at the very heart of Christianity, so that no one who denied that Jesus had come in the flesh was sent from God.

As we look through the New Testament, we see several reasons why Jesus had to be fully man if he was going to be the Messiah and earn our salvation. We can list seven of those reasons here.

**a. For Representative Obedience:** As we noted in the chapter on the covenants between God and man above,[11] Jesus was our representative and obeyed for us where Adam had failed and disobeyed. We see this in the parallels between Jesus' temptation (Luke 4:1–13) and the time of testing for Adam and Eve in the garden (Gen. 2:15–3:7). It is also clearly reflected in Paul's discussion of the parallels between Adam and Christ, in Adam's disobedience and Christ's obedience:

> Then as one man's trespass led to condemnation for all men, so *one man's act of righteousness* leads to acquittal and life for all men. For as by one man's disobedience many were made sinners, so *by one man's obedience* many will be made righteous. (Rom. 5:18–19)

This is why Paul can call Christ "the last Adam" (1 Cor. 15:45) and can call Adam the "first man" and Christ the "second man" (1 Cor. 15:47). Jesus had to be a man in order to be our representative and obey in our place.

**b. To Be a Substitute Sacrifice:** If Jesus had not been a man, he could not have died in our place and paid the penalty that was due to us. The author of Hebrews tells us that "For surely it is not with angels that he is concerned but with the descendants of Abraham. Therefore he *had to* be made like his brethren in every respect, so that he might become a merciful and faithful high priest in the service of God, to make expiation [more accurately, 'propitiation'] for the sins of the people" (Heb. 2:16–17; cf. v. 14). Jesus had to become a man, not an angel, because God was concerned with saving men, not with saving angels. But to do this he "*had to*" be made like us in every way, so that he might become "the propitiation" for us, the sacrifice that is an acceptable substitute for us. Though

---

[10]The word *docetism* comes from the Greek verb *dokeō*, "to seem, to appear to be." Any theological position that says that Jesus was not really a man, but only appeared to be a man, is called a "docetic" position. Behind docetism is an assumption that the material creation is inherently evil, and therefore the Son of God could not have been united to a true human nature. No prominent church leader ever advocated docetism, but it was a troublesome heresy that had various supporters in the first four centuries of the church. Modern evangelicals who neglect to teach on the full humanity of Christ can unwittingly support docetic tendencies in their hearers.

[11]See chapter 25, p. 518; also chapter 27, pp. 570–71.

this idea will be discussed more fully in chapter 27, on the atonement, it is important here to realize that unless Christ was fully man, he could not have died to pay the penalty for man's sins. He could not have been a substitute sacrifice for us.

**c. To Be the One Mediator Between God and Men:** Because we were alienated from God by sin, we needed someone to come between God and ourselves and bring us back to him. We needed a mediator who could represent us to God and who could represent God to us. There is only one person who has ever fulfilled that requirement: "There is one God, and *there is one mediator* between God and men, the man Christ Jesus" (1 Tim. 2:5). In order to fulfill this role of mediator, Jesus had to be fully man as well as fully God.

**d. To Fulfill God's Original Purpose for Man to Rule Over Creation:** As we saw in the discussion of the purpose for which God created man,[12] God put mankind on the earth to subdue it and rule over it as God's representatives. But man did not fulfill that purpose, for he instead fell into sin. The author of Hebrews realizes that God intended everything to be in subjection to man, but he admits, "As it is, we do not yet see everything in subjection to him" (Heb. 2:8). Then when Jesus came as a man, he was able to obey God and thereby have the right to rule over creation *as a man,* thus fulfilling God's original purpose in putting man on the earth. Hebrews recognizes this when it says that now "we see Jesus" in the place of authority over the universe, "crowned with glory and honor" (Heb. 2:9; cf. the same phrase in v. 7). Jesus in fact has been given "all authority in heaven and on earth" (Matt. 28:18), and God has "put all things under his feet and has made him the head over all things for the church" (Eph. 1:22). Indeed, we shall someday reign with him on his throne (Rev. 3:21) and experience, in subjection to Christ our Lord, the fulfillment of God's purpose that we reign over the earth (cf. Luke 19:17, 19; 1 Cor. 6:3). Jesus had to be a man in order to fulfill God's original purpose that man rule over his creation.

**e. To Be Our Example and Pattern in Life:** John tells us, "He who says he abides in him ought to walk *in the same way in which he walked*" (1 John 2:6), and reminds us that "when he appears we shall be like him," and that this hope of future conformity to Christ's character even now gives increasing moral purity to our lives (1 John 3:2–3). Paul tells us that we are continually being "changed into his likeness" (2 Cor. 3:18), thus moving toward the goal for which God saved us, that we might "be conformed to the image of his Son" (Rom. 8:29). Peter tells us that especially in suffering we have to consider Christ's example: "Christ also suffered for you, *leaving you an example,* that you should follow in his steps" (1 Peter 2:21). Throughout our Christian life, we are to run the race set before us "looking to Jesus the pioneer and perfecter of our faith" (Heb. 12:2). If we become discouraged by the hostility and opposition of sinners, we are to "consider him who endured from sinners such hostility against himself" (Heb. 12:3). Jesus is also our example in death. Paul's goal is to become "*like him* in his

---

[12]See chapter 15, pp. 272–73, and chapter 21, pp. 447–48.

death" (Phil. 3:10; cf. Acts 7:60; 1 Peter 3:17–18 with 4:1). Our goal should be to be like Christ all our days, up to the point of death, and to die with unfailing obedience to God, with strong trust in him, and with love and forgiveness to others. Jesus had to become a man like us in order to live as our example and pattern in life.

**f. To Be the Pattern for Our Redeemed Bodies:** Paul tells us that when Jesus rose from the dead he rose in a new body that was "imperishable . . . raised in glory . . . raised in power . . . raised a spiritual body" (1 Cor. 15:42–44). This new resurrection body that Jesus had when he rose from the dead is the pattern for what our bodies will be like when we are raised from the dead, because Christ is "the first fruits" (1 Cor. 15:23)—an agricultural metaphor that likens Christ to the first sample of the harvest, showing what the other fruit from that harvest would be like. We now have a physical body like Adam's, but we will have one like Christ's: "Just as we have borne the image of the man of dust, we shall also bear the image of the man of heaven" (1 Cor. 15:49). Jesus had to be raised as a man in order to be the "first-born from the dead" (Col. 1:18), the pattern for the bodies that we would later have.

**g. To Sympathize As High Priest:** The author of Hebrews reminds us that "because he himself has suffered and been tempted, he is able to help those who are tempted" (Heb. 2:18; cf. 4:15–16). If Jesus had not been a man, he would not have been able to know *by experience* what we go through in our temptations and struggles in this life. But because he has lived as a man, he is able to sympathize more fully with us in our experiences.[13]

**6. Jesus Will Be a Man Forever.** Jesus did not give up his human nature after his death and resurrection, for he appeared to his disciples as a man after the resurrection, even with the scars of the nail prints in his hands (John 20:25–27). He had "flesh and bones" (Luke 24:39) and ate food (Luke 24:41–42). Later, when he was talking with his disciples, he was taken up into heaven, still in his resurrected human body, and two angels promised that he would return in the same way: "This Jesus, who was taken up from you into heaven, *will come in the same way* as you saw him go into heaven" (Acts 1:11). Still later, Stephen gazed into heaven and saw Jesus as "the Son of man standing at the right hand of God"

---

[13]This is a difficult concept for us to understand, because we do not want to say that Jesus acquired additional knowledge or information by becoming man: certainly as omniscient God he knew every fact there was to know about the experience of human suffering. But the book of Hebrews does say, "*Because* he himself has suffered and been tempted, he is able to help those who are tempted" (Heb. 2:18), and we must insist that that statement is true—there is a relationship between Jesus' suffering and his ability to sympathize with us and help us in temptation. Apparently the author is speaking not of any additional factual or intellectual knowledge, but of an ability to recall a personal experience that he had himself gone through, an ability he would not have if he had not had that personal experience. Some faint parallel to this might be seen in the fact that a man who is a medical doctor, and has perhaps even written a textbook on obstetrics, might know far more *information* about childbirth than any of his patients. Yet, because he is a man, he will never share in that actual experience. A woman who has herself had a baby (or, to give a closer parallel, a woman physician who first writes a textbook and then has a baby herself) can sympathize much more fully with other women who are having babies.

(Acts 7:56). Jesus also appeared to Saul on the Damascus Road and said, "I am Jesus, whom you are persecuting" (Acts 9:5)—an appearance that Saul (Paul) later coupled with the resurrection appearances of Jesus to others (1 Cor. 9:1; 15:8). In John's vision in Revelation, Jesus still appears as "one like a son of man" (Rev. 1:13), though he is filled with great glory and power, and his appearance causes John to fall at his feet in awe (Rev. 1:13–17). He promises one day to drink wine again with his disciples in his Father's kingdom (Matt. 26:29) and invites us to a great marriage supper in heaven (Rev. 19:9). Moreover, Jesus will continue forever in his offices as prophet, priest, and king, all of them carried out by virtue of the fact that he is both God and man forever.[14]

All of these texts indicate that Jesus did not *temporarily* become man, but that his divine nature was *permanently* united to his human nature, and he lives forever not just as the eternal Son of God, the second person of the Trinity, but also as Jesus, the man who was born of Mary, and as Christ, the Messiah and Savior of his people. Jesus will remain fully God and fully man, yet one person, forever.

## B. The Deity of Christ

To complete the biblical teaching about Jesus Christ, we must affirm not only that he was fully human, but also that he was fully divine. Although the word does not explicitly occur in Scripture, the church has used the term *incarnation* to refer to the fact that Jesus was God in human flesh. The *incarnation* was the act of God the Son whereby he took to himself a human nature.[15] The scriptural proof for the deity of Christ is very extensive in the New Testament. We shall examine it under several categories.[16]

**1. Direct Scriptural Claims.** In this section we examine direct statements of Scripture that Jesus is God or that he is divine.[17]

**a. The Word God (*Theos*) Used of Christ:** Although the word *theos*, "God," is usually reserved in the New Testament for God the Father, nonetheless, there are several passages where it is also used to refer to Jesus Christ. In all of these passages the word "God" is used in the strong sense to refer to the one who is the Creator of heaven and earth, the ruler over all. These passages include John 1:1; 1:18 (in older and better manuscripts); 20:28; Romans 9:5; Titus 2:13; Hebrews 1:8 (quoting Ps. 45:6); and 2 Peter 1:1.[18] As these passages have been discussed

---

[14]See chapter 29, pp. 624–33, on the offices of Christ.

[15]The Latin word *incarnāre* means "to make flesh," and is derived from the prefix *in-* (which has a causative sense, "to cause something to be something") and the stem *caro, carnis-*, "flesh."

[16]In the following section I have not distinguished between claims to deity made by Jesus himself and claims made about him by others: while such a distinction is helpful for tracing development in people's understanding of Christ, for our present purposes both kinds of statements are found in our canonical New Testament Scriptures and are valid sources for building Christian doctrine.

[17]An excellent discussion of New Testament evidence for the deity of Christ, drawn especially from the titles of Christ in the New Testament, is found in Donald Guthrie, *New Testament Theology* (Leicester and Downers Grove, Ill.: InterVarsity Press, 1981), pp. 235–365.

[18]Titus 1:3, in connection with the fact that v. 4 calls Christ Jesus "our Savior" and the fact that it was Jesus Christ who commissioned Paul to preach the gospel, might also be considered another example of the use of the word *God* to refer to Christ.

in some detail in the chapter on the Trinity,[19] the discussion will not be repeated here. It is enough to note that there are at least these seven clear passages in the New Testament that explicitly refer to Jesus as God.

One Old Testament example of the name *God* applied to Christ is seen in a familiar messianic passage: "For to us a child is born, to us a son is given; and the government will be upon his shoulder, and his name will be called 'Wonderful Counselor, *Mighty God* . . .'" (Isa. 9:6).

**b. The Word *Lord* (*Kyrios*) Used of Christ:** Sometimes the word *Lord* (Gk. *kyrios*) is used simply as a polite address to a superior, roughly equivalent to our word *sir* (see Matt. 13:27; 21:30; 27:63; John 4:11). Sometimes it can simply mean "master" of a servant or slave (Matt. 6:24; 21:40). Yet the same word is also used in the Septuagint (the Greek translation of the Old Testament, which was commonly used at the time of Christ) as a translation for the Hebrew *yhwh*, "Yahweh," or (as it is frequently translated) "the LORD," or "Jehovah." The word *kyrios* is used to translate the name of the Lord 6,814 times in the Greek Old Testament. Therefore, any Greek-speaking reader at the time of the New Testament who had any knowledge at all of the Greek Old Testament would have recognized that, in contexts where it was appropriate, the word "Lord" was the name of the one who was the Creator and Sustainer of heaven and earth, the omnipotent God.

Now there are many instances in the New Testament where "Lord" is used of Christ in what can only be understood as this strong Old Testament sense, "the Lord" who is Yahweh or God himself. This use of the word "Lord" is quite striking in the word of the angel to the shepherds of Bethlehem: "For to you is born this day in the city of David a Savior, who is Christ *the Lord*" (Luke 2:11). Though these words are familiar to us from frequent reading of the Christmas story, we should realize how surprising it would be to any first-century Jew to hear that someone born as a baby was the "Christ" (or "Messiah"),[20] and, moreover, that this one who was the Messiah was also "the Lord"—that is, the Lord God himself! The amazing force of the angel's statement, which the shepherds could hardly believe, was to say, essentially, "Today in Bethlehem a baby has been born who is your Savior and your Messiah, and who is also God himself." It is not surprising that "all who heard it wondered at what the shepherds told them" (Luke 2:18).

When Mary comes to visit Elizabeth several months before Jesus is to be born, Elizabeth says, "Why is this granted me, that the mother of *my Lord* should come to me?" (Luke 1:43). Because Jesus was not even born, Elizabeth could not be using the word "Lord" to mean something like human "master." She must rather be using it in the strong Old Testament sense, giving an amazing sense to the sentence: "Why is this granted me, that the mother of the Lord God himself should come to me?" Though this is a very strong statement, it is difficult to understand the word "Lord" in this context in any weaker sense.

---

[19]See chapter 14, pp. 233–37, for discussion of passages that refer to Jesus as "God." See also Murray J. Harris, *Jesus as God* (Grand Rapids: Baker, 1992), for the most extensive exegetical treatment ever published dealing with New Testament passages that refer to Jesus as "God."

[20]The word *Christ* is the Greek translation of the Hebrew word *Messiah*.

We see another example when Matthew says that John the Baptist is the one who cries out in the wilderness, "Prepare the way of *the Lord*, make his paths straight" (Matt. 3:3). In doing this John is quoting Isaiah 40:3, which speaks about the Lord God himself coming among his people. But the context applies this passage to John's role of preparing the way for Jesus to come. The implication is that when Jesus comes, *the Lord himself* will come.

Jesus also identifies himself as the sovereign Lord of the Old Testament when he asks the Pharisees about Psalm 110:1, "The Lord said to *my Lord*, Sit at my right hand, till I put your enemies under your feet" (Matt. 22:44). The force of this statement is that "God the Father said to God the Son [David's Lord], 'Sit at my right hand. . . .'" The Pharisees know he is talking about himself and identifying himself as one worthy of the Old Testament title *kyrios*, "Lord."

Such usage is seen frequently in the Epistles, where "the Lord" is a common name to refer to Christ. Paul says "there is one God, the Father, from whom are all things and for whom we exist, and *one Lord*, Jesus Christ, through whom are all things and through whom we exist" (1 Cor. 8:6; cf. 12:3, and many other passages in the Pauline epistles).

A particularly clear passage is found in Hebrews 1, where the author quotes Psalm 102, which speaks about the work of the Lord in creation and applies it to Christ:

> You, Lord, founded the earth in the beginning,
> and the heavens are the work of your hands;
> they will perish, but you remain;
> they will all grow old like a garment,
> like a mantle you will roll them up,
> and they will be changed.
> But you are the same,
> and your years will never end. (Heb. 1:10–12)

Here Christ is explicitly spoken of as the eternal Lord of heaven and earth who created all things and will remain the same forever. Such strong usage of the term "Lord" to refer to Christ culminates in Revelation 19:16, where we see Christ returning as conquering King, and "On his robe and on his thigh he has a name inscribed, King of kings and *Lord of lords.*"

**c. Other Strong Claims to Deity:** In addition to the uses of the word *God* and *Lord* to refer to Christ, we have other passages that strongly claim deity for Christ. When Jesus told his Jewish opponents that Abraham had seen his (Christ's) day, they challenged him, "You are not yet fifty years old, and have you seen Abraham?" (John 8:57). Here a sufficient response to prove Jesus' eternity would have been, "Before Abraham was, I was." But Jesus did not say this. Instead, he made a much more startling assertion: "Truly, truly, I say to you, before Abraham was, *I am*" (John 8:58). Jesus combined two assertions whose sequence seemed to make no sense: "Before something in the past happened [Abraham was], something in the present happened [I am]." The Jewish leaders recognized at once that he was not speaking in riddles or uttering nonsense: when he said, "I am," he was repeating the very words God used when he identified himself to Moses as "*I*

AM WHO I AM" (Ex. 3:14). Jesus was claiming for himself the title "I AM," by which God designates himself as the eternal existing One, the God who is the source of his own existence and who always has been and always will be. When the Jews heard this unusual, emphatic, solemn statement, they knew that he was claiming to be God. "So they took up stones to throw at him; but Jesus hid himself, and went out of the temple" (John 8:59).[21]

Another strong claim to deity is Jesus' statement at the end of Revelation, "I am the Alpha and the Omega, the first and the last, the beginning and the end" (Rev. 22:13). When this is combined with the statement of God the Father in Revelation 1:8, "I am the Alpha and the Omega," it also constitutes a strong claim to equal deity with God the Father. Sovereign over all of history and all of creation, Jesus is the beginning and the end.

In John 1:1, John not only calls Jesus "God" but also refers to him as "the Word" (Gk. *logos*). John's readers would have recognized in this term *logos* a dual reference, both to the powerful, creative Word of God in the Old Testament by which the heavens and earth were created (Ps. 33:6) and to the organizing or unifying principle of the universe, the thing that held it together and allowed it to make sense, in Greek thinking.[22] John is identifying Jesus with both of these ideas and saying that he is not only the powerful, creative Word of God and the organizing or unifying force in the universe, but also that he became man: "The Word became flesh and dwelt among us, full of grace and truth; we have beheld his glory, glory as of the only Son from the Father" (John 1:14). Here is another strong claim to deity coupled with an explicit statement that Jesus also became man and moved among us as a man.

Further evidence of claims to deity can be found in the fact that Jesus calls himself "*the* Son of man." This title is used eighty-four times in the four gospels but only by Jesus and only to speak of himself (note, e.g., Matt. 16:13 with Luke 9:18). In the rest of the New Testament, the phrase "*the* Son of man" (with the definite article "the") is used only once, in Acts 7:56, where Stephen refers to Christ as the Son of Man. This unique term has as its background the vision in Daniel 7 where Daniel saw one like a "Son of Man" who "came to the Ancient of Days" and was given "dominion and glory and kingdom, *that all peoples, nations, and languages should serve him; his dominion is an everlasting dominion,* which shall not pass away" (Dan. 7:13–14). It is striking that this "son of man" came "with the clouds of heaven" (Dan. 7:13). This passage clearly speaks of someone who had heavenly origin and who was given *eternal rule* over the *whole world.* The high priests did not miss the point of this passage when Jesus said, "Hereafter you will see the Son of man *seated at the right hand of Power, and coming on the clouds of heaven*" (Matt. 26:64). The reference to Daniel 7:13–14 was unmistakable, and the high priest and his council knew that Jesus was claiming to be the eternal world ruler of heavenly origin spoken of in Daniel's vision. Immediately they said, "He has uttered blasphemy. . . . He deserves death" (Matt. 26:65–66). Here

---

[21]The other "I am" sayings in John's gospel, where Jesus claims to be the bread of life (6:35), the light of the world (8:12), the door of the sheep (10:7), the good shepherd (10:11), the resurrection and the life (11:25), the way, the truth, and the life (14:6), and the true vine (15:1), also contribute to the overall picture of deity that John paints of Christ: see Donald Guthrie, *New Testament Theology*, pp. 330–32.

[22]See Donald Guthrie, *New Testament Theology*, esp. p. 326.

Jesus finally made explicit the strong claims to eternal world rule that were earlier hinted at in his frequent use of the title "the Son of man" to apply to himself.

Though the title "Son of God" can sometimes be used simply to refer to Israel (Matt. 2:15), or to man as created by God (Luke 2:38), or to redeemed man generally (Rom. 8:14, 19, 23), there are nevertheless instances in which the phrase "Son of God" refers to Jesus as the heavenly, eternal Son who is equal to God himself (see Matt. 11:25–30; 17:5; 1 Cor. 15:28; Heb. 1:1–3, 5, 8). This is especially true in John's gospel where Jesus is seen as a unique Son from the Father (John 1:14, 18, 34, 49) who fully reveals the Father (John 8:19; 14:9). As Son he is so great that we can trust in him for eternal life (something that could be said of no created being: John 3:16, 36; 20:31). He is also the one who has all authority from the Father to give life, pronounce eternal judgment, and rule over all (John 3:36; 5:20–22, 25; 10:17; 16:15). As Son he has been sent by the Father, and therefore he existed before he came into the world (John 3:37; 5:23; 10:36).

The first three verses of Hebrews are emphatic in saying that the Son is the one whom God "appointed the heir of all things, through whom also he created the world" (Heb. 1:2). This Son, says the writer, "reflects the glory of God and bears the very stamp [lit., is the 'exact duplicate,' Gk. *charaktēr*) of his nature, upholding the universe by his word of power" (Heb. 1:3). Jesus is the exact duplicate of the "nature" (or being, Gk. *hypostasis*) of God, making him exactly equal to God in every attribute. Moreover, he continually upholds the universe "by his word of power," something that only God could do.

These passages combine to indicate that the title "Son of God" *when applied to Christ* strongly affirms his deity as the eternal Son in the Trinity, one equal to God the Father in all his attributes.

**2. Evidence That Jesus Possessed Attributes of Deity.** In addition to the specific affirmations of Jesus' deity seen in the many passages quoted above, we see many examples of actions in Jesus' lifetime that point to his divine character.

Jesus demonstrated his *omnipotence* when he stilled the storm at sea with a word (Matt. 8:26–27), multiplied the loaves and fish (Matt. 14:19), and changed water into wine (John 2:1–11). Some might object that these miracles just showed the power of the Holy Spirit working through him, just as the Holy Spirit could work through any other human being, and therefore these do not demonstrate Jesus' own deity. But the contextual explanations of these events often point not to what they demonstrate about the power of the Holy Spirit but to what they demonstrate about Jesus himself. For instance, after Jesus turned water into wine, John tells us, "This, the first of his miraculous signs, Jesus did at Cana in Galilee, and *manifested his glory;* and his disciples believed in him" (John 2:11). It was not the glory of the Holy Spirit that was manifested but the glory of Jesus himself, as his divine power worked to change water into wine. Similarly, after Jesus stilled the storm on the Sea of Galilee, the disciples did not say, "How great is the power of the Holy Spirit working through this prophet," but rather, "What sort of man is this, that even winds and sea *obey him?*" (Matt. 8:27). It was the authority of Jesus himself to which the winds and the waves were subject, and this could only be the authority of God who rules over the seas and has power to still the waves (cf. Ps. 65:7; 89:9; 107:29).[23]

Jesus asserts his *eternity* when he says, "Before Abraham was, I am" (John 8:58, see discussion above), or, "I am the Alpha and the Omega" (Rev. 22:13).

The *omniscience* of Jesus is demonstrated in his knowing people's thoughts (Mark 2:8) and seeing Nathaniel under the fig tree from far away (John 1:48), and knowing "from the first who those were that did not believe, and who it was that would betray him" (John 6:64). Of course, the revelation of individual, specific events or facts is something that God could give to anyone who had a gift of prophecy in the Old or New Testaments. But Jesus' knowledge was much more extensive than that. He knew "who those were that did not believe," thus implying that he knew the belief or unbelief that was in the hearts of all men. In fact, John says explicitly that Jesus "*knew all men* and needed no one to bear witness of man" (John 2:25). The disciples could later say to him, "Now we know that *you know all things*" (John 16:30). These statements say much more than what could be said of any great prophet or apostle of the Old Testament or New Testament, for they imply omniscience on the part of Jesus.[24]

Finally, after his resurrection, when Jesus asked Peter if he loved him, Peter answered, "Lord, *you know everything;* you know that I love you" (John 21:17). Here Peter is saying much more than that Jesus knows his heart and knows that he loves him. He is rather making a general statement ("You know everything") and from it he is drawing a specific conclusion ("You know that I love you"). Peter is confident that Jesus knows what is in the heart of every person, and therefore he is sure that Jesus knows his own heart.

The divine attribute of *omnipresence* is not directly affirmed to be true of Jesus during his earthly ministry. However, while looking forward to the time that the church would be established, Jesus could say, "Where two or three are gathered in my name, *there am I* in the midst of them" (Matt. 18:20). Moreover, before he left the earth, he told his disciples, "I am with you always, to the close of the age" (Matt. 28:20).[25]

That Jesus possessed divine *sovereignty,* a kind of authority possessed by God alone, is seen in the fact that he could forgive sins (Mark 2:5–7). Unlike the Old Testament prophets who declared, "Thus says the LORD," he could preface his statements with the phrase, "But *I say to you*" (Matt. 5:22, 28, 32, 34, 39, 44)— an amazing claim to his own authority. He could speak with the authority of God himself because he was himself fully God. He had "all things" delivered into his hands by the Father and the authority to reveal the Father to whomever he chose (Matt. 11:25–27). Such is his authority that the future eternal state of everyone in the universe depends on whether they believe in him or reject him (John 3:36).

Jesus also possessed the divine attribute of *immortality,* the inability to die. We

[23]I recognize that other passages attribute some of Christ's miracles to the Holy Spirit—see Matt. 12:28; Luke 4:14, 18, 40.

[24]See below, pp. 560–63, on Mark 13:32, and on the question of how omniscience can be consistent with Christ's learning things as a man.

[25]I do not mean to imply that these verses show that Jesus' human nature was omnipresent. Jesus' human nature, including his physical body, was never more than one place at one time. It is probably best to understand these verses to refer to Jesus' divine nature (see below, pp. 556–61, for discussion of the distinction between Christ's two natures).

see this indicated near the beginning of John's gospel, when Jesus says to the Jews, "Destroy this temple, and in three days *I will raise it up*" (John 2:19). John explains that he was not speaking about the temple made with stones in Jerusalem, "but he spoke of the temple of *his body*. When therefore he was raised from the dead, his disciples remembered that he had said this; and they believed the scripture and the word which Jesus had spoken" (John 2:21–22). We must insist of course that Jesus really did die: this very passage speaks of the time when "he was raised from the dead." But it is also significant that Jesus predicts that he will have an active role in his own resurrection: "*I will raise it up*." Although other Scripture passages tell us that God the Father was active in raising Christ from the dead, here he says that he himself will be active in his resurrection.

Jesus claims the power to lay down his life and take it up again in another passage in John's gospel: "For this reason the Father loves me, because I lay down my life, that I may take it again. No one takes it from me, but I lay it down on my own accord. I have power to lay it down, and I have power to take it again; this charge I have received from my Father" (John 10:17–18). Here Jesus speaks of a power no other human being has had—the power to lay down his own life *and* the power to take it up again. Once again, this is an indication that Jesus possessed the divine attribute of immortality. Similarly, the author of Hebrews says that Jesus "has become a priest, not according to a legal requirement concerning bodily descent but by the power of *an indestructible life*" (Heb. 7:16). (The fact that immortality is a unique characteristic of God alone is seen in 1 Tim. 6:16, which speaks of God as the one "who alone has immortality.")

Another clear attestation to the deity of Christ is the fact that he is counted *worthy to be worshiped*, something that is true of no other creature, including angels (see Rev. 19:10), but only God alone. Yet Scripture says of Christ that "God has highly exalted him and bestowed on him the name which is above every name, that at the name of Jesus every knee should bow, in heaven and on earth and under the earth, and every tongue confess that Jesus Christ is Lord, to the glory of God the Father" (Phil. 2:9–11). Similarly, God commands the angels to worship Christ, for we read, "When he brings the first-born into the world, he says, 'Let all God's angels worship him'" (Heb. 1:6).

John is allowed a glimpse of the worship that occurs in heaven, for he sees thousands and thousands of angels and heavenly creatures around God's throne saying, "Worthy is the Lamb who was slain, to receive power and wealth and wisdom and might and honor and glory and blessing!" (Rev. 5:12). Then he hears "*every creature* in heaven and on earth and under the earth and in the sea, and all therein, saying, 'To him who sits upon the throne *and to the Lamb* be blessing and honor and glory and might for ever and ever!'" (Rev. 5:13). Christ is here called "the Lamb who was slain," and he is accorded the universal worship offered to God the Father, thus clearly demonstrating his equality in deity.[26]

## 3. Did Jesus Give Up Some of His Divine Attributes While on Earth? (The Kenosis Theory). Paul writes to the Philippians,

---

[26]See also Matt. 28:17 where Jesus accepted worship from his disciples after his resurrection.

Have this mind among yourselves, which is yours in Christ Jesus, who, though he was in the form of God, did not count equality with God a thing to be grasped, but *emptied himself*, taking the form of a servant, being born in the likeness of men. (Phil. 2:5–7)

Beginning with this text, several theologians in Germany (from about 1860–1880) and in England (from about 1890–1910) advocated a view of the incarnation that had not been advocated before in the history of the church. This new view was called the "kenosis theory," and the overall position it represented was called "kenotic theology." The *kenosis theory* holds that Christ gave up some of his divine attributes while he was on earth as a man. (The word *kenosis* is taken from the Greek verb *kenoō*, which generally means "to empty," and is translated "emptied himself" in Phil. 2:7.) According to the theory Christ "emptied himself" of some of his divine attributes, such as omniscience, omnipresence, and omnipotence, while he was on earth as a man. This was viewed as a voluntary self-limitation on Christ's part, which he carried out in order to fulfill his work of redemption.[27]

But does Philippians 2:7 teach that Christ emptied himself of some of his divine attributes, and does the rest of the New Testament confirm this? The evidence of Scripture points to a negative answer to both questions. We must first realize that no recognized teacher in the first 1,800 years of church history, including those who were native speakers of Greek, thought that "emptied himself" in Philippians 2:7 meant that the Son of God gave up some of his divine attributes. Second, we must recognize that the text does not say that Christ "emptied himself of some powers" or "emptied himself of divine attributes" or anything like that. Third, the text *does* describe what Jesus did in this "emptying": he did not do it by giving up any of his attributes but rather by "taking the form of a servant," that is, by coming to live as a man, and "being found in human form he humbled himself and became obedient unto death, even death on a cross" (Phil. 2:8). Thus, the context itself interprets this "emptying" as equivalent to "humbling himself" and taking on a lowly status and position. Thus, the NIV, instead of translating the phrase, "He *emptied* himself," translates it, "but *made himself nothing*" (Phil. 2:7 NIV). The emptying includes change of role and status, not essential attributes or nature.

A fourth reason for this interpretation is seen in Paul's purpose in this context. His purpose has been to persuade the Philippians that they should "do nothing from selfishness or conceit, but in humility count others better than yourselves" (Phil. 2:3), and he continues by telling them, "Let each of you look not only to his own interests, but also to the interests of others" (Phil. 2:4). To persuade them to be humble and to put the interests of others first, he then holds up the example of Christ: "Have this mind among yourselves, which is yours in Christ Jesus, who, though he was in the form of God, did not count equality with God a thing to be grasped, but emptied himself, taking the form of a servant . . ." (Phil. 2:5–7).

Now in holding up Christ as an example, he wants the Philippians to imitate Christ. But certainly he is not asking the Philippian Christians to "give up" or "lay

---

[27]A very clear overview of the history of kenotic theology is found in the article "Kenosis, a Kenotic Theology" by S. M. Smith, in *EDT*, pp. 600–602. Surprisingly (for the volume in which his essay appears), Smith ends up endorsing kenotic theology as a valid form of orthodox, biblical faith (p. 602)!

aside" any of their essential attributes or abilities! He is not asking them to "give up" their intelligence or strength or skill and become a diminished version of what they were. Rather, he is asking them to put the interests of others first: "Let each of you look not only to his own interests, but also to the interests of others" (Phil. 2:4). And because that is his goal, it fits the context to understand that he is using Christ as the supreme example of one who did just that: he put the interests of others first and was willing to give up some of the privilege and status that was his as God.

Therefore, the best understanding of this passage is that it talks about Jesus giving up the *status* and *privilege* that was his in heaven: he "did not count equality with God a thing to be grasped" (or "clung to for his own advantage"), but "emptied himself" or "humbled himself" for our sake, and came to live as a man. Jesus speaks elsewhere of the "glory" he had with the Father "before the world was made" (John 17:5), a glory that he had given up and was going to receive again when he returned to heaven. And Paul could speak of Christ who, "though he was rich, yet for your sake he became poor" (2 Cor. 8:9), once again speaking of the privilege and honor that he deserved but temporarily gave up for us.

The fifth and final reason why the "kenosis" view of Philippians 2:7 must be rejected is the larger context of the teaching of the New Testament and the doctrinal teaching of the entire Bible. If it were true that such a momentous event as this happened, that the eternal Son of God ceased for a time to have all the attributes of God—ceased, for a time, to be omniscient, omnipotent, and omnipresent, for example—then we would expect that such an incredible event would be taught clearly and repeatedly in the New Testament, not found in the very doubtful interpretation of one word in one epistle. But we find the opposite of that: we do not find it stated anywhere else that the Son of God ceased to have some of the attributes of God that he had possessed from eternity. In fact, if the kenosis theory were true (and this is a foundational objection against it), then we could no longer affirm Jesus was fully God while he was here on earth.[28] The kenosis theory ultimately denies the full deity of Jesus Christ and makes him something less than fully God. S. M. Smith admits, "All forms of classical orthodoxy either explicitly reject or reject in principle kenotic theology."[29]

It is important to realize that the major force persuading people to accept kenotic theory was not that they had discovered a better understanding of Philippians 2:7 or any other passage of the New Testament, but rather the increasing discomfort people were feeling with the formulations of the doctrine of Christ in historic, classical orthodoxy. It just seemed too incredible for modern rational and "scientific" people to believe that Jesus Christ could be truly human and fully, absolutely God at the same time.[30] The kenosis theory began to sound

---

[28]Sometimes the word *kenosis* is used in a weaker sense not to apply to the kenosis theory in its full sense, but simply to refer to a more orthodox understanding of Phil. 2:7, in which it means simply that Jesus gave up his glory and privilege for a time while he was on earth. (This is essentially the view we have advocated in this text.) But it does not seem at all wise to use the term "kenosis" to refer to such a traditional understanding of Phil. 2:7, for it is too easily confused with the full-blown kenosis doctrine that essentially denies the full deity of Christ. To take a term that formally applies to a false doctrinal teaching and then use it to apply to a scripturally sound position is just confusing to most people.

[29]S. M. Smith, "Kenosis, A Kenotic Theology," p. 601.

[30]Smith points out that one of the primary influences leading some to adopt kenotic theology was the growth of modern psychology in the nineteenth century: "The age was learning to think in terms

more and more like an acceptable way to say that (in some sense) Jesus was God, but a kind of God who had for a time given up some of his Godlike qualities, those that were most difficult for people to accept in the modern world.

**4. Conclusion: Christ Is Fully Divine.** The New Testament, in hundreds of explicit verses that call Jesus "God" and "Lord" and use a number of other titles of deity to refer to him, and in many passages that attribute actions or words to him that could only be true of God himself, affirms again and again the full, absolute deity of Jesus Christ. "In him *all the fulness of God* was pleased to dwell" (Col. 1:19), and "in him the whole fulness of deity dwells bodily" (Col. 2:9). In an earlier section we argued that Jesus is truly and fully man. Now we conclude that he is truly and fully God as well. His name is rightly called "Emmanuel," that is, "God with us" (Matt. 1:23).

**5. Is The Doctrine of the Incarnation "Unintelligible" Today?** Throughout history there have been objections to the New Testament teaching on the full deity of Christ. One recent attack on this doctrine deserves mention here because it created a large controversy, since the contributors to the volume were all recognized church leaders in England. The book was called *The Myth of God Incarnate,* edited by John Hick (London: SCM, 1977). The title gives away the thesis of the book: the idea that Jesus was "God incarnate" or "God come in the flesh" is a "myth"—a helpful story, perhaps, for the faith of earlier generations, but not one that can really be believed by us today.

The argument of the book begins with some foundational assumptions: (1) the Bible does not have absolute divine authority for us today (p. i), and (2) Christianity, like all human life and thought, is evolving and changing over time (p. ii). The basic claims of the book are laid out in the first two chapters. In chapter 1, Maurice Wiles argues that it is possible to have Christianity without the doctrine of the incarnation. The church has given up earlier doctrines, such as the "real presence" of Christ in the Lord's Supper, the inerrancy of Scripture, and the virgin birth; therefore, it is possible to give up the traditional doctrine of the incarnation and still keep the Christian faith as well (pp. 2–3). Moreover, the doctrine of the incarnation is not directly presented in Scripture but originated in a setting where belief in the supernatural was credible; nevertheless, it has never been a coherent or intelligible doctrine through the history of the church (pp. 3–5).

---

of the categories of psychology. Consciousness was a central category. If at our 'center' is our consciousness, and if Jesus was both omniscient God and limited man, then he had two centers and was thus fundamentally not one of us. Christology was becoming inconceivable for some" (ibid., pp. 600–601). In other words, pressures of modern psychological study were making belief in the combination of full deity and full humanity in the one person of Christ difficult to explain or even intellectually embarrassing: how could someone be so different from us and still be truly a man?

Yet we might respond that modern psychology is inherently limited in that its only object of study is simple human beings. No modern psychologist has ever studied anyone who was perfectly free from sin (as Christ was) and who was both fully God and fully man (as Christ was). If we limit our understanding to what modern psychology tells us is "possible" or "conceivable," then we will have neither a sinless Christ nor a divine Christ. In this as in many other points of doctrine, our understanding of what is "possible" must be determined not by modern empirical study of a finite, fallen world, but by the teachings of Scripture itself.

Regarding the New Testament teaching, Francis Young, in chapter 2, argues that the New Testament contains the writings of many diverse witnesses who tell of their own understanding of Christ, but that no single or unified view of Christ can be gained from the entire New Testament; the early church's understanding of the person of Christ was developing in various directions over time. Young concludes that the situation is similar today: within the Christian church many diverse *personal responses* to the story of Jesus Christ are acceptable for us as well, and that would certainly include the response that sees Christ as a man in whom God was uniquely at work but not by any means a man who was also fully God.[31]

From the standpoint of evangelical theology, it is significant to note that this forthright rejection of Jesus' deity could only be advocated upon a prior assumption that the New Testament is not to be accepted as an absolute divine authority for us, truthful at every point. This question of authority is, in many cases, the great dividing line in conclusions about the person of Christ. Second, much of the criticism of the doctrine of the incarnation focused on the claim that it was not "coherent" or "intelligible." Yet at root this is simply an indication that the authors are unwilling to accept anything that does not appear to fit in with their "scientific" worldview in which the natural universe is a closed system not open to such divine intrusions as miracles and the incarnation. The assertion that "Jesus was fully God and fully man in one person," though not a contradiction, is a paradox that we cannot fully understand in this age and perhaps not for all eternity, but this does not give us the right to label it "incoherent" or "unintelligible." The doctrine of the incarnation as understood by the church throughout history has indeed been coherent and intelligible, though no one maintains that it provides us with an exhaustive explanation of how Jesus is both fully God and fully man. Our proper response is not to reject the clear and central teaching of Scripture about the incarnation, but simply to recognize that it will remain a paradox, that this is all that God has chosen to reveal to us about it, and that it is true. If we are to submit ourselves to God and to his words in Scripture, then we must believe it.

**6. Why Was Jesus' Deity Necessary?** In the previous section we listed several reasons why it was necessary for Jesus to be fully man in order to earn our redemption. Here it is appropriate to recognize that it is crucially important to insist on the full deity of Christ as well, not only because it is clearly taught in Scripture, but also because (1) only someone who is infinite God could bear the full penalty for all the sins of all those who would believe in him—any finite creature would have been incapable of bearing that penalty; (2) salvation is from the Lord (Jonah 2:9 NASB), and the whole message of Scripture is designed to show that no human being, no creature, could ever save man—only God himself could; and (3) only someone who was truly and fully God could be the one mediator between God and man (1 Tim. 2:5), both to bring us back to God and also to reveal God most fully to us (John 14:9).

---

[31]The book was quickly answered by another series of essays, *The Truth of God Incarnate*, ed. Michael Green (Sevenoaks, Kent, U.K.: Hodder and Stoughton, and Grand Rapids: Eerdmans, 1977). Later the authors of *The Myth of God Incarnate* and several of their critics published the proceedings of a three-day meeting in a third book: Michael Golder, ed., *Incarnation and Myth: The Debate Continued* (London: SCM, 1979).

Thus, if Jesus is not fully God, we have no salvation and ultimately no Christianity. It is no accident that throughout history those groups that have given up belief in the full deity of Christ have not remained long within the Christian faith but have soon drifted toward the kind of religion represented by Unitarianism in the United States and elsewhere. "No one who denies the Son has the Father" (1 John 2:23). "Any one who goes ahead and does not abide in the doctrine of Christ does not have God; he who abides in the doctrine has both the Father and the Son" (2 John 9).

## C. The Incarnation: Deity and Humanity in the One Person of Christ

The biblical teaching about the full deity and full humanity of Christ is so extensive that both have been believed from the earliest times in the history of the church. But a precise understanding of how full deity and full humanity could be combined together in one person was formulated only gradually in the church and did not reach the final form until the Chalcedonian Definition in A.D. 451. Before that point, several inadequate views of the person of Christ were proposed and then rejected. One view, Arianism, which held that Jesus was not fully divine, was discussed above in the chapter on the doctrine of the Trinity.[32] But three other views that were eventually rejected as heretical should be mentioned at this point.

### 1. Three Inadequate Views of the Person of Christ.

**a. Apollinarianism:** Apollinaris, who became bishop in Laodicea about A.D. 361, taught that the one person of Christ had a human body but not a human mind or spirit, and that the mind and spirit of Christ were from the divine nature of the Son of God. This view may be represented as in figure 26.1.

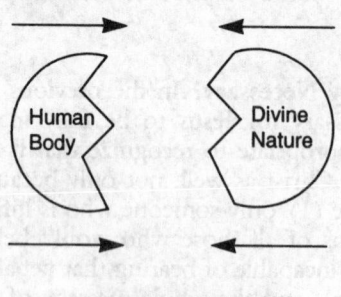

APOLLINARIANISM
Figure 26.1

But the views of Apollinaris were rejected by the leaders of the church at that time, who realized that it was not just our human body that needed salvation and needed to be represented by Christ in his redemptive work, but our human minds and spirits (or souls) as well: Christ had to be fully and truly man if he was to save

---

[32]See the discussion of Arianism in chapter 14, pp. 243–48.

us (Heb. 2:17). Apollinarianism was rejected by several church councils, from the Council of Alexandria in A.D. 362 to the Council of Constantinople in A.D. 381.

**b. Nestorianism:** Nestorianism is the doctrine that there were two separate persons in Christ, a human person and a divine person, a teaching that is distinct from the biblical view that sees Jesus as one person. Nestorianism may be diagramed as in figure 26.2.

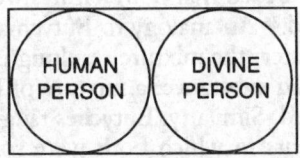

**NESTORIANISM**
*Figure 26.2*

Nestorius was a popular preacher at Antioch, and from A.D. 428 was bishop of Constantinople. Although Nestorius himself probably never taught the heretical view that goes by his name (the idea that Christ was two persons in one body, rather than one person), through a combination of several personal conflicts and a good deal of ecclesiastical politics, he was removed from his office of bishop and his teachings were condemned.[33]

It is important to understand why the church could not accept the view that Christ was two distinct persons. Nowhere in Scripture do we have an indication that the human nature of Christ, for example, is an independent person, deciding to do something contrary to the divine nature of Christ. Nowhere do we have an indication of the human and divine natures talking to each other or struggling within Christ, or any such thing. Rather, we have a consistent picture of a single person acting in wholeness and unity. Jesus always speaks as "I," not as "we,"[34] though he can refer to himself and the Father together as "we" (John 14:23). The Bible always speaks of Jesus as "he," not as "they." And, though we can sometimes distinguish actions of his divine nature and actions of his human nature in order to help us understand some of the statements and actions recorded in Scripture, the Bible itself does not say "Jesus' human nature did this" or "Jesus' divine nature did that," as though they were separate persons, but always talks about what the *person* of Christ did. Therefore, the church continued to insist that Jesus was one person, although possessing both a human nature and a divine nature.

---

[33]Harold O. J. Brown says, "Nestorius' incarnate person was a single person, not two as his critics thought, but he could not convince others that it was so. Consequently he has gone down in history as a great heretic although what he actually believed was reaffirmed at Chalcedon" (*Heresies*, p. 176). Brown's extensive discussion of Nestorianism and related issues on pp. 172–84 is very helpful.

[34]There is an unusual usage in John 3:11, where Jesus suddenly shifts to the plural, "Truly, truly, I say to you, *we* speak of what we know, and bear witness to what we have seen." Jesus may have been referring to himself and some disciples with him who are not mentioned, in contrast with the "we" of the Jewish rulers that Nicodemus alluded to when he opened the conversation: "Rabbi, *we* know that you are a teacher come from God" (John 3:2). Or Jesus may have been speaking of himself together with the witness of the Holy Spirit, whose work is the subject of the conversation (vv. 5–9). In any case, Jesus is not referring to himself as "we," but calls himself "I" in that very sentence. See discussion in Leon Morris, *The Gospel According to John*, pp. 221–22.

**c. Monophysitism (Eutychianism):** A third inadequate view is called *monophysitism,* the view that Christ had one nature only (Gk. *monos,* "one," and *physis,* "nature"). The primary advocate of this view in the early church was Eutyches (c. A.D. 378–454), who was the leader of a monastery at Constantinople. Eutyches taught the opposite error from Nestorianism, for he denied that the human nature and divine nature in Christ remained fully human and fully divine. He held rather that the human nature of Christ was taken up and absorbed into the divine nature, so that both natures were changed somewhat and *a third kind of nature* resulted.[35] An analogy to Eutychianism can be seen if we put a drop of ink in a glass of water: the mixture resulting is neither pure ink nor pure water, but some kind of third substance, a mixture of the two in which both the ink and the water are changed. Similarly, Eutyches taught that Jesus was a mixture of divine and human elements in which both were somewhat modified to form one new nature. This may be represented as in figure 26.3.

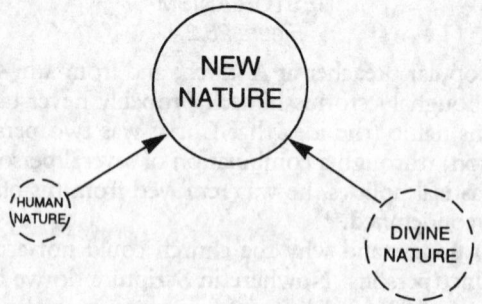

**EUTYCHIANISM**
*Figure 26.3*

Monophysitism also rightly caused great concern in the church, because, by this doctrine, Christ was neither truly God nor truly man. And if that was so, he could not truly represent us as a man nor could he be true God and able to earn our salvation.

**2. The Solution to the Controversy: The Chalcedonian Definition of A.D. 451.** In order to attempt to solve the problems raised by the controversies over the person of Christ, a large church council was convened in the city of Chalcedon near Constantinople (modern Istanbul), from October 8 to November 1, A.D. 451. The resulting statement, called the Chalcedonian Definition, guarded against Apollinarianism, Nestorianism, and Eutychianism. It has been taken as the standard, orthodox definition of the biblical teaching on the person of Christ since that day by Catholic, Protestant, and Orthodox branches of Christianity alike.[36]

---

[35]A variant form of Eutychianism held that the human nature was simply lost in the divine, so that the resulting single nature was the divine nature only.

[36]However, it should be noted that three localized groups of ancient churches rejected the Chalcedonian definition and still endorse monophysitism to this day: the Ethiopian Orthodox church, the Coptic Orthodox church (in Egypt), and the Syrian Jacobite church. See H. D. McDonald, "Monophysitism," in *NDT,* pp. 442–43.

The statement is not long, and we may quote it in its entirety:[37]

We, then, following the holy Fathers, all with one consent, teach men to confess one and the same Son, our Lord Jesus Christ, the same perfect in Godhead and also perfect in manhood; truly God and truly man, of a reasonable [rational] soul and body; *consubstantial [coessential] with the Father according to the Godhead, and consubstantial with us according to the Manhood;* in all things like unto us, without sin; begotten before all ages of the Father according to the Godhead, and in these latter days, for us and for our salvation, born of the Virgin Mary, the Mother of God, according to the Manhood; one and the same Christ, Son, Lord, Only-begotten, to be acknowledged in *two natures, inconfusedly, unchangeably, indivisibly, inseparably;* the distinction of natures being by no means taken away by the union, but rather *the property of each nature being preserved,* and concurring in *one Person* and one Subsistence, not parted or divided into two persons, but one and the same Son, and only begotten, God, the Word, the Lord Jesus Christ, as the prophets from the beginning [have declared] concerning him, and the Lord Jesus Christ himself has taught us, and the Creed of the holy Fathers has been handed down to us.

Against the view of Apollinaris that Christ did not have a human mind or soul, we have the statement that he was *"truly man,* of a *reasonable soul* and body . . . *consubstantial with us* according to the Manhood; in all things like unto us." (The word *consubstantial* means "having the same nature or substance.")

In opposition to the view of Nestorianism that Christ was two persons united in one body, we have the words *"indivisibly, inseparably* . . . concurring in *one Person* and one Subsistence, not parted or divided into two persons."

Against the view of Monophysitism that Christ had only one nature, and that his human nature was lost in the union with the divine nature, we have the words "to be acknowledged in *two natures, inconfusedly, unchangeably* . . . the distinction of natures being by no means taken away by the union, but rather *the property of each nature being preserved."* The human and the divine natures were not confused or changed when Christ became man, but the human nature remained a truly human nature, and the divine nature remained a truly divine nature.

Figure 26.4 may be helpful in showing this, in contrast to the earlier diagrams. It indicates that the eternal Son of God took to himself a truly human nature, and that Christ's divine and human natures remain distinct and retain their own properties, yet they are eternally and inseparably united together in one person.

Some have said that the Chalcedonian Definition really did not define for us in any positive way what the person of Christ actually *is,* but simply told us several things that it *is not.* In this way some have said that it is not a very helpful definition. But such an accusation is misleading and inaccurate. The definition actually did a great deal to help us understand the biblical teaching correctly. It taught that Christ definitely has two natures, a human nature and a divine nature. It taught that his divine nature is exactly the same as that of the Father ("consubstantial with the Father according to the Godhead"). And it maintained that the human nature is exactly like our human nature, yet without sin ("consubstantial with us according to the Manhood; in all things like unto us, without sin"). Moreover, it affirmed that in the person of Christ the human nature retains its distinctive characteristics and the divine nature retains its distinctive

---

[37]English translation taken from Philip Schaff, *Creeds of Christendom,* 2:62–63.

characteristics ("the distinction of natures being by no means taken away by the union, but rather *the property of each nature being preserved*"). Finally, it affirmed that, whether we can understand it or not, these two natures are united together in the one person of Christ.

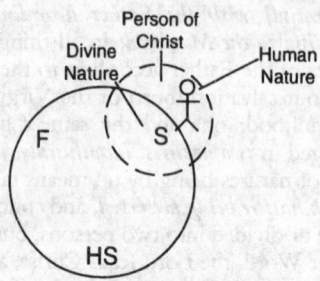

**CHALCEDONIAN CHRISTOLOGY**
*Figure 26.4*

When the Chalcedonian Definition says that the two natures of Christ occur together "in one Person and one *Subsistence*," the Greek word translated as "Subsistence" is the word *hypostasis*, "being." Hence the union of Christ's human and divine natures in one person is sometimes called the *hypostatic union*. This phrase simply means the union of Christ's human and divine natures in one being.

**3. Combining Specific Biblical Texts on Christ's Deity and Humanity.** When we examine the New Testament, as we did above in the sections on Jesus' humanity and deity, there are several passages that seem difficult to fit together (How could Jesus be omnipotent and yet weak? How could he leave the world and yet be present everywhere? How could he learn things and yet be omniscient?). As the church struggled to understand these teachings, it finally came up with the Chalcedonian Definition, which spoke of two distinct natures in Christ that retain their own properties yet remain together in one person. This distinction, which helps us in our understanding of the biblical passages mentioned earlier, also seems to be demanded by those passages.

**a. One Nature Does Some Things That the Other Nature Does Not Do:** Evangelical theologians in previous generations have not hesitated to distinguish between things done by Christ's human nature but not by his divine nature, or by his divine nature but not by his human nature. It seems that we have to do this if we are willing to affirm the Chalcedonian statement about "the *property of each nature* being preserved." But few recent theologians have been willing to make such distinctions, perhaps because of a hesitancy to affirm something we cannot understand.

When we are talking about Jesus' human nature, we can say that he ascended to heaven and is no longer in the world (John 16:28; 17:11; Acts 1:9–11).[38] But

---

[38]Lutheran theologians, following Martin Luther, have sometimes claimed that Jesus' human nature, even his human body, is also everywhere present or "ubiquitous." But this position has not been

with respect to his divine nature, we can say that Jesus is everywhere present: "Where two or three are gathered in my name, *there am I* in the midst of them" (Matt. 18:20); "I am with you always, to the close of the age" (Matt. 28:20); "If a man loves me, he will keep my word, and my Father will love him, and *we* will come to him and make our home with him" (John 14:23). So we can say that both things are true about the *person* of Christ—he has returned to heaven, *and* he is also present with us.

Similarly, we can say that Jesus was about thirty years old (Luke 3:23), if we are speaking with respect to his human nature, but we can say that he eternally existed (John 1:1–2; 8:58) if we are speaking of his divine nature.

In his human nature, Jesus was weak and tired (Matt. 4:2; 8:24; Mark 15:21; John 4:6), but in his divine nature he was omnipotent (Matt. 8:26–27; Col. 1:17; Heb. 1:3). Particularly striking is the scene on the Sea of Galilee where Jesus was asleep in the stern of the boat, presumably because he was weary (Matt. 8:24). But he was able to arise from his sleep and calm the wind and sea with a word (Matt. 8:26–27)! Tired yet omnipotent! Here Jesus' weak human nature completely hid his omnipotence until that omnipotence broke forth in a sovereign word from the Lord of heaven and earth.

If someone asks whether Jesus, when he was asleep in the boat, was also "continually carrying along all things by his word of power" (Heb. 1:3, author's translation), and whether all things in the universe were being held together by him at that time (see Col. 1:17), the answer must be yes, for those activities have always been and will always be the particular responsibility of the second person of the Trinity, the eternal Son of God. Those who find the doctrine of the incarnation "inconceivable" have sometimes asked whether Jesus, when he was a baby in the manger at Bethlehem, was also "upholding the universe." To this question the answer must also be yes: Jesus was not just potentially God or someone in whom God uniquely worked, but was *truly and fully God,* with all the attributes of God. He was "a Savior, who is Christ *the Lord*" (Luke 2:11). Those who reject this as impossible simply have a different definition of what is "possible" than God has, as revealed in Scripture.[39] To say that we cannot

---

adopted by any other segment of the Christian church, and it seems to have been a position that Luther himself took mainly in an attempt to justify his view that Christ's body was actually present in the Lord's Supper (not in the elements themselves, but with them).

[39]A. N. S. Lane explicitly denies the Chalcedonian view of Christ on the ground that it cannot be: "Omniscience and ignorance, omnipotence and impotence cannot coexist. The former swamps the latter" ("Christology Beyond Chalcedon," in *Christ the Lord: Studies in Christology Presented to Donald Guthrie,* edited by Harold H. Rowden (Leicester and Downers Grove, Ill.: InterVarsity Press, 1982), p. 270. He says that Christ "explicitly denied his omniscience (Mt. 24:36 = Mk. 13:32) but even the clear words of Christ have not sufficed to counter the pull of docetism. . . . The affirmation of the omniscience of the historical Jesus has no biblical basis and indeed runs counter to the clear teaching of the Gospels. . . . It has serious theological implications in that it undermines his true humanity as taught in Scripture" (p. 271).

But (see pp. 560–63, below) Matt. 24:36 and Mark 13:32 are certainly capable of being understood to refer to Jesus' knowledge in his human nature. And when Lane says that omniscience and ignorance "cannot coexist" he is simply pitting one part of a biblical paradox against another and then asserting that one part is impossible. On what grounds are we justified in saying that an omniscient divine nature and a human nature with limited knowledge "cannot coexist,"? Or that an omnipotent divine nature and a weak human nature "cannot coexist"? Such assertions fundamentally deny that infinite deity and finite humanity can exist together in the same person—in other words,

understand this is appropriate humility. But to say that it is not possible seems more like intellectual arrogance.

In a similar way, we can understand that in his human nature, Jesus died (Luke 23:46; 1 Cor. 15:3). But with respect to his divine nature, he did not die, but was able to raise himself from the dead (John 2:19; 10:17–18; Heb. 7:16). Yet here we must give a note of caution: it is true that when Jesus died his physical body died and his human soul (or spirit) was separated from his body and passed into the presence of God the Father in heaven (Luke 23:43, 46). In this way he experienced a death that is like the one we as believers experience if we die before Christ returns. And it is not correct to say that Jesus' divine nature died, or could die, if "die" means a cessation of activity, a cessation of consciousness, or a diminution of power. Nevertheless, by virtue of union with Jesus' human nature, his divine nature somehow tasted something of what it was like to go through death. The *person* of Christ experienced death. Moreover, it seems difficult to understand how Jesus' human nature alone could have borne the wrath of God against the sins of millions of people. It seems that Jesus' divine nature had somehow to participate in the bearing of wrath against sin that was due to us (though Scripture nowhere explicitly affirms this). Therefore, even though Jesus' divine nature did not actually die, Jesus went through the experience of death as a whole person, and both human and divine natures somehow shared in that experience. Beyond that, Scripture does not enable us to say more.

The distinction between Jesus' human and divine natures also helps us understand Jesus' temptations. With respect to his human nature, he certainly was tempted in every way as we are, yet without sin (Heb. 4:15). Yet with respect to his divine nature, he was not tempted, because God cannot be tempted with evil (James 1:13).

At this point it seems necessary to say that Jesus had two distinct wills, a human will and a divine will, and that the wills belong to the two distinct natures of Christ, not to the person. In fact, there was a position, called the *monothelite* view, which held that Jesus had only "one will," but that was certainly a minority view in the church, and it was rejected as heretical at a church council in Constantinople in A.D. 681. Since then the view that Christ had two wills (a human will and a divine will) has been generally, but not universally, held through the church. In fact, Charles Hodge says:

> The decision against Nestorius, in which the unity of Christ's person was asserted; that against Eutyches, affirming the distinction of natures; and that against the Monothelites, declaring that the possession of a human nature involves of necessity the possession of a human will, have been received as the true faith by the Church universal, the Greek, Latin, and Protestant.[40]

Hodge explains that the church thought that "to deny Christ a human will, was to deny he had a human nature, or was truly a man. Besides, it precluded the possibility of his having been tempted, and therefore contradicted the Scriptures, and separated him so far from his people he could not sympathize with them in

---

they deny that Jesus could be *fully* God and *fully* man at the same time. In this way, they deny the essence of the incarnation.

[40]Charles Hodge, *Systematic Theology*, 2:405.

their temptations."[41] Moreover, Hodge notes that along with the idea that Christ had two wills is the related idea that he had two centers of consciousness or intelligence: "As there are two distinct natures, human and divine, there are of necessity two intelligences and two wills, the one fallible and finite, the other immutable and infinite."[42]

This distinction of two wills and two centers of consciousness helps us understand how Jesus could learn things and yet know all things. On the one hand, with respect to his human nature, he had limited knowledge (Mark 13:32; Luke 2:52). On the other hand, Jesus clearly knew all things (John 2:25; 16:30; 21:17). Now this is only understandable if Jesus learned things and had limited knowledge with respect to his human nature but was always omniscient with respect to his divine nature, and therefore he was able any time to "call to mind" whatever information would be needed for his ministry. In this way we can understand Jesus' statement concerning the time of his return: "But of that day or that hour no one knows, not even the angels in heaven, nor the Son, but only the Father" (Mark 13:32). This ignorance of the time of his return was true of Jesus' human nature and human consciousness only, for in his divine nature he was certainly omniscient and certainly knew the time when he would return to the earth.[43]

At this point someone may object that if we say that Jesus had two centers of consciousness and two wills, that *requires* that he was two distinct persons, and we have really fallen into the error of "Nestorianism." But in response, it must simply be affirmed that two wills and two centers of consciousness *do not* require that Jesus be two distinct persons. It is mere assertion without proof to say that they do. If someone responds that he or she *does not understand* how Jesus could have two centers of consciousness and still be one person, then that fact may certainly be admitted by all. But failing to understand something does not mean that it is impossible, only that our understanding is limited. The great majority of the church throughout its history has said that Jesus had two wills and centers of consciousness, yet he remained one person. Such a formulation is not impossible, merely a mystery that we do not now fully understand. To adopt any other solution would create a far greater problem: it would require that we give up either the full deity or the full humanity of Christ, and that we cannot do.[44]

---

[41]Ibid., pp. 404–5.

[42]Ibid., p. 405.

[43]In commenting on Mark 13:32, John Calvin, H. B. Swete, an Anglican commentator (*The Gospel According to St. Mark* [London: Macmillan, 1913], p. 316), and R. C. H. Lenski, a Lutheran commentator (*The Interpretation of St. Mark's Gospel* [Minneapolis: Augsburg, 1961 (reprint)], p. 590), all attribute this ignorance of Jesus to his human nature only, not to his divine nature.

[44]At this point an analogy from our human experience may be somewhat helpful. Anyone who has run in a race knows that near the end of the race there are conflicting desires within. On the one hand, the runner's lungs and legs and arms seem to be crying out, "Stop! Stop!" There is a clear desire to stop because of the physical pain. On the other hand, something in the runner's mind says, "Go on! Go on! I want to win!" We have all known similar instances of conflicting desires within. Now if we, being ordinary human beings, can have differing or distinct desires within us and yet be one person, how much more possible is that for one who was both man and God at the same time? If we say we do not understand how that could be, we simply admit our ignorance of the situation, for none of us has ever experienced what it is like to be both God and man at the same time, nor will we ever have such an experience ourselves. We should not say it is impossible, but, if we are convinced that New Testament texts lead us to this conclusion, we should accept it and agree with it.

**b. Anything Either Nature Does, the Person of Christ Does:** In the previous section we mentioned a number of things that were done by one nature but not the other in the person of Christ. Now we must affirm that anything that is true of the human or the divine nature is true of the person of Christ. Thus Jesus can say, "Before Abraham was, I am" (John 8:58). He does not say, "Before Abraham was, my divine nature existed," because he is free to talk about anything done by his divine nature alone or his human nature alone as something that *he* did.

In the human sphere, this is certainly true of our conversation as well. If I type a letter, even though my feet and toes had nothing to do with typing the letter, I do not tell people, "My fingers typed a letter and my toes had nothing to do with it" (though that is true). Rather, I tell people, "*I* typed a letter." That is true because anything that is done by one part of me is done by *me*.

Thus, "*Christ* died for our sins" (1 Cor. 15:3). Even though actually only his human body ceased living and ceased functioning, it was nonetheless *Christ* as a person who died for our sin. This is simply a means of affirming that whatever can be said of one nature or the other can be said of the *person* of Christ.

Therefore it is correct for Jesus to say, "I am leaving the world" (John 16:28), or "I am no more in the world" (John 17:11), but at the same time to say, "I am with you always" (Matt. 28:20). Anything that is done by one nature or the other is done by the *person* of Christ.

**c. Titles That Remind Us One Nature Can Be Used of the Person Even When the Action Is Done By the Other Nature:** The New Testament authors sometimes use titles that remind us of either the human nature or the divine nature in order to speak of the person of Christ, even though the action mentioned may be done only by the other nature than the one we might think of from the title. For example, Paul says that if the rulers of this world had understood the wisdom of God, "they would not have crucified *the Lord of glory*" (1 Cor. 2:8). Now when we see the phrase "the Lord of glory" it reminds us specifically of Jesus' divine nature. But Paul uses this title (probably intentionally to show the horrible evil of the crucifixion) to say that Jesus was "crucified." Even though Jesus' divine nature was not crucified, it was true of Jesus as a *person* that he was crucified, and Paul affirms that about him even though he uses the title "the Lord of glory."

Similarly, when Elizabeth calls Mary "the mother of *my Lord*" (Luke 1:43), the name "my Lord" is a title that reminds us of Christ's divine nature. Yet Mary of course is not the mother of Jesus' divine nature, which has always existed. Mary is simply the mother of the human nature of Christ. Nevertheless, Elizabeth can call her "the mother of my Lord" because she is using the title "Lord" to refer to the person of Christ. A similar expression occurs in Luke 2:11: "For to you *is born* this day in the city of David a Savior, who is Christ *the Lord*."

In this way, we can understand Mark 13:32, where Jesus says no one knows the time of his return, "not even the angels in heaven, *nor the Son*, but only the Father." Though the term "the Son" specifically reminds us of Jesus' heavenly, eternal sonship with God the Father, it is really used here not to speak specifically of his divine nature, but to speak generally of him as a person, and to affirm something that is in fact true of his human nature only.[45] And it is true that in one important sense (that is, with respect to his human nature) Jesus did not know the time when he would return.

**d. Brief Summary Sentence:** Sometimes in the study of systematic theology, the following sentence has been used to summarize the incarnation: "Remaining what he was, he became what he was not." In other words, while Jesus continued "remaining" what he was (that is, fully divine) he also became what he previously had not been (that is, fully human as well). Jesus did not give up any of his deity when he became man, but he did take on humanity that was not his before.

**e. "Communication" of Attributes:** Once we have decided that Jesus was fully man and fully God, and that his human nature remained *fully* human and his divine nature remained *fully* divine, we can still ask whether there were some qualities or abilities that were given (or "communicated") from one nature to the other. It seems there were.

**(1) From the Divine Nature to the Human Nature**

Although Jesus' human nature did not change its essential character, because it was united with the divine nature in the one person of Christ, Jesus' human nature gained (a) a worthiness to be worshiped and (b) an inability to sin, both of which did not belong to human beings otherwise.[46]

**(2) From the Human Nature to the Divine Nature**

Jesus' human nature gave him (a) an ability to experience suffering and death; (b) an ability to understand by experience what we are experiencing; and (c) an ability to be our substitute sacrifice, which Jesus as God alone could not have done.

**f. Conclusion:** At the end of this long discussion, it may be easy for us to lose sight of what is actually taught in Scripture. It is by far the most amazing miracle of the entire Bible—far more amazing than the resurrection and more amazing even than the creation of the universe. The fact that the infinite, omnipotent, eternal Son of God could become man and join himself to a human nature forever, so that infinite God became one person with finite man, will remain for eternity the most profound miracle and the most profound mystery in all the universe.

---

[45]Similar usage is perhaps seen in John 3:13 and Acts 20:28 (in this latter verse some manuscripts read "with his own blood").

[46]See above, p. 558, note 38, on the Lutheran view that ubiquity was also communicated from the divine nature to the human.

## QUESTIONS FOR PERSONAL APPLICATION

1. After reading this chapter, are there specific ways in which you now think of Jesus as being more like you than you did before? What are these? How can a clearer understanding of Jesus' humanity help you face temptations? How can it help you to pray? What are the most difficult situations in your life right now? Can you think of any similar situations that Jesus might have faced? Does that encourage you to pray confidently to him? Can you picture what it would have been like if you had been present when Jesus said, "Before Abraham was, I am"? What would you have felt? Honestly, what would your response have been? Now try visualizing yourself as present when Jesus made some of the other "I am" statements recorded in John's gospel.[47]

2. After reading this chapter, is there anything that you understand more fully about the deity of Jesus? Can you describe (and perhaps identify with) what the disciples must have felt as they came to a growing realization of who Jesus actually was? Do you think Jesus is the one person you would be able to trust with your life for all eternity? Will you be happy to join with thousands of others in worshiping around his throne in heaven? Do you delight in worshiping him now?

## SPECIAL TERMS

| | |
|---|---|
| Apollinarianism | kenosis theory |
| Arianism | Logos |
| Chalcedonian Definition | Lord |
| communication of attributes | monophysitism |
| docetism | monothelite view |
| Eutychianism | Nestorianism |
| God | Son of God |
| hypostatic union | Son of Man |
| impeccability | virgin birth |
| incarnation | |

## BIBLIOGRAPHY

(For an explanation of this bibliography see the note on the bibliography to chapter 1, p. 38. Complete bibliographical data may be found on pp. 1223–29.)

### Sections in Evangelical Systematic Theologies

1. Anglican (Episcopalian)
   - 1882–92    Litton, 178–218
   - 1930    Thomas, 32–49, 223–28
2. Arminian (Wesleyan or Methodist)
   - 1875–76    Pope, 2:106–51, 188–96, 254–62

---

[47]See the list of "I am" statements at p. 546, note 21, above.

                1892–94    Miley, 2:4–62
                  1940    Wiley, 2:143–86
                  1960    Purkiser, 164–82
                  1983    Carter, 1:331–74
                1987–90    Oden, 2:1–314, 527–42
3. Baptist
                  1767    Gill, 1:537–69
                  1887    Boyce, 258–91
                  1907    Strong, 669–700
                  1917    Mullins, 154–202
                1976–83    Henry, 3:9–215
                1983–85    Erickson, 661–758
                1987–94    Lewis/Demarest, 2:251–370
4. Dispensational
                  1947    Chafer, 1:318–96; 5:3–176
                  1949    Thiessen, 206–28
                  1986    Ryrie, 235–53, 260–66
5. Lutheran
                1917–24    Pieper, 2:55–279
                  1934    Mueller, 255–86
6. Reformed (or Presbyterian)
                  1559    Calvin, 1:423–94 (2.9–14)
                1724–58    Edwards, 2:499–510, 949–55
                  1861    Heppe, 410–47
                1871–73    Hodge, 1:483–521; 2:378–454
                  1878    Dabney, 464–99
                1887–1921  Warfield, *BTS*, 157–237; *SSW*, 1:139–66; *BD*, 71–100,
                           175–212; *PWC*, 4–319; *LG*, 1–304; *CC*, 3–389, 447–58
                  1889    Shedd, 2a:261–349; 3:378–400
                1937–66    Murray, *CW*, 1:29–35, 340–43; *CW*, 2:132–41; *CW*,
                           4:58–91
                  1938    Berkhof, 305–30
                  1962    Buswell, 2:17–32, 40–70
7. Renewal (or charismatic/Pentecostal)
                1988–92    Williams, 1:305–52

## Sections in Representative Roman Catholic Systematic Theologies

1. Roman Catholic: Traditional
                  1955    Ott, 125–75
2. Roman Catholic: Post-Vatican II
                  1980    McBrien, 1:267–546

## Other Works

Anselm. "The Incarnation of the Word." In *Anselm of Canterbury*. Vol. 3. Toronto: Edwin Mellen, 1976.

————. *Why God Became Man: and The Virgin Conception and Original Sin*. Trans. by Joseph M. Colleran. Albany, N.Y.: Magi, 1969.

Athanasius. *On the Incarnation*. Translated by a religious of C.S.M.V. New York: Macmillan, 1946.

Berkouwer, G. C. *The Person of Christ*. Trans. by John Vriend. Grand Rapids: Eerdmans, 1954.

Bray, G. L. *Creeds, Councils and Christ*. Leicester: Inter-Varsity Press, 1984.

————. "Christology." In *NDT*, pp. 137–40.

Brown, Harold O. J. *Heresies: The Image of Christ in the Mirror of Heresy and Orthodoxy From the Apostles to the Present*. Garden City, N.Y.: Doubleday, 1984.

Bruce, F. F. *Jesus: Lord and Savior*. The Jesus Library, ed. by Michael Green. Downers Grove, Ill.: InterVarsity Press, 1986.

Erickson, Millard. *The Word Became Flesh: A Contemporary Incarnational Christology*. Grand Rapids: Baker, 1991.

Guthrie, Donald. *Jesus the Messiah*. Grand Rapids: Zondervan, 1972.

————. *New Testament Theology*. Leicester and Downers Grove, Ill.: InterVarsity Press, 1981, pp. 219–365.

Harris, Murray J. *Jesus As God*. Grand Rapids: Baker, 1992.

Hughes, Philip Edgcumbe. *The True Image: The Origin and Destiny of Man in Christ*. Grand Rapids: Eerdmans, and Leicester: Inter-Varsity Press, 1989, pp. 211–414.

Longenecker, Richard. *The Christology of Early Jewish Christianity*. London: SCM, 1970.

Marshall, I. Howard. *I Believe in the Historical Jesus*. Grand Rapids: Eerdmans, 1977.

McGrath, Alister E. *Understanding Jesus: Who He Is and Why He Matters*. Grand Rapids: Zondervan, 1987.

Moule, C. F. D. *The Origin of Christology*. Cambridge: Cambridge University Press, 1977.

Payne, Philip B. "Jesus' Implicit Claim to Deity in His Parables." *TrinJ*, vol. 2, n.s., no. 1 (Spring 1981), pp. 3–23.

Reymond, Robert L. *Jesus, Divine Messiah*. Phillipsburg, N.J.: Presbyterian and Reformed, 1990.

Runia, Klaas. *The Present-Day Christological Debate*. Leicester: Inter-Varsity Press, 1984.

Sproul, R. C. *The Glory of Christ*. Wheaton, Ill.: Tyndale, 1990.

Stein, R. H. "Jesus Christ." In *EDT*, pp. 582–85.

Wallace, R. S. "Christology." In *EDT*, pp. 221–27.

Walvoord, John F. *Jesus Christ Our Lord*. Chicago: Moody, 1969.

Wells, David F. *The Person of Christ: A Biblical and Historical Analysis of the Incarnation*. Westchester, Ill.: Crossway, 1984.

## SCRIPTURE MEMORY PASSAGE

**John 1:14:** *And the Word became flesh and dwelt among us, full of grace and truth; we have beheld his glory, glory as of the only Son from the Father.*

## HYMN

### "Fairest Lord Jesus"

Fairest Lord Jesus, ruler of all nature,
Son of God and Son of Man!
Thee will I cherish, thee will I honor,
Thou, my soul's glory, joy, and crown.

Fair are the meadows, fair are the woodlands,
Robed in the blooming garb of spring:
Jesus is fairer, Jesus is purer,
Who makes the woeful heart to sing.

Fair is the sunshine, fair is the moonlight,
And all the twinkling, starry host:
Jesus shines brighter, Jesus shines purer
Than all the angels heav'n can boast.

Beautiful Savior! Lord of the nations!
Son of God and Son of Man!
Glory and honor, praise, adoration,
Now and forever more be thine.

FROM *MÜNSTER GESANGBUCH*, 1677, TRANSLATED 1850, 1873

# Chapter 27

# The Atonement

*Was it necessary for Christ to die? Did Christ's*
*entire earthly life earn any saving benefits*
*for us? The cause and nature of the atonement.*
*Did Christ descend into hell?*

## EXPLANATION AND SCRIPTURAL BASIS

We may define the atonement as follows: *The atonement is the work Christ did in his life and death to earn our salvation.* This definition indicates that we are using the word *atonement* in a broader sense than it is sometimes used. Sometimes it is used to refer only to Jesus' dying and paying for our sins on the cross. But, as will be seen below, since saving benefits also come to us from Christ's life, we have included that in our definition as well.[1]

### A. The Cause of the Atonement

What was the ultimate cause that led to Christ's coming to earth and dying for our sins? To find this we must trace the question back to something in the character of God himself. And here Scripture points to two things: the *love* and *justice* of God.

The love of God as a cause of the atonement is seen in the most familiar passage in the Bible: "For God *so loved the world* that he gave his only Son, that whoever believes in him should not perish but have eternal life" (John 3:16). But the justice of God also required that God find a way that the penalty due to us for our sins would be paid (for he could not accept us into fellowship with himself unless the penalty was paid). Paul explains that this was why God sent Christ to be a "propitiation" (Rom. 3:25 NASB) (that is, a sacrifice that bears God's wrath so that God becomes "propitious" or favorably disposed toward us): it was *"to show God's righteousness,* because in his divine forbearance he had passed over former sins" (Rom. 3:25). Here Paul says that God had been forgiving sins in the Old Testament but no penalty had been paid—a fact that would make people wonder whether God was indeed just and ask how he could forgive sins without a penalty. No God who was truly just could do that, could he? Yet when God sent Christ to

---

[1]Of course, there are also saving benefits that come to us from Christ's resurrection and ascension, from his continuing high priestly work of intercession for us, and from his second coming. These are discussed as separate topics in subsequent chapters of this book. For the sake of clarity, I have here included under the title "atonement" only those things that Christ did for our salvation during his earthly life and in his death.

568

die and pay the penalty for our sins, "it was to prove at the present time that he himself is righteous and that he justifies him who has faith in Jesus" (Rom. 3:26).

Therefore both the love and the justice of God were the ultimate cause of the atonement. It is not helpful for us to ask which is more important, however, because without the love of God, he would never have taken any steps to redeem us, yet without the justice of God, the specific requirement that Christ should earn our salvation by dying for our sins would not have been met. Both the love and the justice of God were equally important.

## B. The Necessity of the Atonement

Was there any other way for God to save human beings than by sending his Son to die in our place?

Before answering this question, it is important to realize that it was not necessary for God to save any people at all. When we appreciate that "God did not spare the angels when they sinned, but cast them into hell and committed them to pits of nether gloom to be kept until the judgment" (2 Peter 2:4), then we realize that God could also have chosen with perfect justice to have left us in our sins awaiting judgment: he could have chosen to save no one, just as he did with the sinful angels. So in this sense the atonement was not absolutely necessary.

But once God, in his love, decided to save some human beings, then several passages in Scripture indicate that there was no other way for God to do this than through the death of his Son. Therefore, the atonement was not absolutely necessary, but, as a "consequence" of God's decision to save some human beings, the atonement was absolutely necessary. This is sometimes called the "consequent absolute necessity" view of the atonement.

In the Garden of Gethsemane Jesus prays, *"If it be possible,* let this cup pass from me; nevertheless, not as I will, but as you will" (Matt. 26:39). We may be confident that Jesus always prayed according to the will of the Father, and that he always prayed with fullness of faith. Thus it seems that this prayer, which Matthew takes pains to record for us, shows that it was *not possible* for Jesus to avoid the death on the cross which was soon to come to him (the "cup" of suffering that he had said would be his). If he was going to accomplish the work that the Father sent him to do, and if people were going to be redeemed for God, then it was necessary for him to die on the cross.

He said something similar after his resurrection, when he was talking with two disciples on the road to Emmaus. They were sad that Jesus had died, but his response was, "O foolish men, and slow of heart to believe all that the prophets have spoken! Was it not *necessary* that the Christ should suffer these things and enter into his glory?" (Luke 24:25–26). Jesus understood that God's plan of redemption (which he explained for the disciples from many Old Testament Scriptures, Luke 24:27) made it necessary for the Messiah to die for the sins of his people.

As we saw above, Paul in Romans 3 also shows that if God were to be righteous, and still save people, he had to send Christ to pay the penalty for sins: "It was to prove at the present time that he himself is righteous and that he justifies him who has faith in Jesus" (Rom. 3:26). The epistle to the Hebrews emphasizes that Christ had to suffer for our sins: "He *had to* be made like his brethren in every respect, so that he might become a merciful and faithful high priest in the service of God, to make expiation [lit. 'propitiation'] for the sins of the people" (Heb. 2:17). The author of Hebrews also argues that since "it is impossible that the blood of bulls and goats should take away sins" (Heb. 10:4), a better sacrifice is required (Heb. 9:23). Only the blood of Christ, that is, his death, would be able really to take away sins (Heb. 9:25–26). There was no other way for God to save us than for Christ to die in our place.

## C. The Nature of the Atonement

In this section we consider two aspects of Christ's work: (1) Christ's obedience for us, in which he obeyed the requirements of the law in our place and was perfectly obedient to the will of God the Father as our representative, and (2) Christ's sufferings for us, in which he took the penalty due for our sins and as a result died for our sins.

It is important to notice that in both of these categories the primary emphasis and the primary influence of Christ's work of redemption is not on us, but on God the Father. Jesus obeyed the Father in our place and perfectly met the demands of the law. And he suffered in our place, receiving in himself the penalty that God the Father would have visited upon us. In both cases, the atonement is viewed as objective; that is, something that has primary influence directly on God himself. Only secondarily does it have application to us, and this is only because there was a definite event in the relationship between God the Father and God the Son that secured our salvation.

**1. Christ's Obedience for Us (Sometimes Called His "Active Obedience").** If Christ had only earned forgiveness of sins for us, then we would not merit heaven. Our guilt would have been removed, but we would simply be in the position of Adam and Eve before they had done anything good or bad and before they had passed a time of probation successfully. To be established in righteousness forever and to have their fellowship with God made sure forever, Adam and Eve had to obey God perfectly over a period of time. Then God would have looked on their faithful obedience with pleasure and delight, and they would have lived with him in fellowship forever.[2]

For this reason, Christ had to live a life of perfect obedience to God in order to earn righteousness for us. He had to obey the law for his whole life on our behalf so that the positive merits of his perfect obedience would be counted for us. Sometimes this is called Christ's "active obedience," while his suffering and dying for our sins is called his "passive obedience."[3] Paul says his goal is that he may be

---

[2]See discussion of the covenant of works in chapter 25, pp. 516–18.

[3]Some have objected that this "active" and "passive" terminology is not entirely satisfactory, because even in paying for our sins Christ was in one sense actively accepting the suffering given him by the Father and was even active in laying down his own life (John 10:18). Moreover, both aspects of Christ's obedience continued through his whole life: his active obedience included faithful obedience from birth up to and including the point of his death; and his suffering on our behalf, which found its climax in the crucifixion, continued through his whole life (see discussion below). Nevertheless, the distinction between active and passive obedience is still useful because it helps us appreciate the two aspects of Christ's work for us. (See the discussion in John Murray, *Redemption Accomplished and*

found in Christ, "*not having a righteousness of [his] own,* based on law, but *that which is through faith in Christ,* the righteousness from God that depends on faith" (Phil. 3:9). It is not just moral neutrality that Paul knows he needs from Christ (that is, a clean slate with sins forgiven), but a positive moral righteousness. And he knows that that cannot come from himself, but must come through faith in Christ. Similarly, Paul says that Christ has been made *"our righteousness"* (1 Cor. 1:30). And he quite explicitly says, "For as by one man's disobedience many were made sinners, so by one man's obedience many will be *made righteous*" (Rom. 5:19).

Some theologians have not taught that Christ needed to achieve a lifelong record of perfect obedience for us. They have simply emphasized that Christ had to die and thereby pay the penalty for our sins.[4] But such a position does not adequately explain why Christ did more than just die for us; he also became our "righteousness" before God. Jesus said to John the Baptist, before he was baptized by him, "It is fitting for us *to fulfil all righteousness*" (Matt. 3:15).

It might be argued that Christ had to live a life of perfect righteousness for his own sake, not for ours, before he could be a sinless sacrifice for us. But Jesus had no need to live a life of perfect obedience for his own sake—he had shared love and fellowship with the Father for all eternity and was in his own character eternally worthy of the Father's good pleasure and delight. He rather had to "fulfill all righteousness" for our sake; that is, for the sake of the people whom he was representing as their head. Unless he had done this for us, we would have no record of obedience by which we would merit God's favor and merit eternal life with him. Moreover, if Jesus had needed only sinlessness and not also a life of perfect obedience, he could have died for us when he was a young child rather than when he was thirty-three years old.

By way of application, we ought to ask ourselves whose lifelong record of obedience we would rather rely on for our standing before God, Christ's or our own? As we think about the life of Christ, we ought to ask ourselves, was it good enough to deserve God's approval? And are we willing to rely on his record of obedience for our eternal destiny?

**2. Christ's Sufferings for Us (Sometimes Called His "Passive Obedience").** In addition to obeying the law perfectly for his whole life on our behalf, Christ also took on himself the sufferings necessary to pay the penalty for our sins.

**a. Suffering for His Whole Life:** In a broad sense the penalty Christ bore in paying for our sins was suffering in both his body and soul throughout his life. Though Christ's sufferings culminated in his death on the cross (see below), his whole life in a fallen world involved suffering. For example, Jesus endured tremendous suffering during the temptation in the wilderness (Matt. 4:1–11), when he was assaulted for forty days by the attacks of Satan.[5] He also suffered in

*Applied* [Grand Rapids: Eerdmans, 1955], pp. 20–24.) R. L. Reymond prefers the terms *preceptive* (for active) and *penal* (for passive), in his article "Obedience of Christ," *EDT,* p. 785.

[4]For example, I could find no discussion of the active obedience of Christ in the seven-volume *Systematic Theology* by Lewis Sperry Chafer (Dallas: Dallas Seminary Press, 1947–48) or in Millard Erickson's *Christian Theology,* pp. 761–800.

[5]In Mark 1:13 the present participle *peirazomenos,* "being tempted," modifies the imperfect main

growing to maturity, "Although he was a Son, he learned obedience through what he *suffered*" (Heb. 5:8). He knew suffering in the intense opposition he faced from Jewish leaders throughout much of his earthly ministry (see Heb. 12:3–4). We may suppose too that he experienced suffering and grief at the death of his earthly father,[6] and certainly he experienced grief at the death of his close friend Lazarus (John 11:35). In predicting the coming of the Messiah, Isaiah said he would be "a *man of sorrows*, and acquainted with grief" (Isa. 53:3).

**b. The Pain of the Cross:** The sufferings of Jesus intensified as he drew near to the cross. He told his disciples of something of the agony he was going through when he said, "My soul is very sorrowful, even to death" (Matt. 26:38). It was especially on the cross that Jesus' sufferings for us reached their climax, for it was there that he bore the penalty for our sin and died in our place. Scripture teaches us that there were four different aspects of the pain that Jesus experienced:

**(1)Physical Pain and Death**

We do not need to hold that Jesus suffered more physical pain than any human being has ever suffered, for the Bible nowhere makes such a claim. But we still must not forget that death by crucifixion was one of the most horrible forms of execution ever devised by man.

Many readers of the Gospels in the ancient world would have witnessed crucifixions and thus would have had a painfully vivid mental picture upon reading the simple words "And they crucified him" (Mark 15:24). A criminal who was crucified was essentially forced to inflict upon himself a very slow death by suffocation. When the criminal's arms were outstretched and fastened by nails to the cross, he had to support most of the weight of his body with his arms. The chest cavity would be pulled upward and outward, making it difficult to exhale in order to be able to draw a fresh breath. But when the victim's longing for oxygen became unbearable, he would have to push himself up with his feet, thus giving more natural support to the weight of his body, releasing some of the weight from his arms, and enabling his chest cavity to contract more normally. By pushing himself upward in this way the criminal could fend off suffocation, but it was extremely painful because it required putting the body's weight on the nails holding the feet, and bending the elbows and pulling upward on the nails driven through the wrists.[7] The criminal's back, which had been torn open repeatedly by a previous flogging, would scrape against the wooden cross with each breath. Thus Seneca (first century A.D.) spoke of a crucified man "drawing the breath of life amid long-drawn-out agony" (Epistle 101, to Lucilius, section 14).

A physician writing in the *Journal of the American Medical Association* in 1986 explained the pain that would have been experienced in death by crucifixion:

---

verb of the clause (*ēn*, "was"), indicating that Jesus was continually being tempted throughout the forty days in which he was in the wilderness.

[6]Although Scripture does not explicitly say that Joseph died during Jesus' life, we hear nothing of him after Jesus is twelve years old: see discussion in chapter 26, p. 537, n. 7.

[7]The Greek word usually translated "hand" (*cheir*: Luke 24:39–40; John 20:20) can sometimes refer to the arm (BAGD, p. 880; LSJ, p. 1983, 2). A nail through the hands would not have been able to support the weight of the body, for the hands would have torn.

Adequate exhalation required lifting the body by pushing up on the feet and by flexing the elbows. . . . However, this maneuver would place the entire weight of the body on the tarsals and would produce searing pain. Furthermore, flexion of the elbows would cause rotation of the wrists about the iron nails and cause fiery pain along the damaged median nerves. . . . Muscle cramps and paresthesias of the outstretched and uplifted arms would add to the discomfort. As a result, each respiratory effort would become agonizing and tiring and lead eventually to asphyxia.[8]

In some cases, crucified men would survive for several days, nearly suffocating but not quite dying. This was why the executioners would sometimes break the legs of a criminal, so that death would come quickly, as we see in John 19:31–33:

> Since it was the day of Preparation, in order to prevent the bodies from remaining on the cross on the sabbath (for that sabbath was a high day), the Jews asked Pilate that their legs might be broken, and that they might be taken away. So the soldiers came and broke the legs of the first, and of the other who had been crucified with him; but when they came to Jesus and saw that he was already dead, they did not break his legs.

### (2) The Pain of Bearing Sin

More awful than the pain of physical suffering that Jesus endured was the psychological pain of bearing the guilt for our sin. In our own experience as Christians we know something of the anguish we feel when we know we have sinned. The weight of guilt is heavy on our hearts, and there is a bitter sense of separation from all that is right in the universe, an awareness of something that in a very deep sense ought not to be. In fact, the more we grow in holiness as God's children, the more intensely we feel this instinctive revulsion against evil.

Now Jesus was perfectly holy. He hated sin with his entire being. The thought of evil, of sin, contradicted everything in his character. Far more than we do, Jesus instinctively rebelled against evil. Yet in obedience to the Father, and out of love for us, Jesus took on himself all the sins of those who would someday be saved. Taking on himself all the evil against which his soul rebelled created deep revulsion in the center of his being. All that he hated most deeply was poured out fully upon him.

Scripture frequently says that our sins were put on Christ: "The LORD has laid on him the iniquity of us all" (Isa. 53:6), and "He *bore the sin* of many" (Isa. 53:12). John the Baptist calls Jesus "the Lamb of God, who takes away the sin of the world" (John 1:29). Paul declares that God made Christ "*to be sin*" (2 Cor. 5:21) and that Christ became "a curse for us" (Gal. 3:13). The author of Hebrews says that Christ was "offered once to bear the sins of many" (Heb. 9:28). And Peter says, "He himself *bore our sins* in his body on the tree" (1 Peter 2:24).[9]

The passage from 2 Corinthians quoted above, together with the verses from

---

[8]William Edwards, M.D., et al., *JAMA* vol. 255, no. 11 (March 21, 1986), p. 1461.

[9]See Grudem, *1 Peter*, pp. 133–34, for a detailed answer to Deissmann's view that 1 Peter 2:24 means that Christ "carried our sins up to the cross" but did not himself bear the guilt for our sins on the cross. Influenced by Deissmann, BAGD, p. 63, 3, surprisingly deny that the verb *anapherō*, which is used in 1 Peter 2:24 can mean "bear," but Polybius 1.36.3 and Thucydides 3.38.3 provide extrabiblical examples of that meaning, and it certainly has that meaning in the LXX of Isa. 53:4, 11, 12, and in the quotation of Isa. 53:12 in Heb. 9:28; cf. LSJ, p. 125, 3.

Isaiah, indicate that it was God the Father who put our sins on Christ. How could that be? In the same way in which Adam's sins were imputed to us,[10] so God *imputed* our sins to Christ; that is, he *thought of them as belonging to Christ,* and, since God is the ultimate judge and definer of what really is in the universe, when God thought of our sins as belonging to Christ then in fact they actually did belong to Christ. This does not mean that God thought that Christ had himself committed the sins, or that Christ himself actually had a sinful nature, but rather that the guilt for our sins (that is, the liability to punishment) was thought of by God as belonging to Christ rather than to us.

Some have objected that it was not fair for God to do this, to transfer the guilt of sin from us to an innocent person, Christ. Yet we must remember that Christ voluntarily took on himself the guilt for our sins, so this objection loses much of its force. Moreover, God himself (Father, Son, and Holy Spirit) is the ultimate standard of what is just and fair in the universe, and he decreed that the atonement would take place in this way, and that it did in fact satisfy the demands of his own righteousness and justice.

### (3) Abandonment

The physical pain of crucifixion and the pain of taking on himself the absolute evil of our sins were aggravated by the fact that Jesus faced this pain alone. In the Garden of Gethsemane, when Jesus took with him Peter, James and John, he confided something of his agony to them: "My soul is very sorrowful, even to death; remain here, and watch" (Mark 14:34). This is the kind of confidence one would disclose to a close friend, and it implies a request for support in his hour of greatest trial. Yet as soon as Jesus was arrested, "all the disciples forsook him and fled" (Matt. 26:56).

Here also there is a very faint analogy in our experience, for we cannot live long without tasting the inward ache of rejection, whether it be rejection by a close friend, by a parent or child, or by a wife or husband. Yet in all those cases there is at least a sense that we could have done something differently, that at least in small part we may be at fault. It was not so with Jesus and the disciples, for, "having loved his own who were in the world, he loved them to the end" (John 13:1). He had done nothing but love them; in return, they all abandoned him.

But far worse than desertion by even the closest of human friends was the fact that Jesus was deprived of the closeness to the Father that had been the deepest joy of his heart for all his earthly life. When Jesus cried out "Eli, Eli, lama sabach-thani?" that is, "My God, my God, why have you forsaken me?" (Matt. 27:46), he showed that he was finally cut off from the sweet fellowship with his heavenly Father that had been the unfailing source of his inward strength and the element of greatest joy in a life filled with sorrow. As Jesus bore our sins on the cross, he was abandoned by his heavenly Father, who is "of purer eyes than to behold evil" (Hab. 1:13). He faced the weight of the guilt of millions of sins alone.

### (4) Bearing the Wrath of God

Yet more difficult than these three previous aspects of Jesus' pain was the pain of bearing the wrath of God upon himself. As Jesus bore the guilt of our sins

---

[10]See chapter 24, pp. 494–96, for a discussion of the imputation of Adam's sin to us.

alone, God the Father, the mighty Creator, the Lord of the universe, poured out on Jesus the fury of his wrath: Jesus became the object of the intense hatred of sin and vengeance against sin which God had patiently stored up since the beginning of the world.

Romans 3:25 tells us that God put forward Christ as a *"propitiation"* (NASB) a word that means "a sacrifice that bears God's wrath to the end and in so doing changes God's wrath toward us into favor." Paul tells us that "This was to show God's righteousness, because in his divine forbearance he had passed over former sins; it was to prove at the present time that he himself is righteous and that he justifies him who has faith in Jesus" (Rom. 3:25–26). God had not simply forgiven sin and forgotten about the punishment in generations past. He had forgiven sins and stored up his righteous anger against those sins. But at the cross the fury of all that stored-up wrath against sin was unleashed against God's own Son.

Many theologians outside the evangelical world have strongly objected to the idea that Jesus bore the wrath of God against sin.[11] Their basic assumption is that since God is a God of love, it would be inconsistent with his character to show wrath against the human beings he has created and for whom he is a loving Father. But evangelical scholars have convincingly argued that the idea of the wrath of God is solidly rooted in both the Old and New Testaments: "The whole of the argument of the opening part of Romans is that all men, Gentiles and Jews alike, are sinners, and that they come under the wrath and the condemnation of God."[12]

Three other crucial passages in the New Testament refer to Jesus' death as a "propitiation": Hebrews 2:17; 1 John 2:2; and 4:10. The Greek terms (the verb *hilaskomai*, "to make propitiation" and the noun *hilasmos*, "a sacrifice of propitiation") used in these passages have the sense of "a sacrifice that turns away the wrath of God—and thereby makes God propitious (or favorable) toward us."[13] This is the consistent meaning of these words outside the Bible where they were well understood in reference to pagan Greek religions. These verses simply mean that Jesus bore the wrath of God against sin.

It is important to insist on this fact, because it is the heart of the doctrine of the atonement. It means that there is an eternal, unchangeable requirement in the holiness and justice of God that sin be paid for. Furthermore, before the atonement ever could have an effect on our subjective consciousness, it first had an effect on God and his relation to the sinners he planned to redeem. Apart from this central truth, the death of Christ really cannot be adequately understood (see discussion of other views of the atonement below).

Although we must be cautious in suggesting any analogies to the experience

---

[11]See the detailed linguistic argument of C. H. Dodd, *The Bible and the Greeks* (London: Hodder and Stoughton, 1935), pp. 82–95. Dodd argues that the idea of propitiation was common in pagan religions but foreign to the thought of Old Testament and New Testament writers.

[12]Leon Morris, "Propitiation," *EDT*, p. 888 (includes brief bibliography). Morris's own work has represented the best of evangelical scholarship on this question: see his *The Apostolic Preaching of the Cross*, 3d ed. (London: Tyndale Press, 1965), pp. 144–213. See also the discussion of the wrath of God in chapter 12, pp. 205–7.

[13]Under the influence of scholars who denied that the idea of propitiation was in the New Testament, the RSV translated *hilasmos* as "expiation," a word that means "an action that cleanses from sin" but includes no concept of appeasing God's wrath.

Christ went through (for his experience was and always will be without precedent or comparison), nonetheless, all our understanding of Jesus' suffering comes in some sense by way of analogous experiences in our life—for that is how God teaches us in Scripture.[14] Once again our human experience provides a very faint analogy that helps us understand what it means to bear the wrath of God. Perhaps as children we have faced the wrath of a human father when we have done wrong, or perhaps as adults we have known the anger of an employer because of a mistake we have made. We are inwardly shaken, disturbed by the crashing of another personality, filled with displeasure, into our very selves, and we tremble. We can hardly imagine the personal disintegration that would threaten if the outpouring of wrath came not from some finite human being but from Almighty God. If even the presence of God when he does not manifest wrath arouses fear and trembling in people (cf. Heb. 12:21, 28–29), how terrible it must be to face the presence of a wrathful God (Heb. 10:31).

With this in mind, we are now better able to understand Jesus' cry of desolation, "My God, my God, why have you forsaken me?" (Matt. 27:46b). The question does not mean, "Why have you left me forever?" for Jesus knew that he was leaving the world, that he was going to the Father (John 14:28; 16:10, 17). Jesus knew that he would rise again (John 2:19; Luke 18:33; Mark 9:31; et al.). It was "for the joy that was set before him" that Jesus "endured the cross, despising the shame, and is seated at the right hand of the throne of God" (Heb. 12:2). Jesus knew that he could still call God "my God." This cry of desolation is not a cry of total despair. Furthermore, "Why have you forsaken me?" does not imply that Jesus wondered why he was dying. He had said, "The Son of man also came not to be served but to serve, and to give his life as a ransom for many" (Mark 10:45). Jesus knew that he was dying for our sins.

Jesus' cry is a quotation from Psalm 22:1, a psalm in which the psalmist asks why God is so far from helping him, why God delays in rescuing him:

> My God, my God, why have you forsaken me?
> Why are you so far from helping me, from the words of my
>     groaning?
> O my God, I cry by day, but you do not answer;
>     and by night, but find no rest. (Ps. 22:1–2)

Yet the psalmist was eventually rescued by God, and his cry of desolation turned into a hymn of praise (vv. 22–31). Jesus, who knew the words of Scripture as his own, knew well the context of Psalm 22. In quoting this psalm, he is quoting a cry of desolation that also has implicit in its context an unremitting faith in the God who will ultimately deliver him. Nevertheless, it remains a very real cry of anguish because the suffering has gone on so long and no release is in sight.

With this context for the quotation it is better to understand the question "Why have you forsaken me?" as meaning, "Why have you left me *for so long*?" This is the sense it has in Psalm 22. Jesus, in his human nature, knew he would have to bear our sins, to suffer and to die. But, in his human consciousness, he probably did not know how long this suffering would take. Yet to bear the guilt of millions of

---

[14]See the discussion of anthropomorphic language in Scripture to teach us about God in chapter 11, pp. 157–60.

sins even for a moment would cause the greatest anguish of soul. To face the deep and furious wrath of an infinite God even for an instant would cause the most profound fear. But Jesus' suffering was not over in a minute—or two—or ten. When would it end? Could there be yet more weight of sin? Yet more wrath of God? Hour after hour it went on—the dark weight of sin and the deep wrath of God poured over Jesus in wave after wave. Jesus at last cried out, "My God, my God, why have you forsaken me?" Why must this suffering go on so long? Oh God, my God, will you ever bring it to an end?

Then at last Jesus knew his suffering was nearing completion. He knew he had consciously borne all the wrath of the Father against our sins, for God's anger had abated and the awful heaviness of sin was being removed. He knew that all that remained was to yield up his spirit to his heavenly Father and die. With a shout of victory Jesus cried out, "It is finished!" (John 19:30). Then with a loud voice he once more cried out, "Father, into your hands I commit my spirit!" (Luke 23:46). And then he voluntarily gave up the life that no one could take from him (John 10:17–18), and he died. As Isaiah had predicted, "he poured out his soul to death" and "bore the sin of many" (Isa. 53:12). God the Father saw "the fruit of the travail of his soul" and was "satisfied" (Isa. 53:11).

### c. Further Understanding of the Death of Christ:

#### (1) The Penalty Was Inflicted By God the Father

If we ask, "Who required Christ to pay the penalty for our sins?" the answer given by Scripture is that the penalty was inflicted by God the Father as he represented the interests of the Trinity in redemption. It was God's justice that required that sin be paid for, and, among the members of the Trinity, it was God the Father whose role was to require that payment. God the Son voluntarily took upon himself the role of bearing the penalty for sin. Referring to God the Father, Paul says, "For our sake he made him to be sin who knew no sin [that is, Christ], so that in him we might become the righteousness of God" (2 Cor. 5:21). Isaiah said, "The LORD has laid on him the iniquity of us all" (Isa. 53:6). He goes on to describe the sufferings of Christ: "Yet it was the will of the LORD to bruise him; he has put him to grief" (Isa. 53:10).

Herein we see something of the amazing love of both God the Father and God the Son in redemption. Not only did Jesus know that he would bear the incredible pain of the cross, but God the Father also knew that he would have to inflict this pain on his own deeply loved Son. "God shows his love for us in that while we were yet sinners Christ died for us" (Rom. 5:8).

#### (2) Not Eternal Suffering but Complete Payment

If we had to pay the penalty for our own sins, we would have to suffer eternally in separation from God.[15] However, Jesus did not suffer eternally. There are two reasons for this difference: (a) If we suffered for our own sins, we would never be able to make ourselves right with God again. There would be no hope because there would be no way to live again and earn perfect righteousness before God, and there would be no way to undo our sinful nature and make it right before

God. Moreover, we would continue to exist as sinners who would not suffer with pure hearts of righteousness before God, but would suffer with resentment and bitterness against God, thus continually compounding our sin. (b) Jesus was able to bear all the wrath of God against our sin and to bear it to the end. No mere man could ever have done this, but by virtue of the union of divine and human natures in himself, Jesus was able to bear all the wrath of God against sin and bear it to the end. Isaiah predicted that God "shall see the fruit of the travail of his soul *and be satisfied*" (Isa. 53:11). When Jesus knew that he had paid the full penalty for our sin, he said, *"It is finished"* (John 19:30). If Christ had not paid the full penalty, there would still be condemnation left for us. But since he has paid the full penalty that is due to us, "There is therefore now no condemnation for those who are in Christ Jesus" (Rom. 8:1).

It should help us at this point to realize that nothing in the eternal character of God and nothing in the laws God had given for mankind required that there be eternal suffering to pay for man's sins. In fact, if there is eternal suffering, it simply shows that the penalty has never been fully paid, and that the evildoer continues to be a sinner by nature. But when Christ's sufferings at last came to an end on the cross, it showed that he had borne the full measure of God's wrath against sin and there was no penalty left to pay. It also showed that he was himself righteous before God. In this way the fact that Christ suffered for a limited time rather than eternally shows that his suffering was a sufficient payment for sins. The author of Hebrews repeats this theme again and again, emphasizing the completion and the finality of Christ's redemptive work:

> Nor was it to offer himself repeatedly, as the high priest enters the Holy Place yearly with blood not his own; for then he would have had to suffer repeatedly since the foundation of the world. But as it is, he has appeared once for all at the end of the age to put away sin by the sacrifice of himself. . . . Christ, having been offered once *to bear the sins of many,* will appear a second time, not to deal with sin but to save those who are eagerly waiting for him. (Heb. 9:25–28)

This New Testament emphasis on the completion and finality of Christ's sacrificial death stands in contrast to the Roman Catholic teaching that in the mass there is a repetition of the sacrifice of Christ.[16] Because of this official teaching of the Roman Catholic Church, many Protestants since the Reformation, and still today, are convinced that they cannot in good conscience actually participate in the Roman Catholic mass, because it would seem to be an endorsement of the Catholic view that the sacrifice of Christ is repeated every time the mass is offered.

The New Testament emphasis on the completion and finality of Christ's sacrifice of himself for us has much practical application, because it assures us that there is no more penalty for sin left for us to pay. The penalty has entirely been paid by Christ, and we should have no remaining fear of condemnation or punishment.

---

[16] Ludwig Ott, *Fundamentals of Catholic Dogma,* p. 408, says, "In the Sacrifice of the Mass and in the Sacrifice of the Cross the Sacrificial Gift and the Primary Sacrificing Priest are identical; only the nature and the mode of the offering are different. . . . according to the Thomistic view, *in every Mass Christ also performs an actual immediate sacrificial activity,* which, however, must not be conceived as a totality of many successive acts but as one single uninterrupted sacrificial act of the Transfigured Christ. The purpose of the Sacrifice is the same in the Sacrifice of the Mass as in the Sacrifice of the Cross; primarily the glorification of God, secondarily atonement, thanksgiving and appeal."

### (3) The Meaning of the Blood of Christ

The New Testament frequently connects the blood of Christ with our redemption. For example, Peter says, "You know that you were ransomed from the futile ways inherited from your fathers, not with perishable things such as silver or gold, but with the precious blood of Christ, like that of a lamb without blemish or spot" (1 Peter 1:18–19).

The blood of Christ is the clear outward evidence that his life blood was poured out when he died a sacrificial death to pay for our redemption—"the blood of Christ" means his death in its saving aspects.[17] Although we may think that Christ's blood (as evidence that his life had been given) would have exclusive reference to the removal of our judicial guilt before God—for this is its primary reference—the New Testament authors also attribute to it several other effects. By the blood of Christ our consciences are cleansed (Heb. 9:14), we gain bold access to God in worship and prayer (Heb. 10:19), we are progressively cleansed from remaining sin (1 John 1:7; cf. Rev. 1:5b), we are able to conquer the accuser of the brethren (Rev. 12:10–11), and we are rescued out of a sinful way of life (1 Peter 1:18–19).[18]

Scripture speaks so much about the blood of Christ because its shedding was very clear evidence that his life was being given in judicial execution (that is, he was condemned to death and died paying a penalty imposed both by an earthly human judge and by God himself in heaven). Scripture's emphasis on the blood of Christ also shows the clear connection between Christ's death and the many sacrifices in the Old Testament that involved the pouring out of the life blood of the sacrificial animal. These sacrifices all pointed forward to and prefigured the death of Christ.

### (4) Christ's Death as "Penal Substitution"

The view of Christ's death presented here has frequently been called the theory of *"penal substitution."* Christ's death was "penal" in that he bore a penalty when he died. His death was also a "substitution" in that he was a substitute for us when he died. This has been the orthodox understanding of the atonement held by evangelical theologians, in contrast to other views that attempt to explain the atonement apart from the idea of the wrath of God or payment of the penalty for sin (see below).

This view of the atonement is sometimes called the theory of *vicarious atonement.* A "vicar" is someone who stands in the place of another or who represents another. Christ's death was therefore "vicarious" because he stood in our place and represented us. As our representative, he took the penalty that we deserve.

### d. New Testament Terms Describing Different Aspects of the Atonement:

The atoning work of Christ is a complex event that has several effects on us. It can therefore be viewed from several different aspects. The New Testament uses different words to describe these; we shall examine four of the more important terms.

---

[17]So Leon Morris, *The Apostolic Preaching of the Cross,* pp. 112–26.
[18]This paragraph has been taken from Wayne Grudem, *The First Epistle of Peter,* p. 84.

The four terms show how Christ's death met the four needs that we have as sinners:

1. We deserve to *die* as the penalty for sin.
2. We deserve to *bear God's wrath* against sin.
3. We are *separated* from God by our sins.
4. We are in *bondage to sin* and to the kingdom of Satan.

These four needs are met by Christ's death in the following ways:

### (1) Sacrifice

To pay the penalty of death that we deserved because of our sins, Christ died as a sacrifice for us. "He has appeared once for all at the end of the age to put away sin by the sacrifice of himself" (Heb. 9:26).

### (2) Propitiation

To remove us from the wrath of God that we deserved, Christ died as a propitiation for our sins. "In this is love, not that we loved God, but that He loved us and sent His Son to be the propitiation for our sins" (1 John 4:10 NASB).

### (3) Reconciliation

To overcome our separation from God, we needed someone to provide reconciliation and thereby bring us back into fellowship with God. Paul says that God "through Christ reconciled us to himself and gave us the ministry of reconciliation; that is, in Christ God was reconciling the world to himself" (2 Cor. 5:18–19).

### (4) Redemption

Because we as sinners are in bondage to sin and to Satan, we need someone to provide redemption and thereby "redeem" us out of that bondage. When we speak of redemption, the idea of a "ransom" comes into view. A ransom is the price paid to redeem someone from bondage or captivity. Jesus said of himself, "For the Son of man also came not to be served but to serve, and to give his life *as a ransom for many*" (Mark 10:45). If we ask to whom the ransom was paid, we realize that the human analogy of a ransom payment does not fit the atonement of Christ in every detail. Though we were in bondage to sin and to Satan, there was no "ransom" paid either to "sin" or to Satan himself, for they did not have power to demand such payment, nor was Satan the one whose holiness was offended by sin and who required a penalty to be paid for sin. As we saw earlier, the penalty for sin was paid by Christ and received and accepted by God the Father. But we hesitate to speak of paying a "ransom" to God the Father, because it was not he who held us in bondage but Satan and our own sins. Therefore at this point the idea of a ransom payment cannot be pressed in every detail. It is sufficient to note that a price was paid (the death of Christ) and the result was that we were "redeemed" from bondage.

We were redeemed from bondage to Satan because "the whole world is in the power of the evil one" (1 John 5:19), and when Christ came he died to "deliver all those who through fear of death were subject to lifelong bondage" (Heb.

2:15). In fact, God the Father "has delivered us from the dominion of darkness and transferred us to the kingdom of his beloved Son" (Col. 1:13).

As for deliverance from bondage to sin, Paul says, "So you also must consider yourselves dead to sin and alive to God in Christ Jesus. . . . For sin will have no dominion over you, since you are not under law but under grace" (Rom. 6:11, 14). We have been delivered from bondage to the guilt of sin and from bondage to its ruling power in our lives.

**e. Other Views of the Atonement:** In contrast to the penal substitution view of the atonement presented in this chapter, several other views have been advocated in the history of the church.

### (1) The Ransom to Satan Theory

This view was held by Origen (c. A.D. 185—c. 254), a theologian from Alexandria and later Caesarea, and after him by some others in the early history of the church. According to this view, the ransom Christ paid to redeem us was paid to Satan, in whose kingdom all people were by virtue of sin.

This theory finds no direct confirmation in Scripture and has few supporters in the history of the church. It falsely thinks of Satan rather than God as the one who required that a payment be made for sin and thus completely neglects the demands of God's justice with respect to sin. It views Satan as having much more power than he actually does, namely, power to demand whatever he wants from God, rather than as one who has been cast down from heaven and has no right to demand anything of God. Nowhere does Scripture say that we as sinners owe anything to Satan, but it repeatedly says that God requires of us a payment for our sins. This view also fails to deal with the texts that speak of Christ's death as a propitiation offered to God the Father for our sins, or with the fact that God the Father represented the Trinity in accepting the payment for sins from Christ (see discussion above).

### (2) The Moral Influence Theory

First advocated by Peter Abelard (1079–1142), a French theologian, the moral influence theory of the atonement holds that God did not require the payment of a penalty for sin, but that Christ's death was simply a way in which God showed how much he loved human beings by identifying with their sufferings, even to the point of death. Christ's death therefore becomes a great teaching example that shows God's love to us and draws from us a grateful response, so that in loving him we are forgiven.

The great difficulty with this viewpoint is that it is contrary to so many passages of Scripture that speak of Christ dying for sin, bearing our sin, or dying as a propitiation. Moreover, it robs the atonement of its objective character, because it holds that the atonement had no effect on God himself. Finally, it has no way of dealing with our guilt—if Christ did not die to pay for our sins, we have no right to trust in him for forgiveness of sins.

### (3) The Example Theory

The example theory of the atonement was taught by the Socinians, the followers of Faustus Socinus (1539–1604), an Italian theologian who settled in Poland in 1578 and attracted a wide following.[19] The example theory, like the moral influence theory, also denies that God's justice requires payment for sin; it says that Christ's death simply provides us with an example of how we should trust and obey God perfectly, even if that trust and obedience leads to a horrible death. Whereas the moral influence theory says that Christ's death teaches us how much God loves us, the example theory says that Christ's death teaches us how we should live. Support for this view could be found in 1 Peter 2:21, "For to this you have been called, because Christ also suffered for you, leaving you an example, that you should follow in his steps."

While it is true that Christ is an example for us even in his death, the question is whether this fact is the complete explanation of the atonement. The example theory fails to account for the many Scriptures that focus on Christ's death as a payment for sin, the fact that Christ bore our sins, and the fact that he was the propitiation for our sins. These considerations alone mean that the theory must be rejected. Moreover, this view really ends up arguing that man can save himself by following Christ's example and by trusting and obeying God just as Christ did. Thus it fails to show how the guilt of our sin can be removed, because it does not hold that Christ actually paid the penalty for our sins or made provision for our guilt when he died.

### (4) The Governmental Theory

The governmental theory of the atonement was first taught by a Dutch theologian and jurist, Hugo Grotius (1583–1645). This theory holds that God did not actually have to require payment for sin, but, since he was omnipotent God, he could have set aside that requirement and simply forgiven sins without the payment of a penalty. Then what was the purpose of Christ's death? It was God's demonstration of the fact that his laws had been broken, that he is the moral lawgiver and governor of the universe, and that some kind of penalty would be required whenever his laws were broken. Thus Christ did not exactly pay the penalty for the actual sins of any people, but simply suffered to show that when God's laws are broken there must be some penalty paid.

The problem with this view again is that it fails to account adequately for all the Scriptures that speak of Christ bearing our sins on the cross, of God laying on Christ the iniquity of us all, of Christ dying specifically for our sins, and of Christ being the propitiation for our sins. Moreover, it takes away the objective character of the atonement by making its purpose not the satisfaction of God's justice but simply that of influencing us to realize that God has laws that must be kept. This view also implies that we cannot rightly trust in Christ's completed work for forgiveness of sin, because he has not actually made payment for those sins. Moreover, it makes the actual earning of forgiveness for us something that happened in God's own mind apart from the death of Christ on the cross—he had already decided to forgive us without requiring any penalty from us and then punished Christ only to demonstrate that he was still the moral governor of the universe. But this means that Christ (in this view) did not actually earn forgiveness

---

[19]The Socinians were anti-trinitarian since they denied the deity of Christ: their thought led to modern Unitarianism.

## THE GRADUAL FORMATION OF THE APOSTLES' CREED

| Ultimate Text of the Western Creed — Pirminius, A.D.750 | CREDO (I believe): | | | |
|---|---|---|---|---|
| | Art. III | | | |
| | Qui Conceptus est | De Spirita Sancto | Natus | Ex Maria Virgine |
| | Who was conceived | By the Holy Ghost | Born | Of the Virgin Mary |
| I. St. Irenæus, A.D.200 | τόν σαρκω-θέντα ὑπὲρ τῆς ἡμετέρας σωτηίας (ἄνθρωπος ἐγένετο) | | (Generationem) | τὴν ἐκ παρθέ-νου γέν-νησιν (ex Virgine) |
| II. Tertullian, A.D.220 | (missum a Patre in Virginem) | (EX SPIRITU Patris Dei et virtute) | NATUM (carnem factum et ex ea natum) | EX VIRGINE MARIA |
| III. St. Cyrpian, A.D.250 | | | | |
| IV. Novatian, A.D.260 | | | | |
| V. Marcellus, A.D.341 | | ἐκ πνεύμα-τος ἁγίου | γεννηθέντα | καὶ Μα-ρίας τῆς παρθένου |
| VI. Rufinus, A.D.390 Aquileja | QUI | de Spiritu SANCTO | natus est | ex Maria Virgine |
| VII. Refinus, Rome, A.D.390 | qui | de Spiritu Sancto · | natus est | ex Maria Virgine |
| VIII. St. Augustine, A.D.400 | qui | de Spiritu Santo also [per Sp. Sanct.] | natus est | ex Maria Virgine also [et] |
| IX. St. Nicetas, A.D.450. | qui | ex Spiritu Sancto | natus est | et Virgine Maria |
| X. Eusebius Gallus, A.D.550(?) | qui CONCEP-TUS EST | de Spiritu Sancto | natus est | ex Maria Virgine |
| XI. Sacramentarium Gallicanum. A.D.650 | qui conceptus est | de Spiritu Sancto | natus est | ex Maria Virgine |

## THE GRADUAL FORMATION OF THE APOSTLES' CREED

| Art. IV | | | | |
|---|---|---|---|---|
| Passus | Sub Pontio Pilato | Crucifixus | Mortuus | Et Sepultus |
| *Suffered* | *Under Pontius Pilate* | *Was crucified* | *Dead* | *And buried* |
| καὶ τὸ πάθος | (SUB PONTIO PILATO) | | | |
| CRUCIFIXUM (passum) | sub Pontio Pilato | | (MORTUUM) | (ET SEPULTUM secundum Scripturas) |
| | | | | |
| | | | | |
| | τὸν ἐπὶ ποντίου πιλάτου | σταυρω-θέντα | | καὶ ταφέντα |
| | sub Pontio Pilate | crucifixus | | et sepultus |
| | sub Pontio Pilato | crucifixus | | et sepultus |
| passus | sub Pontio Pilato | crucifixus | | et sepultus |
| passus | sub Pontio Pilato | | | |
| | | | mortuus | et sepultus |
| passus | sub Pontio Pilato | crucifixus | mortuus | et sepultus |

## THE GRADUAL FORMATION OF THE APOSTLES' CREED

| Art. V | | | | Art. VI | |
|---|---|---|---|---|---|
| Descendit ad Inferna <br> *He descended into hell* | Tertia die <br> *The third day* | Resurrexit <br> *He rose again* | A mortuis <br> *From the dead* | Ascendit ad coelos <br> *He ascended into heaven* | Sedet ad dexteram <br> *And sitteth at the right hand* |
| | | καὶ τὴν ἔγερσιν (et resurgens) | εκ νεκρῶν | εἰς τοὺς οὐρανοὺς ἀνάληφιν (et in claritate receptus) | |
| | TERTIA DIE | resuscitatum (a Patre) <br><br> (resurrexisse) | E MORTUIS | receptum in coelis (in coelos resumptum) (in coelos ereptum) | SEDENTEM nunc AD DEX-TERAM |
| | | | | | |
| | | | | | |
| | καὶ τῇ τρίτῃ ἡμέρᾳ | ἀνα-στάντα | ἐκ τῶν νεκρῶν | ἀναβάντα εἰς τοὺς οὐρανούς | καὶ κα-θημένον ἐν δεξίᾳ |
| DESCENDIT in INFERNA | tertia die | RESURREXIT | A mortuis | ASCENDIT in COELOS | SEDET ad dexteram |
| | tertia die | resurrexit | a mortuis | ascendit in coelos | SEDET ad dexteram |
| | tertio die | resurrexit | a mortuis | ascendit in coelos | sedet ad dexteram |
| | tertio die | resurrexit | vivus a mortuis | ascendit in coelos | sedet ad dexteram |
| | tertia die | resurrexit | a mortuis | ascendit AD coelos | sedet ad dexteram |
| Descendit AD Inferna | tertia die | resurrexit | a mortuis | ascendit ad coelos | sedet ad dexteram |

or salvation for us, and thus the value of his redemptive work is greatly minimized. Finally, this theory fails to take adequate account of the unchangeableness of God and the infinite purity of his justice. To say that God can forgive sins without requiring any penalty (in spite of the fact that throughout Scripture sin always requires the payment of a penalty) is seriously to underestimate the absolute character of the justice of God.

**f. Did Christ Descend Into Hell?:**[20] It is sometimes argued that Christ descended into hell after he died. The phrase "he descended into hell" does not occur in the Bible. But the widely used Apostles' Creed reads, "was crucified, dead, and buried, he descended into hell; the third day he rose again from the dead." Does this mean that Christ endured further suffering after his death on the cross? As we shall see below, an examination of the biblical evidence indicates that he did not. But before looking at the relevant biblical texts, it is appropriate to examine the phrase "he descended into hell" in the Apostles' Creed.

### (1) The Origin of the Phrase, "He Descended Into Hell"

A murky background lies behind much of the history of the phrase itself. Its origins, where they can be found, are far from praiseworthy. The great church historian Philip Schaff has summarized the development of the Apostles' Creed in an extensive chart, part of which is reproduced on pages 583–85.[21]

This chart shows that, unlike the Nicene Creed and the Chalcedonian Definition, the Apostles' Creed was not written or approved by a single church council at one specific time. Rather, it gradually took shape from about A.D. 200 to 750.

It is surprising to find that the phrase "he descended into hell" was not found in any of the early versions of the Creed (in the versions used in Rome, in the rest of Italy, and in Africa) until it appeared in one of two versions from Rufinus in A.D. 390. Then it was not included again in any version of the Creed until A.D. 650. Moreover, Rufinus, the only person who included it before A.D. 650, did not think that it meant that Christ descended into hell, but understood the phrase simply to mean that Christ was "buried."[22] In other words, he took it to mean that Christ "descended into the grave." (The Greek form has *hadēs,* which can mean just "grave," not *geenna,* "hell, place of punishment."). We should also note that the phrase only appears in one of the two versions of the Creed that we have from Rufinus: it was not in the Roman form of the Creed that he preserved.

---

[20]The following section is taken from Wayne Grudem, "He Did Not Descend Into Hell: A Plea for Following Scripture Instead of the Apostles' Creed," *JETS* vol. 34, no. 1 (March, 1991), pp. 103–13.
[21]This chart is taken from *The Creeds of Christendom,* 2:52–55.
[22]See Schaff, *Creeds,* 1,21, n. 6; see also 46, n. 2. Schaff notes that the phrase was found somewhat earlier (around A.D. 360), but then it was not in any orthodox creeds or any versions of the Apostles' Creed but in some creeds of the Arians—people who denied the full deity of Christ, holding that the Son was created by the Father (see Schaff, *Creeds,* 2.46, n. 2). (Schaff does not give documentation for this reference to Arian creeds.)
It should be noted that Schaff throughout his *Creeds of Christendom* has several editorial comments defending an actual descent of Christ into hell after his death on the cross. Thus, for example, he says that "Rufinus himself, however, misunderstood it by making it to mean the same as buried" (1.21, n. 6)—thus Schaff assumes that to understand the phrase to mean "he descended into the grave" is to misunderstand it (see also 2.46, n. 2; 3.321, n. 1).

This means, therefore, that until A.D. 650 no version of the Creed included this phrase with the intention of saying that Christ "descended into hell"—the only version to include the phrase before A.D. 650 gives it a different meaning. At this point one wonders if the term *apostolic* can in any sense be applied to this phrase, or if it really has a rightful place in a creed whose title claims for itself descent from the earliest apostles of Christ.

This survey of the historical development of the phrase also raises the possibility that when the phrase first began to be more commonly used, it may have been in other versions (now lost to us) that did not have the expression "and buried." If so, it probably would have meant to others just what it meant to Rufinus: "descended into the grave." But later when the phrase was incorporated into different versions of the Creed that already had the phrase "and buried," some other explanation had to be given to it. This mistaken insertion of the phrase after the words "and buried"—apparently done by someone around A.D. 650—led to all sorts of attempts to explain "he descended into hell" in some way that did not contradict the rest of Scripture.

Some have taken it to mean that Christ suffered the pains of hell while on the cross. Calvin, for example, says that "Christ's descent into hell" refers to the fact that he not only died a bodily death but that "it was expedient at the same time for him to undergo the severity of God's vengeance, to appease his wrath and satisfy his just judgment."[23]

Similarly, the Heidelberg Catechism, Question 44, asks,

Why is it added: He descended into Hades?

Answer: That in my greatest temptations I may be assured that Christ, my Lord, by his inexpressible anguish, pains, and terrors which he suffered in his soul on the cross and before, has redeemed me from the anguish and torment of hell.[24]

But is this a satisfactory explanation of the phrase, "he descended into hell"? While it is true that Christ suffered the outpouring of God's wrath on the cross, this explanation does not really fit the phrase in the Apostles' Creed—"descended" hardly represents this idea, and the placement of the phrase after "was crucified, dead, and buried" makes this an artificial and unconvincing interpretation.

Others have understood it to mean that Christ continued in the "state of death" until his resurrection. The Westminster Larger Catechism, Question 50, says,

Christ's humiliation after his death consisted in his being buried, and continuing in the state of the dead, and under the power of death till the third day; which hath been otherwise expressed in these words, He descended into hell.

Though it is true that Christ continued in the state of death until the third day, once again it is a strained and unpersuasive explanation of "he descended into hell," for the placement of the phrase would then give the awkward sense, "he was crucified, dead, and buried; he descended to being dead." This interpretation does not explain what the words first meant in this sequence but is rather an unconvincing attempt to salvage some theologically acceptable sense out of them.

---

[23]John Calvin, *Institutes of the Christian Religion*, 1.515 (2.16.10).
[24]Schaff, *Creeds*, 3.321.

Moreover, the English word "hell" has no such sense as simply "being dead" (though the Greek word *hadēs* can mean this), so this becomes a doubly artificial explanation for English-speaking people.

Finally, some have argued that the phrase means just what it appears to mean on first reading: that Christ actually did descend into hell after his death on the cross. It is easy to understand the Apostles' Creed to mean just this (indeed, that is certainly the natural sense), but then another question arises: Can this idea be supported from Scripture?

### (2) Possible Biblical Support for a Descent Into Hell

Support for the idea that Christ descended into hell has been found primarily in five passages: Acts 2:27; Romans 10:6–7; Ephesians 4:8–9; 1 Peter 3:18–20; and 1 Peter 4:6. (A few other passages have been appealed to, but less convincingly.)[25] On closer inspection, do any of those passages clearly establish this teaching?

*(a) Acts 2:27.* This is part of Peter's sermon on the Day of Pentecost, where he is quoting Psalm 16:10. In the King James Version the verse reads: "because thou wilt not *leave my soul in hell,* neither wilt thou suffer thine Holy One to see corruption."

Does this mean that Christ entered hell after he died? Not necessarily; because another sense is certainly possible for these verses. The word "hell" here represents a New Testament Greek term (*hadēs*) and an Old Testament Hebrew term (*šeʾôl,* popularly translated as sheol) that can mean simply "the grave" or "death" (the state of being dead). Thus, the NIV translates: "Because you will not *abandon me to the grave,* nor will you let your Holy One see decay" (Acts 2:27). This sense is preferable because the context emphasizes that Christ's body rose from the grave, unlike David's, which remained in the grave. The reasoning is: "My body also will live in hope" (v. 26), "because you will not abandon me to the grave" (v. 27). Peter is using David's psalm to show that Christ's body did not decay—he is therefore unlike David, who "died and was buried, and his tomb is here to this day" (v. 29 NIV). Therefore this passage about Christ's resurrection from the grave does not convincingly support the idea that Christ descended into hell.

*(b) Romans 10:6–7.* These verses contain two rhetorical questions, again Old Testament quotations (from Deut. 30:13): "Do not say in your heart, 'Who will ascend into heaven?' (that is, to bring Christ down) or 'Who will descend into the abyss?' (that is, to bring Christ up from the dead)." But this passage hardly teaches that Christ descended into hell. The point of the passage is that Paul is telling people not to ask these questions, because Christ is not far away—he is near—and faith in him is as near as confessing with our mouth and believing in our heart (v. 9). These prohibited questions are questions of unbelief, not assertions of what Scripture teaches. However, some may object that Paul would not have anticipated that his readers would ask such questions unless it was widely known that Christ did in fact descend "into the abyss." However, even if this were true, Scripture would not be saying or implying that Christ went into "hell" (in the

---

[25]For example, Matt. 12:40, which says that Christ will be three days and nights "in the heart of the earth," simply refers to the fact that he was in the grave between his death and resurrection (cf., in the LXX, Ps. 45[46]:2 with Jonah 2:3).

sense of a place of punishment for the dead, ordinarily expressed by Gk. *geenna*), but rather that he went into "the abyss" (Gk. *abyssos*, a term which often in the LXX is used of the depths of the ocean [Gen. 1:2; 7:11; 8:2; Deut. 8:7; Ps. 106(107):26], but it can also apparently refer just to the realm of the dead [Ps. 70(71):20]).[26]

Paul here uses the word "deep" (*abyssos*) as a contrast to "heaven" in order to give the sense of a place that is unreachable, inaccessible to human beings. The contrast is not, "Who shall go to find Christ in a place of great blessing (heaven) or a place of great punishment (hell)?" but rather, "Who shall go to find Christ in a place that is inaccessibly high (heaven) or in a place that is inaccessibly low (the deep, or the realm of death)?" No clear affirmation or denial of a "descent into hell" can be found in this passage.

(c) *Ephesians 4:8–9*. Here Paul writes, "In saying, 'He ascended,' what does it mean but that he had also descended into the lower parts of the earth?"

Does this mean that Christ "descended" to hell? It is at first unclear what is meant by "the lower parts of the earth," but another translation seems to give the best sense: "What does 'he ascended' mean except that he also descended to the *lower, earthly regions*?" (NIV). Here the NIV takes "descended" to refer to Christ's coming to earth as a baby (the Incarnation). The last four words are an acceptable understanding of the Greek text, taking the phrase "the lower regions *of* the earth" to mean "lower regions *which are* the earth" (the grammatical form in Greek would then be called a genitive of apposition). We do the same thing in English— for example, in the phrase "the city of Chicago," we mean "the city which is Chicago."

The NIV rendering is preferable in this context because Paul is saying that the Christ who went up to heaven (in his ascension) is the same one who earlier came down from heaven (v. 10). That "descent" from heaven occurred, of course, when Christ came to be born as a man. So the verse speaks of the incarnation, not of a descent into hell.[27]

(d) *1 Peter 3:18–20*. For many people this is the most puzzling passage on this entire subject. Peter tells us that Christ was "put to death in the flesh but made alive in the spirit; *in which he went and preached to the spirits in prison,* who formerly did not obey, when God's patience waited in the days of Noah, during the building of the ark" (RSV).

**Does this refer to Christ preaching in hell?**

Some have taken "he went and preached to the spirits in prison" to mean that Christ went into hell and preached to the spirits who were there—either

---

[26]1 Clem. 28:3 uses *abyssos* instead of the Septuagint's *hadēs* to translate Ps. 139:8, "If I make my bed in Sheol, thou art there!" In the New Testament, the term is used only in Luke 8:31; Rom. 10:7; and seven times in Revelation (there it refers to the "bottomless pit"). Therefore, although the term can refer to the abode of condemned demons (as in Revelation), this is not its common sense in the LXX or a necessary sense in its New Testament usage. The primary force of the term is a place that is deep, unfathomable to human beings, ordinarily unable to be reached by them. (C. E. B. Cranfield, *A Critical and Exegetical Commentary on the Epistle to the Romans,* 2.525, notes that *abyssos* is the ordinary LXX translation for Hebrew *tehōm,* and that *tehōm* is used in the Mishnah [Pesahim 7:7; Nazir 9:2] to refer to a grave that had been unknown.)

[27]Referring to Eph. 4:9, H. Bietenhard says, "In modern exposition the reference of this passage to the *descensus ad inferos* ("he descended into hell" in the Apostles' Creed) is almost without exception rejected" (*NIDNTT,* 2:210).

proclaiming the gospel and offering a second chance to repent, or just proclaiming that he had triumphed over them and that they were eternally condemned.

But these interpretations fail to explain adequately either the passage itself or its setting in this context. Peter does not say that Christ preached to spirits generally, but only to those "who formerly did not obey . . . *during the building of the ark.*" Such a limited audience—those who disobeyed during the building of the ark—would be a strange group for Christ to travel to hell and preach to. If Christ proclaimed his triumph, why only to these sinners and not to all? And if he offered a second chance for salvation, why only to these sinners and not to all? Even more difficult for this view is the fact that Scripture elsewhere indicates that there is no opportunity for repentance after death (Luke 16:26; Heb. 10:26–27).

Moreover, the context of 1 Peter 3 makes "preaching in hell" unlikely. Peter is encouraging his readers to witness boldly to hostile unbelievers around them. He just told them to "always be prepared to give an answer to everyone who asks you" (1 Peter 3:15 NIV). This evangelistic motif would lose its urgency if Peter were teaching a second chance for salvation after death. And it would not fit at all with a "preaching" of condemnation.

**Does it refer to Christ preaching to fallen angels?**

To give a better explanation for these difficulties, several commentators have proposed taking "spirits in prison" to mean demonic spirits, the spirits of fallen angels, and have said that Christ proclaimed condemnation to these demons. This (it is claimed) would comfort Peter's readers by showing them that the demonic forces oppressing them would also be defeated by Christ.

However, Peter's readers would have to go through an incredibly complicated reasoning process to draw this conclusion when Peter does not explicitly teach it. They would have to reason from (1) some demons who sinned long ago were condemned, to (2) other demons are now inciting your human persecutors, to (3) those demons will likewise be condemned someday, to (4) therefore your persecutors will finally be judged as well. Finally Peter's readers would get to Peter's point: (5) Therefore don't fear your persecutors.

Those who hold this "preaching to fallen angels" view must assume that Peter's readers would "read between the lines" and conclude all this (points 2–5) from the simple statement that Christ "preached to the spirits in prison, who formerly did not obey" (1 Peter 3:19–20). But does it not seem too farfetched to say that Peter knew his readers would read all this into the text?

Moreover, Peter emphasizes hostile *persons,* not demons, in the context (1 Peter 3:14, 16). And where would Peter's readers get the idea that angels sinned "during the building of the ark"? There is nothing of that in the Genesis story about the building of the ark. And (in spite of what some have claimed), if we look at all the traditions of Jewish interpretation of the flood story, we find no mention of angels sinning specifically "during the building of the ark."[28] Therefore the view that Peter is speaking of Christ's proclamation of judgment to fallen angels is really not persuasive either.

---

[28]For an extensive discussion of Jewish interpretations of the sin of the "sons of God" in Gen. 6:2, 4, and of the identity of those who sinned while the ark was being built, see "Christ Preaching Through Noah: 1 Peter 3:19–20 in the Light of Dominant Themes in Jewish Literature," in Wayne Grudem, *The First Epistle of Peter,* pp. 203–39. (This appendix has a lengthy discussion of 1 Peter 3:19–20, which I have only briefly summarized here.)

**Does it refer to Christ's proclaiming release to Old Testament saints?**

Another explanation is that Christ, after his death, went and proclaimed release to Old Testament believers who had been unable to enter heaven until the completion of Christ's redemptive work.

But again we may question whether this view adequately accounts for what the text actually says. It does not say that Christ preached to those who were believers or faithful to God, but to those "who formerly *did not obey*"—the emphasis is on their disobedience. Moreover, Peter does not specify Old Testament believers generally, but only those who were disobedient "in the days of Noah, during the building of the ark" (1 Peter 3:20).

Finally, Scripture gives us no clear evidence to make us think that full access to the blessings of being in God's presence in heaven were withheld from Old Testament believers when they died—indeed, several passages suggest that believers who died before Christ's death did enter into the presence of God at once because their sins were forgiven by trusting in the Messiah who was to come (Gen. 5:24; 2 Sam. 12:23; Pss. 16:11; 17:15; 23:6; Eccl. 12:7; Matt. 22:31–32; Luke 16:22; Rom. 4:1–8; Heb. 11:5).

**A more satisfying explanation.**

The most satisfactory explanation of 1 Peter 3:19–20 seems rather to be one proposed (but not really defended) long ago by Augustine: the passage refers not to something Christ did between his death and resurrection, but to what he did "in the spiritual realm of existence" (or "through the Spirit") *at the time of Noah.* When Noah was building the ark, Christ "in spirit" was preaching through Noah to the hostile unbelievers around him.[29]

This view gains support from two other statements of Peter. In 1 Peter 1:11, he says that the "Spirit of Christ" was speaking in the Old Testament prophets. This suggests that Peter could readily have thought that the "Spirit of Christ" was speaking through Noah as well. Then in 2 Peter 2:5, he calls Noah a *"preacher* of righteousness"* (NIV), using the noun (*kēryx*) that comes from the same root as the verb "preached" (*ekēryxen*) in 1 Peter 3:19. So it seems likely that when Christ "preached to the spirits in prison" he did so through Noah in the days before the flood.

The people to whom Christ preached through Noah were unbelievers on the earth at the time of Noah, but Peter calls them "spirits in prison" because they are now in the prison of hell—even though they were not just "spirits" but persons on earth when the preaching was done. (The NASB says Christ preached "to the spirits now in prison.") We can speak the same way in English: "I knew President Clinton when he was a college student" is an appropriate statement, even though he was not president when he was in college. The sentence means, "I knew the man who is now President Clinton when he was still a student in college." So "Christ preached to the spirits in prison" means "Christ preached to people who are now spirits in prison when they were still persons on earth."[30]

This interpretation is very appropriate to the larger context of 1 Peter 3:13–

---

[29]This section is a brief summary of a more extensive discussion of this passage in Wayne Grudem, *The First Epistle of Peter,* pp. 157–62 and 203–39.

[30]My student Tet-Lim Yee has called my attention to another very similar expression elsewhere in Scripture: Naomi speaks of how kindly Ruth and Orpah "have dealt with the dead" (Ruth 1:8), referring to their treatment of their husbands while the husbands were still alive.

22. The parallel between the situation of Noah and the situation of Peter's readers is clear at several points:

| Noah | Peter's readers |
|---|---|
| Righteous minority | Righteous minority |
| Surrounded by hostile unbelievers | Surrounded by hostile unbelievers |
| God's judgment was near | God's judgment may come soon (1 Peter 4:5, 7; 2 Peter 3:10) |
| Noah witnessed boldly (by Christ's power) | They should witness boldly by Christ's power (1 Peter 3:14, 16–17; 3:15; 4:11) |
| Noah was finally saved | They will finally be saved (1 Peter 3:13–14; 4:13; 5:10) |

Such an understanding of the text seems to be by far the most likely solution to a puzzling passage. Yet this means that our fourth possible support for a descent of Christ into hell also turns up negative—the text speaks rather of something Christ did on earth at the time of Noah.

*(e) 1 Peter 4:6.* This fifth and final passage says, "For this is why the gospel was preached even to the dead, that though judged in the flesh like men, they might live in the spirit like God."

Does this verse mean that Christ went to hell and preached the gospel to those who had died? If so, it would be the only passage in the Bible that taught a "second chance" for salvation after death and would contradict passages such as Luke 16:19–31 and Hebrews 9:27, which clearly seem to deny this possibility. Moreover, the passage does not explicitly say that Christ preached to people after they had died, and could rather mean that the gospel in general was preached (this verse does not even say that Christ preached) to people who are now dead, but that it was preached to them while they were still alive on earth.

This is a common explanation, and it seems to fit this verse much better. It finds support in the second word of the verse, "this," which refers back to the final judgment mentioned at the end of verse 5. Peter is saying that it was because of the final judgment that the gospel was preached to the dead.

This would comfort the readers concerning their Christian friends who had already died. They may have wondered, "Did the gospel benefit them, since it didn't save them from death?" Peter answers that the reason the gospel was preached to those who had died was not to save them from physical death (they were "judged in the flesh like men") but to save them from final judgment (they will "live in the spirit like God"). Therefore, the fact that they had died did not indicate that the gospel had failed in its purpose—for they would surely live forever in the spiritual realm.

Thus, "the dead" are people who have died and are now dead, even though they were alive and on earth when the gospel was preached to them. (The NIV translates, "For this is the reason the gospel was preached even to *those who are now dead,*" and NASB has "those who are dead.") This avoids the doctrinal problem of a "second chance" of salvation after death and fits both the wording and the context of the verse.

We conclude, therefore, that this last passage, when viewed in its context, turns out to provide no convincing support for the doctrine of a descent of Christ into hell.

At this point, people on all sides of the question of whether Christ actually descended into hell should be able to agree at least that the idea of Christ's "descent into hell" is not taught clearly or explicitly in any passage of Scripture. And many people (including the present author) will conclude that this idea is not taught in Scripture at all. But beyond the question of whether any passage positively teaches this idea, we must ask whether it is contrary to any passages of Scripture.

### (3) Biblical Opposition to a "Descent Into Hell"

In addition to the fact that there is little if any biblical support for a descent of Christ into hell, there are some New Testament texts that argue against the possibility of Christ's going to hell after his death.

Jesus' words to the thief on the cross, "Today you will be with me in Paradise" (Luke 23:43), imply that after Jesus died his soul (or spirit) went immediately to the presence of the Father in heaven, even though his body remained on earth and was buried. Some people deny this by arguing that "Paradise" is a place distinct from heaven, but in both of the other New Testament uses the word clearly means "heaven": in 2 Corinthians 12:4 it is the place to which Paul was caught up in his revelation of heaven, and in Revelation 2:7 it is the place where we find the tree of life—which is clearly heaven in Revelation 22:2 and 14.[31]

In addition, the cry of Jesus, "It is finished" (John 19:30) strongly suggests that Christ's suffering was finished at that moment and so was his alienation from the Father because of bearing our sin. This implies that he would not descend into hell, but would go at once into the Father's presence.

Finally, the cry, "Father, into your hands I commit my spirit" (Luke 23:46), also suggests that Christ expected (correctly) the immediate end of his suffering and estrangement and the welcoming of his spirit into heaven by God the Father (note Stephen's similar cry in Acts 7:59).

These texts indicate, then, that Christ in his death experienced the same things believers in this present age experience when they die: his dead body remained on earth and was buried (as ours will be), but his spirit (or soul) passed immediately into the presence of God in heaven (just as ours will). Then on the first Easter morning, Christ's spirit was reunited with his body and he was raised from the dead—just as Christians who have died will (when Christ returns) be reunited to their bodies and raised in their perfect resurrection bodies to new life.[32]

---

[31]Further support for this idea is found in the fact that though the word *paradeisos*, "paradise," could simply mean "pleasant garden" (esp. used in the LXX of the Garden of Eden), it also frequently meant "heaven" or "a place of blessedness in the presence of God": see Isa. 51:3; Ezek. 28:13; 31:8–9; T. Levi 18:10; 1 Enoch 20:7; 32:3; Sib. Or. 3:48. This was increasingly the sense of the term in intertestamental Jewish literature (for several more references see Joachim Jeremias, *paradeisos*, *TDNT* 5 [1967], pp. 765–73, esp. 767, nn. 16–23).

[32]John 20:17 ("Do not hold me, for I have not yet ascended to the Father") is best understood to mean that Jesus in his new resurrected state, with a resurrection body, had not yet ascended back to heaven; therefore, Mary should not try to hold on to Jesus' body. The perfect tense of *anabebēka*, "ascended," gives the sense, "I have not yet ascended and remained in the place where I ascended" or "I

This fact has pastoral encouragement for us: we need not fear death, not only because eternal life lies on the other side, but also because we know that our Savior himself has gone through exactly the same experience we will go through—he has prepared, even sanctified the way, and we follow him with confidence each step of that way. This is much greater comfort regarding death than could ever be given by any view of a descent into hell.

### (4) Conclusion Regarding the Apostles' Creed and the Question of Christ's Possible Descent Into Hell

Does the phrase "he descended into hell" deserve to be retained in the Apostles' Creed alongside the great doctrines of the faith on which all can agree? The single argument in its favor seems to be the fact that it has been around so long. But an old mistake is still a mistake—and as long as it has been around there has been confusion and disagreement over its meaning.

On the other side, there are several compelling reasons against keeping the phrase. It has no clear warrant from Scripture and indeed seems to be contradicted by some passages in Scripture. It has no claim to being "apostolic" and no support (in the sense of a "descent into hell") from the first six centuries of the church. It was not in the earliest versions of the Creed and was only included in it later because of an apparent misunderstanding about its meaning. Unlike every other phrase in the Creed, it represents not some major doctrine on which all Christians agree, but rather a statement about which most Christians seem to disagree.[33] It is at best confusing and in most cases misleading for modern Christians. My own judgment is that there would be all gain and no loss if it were dropped from the Creed once for all.

Concerning the doctrinal question of whether Christ did descend into hell after he died, the answer from several passages of Scripture seems clearly to be no.

## D. The Extent of the Atonement

One of the differences between Reformed theologians and other Catholic and Protestant theologians has been the question of the extent of the atonement. The question may be put this way: when Christ died on the cross, did he pay for the sins of the entire human race or only for the sins of those who he knew would ultimately be saved?

Non-Reformed people argue that the gospel offer in Scripture is repeatedly made to all people, and for this offer to be genuine, the payment for sins must have already been made and must be actually available for all people. They also say that if the people whose sins Christ paid for are limited, then the free offer of the gospel also is limited, and the offer of the gospel cannot be made to all mankind without exception.

On the other hand, Reformed people argue that if Christ's death actually paid for the sins of every person who ever lived, then there is no penalty left for *anyone*

---

am not yet in the ascended state" (the latter phrase is from D. A. Carson, *The Gospel According to John* [Leicester: Inter-Varsity Press, and Grand Rapids: Eerdmans, 1991], p. 644).

[33]Randall E. Otto adopts a similar recommendation: "To include such a mysterious article in the creed, which is supposed to be a summary of the basic and vital tenets of the faith, seems very unwise" ("*Descendit in Inferna:* A Reformed Review of a Doctrinal Conundrum," *WTJ* 52 [1990], p. 150).

to pay, and it necessarily follows that all people will be saved, without exception. For God could not condemn to eternal punishment anyone whose sins are already paid for: that would be demanding double payment, and it would therefore be unjust. In answer to the objection that this compromises the free offer of the gospel to every person, Reformed people answer that we do not know who they are who will come to trust in Christ, for only God knows that. As far as we are concerned, the free offer of the gospel is to be made to everybody without exception. We also know that everyone who repents and believes in Christ will be saved, so all are called to repentance (cf. Acts 17:30). The fact that God foreknew who would be saved, and that he accepted Christ's death as payment for their sins only, does not inhibit the free offer of the gospel, for who will respond to it is hidden in the secret counsels of God. That we do not know who will respond no more constitutes a reason for not offering the gospel to all than not knowing the extent of the harvest prevents the farmer from sowing seed in his fields.

Finally, Reformed people argue that God's purposes in redemption are agreed upon within the Trinity and they are certainly accomplished. Those whom God planned to save are the same people for whom Christ also came to die, and to those same people the Holy Spirit will certainly apply the benefits of Christ's redemptive work, even awakening their faith (John 1:12; Phil. 1:29; cf. Eph. 2:2) and calling them to trust in him. What God the Father purposed, God the Son and the Holy Spirit agreed to and surely carried out.

**1. Scripture Passages Used to Support the Reformed View.** Several Scripture passages speak of the fact that Christ died for his people. "The good shepherd lays down his life *for the sheep*" (John 10:11). "I lay down my life for the sheep" (John 10:15). Paul speaks of "the church of God which he obtained with the blood of his own Son" (Acts 20:28). He also says, "He who did not spare his own Son but gave him up for us all, will he not also give us all things with him?" (Rom. 8:32). This passage indicates a connection between God's purpose in giving up his Son "for us all" and giving us "all things" that pertain to salvation as well. In the next sentence Paul clearly limits the application of this to those who will be saved because he says, "Who shall bring any charge against God's elect?" (Rom. 8:33) and in the next verse mentions Christ's death as a reason why no one shall bring a charge against the elect (8:34). In another passage, Paul says, "Husbands, love your wives, as Christ loved the church and gave himself up *for her*" (Eph. 5:25).

Moreover, Christ during his earthly ministry is aware of a group of people whom the Father has given to him. "All that the Father gives me will come to me; and him who comes to me I will not cast out . . . this is the will of him who sent me, that I should lose nothing of all that he has given me, but raise it up at the last day" (John 6:37–39). He also says, "I am not praying for the world but for those whom you have given me, for they are yours" (John 17:9). He then goes on from this specific reference to the disciples to say, "I do not pray for these only, but also for those who believe in me through their word" (John 17:20).

Finally, some passages speak of a definite transaction between the Father and the Son when Christ died, a transaction that had specific reference to those who would believe. For example, Paul says, "God shows his love for us in that while we were yet sinners Christ died *for us*" (Rom. 5:8). He adds, "For if while we were enemies *we were reconciled to God by the death of his Son,* much more, now that we are reconciled, shall we be saved by his life" (Rom. 5:10). This reconciliation to God occurred with respect to the specific people who would be saved, and it occurred "while we were enemies." Similarly, Paul says, *"For our sake* he made him to be sin who knew no sin, so that in him we might become the righteousness of God" (2 Cor. 5:21; cf. Gal. 1:4; Eph. 1:7). And "Christ redeemed *us* from the curse of the law, having become a curse *for us"* (Gal. 3:13).

Further support for the Reformed view is found in the consideration that all the blessings of salvation, including faith, repentance, and all of the works of the Holy Spirit in applying redemption, were also secured by Christ's redemptive work specifically for his people. Those for whom he earned forgiveness also have had those other benefits earned for them (cf. Eph. 1:3–4; 2:8; Phil. 1:29).[34]

What I have called "the Reformed view" in this section is commonly referred to as "limited atonement."[35] However, most theologians who hold this position today do not prefer the term "limited atonement" because it is so easily subject to misunderstanding, as if this view somehow held that Christ's atoning work was deficient in some way. The term that is usually preferred is *particular redemption,* since this view holds that Christ died for particular people (specifically, those who would be saved and whom he came to redeem), that he foreknew each one of them individually (cf. Eph. 1:3–5) and had them individually in mind in his atoning work.[36]

The opposite position, that Christ's death actually paid for the sins of all people who ever lived, is called "general redemption" or "unlimited atonement."

## 2. Scripture Passages Used to Support the Non-Reformed View (General Redemption or Unlimited Atonement). 
A number of Scripture passages indicate that in some sense Christ died for the whole world. John the Baptist said, "Behold, the Lamb of God, who takes away the sin *of the world!"* (John 1:29). And John 3:16 tells us that "God so loved the world that he gave his only Son, that whoever believes in him should not perish but have eternal life." Jesus said, "The

---

[34]I am not aware of any Arminians who hold what I have called the "Reformed view," the view that is commonly called "particular redemption" or "limited atonement." But it does not seem logically impossible for someone to hold a traditional Arminian position (that God foreknew who would believe and predestined them on the basis of that foreknowledge) coupled with the belief that Christ's death actually paid the penalty for the sins of those who God knew would believe and not for any others. This is just to say that, while "limited atonement" is necessarily part of a Reformed viewpoint because it logically follows from the overall sovereignty of God in the entire work of redemption, one could (in theory at least) hold to "limited atonement" and not adopt a Reformed position on other points concerning God's sovereignty in life generally or in salvation in particular.

[35]Thus, it is the "L" in the acronym "TULIP," which represents the so-called "five points of Calvinism," five doctrinal positions that distinguish Calvinists or Reformed theologians from many other Protestants. The five points represented by the word are: Total depravity, Unconditional election, Limited atonement, Irresistible grace, and Perseverance of the saints. (This book advocates these five doctrinal points, but it attempts in each case to point out the arguments in favor of an opposing position and to provide an appropriate bibliography representing both views; for the individual points see the following chapters: 24 [T], 32 [U], 27 [L], 34 [I], and 40 [P].)

[36]Reformed people argue that it is the other view that really limits the power of the atonement because on that view the atonement does not actually guarantee salvation for God's people but only makes salvation possible for all people. In other words, if the atonement is not limited with respect to the number of people to which it applies, then it must be limited with respect to what it actually accomplishes.

bread which I shall give for the life of the world is my flesh" (John 6:51). Paul says that in Christ "God was reconciling *the world* to himself" (2 Cor. 5:19). We read of Christ that "he is the expiation [lit. 'propitiation'] for our sins, and not for ours only but also for the sins of *the whole world*" (1 John 2:2). Paul writes that Christ Jesus "gave himself as a ransom *for all*" (1 Tim. 2:6). And the author of Hebrews says that Jesus was for a little while made lower than the angels "so that by the grace of God he might taste death for every one" (Heb. 2:9).

Other passages appear to speak of Christ dying for those who will not be saved. Paul says, "Do not let what you eat cause the ruin of one for whom Christ died" (Rom. 14:15). In a similar context he tells the Corinthians not to eat publicly at an idol's temple because they might encourage those who are weak in their faith to violate their consciences and eat food offered to idols. He then says, "And so by your knowledge this weak man is destroyed, the brother *for whom Christ died*" (1 Cor. 8:11). Peter writes about false teachers as follows: "But false prophets also arose among the people, just as there will be false teachers among you, who will secretly bring in destructive heresies, *even denying the Master who bought them,* bringing upon themselves swift destruction" (2 Peter 2:1; cf. Heb. 10:29).

**3. Some Points of Agreement and Some Conclusions About Disputed Texts.**
It would be helpful first to list the points on which both sides agree:

1. Not all will be saved.

2. A free offer of the gospel can rightly be made to every person ever born. It is completely true that "whoever will" may come to Christ for salvation, and no one who comes to him will be turned away. This free offer of the gospel is extended in good faith to every person.

3. All agree that Christ's death in itself, because he is the infinite Son of God, has infinite merit and is in itself sufficient to pay the penalty of the sins of as many or as few as the Father and the Son decreed. The question is not about the intrinsic merits of Christ's sufferings and death, but about the number of people for whom the Father and the Son thought Christ's death to be sufficient payment at the time Christ died.

Beyond these points of agreement, however, a difference remains concerning the following question: "When Christ died, did he *actually pay the penalty* only for the sins of those who would believe in him, or for the sins of every person who ever lived?" On this question it seems that those who hold to particular redemption have stronger arguments on their side. First, an important point that is not generally answered by advocates of the general redemption view is that people who are eternally condemned to hell suffer the penalty for all of their own sins, and therefore their penalty could not have been fully taken by Christ. Those who hold the general redemption view sometimes answer that people suffer in hell because of the sin of rejecting Christ, even though their other sins were paid for. But this is hardly a satisfactory position, for (1) some have never rejected Christ because they have never heard of him, and (2) the emphasis of Scripture when it speaks of eternal punishment is not on the fact that the people suffer because they have rejected Christ, but on the fact that they suffer because of their own sins in this life (see Rom. 5:6–8, 13–16, et al.). This significant point seems to tip the argument decisively in favor of the particular redemption position.

Another significant point in favor of particular redemption is the fact that Christ completely earned our salvation, paying the penalty for all our sins. He did not just redeem us potentially, but actually redeemed us as individuals whom he loved. A third weighty point in favor of particular redemption is that there is eternal unity in the counsels and plans of God and in the work of the Father, Son, and Holy Spirit in accomplishing their plans (see Rom. 8:28–30).

With regard to Scripture passages used to support general redemption, the following may be said: Several passages that speak about "the world" simply mean that sinners generally will be saved, without implying that every single individual in the world will be saved. So the fact that Christ is the Lamb of God who takes away the sin of the world (John 1:29) does not mean (on anybody's interpretation) that Christ actually removes the sins of every single person in the world, for both sides agree that not all are saved. Similarly, the fact that God was in Christ reconciling the world to himself (2 Cor. 5:19) does not mean that every single person in the world was reconciled to God, but that sinners generally were reconciled to God. Another way of putting these two passages would be to say that Jesus was the Lamb of God who takes away the sin of sinners, or that God was in Christ reconciling sinners to himself. This does not mean that all sinners will be saved or were reconciled, but simply that these groups in general, but not necessarily every single person in them, were the objects of God's redeeming work: it essentially means that "God so loved sinners that he gave his only Son . . ." without implying that every sinner in the whole world will be saved.

The passages that speak about Christ dying "for" the whole world are best understood to refer to the free offer of the gospel that is made to all people. When Jesus says, "The bread which I shall give *for the life of the world* is my flesh" (John 6:51), it is in the context of speaking of himself as the Bread that came down from heaven, which is offered to people and which they may, if they are willing, receive for themselves. Earlier in the same discussion Jesus said that "the bread of God is that which comes down from heaven, and gives life to the world" (John 6:33). This may be understood in the sense of bringing redeeming life into the world but not meaning that every single person in the world will have that redeeming life. Jesus then speaks of himself as inviting others to come and take up this living bread: "He who comes to me shall not hunger, and he who believes in me shall never thirst. . . . This is the bread which comes down from heaven, that a man may eat of it and not die. I am the living bread which came down from heaven; if any one eats of this bread, he will live for ever; and the bread which I shall give for the life of the world is my flesh" (John 6:35, 50–51). Jesus gives his flesh to bring life into the world and to offer life to the world, but to say that Jesus came to offer eternal life to the world (a point on which both sides agree) is not to say that he actually paid the penalty for the sins of everyone who would ever live, for that is a separate question.

When John says that Christ "is the propitiation for our sins, and not for ours only but also for the sins of the whole world" (1 John 2:2, author's translation), he may simply be understood to mean that Christ is the atoning sacrifice that the gospel now *makes available for* the sins of everyone in the world. The preposition "for" (Gk. *peri* plus genitive) is ambiguous with respect to the specific sense in which Christ is the propitiation "for" the sins of the world. *Peri* simply means "concerning" or "with respect to" but is not specific enough to define the exact way in which Christ is the sacrifice with respect to the sins of the world. It would be entirely consistent with the language of the verse to think that John is simply saying that Christ is the atoning sacrifice who is available to pay for the sins of anyone in the world.[37] Likewise, when Paul says that Christ "gave himself as a ransom *for all*" (1 Tim. 2:6), we are to understand this to mean a ransom available for all people, without exception.[38]

When the author of Hebrews says that Christ was made lower than the angels "so that by the grace of God he might taste death for every one" (Heb. 2:9), the passage is best understood to refer to every one of Christ's people, every one who is redeemed. It does not say everyone "in the whole world" or any such expression, and in the immediate context the author is certainly speaking of those who are redeemed (see "bringing many sons to glory" [v. 10]; "those who are sanctified" [v. 11]; and "the children God has given me" [v. 13]). The Greek word *pas*, here translated "every one," is also used in a similar sense to mean "all of God's people" in Hebrews 8:11, "for *all* shall know me," and in Hebrews 12:8, "If you are left without discipline, in which *all* have participated, then you are illegitimate children and not sons." In both cases the "all" is not explicitly restricted by a specific phrase such as "all of God's people," but this is clearly the sense in the overall context. Of course, in other contexts, the same word "all" can mean "all people without exception," but this must be determined from the individual context in each case.

When Paul speaks in Romans 14:15 and 1 Corinthians 8:11 about the possibility of destroying one for whom Christ died, it seems best here as well to think of the word "for" in the sense that Christ died "*to make salvation available for*" these people or "to bring the free offer of the gospel to" these people who are associated with the fellowship of the church. He does not seem to have in mind the specific question of the inter-trinitarian decision regarding whose sins the Father counted Christ's death as a payment for. Rather, he is speaking of those to whom the gospel has been offered. In another passage, when Paul calls the weak man a "brother for whom Christ died" in 1 Corinthians 8:11, he is not necessarily pronouncing on the inward spiritual condition of a person's heart, but is probably just speaking according to what is often called the "judgment of charity" by which people who are participating in the fellowship of the church can rightly be referred to as brothers and sisters.[39]

---

[37]Compare a similar sense for the phrase "for sins" (Gk. *peri harmartiōn*) in Heb. 10:26 where the author says that if someone continues on sinning deliberately after receiving the knowledge of the truth "there no longer remains a sacrifice for sins." This does not mean that Christ's sacrifice no longer exists, but it is no longer available for that person who has willfully spurned it and put himself beyond the realm of willing repentance. Here "sacrifice for sins" means "a sacrifice available to be claimed for the payment of sins." In the same way 1 John 2:2 can mean "the propitiation *available for* the sins of the whole world [esp. with reference to Gentiles as well as Jews]."

[38]When Paul says that God "is the Savior of all men, especially of those who believe" (1 Tim. 4:10), he is referring to God the Father, not to Christ, and probably uses the word "Savior" in the sense of "one who preserves people's lives and rescues them from danger" rather than the sense of "one who forgives their sins," for surely Paul does not mean that every single person will be saved. However, another possible meaning is that God "is the Savior of all sorts of people—that is, of people who believe" (for a defense of this view see George W. Knight III, *The Pastoral Epistles*, pp. 203–4).

[39]Another possible interpretation of these two passages is that "destroy" means ruin the ministry or Christian growth of someone who will nonetheless remain a believer but whose principles will be compromised. That sense would certainly fit the context well in both cases, but one argument against it

When Peter speaks of false teachers who bring in destructive heresies, "even denying the Master who bought them" (2 Peter 2:1), it is unclear whether the word "Master" (Gk. *despotēs*) refers to Christ (as in Jude 4) or to God the Father (as in Luke 2:29; Acts 4:24; Rev. 6:10). In either case, the Old Testament allusion is probably to Deuteronomy 32:6, where Moses says to the rebellious people who have turned away from God, "Is not he your Father *who has bought you?*" (author's translation).[40] Peter is drawing an analogy between the past false prophets who arose among the Jews and those who will be false teachers within the churches to which he writes: "But false prophets also arose among the people, just as there will be false teachers among you, who will secretly bring in destructive heresies, even denying the Master who bought them" (2 Peter 2:1). In line with this clear reference to false prophets in the Old Testament, Peter also alludes to the fact that the rebellious Jews turned away from God who "bought" them out of Egypt in the exodus. From the time of the exodus onward, any Jewish person would have considered himself or herself one who was "bought" by God in the exodus and therefore a person of God's own possession. In this sense, the false teachers arising among the people were denying God their Father, to whom they rightfully belonged.[41] So the text means not that Christ had redeemed these false prophets, but simply that they were rebellious Jewish people (or church attenders in the same position as the rebellious Jews) who were rightly owned by God because they had been brought out of the land of Egypt (or their forefathers had), but they were ungrateful to him. Christ's specific redemptive work on the cross is not in view in this verse.[42]

With regard to the verses that talk of Christ's dying for his sheep, his church, or his people, non-Reformed people may answer that these passages do not deny that he died to pay the penalty for others as well. In response, while it is true that they do not explicitly deny that Christ died for others as well, their frequent reference to his death for his people would at least strongly suggest that this is a correct inference. Even if they do not absolutely imply such a particularizing of redemption, these verses do at least seem to be most naturally interpreted in this way.

In conclusion, it seems to me that the Reformed position of "particular redemption" is most consistent with the overall teaching of Scripture. But once that has been said, several points of caution need to be raised.

---

is that the Greek word *apollymi*, "destroy," which is used in both cases, seems a stronger word than would be appropriate if that were Paul's intention. The same word is used often of eternal destruction (see John 3:16; Rom. 2:12; 1 Cor. 1:18; 15:18; 2 Cor. 2:15; 4:3; 2 Peter 3:9). However, the context of 1 Cor. 8:11 may indicate a different sense than these other passages, for this verse does not talk about God "destroying" someone but about other human beings doing something to "destroy" another—which suggests a weaker sense for the term here.

[40]Though the Septuagint does not use Peter's term *agorazō* but rather *kataomai*, the words are synonymous in many cases, and both can mean "buy, purchase"; the Hebrew term in Deut. 32:6 is *qānāh*, which frequently means "purchase, buy" in the Old Testament.

[41]This is the view taken by John Gill, *The Cause of God and Truth* (Grand Rapids: Baker, 1980; repr. of 1855 ed.; first published 1735), p. 61. Gill discusses other possible interpretations of the passage, but this seems most persuasive. We should realize that in both of his epistles, Peter very frequently portrays the churches to which he is writing in terms of the rich imagery of the people of God in the Old Testament: see W. Grudem, *The First Epistle of Peter*, p. 113.

[42]The Greek word *despotēs*, "Master," is elsewhere used of God in contexts that emphasize his role as Creator and Ruler of the world (Acts 4:24; Rev. 6:10).

**4. Points of Clarification and Caution Regarding This Doctrine.** It is important to state some points of clarification and also some areas in which we can rightly object to the way in which some advocates of particular redemption have expressed their arguments. It is also important to ask what the pastoral implications are for this teaching.

1. It seems to be a mistake to state the question as Berkhof does[43] and focus on the purpose of the Father and the Son, rather than on what actually happened in the atonement. If we confine the discussion to the purpose of the atonement, then this is just another form of the larger dispute between Calvinists and Arminians over whether God's purpose is (a) to save all people, a purpose that is frustrated by man's will to rebel—the Arminian position—or whether God's purpose is (b) to save those whom he has chosen—the Calvinist position. This question will not be decided at the narrow point of the question of the extent of the atonement, for the specific scriptural texts on that point are too few and can hardly be said to be conclusive on either side. One's decisions on these passages will tend to be determined by one's view of the larger question as to what Scripture as a whole teaches about the nature of the atonement and about the broader issues of God's providence, sovereignty, and the doctrine of election. Whatever decisions are made on those larger topics will apply specifically to this point, and people will come to their conclusions accordingly.

Rather than focusing on the purpose of the atonement, therefore, the question is rightfully asked about the atonement itself: Did Christ pay for the sins of all unbelievers who will be eternally condemned, and did he pay for their sins fully and completely on the cross? It seems that we have to answer no to that question.

2. The statements "Christ died for his people only" and "Christ died for all people" are both true in some senses, and too often the argument over this issue has been confused because of various senses that can be given to the word "for" in these two statements.

The statement "Christ died for his people only" can be understood to mean that "Christ died to actually pay the penalty for all the sins of his people only." In that sense it is true. But when non-Reformed people hear the sentence "Christ died for his people only," they often hear in it, "Christ died so that he could make the gospel available only to a chosen few," and they are troubled over what they see as a real threat to the free offer of the gospel to every person. Reformed people who hold to particular redemption should recognize the potential for misunderstanding that arises with the sentence "Christ died for his people only," and, out of concern for the truth and out of pastoral concern to affirm the free offer of the gospel and to avoid misunderstanding in the body of Christ, they should be more precise in saying exactly what they mean. The simple sentence, "Christ died for his people only," while true in the sense explained above, is seldom understood in that way when people unfamiliar with Reformed doctrine hear it, and it therefore is better not to use such an ambiguous sentence at all.

On the other hand, the sentence, "Christ died for all people," is true if it means, "Christ died to make salvation available to all people" or if it means, "Christ died

---

[43]Berkhof says, "The question does relate to the design of the atonement. Did the Father in sending Christ, and did Christ in coming into the world, to make atonement for sin, do this with the design or for the purpose of saving only the elect or all men? That is the question, and that only is the question" (*Systematic Theology,* p. 394).

to bring the free offer of the gospel to all people." In fact, this is the kind of language Scripture itself uses in passages like John 6:51; 1 Timothy 2:6; and 1 John 2:2.[44] It really seems to be only nit-picking that creates controversies and useless disputes when Reformed people insist on being such purists in their speech that they object any time someone says that "Christ died for all people." There are certainly acceptable ways of understanding that sentence that are consistent with the speech of the scriptural authors themselves.

Similarly, I do not think we should rush to criticize an evangelist who tells an audience of unbelievers, "Christ died for your sins," if it is made clear in the context that it is necessary to trust in Christ before one can receive the benefits of the gospel offer. In that sense the sentence is simply understood to mean "Christ died to offer you forgiveness for your sins" or "Christ died to make available forgiveness for your sins." The important point here is that sinners realize that salvation is available for everyone and that payment of sins is available for everyone.

At this point some Reformed theologians will object and will warn us that if we say to unbelievers, "Christ died for your sins," the unbelievers will draw the conclusion, "Therefore I am saved no matter what I do." But this does not seem to be a problem in actual fact, for whenever evangelicals (Reformed or non-Reformed) speak about the gospel to unbelievers, they are always very clear on the fact that the death of Christ has no benefit for a person unless that person believes in Christ. Therefore, the problem seems to be more something that Reformed people *think* unbelievers should believe (if they were consistent in reasoning back into the secret counsels of God and the relationship between the Father and Son in the counsels of the Trinity at the point of Christ's propitiatory sacrifice on the cross). But unbelievers simply do not reason that way: they know that they must exercise faith in Christ before they will experience any benefits from his saving work. Moreover, it is far more likely that people will understand the sentence "Christ died for your sins" in the doctrinally correct sense that "Christ died in order to offer you forgiveness for your sins" rather than in the doctrinally incorrect sense, "Christ died and completely paid the penalty already for all your sins."[45]

3. In terms of the practical, pastoral effects of our words, both those who hold to particular redemption and those who hold to general redemption agree at several key points:

a. Both sincerely want to avoid implying that people will be saved whether they believe in Christ or not. Non-Reformed people sometimes accuse Reformed people of saying that the elect will be saved irrespective of responding to the gospel, but this is clearly a misrepresentation of the Reformed position. On the other hand, Reformed people think that those who hold to general redemption are in danger of implying that everybody will be saved whether they believe in Christ or not. But this is not a position that non-Reformed people actually hold, and it is always precarious to criticize people for a position that they do not say

---

[44]Berkhof says that 1 Tim. 2:2 refers to "the revealed will of God that both Jews and Gentiles should be saved" (ibid., p. 396).

[45]I am not here arguing that we should be careless in our language; I am arguing that we should not rush to criticize when other Christians unreflectively use ambiguous language without intending to contradict any teaching of Scripture.

they hold, just because you think that they should hold that position if they were consistent with their other views.

b. Both sides want to avoid implying that there might be some people who come to Christ for salvation but are turned away because Christ did not die for them. No one wants to say or imply to an unbeliever, "Christ might have died for your sins (and then again he might not have!)." Both sides want to clearly affirm that all who come to Christ for salvation will in fact be saved. "Him who comes to me I will not cast out" (John 6:37).

c. Both sides want to avoid implying that God is hypocritical or insincere when he makes the free offer of the gospel. It is a genuine offer, and it is always true that all who wish to come to Christ for salvation and who do actually come to him will be saved.

d. Finally, we may ask why this matter is so important after all. Although Reformed people have sometimes made belief in particular redemption a test of doctrinal orthodoxy, it would be healthy to realize that Scripture itself never singles this out as a doctrine of major importance, nor does it once make it the subject of any explicit theological discussion. Our knowledge of the issue comes only from incidental references to it in passages whose concern is with other doctrinal or practical matters. In fact, this is really a question that probes into the inner counsels of the Trinity and does so in an area in which there is very little direct scriptural testimony—a fact that should cause us to be cautious. A balanced pastoral perspective would seem to be to say that this teaching of particular redemption *seems* to us to be true, that it gives logical consistency to our theological system, and that it can be helpful in assuring people of Christ's love for them individually and of the completeness of his redemptive work for them; but that it also is a subject that almost inevitably leads to some confusion, some misunderstanding, and often some wrongful argumentativeness and divisiveness among God's people—all of which are negative pastoral considerations. Perhaps that is why the apostles such as John and Peter and Paul, in their wisdom, placed almost no emphasis on this question at all. And perhaps we would do well to ponder their example.

## QUESTIONS FOR PERSONAL APPLICATION

1. In what ways has this chapter enabled you to appreciate Christ's death more than you did before? Has it given you more or less confidence in the fact that your sins have actually been paid for by Christ?

2. If the ultimate cause of the atonement is found in the love and justice of God, then was there anything in you that required God to love you or to take steps to save you (when he looked forward and thought of you as a sinner in rebellion against him)? Does your answer to this question help you to appreciate the character of God's love for you as a person who did not at all deserve that love? How does that realization make you feel in your relationship to God?

3. Do you think that Christ's sufferings were enough to pay for your sins? Are you willing to rely on his work to pay for all your sins? Do you think he is a sufficient Savior, worthy of your trust? When he invites you, "Come to me . . . and I will give you rest" (Matt. 11:28), do you now trust him? Will you now and always rely on him with your whole heart for complete salvation?

4. If Christ bore all the guilt for our sins, all the wrath of God against sin, and all the penalty of the death that we deserved, then will God ever turn his wrath against you as a believer (see Rom. 8:31–39)? Can any of the hardships or sufferings that you experience in life be due to the wrath of God against you? If not, then why do we as Christians experience difficulties and sufferings in this life (see Rom. 8:28; Heb. 12:3–11)?

5. Do you think Christ's life was good enough to deserve God's approval? Are you willing to rely on it for your eternal destiny? Is Jesus Christ a reliable enough and good enough Savior for you to trust him? Which would you rather trust in for your eternal standing before God: your own life or Christ's?

6. If Christ has indeed redeemed you from bondage to sin and to the kingdom of Satan, are there areas of your life in which you could more fully realize this to be true? Could this realization give you more encouragement in your Christian life?

7. Do you think it was fair for Christ to be your substitute and to pay your penalty? When you think about him acting as your substitute and dying for you, what attitude and emotion is called forth in your heart?

## SPECIAL TERMS

| | |
|---|---|
| active obedience | particular redemption |
| atonement | passive obedience |
| blood of Christ | penal substitution |
| consequent absolute necessity | propitiation |
| example theory | ransom to Satan theory |
| general redemption | reconciliation |
| governmental theory | redemption |
| impute | sacrifice |
| limited atonement | unlimited atonement |
| moral influence theory | vicarious atonement |

## BIBLIOGRAPHY

(For an explanation of this bibliography see the note on the bibliography to chapter 1, p. 38. Complete bibliographical data may be found on pp. 1223–29.)

## Sections in Evangelical Systematic Theologies

1. Anglican (Episcopalian)
   - 1882-92     Litton, 221-36
   - 1930        Thomas, 49-72, 414-26
2. Arminian (Wesleyan or Methodist)
   - 1847        Finney, 258-82
   - 1875-76     Pope, 2:141-88, 263-316
   - 1892-94     Miley, 2:65-240
   - 1940        Wiley, 2:217-300
   - 1960        Purkiser, 243-68
   - 1983        Carter, 1:483-505
   - 1983-       Cottrell, 3:401-60
   - 1987-90     Oden, 2:317-450
3. Baptist
   - 1767        Gill, 1:562-83; 2:1-68
   - 1887        Boyce, 295-341
   - 1907        Strong, 701-6, 713-75
   - 1917        Mullins, 304-37
   - 1983-85     Erickson, 761-841
   - 1987-94     Lewis/Demarest, 2:371-436
4. Dispensational
   - 1947        Chafer, 3:35-164, 183-205; 5:177-230
   - 1949        Thiessen, 229-42
   - 1986        Ryrie, 275-309, 318-23
5. Lutheran
   - 1917-24     Pieper, 2:280-330, 342-82
   - 1934        Mueller, 287-95, 305-13
6. Reformed (or Presbyterian)
   - 1559        Calvin, 1:503-34 (2.16-17)
   - 1724-58     Edwards, 1:574-80; 2:766-78
   - 1861        Heppe, 448-87, 488-94
   - 1871-73     Hodge, 2:480-591, 610-25
   - 1878        Dabney, 485-553
   - 1887-1921   Warfield, *SSW*, 1:167-77; *SSW*, 2:308-20; *BD*, 327-438; *PWC*, 325-530; *CC*, 393-444
   - 1889        Shedd, 2b:353-489; 3:401-70
   - 1937-66     Murray, *CW*, 1:36-39, 59-85; 2:142-57; *RAA*, 9-57
   - 1938        Berkhof, 331-43, 361-99
   - 1962        Buswell, 2:70-133
7. Renewal (or charismatic/Pentecostal)
   - 1988-92     Williams, 1:353-80

## Sections in Representative Roman Catholic Systematic Theologies

1. Roman Catholic: Traditional
   1955    Ott, 175–79, 182–92, 211–19
2. Roman Catholic: Post-Vatican II
   1980    McBrien, 1:417–23; 2:865–901

## Other Works

Bauckham, Richard J. "Descent into Hell." In *NDT*, pp. 194–95.

Berkouwer, G. C. *The Work of Christ*. Trans. by Cornelius Lambregtse. Grand Rapids: Eerdmans, 1965.

Brown, John. *The Sufferings and Glories of the Messiah*. Evanston, Ind.: Sovereign Grace Publishers, 1959 (reprint of 1852 edition).

Campbell, John McLeod. *The Nature of the Atonement*. 6th ed. London and New York: Macmillan, 1886 (first published in 1856).

Elwell, Walter. "Atonement, Extent of the." In *EDT*, pp. 98–100.

Green, Michael. *The Empty Cross of Jesus*. The Jesus Library, ed. by Michael Green. Downers Grove, Ill.: InterVarsity Press, 1984.

Grensted, L. W. *A Short History of the Doctrine of the Atonement*. Manchester: University Press, and London: Longmans, 1962.

Hodge, Archibald A. *The Atonement*. London: T. Nelson, 1868.

McDonald, H. D. *The Atonement of the Death of Christ*. Grand Rapids: Baker, 1985.

McGrath, Alister E. *Luther's Theology of the Cross: Martin Luther's Theological Breakthrough*. Oxford: Basil Blackwell, 1985.

————. *The Mystery of the Cross*. Grand Rapids: Zondervan, 1988.

————. *What Was God Doing on the Cross?* Grand Rapids: Zondervan, 1993.

Martin, Hugh. *The Atonement: In Its Relations to the Covenant, the Priesthood, the Intercession of Our Lord*. Philadelphia: Smith and English, 1871.

Morey, Robert A. *Studies in the Atonement*. Southbridge, Mass.: Crowne, 1989.

Morris, Leon. *The Apostolic Preaching of the Cross*. 3d ed. Grand Rapids: Eerdmans, 1965.

————. "Atonement." In *EDT*, p. 97.

————. *The Atonement: Its Meaning and Significance*. Leicester and Downers Grove, Ill: InterVarsity Press, 1983.

————. "Atonement, Theories of the." In *EDT*, pp. 100–102.

————. *The Cross in the New Testament*. Grand Rapids: Eerdmans, 1965.

————. *The Cross of Jesus*. Grand Rapids: Eerdmans, and Exeter: Paternoster, 1988.

Murray, John. *Redemption Accomplished and Applied*. Grand Rapids: Eerdmans, 1955, pp. 9–78.

Owen, John. *The Death of Death in the Death of Christ*. Carlisle, Pa.: Banner of Truth, 1959.

Smeaton, George. *The Doctrine of the Atonement as Taught by Christ Himself*. Grand Rapids: Zondervan, 1953 (reprint of 1871 edition).

Smeaton, George. *The Apostles' Doctrine of the Atonement*. Grand Rapids: Zondervan, 1957 (reprint of 1870 edition).

Stott, John R. W. *The Cross of Christ*. Leicester and Downers Grove, Ill.: InterVarsity Press, 1986.

Turretin, Francis. *The Atonement of Christ*. Trans. by James R. Willson. Grand Rapids: Baker, 1978 (reprint of 1859 edition; first published in Latin in 1674).

Wallace, Ronald S. *The Atoning Death of Christ*. Westchester, Ill.: Crossway, 1981.

## SCRIPTURE MEMORY PASSAGE

**Romans 3:23–26:** *Since all have sinned and fall short of the glory of God, they are justified by his grace as a gift, through the redemption which is in Christ Jesus, whom God put forward as an expiation [lit. 'propitiation'] by his blood, to be received by faith. This was to show God's righteousness, because in his divine forbearance he had passed over former sins; it was to prove at the present time that he himself is righteous and that he justifies him who has faith in Jesus.*

## HYMN

"When I Survey the Wondrous Cross"

When I survey the wondrous cross
    On which the Prince of Glory died,
My richest gain I count but loss,
    And pour contempt on all my pride.

Forbid it, Lord, that I should boast,
    Save in the death of Christ my God:
All the vain things that charm me most,
    I sacrifice them to his blood.

See, from his head, his hands, his feet,
    Sorrow and love flow mingled down:
Did e'er such love and sorrow meet,
    Or thorns compose so rich a crown?

His dying crimson, like a robe,
    Spread o'er his body on the tree;
Then am I dead to all the globe,
    And all the globe is dead to me.

Were the whole realm of nature mine,
    That were a present far too small;
Love so amazing, so divine,
    Demands my soul, my life, my all.

AUTHOR: ISAAC WATTS, 1707

# Chapter 28

# Resurrection and Ascension

*What was Christ's resurrection body like? What is its significance for us? What happened to Christ when he ascended into heaven? What is meant by the states of Jesus Christ?*

## EXPLANATION AND SCRIPTURAL BASIS

### A. Resurrection

**1. New Testament Evidence.** The Gospels contain abundant testimony to the resurrection of Christ (see Matt. 28:1–20; Mark 16:1–8; Luke 24:1–53; John 20:1–21:25). In addition to these detailed narratives in the four gospels, the book of Acts is a story of the apostles' proclamation of the resurrection of Christ and of continued prayer to Christ and trust in him as the one who is alive and reigning in heaven. The Epistles depend entirely on the assumption that Jesus is a living, reigning Savior who is now the exalted head of the church, who is to be trusted, worshiped, and adored, and who will some day return in power and great glory to reign as King over the earth. The book of Revelation repeatedly shows the risen Christ reigning in heaven and predicts his return to conquer his enemies and reign in glory. Thus the entire New Testament bears witness to the resurrection of Christ.[1]

**2. The Nature of Christ's Resurrection.** Christ's resurrection was not simply a coming back from the dead, as had been experienced by others before, such as Lazarus (John 11:1–44), for then Jesus would have been subject to weakness and aging and eventually would have died again just as all other human beings die. Rather, when he rose from the dead Jesus was the "first fruits"[2] (1 Cor. 15:20, 23)

---

[1]The historical arguments for the resurrection of Christ are substantial and have persuaded many skeptics who started to examine the evidence for the purpose of disproving the resurrection. The best-known account of such a change from skepticism to belief is Frank Morison, *Who Moved the Stone?* (London: Faber and Faber, 1930; reprint, Grand Rapids: Zondervan, 1958). A widely used booklet summarizing the arguments is J. N. D. Anderson, *The Evidence for the Resurrection* (London and Downers Grove, Ill.: InterVarsity Press, 1966). (Both Morison and Anderson were trained as lawyers.) More recent and detailed presentations are found in William Lane Craig, *The Son Rises: The Historical Evidence for the Resurrection of Jesus* (Chicago: Moody, 1981); Gary Habermas and Anthony Flew, *Did Jesus Rise From the Dead? The Resurrection Debate*, ed. Terry L. Miethe (New York: Harper and Row, 1987); Gary Habermas, "Resurrection of Christ," in *EDT*, pp. 938–41. An extensive compilation of arguments and quotations from recognized scholars affirming the overwhelming reliability of the evidence for Christ's resurrection is found in Josh McDowell, *Evidence that Demands a Verdict*, rev. ed., vol. 1 (San Bernardino, Calif.: Here's Life Publishers, 1979), pp. 179–263.

[2]See discussion of the term "first fruits" on p. 615, below.

of a new kind of human life, a life in which his body was made perfect, no longer subject to weakness, aging, or death, but able to live eternally.

It is true that two of Jesus' disciples did not recognize him when they walked with him on the road to Emmaus (Luke 24:13–32), but Luke specifically tells us that this was because "their eyes were kept from recognizing him" (Luke 24:16), and later "their eyes were opened and they recognized him" (Luke 24:31). Mary Magdalene failed to recognize Jesus only for a moment (John 20:14–16), but it may have been still quite dark and she was not at first looking at him—she had come the first time "while it was still dark" (John 20:1), and she "turned" to speak to Jesus once she recognized him (John 20:16).

On other occasions the disciples seemed to have recognized Jesus fairly quickly (Matt. 28:9, 17; John 20:19–20, 26–28; 21:7, 12). When Jesus appeared to the eleven disciples in Jerusalem, they were initially startled and frightened (Luke 24:33, 37), yet when they saw Jesus' hands and his feet and watched him eat a piece of fish, they were convinced that he had risen from the dead. These examples indicate that there was a considerable degree of continuity between the physical appearance of Jesus before his death and after his resurrection. Yet Jesus did not look exactly as he had before he died, for in addition to the initial amazement of the disciples at what they apparently thought could not happen, there was probably sufficient difference in his physical appearance for Jesus not to be immediately recognized. Perhaps that difference in appearance was simply the difference between a man who had lived a life of suffering, hardship, and grief, and one whose body was restored to its full youthful appearance of perfect health: though Jesus' body was still a physical body, it was raised as a transformed body, never able again to suffer, be weak or ill, or die; it had "put on immortality" (1 Cor. 15:53). Paul says the resurrection body is raised "imperishable . . . in glory . . . in power . . . a spiritual body" (1 Cor. 15:42–44).[3]

The fact that Jesus had a physical body that could be touched and handled after the resurrection is seen in that the disciples "took hold of his feet" (Matt. 28:9), that he appeared to the disciples on the road to Emmaus to be just another traveler on the road (Luke 24:15–18, 28–29), that he took bread and broke it (Luke 24:30), that he ate a piece of broiled fish to demonstrate clearly that he had a physical body and was not just a spirit, that Mary thought him to be a gardener (John 20:15), that "he showed them his hands and his side" (John 20:20), that he invited Thomas to touch his hands and his side (John 20:27), that he prepared breakfast for his disciples (John 21:12–13), and that he explicitly told them, "See my hands and my feet, that it is I myself; handle me, and see; for *a spirit has not*

---

[3]By "spiritual body" Paul does not mean "immaterial," but rather "suited to and responsive to the guidance of the Spirit." In the Pauline epistles, the word "spiritual" (Gk. *pneumatikos*) never means "nonphysical" but rather "consistent with the character and activity of the Holy Spirit" (see, e.g., Rom. 1:11; 7:14; 1 Cor. 2:13, 15; 3:1; 14:37; Gal. 6:1 ["you who are spiritual"]; Eph. 5:19). The RSV translation, "It is sown a *physical* body, it is raised a *spiritual* body," is very misleading, because Paul does not use the word that was available to him if he had meant to speak of a physical body (Gk. *sōmatikos*), but rather uses the word *psychikos*, which means, in this context, "natural" (so NIV, NASB), that is, a body that is living in its own life and strength and in the characteristics of this present age but is not fully subject to and conforming to the character and will of the Holy Spirit. Therefore, a clearer paraphrase would be, "It is sown a *natural* body subject to the characteristics and desires of this age, and governed by its own sinful will, but it is raised a *spiritual* body, completely subject to the will of the Holy Spirit and responsive to the Holy Spirit's guidance." Such a body is not at all "nonphysical," but it is a physical body raised to the degree of perfection for which God originally intended it.

*flesh and bones as you see that I have*" (Luke 24:39). Peter said that the disciples "ate and drank with him after he rose from the dead" (Acts 10:41).

It is true that Jesus apparently was able to appear and disappear out of sight quite suddenly (Luke 24:31, 36; John 20:19, 26). Yet we should be careful not to draw too many conclusions from this fact, for not all the passages affirm that Jesus could suddenly appear or disappear; some just say that Jesus came and stood among the disciples. When Jesus suddenly vanished from the sight of the disciples in Emmaus, this may have been a special miraculous occurrence, such as happened when "the Spirit of the Lord caught up Philip; and the eunuch saw him no more" (Acts 8:39). Nor should we make too much of the fact that Jesus came and stood among the disciples on two occasions when the doors were "shut"[4] (John 20:19, 26), for no text says that Jesus "passed through walls" or anything like that. Indeed, on another occasion in the New Testament where someone needed to pass through a locked door, the door miraculously opened (see Acts 12:10).[5]

Murray Harris has recently proposed an alternative interpretation to the verses quoted above, especially the verses showing Jesus appearing and disappearing at different times: he says that these verses show that while Jesus could sometimes materialize into a physical body, his customary existence was in a nonphysical or nonfleshly form of his "spiritual body." Moreover, when he ascended into heaven after forty days, Jesus permanently gave up any more materializing into a physical body. Professor Harris says:

> The resurrection of Jesus was not his transformation into an immaterial body but his acquisition of a "spiritual body" which could materialize or dematerialize at will. When, on occasion, Jesus chose to appear to various persons in material form, this was just as really the "spiritual body" of Jesus as when he was not visible or tangible. . . . After the forty days, when his appearances on earth were ended, Jesus assumed the sole mode of being visible to the inhabitants of heaven but having a nonfleshly body. . . . In his risen state he transcended the normal laws of physical existence. He was no longer bound by material or spatial limitations.[6]

It is important to realize that Harris definitely affirms the physical, bodily resurrection of Jesus from the dead.[7] He says that the same body that died was also raised, but then it was transformed into a "spiritual body" with new properties.[8]

---

[4]The Greek perfect participle *kekleismenon* may mean either that the doors were "shut" or that they were "locked."

[5]I do not wish to argue that it is impossible that Jesus' resurrection body somehow passed through the door or the wall to enter the room, only that no verse in the Bible says that. It is possible, but the possibility does not deserve the status of an assured conclusion that it has reached in much popular preaching and much evangelical scholarship—it is just one possible inference from these verses, among several. Leon Morris says, "Some suggest that Jesus came right through the closed door, or that the door opened of its own accord or the like. But Scripture says nothing of the mode of Jesus' entry into the room and we do well not to attempt too exact a definition" (*The Gospel According to John*, p. 844). The problem with an affirmation that Jesus passed through walls is that it may cause people to think of Jesus' resurrection body as somehow nonmaterial, and this is contrary to the explicit affirmations of material characteristics that we have in several New Testament texts.

[6]Murray Harris, *From Grave to Glory: Resurrection in the New Testament* (Grand Rapids: Zondervan, 1990), pp. 142–43.

[7]See Harris, ibid., pp. 351 and 353 (where he "unequivocally" affirms "the literal, physical resurrection of Jesus from the dead") and p. 365 ("I am happy to affirm that our Lord rose from the dead in the actual physical body he possessed before his death").

[8]He understands "spiritual" not to mean "nonphysical" but rather "animated and guided by the spirit" (or possibly "Spirit"), p. 195.

In response, while I do not consider this a doctrinal question of major significance (since it is simply a question about the nature of the resurrection body, about which we now know very little),[9] I nevertheless think the New Testament provides some persuasive evidence that would lead us to differ with Harris's view. Harris agrees that at several times Jesus had a physical body that could eat food and be touched and that had flesh and bones. He even agrees that at Jesus' ascension into heaven, "It was a real Jesus of 'flesh and bones' (Luke 24:39) who was taken up before the eyes of his disciples."[10] The only question is whether this body of Jesus at other times existed in nonphysical, nonfleshly form, as Harris claims. To answer that, we have to ask whether the New Testament texts about Jesus appearing and disappearing require this conclusion. It does not seem that they do.

Luke 24:31, which says that after Jesus broke bread and gave it to the two disciples, "he *disappeared* from their sight" (NIV), does not require this. The Greek expression used here for "disappeared" (*aphantos egeneto*) does not occur elsewhere in the New Testament, but when found in Diodorus Siculus (a historian who wrote from 60–30 B.C.), it is used once of a man named Amphiaraus who, with his chariot, fell into a chasm and "disappeared from sight," and the same expression is used in another place to talk about Atlas who was blown off a mountaintop by high winds and "disappeared."[11] In neither case does the expression mean that the person became immaterial or even invisible, but only that he was moved to a place hidden from people's sight.[12] So in Luke 24:31, all we can conclude is that the disciples no longer saw Jesus—perhaps the Spirit of the Lord took him away (as with Philip in Acts 8:39), or perhaps he was just hidden again from their sight (as with Moses and Elijah on the Mount of Transfiguration, Matt. 17:8, or as with the heavenly army around Elisha, 2 Kings 6:17, or [apparently] as with the disciples walking past the prison guards in Acts 5:19–23; 12:6, 10). In neither case do we need to conclude that Jesus' physical body became nonphysical, any more than we need to conclude that the disciples' bodies became nonphysical when they walked past the guards (Acts 5:23; 12:10) and escaped from prison. So Luke 24:31 does not say that any transformation happened to Jesus' body; it merely says that the disciples could no longer see him.[13]

---

[9]See the lengthy report about Harris's view and those who have criticized it (and sometimes misrepresented it) in *CT,* April 5, 1993, pp. 62–66. Norman Geisler and some others have accused Harris of teaching serious heresy, but in this article, J. I. Packer says that "both Harris and Geisler appear to be orthodox, and both of them equally so" (pp. 64–65). A report from three other evangelical theologians, Millard Erickson, Bruce Demarest, and Roger Nicole, says that Harris's views are "somewhat novel" but "are compatible with the doctrinal position [of Trinity Evangelical Divinity School, where Harris teaches, and] . . . of the wider evangelical movement" (p. 63).

[10]Harris, *From Grave to Glory,* p. 422.

[11]Diod. Sic. 4.65.9 (of Amphiaraus) and 3.60.3 (of Atlas).

[12]Another occurrence of the word *aphantos* has a similar sense: Plutarch (ca. A.D. 50–ca. 120) reports someone who said that if there is a "mid-center" of the earth or ocean, "it is known to the gods, but is hidden (*aphantos*) from mortals" (*Moralia* 409F). The sense is not "immaterial" but "hidden from sight, not visible."

[13]Compare Luke 24:16, where it says that Jesus drew near to the disciples on the Emmaus Road, but "their eyes were kept from recognizing him." If God could cause the disciples' eyes to be partially blinded so that they could see Jesus but not recognize him, then certainly a few minutes later he could cause their eyes to be more fully blinded so they could not see him at all. The possibilities are too

As for the claim that Jesus passed through material substances, this is not substantiated in the New Testament. As explained above, the fact that Jesus appeared in a room when the doors had been shut or locked (John 20:19, 26) may or may not mean that he passed through a door or wall. Especially relevant here is the first deliverance of the apostles from prison: they did not walk through the doors, but "an angel of the Lord opened the prison doors and brought them out" (Acts 5:19); yet the next morning the prison officers reported, "We found the prison securely locked and the sentries standing at the doors, but when we opened it we found no one inside" (Acts 5:23). The angel had opened the doors, the apostles had passed through, and the angel had closed and locked the doors again. Similarly, when Peter was rescued from prison, he did not dematerialize in order to pass through the locked chains around him, but "the chains fell off his hands" (Acts 12:7).[14] In the same way, it is certainly possible that the door miraculously opened for Jesus or even that he had entered the room with the disciples but was temporarily hidden from their eyes.

With regard to the nature of Jesus' resurrection body, much more decisive than the texts about Jesus' appearing and disappearing are the texts that show that Jesus clearly had a physical body with "flesh and bones" (Luke 24:39), which could eat and drink, break bread, prepare breakfast, and be touched. Unlike the texts on Jesus' appearing and disappearing, these texts are not capable of an alternative explanation that denies Jesus' physical body—Harris himself agrees that in these texts Jesus had a body of flesh and bones. But what were these physical appearances intended to teach the disciples if not that Jesus' resurrection body was definitely a physical body? If Jesus rose from the dead in the same physical body that had died, and if he repeatedly appeared to the disciples in that physical body, eating and drinking with them (Acts 10:41) over forty days, and if he ascended into heaven in that same physical body (Acts 1:9), and if the angel immediately told the disciples that "this Jesus, who was taken up from you into heaven, will come in the same way as you saw him go into heaven" (Acts 1:11), then Jesus was clearly teaching them that his resurrection body was *a physical body*. If the "customary form" of his resurrection body was nonphysical, then in these repeated physical appearances Jesus would be guilty of misleading the disciples (and all subsequent readers of the New Testament) into thinking that his resurrection body remained physical when it did not. If he was customarily nonphysical and was going to become nonphysical forever at the ascension, then it would be very misleading for Jesus to say, "See my hands and my feet, that it is I myself; handle

---

complex and our knowledge is too limited for us to insist that these texts require that Jesus became nonphysical.

[14]Harris says that Jesus passed through a sealed tomb, according to Matt. 28:2, 6, but the verses can just as easily mean that the stone was first rolled away, and then Jesus came out (cf. Luke 24:2). Similarly, John 20:4–7 only says that the grave cloths were lying where Jesus' body had been but does not require that Jesus' body passed through the linen cloths: it could as readily mean that Jesus (or an angel) removed the cloths and placed them neatly in the tomb. Acts 10:40 says that Jesus was made "manifest" or visible to chosen witnesses (that is, they saw him), but again it says nothing about him materializing or being immaterial. In all of these verses, Harris seems to me to be concluding too much from too little data.

Finally, even if Jesus did pass through the door or the wall (as many Christians have concluded), this does not require us to say that his body was customarily nonmaterial, but could well be explained as a special miracle or as a property of resurrection bodies that we do not now understand, but that does not require that they be nonphysical or nonmaterial.

me, and see; for a spirit has not flesh and bones as you see that I have" (Luke 24:39). He did not say, ". . . flesh and bones, as you see that I temporarily have"! It would have been wrong to teach the disciples that he had a physical body when in his customary mode of existence he really did not.

If Jesus had wanted to teach them that he could materialize and dematerialize at will (as Harris argues), then he could easily have dematerialized before their eyes, so that they could clearly record this event. Or he could easily have passed through a wall while they watched, rather than just suddenly standing among them. In short, if Jesus and the New Testament authors had wanted to teach us that the resurrection body was customarily and essentially nonmaterial, they could have done so, but instead they gave many clear indications that it was customarily physical and material, even though it was a body that was perfected, made forever free from weakness, sickness, and death.

Finally, there is a larger doctrinal consideration. The physical resurrection of Jesus, and his eternal possession of a physical resurrection body, give clear affirmation of the goodness of the material creation that God originally made: "And God saw everything that he had made, and behold, *it was very good*" (Gen. 1:31). We as resurrected men and women will live forever in "new heavens and a new earth in which righteousness dwells" (2 Peter 3:13). We will live in a renewed earth that "will be set free from its bondage to decay" (Rom. 8:21) and become like a new Garden of Eden. There will be a new Jerusalem, and people "shall bring into it the glory and the honor of the nations" (Rev. 21:26), and there will be "the river of the water of life, bright as crystal, flowing from the throne of God and of the Lamb through the middle of the street of the city; also, on either side of the river, the tree of life with its twelve kinds of fruit, yielding its fruit each month" (Rev. 22:1–2). In this very material, physical, renewed universe, it seems that we will need to live as human beings with physical bodies, suitable for life in God's renewed physical creation. Specifically, Jesus' physical resurrection body affirms the goodness of God's original creation of man not as a mere spirit like the angels, but as a creature with a physical body that was "very good." We must not fall into the error of thinking that nonmaterial existence is somehow a better form of existence for creatures:[15] when God made us as the pinnacle of his creation, he gave us physical bodies. In a perfected physical body Jesus rose from the dead, now reigns in heaven, and will return to take us to be with himself forever.

**3. Both the Father and the Son Participated in the Resurrection.** Some texts affirm that God the Father specifically raised Christ from the dead (Acts 2:24; Rom. 6:4; 1 Cor. 6:14; Gal. 1:1; Eph. 1:20), but other texts speak of Jesus as participating in his own resurrection. Jesus says: "The reason my Father loves me is that I lay down my life—only to take it up again. No one takes it from me, but I lay it down of my own accord. I have authority to lay it down and authority to take it up again. This command I received from my Father" (John 10:17–18 NIV; cf. 2:19–21). It is best to conclude that both the Father and the Son were

---

[15]Professor Harris also wants to avoid this error, for he says, "There can be no dualism between spirit and matter. No New Testament writer envisages the salvation of the soul or spirit with the visible material world abandoned to oblivion" (p. 251). Yet I am concerned that his position may lead others to a depreciation of the value of the material creation and of the goodness of our physical bodies as created by God.

involved in the resurrection.[16] Indeed, Jesus says, "I am the resurrection and the life" (John 11:25; cf. Heb. 7:16).[17]

## 4. Doctrinal Significance of the Resurrection.

**a. Christ's Resurrection Insures Our Regeneration:** Peter says that "we have been born anew to a living hope through the resurrection of Jesus Christ from the dead" (1 Peter 1:3). Here he explicitly connects Jesus' resurrection with our regeneration or new birth. When Jesus rose from the dead he had a new quality of life, a "resurrection life" in a human body and human spirit that were perfectly suited for fellowship and obedience to God forever. In his resurrection, Jesus earned for us a new life just like his. We do not receive all of that new "resurrection life" when we become Christians, for our bodies remain as they were, still subject to weakness, aging, and death. But in our spirits we are made alive with new resurrection power.[18] Thus it is through his resurrection that Christ earned for us the new kind of life we receive when we are "born again." This is why Paul can say that God "made us alive together with Christ (by grace you have been saved), and *raised us up with him*" (Eph. 2:5–6; cf. Col. 3:1). When God raised Christ from the dead he thought of us as somehow being raised "with Christ" and therefore deserving of the merits of Christ's resurrection. Paul says his goal in life is "that I may know him and the power of his resurrection . . ." (Phil. 3:10). Paul knew that even in this life the resurrection of Christ gave new power for Christian ministry and obedience to God.

Paul connects the resurrection of Christ with the spiritual power at work within us when he tells the Ephesians that he is praying that they would know "what is the immeasurable greatness of his power in us who believe, according to the working of his great might which he accomplished in Christ when he raised him from the dead and made him sit at his right hand in the heavenly places" (Eph. 1:19–20). Here Paul says that the power by which God raised Christ from the dead is the same power at work within us. Paul further sees us as raised in Christ when he says, "We were buried therefore with him by baptism into death, so that as Christ was raised from the dead by the glory of the Father, we too might walk in newness of life. . . . So you also must consider yourselves dead to sin and alive to God in Christ Jesus" (Rom. 6:4, 11). This new resurrection power in us includes *power to gain more and more victory over remaining sin* in our lives—"sin will have no dominion over you" (Rom. 6:14; cf. 1 Cor. 15:17)—even though we will never be perfect in this life. This resurrection power also includes *power for ministry in the work of the kingdom*. It was after Jesus' resurrection that he promised his disciples, "You shall receive power when the Holy Spirit has come upon you; and you shall be my witnesses in Jerusalem and in all Judea and Samaria and to the end of the earth" (Acts 1:8). This new, intensified power for proclaiming the gospel and working miracles and triumphing over the opposition of the enemy

---

[16]See the discussion of the participation of the Father and the Son in the resurrection in chapter 26, pp. 548–49.

[17]Because the works of God are usually works of the entire Trinity, it is probably true to say that the Holy Spirit also was involved in raising Jesus from the dead, but no text of Scripture affirms that explicitly (but see Rom. 8:11).

[18]See chapter 34, pp. 699–708, for a discussion of regeneration.

was given to the disciples after Christ's resurrection from the dead and was part of the new resurrection power that characterized their Christian lives.

**b. Christ's Resurrection Insures Our Justification:** In only one passage does Paul explicitly connect Christ's resurrection with our justification (or our receiving a declaration that we are not guilty but righteous before God).[19] Paul says that Jesus "was put to death for our trespasses and *raised for our justification*" (Rom. 4:25). When Christ was raised from the dead, it was God's declaration of approval of Christ's work of redemption. Because Christ "humbled himself and became obedient unto death, even death on a cross" (Phil. 2:8), "God has highly exalted him . . ." (Phil. 2:9). By raising Christ from the dead, God the Father was in effect saying that he approved of Christ's work of suffering and dying for our sins, that his work was completed, and that Christ no longer had any need to remain dead. There was no penalty left to pay for sin, no more wrath of God to bear, no more guilt or liability to punishment—all had been completely paid for, and no guilt remained. In the resurrection, God was saying to Christ, "I approve of what you have done, and you find favor in my sight."

This explains how Paul can say that Christ was "raised for our justification" (Rom. 4:25). If God "raised us up with him" (Eph. 2:6), then, by virtue of our union with Christ, God's declaration of approval of Christ is also his declaration of approval of us. When the Father in essence said to Christ, "All the penalty for sins has been paid and I find you not guilty but righteous in my sight," he was thereby making the declaration that would also apply to us once we trusted in Christ for salvation. In this way Christ's resurrection also gave final proof that he had earned our justification.

**c. Christ's Resurrection Insures That We Will Receive Perfect Resurrection Bodies As Well:** The New Testament several times connects Jesus' resurrection with our final bodily resurrection. "And God raised the Lord and will also raise us up by his power" (1 Cor. 6:14). Similarly, "he who raised the Lord Jesus will raise us also with Jesus and bring us with you into his presence" (2 Cor. 4:14). But the most extensive discussion of the connection between Christ's resurrection and our own is found in 1 Corinthians 15:12–58. There Paul says that Christ is the "first fruits of those who have fallen asleep" (1 Cor. 15:20). In calling Christ the "first fruits" (Gk. *aparchē*), Paul uses a metaphor from agriculture to indicate that we will be like Christ. Just as the "first fruits" or the first taste of the ripening crop show what the rest of the harvest will be like for that crop, so Christ as the "first fruits" shows what our resurrection bodies will be like when, in God's final "harvest," he raises us from the dead and brings us into his presence.[20]

After Jesus' resurrection, he still had the nail prints in his hands and feet and the mark from the spear in his side (John 20:27). People sometimes wonder if that indicates that the scars of serious injuries that we have received in this life will also remain on our resurrection bodies. The answer is that we probably will not have any scars from injuries or wounds received in this life, but our bodies will be made

---

[19]See chapter 36, pp. 722–35, on justification.

[20]See chapter 42, pp. 831–35, for a more detailed discussion of the nature of our resurrection bodies.

perfect, "incorruptible" and raised "in glory." The scars from Jesus' crucifixion are unique because they are an eternal reminder of his sufferings and death for us.[21] The fact that he retains those scars does not necessarily mean that we shall retain ours. Rather, all will be healed, and all will be made perfect and whole.

**5. Ethical Significance of the Resurrection.** Paul also sees that the resurrection has application to our obedience to God in this life. After a long discussion of the resurrection, Paul concludes by encouraging his readers, "*Therefore,* my beloved brethren, be steadfast, immovable, always abounding in the work of the Lord, knowing that in the Lord your labor is not in vain" (1 Cor. 15:58). It is because Christ was raised from the dead, and we too shall be raised from the dead, that we should continue steadfastly in the Lord's work. This is because everything that we do to bring people into the kingdom and build them up will indeed have eternal significance, because we shall all be raised on the day when Christ returns, and we shall live with him forever.

Second, Paul encourages us, when we think about the resurrection, to focus on our future heavenly reward as our goal. He sees the resurrection as a time when all the struggles of this life will be repaid. But if Christ has not been raised and if there is no resurrection, then "your faith is futile and you are still in your sins. Then those also who have fallen asleep in Christ have perished. If for this life only we have hoped in Christ, we are of all men most to be pitied" (1 Cor. 15:17–19; cf. v. 32). But because Christ has been raised, and because we have been raised with him, we are to seek for a heavenly reward and set our mind on things of heaven:

> If then you have been raised with Christ, *seek the things that are above,* where Christ is, seated at the right hand of God. Set your minds on things that are above, not on things that are on earth. For you have died, and your life is hid with Christ in God. When Christ who is our life appears, then you also will appear with him in glory. (Col. 3:1–4)

A third ethical application of the resurrection is the obligation to stop yielding to sin in our lives. When Paul says we are to consider ourselves "dead to sin and alive to God in Christ Jesus" by virtue of the resurrection of Christ and his resurrection power within us (Rom. 6:11), he then goes on immediately to say,"*Let not sin therefore reign* in your mortal bodies. . . . Do not yield your members to sin" (Rom. 6:12–13). The fact that we have this new resurrection power over the domination of sin in our lives is used by Paul as a reason to exhort us not to sin any more.

## B. Ascension Into Heaven

**1. Christ Ascended to a Place.** After Jesus' resurrection, he was on earth for forty days (Acts 1:3), then he led them out to Bethany, just outside Jerusalem, and

---

[21]In fact, the evidences of the severe beating and disfigurement that Jesus suffered before his crucifixion were probably all healed, and only the scars in his hands, feet, and side remained as testimony to his death for us: Jesus was raised "in glory" (cf. 1 Cor. 15:43), not in horrible disfigurement just barely brought back to life.

"lifting up his hands, he blessed them. While he blessed them, he parted from them, and was carried up into heaven" (Luke 24:50–51).

A similar account is given by Luke in the opening section of Acts:

And when he had said this, as they were looking on, he was lifted up, and a cloud took him out of their sight. And while they were gazing into heaven as he went, behold, two men stood by them in white robes, and said, "Men of Galilee, why do you stand looking into heaven? This Jesus, who was taken up from you into heaven, will come in the same way as you saw him go into heaven." (Acts 1:9–11)

These narratives describe an event that is clearly designed to show the disciples that Jesus went to a place. He did not suddenly disappear from them, never to be seen by them again, but gradually ascended as they were watching, and then a cloud (apparently the cloud of God's glory) took him from their sight. But the angels immediately said that he would come back *in the same way* in which he had gone into heaven. The fact that Jesus had a resurrection body that was subject to spatial limitations (it could be at only one place at one time) means that Jesus went *somewhere* when he ascended into heaven.

It is surprising that even some evangelical theologians hesitate to affirm that heaven is a place or that Jesus ascended to a definite location somewhere in the space-time universe. Admittedly we cannot now see where Jesus is, but that is not because he passed into some ethereal "state of being" that has no location at all in the space-time universe, but rather because our eyes are unable to see the unseen spiritual world that exists all around us. There are angels around us, but we simply cannot see them because our eyes do not have that capacity: Elisha was surrounded by an army of angels and chariots of fire protecting him from the Syrians at Dothan, but Elisha's servant was not able to see those angels until God opened his eyes so that he could see things that existed in that spiritual dimension (2 Kings 6:17). Similarly, when Stephen was dying, God gave him a special ability to see the world that is now hidden from our eyes, for he "gazed into heaven and saw the glory of God, and Jesus standing at the right hand of God; and he said, 'Behold, I see the heavens opened, and the Son of man standing at the right hand of God'" (Acts 7:55–56). And Jesus himself said, "In my Father's house are many rooms; if it were not so, would I have told you that I go to prepare *a place* for you? And when I go and prepare a place for you, I will come again and will take you to myself, that where I am you may be also" (John 14:2–3).

Of course we cannot now say exactly where heaven is. Scripture often pictures people as ascending up into heaven (as Jesus did, and Elijah) or coming down from heaven (as the angels in Jacob's dream, Gen. 28:12), so we are justified in thinking of heaven as somewhere "above" the earth. Admittedly the earth is round and it rotates, so where heaven is we are simply unable to say more precisely— Scripture does not tell us. But the repeated emphasis on the fact that Jesus went somewhere (as did Elijah, 2 Kings 2:11), and the fact that the New Jerusalem will come down out of heaven from God (Rev. 21:2), all indicate that there is clearly a localization of heaven in the space-time universe. Those who do not believe in Scripture may scoff at such an idea and wonder how it can be so, just as the first Russian cosmonaut who came back from space and declared that he did not see God or heaven anywhere, but that simply points to the blindness of their eyes toward the unseen spiritual world; it does not indicate that heaven does not exist in a certain place. In fact, the ascension of Jesus into heaven is designed to teach us that heaven does exist as a place in the space-time universe. (See chapter 57 for a further discussion of the nature of heaven.)

**2. Christ Received Glory and Honor That Had Not Been His Before As the God-Man.** When Jesus ascended into heaven he received glory, honor, and authority that had never been his before as one who was both God and man. Before Jesus died, he prayed, "Father, glorify me in your own presence with the glory which I had with you before the world was made" (John 17:5).[22] In his sermon at Pentecost Peter said that Jesus was "exalted at the right hand of God" (Acts 2:33), and Paul declared that "God has highly exalted him" (Phil. 2:9), and that he was "taken up in glory" (1 Tim. 3:16; cf. Heb. 1:4). Christ is now in heaven with the angelic choirs singing praise to him with the words, "Worthy is the Lamb who was slain, to receive power and wealth and wisdom and might and honor and glory and blessing!" (Rev. 5:12).[23]

**3. Christ Was Seated at God's Right Hand (Christ's Session).** One specific aspect of Christ's ascension into heaven and receiving of honor was the fact that he *sat down* at the right hand of God. This is sometimes called his *session* at God's right hand.[24]

The Old Testament predicted that the Messiah would sit at the right hand of God: "The LORD says to my lord: 'Sit at my right hand, till I make your enemies your footstool'" (Ps. 110:1). When Christ ascended back into heaven he received the fulfillment of that promise: "When he had made purification for sins, he *sat down* at the right hand of the Majesty on high" (Heb. 1:3). This welcoming into the presence of God and sitting at God's right hand is a dramatic indication of the completion of Christ's work of redemption. Just as a human being will sit down at the completion of a large task to enjoy the satisfaction of having accomplished it, so Jesus sat at the right hand of God, visibly demonstrating that his work of redemption was completed.

In addition to showing the completion of Christ's work of redemption, the act of sitting at God's right hand is an indication that he received authority over the universe. Paul says that God "raised him from the dead and made him sit at his right hand in the heavenly places, far above all rule and authority and power and dominion, and above every name that is named" (Eph. 1:20–21). Similarly, Peter says that Jesus "has gone into heaven and is at the right hand of God, with angels, authorities, and powers subject to him" (1 Peter 3:22). Paul also alludes to Psalm 110:1 when he says that Christ "must reign until he has put all his enemies under his feet" (1 Cor. 15:25).

One additional aspect of the authority that Christ received from the Father when he sat at his right hand was the authority to pour out the Holy Spirit on the

---

[22]This verse shows that the glory Jesus received had been his before as eternal Son of God, but it had not been his before in his incarnate form as God-man.

[23]Some Lutheran theologians have also said that when Jesus ascended into heaven his human nature became ubiquitous (everywhere present): see the discussion in chapter 26, p. 558, n. 38.

[24]The word *session* formerly meant "the act of sitting down," but it no longer has that meaning in ordinary English usage today.

church. Peter says on the Day of Pentecost, "Being therefore exalted at the right hand of God, and having *received from the Father the promise of the Holy Spirit,* he has poured out this which you see and hear" (Acts 2:33).

The fact that Jesus now sits at the right hand of God in heaven does not mean that he is perpetually "fixed" there or that he is inactive. He is also seen as standing at God's right hand (Acts 7:56) and as walking among the seven golden lampstands in heaven (Rev. 2:1). Just as a human king sits on his royal throne at his accession to the kingship, but then engages in many other activities throughout each day, so Christ sat at the right hand of God as a dramatic evidence of the completion of his redemptive work and his reception of authority over the universe, but he is certainly engaged in other activities in heaven as well.

**4. Christ's Ascension Has Doctrinal Significance for Our Lives.** Just as the resurrection has profound implications for our lives, so Christ's ascension has significant implications for us. First, since we are united with Christ in every aspect of his work of redemption,[25] Christ's going up into heaven foreshadows our future ascension into heaven with him. "We who are alive, who are left, shall be caught up together with them in the clouds to meet the Lord in the air; and so we shall always be with the Lord" (1 Thess. 4:17). The author of Hebrews wants us to run the race of life with the knowledge that we are following in Jesus' steps and will eventually arrive at the blessings of life in heaven that he is now enjoying: "Let us run with perseverance the race that is set before us, looking to Jesus the pioneer and perfecter of our faith, who for the joy that was set before him endured the cross, despising the shame, and is seated at the right hand of the throne of God" (Heb. 12:1–2). And Jesus himself says that he will one day take us to be with himself (John 14:3).

Second, Jesus' ascension gives us assurance that our final home will be in heaven with him. "In my Father's house are many rooms; if it were not so, would I have told you that I go to prepare a place for you? And when I go and prepare a place for you, I will come again and will take you to myself, that where I am you may be also" (John 14:2–3). Jesus was a man like us in every way yet without sin, and he has gone before us so that eventually we might follow him there and live with him forever. The fact that Jesus has already ascended into heaven and achieved the goal set before him gives great assurance to us that we will eventually go there also.

Third, because of our union with Christ in his ascension, we are able to share now (in part) in Christ's authority over the universe, and we will later share in it more fully. This is what Paul points to when he says that God "raised us up with him, and made us *sit with him in the heavenly places* in Christ Jesus" (Eph. 2:6). We are not physically present in heaven, of course, for we remain here on earth at the present time. But if Christ's session at God's right hand refers to his reception of authority, then the fact that God has made us sit with Christ means that we share in some measure in the authority that Christ has, authority to contend against "the spiritual hosts of wickedness in the heavenly places" (Eph. 6:12; cf. vv. 10–18) and to do battle with weapons that "have divine power to destroy strongholds" (2 Cor. 10:4). This sharing in Christ's authority over the universe will be made more fully our possession in the age to come: "Do you not know that we are to

---

[25]See the discussion of union with Christ in chapter 43, pp. 840–50.

judge angels?" (1 Cor. 6:3). Moreover, we will share with Christ in his authority over the creation that God has made (Heb. 2:5–8).[26] Jesus promises, "He who conquers and who keeps my works until the end, I will give him power over the nations, and he shall rule them with a rod of iron, as when earthen pots are broken in pieces, even as I myself have received power from my Father" (Rev. 2:26–27). He also promises, "He who conquers, I will grant him to sit with me on my throne, as I myself conquered and sat down with my Father on his throne" (Rev. 3:21). These are amazing promises of our future sharing in Christ's sitting at the right hand of God, promises that we will not fully understand until the age to come.

## C. States of Jesus Christ

In talking about the life, death, and resurrection of Christ, theologians have sometimes talked about the "states of Jesus Christ." By this they mean the different relationships Jesus had to God's law for mankind, to the possession of authority, and to receiving honor for himself. Generally two states (humiliation and exaltation) are distinguished. Thus, the doctrine of "the twofold state of Christ" is the teaching that Christ experienced first the state of humiliation, then the state of exaltation.

Within the humiliation of Christ are included his incarnation, suffering, death, and burial. Sometimes a fifth aspect (descent into hell) is included, but as explained above, the position taken in this book is that that concept is not supported in Scripture.

In the exaltation of Christ, there are also four aspects: his resurrection, ascension into heaven, session at the right hand of God, and return in glory and power. Many systematic theologies use the state of humiliation and the state of exaltation as broad categories to organize their discussion of Jesus' work.[27]

## QUESTIONS FOR PERSONAL APPLICATION

1. As you read this chapter, what aspects of the Bible's teaching about a resurrection body were new to your understanding? Can you think of some characteristics of the resurrection body that you especially look forward to? How does the thought of having such a body make you feel?

2. What things would you like to do now but find yourself unable to do because of the weakness or limitations of your own physical body? Do you think these activities would be appropriate to your life in heaven? Will you be able to do them then?

3. When you were born again, you received new spiritual life within. If you think of this new spiritual life as part of the resurrection power of Christ working within you, how does that give you encouragement in living the Christian life and in ministering to people's needs?

---

[26]See discussion of Heb. 2:5–8 in chapter 26, p. 541; see also pp. 272–73.

[27]Although this is a useful method of organization, I have not used it in this book. However, all of the topics included in discussions of these two states have been covered in this and other chapters of this book. For more detailed discussion, see W. Grudem, "States of Jesus Christ," *EDT*, pp. 1052–54.

4. The Bible says that you are now seated with Christ in the heavenly places (Eph. 2:6). As you meditate on this fact, how will it affect your prayer life and your engaging in spiritual warfare against demonic forces?

5. When you think of Christ now in heaven, does it cause you to focus more attention on things that will have eternal significance? Does it increase your assurance that you will someday be with him in heaven? How do you feel about the prospect of reigning with Christ over the nations and over angels as well?

## SPECIAL TERMS

ascension
exaltation of Christ
humiliation of Christ
incorruptible
raised in glory

raised in power
resurrection
session
spiritual body
states of Jesus Christ

## BIBLIOGRAPHY

(For an explanation of this bibliography see the note on the bibliography to chapter 1, p. 38. Complete bibliographical data may be found on pp. 1223–29.)

### Sections in Evangelical Systematic Theologies

1. Anglican (Episcopalian)
   1882–92    Litton, 195–96
   1930       Thomas, 73–87
2. Arminian (Wesleyan or Methodist)
   1875–76    Pope, 3:401–6
   1987–90    Oden, 451–526
3. Baptist
   1767       Gill, 1:583–602
   1907       Strong, 706–10, 1015–23
   1917       Mullins, 44–46, 158–64, 472–78
   1983–85    Erickson, 769–79
   1987–94    Lewis/Demarest, 2:437–96
4. Dispensational
   1947       Chafer, 5:231–79
   1949       Thiessen, 243–50
   1986       Ryrie, 267–74
5. Lutheran
   1917–24    Pieper, 2:324–30
   1934       Mueller, 295–300
6. Reformed (or Presbyterian)
   1861       Heppe, 488–509

|          |                                      |
|----------|--------------------------------------|
| 1871–73  | Hodge, 2:626–38                      |
| 1887–1921| Warfield, *SSW*, 1:178–202; *PWC*, 535–48 |
| 1937–66  | Murray, *CW*, 1:40–43; *CW*, 4:82–91 |
| 1938     | Berkhof, 344–55                      |
| 1962     | Buswell, 2:32–40                     |

7. Renewal (or charismatic/Pentecostal)

| 1988–92 | Williams, 1:381–413 |
|---------|---------------------|

## Sections in Representative Roman Catholic Systematic Theologies

1. Roman Catholic: Traditional

| 1955 | Ott, 192–96 |
|------|-------------|

2. Roman Catholic: Post-Vatican II

| 1980 | McBrien, 1:405–17 |
|------|-------------------|

## Other Works

Bray, G. L. "Ascension and Heavenly Session of Christ." In *NDT*, pp. 46–47.

Craig, William Lane. *The Son Rises: The Historical Evidence for the Resurrection of Jesus*. Chicago: Moody, 1981.

Fuller, Daniel P. *Easter Faith and History*. Grand Rapids: Eerdmans, 1965.

Gaffin, Richard B., Jr. *Resurrection and Redemption: A Study in Paul's Soteriology.* Formerly, *The Centrality of the Resurrection: A Study in Paul's Soteriology*. Phillipsburg, N.J.: Presbyterian and Reformed, 1978.

Habermas, G. R. "Resurrection of Christ." In *EDT*, pp. 938–41.

———, and Anthony Flew. *Did Jesus Rise From the Dead? The Resurrection Debate*. Edited by Terry L. Miethe. New York: Harper and Row, 1987.

Harris, Murray J. *From Grave to Glory: Resurrection in the New Testament, Including a Response to Norman L. Geisler*. Grand Rapids: Zondervan, 1990.

———. "Resurrection, General." In *NDT*, pp. 581–82.

Ladd, George E. *I Believe in the Resurrection of Jesus*. Grand Rapids: Eerdmans, 1975.

Macleod, D. "Resurrection of Christ." In *NDT*, pp. 582–85.

Morison, Frank. *Who Moved the Stone?* London: Faber and Faber, 1930; reprint, Grand Rapids: Zondervan, 1958.

O'Donovan, Oliver. *Resurrection and Moral Order*. Leicester: Inter-Varsity Press, 1986.

Ross, A. "Ascension of Christ." In *EDT*, pp. 86–87.

Swete, Henry Barclay. *The Ascended Christ: A Study in the Earliest Christian Teaching*. London: Macmillan, 1910.

Tenney, Merrill C. *The Reality of the Resurrection*. New York: Harper and Row, 1963.

Toon, Peter. *The Ascension of Our Lord*. Nashville: Thomas Nelson, 1984.

Wenham, John. *The Easter Enigma*. London: Paternoster, 1984.

## SCRIPTURE MEMORY PASSAGE

**1 Corinthians 15:20–23:** *But in fact Christ has been raised from the dead, the first fruits of those who have fallen asleep. For as by a man came death, by a man has come also the resurrection of the dead. For as in Adam all die, so also in Christ shall all be made alive. But each in his own order: Christ the first fruits, then at his coming those who belong to Christ.*

## HYMN

### "Christ the Lord Is Risen Today"

"Christ the Lord is risen today," al-le-lu-ia!
Sons of men and angels say; al-le-lu-ia!
Raise your joys and triumphs high; al-le-lu-ia!
Sing, ye heav'ns, and earth reply; al-le-lu-ia!

Vain the stone, the watch, the seal; al-le-lu-ia!
Christ has burst the gates of hell: al-le-lu-ia!
Death in vain forbids him rise; al-le-lu-ia!
Christ hath opened paradise. Al-le-lu-ia!

Lives again our glorious King; al-le-lu-ia!
Where, O death, is now thy sting? Al-le-lu-ia!
Once he died, our souls to save; al-le-lu-ia!
Where thy victory, O grave? Al-le-lu-ia!

Soar we now where Christ has led, al-le-lu-ia!
Following our exalted Head; al-le-lu-ia!
Made like him, like him we rise; al-le-lu-ia!
Ours the cross, the grave, the skies. Al-le-lu-ia!

Hail, the Lord of earth and heav'n! Al-le-lu-ia!
Praise to thee by both be giv'n; al-le-lu-ia!
Thee we greet triumphant now; al-le-lu-ia!
Hail, the resurrection thou! Al-le-lu-ia!

AUTHOR: CHARLES WESLEY, 1739

# Chapter 29

# The Offices of Christ

## How is Christ prophet, priest, and king?

### EXPLANATION AND SCRIPTURAL BASIS

There were three major offices among the people of Israel in the Old Testament: the *prophet* (such as Nathan, 2 Sam. 7:2), the *priest* (such as Abiathar, 1 Sam. 30:7), and the *king* (such as King David, 2 Sam. 5:3). These three offices were distinct. The prophet spoke God's words to the people; the priest offered sacrifices, prayers, and praises to God on behalf of the people; and the king ruled over the people as God's representative. These three offices foreshadowed Christ's own work in different ways. Therefore we can look again at Christ's work, now thinking about the perspective of these three offices or categories.[1] Christ fulfills these three offices in the following ways: as *prophet* he reveals God to us and speaks God's words to us; as *priest* he both offers a sacrifice to God on our behalf and is himself the sacrifice that is offered; and as *king* he rules over the church and over the universe as well. We now turn to discuss each of these offices in more detail.

### A. Christ as Prophet

The Old Testament prophets spoke God's words to the people. Moses was the first major prophet, and he wrote the first five books of the Bible, the Pentateuch. After Moses there was a succession of other prophets who spoke and wrote God's words.[2] But Moses predicted that sometime another prophet like himself would come.

> The LORD your God will raise up for you a *prophet like me* from among you, from your brethren—him you shall heed—just as you desired of the LORD your God. . . . And the LORD said to me . . . "I will raise up for them a prophet like you from among their brethren; and I will put my words in his mouth, and he shall speak to them all that I command him." (Deut. 18:15–18)

However, when we look at the gospels we see that Jesus is not *primarily* viewed as a prophet or as *the* prophet like Moses, though there are occasional references to

---

[1]John Calvin (1509–64) was the first major theologian to apply these three categories to the work of Christ (see his *Institutes of the Christian Religion*, Book 2, Chapter 15). The categories have been adapted by many subsequent theologians as a helpful way of understanding various aspects of Christ's work.

[2]See the discussion of the writing of the books in the Old Testament canon in chapter 3, pp. 54–60.

this effect. Often those who call Jesus a "prophet" know very little about him. For instance, various opinions of Jesus were circulating: "Some say John the Baptist, others say Elijah, and others Jeremiah *or one of the prophets*" (Matt. 16:14; cf. Luke 9:8). When Jesus raised the son of the widow of Nain from the dead, the people were afraid and said, "A great *prophet* has arisen among us!" (Luke 7:16). When Jesus told the Samaritan woman at the well something of her past life, she immediately responded, "Sir, I perceive that you are *a prophet*" (John 4:19). But she did not then know very much at all about him. The reaction of the man born blind who was healed in the temple was similar: "He is a prophet" (John 9:17; note that his belief in Jesus' messiahship and deity did not come until v. 37, after a subsequent conversation with Jesus).[3] Therefore, "prophet" is not a primary designation of Jesus or one used frequently by him or about him.

Nevertheless, there was still an expectation that *the* prophet like Moses would come (Deut. 18:15, 18). For instance, after Jesus had multiplied the loaves and fish, some people exclaimed, "This is indeed *the prophet* who is to come into the world!" (John 6:14; cf. 7:40). Peter also identified Christ as the prophet predicted by Moses (see Acts 3:22–24, quoting Deut. 18:15). So Jesus is indeed the prophet predicted by Moses.

Nevertheless, it is significant that in the Epistles Jesus is never called a prophet or *the* prophet. This is especially significant in the opening chapters of Hebrews, because there was a clear opportunity to identify Jesus as a prophet if the author had wished to do so. He begins by saying, "In many and various ways God spoke of old to our fathers *by the prophets;* but in these last days he has spoken to us *by a Son*" (Heb. 1:1–2). Then after discussing the greatness of the Son, in chapters 1–2, the author concludes this section not by saying, "Therefore, consider Jesus, the greatest prophet of all," or something like that, but rather by saying, "Therefore, holy brethren, who share in a heavenly call, consider Jesus, *the apostle* and high priest of our confession" (Heb. 3:1).

Why did the New Testament epistles avoid calling Jesus a prophet? Apparently because, although Jesus is the prophet whom Moses predicted, yet he is also far greater than any of the Old Testament prophets, in two ways:

1. He is the one *about whom* the prophecies in the Old Testament were made. When Jesus spoke with the two disciples on the road to Emmaus, he took them through the entire Old Testament, showing how the prophecies pointed to him: "And beginning with Moses *and all the prophets,* he interpreted to them in all the scriptures the things concerning himself" (Luke 24:27). He told these disciples that they were "slow of heart to believe *all that the prophets had spoken,*" showing that it was "necessary that the Christ should suffer these things and enter into his glory" (Luke 24:25–26; cf. 1 Peter 1:11, which says that the Old Testament prophets were "predicting the sufferings of Christ and the subsequent glory"). Thus, the Old Testament prophets looked *forward* to Christ in what they wrote, and the New Testament apostles looked *back* to Christ and interpreted his life for the benefit of the church.

2. Jesus was not merely a messenger of revelation from God (like all the other

---

[3]In Luke 24:19 the two travelers on the road to Emmaus also refer to Jesus as a "prophet," thus putting him in a general category of religious leaders sent from God, perhaps for the benefit of the stranger whom they presumed to have little knowledge of the events surrounding Jesus' life.

prophets), but was himself the *source* of revelation from God. Rather than saying, as all the Old Testament prophets did, "Thus says the LORD," Jesus could begin divinely authoritative teaching with the amazing statement, "But I *say* unto you" (Matt. 5:22; et al.). The word of the LORD *came to* the Old Testament prophets, but Jesus spoke on his own authority as the eternal Word of God (John 1:1) who perfectly revealed the Father to us (John 14:9; Heb. 1:1–2).

In the broader sense of *prophet,* simply meaning one who reveals God to us and speaks to us the words of God, Christ is of course truly and fully a prophet. In fact, he is the one whom all the Old Testament prophets prefigured in their speech and in their actions.

## B. Christ as Priest

In the Old Testament, the priests were appointed by God to offer sacrifices. They also offered prayers and praise to God on behalf of the people. In so doing they "sanctified" the people or made them acceptable to come into God's presence, albeit in a limited way during the Old Testament period. In the New Testament Jesus becomes our great high priest. This theme is developed extensively in the letter to the Hebrews, where we find that Jesus functions as priest in two ways.

**1. Jesus Offered a Perfect Sacrifice for Sin.** The sacrifice which Jesus offered for sins was not the blood of animals such as bulls or goats: "For it is impossible that the blood of bulls and goats should take away sins" (Heb. 10:4). Instead, Jesus offered himself as a perfect sacrifice: "But as it is, he has appeared once for all at the end of the age to put away sin *by the sacrifice of himself*" (Heb. 9:26). This was a completed and final sacrifice, never to be repeated, a theme frequently emphasized in the book of Hebrews (see 7:27; 9:12, 24–28; 10:1–2, 10, 12, 14; 13:12). Therefore Jesus fulfilled all the expectations that were prefigured, not only in the Old Testament sacrifices, but also in the lives and actions of the priests who offered them: he was both the sacrifice and the priest who offered the sacrifice. Jesus is now the "great high priest who has passed through the heavens" (Heb. 4:14) and who has appeared "in the presence of God on our behalf" (Heb. 9:24), since he has offered a sacrifice that ended for all time the need for any further sacrifices.

**2. Jesus Continually Brings Us Near to God.** The Old Testament priests not only offered sacrifices, but also in a representative way they came into the presence of God from time to time on behalf of the people. But Jesus does much more than that. As our perfect high priest, he continually *leads us* into God's presence so that we no longer have need of a Jerusalem temple, or of a special priesthood to stand between us and God. And Jesus does not come into the inner part (the holy of holies) of the earthly temple in Jerusalem, but he has gone into the heavenly equivalent to the holy of holies, the very presence of God himself in heaven (Heb. 9:24). Therefore we have a hope that follows him there: "We have this as a sure and steadfast anchor of the soul, a hope that *enters into the inner shrine behind the curtain,* where Jesus has gone as a forerunner on our behalf, having become a high priest for ever" (Heb. 6:19–20). This means that we have a far greater privilege than those people who lived at the time of the Old Testament temple. They could not even enter into the first room of the temple, the holy place, for only the priests could go there. Then into the inner room of the temple, the holy of holies, only the high priest could go, and he could only enter there once a year (Heb 9:1–7). But when Jesus offered a perfect sacrifice for sins, the curtain or veil of the temple that closed off the holy of holies was torn in two from top to bottom (Luke 23:45), thus indicating in a symbolic way on earth that the way of access to God in heaven was opened by Jesus' death. Therefore the author of Hebrews can make this amazing exhortation to all believers:

> Therefore, brethren, since we have confidence to *enter the sanctuary* [lit. 'the holy places,' meaning both the 'holy place' and the 'holy of holies' itself] by the blood of Jesus . . . and since we have a great priest over the house of God, *let us draw near with a true heart in full assurance of faith*. (Heb. 10:19–22)

Jesus has opened for us the way of access to God so that we can continually "draw near" into God's very presence without fear but with "confidence" and in "full assurance of faith."

**3. Jesus as Priest Continually Prays for Us.** One other priestly function in the Old Testament was to pray on behalf of the people. The author of Hebrews tells us that Jesus also fulfills this function: "He is able for all time to save those who draw near to God through him, since he always lives *to make intercession for them*" (Heb. 7:25). Paul affirms the same point when he says Christ Jesus is the one "who indeed *intercedes for us*" (Rom. 8:34).

Some have argued that this work of high priestly intercession is only the act of remaining in the Father's presence as a continual reminder that he himself has paid the penalty for all our sins. According to this view, Jesus does not actually make specific prayers to God the Father about individual needs in our lives, but "intercedes" only in the sense of remaining in God's presence as our high priestly representative.

However, this view does not seem to fit the actual language used in Romans 8:34 and Hebrews 7:25. In both cases, the word *intercede* translates the Greek term *entygchanō*. This word does not mean merely "to stand as someone's representative before another person," but clearly has the sense of making specific requests or petitions before someone. For example, Festus uses this word to say to King Agrippa, "You see this man about whom the whole Jewish people *petitioned* me" (Acts 25:24). Paul also uses it of Elijah when he "*pleads* with God against Israel" (Rom. 11:2). In both cases the requests are very specific, not just general representations.[4]

We may conclude, then, that both Paul and the author of Hebrews are saying that Jesus continually lives in the presence of God to make specific requests and to bring specific petitions before God on our behalf. This is a role that Jesus, as God-

---

[4]Literature outside the New Testament provides further examples of *entygchanō* used to mean "to bring requests or petitions." See, e.g., Wisd. 8:20 ("I *asked* the Lord, and made petition to him"); 1 Macc. 8:32; 3 Macc. 6:37 ("They *requested* the King, that he send them back to their home"); 1 Clem. 56:1; Epistle of Polycarp to the Philippians 4:3; Josephus, *Antiquities* 12:18; 16:170 (the Jews in Cyrene *petition* Marcus Agrippa concerning people in their land who are falsely collecting taxes). More examples could be found as well (cf. also Rom. 8:27, and, using a cognate word, v. 26).

man, is uniquely qualified to fulfill. Although God could care for all our needs in response to direct observation (Matt. 6:8), yet it has pleased God, in his relationship to the human race, to decide to act instead in response to prayer, apparently so that the faith shown through prayer might glorify him. It is especially the prayers of men and women created in his image that are pleasing in God's sight. In Christ, we have a true man, a perfect man, praying and thereby continually glorifying God through prayer. Thus, human manhood is raised to a highly exalted position: "There is one God, and there is one mediator between God and men, *the man* Christ Jesus" (1 Tim. 2:5).

Yet in his human nature alone Jesus could not of course be such a great high priest for all his people all over the world. He could not hear the prayers of persons far away, nor could he hear prayers that were only spoken in a person's mind. He could not hear all requests simultaneously (for in the world at any one moment there are millions of people praying to him). Therefore, in order to be the perfect high priest who intercedes for us, he must be God as well as man. He must be one who in his divine nature can both know all things and bring them into the presence of the Father. Yet because he became and continues to be man he has the right to represent us before God and he can express his petitions from the viewpoint of a sympathetic high priest, one who understands by experience what we go through.

Therefore, Jesus is the only person in the whole universe for all eternity who can be such a heavenly high priest, one who is truly God and truly man, exalted forever above the heavens.

The thought that Jesus is continually praying for us should give us great encouragement. He always prays for us according to the Father's will, so we can know that his requests will be granted. Berkhof says:

> It is a consoling thought that Christ is praying for us, even when we are negligent in our prayer life; that He is presenting to the Father those spiritual needs which were not present to our minds and which we often neglect to include in our prayers; and that He prays for our protection against the dangers of which we are not even conscious, and against the enemies which threaten us, though we do not notice it. He is praying that our faith may not cease, and that we may come out victoriously in the end.[5]

## C. Christ as King

In the Old Testament the king has authority to rule over the nation of Israel. In the New Testament, Jesus was born to be King of the Jews (Matt. 2:2), but he refused any attempt by people to try to make him an earthly king with earthly military and political power (John 6:15). He told Pilate, "My kingship is not of this world; if my kingship were of this world, my servants would fight, that I might not be handed over to the Jews; but my kingship is not from the world" (John 18:36). Nonetheless, Jesus did have a kingdom whose arrival he announced in his preaching (Matt. 4:17, 23; 12:28, et al.). He is in fact the true king of the new people of God. Thus, Jesus refused to rebuke his disciples who cried out at

---

[5]Berkhof, *Systematic Theology*, p. 403.

his triumphal entry into Jerusalem, "Blessed is *the King* who comes in the name of the Lord!" (Luke 19:38; cf. vv. 39–40; also Matt. 21:5; John 1:49; Acts 17:7).

After his resurrection, Jesus was given by God the Father far greater authority over the church and over the universe. God raised him up and "made him sit at his right hand in the heavenly places, *far above all rule and authority and power and dominion,* and above every name that is named, not only in this age but also in that which is to come; and he has put all things under his feet and has made him the head over all things for the church" (Eph. 1:20–22; Matt. 28:18; 1 Cor. 15:25). That authority over the church and over the universe will be more fully recognized by people when Jesus returns to earth in power and great glory to reign (Matt. 26:64; 2 Thes. 1:7–10; Rev. 19:11–16). On that day he will be acknowledged as "*King of kings* and Lord of lords" (Rev. 19:16) and every knee shall bow to him (Phil. 2:10).

### D. Our Roles as Prophets, Priests, and Kings

If we look back at the situation of Adam before the fall and forward to our future status with Christ in heaven for eternity, we can see that these roles of prophet, priest, and king had parallels in the experience that God originally intended for man, and will be fulfilled in our lives in heaven.

In the Garden of Eden, Adam was a "prophet" in that he had true knowledge of God and always spoke truthfully about God and about his creation. He was a "priest" in that he was able freely and openly to offer prayer and praise to God. There was no need of a sacrifice to pay for sins, but in another sense of sacrifice Adam and Eve's work would have been offered to God in gratitude and thanksgiving, and so would have been a "sacrifice" of another sort (cf. Heb. 13:15). Adam and Eve were also "kings" (or king and queen) in the sense of having been given dominion and rule over the creation (Gen. 1:26–28).

After sin entered into the world, fallen human beings no longer functioned as prophets, for they believed false information about God and spoke falsely about him to others. They no longer had priestly access to God because sin cut them off from his presence. Instead of ruling over the creation as kings, they were subject to the harshness of the creation and tyrannized by flood, drought, and unproductive land, as well as by tyrannical human rulers. The nobility of man as God had created him—to be a true prophet, priest, and king—was lost through sin.

There was a partial recovery of the purity of these three roles in the establishment of the three offices of prophet, priest, and king in the kingdom of Israel. From time to time godly men occupied these offices. But there were also false prophets, dishonest priests, and ungodly kings, and the original purity and holiness with which God intended man to fulfill these offices were never fully realized.

When Christ came, we saw for the first time the fulfillment of these three roles, since he was the perfect prophet, who most fully declared God's words to us, the perfect high priest, who offered the supreme sacrifice for sins and who brought his people near to God, and the true and rightful king of the universe, who will reign forever with a scepter of righteousness over the new heavens and new earth.

But amazingly we as Christians even now begin to imitate Christ in each of these roles, though in a subordinate way. We have a "prophetic" role as we proclaim the gospel to the world and thereby bring God's saving Word to people. In fact, whenever we speak truthfully about God to believers or to unbelievers we are fulfilling a "prophetic" function (using the word *prophetic* in a very broad sense).

We are also priests, because Peter calls us "a royal priesthood" (1 Peter 2:9). He invites us to be built into a spiritual temple and "to be a holy priesthood" as well as "to offer spiritual sacrifices acceptable to God through Jesus Christ" (1 Peter 2:5). The author of Hebrews also views us as priests who are able to enter into the holy of holies (Heb. 10:19, 22) and able to "continually offer up a sacrifice of praise to God, that is, the fruit of lips that acknowledge his name" (Heb. 13:15). He also tells us that our good works are sacrifices pleasing to God: "Do not neglect to do good and to share what you have, for such *sacrifices* are pleasing to God" (Heb. 13:16). Paul also has a priestly role in mind for us when he writes, "I appeal to you therefore, brethren, by the mercies of God, to present your bodies *as a living sacrifice,* holy and acceptable to God, which is your spiritual worship" (Rom. 12:1).

We also share in part now in the kingly reign of Christ, since we have been raised to sit with him in the heavenly places (Eph. 2:6), thus sharing to some degree in his authority over evil spiritual forces that may be arrayed against us (Eph. 6:10–18; James 4:7; 1 Peter 5:9; 1 John 4:4). God has even now committed to us authority over various areas in this world or in the church, giving to some authority over much and to some authority over little. But when the Lord returns those who have been faithful over little will be given authority over much (Matt. 25:14–30).

When Christ returns and rules over the new heavens and new earth, we will once again be true "prophets" because our knowledge will then be perfect and we shall know as we are known (1 Cor. 13:12). Then we will speak only truth about God and about his world, and in us the original prophetic purpose which God had for Adam will be fulfilled. We will be priests forever, for we will eternally worship and offer prayer to God as we behold his face and dwell in his presence (Rev. 22:3–4). We will continually offer ourselves and all that we do or have as sacrifices to our most worthy king.

Yet we shall also, in subjection to God, share in ruling over the universe, for with him we shall "reign forever and ever" (Rev. 22:5). Jesus says, "He who conquers, I will grant him *to sit with me on my throne,* as I myself conquered and sat down with my Father on his throne" (Rev. 3:21). In fact, Paul tells the Corinthians, "Do you not know that *the saints will judge the world?* . . . Do you not know that *we are to judge angels?*" (1 Cor. 6:2–3). Therefore for all eternity, we shall forever function as subordinate prophets, priests, and kings, yet always subject to the Lord Jesus, the supreme prophet, priest, and king.

# QUESTIONS FOR PERSONAL APPLICATION

1. Can you see some ways in which an understanding of Christ's role as prophet, priest, and king will help you understand more fully the functions of prophets, priests, and kings in the Old Testament? Read the description of Solomon's kingdom in 1 Kings 4:20–34 and 1 Kings 10:14–29. Do you see in Solomon's kingdom any foreshadowing of the three offices of Christ? Any foreshadowing of Christ's eternal kingdom? Do you think that you have greater or lesser privileges living now as a member of the church in the new covenant age?

2. Can you see any fulfillment of the role of prophet in your life now? Of the role of priest? Of the role of king? How could each of these functions be developed in your life?

# SPECIAL TERMS

intercession
king

priest
prophet

# BIBLIOGRAPHY

(For an explanation of this bibliography see the note on the bibliography to chapter 1, p. 38. Complete bibliographical data may be found on pp. 1223–29.)

## Sections in Evangelical Systematic Theologies

1. Anglican (Episcopalian)
    1882–92    Litton, 219–38
2. Arminian (Wesleyan or Methodist)
    1875–76    Pope, 2:197–262
    1940    Wiley, 2:187–216
    1983    Carter, 1:363–64
3. Baptist
    1767    Gill, 1:602–44
    1887    Boyce, 291–95
    1907    Strong, 710–76
    1917    Mullins, 303–4
    1983–85    Erickson, 762–63
4. Dispensational
    1947    Chafer, 3:17–30
    1986    Ryrie, 254–59
5. Lutheran
    1917–24    Pieper, 2:330–96
    1934    Mueller, 301–18
6. Reformed (or Presbyterian)

| 1559 | Calvin, 1:494–503 (2.15) |
| 1871–73 | Hodge, 2:455–90, 592–609 |
| 1878 | Dabney, 475–77, 483–87 |
| 1937–66 | Murray, *CW,* 1:44–58 |
| 1938 | Berkhof, 356–66, 406–12 |

## Sections in Representative Roman Catholic Systematic Theologies

1. Roman Catholic: Traditional
   1955    Ott, 179–91
2. Roman Catholic: Post–Vatican II
   1980    McBrien (no explicit treatment)

### Other Works

Baker, J. P. "Offices of Christ." In *NDT,* pp. 476–77.

Letham, Robert. *The Work of Christ.* Downers Grove, Ill.: InterVarsity Press, 1993.

Reymond, R. L. "Offices of Christ." In *EDT,* p. 793.

### SCRIPTURE MEMORY PASSAGE

**1 Peter 2:9–10:** *But you are a chosen race, a royal priesthood, a holy nation, God's own people, that you may declare the wonderful deeds of him who called you out of darkness into his marvelous light. Once you were no people but now you are God's people; once you had not received mercy but now you have received mercy.*

### HYMN

#### "Rejoice the Lord Is King"

This powerful hymn encourages us to rejoice at Christ's present and future kingship. (An excellent hymn about Christ's role as priest is "Arise, My Soul, Arise," also by Charles Wesley, and this may be used as an alternative hymn. Another alternative is "How Sweet the Name of Jesus Sounds," by John Newton, esp. v. 4.)

Rejoice, the Lord is King: your Lord and King adore;
    Rejoice, give thanks and sing, and triumph evermore:
Lift up your heart, lift up your voice;
    Rejoice, again I say, rejoice.

Jesus, the Savior, reigns, the God of truth and love;
    When he had purged our stains, he took his seat above:
Lift up your heart, lift up your voice;
    Rejoice, again I say, rejoice.

His kingdom cannot fail, he rules o'er earth and heav'n;
    The keys of death and hell are to our Jesus giv'n:
Lift up your heart, lift up your voice;
    Rejoice, again I say, rejoice.

He sits at God's right hand till all his foes submit,
  And bow to his command, and fall beneath his feet:
Lift up your heart, lift up your voice;
  Rejoice, again I say, rejoice.

AUTHOR: CHARLES WESLEY, 1746

# Chapter 30

# The Work of the Holy Spirit

*What are the distinctive activities of the Holy Spirit throughout the history of the Bible?*

## EXPLANATION AND SCRIPTURAL BASIS

In the previous chapters we have discussed at some length the person and work of God the Father, and, more recently, the person and work of God the Son, Jesus Christ. We have also examined the biblical evidence for the deity and distinct personality of the Holy Spirit (in connection with the doctrine of the Trinity). It is appropriate now in this chapter that we focus on the distinctive work of the Holy Spirit. Among the different activities of the members of the Trinity, what activities are said to be especially the work of God the Holy Spirit?

We should realize at the outset that other chapters in this book deal more or less directly with certain aspects of the Holy Spirit's work. The chapters on baptism in and filling with the Holy Spirit (39) and the gifts of the Holy Spirit (52–53) deal almost entirely with specific works of the Holy Spirit. Moreover, the chapters on the authority of Scripture (4), prayer (18), the gospel call (33), regeneration (34), sanctification (38), perseverance (40), glorification (42), church discipline (46), the means of grace within the church (48), and worship (51) all treat various aspects of the Holy Spirit's work in the world, and especially in the lives of believers. Nonetheless, in this chapter we shall attempt to gain an overview of the teaching of all of Scripture on the work of the Holy Spirit in order to understand more fully what kinds of activities have been especially delegated to the Holy Spirit by God the Father and God the Son.

We may define the work of the Holy Spirit as follows: *The work of the Holy Spirit is to manifest the active presence of God in the world, and especially in the church.* This definition indicates that the Holy Spirit is the member of the Trinity whom the Scripture most often represents as being *present* to do God's work in the world. Although this is true to some extent throughout the Bible, it is particularly true in the new covenant age. In the Old Testament, the presence of God was many times manifested in the glory of God and in theophanies, and in the gospels Jesus himself manifested the presence of God among men. But after Jesus ascended into heaven, and continuing through the entire church age, the Holy Spirit is now the *primary* manifestation of the presence of the Trinity among us. He is the one who is most prominently *present* with us now.[1]

---

[1] In this discussion, when I use the word "present" I mean "present to bless," as discussed in the

From the very beginning of creation we have an indication that the Holy Spirit's work is to complete and sustain what God the Father has planned and what God the Son has begun, for in Genesis 1:2, "the *Spirit of God* was moving over the face of the waters." And at Pentecost, with the beginning of the new creation in Christ, it is the Holy Spirit who comes to grant power to the church (Acts 1:8; 2:4, 17–18). Because the Holy Spirit is the person of the Trinity through whom God particularly manifests his presence in the new covenant age, it is appropriate that Paul should call the Holy Spirit the "first fruits" (Rom. 8:23) and the "guarantee" (or "down payment," 2 Cor. 1:22; 5:5) of the full manifestation of God's presence that we will know in the new heavens and new earth (cf. Rev. 21:3–4).

Even in the Old Testament, it was predicted that the presence of the Holy Spirit would bring abundant blessings from God: Isaiah predicted a time when the Spirit would bring great renewal.

> For the palace will be forsaken, the populous city deserted . . . *until the Spirit is poured upon us from on high,* and the wilderness becomes a fruitful field, and the fruitful field is deemed a forest. Then justice will dwell in the wilderness, and righteousness abide in the fruitful field. And the effect of righteousness will be peace, and the result of righteousness, quietness and trust for ever. My people will abide in a peaceful habitation, in secure dwellings, and in quiet resting places. (Isa. 32:14–18)

Similarly, God prophesied through Isaiah to Jacob, "For I will pour water on the thirsty land, and streams on the dry ground; *I will pour my Spirit upon your descendants,* and my blessing on your offspring" (Isa. 44:3).

By contrast, the departure of the Holy Spirit removed the blessing of God from a people: "But they rebelled and *grieved his holy Spirit;* therefore he turned to be their enemy, and himself fought against them" (Isa. 63:10). Nonetheless, several prophecies in the Old Testament predicted a time when the Holy Spirit would come in greater fullness, a time when God would make a new covenant with his people (Ezek. 36:26–27; 37:14; 39:29; Joel 2:28–29).

In what specific ways does the Holy Spirit bring God's blessing? We may distinguish four aspects of the work of the Holy Spirit to bring evidence of God's presence and to bless: (1) the Holy Spirit *empowers;* (2) the Holy Spirit *purifies;* (3) the Holy Spirit *reveals;* (4) the Holy Spirit *unifies.* We will examine each of these four activities below. Finally, we must recognize that these activities of the Holy Spirit are not to be taken for granted, and they do not just happen automatically among God's people. Rather, the Holy Spirit reflects the pleasure or displeasure of God with the faith and obedience—or unbelief and disobedience—of God's people. Because of this, we need to look at a fifth aspect of the Holy Spirit's activity: (5) the Holy Spirit *gives stronger or weaker evidence* of the presence and blessing of God, according to our response to him.

---

section on God's omnipotence in chapter 11. Of course, since he is fully God, the *being* of the Holy Spirit is always present everywhere (he is omnipresent), but he does not always show his presence in activities that bring blessing (see chapter 11, pp. 173–77).

## A. The Holy Spirit Empowers

**1. He Gives Life.** In the realm of nature it is the role of the Holy Spirit to give life to all animate creatures, whether on the ground or in the sky and sea, for "When you send forth your Spirit, they are created" (Ps. 104:30). Conversely, if God "should take back his spirit to himself, and gather to himself his breath, all flesh would perish together, and man would return to dust" (Job 34:14–15). Here we see the role of the Spirit in the giving and sustaining of human and animal life.

Parallel with this is the role of the Holy Spirit to give us new life in regeneration.[2] Jesus told Nicodemus, "That which is born of the flesh is flesh, and that which is *born of the Spirit* is spirit. Do not marvel that I said to you, 'You must be born anew'" (John 3:6–7; cf. vv. 5, 8; 6:63; 2 Cor. 3:6). He also said, "It is *the Spirit who gives life;* the flesh profits nothing" (John 6:63 NASB; cf. 2 Cor. 3:6; Acts 10:44–47; Titus 3:5).[3] Consistent with this life-giving function of the Holy Spirit is the fact that it was the Holy Spirit who conceived Jesus in the womb of Mary his mother (Matt. 1:18, 20; Luke 1:35). And on the day when Christ returns, it is the same Holy Spirit who will complete this life-giving work by giving new resurrection life to our mortal bodies: "If the Spirit of him who raised Jesus from the dead dwells in you, he who raised Christ Jesus from the dead will give life to your mortal bodies also *through his Spirit* which dwells in you" (Rom. 8:11).

**2. He Gives Power for Service.**

**a. Old Testament:** In the Old Testament, the Holy Spirit frequently empowered people for special service. He empowered Joshua with leadership skills and wisdom (Num. 27:18; Deut. 34:9), and empowered the judges to deliver Israel from their oppressors (note how "the Spirit of the LORD came upon" Othniel in Judg. 3:10, Gideon in 6:34, Jephthah in 11:29, and Samson in 13:25; 14:6, 19; 15:14). The Holy Spirit came mightily upon Saul to arouse him to battle against the enemies of Israel (1 Sam. 11:6), and when David was anointed as king, "the Spirit of the LORD came mightily upon David from that day forward" (1 Sam. 16:13), equipping David to fulfill the task of kingship to which God had called him.[4] In a slightly different kind of empowering, the Holy Spirit endowed Bezalel with artistic skills for the construction of the tabernacle and its equipment (Ex. 31:3; 35:31), and with the ability to teach these skills to others (Ex. 35:34).[5]

---

[2] See the discussion of regeneration in chapter 34, pp. 699–708. Moreover, as we argue in chapter 39, the phrase "baptism in the Holy Spirit" is used by the New Testament (for example, in 1 Cor. 12:13) to speak of the Holy Spirit's work at the time we become Christians (though many evangelicals today, especially in charismatic and Pentecostal groups, would understand "baptism in the Holy Spirit" to refer to something the Holy Spirit does after conversion).

[3] Related to the life-giving work of the Holy Spirit is the fact that he also seals his work to us so that he keeps true believers from falling away from God and losing their salvation (Eph. 1:13).

[4] It is apparently in the sense of equipping for kingship that David asks that the Holy Spirit not be withdrawn from him when he prays, "Cast me not away from your presence, and *take not your holy Spirit from me*" (Ps. 51:11). Just as the Holy Spirit in his role of anointing Saul for kingship had departed from Saul at the same time as he came upon David (cf. 1 Sam. 16:13 with v. 14), so David, after his sin with Bathsheba (see Ps. 51, title), prayed that the Holy Spirit would not similarly be taken from him.

[5] The Holy Spirit also empowered the Old Testament prophets by giving them revelations to speak, but I have included that function under Section C below ("The Holy Spirit Reveals").

The Holy Spirit also protected God's people and enabled them to overcome their enemies. For example, God put his Spirit in the midst of them at the time of the exodus (Isa. 63:11–12) and later, after their return from exile, put his Spirit in the midst of them to protect them and keep them from fear (Hag. 2:5). When Saul was attempting to capture David by force, the Holy Spirit came upon Saul's messengers (1 Sam. 19:20) and eventually upon Saul himself (v. 23), causing them involuntarily to fall to the ground and to prophesy for hours, thus defeating Saul's purpose and humiliating him in response to his malicious show of force against David and Samuel. In a similar way, while Ezekiel was prophesying judgment by the power of the Holy Spirit against some of the leaders of Israel (Ezek. 11:5), one of the leaders named Pelatiah actually died (Ezek. 11:13). In this way the Holy Spirit brought immediate judgment on him.

Finally, the Old Testament predicted a time when the Holy Spirit would anoint a Servant-Messiah in great fullness and power:

> And the *Spirit of the* LORD *shall rest upon him,* the spirit of wisdom and understanding, the spirit of counsel and might, the spirit of knowledge and the fear of the LORD. And his delight shall be in the fear of the LORD. (Isa. 11:2–3)

Isaiah prophesied that God would say of this coming Servant, "I have put my Spirit upon him" (Isa. 42:1), and he himself would say, "The Spirit of the Lord GOD is upon me, because the LORD has anointed me" (Isa. 61:1; cf. Luke 4:18).

Before leaving this discussion of the empowering of the Holy Spirit in the Old Testament, we should note that it sometimes is said that there was no work of the Holy Spirit *within* people in the Old Testament. This idea has mainly been inferred from Jesus' words to the disciples in John 14:17, "He dwells with you, and will be *in* you." But we should not conclude from this verse that there was no work of the Holy Spirit within people before Pentecost. Although the Old Testament does not frequently speak of people who had the Holy Spirit in them or who were filled with the Holy Spirit, there are a few examples: Joshua is said to have the Holy Spirit within him (Num. 27:18; Deut. 34:9), as are Ezekiel (Ezek. 2:2; 3:24), Daniel (Dan. 4:8–9, 18; 5:11), and Micah (Mic. 3:8).[6] This means that when Jesus says to his disciples that the Holy Spirit "dwells with you and will be in you" (John 14:17), he cannot mean that there was an absolute "within/without" difference between the old and new covenant work of the Holy Spirit. Nor can John 7:39 ("as yet the Spirit had not been given, because Jesus was not yet glorified") mean that there was *no* activity of the Holy Spirit in people's lives before Pentecost. Both of these passages must be different ways of saying that the more powerful, fuller work of the Holy Spirit that is characteristic of life after Pentecost had not yet begun in the lives of the disciples. The Holy Spirit had not come within them in the way in which God had promised to put the Holy Spirit within his people when the new covenant would come (see Ezek. 36:26, 27; 37:14), nor had the Holy Spirit been poured out in the great abundance and fullness that would characterize the new covenant age (Joel 2:28–29). In this powerful new covenant sense, the Holy Spirit was not yet at work within the disciples.[7]

---

[6]Before Pentecost in the New Testament we also find that John the Baptist (Luke 1:15), Elizabeth (Luke 1:41), and Zechariah (Luke 1:67) were all said to be filled with the Holy Spirit.

[7]See chapter 39, pp. 770–72, for a fuller discussion of the differences between the work of the Holy Spirit in the old covenant and in the new covenant.

**b. New Testament:** The empowering work of the Holy Spirit in the New Testament is seen first and most fully in his anointing and empowering of Jesus as the Messiah. The Holy Spirit descended upon Jesus at his baptism (Matt. 3:16; Mark 1:11; Luke 3:22). John the Baptist said, "I saw the Spirit descend as a dove from heaven, and it remained on him" (John 1:32). Therefore Jesus entered into the temptation in the wilderness "full of the Holy Spirit" (Luke 4:1), and after his temptation, at the beginning of his ministry, "Jesus returned *in the power of the Spirit* into Galilee" (Luke 4:14). When Jesus came to preach in the synagogue at Nazareth, he declared that Isaiah's prophecy was fulfilled in himself: "The Spirit of the Lord is upon me, because he has anointed me to preach good news to the poor. He has sent me to proclaim release to the captives and recovering of sight to the blind, to set at liberty those who are oppressed, to proclaim the acceptable year of the Lord" (Luke 4:18–19). The power of the Holy Spirit in Jesus' life was then seen in his subsequent miracles, as he cast out demons with a word and healed all who came to him (Luke 4:36, 40–41). The Holy Spirit was pleased to dwell in Jesus and empower him, for he fully delighted in the absolute moral purity of Jesus' life. In the context of talking about his own ministry, and the Father's blessing on that ministry, Jesus says, "It is not by measure that he gives the Spirit; the Father loves the Son, and has given all things into his hand" (John 3:34–35). Jesus had an anointing of the Holy Spirit without measure, and this anointing "remained on him" (John 1:32; cf. Acts 10:38).

The Holy Spirit also empowered Jesus' disciples for various kinds of ministry. Jesus had promised them, "You shall *receive power when the Holy Spirit has come upon you;* and you shall be my witnesses in Jerusalem and in all Judea and Samaria and to the end of the earth" (Acts 1:8).[8] There are several specific examples of the Holy Spirit's empowering the early Christians to work miracles as they proclaimed the gospel (note Stephen in Acts 6:5, 8; and Paul in Rom. 15:19; 1 Cor. 2:4). But the Holy Spirit also gave great power to the preaching of the early church so that when the disciples were filled with the Holy Spirit they proclaimed the Word boldly and with great power (Acts 4:8, 31; 6:10; 1 Thess. 1:5; 1 Peter 1:12). In general, we can say that the Holy Spirit speaks through the gospel message as it is effectively proclaimed to people's hearts. The New Testament ends with an invitation from both the Holy Spirit and the church, who together call people to salvation: "The Spirit and the Bride say, 'Come.' And let him who hears say, 'Come'" (Rev. 22:17). In fact, not only in the preaching of the gospel message, but also in the reading and teaching of Scripture, the Holy Spirit continues to

---

[8]The word here translated "power" (*dynamis*) occurs nine other times in Acts. In one case (4:33), it is unclear whether this "power" refers to powerful preaching that convicted the hearers or to miraculous signs that accompanied the preaching. But in the other eight examples (2:22; 3:12; 4:7; 6:8; 8:10 [in this verse referring to pagan miracle-working power], 13; 10:38; 19:11) it refers to *power to work miracles*. This meaning of the term *dynamis* is further confirmed by its frequent use in Luke's gospel to refer to miracle-working power. Therefore when Jesus promised the disciples in Acts 1:8 that they would receive "power" when the Holy Spirit came upon them, it seems likely that they would have understood him to mean at least the power of the Holy Spirit to work miracles that would attest to the truthfulness of the gospel. Because the immediate context of the sentence talks about being witnesses for Jesus, they may also have understood him to mean that they would receive the power of the Holy Spirit to work through their preaching and bring conviction of sins and awaken faith in people's hearts. This power in their preaching was evident in subsequent events, as when Peter's hearers "were cut to the heart" (Acts 2:37), or when "many of those who heard the word believed; and the number of the men came to about five thousand" (Acts 4:4).

speak to people's hearts each day (see Heb. 3:7 and 10:15, where the author quotes an Old Testament passage and says that the Holy Spirit is now speaking that passage to his readers).

Another aspect of empowering Christians for service is the Holy Spirit's activity of giving spiritual gifts to equip Christians for ministry. After listing a variety of spiritual gifts, Paul says, "But *one and the same Spirit works all these things*, distributing to each one individually just as He wills" (1 Cor. 12:11 NASB). Since the Holy Spirit is the one who shows or manifests God's presence in the world, it is not surprising that Paul can call spiritual gifts "manifestations" of the Holy Spirit (1 Cor. 12:7).[9] When spiritual gifts are active, it is another indication of the presence of God the Holy Spirit in the church.[10]

In the prayer lives of individual believers, we find that the Holy Spirit empowers prayer and makes it effective. "We do not know how to pray as we ought, but the Spirit himself intercedes for us with sighs too deep for words" (Rom. 8:26).[11] And Paul says that we "have access in one Spirit to the Father" (Eph. 2:18). One specific kind of prayer that the New Testament says is empowered by the Holy Spirit is the gift of prayer in tongues (1 Cor. 12:10–11; 14:2, 14–17).[12]

Yet another aspect of the Holy Spirit's work in empowering Christians for service is empowering people to overcome spiritual opposition to the preaching of the gospel and to God's work in people's lives. This power in spiritual warfare was first seen in the life of Jesus, who said, "If it is *by the Spirit of God* that I cast out demons, then the kingdom of God has come upon you" (Matt. 12:28). When Paul came to Cyprus he encountered opposition from Elymas the magician, but he, "*filled with the Holy Spirit*, looked intently at him and said, 'You son of the devil, you enemy of all righteousness, full of all deceit and villainy, will you not stop making crooked the straight paths of the Lord? And now, behold, the hand of the Lord is upon you, and you shall be blind and unable to see the sun for a time.' Immediately mist and darkness fell upon him and he went about seeking people to lead him by the hand" (Acts 13:9–11). The gift of "distinguishing between spirits" (1 Cor. 12:10), given by the Holy Spirit, is also to be a tool in this warfare against the forces of darkness, as is the Word of God, which functions as the "sword of the Spirit" (Eph. 6:17) in spiritual conflict.

## B. The Holy Spirit Purifies

Since this member of the Trinity is called the *Holy* Spirit, it is not surprising to find that one of his primary activities is to cleanse us from sin and to "sanctify us" or make us more holy in actual conduct of life. Even in the lives of unbelievers there is some restraining influence of the Holy Spirit as he convicts the world of sin (John 16:8–11; Acts 7:51). But when people become Christians the Holy

---

[9]The Greek word translated "manifestation" is *phanerōsis*, which means something that discloses, something that makes publicly evident or clear. The related adjective *phaneros* means "visible, clear, plainly to be seen, open, plain, evident, known" (BAGD, p. 852).

[10]The Holy Spirit also empowers obedience to God during the Christian life (see discussion below on the Holy Spirit's work of purification).

[11]See discussion of Rom. 8:26 in chapter 18, pp. 381–82, and chapter 53, pp. 1078–80.

[12]See discussion of speaking in tongues in chapter 53, pp. 1069–80.

Spirit does an initial cleansing work in them, making a decisive break with the patterns of sin that were in their lives before.[13] Paul says of the Corinthians, "You were washed, *you were sanctified,* you were justified in the name of the Lord Jesus Christ and *in the Spirit of our God*" (1 Cor. 6:11; see also Titus 3:5). This cleansing and purifying work of the Holy Spirit is apparently what is symbolized by the metaphor of fire when John the Baptist says that Jesus will baptize people "with the Holy Spirit and with fire" (Matt. 3:11; Luke 3:16).

After the initial break with sin that the Holy Spirit brings about in our lives at conversion, he also produces in us growth in holiness of life. He brings forth the *"fruit of the Spirit"* within us ("love, joy, peace, patience, kindness, goodness, faithfulness, gentleness, self-control," Gal. 5:22–23), those qualities that reflect the character of God. As we continually "are being changed into his likeness from one degree of glory to another," we should be reminded that "this comes from the Lord who is the Spirit" (2 Cor. 3:18). Sanctification comes by the power of the Holy Spirit (2 Thess. 2:13; 1 Peter 1:2; cf. Rom. 8:4, 15–16), so that it is *"by the Spirit"* that we are able to "put to death the deeds of the body" and grow in personal holiness (Rom. 8:13; see 7:6; Phil. 1:19).[14]

Some people today say a purifying (or healing) work of the Holy Spirit occurs when they are "slain in the Spirit," an experience in which they suddenly fall to the ground in a semi-conscious state and remain there for minutes or hours. Although the phrase "slaying in the Spirit" is nowhere in Scripture, there are instances when people fell to the ground, or fell into a trance, in the presence of God.[15] Contemporary experiences should be evaluated according to what lasting results ("fruit") they bear in people's lives (see Matt. 7:15–20; 1 Cor. 14:12, 26c).

## C. The Holy Spirit Reveals

**1. Revelation to Prophets and Apostles.** In chapter 4 we discussed in great detail the work of the Holy Spirit in revealing God's words to the Old Testament prophets and New Testament apostles, in many cases so that these words could be put into Scripture (see, for example, Num. 24:2; Ezek. 11:5; Zech. 7:12; et al.). The whole of the Old Testament Scriptures came about because "men spoke from God as they were carried along by the Holy Spirit" (2 Peter 1:21 NIV). Several other passages mention this work of the Holy Spirit in Old Testament prophets (see Matt. 22:43; Acts 1:16; 4:25; 28:25; 1 Peter 1:21). The New Testament apostles and others who wrote words of New Testament Scripture were also guided "into all the truth" by the Holy Spirit (John 16:13), who also spoke to the apostles what he heard from the Father and the Son, and declared to them "the things that are to come" (John 16:3; cf. Eph. 3:5). Others who were filled with the Holy Spirit also spoke or sang words that became part of Scripture, such as Elizabeth (Luke 1:41), Zechariah (Luke 1:67), and Simeon (Luke 2:25).

---

[13]See discussion of this in John Murray, "Definitive Sanctification," in *Collected Writings of John Murray* (Edinburgh and Carlisle, Pa.: Banner of Truth, 1977), pp. 277–84.

[14]See chapter 38, pp. 746–62, for a more extensive discussion of sanctification.

[15]See Gen. 15:12; Exod. 40:35; 1 Sam. 19:24; 1 Kings 8:11; Ezek. 1:28; 3:23; Dan. 8:27; John 18:6; Acts 9:4; 10:10; Rev. 1:17; 4:10 (compare angelic encounters in Dan. 8:17–18; 10:7–17).

**2. He Gives Evidence of God's Presence.** Sometimes it has been said that the work of the Holy Spirit is not to call attention to himself but rather to give glory to Jesus and to God the Father. But this seems to be a false dichotomy, not supported by Scripture. Of course the Holy Spirit does glorify Jesus (John 16:14) and bear witness to him (John 15:26; Acts 5:32; 1 John 2:3; 1 John 4:2). But this does not mean that he does not make his own actions and words known! The Bible has hundreds of verses *talking about the work of the Holy Spirit,* making his work known, and the Bible is itself spoken or inspired by the Holy Spirit!

Moreover, *the Holy Spirit frequently made himself known by phenomena that indicated his activity,* both in the Old Testament and in the New Testament periods. This was true when the Holy Spirit came upon the seventy elders with Moses and they prophesied (Num. 11:25–26), and when the Holy Spirit came upon the judges to enable them to do great works of power (Judg. 14:6, 19; 15:14, et al.). In these instances people could see the effect of the Holy Spirit coming on the Lord's servants. This was also true when the Holy Spirit came mightily upon Saul and he prophesied with a band of prophets (1 Sam. 10:6, 10), and it was frequently true when he empowered the Old Testament prophets to give public prophecies.

The Holy Spirit also made his presence evident in a visible way when he descended as a dove on Jesus (John 1:32), or came as a sound of a rushing wind and with visible tongues of fire on the disciples at Pentecost (Acts 2:2–3). In addition, when people had the Holy Spirit poured out on them and began to speak in tongues or praise God in a remarkable and spontaneous way (see Acts 2:4; 10:44–46; 19:6), the Holy Spirit certainly made his presence known as well. And Jesus promised that the Holy Spirit within us would be so powerful he would be like a river of living water flowing out from our inmost beings (see John 7:39)—a simile that suggests that people would be aware of a presence that would somehow be perceptible.

In the lives of individual believers, the Holy Spirit does not entirely conceal his work, but makes himself known in various ways. He bears witness with our spirit that we are children of God (Rom. 8:16), and cries, "Abba! Father!" (Gal. 4:6). He provides a guarantee or a down payment of our future fellowship with him in heaven (2 Cor. 1:22; 5:5), and reveals his desires to us so that we can be led by those desires and follow them (Rom. 8:4–16; Gal. 5:16–25). He gives gifts that manifest his presence (1 Cor. 12:7–11). And from time to time he works miraculous signs and wonders that strongly attest to the presence of God in the preaching of the gospel (Heb. 2:4; cf. 1 Cor. 2:4; Rom. 15:19).

It seems more accurate, therefore, to say that although the Holy Spirit does glorify Jesus, he also frequently calls attention to his work and *gives recognizable evidences that make his presence known.* Indeed, it seems that one of his primary purposes in the new covenant age is *to manifest the presence of God,* to give indications that make the presence of God known. And when the Holy Spirit works in various ways that can be perceived by believers and unbelievers, this encourages people's faith that God is near and that he is working to fulfill his purposes in the church and to bring blessing to his people.

**3. He Guides and Directs God's People.** Scripture gives many examples of direct guidance from the Holy Spirit to various people. In fact, in the Old Testament, God said that it was sin for the people to enter into agreements with others when those agreements were "not of my Spirit" (Isa. 30:1). Apparently the people had been deciding on the basis of their own wisdom and common sense rather than seeking the guidance of God's Holy Spirit before they entered into such agreements. In the New Testament, the Holy Spirit led Jesus into the wilderness for his period of temptation (Matt. 4:1; Luke 4:1); in fact, so strong was this leading of the Holy Spirit that Mark can say that "The Spirit immediately drove him out into the wilderness" (Mark 1:12).[16]

In other contexts the Holy Spirit gave direct words of guidance to people, saying to Philip, for example, "Go up and join this chariot" (Acts 8:29), or telling Peter to go with three men who came to him from Cornelius' household (Acts 10:19–20; 11:12), or directing the Christians at Antioch, "Set apart for me Barnabas and Saul for the work to which I have called them" (Acts 13:2).

Also in the category of "giving guidance," but of a much more direct and compelling kind, are several examples where the Holy Spirit actually transported a person from one place to another. This was so when "the Spirit of the Lord caught up Philip; and the eunuch saw him no more. . . . But Philip was found at Azotus" (Acts 8:39–40)—the guidance in this case could hardly have been more clear! But similar things happened to some Old Testament prophets, for those who knew Elijah seemed to expect that the Spirit of God would snatch him up and transport him somewhere (1 Kings 18:12; 2 Kings 2:16: "It may be that the Spirit of the LORD has caught him up and cast him upon some mountain or into some valley"). The Spirit of the Lord several times, Ezekiel says, "lifted me up" and brought him to one place or another (Ezek. 11:1; 37:1; 43:5), an experience that was also part of John's later visions in Revelation (Rev. 17:3; 21:10).[17]

But in the vast majority of cases the leading and guiding by the Holy Spirit is not nearly as dramatic as this. Scripture talks rather about a day-to-day guidance by the Holy Spirit—being "led" by the Holy Spirit (Rom. 8:14; Gal. 5:18), and walking according to the Spirit (Rom. 8:4; Gal. 5:16). Now it is possible to understand Paul here to be referring only to obedience to the moral commands of Scripture, but this interpretation seems quite unlikely, especially since the entire context is dealing with emotions and desires which we perceive in a more subjective way, and because Paul here contrasts being led by the Spirit with following the desires of the flesh or the sinful nature:

> But I say, *walk by the Spirit,* and do not gratify the desires of the flesh. For the desires of the flesh are against the Spirit, and the *desires of the Spirit* are against the flesh. . . . Now the works of the flesh are plain: fornication, impurity, licentiousness, idolatry, sorcery, enmity, strife, jealousy, anger. . . . But the fruit of the Spirit is love, joy, peace, patience, kindness, goodness, faithfulness, gentleness, self-control. . . . If we live by the Spirit, let us also walk by the Spirit. Let us have no self-conceit, no provoking of one another, no envy of one another. (Gal. 5:16–26)

---

[16]The verb here translated "drove out" is a strong term, *ekballō*, which means "drive out, expel," and more literally can mean "throw out."

[17]It is possible that Ezekiel and John are speaking of transportation in a vision (as in Ezek. 8:3 and 11:24) rather than literal physical travel. Paul allows for both possibilities in 2 Cor. 12:2–3.

The contrast between "desires of the flesh" and "desires of the Spirit" implies that our lives should be responding moment by moment to the desires of the Holy Spirit, not to the desires of the flesh. Now it may be that a large part of responding to those desires is the intellectual process of understanding what love, joy, peace (and so forth) are, and then acting in a loving or a joyful or peaceful way. But this can hardly constitute the whole of such guidance by the Spirit because these emotions are not simply things we think about; they are things we also feel and sense at a deeper level. In fact, the word translated "desires" (Gk. *epithymia*) is a word that refers to strong human desires, not simply to intellectual decisions. Paul implies that we are to follow these desires as they are produced by the Holy Spirit in us. Moreover, the idea of being "led" by the Holy Spirit (Gal. 5:18) implies an active *personal* participation by the Holy Spirit in guiding us. This is something more than our reflecting on biblical moral standards, and includes an involvement by the Holy Spirit in relating to us as persons and leading and directing us.

There are specific examples of the Holy Spirit guiding people directly in the book of Acts. After the decision of the Jerusalem council, the leaders wrote in their letter to the churches, "It has *seemed good to the Holy Spirit* and to us to lay upon you no greater burden than these necessary things" (Acts 15:28). This verse suggests that the council must have had a sense of the good pleasure of the Holy Spirit in these areas: they knew what "seemed good to the Holy Spirit." On Paul's second missionary journey, Luke writes that they were "forbidden by the Holy Spirit to speak the word in Asia" and then that "they attempted to go into Bithynia, but the Spirit of Jesus did not allow them" (Acts 16:6–7). Of course, no written principle from the Old Testament Scriptures would have led them to conclude that they could not preach in Asia or Bithynia. The Holy Spirit must rather have communicated his direct guidance to them in some specific way, whether through words heard audibly or in the mind, or through strong subjective impressions of a lack of the Holy Spirit's presence and blessing as they attempted to travel to these different areas. Later, when Paul is on his way to Jerusalem, he says, "I am going to Jerusalem, *bound in the Spirit*, not knowing what shall befall me there; except that the Holy Spirit testifies to me in every city that imprisonment and afflictions await me" (Acts 20:22–23). Paul did not think he had another choice—so clearly did the Holy Spirit manifest his presence and desires to him, that Paul could speak of having been "bound" in the Spirit.[18]

In other cases the Holy Spirit gave guidance to establish people in various ministries or church offices. So the Holy Spirit said to some in the church at Antioch, "Set apart for me Barnabas and Saul for the work to which I have called them" (Acts 13:2). And Paul could say that the Holy Spirit had established the elders of the Ephesian church in their office because he said, "Take heed to yourselves and to all the flock, in which the Holy Spirit has made you overseers"

---

[18]The word translated "bound" is a perfect passive participle of *deō*, and signifies an earlier completed event (perhaps a strong conviction from the Holy Spirit that settled Paul's mind on the trip to Jerusalem once for all), but an event that also has continuing results in the present, so that Paul remained "bound" when he spoke (the event still influenced Paul so strongly that he had no other choice but to continue forward toward Jerusalem).

(Acts 20:28). Finally, the Holy Spirit did provide some guidance through the means of spiritual gifts such as prophecy (1 Cor. 14:29–33).[19]

**4. He Provides a Godlike Atmosphere When He Manifests His Presence.** Because the Holy Spirit is fully God, and shares all the attributes of God, his influence will be to bring a Godlike character or atmosphere to the situations in which he is active. Because he is the *Holy* Spirit he will at times bring about a conviction of sin, righteousness, and judgment (John 16:8–11). Because God is love, the Holy Spirit pours God's love into our hearts (Rom. 5:5; 15:30; Col. 1:8) and often the strongly manifested presence of the Holy Spirit will create an atmosphere of love. Because God is "not a God of confusion but of peace" (1 Cor. 14:33), the Holy Spirit brings an atmosphere of peace into situations: "The kingdom of God is not food and drink, but righteousness and peace and joy in the Holy Spirit" (Rom. 14:17; cf. Gal. 5:22). This last verse also teaches that the Holy Spirit imparts an atmosphere of joy (see also Acts 13:52; 1 Thess. 1:6). Although the list is not exhaustive, Paul summarized many of these Godlike qualities that the Holy Spirit produces when he listed the various elements of the fruit of the Spirit in Galatians 5:22–23.

Other elements of the atmosphere that the Holy Spirit can impart are truth (John 14:17; 15:26; 16:13; 1 John 5:7), wisdom (Deut. 34:9; Isa. 11:2), comfort (Acts 9:31), freedom (2 Cor. 3:17), righteousness (Rom. 14:17), hope (Rom. 15:13; cf. Gal. 5:5), an awareness of sonship or adoption (Rom. 8:15–16; Gal. 4:5–6), and even glory (2 Cor. 3:8). The Holy Spirit also brings unity (Eph. 4:3), and power (Acts 1:18; 1 Cor. 2:4; 2 Tim. 1:7; cf. Acts 1:8). All of these elements of the Holy Spirit's activity indicate the various aspects of an atmosphere in which he makes his own presence—and thereby his own character—known to the people.

**5. He Gives Us Assurance.** The Holy Spirit bears witness "with our spirits that we are children of God" (Rom. 8:16), and gives evidence of the work of God within us: "And by this we know that he abides in us, by the Spirit which he has given us" (1 John 3:24). "By this we know that we abide in him and he in us, *because he has given us of his own Spirit*" (1 John 4:13). The Holy Spirit not only witnesses to us that we are God's children, but also witnesses that God abides in us and that we are abiding in him. Once again more than our intellect is involved: the Spirit works to give us assurance at the subjective level of spiritual and emotional perception as well.

**6. He Teaches and Illumines.** Another aspect of the Holy Spirit's revealing work is teaching certain things to God's people and illumining them so that they can understand things. Jesus promised this teaching function especially to his disciples

---

[19]However, it is always dangerous to follow spontaneous prophecies alone for guidance in this church age, since we are never to think of any prophecies as inerrant or 100 percent accurate today. Mistakes can especially come in the area of personal guidance. But all that does not allow us to say that there can be no guidance that comes through prophecy. See further discussion about subjective guidance in general and the gift of prophecy in particular in chapter 8, p. 128, and chapter 53, pp. 1049–61.

when he said that the Holy Spirit "will *teach* you all things, and bring to your remembrance all that I have said to you" (John 14:26), and said, "he will guide you into all the truth" (John 16:13). Moreover, he promised that when his disciples were put on trial because of persecution, the Holy Spirit would teach them at that time what to say (Luke 12:12; cf. Matt. 10:20; Mark 13:11).. At other times the Holy Spirit revealed specific information to people—showing Simeon that he would not die until he saw the Messiah, for example (Luke 2:26), or revealing to Agabus that a famine would occur (Acts 11:28) or that Paul would be taken captive in Jerusalem (Acts 21:11). In other cases the Holy Spirit revealed to Paul that he would suffer in Jerusalem (Acts 20:23; 21:4) and expressly said to Paul things that would happen in the latter days (1 Tim. 4:1), and revealed to him what God has prepared for those who love him (1 Cor. 2:10).

The illuminating work of the Holy Spirit is seen in the fact that he enables us to understand: "We have received not the spirit of the world, but the Spirit which is from God, *that we might understand* the gifts bestowed on us by God" (1 Cor. 2:12). Therefore, "The unspiritual man does not receive the gifts (literally, things) of the Spirit of God" but "The spiritual man judges all things" (1 Cor. 2:14–15). We should pray that the Holy Spirit would give us his illumination and thereby help us to understand rightly when we study Scripture or when we ponder situations in our lives. Although he did not mention the Holy Spirit specifically, the psalmist prayed for such illumination when he asked God, "Open my eyes, that I may behold wondrous things out of your law" (Ps. 119:18). Similarly, Paul prayed for the Christians in and around Ephesus,

> . . . that the God of our Lord Jesus Christ, the Father of glory, may give you a spirit [or: "the Spirit," NIV] of wisdom and of revelation in the knowledge of him, having the eyes of your hearts enlightened, that you may know what is the hope to which he has called you, what are the riches of his glorious inheritance in the saints, and what is the immeasurable greatness of his power in us who believe, according to the working of his great might. (Eph. 1:17–19)

### D. The Holy Spirit Unifies

When the Holy Spirit was poured out on the church at Pentecost, Peter proclaimed that the prophecy of Joel 2:28–32 was fulfilled:

> But this is what was spoken by the prophet Joel:
>
> "And in the last days it shall be, God declares,
> that I will pour out my Spirit upon all flesh,
> and your sons and your daughters shall prophesy,
> and your young men shall see visions,
> and your old men shall dream dreams;
> yes, and on my menservants and my maidservants in those days
> I will pour out my Spirit; and they shall prophesy." (Acts 2:16–18)

There is an emphasis on the Holy Spirit coming on a community of believers— not just a leader like Moses or Joshua, but sons and daughters, old men and young men, menservants and maidservants—all will receive the outpouring of the Holy Spirit in this time.[20]

In the event of Pentecost, the Holy Spirit created a new community which was the church. The community was marked by unprecedented unity, as Luke reminds us:

> And all who believed were together and had all things in common; and they sold their possessions and goods and distributed them to all, as any had need. And day by day, attending the temple together and breaking bread in their homes, they partook of food with glad and generous hearts, praising God and having favor with all the people. (Acts 2:44–47)

Paul blesses the Corinthian church with a blessing that seeks the unifying fellowship of the Holy Spirit for all of them when he says, "The grace of the Lord Jesus Christ and the love of God and the *fellowship of the Holy Spirit*[21] be with you all" (2 Cor. 13:14). It is significant that in this trinitarian verse he especially attributes the deepening of fellowship among believers not to the Father or the Son but to the Holy Spirit, a statement consistent with the overall unifying work of the Spirit in the church.

This unifying function of the Holy Spirit is also evident when Paul tells the Philippians, "If therefore there is any encouragement in Christ, if there is any consolation of love, if there is any *fellowship of the Spirit* . . . make my joy complete by being of the same mind, maintaining the same love, united in spirit, intent on one purpose" (Phil. 2:1–2 NASB).[22] In a similar way, when he emphasizes the new unity between Jews and Gentiles in the church, he says that "through him we both have access in one Spirit to the Father" (Eph. 2:18), and says that in the Lord they are built into the one new house of God "in the Spirit" (Eph. 2:22). When he wants to remind them of the unity they should have as Christians he exhorts them to be "eager to maintain *the unity of the Spirit* in the bond of peace" (Eph. 4:3).

Paul's discussion of spiritual gifts also repeats this theme of the unifying work of the Holy Spirit. Whereas we might think that people who have differing gifts would not readily get along well with each other, Paul's conclusion is just the opposite: differing gifts draw us together, because we are forced to depend on each other. "The eye cannot say to the hand, 'I have no need of you,' nor again the head to the feet, 'I have no need of you'" (1 Cor. 12:21). These differing gifts, Paul tells us, are empowered by "one and the same Spirit, who apportions to each one individually as he wills" (1 Cor. 12:11), so that in the church, "To each is given the *manifestation of the Spirit* for the common good" (1 Cor. 12:7). In fact, "in one Spirit we were all baptized into one body—Jews or Greeks, slaves or

---

[20]This was also a fulfillment of Moses' wish that the Lord would put his Spirit on all his people (Num. 11:29), and of the vision of the valley of dry bones revived by the Spirit in Ezek. 37. See also Donald Guthrie, *New Testament Theology*, pp. 512–13, 540, 562.

[21]The word *koinōnia*, "fellowship," could also mean "participation in the Holy Spirit," but it would make little sense for Paul to wish for them something they already had as believers (participation in the Holy Spirit). It is better to translate the verse, "fellowship of the Holy Spirit," thus emphasizing a blessing from the Holy Spirit that Paul hoped would increase in the Corinthian church.

[22]The Greek word *koinōnia* is also best translated "fellowship" here because Paul's purpose in Phil. 2:1–11 is to encourage unity in the Philippian church. (See the preceding footnote also.)

free—and all were made to drink of one Spirit" (1 Cor. 12:13, author's translation).[23]

The idea that the Holy Spirit unifies the church is also evident in the fact that "strife . . . disputes, dissensions, factions" (Gal. 5:20 NASB) are desires of the flesh that are opposed to being "led by the Spirit" (Gal. 5:18; cf. v. 25). The Holy Spirit is the one who produces love in our hearts (Rom. 5:5; Gal. 5:22; Col. 1:8), and this love "binds everything together in perfect harmony" (Col. 3:14). Therefore when the Holy Spirit is working strongly in a church to manifest God's presence, one evidence will be a beautiful harmony in the church community and overflowing love for one another.

### E. The Holy Spirit Gives Stronger or Weaker Evidence of the Presence and Blessing of God According to Our Response to Him

Many examples in both the Old and New Testament indicate that the Holy Spirit will bestow or withdraw blessing according to whether or not he is pleased by the situation he sees. It is noteworthy that Jesus was completely without sin and the Holy Spirit "remained on him" (John 1:32) and was given to him without measure (John 3:34). In the Old Testament the Holy Spirit came mightily upon Samson several times (Judg. 13:25; 14:6, 19; 15:14), but ultimately left him when he persisted in sin (Judg. 16:20). Similarly, when Saul persisted in disobedience the Holy Spirit departed from him (1 Sam. 16:14). And when the people of Israel rebelled and grieved the Holy Spirit he turned against them (Isa. 63:10).

Also in the New Testament the Holy Spirit can be grieved and cease to bring blessing in a situation. Stephen rebuked the Jewish leaders, saying, "You always *resist the Holy Spirit*" (Acts 7:51). Paul warns the Ephesian Christians, "Do not *grieve the Holy Spirit of God,* in whom you were sealed for the day of redemption" (Eph. 4:30), and exhorts the Thessalonian church, "Do not *quench the Spirit*" (1 Thess. 5:19; cf. the metaphor of delaying to open the door and thereby disappointing one's lover in Song of Sol. 5:3, 6). In a similar vein, Paul gives a serious warning to Christians not to defile their bodies by joining them to a prostitute because the Holy Spirit lives within their bodies: "Do you not know that your body is a temple of the Holy Spirit within you, which you have from God? You are not your own; you were bought with a price. So glorify God in your body" (1 Cor. 6:19–20).

Even more serious than grieving or quenching the Holy Spirit is a deeper, more hardened disobedience to him that brings strong judgment. When Peter rebuked Ananias, "Why has Satan filled your heart to lie to the Holy Spirit and to keep back part of the proceeds of the land?" (Acts 5:3), he fell down dead. Similarly, when Peter said to Ananias's wife Sapphira, "How is it that you have agreed together to tempt the Spirit of the Lord?" (Acts 5:9), she immediately fell down dead as well. The book of Hebrews warns those who are in danger of falling away that severe punishment is deserved by the man "who has spurned the Son of God, and profaned the blood of the covenant by which he was sanctified, and *outraged*

---

[23]See the extended discussion of this verse in chapter 39, pp. 766–69.

*the Spirit of grace*" (Heb. 10:29). For such a person there only remains "a fearful prospect of judgment" (Heb. 10:27).[24]

Finally, there remains one more level of offense against the Holy Spirit. This kind of offense is even more serious than grieving him or acting with the hardened disobedience to him that brings discipline or judgment. It is possible so to offend the Holy Spirit that his convicting work will not be brought to bear again in a person's life.

> Every sin and blasphemy will be forgiven men, but the *blasphemy against the Spirit* will not be forgiven. And whoever says a word against the Son of man will be forgiven; but whoever speaks against the Holy Spirit will not be forgiven, either in this age or in the age to come. (Matt. 12:31–32; cf. Mark 3:29; Luke 12:10)

These statements are made in a context in which the Pharisees willfully and maliciously attribute to Satan the powerful work of the Holy Spirit that was evident in the ministry of Jesus. Since the Holy Spirit so clearly manifested the presence of God, those who willfully and maliciously spoke against him and attributed his activity instead to the power of Satan were guilty, Jesus said, "of an eternal sin" (Mark 3:29).[25]

All of these passages indicate that we must be very careful not to grieve or offend the Holy Spirit. He will not force himself on us against our wills (see 1 Cor. 14:32), but if we resist and quench and oppose him, then his empowering will depart and he will remove much of the blessing of God from our lives.

On the other hand, in the life of Christians whose conduct is pleasing to God, the Holy Spirit will be present to bring great blessing. The Holy Spirit was "poured out" in fullness at Pentecost (see Acts 2:17–18) and he now dwells within all true believers, making them temples of the living God (1 Cor. 3:16; 6:19–20). We can know close fellowship and partnership with the Holy Spirit in our lives (2 Cor. 3:14; Phil. 2:1). He entrusts gifts (1 Cor. 12:11) and truth (2 Tim. 1:14) and ministries (Acts 20:28) to us. In fact, so full and abundant will be his presence that Jesus could promise that he will flow out of our inmost being like "rivers of living water" (John 7:38–39). Peter promises that his presence especially rests on those who suffer for the sake of Christ: "If you are reproached for the name of Christ, you are blessed, because the spirit of glory and of God rests upon you" (1 Peter 4:14).

Therefore it is important that all our ministry be done *in the Holy Spirit,* that is, that we consciously dwell in the Godlike atmosphere created by the Holy Spirit— the atmosphere of power, love, joy, truth, holiness, righteousness, and peace. But greater than these characteristics of the atmosphere created by the Holy Spirit is the sense of the presence of the Holy Spirit himself—*to be in the Holy Spirit is really to be in an atmosphere of God's manifested presence.* This is why people in the New Testament can walk in the comfort of the Holy Spirit (Acts 9:31), and why it is possible just to be "in the Spirit" as John was on the Lord's day (Rev. 1:10; cf. 4:2).

It is surprising how many particular activities are said in the New Testament to be done "in" the Holy Spirit: it is possible to *rejoice* in the Holy Spirit (Luke

---

[24]This passage could also be put in the next category, discussed in the following paragraph.
[25]See chapter 24, pp. 507–9, for a fuller discussion of the unpardonable sin.

10:21), to *resolve* or decide something in the Holy Spirit (Acts 19:21), to have one's *conscience bear witness* in the Holy Spirit (Rom. 9:1), to have *access to God* in the Holy Spirit (Eph. 2:18), to *pray* in the Holy Spirit (Eph. 6:18; Jude 20), and to *love* in the Holy Spirit (Col. 1:8). In the light of these texts, we might ask ourselves, for how many of these activities during each day are we consciously aware of the Holy Spirit's presence and blessing?

It is also possible to be filled with the Holy Spirit (Eph. 5:18; cf. Luke 1:15, 41, 67; 4:1; Acts 2:4; 4:8; 6:3, 5; 7:55; 9:17; 11:24; 13:9). To be filled with the Holy Spirit is to be filled with the immediate presence of God himself, and it therefore will result in feeling what God feels, desiring what God desires, doing what God wants, speaking by God's power, praying and ministering in God's strength, and knowing with the knowledge which God himself gives.[26] In times when the church experiences revival the Holy Spirit produces these results in people's lives in especially powerful ways.

Therefore in our Christian lives it is important that we depend on the Holy Spirit's power, recognizing that any significant work is done "Not by might, nor by power, *but by my Spirit,* says the LORD of hosts" (Zech. 4:6). Paul is emphatic in telling the Galatians that the Holy Spirit was received by faith in the beginning of their Christian life (Gal. 3:2) and would continue to work according to their faith in their lives subsequent to conversion: "Having begun with the Spirit, are you now ending with the flesh? . . . Does he who supplies the Spirit to you and works miracles among you do so by works of the law, or by hearing with faith?" (Gal. 3:3, 5).

Therefore we are to walk according to the guidance of the Holy Spirit (Rom. 8:12–16; Gal. 5:16–26) and set our minds on the things of the Spirit (Rom. 8:4–6). All our ministry, whatever form it may take, is to be done in the power of the Holy Spirit.

## QUESTIONS FOR PERSONAL APPLICATION

1. In the past, has it been hard for you to think of the Holy Spirit as a person rather than simply as a presence or force? What items (if any) in this chapter have helped you think more readily of the Holy Spirit as a person? Do you think that you have a consciousness of relating to the Holy Spirit as a person who is distinct from God the Father and God the Son? What might help you be more aware of this distinction among the members of the Trinity as they relate to you?

2. Do you perceive any difference in the way the Father, Son, and Holy Spirit relate to you in your Christian life? If so, can you explain what that difference is or how you are aware of it?

3. Have you ever been especially aware of the Holy Spirit's empowering in a specific situation of ministry? (This could have been while doing evangelism or counseling, Bible teaching or preaching, prayer or worship, or in some other ministry situation.) How did you perceive the presence of the Holy Spirit at that time, or what made you aware of his presence?

---

[26]See chapter 39, pp. 781–84, for more extensive discussion of being filled with the Holy Spirit.

4. In your own experience, in what ways does the guidance of the Holy Spirit come to you? Is it primarily (or exclusively) through the words of Scripture? If so, are there times when certain Scripture passages seem to come alive or speak with great relevance and forcefulness to you at the moment? How do you know when this is happening? If the Holy Spirit's guidance has come to you in other ways in addition to speaking through the words of Scripture, what have those other ways been?

5. Do you have a sense from time to time of the pleasure or displeasure of the Holy Spirit at some course of action that you are taking? Is there anything in your life right now that is grieving the Holy Spirit? What do you plan to do about it?

6. Did the Holy Spirit immediately leave Samson when he began to sin (see Judg. 13:25; 14:6, 19; 15:14)? Why or why not? Is the presence of spiritual power in someone's ministry a guarantee that the Holy Spirit is pleased with all of that person's life?

## SPECIAL TERMS

blasphemy against the Holy Spirit
filled with the Holy Spirit
Holy Spirit

in the Holy Spirit
manifestation of God's active presence

## BIBLIOGRAPHY

(For an explanation of this bibliography see the note on the bibliography to chapter 1, p. 38. Complete bibliographical data may be found on pp. 1223–29.)

### Sections in Evangelical Systematic Theologies

1. Anglican (Episcopalian)
       1882–92    Litton, 242–47
       1930       Thomas, 90–99
2. Arminian (Wesleyan or Methodist)
       1875–76    Pope, 2:321–36
       1940       Wiley, 2:303–33
       1960       Purkiser, 183–203
       1983       Carter, 1:415–72
3. Baptist
       1917       Mullins, 359–65
       1976–83    Henry, 4:476–93; 6:370–401
       1983–85    Erickson, 845–83
4. Dispensational
       1947       Chafer, 1:397–414; 6:26–298
       1949       Thiessen, 251–56
       1986       Ryrie, 341–90

5. Lutheran

    1917–24    Pieper (no extensive treatment, but see extensive index entries: 4:391–99)

    1934    Mueller, 443

6. Reformed (or Presbyterian)

    1559    Calvin, 2:537–42 (3.1)

    1887–1921    Warfield, *SSW*, 1:203–22; *BD*, 101–32

    1937–66    Murray, *CW*, 1:138–42, 186–92; *CW*, 3:210–14

    1938    Berkhof, 423–31

7. Renewal (or charismatic/Pentecostal)

    1988–92    Williams, 2:137–207, 237–70

## Sections in Representative Roman Catholic Systematic Theologies

1. Roman Catholic: Traditional

    1955    Ott (no explicit treatment)

2. Roman Catholic: Post-Vatican II

    1980    McBrien (no explicit treatment)

## Other Works

Bruner, Frederick Dale. *A Theology of the Holy Spirit*. Grand Rapids: Eerdmans, 1970.

Carson, D. A. *Showing the Spirit: A Theological Exposition of 1 Corinthians 12–14*. Grand Rapids: Baker, 1987.

Carter, Charles. *The Person and Ministry of the Holy Spirit*. Grand Rapids: Baker, 1974.

Caulley, T. S. "Holy Spirit." In *EDT*, pp. 521–27.

Gaffin, Richard B., Jr. "The Holy Spirit." *WTJ* 43:1 (Fall 1980), pp. 58–78.

Green, Michael. *I Believe in the Holy Spirit*. Grand Rapids: Eerdmans, 1975.

Hawthorne, Gerald. *The Presence and the Power: The Significance of the Holy Spirit in the Life and Ministry of Jesus*. Dallas: Word, 1991.

Hoekema, Anthony A. "The Role of the Holy Spirit." In *Saved By Grace*. Grand Rapids: Eerdmans, and Exeter: Paternoster, 1989, pp. 28–53.

Horton, S. M. *What the Bible Says About the Holy Spirit*. Springfield, Mo.: Gospel Publishing House, 1976.

Ladd, George E. *The Presence of the Future: The Eschatology of Biblical Realism*. Grand Rapids: Eerdmans, 1974.

Moule, C. F. D. *The Holy Spirit*. Grand Rapids: Eerdmans, 1978.

Pache, Rene. *The Person and Work of the Holy Spirit*. Chicago: Moody, 1954.

Packer, J. I. "Holy Spirit." In *NDT*, pp. 316–19.

———. *Keep in Step with the Spirit*. Old Tappan, N.J.: Revell, 1984.

Palmer, Edwin H. *The Person and Ministry of the Holy Spirit*. Grand Rapids: Baker, 1958.

Ryrie, C. C. *The Holy Spirit*. Chicago: Moody, 1965.

Smeaton, G. *The Doctrine of the Holy Spirit*. 2d ed. Edinburgh: T. and T. Clark, 1889.

Sproul, R. C. *The Mystery of the Holy Spirit*. Wheaton, Ill.: Tyndale, 1990.

Stott, John R. W. *Baptism and Fullness: The Work of the Holy Spirit Today*. Downers Grove, Ill.: InterVarsity Press, 1964.

Swete, Henry B. *The Holy Spirit in the New Testament*. 2d ed. London: Macmillan, 1910.

White, John. *When the Spirit Comes with Power*. Downers Grove, Ill.: InterVarsity Press, 1988.

Wood, Leon J. *The Holy Spirit in the Old Testament*. Grand Rapids: Zondervan, 1976.

## SCRIPTURE MEMORY PASSAGE

**Romans 8:12–14:** *So then, brethren, we are debtors, not to the flesh, to live according to the flesh—for if you live according to the flesh you will die, but if by the Spirit you put to death the deeds of the body you will live. For all who are led by the Spirit of God are sons of God.*

## HYMN

### "Come, O Creator Spirit"

This is one of the oldest hymns in any hymnal, written by an anonymous author in the tenth century or earlier. It directly addresses the Holy Spirit and asks him to come and bring blessing in our hearts, filling us with joy and love and praise, and giving us protection from the enemy and peace in our lives.

Come, O Creator Spirit blest,
    And in our hearts take up thy rest;
Spirit of grace, with heav'nly aid
    Come to the souls whom thou hast made.

Thou art the Comforter, we cry,
    Sent to the earth from God Most High,
Fountain of life and fire of love,
    And our anointing from above.

Bringing from heav'n our sev'n-fold dow'r,
    Sign of our God's right hand of pow'r,
O blessed Spirit, promised long,
    Thy coming wakes the heart to song.

Make our dull minds with rapture glow,
    Let human hearts with love o'erflow;
And, when our feeble flesh would fail,
    May thine immortal strength prevail.

Far from our souls the foe repel,
    Grant us in peace henceforth to dwell;
Ill shall not come, nor harm betide,
    If only thou wilt be our guide.

Show us the Father, Holy One,
  Help us to know th' eternal Son;
Spirit divine, for evermore
  Thee will we trust and thee adore.

ANON., TENTH CENTURY

Alternative hymn:
"Spirit of God, Descend Upon My Heart"

Spirit of God, descend upon my heart;
  Wean it from earth, through all its pulses move;
Stoop to my weakness, mighty as thou art,
  And make me love thee as I ought to love.

Hast thou not bid us love thee, God and King?
  All, all thine own, soul, heart, and strength and mind.
I see thy cross - there teach my heart to cling:
  O let me seek thee, and O let me find.

Teach me to feel that thou art always nigh;
  Teach me the struggles of the soul to bear,
To check the rising doubt, the rebel sigh;
  Teach me the patience of unanswered prayer.

Teach me to love thee as thine angels love,
  One holy passion filling all my frame;
The baptism of the heav'n descended Dove,
  My heart an altar, and thy love the flame.

AUTHOR: GEORGE CROLY, 1854

# Part 5

# The Doctrine of the Application of Redemption

# Chapter 31

# Common Grace

*What are the undeserved blessings that God gives to all people, both believers and unbelievers?*

## EXPLANATION AND SCRIPTURAL BASIS

### A. Introduction and Definition

When Adam and Eve sinned, they became worthy of eternal punishment and separation from God (Gen. 2:17). In the same way, when human beings sin today they become liable to the wrath of God and to eternal punishment: "The wages of sin is death" (Rom. 6:23). This means that once people sin, God's justice would require only one thing—that they be eternally separated from God, cut off from experiencing *any* good from him, and that they live forever in hell, receiving only his wrath eternally. In fact, this was what happened to angels who sinned, and it could justly have happened to us as well: "*God did not spare the angels when they sinned,* but cast them into hell and committed them to pits of nether gloom to be kept until the judgment" (2 Peter 2:4).

But in fact Adam and Eve did not die at once (though the sentence of death *began* to be worked out in their lives on the day they sinned). The full execution of the sentence of death was delayed for many years. Moreover, millions of their descendants even to this day do not die and go to hell as soon as they sin, but continue to live for many years, enjoying countless blessings in this world. How can this be? *How can God continue to give blessings to sinners who deserve only death*— not only to those who will ultimately be saved, but also to millions who will never be saved, whose sins will never be forgiven?

The answer to these questions is that God bestows *common grace*. We may define common grace as follows: *Common grace is the grace of God by which he gives people innumerable blessings that are not part of salvation.* The word *common* here means something that is common to all people and is not restricted to believers or to the elect only.

In distinction from common grace, the grace of God that brings people to salvation is often called "saving grace." Of course, when we talk about "common grace" and "saving grace" we are not implying that there are two different kinds of grace in God himself, but only that God's grace manifests itself in the world in two different ways. Common grace is different from saving grace in its *results* (it does not bring about salvation), in its *recipients* (it is given to believers and unbelievers alike), and in its *source* (it does not directly flow from Christ's atoning work, since

657

Christ's death did not earn any measure of forgiveness for unbelievers, and therefore did not merit the blessings of common grace for them either). However, on this last point it should be said that common grace does flow *indirectly* from Christ's redemptive work, because the fact that God did not judge the world at once when sin entered it was primarily or perhaps exclusively due to the fact that he planned eventually to save some sinners through the death of his Son.[1]

## B. Examples of Common Grace

If we look at the world around us and contrast it with the fires of hell that the world deserves, we can immediately see abundant evidence of God's common grace in thousands of examples in everyday life. We can distinguish several specific categories in which this common grace is seen.

**1. The Physical Realm.** Unbelievers continue to live in this world solely because of God's common grace—every breath that people take is of grace, for the wages of sin is death, not life. Moreover, the earth does not produce only thorns and thistles (Gen. 3:18), or remain a parched desert, but by God's common grace it produces food and materials for clothing and shelter, often in great abundance and diversity. Jesus said, "Love your enemies and pray for those who persecute you, so that you may be sons of your Father who is in heaven; for *he makes his sun rise on the evil and on the good, and sends rain on the just and on the unjust*" (Matt. 5:44–45). Here Jesus appeals to God's abundant common grace as an encouragement to his disciples that they too should bestow love and prayer for blessing on unbelievers (cf. Luke 6:35–36). Similarly, Paul told the people of Lystra, "In past generations he allowed all the nations to walk in their own ways; yet he did not leave himself without witness, for he did good and *gave you from heaven rains and fruitful seasons, satisfying your hearts with food and gladness*" (Acts 14:16–17).

The Old Testament also speaks of the common grace of God that comes to unbelievers as well as to believers. One specific example is Potiphar, the Egyptian captain of the guard who purchased Joseph as a slave: "*The LORD blessed the Egyptian's house* for Joseph's sake; the blessing of the LORD was upon all that he had, in house and field" (Gen. 39:5). David speaks in a much more general way about all the creatures God has made: "The LORD is good to all, and his compassion is over all that he has made. . . . The eyes of all look to you, and you give them their food in due season. You open your hand, you satisfy the desire of every living thing" (Ps. 145:9, 15–16).

These verses are another reminder that the goodness that is found in the whole creation is due to God's goodness and compassion.

We even see evidence of God's common grace in the beauty of the natural world. Though nature itself is in "bondage to decay" and has been "subjected to futility" (Rom. 8:21, 20) because of the curse of the fall (Gen. 3:17–19), much beauty still remains in the natural world. The beauty of multicolored flowers, of

---

[1]It should be noted that I have put this chapter on common grace in part 5 of this book, "The Doctrine of the Application of Redemption," not because common grace flows directly from Christ's redemptive work (it does not), but because it has a role of preparing for and assisting in God's work of the application of redemption to believers.

grass and woodlands, of rivers and lakes and mountains and ocean shores, still remains as a daily testimony to the continuing common grace of God. Unbelievers deserve to enjoy none of this beauty, but by God's grace they can enjoy much of it for their whole lives.

**2. The Intellectual Realm.** Satan is "a liar and the father of lies" and "there is no truth in him" (John 8:44), because he is fully given over to evil and to the irrationality and commitment to falsehood that accompanies radical evil. But human beings in the world today, even unbelievers, are not totally given over to lying, irrationality, and ignorance. All people are able to have some grasp of truth; indeed, some have great intelligence and understanding. This also must be seen as a result of God's grace. John speaks of Jesus as "the true light that *enlightens every man*" (John 1:9), for in his role as creator and sustainer of the universe (not particularly in his role as redeemer) the Son of God allows enlightenment and understanding to come to all people in the world.[2]

God's common grace in the intellectual realm is seen in the fact that all people have a knowledge of God: "Although *they knew God* they did not honor him as God or give thanks to him" (Rom. 1:21). This means that there is a sense of God's existence and often a hunger to know God that he allows to remain in people's hearts, even though it often results in many differing man-made religions. Therefore, even when speaking to people who held to false religions, Paul could find a point of contact regarding knowledge of God's existence, as he did when speaking to the Athenian philosophers: "Men of Athens, I perceive that in every way you are very religious. . . . What therefore you worship as unknown, this I proclaim to you" (Acts 17:22–23).

The common grace of God in the intellectual realm also results in an ability to grasp truth and distinguish it from error, and to experience growth in knowledge that can be used in the investigation of the universe and in the task of subduing the earth. This means that *all science and technology carried out by non-Christians is a result of common grace,* allowing them to make incredible discoveries and inventions, to develop the earth's resources into many material goods, to produce and distribute those resources, and to have skill in their productive work. In a practical sense this means that every time we walk into a grocery store or ride in an automobile or enter a house we should remember that we are experiencing the results of the abundant common grace of God poured out so richly on all mankind.

---

[2]Since the context of John 1 is talking about Christ coming into the world, it is better to take the phrase "was coming into the world" to modify the true light, Christ (so RSV, NASB, NIV), rather than every man (so KJV, NASB mg., NIV mg.), though both are grammatically possible. In either case, the verse still says that Christ enlightens every man. Though some have argued that this enlightening is just the shining of the light of Christ's incarnate presence in the world (so D. A. Carson, *The Gospel According to John*, pp. 123–24), it is more likely that this enlightening is the light of general revelation that all people receive, the ability to observe and understand many true facts about God and the universe (so Leon Morris, *The Gospel According to John*, pp. 94–95). This is because (1) when John specifies that Christ "enlightens *every man*" (rather than "all men" or "the world") he suggests to us that this enlightening takes place for every individual, which would be true of general knowledge, but not of knowledge of Christ. (2) This sense allows the word "enlightens" to speak of an *actual* enlightening, not just a potential one. Christ here is said to enlighten, not just to offer enlightenment. (3) This sense heightens the ironic contrast in vv. 9–10 though Christ gives knowledge to all men, and though he created all men, yet they did not know him or receive him.

**3. The Moral Realm.** God also by common grace restrains people from being as evil as they could be. Once again the demonic realm, totally devoted to evil and destruction, provides a clear contrast with human society in which evil is clearly restrained. If people persist hard-heartedly and repeatedly in following sin over a course of time, God will eventually "give them up" to greater and greater sin (cf. Ps. 81:12; Rom. 1:24, 26, 28), but in the case of most human beings they do not fall to the depths to which their sin would otherwise take them, because God intervenes and puts restraints on their conduct. One very effective restraint is the force of conscience: Paul says, "When Gentiles who have not the law do by nature what the law requires, they are a law to themselves, even though they do not have the law. They show that *what the law requires is written on their hearts,* while *their conscience also bears witness* and their conflicting thoughts accuse or perhaps excuse them" (Rom. 2:14–15).

This inward sense of right and wrong that God gives to all people means that they will frequently approve of moral standards that reflect many of the moral standards in Scripture. Even those who are given up to the most base sin, Paul says, "Know God's decree that those who do such things deserve to die" (Rom. 1:32). And in many other cases this inward sense of conscience leads people to establish laws and customs in society that are, in terms of the outward behavior they approve or prohibit, quite like the moral laws of Scripture: people often establish laws or have customs that respect the sanctity of marriage and the family, protect human life, and prohibit theft and falsehood in speech.[3] Because of this, people will frequently live in ways that are morally upright and outwardly conform to the moral standards found in Scripture. Though their moral behavior cannot earn merit with God (since Scripture clearly says that "no man is justified before God by the law," Gal. 3:11, and "All have turned aside, together they have gone wrong; no one does good, not even one," Rom. 3:12), nevertheless in some sense less than earning God's eternal approval or merit, unbelievers do "do good." Jesus implies this when he says, "If you do good to those *who do good to you,* what credit is that to you? For *even sinners do the same*" (Luke 6:33; cf. 2 Kings 12:2 and 2 Chron. 24:2, where Joash is said to have done good during his reign as king, with 2 Chron. 24:17–25, where he did such evil as to make it apparent that there was not saving faith in his life). Of course, in areas where the gospel has had great influence and the church is strong, it will have a stronger moral influence on society than in places where the gospel has never reached, or where it has little restraining influence (for example, in cannibalistic societies—or even in modern Western society where belief in the gospel and moral absolutes have both been abandoned by the dominant culture).

God also demonstrates his common grace by giving *warnings of final judgment in the operation of the natural world.* God has so ordered the world that living according to his moral standards very often brings rewards in the natural realm, and violating God's standards often brings destruction to people, in both cases indicating the eventual direction of the final judgment: Honesty, hard work, showing love and kindness to others, and faithfulness in marriage and family will

---

[3]Of course, the operation of conscience is never perfect in sinful people in this life (as Paul realizes in Rom. 2:15), so societies will vary in the degree to which they approve differing aspects of God's moral laws. Nevertheless, significant resemblance to the moral laws of Scripture is found in the laws and customs of every human society.

(except in the most corrupt societies) bring much more material and emotional reward in this life than dishonesty, laziness, cruelty, marital infidelity, and other wrongs such as drunkenness, drug abuse, theft, and so forth. These normal consequences of sin or righteousness should serve as a warning of judgment to come, and, in this way, they are also examples of God's common grace.

**4. The Creative Realm.** God has allowed significant measures of skill in artistic and musical areas, as well as in other spheres in which creativity and skill can be expressed, such as athletics, cooking, writing, and so forth. Moreover, God gives to us an ability to appreciate beauty in many areas of life. And in this area as well as in the physical and intellectual realm, the blessings of common grace are sometimes poured out on unbelievers even more abundantly than on believers. Yet in all cases it is a result of the grace of God.

**5. The Societal Realm.** God's grace is also evident in the existence of various organizations and structures in human society. We see this first in the human family, evidenced in the fact that Adam and Eve remained husband and wife after the fall and then had children, both sons and daughters (Gen. 5:4). Adam and Eve's children married and formed families for themselves (Gen. 4:17, 19, 26). The human family persists today, not simply as an institution for believers, but for all people.

Human government is also a result of common grace. It was instituted in principle by God after the flood (see Gen. 9:6), and is clearly stated to be given by God in Romans 13:1: "There is no authority except from God, and those that exist have been instituted by God." It is clear that government is a gift from God for mankind generally, for Paul says the ruler is "God's servant for your good" and that he is "the servant of God to execute his wrath on the wrongdoer" (Rom. 13:4). One of the primary means God uses to restrain evil in the world is human government. Human laws and police forces and judicial systems provide a powerful deterrent to evil actions, and these are necessary, for there is much evil in the world that is irrational and that can only be restrained by force, because it will not be deterred by reason or education. Of course, the sinfulness of man can also affect governments themselves, so that they become corrupt and actually encourage evil rather than encourage good. This is just to say that human government, like all the other blessings of common grace that God gives, can be used either for good or for evil purposes.

Other organizations in human society include educational institutions, businesses and corporations, voluntary associations (such as many charitable and public service groups), and countless examples of ordinary human friendship. All of these function to bring some measure of good to human beings, and all are expressions of the common grace of God.

**6. The Religious Realm.** Even in the realm of human religion, God's common grace brings some blessings to unbelieving people. Jesus tells us, "Love your enemies and *pray for those who persecute you*" (Matt. 5:44), and since there is no restriction in the context simply to pray for their salvation, and since the command to pray for our persecutors is coupled with a command to love them, it seems reasonable to conclude that God intends to answer our prayers even for our persecutors with regard to many areas of life. In fact, Paul specifically commands that we pray "for kings and all who are in high positions" (1 Tim. 2:1–2). When we seek good for unbelievers it is consistent with God's own practice of granting sunshine and rain "on the just and on the unjust" (Matt. 5:45) and also consistent with the practice of Jesus during his earthly ministry when he healed every person who was brought to him (Luke 4:40). There is no indication that he required all of them to believe in him or to agree that he was the Messiah before he granted physical healing to them.

Does God answer the prayers of unbelievers? Although God has not promised to answer the prayers of unbelievers as he has promised to answer the prayers of those who come in Jesus' name, and although he has no obligation to answer the prayers of unbelievers, nonetheless, God may out of his common grace still hear and grant the prayers of unbelievers, thus demonstrating his mercy and goodness in yet another way (cf. Ps. 145:9, 15; Matt. 7:22; Luke 6:35–36). This is apparently the sense of 1 Timothy 4:10, which says that God is "the Savior of all men, especially of those who believe." Here "Savior" cannot be restricted in meaning to "one who forgives sins and gives eternal life," because these things are not given to those who do not believe; "Savior" must have a more general sense here, namely, "one who rescues from distress, one who delivers." In cases of trouble or distress God often does hear the prayers of unbelievers, and graciously delivers them from their trouble. Moreover, even unbelievers often have a sense of gratitude toward God for the goodness of creation, for deliverance from danger, and for the blessings of family, home, friendships, and country. In addition, unbelievers who come in close contact with the church and perhaps associate with it for a time can have some religious experiences that seem very close to the experience of those who are saved (see Heb. 4:4–6; Matt. 7:22–23).[4]

Finally, even the proclamation of the gospel to those who do not ultimately accept it is a clear declaration of the mercy and grace of God, which gives clear witness to the fact that God does not delight in the death or condemnation of any of his creatures (cf. Ezek. 33:11; 1 Tim. 2:4).

**7. Common Grace and Special Grace Influence Each Other.** Common grace, of course, influences and enriches the church, since apart from God's common grace given to carpenters and other kinds of craftsmen, there would be no church buildings; apart from common grace given to printers and typesetters and bookbinders (and even to those who work in paper mills or cut trees from forests to make paper), there would be no Bibles. In countless ways in everyday activities the church benefits from common grace.

On the other hand, the special grace that God gives to those who are saved brings more of the blessings of common grace to unbelievers living in the realm of the church's influence. Unbelievers benefit from the example of Christian lives that they see in society, from the prayers and the acts of mercy that Christians do for the community, from the knowledge of the teachings of Scripture and its wisdom in which they find some intellectual and moral benefit, and from the influence on laws, customs, and beliefs of a society that comes through the social and political

---

[4]See the extended discussion of Heb. 6:4–6 in chapter 40, pp. 796–801.

activities of Christians. Historically it has often been the powerful presence of those whose lives were changed by the gospel that has resulted in freedom for slaves (in the British colonies and the United States), rights for women, widespread public education, technological and scientific progress, increased productivity in the economy, a high value placed on work and thrift and honesty, and so forth.

**8. Common Grace Does Not Save People.** In spite of all of this, we must realize that common grace is different from saving grace. Common grace does not change the human heart or bring people to genuine repentance and faith—it cannot and does not save people (though in the intellectual and moral sphere it can give some preparation to make people more disposed toward accepting the gospel). Common grace restrains sin but does not change anyone's foundational disposition to sin, nor does it in any significant measure purify fallen human nature.[5]

We must also recognize that the actions of unbelievers performed by virtue of common grace do not in themselves merit God's approval or favor. These actions do not spring from faith ("Whatever does not proceed from faith is sin," Rom. 14:23), nor are they motivated by a love for God (Matt. 22:37), but rather love of self in some form or another. Therefore, although we may readily say that the works of unbelievers that externally conform to the laws of God are "good" in some sense, they nonetheless are not good in terms of meriting God's approval nor of making God obligated to the sinner in any way.

Finally, we should recognize that unbelievers often receive more common grace than believers—they may be more skillful, harder working, more intelligent, more creative, or have more of the material benefits of this life to enjoy. This in no way indicates that they are more favored by God in an absolute sense or that they will gain any share in eternal salvation, but only that God distributes the blessings of common grace in various ways, often granting very significant blessings to unbelievers. In all of this, they should, of course, acknowledge God's goodness (Acts 14:17), and should recognize that God's revealed will is that "God's kindness" should eventually lead them "to repentance" (Rom. 2:4).

## C. Reasons for Common Grace

Why does God bestow common grace on undeserving sinners who will never come to salvation? We can suggest at least four reasons.

---

[5]The viewpoint on common grace presented in this chapter is consistent with the Reformed or Calvinistic perspective of the book as a whole, a perspective that has been argued for more specifically in discussing God's sovereignty (chapter 13, pp. 211–18), God's providence (chapter 16), sin (chapter 24), and election, the gospel call, and regeneration (chapters 32–34). We should note, however, that an Arminian understanding of common grace would be different at this point; it would say that common grace gives to every person the *ability* to turn to God in faith and repentance, and in fact *influences* the sinner to do this unless he or she specifically resists it. Therefore, on an Arminian understanding, common grace has a function that much more clearly relates to saving grace—in fact, common grace is simply an early expression of the totality of saving grace. This position (that the ability to repent and believe is given to all people) is discussed in chapter 32 on election and chapters 33 and 34 on the gospel call and regeneration.

**1. To Redeem Those Who Will Be Saved.** Peter says that the day of judgment and final execution of punishment is being delayed because there are yet more people who will be saved: "The Lord is not slow about his promise as some count slowness, but is forbearing toward you, *not wishing that any should perish, but that all should reach repentance.* But the day of the Lord will come like a thief" (2 Peter 3:9–10). In fact, this reason was true from the beginning of human history, for if God wanted to save any people out of the whole mass of sinful humanity, he could not have destroyed all sinners immediately (for then there would be no human race left). He chose rather to allow sinful humans to live for some time, so that they might have an opportunity to repent, and also so that they would bear children and enable subsequent generations to live and then hear the gospel and repent.

**2. To Demonstrate God's Goodness and Mercy.** God's goodness and mercy are not only seen in the salvation of believers, but also in the blessings he gives to undeserving sinners. When God "is kind to the ungrateful and the selfish" (Luke 6:35), his kindness is revealed in the universe, to his glory. David says, "The LORD is *good to all,* and his compassion is over all that he has made" (Ps. 145:9). In the story of Jesus talking with the rich young ruler, we read, "And Jesus looking upon him *loved him*" (Mark 10:21), even though the man was an unbeliever and would in a moment turn away from Jesus because of his great possessions. Berkhof says that God "showers untold blessings upon all men and also clearly indicates that these are the expressions of a favorable disposition in God, which falls short however of the positive volition to pardon their sin, to lift their sentence, and to grant them salvation."[6]

It is not unjust for God to delay the execution of punishment upon sin and to give temporary blessings to human beings, because the punishment is not forgotten, but just delayed. In delaying punishment, God shows clearly that he has no pleasure in executing final judgment, but rather delights in the salvation of men and women. "As I live, says the Lord GOD, I have no pleasure in the death of the wicked, but that the wicked turn back from his way and live" (Ezek. 33:11). God "desires all men to be saved and to come to the knowledge of the truth" (1 Tim. 2:4). In all of this the delay of punishment gives clear evidence of God's mercy and goodness and love.

**3. To Demonstrate God's Justice.** When God repeatedly invites sinners to come to faith and when they repeatedly refuse his invitations, the justice of God in condemning them is seen much more clearly. Paul warns that those who persist in unbelief are simply storing up more wrath for themselves: "By your hard and impenitent heart you are storing up wrath for yourself on the day of wrath when God's righteous judgment will be revealed" (Rom. 2:5). On the day of judgment "every mouth" will be "stopped" (Rom. 3:19) and no one will be able to object that God has been unjust.

---

[6]Berkhof, *Systematic Theology*, p. 445.

**4. To Demonstrate God's Glory.** Finally, God's glory is shown in many ways by the activities of human beings in all the areas in which common grace is operative. In developing and exercising dominion over the earth, men and women demonstrate and reflect the wisdom of their Creator, demonstrate God-like qualities of skill and moral virtue and authority over the universe, and so forth. Though all of these activities are tainted by sinful motives, they nonetheless reflect the excellence of our Creator and therefore bring glory to God, not fully or perfectly, but nonetheless significantly.

### D. Our Response to the Doctrine of Common Grace

In thinking about the varying kinds of goodness seen in the lives of unbelievers because of God's abundant common grace, we should keep three points in mind:

**1. Common Grace Does Not Mean That Those Who Receive It Will Be Saved.** Even exceptionally large amounts of common grace do not imply that those who receive it will be saved. Even the most skilled, most intelligent, most wealthy and powerful people in the world still need the gospel of Jesus Christ or they will be condemned for eternity! Even the most moral and kind of our neighbors still need the gospel of Jesus Christ or they will be condemned for eternity! They may appear outwardly to have no needs, but Scripture still says that unbelievers are "enemies" of God (Rom. 5:10; cf. Col. 1:21; James 4:4) and are "against" Christ (Matt. 12:30). They "live as enemies of the cross of Christ" and have their "minds set on earthly things" (Phil. 3:18–19) and are "by nature children of wrath, like the rest of mankind" (Eph. 2:3).

**2. We Must Be Careful Not to Reject the Good Things That Unbelievers Do as Totally Evil.** By common grace, unbelievers do *some* good, and we should see God's hand in it and be thankful for common grace as it operates in every friendship, every act of kindness, every way in which it brings blessing to others. All of this—though the unbeliever does not know it—is ultimately from God and he deserves the glory for it.

**3. The Doctrine of Common Grace Should Stir Our Hearts to Much Greater Thankfulness to God.** When we walk down a street and see houses and gardens and families dwelling in security, or when we do business in the marketplace and see the abundant results of technological progress, or when we walk through the woods and see the beauty of nature, or when we are protected by government,[7] or when we are educated from the vast storehouse of human knowledge, we should realize not only that God in his sovereignty is ultimately responsible for all of these blessings, but also that God has granted them all to sinners who are *totally undeserving* of any of them! These blessings in the world are not only evidence of God's power and wisdom, they are also continually a manifestation of his abundant *grace*. The realization of this fact should cause our hearts to swell with thanksgiving to God in every activity of life.

---

[7]Paul explicitly directs us to offer to God "thanksgivings" for "kings and all who are in high positions" (1 Tim. 2:1–2).

## QUESTIONS FOR PERSONAL APPLICATION

1. Before you read this chapter, did you have a different viewpoint on whether unbelievers deserved the ordinary benefits of the world around them? How has your perspective changed, if at all?

2. Do you know of examples where God has answered the prayers of unbelievers who were in difficulty, or answered your prayers for the needs of an unbelieving friend? Has it provided an opening for sharing the gospel? Did the unbeliever eventually come to salvation in Christ? Do you think that God often uses the blessings of common grace as a means to prepare people to receive the gospel?

3. In what ways will this doctrine change the way you relate to an unbelieving neighbor or friend? Will it tend to make you thankful for the good that you see in their lives? How do you think this might affect your relationship with that person in a more general sense?

4. As you look around the place where you are at this moment, can you name at least twenty different examples of common grace that you can see? How does that make you feel?

5. Has this chapter changed the way you view creative activities such as music, art, architecture, or poetry, or (something that is very similar) the creativity expressed in athletic activities?

6. If you are kind to an unbeliever and he or she never comes to accept Christ, has it done any good in God's sight (see Matt. 5:44–45; Luke 6:32–36)? What good has it done? Why do you think that God is good even to those who will never be saved—in what way does it further his purposes for the universe? Do you think we have any obligation to give more effort to showing good to believers than to unbelievers? Can you name any passages of Scripture that help in answering this question?

## SPECIAL TERMS

common grace
special grace

## BIBLIOGRAPHY

(For an explanation of this bibliography see the note on the bibliography to chapter 1, p. 38. Complete bibliographical data may be found on pp. 1223–29.) Note: This subject is not often treated in a separate section in systematic theologies, but see the few sections listed below in the following works:

### Sections in Evangelical Systematic Theologies

1. Anglican (Episcopalian)
          1930      Thomas, 210–14
5. Lutheran
          1934      Mueller, 242–54

6. Reformed (or Presbyterian)

|        |                      |
|--------|----------------------|
| 1871–73 | Hodge, 2:654–74 |
| 1937–66 | Murray, *CW,* 2:93–119 |
| 1938 | Berkhof, 432–46 |

## Sections in Representative Roman Catholic Systematic Theologies

1. Roman Catholic: Traditional

|      |             |
|------|-------------|
| 1955 | Ott, 238–42 |

## Other Works

Hoekema, Anthony A. "The Restraint of Sin." In *Created In God's Image*. Grand Rapids: Eerdmans, and Exeter: Paternoster, 1986, pp. 187–202.

Hughes, P. E. "Grace." In *EDT*, pp. 479–82.

Kearsley, R. "Grace." In *NDT*, pp. 280–81.

Van Til, Cornelius. *Common Grace and the Gospel*. Nutley, N.J.: Presbyterian and Reformed, 1972.

Van Til, Cornelius. *In Defense of the Faith*, vol. 5: *An Introduction to Systematic Theology*. n.p.: Presbyterian and Reformed Publishing Co., 1976, pp. 75–99, 253–62.

## SCRIPTURE MEMORY PASSAGE

**Luke 6:35–36:** *But love your enemies, and do good, and lend, expecting nothing in return; and your reward will be great, and you will be sons of the Most High; for he is kind to the ungrateful and the selfish. Be merciful, even as your Father is merciful.*

## HYMN

### "All People That on Earth Do Dwell"

This very old setting of Psalm 100 is a call to all people on earth to praise God because of his abundant goodness.

All people that on earth do dwell,
Sing to the Lord with cheerful voice;
Him serve with fear, his praise forthtell,
Come ye before him and rejoice.

The Lord ye know is God indeed;
Without our aid he did us make;
We are his folk, he doth us feed,
And for his sheep he doth us take.

O enter then his gates with praise,
Approach with joy his courts unto;
Praise, laud, and bless his name always,
For it is seemly so to do.

For why? The Lord our God is good,
  His mercy is forever sure;
His truth at all times firmly stood,
  And shall from age to age endure.

AUTHOR: WILLIAM KETHE, 1561

# Chapter 32

# Election and Reprobation

*When and why did God choose us?*
*Are some not chosen?*

In the earlier chapters we talked about the fact that we all have sinned and deserve eternal punishment from God, and the fact that Christ died and *earned* salvation for us. But now in this unit (chapters 32–43) we will look at the way God *applies* that salvation to our lives. We begin in this chapter with God's work of election, that is, his decision to choose us to be saved before the foundation of the world. This act of election is, of course, not (strictly speaking) part of the *application* of salvation to us, since it came before Christ earned our salvation when he died on the cross. But we treat election at this point because it is chronologically the *beginning* of God's dealing with us in a gracious way. Therefore, it is rightly thought of as the first step in the process of God's bringing salvation to us individually.[1]

Other steps in God's work of applying salvation to our lives include our hearing the gospel call, our being regenerated by the Holy Spirit, our responding in faith and repentance, and God forgiving us and giving us membership in his family, as well as granting us growth in the Christian life and keeping us faithful to himself throughout life. At the end of our life we die and go into his presence, then when Christ returns we receive resurrection bodies, and the process of acquiring salvation is complete.

Various theologians have given specific terms to a number of these events, and have often listed them in a specific order in which they believe that they occur in our lives. Such a list of the events in which God applies salvation to us is called the *order of salvation,* and is sometimes referred to by a Latin phrase, *ordo salutis,* which simply means "order of salvation." Before discussing any of these elements in the application of salvation to our lives, we can give a complete list here of the elements that will be treated in the following chapters:

---

[1]This chapter could be placed elsewhere in the sequence of topics treated. It could be placed immediately after chapter 16, on God's providence, for example, since election is just one aspect of God's providential control of the world. Or it could be placed in chapter 25, as part of the treatment of the covenant of grace between God and man. Or it could be placed in chapter 40, as part of the discussion of perseverance, especially related to the question of assurance of salvation, since God's choice of us to be saved gives great assurance that he will fulfill his purposes. But I have chosen to place it here at the beginning of the chapters that discuss God's personal dealing with us in grace. (Note the similar ordering of topics by Paul in Rom. 8:29-30.)

"The Order of Salvation"
1. Election (God's choice of people to be saved)
2. The gospel call (proclaiming the message of the gospel)
3. Regeneration (being born again)
4. Conversion (faith and repentance)
5. Justification (right legal standing)
6. Adoption (membership in God's family)
7. Sanctification (right conduct of life)
8. Perseverance (remaining a Christian)
9. Death (going to be with the Lord)
10. Glorification (receiving a resurrection body)

We should note here that items 2–6 and part of 7 are all involved in "becoming a Christian." Numbers 7 and 8 work themselves out in this life, number 9 occurs at the end of this life, and number 10 occurs when Christ returns.[2]

We begin our discussion of the order of salvation with the first element, election. In connection with this we will also discuss at the end of this chapter the question of "reprobation," the decision of God to pass over those who will not be saved, and to punish them for their sins. As will be explained below, election and reprobation are different in several important respects, and it is important to distinguish these so that we do not think wrongly about God or his activity.

The term *predestination* is also frequently used in this discussion. In this textbook, and in Reformed theology generally, *predestination* is a broader term and includes the two aspects of election (for believers) and reprobation (for unbelievers). However, the term *double predestination* is not a helpful term because it gives the impression that both election and reprobation are carried out in the same way by God and have no essential differences between them, which is certainly not true. Therefore, the term *double predestination* is not generally used by Reformed theologians, though it is sometimes used to refer to Reformed teaching by those who criticize it. The term *double predestination* will not be used in this book to refer to election and reprobation, since it blurs the distinctions between them and does not give an accurate indication of what is actually being taught.

## EXPLANATION AND SCRIPTURAL BASIS

We may define election as follows: *Election is an act of God before creation in which he chooses some people to be saved, not on account of any foreseen merit in them, but only because of his sovereign good pleasure.*

There has been much controversy in the church and much misunderstanding over this doctrine. Many of the controversial questions regarding man's will and responsibility and regarding the justice of God with respect to human choices have been discussed at some length in connection with God's providence (chapter 16).

---

[2]For a discussion of the order of events in this list, see John Murray, *Redemption Accomplished and Applied* (Grand Rapids: Eerdmans, 1955), pp. 79–87. New approaches to a synthesis of Pauline themes in the order of salvation are found in Vern Poythress, "Using Multiple Thematic Centers in Theological Synthesis: Holiness as a Test Case in Developing a Pauline Theology" (unpublished manuscript available from the Campus Bookstore, Westminster Theological Seminary, P.O. Box 27009, Philadelphia, PA, 19118).

We will focus here only on those additional questions that apply specifically to the question of election.

Our approach in this chapter will be first simply to cite a number of passages from the New Testament that discuss election. Then we will attempt to understand the purpose of God that the New Testament authors see in the doctrine of election. Finally, we will attempt to clarify our understanding of this doctrine and answer some objections, and also to consider the doctrine of reprobation.

## A. Does the New Testament Teach Predestination?

Several passages in the New Testament seem to affirm quite clearly that God ordained beforehand those who would be saved. For example, when Paul and Barnabas began to preach to the Gentiles in Antioch in Pisidia, Luke writes, "And when the Gentiles heard this, they were glad and glorified the word of God; and *as many as were ordained to eternal life believed*" (Acts 13:48). It is significant that Luke mentions the fact of election almost in passing. It is as if this were the normal occurrence when the gospel was preached. How many believed? "As many as were ordained to eternal life believed."

In Romans 8:28–30, we read:

> We know that in everything God works for good with those who love him, who are called according to his purpose. *For those whom he foreknew he also predestined to be conformed to the image of his Son,* in order that he might be the first-born among many brethren. *And those whom he predestined he also called; and those whom he called he also justified; and those whom he justified he also glorified.*[3]

In the following chapter, when talking about God's chosing Jacob and not Esau, Paul says it was not because of anything that Jacob or Esau had done, but simply in order that God's purpose of election might continue.

> Though they were not yet born and had done nothing either good or bad, *in order that God's purpose of election might continue,* not because of works but because of his call, she was told, "The elder will serve the younger." As it is written, "Jacob I loved, but Esau I hated." (Rom. 9:11–13)

Regarding the fact that some of the people of Israel were saved, but others were not, Paul says: "Israel failed to obtain what it sought. *The elect* obtained it, but the rest were hardened" (Rom. 11:7). Here again Paul indicates two distinct groups within the people of Israel. Those who were "the elect" obtained the salvation that they sought, while those who were not the elect simply "were hardened."

Paul talks explicitly about God's choice of believers before the foundation of the world in the beginning of Ephesians.

---

[3]Clark Pinnock says that this text does not speak of predestination to salvation, but rather to a certain privilege, that of being conformed to Jesus Christ: "There is no predestination to salvation or damnation in the Bible. There is only a predestination for those who are already children of God with respect to certain privileges out ahead of them" (p. 18). But such a view does not do justice to Rom. 8:29–30, because those who are said to be predestined in this verse are not yet children of God, because Paul here speaks of predestination before calling or justification. Moreover, the privilege of being conformed to the image of Christ is not just for some Christians, but for all.

"*He chose us in him before the foundation of the world,* that we should be holy and blameless before him. *He destined us in love* to be his sons through Jesus Christ, according to the purpose of his will, to the praise of his glorious grace." (Eph. 1:4–6)

Here Paul is writing to believers and he specifically says that God "chose us" in Christ, referring to believers generally. In a similar way, several verses later he says, "We who first hoped in Christ have been *destined and appointed* to live for the praise of his glory" (Eph. 1:12).

He writes to the Thessalonians, "For we know, brethren beloved by God, that *he has chosen you;* for our gospel came to you not only in word, but also in power and in the Holy Spirit and with full conviction" (1 Thess. 1:4–5).

Paul says that the fact that the Thessalonians *believed* the gospel when he preached it ("for our gospel came to you . . . in power . . . and with full conviction") *is the reason he knows that God chose them.* As soon as they came to faith Paul concluded that long ago God had chosen them, and therefore they had believed when he preached. He later writes to the same church, "We are bound to give thanks to God always for you, brethren beloved by the Lord, because *God chose you from the beginning to be saved,* through sanctification by the Spirit and belief in the truth" (2 Thess. 2:13).

Although the next text does not specifically mention the election of human beings, it is interesting at this point also to notice what Paul says about angels. When he gives a solemn command to Timothy, he writes, "In the presence of God and of Christ Jesus and of *the elect angels* I charge you to keep these rules without favor" (1 Tim. 5:21). Paul is aware that there are good angels witnessing his command and witnessing Timothy's response to it, and he is so sure that it is God's act of election that has affected every one of those good angels that he can call them *"elect angels."*

When Paul talks about the reason why God saved us and called us to himself, he explicitly denies that it was because of our works, but points rather to God's own purpose and his unmerited grace in eternity past. He says God is the one "who saved us and called us with a holy calling, not in virtue of our works but in virtue of *his own purpose* and the *grace which he gave us in Christ Jesus ages ago*" (2 Tim. 1:9).

When Peter writes an epistle to hundreds of Christians in many churches in Asia Minor, he writes, "To *God's elect* . . . scattered throughout Pontus, Galatia, Cappadocia, Asia and Bithynia" (1 Peter 1:1 NIV). He later calls them "a *chosen race*" (1 Peter 2:9).

In John's vision in Revelation, those who do not give in to persecution and begin to worship the beast are persons whose names have been written in the book of life before the foundation of the world: "And authority was given it over every tribe and people and tongue and nation, and all who dwell on earth will worship it, *every one whose name has not been written before the foundation of the world in the book of life* of the Lamb that was slain" (Rev. 13:7–8)[4] In a similar

---

[4]Grammatically the phrase "before the foundation of the world" could modify either "whose name has not been written" (as here, in the RSV; also in the NASB and NIV mg.), or "the lamb that was slain" (so KJV, NIV). But the parallel expression in Rev. 17:8, "whose names have not been *written in the book of life from the foundation of the world,*" seems decisive, and there only one sense is possible (the parallel wording is striking in the Greek text, since the two verses share eleven identical words in talking about

way, we read of the beast from the bottomless pit in Revelation 17: "The dwellers on earth *whose names have not been written in the book of life from the foundation of the world,* will marvel to behold the beast, because it was and is not and is to come" (Rev. 17:8).

## B. How Does the New Testament Present the Teaching of Election?

After reading this list of verses on election, it is important to view this doctrine in the way the New Testament itself views it.

**1. As a Comfort.** The New Testament authors often present the doctrine of election as a comfort to believers. When Paul assures the Romans that "in everything God works for good with those who love him, who are called according to his purpose" (Rom. 8:28), he gives God's work of predestination as a reason why we can be assured of this truth. He explains in the next verse, "*For* those whom he foreknew he also predestined to be conformed to the image of his Son . . . And those whom he predestined he also called . . . justified . . . glorified" (Rom. 8:29–30). Paul's point is to say that God has *always* acted for the good of those whom he called to himself. If Paul looks into the distant past before the creation of the world, he sees that God foreknew and predestined his people to be conformed to the image of Christ.[5] If he looks at the recent past he finds that God called and justified his people whom he had predestined. And if he then looks toward the future when Christ returns, he sees that God has determined to give perfect, glorified bodies to those who believe in Christ. From eternity to eternity God has acted with the good of his people in mind. But if God has *always* acted for our good and will in the future act for our good, Paul reasons, then *will he not also in our present circumstances* work every circumstance together for our good as well? In this way predestination is seen as a comfort for believers in the everyday events of life.

**2. As a Reason to Praise God.** Paul says, "He destined us in love to be his sons through Jesus Christ, according to the purpose of his will, *to the praise of his glorious grace*" (Eph. 1:5–6). Similarly, he says, "We who first hoped in Christ have been destined and appointed to live *for the praise of his glory*" (Eph. 1:12).
Paul tells the Christians at Thessalonica, "*We give thanks to God* always for you all. . . . *For we know,* brethren beloved by God, *that he has chosen you*" (1 Thess. 1:2, 4). The reason Paul can give thanks to God for the Thessalonian Christians is that he knows God is ultimately responsible for their salvation and has in fact chosen them to be saved. This is made even clearer in 2 Thessalonians 2:13: "But *we are bound to give thanks to God* always for you, brethren beloved by the Lord,

---

people whose names are written in the book of life). Moreover, the RSV/NASB reading makes much better sense in light of the rest of Scripture: the Bible often talks about God choosing us before the foundation of the world, but nowhere else does Scripture say that Christ was slain from the foundation of the world—a statement that simply is not true in any literal sense, because Christ was not slain until he died on the cross. Therefore, on the NIV/KJV reading, the verse must be interpreted to mean something like, "God *planned* from the foundation of the world that Christ would be slain"—but that is not what the text actually says, on either reading.
[5]See the discussion below (pp. 676–77) on the meaning of "foreknow" here.

*because God chose you* from the beginning to be saved." Paul was obligated to give thanks to God for the Christians at Thessalonica because he knew that their salvation was ultimately due to God's choice of them. Therefore it is appropriate for Paul to thank God for them rather than praising them for their own saving faith.

Understood in this way, the doctrine of election does increase praise given to God for our salvation and seriously diminishes any pride that we might feel if we thought that our salvation was due to something good in us or something for which we should receive credit.

**3. As an Encouragement to Evangelism.** Paul says, "I endure everything for the sake of the elect, that they also may obtain salvation in Christ Jesus with its eternal glory" (2 Tim. 2:10). He knows that God has chosen some people to be saved, and he sees this as an encouragement to preach the gospel, even if it means enduring great suffering. Election is Paul's guarantee that there will be some success for his evangelism, for he knows that some of the people he speaks to will be the elect, and they will believe the gospel and be saved. It is as if someone invited us to come fishing and said, "I guarantee that you will catch some fish— they are hungry and waiting."

## C. Misunderstandings of the Doctrine of Election

**1. Election Is Not Fatalistic or Mechanistic.** Sometimes those who object to the doctrine of election say that it is "fatalism" or that it presents a "mechanistic system" for the universe. Two somewhat different objections are involved here. By "fatalism" is meant a system in which human choices and human decisions really do not make any difference. In fatalism, no matter what we do, things are going to turn out as they have been previously ordained. Therefore, it is futile to attempt to influence the outcome of events or the outcome of our lives by putting forth any effort or making any significant choices, because these will not make any difference any way. In a true fatalistic system, of course, our humanity is destroyed for our choices really mean nothing, and the motivation for moral accountability is removed.

In a mechanistic system the picture is one of an impersonal universe in which all things that happen have been inflexibly determined by an impersonal force long ago, and the universe functions in a mechanical way so that human beings are more like machines or robots than genuine persons. Here also genuine human personality would be reduced to the level of a machine that simply functions in accordance with predetermined plans and in response to predetermined causes and influences.

By contrast to the mechanistic picture, the New Testament presents the entire outworking of our salvation as something brought about by a *personal* God in relationship with *personal* creatures. God "destined us *in love* to be his sons through Jesus Christ" (Eph. 1:5). God's act of election was neither impersonal nor mechanistic, but was permeated with personal love for those whom he chose. Moreover, the personal care of God for his creatures, even those who rebel against him, is seen clearly in God's plea through Ezekiel, "As I live, says the Lord GOD, *I have no pleasure in the death of the wicked, but that the wicked turn from his way and live;* turn back, turn back from your evil ways; for why will you die, O house of Israel?" (Ezek. 33:11).

When talking about our response to the gospel offer, Scripture continually views us not as mechanistic creatures or robots, but as *genuine persons,* personal creatures who make willing choices to accept or reject the gospel.[6] Jesus invites everyone, "*Come to me,* all who labor and are heavy laden, and I will give you rest" (Matt. 11:28). And we read the invitation at the end of Revelation: "The Spirit and the Bride say, 'Come.' And let him who hears say, 'Come.' And let him who is thirsty come, let *him who desires* take the water of life without price" (Rev. 22:17). This invitation and many others like it are addressed to genuine persons who are capable of hearing the invitation and responding to it by a decision of their wills. Regarding those who will not accept him, Jesus clearly emphasizes their hardness of heart and their stubborn refusal to come to him: "Yet you *refuse* to come to me that you may have life" (John 5:40). And Jesus cries out in sorrow to the city that had rejected him, "O Jerusalem, Jerusalem, killing the prophets and stoning those who are sent to you! How often would I have gathered your children together as a hen gathers her brood under her wings, *and you would not!*" (Matt. 23:37).

In contrast to the charge of fatalism, we also see a much different picture in the New Testament. Not only do we make willing choices as real persons, but these choices are also *real choices* because they do affect the course of events in the world. They affect our own lives and they affect the lives and destinies of others. So, "*He who believes in him* is not condemned; *he who does not believe* is condemned already, because he has not believed in the name of the only Son of God" (John 3:18). Our personal decisions to believe or not believe in Christ have eternal consequences in our lives, and Scripture is quite willing to talk about our decision to believe or not believe as the factor that decides our eternal destiny.

The implication of this is that we certainly must preach the gospel, and people's eternal destiny hinges on whether we proclaim the gospel or not. Therefore when the Lord one night told Paul, "Do not be afraid, but speak and do not be silent; for I am with you, and no man shall attack you to harm you; for *I have many people in this city*" (Acts 18:9–10), Paul did not simply conclude that the "many people" who belong to God would be saved whether he stayed there preaching the gospel or not. Rather, "*he stayed a year and six months,* teaching the word of God among them" (Acts 18:11)—this was longer than Paul stayed in any other city except Ephesus during his three missionary journeys. When Paul was told that God had many elect people in Corinth, he stayed a long time and preached, in order that those elect people might be saved! Paul is quite clear about the fact that unless people preach the gospel others will not be saved:

> But how are men to call upon him in whom they have not believed? *And how are they to believe in him of whom they have never heard? And how are they to hear without a preacher?* . . . So faith comes from what is heard, and what is heard comes by the preaching of Christ. (Rom. 10:14, 17)

---

[6]See chapter 16, pp. 320–22, 334, 340–47, for a more extensive discussion of how we can be genuine persons and make real choices when God has beforehand ordained what we do.

Did Paul know before he went to a city who was elected by God for salvation and who was not? No, he did not. That is something that God does not show to us ahead of time. But once people come to faith in Christ then we can be confident that God had earlier chosen them for salvation. This is exactly Paul's conclusion regarding the Thessalonians; he says that he knows that God chose them because when he preached to them, the gospel came in power and with full conviction: "For we know, brethren beloved by God, that he has chosen you; *for our gospel came to you* not only in word, but also in *power* and in the *Holy Spirit* and *with full conviction*" (1 Thess. 1:4–5). Far from saying that whatever he did made no difference, and that God's elect would be saved whether he preached or not, Paul endured a life of incredible hardship in order to bring the gospel to those whom God had chosen. At the end of a life filled with suffering he said, "Therefore *I endure everything for the sake of the elect, that they also may obtain salvation* in Christ Jesus with its eternal glory" (2 Tim. 2:10).

**2. Election Is Not Based on God's Foreknowledge of Our Faith.** Quite commonly people will agree that God predestines some to be saved, but they will say that he does this by looking into the future and seeing who will believe in Christ and who will not. If he sees that a person is going to come to saving faith, then he will predestine that person to be saved, *based on foreknowledge of that person's faith.* If he sees that a person will not come to saving faith, then he does not predestine that person to be saved. In this way, it is thought, the ultimate reason why some are saved and some are not lies *within the people themselves,* not within God. All that God does in his predestining work is to give confirmation to the decision he knows people will make on their own. The verse commonly used to support this view is Romans 8:29: "For those *whom he foreknew* he also predestined to be conformed to the image of his Son."[7]

**a. Foreknowledge of Persons, Not Facts:** But this verse can hardly be used to demonstrate that God based his predestination on foreknowledge of *the fact that a person would believe*. The passage speaks rather of the fact that God knew *persons* ("*those whom* he foreknew"), not that he knew some *fact about them,* such as the fact that they would believe. It is a personal, relational knowledge that is spoken of here: God, looking into the future, thought of certain people in saving relationship to him, and in that sense he "knew them" long ago. This is the sense in which Paul can talk about God's "knowing" someone, for example, in 1 Corinthians 8:3: "But if one loves God, one is *known by him.*" Similarly, he says, "but now that you have come to know God, or rather *to be known by God* . . ." (Gal. 4:9). When people *know* God in Scripture, or when God *knows* them, it is personal knowledge that involves a saving relationship. Therefore in Romans 8:29, "those whom he *foreknew*" is best understood to mean, "those whom he long ago *thought of in a saving relationship to himself.*" The text actually says nothing

---

[7]The idea that predestination is based on God's foreknowledge of those who would believe is argued in Jack W. Cottrell, "Conditional Election," in *Grace Unlimited*, pp. 51–73. Cottrell says, "Through his foreknowledge God sees who will believe upon Jesus Christ as Savior and Lord, and become united with him in Christian baptism; then even before the creation of the world he predestines these believers to share the glory of the risen Christ" (p. 62).

about God foreknowing or foreseeing that certain people would believe, nor is that idea mentioned in any other text of Scripture.[8]

Sometimes people say that God elected *groups* of people, but not individuals to salvation. In some Arminian views, God just elected the church as a group, while the Swiss theologian Karl Barth (1886–1968) said that God elected Christ, and all people in Christ. But Romans 8:29 talks about certain people whom God foreknew ("*those whom* he foreknew"), not just undefined or unfilled groups. And in Ephesians Paul talks about certain people whom God chose, including himself: "He *chose us* in him before the foundation of the world" (Eph. 1:4). To talk about God choosing a group with no people in it is not biblical election at all. But to talk about God choosing a group of people means that he chose specific individuals who constituted that group.[9]

**b. Scripture Never Speaks of Our Faith As the Reason God Chose Us:** In addition, when we look beyond these specific passages that speak of foreknowledge and look at verses that talk about the *reason* God chose us, we find that Scripture never speaks of our faith or the fact that we would come to believe in Christ as the reason God chose us. In fact, Paul seems explicitly to exclude the consideration of what people would do in life from his understanding of God's choice of Jacob rather than Esau: he says, "Though they were not yet born and had done nothing either good or bad, *in order that God's purpose of election might continue,* not because of works but because of his call, she was told, 'The elder will serve the younger.' As it is written, 'Jacob I loved, but Esau I hated'" (Rom. 9:11–13). Nothing that Jacob or Esau would do in life influenced God's decision; it was simply in order that his purpose of election might continue.

When discussing the Jewish people who have come to faith in Christ, Paul says, "So too at the present time there is a remnant, *chosen by grace.* But if it is by grace, it is no longer on the basis of works" (Rom. 11:5–6). Here again Paul emphasizes God's grace and the complete absence of human merit in the process of election. Someone might object that faith is not viewed as a "work" in Scripture and therefore faith should be excluded from the quotation above ("It is no longer on the basis of *works*"). Based on this objection, Paul could actually mean, "But if it is by grace, it is no longer on the basis of works, but rather on the basis of whether someone would believe." However, this is unlikely in this context: Paul is not contrasting human faith and human works; he is contrasting God's sovereign choosing of people with *any* human activity, and he points to God's sovereign will as the ultimate basis for God's choice of the Jews who have come to Christ.

Similarly, when Paul talks about election in Ephesians, there is no mention of any foreknowledge of the fact that we would believe, or any idea that there was anything worthy or meritorious in us (such as a tendency to believe) that was the basis for God's choosing us. Rather, Paul says, "He destined us *in love* to be his sons through Jesus Christ, *according to the purpose of his will,* to the praise of his glorious grace *which he freely bestowed on us* in the Beloved" (Eph. 1:5–6). Now if

---

[8]Rom. 11:2 similarly speaks of God's foreknowing *persons,* not facts about people or the fact that they would believe: "God has not rejected his people *whom he foreknew.*"

[9]In answer to Barth's view that all are chosen in Christ, see the discussion below on reprobation (the fact that some are not chosen), and chapter 7, pp. 116–18, and chapter 56, pp. 1148–53, on the fact that those who do not believe in Christ will not be saved.

God's grace is to be praised for election, and not human ability to believe or decision to believe, then once again it is consistent for Paul to mention nothing of human faith but only to mention God's predestining activity, his purpose and will, and his freely given grace.

Again in 2 Timothy, Paul says that God "saved us and called us with a holy calling, not in virtue of our works but *in virtue of his own purpose* and the grace which he gave us in Christ Jesus ages ago" (2 Tim. 1:9). Once again God's sovereign purpose is seen as the ultimate reason for our salvation, and Paul connects this with the fact that God gave us grace in Christ Jesus ages ago— another way of speaking of the truth that God freely gave favor to us when he chose us without reference to any foreseen merit or worthiness on our part.

**c. Election Based on Something Good in Us (Our Faith) Would Be the Beginning of Salvation by Merit:** Yet another kind of objection can be brought against the idea that God chose us because he foreknew that we would come to faith. If the *ultimate* determining factor in whether we will be saved or not is our own decision to accept Christ, then we shall be more inclined to think that we deserve some credit for the fact that we were saved: in distinction from other people who continue to reject Christ, we were wise enough in our judgment or good enough in our moral tendencies or perceptive enough in our spiritual capacities to decide to believe in Christ. But once we begin to think this way then we seriously diminish the glory that is to be given to God for our salvation. We become uncomfortable speaking like Paul who says that God "destined us . . . *according to the purpose of his will*, to the praise of his glorious *grace*" (Eph. 1:5–6), and we begin to think that God "destined us . . . according to the fact that he knew that we would have enough tendencies toward goodness and faith within us that we would believe." When we think like this we begin to sound very much unlike the New Testament when it talks about election or predestination. By contrast, if election is solely based on God's own good pleasure and his sovereign decision to love us in spite of our lack of goodness or merit, then certainly we have a profound sense of appreciation to him for a salvation that is totally undeserved, and we will forever be willing to praise his "glorious grace" (Eph. 1:6).

In the final analysis, the difference between two views of election can be seen in the way they answer a very simple question. Given the fact that in the final analysis some people will choose to accept Christ and some people will not, the question is, "What makes people differ?" That is, what *ultimately* makes the difference between those who believe and those who do not? If our answer is that it is ultimately based on something God does (namely, his sovereign election of those who would be saved), then we see that salvation at its most foundational level is based on *grace alone*. On the other hand, if we answer that the ultimate difference between those who are saved and those who are not is because of *something in man* (that is, a tendency or disposition to believe or not believe), then salvation ultimately depends on a combination of grace plus human ability.[10]

---

[10]The fact that the Arminian position ultimately makes something in man the determining factor in whether people are saved or not is seen clearly in the statement of I. Howard Marshall: "The effect of the call of God is to place man in a position where he can say 'yes' or 'no' (which he could not do before God called him; till then he was in a continuous attitude of 'no')" ("Predestination in the New Testament," in *Grace Unlimited*, p. 140). In this statement of Marshall's we see that the final

**d. Predestination Based on Foreknowledge Still Does Not Give People Free Choice:** The idea that God's predestination of some to believe is based on foreknowledge of their faith encounters still another problem: upon reflection, this system turns out to give no real freedom to man either. For if God can look into the future and see that person A *will* come to faith in Christ, and that person B *will not* come to faith in Christ, then those facts are already *fixed*, they are already *determined*. If we assume that God's knowledge of the future is *true* (which it must be), then it is absolutely certain that person A will believe and person B will not. There is no way that their lives could turn out any differently than this. Therefore it is fair to say that their destinies are still *determined*, for they could not be otherwise. But *by what* are these destinies determined? If they are determined by God himself, then we no longer have election based ultimately on foreknowledge of faith, but rather on God's sovereign will. But if these destinies are not determined by God, then who or what determines them? Certainly no Christian would say that there is some powerful being other than God controlling people's destinies. Therefore it seems that the only other possible solution is to say they are determined by some impersonal force, some kind of fate, operative in the universe, making things turn out as they do. But what kind of benefit is this? We have then sacrificed election in love by a personal God for a kind of determinism by an impersonal force and God is no longer to be given the ultimate credit for our salvation.

**e. Conclusion: Election Is Unconditional:** It seems best, for the previous four reasons, to reject the idea that election is based on God's foreknowledge of our faith. We conclude instead that the reason for election is simply God's sovereign choice—he "destined us in love to be his sons" (Eph. 1:5). God chose us simply because he decided to bestow his love upon us. It was not because of any foreseen faith or foreseen merit in us.

This understanding of election has traditionally been called "unconditional election."[11] It is "unconditional" because it is not *conditioned upon* anything that God sees in us that makes us worthy of his choosing us.[12]

---

determinant of whether people are saved or not is whether they say yes or no to God's call, and therefore salvation still ultimately depends on something in man, an ability or tendency within him that persuades him to say yes rather than no.

[11]Unconditional election is the "U" in the acronym TULIP, which stands for "the five points of Calvinism." The other letters stand for *Total* depravity (see chapter 24, pp. 497–98), *Limited* atonement (see chapter 27, pp. 594–603), *Irresistible* grace (see chapter 34, p. 700), and *Perseverance* of the saints (see chapter 40, pp. 788–803). See also p. 596, n. 35.

[12]Regarding the doctrine of election, there has been a dispute in Reformed circles (those who hold to election as presented here) between two positions known as *supralapsarianism* and *infralapsarianism*. The difference concerns what happened in God's mind before the foundation of the world. It does not concern something that happened in time, but rather it concerns the *logical* order of God's thoughts. The question is whether, in logical order, (a) God decided first that he would *save some people* and second that he would *allow sin* into the world so that he could save them from it (the supralapsarian position), or whether it was the other way around, so that (b) God first decided that he would *allow sin* into the world and second decided that he would *save some people* from it (the infralapsarian position). The word *supralapsarian* means "before the fall," and the word *infralapsarian* means "after the fall." The discussion is complex and highly speculative because there is very little direct biblical data to help us with it. Good arguments have been advanced in support of each view, and there is probably some element of truth in each one. But in the last analysis it seems wiser to say that Scripture does not give us enough data to probe into this mystery, and, moreover, it does not seem very edifying to do so.

## D. Objections to the Doctrine of Election

It must be said that the doctrine of election as presented here is by no means universally accepted in the Christian church, either in Catholicism or Protestantism. There is a long history of acceptance of the doctrine as here presented, but many others have objected to it as well. Among current evangelicals, those in more Reformed or Calvinistic circles (conservative Presbyterian denominations, for example) will accept this view, as will many Lutherans and Anglicans (Episcopalians) and a large number of Baptists and people in independent churches. On the other hand, it will be rejected quite decisively by nearly all Methodists, as well as by many others in Baptist, Anglican, and independent churches.[13] While a number of the objections to election are more specific forms of objection to the doctrine of providence presented in chapter 16, and have been answered in more detail there, a few particular objections should be mentioned here.

**1. Election Means That We Do Not Have a Choice in Whether We Accept Christ or Not.** According to this objection, the doctrine of election denies all the gospel invitations that appeal to the will of man and ask people to make a choice in whether to respond to Christ's invitation or not. In response to this, we must affirm that the doctrine of election is fully able to accommodate the idea that we have a voluntary choice and we make willing decisions in accepting or rejecting Christ. Our choices are voluntary because they are what we want to do and what we decide to do.[14] This does not mean that our choices are absolutely free, because (as explained in chapter 16, on providence), God can work sovereignly through our desires so that he guarantees that our choices come about as he has ordained, but this can still be understood as a real choice because God has created us and he ordains that such a choice is real. In short, we can say that God causes us to choose Christ voluntarily. The mistaken assumption underlying this objection is that a choice must be absolutely free (that is, not in any way caused by God) in order for it to be a genuine human choice.

In fact, I have decided to mention the discussion in this textbook at this point only because the words "supralapsarian" and "infralapsarian" are sometimes used in theological circles as symbols for the most abstract and obscure of theological discussions, and it seemed to me appropriate simply to inform the reader of the nature of this dispute and the meaning of these terms. For those interested, a further discussion is found in Berkhof, *Systematic Theology,* pp. 118–25.

[13]For a full discussion of objections to election, the reader may refer to two excellent recent collections of essays from what is called an "Arminian" perspective, a perspective that rejects the view of election advocated in this chapter: see Clark H. Pinnock, ed., *Grace Unlimited* (Minneapolis: Bethany Fellowship, 1975), and Clark H. Pinnock, ed., *The Grace of God, the Will of Man: A Case for Arminianism.* In response to these two books, Tom Schreiner and Bruce Ware have edited a substantial collection of essays from Reformed scholars, with a proposed title *The Grace of God, the Bondage of the Will: A Case for Calvinism* (forthcoming; projected from Baker Book House, Grand Rapids, in 1995).

[14]Grant R. Osborne, "Exegetical Notes on Calvinist Texts," in *Grace Unlimited,* pp. 167–89, several times points out evidence of human volition or human choice involved in the immediate context of texts that talk about election or predestination. A representative example is seen on p. 175, where Osborne discusses Acts 13:48, "as many as were ordained to eternal life believed." Osborne responds, "While we agree that the basic thrust is divine election, this does not negate the presence of human volition, as seen in the context" (p. 175). Such a response seems to assume that a Reformed view denies human volition or choice. But it must be answered that the Reformed position as traditionally argued certainly allows for genuine human volition or human will in choices that are made, and simply says that God is so wise and powerful that he *ordains* that we respond *willingly.* Osborne does not directly interact with this position.

## 2. On This Definition of Election, Our Choices Are Not Real Choices.

Continuing the discussion in the previous paragraph, someone might object that if a choice is caused by God, it may appear to us to be voluntary and willed by us, but it is nonetheless not a genuine or real choice, because it is not absolutely free. Once again we must respond by challenging the assumption that a choice must be absolutely free in order to be genuine or valid. If God makes us in a certain way and then tells us that our voluntary choices are real and genuine choices, then we must agree that they are. God is the definition of what is real and genuine in the universe. By contrast, we might ask where Scripture ever says that our choices have to be free from God's influence or control in order to be real or genuine choices. It does not seem that Scripture ever speaks in this way.

## 3. The Doctrine of Election Makes Us Puppets or Robots, Not Real Persons.

According to this objection, if God really causes everything that we choose with regard to salvation, then we are no longer real persons. Once again it must be answered that God has created us and we must allow him to define what genuine personhood is. The analogy of a "puppet" or a "robot" reduces us to a sub-human category of things that have been created by man. But genuine human beings are far greater than puppets or robots, because we do have a genuine will and we do make voluntary decisions based on our own preferences and wants. In fact, it is this ability to make willing choices that is one thing that distinguishes us from much of the lower creation. We are real people created in God's image, and God has allowed us to make genuine choices that have real effects on our lives.

## 4. The Doctrine of Election Means That Unbelievers Never Had a Chance to Believe.

This objection to election says that if God had decreed from eternity that some people would not believe, then there was no genuine chance for them to believe, and the entire system functions unfairly. Two responses can be made to this objection. First, we must note that the Bible does not allow us to say that unbelievers had no chance to believe. When people rejected Jesus he always put the blame on their willful choice to reject him, not on anything decreed by God the Father. "Why do you not understand what I say? It is because you cannot bear to hear my word. You are of your father the devil, and your *will* is to do your father's desires" (John 8:43–44). He says to Jerusalem, "How often would I have gathered your children together . . . *and you would not!*" (Matt. 23:37). He said to the Jews who rejected him, "You *refuse to come to me* that you may have life" (John 5:40). Romans 1 makes it plain that all people are confronted with a revelation from God of such clarity that they are "without excuse" (Rom. 1:20). This is the consistent pattern in Scripture: people who remain in unbelief do so because they are unwilling to come to God, and the blame for such unbelief always lies with the unbelievers themselves, never with God.

At a second level, the answer to this question must simply be Paul's answer to a similar objection: "But who are you, a man, to answer back to God? Will what is molded say to its molder, 'Why have you made me thus?'" (Rom. 9:20).

**5. Election Is Unfair.** Sometimes people regard the doctrine of election as unfair, since it teaches that God chooses some to be saved and passes over others, deciding not to save them. How can this be fair?

Two responses may be given at this point. First, we must remember that *it would be perfectly fair for God not to save anyone,* just as he did with the angels: "God did not spare the angels when they sinned, but cast them into hell and committed them to pits of nether gloom to be kept until the judgment" (2 Peter 2:4).[15] What would be perfectly fair for God would be to do with human beings as he did with angels, that is, to save none of those who sinned and rebelled against him. But if he does save *some at all,* then this is a demonstration of grace that goes far beyond the requirements of fairness and justice.

But at a deeper level this objection would say that it is not fair for God to create some people who he knew would sin and be eternally condemned, and whom he would not redeem. Paul raises this objection in Romans 9. After saying that God "has mercy upon whomever he wills, and he hardens the heart of whomever he wills" (Rom. 9:18),[16] Paul then raises this precise objection: "You will say to me then, 'Why does he still find fault? For who can resist his will?'" (Rom. 9:19). Here is the heart of the "unfairness" objection against the doctrine of election. If each person's ultimate destiny is determined by God, not by the person himself or herself (that is, even when people make willing choices that determine whether they will be saved or not, if God is actually behind those choices somehow causing them to occur), then how can this be fair?

Paul's response is not one that appeals to our pride, nor does he attempt to give a philosophical explanation of why this is just. He simply calls on God's rights as the omnipotent Creator:

> But who are you, a man, to answer back to God? Will what is molded say to its molder, "Why have you made me thus?" Has the potter no right over the clay, to make out of the same lump one vessel for beauty and another for menial use? What if God, desiring to show his wrath and to make known his power, has endured with much patience the vessels of wrath made for destruction, in order to make known the riches of his glory for the vessels of mercy, which he has prepared beforehand for glory, even us whom he has called, not from the Jews only but also from the Gentiles? (Rom. 9:20–24)[17]

---

[15]See chapter 19, p. 403, for a discussion of the fact that it would be fair for God to save no one.

[16]One Arminian view of this verse is given by Jack Cottrell. He argues that Rom. 9:18, "He has mercy upon whomever he will, and he hardens the heart of whomever he will," refers not to God's choice of people for salvation, but to God's choice of people for certain kinds of service: "He chooses whom he pleases for service, not salvation" ("The Nature of the Divine Sovereignty," in *The Grace of God, the Will of Man,* p. 114). This is not a convincing interpretation, however, because the entire context definitely concerns salvation: Paul says, "I have great sorrow and unceasing anguish in my heart" and "I could wish that I myself were accursed and cut off from Christ for the sake of my brethren, my kinsmen by race" (Rom. 9:2, 3), not because the Jews were not chosen for some particular service, but because they were not saved! He speaks in v. 8 not of those who were chosen for service and those who were not, but of those who are "children of God" and those who are not. And he speaks in v. 22 not of some who missed an opportunity for service, but of "vessels of wrath made for destruction." Salvation is in view in the entire context.

[17]James D. Strauss, "God's Promise and Universal History: The Theology of Romans 9," in *Grace Unlimited,* argues that in Romans 9 "vessels of wrath *made for destruction*" should rather be translated "fitted themselves" for wrath (p. 200). But he gives no examples of a genuine reflexive use of the verb *katartizō,* which would be required here. BAGD, pp. 417–18, note that the *passive* can be used intransitively (as here if we translate "made for destruction," as the RSV), but they give no example of an

Paul simply says that there is a point beyond which we cannot answer back to God or question his justice. He has done what he has done according to his sovereign will. He is the Creator; we are the creatures, and we ultimately have no basis from which to accuse him of unfairness or injustice.[18] When we read these words of Paul we are confronted with a decision whether or not to accept what God says here, and what he does, simply because he is God and we are not. It is a question that reaches deep into our understanding of ourselves as creatures and of our relationship to God as our Creator.

This objection of unfairness takes a slightly different form when people say that it is *unfair of God to save some people and not to save all*. This objection is based on an idea of justice among human beings that we sense intuitively. We recognize in human affairs that it is right to treat equal people in an equal way. Therefore it seems intuitively appropriate to us to say that if God is going to save *some* sinners he ought to save *all* sinners. But in answer to this objection it must be said that we really have no right to impose on God our intuitive sense of what is appropriate among human beings. Whenever Scripture begins to treat this area it goes back to God's sovereignty as Creator and says he has a right to do with his creation as he wills (see Rom. 9:19–20, quoted above).[19] If God ultimately decided to create some creatures to be saved and others not to be saved, then that was his sovereign choice, and we have no moral or scriptural basis on which we can insist that it was not fair.

**6. The Bible Says That God Wills to Save Everyone.** Another objection to the doctrine of election is that it contradicts certain passages of Scripture that say that God wills for all to be saved. Paul writes of God our Savior, *"who desires all men to be saved and to come to the knowledge of the truth"* (1 Tim. 2:4). And Peter says, "The Lord is not slow about his promise as some count slowness, but is forbearing toward you, *not wishing that any should perish, but that all should reach repentance"* (2 Peter 3:9). Do not these passages contradict the idea that God has only chosen certain people to be saved?

One common solution to this question (from the Reformed perspective advocated in this book) is to say that these verses speak of God's *revealed will* (telling us what we should do), not his *hidden will* (his eternal plans for what will happen).[20] The verses simply tell us that God invites and commands every person

---

active or middle voice of this verb being used without a direct object. Moreover, Strauss' suggestion, "fitted themselves" for wrath, would not really fit the picture of a potter making vessels of various sorts, for pots do not make themselves, but the potter makes them.

Another objection brought by Strauss is to say that the potter and clay imagery in Rom. 9:20–23 is derived from Old Testament passages that emphasize God's call for people freely to choose repentance and faith. He says that this negates the idea of sovereign predestining on God's part (p. 199). But here Strauss simply misunderstands the Reformed position, which never denies human responsibility or human willingness in making choices.

[18]For further discussion, see John Piper, *The Justification of God: An Exegetical and Theological Study of Romans 9:1–23* (Grand Rapids: Baker, 1983).

[19]I. Howard Marshall, "Predestination in the New Testament," (in *Grace Unlimited*, p. 136), specifically says, "I cannot see how it can be just arbitrarily to save one guilty sinner and not another." But that seems to be precisely Paul's point in Rom. 9:18–20: God does save some and decide not to save others, and we have no right, as creatures, to say that this is unjust.

[20]For a discussion of the difference between God's revealed will and his secret will, see chapter 13, pp. 213–16; also chapter 16, pp. 327–30. See also John Piper, "Are There Two Wills in God? Divine

to repent and come to Christ for salvation, but they do not tell us anything about God's secret decrees regarding who will be saved.

The Arminian theologian Clark Pinnock objects to the idea that God has a secret and a revealed will—he calls it "the exceedingly paradoxical notion of two divine wills regarding salvation."[21] But Pinnock never really answers the question of why all are not saved (from an Arminian perspective). Ultimately Arminians *also* must say that God *wills* something more strongly than he wills the salvation of all people, *for in fact all are not saved.* Arminians claim that the reason why all are not saved is that God wills to preserve the free will of man *more than* he wills to save everyone. But is this not also making a distinction in two aspects of the will of God? On the one hand God wills that all be saved (1 Tim. 2:5–6; 2 Peter 3:9). But on the other hand he wills to preserve man's absolutely free choice. In fact, he wills the second thing *more than* the first. But this means that Arminians also must say that 1 Timothy 2:5–6 and 2 Peter 3:9 do not say that God wills the salvation of everyone in an absolute or unqualified way—they too must say that the verses only refer to one kind or one aspect of God's will.

Here the difference between the Reformed and the Arminian conception of God's will is clearly seen. Both Calvinists and Arminians agree that God's commands in Scripture reveal to us what he wants us to do, and both agree that the commands in Scripture invite us to repent and trust in Christ for salvation. Therefore, in one sense both agree that God wills that we be saved—it is the will that he reveals to us explicitly in the gospel invitation.

But both sides must also say that there is something else that God deems more important than saving everyone. Reformed theologians say that God deems *his own glory* more important than saving everyone, and that (according to Rom. 9) God's glory is also furthered by the fact that some are not saved. Arminian theologians also say that something else is more important to God than the salvation of all people, namely, the preservation of *man's free will.* So in a Reformed system God's highest value is his own glory, and in an Arminian system God's highest value is the free will of man. These are two distinctly different conceptions of the nature of God, and it seems that the Reformed position has much more explicit biblical support than the Arminian position does on this question.[22]

## E. The Doctrine of Reprobation

When we understand election as God's sovereign choice of some persons to be saved, then there is necessarily another aspect of that choice, namely, God's

---

Election and God's Desire for All to Be Saved," in *The Grace of God, the Bondage of the Will,* ed. Tom Schreiner and Bruce Ware.

[21]Clark Pinnock, "Introduction," in *Grace Unlimited,* p. 13.

[22]See chapter 15, pp. 271–73, and chapter 21, pp. 440–41, on the fact that God created us and the whole universe for his own glory. An Arminian may object to putting the difference this way, and may say that God is more glorified when we choose him out of an absolutely free will, but this is simply a doubtful assumption based on intuition or human analogy, and has no specific support from Scripture. Moreover, to be consistent it seems the Arminian would also have to take account of the millions who do not choose God, and would have to say that God is also more glorified by the free choices of the millions who freely decide against God—otherwise, why would God allow them to persist in this free choice of rebellion?

sovereign decision to pass over others and not to save them. This decision of God in eternity past is called reprobation. *Reprobation is the sovereign decision of God before creation to pass over some persons, in sorrow deciding not to save them, and to punish them for their sins, and thereby to manifest his justice.*

In many ways the doctrine of reprobation is the most difficult of all the teachings of Scripture for us to think about and to accept, because it deals with such horrible and eternal consequences for human beings made in the image of God. The love that God gives us for our fellow human beings and the love that he commands us to have toward our neighbor cause us to recoil against this doctrine, and it is right that we feel such dread in contemplating it.[23] It is something that we would not want to believe, and would not believe, unless Scripture clearly taught it.

But are there Scripture passages that speak of such a decision by God? Certainly there are some. Jude speaks of some persons "who *long ago were designated for this condemnation,* ungodly persons who pervert the grace of our God into licentiousness and deny our only Master and Lord, Jesus Christ" (Jude 4).

Moreover, Paul, in the passage referred to above, speaks in the same way of Pharaoh and others:

For the Scripture says to Pharaoh, "I have raised you up for the very purpose of showing my power in you, so that my name may be proclaimed in all the earth." So then he has mercy upon whomever he wills, and he hardens the heart of whomever he wills. . . . What if God, desiring to show his wrath and to make known his power, has endured with much patience the vessels of wrath made for destruction? (Rom. 9:17–22)

Regarding the results of the fact that God failed to choose all for salvation, Paul says, "The elect obtained it, but the rest were hardened" (Rom. 11:7). And Peter says of those who reject the gospel, "they stumble because they disobey the word, *as they were destined to do*" (1 Peter 2:8).[24]

In spite of the fact that we recoil against this doctrine, we must be careful of our attitude toward God and toward these passages of Scripture. We must never begin to wish that the Bible was written in another way, or that it did not contain these verses. Moreover, if we are convinced that these verses teach reprobation, then we are obligated both to believe it and accept it as fair and just of God, even though it still causes us to tremble in horror as we think of it. In this context it may surprise us to see that Jesus can thank God *both* for hiding the knowledge of salvation from some and for revealing it to others: "Jesus declared, 'I thank you, Father, Lord of heaven and earth, that you have hidden these things from the wise and understanding and revealed them to babes; yea, Father, for such was your gracious will'" (Matt. 11:25–26).

Moreover, we must recognize that somehow, in God's wisdom, the fact of reprobation and the eternal condemnation of some will show God's justice and

---

[23]John Calvin himself says of reprobation, "The decree is dreadful indeed, I confess." Calvin, *Institutes,* 3.23.7 (2:955); but it should be noted that his Latin word *horribilis* does not mean "hateful" but rather "fearful, awe-inspiring."

[24]See discussion of this verse in Wayne Grudem, *1 Peter,* pp. 107–10. The verse does not simply say that God destined the *fact* that those who disobey would stumble, but speaks rather of God destining certain *people* to disobey and stumble: "as they were destined to do." (The Greek verb *etethēsan,* "they were destined," requires a plural subject.)

also result in his glory. Paul says, "What if God, *desiring to show his wrath and to make known his power,* has endured with much patience the vessels of wrath made for destruction" (Rom. 9:22). Paul also notes that the fact of such punishment on the "vessels of wrath" serves to show the greatness of God's mercy toward us: God does this "in order to make known the riches of his glory for the vessels of mercy" (Rom. 9:23).

We also must remember that *there are important differences between election and reprobation as they are presented in the Bible.* Election to salvation is viewed as a cause for rejoicing and praise to God, who is worthy of praise and receives all the credit for our salvation (see Eph. 1:3–6; 1 Peter 1:1–3). God is viewed as actively choosing us for salvation, and doing so in love and with delight. But reprobation is viewed as something that brings God sorrow, not delight (see Ezek. 33:11), and the blame for the condemnation of sinners is always put on the people or angels who rebel, never on God himself (see John 3:18–19; 5:40). So in the presentation of Scripture the cause of election lies in God, and the cause of reprobation lies in the sinner. Another important difference is that the ground of election is God's grace, whereas the ground of reprobation is God's justice. Therefore "double predestination" is not a helpful or accurate phrase, because it neglects these differences between election and reprobation.

The sorrow of God at the death of the wicked ("I have no pleasure in the death of the wicked, but that the wicked turn from his way and live," Ezek. 33:11) helps us understand how appropriate it was that Paul himself felt great sorrow when he thought about the unbelieving Jews who had rejected Christ. Paul says:

> I am speaking the truth in Christ, I am not lying; my conscience bears me witness in the Holy Spirit, that *I have great sorrow and unceasing anguish in my heart.* For I could wish that I myself were accursed and cut off from Christ for the sake of my brethren, my kinsmen by race. They are Israelites. . . . (Rom. 9:1–4)

We ought also to feel this great sorrow as well when we think about the fate of unbelievers.

But it might be objected at this point, if God genuinely feels sorrow at the punishment of the wicked, then why does he allow it or even decree that it will come about? The answer must be that God knows that this will ultimately result in greater glory for himself. It will show his power and wrath and justice and mercy in a way that could not otherwise be demonstrated. Certainly in our own human experience it is possible to do something that causes us great sorrow but which we know will result in long-term greater good. And so, after this faint human analogy, we may somewhat understand that God can decree something that causes him sorrow yet ultimately will further his glory.

## F. Practical Application of the Doctrine of Election

In terms of our own relationship with God, the doctrine of election does have significant practical application. When we think of the biblical teaching on both election and reprobation, it is appropriate to apply it to our own lives individually. It is right for each Christian to ask of himself or herself, "Why am I a Christian? What is the final reason why God decided to save me?"

The doctrine of election tells us that I am a Christian simply because God in eternity past decided to set his love on me. But why did he decide to set his love on me? Not for anything good in me, but simply because he decided to love me. There is no more ultimate reason than that.

It humbles us before God to think in this way. It makes us realize that we have no claim on God's grace whatsoever. Our salvation is totally due to grace alone. Our only appropriate response is to give God eternal praise.

## QUESTIONS FOR PERSONAL APPLICATION

1. Do you think that God chose you individually to be saved before he created the world? Do you think he did it on the basis of the fact that he knew you would believe in Christ, or was it "unconditional election," not based on anything that he foresaw in you that made you worthy of his love? No matter how you answered the previous question, explain how your answer makes you feel when you think about yourself in relationship to God.

2. Does the doctrine of election give you any comfort or assurance about your future?

3. After reading this chapter, do you honestly feel that you would like to give thanks or praise to God for choosing you to be saved? Do you sense any unfairness in the fact that God did not decide to save everyone?

4. If you agree with the doctrine of election as presented in this chapter, does it diminish your sense of individual personhood or make you feel somewhat like a robot or a puppet in God's hands? Do you think it should make you feel this way?

5. What effect do you think this chapter will have on your motivation for evangelism? Is this a positive or negative effect? Can you think of ways in which the doctrine of election can be used as a positive encouragement to evangelism (see 1 Thess. 1:4–5; 2 Tim. 2:10)?

6. Whether you adopt a Reformed or Arminian perspective on the question of election, can you think of some positive benefits in the Christian life that those who hold the *opposite* position from yours seem more frequently to experience than you do? Even though you do not agree with the other position, can you list some helpful concerns or practical truths about the Christian life that you might learn from that position? Is there anything that Calvinists and Arminians could do to bring about greater understanding and less division on this question?

## SPECIAL TERMS

| | |
|---|---|
| determinism | foreknowledge |
| election | predestination |
| fatalism | reprobation |

# BIBLIOGRAPHY

(For an explanation of this bibliography see the note on the bibliography to chapter 1, p. 38. Complete bibliographical data may be found on pp. 1223–29.)

## Sections in Evangelical Systematic Theologies

1. Anglican (Episcopalian)
   - 1930        Thomas, 236–57
   - 1882–92     Litton, 351–63
2. Arminian (Wesleyan or Methodist)
   - 1847        Finney, 481–515
   - 1875–76     Pope, 2:363–67
   - 1892–94     Miley, 2:254–308
   - 1940        Wiley, 2:335–57
   - 1983–       Cottrell, 2:331–502
3. Baptist
   - 1767        Gill, 1:251–88, 300–306
   - 1887        Boyce, 341–67
   - 1907        Strong, 779–90
   - 1917        Mullins, 338–358
   - 1976–83     Henry, 6:76–107
   - 1983–85     Erickson, 907–28
4. Dispensational
   - 1947        Chafer, 3:165–82
   - 1949        Thiessen, 257–63
   - 1986        Ryrie, 310–18
5. Lutheran
   - 1917–24     Pieper, 3:473–506
   - 1934        Mueller, 585–612
6. Reformed (or Presbyterian)
   - 1559        Calvin, 2:920–86 (3.21–24)
   - 1861        Heppe, 150–89
   - 1871–73     Hodge, 2:313–53
   - 1878        Dabney, 223–46
   - 1887–1921   Warfield, BTS, 270–333; SSW, 1:103–11, 285–98; BD, 3–70; PS, 13–112
   - 1937–66     Murray, CW, 1:119–23; CW, 2:123–31; RAA, 79–87
   - 1938        Berkhof, 109–25
   - 1962        Buswell, 2:133–56
7. Renewal (or charismatic/Pentecostal)
   - 1988–92     Williams, 2:13–22

## Sections in Representative Roman Catholic Systematic Theologies

1. Roman Catholic: Traditional
   1955    Ott, 242–46
2. Roman Catholic: Post-Vatican II
   1980    McBrien (no explicit treatment)

## Other Works

Basinger, David, and Randall Basinger, eds. *Predestination and Free Will.* Downers Grove, Ill.: InterVarsity Press, 1985.

Berkouwer, G. C. *Divine Election.* Trans. by Hugo Bekker. Grand Rapids: Eerdmans, 1960.

Carson, D. A. *Divine Sovereignty and Human Responsibility: Biblical Perspectives in Tension.* Atlanta: John Knox Press, 1981.

Coppedge, Allan. *John Wesley in Theological Debate.* Wilmore, Ky.: Wesley Heritage Press, 1987.

Feinberg, John S. "God Ordains All Things." In *Predestination and Free Will: Four Views of Divine Sovereignty and Human Freedom.* David Basinger & Randall Basinger, eds. Downers Grove, Ill.: InterVarsity Press, 1986.

Godfrey, William R. "Predestination." In *NDT,* pp. 528–30.

Klein, William W. *The New Chosen People: A Corporate View of Election.* Grand Rapids: Zondervan, 1990.

Klooster, F. H. "Elect, Election." In *EDT,* pp. 348–49.

Nettles, Thomas. *By His Grace and for His Glory: A Historical, Theological and Practical Study of the Doctrines of Grace in Baptist Life.* Grand Rapids: Baker Book House, 1986.

Packer, J. I. "Election." In *IBD,* Vol. 1, pp. 435–38.

Pinnock, Clark H., ed. *Grace Unlimited.* Minneapolis: Bethany, 1975.

———. *The Grace of God, the Will of Man: A Case for Arminianism.* Grand Rapids: Zondervan, 1989.

Piper, John. *The Justification of God: An Exegetical and Theological Study of Romans 9:1–23.* Grand Rapids: Baker, 1983.

Poythress, Vern. "Using Multiple Thematic Centers in Theological Synthesis: Holiness as a Test Case in Developing a Pauline Theology." Unpublished manuscript available from the Campus Bookstore, Westminster Theological Seminary, P.O. Box 27009, Philadelphia, PA, 19118. (a study on Pauline themes used to describe the application of redemption)

Reid, W. S. "Reprobation." In *EDT,* p. 937.

Schreiner, Thomas, and Bruce Ware, editors. *The Grace of God, the Bondage of the Will: A Case for Calvinism* (proposed title). 2 vols. Forthcoming: Grand Rapids: Baker, projected in 1995.

Shank, R. *Elect in the Son: A Study of the Doctrine of Election.* Springfield, Mo.: Westcott, 1970.

Sproul, R. C. *Chosen by God.* Wheaton, Ill.: Tyndale, 1986.

Steele, David N. and Curtis C. Thomas. *The Five Points of Calvinism—Defined, Defended, Documented.* International Library of Philosophy and Theology:

Biblical and Theological Studies, ed. J. Marcellus Kik. Phillipsburg, N.J.: Presbyterian and Reformed, 1963.

Storms, C. Samuel. *Chosen for Life: An Introductory Guide to the Doctrine of Divine Election.* Grand Rapids: Baker, 1987.

Warfield, B. B. *The Plan of Salvation.* Grand Rapids: Eerdmans, 1942.

————. "Predestination." In *Biblical and Theological Studies.* Philadelphia: Presbyterian and Reformed, 1952.

## SCRIPTURE MEMORY PASSAGE

**Ephesians 1:3–6:** *Blessed be the God and Father of our Lord Jesus Christ, who has blessed us in Christ with every spiritual blessing in the heavenly places, even as he chose us in him before the foundation of the world, that we should be holy and blameless before him. He destined us in love to be his sons through Jesus Christ, according to the purpose of his will, to the praise of his glorious grace which he freely bestowed on us in the Beloved.*

## HYMN

### "When This Passing World Is Done"

This hymn reminds us that when we are once in heaven and look back on our life we will realize how much more we owe to God's mercy and grace than we ever realized in this life. The last stanza especially emphasizes the fact that our election is not based on anything good in ourselves: "Chosen not for good in me."

When this passing world is done,
　　When has sunk yon glaring sun,
When we stand with Christ in glory,
　　Looking o'er life's finished story,
Then, Lord, shall I fully know,
　　Not till then, how much I owe.

When I hear the wicked call
　　On the rocks and hills to fall,
When I see them start to shrink
　　On the fiery deluge brink,
Then, Lord, shall I fully know,
　　Not till then, how much I owe.

When I stand before the throne,
　　Dressed in beauty not my own,
When I see thee as thou art,
　　Love thee with unsinning heart,
Then, Lord, shall I fully know,
　　Not till then, how much I owe.

When the praise of heav'n I hear,
　　Loud as thunders to the ear,
Loud as many waters' noise,
　　Sweet as harp's melodious voice,

Then, Lord, shall I fully know,
   Not till then, how much I owe.

Chosen not for good in me,
   Wakened up from wrath to flee,
Hidden in the Savior's side,
   By the Spirit sanctified,
Teach me, Lord, on earth to show,
   By my love, how much I owe.

AUTHOR: ROBERT MURRAY MCCHEYNE, 1837

# Chapter 33

# The Gospel Call and Effective Calling

*What is the gospel message? How does it become effective?*

## EXPLANATION AND SCRIPTURAL BASIS

When Paul talks about the way that God brings salvation into our lives, he says, "Those whom he *predestined* he also *called;* and those whom he called he also *justified;* and those whom he justified he also *glorified*" (Rom. 8:30). Here Paul points to a definite order in which the blessings of salvation come to us. Although long ago, before the world was made, God "predestined" us to be his children and to be conformed to the image of his Son, Paul points to the fact that in the actual outworking of his purpose in our lives God "called" us (here in this context, God the Father is specifically in view). Then Paul immediately lists justification and glorification, showing that these come after calling. Paul indicates that there is a definite order in God's saving purpose (though not every aspect of our salvation is mentioned here). So we will begin our discussion of the different parts of our experience of salvation with the topic of calling.

## A. Effective Calling

When Paul says, "Those whom he predestined *he* also called; and those whom *he* called he also justified" (Rom. 8:30), he indicates that calling is an act of God. In fact, it is specifically an act of God the Father, for he is the one who predestines people "to be conformed to the image of his Son" (Rom. 8:29). Other verses describe more fully what this calling is. When God calls people in this powerful way, he calls them "out of darkness into his marvelous light" (1 Peter 2:9); he calls them "into the fellowship of his Son" (1 Cor. 1:9; cf. Acts 2:39) and "into his own kingdom and glory" (1 Thess. 2:12; cf. 1 Peter 5:10; 2 Peter 1:3). People who have been called by God "belong to Jesus Christ" (Rom. 1:6). They are called to "be saints" (Rom. 1:7; 1 Cor. 1:2), and have come into a realm of peace (1 Cor. 7:15; Col. 3:15), freedom (Gal. 5:13), hope (Eph. 1:18; 4:4), holiness (1 Thess. 4:7), patient endurance of suffering (1 Peter 2:20–21; 3:9), and eternal life (1 Tim. 6:12).

These verses indicate that no powerless, merely human calling is in view. This calling is rather a kind of "summons" from the King of the universe and it has such power that it brings about the response that it asks for in people's hearts. It is an act of God that *guarantees* a response, because Paul specifies in Romans 8:30 that all who were "called" were also "justified."[1] This calling has the capacity to draw us out of the kingdom of darkness and bring us into God's kingdom so we can join in full fellowship with him: "God is faithful, by whom you were *called into the fellowship of his Son*, Jesus Christ our Lord" (1 Cor. 1:9).[2]

This powerful act of God is often referred to as *effective calling*, to distinguish it from the general gospel invitation that goes to all people and which some people reject. This is not to say that human gospel proclamation is not involved. In fact, God's effective calling comes *through* the human preaching of the gospel, because Paul says, "To this he called you *through our gospel*, so that you may obtain the glory of our Lord Jesus Christ" (2 Thess. 2:14). Of course, there are many who hear the general call of the gospel message and do not respond. But in some cases the gospel call is made so effective by the working of the Holy Spirit in people's hearts that they do respond; we can say that they have received "effective calling."[3]

We may define effective calling as follows: *Effective calling is an act of God the Father, speaking through the human proclamation of the gospel, in which he summons people to himself in such a way that they respond in saving faith.*

It is important that we not give the impression that people will be saved by the power of this call *apart from* their own willing response to the gospel (see chapter 35 on the personal faith and repentance that are necessary for conversion). Although it is true that effective calling awakens and brings forth a response from us, we must always insist that this response still has to be a voluntary, willing response in which the individual person puts his or her trust in Christ.

This is why prayer is so important to effective evangelism. Unless God works in peoples' hearts to make the proclamation of the gospel effective, there will be no genuine saving response. Jesus said, "No one can come to me unless the Father who sent me draws him" (John 6:44).

An example of the gospel call working effectively is seen in Paul's first visit to Philippi. When Lydia heard the gospel message, "The Lord *opened her heart* to give heed to what was said by Paul" (Acts 16:14).

In distinction from effective calling, which is entirely an act of God, we may talk about the *gospel call* in general which comes through human speech. This gospel call is offered to all people, even those who do not accept it. Sometimes this gospel call is referred to as *external calling* or *general calling*. By contrast, the effective calling of God that actually brings about a willing response from the person who hears it is sometimes called *internal calling*. The gospel call is general and external and often rejected, while the effective call is particular, internal, and *always* effective. However, this is not to diminish the importance of the gospel call—it is the means God has appointed through which effective calling will come. Without the gospel call, no one could respond and be saved! "How are they to believe in him of whom they have never heard?" (Rom. 10:14). Therefore it is important to understand exactly what the gospel call is.

---

[1]See the discussion of justification in chapter 36.

[2]1 Thess. 2:12 speaks of God "who *calls you into* his own kingdom and glory," but the sense would even more closely parallel 1 Cor. 1:9 if we adopt the well-attested textual variant *kalesantos* (aorist participle) and translated, "who *has called you into* his own kingdom and glory."

[3]The older term used for "effective calling" was "effectual calling," but the term *effectual* is not as commonly used in English today.

## B. The Elements of the Gospel Call

In human preaching of the gospel, three important elements must be included.

**1. Explanation of the Facts Concerning Salvation.** Anyone who comes to Christ for salvation must have at least a basic understanding of who Christ is and how he meets our needs for salvation. Therefore an explanation of the facts concerning salvation must include at least the following:

1. All people have sinned (Rom. 3:23).
2. The penalty for our sin is death (Rom. 6:23).
3. Jesus Christ died to pay the penalty for our sins (Rom. 5:8).

But understanding those facts and even agreeing that they are true is not enough for a person to be saved. There must also be an invitation for a personal response on the part of the individual who will repent of his or her sins and trust personally in Christ.

**2. Invitation to Respond to Christ Personally in Repentance and Faith.** When the New Testament talks about people coming to salvation it speaks in terms of a personal response to an invitation from Christ himself. That invitation is beautifully expressed, for example, in the words of Jesus:

> *Come to me,* all you who are weary and burdened, and I will give you rest. Take my yoke upon you and learn from me, for I am gentle and humble in heart, and you will find rest for your souls. For my yoke is easy and my burden is light. (Matt. 11:28–30 NIV)

It is important to make clear that these are not just words spoken a long time ago by a religious leader in the past. Every non-Christian hearing these words should be encouraged to think of them as words that Jesus Christ is *even now,* at *this very moment,* speaking to him or to her individually. Jesus Christ is a Savior who is now alive in heaven, and each non-Christian should think of Jesus as speaking directly to him or her, saying, "*Come to me* . . . and I will give you rest" (Matt. 11:28). This is a genuine *personal* invitation that seeks a personal response from each one who hears it.

John also talks about the need for personal response when he says, "He came to his own home, and his own people received him not. *But to all who received him,* who believed in his name, he gave power to become children of God" (John 1:11–12). In emphasizing the need to "receive" Christ, John, too, points to the necessity of an individual response. To those inside a lukewarm church who do not realize their spiritual blindness the Lord Jesus again issues an invitation that calls for personal response: "Behold, I stand at the door and knock; if any one hears my voice and opens the door, I will come in to him and eat with him, and he with me" (Rev. 3:20).

Finally, just five verses from the end of the entire Bible, there is another invitation from the Holy Spirit and the church to come to Christ: "The Spirit and the Bride say, 'Come.' And let him who hears say, 'Come.' And let him who is thirsty come, let him who desires take the water of life without price" (Rev. 22:17).

But what is involved in coming to Christ? Although this will be explained more fully in chapter 35, it is sufficient to note here that if we come to Christ and trust him to save us from our sin, we cannot any longer cling to sin but must willingly renounce it in genuine repentance. In some cases in Scripture both repentance and faith are mentioned together when referring to someone's initial conversion (Paul said that he spent his time "testifying both to Jews and to Greeks of *repentance* to God and of *faith* in our Lord Jesus Christ," Acts 20:21). But at other times only repentance of sins is named and saving faith is assumed as an accompanying factor ("that *repentance* and forgiveness of sins should be preached in his name to all nations" [Luke 24:47; cf. Acts 2:37–38; 3:19; 5:31; 17:30; Rom. 2:4; 2 Cor. 7:10; et al.]). Therefore, any genuine gospel proclamation must include an invitation to make a conscious decision to forsake one's sins and come to Christ in faith, asking Christ for forgiveness of sins. If either the need to repent of sins or the need to trust in Christ for forgiveness is neglected, there is not a full and true proclamation of the gospel.[4]

But what is promised for those who come to Christ? This is the third element of the gospel call.

**3. A Promise of Forgiveness and Eternal Life.** Although the words of personal invitation spoken by Christ do have promises of rest, and power to become children of God, and partaking of the water of life, it is helpful to make explicit just what Christ promises to those who come to him in repentance and faith. The primary thing that is promised in the gospel message is the promise of forgiveness of sins and eternal life with God. "For God so loved the world that he gave his only Son, that whoever believes in him *should not perish but have eternal life*" (John 3:16). And in Peter's preaching of the gospel he says, "Repent therefore, and turn again, *that your sins may be blotted out*" (Acts 3:19; cf. 2:38).

Coupled with the promise of forgiveness and eternal life should be an assurance that Christ will accept all who come to him in sincere repentance and faith seeking salvation: "Him who comes to me I will not cast out" (John 6:37).

## C. The Importance of the Gospel Call

The doctrine of the gospel call is important, because if there were no gospel call we could not be saved. "How are they to believe in him of whom they have never heard?" (Rom. 10:14).

The gospel call is important also because through it God addresses us in the fullness of our humanity. He does not save us "automatically" without seeking for a response from us as whole persons. Rather, he addresses the gospel call to our intellects, our emotions, and our wills. He speaks to our intellects by explaining the facts of salvation in his Word. He speaks to our emotions by issuing a heartfelt personal invitation to respond. He speaks to our wills by asking us to hear his invitation and respond willingly in repentance and faith—to decide to turn from our sins and receive Christ as Savior and rest our hearts in him for salvation.

---

[4]See chapter 35, pp. 713–17, for a fuller discussion of the need for both genuine repentance and genuine faith, and a discussion of the question of whether someone can be saved by "accepting Jesus as Savior but not as Lord."

# QUESTIONS FOR PERSONAL APPLICATION

1. Can you remember the first time you heard the gospel and responded to it? Can you describe what it felt like in your heart? Do you think the Holy Spirit was working to make that gospel call effective in your life? Did you resist it at the time?

2. In your explanation of the gospel call to other people, have some elements been missing? If so, what difference would it make if you added those elements to your explanation of the gospel? Do you think those elements are important to add? What is the one thing most needed to make your proclamation of the gospel more effective?

3. Before reading this chapter, had you thought of Jesus in heaven speaking the words of the gospel invitation personally to people even today? If non-Christians do begin to think of Jesus speaking to them in this way, how do you think it will affect their response to the gospel?

4. Do you understand the elements of the gospel call clearly enough to present them to others? Could you easily turn in the Bible to find four or five appropriate verses that would explain the gospel call clearly to people? (Memorizing the elements of the gospel call and the verses that explain it should be one of the first disciplines of anyone's Christian life.)

## SPECIAL TERMS

effective calling                          the gospel call
external calling                          internal calling

## BIBLIOGRAPHY

(For an explanation of this bibliography see the note on the bibliography to chapter 1, p. 38. Complete bibliographical data may be found on pp. 1223–29.)

### Sections in Evangelical Systematic Theologies

1. Anglican (Episcopalian)
    1882–92    Litton, 239–55
2. Arminian (Wesleyan or Methodist)
    1875–76    Pope, 336–57
    1940    Wiley, 2:334–57
    1960    Purkiser, 269–78
3. Baptist
    1767    Gill, 1:530–37; 2:121–31
    1887    Boyce, 367–73
    1907    Strong, 790–93
    1917    Mullins, 365–68
    1983–85    Erickson, 929–33
4. Dispensational

       1947    Chafer, 3:210–24, 371–93
       1949    Thiessen, 257–63
       1986    Ryrie, 324–25, 335–39
5. Lutheran
   1917–24    Pieper, 2:423–26, 502; 3:220–52
       1934    Mueller, 364–65, 470–85
6. Reformed (or Presbyterian)
       1559    Calvin, 1:537–42 (3.1)
       1861    Heppe, 510–42
   1871–73    Hodge, 2:639–732
       1878    Dabney, 553–79
   1937–66    Murray, *CW*, 1:124–34, 143–65; *CW*, 2:161–66; *CW*, 4:113–32; *RAA*, 88–94
       1938    Berkhof, 454–64
       1962    Buswell, 2:157–68
7. Renewal (or charismatic/Pentecostal)
   1988–92    Williams, 2:13–33

### Sections in Representative Roman Catholic Systematic Theologies

1. Roman Catholic: Traditional
       1955    Ott (no explicit treatment)
2. Roman Catholic: Post-Vatican II
       1980    McBrien (no explicit treatment)

### Other Works

Aldrich, Joseph C. *Life-Style Evangelism: Crossing Traditional Boundaries to Reach the Unbelieving World.* Portland: Multnomah, 1981.
Alleine, Joseph. *Sure Guide to Heaven.* Carlisle, Pa.: Banner of Truth, 1978. First published in 1672 as *An Alarm to the Unconverted.*
Baxter, Richard. *A Call to the Unconverted to Turn and Live.* Reprint: Grand Rapids: Zondervan, 1953.
Coleman, Robert E. *The Master Plan of Evangelism.* Old Tappan, N.J.: Revell, 1963.
Hoekema, Anthony A. *Saved by Grace.* Grand Rapids: Eerdmans, and Exeter: Paternoster, 1989, pp. 68–92.
Kevan, Ernest F. *Salvation.* Phillipsburg, N.J.: Presbyterian and Reformed, 1973.
Little, Paul. *How to Give Away Your Faith.* Revised by Marie Little. Downers Grove, Ill.: InterVarsity Press, 1988.
Kennedy, D. James. *Evangelism Explosion.* 3d ed. Wheaton, Ill.: Tyndale, 1983.
MacArthur, John F., Jr. *The Gospel According to Jesus.* Grand Rapids: Zondervan, 1988.
Murray, John. "Effectual Calling." In *Redemption Accomplished and Applied.* Grand Rapids: Eerdmans, 1955, pp. 88–94.

Packer, J. I. "Call, Calling." In *EDT,* p. 184.

————. *Evangelism and the Sovereignty of God.* Downers Grove, Ill.: InterVarsity Press, 1961.

Wells, David F. *God the Evangelist: How the Holy Spirit Works to Bring Men and Women to Faith.* Grand Rapids: Eerdmans, 1987.

## SCRIPTURE MEMORY PASSAGE

**Matthew 11:28–30:** *Come to me, all who labor and are heavy laden, and I will give you rest. Take my yoke upon you, and learn from me; for I am gentle and lowly in heart, and you will find rest for your souls. For my yoke is easy, and my burden is light.*

## HYMN

### "I Heard the Voice of Jesus Say"

I heard the voice of Jesus say, "Come unto me and rest;
    Lay down, thou weary one, lay down thy head upon my breast."
I came to Jesus as I was, weary and worn and sad,
    I found in him a resting place, and he has made me glad.

I heard the voice of Jesus say, "Behold, I freely give
    The living water; thirsty one, stoop down and drink, and live."
I came to Jesus, and I drank of that life-giving stream;
    My thirst was quenched, my soul revived, and now I live in him.

I heard the voice of Jesus say, "I am this dark world's light;
    Look unto me, thy morn shall rise, and all thy day be bright."
I looked to Jesus, and I found in him my star, my sun;
    And in that light of life I'll walk, till trav'lling days are done.

AUTHOR: HORATIUS BONAR, 1846

# Chapter 34

# Regeneration

*What does it mean to be born again?*

## EXPLANATION AND SCRIPTURAL BASIS

We may define regeneration as follows: *Regeneration is a secret act of God in which he imparts new spiritual life to us.* This is sometimes called "being born again" (using language from John 3:3–8).

### A. Regeneration Is Totally a Work of God

In some of the elements of the application of redemption that we discuss in subsequent chapters, we play an active part (this is true, for example, of conversion, sanctification and perseverance). But in the work of regeneration we play no active role at all. It is instead totally a work of God. We see this, for example, when John talks about those to whom Christ gave power to become children of God—they "were born, not of blood nor of the will of the flesh nor of the will of man, but of God" (John 1:13). Here John specifies that children of God are those who are "born . . . of God" and our human will ("the will of man") does not bring about this kind of birth.

The fact that we are passive in regeneration is also evident when Scripture refers to it as being "born" or being "born again" (cf. James 1:18; 1 Peter 1:3; John 3:3–8). We did not choose to be made physically alive and we did not choose to be born—it is something that happened to us; similarly, these analogies in Scripture suggest that we are entirely passive in regeneration.

This sovereign work of God in regeneration was also predicted in the prophecy of Ezekiel. Through him God promised a time in the future when he would give new spiritual life to his people:

> A *new heart* I will give you, and a *new spirit I will put within you;* and I will take out of your flesh the heart of stone and give you a heart of flesh. And I will put my spirit within you, and cause you to walk in my statutes and be careful to observe my ordinances. (Ezek. 36:26–27)

Which member of the Trinity is the one who causes regeneration? When Jesus speaks of being "born of the Spirit" (John 3:8), he indicates that it is especially God the Holy Spirit who produces regeneration. But other verses also indicate the involvement of God the Father in regeneration: Paul specifies that it is God who "made us alive together with Christ" (Eph. 2:5; cf. Col. 2:13). And James says that it is the "Father of lights" who gave us new birth: "Of his own will *he brought us forth* by the word of truth that we should be a kind of first fruits of his creatures" (James 1:17–18).[1] Finally, Peter says that God "according to his abundant mercy *has given us new birth* . . . through the resurrection of Jesus Christ from the dead" (1 Peter 1:3, author's translation). We can conclude that both God the Father and God the Holy Spirit bring about regeneration.

What is the connection between effective calling[2] and regeneration? As we will see later in this chapter, Scripture indicates that regeneration must come before we can respond to effective calling with saving faith. Therefore we can say that regeneration comes before the *result* of effective calling (our faith). But it is more difficult to specify the exact relationship in time between regeneration and the human proclamation of the gospel through which God works in effective calling. At least two passages suggest that God regenerates us at the same time as he speaks to us in effective calling: Peter says, "You have been *born anew,* not of perishable seed but of imperishable, *through the living and abiding word of God.* . . . That word is the good news which was preached to you" (1 Peter 1:23, 25). And James says, "He chose to *give us birth through the word of truth*" (James 1:18 NIV). As the gospel comes to us, God speaks through it to summon us to himself (effective calling) and to give us new spiritual life (regeneration) so that we are enabled to respond in faith. Effective calling is thus God the Father *speaking powerfully to us,* and regeneration is God the Father and God the Holy Spirit *working powerfully in us,* to make us alive. These two things must have happened simultaneously as Peter was preaching the gospel to the household of Cornelius, for while he was still preaching "the Holy Spirit fell on all who heard the word" (Acts 10:44).

Sometimes the term *irresistible grace*[3] is used in this connection. It refers to the fact that God effectively calls people and also gives them regeneration, and both actions guarantee that we will respond in saving faith. The term *irresistible grace* is subject to misunderstanding, however, since it *seems* to imply that people do not make a voluntary, willing choice in responding to the gospel—a wrong idea, and a wrong understanding of the term *irresistible grace.* The term does preserve something valuable, however, because it indicates that God's work reaches into our hearts to bring about a response that is absolutely certain—even though we respond voluntarily.[4]

[1]When James says that God "brought us forth," he uses language that ordinarily applies to physical birth (being brought forth out of our mothers' wombs, and into the world) and applies it to spiritual birth.

[2]See chapter 33, pp. 692–94, on effective calling.

[3]This is the "I" in the "five points of Calvinism" represented by the acronym TULIP. The other letters stand for Total depravity (see chapter 24, pp. 497–98), Unconditional election (see chapter 32, pp. 676–79), Limited atonement (see chapter 27, pp. 594–603), and Perseverance of the saints (see chapter 40, pp. 788–803) See also p. 596, n. 35.

[4]Some people will object here that God cannot *guarantee* a response that is still willing and voluntary on our part. But this objection simply inserts into the discussion a definition of "voluntary" or "willing" that is not itself supported by Scripture; see discussion in chapter 16, pp. 320–22, 334, 340–47, on God's providence in relation to our voluntary decisions.

## B. The Exact Nature of Regeneration Is Mysterious to Us

Exactly what happens in regeneration is mysterious to us. We know that somehow we who were spiritually dead (Eph. 2:1) have been made alive to God and in a very real sense we have been "born again" (John 3:3, 7; Eph. 2:5; Col. 2:13). But we don't understand how this happens or what exactly God does to us to give us this new spiritual life. Jesus says, "The wind blows where it wills, and you hear the sound of it, but you do not know whence it comes or whither it goes; so it is with every one who is born of the Spirit" (John 3:8).

Scripture views regeneration as something that affects us as whole persons. Of course, our "spirits are alive" to God after regeneration (Rom. 8:10), but that is simply because we as *whole persons* are affected by regeneration. It is not just that our spirits were dead before—*we* were dead to God in trespasses and sins (see Eph. 2:1). And it is not correct to say that the only thing that happens in regeneration is that our spirits are made alive (as some would teach),[5] for *every part of us* is affected by regeneration: "If any one is in Christ, *he is a new creation;* the old has passed away, behold, the new has come" (2 Cor. 5:17).

Because regeneration is a work of God within us in which he gives us new life it is right to conclude that it is an *instantaneous event*. It happens only once. At one moment we are spiritually dead, and then at the next moment we have new spiritual life from God. Nevertheless, we do not always know exactly when this instantaneous change occurs. Especially for children growing up in a Christian home, or for people who attend an evangelical church or Bible study over a period of time and grow gradually in their understanding of the gospel, there may not be a dramatic crisis with a radical change of behavior from "hardened sinner" to "holy saint," but there will be an instantaneous change nonetheless, when God through the Holy Spirit, in an unseen, invisible way, awakens spiritual life within. The change will *become evident* over time in patterns of behavior and desires that are pleasing to God.

In other cases (in fact, probably most cases when adults become Christians) regeneration takes place at a clearly recognizable time at which the person realizes that previously he or she was separated from God and spiritually dead, but immediately afterward there was clearly new spiritual life within. The results can usually be seen at once—a heartfelt trusting in Christ for salvation, an assurance of sins forgiven, a desire to read the Bible and pray (and a sense that these are meaningful spiritual activities), a delight in worship, a desire for Christian fellowship, a sincere desire to be obedient to God's Word in Scripture, and a desire to tell others about Christ. People may say something like this: "I don't know exactly what happened, but before that moment I did not trust in Christ for salvation. I was still wondering and questioning in my mind. But after that moment I realized that I did trust in Christ and he was my Savior. Something happened in my heart."[6] Yet even in these cases we are not quite sure exactly what

---

[5]This view of regeneration usually depends on viewing man as trichotomous or consisting of three parts (body, soul and spirit), a position we discussed in chapter 23 above (pp. 472–83). But if we reject trichotomy and see "soul" and "spirit" as synonyms in Scripture that speak of the immaterial part of our nature, then such an explanation is not persuasive. Even for those who accept trichotomy, the Scriptures that speak of us as a new creation and that say that *we* have been born again (not just our spirits), should be good reason for seeing more in regeneration than merely making our spirits alive.

[6]C. S. Lewis tells the story of his own conversion: "I know very well when, but hardly how, the final

has happened in our hearts. It is just as Jesus said with respect to the wind—we hear its sound and we see the result, but we cannot actually see the wind itself. So it is with the working of the Holy Spirit in our hearts.

## C. In This Sense of "Regeneration," It Comes Before Saving Faith

Using the verses quoted above, we have defined regeneration to be the act of God awakening spiritual life within us, bringing us from spiritual *death* to spiritual *life*. On this definition, it is natural to understand that regeneration comes before saving faith. It is in fact this work of God that gives us the spiritual *ability* to respond to God in faith. However, when we say that it comes "before" saving faith, it is important to remember that they usually come so close together that it will ordinarily seem to us that they are happening at the same time. As God addresses the effective call of the gospel to us, he regenerates us and we respond in faith and repentance to this call. So *from our perspective* it is hard to tell any difference in time, especially because regeneration is a spiritual work that we cannot perceive with our eyes or even understand with our minds.

Yet there are several passages that tell us that this secret, hidden work of God in our spirits does in fact come before we respond to God in saving faith (though often it may be only seconds before we respond). When talking about regeneration with Nicodemus, Jesus said, "Unless one is born of water and the Spirit, *he cannot enter the kingdom of God*" (John 3:5). Now we enter the kingdom of God when we become Christians at conversion. But Jesus says that we have to be born "of the Spirit" before we can do that.[7] Our inability to come to Christ on our own, without an initial work of God within us, is also emphasized when Jesus says, "No one can come to me unless the Father who sent me draws him" (John

---

step was taken. I was driven to Whipsnade one sunny morning. When we set out I did not believe that Jesus Christ is the Son of God, and when we reached the zoo I did. Yet I had not exactly spent the journey in thought. Nor in great emotion" (*Surprised by Joy* [New York: Harcourt, Brace and World, 1955], p. 237).

[7]When Jesus talks about being "born of water" here, the most likely interpretation of this is that he is referring to *spiritual cleansing from sin,* which Ezekiel prophesied when he said, "I will sprinkle clean water upon you, and you shall be clean from all your uncleannesses, and from all your idols I will cleanse you. A new heart I will give you, and a new spirit I will put within you" (Ezek. 36:25–26). Here the water symbolizes spiritual cleansing from sin, just as the new heart and new spirit speak of the new spiritual life that God will give. Ezekiel is prophesying that God will give an internal cleansing from the pollution of sin in the heart at the same time as he awakens new spiritual life within his people. The fact that these two ideas are connected so closely in this well-known prophecy from Ezekiel, and the fact that Jesus assumes that Nicodemus should have understood this truth ("Are you a teacher of Israel, and yet you do not understand this?" [John 3:10]), together with the fact that throughout the conversation Jesus is talking about intensely spiritual concerns, all suggest that this is the most likely understanding of the passage. Another suggestion has been that "born of water" refers to physical birth and the "water" (or amniotic fluid) that accompanies it, but it would hardly be necessary for Jesus to specify that one has to be born in this way when he is talking about spiritual birth, and it is questionable whether first-century Jews would have understood the phrase in this way either. Another interpretation is that Jesus is referring to the water of baptism here, but baptism or any other similar ceremony is not in view in this passage (and it would have been anachronistic for Jesus to speak of Christian baptism here, since that did not begin until Pentecost); moreover, this would make Jesus teach that a physical act of baptism is necessary for salvation, something that would contradict the New Testament emphasis on salvation by faith alone as necessary for salvation, and something which, if it were true, we would certainly expect to find taught much more explicitly in the other New Testament passages that clearly deal with baptism (see chapter 49 on baptism).

6:44), and "No one can come to me unless it is granted him by the Father" (John 6:65). This inward act of regeneration is described beautifully when Luke says of Lydia, *"The Lord opened her heart* to give heed to what was said by Paul" (Acts 16:14). First the Lord opened her heart, then she was able to give heed to Paul's preaching and to respond in faith.

By contrast, Paul tells us, "The man without the Spirit (literally, the "natural man") does not accept the things that come from the Spirit of God, for they are foolishness to him, and he cannot understand them, because they are spiritually discerned" (1 Cor. 2:14 NIV). He also says of people apart from Christ, "no one understands, No one seeks for God" (Rom. 3:11).

The solution to this spiritual deadness and inability to respond only comes when God gives us new life within. "But God, who is rich in mercy, out of the great love with which he loved us, even *when we were dead through our trespasses,* made us alive together with Christ" (Eph. 2:4–5). Paul also says, *"When you were dead in your sins* and in the uncircumcision of your sinful nature, *God made you alive with Christ"* (Col. 2:13 NIV).[8]

The idea that regeneration comes before saving faith is not always understood by evangelicals today. Sometimes people will even say something like, "If you believe in Christ as your Savior, then (after you believe) you will be born again." But Scripture itself never says anything like that. This new birth is viewed by Scripture as something that God does within us in order to enable us to believe.

The reason that evangelicals often think that regeneration comes after saving faith is that they *see the results* (love for God and his Word, and turning from sin) *after* people come to faith, and they think that regeneration must therefore have come after saving faith. Yet here we must decide on the basis of what Scripture tells us, because regeneration itself is not something we see or know about directly: "The wind blows where it wills, and you hear the sound of it, but you do not know whence it comes or whither it goes; so it is with every one who is born of the Spirit" (John 3:8).

Because Christians often tend to focus on the *results* of regeneration, rather than the hidden spiritual act of God itself, some evangelical statements of faith have contained wording that suggests that regeneration comes after saving faith. So, for example, the statement of faith of the Evangelical Free Church of America (which has been adapted by a number of other evangelical organizations) says,

We believe that the true Church is composed of all such persons who *through saving faith* in Jesus Christ *have been regenerated* by the Holy Spirit and are united together in the body of Christ of which He is the Head. (paragraph 8)

[8]The RSV translates Col. 2:13 with a relative clause: "And you, *who were dead* in trespasses and the uncircumcision of your flesh, God made alive together with him," but the Greek text has no relative pronoun (*hous*), which Paul could easily have used, but rather has a participial phrase with the present participle *ontas,* "being," giving a nuance of continuing activity that occurred *at the same time* that the action of the main verb ("made alive") took place. Thus, the NIV expresses the appropriate sense: at the time when we were continuing in the state of being dead in our sins, God made us alive. No matter whether we translate the participle as concessive, causative, or expressing attendant circumstances, or with any other sense possible to the participle, this temporal nuance of time simultaneous with the main verb would still be present as well. Yet the NIV, in translating it as an explicitly temporal participle ("*when* you were dead") seems to have given the best rendering of the intended sense of the verse.

Here the word "regeneration" apparently means the *outward evidence of regeneration* that is seen in a changed life, evidence that certainly does come after saving faith. Thus "being born again" is thought of not in terms of the initial impartation of new life, but in terms of the *total life change that results* from that impartation. If the term "regeneration" is understood in this way, then it would be true that regeneration comes after saving faith.

Nevertheless, if we are to use language that closely conforms to the actual wording of Scripture, it would be better to restrict the word "regeneration" to the instantaneous, *initial* work of God in which he imparts spiritual life to us. Then we can emphasize that we do not see regeneration itself but only the results of it in our lives, and that faith in Christ for salvation is the first result that we see. In fact, we can never know that we have been regenerated until we come to faith in Christ, for that is the outward evidence of this hidden, inward work of God. Once we do come to saving faith in Christ, we know that we have been born again.

By way of application, we should realize that the explanation of the gospel message in Scripture does not take the form of a command, "Be born again and you will be saved," but rather, "Believe in Jesus Christ and you will be saved."[9] This is the consistent pattern in the preaching of the gospel throughout the book of Acts, and also in the descriptions of the gospel given in the Epistles.

## D. Genuine Regeneration Must Bring Results in Life

In an earlier section we saw a beautiful example of the first result of regeneration in a person's life, when Paul spoke the gospel message to Lydia and "the Lord opened her heart to give heed to what was said by Paul" (Acts 16:14; cf. John 6:44, 65; 1 Peter 1:3). Similarly, John says, "Everyone who believes that Jesus is the Christ *is born of God*" (1 John 5:1 NIV).[10] But there are also other results of regeneration, many of which are specified in John's first epistle. For example, John says, "No one who is born of God will continue to sin, because God's seed remains in him; he *cannot go on sinning,* because he has been born of God" (1 John 3:9 NIV). Here John explains that a person who is born again has that spiritual "seed" (that life-generating and growing power) within him, and that this keeps the person living a life free of continual sin. This does not of course mean that the person will have a perfect life, but only that the pattern of life will not be one of continuing indulgence in sin. When people are asked to characterize a regenerated person's life, the adjective that comes to mind should not be "sinner," but rather something like "obedient to Christ" or "obedient to Scripture." We should notice that John says this is true of everyone who is truly born again: "*No*

---

[9]It is true that Jesus tells Nicodemus that he needs to be born again (John 3:7: "Do not marvel that I said to you, 'You must be born anew' "), but this is not a command to Nicodemus to do something that no one can ever do (that is, give himself new spiritual life). It is an indicative sentence, not an imperative sentence. It is a statement of fact designed to point out to Nicodemus his total spiritual need and lack of ability on his own to enter the kingdom of God. A little later, when Jesus begins to speak about the response that is expected from Nicodemus, he speaks about the personal response of faith as the thing necessary: "So must the Son of man be lifted up, that *whoever believes in him* may have eternal life" (John 3:14–15).

[10]The perfect participle translated here "is born" could more explicitly be translated "has been born and continues in the new life that resulted from that event."

*one* who is born of God will continue to sin." Another way of looking at this is to say that "every one who does what is right has been born of him" (1 John 2:29).

A genuine, Christlike *love* will be one specific result in life: "Everyone who loves has been born of God and knows God" (1 John 4:7 NIV). Another effect of the new birth is *overcoming the world:* "And his commands are not burdensome, for everyone born of God has overcome the world" (1 John 5:3–4 NIV). Here John explains that regeneration gives the ability to overcome the pressures and temptations of the world that would otherwise keep us from obeying God's commandments and following his paths. John says that we will overcome these pressures and therefore it will not be "burdensome" to obey God's commands but, he implies, it will rather be joyful. He goes on to explain that the process through which we gain victory over the world is continuing in faith: "This is the victory that has overcome the world, even our faith" (1 John 5:4 NIV).

Finally, John notes that another result of regeneration is *protection from Satan* himself: "We know that anyone born of God does not continue to sin; the one who was born of God [that is, Jesus] keeps him safe, *and the evil one cannot harm him*" (1 John 5:18 NIV). Though there may be attacks from Satan, John reassures his readers that "the one who is in you is greater than the one who is in the world" (1 John 4:4 NIV), and this greater power of the Holy Spirit within us keeps us safe from ultimate spiritual harm by the evil one.

We should realize that John emphasizes these as *necessary* results in the lives of those who are born again. If there is genuine regeneration in a person's life, he or she *will* believe that Jesus is the Christ, and *will* refrain from a life pattern of continual sin, and *will* love his brother, and *will* overcome the temptations of the world, and *will* be kept safe from ultimate harm by the evil one. These passages show that it is impossible for a person to be regenerated and not become truly converted.[11]

Other results of regeneration are listed by Paul where he speaks of the *"fruit of the Spirit,"* that is, the result in life that is produced by the power of the Holy Spirit working within every believer: "But the fruit of the Spirit is love, joy, peace, patience, kindness, goodness, faithfulness, gentleness, self-control" (Gal. 5:22–23). If there is true regeneration then these elements of the fruit of the Spirit will be more and more evident in that person's life. But by contrast, those who are unbelievers, including those who are pretending to be believers but are not, will clearly lack of these character traits in their lives. Jesus told his disciples:

> Beware of false prophets, who come to you in sheep's clothing but inwardly are ravenous wolves. *You will know them by their fruits.* Are grapes gathered from thorns, or figs from thistles? So, every sound tree bears good fruit, but the bad tree bears evil fruit. A sound tree cannot bear evil fruit, nor can a bad tree bear good fruit. Every tree that does not bear good fruit is cut down and thrown into the fire. Thus you will know them by their fruits. (Matt. 7:15–20)

Neither Jesus nor Paul nor John point to activity in the church or miracles as evidence of regeneration. They rather point to character traits in life. In fact, immediately after the verses quoted above Jesus warns that on the day of

---

[11]Since we indicated above that a person is first regenerated, and then subsequently comes to saving faith, there will be a brief time in which someone is regenerated and the results (faith, love, etc.) are not yet seen. But John is saying that the results *will* follow; they are inevitable once someone is born again.

judgment many will say to him, "Lord, Lord, did we not prophesy in your name, and cast out demons in your name, and do many mighty works in your name?" But he will declare to them, "I *never knew you;* depart from me, you evildoers" (Matt. 7:22–23). Prophecy, exorcism, and many miracles and mighty works in Jesus' name (to say nothing of other kinds of intensive church activity in the strength of the flesh over perhaps decades of a person's life) do not provide convincing evidence that a person is truly born again. Apparently all these can be produced in the natural man or woman's own strength, or even with the help of the evil one. But genuine love for God and his people, heartfelt obedience to his commands, and the Christlike character traits that Paul calls the fruit of the Spirit, demonstrated consistently over a period of time in a person's life, simply *cannot* be produced by Satan or by the natural man or woman working in his or her own strength. These can only come about by the Spirit of God working within and giving us new life.

## QUESTIONS FOR PERSONAL APPLICATION

1. Have you been born again? Is there evidence of the new birth in your life? Do you remember a specific time when regeneration occurred in your life? Can you describe how you knew that something had happened?

2. If you (or friends who come to you) are not sure whether you have been born again, what would Scripture encourage you to do in order to gain greater assurance (or to be truly born again for the first time)? (Note: further discussion of repentance and saving faith is given in the next chapter.)

3. Have you thought before that regeneration is prior to saving faith? Are you convinced of it now, or is there still some question in your mind?

4. What do you think about the fact that your regeneration was totally a work of God, and that you contributed nothing to it? How does it make you feel toward yourself? How does it make you feel toward God? By way of analogy, how do you feel about the fact that when you were born physically you had no choice in the matter?

5. Are there areas where the results of regeneration are not very clearly seen in your own life? Do you think it is possible for a person to be regenerated and then stagnate spiritually so that there is little or no growth? What circumstances might a person live in that would lead to such spiritual stagnation and lack of growth (if that is possible), even though the person was truly born again? To what degree does the kind of church one attends, the teaching one receives, the kind of Christian fellowship one has, and the regularity of one's personal time of Bible reading and prayer, affect one's own spiritual life and growth?

6. If regeneration is entirely a work of God and human beings can do nothing to bring it about, then what good does it do to preach the gospel to people at all? Is it somewhat absurd or even cruel to preach the gospel and ask for a response from people who cannot respond because they are spiritually dead? How do you resolve this question?

## SPECIAL TERMS

born again
born of the Spirit
born of water

irresistible grace
regeneration

## BIBLIOGRAPHY

(For an explanation of this bibliography see the note on the bibliography to chapter 1, p. 38. Complete bibliographical data may be found on pp. 1223–29.)

### Sections in Evangelical Systematic Theologies

1. Anglican (Episcopalian)
   - 1882–92    Litton, 320–28
2. Arminian (Wesleyan or Methodist)
   - 1847    Finney, 282–364
   - 1892–94    Miley, 2:327–36
   - 1960    Purkiser, 292–97
3. Baptist
   - 1767    Gill, 2:107–21
   - 1887    Boyce, 373–82
   - 1907    Strong, 809–29
   - 1917    Mullins, 385–89
   - 1983–85    Erickson, 932–33, 942–46
4. Dispensational
   - 1947    Chafer, 6:104–21
   - 1949    Thiessen, 271–76
   - 1986    Ryrie, 325–26
5. Lutheran
   - 1917–24    Pieper, 2:498–501
   - 1934    Mueller, 363–64
6. Reformed (or Presbyterian)
   - 1559    Calvin, 1:592–621 (3.3)
   - 1724–58    Edwards, 543–65, 849–55
   - 1861    Heppe, 518–27
   - 1871–73    Hodge, 2:682–732; 3:3–40
   - 1878    Dabney, 579–99
   - 1887–1921    Warfield, *BTS*, 351–74; *SSW*, 2:321–24
   - 1889    Shedd, 2b, 490–528
   - 1937–66    Murray, *CW*, 2:167–201; *RAA*, 95–105
   - 1938    Berkhof, 465–79
   - 1962    Buswell, 2:168–75

7. Renewal (or charismatic/Pentecostal)
     1988–92     Williams, 2:35–59

## Sections in Representative Roman Catholic Systematic Theologies

1. Roman Catholic: Traditional
          1955     Ott, 219–49
2. Roman Catholic: Post-Vatican II
          1980     McBrien, 2:991–1005

### Other Works

Hoekema, Anthony A. "Regeneration." In *Saved by Grace*. Grand Rapids: Eerdmans, and Exeter: Paternoster, 1989, pp. 93–112.
Kevan, E. F. *Salvation*. Phillipsburg, N.J.: Presbyterian and Reformed, 1973.
Packer, J. I. "Regeneration." In *EDT*, pp. 924–26.
Toon, Peter. *Born Again: A Biblical and Theological Study of Regeneration*. Grand Rapids: Baker, 1987.

### SCRIPTURE MEMORY PASSAGE

**John 3:5–8:** *Jesus answered, "Truly, truly, I say to you, unless one is born of water and the Spirit, he cannot enter the kingdom of God. That which is born of the flesh is flesh, and that which is born of the Spirit is spirit. Do not marvel that I said to you, 'You must be born anew.' The wind blows where it wills, and you hear the sound of it, but you do not know whence it comes or whither it goes; so it is with every one who is born of the Spirit."*

### HYMN

#### "I Sought the Lord, and Afterward I Knew"

This hymn beautifully expresses thanks to God for the fact that, though we did not know it, he sought us, worked in our hearts in a mysterious way, and enabled us to believe, before we came to trust in him.

> I sought the Lord, and afterward I knew
> He moved my soul to seek him, seeking me;
> It was not I that found, O Savior true,
> No, I was found of thee.
>
> Thou didst reach forth thy hand and mine enfold;
> I walked and sank not on the storm–vexed sea,
> 'Twas not so much that I on thee took hold,
> As thou, dear Lord, on me.
>
> I find, I walk, I love, but, O the whole
> Of love is but my answer, Lord, to thee;
> For thou wert long beforehand with my soul,
> Always thou lovedst me.

ANON., C. 1904

# Chapter 35

# Conversion
# (Faith and Repentance)

*What is true repentance? What is saving faith? Can people accept Jesus as Savior and not as Lord?*

The last two chapters have explained how God himself (through the human preaching of the Word) issues the gospel call to us and, by the work of the Holy Spirit, regenerates us, imparting new spiritual life within. In this chapter we examine our response to the gospel call. We may define conversion as follows: *Conversion is our willing response to the gospel call, in which we sincerely repent of sins and place our trust in Christ for salvation.*

The word *conversion* itself means "turning"—here it represents a spiritual turn, a turning *from* sin *to* Christ. The turning from sin is called *repentance*, and the turning to Christ is called *faith*. We can look at each of these elements of conversion, and in one sense it does not matter which one we discuss first, for neither one can occur without the other, and they must occur together when true conversion takes place. For the purposes of this chapter, we shall examine saving faith first, and then repentance.

## A. True Saving Faith Includes Knowledge, Approval, and Personal Trust

**1. Knowledge Alone Is Not Enough.** Personal saving faith, in the way Scripture understands it, involves more than mere knowledge. Of course *it is necessary that we have some knowledge of who Christ is and what he has done*, for "how are they to believe in him of whom they have never heard?" (Rom. 10:14). But knowledge about the *facts* of Jesus' life, death, and resurrection for us is not enough, for people can know facts but rebel against them or dislike them. For example, Paul tells us that many people know God's laws but dislike them: "Though they *know* God's decree that those who do such things deserve to die, they not only do them but approve those who practice them" (Rom. 1:32). Even the demons know who God is and know the facts about Jesus' life and saving works, for James says, "You believe that God is one; you do well. Even the demons believe—and shudder" (James 2:19). But that knowledge certainly does not mean that the demons are saved.

**2. Knowledge and Approval Are Not Enough.** Moreover, merely knowing the facts and *approving* of them or *agreeing* that they are true is not enough.

709

Nicodemus knew that Jesus had come from God, for he said, "Rabbi, we know that you are a teacher come from God; for no one can do these signs that you do, unless God is with him" (John 3:2). Nicodemus had evaluated the facts of the situation, including Jesus' teaching and his remarkable miracles, and had drawn a correct conclusion from those facts: Jesus was a teacher come from God. But this alone did not mean that Nicodemus had saving faith, for he still had to put his trust in Christ for salvation; he still had to "believe in him." King Agrippa provides another example of knowledge and approval without saving faith. Paul realized that King Agrippa knew and apparently viewed with approval the Jewish Scriptures (what we now call the Old Testament). When Paul was on trial before Agrippa, he said, "King Agrippa, do you believe the prophets? I know that *you believe*" (Acts 26:27). Yet Agrippa did not have saving faith, for he said to Paul, "In a short time you think to make me a Christian!" (Acts 26:28).

**3. I Must Decide to Depend on Jesus to Save Me Personally.** In addition to knowledge of the facts of the gospel and approval of those facts, in order to be saved, I must decide to depend on Jesus to save me. In doing this I move from being an interested observer of the facts of salvation and the teachings of the Bible to being someone who enters into a new relationship with Jesus Christ as a living person. We may therefore define saving faith in the following way: *Saving faith is trust in Jesus Christ as a living person for forgiveness of sins and for eternal life with God.*

This definition emphasizes that saving faith is not just a belief in facts but *personal trust in Jesus* to save *me*. As we will explain in the following chapters, much more is involved in salvation than simply forgiveness of sins and eternal life, but someone who initially comes to Christ seldom realizes the extent of the blessings of salvation that will come. Moreover, we may rightly summarize the two major concerns of a person who trusts in Christ as "forgiveness of sins" and "eternal life with God." Of course, eternal life with God involves such matters as a declaration of righteousness before God (part of justification, as explained in the next chapter), adoption, sanctification, and glorification, but these things may be understood in detail later. The main thing that concerns an unbeliever who comes to Christ is the fact that sin has separated him or her from the fellowship with God for which we were made. The unbeliever comes to Christ seeking to have sin and guilt removed and to enter into a genuine relationship with God that will last forever.

The definition emphasizes *personal trust* in Christ, not just belief in facts about Christ. Because saving faith in Scripture involves this personal trust, the word "trust" is a better word to use in contemporary culture than the word "faith" or "belief." The reason is that we can "believe" something to be true with no personal commitment or dependence involved in it. I can *believe* that Canberra is the capital of Australia, or that 7 times 6 is 42, but have no personal commitment or dependence on anyone when I simply believe those facts. The word *faith*, on the other hand, is sometimes used today to refer to an almost irrational commitment to something in spite of strong evidence to the contrary, a sort of irrational decision to believe something that we are quite sure is *not* true! (If your favorite football team continues to lose games, someone might encourage you to "have faith" even though all the facts point the opposite direction.) In these two popular senses, the word "belief" and the word "faith" have a meaning contrary to the biblical sense.[1]

The word *trust* is closer to the biblical idea, since we are familiar with trusting persons in everyday life. The more we come to know a person, and the more we see in that person a pattern of life that warrants trust, the more we find ourselves able to place trust in that person to do what he or she promises, or to act in ways that we can rely on. This fuller sense of personal trust is indicated in several passages of Scripture in which initial saving faith is spoken of in very personal terms, often using analogies drawn from personal relationships. John says, "To all who *received him,* who believed in his name, he gave power to become children of God" (John 1:12). Much as we would receive a guest into our homes, John speaks of receiving Christ.

John 3:16 tells us that "whoever *believes in him* should not perish but have eternal life." Here John uses a surprising phrase when he does not simply say, "whoever *believes him*" (that is, believes that what he says is true and able to be trusted), but rather, "whoever *believes in him.*" The Greek phrase *pisteuō eis auton* could also be translated "believe *into* him" with the sense of trust or confidence that goes *into* and rests *in* Jesus as a person. Leon Morris can say, "Faith, for John, is an activity which takes men right out of themselves and makes them one with Christ." He understands the Greek phrase *pisteuō eis* to be a significant indication that New Testament faith is not just intellectual assent but includes a "moral element of personal trust."[2] Such an expression was rare or perhaps nonexistent in the secular Greek found outside the New Testament, but it was well suited to express the personal trust in Christ that is involved in saving faith.

Jesus speaks of "coming to him" in several places. He says, "All that the Father gives me will *come to me;* and him who comes to me I will not cast out" (John 6:37). He also says, "If any one thirst, let him *come to me* and drink" (John 7:37). In a similar way, he says, "*Come to me,* all who labor and are heavy laden, and I will give you rest. Take my yoke upon you, and learn from me; for I am gentle and lowly in heart, and you will find rest for your souls. For my yoke is easy, and my burden is light" (Matt. 11:28–30). In these passages we have the idea of coming to Christ and asking for acceptance, for living water to drink, and for rest and instruction. All of these give an intensely personal picture of what is involved in saving faith. The author of Hebrews also asks us to think of Jesus as now alive in heaven, ready to receive us: "He is able for all time to save those who draw near to God through him, since *he always lives* to make intercession for them" (Heb. 7:25). Jesus is pictured here (as many times in the New Testament) as one who is now alive in heaven, always able to help those who come to him.

Reformed theologian J. I. Packer quotes the following paragraphs from the

---

[1]Of course, the words *believe/belief* and *faith* occur frequently in the Bible, and we should not completely give up using them in a proper biblical sense just because our culture sometimes gives them an incorrect sense. My point is simply that when explaining the gospel to an unbeliever, the word *trust* seems to be most likely to convey the biblical sense today.

[2]Leon Morris, *The Gospel According to John,* p. 336, with reference to the longer discussion by C. H. Dodd, *The Interpretation of the Fourth Gospel* (Cambridge: Cambridge University Press, 1953), pp. 179–86, and a note that Dodd finds no parallel to the use of *pisteuō* followed by the preposition *eis,* to refer to trust in a person, in secular Greek. The expression rather is a literal translation of the expression "to believe in" from the Hebrew Old Testament.

British Puritan writer John Owen, describing the invitation of Christ to respond in personal faith:

> This is somewhat of the word which he now speaks unto you: Why will ye die? why will ye perish? why will ye not have compassion on your own souls? Can your hearts endure, or can your hands be strong, in the day of wrath that is approaching? . . . Look unto me, and be saved; come unto me, and I will ease you of all sins, sorrows, fears, burdens, and give rest to your souls. Come, I entreat you; lay aside all procrastinations, all delays; put me off no more; eternity lies at the door . . . do not so hate me as that you will rather perish than accept of deliverance by me.
>
> These and the like things doth the Lord Christ continually declare, proclaim, plead and urge upon the souls of sinners. . . . He doth it in the preaching of the word, as if he were present with you, stood amongst you, and spake personally to every one of you. . . . He hath appointed the ministers of the gospel to appear before you, and to deal with you in his stead, avowing as his own the invitations which are given you in his name. (2 Cor. 5:19–20)[3]

With this understanding of true New Testament faith, we may now appreciate that when a person comes to trust in Christ, all three elements must be present. There must be some basic knowledge or *understanding* of the facts of the gospel. There must also be *approval* of, or agreement with, these facts. Such agreement includes a conviction that the facts spoken of the gospel are true, especially the fact that I am a sinner in need of salvation and that Christ alone has paid the penalty for my sin and offers salvation to me. It also includes an awareness that I need to trust in Christ for salvation and that he is the only way to God, and the only means provided for my salvation. This approval of the facts of the gospel will also involve a desire to be saved through Christ. But all this still does not add up to true saving faith. That comes only when I make a decision of my will to depend on, or put my *trust* in, Christ as *my* Savior. This personal decision to place my trust in Christ is something done with my heart, the central faculty of my entire being that makes commitments for me as a whole person.

**4. Faith Should Increase as Our Knowledge Increases.** Contrary to the current secular understanding of "faith," true New Testament faith is not something that is made stronger by ignorance or by believing against the evidence. Rather, saving faith is consistent with knowledge and true understanding of facts. Paul says, "Faith comes from hearing, and hearing by the word of Christ" (Rom. 10:17 NASB). When people have true information about Christ, they are better able to put their trust in him. Moreover, the more we know about him and about the character of God that is completely revealed in him, the more fully we are able to put our trust in him. Thus faith is not weakened by knowledge but should increase with more true knowledge.

In the case of saving faith in Christ, our knowledge of him comes by believing a reliable testimony about him. Here, the reliable testimony that we believe is the words of Scripture. Since they are God's very words, they are completely reliable, and we gain true knowledge of Christ through them. This is why "Faith comes from hearing, and hearing by the word of Christ" (Rom. 10:17 NASB). In everyday life, we come to believe many things when we hear testimony from a person we

---

[3]J. I. Packer, *Evangelism and the Sovereignty of God*, p. 104.

consider to be reliable or trustworthy. This kind of decision is even more justified here, when the actual words of God provide that testimony and we believe it.

## B. Faith and Repentance Must Come Together

We may define repentance as follows: *Repentance is a heartfelt sorrow for sin, a renouncing of it, and a sincere commitment to forsake it and walk in obedience to Christ.*

This definition indicates that repentance is something that can occur at a specific point in time, and is not equivalent to a demonstration of change in a person's pattern of life. Repentance, like faith, is an intellectual *understanding* (that sin is wrong), an emotional *approval* of the teachings of Scripture regarding sin (a sorrow for sin and a hatred of it), and a *personal decision* to turn from it (a renouncing of sin and a decision of the will to forsake it and lead a life of obedience to Christ instead). We cannot say that someone has to actually *live* that changed life over a period of time before repentance can be genuine, or else repentance would be turned into a kind of obedience that we could *do* to merit salvation for ourselves. Of course, genuine repentance will result in a changed life. In fact, a truly repentant person will begin at once to live a changed life, and we can call that changed life the fruit of repentance. But we should never attempt to require that there be a period of time in which a person actually lives a changed life before we give assurance of forgiveness. Repentance is something that occurs in the heart and involves the whole person in a decision to turn from sin.

It is important to realize that mere sorrow for one's actions, or even deep remorse over one's actions, does not constitute genuine repentance unless it is accompanied by a sincere decision to forsake sin that is being committed against God. Paul preached about "repentance *to God* and of faith in our Lord Jesus Christ" (Acts 20:21). He says that he rejoiced over the Corinthians, "not because you were grieved, but because you were *grieved into repenting. . . . For godly grief produces a repentance that leads to salvation and brings no regret, but worldly grief produces death*" (2 Cor. 7:9–10). A worldly sort of grief may involve great sorrow for one's actions and probably also fear of punishment but no genuine renouncing of sin or commitment to forsake it in one's life. Hebrews 12:17 tells us that Esau wept over the consequences of his actions but did not truly repent. Moreover, as 2 Corinthians 7:9–10 indicates, even true godly grief is just one factor that leads to genuine repentance, but such grief is not itself the sincere decision of the heart in the presence of God that makes genuine repentance.

Scripture puts repentance and faith together as different aspects of the one act of coming to Christ for salvation. It is not that a person first turns from sin and next trusts in Christ, or first trusts in Christ and then turns from sin, but rather that both occur at the same time. When we turn to Christ *for* salvation from our sins, we are simultaneously turning *away* from the sins that we are asking Christ to save us from. If that were not true our turning to Christ for salvation from sin could hardly be a genuine turning to him or trusting in him.

The fact that repentance and faith are simply two different sides of the same coin, or two different aspects of the one event of conversion, may be seen in figure 35.1.

In this diagram, the person who genuinely turns to Christ for salvation must at the same time release the sin to which he or she has been clinging and turn away from that sin in order to turn to Christ. Thus, neither repentance nor faith comes first; they must come together. John Murray speaks of "penitent faith" and "believing repentance."[4]

CONVERSION IS A SINGLE ACTION OF TURNING FROM SIN IN
REPENTANCE AND TURNING TO CHRIST IN FAITH
*Figure 35.1*

Therefore, it is clearly contrary to the New Testament evidence to speak about the possibility of having true saving faith without having any repentance for sin. It is also contrary to the New Testament to speak about the possibility of someone accepting Christ "as Savior" but not "as Lord," if that means simply depending on him for salvation but not committing oneself to forsake sin and to be obedient to Christ from that point on.

Some prominent voices within evangelicalism have differed with this point, arguing that a gospel presentation that requires *repentance* as well as faith is really preaching salvation by works. They argue that the view advocated in this chapter, that repentance and faith must go together, is a false gospel of "lordship salvation." They would say that saving faith *only* involves trusting Christ as Savior, and that submitting to him as Lord is an optional later step that is unnecessary for salvation. For many who teach this view, saving faith only requires an intellectual agreement with the facts of the gospel.[5]

---

[4]John Murray, *Redemption Accomplished and Applied*, p. 113.

[5]The source of this view of the gospel is apparently Lewis Sperry Chafer, especially in his *Systematic Theology*, vol. 3, where he says, "The New Testament does not impose repentance upon the unsaved as a condition of salvation" (p. 376). Chafer recognizes that many verses call upon people to repent, but he simply defines repentance away as a "change of mind" that does not include sorrow for sin or turning from sin (pp. 372–75). Thus he can say, "Repentance, which is a change of mind, is included in believing" (p. 375). He argues that "the added demand that the unsaved must dedicate themselves to do God's will in their daily life, as well as to believe upon Christ" is a "confusing intrusion into the doctrine that salvation is conditioned alone upon believing" (p. 384). Chafer provides a basis for the view that people must first accept Christ as Savior, and later as Lord, when he says that the preacher has the obligation "of preaching the Lordship of Christ to Christians exclusively, and the Saviorhood of Christ to those who are unsaved" (p. 387). The most vocal contemporary proponent of this view has been Dallas Seminary professor Zane C. Hodges: see his book *The Gospel Under Siege* (Dallas: Redención Viva, 1981).

When Jesus invites sinners, "Come to me, all who labor and are heavy laden, and I will give you rest," he immediately adds, *"Take my yoke upon you,* and *learn from me"* (Matt. 11:28-29). To come to him includes taking his yoke upon us, being subject to his direction and guidance, learning from him and being obedient to him. If we are unwilling to make such a commitment, then we have not truly placed our trust in him.

When Scripture speaks of trusting in God or in Christ, it frequently connects such trust with genuine repentance. For example, Isaiah gives an eloquent testimony that is typical of the message of many of the Old Testament prophets:

> Seek the LORD while he may be found,
> call upon him while he is near;
> let the wicked *forsake his way,*
> and the unrighteous man his thoughts;
> let him *return to the LORD,* that he may have mercy on him,
> and to our God, for he will abundantly pardon. (Isa. 55:6-7)

Here both repentance from sin and coming to God for pardon are mentioned. In the New Testament, Paul summarizes his gospel ministry as one of "testifying both to Jews and to Greeks of *repentance* to God and of *faith* in our Lord Jesus Christ" (Acts 20:21). The author of Hebrews includes as the first two elements in a list of elementary doctrines *"repentance* from dead works" and *"faith* toward God" (Heb. 6:1).

Of course sometimes faith alone is named as the thing necessary for coming to Christ for salvation (see John 3:16; Acts 16:31; Rom. 10:9; Eph. 2:8-9, et al.). These are familiar passages and we emphasize them often when explaining the

---

But not all at Dallas Seminary or all within Dispensational theology would hold this view. A controversy over this point erupted in American evangelicalism when John MacArthur, himself a Dispensationalist, published *The Gospel According to Jesus* (Grand Rapids: Zondervan, 1988, rev. ed. 1994). This excellent book (with enthusiastic forewords by J. I. Packer and James Montgomery Boice) strongly criticized the views of writers like Chafer and Hodges on evangelism and the nature of saving faith. MacArthur argued very convincingly from many New Testament passages that one cannot truly accept Christ as Savior without also accepting him as Lord, or, in other words, that there can be no true saving faith without genuine repentance as well. He said that any other view preaches a cheap gospel that offers unconverted people false security, telling them they are saved simply because they agreed that the facts of the gospel were true or prayed a prayer, but they had no true repentance and no real change of life. MacArthur argued that such unbiblical evangelism has never been the teaching of the church through history, and that the weakened gospel heard so often today has resulted in a whole generation of professing Christians whose lives are no different from the surrounding culture and who are really not saved at all. Hodges quickly responded to MacArthur with another book, *Absolutely Free! A Biblical Reply to Lordship Salvation* (Dallas: Redención Viva, and Grand Rapids: Zondervan, 1989).

As I have argued in this chapter, it seems to me clear that MacArthur is certainly right to maintain that true saving faith in New Testament terms is more than mere intellectual assent to facts; it must include a heartfelt coming to Christ in personal dependence on him for salvation, combined with a heartfelt repentance from sin. It is misleading to brand this teaching "Lordship salvation" as if it were some new doctrine, or as if there were any other kind of salvation—MacArthur is teaching what has been the historic position of Christian orthodoxy on this matter, as he demonstrates in an appendix to his book (pp. 221-37). This position is not salvation by works, but simply states the gospel of *free* grace, and salvation by grace through faith in all its biblical fullness. The change of life that will result from genuine conversion does not save us, but it will certainly result if our faith is genuine, for "faith by itself, if it has no works, is dead" (James 2:17).

The Sandemanians were a small group of evangelical churches who taught a view similar to Zane Hodges in England and the United States from 1725 until they died out around 1900; see R. E. D. Clark, "Sandemanians," in *NIDCC,* p. 877.

gospel to others. But what we do not often realize is the fact that there are many other passages where *only repentance* is named, for it is simply assumed that true repentance will also involve faith in Christ for forgiveness of sins. The New Testament authors understood so well that genuine repentance and genuine faith had to go together that they often simply mentioned repentance alone with the understanding that faith would also be included, because turning *from* sins in a genuine way is impossible apart from a genuine turning *to* God. Therefore, just before Jesus ascended into heaven, he told his disciples, "Thus it is written, that the Christ should suffer and on the third day rise from the dead, and that *repentance* and forgiveness of sins should be preached in his name to all nations" (Luke 24:46–47). Saving faith is implied in the phrase "forgiveness of sins," but it is not explicitly named.

The preaching recorded in the book of Acts shows the same pattern. After Peter's sermon at Pentecost, the crowd asked, "Brethren, what shall we do?" Peter replied, "*Repent,* and be baptized every one of you in the name of Jesus Christ for the forgiveness of your sins" (Acts 2:37–38).[6] In his second sermon Peter spoke to his hearers in a similar way, saying, "*Repent* therefore, and turn again, that your sins may be blotted out, that times of refreshing may come from the presence of the Lord" (Acts 3:19). Later, when the apostles were on trial before the Sanhedrin, Peter spoke of Christ, saying, "God exalted him at his right hand as Leader and Savior, to give *repentance* to Israel and forgiveness of sins" (Acts 5:31). And when Paul was preaching on the Areopagus in Athens to an assembly of Greek philosophers, he said, "The times of ignorance God overlooked, but now *he commands all men everywhere to repent*" (Acts 17:30). He also says in his epistles, "Do you not know that God's kindness is meant to lead you to repentance?" (Rom. 2:4), and he speaks of "a *repentance* that leads to salvation" (2 Cor. 7:10).

We also see that when Jesus encounters people personally he requires them to turn from their sin before they come to follow him. Whether it be speaking to the rich young ruler and asking that he give up his possessions (Luke 18:18–30), coming to the house of Zacchaeus and declaring that salvation had come to him that day because he had given half his goods to the poor and had repaid fourfold anything that he had stolen (Luke 19:1–10), speaking to the woman at the well and asking her to call her husband (John 4:16), or speaking to Nicodemus and rebuking his rabbinic unbelief and pride in his own knowledge (John 3:1–21), Jesus consistently puts his finger on the area of sin most influential in that person's life. In fact, we may ask whether anyone in the gospels ever came to sincere faith in Christ without repenting of his or her sins.

When we realize that genuine saving faith must be accompanied by genuine repentance for sin, it helps us to understand why some preaching of the gospel has such inadequate results today. If there is no mention of the need for repentance, sometimes the gospel message becomes only, "Believe in Jesus Christ and be saved" without any mention of repentance at all.[7] But this watered-down version

---

[6]See chapter 49, pp. 973–75, 981, on the question of whether baptism is necessary for salvation.

[7]It is true that Paul tells the Philippian jailer in Acts 16:31, "Believe in the Lord Jesus, and you will be saved, you and your household." However, even that sentence includes an acknowledgment that Jesus is "Lord," and, moreover, the next sentence makes it clear that Paul said much more to the man than this brief sentence, for we read, "And they spoke the word of the Lord to him and to all that were in his house" (Acts 16:32).

of the gospel does not ask for a wholehearted commitment to Christ—commitment *to* Christ, if genuine, must include a commitment to turn *from* sin. Preaching the need for faith without repentance is preaching only half of the gospel. It will result in many people being deceived, thinking that they have heard the Christian gospel and tried it, but nothing has happened. They might even say something like, "I accepted Christ as Savior over and over again and it never worked." Yet they never really did receive Christ as their Savior, for he comes to us in his majesty and invites us to receive him as he is—the one who deserves to be, and demands to be, absolute Lord of our lives as well.

Finally, what shall we say about the common practice of asking people to *pray* to receive Christ as their personal Savior and Lord? Since personal faith in Christ must involve an actual decision of the will, it is often very helpful to *express* that decision in spoken words, and this could very naturally take the form of a prayer to Christ in which we tell him of our sorrow for sin, our commitment to forsake it, and our decision actually to put our trust in him. Such a spoken prayer does not in itself save us, but the attitude of heart that it represents does constitute true conversion, and the decision to speak that prayer can often be the point at which a person truly comes to faith in Christ.

## C. Both Faith and Repentance Continue Throughout Life

Although we have been considering initial faith and repentance as the two aspects of conversion at the beginning of the Christian life, it is important to realize that faith and repentance are not confined to the beginning of the Christian life. They are rather attitudes of heart that continue throughout our lives as Christians. Jesus tells his disciples to pray daily, "And forgive us our sins as we also have forgiven those who sin against us" (Matt. 6:12, author's translation), a prayer that, if genuine, will certainly involve daily sorrow for sin and genuine repentance. And the risen Christ says to the church in Laodicea, "Those whom I love, I reprove and chasten; so be zealous *and repent*" (Rev. 3:19; cf. 2 Cor. 7:10).

With regard to faith, Paul tells us, "So faith, hope, love abide, these three; but the greatest of these is love" (1 Cor. 13:13). He certainly means that these three abide throughout the course of this life, but he probably also means that they abide for all eternity: if faith is trusting God to provide all our needs, then this attitude will never cease, not even in the age to come. But in any case, the point is clearly made that faith continues throughout this life. Paul also says, "The life I now live in the flesh I live *by faith in the Son of God*, who loved me and gave himself for me" (Gal. 2:20).

Therefore, although it is true that *initial* saving faith and *initial* repentance occur only once in our lives, and when they occur they constitute true conversion, nonetheless, the heart attitudes of repentance and faith only begin at conversion. These same attitudes should continue throughout the course of our Christian lives. Each day there should be heartfelt repentance for sins that we have committed, and faith in Christ to provide for our needs and to empower us to live the Christian life.

## QUESTIONS FOR PERSONAL APPLICATION

1. Have you come to trust in Christ personally, or are you still at the point of intellectual knowledge and emotional approval of the facts of salvation without having personally put your trust in Christ? If you have not put your trust in Christ yet, what do you think it is that is making you hesitate?

2. Did this chapter help you think of faith in Christ in more personal terms? If so, how might that increase your own level of faith? Do you think that it might be easier for young children than for adults to think of trust in Christ as trust in a real *person* who is alive today? Why or why not? What does this tell you about the way Christian parents should teach their children about Jesus?

3. If your knowledge about God has increased through reading this book, has your faith in God increased along with that knowledge? Why or why not? If your faith has not increased along with your knowledge, what can you do to encourage your faith to grow more than it has?

4. In terms of human relationships, do you trust a person more when you do not know that person very well or after you have come to know him or her quite well (assuming that the person is essentially a trustworthy and reliable person)? What does that fact tell you about how your trust in God might increase? What things might you do during the day to come to know God better, and to come to know Jesus and the Holy Spirit better?

5. Did you feel a sincere sorrow for sin when you first came to Christ? Can you describe what it felt like? Did it lead you to a genuine commitment to forsake sin? How long was it before you noticed a change in your pattern of life?

6. Have you ever truly repented of sin, or do you think you have been taught a watered-down gospel that did not include repentance? Do you think it is possible for someone genuinely to trust in Christ for forgiveness of sins without also sincerely repenting for sins? Do you think that genuine repentance usually involves only a sincere feeling of sorrow for sin in general, or does it involve genuine sorrow for specific sins, and turning from those specific sins?

7. Have faith and repentance remained a continuing part of your Christian life, or have those attitudes of heart grown somewhat weak in your life? What has been the result in your Christian life?

## SPECIAL TERMS

faith
repentance
trust

# BIBLIOGRAPHY

(For an explanation of this bibliography see the note on the bibliography to chapter 1, p. 38. Complete bibliographical data may be found on pp. 1223–29.)

## Sections in Evangelical Systematic Theologies

1. Anglican (Episcopalian)

| | |
|---|---|
| 1882–92 | Litton, 288–300 |

2. Arminian (Wesleyan or Methodist)

| | |
|---|---|
| 1847 | Finney, 364–82 |
| 1875–76 | Pope, 2:367–85 |
| 1940 | Wiley, 2:357–78 |
| 1983 | Carter, 1:496–99 |

3. Baptist

| | |
|---|---|
| 1767 | Gill, 2:131–41 |
| 1887 | Boyce, 373–94 |
| 1907 | Strong, 829–49 |
| 1917 | Mullins, 368–85 |
| 1983–85 | Erickson, 933–42 |

4. Dispensational

| | |
|---|---|
| 1947 | Chafer, 3:371–93 |
| 1949 | Thiessen, 264–70 |
| 1986 | Ryrie, 324–27 |

5. Lutheran

| | |
|---|---|
| 1917–24 | Pieper, 2:422–503 |
| 1934 | Mueller, 319–66 |

6. Reformed (or Presbyterian)

| | |
|---|---|
| 1559 | Calvin, 1:340–67, 423–28 (2.6–7, 9; 3.2–5), 542–684 |
| 1724–58 | Edwards, 2:578–96 |
| 1861 | Heppe, 526–42 |
| 1871–73 | Hodge, 3:41–113 |
| 1878 | Dabney, 600–612, 651–60 |
| 1887–1921 | Warfield, BTS, 375–403; SSW, 1:267–82; SSW, 2:655–59; BD, 467–510 |
| 1889 | Shedd, 2b:529–37 |
| 1937–66 | Murray, CW, 2:235–74; RAA, 106–16 |
| 1938 | Berkhof, 480–509 |
| 1962 | Buswell, 2:175–86 |

7. Renewal (or charismatic/Pentecostal)

| | |
|---|---|
| 1988–92 | Williams, 2:28–31 |

## Sections in Representative Roman Catholic Systematic Theologies

1. Roman Catholic: Traditional
    1955     Ott, 252–54
2. Roman Catholic: Post-Vatican II
    1980     McBrien, 1:31–46

## Other Works

Berkouwer, G. C. *Faith and Justification*. Trans. by Lewis B. Smedes. Grand Rapids: Eerdmans, 1954.

Boice, James Montgomery. *Christ's Call to Discipleship*. Chicago: Moody, 1986.

Chantry, Walter. *Today's Gospel: Authentic or Synthetic?* Carlisle, Pa.: Banner of Truth, 1970.

Hodges, Zane C. *Absolutely Free! A Biblical Reply to Lordship Salvation*. Dallas: Redención Viva, and Grand Rapids: Zondervan, 1989.

———. *The Gospel Under Siege: A Study on Faith and Works*. Dallas: Redención Viva, 1981.

Hoekema, Anthony A. *Saved by Grace*. Grand Rapids: Eerdmans, and Exeter: Paternoster, 1989, pp. 113–51.

Kromminga, C. G. "Repentance." In *EDT*, pp. 936–37.

MacArthur, John F., Jr. *The Gospel According to Jesus*. Grand Rapids: Zondervan, 1988.

Machen, J. Gresham. *What Is Faith?* Grand Rapids: Eerdmans, 1925.

Morris, Leon. "Faith." In *IBD*. Vol. 1, pp. 496–98.

Murray, John. "Faith and Repentance." In *Redemption Accomplished and Applied*. Grand Rapids: Eerdmans, 1955, pp. 106–16.

———. "Repentance." In *The New Bible Dictionary*. Ed. by J. D. Douglas. London: Tyndale Press, and Grand Rapids: Eerdmans, 1962, pp. 1083–84.

Packer, J. I. "Evangelicals and the Way of Salvation: New Challenges to the Gospel–Universalism and Justification by Faith." In *Evangelical Affirmations*. Ed. by Kenneth S. Kantzer and Carl F. H. Henry. Grand Rapids: Zondervan, 1990, pp. 107–36.

———. *Evangelism and the Sovereignty of God*. London: Inter-Varsity Press, 1961.

———. "Faith." In *EDT,* pp. 399–402.

Ryrie, Charles C. *So Great Salvation: What It Means to Believe in Jesus Christ*. Wheaton, Ill.: Scripture Press, 1989.

Watson, Thomas. *The Doctrine of Repentance*. Carlisle, Pa.: Banner of Truth, 1987.

## SCRIPTURE MEMORY PASSAGE

**John 3:16:** *For God so loved the world that he gave his only Son, that whoever believes in him should not perish but have eternal life.*

# HYMN

## "Just As I Am"

Just as I am, without one plea
  But that thy blood was shed for me,
And that thou bidd'st me come to thee,
    O Lamb of God, I come, I come.

Just as I am, and waiting not
  To rid my soul of one dark blot,
To thee, whose blood can cleanse each spot,
    O Lamb of God, I come, I come.

Just as I am, though tossed about
  With many a conflict, many a doubt,
Fightings and fears within, without,
    O Lamb of God, I come, I come.

Just as I am, poor, wretched, blind;
  Sight, riches, healing of the mind,
Yea, all I need, in thee to find,
    O Lamb of God, I come, I come.

Just as I am! Thou wilt receive,
  Wilt welcome, pardon, cleanse, relieve;
Because thy promise I believe,
    O Lamb of God, I come, I come.

Just as I am! Thy love unknown
  Has broken ev'ry barrier down;
Now, to be thine, yea, thine alone,
    O Lamb of God, I come, I come.

AUTHOR: CHARLOTTE ELLIOT, 1836

# Chapter 36

# Justification (Right Legal Standing Before God)

## How and when do we gain right legal standing before God?

## EXPLANATION AND SCRIPTURAL BASIS

In the previous chapters we talked about the gospel call (in which God calls us to trust in Christ for salvation), regeneration (in which God imparts new spiritual life to us), and conversion (in which we respond to the gospel call in repentance for sin and faith in Christ for salvation). But *what about the guilt of our sin?* The gospel call invited us to trust in Christ for forgiveness of sins. Regeneration made it possible for us to respond to that invitation. In conversion we did respond, trusting in Christ for forgiveness of sins. Now the next step in the process of applying redemption to us is that God must respond to our faith and do what he promised, that is, actually declare our sins to be forgiven. This must be a *legal declaration* concerning our relationship to God's laws, stating that we are completely forgiven and no longer liable to punishment.

A right understanding of justification is absolutely crucial to the whole Christian faith. Once Martin Luther realized the truth of justification by faith alone, he became a Christian and overflowed with the new-found joy of the gospel. The primary issue in the Protestant Reformation was a dispute with the Roman Catholic Church over justification. If we are to safeguard the truth of the gospel for future generations, we must understand the truth of justification. Even today, a true view of justification is the dividing line between the biblical gospel of salvation by faith alone and all false gospels of salvation based on good works.

When Paul gives an overview of the process by which God applies salvation to us, he mentions justification explicitly: "Those whom he predestined he also called; and those whom he called he also *justified;* and those whom he justified he also glorified" (Rom. 8:30). As we explained in a previous chapter, the word *called* here refers to the effective calling of the gospel, which includes regeneration and brings forth the response of repentance and faith (or conversion) on our part. After effective calling and the response that it initiates on our part, the next step in the application of redemption is "justification." Here Paul mentions that this is something that God himself does: "Those whom he called *he also justified.*"

Moreover, Paul quite clearly teaches that this justification comes *after* our faith and *as God's response to* our faith. He says that God "justifies him who *has faith* in Jesus" (Rom. 3:26), and that "a man is justified *by faith* apart from works of law" (Rom. 3:28). He says, "Since we are justified *by faith,* we have peace with God

722

through our Lord Jesus Christ" (Rom. 5:1). Moreover, "a man is not justified by works of the law but *through faith* in Jesus Christ" (Gal. 2:16).

Just what is justification? We may define it as follows: *Justification is an instantaneous legal act of God in which he (1) thinks of our sins as forgiven and Christ's righteousness as belonging to us, and (2) declares us to be righteous in his sight.*

In explaining the elements of this definition, we will look first at the second half of it, the aspect of justification in which God "declares us to be righteous in his sight." The reason for treating these items in reverse order is that the emphasis of the New Testament in the use of the word *justification* and related terms is on the second half of the definition, the legal declaration by God. But there are also passages that show that this declaration is based on the fact that God first thinks of righteousness as belonging to us. So both aspects must be treated, even though the New Testament terms for justification focus on the legal declaration by God.

## A. Justification Includes a Legal Declaration By God

The use of the word *justify* in the Bible indicates that justification is a legal declaration by God. The verb *justify* in the New Testament (Gk. *dikaioō*) has a range of meanings, but a very common sense is "to declare righteous." For example, we read, "When they heard this all the people and the tax collectors *justified* God, having been baptized with the baptism of John" (Luke 7:29). Of course the people and the tax collectors did not *make* God to be righteous—that would be impossible for anyone to do. Rather they *declared* God to be righteous. This is also the sense of the term in passages where the New Testament talks about us being declared righteous by God (Rom. 3:20, 26, 28; 5:1; 8:30; 10:4, 10; Gal. 2:16; 3:24). This sense is particularly evident, for example, in Romans 4:5: "And to one who does not work but trusts him who *justifies the ungodly,* his faith is reckoned as righteousness." Here Paul cannot mean that God "makes the ungodly to be righteous" (by changing them internally and making them morally perfect), for then they would have merit or works of their own to depend on. Rather, he means that God declares the ungodly to be righteous in his sight, not on the basis of their good works, but in response to their faith.

The idea that justification is a legal declaration is quite evident also when justification is contrasted with condemnation. Paul says, "Who shall bring any charge against God's elect? It is God who *justifies;* who is to condemn?" (Rom. 8:33–34). To "condemn" someone is to declare that person guilty. The opposite of condemnation is justification, which, in this context, must mean "to declare someone not guilty." This is also evident from the fact that God's act of justifying is given as Paul's answer to the possibility of someone bringing an accusation or "charge" against God's people: such a declaration of guilt cannot stand in the face of God's declaration of righteousness.

Some Old Testament examples of the word *justify* (Gk. *dikaioō* in the Septuagint, when translating the hiphil of *tsādak*, "to justify") add support to this understanding. For example, we read of judges who "*justify the righteous* and condemn the wicked" (Deut. 25:1 NASB). Now in this case "justify" must mean "declare to be righteous or not guilty," just as "condemn" means "declare to be guilty." It would make no sense to say that "justify" here means "to make someone to be good internally," for judges simply do not and cannot make people to be good on the inside. Nor does a judge's act of condemning the wicked make that person to be evil on the inside; it simply declares that the person is guilty with respect to the particular crime that has been brought before the court (cf. Ex. 23:7; 1 Kings 8:32; 2 Chron. 6:23). Similarly, Job refuses to say that his comforters were right in what they said: "Far be it from me that I should *declare you right*" (Job 27:5 NASB, using the same Hebrew and Greek terms for "justify"). The same idea is found in Proverbs: "He who *justifies* the wicked and he who condemns the righteous are both alike an abomination to the LORD" (Prov. 17:15). Here the idea of legal declaration is especially strong. Certainly it would not be an abomination to the LORD if "justify" meant "to *make* someone good or righteous inside." In that case, to "justify the wicked" would be a very good thing in God's sight. But if "justify" means "declare to be righteous," then it is perfectly clear why "he who justifies the wicked" is "an abomination to the LORD." Similarly, Isaiah condemns those "who *justify* the wicked for a bribe" (Isa. 5:23 NASB); again, "justify" must mean "declare to be righteous" (here used in the context of a legal declaration).

In this sense of "*declare* to be righteous" or "*declare* to be not guilty" Paul frequently uses the word to speak of God's justification of us, his declaration that we, though guilty sinners, are nonetheless righteous in his sight. It is important to emphasize that this legal declaration in itself does not change our internal nature or character at all. In this sense of "justify," God issues a legal declaration about us. This is why theologians have also said that justification is *forensic*, where the word *forensic* means "having to do with legal proceedings."

John Murray makes an important distinction between regeneration and justification:

> Regeneration is an act of God in us; justification is a judgment of God with respect to us. The distinction is like that of the distinction between the act of a surgeon and the act of a judge. The surgeon, when he removes an inward cancer, does something in us. That is not what a judge does—he gives a verdict regarding our judicial status. If we are innocent he declares accordingly.
>
> The purity of the gospel is bound up with the recognition of this distinction. If justification is confused with regeneration or sanctification, then the door is opened for the perversion of the gospel at its center. Justification is still the article of the standing or falling of the Church.[1]

## B. God Declares Us to Be Just in His Sight

In God's legal declaration of justification, he specifically declares that we are just *in his sight*. This declaration involves two aspects. First, it means that he declares that we have no penalty to pay for sin, including past, present, and future sins. After a long discussion of justification by faith alone (Rom. 4:1–5:21), and a parenthetical discussion on remaining sin in the Christian life, Paul returns to his main argument in the book of Romans and tells what is true of those who have been justified by faith: "There is therefore now *no condemnation* for those who are in Christ Jesus" (Rom. 8:1). In this sense those who are justified have no penalty to pay for sin. This means that we are not subject to any charge of guilt or

---

[1]John Murray, *Redemption Accomplished and Applied*, p. 121.

condemnation: "Who shall bring any charge against God's elect? It is God who *justifies;* who is to condemn?" (Rom. 8:33–34).

The idea of full forgiveness of sins is prominent when Paul discusses justification by faith alone in Romans 4. Paul quotes David as pronouncing a blessing on one "to whom God reckons righteousness apart from works." He then recalls how David said, "Blessed are those *whose iniquities are forgiven,* and whose sins are covered; blessed is the man against whom the Lord will not reckon his sin" (Rom. 4:6–8). This justification therefore clearly involves the forgiveness of sins. David spoke similarly in Psalm 103:12, "As far as the east is from the west, so far does he remove our transgressions from us" (cf. v. 3).

But if God merely declared us to be *forgiven from our past sins,* that would not solve our problems entirely, for it would only make us morally neutral before God. We would be in the state that Adam was in before he had done anything right or wrong in God's sight—he was not guilty before God, but neither had he earned a record of righteousness before God. This first aspect of justification, in which God declares that our sins are forgiven, may be represented as in figure 36.1, in which the minus signs represent sins on our account that are completely forgiven in justification.

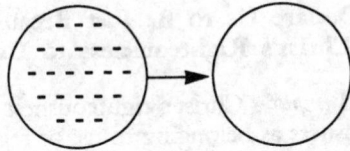

**FORGIVENESS OF PAST SINS IS ONE PART OF JUSTIFICATION**
*Figure 36.1*

However, such a movement is not enough to earn us favor with God. We must rather move from a point of moral neutrality to a point of having positive righteousness before God, the righteousness of a life of perfect obedience to him. Our need may therefore be represented as in figure 36.2, in which the plus signs indicate a record of righteousness before God.

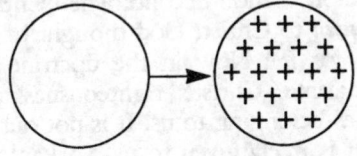

**IMPUTATION OF CHRIST'S RIGHTEOUSNESS TO US**
**IS THE OTHER PART OF JUSTIFICATION**
*Figure 36.2*

Therefore the second aspect of justification is that God must declare us not to be merely *neutral* in his sight but actually to be *righteous* in his sight. In fact, he must declare us to have the merits of perfect righteousness before him. The Old

Testament sometimes spoke of God as giving such righteousness to his people even though they had not earned it themselves. Isaiah says, "He has clothed me with the garments of salvation, *he has covered me with the robe of righteousness*" (Isa. 61:10). But Paul speaks more specifically about this in the New Testament. As a solution to our need for righteousness, Paul tells us that "the righteousness of God has been manifested apart from law, although the law and the prophets bear witness to it, *the righteousness of God through faith in Jesus Christ* for all who believe" (Rom. 3:21–22). He says, "Abraham believed God, and *it was reckoned to him as righteousness*" (Rom. 4:3; quoting Gen. 15:6). This came about through the obedience of Christ, for Paul says at the end of this extensive discussion of justification by faith that "by one man's obedience many will be *made righteous*" (Rom. 5:19). The second aspect of God's declaration in justification, then, is that we have the merits of perfect righteousness before him.

But questions arise: How can God declare that we have no penalty to pay for sin, and that we have the merits of perfect righteousness, if we are in fact guilty sinners? How can God declare us to be not guilty but righteous when in fact *we are unrighteous*? These questions lead to our next point.

## C. God Can Declare Us to Be Just Because He Imputes Christ's Righteousness to Us

When we say that God *imputes* Christ's righteousness to us it means that God *thinks of* Christ's righteousness as belonging to us, or regards it *as belonging to* us. He "reckons" it to our account. We read, "Abraham believed God, and *it was reckoned to him as righteousness*" (Rom. 4:3, quoting Gen. 15:6). Paul explains, "To one who does not work but trusts him who justifies the ungodly, his faith *is reckoned* as righteousness. So also David pronounces a blessing upon the man to whom *God reckons righteousness* apart from works" (Rom. 4:6). In this way, Christ's righteousness became ours. Paul says that we are those who received "the free gift of righteousness" (Rom. 5:17).

This is the third time in studying the doctrines of Scripture that we have encountered the idea of *imputing* guilt or righteousness to someone else. First, when Adam sinned, his guilt was imputed to us; God the Father viewed it as belonging to us, and therefore it did.[2] Second, when Christ suffered and died for our sins, our sin was *imputed* to Christ; God thought of it as belonging to him, and he paid the penalty for it.[3] Now in the doctrine of justification we see imputation for the third time. Christ's righteousness is *imputed* to us, and therefore God *thinks of it* as belonging to us. It is not our own righteousness but Christ's righteousness that is freely given to us. So Paul can say that God made Christ to be "our wisdom, *our righteousness* and sanctification and redemption" (1 Cor. 1:30). And Paul says that his goal is to be found in Christ, "not having a righteousness of my own, based on law, but that which is through faith in Christ, *the righteousness from God* that depends on faith" (Phil. 3:9). Paul knows that the

---

[2]See chapter 24, pp. 494–96, on the idea of Adam's sin being imputed to us.

[3]See chapter 27, pp. 573–74, on the fact that our guilt was imputed to Christ. Paul says, "God made him who had no sin to be sin for us, so that in him we might become the righteousness of God" (2 Cor. 5:21 NIV).

righteousness he has before God is not anything of his own doing; it is the righteousness of God that comes through Jesus Christ (cf. Rom. 3:21–22).[4]

It is essential to the heart of the gospel to insist that God declares us to be just or righteous not on the basis of our actual condition of righteousness or holiness, but rather on the basis of Christ's perfect righteousness, which he thinks of as belonging to us. This was the heart of the difference between Protestantism and Roman Catholicism at the Reformation. Protestantism since the time of Martin Luther has insisted that justification does *not* change us internally and it is *not* a declaration based in any way on any goodness that we have in ourselves. If justification changed us internally and then declared us to be righteous based on how good we actually were, then (1) we could never be declared perfectly righteous in this life, because there is always sin that remains in our lives, and (2) there would be no provision for forgiveness of past sins (committed before we were changed internally), and therefore we could never have confidence that we are right before God. We would lose the confidence that Paul has when he says, "Therefore, *since we are justified by faith*, we have peace with God through our Lord Jesus Christ" (Rom. 5:1).[5] If we thought of justification as based on something that we are internally we would never have the confidence to say with Paul, "There is therefore now *no condemnation* for those who are in Christ Jesus" (Rom. 8:1). We would have no assurance of forgiveness with God, no confidence to draw near to him "with a true heart in full assurance of faith" (Heb. 10:22). We would not be able to speak of "the *free gift* of righteousness" (Rom. 5:17), or say that "the *free gift* of God is eternal life in Christ Jesus our Lord" (Rom. 6:23).

The traditional Roman Catholic understanding of justification is very different from this. The Roman Catholic Church understands justification as something that changes us internally and makes us more holy within. "According to the teaching of the Council of Trent, justification is 'sanctifying and renewing of the inner man.'"[6] In order for justification to begin, one must first be baptized and

---

[4]One sometimes hears the popular explanation that *justified* means "just-as-if-I'd-never-sinned." The definition is a clever play on words and contains an element of truth (for the justified person, like the person who has never sinned, has no penalty to pay for sin). But the definition is misleading in two other ways because (1) it mentions nothing about the fact that Christ's righteousness is reckoned to my account when I am justified; to do this it would have to say also "just-as-if-I'd-lived-a-life-of-perfect-righteousness." (2) But more significantly, it cannot adequately represent the fact that I will *never* be in a state that is "just-as-if-I'd-never-sinned," because I will *always* be conscious of the fact that I *have* sinned and that I am not an innocent person but a guilty person who has been forgiven. This is very different from "just as if I had never sinned"! Moreover, it is different from "just as if I had lived a life of perfect righteousness," because I will forever know that I *have not* lived a life of perfect righteousness, but that Christ's righteousness is given to me by God's grace.

Therefore both in the forgiveness of sins and in the imputation of Christ's righteousness, my situation is far different from what it would be if I had never sinned and had lived a perfectly righteous life. For all eternity I will remember that I am a forgiven *sinner*, and that my righteousness is not based on my own merit, but on the grace of God in the saving work of Jesus Christ. None of that rich teaching at the heart of the gospel will be understood by those who are encouraged to go through their lives thinking "justified" means "just-as-if-I'd-never-sinned."

[5]The aorist passive participle *dikaōthentes* placed before the main verb conveys the sense of a completed event prior to the present tense main verb, "We have peace," giving the sense, "Since we *have been justified* by faith, we have peace."

[6]Ludwig Ott, *Fundamentals of Catholic Dogma*, p. 257; also quoted with approval on p. 250. It should be noted that Ott represents more traditional, pre-Vatican II Roman Catholicism, and that many contemporary Roman Catholics have sought an understanding of justification that is closer to a Protestant view.

then (as an adult) continue to have faith: "The instrumental cause ... . of the first justification is the Sacrament of Baptism."[7] But "the justification of an adult is not possible without Faith. . . . As far as the content of justifying faith is concerned, the so-called fiducial faith does not suffice. What is demanded is theological or dogmatic faith (confessional faith) which consists in the firm acceptance of the Divine truths of Revelation."[8] Thus baptism is the means by which justification is first obtained, and then faith is necessary if an adult is to receive justification or to continue in the state of justification. Ott explains that "the so-called fiduciary faith" is not enough—meaning that the faith that simply trusts in Christ for forgiveness of sins is not enough. It must be a faith that accepts the content of the teaching of the Catholic Church, "theological or dogmatic faith."

The Roman Catholic view may be said to understand justification as based not on *imputed* righteousness but on *infused* righteousness—that is, righteousness that God actually *puts into us* and that changes us internally and in terms of our actual moral character. Then he gives us varying measures of justification according to the measure of righteousness that has been infused or placed within us.

The result of this Roman Catholic view of justification is that people cannot be sure if they are in a "state of grace" where they experience God's complete acceptance and favor. The Catholic Church teaches that people cannot be certain that they are in this "state of grace" unless they receive a special revelation from God to this effect. The Council of Trent declared,

> If one considers his own weakness and his defective disposition, he may well be fearful and anxious as to the state of grace, as nobody knows with the certainty of faith, which permits of no error, that he has achieved the grace of God.

To this statement Ott adds the comment,

> The reason for the uncertainty of the state of grace lies in this, that without a special revelation nobody can with certainty of faith know whether or not he has fulfilled all the conditions which are necessary for the achieving of justification. The impossibility of the certainty of faith, however, by no means excludes a high moral certainty supported by the testimony of conscience.[9]

Moreover, since the Roman Catholic Church views justification as including something that God does within us, it follows that people can experience varying degrees of justification. We read, "The degree of justifying grace is not identical in all the just" and "grace can be increased by good works."[10] Ott explains how this Catholic view differs from that of the Protestant Reformers: "As the Reformers wrongly regarded justification as a merely external imputation of Christ's justice, they were obliged also to hold that justification is identical in all men. The Council of Trent, however, declared that the measure of the grace of justification received varies in the individual person who is justified, according to the measure of God's free distribution and to the disposition and the co-operation of the recipient himself."[11]

---

[7]Ibid., p. 251.
[8]Ibid., pp. 252–53.
[9]Ibid., pp. 261–62.
[10]Ibid., p. 262.
[11]Ibid., p. 262.

Finally, the logical consequence of this view of justification is that our eternal life with God is not based on God's grace alone, but partially on our merit as well: "For the justified eternal life is both a gift of grace promised by God and a reward for his own good works and merits. . . . Salutary works are, at the same time, gifts of God and meritorious acts of man."[12]

To support this view of justification from Scripture, Ott repeatedly mingles passages from the New Testament that talk not only of justification, but also of many other aspects of the Christian life, such as regeneration (which God works in us), sanctification (which is a process in the Christian life and which of course does vary from individual to individual), the possession and use of various spiritual gifts in the Christian life (which differ from individual to individual) and eternal reward (which also varies according to the individual). To classify all of these passages under the category of "justification" only blurs the issue and ultimately makes forgiveness of sins and right legal standing before God a matter of our own merit, not a free gift from God. Therefore, this blurring of distinctions ultimately destroys the heart of the gospel.

That is what Martin Luther so clearly saw and that is what gave such motivation to the Reformation. When the good news of the gospel truly became the good news of totally free salvation in Jesus Christ, then it spread like wildfire throughout the civilized world. But this was simply a recovery of the original gospel, which declares, "The wages of sin is death, but the *free gift of God* is eternal life in Christ Jesus our Lord" (Rom. 6:23), and insists that "There is therefore now *no condemnation* for those who are in Christ Jesus" (Rom. 8:1).

## D. Justification Comes to Us Entirely by God's Grace, Not on Account of Any Merit in Ourselves

After Paul explains in Romans 1:18–3:20 that no one will ever be able to make himself righteous before God ("For no human being will be justified in his sight by works of the law," Rom. 3:20), then Paul goes on to explain that "since all have sinned and fall short of the glory of God, they are justified *by his grace as a gift,* through the redemption which is in Christ Jesus" (Rom. 3:23–24). God's "grace" means his "unmerited favor." Because we are completely unable to earn favor with God, the only way we could be declared righteous is if God freely provides salvation for us by grace, totally apart from our work. Paul explains, "For *by grace* you have been saved through faith; and this is not your own doing, it is the gift of God—not because of works, lest any man should boast" (Eph. 2:8–9; cf. Titus 3:7). Grace is clearly put in contrast to works or merit as the reason why God is willing to justify us. God did not have any obligation to impute our sin to Christ or to impute Christ's righteousness to us; it was only because of his unmerited favor that he did this.

In distinction from the Roman Catholic teaching that we are justified by God's grace *plus some merit of our own,* as we make ourselves fit to receive the grace of justification and as we grow in this state of grace though our good works, Luther and the other Reformers insisted that justification comes by grace *alone,* not by grace plus some merit on our part.

---

[12]Ibid., p. 264.

## E. God Justifies Us Through Our Faith in Christ

When we began this chapter we noted that justification comes after saving faith. Paul makes this sequence clear when he says, "We have believed in Christ Jesus, *in order to be justified* by faith in Christ, and not by works of the law, because by works of the law shall no one be justified" (Gal. 2:16). Here Paul indicates that faith comes first and it is for the purpose of being justified. He also says that Christ is "to be received by faith" and that God "justifies him who has *faith* in Jesus" (Rom. 3:25, 26). The entire chapter of Romans 4 is a defense of the fact that we are justified by faith, not by works, just as Abraham and David themselves were. Paul says, "We are justified *by faith*" (Rom. 5:1).

Scripture never says that we are justified because of the inherent goodness of our faith, as if our faith has merit before God. It never allows us to think that our faith in itself earns favor with God. Rather, Scripture says that we are justified "by means of" our faith, understanding faith to be the instrument through which justification is given to us, but not at all an activity that earns us merit or favor with God. Rather, we are justified solely because of the merits of Christ's work (Rom. 5:17–19).[13]

But we may ask why God chose *faith* to be the attitude of heart by which we would obtain justification. Why could God not have decided to give justification to all those who sincerely show love? Or who show joy? Or contentment? Or humility? Or wisdom? Why did God choose *faith* as the means by which we receive justification?

It is apparently because *faith* is the one attitude of heart that is the exact opposite of depending on ourselves. When we come to Christ in faith we essentially say, "I give up! I will not depend on myself or my own good works any longer. I know that I can never make myself righteous before God. Therefore, Jesus, I trust you and depend on you completely to give me a righteous standing before God." In this way, faith is the exact opposite of trusting in ourselves, and therefore it is the attitude that perfectly fits salvation that depends not at all on our own merit but entirely on God's free gift of grace. Paul explains this when he says, "That is why it depends *on faith, in order that the promise may rest on grace* and be guaranteed to all his descendants" (Rom. 4:16). This is why the Reformers from Martin Luther on were so firm in their insistence that justification comes not through faith plus some merit or good work on our part, but only *through faith alone.* "For by grace you have been saved *through faith;* and this[14] is not your own

---

[13]One example from ordinary life might be seen in receiving a paycheck for work that has been done for an employer. The "means" or "instrument" that I use to get this paycheck is the act of reaching out my hand and taking an envelope from my mail box, then opening it and pulling out the check. But my employer does not pay me for doing any of those actions. The pay is entirely for work that I did prior to that. Actually taking the check did not earn me one cent of the money I received—it was simply the *instrument* or *means* I used to take the payment into my possession. Similarly, faith is the *instrument* we use to receive justification from God, but it in itself gains us no merit with God. (The analogy is helpful but it is not perfect, because I had previously worked to earn the money, whereas justification is based on the work of Christ. The analogy would be closer if I had worked and then died, and my wife then picked up the paycheck from my mail box.)

[14]The word translated "this" is the neuter pronoun *touto,* which refers not to "faith" or to "grace" specifically in the previous clause (for they are both feminine nouns in Greek, and would require feminine pronouns), but to the entire idea expressed in the preceding phrase, the idea that you have been saved by grace through faith.

doing, it is the gift of God—not because of works, lest any man should boast" (Eph. 2:8–9). Paul repeatedly says that "no human being will be justified in his sight by works of law" (Rom. 3:20); the same idea is repeated in Galatians 2:16; 3:11; 5:4.

But is this consistent with the epistle of James? What can James mean when he says, "You see that a man is *justified by works* and not by faith alone" (James 2:24). Here we must realize that James is using the word *justified* in a different sense from the way Paul uses it. In the beginning of this chapter we noted that the word *justify* has a range of meanings, and that one significant sense was "declare to be righteous," but we should also notice that the Greek word *dikaioō* can also mean "demonstrate or show to be righteous." For instance, Jesus said to the Pharisees, "You are those who *justify* yourselves before men, but God knows your hearts" (Luke 16:15). The point here was not that the Pharisees went around making legal declarations that they were "not guilty" before God, but rather that they were always attempting to *show others* that they were righteous by their outward deeds. Jesus knew that the truth was otherwise: "But God knows your hearts" (Luke 16:15). Similarly, the lawyer who put Jesus to a test by asking what he should do to inherit eternal life answered Jesus' first question well. But when Jesus told him, "Do this, and you will live," he was not satisfied. Luke tells us, "But he, *desiring to justify himself,* said to Jesus, 'And who is my neighbor?' " (Luke 10:28–29). Now he was not desiring to give a legal pronouncement about himself that he was not guilty in God's sight; rather, he was desiring to "show himself righteous" before others who were listening. Other examples of the word *justify* meaning "show to be righteous" can be found in Matthew 11:19; Luke 7:35; Romans 3:4.

Our interpretation of James 2 depends not only on the fact that "show to be righteous" is an acceptable sense for the word *justified,* but also on the consideration that this sense fits well in the context of James 2. When James says, "Was not Abraham our father *justified by works,* when he offered his son Isaac upon the altar?" (v. 21) he is referring to something later in Abraham's life, the story of the sacrifice of Isaac, which occurred in Genesis 22. This is long after the time recorded in Genesis 15:6 where Abraham believed God "and he reckoned it to him as righteousness." Yet this earlier incident at the beginning of Abraham's covenantal relationship with God is the one that Paul quotes and repeatedly refers to in Romans 4. Paul is talking about the time God justified Abraham once for all, reckoning righteousness to him as a result of his faith in God. But James is talking about something far later, after Abraham had waited many years for the birth of Isaac, and then after Isaac had grown old enough to carry wood up the mountain for a sacrifice. At that point Abraham was "shown to be righteous" by his works, and in that sense James says that Abraham was "justified by works, when he offered his son Isaac upon the altar" (James 2:21).[15]

The larger concern of James in this section also fits this understanding. James is concerned to show that mere intellectual agreement with the gospel is a "faith" that is really no faith at all. He is concerned to argue against those who say they have faith but show no change in their lives. He says, "Show me your faith apart

[15]James does quote the text, "Abraham believed God, and it was reckoned to him as righteousness" in v. 23, but he says that Scripture "was fulfilled" when Abraham offered his son, apparently meaning that the earlier declaration of righteousness was then worked out and its results were seen to be true in Abraham's life when he offered Isaac on the altar.

from your works, and I by my works will show you my faith" (James 2:18). "For as the body apart from the spirit is dead, so faith apart from works is dead" (James 2:26). James is simply saying here that "faith" that has no results or "works" is not real faith at all; it is "dead" faith. He is not denying Paul's clear teaching that justification (in the sense of a declaration of right legal standing before God) is by faith alone apart from works of the law; he is simply affirming a different truth, namely, that "justification" in the sense of an outward showing that one is righteous only occurs as we see evidence in a person's life. To paraphrase, James is saying that a person is "*shown to be righteous* by his works, and not by his faith alone." This is something with which Paul also would certainly agree (2 Cor. 13:5; Gal. 5:19–24).

The practical implications of the doctrine of justification by faith alone are very significant. First, this doctrine enables us to offer genuine *hope* to unbelievers who know they could never make themselves righteous before God: if salvation is a free gift to be received through faith *alone,* then anyone who hears the gospel may hope that eternal life is freely offered and may be obtained.

Second, this doctrine gives us confidence that God will never make us pay the penalty for sins that have been forgiven on Christ's merits. Of course, we may continue to suffer the ordinary *consequences* of sin (an alcoholic who quits drinking may still have physical weakness for the rest of his or her life, and a thief who is justified may still have to go to jail to pay the penalty for his or her crime). Moreover, God may *discipline* us if we continue to act in ways that are disobedient to him (see Heb. 12:5–11), doing this out of love and for our own good. But God can never nor will ever *take vengeance* on us for past sins or *make us pay the penalty* that is due for them or *punish us out of wrath* and *for the purpose of doing us harm.* "There is therefore now no condemnation for those that are in Christ Jesus" (Rom 8:1). This fact should give us a great sense of joy and confidence before God that we are accepted by him and that we stand before him as "not guilty" and "righteous" forever.

## QUESTIONS FOR PERSONAL APPLICATION

1. Are you confident that God has declared you "not guilty" forever in his sight? Do you know when that happened in your own life? Did you do or think anything that resulted in God's justifying of you? Did you do anything to deserve justification? If you are not sure that God has justified you fully and for all time, is there something you need to do before that will happen? What would persuade you that God has certainly justified you?

2. If you think of yourself standing before God on the day of judgment, would you think that it is enough simply to have your sins all forgiven, or would you also feel a need to have the righteousness of Christ reckoned to your account?

3. Do you think the difference between the Roman Catholic and Protestant understanding of justification is an important one? Describe how you would feel about your relationship to God if you held the Roman Catholic view of justification. Do modern Roman Catholics you know seem to hold to this traditional Roman Catholic view of justification, or do they have another view?

4. Have you ever wondered if God is still continuing to punish you from time to time for sins you have done in the past, even long ago? How does the doctrine of justification help you deal with those feelings?

## SPECIAL TERMS

| | |
|---|---|
| forensic | infused righteousness |
| impute | justification |

## BIBLIOGRAPHY

(For an explanation of this bibliography see the note on the bibliography to chapter 1, p. 38. Complete bibliographical data may be found on pp. 1223–29.)

### Sections In Evangelical Systematic Theologies

1. Anglican (Episcopalian)
     1882–92   Litton, 265–320
        1930   Thomas, 184–98, 210–20
2. Arminian (Wesleyan or Methodist)
        1847   Finney, 382–402
     1875–76   Pope, 2:358–62, 402–51
     1892–94   Miley, 2:309–26
        1940   Wiley, 2:379–401
        1960   Purkiser, 287–92
3. Baptist
        1767   Gill, 1:291–300; 2:68–93
        1887   Boyce, 394–404
        1907   Strong, 846–68
        1917   Mullins, 389–401
     1983–85   Erickson, 954–61
4. Dispensational
        1947   Chafer, 3:238–46
        1949   Thiessen, 271–76
        1986   Ryrie, 298–300
5. Lutheran
     1917–24   Pieper, 2:3–54, 503–57
        1934   Mueller, 242–54, 367–83
6. Reformed (or Presbyterian)
        1559   Calvin, I, 725–833 (3.11–18)
        1861   Heppe, 543–64
     1871–73   Hodge, 3:114–212
        1878   Dabney, 618–50
     1887–1921 Warfield, *BTS*, 262–68

    1889      Shedd, 2b:538–52
 1937–66      Murray, *CW*, 2:202–22; *RAA*, 117–31
    1938      Berkhof, 510–26
    1962      Buswell, 2:187–96
7. Renewal (or charismatic/Pentecostal)
 1988–92      Williams, 2:61–82

## Sections in Representative Roman Catholic Systematic Theologies

1. Roman Catholic: Traditional
    1955      Ott, 250–69

## Other Works

Berkouwer, G. C. *Faith and Justification*. Trans. by Lewis B. Smedes. Grand Rapids: Eerdmans, 1954.

Carson, D. A., ed. *Right With God: Justification in the Bible and the World*. Grand Rapids: Baker, 1992.

Hoekema, Anthony A. "Justification." In *Saved by Grace*. Grand Rapids: Eerdmans, and Exeter: Paternoster, 1989, pp. 152–91.

McGrath, Alister E. *Iustitia Dei: A History of the Christian Doctrine of Justification*. 2 vols. Cambridge: Cambridge University Press, 1986.

————. *Justification by Faith: An Introduction*. Grand Rapids: Zondervan, 1988.

Morris, Leon. *The Apostolic Preaching of the Cross*. 3d ed. Grand Rapids: Eerdmans, 1965, pp. 251–98.

Murray, John. "Justification." In *Redemption Accomplished and Applied*. Grand Rapids: Eerdmans, 1955, pp. 117–31.

Packer, J. I. et al. *Here We Stand: Justification by Faith Today*. London: Hodder and Stoughton, 1986.

————. "Justification." In *EDT*, pp. 593–97.

Pink, A. W. *The Doctrines of Election and Justification*. Grand Rapids: Baker, 1974.

Wright, N. T. "Justification." In *NDT*, pp. 359–61.

Ziesler, J.A. *The Meaning of Righteous in Paul*. Cambridge: Cambridge University, 1972.

## SCRIPTURE MEMORY PASSAGE

**Romans 3:27–28:** *Then what becomes of our boasting? It is excluded. On what principle? On the principle of works? No, but on the principle of faith. For we hold that a man is justified by faith apart from works of law.*

## HYMN

### "Jesus, Thy Blood and Righteousness"

Jesus, thy blood and righteousness
  My beauty are, my glorious dress;
'Midst flaming worlds, in these arrayed,
  With joy shall I lift up my head.

Bold shall I stand in thy great day;
  For who aught to my charge shall lay?
Fully absolved through these I am
  From sin and fear, from guilt and shame.

When from the dust of death I rise
  To claim my mansion in the skies,
Ev'n then this shall be all my plea,
  Jesus hath lived, hath died, for me.

Jesus, be endless praise to thee,
  Whose boundless mercy hath for me—
For me a full atonement made,
  An everlasting ransom paid.

O let the dead now hear thy voice;
  Now bid thy banished ones rejoice;
Their beauty this, their glorious dress,
  Jesus, thy blood and righteousness.

AUTHOR: COUNT NIKOLAUS LUDWIG VON ZINZENDORF, 1739
(TRANS. JOHN WESLEY, 1740, ALT.)

# Chapter 37

# Adoption (Membership in God's Family)

*What are benefits of being a member of God's family?*

## EXPLANATION AND SCRIPTURAL BASIS

In regeneration God gives us new spiritual life within. In justification God gives us right legal standing before him. But in adoption God makes us members of his family. Therefore, the biblical teaching on adoption focuses much more on the personal relationships that salvation gives us with God and with his people.

### A. Scriptural Evidence for Adoption

We may define adoption as follows: *Adoption is an act of God whereby he makes us members of his family.*

John mentions adoption at the beginning of his gospel, where he says, "But to all who received him, who believed in his name, he gave power *to become children of God*" (John 1:12). By contrast, those who do not believe in Christ are not children of God or adopted into his family, but are "children of wrath" (Eph. 2:3) and "sons of disobedience" (Eph. 2:2; 5:6). Although those Jews who rejected Christ tried to claim that God was their father (John 8:41), Jesus told them, "If God were your Father, you would love me. . . . You are of your father the devil, and your will is to do your father's desires" (John 8:42–44).

The New Testament epistles bear repeated testimony to the fact that we are now God's children in a special sense, members of his family. Paul says:

> For all who are led by the Spirit of God are *sons of God*. For you did not receive the spirit of slavery to fall back into fear, but you have received the *spirit of sonship*. When we cry, "Abba! Father!" it is the Spirit himself bearing witness with our spirit that we are *children of God,* and if children, then heirs, heirs of God and fellow heirs with Christ, provided we suffer with him in order that we may also be glorified with him. (Rom. 8:14–17)

But if we are God's children, are we then related to one another as family members? Certainly so. In fact, this adoption into God's family makes us partakers together in *one family* even with the believing Jews of the Old Testament, for Paul says that we are Abraham's children as well: "Not all are children of Abraham because they are his descendants; but 'Through Isaac shall your descendants be named.' This means that it is not the children of the flesh who are the children of

God, but the children of the promise are reckoned as descendants" (Rom. 9:7–8). He further explains in Galatians, "Now we, brethren, like Isaac, are children of promise . . . we are not children of the slave but of the free woman" (Gal. 4:28, 31; cf. 1 Peter 3:6, where Peter sees believing women as daughters of Sarah in the new covenant).

Paul explains that this status of adoption as God's children was not fully realized in the old covenant. He says that "before faith came, we were confined under the law . . . the law was our custodian until Christ came, that we might be justified by faith. But now that faith has come, we are no longer under a custodian; for *in Christ Jesus you are all sons of God, through faith*" (Gal. 3:23–26). This is not to say that the Old Testament completely omitted talk of God as our Father, for God did call himself the Father of the children of Israel and called them his children in several places (Ps. 103:13; Isa. 43:6–7; Mal. 1:6; 2:10). But even though there was a consciousness of God as Father to the people of Israel, the full benefits and privileges of membership in God's family, and the full realization of that membership, did not come until Christ came and the Spirit of the Son of God was poured into our hearts, bearing witness with our spirit that we were God's children.

What evidence do we see in our lives that we are God's children? Paul sees clear evidence in the fact that the Holy Spirit bears witness in our hearts that we are God's children: "But when the time had fully come, God sent forth his Son, born of woman, born under the law, to redeem those who were under the law, so that we might receive *adoption as sons*. And because *you are sons,* God has sent the Spirit of his Son into our hearts, crying, 'Abba! Father!' So through God you are no longer a slave *but a son,* and *if a son then an heir*" (Gal. 4:4–7).

John's first epistle places much emphasis on our status as children of God: "See what love the Father has given us, that we should be called *children of God;* and so we are. . . . Beloved, we are God's children now" (1 John 3:1–2; John frequently calls his readers "children" or "little children").[1]

Although Jesus does call us his "brothers" (Heb. 2:12 NIV) and he is therefore in one sense our older brother in God's family (cf. Heb. 2:14), and can be called "the firstborn among many brethren" (Rom. 8:29), he is nevertheless careful to make a clear distinction between the way in which God is our heavenly Father and the way in which he relates to God the Father. He says to Mary Magdalene, "I am ascending *to my Father and your Father,* to my God and your God" (John 20:17), thus making a clear distinction between the far greater and eternal sense in which God is his Father, and the sense in which God is our Father.

Although the New Testament says that we are *now* God's children (1 John 3:2), we should also note that there is another sense in which our adoption is still future because we will not receive the full benefits and privileges of adoption until Christ returns and we have new resurrection bodies. Paul speaks of this later, fuller sense of adoption when he says, "Not only the creation, but we ourselves, who have the first fruits of the Spirit, groan inwardly as we wait for adoption as sons, *the redemption of our bodies*" (Rom. 8:23). Here Paul sees the receiving of new

[1]There are several other passages that speak about our status as God's children or our membership in his family (see Matt. 5:48; 7:11; 2 Cor. 6:18; Eph. 5:1; Phil. 2:15; Heb. 2:13–14; 12:5–11; 1 Peter 1:14; 1 John 3:10).

resurrection bodies as the fulfillment of our privileges of adoption, so much so that he can refer to it as our "adoption as sons."

## B. Adoption Follows Conversion and Is an Outcome of Saving Faith

We might initially think that we would become God's children by regeneration, since the imagery of being "born again" in regeneration makes us think of children being born into a human family. But the New Testament never connects adoption with regeneration: indeed, the idea of *adoption* is opposite to the idea of being born into a family!

Rather, the New Testament connects adoption with saving faith, and says that in response to our trusting in Christ, God has adopted us into his family. Paul says, "In Christ Jesus you are all *sons of God, through faith*" (Gal. 3:23–26). And John writes, "But to all who received him, who *believed in his name,* he gave power *to become children of God*" (John 1:12).[2] These two verses make it clear that adoption follows conversion and is God's response to our faith.

One objection to this might be brought from Paul's statement, "*Because you are sons,* God has sent the Spirit of his Son into our hearts, crying, 'Abba! Father!'" (Gal. 4:6). Someone might understand this verse to mean that first God adopted us as sons and second he gave us the Holy Spirit to bring regeneration to our hearts. But a few verses earlier Paul had said that we have become sons of God "through faith" (Gal. 3:26). Therefore Paul's statement in Galatians 4:6 is best understood not to refer to the giving of the Holy Spirit in regeneration, but rather to an additional activity of the Holy Spirit in which he begins to bear witness with our spirit and to assure us that we are members of God's family. This work of the Holy Spirit gives us *assurance* of our adoption, and it is in this sense that Paul says that, after we have become sons, God causes his Holy Spirit within our hearts to cry, "Abba! Father!" (cf. Rom 8:15–16).

## C. Adoption Is Distinct From Justification

Although adoption is a privilege that comes to us at the time we become Christians (John 1:12; Gal 3:26; 1 John 3:1–2), nevertheless, it is a privilege that is distinct from justification and distinct from regeneration. In regeneration we are made spiritually alive, able to relate to God in prayer and worship and able to hear his Word with receptive hearts. But it is possible that God could have creatures who are spiritually alive and yet are not members of his family and do not share the special privileges of family members—angels, for example, apparently fall into that category.[3] Therefore, it would have been possible for God to decide to give us regeneration without the great privileges of adoption into his family.

---

[2]It is true that in John 1:13 he specifies that these were people who were born "of God," but this is simply giving additional information about them (namely, that they had been regenerated by God). That does not negate the fact that it was to those who "believed in his name" that Christ gave power to become children of God.

[3]Although both good and evil angels are in one place in Scripture called "the sons of God" (Job 1:6), this is apparently a reference to the status of sonship that comes by the fact that God created them. It does not seem to indicate that angels generally (especially evil angels) share in any of the family privileges that we receive as God's children. In fact, Heb. 2:14–16 makes a clear distinction between our status as God's children and the status of angels. Moreover, angels are nowhere else referred to as

Moreover, God could have given us justification without the privileges of adoption into his family, for he could have forgiven our sins and given us right legal standing before him without making us his children. It is important to realize this because it helps us to recognize how great are our privileges in adoption. Regeneration has to do with our spiritual life within. Justification has to do with our standing before God's law. But adoption has to do with our *relationship* with God as our Father, and in adoption we are given many of the greatest blessings that we will know for all eternity. When we begin to realize the excellence of these blessings, and when we appreciate that God has no obligation to give us any of them, then we will be able to exclaim with the apostle John, "See *what love* the Father has given us, that we should be called children of God; and so we are" (1 John 3:1).

## D. The Privileges of Adoption

The benefits or privileges that accompany adoption are seen, first, in the way God relates to us, and then also in the way we relate to one another as brothers and sisters in God's family.

One of the greatest privileges of our adoption is being able to speak to God and *relate to him as a* good and loving *Father*. We are to pray, "Our Father who art in heaven" (Matt. 6:9), and we are to realize that we are "no longer slaves, but sons" (Gal. 4:7). Therefore, we now relate to God not as a slave relates to a slave master, but as a child relates to his or her father. In fact, God gives us an *internal witness from the Holy Spirit* that causes us instinctively to call God our Father. "When we cry, 'Abba! Father!' it is the Spirit himself bearing witness with our spirit that we are children of God" (Rom. 8:15–16). This relationship to God as our Father is the foundation of many other blessings of the Christian life, and it becomes the primary way in which we relate to God. Certainly it is true that God is our Creator, our judge, our Lord and Master, our teacher, our provider and protector, and the one who by his providential care sustains our existence. But the role that is most intimate, and the role that conveys the highest privileges of fellowship with God for eternity, is his role as our heavenly Father.

The fact that God relates to us as Father shows very clearly that he *loves us* (1 John 3:1), that he *understands us* ("As a father has compassion on his children, so the LORD has compassion on those who fear him; for he knows how we are formed, he remembers that we are dust" [Ps. 103:13–14 NIV]), and that he *takes care of our needs* ("For the Gentiles seek all these things; and your heavenly Father knows that you need them all," Matt. 6:32). Moreover, in his role as our Father, God *gives us many good gifts:* "If you then, who are evil, know how to give good gifts to your children, how much more will your Father who is in heaven give good things to those who ask him!" (Matt. 7:11). He especially *gives us* the gift of *the Holy Spirit* to comfort us and to empower us for ministry and for living the Christian life (Luke 11:13).[4] In fact, it is not only gifts in this life that God gives

---

members of God's familyor said to have the family privileges that belong to us as God's children. (It is unlikely that Gen. 6:2–4 refers to angels; see Wayne Grudem, *The First Epistle of Peter,* pp. 211–15.)

[4]In this verse Jesus says, "If you then, who are evil, know how to give good gifts to your children, how much more will the heavenly Father give the Holy Spirit to those who ask him!" Here he seems to

to us, but he also gives us a great *inheritance in heaven*, because we have become joint heirs with Christ. Paul says, "You are no longer a slave, but a son, and if a son then an heir" (Gal. 4:7); we are in fact "heirs of God and fellow heirs with Christ" (Rom. 8:17). As heirs we have the rights to a great eternal "inheritance which is imperishable, undefiled, and unfading, kept in heaven for you" (1 Peter 1:4). All the great privileges and blessings of heaven are laid up for us and put at our disposal because we are children of the King, members of the royal family, princes and princesses who will reign with Christ over the new heavens and new earth (Rev. 2:26–27; 3:21). As a foretaste of this great privilege, angels are even now sent to minister to us and serve us (Heb. 1:14).

It is in the context of this relationship with God as our heavenly Father that we are to understand the prayer that Jesus told his disciples to pray daily, "*Our Father* who art in heaven . . . *forgive us our sins*, as we also have forgiven those who sin against us" (Matt. 6:9–12, author's translation). This daily prayer for forgiveness of sins is not a prayer that God would give us justification again and again throughout our lives, for justification is a one-time event that occurs immediately after we trust in Christ with saving faith. Rather, the prayer for forgiveness of sins each day is a prayer that God's fatherly relationship with us, which has been disrupted by sin that displeased him, be restored, and that he relate to us once again as a Father who delights in his children whom he loves. The prayer, "Forgive us our sins," therefore, is one in which we are relating not to God as eternal judge of the universe, but to God as a Father. It is a prayer in which we wish to restore the open fellowship with our Father that has been broken because of sin (see also 1 John 1:9; 3:19–22).

The privilege of being *led by the Holy Spirit* is also a benefit of adoption. Paul indicates that this is a moral benefit whereby the Holy Spirit puts in us desires to obey God and live according to his will. He says, "All who are *led by the Spirit of God* are *sons of God*" (Rom. 8:14), and he gives this as the *reason* Christians should "put to death the deeds of the body" by means of the Holy Spirit working within them (v. 13; note "for" at the beginning of v. 14). He sees the Holy Spirit as leading and guiding God's children in paths of obedience to God.

Another privilege of adoption into God's family, though we do not always recognize it as a privilege, is the fact that God *disciplines us* as his children. "My son, do not regard lightly the discipline of the Lord, nor lose courage when you are punished by him. For the Lord disciplines him whom he loves, and chastises every son whom he receives" (Heb. 12:5–6, quoting Prov. 3:11–12). The author of Hebrews explains, "God is treating you as sons; for what son is there whom his father does not discipline? . . . he disciplines us for our good, that we may share his holiness" (Heb. 12:7, 10). Just as earthly children grow in obedience and righteousness when they are disciplined properly by their earthly fathers, so we grow in righteousness and holiness when we are disciplined by our heavenly Father.

Related to the fatherly discipline of God is the fact that, as children of God and joint heirs with Christ, we have the *privilege of sharing both in his sufferings and in his subsequent glory*. Just as it was "necessary that the Christ should suffer these

mean not the gift of the Holy Spirit dwelling within as he comes at regeneration, but the gift of further empowering for ministry, for gifts to be used in ministry, or for Christian living.

things and enter into his glory" (Luke 24:26), so God gives us the privilege of walking the same path that Christ walked, enduring sufferings in this life that we may also receive great glory in the life to come: "if children, then heirs, heirs of God and fellow heirs with Christ, *provided we suffer with him* in order that we may also be *glorified with him*" (Rom. 8:17).

In addition to these great privileges that concern our relationship to God and fellowship with him, we also have privileges of adoption that affect the way that we relate to each other and affect our own personal conduct. Because we are God's children, our relationship with each other is far deeper and more intimate than the relationship that angels, for example, have to one another, for we are all *members of one family*. Many times the New Testament refers to Christians as "brothers" and "sisters" in Christ (Rom. 1:13; 8:12; 1 Cor. 1:10; 6:8; James 1:2; Matt. 12:50; Rom. 16:1; 1 Cor. 7:15; Philem. 1:2; James 2:15). In addition to this, the many verses in which entire churches are referred to as "brothers" should not be understood to refer to the men in the congregation only, but are rather generic references to the whole church, and, except where the context explicitly indicates otherwise, should be taken to mean "brothers and sisters in the Lord." The designation "brother" is so common in the epistles that it seems to be the predominant way in which the New Testament authors refer to the other Christians to whom they are writing. This indicates the strong consciousness they had of the nature of the church as the family of God. In fact, Paul tells Timothy to relate to the church at Ephesus, and to the individuals within the church, as he would relate to members of a large family: "Do not rebuke an older man but exhort him as you would a *father;* treat younger men like *brothers,* older women like *mothers,* younger women like *sisters,* in all purity" (1 Tim. 5:1–2).[5]

This concept of the church as God's family should give us a new perspective on the work of the church; it is "family work," and the various members of the family never should compete with each other or hinder one another in their efforts, but should encourage one another and be thankful for whatever good or whatever progress comes to any member of the family, for all are contributing to the good of the family and the honor of God our Father. In fact, just as members of an earthly family often have times of joy and fellowship when they work together on a single project, so our times of working together in building up the church ought to be times of great joy and fellowship with one another. Moreover, just as members of an earthly family honor their parents and fulfill the purpose of a family most when they eagerly welcome any brothers or sisters who are newly adopted into that family, so we ought to welcome new members of the family of Christ eagerly and with love.

Another aspect of our membership in God's family is that we, as God's children, are to *imitate our Father* in heaven in all our conduct. Paul says, "be imitators of God, as beloved children" (Eph. 5:1). Peter echoes this theme when he says, "As obedient children, do not be conformed to the passions of your former ignorance, but as he who called you is holy, be holy yourselves in all your conduct; since it is written, 'You shall be holy, for I am holy'" (1 Peter 1:14–16). Both Peter and

---

[5]An extensive analysis of the New Testament teaching on the church as a family is found in Vern S. Poythress, "The Church as a Family: Why Male Leadership in the Family Requires Male Leadership in the Church as Well," in W. Grudem and J. Piper, eds., *Recovering Biblical Manhood and Womanhood,* pp. 233–47.

Paul realize that it is natural for children to imitate their earthly fathers. They appeal to this natural sense that children have in order to remind us that we are to imitate our heavenly Father—indeed, this should be something we naturally want to do and delight in. If God our Father in heaven is holy, we should be holy as obedient children.

When we walk in paths of righteous conduct we *honor our heavenly Father* and bring glory to him. When we act in a way that is pleasing to God, we are to do so that others "may see your good works and give glory to your Father who is in heaven" (Matt. 5:16). Paul encourages the Philippians to maintain pure conduct before unbelievers "that you may be blameless and innocent, *children of God* without blemish in the midst of a crooked and perverse generation, among whom you shine as lights in the world" (Phil. 2:15). Indeed, a consistent pattern of moral conduct is also evidence that we are truly children of God. John says, "By this it may be seen who are the children of God, and who are the children of the devil: whoever does not do right is not of God, nor he who does not love his brother" (1 John 3:10).

## QUESTIONS FOR PERSONAL APPLICATION

1. Look back over the list of privileges that come with our adoption as God's children. Had you previously thought of these as automatically yours because you had been born again? Can you describe what our eternal life would be like if we had regeneration and justification and many of the other privileges that come with salvation, but no adoption into God's family? Now how do you feel about the fact that God has adopted you into his family compared with the way you felt before reading this chapter?

2. Has your relationship with your own human family become better or more difficult as a result of your becoming a Christian? If your relationship with your earthly family has become more difficult, how have you found Mark 10:29–30 to be true in your life as a Christian?

3. Sometimes people who have had unloving or cruel earthly fathers have found that their background creates difficulty in their thinking about God and relating to him as a heavenly Father. How can Hebrews 12:10, Matthew 7:11, and Luke 11:13, which contrast sinful earthly fathers with our perfect Father in heaven, be of help in that situation? Might 1 Peter 1:18 be helpful in this situation as well? What can a person who has had a cruel and unloving earthly father do to gain a better and better appreciation of who God is and what kind of Father he is? Do you think that any of the people who became Christians in the first century had cruel and unloving fathers, or no living fathers at all? What teachings of the Old Testament would have helped them at this point? Do you think that people who have had evil earthly fathers have a God-given inward sense of what a good father would be like?

4. Think of the people who are members of your church. Has this chapter helped you to think of them more as your brothers and sisters (or if they are older, as those who are like "fathers" and "mothers" to you)? How do you think an added appreciation of this idea of the church as a family would be helpful to your church? How could you encourage a greater appreciation of this idea?

5. Does your church have any sense of competition with other churches that might be overcome by greater appreciation of the doctrine of adoption?

6. In the human family, when one of the children commits a crime and is publicly punished for it, the entire family suffers shame. On the other hand, when a family member is honored for an outstanding achievement, the entire family is proud and rejoices. How does this analogy of events in a human family make you feel about your own personal level of holiness in life, and the way it reflects on the other members of your spiritual family? How does it make you feel about the need for personal holiness among your brothers and sisters in the church? Do you personally have a strong inward desire to imitate your heavenly Father in your conduct (Eph. 5:1; 1 Peter 1:14–16)?

7. Do you sense the Holy Spirit within you bearing witness with your spirit that your are a child of God (Rom. 8:15–16; Gal. 4:6)? Can you describe what that sense is like?

8. Do you sense any discrimination against Christians of other races or other social or economic positions? Can you understand how the doctrine of adoption should obliterate such distinctions in the church (see Gal. 3:26–28)? Can you also see how the doctrine of adoption means that neither men nor women should think of the other sex as more important or less important in the church (see Gal. 3:28)?

## SPECIAL TERM

adoption

## BIBLIOGRAPHY

(For an explanation of this bibliography see the note on the bibliography to chapter 1, p. 38. Complete bibliographical data may be found on pp. 1223–29.
Note: Many systematic theologies do not treat adoption as a separate topic, but include a discussion of the privileges of adoption in a discussion of justification and its results.)

### Sections in Evangelical Systematic Theologies

1. Anglican (Episcopalian)
    1882–92     Litton (no explicit treatment)
2. Arminian (Wesleyan or Methodist)
    1875–76     Pope, 3:1–27

|      | 1892–94 | Miley, 2:337–38 |
|      | 1940    | Wiley, 2:402–39 |
|      | 1960    | Purkiser, 297–98 |

3. Baptist

|      | 1767    | Gill, 1:288–91; 2:93–107 |
|      | 1887    | Boyce, 404–9 |
|      | 1917    | Mullins, 401–9 |
|      | 1983–85 | Erickson, 961–66 |

4. Dispensational

|      | 1947    | Chafer, 3:241–43 |
|      | 1949    | Thiessen, 278–82 |
|      | 1986    | Ryrie, 301–2, 306–7 |

5. Lutheran

|      | 1917–24 | Pieper, 2:408–9 |

6. Reformed (or Presbyterian)

|      | 1937–66 | Murray, CW, 2:223–34; RAA, 132–40 |
|      | 1962    | Buswell, 2:212–13 |

## Sections in Representative Roman Catholic Systematic Theologies

1. Roman Catholic: Traditional

|      | 1955 | Ott (no explicit treatment) |

2. Roman Catholic: Post-Vatican II

|      | 1980 | McBrien (no explicit treatment) |

### Other Works

Davids, P. H. "Adoption." In EDT, p. 13.

Murray, John. "Adoption." In Redemption Accomplished and Applied. Grand Rapids: Eerdmans, 1955, pp. 132–40.

## SCRIPTURE MEMORY PASSAGE

**Romans 8:14–17:** *For all who are led by the Spirit of God are sons of God. For you did not receive the spirit of slavery to fall back into fear, but you have received the spirit of sonship. When we cry, "Abba! Father!" it is the Spirit himself bearing witness with our spirit that we are children of God, and if children, then heirs, heirs of God and fellow heirs with Christ, provided we suffer with him in order that we may also be glorified with him.*

## HYMN

"Children of the Heavenly Father"

Children of the heav'nly Father
    Safely in his bosom gather;
Nestling bird nor star in heaven
    Such a refuge e'er was given.

God his own doth tend and nourish,
    In his holy courts they flourish;
From all evil things he spares them,
    In his mighty arms he bears them.

Neither life nor death shall ever
    From the Lord his children sever;
Unto them his grace he showeth,
    And their sorrows all he knoweth.

Praise the Lord in joyful numbers,
    Your Protector never slumbers;
At the will of your Defender
    Every foeman must surrender.

Though he giveth or he taketh,
    God his children ne'er forsaketh;
His the loving purpose solely
    To preserve them pure and holy.

AUTHOR: CAROLINE V. SANDELL BERG, C. 1855
(TRANS. ERNST W. OLSON, 1925)

# Chapter 38

# Sanctification (Growth in Likeness to Christ)

*How do we grow in Christian maturity? What are the blessings of Christian growth?*

## EXPLANATION AND SCRIPTURAL BASIS

The previous chapters have discussed several acts of God that occur at the beginning of our Christian lives: the gospel call (which God addresses to us), regeneration (by which God imparts new life to us), justification (by which God gives us right legal standing before him), and adoption (in which God makes us members of his family). We have also discussed conversion (in which we repent of sins and trust in Christ for salvation). These events all occur at the beginning of our Christian lives.[1]

But now we come to a part of the application of redemption that is a *progressive* work that continues throughout our earthly lives. It is also a work in which *God and man cooperate,* each playing distinct roles. This part of the application of redemption is called sanctification: *Sanctification is a progressive work of God and man that makes us more and more free from sin and like Christ in our actual lives.*

## A. Differences Between Justification and Sanctification

The following table specifies several differences between justification and sanctification:

| Justification | Sanctification |
|---|---|
| Legal standing | Internal condition |
| Once for all time | Continuous throughout life |
| Entirely God's work | We cooperate |
| Perfect in this life | Not perfect in this life |
| The same in all Christians | Greater in some than in others |

As this chart indicates, sanctification is something that continues throughout our Christian life. The ordinary course of a Christian's life will involve continual

---

[1]Although the initial saving faith by which we are justified occurs only at the time of conversion, faith and repentance do continue throughout our lives as well (see chapter 35, pp. 717–18). Similarly, although regeneration, justification, and adoption are instantaneous one-time events that occur at the beginning of the Christian life, the results of all of these continue throughout life: we continue to have the spiritual life we receive from regeneration, the legal standing we receive from justification, and the membership in God's family we receive from adoption.

growth in sanctification, and it is something that the New Testament encourages us to give effort and attention to.

## B. Three Stages of Sanctification

**1. Sanctification Has a Definite Beginning at Regeneration.** A definite moral change occurs in our lives at the point of regeneration, for Paul talks about the "washing of regeneration and renewal in the Holy Spirit" (Titus 3:5). Once we have been born again we cannot continue to sin as a habit or a pattern of life (1 John 3:9), because the power of new spiritual life within us keeps us from yielding to a life of sin.

This initial moral change is the first stage in sanctification. In this sense, there is some overlap between regeneration and sanctification, for this moral change is actually a part of regeneration. But when we view it from the standpoint of moral change within us, we can also see it as the first stage in sanctification. Paul looks back on a completed event when he says to the Corinthians, "But you were washed, *you were sanctified,* you were justified in the name of the Lord Jesus Christ and in the Spirit of our God" (1 Cor. 6:11). Similarly, in Acts 20:32 Paul can refer to Christians as "all those who are sanctified."[2]

This initial step in sanctification involves a definite break from the ruling power and love of sin, so that the believer is no longer ruled or dominated by sin and no longer loves to sin. Paul says, "So you also must *consider yourselves dead to sin* and alive to God in Christ Jesus. . . . For *sin will have no dominion over you*" (Rom. 6:11, 14). Paul says that Christians have been "set free from sin" (Rom. 6:18). In this context, to be dead to sin or to be set free from sin involves the power to overcome acts or patterns of sinful behavior in one's life. Paul tells the Romans not to let sin "reign in your mortal bodies," and he also says, "Do not yield your members to sin as instruments of wickedness, but yield yourselves to God" (Rom. 6:12–13). To be dead to the ruling power of sin means that we as Christians, by virtue of the power of the Holy Spirit and the resurrection life of Christ working within us, have power to overcome the temptations and enticements of sin. Sin will no longer be our master, as once it was before we became Christians.

In practical terms, this means that we must affirm two things to be true. On the one hand, we will never be able to say, "I am completely free from sin," because our sanctification will never be completed (see below). But on the other hand, a Christian should never say (for example), "This sin has defeated me. I give up. I have had a bad temper for thirty-seven years, and I will have one until the day I die, and people are just going to have to put up with me the way I am!" To say this is to say that sin has gained dominion. It is to allow sin to reign in our bodies. It is to admit defeat. It is to deny the truth of Scripture, which tells us, "You also must consider yourselves dead to sin and alive to God in Christ Jesus" (Rom. 6:11). It is to deny the truth of Scripture that tells us that "sin will have no dominion over you" (Rom. 6:14).

This initial break with sin, then, involves a reorientation of our desires so that

---

[2]The Greek expression is *tois hēgiasmenois,* a substantival perfect passive participle that expresses both a completed past activity (they were sanctified) and a continuing result (they continue to experience the sanctifying influence of that past action).

we no longer have a dominant love for sin in our lives. Paul knows that his readers were formerly slaves to sin (as all unbelievers are), but he says that they are enslaved no longer. "You who were once slaves of sin have become obedient from the heart to the standard of teaching to which you were committed, and, having been set free from sin, have become slaves of righteousness" (Rom. 6:17–18). This change of one's primary love and primary desires occurs at the beginning of sanctification.[3]

**2. Sanctification Increases Throughout Life.** Even though the New Testament speaks about a definite beginning to sanctification, it also sees it as a process that continues throughout our Christian lives. This is the primary sense in which sanctification is used in systematic theology and in Christian conversation generally today.[4] Although Paul says that his readers have been set free from sin (Rom. 6:18) and that they are "dead to sin and alive to God" (Rom. 6:11), he nonetheless recognizes that sin remains in their lives, so he tells them not to let it reign and not to yield to it (Rom. 6:12–13). Their task, therefore, as Christians is to grow more and more in sanctification, just as they previously grew more and more in sin: "Just as you once yielded your members to impurity and to greater and greater iniquity, so now yield your members to righteousness for sanctification" (Rom. 6:19; the words "just as . . . so now" [Gk. *hōsper . . . houtōs*] indicate that Paul wants them to do this in the same way: "just as" they previously yielded to more and more sin, "in just the same way" they are now to yield themselves to more and more righteousness for sanctification).

Paul says that throughout the Christian life "we all . . . are being changed into his likeness from one degree of glory to another" (2 Cor. 3:18). We are progressively becoming more and more like Christ as we go on in the Christian

---

[3]Some may wish to add to this section one or more passages from Hebrews that speak about our sanctification as having been completed in the past. For example, the author says that by the will of God "we have been sanctified through the offering of the body of Jesus Christ once for all" (Heb. 10:10). The Greek expression is a periphrastic perfect passive participle, *hēgiasmenoi esmen*, which speaks of a continuing present situation that results from a completed past action: "We are continually in the state of 'having been sanctified' (and we continue to feel the results of that previous act of sanctification)."

But in Hebrews the term *sanctify* (Gk. *hagiazō*) is related more to the Old Testament background of ceremonial purity or holiness as necessary for access to God's presence, and therefore "sanctified" in Hebrews means "made holy and righteous in God's sight and therefore fit to draw near to God in worship." As such, "sanctified" in Hebrews is roughly equivalent to "justified" in Paul's vocabulary. This sense of "sanctified" can be seen in Heb. 9:13; 10:10; 13:12. These passages speak of a ceremonial kind of purification that allows access to God, and, as such, "sanctification" here applies to the beginning of the Christian life. Nevertheless, the focus is more on access to God in worship, while the Pauline emphasis is on justification from the penalty of sin that was due under God's law.

[4]There is a different usage of the word *sanctified* in the Wesleyan/Holiness tradition within Protestantism. In these circles the experience of sanctification is sometimes viewed as a single event subsequent to conversion in which a Christian attains a higher level of holiness, a level sometimes known as "entire sanctification" or "sinless perfection." Within this tradition, sanctification is seen as an experience one seeks for in the Christian life and is sometimes able to attain. (See the systematic theologies listed under the category "Arminian" in the bibliography at the end of this chapter.) Therefore, while most Protestants would say, "I am being sanctified," some within the Wesleyan/Holiness tradition would say, "I *have been* sanctified," referring not to the initial break with sin that comes with conversion, but to a subsequent experience in which they began to know freedom from conscious sin in their lives. The difficulties with this position are outlined in section 4 below, "Sanctification Is Never Completed in This Life."

life. Therefore he says, "Forgetting what lies behind and straining forward to what lies ahead, *I press on* toward the goal for the prize of the upward call of God in Christ Jesus" (Phil. 3:13–14)—this is in the context of saying that he is not already perfect but he presses on to achieve all of the purposes for which Christ has saved him (vv. 9–12).

Paul tells the Colossians that they should not lie to one another, since they have "put on the new nature, which is *being renewed* in knowledge after the image of its creator" (Col. 3:10), thus showing that sanctification even involves increasing likeness to God in our thoughts as well as our words and deeds. The author of Hebrews tells his readers to "lay aside every weight, and sin which clings so closely" (Heb. 12:1), and to *"strive for . . . the holiness* without which no one will see the Lord" (Heb. 12:14). James encourages his hearers, "Be doers of the word, and not hearers only" (James 1:22), and Peter tells his readers, "Be holy yourselves in all your conduct" (1 Peter 1:15).

It is not necessary to list multiple additional quotations, because much of the New Testament is taken up with instructing believers in various churches on how they should grow in likeness to Christ. All of the moral exhortations and commands in the New Testament epistles apply here, because they all exhort believers to one aspect or another of greater sanctification in their lives. It is the expectation of all the New Testament authors that our sanctification will increase throughout our Christian lives.

**3. Sanctification Is Completed at Death (for Our Souls) and When the Lord Returns (for Our Bodies).** Because there is sin that still remains in our hearts even though we have become Christians (Rom. 6:12–13; 1 John 1:8), our sanctification will never be completed in this life (see below). But once we die and go to be with the Lord, then our sanctification is completed in one sense, for our souls are set free from indwelling sin and are made perfect. The author of Hebrews says that when we come into the presence of God to worship we come "to the spirits of just men *made perfect"* (Heb. 12:23). This is only appropriate because it is in anticipation of the fact that "nothing unclean shall enter" into the presence of God, the heavenly city (Rev. 21:27).

However, when we appreciate that sanctification involves the whole person, including our bodies (see 2 Cor. 7:1; 1 Thess. 5:23), then we realize that sanctification will not be entirely completed until the Lord returns and we receive new resurrection bodies. We await the coming of our Lord Jesus Christ from heaven, and he "will change our lowly body to be like his glorious body" (Phil. 3:21). It is "at his coming" (1 Cor. 15:23) that we will be made alive with a resurrection body and then we shall fully "bear the image of the Man of heaven" (1 Cor. 15:49).[5]

We may diagram the process of sanctification as in figure 38.1, showing that we are slaves to sin prior to conversion, (1) that there is a definite beginning to sanctification at the point of conversion, (2) that sanctification should increase throughout the Christian life, and (3) that sanctification is made perfect at death. (The completion of sanctification when we receive resurrection bodies is omitted from this chart for the sake of simplicity.)

---

[5]See chapter 42 on glorification (that is, receiving a resurrection body when Christ returns).

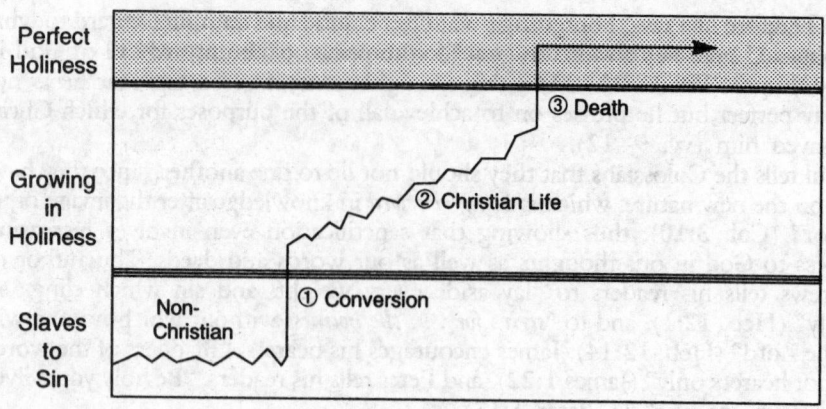

**THE PROCESS OF SANCTIFICATION**
*Figure 38.1*

I have shown the progress of sanctification as a jagged line on this chart, indicating that growth in sanctification is not always one-directional in this life, but that progress in sanctification occurs at some times, while at other times we realize that we are regressing somewhat. In the extreme case, a believer who makes very little use of the means of sanctification, but rather has bad teaching, lacks good Christian fellowship, and pays little attention to God's Word and prayer, may actually go for many years with very little progress in sanctification at all—but this is certainly not the normal or expected pattern of the Christian life. It is in fact highly abnormal.

**4. Sanctification Is Never Completed in This Life.** There have always been some in the history of the church who have taken commands such as Matthew 5:48 ("You, therefore, *must be perfect*, as your heavenly Father is perfect") or 2 Corinthians 7:1 ("let us cleanse ourselves from every defilement of body and spirit, and *make holiness perfect* in the fear of God") and reasoned that since God gives us these commands, he must also give us the ability to obey them perfectly. Therefore, they have concluded, it is possible for us to attain a state of sinless perfection in this life. Moreover, they point to Paul's prayer for the Thessalonians, "May the God of peace himself sanctify you wholly" (1 Thess. 5:23), and infer that Paul's prayer may well have been fulfilled for some of the Thessalonian Christians. In fact, John even says, "No one who abides in him sins" (1 John 3:6)! Do these verses not point to the possibility of sinless perfection in the life of some Christians? In this discussion, I will use the term *perfectionism* to refer to this view that sinless perfection is possible in this life.

On closer inspection, these passages do not support the perfectionist position. First, it is simply not taught in Scripture that when God gives a command, he also gives the ability to obey it in every case.[6] God commands all people everywhere to obey all of his moral laws and holds them accountable for failing to obey them, even though unredeemed people are sinners and, as such, dead in trespasses and sins, and thus unable to obey God's commands. When Jesus commands us to be perfect as our Father in heaven is perfect (Matt. 5:48), this simply shows that God's own absolute moral purity is the standard toward which we are to aim and the standard for which God holds us accountable. The fact that we are unable to attain that standard does not mean that it will be lowered; rather, it means that we need God's grace and forgiveness to overcome our remaining sin. Similarly, when Paul commands the Corinthians to make holiness perfect in the fear of the Lord (2 Cor. 7:1), or prays that God would sanctify the Thessalonians wholly (1 Thess. 5:23), he is pointing to the goal that he desires them to reach. He does not imply that any reach it, but only that this is the high moral standard toward which God wants all believers to aspire.

John's statement that "No one who abides in him sins" (1 John 3:6) does not teach that some of us attain perfection, because the present-tense Greek verbs are better translated as indicating continual or habitual activity: "No one who lives in him *keeps on sinning*. No one who *continues to sin* has either seen him or known him" (1 John 3:6 NIV). This is similar to John's statement a few verses later, "No one who is born of God will continue to sin, because God's seed remains in him; he cannot go on sinning, because he has been born of God" (1 John 3:9 NIV). If these verses were taken to prove sinless perfection, they would have to prove it for all Christians, because they talk about what is true of everyone born of God, and everyone who has seen Christ and known him.[7]

Therefore, there do not seem to be any convincing verses in Scripture that teach that it is possible for anyone to be completely free of sin in this life. On the other hand, there are passages in both the Old and New Testaments that clearly teach that we cannot be morally perfect in this life. In Solomon's prayer at the dedication of the temple, he says, "If they sin against you—for *there is no man who does not sin*" (1 Kings 8:46). Similarly, we read a rhetorical question with an implied negative answer in Proverbs 20:9: "Who can say, 'I have made my heart clean; I am pure from my sin'?" And we read the explicit statement in Ecclesiastes 7:20, "*Surely there is not a righteous man on earth who does good and never sins.*"

In the New Testament, we find Jesus commanding his disciples to pray, "Give us this day our daily bread; and *forgive us our sins,* as we also have forgiven those who sin against us" (Matt. 6:11–12, author's translation). Just as the prayer for daily bread provides a model for a prayer that should be repeated each day, so the prayer for the forgiveness of sins is included in the type of prayer that should be made each day in a believer's life.

As we noted above, when Paul talks about the new power over sin that is given to a Christian, he does not say that there will be no sin in the Christian's life, but simply tells the believers not to let sin "reign" in their bodies nor to "yield" their members to sin (Rom. 6:12–13). He does not say that they will not sin, but says that sin will not dominate or "have . . . dominion" over them (Rom. 6:14). The

---

[6]See chapter 24, p. 499, for a discussion of the fact that God's commands in Scripture do not always imply that we have the ability to obey them.

[7]1 John 5:18 is to be understood in a similar way.

very fact that he issues these directions shows his realization that sin will continue to be present in the lives of believers throughout their time on earth. Even James the brother of our Lord could say, *"We all make many mistakes"* (James 3:2), and if James himself can say this, then we certainly should be willing to say it as well. Finally, in the same letter in which John declares so frequently that a child of God will not continue in a pattern of sinful behavior, he also says clearly, "If we say we have no sin, we deceive ourselves, and the truth is not in us" (1 John 1:8). Here John explicitly excludes the possibility of being completely free from sin in our lives. In fact, he says that anyone who claims to be free from sin is simply deceiving himself, and the truth is not in him.[8]

But once we have concluded that sanctification will never be completed in this life, we must exercise pastoral wisdom and caution in the way we use this truth. Some may take this fact and use it as an excuse not to strive for holiness or grow in sanctification—a procedure exactly contrary to dozens of New Testament commands. Others may think about the fact that we cannot be perfect in this life and lose hope of making any progress in the Christian life—an attitude that is also contrary to the clear teaching of Romans 6 and other passages about the resurrection power of Christ in our lives enabling us to overcome sin. Therefore, although sanctification will never be completed in this life, we must also emphasize that it should never stop increasing in this life.

Moreover, as Christians grow in maturity, the kinds of sin that remain in their lives are often not so much sins of words or deeds that are outwardly noticeable to others, but inward sins of attitudes and motives of the heart—desires such as pride and selfishness, lack of courage or faith, lack of zeal in loving God with our whole hearts and our neighbors as ourselves, and failure to fully trust God for all that he promises in every situation. These are real sins! They show how far short we fall of the moral perfection of Christ.

However, recognizing the nature of these sins that will persist even in more mature Christians also helps to guard against misunderstanding when we say that no one will be perfect and free from sin in this life. It is certainly possible that many mature Christians at many times during the day are free from conscious or willful acts of disobedience to God in their words or their deeds. In fact, if Christian leaders are to "set the believers an *example* in speech and conduct, in love, in faith, in purity" (1 Tim. 4:12), then it will frequently be true that their lives will be free from words or deeds that others will count as blameworthy. But this is far removed from attaining total freedom from sin in our motives and in the thoughts and intents of our hearts.

John Murray notes that when Isaiah the prophet came into the presence of God he could only cry out, "Woe is me! For I am lost; for I am a man of unclean lips, and I dwell in the midst of a people of unclean lips; for my eyes have seen the King, the LORD of hosts!" (Isa. 6:5). And when Job, whose righteousness was earlier commended in the story about his life, came into the presence of almighty God, he could only say, "I had heard of you by the hearing of the ear, but now my eye sees you; therefore I despise myself, and repent in dust and ashes" (Job 42:5–

---

[8]See chapter 24, p. 498, n. 16, for a discussion of the view that 1 John 1:8 does not necessarily apply to all Christians.

6). Murray concludes from these examples and from the testimony of other saints through the history of the church:

> Indeed, the more sanctified the person is, the more conformed he is to the image of his Savior, the more he must recoil against every lack of conformity to the holiness of God. The deeper his apprehension of the majesty of God, the greater the intensity of his love to God, the more persistent his yearning for the attainment of the prize of the high calling of God in Christ Jesus, the more conscious will he be of the gravity of the sin that remains and the more poignant will be his detestation of it. . . . Was this not the effect in all the people of God as they came into closer proximity to the revelation of God's holiness?[9]

## C. God and Man Cooperate in Sanctification

Some (such as John Murray)[10] object to saying that God and man "cooperate" in sanctification, because they want to insist that God's work is primary and our work in sanctification is only a secondary one (see Phil. 2:12–13). However, if we explain the nature of God's role and our role in sanctification clearly, it does not seem inappropriate to say that God and man cooperate in sanctification. God works in our sanctification and we work as well, and we work for the same purpose. We are not saying that we have equal roles in sanctification or that we both work in the same way, but simply that we cooperate with God in ways that are appropriate to our status as God's creatures. And the fact that Scripture emphasizes the role that we play in sanctification (with all the moral commands of the New Testament), makes it appropriate to teach that God calls us to cooperate with him in this activity.[11]

**1. God's Role in Sanctification.** Since sanctification is primarily a work of God, it is appropriate that Paul prays, "May the God of peace himself sanctify you wholly" (1 Thess. 5:23). One specific role of God the Father in this sanctification is his process of disciplining us as his children (see Heb. 12:5–11). Paul tells the Philippians, *"God is at work in you,* both to will and to work for his good pleasure" (Phil. 2:13), thus indicating something of the way in which God sanctifies them—both by causing them to want his will and by giving them power to do it. The author of Hebrews speaks of the role of the Father and the role of the Son in a familiar benediction: "Now may the God of peace . . . equip you with everything good that you may do his will, working in you that which is pleasing in his sight, through Jesus Christ; to whom be glory for ever and ever" (Heb. 13:20–21).

The role of God the Son, Jesus Christ, in sanctification is, first, that he *earned* our sanctification for us. Therefore Paul could say that God made Christ to be "our wisdom, our righteousness and sanctification and redemption" (1 Cor.

---

[9]John Murray, *Redemption Accomplished and Applied,* p. 145.

[10]Ibid., pp. 148–49.

[11]On the other hand, if we wish to say that sanctification is entirely God's work, and that we use the means of sanctification in order to contribute to it (or some similar expression), the meaning is the same. I am simply concerned that if we say sanctification is entirely God's work, we can be misunderstood and encourage an excessively passive role on the part of Christians, who may be led to think that they need to do nothing in the process of sanctification in their lives.

1:30). Moreover, in the process of sanctification, Jesus is also our *example,* for we are to run the race of life "looking to Jesus the pioneer and perfecter of our faith" (Heb. 12:2). Peter tells his readers, "Christ also suffered for you, leaving you an example, that you should follow in his steps" (1 Peter 2:21). And John says, "He who says he abides in him ought to walk in the same way in which he walked" (1 John 2:6).

But it is specifically God the Holy Spirit who works within us to change us and sanctify us, giving us greater holiness of life. Peter speaks of the "sanctification of the Spirit" (1 Peter 1:2, author's translation), and Paul speaks of "sanctification by the Spirit" (2 Thess. 2:13). It is the Holy Spirit who produces in us the "fruit of the Spirit" (Gal. 5:22–23), those character traits that are part of greater and greater sanctification. If we grow in sanctification we "walk by the Spirit" and are "led by the Spirit" (Gal. 5:16–18; cf. Rom. 8:14), that is, we are more and more responsive to the desires and promptings of the Holy Spirit in our life and character. The Holy Spirit is the spirit of holiness, and he produces holiness within us.[12]

## 2. Our Role in Sanctification.

The role that we play in sanctification is both a *passive* one in which we depend on God to sanctify us, and an *active* one in which we strive to obey God and take steps that will increase our sanctification. We can now consider both of these aspects of our role in sanctification.

First, what may be called the "passive" role that we play in sanctification is seen in texts that encourage us to trust God or to pray and ask that he sanctify us. Paul tells his readers, "*Yield yourselves to God* as men who have been brought from death to life" (Rom. 6:13; cf. v. 19), and he tells the Roman Christians, "Present your bodies as a living sacrifice, holy and acceptable to God" (Rom. 12:1). Paul realizes that we are dependent on the Holy Spirit's work to grow in sanctification, because he says, "If *by the Spirit* you put to death the deeds of the body you will live" (Rom. 8:13).

Unfortunately today, this "passive" role in sanctification, this idea of yielding to God and trusting him to work in us "to will and to work for his good pleasure" (Phil. 2:13), is sometimes so strongly emphasized that it is the only thing people are told about the path of sanctification. Sometimes the popular phrase "let go and let God" is given as a summary of how to live the Christian life. But this is a tragic distortion of the doctrine of sanctification, for it only speaks of one half of the part we must play, and, by itself, will lead Christians to become lazy and to neglect the active role that Scripture commands them to play in their own sanctification.

That active role which we are to play is indicated by Romans 8:13, where Paul says, "If by the Spirit *you* put to death the deeds of the body you will live." Here Paul acknowledges that it is "by the Spirit" that we are able to do this. But he also says we must do it! It is not the Holy Spirit who is commanded to put to death the deeds of the flesh, but Christians! Similarly, Paul tells the Philippians, "Therefore, my beloved, as you have always obeyed, so now, not only as in my presence but much more in my absence, *work out your own salvation* with fear and trembling; for God is at work in you, both to will and to work for his good

---

[12]See chapter 30, pp. 642–43, for a further discussion of the work of the Holy Spirit in sanctification.

pleasure" (Phil. 2:12–13). Paul encourages them to obey even more than they did when he was present. He says that obedience is the way in which they "work out [their] own salvation," meaning that they will "work out" the further realization of the benefits of salvation in their Christian life.[13] The Philippians are to work at this growth in sanctification, and to do it solemnly and with reverence ("with fear and trembling"), for they are doing it in the presence of God himself. But there is more: the reason why they are to work and to expect that their work will yield positive results is that "God is at work in you"—the prior and foundational work of God in sanctification means that their own work is empowered by God; therefore it will be worthwhile and will bear positive results.

There are many aspects to this active role that we are to play in sanctification. We are to "*Strive . . . for* the *holiness* without which no one will see the Lord" (Heb. 12:14); we are to "*abstain from immorality*" and so obey the will of God, which is our "sanctification" (1 Thess. 4:3). John says that those who hope to be like Christ when he appears will actively work at purification in this life: "And every one who thus hopes in him *purifies himself* as he is pure" (1 John 3:3). Paul tells the Corinthians to "*shun immorality*" (1 Cor. 6:18), and not to have partnership with unbelievers (2 Cor. 6:14). He then says, "Let us *cleanse ourselves* from every defilement of body and spirit, and make holiness perfect in the fear of God" (2 Cor. 7:1). This kind of striving for obedience to God and for holiness may involve great effort on our part, for Peter tells his readers to "*make every effort*" to grow in character traits that accord with godliness (2 Peter 1:5). Many specific passages of the New Testament encourage detailed attention to various aspects of holiness and godliness in life (see Rom. 12:1–13:14; Eph. 4:17–6:20; Phil. 4:4–9; Col. 3:5–4:6; 1 Peter 2:11–5:11; et al.). We are continually to build up patterns and habits of holiness, for one measure of maturity is that mature Christians "have their faculties trained by practice to distinguish good from evil" (Heb. 5:14).

The New Testament does not suggest any short-cuts by which we can grow in sanctification, but simply encourages us repeatedly to give ourselves to the old-fashioned, time-honored means of Bible reading and meditation (Ps. 1:2; Matt. 4:4; 17:17), prayer (Eph. 6:18; Phil. 4:6), worship (Eph. 5:18–20), witnessing (Matt. 28:19–20), Christian fellowship (Heb. 10:24–25), and self-discipline or self-control (Gal. 5:23; Titus 1:8).

It is important that we continue to grow both in our passive trust in God to sanctify us and in our active striving for holiness and greater obedience in our lives. If we neglect active striving to obey God, we become passive, lazy Christians. If we neglect the passive role of trusting God and yielding to him, we become proud and overly confident in ourselves. In either case, our sanctification will be greatly deficient. We must maintain faith and diligence to obey at the same time. The old hymn wisely says, "*Trust and obey,* for there's no other way, to be happy in Jesus, but to trust and obey."[14]

---

[13]This verse does not use the word "salvation" to refer to initial justification, but to the ongoing process of experiencing more and more of the blessings of salvation; here, "salvation" is roughly equivalent to "sanctification."

[14]Comparing our life to a tree with two large roots, John Livingstone said, "Satan strikes . . . either at the root of faith or at the root of diligence" (quoted in D. M. M'Intyre, *The Hidden Life of Prayer* [Minneapolis: Bethany Fellowship, 1969], p. 39).

One more point must be added to this discussion of our role in sanctification: sanctification is usually a corporate process in the New Testament. It is something that happens in community. We are admonished, "Let us consider how to *stir up one another to love and good works,* not neglecting to meet together, as is the habit of some, but encouraging one another, and all the more as you see the Day drawing near" (Heb. 10:24–25). Together Christians are "built into a spiritual house, to be a holy priesthood" (1 Peter 2:5); together they are "a holy nation" (1 Peter 2:9); together they are to "encourage one another and build one another up" (1 Thess. 5:11). Paul says that "to lead a life worthy of the calling to which you have been called" (Eph. 4:1) is to live in a special way in community—"with all lowliness and meekness, with patience, forbearing one another in love, eager to maintain the unity of the Spirit in the bond of peace" (Eph. 4:2–3). When that happens, the body of Christ functions as a unified whole, with each part "working properly," so that corporate sanctification occurs as it "makes bodily growth and upbuilds itself in love" (Eph. 4:16; cf. 1 Cor. 12:12–26; Gal. 6:1–2). It is significant that the fruit of the Spirit includes many things that build community ("love, joy, peace, patience, kindness, goodness, faithfulness, gentleness, self-control," Gal. 5:22–23), whereas "the works of the flesh" destroy community ("fornication, impurity, licentiousness, idolatry, sorcery, enmity, strife, jealousy, anger, selfishness, dissension, party spirit, envy, drunkenness, carousing, and the like," Gal. 5:19–21).

### D. Sanctification Affects the Whole Person

We see that sanctification affects our *intellect* and our knowledge when Paul says that we have put on the new nature "which is being renewed in *knowledge* after the image of its creator" (Col. 3:10). He prays that the Philippians may see their love "abound more and more, with knowledge and all discernment" (Phil. 1:9). And he urges the Roman Christians to be "transformed by the renewal of your mind" (Rom. 12:2). Although our knowledge of God is more than intellectual knowledge, there is certainly an intellectual component to it, and Paul says that this knowledge of God should keep increasing throughout our lives: a life "worthy of the Lord, fully pleasing to him" is one that is continually "increasing in the knowledge of God" (Col. 1:10). The sanctification of our intellects will involve growth in wisdom and knowledge as we increasingly "take every thought captive to obey Christ" (2 Cor. 10:5) and find that our thoughts are more and more the thoughts that God himself imparts to us in his Word.

Moreover, growth in sanctification will affect our *emotions.* We will see increasingly in our lives emotions such as "love, joy, peace, patience" (Gal. 5:22). We will be able increasingly to obey Peter's command "to abstain from the passions of the flesh that wage war against your soul" (1 Peter 2:11). We will find it increasingly true that we do not "love the world or things in the world" (1 John 2:15), but that we, like our Savior, delight to do God's will. In ever-increasing measure we will become "obedient from the heart" (Rom. 6:17), and we will "put away" the negative emotions involved in "bitterness and wrath and anger and clamor and slander" (Eph. 4:31).

Moreover, sanctification will have an effect on our *will,* our decision-making faculty, because God is at work in us, "to *will* and to work for his good pleasure"

(Phil. 2:13). As we grow in sanctification, our will will be more and more conformed to the will of our heavenly Father.

Sanctification will also affect our *spirit,* the nonphysical part of our beings. We are to "cleanse ourselves from every defilement of body and *spirit,* and make holiness perfect in the fear of God" (2 Cor. 7:1), and Paul says that a concern about the affairs of the Lord will mean taking thought for "how to be holy in body and *spirit*" (1 Cor. 7:34).[15]

Finally, sanctification affects our *physical bodies.* Paul says, "May the God of peace himself sanctify you wholly; and may your spirit and soul *and body* be kept sound and blameless at the coming of our Lord Jesus Christ" (1 Thess. 5:23). Moreover, Paul encourages the Corinthians, "Let us cleanse ourselves from every defilement of *body* and spirit, and make holiness perfect in the fear of God" (2 Cor. 7:1; cf. 1 Cor. 7:34). As we become more sanctified in our bodies, our bodies become more and more useful servants of God, more and more responsive to the will of God and the desires of the Holy Spirit (cf. 1 Cor. 9:27).[16] We will not let sin reign in our bodies (Rom. 6:4) nor allow our bodies to participate in any way in immorality (1 Cor. 6:13), but will treat our bodies with care and will recognize that they are the means by which the Holy Spirit works through us in this life. Therefore they are not to be recklessly abused or mistreated, but are to be made useful and able to respond to God's will: "Do you not know that your body is a temple of the Holy Spirit within you, which you have from God? You are not your own; you were bought with a price. So glorify God in your body" (1 Cor. 6:19–20).

## E. Motives for Obedience to God in the Christian Life

Christians sometimes fail to recognize the wide range of motives for obedience to God that are found in the New Testament. (1) It is true that a desire to please God and express our love to him is a very important motive for obeying him— Jesus says, "If you love me, you will keep my commandments" (John 14:15), and, "He who has my commandments and keeps them, he it is who loves me" (John 14:21; cf. 1 John 5:3). But many other motives are also given to us: (2) the need to keep a clear conscience before God (Rom. 13:5; 1 Tim. 1:5, 19; 2 Tim. 1:3; 1 Peter 3:16); (3) the desire to be a "vessel for noble use" and have increased effectiveness in the work of the kingdom (2 Tim. 2:20–21); (4) the desire to see unbelievers come to Christ through observing our lives (1 Peter 3:1–2, 15–16); (5) the desire to receive present blessings from God on our lives and ministries (1 Peter 3:9–12); (6) the desire to avoid God's displeasure and discipline on our lives (sometimes called "the fear of God") (Acts 5:11; 9:31; 2 Cor. 5:11; 7:1; Eph. 4:30; Phil. 2:12; 1 Tim. 5:20; Heb. 12:3–11; 1 Peter 1:17; 2:17; cf. the state of unbelievers in Rom. 3:8); (7) the desire to seek greater heavenly reward

---

[15]See chapter 23, pp. 473–77, for a discussion of the fact that "soul" and "spirit" are used roughly synonymously in the Bible.

[16]Of course, physical weakness will inevitably come with old age, and sometimes comes earlier due to infirmity, but this can be consistent with increased sanctification as God's power is "made perfect in weakness" (2 Cor. 12:9). Paul clearly teaches this when he says, "We have this treasure in earthen vessels, to show that the transcendent power belongs to God and not to us" (2 Cor. 4:7), and, "We do not lose heart. Though our outer nature is wasting away, our inner nature is being renewed every day" (2 Cor. 4:16).

(Matt. 6:19–21; Luke 19:17–19; 1 Cor. 3:12–15; 2 Cor. 5:9–10);[17] (8) the desire for a deeper walk with God (Matt. 5:8; John 14:21; 1 John 1:6; 3:21–22; and, in the Old Testament, Ps. 66:18; Isa. 59:2); (9) the desire that angels would glorify God for our obedience (1 Tim. 5:21; 1 Peter 1:12); (10) the desire for peace (Phil. 4:9) and joy (Heb. 12:1–2) in our lives; and (11) the desire to do what God commands, simply because his commands are right, and we delight in doing what is right (Phil. 4:8; cf. Ps. 40:8).

## F. The Beauty and Joy of Sanctification

It would not be right to end our discussion without noting that sanctification brings great joy to us. The more we grow in likeness to Christ, the more we will personally experience the "joy" and "peace" that are part of the fruit of the Holy Spirit (Gal. 5:22), and the more we will draw near to the kind of life that we will have in heaven. Paul says that as we become more and more obedient to God, "the return you get is sanctification and its end, eternal life" (Rom. 6:22). He realizes that this is the source of our true joy. "For the kingdom of God is not food and drink but righteousness and peace and joy in the Holy Spirit" (Rom. 14:17). As we grow in holiness we grow in conformity to the image of Christ, and more and more of the beauty of his character is seen in our own lives. This is the goal of perfect sanctification which we hope and long for, and which will be ours when Christ returns. "And every one who thus hopes in him purifies himself as he is pure" (1 John 3:3).

## QUESTIONS FOR PERSONAL APPLICATION

1. Can you remember in your own experience the definite beginning to sanctification that occurred when you became a Christian? Did you sense a clear break from the ruling power and love of sin in your life? Do you really believe that you are even now dead to the ruling power and love of sin in your life? How can this truth of the Christian life be of help to you in specific areas of your life where you still need to grow in sanctification?

2. As you look back over the last few years of your Christian life, can you see a pattern of definite growth in sanctification? What are some things that you used to delight in which no longer interest you? What are some things that you used to have no interest in that now hold great interest for you?

3. As you have grown to greater maturity and holiness in the Christian life, have you become more conscious of the weight of sin that remains in your heart? If not, why has this not been so? Do you think that it would be helpful if you had a greater consciousness of the sin that remains in your own life? If you had this, what difference would it make in your own life?

---

[17]See chapter 56, pp. 1143–45, for a discussion of degrees of reward in heaven.

4. How would it affect your life if you thought more about the fact that the Holy Spirit is continually at work in you to increase your sanctification? In living the Christian life, have you maintained a balance between your passive role and your active role in sanctification, or have you tended to emphasize one aspect over the other, and why? What might you do to correct this imbalance, if there is one in your life?

5. Have you thought previously that sanctification affects your intellect and the way you think? What areas of your intellect still need quite a bit of growth in sanctification? With regard to your emotions, in what areas do you know that God still needs to work to bring about greater sanctification? Are there areas or aspects of sanctification that need to be improved with respect to your physical body and its obedience to God's purposes?

6. Are there areas where you have struggled for years to grow in sanctification, but with no progress at all in your life? Has this chapter helped you regain hope for progress in those areas? (For Christians who have serious discouragement over lack of progress in sanctification, it is very important to talk personally to a pastor or other mature Christian about this situation, rather than letting it go on for a long period of time.)

7. Overall, has this chapter been an encouragement or discouragement to you in your Christian life?

## SPECIAL TERMS

perfectionism
sanctification
sinless perfection

## BIBLIOGRAPHY

(For an explanation of this bibliography see the note on the bibliography to chapter 1, p. 38. Complete bibliographical data may be found on pp. 1223–29.)

### Sections in Evangelical Systematic Theologies

1. Anglican (Episcopalian)
    1882–92    Litton, 330–45
      1930    Thomas, 199–209, 223–35
2. Arminian (Wesleyan or Methodist)
      1847    Finney, 423–81
    1875–76    Pope, 3:27–100
    1892–94    Miley, 2:355–84
      1940    Wiley, 2:440–517; 3:7–102
      1960    Purkiser, 305–92, 428–41
      1983    Carter, 1:521–69

3. Baptist

|  |  |
|---|---|
| 1767 | Gill, 2:93–107, 141–51, 364–557 |
| 1887 | Boyce, 409–25 |
| 1907 | Strong, 869–81 |
| 1917 | Mullins, 417–32 |
| 1983–85 | Erickson, 967–84 |

4. Dispensational

|  |  |
|---|---|
| 1947 | Chafer, 3:355–63; 6:162–298 |
| 1949 | Thiessen, 283–89 |
| 1986 | Ryrie, 300–306 |

5. Lutheran

|  |  |
|---|---|
| 1917–24 | Pieper, 3:3–86 |
| 1934 | Mueller, 384–435 |

6. Reformed (or Presbyterian)

|  |  |
|---|---|
| 1559 | Calvin, 1:684–725, 833–49 (3.6–10, 19) |
| 1724–58 | Edwards, 2:173–85 |
| 1861 | Heppe, 565–80 |
| 1871–73 | Hodge, 3:213–465 |
| 1878 | Dabney, 674–87 |
| 1887–1921 | Warfield, SSW, 2:325–28; Perf., 3–464 |
| 1889 | Shedd, 2b:553–60 |
| 1937–66 | Murray, CW, 2:277–317; RAA, 141–51 |
| 1938 | Berkhof, 527–44 |
| 1962 | Buswell, 2:196–215 |

7. Renewal (or charismatic/Pentecostal)

|  |  |
|---|---|
| 1988–92 | Williams, 2:83–117, 411–45 |

## Sections in Representative Roman Catholic Systematic Theologies

1. Roman Catholic: Traditional

|  |  |
|---|---|
| 1955 | Ott, 254–69 |

2. Roman Catholic: Post-Vatican II

|  |  |
|---|---|
| 1980 | McBrien, 2:903–1099 |

## Other Works

Alexander, Donald L., ed. *Christian Spirituality: Five Views of Sanctification*. Downers Grove, Ill.: InterVarsity Press, 1988.

Berkouwer, G. C. *Faith and Sanctification*. Trans. by John Vriend. Grand Rapids: Eerdmans, 1952.

Bockmuehl, Klaus. "Sanctification." In *NDT*, pp. 613–16.

Chafer, Lewis Sperry. *He That Is Spiritual*. Rev. ed. Grand Rapids: Zondervan, 1967.

Coppedge, Allan. *The Biblical Principles of Discipleship*. Grand Rapids: Francis Asbury Press, 1989.

Downs, Perry G. *Teaching for Spiritual Growth: An Introduction to Christian Education*. Grand Rapids: Zondervan, 1994.

Hoekema, Anthony A. "Sanctification." In *Saved by Grace*. Grand Rapids: Eerdmans and Exeter: Paternoster, 1989, pp. 192–233.

Murray, John. "Sanctification." In *Redemption Accomplished and Applied*. Grand Rapids: Eerdmans, 1955, pp. 141–50.

Packer, J. I. *Keep in Step With the Spirit*. Old Tappan, N.J.: Revell, 1984.

Prior, K. *The Way of Holiness*. Downers Grove, Ill.: InterVarsity Press, 1967.

Ryle, J. C. *Holiness: Its Nature, Hindrances, Difficulties and Roots*. Westwood, N.J.: Revell, n.d.

White, R. E. O. "Sanctification." In *EDT*, pp. 969–71.

Willard, Dallas. *The Spirit of the Disciplines: Understanding How God Changes Lives*. San Francisco: Harper and Row, 1988.

Ziesler, J. A. *The Meaning of Righteousness in Paul*. Cambridge: Cambridge University Press, 1972.

## SCRIPTURE MEMORY PASSAGE

**Romans 6:11–14:** *So you also must consider yourselves dead to sin and alive to God in Christ Jesus. Let not sin therefore reign in your mortal bodies, to make you obey their passions. Do not yield your members to sin as instruments of wickedness, but yield yourselves to God as men who have been brought from death to life, and your members to God as instruments of righteousness. For sin will have no dominion over you, since you are not under law but under grace.*

## HYMN

"Take Time to Be Holy"

Take time to be holy, speak oft with thy Lord;
　　Abide in him always, and feed on his Word.
Make friends of God's children; help those who are weak;
　　Forgetting in nothing his blessing to seek.

Take time to be holy, the world rushes on;
　　Spend much time in secret with Jesus alone.
By looking to Jesus, like him thou shalt be;
　　Thy friends in thy conduct his likeness shall see.

Take time to be holy, let him be thy guide,
　　And run not before him, whatever betide;
In joy or in sorrow, still follow thy Lord,
　　And, looking to Jesus, still trust in his Word.

Take time to be holy, be calm in thy soul;
　　Each thought and each motive beneath his control;
Thus led by his Spirit to fountains of love,
　　Thou soon shalt be fitted for service above.

AUTHOR: WILLIAM D. LONGSTAFF, 1887

Alternate hymn: "Trust and Obey"

# Chapter 39

# Baptism in and Filling With the Holy Spirit

*Should we seek a "baptism in the Holy Spirit" after conversion? What does it mean to be filled with the Holy Spirit?*

Systematic theology books have not traditionally included a chapter on baptism in the Holy Spirit or filling with the Holy Spirit as part of the study of the "order of salvation," the study of the various steps in which the benefits of salvation are applied to our lives.[1] But with the spread of Pentecostalism that began in 1901, the widespread influence of the charismatic movement in the 1960's and 1970's, and the remarkable growth of Pentecostal and charismatic[2] churches worldwide from 1970 to the present, the question of a "baptism in the Holy Spirit" distinct

---

[1] See chapter 32, p. 670, for a list of the elements in the order of salvation.

[2] I am using the terms *Pentecostal* and *charismatic* in the following way: *Pentecostal* refers to any denomination or group that traces its historical origin back to the Pentecostal revival that began in the United States in 1901 and that holds to the doctrinal positions (a) that baptism in the Holy Spirit is ordinarily an event subsequent to conversion, and (b) that baptism in the Holy Spirit is made evident by the sign of speaking in tongues, and (c) that all the spiritual gifts mentioned in the New Testament are to be sought and used today. Pentecostal groups usually have their own distinct denominational structures, the most prominent of which is the Assemblies of God.

*Charismatic* refers to any groups (or people) that trace their historical origin to the charismatic renewal movement of the 1960s and 1970s, seek to practice all the spiritual gifts mentioned in the New Testament (including prophecy, healing, miracles, tongues, interpretation, and distinguishing between spirits), and allow differing viewpoints on whether baptism in the Holy Spirit is subsequent to conversion and whether tongues is a sign of baptism in the Holy Spirit. Charismatics will very often refrain from forming their own denomination, but will view themselves as a force for renewal within existing Protestant and Roman Catholic churches. There is no representative charismatic denomination in the United States today, but the most prominent charismatic spokesman is probably Pat Robertson with his Christian Broadcasting Network, the television program "The 700 Club," and Regent University (formerly CBN University).

In the 1980s yet a third renewal movement arose, called the *"third wave"* by missions professor C. Peter Wagner at Fuller Seminary (he referred to the Pentecostal renewal as the first wave of the Holy Spirit's renewing work in the modern church, and the charismatic movement as the second wave). "Third wave" people encourage the equipping of all believers to use New Testament spiritual gifts today, and say that the proclamation of the gospel should ordinarily be accompanied by "signs, wonders, and miracles," according to the New Testament pattern. They teach, however, that baptism in the Holy Spirit happens to all Christians at conversion, and that subsequent experiences are better called "filling" with the Holy Spirit. The most prominent representative of the "third wave" is John Wimber, senior pastor of the Vineyard Christian Fellowship in Anaheim, California, and leader of the Association of Vineyard Churches. Wimber's two most influential books, *Power Evangelism* (San Francisco: Harper and Row, 1986; rev. ed., 1992) and *Power Healing* (San Francisco: Harper and Row, 1987), both co-authored by Kevin Springer, are widely recognized as representative of distinctive "third wave" emphases.

The definitive reference work for these movements is now Stanley M. Burgess and Gary B. McGee, eds., *Dictionary of Pentecostal and Charismatic Movements* (Grand Rapids: Zondervan, 1988).

from regeneration has come into increasing prominence. I have put this chapter at this point in our study of the application of redemption for two reasons: (1) A proper understanding of this question must assume an understanding of regeneration, adoption, and sanctification, all of which have been discussed in previous chapters. (2) All the previous chapters on the application of redemption have discussed events that occur (or in the case of sanctification, that begin) at the point at which a person becomes a Christian. But this question concerns an event that occurs either at the point of conversion (according to one view) or sometime after conversion (according to another view). Moreover, people on both sides of the question agree that some kind of second experience has happened to many people after their conversion, and therefore one very important question is how to understand this experience in the light of Scripture and what scriptural categories properly apply to it.

## EXPLANATION AND SCRIPTURAL BASIS

### A. The Traditional Pentecostal Understanding

The topic of this chapter has become important today because many Christians say that they have experienced a "baptism in the Holy Spirit" that came after they became Christians and that brought great blessing in their lives. They claim that prayer and Bible study have become much more meaningful and effective, that they have discovered new joy in worship, and they often say that they have received new spiritual gifts (especially, and most frequently, the gift of speaking in tongues).

This traditional Pentecostal or charismatic position is supported from Scripture in the following way:

(1) Jesus' disciples were born-again believers long before the day of Pentecost, perhaps during Jesus' life and ministry, but certainly by the time that Jesus, after his resurrection, "breathed on them, and said to them, 'Receive the Holy Spirit'" (John 20:22).

(2) Jesus nevertheless commanded his disciples "not to depart from Jerusalem, but to wait for the promise of the Father" (Acts 1:4), telling them, "Before many days you shall be *baptized with the Holy Spirit*" (Acts 1:5). He told them, "You shall receive power when the Holy Spirit has come upon you" (Acts 1:8). The disciples then obeyed Jesus' command and waited in Jerusalem for the Holy Spirit to come upon them so that they would receive new empowering for witness and ministry.

(3) When the disciples had waited for ten days, the day of Pentecost came, tongues of fire rested above their heads, "And they were all filled with the Holy Spirit and began to speak in other tongues, as the Spirit gave them utterance" (Acts 2:4). This clearly shows that they received a baptism in (or with)[3] the Holy

---

[3]It does not matter much whether we translate the Greek phrase *en pneumati* as "in the Spirit" or "with the Spirit" because both are acceptable translations, and people on all sides of this topic seem to use those two expressions rather interchangeably. I have used "in the Holy Spirit" ordinarily throughout this chapter, but the RSV translation which I quote here generally prefers to use "with the Holy Spirit." I do not make any distinction between these two phrases in the discussion of this chapter. (But see below, pp. 767–68, for a discussion of the frequent claim by Pentecostals that baptism *by* the Holy Spirit [as in 1 Cor. 12:13] is a different event than baptism *in* [or with] the Holy Spirit.)

Spirit. Although the disciples were born again long before Pentecost, at Pentecost they received a "baptism with the Holy Spirit" (Acts 1:5 and 11:16 refer to it this way) that was subsequent to conversion and resulted in great empowering for ministry as well as speaking in tongues.[4]

(4) Christians today, like the apostles, should ask Jesus for a "baptism in the Holy Spirit" and thus follow the pattern of the disciples' lives.[5] If we receive this baptism in the Holy Spirit, it will result in much more power for ministry for our own lives, just as it did in the lives of the disciples, and will often (or always, according to some teachers) result in speaking in tongues as well.

(5) Support for this pattern—in which people are first born again and then later are baptized in the Holy Spirit—is seen in several other instances in the book of Acts. It is seen, for example, in Acts 8, where the people of Samaria first became Christians when they "believed Philip as he preached good news about the kingdom of God and the name of Jesus Christ" (Acts 8:12), but only later received the Holy Spirit when the apostles Peter and John came from Jerusalem and prayed for them (Acts 8:14–17).[6]

Another example is found in Acts 19, where Paul came and found "some disciples" at Ephesus (Acts 19:1). But, "when Paul had laid his hands upon them, the Holy Spirit came on them; and they spoke with tongues and prophesied" (Acts 19:6).

All of these examples (Acts 2, 8, sometimes 10, and 19)[7] are cited by Pentecostals in order to show that a "baptism in the Holy Spirit" subsequent to conversion was a very common occurrence for New Testament Christians. Therefore, they reason, if it was common for Christians in Acts to have this second experience sometime after conversion, should it not be common for us today as well?

We can analyze this issue of the baptism in the Holy Spirit by asking three questions: (1) What does the phrase "baptism in the Holy Spirit" mean in the New Testament? (2) How should we understand the "second experiences" that came to born-again believers in the book of Acts? (3) Are there other biblical expressions, such as "filling with the Holy Spirit," that are better suited to describe an empowering with the Holy Spirit that comes after conversion?

---

[4]Most Pentecostal discussions of baptism in the Holy Spirit include the view that speaking in tongues is a "sign" that one has been baptized in the Holy Spirit, and that this sign will be given to all who have been baptized in the Holy Spirit, even though not all will later have the gift of speaking in tongues as a continuing gift in their lives.

[5]I personally heard such teaching on baptism in the Holy Spirit as a first-year university student in 1967, and later privately prayed, as instructed, first repenting of all known sin and once again yielding every area of my life to God, then asking Jesus to baptize me in the Holy Spirit. Though my understanding of that experience has since changed, so that I would explain it in different terms (see below), the result in my life was undoubtedly a positive and lasting one, including a much deeper love for Christ and much greater effectiveness in personal ministry.

[6]Another example sometimes cited is that of Cornelius in Acts 10. He was a devout man who prayed constantly to God (Acts 10:2), but when Peter came and preached to him and his household, Peter and those with him were amazed "because the gift of the Holy Spirit had been poured out even on the Gentiles. For they heard them speaking in tongues and extolling God" (Acts 10:45–46).

[7]The case of Paul in Acts 9:17 is sometimes mentioned as well, but it is not as clear-cut, since his violent persecution of the church prior to that time indicates that he was not born again before the Damascus Road experience. But some have seen a similar pattern in the distinction between his conversion on the Damascus Road and his receiving the Holy Spirit at the hands of Ananias three days later.

## B. What Does "Baptism in the Holy Spirit" Mean in the New Testament?

There are only seven passages in the New Testament where we read of someone being baptized in the Holy Spirit. (The English translations quoted here use the word *with* rather than *in.*)[8] The seven passages follow:

In the first four verses, John the Baptist is speaking of Jesus and predicting that he will baptize people in (or with) the Holy Spirit:

> Matthew 3:11: "I baptize you with water for repentance, but he who is coming after me is mightier than I, whose sandals I am not worthy to carry; he will *baptize you with the Holy Spirit* and with fire."

> Mark 1:8: "I have baptized you with water; but he will *baptize you with the Holy Spirit.*"

> Luke 3:16: "I baptize you with water; but he who is mightier that I is coming, the thong of whose sandals I am not worthy to untie; he will *baptize you with the Holy Spirit* and with fire."

> John 1:33: "He who sent me to baptize with water said to me, 'He on whom you see the Spirit descend and remain, this is he who *baptizes with the Holy Spirit.*'"

It is hard to draw any conclusions from these four passages with respect to what baptism with the Holy Spirit really is. We discover that Jesus is the one who will carry out this baptism and he will baptize his followers. But no further specification of this baptism is given.

The next two passages refer directly to Pentecost:

> Acts 1:5: [Here Jesus says,] "John baptized with water, but before many days you shall be *baptized with the Holy Spirit.*"

> Acts 11:16: [Here Peter refers back to the same words of Jesus that were quoted in the previous verse. He says,] "I remembered the word of the Lord, how he said, 'John baptized with water, but you shall be *baptized with the Holy Spirit.*'"

These two passages show us that whatever we may understand baptism in the Holy Spirit to be, it certainly happened at the day of Pentecost as recorded in Acts 2, when the Holy Spirit fell in great power on the disciples and those with them, and they spoke in other tongues, and about three thousand people were converted (Acts 2:14).

It is important to realize that all six of these verses use almost exactly the same expression in Greek, with the only differences being some variation in word order or verb tense to fit the sentence, and with one example having the preposition understood rather than expressed explicitly.[9]

The only remaining reference in the New Testament is in the Pauline epistles:

> 1 Corinthians 12:13 (NIV mg): "For we were all *baptized in one Spirit* into one body—whether Jews or Greeks, slave or free—and we were all given the one Spirit to drink."

---

[8]See above, footnote 3.

[9]The expression used in all six passages is the verb *baptizō* ("baptize") plus the prepositional phrase *en pneumati hagiō* ("in [or with] the Holy Spirit"), except that Mark omits the preposition *en.* Even so, there is no difference in meaning, because the dative noun alone can take the same sense as the preposition *en* plus the dative noun. Matthew and Luke also add "and with fire."

Now the question is whether 1 Corinthians 12:13 refers to the same activity as these other six verses. In many English translations it appears to be different, for many translations are similar to the RSV, which says, "For *by one Spirit* we were all baptized into one body." Those who support the Pentecostal view of baptism in the Holy Spirit after conversion are quite eager to see this verse as referring to something other than baptism in the Holy Spirit, and they frequently emphasize the difference that comes out in the English translations. In all the other six verses, Jesus is the one who baptizes people and the Holy Spirit is the "element" (parallel to water in physical baptism) in which or with which Jesus baptizes people. But here in 1 Corinthians 12:13 (so the Pentecostal explanation goes) we have something quite different—here the person doing the baptizing is not Jesus but the Holy Spirit. Therefore, they say, 1 Corinthians 12:13 should not be taken into account when we ask what the New Testament means by "baptism in the Holy Spirit."

This point is very important to the Pentecostal position, because, if we admit that 1 Corinthians 12:13 refers to baptism *in* the Holy Spirit, then it is very hard to maintain that it is an experience that comes after conversion. In this verse Paul says that this baptism in/with/by the Holy Spirit made us members of the body of Christ—"We were all baptized *in* one Spirit into one body" (1 Cor. 12:13 NIV mg). But if this really is a "baptism in the Holy Spirit," the same as the event that was referred to in the previous six verses, then Paul is saying that it happened to all the Corinthians *when they became members of the body of Christ; that is, when they became Christians.* For it was that baptism that resulted in their being members of the body of Christ, the church. Such a conclusion would be very difficult for the Pentecostal position that holds that baptism in the Holy Spirit is something that occurs after conversion, not at the same time.

Is it possible to sustain the Pentecostal view that the other six verses refer to a baptism *by Jesus* in which he baptizes us in (or with) the Holy Spirit, but that 1 Corinthians 12:13 refers to something different, to a baptism *by the Holy Spirit?* Although the distinction seems to make sense from some English translations, it really cannot be supported by an examination of the Greek text, for there the expression is almost identical to the expressions we have seen in the other six verses. Paul says *en heni pneumati . . . ebaptisthemen* ("in one Spirit . . . we were baptized"). Apart from one small difference (he refers to "one Spirit" rather than "the Holy Spirit"),[10] all the other elements are the same: the verb is *baptizō,* and the prepositional phrase contains the same words (*en* plus the dative noun *pneumati*). If we translate this same Greek expression "baptize *in* the Holy Spirit" (or "baptize *with* the Holy Spirit") in the other six New Testament occurrences where we find it, then it seems only proper that we translate it in the same way in this seventh occurrence. And no matter how we translate, it seems hard to deny that the original readers would have seen this phrase as referring to the same thing as the other six verses, because for them the words were the same.

But why have modern English translations translated this verse to say, "By one Spirit we were all baptized into one body," thus giving apparent support to the Pentecostal interpretation? We should first note that the NASB gives "in" as a

---

[10]In this context, in which he is talking repeatedly about the Holy Spirit and spiritual gifts, there can be little doubt that he is referring to the Holy Spirit.

marginal translation, and the NIV margin gives both "with" and "in" as alternatives. The reason these translations have chosen the word "by" has apparently been a desire to avoid an appearance of two locations for the baptism in the same sentence. The sentence already says that this baptism was "into one body," and perhaps the translators thought it seemed awkward to say, *"in* one Spirit we were all baptized *into* one body." But this should not be seen as a great difficulty, for Paul says, referring to the Israelites, "all were baptized *into* Moses *in* the cloud and *in* the sea" (1 Cor. 10:2)—a very closely parallel expression where the cloud and the sea are the "elements" that surrounded or overwhelmed the people of Israel and *Moses* means the new life of participation in the Mosaic covenant and the fellowship of God's people (led by Moses) that the Israelites found themselves in after they had passed through the cloud and the sea. It is not that there were two locations for the same baptism, but one was the element in which they were baptized and the other was the location in which they found themselves after the baptism. This is very similar to 1 Corinthians 12:13: the Holy Spirit was the *element* in which they were baptized, and the body of Christ, the church, was the *location* in which they found themselves after that baptism.[11] It thus seems appropriate to conclude that 1 Corinthians 12:13 also refers to baptism "in" or "with" the Holy Spirit, and is referring to the same thing as the other six verses mentioned.

But this has a significant implication for us: it means that, as far as the apostle Paul was concerned, *baptism in the Holy Spirit occurred at conversion*. He says that all the Corinthians were baptized in the Holy Spirit and the result was that they became members of the body of Christ: "For we were all baptized in one Spirit into one body" (1 Cor. 12:13 NIV mg). "Baptism in the Holy Spirit," therefore, must refer to the activity of the Holy Spirit at the beginning of the Christian life when he gives us new spiritual life (in regeneration) and cleanses us and gives a clear break with the power and love of sin (the initial stage of sanctification). In this way "baptism in the Holy Spirit" refers to all that the Holy Spirit does at the beginning of our Christian lives. But this means that it cannot refer to an experience after conversion, as the Pentecostal interpretation would have it.[12]

---

[11]In addition to the fact that this Greek phrase found in 1 Cor. 12:13 is translated to refer to baptism in the Holy Spirit in all the other six occurrences, there is a grammatical argument that supports the translation "*in* one Spirit we were all baptized into one body" in 1 Cor. 12:13: if Paul had wanted to say that we were baptized *by* the Holy Spirit, he would have used a different expression. To be baptized "by" someone in the New Testament is always expressed by the preposition *hypo* followed by a genitive noun. This is the way New Testament writers say that people were baptized in the Jordan River "by" John the Baptist (Matt. 3:6; Mark 1:5; Luke 3:7) or that Jesus was baptized "by" John (Matt. 3:13; Mark 1:9), or that the Pharisees had not been baptized "by" John (Luke 7:30), or that John the Baptist told Jesus, "I need to be baptized by you" (Matt. 3:14). Therefore, if Paul had wanted to say that the Corinthians had all been baptized *by* the Holy Spirit he would have used *hypo* plus the genitive, not *en* plus the dative. (It is common in the New Testament for the agent who performs the action expressed by a passive verb to be named using *hypo* plus the genitive.) Further support for the view that 1 Cor. 12:13 means "in (or with) one Spirit" is found in M. J. Harris, "Prepositions and Theology in the Greek New Testament," in *NIDNTT*, vol. 3, p. 1210.

[12]Howard M. Ervin, *Conversion-Initiation and the Baptism in the Holy Spirit* (Peabody, Mass.: Hendrickson, 1984), pp. 98–102, admits that 1 Cor. 12:13, however it is translated, does refer to the beginning of the Christian life (he says it is "initiatory," p. 101), but then he says that the next phrase, "we were made to drink of one Spirit" (his translation) refers to a subsequent empowering for service. He also says that Paul's use of the phrase "baptism in the Holy Spirit" is different from the sense the phrase takes in the other six occurrences in the New Testament. Thus, he apparently grants the non-

But how, then, do we understand the references to baptism in the Holy Spirit in Acts 1:5 and 11:6, both of which refer to the day of Pentecost? Were these not instances where the disciples, having previously been regenerated by the Holy Spirit, now experienced a new empowering from the Holy Spirit that enabled them to minister effectively?

It is true that the disciples were "born again" long before Pentecost, and in fact probably long before Jesus breathed on them and told them to receive the Holy Spirit in John 20:22.[13] Jesus had said, "No one can come to me unless the Father who sent me draws him" (John 6:44), but the disciples certainly had come to Jesus and had followed him (even though their understanding of who he was increased gradually over time). Certainly when Peter said to Jesus, "You are the Christ, the Son of the living God" (Matt. 16:16), it was evidence of some kind of regenerating work of the Holy Spirit in his heart. Jesus told him, "Flesh and blood has not revealed this to you, but my Father who is in heaven" (Matt. 16:17). And Jesus had said to the Father regarding his disciples, "I have given them the words which you gave me, and *they have received them* and know in truth that I came from you; and they have believed that you sent me. . . . *I have guarded them,* and *none of them is lost* but the son of perdition, that the scripture might be fulfilled" (John 17:8, 12). The disciples had "little faith" (Matt. 8:26) at times, but they did have faith! Certainly they were regenerated long before the day of Pentecost.[14]

---

Pentecostal interpretation of 1 Cor. 12:13, but still says that Paul uses the same phrase with different meaning. Yet this argument does not seem persuasive. It would be very unlikely if Luke, who was Paul's traveling companion throughout much of his missionary activity, and who was probably with Paul in Rome when he wrote the book of Acts (Acts 28:30–31), would use a phrase in a different sense than Paul, or that Paul would use this phrase in a different sense than the sense in which it was so prominently used by Matthew, Mark, Luke and John.

Another attempt to avoid our conclusion on 1 Cor. 12:13 is found in John P. Baker, *Baptized in One Spirit* (Plainfield, N.J.: Logos Books, 1970), pp. 18–25, where he argues that 1 Cor. 12:13 does not mean that we were baptized *into* one body, but that we were baptized "*for* the one body of Christ" (p. 24). But Baker's argument is not convincing, because the word "for" at the beginning of v. 13 shows that it must be an argument that supports v. 12, where Paul says that we are many members, but one body. Yet in order for v. 13 to show that all Christians are a part of one body, it is necessary for v. 13 to communicate why we are *all* members of one body, and Paul does this by showing that we are all baptized into one body. Baker's view, that this happens only to some "who are already members *of* the body of Christ to enable them to function effectively" (p. 24), is not convincing in view of Paul's statement that "all" Christians were baptized into one body. Moreover, baptism *for the benefit of* one body (which is essentially what Baker takes it to mean) gives a very unusual sense to the preposition *eis*—if Paul had meant this, we would have expected something like *heneka,* "for the sake of," or *hyper* plus the genitive, meaning "in behalf, for the sake of."

[13]When Jesus breathed on his disciples and said to them, "Receive the Holy Spirit" (John 20:22), it probably was an acted-out prophecy of what would happen to them at Pentecost. In this same context—in fact, in the verse immediately preceding—Jesus had told them something that would not happen until Pentecost: "As the Father has sent me, *even so I send you*" (John 20:21). But even though he said this before he had ascended into heaven, he did not really send them out to preach the gospel until the Day of Pentecost had come. Therefore his words were looking forward to what would happen at Pentecost. It is best to understand the words in the next sentence, "Receive the Holy Spirit," in the same way—he was speaking in advance of something that would happen on the Day of Pentecost. On that day they would receive the new covenant fullness and power of the Holy Spirit, a much greater empowering of the Holy Spirit than what they had experienced before.

[14]I do not mean to say that believers' experience of regeneration in the old covenant was exactly the same as that of new covenant believers. While considerations listed in the following discussion indicate a less-powerful work of the Holy Spirit in the old covenant, defining the nature of the differences is difficult, since Scripture gives us little explicit information about it. But the fact that there was any saving faith at all in old covenant believers requires us to think that there was some kind of

But we must realize that the day of Pentecost is much more than an individual event in the lives of Jesus' disciples and those with them. The day of Pentecost was the point of transition between the old covenant work and ministry of the Holy Spirit and the new covenant work and ministry of the Holy Spirit. Of course the Holy Spirit was at work throughout the Old Testament, hovering over the waters of the first day of creation (Gen. 1:2), empowering people for service to God and leadership and prophecy (Ex. 31:3; 35:31; Deut. 34:9; Judg. 14:6; 1 Sam. 16:13; Ps. 51:11, et al.). But during that time the work of the Holy Spirit in individual lives was, in general, a work of lesser power.

There are several indications of a less powerful and less extensive work of the Holy Spirit in the old covenant: the Holy Spirit only came to a few people with significant power for ministry (Num. 11:16–17, for example), but Moses longed for the day when the Holy Spirit would be poured out on all of God's people: "Would that all the LORD's people were prophets, that the LORD would put his spirit upon them!" (Num. 11:29). The equipping of the Holy Spirit for special ministries could be lost, as it was in the life of Saul (1 Sam. 16:14), and as David feared that it might be in his own life (Ps. 51:11). In terms of spiritual power in the lives of the people of God, there was little power over the dominion of Satan, resulting in very little effective evangelism of the nations around Israel, and no examples of ability to cast out demons.[15] The old covenant work of the Holy Spirit was almost completely confined to the nation of Israel, but in the new covenant there is created a new "dwelling place of God" (Eph. 2:22), the church, which unites both Gentiles and Jews in the body of Christ.

Moreover, the Old Testament people of God looked forward to a "new covenant" age when the work of the Holy Spirit would be much more powerful and much more widespread (Num. 11:29; Jer. 31:31–33; Ezek. 36:26–27; Joel 2:28–29).[16]

When the New Testament opens, we see John the Baptist as the last of the Old Testament prophets. Jesus said, "Among those born of women there has risen no one greater than John the Baptist; yet he who is least in the kingdom of heaven is greater than he . . . all the prophets and the law prophesied until John; and if you are willing to accept it, he is Elijah who is to come" (Matt. 11:11–14). John knew that he baptized with water, but Jesus would baptize with the Holy Spirit (John 3:16). John the Baptist, then, still was living in an "old covenant" experience of the working of the Holy Spirit.

In the life of Jesus, we first see the new covenant power of the Holy Spirit at work. The Holy Spirit descends on him at his baptism (Luke 3:21–22), and after

---

regenerating work of the Holy Spirit in them, enabling them to believe. (See the discussion of regeneration in chapter 34.)

[15]The closest thing to casting out demons in the Old Testament is the situation where the evil spirit troubling Saul departed from him whenever David played his lyre (1 Sam. 16:23), but this is hardly equivalent to the effective and lasting casting out of demons of which we see in the New Testament age.

[16]Of course, there were examples in the Old Testament where certain leaders were remarkably gifted by God and empowered by the Holy Spirit—Moses, David, Daniel, many of the writing prophets, and even Samson received unusual empowering from the Holy Spirit for specific ministries. But their experiences were not typical of the vast numbers of God's people who were saved by faith as they looked forward to the promised Messiah's coming, but who did not have the outpouring of the Holy Spirit in the new covenant power that we experience today.

his temptation Jesus "returned *in the power of the Spirit* into Galilee" (Luke 4:14). Then we begin to see what this new covenant power of the Holy Spirit will look like, because Jesus casts out demons with a word, heals all who are brought to him, and teaches with authority that people had not heard before (see Luke 4:16–44, et al.).

The disciples, however, do not receive this full new covenant empowering for ministry until the Day of Pentecost, for Jesus tells them to wait in Jerusalem, and promises, "*You shall receive power* when the Holy Spirit has come upon you" (Acts 1:8). This was a transition in the lives of the disciples as well (see John 7:39; 14:17; 16:7; Acts 2:16). The promise of Joel that the Holy Spirit would come in new covenant fullness was fulfilled (Acts 2:16) as Jesus returned to heaven and then was given authority to pour out the Holy Spirit in new fullness and power (Acts 2:33).

What was the result in the lives of the disciples? These believers, who had had an old-covenant less-powerful experience of the Holy Spirit in their lives, received on the Day of Pentecost a more-powerful new-covenant experience of the Holy Spirit working in their lives.[17] They received much greater "power" (Acts 1:8), power for living the Christian life and for carrying out Christian ministry.

This transition from an old covenant experience of the Holy Spirit to a new covenant experience of the Holy Spirit can be seen in figure 39.1.[18]

In this diagram, the thinner line at the bottom represents the less-powerful work of the Holy Spirit in individuals' lives during the old covenant. The thicker line that begins at Pentecost shows the more-powerful work of the Holy Spirit in people's lives after that time. The lines for "this age" and "the age to come" overlap now because the powers of the age to come have broken into this present evil age, so that Christians live during an "overlap of the ages." The dotted lines prior to Pentecost indicate that in the life of Jesus the more-powerful work of the Holy Spirit had already begun in a way that anticipated (and even surpassed) what would come at Pentecost.[19]

This new covenant power gave the disciples more effectiveness in their witness and their ministry (Acts 1:8; Eph. 4:8, 11–13), much greater power for victory over the influence of sin in the lives of all believers (note the emphasis on the power of Christ's resurrection at work within us in Rom. 6:11–14; 8:13–14; Gal. 2:20; Phil. 3:10), and power for victory over Satan and demonic forces that would attack believers (2 Cor. 10:3–4; Eph. 1:19–21; 6:10–18; 1 John 4:4).

---

[17]Ervin, *Conversion-Initiation*, pp. 14, 15–19, objects that the new covenant did not begin at Pentecost but earlier at the time of Jesus' death. This is certainly true, but it misses the point. We are not arguing that the new covenant itself began at the day of Pentecost, but the new covenant experience of the Holy Spirit began at Pentecost, because it was there that Jesus poured out the Holy Spirit in new covenant fullness and power (Acts 2:33; cf. 1:4–5).

Ervin also objects that the disciples at Pentecost received "power-in-mission" from the Holy Spirit, not entrance into the new covenant (pp. 17–18). But here Ervin has put forth a false dichotomy: it is not either/or, but both/and: at Pentecost the disciples both entered into a new covenant experience of the Holy Spirit and (of course) received a new empowering for ministry with that experience of the Holy Spirit.

[18]I have adapted this diagram from George Ladd, *A Theology of the New Testament* (Grand Rapids: Eerdmans, 1974), pp. 68–69.

[19]Because of their association with Jesus, the disciples also received some foretaste of the post-Pentecostal power of the Holy Spirit when they healed the sick and cast out demons (cf. Luke 9:1; 10:1, 8, 17–20, and many other verses).

This new covenant power of the Holy Spirit also resulted in a wide and hitherto unknown distribution of gifts for ministry to all believers (Acts 2:16–18; 1 Cor. 12:7, 11; 1 Peter 4:10; cf. Num. 11:17, 24–29). These gifts also had corporate implications because they were intended not to be used individualistically but for the corporate building up of the body of Christ (1 Cor. 12:7; 14:12). It also meant that the gospel was no longer effectively limited to the Jews only, but that all races and all nations would hear the gospel in power and would be united into the church, to the glory of God (Eph. 2:11–3:10).[20] The Day of Pentecost was certainly a remarkable time of transition in the whole history of redemption as recorded in Scripture. It was a remarkable day in the history of the world, because on that day the Holy Spirit began to function among God's people with new covenant power.

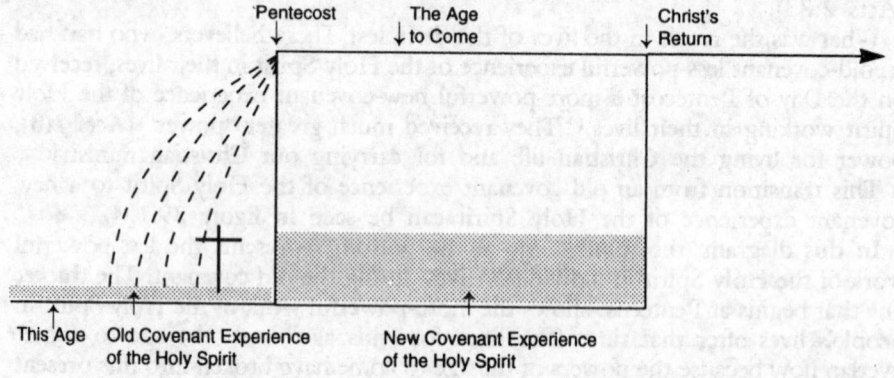

AT PENTECOST BELIEVERS EXPERIENCED A TRANSITION FROM AN OLD COVENANT EXPERIENCE OF THE HOLY SPIRIT TO A MORE POWERFUL, NEW COVENANT EXPERIENCE OF THE HOLY SPIRIT
*Figure 39.1*

But this fact helps us understand what happened to the disciples at Pentecost. They received this remarkable new empowering from the Holy Spirit *because they were living at the time of the transition between the old covenant work of the Holy Spirit and the new covenant work of the Holy Spirit*. Though it was a "second experience" of the Holy Spirit, coming as it did long after their conversion, it is not to be taken as a pattern for us, for we are not living at a time of transition in the work of the Holy Spirit. In their case, believers with an old covenant empowering from the Holy Spirit became believers with a new covenant empowering from the Holy Spirit. But we today do not first become believers with a weaker, old covenant work of the Holy Spirit in our hearts and wait until some later time to receive a new covenant work of the Holy Spirit. Rather, we are in the same position as those who became Christians in the church at Corinth: when we become

[20]When the Holy Spirit came in power he ordinarily came to groups of people rather than to isolated individuals (so Acts 2:4; 8:17; 10:44; 19:6; but the conversion of Saul is different: see Acts 9:17–18). A new community, filled with love for one another, was the evident result of the outpouring of the Holy Spirit in this way (see Acts 2:41–47).

Christians we are all *"baptized in one Spirit* into one body" (1 Cor. 12:13)—just as the Corinthians were, and just as were the new believers in many churches who were converted when Paul traveled on his missionary journeys.

In conclusion, the disciples certainly did experience "a baptism in the Holy Spirit" after conversion on the Day of Pentecost, but this happened because they were living at a unique point in history, and this event in their lives is therefore not a pattern that we are to seek to imitate.

What shall we say about the phrase "baptism in the Holy Spirit"? It is a phrase that the New Testament authors use to speak of coming into the new covenant power of the Holy Spirit. It happened at Pentecost for the disciples, but it happened at conversion for the Corinthians and for us.[21]

It is not a phrase the New Testament authors would use to speak of any post-conversion experience of empowering by the Holy Spirit.

## C. How Should We Understand the "Second Experiences" in Acts?

But even if we have correctly understood the experience of the disciples at Pentecost as recorded in Acts 2, are there not other examples of people who had a "second experience" of empowering of the Holy Spirit after conversion, such as those in Acts 8 (at Samaria), Acts 10 (Cornelius' household), and Acts 19 (the Ephesian disciples)?

These are not really convincing examples to prove the Pentecostal doctrine of baptism in the Holy Spirit either. First, the expression "baptism in the Holy Spirit" is not ordinarily used to refer to any of these events,[22] and this should give us some hesitation in applying this phrase to them. But more importantly, a closer look at each case shows more clearly what was happening in these events.

In Acts 8:4–25 the Samaritan people "believed Philip as he preached good news about the kingdom of God and the name of Jesus Christ" and "they were baptized, both men and women" (Acts 8:12). Some have argued that this was not genuine saving faith on the part of the Samaritans.[23] However, there is no indication in the text that Philip had a deficient understanding of the gospel (he had been prominent in the Jerusalem church) or that Philip himself thought that their faith in Christ was inadequate, for he allowed them to be baptized (Acts 8:12).

---

[21]My student James Renehan has argued (in a lengthy paper) that baptism in the Holy Spirit, while occurring at the same time as conversion, should nevertheless be considered a distinct element in the "order of salvation" (the list of things that happen to us in experiencing salvation; see chapter 32, p. 670). He notes that baptism in the Holy Spirit is not exactly the same as any of the other elements in the order of salvation (such as regeneration or conversion), and may also be called "receiving the Holy Spirit" (see Acts 8:15–16; 19:2, 6; Rom. 8:9, 11; Gal. 3:2). Renehan's idea is clearly not the charismatic doctrine of a baptism in the Holy Spirit subsequent to conversion (for he would say it always accompanies genuine conversion and always occurs at the same time as conversion). The suggestion is an interesting one and, while I have not presently adopted it in this chapter, I think it deserves further consideration. It would not be inconsistent with my overall argument in this chapter.

[22]The only exception is Acts 11:15–17. While this passage does not explicitly call the falling of the Holy Spirit on Cornelius' household a "baptism in the Holy Spirit," when Peter says, "the Holy Spirit fell on them *just as on us at the beginning,"* and then recalls Jesus' words about baptism in the Holy Spirit, he clearly implies that the members of Cornelius's household were baptized in the Holy Spirit when he preached to them (see Acts 10:44–48).

[23]This is the argument of James Dunn, *Baptism in the Holy Spirit* (London: SCM, 1970), pp. 55–72.

A better understanding of this event would be that God, in his providence, sovereignly waited to give the new covenant empowering of the Holy Spirit to the Samaritans directly through the hands of the apostles (Acts 8:14–17)[24] so that it might be evident to the highest leadership in the Jerusalem church that the Samaritans were not second-class citizens but full members of the church. This was important because of the historical animosity between Jews and Samaritans ("Jews have no dealings with Samaritans," John 4:9), and because Jesus had specified that the spread of the gospel to Samaria would be the next major step after it had been preached in Jerusalem and the region of Judea that surrounded Jerusalem: "You shall be my witnesses in Jerusalem and in all Judea *and Samaria* and to the end of the earth" (Acts 1:8). Thus, the event in Acts 8 was a kind of "Samaritan Pentecost," a special outpouring of the Holy Spirit on the people of Samaria, who were a mixed race of Jewish and Gentile ancestry, so that it might be evident to all that the full new covenant blessings and power of the Holy Spirit had come to this group of people as well, and were not confined to Jews only. Because this is a special event in the history of redemption, as the pattern of Acts 1:8 is worked out in the book of Acts, it is not a pattern for us to repeat today. It is simply part of the transition between the old covenant experience of the Holy Spirit and the new covenant experience of the Holy Spirit.

The situation in Acts 10 is less complicated, because it is not even clear that Cornelius was a genuine believer before Peter came and preached the gospel to him. Certainly he had not trusted in Christ for salvation. He is rather a Gentile who was one of the first examples of the way in which the gospel would go "to the end of the earth" (Acts 1:8).[25] Certainly Cornelius had not first believed in Christ's death and resurrection to save him and then later come into a second experience after his conversion.

In Acts 19, once again we encounter a situation of some people who had not really heard the gospel of salvation through Christ. They had been baptized into the baptism of John the Baptist (Acts 19:3), so they were probably people who had heard John the Baptist preach, or had talked to others who had heard John the Baptist preach, and had been baptized "into John's baptism" (Acts 19:3) as a sign that they were repenting of their sins and preparing for the Messiah who was to come. They certainly had not heard of Christ's death and resurrection, for they had not even heard that there was a Holy Spirit (Acts 19:2)!—a fact that no one who was present at Pentecost or who had heard the gospel after Pentecost could have failed to know. It is likely that they had not even heard that Jesus had come and lived and died, because Paul had to explain to them, "John baptized with the baptism of repentance, telling the people to believe in the one who was to come after him, *that is, Jesus*" (Acts 19:4). Therefore these "disciples" in Ephesus did not have new covenant understanding or new covenant faith, and they certainly did not have a new covenant empowering of the Holy Spirit—they were "disciples" only in the sense of followers of John the Baptist who were still waiting for the

[24]In this section I am largely following the careful discussion of John Stott, *Baptism and Fulness,* 2d ed. (Leicester and Downers Grove, Ill.: InterVarsity Press, 1976), pp. 31–34.

[25]Even if we did regard him as someone who first had a kind of old covenant faith in the Jewish Messiah who was to come, this would only show that he is one more example of someone who first had an old covenant experience of the Holy Spirit and then came into a new covenant experience of the Holy Spirit.

Messiah. When they heard of him they believed in him, and then received the power of the Holy Spirit that was appropriate to the gospel of the risen Lord Jesus Christ.

Because of this, these disciples at Ephesus are certainly not a pattern for us today either, for we do not first have faith in a Messiah that we are waiting for, and then later learn that Jesus has come and lived and died and risen again. We come into an understanding of the gospel of Christ immediately, and we, like the Corinthians, enter immediately into the new covenant experience of the power of the Holy Spirit.[26]

It seems therefore that there are no New Testament texts that encourage us to seek for a second experience of "baptism in the Holy Spirit" that comes after conversion.

## D. What Terms Shall We Use to Refer to an Empowering by the Holy Spirit That Comes After Conversion?

The previous sections have argued that "baptism in the Holy Spirit" is not the term the New Testament authors would use to speak of a post-conversion work of the Spirit, and that the examples of "second experiences" of receiving the Holy Spirit in the book of Acts are not patterns for us to imitate in our Christian lives. But the question remains, "What is actually happening to the millions of people who claim that they have received this 'baptism in the Holy Spirit' and that it has brought much blessing to their lives? Could it be that this has been a genuine work of the Holy Spirit but that the biblical categories and biblical examples used to illustrate it have been incorrect? Might it be that there are other biblical expressions and biblical teachings that point to this kind of work of the Holy Spirit after conversion and help us understand it more accurately?" I think there are, but before we look at these, it is appropriate to comment on the importance of having a correct understanding at this point.

**1. Harm Comes to the Church From Teaching Two-Class Christianity.** At various times in the history of the church Christians have attempted to divide the church into two categories of believers. This is in effect what happens with the Pentecostal doctrine of baptism in the Holy Spirit. It might be pictured as in figure 39.2, which shows the world divided into Christians and non-Christians, and then shows Christians divided into two categories, ordinary believers and Spirit-baptized believers.

But such a division of Christians into two categories is not a unique understanding that is found only in Pentecostal teaching in the twentieth century. In fact, much Pentecostal teaching came out of earlier holiness groups that had

---

[26]Regarding Acts 19:1–7, Ervin, *Conversion-Initiation,* pp. 55–59, objects that these disciples were first baptized and then, when Paul laid his hands on them, they were empowered with the Holy Spirit. We may admit that this is true, but the two events were so closely connected in time that it is hard to make a clear separation between them, and they certainly do not fit the common Pentecostal pattern of instruction and prayer, sometimes weeks or months or years after conversion, seeking a subsequent baptism in the Holy Spirit. If we had asked them later if their baptism in the Holy Spirit was "subsequent" to their conversion, they would probably have said that it was at the same time, so closely connected were these events in the actual historical sequence.

taught that Christians could either be ordinary believers or "sanctified" believers. Other groups have divided Christians using different categories, such as ordinary believers and those who are "Spirit filled," or ordinary believers and those who are "disciples," or "carnal" and "spiritual" Christians. In fact, the Roman Catholic Church has long had not two but three categories: ordinary believers, priests, and saints. All of these divisions into different categories of Christians can be seen in figure 39.3.[27]

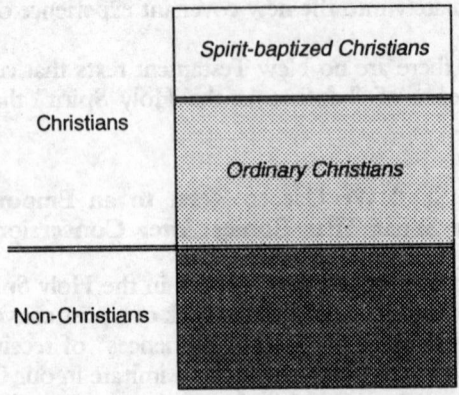

CHRISTIANS DIVIDED INTO TWO CATEGORIES:
ORDINARY AND SPIRIT-BAPTIZED
Figure 39.2

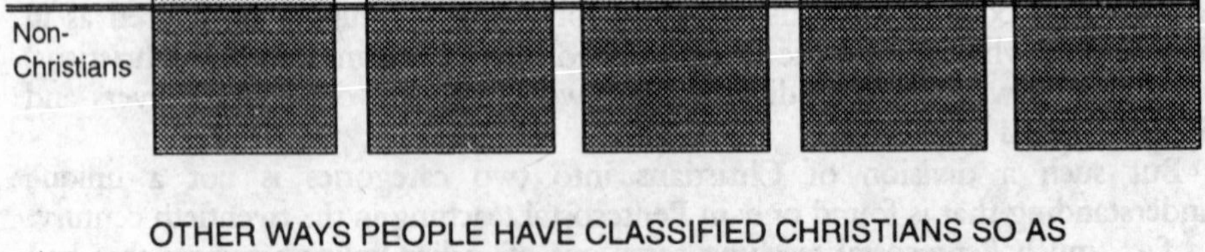

| | Spirit-filled Christians | Spiritual Christians | "Sanctified" Christians | "Disciples" | Saints |
| | | | | | Priests |
| Christians | | | | | |
| | Ordinary Christians | Carnal Christians | Ordinary Christians | Ordinary Christians | Ordinary Christians |
| Non-Christians | | | | | |

OTHER WAYS PEOPLE HAVE CLASSIFIED CHRISTIANS SO AS
TO DIVIDE THEM INTO TWO (OR THREE) CATEGORIES
Figure 39.3

Although those who teach the classical Pentecostal view of baptism in the Holy Spirit may deny that they are attempting to divide Christians into two categories,

---

[27]I have not included in this diagram another division that is sometimes reflected, not in any official teaching, but in attitude and practice, in Reformed circles: the division between ordinary Christians and those who are "truly Reformed."

such a division is implicit every time they ask whether someone has been baptized in the Holy Spirit or not. Such a question strongly suggests that there are two groups of Christians, those who have had this experience of "baptism in the Holy Spirit" and those who have not.

What is the problem with viewing Christians as existing in two categories like this? The problem is that it contributes to a "we-they" mentality in churches, and leads to jealousy, pride, and divisiveness. No matter how much these people who have received this special empowering of the Holy Spirit try to be thoughtful and considerate of those who have not, if they genuinely love their fellow brothers and sisters in Christ, and if this has been a very helpful experience in their own Christian lives, they cannot help but give the impression that they would like others to share this experience as well. Even if they are not proud in their hearts (and it seems to me that most are not) with respect to this experience, such a conviction that there is a second category of Christians will inevitably give an impression of pride or spiritual superiority. Yet there will very likely be a sense of jealousy on the part of those who have not had such an experience. In this way, a view of two groups within the church is fostered, and the repeated charge of divisiveness that is made against the charismatic movement is given some credibility. In fact, divisions often do occur in churches.

The major objection to this position is that the New Testament itself teaches no such two-level or two-class Christianity. Nowhere in the Epistles do we read of Paul or Peter telling a church that is having problems, "You all need to be baptized in the Holy Spirit." Nowhere do we hear of the risen Lord Jesus speaking to the troubled and weak churches in Revelation 2–3, "Ask me to baptize you in the Holy Spirit." It is hard to avoid the conclusion that the two-level or two-class view taught by all of these groups throughout history does not have a solid foundation in the New Testament itself.

**2. There Are Many Degrees of Empowering, Fellowship With God, and Personal Christian Maturity.** Is there a better model for understanding the varying degrees of maturity and power and fellowship with God that Christians experience? If we are willing to eliminate the categories that make us think of Christians in one group or another, a better model is possible, as represented in figure 39.4.

This chart shows the world as divided into non-Christians and Christians, but among Christians there are not categories into which we can place believers and divide them into set groups. Rather, there are Christians at all points along a scale of increasing Christian maturity (sanctification), increasing closeness of fellowship in their walk with God (an aspect of adoption), and greater experiences of the power of the Holy Spirit at work in their lives and ministries.

The Christian life should be one of *growth in all of these areas* as we progress throughout life. For many people that growth will be gradual and progressive, and will extend over all the years of their lives. We could represent it by the arrow in figure 39.5.[28]

---

[28]To be more precise we need to recognize that we can grow in some aspects of the Christian life without growing in others, and a single chart is therefore inadequate to show all of this. For example, Christians can grow in power but not in holiness (as the Corinthian church had done), or people can

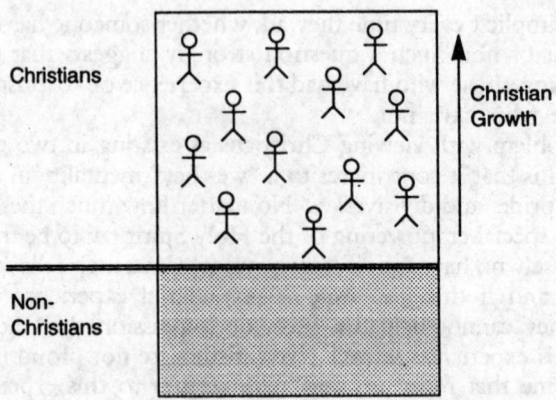

**A BETTER PICTURE: CHRISTIANS HAVE EXPERIENCED
VARYING DEGREES OF GROWTH, BUT THEY SHOULD NOT
BE DIVIDED INTO TWO DISTINCT CATEGORIES**
*Figure 39.4*

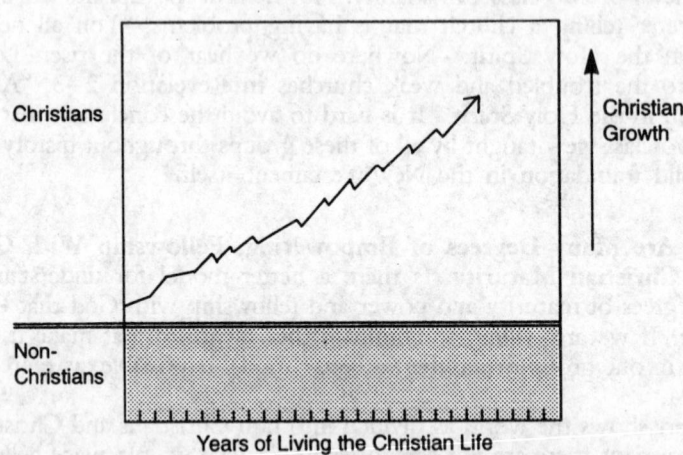

**FOR MOST CHRISTIANS GROWTH WILL BE GRADUAL AND
PROGRESSIVE AND WILL EXTEND OVER THEIR WHOLE LIVES**
*Figure 39.5*

---

grow in knowledge but not in power, or knowledge but not in holiness of life (something that tragically happens to some—but certainly not all—students in theological seminaries, and to some pastors who place excessive emphasis on academic pursuits). Or a person can grow in personal fellowship with God but not in knowledge of Scripture (something that happens with an extensive "pietistic" emphasis). Or someone can grow in holiness of life but not in power or use of spiritual gifts. All sorts of combinations like this are possible, but we would need several charts to show them in a schematic way. For the sake of simplicity I have simply represented "Christian growth" in general on this chart.

**a. How Should We Understand Contemporary Experience?** What then has happened to people who say they have experienced a "baptism in the Holy Spirit" that has brought great blessing to their lives? We must understand first what is commonly taught about the need to prepare for baptism in the Holy Spirit. Very often people will be taught that they should confess all known sins, repent of any remaining sin in their lives, trust Christ to forgive those sins, commit every area of their lives to the Lord's service, yield themselves fully to him, and believe that Christ is going to empower them in a new way and equip them with new gifts for ministry. Then after that preparation, they are encouraged to ask Jesus in prayer to baptize them in the Holy Spirit. But what does this preparation do? It is a guaranteed prescription for significant growth in the Christian life! Such confession, repentance, renewed commitment, and heightened faith and expectation, if they are genuine, can only bring positive results in a person's life. If any Christian is sincere in these steps of preparation to receive baptism in the Holy Spirit, there will certainly be growth in sanctification and deeper fellowship with God. In addition to that, we may expect that at many of these times the Holy Spirit will graciously bring a measure of the additional fullness and empowering that sincere Christians are seeking, even though their theological understanding and vocabulary may be imperfect in the asking. If this happens, they may well realize increased power for ministry and growth in spiritual gifts as well. We could say that a person has moved from point A to point B in figure 39.6 and has made one very large step forward in the Christian life.

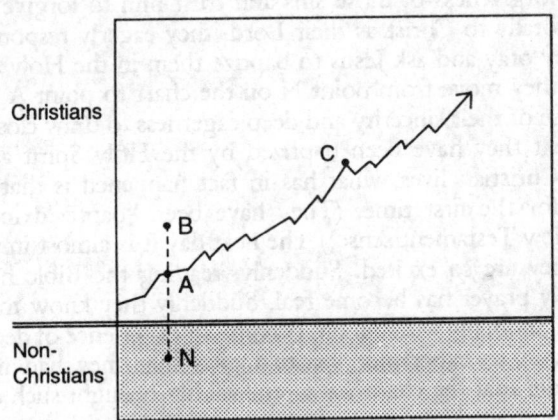

A SINGLE EXPERIENCE MAY RESULT IN A LARGE
STEP OF GROWTH IN THE CHRISTIAN LIFE
*Figure 39.6*

Of course prayer and Bible study and worship will seem more meaningful. Of course there will be more fruitfulness in evangelism and other kinds of ministry. But it is important to recognize that someone who moves from point A to point B on the chart is not now in a separate category of Christians, such as a group of those who have been "baptized in the Holy Spirit" and who are therefore different from those who have not had such an experience. There might be another

Christian in the same church who has never had such a large step of growth but who has nonetheless been making steady progress for the last forty years of his or her Christian life and has come to point C on the chart above. Though that person has never had a single experience that Pentecostals would call a "baptism in the Holy Spirit," he or she is still much farther along the path of Christian growth than the younger Christian who has recently been "baptized in the Holy Spirit" (according to Pentecostal terminology) and moved from point A to point B. Although the Christian who moved from point A to point B is not farther along in the Christian life than another person who is at point C, the person who moved to point B is certainly farther along *than he or she was before,* and this is certainly a positive result in his or her life. Thus, with this understanding of the Christian life, we have no divisions of Christians into two categories.

Before we leave this chart, one more observation should be made: in many cases the charismatic movement has brought teaching on the baptism of the Holy Spirit into more liberal churches where, for many years, there has not been a clear proclamation of the gospel of salvation by faith in Christ alone, and where people have not been taught that they can believe the Bible completely as God's Word to us. In such cases, many of the people in those churches have never experienced saving faith—they are at point N on the chart above, actually non-Christians and not born again.[29] Now when a representative of a charismatic renewal comes to these churches and tells them that they can experience new vitality in their Christian lives, and then tells them that the preparation is to repent of all known sins, ask Christ for forgiveness of those sins and trust him to forgive them, and commit their lives totally to Christ as their Lord, they eagerly respond to those directions. Then they pray and ask Jesus to baptize them in the Holy Spirit. The actual result is that they move from point N on the chart to point A or perhaps even point B, because of their sincerity and deep eagerness to draw closer to God. While they think that they have been baptized by the Holy Spirit as a second experience in their Christian lives, what has in fact happened is that they have become Christians for the first time. (They have been "baptized in the Holy Spirit" in the true New Testament sense!) The next day it is almost impossible to keep them silent, they are so excited. Suddenly, reading the Bible has become meaningful. Suddenly prayer has become real. Suddenly they know the presence of God in their lives. Suddenly worship has become an experience of deep joy, and often they have begun to experience spiritual gifts that they had not known before. It is no wonder that the charismatic renewal has brought such excitement (and often much controversy) to many Roman Catholic parishes and to many mainline, more liberal Protestant denominations. Though we may differ with the way this teaching is actually presented, no one should fault the good results that have come about as a result of it in these churches.

**b. What Terms Should We Use Today?** Now we can understand why our use of terms to describe this experience and the category of understanding we put it in are so important. If we use the traditional Pentecostal terminology of "baptism of

---

[29]However, in many cases, both in some Protestant churches and in Roman Catholic churches, people have been told that they received Christ and became Christians at their baptism when they were infants.

the Holy Spirit," then we almost inevitably end up with two-category Christianity, for this is seen as a common experience that *can* and indeed *should* happen to Christians at one point in time, and, once it has happened, does not need to be repeated. It is seen as a single experience of empowering for ministry that is distinct from the experience of becoming a Christian, and people either have received that experience or they have not. Especially when the experience is described in terms of what happened to the disciples at Pentecost in Acts 2 (which was clearly a one-time experience for them), the Samaritans in Acts 8, and the Ephesian disciples in Acts 19, it is clearly implied that this is a one-time event that empowers people for ministry but that also puts them in a separate category or group than the one they were in before this experience. The use of the term *"the baptism in the Holy Spirit"* inevitably implies two groups of Christians.

But if we are correct in understanding the experience that has come to millions of people in the charismatic renewal as a large step of growth in their Christian lives, then some other term than "baptism in the Holy Spirit" would seem to be more appropriate. There might be several terms that we could use, so long as they allow for repetition, varying degrees of intensity, and further development beyond that one experience, and so long as they do not suggest that all truly obedient Christians should have the same experience.[30] We have already used one expression, "*a large step of growth* in several aspects of the Christian life." Because this phrase speaks of "*a* large step of growth" it cannot be misunderstood to refer to a single experience that puts Christians in a new category. And because it is referred to as a large step of growth, it clearly implies that others may experience such growth in smaller steps over a longer period of time but reach the same point in the Christian life.[31]

Another term that may be helpful is "a new *empowering for ministry*." It is certainly true that many who have received such a charismatic experience do find new power for ministry in their Christian lives, including the ability to use spiritual gifts that had not been theirs before. However, the problem with this phrase is that it does not say anything about the deepened fellowship with God, the greater effectiveness in prayer and Bible study, and the new joy in worship that often also result from this experience.

**c. What Is "Being Filled With the Spirit"?** Yet an even more commonly used term in the New Testament is *"being filled with the Holy Spirit."* Because of its frequent use in contexts that speak of Christian growth and ministry, *this seems to me to be the best term to use* to describe genuine "second experiences" today (or third or fourth experiences, etc.). Paul tells the Ephesians, "Do not get drunk with wine, for that is debauchery; but *be filled with the Spirit*" (Eph. 5:18). He uses a present tense imperative verb that could more explicitly be translated, "Be continually being filled with the Holy Spirit," thus implying that this is something that should repeatedly be happening to Christians. Such fullness of the Holy Spirit will result in *renewed worship and thanksgiving* (Eph. 5:19–20), and in renewed

---

[30]The same criteria could be used to find replacement terms for some of the other "two-category" views mentioned above, or else to explain the terms that are used so as to avoid misunderstanding.
[31]Paul does say that we "are to grow up *in every way* into him who is the head, into Christ" (Eph. 4:15).

relationships to others, especially those in authority over us or those under our authority (Eph. 5:21—6:9). In addition, since the Holy Spirit is the Spirit who sanctifies us, such a filling will often result in *increased sanctification*. Furthermore, since the Holy Spirit is the one who empowers us for Christian service and gives us spiritual gifts, such filling will often result in *increased power for ministry* and increased effectiveness and perhaps diversity in the use of *spiritual gifts*.

We see examples of repeated filling with the Holy Spirit in the book of Acts. In Acts 2:4, the disciples and those with them were "all *filled with the Holy Spirit*." Later, when Peter was standing before the Sanhedrin, we read, "Then Peter, *filled with the Holy Spirit*, said to them . . ." (Acts 4:8). But a little later, when Peter and the other apostles had returned to the church to tell what had happened (Acts 4:23) they joined together in prayer. After they had prayed they were again filled with the Holy Spirit, a sequence of events that Luke makes clear: "*After* they prayed, the place where they were meeting was shaken. And they were all *filled with the Holy Spirit* and spoke the word of God boldly*" (Acts 4:31 NIV). Even though Peter had been filled with the Holy Spirit at Pentecost (Acts 2:4) and had later been filled with the Holy Spirit before speaking to the Sanhedrin (Acts 4:8), he was once again filled with the Holy Spirit after the group of Christians he was meeting with had prayed.

Therefore, it is appropriate to understand filling with the Holy Spirit *not as a one-time event* but as *an event that can occur over and over again* in a Christian's life. It may involve a momentary empowering for a specific ministry (such as apparently happened in Acts 4:8; 7:55), but it may also refer to a long-term characteristic of a person's life (see Acts 6:3; 11:24). In either case such filling can occur many times in a person's life: even though Stephen, as an early deacon (or apostolic assistant), was a man "full of the Spirit and of wisdom" (Acts 6:3, 5), when he was being stoned he apparently received a fresh new filling of the Holy Spirit in great power (Acts 7:55).

Someone might object that a person who is already "full" of the Holy Spirit cannot become more full—if a glass is full of water no more water can be put into it. But a water glass is a poor analogy for us as real people, for God is able to cause us to grow and to be able to contain much more of the Holy Spirit's fullness and power. A better analogy might be a balloon, which can be "full" of air even though it has very little air in it. When more air is blown in, the balloon expands and in a sense it is "more full." So it is with us: we can be filled with the Holy Spirit and at the same time be able to receive much more of the Holy Spirit as well. It was only Jesus himself to whom the Father gave the Spirit without measure (John 3:34).

The divisiveness that comes with the term "*baptism in the Holy Spirit*" could easily be avoided by using any of the alternative terms mentioned in this section. People could be thankful for "a new fullness of the Holy Spirit" or "a new empowering for ministry" or "a significant step in growth" in some aspect of another Christian's life. There would be no separating into "we" and "they," for we would recognize that we are all part of one body with no separate categories.[32]

---

[32]It is my personal opinion that most of the divisiveness that has come with the influence of charismatic renewal in many churches has not come because of spiritual gifts but because of a misunderstanding of what is happening and the implications of two groups of Christians that come with the term "baptism in the Holy Spirit."

In fact, many charismatics and even some traditional Pentecostals today are using the term "baptism in the Holy Spirit" far less frequently, preferring to use other terms such as "being filled with the Holy Spirit" instead.[33]

Moreover, many people who have had no single dramatic experience (such as what Pentecostals have called a baptism in the Holy Spirit) have nonetheless begun to experience new freedom and joy in worship (often with the advent of modern worship or praise songs in their churches), and to use a wider variety of spiritual gifts with effectiveness and edification for themselves and their churches (including gifts such as healing, prophecy, working of miracles, discernment of spirits, and the ability to exercise authority over demonic forces with prayer and a word of rebuke spoken directly to the evil spirits). Sometimes the gift of speaking in tongues and the gift of interpretation have been used as well, but in other cases they have not. All of this is to say that the differences between Pentecostals and charismatics on the one hand, and more traditional and mainstream evangelical Christians on the other hand, seem to me to be breaking down more and more, and there are fewer and fewer differences between them.

Someone may object that it is specifically this experience of praying for a baptism in the Holy Spirit that catapults people into a new level of power in ministry and effectiveness in use of spiritual gifts. Since this experience has been so helpful in the lives of millions of people, should we so quickly dismiss it? In response, it must be said that, if the terminology "baptism in the Holy Spirit" is changed for something more representative of New Testament teaching, there should be no objection at all to people coming into churches, and to encouraging people to prepare their hearts for spiritual renewal by sincere repentance and renewed commitment to Christ and by believing that the Holy Spirit can work much more powerfully in their lives.[34] There is nothing wrong with teaching people to pray and to seek this greater infilling of the Holy Spirit, or to expect and ask the Lord for an outpouring of more spiritual gifts in their lives, for the benefit of the body of Christ (see 1 Cor. 12:31; 14:1, 12). In fact, most evangelical Christians in every denomination genuinely long for greater power in ministry, greater joy in worship, and deeper fellowship with God. Many would also welcome increased understanding of spiritual gifts, and encouragement to grow in the use of them. If Pentecostal and charismatic Christians would be willing to

---

[33]John Wimber, who does not like to identify himself as a Pentecostal or a charismatic, says with much wisdom, "I have discovered that the argument concerning the baptism of the Spirit usually comes down to a question of labels. Good medicine may be incorrectly labeled, which is probably true in this case. The Pentecostals' experience of God is better than their explanation of it" (John Wimber with Kevin Springer, *Power Evangelism*, p. 145). In recent years I have noticed in personal conversation with professors at institutions affiliated with the charismatic movement that there is an increasing tendency to talk about filling with the Holy Spirit rather than baptism in the Holy Spirit to represent what has happened to those within the charismatic movement.

[34]My student Jack Mattern, though not himself a charismatic, has told me that in over a decade of working with students on university campuses, he has found a great hunger among Christians to know how they may be filled with the Holy Spirit. He rightly points out that effective teaching on this area must include the need (1) to yield our lives fully to God (Rom. 12:1; Gal. 2:20), (2) to depend fully on God for power to live the Christian life (Rom. 8:13; Gal. 2:20; 3:2–3), and (3) to obey the Lord's commands in our lives (1 John 2:6). These elements are similar to the steps of preparation mentioned above in the discussion of common charismatic teaching. In any case, to these steps could certainly be added a prayer that the Holy Spirit would fill us, in accordance with the will of God as expressed in Eph. 5:18. There should be no objection to teaching Christians to pray daily in accordance with these principles.

teach on these things without the additional baggage of two-level Christianity that is implied by the term "baptism in the Holy Spirit," they might find a new era of greatly increased effectiveness in bringing teaching on these other areas of the Christian life to evangelicals generally.

**3. Being Filled With the Holy Spirit Does Not Always Result in Speaking in Tongues.** One remaining point needs to be made with respect to the experience of being filled with the Holy Spirit. Because there were several cases in Acts where people received the new covenant power of the Holy Spirit and began to speak with tongues at the same time (Acts 2:4; 10:46; 19:6; probably also implied in 8:17–19 because of the parallel with the experience of the disciples in Acts 2), Pentecostal teaching has commonly maintained that the outward sign of baptism in the Holy Spirit is speaking in tongues (that is, speaking in languages that are not understood by and have not been learned by the person speaking, whether known human languages or other kinds of angelic or heavenly or miraculously given languages).[35]

But it is important to realize that there are many cases where being filled with the Holy Spirit *did not* result in speaking in tongues. When Jesus was filled with the Spirit in Luke 4:1, the result was strength to overcome the temptations of Satan in the wilderness. When the temptations were ended, and Jesus "returned in the power of the Spirit into Galilee" (Luke 4:14), the results were miracles of healing, casting out of demons, and teaching with authority. When Elizabeth was filled with the Holy Spirit, she spoke a word of blessing to Mary (Luke 1:41–45). When Zechariah was filled with the Holy Spirit, he prophesied (Luke 1:67–79). Other results of being filled with the Holy Spirit were powerful preaching of the gospel (Acts 4:31), (perhaps) wisdom and Christian maturity and sound judgment (Acts 6:3), powerful preaching and testimony when on trial (Acts 4:8), a vision of heaven (Acts 7:55), and (apparently) faith and maturity of life (Acts 11:24). Several of these cases may also imply the fullness of the Holy Spirit to empower some kind of ministry, especially in the context of the book of Acts, where the empowering of the Holy Spirit is frequently seen to result in miracles, preaching, and works of great power.[36]

Therefore, while an experience of being filled with the Holy Spirit may result in the gift of speaking in tongues, or in the use of some other gifts that had not previously been experienced, it also may come without the gift of speaking in tongues. In fact, many Christians throughout history have experienced powerful infillings of the Holy Spirit that have not been accompanied by speaking in tongues. With regard to this gift as well as all other gifts, we must simply say that the Holy Spirit "apportions each one individually as he wills" (1 Cor. 12:11).

## QUESTIONS FOR PERSONAL APPLICATION

1. Before reading this chapter, what was your understanding of "baptism in the Holy Spirit"? How has your understanding changed, if at all?

---

[35]See chapter 53, pp. 1069–80, for a discussion of speaking in tongues.

[36]Scripture does not specify what result there was in the life of John the Baptist, who was "filled with the Holy Spirit, even from his mother's womb" (Luke 1:15), but "the hand of the Lord was with him" (Luke 1:66), and "the child grew and became strong in spirit" (Luke 1:80).

2. Has your own Christian life included one or more events that you could call "a large step of growth" in some area or another in the Christian life? Or has it rather been one of small but continuing steps in sanctification, in fellowship with God, and in use of spiritual gifts and power in ministry?

3. Have you known people who have claimed they received a "baptism in the Holy Spirit" after conversion? In your evaluation, has the result in their lives been mostly positive, or mostly negative, or has it been rather mixed? If you have had such an experience yourself, do you think that understanding it as a one-time "baptism in the Holy Spirit" was essential to the experience, or could the same results have come in your Christian life if it had been called "being filled with the Holy Spirit"? Do you think it would be right to seek for an experience of filling with the Holy Spirit in your own life now? How might someone go about doing this?

4. We all realize that it is possible to overemphasize something good in the Christian life to such an extent that our lives become unbalanced and not as effective in ministry as they might be. If we think of the various ways in which we can grow in the Christian life (knowledge of the Word and sound doctrine, prayer, love for God, love for other Christians and for non-Christians, trust in God each day, worship, holiness of life, use of spiritual gifts, effective power of the Holy Spirit in our witness and ministry, daily fellowship with God, etc.), in what areas do you think you need to ask God for more growth in your own life? Would it be appropriate to ask him for a new fullness of the Holy Spirit to accompany growth in those areas?

5. With regard to this topic of baptism in or being filled with the Holy Spirit, do you think that evangelical churches generally have been moving toward more divisiveness or more unity on this issue?

## SPECIAL TERMS

baptism by the Holy Spirit
baptism in the Holy Spirit
baptism with the Holy Spirit
being filled with the Holy Spirit
Pentecost
new covenant experience of the Holy Spirit
old covenant experience of the Holy Spirit
two-class Christianity

## BIBLIOGRAPHY

(For an explanation of this bibliography see the note on the bibliography to chapter 1, p. 38. Complete bibliographical data may be found on pp. 1223–29.) Note: Very few systematic theologies have included explicit treatment of this topic, since it has only become a controversial issue in this century.)

### Sections In Evangelical Systematic Theologies

2. Arminian (Wesleyan or Methodist)
   1983    Carter, 1:435–47

3. Baptist
   1983–85    Erickson, 879–80
4. Dispensational
   1947    Chafer, 6:138–61
   1986    Ryrie, 362–66
6. Reformed (or Presbyterian)
   1962    Buswell, 2:208–12
7. Renewal (or charismatic/Pentecostal)
   1988–92    Williams, 2:177–79, 181–207, 271–321

**Sections in Representative Roman Catholic Systematic Theologies**

(no explicit treatment)

**Other Works**

Bennett, Dennis and Rita. *The Holy Spirit and You*. Plainfield, N.J.: Logos, 1971.

Bruner, Frederick Dale. *A Theology of the Holy Spirit: The Pentecostal Experience and the New Testament Witness*. Grand Rapids: Eerdmans, 1970.

Dunn, James D. G. *Baptism in the Holy Spirit*. London: SCM, 1970.

Ervin, Howard M. *Conversion-Initiation and the Baptism in the Holy Spirit: A Critique of James D. G. Dunn, "Baptism in the Holy Spirit."* Peabody, Mass.: Hendrickson, 1984.

————. *Spirit Baptism*. Peabody, Mass.: Hendriksen, 1987.

Gaffin, Richard. *Perspectives on Pentecost*. Phillipsburg, N.J.: Presbyterian and Reformed, 1979.

Green, Michael. *Baptism: Its Purpose, Practice and Power*. Downers Grove, Ill.: InterVarsity Press, 1987, pp. 127–41.

————. "The Spirit's Baptism." In *I Believe in the Holy Spirit*. London: Hodder and Stoughton, and Grand Rapids: Eerdmans, 1975, pp. 123–47.

Hoekema, Anthony A. *Holy Spirit Baptism*. Grand Rapids: Eerdmans, (1972).

Lloyd-Jones, Martyn. *Joy Unspeakable: Power and Renewal in the Holy Spirit*. Ed. by Christopher Catherwood. Wheaton, Ill.: Shaw, 1984.

McGee, Gary B., ed. *Initial Evidence*. Peabody, Mass.: Hendrickson, 1991.

Packer, J. I. "Baptism in the Spirit." In *NDT*, pp. 73–74.

————. *Keep in Step With the Spirit*. Old Tappan, N.J.: Revell, and Leicester: Inter-Varsity Press, 1984.

Stott, John. *Baptism and Fulness*. Leicester and Downers Grove, Ill.: InterVarsity Press, 1976.

Unger, Merrill F. *The Baptizing Work of the Holy Spirit*. Wheaton, Ill.: Van Kampen Press, 1953.

White, R. E. O. "Baptism of the Spirit." In *EDT*, pp. 121–22.

**SCRIPTURE MEMORY PASSAGE**

**1 Corinthians 12:12–13:** *For just as the body is one and has many members, and all the members of the body, though many, are one body, so it is with Christ. For by [or "in"]* *one Spirit we were all baptized into one body—Jews or Greeks, slaves or free—and all were made to drink of one Spirit.*

## HYMN

### "Spirit of God, Descend Upon My Heart"

Spirit of God, descend upon my heart;
  Wean it from earth, through all its pulses move;
Stoop to my weakness, mighty as thou art,
  And make me love thee as I ought to love.

Hast thou not bid us love thee, God and King?
  All, all thine own, soul, heart, and strength and mind.
I see thy cross—there teach my heart to cling:
  O let me seek thee, and O let me find.

Teach me to feel that thou art always nigh;
  Teach me the struggles of the soul to bear,
To check the rising doubt, the rebel sigh;
  Teach me the patience of unanswered prayer.

Teach me to love thee as thine angels love,
  One holy passion filling all my frame;
The baptism of the heav'n descended dove
  My heart an altar, and thy love the flame.

AUTHOR: GEORGE CROLY, 1854

Alternative hymn: "Spirit of the Living God"

# Chapter 40

# The Perseverance of the Saints (Remaining a Christian)

*Can true Christians lose their salvation? How can we know if we are truly born again?*

## EXPLANATION AND SCRIPTURAL BASIS

Our previous discussion has dealt with many aspects of the full salvation that Christ has earned for us and that the Holy Spirit now applies to us. But how do we know that we shall continue to be Christians throughout our lives? Is there anything that will keep us from falling away from Christ, anything to guarantee that we will remain Christians until we die and that we will in fact live with God in heaven forever? Or might it be that we will turn away from Christ and lose the blessings of our salvation? The topic of the perseverance of the saints speaks to these questions. *The perseverance of the saints means that all those who are truly born again will be kept by God's power and will persevere as Christians until the end of their lives, and that only those who persevere until the end have been truly born again.*

This definition has two parts to it. It indicates first that there is assurance to be given to those who are truly born again, for it reminds them that God's power will keep them as Christians until they die, and they will surely live with Christ in heaven forever. On the other hand, the second half of the definition makes it clear that continuing in the Christian life is one of the evidences that a person is truly born again. It is important to keep this aspect of the doctrine in mind as well, lest false assurance be given to people who were never really believers in the first place.

It should be noted that this question is one on which evangelical Christians have long had significant disagreement. Many within the Wesleyan/Arminian tradition have held that it is possible for someone who is truly born again to lose his or her salvation, while Reformed Christians have held that that is not possible for someone who is *truly* born again.[1] Most Baptists have followed the Reformed tradition at this point; however, they have frequently used the term *"eternal security"* or the *"eternal security of the believer"* rather than the term *"perseverance of the saints."*

## A. All Who Are Truly Born Again Will Persevere to the End

There are many passages that teach that those who are truly born again, who are genuinely Christians, will continue in the Christian life until death and will then go to be with Christ in heaven. Jesus says,

---

[1]The doctrine of the perseverance of the saints is represented by "P" in the acronym TULIP, which is often used to summarize the "five points of Calvinism." (See full list at p. 679, n. 11.)

I have come down from heaven, not to do my own will, but the will of him who sent me; and this is the will of him who sent me, that I should lose nothing of all that he has given me, but raise it up at the last day. For this is the will of my Father, that *every one who* sees the Son and *believes in* him should have eternal life; and *I will raise him up at the last day.* (John 6:38–40)

Here Jesus says that everyone who believes in him will have eternal life. He says that he will raise that person up at the last day—which, in this context of believing in the Son and having eternal life, clearly means that Jesus will raise that person up to eternal life with him (not just raise him up to be judged and condemned). It seems hard to avoid the conclusion that everyone who truly believes in Christ will remain a Christian up to the day of final resurrection into the blessings of life in the presence of God.[2] Moreover, this text emphasizes that Jesus does the will of the Father, which is that he should *"lose nothing* of all that he has given me" (John 6:39). Once again, those given to the Son by the Father will not be lost.

Another passage emphasizing this truth is John 10:27–29, in which Jesus says:

My sheep hear my voice, and I know them, and they follow me; and I give them eternal life, and *they shall never perish,* and no one shall snatch them out of my hand. My Father, who has given them to me, is greater than all, and no one is able to snatch them out of the Father's hand.

Here Jesus says that those who follow him, those who are his sheep, are given eternal life. He further says that "no one shall snatch them out of my hand" (v. 28). Now some have objected to this that even though no one else can take Christians out of Christ's hand, we might remove ourselves from Christ's hand. But that seems to be pedantic quibbling over words—does not "no one" also include the person who is in Christ's hand? Moreover, we know that our own hearts are far from trustworthy. Therefore if the possibility remained that we could remove ourself from Christ's hand, the passage would hardly give the assurance that Jesus intends by it.

But more importantly, the most forceful phrase in the passage is *"they shall never perish"* (v. 28). The Greek construction (*ou mē* plus aorist subjunctive) is especially emphatic and might be translated more explicitly, "and they shall certainly not perish forever." This emphasizes that those who are Jesus' "sheep" and who follow

---

[2]Grant R. Osborne, "Exegetical Notes on Calvinist Texts," in *Grace Unlimited*, pp. 170–71, does not give an alternative explanation for Jesus' statement, "I will raise him up at the last day," when he deals with this passage. But he does say that in this context v. 35 emphasizes the fact that eternal life is dependent on the individual person "coming and believing" in Christ (p. 171) and that the present tense verbs used for "believe" in these passages imply not merely an initial decision of faith, but rather continuing in that state.

I regret having to differ with my friend and colleague on this question, but there is something to be said in response: while no one would deny that it is necessary for people themselves to believe in Christ for eternal life, and while it is also true that Jesus here speaks not just of initial saving faith but of a faith that continues over time, the verse does not go so far as to specify that "everyone who believes continuously *until his or her death* will have eternal life," but rather simply says that "he who is *presently in a state of believing* in Christ" will have eternal life and Jesus will raise him up at the last day. The verse speaks about all who presently are in a state of believing in Christ, and it says that all of them will be raised up by Christ at the last day. No further objections to this specific verse are given in Osborne's second essay, "Soteriology in the Gospel of John," in *The Grace of God, the Will of Man*, p. 248.

him, and to whom he has given eternal life, shall never lose their salvation or be separated from Christ—they shall "never perish."[3]

There are several other passages that say those who believe have "eternal life." One example is John 3:36: "He who believes in the Son *has eternal life*" (cf. also John 5:24; 6:4–7; 10:28; 1 John 5:13). Now if this is truly eternal life that believers have, then it is life that lasts forever with God. It is a gift of God that comes with salvation (it is put in contrast to condemnation and eternal judgment in John 3:16–17, 36; 10:28). Arminians have objected that "eternal life" is simply a quality of life, a type of life in relationship with God, which one can have for a time and then lose. But this objection does not seem to be convincing in view of the clear nuance of unending time involved in the adjective *eternal* (Gk. *aiōnios*, "eternal, without end").[4] Certainly there is a special quality about this life, but the emphasis in the adjective *eternal* is on the fact that it is the opposite of death; it is the opposite of judgment and separation from God; it is life that goes on forever in the presence of God. And he who believes in the Son has this "*eternal* life" (John 3:36).

Evidence in Paul's writings and the other New Testament epistles also indicates that those who are truly born again will persevere to the end. There remains "no condemnation for those who are in Christ Jesus" (Rom. 8:1); therefore, it would be unjust for God to give any kind of eternal punishment to those who are Christians—no condemnation remains for them, for the entire penalty for their sins has been paid.

Then in Romans 8:30, Paul emphasizes the clear connection between God's eternal purposes in predestination and his working out of those purposes in life, together with his final realization of those purposes in "glorifying" or giving final resurrection bodies to those whom he has brought into union with Christ: "And those whom he predestined he also called; and those whom he called he also justified; and those whom he justified he also glorified." Here Paul sees the future event of glorification as such a certainty in God's settled purpose that he can speak of it as if it were already accomplished ("he also glorified"). This is true of all those who are called and justified—that is, all those who truly become Christians.

Further evidence that God keeps those who are born again safe for eternity is the "seal" that God places upon us. This "seal" is the Holy Spirit within us, who

---

[3]The Greek word used here for "perish" is *apollymi*, the same term John uses in John 3:16 to say that "whoever believes in him should not perish but have eternal life."

Grant Osborne, in "Exegetical Notes on Calvinist Texts," p. 172, says that this verse must not be interpreted apart from the teaching about the vine and the branches in John 15:1–7, but he gives no alternative explanation for the phrase "they shall never perish," and gives no reason why we should fail to understand it to mean that these people will certainly have life with God forever in heaven. In his subsequent article, "Soteriology in the Gospel of John," Osborne again mentions John 10:28, but gives no alternative explanation for it other than to say that this passage emphasizes God's sovereignty, but other passages in John emphasize the faith-response that works together with God's sovereignty. These articles do not seem to provide a reason why we should not understand these words in an ordinary sense, indicating that one who believes in Christ will certainly never fall away.

Of course, those who believe in the doctrine of the perseverance of the saints (such as myself) would affirm that the *way* God keeps us safe is by causing us to continue to believe in Christ (see discussion below), so to say that Scripture also emphasizes the necessity of continuing in faith is not to object to the doctrine of perseverance of the saints as it has been expressed by Reformed theologians frequently in the history of the church. In other words, there is a way to believe in both sets of texts without concluding that people who are truly born again can lose their salvation.

[4]*BAGD*, p. 28.

also acts as God's "guarantee" that we will receive the inheritance promised to us: "In him you also, who have heard the word of truth, the gospel of your salvation, and have believed in him, were *sealed with the promised Holy Spirit,* which is the *guarantee* of our inheritance until we acquire possession of it, to the praise of his glory" (Eph. 1:13–14). The Greek word translated "guarantee" in this passage (*arrabōn*) is a legal and commercial term that means "first installment, deposit, down payment, pledge" and represents "a payment which obligates the contracting party to make further payments."[5] When God gave us the Holy Spirit within, he committed himself to give all the further blessings of eternal life and a great reward in heaven with him. This is why Paul can say that the Holy Spirit is the *"guarantee* of our inheritance until we acquire possession of it" (Eph. 1:14). All who have the Holy Spirit within them, all who are truly born again, have God's unchanging promise and guarantee that the inheritance of eternal life in heaven will certainly be theirs. God's own faithfulness is pledged to bring it about.[6]

Another example of assurance that believers will persevere to the end is found in Paul's statement to the Philippians: "I am sure that he who began a good work in you will bring it to completion at the day of Jesus Christ" (Phil. 1:6). It is true that the word "you" here is plural (Gk. *hymas*), and thus he is referring to Christians in the Philippian church generally, but he is still talking about the specific believers to whom he is writing, and saying that God's good work that began in them will continue and will be completed at the day Christ returns.[7] Peter tells his readers that they are those "who *by God's power are guarded* through faith for a salvation ready to be revealed in the last time" (1 Peter 1:5). The word *guarded* (Gk. *phroureō*) can mean both "kept from escaping" and "protected from attack," and perhaps both kinds of guarding are intended here: God is preserving believers from escaping out of his kingdom, and he is protecting them from external attacks.

The present participle that Peter uses gives the sense "You are continually being guarded."[8] He stresses that this is by God's power. Yet God's power does not work apart from the personal faith of those being guarded, but through their

---

[5]Ibid., p. 109.

[6]Osborne, "Exegetical Notes on Calvinist Texts," p. 181, answers this verse by saying that Paul also teaches personal responsibility, since "the Christian is warned not to 'grieve' the Spirit (cf. 1 Thess. 4:8)" and "the danger of apostasy is real, and he dare not 'grieve' the Spirit." But once again this objection provides no alternative interpretation to the verse at hand, but simply refers to other verses that teach personal responsibility, a fact that a Reformed theologian would also be eager to affirm.

Arminian theologians frequently assume that if they affirm human responsibility and the need for continuing in faith they have thereby negated the idea that God's sovereign keeping and protection is absolutely certain and eternal life is guaranteed. But they often to do this without providing any other convincing interpretations for the texts cited to demonstrate the doctrine of perseverance of the saints, or any explanation that would show why we should not take these words as absolute guarantees that those who are born again will certainly persevere to the end. Rather than assuming that passages on human responsibility negate the idea of God's sovereign protection, it seems better to adopt the Reformed position that says that God's sovereign protection is consistent with human responsibility, because it works through human responsibility and guarantees that we will respond by maintaining the faith that is necessary to persevere.

[7]Osborne rightly rejects the idea that this refers only to the fact that the church will continue. He says, "Paul does intend that the promise extend to the individual. He will be kept by God with a view to the final salvation, but this does not obviate the need for perseverance" ("Exegetical Notes on Calvinist Texts," p. 182).

[8]The following three paragraphs are taken from W. Grudem, *The First Epistle of Peter* (Leicester: Inter-Varsity Press, and Grand Rapids: Eerdmans, 1988), pp. 58–59.

faith. ("Faith," *pistis*, is regularly a personal activity of individual believers in Peter's epistles; see 1 Peter 1:7, 9, 21; 5:9; 2 Peter 1:1, 5; and commonly in the New Testament.) The parallel examples of God working "through" someone or something in Peter's writings (1 Peter 1:3, 23: 2 Peter 1:4, and probably also 1 Peter 1:12; 2:14; 3:1) suggest that the believer's personal faith or trust in God is the means God uses to guard his people. Thus we might give the sense of the verse by saying that "God is continually using his power to guard his people by means of their faith," a statement that seems to imply that God's power in fact energizes and continually sustains individual, personal faith.[9]

This guarding is not for a temporary goal but for a salvation ready to be revealed in the last time. "Salvation" is used here not of past justification or of present sanctification (speaking in theological categories) but of the future full possession of all the blessings of our redemption—of the final, complete fulfillment of our salvation (cf. Rom. 13:11; 1 Peter 2:2). Though already prepared or "ready," it will not be "revealed" by God to mankind generally until the "last time," the time of final judgment.

This last phrase makes it difficult if not impossible to see any end to God's guarding activity. If God's guarding has as its purpose the preservation of believers until they receive their full, heavenly salvation, then it is safe to conclude that God will accomplish that purpose and they will in fact attain that final salvation. Ultimately their attainment of final salvation depends on God's power. Nevertheless, God's power continually works "through" their faith. Do they wish to know whether God is guarding them? If they continue to trust God through Christ, God is working and guarding them, and he should be thanked.

This emphasis on God's guarding in combination with our faith provides a natural transition to the second half of the doctrine of perseverance.

## B. Only Those Who Persevere to the End Have Been Truly Born Again

While Scripture repeatedly emphasizes that those who are truly born again will persevere to the end and will certainly have eternal life in heaven with God, there are other passages that speak of the necessity of continuing in faith throughout life. They make us realize that what Peter said in 1 Peter 1:5 is true, namely, that God does not guard us *apart from* our faith, but only by working *through* our faith so that he enables us to continue to believe in him. In this way, those who continue to trust in Christ gain assurance that God is working in them and guarding them.

One example of this kind of passage is John 8:31–32: "Jesus then said to the Jews who had believed in him, '*If you continue in my word*, you are truly my disciples, and you will know the truth, and the truth will make you free.'" Jesus is here giving a warning that one evidence of genuine faith is continuing in his word, that is, continuing to believe what he says and living a life of obedience to his

---

[9]The translation by J. N. D. Kelly, "as a result of . . . faith," is an extremely unlikely rendering of the very common construction *dia* with the genitive (the few examples of this construction meaning "as a result of" which are suggested in, *BAGD*, p. 180, IV, are all ambiguous, and Kelly himself gives no examples: see J. N. D. Kelly, *A Commentary on the Epistles of Peter and Jude*, Black's New Testament Commentaries [London: Black, 1969], p. 52).

commands. Similarly, Jesus says, *"He who endures to the end will be saved"* (Matt. 10:22), as a means of warning people not to fall away in times of persecution.

Paul says to the Colossian Christians that Christ has reconciled them to God, "in order to present you holy and blameless and irreproachable before him, *provided that you continue in the faith,* stable and steadfast, not shifting from the hope of the gospel which you heard" (Col. 1:22–23). It is only natural that Paul and the other New Testament writers would speak this way, for they are addressing groups of people who profess to be Christians, without being able to know the actual state of every person's heart. There may have been people at Colossae who had joined in the fellowship of the church, and perhaps even professed that they had faith in Christ and had been baptized into membership of the church, but who never had true saving faith. How is Paul to distinguish such people from true believers? How can he avoid giving them false assurance, assurance that they will be saved eternally when in fact they will not, unless they come to true repentance and faith? Paul knows that those whose faith is not real will eventually fall away from participation in the fellowship of the church. Therefore he tells his readers that they will ultimately be saved, *"provided that you continue in the faith"* (Col. 1:23). Those who continue show thereby that they are genuine believers. But those who do not continue in the faith show that there was no genuine faith in their hearts in the first place.

A similar emphasis is seen in Hebrews 3:14 (NASB): "For we have become partakers of Christ, *if we hold fast the beginning of our assurance firm to the end."* This verse provides an excellent perspective on the doctrine of perseverance. How do we know if "we have become partakers of Christ"? How do we know if this being joined to Christ has happened to us at some time in the past?[10] One way in which we know that we have come to genuine faith in Christ is if we continue in faith until the end of our lives.

Attention to the context of Hebrews 3:14 will keep us from using this and other similar passages in a pastorally inappropriate way. We must remember that there are other evidences elsewhere in Scripture that give Christians assurance of salvation,[11] so *we should not think that assurance that we belong to Christ is impossible until we die.* However, continuing in faith is the one means of assurance that is named here by the author of Hebrews. He mentions this to warn his readers that they should not fall away from Christ, because he is writing to a situation where such a warning is needed. The beginning of that section, just two verses earlier, said, "Take care, brethren, lest there be in any of you an evil, unbelieving heart, leading you to fall away from the living God" (Heb. 3:12). In fact, in all of the passages where continuing to believe in Christ to the end of our lives is mentioned as one indication of genuine faith, the purpose is never to make those who are presently trusting in Christ worry that some time in the future they might fall away (and we should never use these passages that way either, for that would be to give wrongful cause for worry in a way that Scripture does not intend). Rather, the purpose is always *to warn those who are thinking of falling away or have fallen away* that if they do this it is a strong indication that they were never saved in the

---

[10]The author uses the perfect tense verb *gegonamen,* "we have become" (at some time in the past, with results that continue into the present).

[11]See the list of evidences of salvation given in section D, pp. 803–6, below.

first place. Thus, the necessity for continuing in faith should just be used as a warning against falling away, a warning that those who fall away give evidence that their faith was never real.

John clearly states that when people fall away from fellowship with the church and from belief in Christ they thereby show that their faith was not real in the first place and that they were never part of the true body of Christ. Speaking of people who have left the fellowship of believers, John says, "They went out from us, but they were not of us; for *if they had been of us, they would have continued with us;* but they went out, that it might be plain that they all are not of us" (1 John 2:19). John says that those who have departed showed by their actions that they "were not of us"—that they were not truly born again.

## C. Those Who Finally Fall Away May Give Many External Signs of Conversion

Is it always clear which people in the church have genuine saving faith and which have only an intellectual persuasion of the truth of the gospel but no genuine faith in their hearts? It is not always easy to tell, and Scripture mentions in several places that *unbelievers* in fellowship with the visible church can give some external signs or indications that make them look or sound like genuine believers. For example, Judas, who betrayed Christ, must have acted almost exactly like the other disciples during the three years he was with Jesus. So convincing was his conformity to the behavior pattern of the other disciples, that at the end of three years of Jesus' ministry, when he said that one of his disciples would betray him, they did not all turn and suspect Judas, but they rather "began to say to him one after another, 'Is it I?' " (Matt. 26:22; cf. Mark 14:19; Luke 22:23; John 13:22). However, Jesus himself knew that there was no genuine faith in Judas' heart, because he said at one point, "Did I not choose you, the twelve, and one of you is a devil?" (John 6:70). John later wrote in his gospel that "Jesus knew from the first who those were that did not believe, and who it was that would betray him" (John 6:64). But the disciples themselves did not know.

Paul also speaks of *"false brethren* secretly brought in" (Gal. 2:4), and says that in his journeys he has been "in danger from *false brethren"* (2 Cor. 11:26). He also says that the servants of Satan *"disguise themselves* as servants of righteousness" (2 Cor. 11:15). This does not mean that all unbelievers in the church who nevertheless give some signs of true conversion are servants of Satan secretly undermining the work of the church, for some may be in process of considering the claims of the gospel and moving toward real faith, others may have heard only an inadequate explanation of the gospel message, and others may not have come under genuine conviction of the Holy Spirit yet. But Paul's statements do mean that some unbelievers in the church will be false brothers and sisters sent to disrupt the fellowship, while others will simply be unbelievers who will eventually come to genuine saving faith. In both cases, however, they give several external signs that make them look like genuine believers.

We can see this also in Jesus' statement about what will happen at the last judgment:

Not every one who says to me, "Lord, Lord," shall enter the kingdom of heaven, but he who does the will of my Father who is in heaven. On that day many will say to me, "Lord, Lord, did we not prophesy in your name, and cast out demons in your name, and do many mighty works in your name?" And then will I declare to them, "*I never knew you;* depart from me, you evildoers." (Matt. 7:21–23)

Although these people prophesied and cast out demons and did "many mighty works" in Jesus' name, the ability to do such works did not guarantee that they were Christians. Jesus says, "I never knew you." He does not say, "I knew you at one time but I no longer know you," nor "I knew you at one time but you strayed away from me," but rather, "I *never* knew you." They never were genuine believers.

A similar teaching is found in the parable of the sower in Mark 4. Jesus says, "Other seed fell on rocky ground, where it had not much soil, and immediately it sprang up, since it had no depth of soil; and when the sun rose it was scorched, and since it had no root it withered away" (Mark 4:5–6). Jesus explains that the seed sown upon rocky ground represents people who "when they hear the word, immediately receive it with joy; and *they have no root in themselves,* but endure for a while; then, when tribulation or persecution arises on account of the word, immediately they fall away" (Mark 4:16–17). The fact that they "have no root in themselves" indicates that there is no source of life within these plants; similarly, the people represented by them have no genuine life of their own within. They have an appearance of conversion and they apparently have become Christians because they receive the word "with joy," but when difficulty comes, they are nowhere to be found—their apparent conversion was not genuine and there was no real saving faith in their hearts.

The importance of continuing in faith is also affirmed in the parable of Jesus as the vine, in which Christians are portrayed as branches (John 15:1–7). Jesus says:

I am the true vine, and my Father is the vinedresser. Every branch of mine that bears no fruit, he takes away, and every branch that does bear fruit he prunes, that it may bear more fruit. . . . If a man does not abide in me, he is cast forth as a branch and withers; and the branches are gathered, thrown into the fire and burned. (John 15:1–2, 6)

Arminians have argued that the branches that do not bear fruit are still true branches on the vine—Jesus refers to "Every branch *of mine* that bears no fruit" (v. 2). Therefore the branches that are gathered and thrown into the fire and burned must refer to true believers that were once part of the vine but fell away and became subject to eternal judgment. But that is not a necessary implication of Jesus' teaching at this point. The imagery of the vine used in this parable is limited in how much detail it can teach. In fact, if Jesus had wanted to teach that there were true and false believers associated with him, and if he wanted to use the analogy of a vine and branches, then the only way he could refer to people who do not have genuine life in themselves would be to speak of branches that bear no fruit (somewhat after the analogy of the seeds that fell on rocky ground and had "no root in themselves" in Mark 4:17). Here in John 15 the branches that do not bear fruit, though they are in some way connected to Jesus and give an outward appearance of being genuine branches, nonetheless give indication of their true state by the fact that they bear no fruit. This is similarly indicated by the fact that the person "does not abide" in Christ (John 15:6) and is cast off as a branch and withers. If we try to press the analogy any further, by saying, for example, that all branches on a vine really are alive or they would not be there in the first place, then we are simply trying to press the imagery beyond what it is able to teach— and in that case there would be nothing in the analogy that could represent false believers in any case. The point of the imagery is simply that those who bear fruit thereby give evidence that they are abiding in Christ; those who do not, are not abiding in him.

Finally, there are two passages in Hebrews that also affirm that those who finally fall away may give many external signs of conversion and may look in many ways like Christians. The first of these, Hebrews 6:4–6, has frequently been used by Arminians as proof that believers can lose their salvation. But on closer inspection such an interpretation is not convincing. The author writes,

> For it is impossible to restore again to repentance those who have once been enlightened, who have tasted the heavenly gift, and have become partakers of the Holy Spirit, and have tasted the goodness of the word of God and the powers of the age to come, if they then commit apostasy, since they crucify the Son of God on their own account and hold him up to contempt. (Heb. 6:4–6)

The author continues with an example from agriculture:

> For land which has drunk the rain that often falls upon it, and brings forth vegetation useful to those for whose sake it is cultivated, receives a blessing from God. But if it bears thorns and thistles, it is worthless and near to being cursed; its end is to be burned. (Heb. 6:7–8)

In this agricultural metaphor, those who receive final judgment are compared to land that bears no vegetation or useful fruit, but rather bears thorns and thistles. When we recall the other metaphors in Scripture where good fruit is a sign of true spiritual life and fruitlessness is a sign of false believers (for example, Matt. 3:8– 10; 7:15–20; 12:33–35), we already have an indication that the author is speaking of people whose most trustworthy evidence of their spiritual condition (the fruit they bear) is negative, suggesting that the author is talking about people who are not genuinely Christians.

Some have objected that the long description of things that have happened to these people who fall away means that they must have been genuinely born again. But that is not a convincing objection when we look at the individual terms used. The author says they have "once been *enlightened*" (Heb. 6:4). But this enlightening simply means that they came to understand the truths of the gospel, not that they responded to those truths with genuine saving faith.[12]

Similarly, the word *once* that is used to speak of those who "have once been

---

[12]The word *enlightened* translates the Greek term *phōtizō*, which refers to learning in general, not necessarily a learning that results in salvation—it is used in John 1:9 of "enlightening" every man that comes into the world, in 1 Cor. 4:5 of the enlightening that comes at the final judgment, and in Eph. 1:18 of the enlightening that accompanies growth in the Christian life. The word is not a "technical term" that means that the people in question were saved.

After completing the following discussion of Hebrews 6:4–6, I wrote a much more extensive study, with additional analysis, supporting data, and interaction with other literature: see Wayne Grudem, "Perseverance of the Saints: A Case Study From Heb. 6:4–6 and the Other Warning Passages of Hebrews," in *The Grace of God, the Bondage of the Will,* vol. 1, ed. Tom Schreiner and Bruce Ware (Grand Rapids: Baker, forthcoming in 1995).

enlightened" is the Greek term *hapax,* which is used, for example, in Philippians 4:16 of the Philippians' sending Paul a gift "*once* and again," and in Hebrews 9:7 of entrance in the Holy of Holies "*once* a year." Therefore, this word does not mean that something happened "once" and can never be repeated, but simply that it happened once, without specifying whether it will be repeated or not.[13]

The text further says that these people "have *tasted* the heavenly gift" and that they "have *tasted* the goodness of the word of God and the powers of the age to come" (Heb. 6:4–5). Inherent in the idea of tasting is the fact that the tasting is temporary and one might or might not decide to accept the thing that is tasted. For example, the same Greek word (*geuomai*) is used in Matthew 27:34 to say that those crucifying Jesus "offered him wine to drink, mingled with gall; but when he *tasted* it, he would not drink it." The word is also used in a figurative sense meaning "come to know something."[14] If we understand it in this figurative sense, as it must be understood here since the passage is not talking about tasting literal food, then it means that these people have come to understand the heavenly gift (which probably means here that they had experienced some of the power of the Holy Spirit at work) and to know something of the Word of God and the powers of the age to come. It does not necessarily mean that they had (or did not have) genuine saving faith, but may simply mean that they came to understand it and have some experience of spiritual power.[15]

The text also further says that these people "have become *partakers* of the Holy Spirit" (Heb. 6:4). The question here is the exact meaning of the word *metochos,* which is here translated "partaker." It is not always clear to English-speaking readers that this term has a range of meaning and may imply very close participation and attachment, or may only imply a loose association with the other person or persons named. For example, the context shows that in Hebrews 3:14 to become a "partaker" of Christ means to have a very close participation with him in a saving relationship.[16] On the other hand, *metochos* can also be used in a much looser sense, simply to refer to associates or companions. We read that when the disciples took in a great catch of fish so that their nets were breaking, "they

---

[13]This is not the same word as *ephapax,* which is more regularly used in the New Testament of nonrepeatable events (Rom. 6:10; Heb. 7:27; 9:12; 10:10).

[14]*BAGD,* p. 157. They mention other examples of *geuomai* ("taste"), such as Herodotus 6.5, where the people of Miletus had "tasted of freedom," but it was certainly not their own possession. They also cite Dio Chrysostom, 32.72, where he speaks of the people of Alexandria in a time when they "had a taste of warfare" in an encounter with Roman troops who were simply harassing them and not actually engaging in genuine war. Josephus, *The Jewish War,* 2.158, speaks about the theological views of the Essenes "whereby they irresistibly attract all who have once *tasted* their philosophy." Here again Josephus makes it clear that those who have "once tasted" have not yet made the Essene philosophy their own, but are simply very strongly attracted to it. By analogy, in Heb. 6 those who have "tasted" the heavenly gift and the word of God and the powers of the age to come may be strongly attracted to these things, or they may not be, but mere tasting does not mean that they have made it their own— quite the contrary, if all the author can say of them is that they have "tasted" these things, it suggests that they have not made what they tasted to be their own.

[15]The word *tasted* is also used in Heb. 2:9 to say that Jesus "tasted death," indicating that he came to know it by experience (but "tasted" is an apt word because he did not remain dead). The same could be true of those who had some experience of heavenly gifts, as can be true even of unbelievers (cf. Matt. 7:22; 1 Cor. 7:14; 2 Peter 2:20–22). In Heb. 6:4–5 these people's experience of the Holy Spirit's power and of the Word of God was of course a *genuine experience* (just as Jesus *genuinely* died), but that by itself does not show that the people had an experience of regeneration.

[16]The same Greek word *metochos* is used in Heb. 3:14, even though the English text of the RSV says "We share in Christ."

beckoned to their *partners* in the other boat to come and help them" (Luke 5:7). Here it simply refers to those who were companions or partners with Peter and the other disciples in their fishing work.[17] Ephesians 5:7 uses a closely related word (*symmetochos*, a compound of *metochos* and the preposition *syn* ["with"]) when Paul warns Christians about the sinful acts of unbelievers and says, "do not associate with them" (Eph. 5:7). He is not concerned that their total nature will be transformed by the unbelievers, but simply that they will associate with them and have their own witness compromised and their own lives influenced to some degree by them.

By analogy, Hebrews 6:4–6 speaks of people who have been *"associated with"* the Holy Spirit, and thereby had their lives influenced by him, but it need not imply that they had a redeeming work of the Holy Spirit in their lives, or that they were regenerated. By similar analogy with the example of the fishing companions in Luke 5:7, Peter and the disciples could be *associated with* them and even to some degree influenced by them without having a thoroughgoing change of life caused by that association. The very word *metochos* allows for a range of influence from fairly weak to fairly strong, for it only means "one who participates with or shares with or accompanies in some activity." This was apparently what had happened to these people spoken of in Hebrews 6, who had been associated with the church and as such associated with the work of the Holy Spirit, and no doubt had been influenced by him in some ways in their lives.[18]

Finally, the text says that it is impossible "to restore again to *repentance*" people who have experienced these things and have then committed apostasy. Some have argued that if this is a repentance to which they need to be restored again, then it must be genuine repentance. But this is not necessarily the case. First, we must realize that "repentance" (Gk. *metanoia*) does not need to refer to inward heart

---

[17]Heb. 1:9 also uses the same word to speak of "comrades" (RSV) or "companions" (NIV, NASB).

[18]The other uses of *metochos* in Hebrews (3:1 and 12:8) do suggest closer association or participation, but even 12:8, which talks about people becoming partakers in discipline, certainly allows for the fact that some may receive that discipline but not be transformed by it. In any case, the evidence is not strong enough to make us think that the author of Hebrews used this word as a "technical term" that always referred to a saving kind of participation (it did not in Heb. 1:9 and 12:8), and our understanding of the sense of the word must be governed by an examination of the range of meaning it can take in the Greek literature of the New Testament and in other literature that shares a similar vocabulary with the writers of the New Testament.

The usage of the Septuagint is also instructive with respect to this word, since in several instances it only refers to companionship, not any kind of regenerating or life-changing experience with God or with the Holy Spirit. For instance, in 1 Kings 20:30, Saul accuses Jonathan of being a "partner" with David. In Ps. 119:63, the psalmist says he is a "companion" of all those who fear God. Eccl. 4:10 says that two are better than one, for if they fall, the one will lift up his "partner." Prov. 28:24, in the translations of Aquila, Symmachus, and Theodotian, uses this word to say that a man who rejects his father or mother is a "companion" of ungodly men. Examples of somewhat stronger association are seen in Esth. 8:13; Prov. 29:10; Hos. 4:17; 3 Macc. 3:21.

The conclusion of this examination of the term *metochos* is that, while it can be used of very close association with saving results in a person's life, it can also be used simply of associating or participating with someone else. Therefore the term itself does not require that the people in Heb. 6:4–6 had saving participation with the Holy Spirit or had been regenerated. It simply means they had in some ways been associated with and influenced by the Holy Spirit.

The people who prophesied and cast out demons and did many mighty works in Jesus' name in Matt. 7:22 are good examples of people who certainly did have some sharing in the work of the Holy Spirit or who had become "partakers" of the Holy Spirit in this sense, but had not been saved: Jesus says, "I never knew you" (Matt. 7:23).

repentance unto salvation. For example, Hebrews 12:17 uses this word to speak of a change of mind that Esau sought concerning the sale of his birthright, and refers to it as "repentance" (*metanoia*). This would not have been a repentance for salvation, but simply a change of mind and an undoing of the transaction regarding his birthright. (Note also the example of Judas' repentance in Matt. 27:3—howbeit with a different Greek word.)

The cognate verb "to repent" (Gk. *metanoeō*) is sometimes used to refer not to saving repentance, but just to sorrow for individual offenses in Luke 17:3–4: "If your brother sins, rebuke him, and *if he repents* forgive him; and if he sins against you seven times in the day, and turns to you seven times, and says, 'I repent,' you must forgive him." We conclude that "repentance" simply means a sorrow for actions that have been done or for sins that have been committed. Whether or not it is a genuine saving repentance, a "repentance unto salvation," may not be always evident right away. The author of Hebrews is not concerned to specify whether it is a genuine repentance or not. He is simply saying that if someone has a sorrow for sin and comes to understand the gospel and experiences these various blessings of the Holy Spirit's work (no doubt in fellowship with the church), and then turns away, it will not be possible to restore such a person again to a place of sorrow for sin. But this does not necessarily imply that the repentance was genuine saving repentance in the first place.

At this point we may ask what kind of person is described by all of these terms. These are no doubt people who have been affiliated closely with the fellowship of the church. They have had some sorrow for sin (repentance). They have clearly understood the gospel (they have been enlightened). They have come to appreciate the attractiveness of the Christian life and the change that comes about in people's lives because of becoming a Christian, and they have probably had answers to prayer in their own lives and felt the power of the Holy Spirit at work, perhaps even using some spiritual gifts in the manner of the unbelievers in Matthew 7:22 (they have become "associated with" the work of the Holy Spirit or have become "partakers" of the Holy Spirit and have tasted the heavenly gift and the powers of the age of come). They have been exposed to the true preaching of the Word and have appreciated much of its teachings (they have tasted the goodness of the Word of God).

But then in spite of all this, if they "commit apostasy" and "crucify the Son of God on their own account and hold him up to contempt" (Heb. 6:6), then they are willfully rejecting all of these blessings and turning decidedly against them. Perhaps all of us have known in our own churches people who (sometimes by their own profession) have long been affiliated with the fellowship of the church but are not themselves born-again Christians. They have thought about the gospel for years and have continued to resist the wooing of the Holy Spirit in their lives, perhaps through an unwillingness to give up lordship of their lives to Jesus and preferring to cling to it themselves.

Now the author tells us that *if these people willfully turn away from all of these temporary blessings,* then it will be impossible to restore them again to any kind of repentance or sorrow for sin. Their hearts will be hardened and their consciences calloused. What more could be done to bring them to salvation? If we tell them Scripture is true they will say that they know it but they have decided to reject it. If we tell them God answers prayer and changes lives they will respond that they know that as well, but they want nothing of it. If we tell them that the Holy Spirit is powerful to work in people's lives and the gift of eternal life is good beyond description, they will say that they understand that, but they want nothing of it. Their repeated familiarity with the things of God and their experience of many influences of the Holy Spirit has simply served to harden them against conversion.

Now the author of Hebrews knows that there are some in the community to which he writes who are in danger of falling away in just this way (see Heb. 2:3; 3:8, 12, 14–15; 4:1, 7, 11; 10:26, 29, 35–36, 38–39; 12:3, 15–17). He wants to warn them that, though they have participated in the fellowship of the church and experienced a number of God's blessings in their lives, yet if they fall away after all that, there is no salvation for them. This does not imply that he thinks that true Christians could fall away—Hebrews 3:14 implies quite the opposite. But he wants them to gain assurance of salvation through their continuing in faith, and thereby implies that if they fall away it would show that they never were Christ's people in the first place (see Heb. 3:6: "We are his house *if* we hold fast our confidence and pride in our hope").

Therefore the author wants to give a severe warning to those in danger of slipping away from their Christian profession. He wants to use the strongest language possible to say, "Here is how far a person can come in experiencing *temporary blessings* and still not really be saved." He is warning them to watch out, because depending on temporary blessings and experiences is not enough. To do this he talks not of any true change of heart or any good fruit produced, but simply about the temporary blessings and experiences that have come to these persons and have given them some understanding of Christianity.

For this reason he immediately passes from this description of those who commit apostasy to a further analogy that shows that these people who fell away never had any genuine fruit in their lives. As we explained above, verses 7–8 speak of these people in terms of *"thorns and thistles,"* the kind of crop that is brought forth on land that has no worthwhile life in itself even though it receives repeated blessings from God (in terms of the analogy, even though rain frequently falls upon it). We should notice here that people who commit apostasy are not compared to a field that once bore good fruit and now does not, but that they are like *land that never bore good fruit,* but only thorns and thistles. The land may look good before the crops start to come up, but the fruit gives the genuine evidence, and it is bad.

Strong support for this interpretation of Hebrews 6:4–8 is found in the verse immediately following. Though the author has been speaking very harshly about the possibility of falling away, he then returns to speak to the situation of the great majority of the hearers, whom he thinks to be genuine Christians. He says, "Though we speak thus, *yet in your case,* beloved, *we feel sure of better things that belong to salvation*" (Heb. 6:9). But the question is "better things" than what? The plural "better things" forms an appropriate contrast to the "good things" that have been mentioned in verses 4–6: the author is convinced that most of his readers have experienced better things than simply the partial and temporary influences of the Holy Spirit and the church talked about in verses 4–6.

In fact, the author talks about these things by saying (literally) that they are "better things, *also belonging to salvation*" (Gk. *kai echomena sōtērias*).[19] These are not only the temporary blessings talked about in verses 4–6, but these are better things, things having not only temporary influence, but "also belonging to salvation." In this way the Greek word *kai* ("also") shows that salvation is something that was not part of the things mentioned in verses 4–6 above. Therefore this word *kai*, which is not explicitly translated in the RSV or NIV (but the NASB comes close),[20] provides a crucial key for understanding the passage. If the author had meant to say that the people mentioned in verses 4–6 were truly saved, then it is very difficult to understand why he would say in verse 9 that he is convinced of *better things* for them, things that belong to salvation, or that have salvation in addition to those things mentioned above. He thus shows that he can use a brief phrase to say that people "have salvation" if he wishes to do so (he does not need to pile up many phrases), and he shows, moreover, that the people whom he speaks of in verses 4–6 are not saved.[21]

What exactly are these "better things"? In addition to salvation mentioned in verse 9, they are things that give real evidence of salvation—genuine fruit in their lives (v. 10), full assurance of hope (v. 11), and saving faith, of the type exhibited by those who inherit the promises (v. 12). In this way he reassures those who are genuine believers—those who show fruit in their lives and show love for other Christians, who show hope and genuine faith that is continuing at the present time, and who are not about to fall away. He wants to reassure these readers (who are certainly the great majority of the ones to whom he writes) while still issuing a strong warning to those among them who may be in danger of falling away.

A similar teaching is found in Hebrews 10:26–31. There the author says, "If we deliberately keep on sinning after we have received the knowledge of the truth, no sacrifice for sins is left" (v. 26 NIV). A person who rejects Christ's salvation and "has treated as an unholy thing the blood of the covenant that sanctified him" (v. 29 NIV) deserves eternal punishment. This again is a strong warning against falling away, but it should not be taken as proof that someone who has truly been born again can lose his or her salvation. When the author talks about the blood of the covenant "that sanctified him," the word *sanctified* is used simply to refer to "external sanctification, like that of the ancient Israelites, by outward connection with God's people."[22] The passage does not talk about someone who is genuinely

---

[19]*BAGD*, p. 334, III, translates the middle participle of *echō* as "hold oneself fast, cling to," and lists Heb. 6:9 as the only New Testament example of this form used "of inner belonging and close association" (cf. *LSJ*, p. 750, C: "hold oneself fast, cling closely"). However, even if we translated the middle voice in the same way as the active, the phrase would mean, "things also having salvation," and my argument in this section would not be affected.

[20]The NASB translates, "*and* things that accompany salvation."

[21]Someone might object that the phrase "better things" does not contrast with the temporary blessings in vv. 4–6, but with the judgment mentioned that is coming to the thorns and thistles who are about to be "burned" in v. 8. But it is unlikely that the author would refer to not being cursed simply as "better things." The comparative "better" (*kreisson*) is used thirteen times in Hebrews, and it regularly contrasts something *better* with something *good* (better covenant, better sacrifice, etc.); similarly, here it suggests a comparison with things that are already good (such as the blessings in vv. 4–6), much more than it suggests a contrast with the horrible fate of eternal judgment in v. 8.

[22]A. H. Strong, *Systematic Theology*, p. 884. Strong mentions an appropriate parallel use of the verb "sanctify" in 1 Cor. 7:14, which speaks about the unbelieving husband being "sanctified" by the believing wife (1 Cor. 7:14, where the same Greek word, *hagiazō*, is used). Outward ceremonial sanctification is also referred in Heb. 9:13; cf. Matt. 23:17, 19.

saved, but someone who has received some beneficial moral influence through contact with the church.[23]

One other passage in John's writings has been claimed to teach the possibility of loss of salvation. In Revelation 3:5, Jesus says, "He who conquers shall be clad thus in white garments, and *I will not blot his name out of the book of life.*" Some have claimed that when Jesus says this he implies that it is possible that he would blot out the names of some people from the book of life, people who had already had their names written in it and were thus already saved. But the fact that Jesus emphatically states that he will *not* do something should not be taken as teaching that he will do that same thing in other cases! The same kind of Greek construction[24] is used to give an emphatic negation in John 10:28, where Jesus says, "I give them eternal life, and *they shall never perish.*" This does not mean that there are some of Jesus' sheep who do not hear his voice and follow him and who will perish; it is simply affirming that his sheep certainly will not perish. Similarly, when God says, "I will never fail you nor forsake you" (Heb. 13:5), it does not imply that he will leave or forsake others; it just emphatically states that he will not leave nor forsake his people. Or, in even a closer parallel, in Matthew 12:32, Jesus says, "Whoever speaks against the Holy Spirit *will not be forgiven,* either in this age *or in the age to come.*" This does not imply that some sins will be forgiven in the age to come (as Roman Catholics claim in support for the doctrine of purgatory)[25]— that is simply an error in reasoning: to say that something will not happen in the age to come does not imply that it might happen in the age to come! In the same way, Revelation 3:5 is just a strong assurance that those who are clad in the white garments and who have remained faithful to Christ will not have their names blotted out of the book of life.[26]

Finally, one passage from the Old Testament is sometimes used to argue that people can lose their salvation: the story of the Holy Spirit departing from King Saul. But Saul should not be taken as an example of someone who lost his salvation, for when "the Spirit of the LORD departed from Saul" (1 Sam. 16:14), it was immediately after Samuel had anointed David king and "the Spirit of the LORD came mightily upon David from that day forward" (1 Sam. 16:13). In fact, the Spirit of the Lord coming upon David is reported in the immediately previous sentence to the one in which we read that the Spirit departed from Saul. This close connection means that Scripture is not here talking about a total loss of all work of the Holy Spirit in Saul's life, but simply about the withdrawing of the Holy Spirit's function of empowering Saul as king.[27] But that does not mean that Saul

[23]Ex. 24:7–8 speaks of the blood of the covenant that set apart the people as God's people even though not all were truly born again. In the context of Heb. 10, such imagery, taken from the Old Testament process of sanctifying a people so that they could come before God to worship, is an appropriate background.
[24]The construction uses *ou mē* plus the aorist subjunctive to express emphatic negation.
[25]See discussion of the doctrine of purgatory in chapter 41, pp. 817–19.
[26]A different kind of book is probably in view in Ex. 32:33, where God says to Moses, "Whoever has sinned against me, him will I blot out of my book." Here the New Testament idea of the "book of life" is not mentioned. Rather, the image is one of God keeping a record of those currently dwelling among his people, much as an earthly king would do. To "blot out" someone's name from such a book would imply that the person had died. Using this imagery, Ex. 32:33 is best understood to mean that God will take the life of anyone who sins against him (see v. 35). Eternal destiny is not in view in this passage.
[27]We should give a similar interpretation to David's prayer in Ps. 51:11: "Take not your holy Spirit

was eternally condemned. It is simply very hard to tell from the pages of the Old Testament whether Saul, throughout his life, was (a) an unregenerate man who had leadership capabilities and was used by God as a demonstration of the fact that someone worthy to be king in the eyes of the world was not thereby suited to be king over the Lord's people, or (b) a regenerate man with poor understanding and a life that increasingly strayed from the Lord.

### D. What Can Give a Believer Genuine Assurance?

If it is true, as explained in the previous section, that those who are unbelievers and who finally fall away may give many external signs of conversion, then what will serve as evidence of genuine conversion? What can give real assurance to a real believer? We can list three categories of questions that a person could ask of himself or herself.

**1. Do I Have a Present Trust in Christ for Salvation?** Paul tells the Colossians that they will be saved on the last day, "provided that you *continue in the faith,* stable and steadfast, not shifting from the hope of the gospel which you heard" (Col. 1:23). The author of Hebrews says, "We share in Christ, if only we hold our first confidence firm to the end" (Heb. 3:14) and encourages his readers to be imitators of those "who *through faith* and patience inherit the promises" (Heb. 6:12). In fact, the most famous verse in the entire Bible uses a present tense verb that may be translated, "whoever continues believing in him" may have eternal life (see John 3:16).

Therefore a person should ask himself or herself, "Do I today have trust in Christ to forgive my sins and take me without blame into heaven forever? Do I have confidence in my heart that he has saved me? If I were to die tonight and stand before God's judgment seat, and if he were to ask me why he should let me into heaven, would I begin to think of my good deeds and depend on them, or would I without hesitation say that I am depending on the merits of Christ and am confident that he is a sufficient Savior?"

This emphasis on *present* faith in Christ stands in contrast to the practice of some church "testimonies" where people repeatedly recite details of a conversion experience that may have happened 20 or 30 years ago. If a testimony of saving faith is genuine, it should be a testimony of faith that is active this very day.

**2. Is There Evidence of a Regenerating Work of the Holy Spirit in My Heart?** The evidence of the work of the Holy Spirit in our hearts comes in many different forms. Although we should not put confidence in the demonstration of miraculous works (Matt. 7:22), or long hours and years of work at some local church (which may simply be building with "wood, hay, straw" [in terms of 1 Cor. 3:12] to further one's own ego or power over others, or to attempt to earn merit with God), there are many other evidences of a real work of the Holy Spirit in one's heart.

from me." David is praying that the Holy Spirit's anointing for kingship would not be removed from him, and that the presence and power of God on his life would not depart; he is not praying against a loss of eternal salvation.

First, there is a subjective testimony of the Holy Spirit within our hearts bearing witness that we are God's children (Rom. 8:15–16; 1 John 4:13). This testimony will usually be accompanied by a sense of being led by the Holy Spirit in paths of obedience to God's will (Rom. 8:14).

In addition, if the Holy Spirit is genuinely at work in our lives, he will be producing the kind of character traits that Paul calls "the fruit of the Spirit" (Gal. 5:22). He lists several attitudes and character traits that are produced by the Holy Spirit: "love, joy, peace, patience, kindness, goodness, faithfulness, gentleness, self-control" (Gal. 5:22–23). Of course, the question is not, "Do I perfectly exemplify all of these characteristics in my life?" but rather, "Are these things a general characteristic of my life? Do I sense these attitudes in my heart? Do others (especially those closest to me) see these traits exhibited in my life? Have I been growing in them over a period of years?" There is no suggestion in the New Testament that any non-Christian, any unregenerate person, can convincingly fake these character traits, especially for those who know the person most closely.

Related to this kind of fruit is another kind of fruit—the results of one's life and ministry as they have influence on others and on the church. There are some people who profess to be Christians but whose influence on others is to discourage them, to drag them down, to injure their faith, and to provoke controversy and divisiveness. The result of their life and ministry is not to build up others and to build up the church, but to tear it down. On the other hand, there are those who seem to edify others in every conversation, every prayer, and every work of ministry they put their hand to. Jesus said, regarding false prophets, "You will know them by their fruits. . . . Every sound tree bears good fruit, but the bad tree bears evil fruit. . . . Thus you will know them by their fruits" (Matt. 7:16–20).

Another evidence of work of the Holy Spirit is continuing to believe and accept the sound teaching of the church. Those who begin to deny major doctrines of the faith give serious negative indications concerning their salvation: "No one who denies the Son has the Father. . . . If what you heard from the beginning abides in you, then you will abide in the Son and in the Father" (1 John 2:23–24). John also says, "Whoever knows God listens to us, and he who is not of God does not listen to us" (1 John 4:6). Since the New Testament writings are the current replacement for the apostles like John, we might also say that whoever knows God will continue to read and to delight in God's Word, and will continue to believe it fully. Those who do not believe and delight in God's Word give evidence that they are not "of God."

Another evidence of genuine salvation is a continuing present relationship with Jesus Christ. Jesus says, "Abide in me, and I in you" and, "If you abide in me, and my words abide in you, ask whatever you will, and it shall be done for you" (John 15:4, 7). This abiding in Christ will include not only day-by-day trust in him in various situations, but also certainly regular fellowship with him in prayer and worship.

Finally, a major area of evidence that we are genuine believers is found in a life of obedience to God's commands. John says, "He who says 'I know him' but disobeys his commandments is a liar, and the truth is not in him; but whoever keeps his word, in him truly love for God is perfected. By this we may be sure that we are in him: he who says he abides in him ought to walk in the same way in which he walked" (1 John 2:4–6). A perfect life is not necessary, of course. John is rather saying that in general our lives ought to be ones of imitation of Christ and likeness to him in what we do and say. If we have genuine saving faith, there will be clear results in obedience in our lives (see also 1 John 3:9–10, 24; 5:18). Thus James can say, "Faith by itself, if it has no works, is dead" and "I by my works will show you my faith" (James 2:17–18). One large area of obedience to God includes love for fellow Christians. "He who loves his brother abides in the light" (1 John 2:10). "We know that we have passed out of death into life, because we love the brethren. He who does not love abides in death" (1 John 3:14, cf. 3:17; 4:7). One evidence of this love is continuing in Christian fellowship (1 John 2:19), and another is giving to a brother in need (1 John 3:17; cf. Matt. 25:31–46).

**3. Do I See a Long-Term Pattern of Growth in My Christian Life?** The first two areas of assurance dealt with present faith and present evidence of the Holy Spirit at work in our lives. But Peter gives one more kind of test that we can use to ask whether we are genuinely believers. He tells us that there are some character traits which, if we keep on increasing in them, will guarantee that we will "never fall" (2 Peter 1:10). He tells his readers to add to their faith "virtue . . . knowledge . . . self-control . . . steadfastness . . . godliness . . . brotherly affection . . . love" (2 Peter 1:5–7). Then he says that these things are to belong to his readers and to continually "abound" in their lives (2 Peter 1:8). He adds that they are to "be the more zealous to confirm your call and election" and says then that "*if you do this* (literally, "these things," referring to the character traits mentioned in vv. 5–7) *you will never fall*" (2 Peter 1:10).

The way that we confirm our call and election, then, is to continue to grow in "these things." This implies that our assurance of salvation can be something that increases over time in our lives. Every year that we add to these character traits in our lives, we gain greater and greater assurance of our salvation. Thus, though young believers can have a quite strong confidence in their salvation, that assurance can increase to even deeper certainty over the years in which they grow toward Christian maturity.[28] If they continue to add these things they will confirm their call and election and will "never fall."

The result of these three questions that we can ask ourselves should be to give strong assurance to those who are genuinely believers. In this way the doctrine of the perseverance of the saints will be a tremendously comforting doctrine. No one who has such assurance should wonder, "Will I be able to persevere to the end of my life and therefore be saved?" Everyone who gains assurance through such a self-examination should rather think, "I am truly born again; therefore, I will certainly persevere to the end, because I am being guarded 'by God's power' working through my faith (1 Peter 1:5) and therefore I will never be lost. Jesus will raise me up at the last day and I will enter into his kingdom forever" (John 6:40).

On the other hand, this doctrine of the perseverance of the saints, if rightly understood, should cause genuine worry, and even fear, in the hearts of any who

---

[28]Cf. 1 Tim. 3:13, which says, that those who have "served well" as deacons gain "great assurance in their faith in Christ Jesus" (NIV).

are "backsliding" or straying away from Christ. Such persons must clearly be warned that only those who persevere to the end have been truly born again. If they fall away from their profession of faith in Christ and life of obedience to him, they may not really be saved—in fact, the *evidence* that they are giving *is that they are not saved,* and they never really were saved. Once they stop trusting in Christ and obeying him (I am speaking in terms of outward evidence) they have no genuine assurance of salvation, and they should consider themselves unsaved, and turn to Christ in repentance and ask him for forgiveness of their sins.

At this point, in terms of pastoral care with those who have strayed away from their Christian profession, we should realize that *Calvinists and Arminians* (those who believe in the perseverance of the saints and those who think that Christians can lose their salvation) *will both counsel a "backslider" in the same way.* According to the Arminian this person was a Christian at one time but is no longer a Christian. According to the Calvinist, such a person never really was a Christian in the first place and is not one now. But in both cases the biblical counsel given would be the same: "You do not appear to be a Christian now—you must repent of your sins and trust in Christ for your salvation!" Though the Calvinist and Arminian would differ on their interpretation of the previous history, they would agree on what should be done in the present.[29]

But here we see why the phrase *eternal security* can be quite misleading. In some evangelical churches, instead of teaching the full and balanced presentation of the doctrine of the perseverance of the saints, pastors have sometimes taught a watered-down version, which in effect tells people that all who have once made a profession of faith and been baptized are "eternally secure." The result is that some people who are not genuinely converted at all may "come forward" at the end of an evangelistic sermon to profess faith in Christ, and may be baptized shortly after that, but then they leave the fellowship of the church and live a life no different from the one they lived before they gained this "eternal security." In this way people are given false assurance and are being cruelly deceived into thinking they are going to heaven when in fact they are not.[30]

## QUESTIONS FOR PERSONAL APPLICATION

1. Do you have assurance that you are truly born again? What evidence do you see in your own life to give you that assurance? Do you think that God wants true believers to go on throughout life worrying about whether they are really born again, or to have firm assurance that they are his people? (See 1 John 5:13.) Have you seen a pattern of growth in your Christian life over time? Are you trusting in your own power to keep on believing in Christ, or in God's power to keep your faith active and alive?

---

[29]Of course, both the Calvinist and the Arminian would allow for the possibility that the "backslidden" person is truly born again and had just fallen into sin and doubt. But both would agree that it is pastorally wise to assume that the person is not a Christian until some evidence of present faith is forthcoming.

[30]Of course, not all who use the phrase *eternal security* make mistakes of this sort, but the phrase is certainly open to such misunderstanding.

2. If you have doubts about whether you are truly born again, what is it in your life that is giving reason for those doubts? What would Scripture encourage you to do to resolve those doubts (see 2 Peter 1:5–11; also Matt. 11:28–30; John 6:37)? Do you think that Jesus now knows about your doubts and understands them? What do you think he would like you to do now to gain greater assurance of salvation?

3. Have you known people, perhaps in your church, whose "fruit" is always destructive or divisive or harmful to the ministry of the church and the faith of others? Do they have very much influence, perhaps even positions of leadership in the church? Do you think that an evaluation of the fruit of one's life and influence on others should be a qualification for church leadership? Is it possible that people would profess agreement with every true Christian doctrine and still not be born again? What are some more reliable evidences of genuine conversion other than intellectual adherence to sound doctrine?

## SPECIAL TERMS

assurance of salvation
eternal security
perseverance of the saints

## BIBLIOGRAPHY

(For an explanation of this bibliography see the note on the bibliography to chapter 1, p. 38. Complete bibliographical data may be found on pp. 1223–29.)

### Sections in Evangelical Systematic Theologies

1. Anglican (Episcopalian)
    1882–92    Litton, 345–51
2. Arminian (Wesleyan or Methodist)
    1847    Finney, 544–619
    1875–76    Pope, 3:100–147
    1892–94    Miley, 2:268–70, 339–54
    1960    Purkiser, 298–304
3. Baptist
    1767    Gill, 2:151–78
    1887    Boyce, 425–37
    1907    Strong, 881–86
    1917    Mullins, 432–38
    1983–85    Erickson, 985–97
4. Dispensational
    1947    Chafer, 3:267–355
    1949    Thiessen, 290–95

                    1986        Ryrie, 328–34
5. Lutheran

          1917–24     Pieper, 3:89–100

          1934        Mueller, 436–40
6. Reformed (or Presbyterian)

          1559        Calvin, 2:968–76 (3.24.4–9)

          1724–58     Edwards, 596–604

          1861        Heppe, 581–89

          1871–73     Hodge, 3:104–13

          1878        Dabney, 687–713

          1937–66     Murray, *RAA* ,151–60

          1938        Berkhof, 545–54
7. Renewal (or charismatic/Pentecostal)

          1988–92     Williams, 2:119–36


## Sections in Representative Roman Catholic Systematic Theologies

(no explicit treatment)

## Other Works

Berkouwer, G. C. *Faith and Perseverance*. Trans. by Robert D. Knudsen. Grand
    Rapids: Eerdmans, 1958.

Carson, D. A. "Reflections on Christian Assurance." In *WTJ* 54 (1992), pp. 1–
    29.

Demarest, B. A. "Assurance." In *EDT*, pp. 91–92.

Grudem, Wayne. "The Perseverance of the Saints: A Case Study From Heb. 6:4–
    6 and the Other Warning Passages of Hebrews." In *The Grace of God, the
    Bondage of the Will*. Vol. 1. Ed. Tom Schreiner and Bruce Ware. Forthcom-
    ing: Grand Rapids: Baker, 1995.

Guthrie, William. *The Christian's Great Interest*. London: Banner of Truth, 1969.
    See esp. Part I, *The Trial of a Saving Interest in Christ*, which was first
    published as a separate book in 1658.

Hoekema, Anthony A. "The Perseverance of True Believers." In *Saved by Grace*.
    Grand Rapids: Eerdmans, and Exeter: Paternoster, 1989, pp. 234–56.

Kearsley, R. "Perseverance." In *NDT*, pp. 506–7.

Marshall, I. H. *Kept by the Power of God*. Minneapolis: Bethany, 1969.

McKnight, Scot. "The Warning Passages of Hebrews," *TrinJ* 13, n.s. (1992), pp.
    21–59.

Murray, John. "Perseverance." In *Redemption Accomplished and Applied*. Grand
    Rapids: Eerdmans, 1955, pp. 151–60.

Shank, Robert. Life in the Son. 2d ed. Minneapolis: Bethany, 1989.

White, R. E. O. "Perseverance." In *EDT*, pp. 844–45.

## SCRIPTURE MEMORY PASSAGE

**John 10:27–28:** *My sheep hear my voice, and I know them, and they follow me; and I give them eternal life, and they shall never perish, and no one shall snatch them out of my hand.*

## HYMN

### "Call Jehovah Thy Salvation"

(Use tune of "Come, Thou Long Expected Jesus.")

Call Jehovah thy salvation, rest beneath th' Almighty's shade,
  In his secret habitation dwell, and never be dismayed:
There no tumult shall alarm thee, thou shalt dread no hidden snare:
  Guile nor violence can harm thee, in eternal safeguard there.

From the sword at noonday wasting, from the noisome pestilence,
  In the depth of midnight blasting, God shall be thy sure defence:
He shall charge his angel legions watch and ward o'er thee to keep;
  Though thou walk through hostile regions, though in desert wilds thou
    sleep.

Since, with pure and firm affection thou on God hast set thy love,
  With the wings of his protection he will shield thee from above:
Thou shalt call on him in trouble, he will hearken, he will save;
  Here for grief reward thee double, crown with life beyond the grave.

AUTHOR: JAMES MONTGOMERY, 1822

# Chapter 41

# Death and the Intermediate State

*What is the purpose of death in the Christian life?*
*What happens to our bodies and souls when we die?*

## EXPLANATION AND SCRIPTURAL BASIS

### A. Why Do Christians Die?

Our treatment of the application of redemption must include a consideration of death and the question of how Christians should view their own death and the death of others. We also must ask what happens to us between the time that we die and the time that Christ returns to give us new resurrection bodies.

**1. Death Is Not a Punishment for Christians.** Paul tells us clearly that there is "no condemnation for those who are in Christ Jesus" (Rom. 8:1). All the penalty for our sins has been paid. Therefore, even though we know that Christians die, we should not view the death of Christians as a punishment from God or in any way a result of a penalty due to us for our sins.[1] It is true that the penalty for sin is death, but that penalty no longer applies to us—not in terms of physical death, and not in terms of spiritual death or separation from God. All of that has been paid for by Christ. Therefore there must be another reason than punishment for our sins if we are to understand why Christians die.

**2. Death Is the Final Outcome of Living in a Fallen World.** In his great wisdom, God decided that he would not apply to us the benefits of Christ's redemptive work all at once. Rather, he has chosen to apply the benefits of salvation to us gradually over time (as we have seen in chapters 33–40). Similarly, he has not chosen to remove all evil from the world immediately, but to wait until the final judgment and the establishment of the new heaven and new earth (see chapters 56 and 57). In short, we still live in a fallen world and our experience of salvation is still incomplete.

The last aspect of the fallen world to be removed will be death. Paul says:

---

[1]Even the death of some Corinthian Christians who had been abusing the Lord's Supper (1 Cor. 11:30) is viewed by Paul as a disciplining or chastening process, not as a result of condemnation: he says, "When we are judged by the Lord, we are being disciplined so that we will not be condemned with the world" (v. 32 NIV).

(In this discussion I am using the word *punishment* to mean retribution from God which is intended to do us harm, and *discipline* to mean hardship through which God intends to do us good.)

Then comes the end, when he delivers the kingdom to God the Father after destroying every rule and every authority and power. For he must reign until he has put all his enemies under his feet. *The last enemy to be destroyed is death.* (1 Cor. 15:26)

When Christ returns,

then shall come to pass the saying that is written:

> "Death is swallowed up in victory."
> "O death, where is your victory?
> O death, where is your sting?" (1 Cor. 15:54–55)

But until that time death remains a reality even in the lives of Christians. Although death does not come to us as a penalty for our individual sins (for that has been paid by Christ), it does come to us as a result of living in a fallen world, where the effects of sin have not all been removed. Related to the experience of death are other results of the fall that harm our physical bodies and signal the presence of death in the world—Christians as well as non-Christians experience aging, illnesses, injuries, and natural disasters (such as floods, violent storms, and earthquakes). Although God often answers prayers to deliver Christians (and also non-Christians) from some of these effects of the fall for a time (and thereby indicates the nature of his coming kingdom), nevertheless, Christians eventually experience all of these things to some measure, and, until Christ returns, all of us will grow old and die. The "last enemy" has not yet been destroyed. And God has chosen to allow us to experience death before we gain all the benefits of salvation that have been earned for us.

**3. God Uses the Experience of Death to Complete Our Sanctification.** Throughout our Christian lives we know that we never have to pay any penalty for sin, for that has all been taken by Christ (Rom. 8:1). Therefore, when we do experience pain and suffering in this life, we should never think it is because God is *punishing* us (for our harm). Sometimes suffering is simply a result of living in a sinful, fallen world, and sometimes it is because God is *disciplining* us (for our good), but in all cases we are assured by Romans 8:28 that "God causes *all things* to work together for good to those who love God, to those who are called according to His purpose" (NASB).

The positive purpose for God's discipline is clear in Hebrews 12, where we read:

> The Lord disciplines him whom he loves. . . . He disciplines us for our good, that we may share his holiness. For the moment all discipline seems painful rather than pleasant; later it yields the peaceful fruit of righteousness to those who have been trained by it. (Heb. 12:6, 10–11)

Not all discipline is in order to correct us from sins that we have committed; it can also be allowed by God to strengthen us in order that we may gain greater ability to trust God and resist sin in the challenging path of obedience. We see this clearly in the life of Jesus, who, though he was without sin, yet "learned obedience *through what he suffered*" (Heb. 5:8).[2] He was made perfect "*through suffering*" (Heb. 2:10). Therefore we should see all the hardship and suffering that comes to us in life as something that God brings to us *to do us good,* strengthening our trust in him and our obedience, and ultimately increasing our ability to glorify him.

Consequently, we should view the aging and weakness and sometimes sickness leading up to death as another kind of discipline that God allows us to go through in order that through this process our sanctification might be furthered and ultimately completed when we go to be in the Lord's presence. The challenge that Jesus gives to the church in Smyrna could really be given to every believer: "*Be faithful unto death,* and I will give you the crown of life" (Rev. 2:10). Paul says his goal in life is that he may become like Christ: "that I may know him and the power of his resurrection, and may share his sufferings, *becoming like him in his death*" (Phil. 3:10). Paul thought about the way in which Jesus died, and made it his goal to exemplify the same characteristics in his life when it came time for him to die—that in whatever circumstances he found himself, he, like Christ, would continue obeying God, trusting God, forgiving others, and caring for the needs of those around him, thus in every way bringing glory to God even in his death. Therefore when in prison, without knowing whether he would die there or come out alive, he could still say, "it is my eager expectation and hope that I shall not be at all ashamed, but that with full courage now as always *Christ will be honored* in my body, whether by life *or by death*" (Phil. 1:20).

The understanding that death is not in any way a punishment for sin, but simply something God brings us through in order to make us more like Christ, should be a great encouragement to us. It should take away from us the fear of death that haunts the minds of unbelievers (cf. Heb. 2:15). Nevertheless, although God will bring good to us through the process of death, we must still remember that death is not natural; it is not right; and in a world created by God it is something that ought not to be. It is an enemy, something that Christ will finally destroy (1 Cor. 15:26).

**4. Our Experience of Death Completes Our Union With Christ.** Another reason why God allows us to experience death, rather than taking us immediately to heaven when we become Christians, is that through death we imitate Christ in what he did and thereby experience closer union with him. Paul can say that we are fellow heirs with Christ "provided we *suffer with him* in order that we may also be glorified with him" (Rom. 8:17). And Peter tells his readers not to be surprised at the fiery testing that comes on them, but encourages them, "rejoice in so far as *you share Christ's sufferings,* that you may also rejoice and be glad when his glory is revealed" (1 Peter 4:13). As we noted above, such union with Christ in suffering includes union with him in death as well (see Phil. 3:10). Jesus is the "pioneer and perfecter of our faith" (Heb. 12:2), and we follow after him as we run the race of life. Peter writes, "Christ also suffered for you, leaving you an example, that you should follow in his steps" (1 Peter 2:21).

**5. Our Obedience to God Is More Important Than Preserving Our Own Lives.** If God uses the experience of death to deepen our trust in him and to

[2]For a discussion of how Jesus learned obedience through what he suffered, see chapter 26, p. 534.

strengthen our obedience to him, then it is important that we remember that the world's goal of preserving one's own physical life at all costs is not the highest goal for a Christian: obedience to God and faithfulness to him in every circumstance is far more important. This is why Paul could say, "I am ready not only to be imprisoned but even to die at Jerusalem for the name of the Lord Jesus" (Acts 21:13; cf. 25:11). He told the Ephesian elders, "I do not account my life of any value nor as precious to myself, if only I may accomplish my course and the ministry which I received from the Lord Jesus, to testify to the gospel of the grace of God" (Acts 20:24).

It was this conviction—that obedience to God is far more important than the preservation of life—that gave Paul courage to go back into the city of Lystra after he had just been stoned and left for dead (Acts 14:20), and then return there again shortly thereafter (Acts 14:21–22). He endured many sufferings and dangers (2 Cor. 11:23–27), often risking his life, in order to obey Christ fully. Therefore he could say at the end of his life, with a note of great triumph, "The time of my departure has come. *I have fought the good fight,* I have finished the race, I have kept the faith" (2 Tim. 4:6–7). This same conviction empowered Old Testament saints to accept martyrdom rather than sin: "Some were tortured, refusing to accept release, that they might rise again to a better life" (literally, "that they might obtain a better resurrection," Heb. 11:35). This conviction also gave Peter and the other apostles courage, when facing the threat of death, to say, "We must obey God rather than men" (Acts 5:29). Certainly this was the point of Jesus' command to the church at Smyrna, "*Be faithful unto death,* and I will give you the crown of life" (Rev. 2:10). We also read that there will be rejoicing in heaven when the faithful saints have conquered the devil "by the blood of the Lamb and by the word of their testimony, for *they loved not their lives even unto death*" (Rev. 12:11).

The persuasion that we may honor the Lord even in our death, and that faithfulness to him is far more important than preserving our lives, has given courage and motivation to martyrs throughout the history of the church. When faced with a choice of preserving their own lives and sinning, or giving up their own lives and being faithful, they chose to give up their own lives—"they loved not their lives even unto death" (Rev. 12:11). Even in times where there is little persecution and little likelihood of martyrdom, it would be good for us to fix this truth in our minds once for all, for if we are willing to give up even our lives for faithfulness to God, we shall find it much easier to give up everything else for the sake of Christ as well.

### B. How Should We Think of Our Own Death and the Death of Others?

**1. Our Own Death.** The New Testament encourages us to view our own death not with fear but with joy at the prospect of going to be with Christ. Paul says, "We would rather be away from the body and at home with the Lord" (2 Cor. 5:8). When he is in prison, not knowing whether he will be executed or released, he can say:

> For to me to live is Christ, and *to die is gain.* If it is to be life in the flesh, that means fruitful labor for me. Yet which I shall choose I cannot tell. I am hard pressed

between the two. *My desire is to depart and be with Christ,* for that is far better. (Phil. 1:21–23)

We also read John's word in Revelation, "And I heard a voice from heaven saying, 'Write this: Blessed are the dead who die in the Lord henceforth.' 'Blessed indeed,' says the Spirit, 'that they may rest from their labors, for their deeds follow them!'" (Rev. 14:13).

Believers need have no fear of death, therefore, for Scripture reassures us that not even "death" will "separate us from the love of God in Christ Jesus our Lord" (Rom. 8:38–39; cf. Ps. 23:4). In fact, Jesus died in order that he might "deliver all those who through fear of death were subject to lifelong bondage" (Heb. 2:15).[3] This verse reminds us that a clear testimony to our lack of fear of death will provide a strong witness for Christians in an age that tries to avoid talking about death and has no answer for it.

**2. The Death of Christian Friends and Relatives.** While we can look forward to our own death with a joyful expectation of being in Christ's presence, our attitude will be somewhat different when we experience the death of Christian friends and relatives. In these cases we will experience genuine sorrow—but mixed with joy that they have gone to be with the Lord.

It is not wrong to express real sorrow at the loss of fellowship with loved ones who have died, and sorrow also for the suffering and hardship that they may have gone through prior to death. Sometimes Christians think it shows lack of faith if they mourn deeply for a brother or sister Christian who has died. But Scripture does not support that view, because when Stephen was stoned, we read that "Devout men buried Stephen, *and made great lamentation over him*" (Acts 8:2). If there ever was certainty that someone went to be with the Lord, it occurred in the case of Stephen. As he died, he said, "Behold, I see the heavens opened, and the Son of man standing at the right hand of God" (Acts 7:56). Then when he was dying, he prayed, "Lord Jesus, receive my spirit," and, "Lord, do not hold this sin against them" (Acts 7:59–60). And this occurred in Jerusalem, with all the apostles still present, those apostles who had seen Jesus himself after he had been raised from the dead. There was no lack of faith on anyone's part that Stephen was in heaven experiencing great joy in the presence of the Lord. Yet in spite of this, "Devout men buried Stephen, *and made great lamentation over him*" (Acts 8:2). Their sorrow showed the genuine grief that they felt at the loss of fellowship with someone whom they loved, and it was not wrong to express this sorrow—it was right. Even Jesus, at the tomb of Lazarus, "wept" (John 11:35), experiencing sorrow at the fact that Lazarus had died, that his sisters and others were experiencing such grief, and also, no doubt, at the fact that there was death in the world at all, for ultimately it is unnatural and ought not to be in a world created by God.

The Ephesian elders, whom Paul had taught personally for three years, later "*wept* and embraced Paul and kissed him, sorrowing most of all because of the word he had spoken, that they should see his face no more" (Acts 20:37–38).

---

[3]Berkhof is certainly correct to say that the burial of Jesus "did not merely serve to prove that Jesus was really dead, but also to remove the terrors of the grave for the redeemed and to sanctify the grave for them" (*Systematic Theology,* p. 340).

And Paul himself, in the same letter in which he expressed such a desire to depart from this life and be with Christ, said that if Epaphroditus had died, he himself would have had *"sorrow upon sorrow"* (Phil. 2:27). Moreover, King David, the man after God's own heart, the man who in his psalms frequently spoke of living forever with God, nonetheless had great sorrow when he learned that Saul and Jonathan had died (2 Sam. 1:11–27).

Nevertheless, the sorrow that we feel is clearly mingled with hope and joy. Paul does not tell the Thessalonians that they should not grieve *at all* concerning their loved ones who have died, but he writes, "that you may not grieve *as others do* who have no hope" (1 Thess. 4:13)—they should not grieve in the same way, with the same bitter despair, that unbelievers have. But certainly they should grieve. He assures them that Christ "died for us so that whether we wake or sleep we might live with him" (1 Thess. 5:10), and thereby encourages them that those who have died have gone to be with the Lord. That is why Scripture can say, "Blessed are the dead who die in the Lord henceforth . . . that they may rest from their labors" (Rev. 14:13). In fact, Scripture even tells us, "Precious in the sight of the LORD is the death of his saints" (Ps. 116:15).

Therefore, though we have genuine sorrow when Christian friends and relatives die, we also can say with Scripture, "O death, where is your victory? O death, where is your sting? . . . Thanks be to God, who gives us the victory through our Lord Jesus Christ" (1 Cor. 15:55–57). Though we mourn, our mourning should be mixed with worship of God and thanksgiving for the life of the loved one who has died. Worship is especially important at this time, as we see in the examples of David and of Job. When David's child died, he stopped praying for the child's health, and worshiped God: "Then David arose from the earth, and washed, and anointed himself, and changed his clothes; and he went into the house of the Lord, *and worshiped"* (2 Sam. 12:20).

Similarly, when Job heard of the death of his ten children,

> Then Job arose, and rent his robe, and shaved his head, and fell upon the ground, *and worshiped.* And he said, "Naked I came from my mother's womb, and naked shall I return; the LORD gave, and the LORD has taken away; blessed be the name of the LORD." (Job 1:20–21)

**3. The Death of Unbelievers.** When unbelievers die, the sorrow we feel is not mingled with the joy of assurance that they have gone to be with the Lord forever. This sorrow, especially regarding those we have been close to, is very deep and real. Paul himself, when thinking about some of his Jewish brothers who had rejected Christ, said, "I am speaking the truth in Christ, I am not lying; my conscience bears me witness in the Holy Spirit, that *I have great sorrow and unceasing anguish in my heart.* For I could wish that I myself were accursed and cut off from Christ for the sake of my brethren, my kinsmen by race" (Rom. 9:1–3).

Yet it also must be said that we often do not have absolute certainty that a person has persisted in refusal to trust in Christ all the way to the point of death. The knowledge of one's impending death often will bring about genuine heart searching on the part of the dying person, and sometimes words of Scripture or words of Christian testimony that have been heard long ago will be recalled and the person may come to genuine repentance and faith. Certainly, we do not have any assurance that this has happened unless there is explicit evidence for it, but it is also good to realize that in many cases we have only probable but not absolute knowledge that those whom we have known as unbelievers have persisted in their unbelief until the point of death. In some cases we simply do not know.

Nevertheless, after a non-Christian has died, it would be wrong to give any indication to others that we think that person has gone to heaven. This would simply be to give misleading information and false assurance, and to diminish the urgency of the need for those who are still alive to trust in Christ. It is much better, as we have opportunity, to focus on the fact that the sorrow that we feel at the loss of someone whom we love causes us to reflect on our own life and destiny as well. In fact, the times when we are able to talk as a friend to the loved ones of an unbeliever who has died are often times when the Lord will open up opportunities to talk about the gospel with those who are still living.

Moreover, it is often very helpful in such circumstances to speak with genuine thankfulness about the good qualities that we have noticed and been encouraged by in the life of the person who has died.[4] A good example of that is seen in David's reaction when King Saul died. Even though Saul had become an evil king and had pursued David and tried to kill him many times, once Saul had died, David spoke freely and publicly about the good things Saul had done:

> Your glory, O Israel, is slain upon your high places! How are the mighty fallen! . . .
> Saul and Jonathan . . . they were swifter than eagles, they were stronger than lions.
> You daughters of Israel, weep over Saul, who clothed you daintily in scarlet, who
> put ornaments of gold upon your apparel. How are the mighty fallen in the midst
> of battle! (2 Sam. 1:19–25)[5]

## C. What Happens When People Die?

**1. The Souls of Believers Go Immediately Into God's Presence.** Death is a temporary cessation of bodily life and a separation of the soul from the body. Once a believer has died, though his or her physical body remains on the earth and is buried, at the moment of death the soul (or spirit) of that believer goes immediately into the presence of God with rejoicing. When Paul thinks about death he says, "We would rather be *away from the body and at home with the Lord*" (2 Cor. 5:8). To be away from the body is to be at home with the Lord. He also says that his desire is "to *depart and be with Christ,* for that is far better" (Phil. 1:23). And Jesus said to the thief who was dying on the cross next to him, "*Today* you will be with me in Paradise" (Luke 23:43).[6] The author of Hebrews says that when Christians come together to worship they come not only into the presence of God in heaven, but also into the presence of "the spirits of just men made

---

[4]It is right to thank God for the benefits of common grace in the lives of unbelievers; see the discussion of common grace in chapter 31.

[5]Even this requires honesty and mature judgment, however, for if we are called upon to perform a funeral service for someone whose life has been widely known as evil and destructive, we do not want to give people the impression that what a person does in this life makes no difference, or that we are ignorant of the noticeably bad qualities of such a person, or we will lose credibility with those who hear us. As an example of the inevitable reaction of people to the death of someone clearly evil, such as Adolf Hitler, note Prov. 11:10, "When the wicked perish there are shouts of gladness."

[6]Paradise is simply another name for heaven: see chapter 27, p. 593.

perfect" (Heb. 12:23).⁷ However, as we shall see in more detail in the next chapter, God will not leave our dead bodies in the earth forever, for when Christ returns the souls of believers will be reunited with their bodies, their bodies will be raised from the dead, and they will live with Christ eternally.

## a. The Bible Does Not Teach the Doctrine of Purgatory:
The fact that the souls of believers go immediately into God's presence means that *there is no such thing as purgatory*. In Roman Catholic teaching, purgatory is the place where the souls of believers go to be further purified from sin until they are ready to be admitted into heaven. According to this view, the sufferings of purgatory are given to God in substitute for the punishment for sins that believers should have received in time, but did not. Speaking of purgatory, Ott says:

> Suffrages operate in such a matter that the satisfactory value of the good works is offered to God in substitution for the temporal punishment for sins which the poor souls still have to render. It operates by way of remission of temporal punishments due to sins.⁸

But this doctrine is not taught in Scripture, and it is in fact contrary to the verses quoted immediately above. The Roman Catholic Church has found support for this doctrine, not in the pages of canonical Scripture as we defined it in chapter 3 above, and as Protestants have accepted it since the Reformation, but in the writings of the Apocrypha,⁹ particularly in 2 Maccabees 12:42–45:

> [Judas Maccabeus, the leader of the Jewish forces] also took a collection, man by man, to the amount of 2,000 drachmas of silver, and sent it to Jerusalem to provide for a sin offering. In doing this he acted very well and honorably, taking into account the resurrection. For if he were not expecting that those who had fallen would rise again, it would have been superfluous and foolish *to pray for the dead*. But if he was looking to the splendid reward that is laid up for those who fall asleep in godliness, it was a holy and pious thought. Therefore *he made atonement for the dead, that they might be delivered from their sin*.

Here it is clear that prayer for the dead is approved, and also making an offering to God to deliver the dead from their sin. But in response it must be said that this literature is not equal to Scripture in authority, and should not be taken as an authoritative source of doctrine. Moreover, it contradicts the clear statements about departing and being with Christ quoted above, and thereby opposes the

---

⁷It must be said, however, that the fact that we go to be with Christ immediately when we die should not be taken as an encouragement to anyone to think that suicide would be right. God says, "You shall not murder" (Ex. 20:13 NIV), and that means that we must not murder ourselves any more than we should murder others.

On the other hand, there are many faithful Christians who in wartime or shipwrecks or other trying circumstances have laid down their own lives for the sake of others, thus fulfilling Jesus' teaching, "Greater love has no man than this, that a man lay down his life for his friends" (John 15:13).

The larger principle is that as long as we remain in this life we are to be faithful to Christ in serving him and in prayer, for he calls us to be "faithful unto death" (Rev. 2:10). And though Paul, in thinking about his own personal desires, wanted to go to be with Christ, he realized that for the sake of the Philippians and for others that he ministered to, to stay alive would be "more necessary" on their behalf (Phil. 1:24).

⁸Ludwig Ott, *Fundamentals of Catholic Dogma*, p. 322.

⁹See chapter 3, pp. 57–59, for a discussion of the reasons why the Apocrypha should not be accepted as part of Scripture.

clear teaching of New Testament Scripture. Furthermore, when it talks about the offering of Judas making "atonement [Gk. *exilasmos* ('propitiation')] for the dead" it contradicts the explicit teaching of the New Testament that Christ alone made atonement for us. Finally, this passage in 2 Maccabees is difficult to square even with Roman Catholic teaching, because it teaches that soldiers who had died in the mortal sin of idolatry (which cannot be forgiven, according to Catholic teaching) should have prayers and sacrifices offered for them with the possibility that they will be delivered from their suffering.

Roman Catholic theology finds support for the doctrine of purgatory primarily in the passage from 2 Maccabees quoted above, and in the teaching of the tradition of the church.[10] Other passages cited by Ott in support of the doctrine of purgatory are 2 Timothy 1:18; Matthew 5:26; 1 Corinthians 3:15; and Matthew 12:32. In 2 Timothy 1:18, Paul says, concerning Onesiphorus, "When he arrived in Rome he searched for me eagerly and found me—may the Lord grant him to find mercy from the Lord on that Day—and you well know all the service he rendered at Ephesus" (2 Tim. 1:17–18). The claim of those who find support for the doctrine of purgatory is that "Onesiphorus . . . apparently was no longer among the living at the time of the Second Epistle to Timothy."[11] This seems to be based on the fact that Paul refers not to Onesiphorus himself but "the household of Onesiphorus" (2 Tim. 1:16); however, that phrase does not prove that Onesiphorus had died, but only that Paul was wishing blessings not only on him but on his entire household. This would not be unusual since Onesiphorus had served in Ephesus where Paul had worked for three years (2 Tim. 1:18; cf. 4:19). To build support for purgatory on the idea that Onesiphorus had already died is simply to build it on an assumption that cannot be supported with clear evidence. (It is not unusual for Paul to express a wish that some Christians would be blessed in the Day of Judgment—see 1 Thess. 5:23.)

In Matthew 12:32, Jesus says, "Whoever speaks against the Holy Spirit will not be forgiven, either in this age or in the age to come." Ott says that this sentence "leaves open the possibility that sins are forgiven not only in this world but in the world to come."[12] However, this is simply an error in reasoning: to say that something will not happen in the age to come does not imply that it might happen in the age to come![13] What is needed to prove the doctrine of purgatory is not a negative statement such as this but a positive statement that says that people suffer for the purpose of continuing purification after they die. But Scripture nowhere says this.

In 1 Corinthians 3:15 Paul says that on the Day of Judgment, the work that everyone has done will be judged and tested by fire, and then says, "*If any man's work is burned up,* he will suffer loss, though he himself will be saved, but only as through fire." But this does not speak of a *person* being burned or suffering punishment, but simply of *his work* as being tested by fire—that which is good will be like gold, silver, and precious stones that will last forever (v. 12). Moreover,

---

[10]Ott, *Fundamentals of Catholic Dogma,* pp. 321–22, 482–85.

[11]Ibid., p. 321.

[12]Ibid., p. 483.

[13]This is a similar mistake to the one made by those who argue that, since Jesus says he will not blot someone's name out of the book of life (Rev. 3:5), it implies that he might blot the names of others out of the book of life (see chapter 40, p. 802).

Ott himself admits that this is something that occurs not during this age but during the day of "the general judgment,"[14] and this further indicates that it can hardly be used as a convincing argument for purgatory. Finally, in Matthew 5:26, after warning people to make friends quickly with their accusers while they are going to the court, lest the accuser hand them to the judge and the judge to the guard and they be put in prison, Jesus then says, "You will never get out till you have paid the last penny." Ott understands this as a parable teaching a "time-limited condition of punishment in the other world."[15] But surely there is no indication in context that this is a parable—Jesus is giving practical teaching about reconciliation of human conflicts and the avoidance of situations that naturally lead to anger and personal injury (see Matt. 5:21–26). Other passages of Scripture that have sometimes been referred to in support of the doctrine of purgatory[16] simply do not speak directly about this idea at all, and can all easily be understood in terms of punishment and deliverance from distress in this life, or of a life of eternal blessing with God in heaven in the life to come.

An even more serious problem with this doctrine is that it teaches that we must add something to the redemptive work of Christ, and that his redemptive work for us was not enough to pay the penalty for all our sins. But this is certainly contrary to the teaching of Scripture.[17] Moreover, in a pastoral sense, the doctrine of purgatory robs believers of the great comfort that should be theirs in knowing that those who have died have immediately gone into the presence of the Lord, and knowing that they also, when they die, will "depart and be with Christ, for that is far better" (Phil. 1:23).

**b. The Bible Does Not Teach the Doctrine of "Soul Sleep":** The fact that souls of believers go immediately into God's presence also means that *the doctrine of soul sleep is incorrect.* This doctrine teaches that when believers die they go into a state of unconscious existence, and the next thing that they are conscious of will be when Christ returns and raises them to eternal life. This doctrine has been taught occasionally by one person or another in the history of the church, including some Anabaptists at the Reformation, and some of the Irvingites in England in the nineteenth century. In fact, one of John Calvin's first writings was a tract against this doctrine, a doctrine that has never found wide acceptance in the church.

Support for the doctrine of soul sleep has generally been found in the fact that Scripture several times speaks of the state of death as "sleep" or "falling asleep" (Matt. 9:24; 27:52; John 11:11; Acts 7:60; 13:36; 1 Cor. 15:6, 18, 20, 51; 1 Thess. 4:13; 5:10). Moreover, certain passages seem to teach that the dead do not have a conscious existence (see Ps. 6:5; 115:17 [but see v. 18!]; Eccl. 9:10; Isa. 38:19). But when Scripture represents death as "sleep" it is simply a metaphorical expression used to indicate that death is only temporary for Christians, just as sleep is temporary. This is clearly seen, for example, when Jesus tells his disciples about the death of Lazarus. He says, "Our friend Lazarus has fallen asleep, but I

---

[14]Ott, *Fundamentals of Catholic Dogma,* p. 483.

[15]Ibid. p. 484.

[16]Berkhof mentions that Roman Catholics have sometimes referred to Isa. 4:4; Mic. 7:8; Zech. 9:11; Mal. 3:2–3; and 1 Cor. 15:29.

[17]See chapter 27, pp. 577–78, on the fact that Christ's death completely paid the penalty for all our sins.

go to awake him out of sleep" (John 11:11). We should notice that Jesus does not here say, "The soul of Lazarus is sleeping," nor, in fact, does any passage in Scripture say that the soul of a person is sleeping or unconscious (a statement that would be necessary to prove the doctrine of soul sleep). Rather Jesus simply says that *Lazarus* has fallen asleep. Then John explains, "Now Jesus had spoken of his death, but they thought that he meant taking rest in sleep. Then Jesus told them plainly, 'Lazarus is dead' " (John 11:12–13). The other passages that speak about people sleeping when they die are likewise to be interpreted as simply a metaphorical expression to teach that death is temporary.

As for the passages that indicate that the dead do not praise God, or that there is a ceasing of conscious activity when people die, these are all to be understood from the perspective of life in this world. From our perspective it appears that once people die, they do not engage in these activities any longer. But Psalm 115 presents the full biblical perspective on this viewpoint. It says, "The dead do not praise the LORD, nor do any that go down into silence." But then it continues in the very next verse with a contrast indicating that those who believe in God will bless the LORD forever: *"But we will bless the LORD from this time forth and for evermore.* Praise the LORD!" (Ps. 115:17–18).

Finally, the passages quoted above demonstrating that the souls of believers go immediately into God's presence and enjoy fellowship with him there (2 Cor. 5:8; Phil. 1:23; Luke 23:43; and Heb. 12:23) all indicate that there is conscious existence and fellowship with God immediately after death for the believer. Jesus did not say, "Today you will no longer have consciousness of anything that is going on," but, "Today *you will be with me in Paradise*" (Luke 23:43). Certainly the conception of paradise understood at that time was not one of unconscious existence but one of great blessing and joy in the presence of God.[18] Paul did not say, "My desire is to depart and be unconscious for a long period of time," but rather, "My desire is to depart *and be with Christ*" (Phil. 1:23)—and he certainly knew that Christ was not an unconscious, sleeping Savior, but one who was actively living and reigning in heaven. To be with Christ was to enjoy the blessing of fellowship in his presence, and that is why to depart and be with him was "far better" (Phil. 1:23). That is why he says, "We would rather be away from the body and at home with the Lord" (2 Cor. 5:8).

The fact that Hebrews 12:1 says, "We are surrounded by so great a cloud of witnesses," just after an entire chapter spent on the discussion of the faith of Old Testament saints who had died (Heb. 11), and the fact that the author encourages us to run the race of life with perseverance because we are surrounded by this great cloud of witnesses, both suggest that those who have died and gone before have some awareness of what is going on in the earth. Scripture says very little about this, probably because it does not want us to speak to those who have died or to pray to them or to contact them in any way (note Saul's great sin in this in 1 Sam. 28:7–25). Nonetheless, Hebrews 12:1–2 does give us this slight hint, probably as an encouragement to us to continue also to be faithful to God as were those who have died and gone to heaven before us. Similarly, at the end of

---

[18]See the other uses of the word *Paradise* in 2 Cor. 12:3 and Rev. 2:7, where the word clearly refers to heaven itself where God is and lives and reigns; see also the discussion of this word in chapter 27, p. 593.

Hebrews 12, the author tells us that when we worship we come into the presence of God in heaven, and we come not to "the spirits of just men who are sleeping in an unconscious state" but "to innumerable angels in festal gathering, and to the assembly of the first-born who are enrolled in heaven, and to a judge who is God of all, and to the spirits of just men made perfect, and to Jesus, the mediator of a new covenant" (Heb. 12:22–24).[19]

Revelation 6:9–11 and 7:9–10 also clearly show the souls or spirits of those who have died and who have gone to heaven praying and worshiping, for they cry out with a loud voice, "O Sovereign Lord, holy and true, how long before you will judge and avenge our blood on those who dwell upon the earth?" (Rev. 6:10), and they are seen "standing before the throne and before the Lamb, clothed in white robes, with palm branches in their hands, and crying out with a loud voice, 'Salvation belongs to our God who sits upon the throne, and to the Lamb!'" (Rev. 7:9–10). All of these passages deny the doctrine of soul sleep, for they make it clear that the souls of believers experience conscious fellowship with God in heaven immediately upon death.

**c. Did Old Testament Believers Enter Immediately Into God's Presence?**
Some have said that, although the souls of believers *since Christ's resurrection* go immediately into God's presence in heaven, the souls of believers who died *before Christ's resurrection* did not enjoy the blessings of heaven but went into a place of waiting for Christ's work of redemption to be complete. Sometimes this is called the *limbus patrum,* or simply limbo.[20] This view has been especially common in Roman Catholic theology, but it has also been held by some Lutherans. Some of the support for this doctrine comes from a particular view of the idea of Christ's descent into hell, which we discussed in an earlier chapter.[21]

Not many Scripture references talk about the state of Old Testament believers after they had died, but those that give us any indication of their state all point in the direction of immediate conscious enjoyment in the presence of God, not of a time of waiting away from God's presence. "Enoch walked with God; and he was not, for *God took him*" (Gen. 5:24; cf. Heb. 11:5). Elijah was not taken to a place on the border of hell, but he "went up by a whirlwind *into heaven*" (2 Kings 2:11; cf. Matt. 17:3, where Moses and Elijah appear, talking with Jesus). And David is confident that he will *"dwell in the house of the LORD for ever"* (Ps. 23:6; cf. 16:10–11; 17:15; 1:15, 18). Moreover, when Jesus answers the Sadducees, he reminds them that God says, "I am the God of Abraham, and the God of Isaac, and the God of Jacob" and then says, "He is not God of the dead, but of the living" (Matt.

[19]The phrase "the communion of saints" in the Apostles' Creed refers to the fact that we have in some sense a communion or fellowship with those who have died and gone before into heaven, an idea that is affirmed in Heb. 12:23. This does not imply that we can be aware of them, but simply that when we worship we join in worship that is already going on in heaven (see chapter 51, pp. 1006–7, on the fact that our worship now is also worship in heaven).

[20]Strictly speaking, Roman Catholic theologians have held that there are two limbos, a place where unbaptized infants go when they die called *limbus infantum,* and a place where Old Testament believers went when they died called *limbus patrum.* The Latin word *limbus* means "border"; these were thought to be places on the border of hell where people were excluded from the presence of God but also did not experience conscious suffering. There is no explicit support in Scripture for either doctrine.

[21]See the discussion of the idea that Christ descended into hell when he died in chapter 27, pp. 586–94.

822          *41 : DEATH AND THE INTERMEDIATE STATE*

22:32), thus implying that Abraham, Isaac, and Jacob were living even at that very moment, and that God was their God. Moreover, in the story of the rich man and Lazarus, Jesus does not say that Lazarus is unconscious, but reports Abraham as saying about Lazarus, "Now he is comforted here" (Luke 16:25). Abraham himself is portrayed as dwelling consciously in a place that is very desirable—that the rich man longed to go to—certainly not a place on the fringe of hell. It is important to notice that since this is before Christ's resurrection, Lazarus was in the same situation as the Old Testament saints.

Therefore it seems likely that Old Testament believers also entered immediately into heaven and enjoyed a time of fellowship with God upon their death. However, it may well have been true that additional rich blessings and much greater rejoining came to them when Christ returned to heaven at his ascension. But this does not mean that they were transported to heaven for the first time, or that that was the first time they enjoyed the blessing of God's presence.

**d. Should We Pray for the Dead?** Finally, the fact that the souls of believers go immediately into God's presence means that *we should not pray for the dead*. Although this idea is taught in 2 Maccabees 12:42–45 (see above), it is nowhere taught in the Bible itself. Moreover, there is no indication that this was the practice of any Christians at the time of the New Testament, nor should it have been. Once *believers* die they enter into God's presence and they are in a state of perfect happiness with him. What good would it do to pray for them anymore? Final heavenly reward will be based on deeds done in this life, as Scripture repeatedly testifies (1 Cor. 3:12–15; 2 Cor. 5:10; et al.).[22] Further, the souls of *unbelievers* who die go to a place of punishment and eternal separation from the presence of God. It would do no good to pray for them either, since their final destiny has been settled by their sin and their rebellion against God in this life. To pray for the dead therefore is simply to pray for something that God has told us has already been decided.[23] Moreover, to teach that we should pray for the dead, or to encourage others to do so, would be to encourage false hope that the destinies of people might be changed after they die, something which Scripture nowhere encourages us to think. It may lead people to much useless anxiety and much time essentially wasted in prayers that will have absolutely no results, and will thereby divert attention from prayers that could be made for events for this life and could have great effect in advancing the work of the kingdom. We should spend time praying according to God's will.

**2. The Souls of Unbelievers Go Immediately to Eternal Punishment.** Scripture never encourages us to think that people will have a second chance to trust in Christ after death. In fact, the situation is quite the contrary. Jesus' story

---

[22]See chapter 56, pp. 1143–45, on degrees of reward in heaven.
[23]Further indication that it is not right to pray for the dead is seen in the fact that David prayed intensely for his little son before that son died, but after he had died, David rose from prayer and washed and changed his clothes and "went into the house of the Lord and worshiped . . . and he ate" (2 Sam. 12:20; cf. v. 23). David realized that once the child had died his task of praying for him was done. When I speak of "praying for the dead" in this section, I mean praying that God would change their status or destiny. Of course there is nothing wrong with *thanking God* for the lives of people after they have died.

about the rich man and Lazarus gives no hope that people can cross from hell to heaven after they have died: though the rich man in hell called out, "Father Abraham, have mercy upon me, and send Lazarus to dip the end of his finger in water and cool my tongue; for I am in anguish in this flame," Abraham replied to him, "Between us and you a great chasm has been fixed, in order that those who would pass from here to you may not be able, and *none may cross from there to us*" (Luke 16:24–26).

The book of Hebrews connects death with the consequence of judgment in close sequence: "just as it is appointed for men to die once, and after that comes judgment . . ." (Heb. 9:27). Moreover, Scripture never represents the final judgment as depending on anything done after we die, but only on what has happened in this life (Matt. 25:31–46; Rom. 2:5–10; cf. 2 Cor. 5:10). Some have argued for a second chance to believe in the gospel on the basis of Christ's preaching to the spirits in prison in 1 Peter 3:18–20 and the preaching of the gospel "even to the dead" in 1 Peter 4:6, but those are inadequate interpretations of the verses in question, and, on closer inspection, do not support such a view.[24]

We should also realize that the idea that there will be a second chance to accept Christ after death is based on the assumption that everyone deserves a chance to accept Christ and that eternal punishment only comes to those who consciously decide to reject him. But certainly that idea is not supported by Scripture: we all are sinners by nature and choice, and no one actually deserves any of God's grace or deserves any opportunity to hear the gospel of Christ—those come only because of God's unmerited favor. Condemnation comes not only because of a willful rejection of Christ, but also because of the sins that we have committed and the rebellion against God that those sins represent (see John 3:18).

The idea that people have a second chance to accept Christ after death would also destroy most motivation for evangelism and missionary activity today, and is not consistent with the intense missionary zeal that was felt by the New Testament church as a whole, and that was especially exemplified in the missionary travels of the apostle Paul.

The fact that there is conscious punishment for unbelievers after they die and that this punishment goes on forever is certainly a difficult doctrine for us to contemplate. But the passages teaching it appear so clear that it seems that we must affirm it if we are to affirm what Scripture teaches. Jesus says that at the day of final judgment he will say to those at his left hand, "Depart from me, you cursed, into the *eternal fire* prepared for the devil and his angels," and he says that "they will go away into *eternal punishment*, but the righteous into eternal life" (Matt. 25:41, 46).[25]

These passages show that we cannot accept as faithful to Scripture the doctrine of *annihilationism*. This is a doctrine that says that unbelievers, either immediately upon death, or else after suffering for a period of time, will simply cease to exist— God will "annihilate" them and they will no longer be. Although the idea initially sounds attractive to us, and it avoids the emotional difficulty connected with affirming eternal conscious punishment for the wicked, such an idea is not

[24]See the discussion of these verses in chapter 27, pp. 589–94; see also W. Grudem, *The First Epistle of Peter,* pp. 155–62, 170–72, 203–39.

[25]See chapter 56, pp. 1140–57, for a discussion of the final judgment and the doctrine of hell.

explicitly affirmed in any passages of Scripture, and seems so clearly to be contradicted by those passages that connect the eternal blessing of the righteous with the eternal punishment of the wicked (Matt. 25:46) and that talk about punishment extending to the wicked day and night forever (Rev. 14:11; 20:10).[26]

Although unbelievers pass into a state of eternal punishment immediately upon death, their bodies will not be raised until the day of final judgment. On that day, their bodies will be raised and reunited with their souls, and they will stand before God's throne for final judgment to be pronounced upon them in the body (see Matt. 25:31-46; John 5:28-29; Acts 24:15; and Rev. 20:12, 15).[27]

## QUESTIONS FOR PERSONAL APPLICATION

1. Have you thought very much about the possibility of your own death? Has there been an element of fear connected with those thoughts? What, if anything, do you fear about death? Do you think that these fears have come from the influence of the world around you or from Scripture? How would the teachings of Scripture encourage you to deal with these fears?

2. Has this chapter changed your feelings about your own death in any way? Can you honestly contemplate it now as something that will bring you nearer to Christ and increase your own trust in God and faithfulness to him? How would you express your hopes regarding your own death?

3. Do you think you would have the courage to refuse to sin even if it meant being thrown to the lions in a Roman coliseum, or burned at the stake during the Reformation, or thrown in prison for years in some foreign country today? Do you think the Christian martyrs throughout history had thought that they would have enough courage when put to the test? What happened to them to equip them for this suffering (read 1 Cor. 10:13)? If you can obtain a copy, you may wish to read the account of the martyrdom of Polycarp, a stirring testimony of faith in God and of God's faithfulness in the second century A.D.[28] Have you settled in your own mind that obedience to Christ is more important than preserving your own life? What would make you hesitant to believe this or act on this conviction?

4. If you have experienced the death of a believer who was close to you, do you think that your reaction to that death was one of sorrow mingled with joy? How has this chapter influenced the way you feel about that situation, if at all?

5. Have you previously believed in the doctrine of purgatory? If you no longer believe in it now, can you describe the way the doctrine made you feel, and the way you now feel emotionally about the fact that that doctrine is not true and there is no such place as purgatory?

---

[26]See chapter 56, pp. 1149-51, for a more extended discussion of annihilationism.

[27]See below, chapter 56, pp. 1140-46.

[28]One version of *The Martyrdom of Polycarp* is available in *The Apostolic Fathers*, 2 vols., ed. Kirsopp Lake, Loeb Classical Library (Cambridge, Mass.: Harvard University Press, 1913), pp. 307-45. It is also available in *The Ante-Nicene Fathers*, ed. A. Roberts and J. Donaldson (10 vols.; Grand Rapids: Eerdmans, 1979 [reprint]).

6. If death itself is viewed as part of the process of sanctification, then how
should we view the process of growing older and weaker in this world? Is
that the way the world views aging? What about you?

## SPECIAL TERMS

annihilationism                    *limbus patrum*
communion of saints                purgatory
death                              soul sleep
limbo

## BIBLIOGRAPHY

(For an explanation of this bibliography see the note on the bibliography to
chapter, p. 38. Complete bibliographical data may be found on pp. 1223–29.)

### Sections in Evangelical Systematic Theologies

1. Anglican (Episcopalian)
    1882–92   Litton, 543–78
    1930   Thomas, 298–310, 508–21
2. Arminian (Wesleyan or Methodist)
    1875–76   Pope, 3:371–86
    1892–94   Miley, 2:430–39
    1940   Wiley, 3:211–42
    1983   Carter, 2:1109–13
3. Baptist
    1767   Gill, 2:179–211
    1887   Boyce, 437–51
    1907   Strong, 982–1003
    1917   Mullins, 458–62
    1983–85   Erickson, 1167–84
4. Dispensational
    1947   Chafer, 4:413–15
    1949   Thiessen, 333–36
    1986   Ryrie, 518–20
5. Lutheran
    1917–24   Pieper, 3:507–15
    1934   Mueller, 613–19
6. Reformed (or Presbyterian)
    1724–58   Edwards, 2:26–36
    1871–73   Hodge, 3:713–70
    1878   Dabney, 817–29
    1889   Shedd, 2b:591–640

        1937–66   Murray, *CW*, 2:401–3; *CW*, 3:242–46
        1938      Berkhof, 668–94
        1962      Buswell, 2:304–23
7. Renewal (or charismatic/Pentecostal)
        1988–92   Williams, 3:400–401, 450

## Sections in Representative Roman Catholic Systematic Theologies

1. Roman Catholic: Traditional
        1955      Ott, 445–50, 473–76, 482–85
2. Roman Catholic: Post-Vatican II
        1980      McBrien, 2:1135–47

## Other Works

Beckwith, Roger T. "Purgatory." In *NDT*, pp. 549–50.

Cooper, John W. *Body, Soul and Life Everlasting: Biblical Anthropology and the Monism-Dualism Debate*. Grand Rapids: Eerdmans, 1989, pp. 81–103, 121–253.

Davids, P. H. "Death." In *EDT*, pp. 299–300.

Feinberg, John S. "1 Peter 3:18–20, Ancient Mythology, and the Intermediate State." *WTJ*. Vol. 48, no. 2 (Fall 1986), pp. 303–36.

Grudem, Wayne. "Christ Preaching Through Noah: 1 Peter 3:19–20 in the Light of Dominant Themes in Jewish Literature." In *The First Epistle of Peter*. Tyndale New Testament Commentaries. Leicester: Inter-Varsity Press, and Grand Rapids: Eerdmans, 1988, pp. 203–39.

Harris, Murray J. "Death." In *NDT*, p. 188.

———. "Intermediate State." In *NDT*, pp. 339–40.

Hoekema, Anthony A. *The Bible and the Future*. Grand Rapids: Eerdmans, 1979, pp. 79–108.

Smith, S. M. "Intermediate State." In *EDT*, pp. 562–64.

## SCRIPTURE MEMORY PASSAGE

**Philippians 1:20–24:** *As it is my eager expectation and hope that I shall not be at all ashamed, but that with full courage now as always Christ will be honored in my body, whether by life or by death. For to me to live is Christ, and to die is gain. If it is to be life in the flesh, that means fruitful labor for me. Yet which I shall choose I cannot tell. I am hard pressed between the two. My desire is to depart and be with Christ, for that is far better. But to remain in the flesh is more necessary on your account.*

## HYMN

"My Jesus I Love Thee"

My Jesus, I love thee, I know thou art mine;
For thee all the follies of sin I resign.

My gracious Redeemer, my Savior art thou;
    If ever I loved thee, my Jesus 'tis now.

I love thee because thou hast first loved me,
    And purchased my pardon on Calvary's tree.
I love thee for wearing the thorns on thy brow;
    If ever I loved thee, my Jesus, 'tis now.

I'll love thee in life, I will love thee in death;
    And praise thee as long as thou lendest me breath;
And say, when the death-dew lies cold on my brow:
    If ever I loved thee, my Jesus, 'tis now.

In mansions of glory and endless delight,
    I'll ever adore thee in heaven so bright;
I'll sing with the glittering crown on my brow:
    If ever I loved thee, my Jesus, 'tis now.

AUTHOR: WILLIAM R. FEATHERSTONE, 1864

# Chapter 42

# Glorification (Receiving a Resurrection Body)

## When will we receive resurrection bodies?
## What will they be like?

### EXPLANATION AND SCRIPTURAL BASIS

When Christ redeemed us he did not just redeem our spirits (or souls)—he redeemed us as whole persons, and this includes the redemption of our bodies. Therefore the application of Christ's work of redemption to us will not be complete until our bodies are entirely set free from the effects of the fall and brought to that state of perfection for which God created them. In fact, the redemption of our bodies will only occur when Christ returns and raises our bodies from the dead. But at this present time, Paul says that we wait for *"the redemption of our bodies,"* and then adds, "for in this hope we were saved" (Rom. 8:23–24). The stage in the application of redemption when we receive resurrection bodies is called *glorification*. Referring to that future day Paul says that we will be *"glorified* with him" (Rom. 8:17). Moreover, when Paul traces the steps in the application of redemption, the last one he names is glorification: "And those whom he predestined he also called; and those whom he called he also justified; and those whom he justified he also *glorified"* (Rom. 8:30).

The day we are glorified will be a day of great victory because on that day the last enemy, death, will be destroyed, just as Scripture predicts: "For he must reign until he has put all his enemies under his feet. The last enemy to be destroyed is death" (1 Cor. 15:25–26). In the context of a discussion of the resurrection of our bodies when Christ returns, Paul says, "Then shall come to pass the saying that is written: 'Death is swallowed up in victory.' 'O death, where is your victory? O death, where is your sting?'" (1 Cor. 15:54–55). When our bodies are raised from the dead we will experience complete victory over the death that came as a result of the fall of Adam and Eve. Then our redemption will be complete.

We may therefore define *glorification* as follows: *Glorification is the final step in the application of redemption. It will happen when Christ returns and raises from the dead the bodies of all believers for all time who have died, and reunites them with their souls, and changes the bodies of all believers who remain alive, thereby giving all believers at the same time perfect resurrection bodies like his own.*

### A. New Testament Evidence for Glorification

The primary New Testament passage on glorification or the resurrection of the body is 1 Corinthians 15:12–58. Paul says, "So also in Christ shall all be made alive. But each in his own order: Christ the first fruits, then *at his coming* those who belong to Christ" (vv. 22–23).[1] Paul discusses the nature of the resurrection body in some detail in verses 35–50, which we will examine in section C below. He then concludes the passage by saying that not all Christians will die, but some who remain alive when Christ returns will simply have their bodies instantaneously changed into new, resurrection bodies that can never grow old or weak and can never die:

> Lo! I tell you a mystery. We shall not all sleep, but *we shall all be changed,* in a moment, in the twinkling of an eye, at the last trumpet. For the trumpet will sound, and the dead will be raised imperishable, and we shall be changed. (1 Cor. 15:51–52)

Paul further explains in 1 Thessalonians that the souls of those who have died and gone to be with Christ will come back and be joined with their bodies on that day, for Christ will bring them with him: "For since we believe that Jesus died and rose again, even so, through Jesus, *God will bring with him those who have fallen asleep*" (1 Thess. 4:14). But here Paul affirms not only that God will bring with Christ those who have died; he also affirms that *"the dead in Christ will rise first"* (1 Thess. 4:16). So these believers who have died with Christ are also raised up to meet Christ (Paul says in v. 17, "We . . . shall be caught up together with them in the clouds to meet the Lord in the air"). This only makes sense if it is the *souls* of believers who have gone into Christ's presence who return with him, and if it is their *bodies* that are raised from the dead to be joined together with their souls, and then to ascend to be with Christ.

In addition to these passages in 1 Corinthians 15 and 1 Thessalonians 4, several other New Testament passages affirm the reality of the doctrine of glorification. Jesus says, "The hour is coming when all who are in the tombs will hear his voice and come forth, those who have done good *to the resurrection of life,* and those who have done evil to the resurrection of judgment" (John 5:28–29).[2] Jesus also says, "This is the will of him who sent me, that I should lose nothing of all that he has given me, but *raise it up at the last day.* For this is the will of my Father, that every one who sees the Son and believes in him should have eternal life; and *I will raise him up at the last day*" (John 6:39–40; cf. vv. 44, 54).

Paul says, "He who raised Christ Jesus from the dead will *give life to your mortal bodies* also through his Spirit which dwells in you" (Rom. 8:11; cf. 2 Cor. 5:1–10). He realizes that Christians should live in eager expectation of Christ's return and of the change in our bodies to be like his own perfect body. He says, "But our commonwealth is in heaven, and from it we await a Savior, the Lord Jesus Christ,

---

[1]Murray J. Harris argues for the possibility of an alternative view, based on his understanding of 2 Cor. 5:1–10: that Christians receive their resurrection bodies immediately after they die. See Harris, *From Grave to Glory: Resurrection in the New Testament,* pp. 207–10. But this view is exceptionally difficult to reconcile with 1 Cor. 15 and 1 Thess. 4: see the discussion in D. A. Carson, "Unity and Diversity in the New Testament: The Possibility of Systematic Theology," in *Scripture and Truth,* pp. 85–86.

[2]Some evangelical Christians hold that believers and unbelievers will be resurrected at the same time (this is the position taken by amillennialists). Others (especially premillennialists) hold that the resurrection of believers occurs before the millennium and the resurrection of the unbelievers for judgment occurs 1,000 years later, after the millennium. See chapter 55 for a discussion of the issues involved, and of this particular verse.

*who will change our lowly body to be like his glorious body,* by the power which enables him even to subject all things to himself" (Phil. 3:20).

## B. Old Testament Support for Glorification

Sometimes people have claimed that the Old Testament has little if any evidence of hope in a future resurrection of the body, but there is in fact more Old Testament evidence for this than we might realize. First, even before Jesus was raised from the dead, the New Testament indicates that many Jewish people living at the time of Christ had some hope of a future bodily resurrection. When Jesus comes to the home of Lazarus after he had died and says to Martha, "Your brother will rise again," Martha responds, "I know that he will rise again *in the resurrection at the last day*" (John 11:23–24). Moreover, when Paul was on trial, he said to Felix that he had a "hope in God which these themselves [his Jewish accusers] accept, that *there will be a resurrection* of both the just and the unjust" (Acts 24:15).

As for the beliefs of those living in the time of the Old Testament, Hebrews 11 tells us that Abraham "looked forward to the city which has foundations, whose builder and maker is God" (Heb. 11:10). We also read that many Old Testament saints "all died in faith, not having received what was promised, but having seen it and greeted it from afar, and having acknowledged that they were strangers and exiles on the earth. . . . But as it is, *they desire a better country, that is, a heavenly one.* Therefore God is not ashamed to be called their God, for he has prepared for them a city" (Heb. 11:13–16). The author even says that Abraham "considered that God was able to raise men even from the dead" (Heb. 11:19).

When we look at the actual teachings of the Old Testament itself, there are indications that Old Testament authors had a strong expectation of the resurrection to come in the future. Job says: "I know that my Redeemer lives, and that in the end he will stand upon the earth. And after my skin has been destroyed, *yet in my flesh I will see God;* I myself will see him with my own eyes—I, and not another" (Job 19:25–26 NIV).[3]

We read in the Psalms, "But God will redeem my soul from the grave; he will surely take me to himself" (Ps. 49:15 NIV; cf. 73:24–25). And we read in Proverbs, "Do not withhold discipline from a child. . . . If you beat him with the rod you will save his life from Sheol" (Prov. 23:13–14). Isaiah says, *"Your dead shall live, their bodies shall rise"* (Isa. 26:19). Daniel has a very explicit prophecy that *"many of those who sleep in the dust of the earth shall awake,* some to everlasting life, and some to shame and everlasting contempt" (Dan. 12:2). (Cf. also Ezekiel's vision of the dry bones in Ezek. 37:1–14.)

Although Old Testament believers certainly did not have as much detail about

---

[3]Several words in this passage are difficult to interpret, and there is scholarly debate over the question of whether Job is looking forward to seeing God in this life (as he does in 42:5) or after his death (note that Job expects his Redeemer to stand upon the earth "in the end," and expects to see God "in my flesh" but this will be "after my skin has been destroyed"). For a summary of the exegetical issues and a persuasive defense of the view that Job is looking forward to a physical resurrection after he dies, see Francis L. Andersen, *Job,* TOTC (Leicester: Inter-Varsity Press, 1976), pp. 193–94. The view that this passage looks forward to seeing God in this life only is largely based on some scholars' convictions that the idea of a future bodily resurrection was not found in Judaism until long after Job was written (but see Heb. 11:10, 19, commenting on Abraham's faith in the resurrection).

the nature of the resurrection or the way it would come about through the resurrection of the Messiah, and although they did not have as clear a basis for confidence in the resurrection as we do in the actual event of the bodily resurrection of Christ, nonetheless there was certainly, as we have seen, an expectation of a future day of bodily resurrection. People who for years had meditated on and believed these statements of Scripture (such as Martha in John 11:24) were prepared to receive the full-fledged New Testament teaching on the resurrection eagerly, for it simply provided more detail and more assurance for what they already had believed.

## C. What Will Our Resurrection Bodies Be Like?

If Christ will raise our bodies from the dead when he returns, and if our bodies will be like his resurrection body (1 Cor. 15:20, 23, 49; Phil. 3:21), then what will our resurrection bodies be like?

Using the example of sowing a seed in the ground and then watching it grow into something much more wonderful, Paul goes on to explain in more detail what our resurrection bodies will be like:

> What is sown is perishable, what is raised is *imperishable*. It is sown in dishonor, it is raised *in glory*. It is sown in weakness, it is raised *in power*. It is sown a physical body, it is raised a *spiritual body*. . . . Just as we have borne the image of the man of dust, we shall also bear the image of the man of heaven. (1 Cor. 15:42–44, 49)

The fact that our new bodies will be "imperishable" means that they will not wear out or grow old or ever be subject to any kind of sickness or disease. They will be completely healthy and strong forever. Moreover, since the gradual process of aging is part of the process by which our bodies now are subject to "corruption," it is appropriate to think that our resurrection bodies will have no sign of aging, but will have the characteristics of youthful but mature manhood or womanhood forever. There will be no evidence of disease or injury, for all will be made perfect.[4] Our resurrection bodies will show the fulfillment of God's perfect wisdom in creating us as human beings who are the pinnacle of his creation and the appropriate bearers of his likeness and image. In these resurrection bodies we will clearly see humanity as God intended it to be.

Paul also says our bodies will be raised "in glory." When this term is contrasted with "dishonor," as it is here, there is a suggestion of the beauty or the attractiveness of appearance that our bodies will have. They will no longer be "dishonorable" or unattractive, but will look "glorious" in their beauty. Moreover, because the word "glory" is so frequently used in Scripture of the bright shining radiance that surrounds the presence of God himself, this term suggests that there will also be a kind of brightness or radiance surrounding our bodies that will be an appropriate outward evidence of the position of exaltation and rule over all creation that God has given to us. This is also suggested in Matthew 13:43, where Jesus says, "Then *the righteous will shine like the sun* in the kingdom of their Father." Similarly, we read in Daniel's vision, "And *those who are wise shall shine like*

---

[4]The fact that the scars of Jesus' nail prints remained on his hands is a special case to remind us of the price he paid for our redemption, and it should not be taken as an indication that any of our scars from physical injuries will remain: see chapter 28, pp. 615–16.

*the brightness of the firmament;* and those who turn many to righteousness, like the stars for ever and ever" (Dan. 12:3, in a passage talking about the final resurrection). Now both of these statements might possibly be understood metaphorically, and in that case they would not indicate that an actual brightness or radiance will surround our resurrection bodies. But there is no reason in the context of either of them that would cause us to see them as metaphorical, and other pieces of evidence argue against doing so. The hints of the age to come that were seen in the shining of the glory of God from the face of Moses (Ex. 34:35), and, in a much greater way, the bright light that shone from Jesus at the transfiguration (Matt. 17:2), together with the fact that we will bear the image of Christ and be like him (1 Cor. 15:49), combine to suggest that there will actually be a visible brightness or radiance that surrounds us when we are in our resurrection bodies.[5]

Our bodies will also be raised "in power" (1 Cor. 15:43). This is in contrast to the "weakness" which we see in our bodies now. Our resurrection bodies will not only be free from disease and aging, they will also be given fullness of strength and power—not infinite power like God, of course, and probably not what we would think of as "superhuman" power in the sense possessed by the "superheroes" in modern fictional children's writing, for example, but nonetheless full and complete human power and strength, the strength that God intended human beings to have in their bodies when he created them. It will therefore be strength that is sufficient to do all that we desire to do in conformity with the will of God.

Finally, Paul says that the body is raised a "spiritual body" (1 Cor. 15:44). In the Pauline epistles, the word "spiritual" (Gk. *pneumatikos*) never means "nonphysical" but rather "consistent with the character and activity of the Holy Spirit" (see, for example, Rom. 1:11; 7:14; 1 Cor. 2:13, 15; 3:1; 14:37; Gal. 6:1 ["you who are spiritual"]; Eph. 5:19). The RSV translation, "It is sown a *physical* body, it is raised a *spiritual* body," is misleading,[6] and a more clear paraphrase would be, "It is sown a *natural* body subject to the characteristics and desires of this age, and governed by its own sinful will, but it is raised a *spiritual* body, completely subject to the will of the Holy Spirit and responsive to the Holy Spirit's guidance." Such a body is not at all "nonphysical," but it is a physical body raised to the degree of perfection for which God originally intended it.

In conclusion, when Christ returns he will give us new resurrection bodies to be like his resurrection body. "When he appears *we shall be like him*" (1 John 3:2; this statement is true not only in an ethical sense but also in terms of our physical bodies; cf. 1 Cor. 15:49; also Rom. 8:29).

In spite of this strong New Testament emphasis on the similarity between our bodies and Jesus' body after the resurrection, some have objected that we will not have physical bodies because Paul says, "*Flesh and blood cannot inherit the kingdom of God,* nor does the perishable inherit the imperishable" (1 Cor. 15:50). This is in the very section in which he has been discussing the resurrection of the dead. But it is surely a misunderstanding to say that this verse implies that we shall not have

---

[5]Jesus' body did not have a bright radiance surrounding it immediately after his resurrection, but when he returned to heaven and received from God the Father the glory that was rightfully his, then "his face was like the sun shining in full strength" (Rev. 1:16). Jesus at his transfiguration gave his disciples only a brief glimpse of the glory that was rightfully his and would be his again in heaven.

[6]See the discussion of the RSV's use of "physical" in 1 Cor. 15:44 in chapter 28, p. 609, n. 3.

physical bodies. When Paul says, "flesh and blood cannot inherit the kingdom of God," what he means by "flesh and blood" is *our present human nature,* particularly our physical bodies, as they are now existing in the likeness of Adam after the fall—that is, subject to weakness, decay, and ultimate death. This is the point he has made in the previous four verses (1 Cor. 15:45–49), in which he has been contrasting Adam with Christ. He explains, "As was the man of dust, so are those who are of the dust" (that is, we ourselves in this present age, 1 Cor. 15:48). Then he explains, "Just as we have borne the image of the man of dust, we shall also bear the image of the man of heaven" (1 Cor. 15:49). By "flesh and blood" here Paul means *"flesh and blood in the present state of existence* with a body like Adam's after the fall, a body is subject to decay and death." He does not mean that we shall exist in a nonphysical state, for the entire heaven and earth will be made new and renewed for us to live in (Rom. 8:18–25), and we ourselves "shall all be changed, in a moment, in the twinkling of an eye, at the last trumpet" (1 Cor. 15:51–52). We will not cease to exist in physical bodies, but we will be changed and we will have an imperishable body, "For this perishable nature must put on the imperishable, and this mortal nature must put on immortality" (1 Cor. 15:53).

Moreover, the repeated instances in which Jesus demonstrated to the disciples that he had a physical body that was able to be touched, that had flesh and bones (Luke 24:39), and that could eat food, show that Jesus' body, which is our pattern, was clearly a physical body that had been made perfect.[7]

What kind of continuity will there be between our present bodies and our future resurrection bodies? Will our bodies look exactly the same and have exactly the same characteristics, or will they be somewhat different, or will they be almost entirely different? Moreover, will our resurrection bodies be made of the same molecules of which our earthly bodies consist, or will they be an entirely new creation from God, or will they be some combination of old and new?

Several passages indicate that Paul expected a considerable measure of continuity between our present earthly bodies and our future resurrection bodies. Paul said, "He who raised Christ Jesus from the dead will give life to *your mortal bodies* also through his Spirit which dwells in you" (Rom. 8:11). He said that Jesus "will change *our lowly body* to be like his glorious body" (Phil. 3:21). And when Paul spoke about the nature of the resurrection body he gave an example of a seed sown in the ground: "What you sow is not the body which is to be, but a bare kernel, perhaps of wheat or of some other grain. But God gives it a body as he has chosen, and to each kind of seed its own body" (1 Cor. 15:37–38). In this example, he draws on common human knowledge that there are differences between what is sown and what is raised (vv. 42–44), but there is also continuity—just as a seed grows into a larger plant, retaining the matter that was in it but taking to itself other materials from the ground as well, so we will have continuity and differences as well. On this analogy we can say that *whatever remains in the grave from our own physical bodies* will be taken by God and transformed and used to make a new resurrection body. But the details of how that will happen remain unclear to us, since Scripture does not specify them—we

---

[7]See chapter 28, pp. 608–13, for a discussion of the nature of Christ's resurrection body.

are to affirm this because Scripture teaches it, even if we cannot fully explain how it can happen.[8]

Another indication of significant continuity between our present bodies and the bodies that we will have is seen in the fact that those believers who remain alive on the day Christ returns will "be changed"—yet their bodies will not be replaced: "We shall not all sleep, but we shall all be *changed,* in a moment, in the twinkling of an eye, at the last trumpet. For the trumpet will sound, and the dead will be raised imperishable, and we shall be changed. For this perishable nature must put on the imperishable, and this mortal nature must put on immortality" (1 Cor. 15:51–53).

We must also clearly note that Christ's own resurrection body, though it differed somewhat from the body he had before he died, so that the disciples did not immediately recognize him in every situation, was similar enough in appearance for the disciples to know who it was rather quickly. There were some instances when they did not immediately recognize him, but this may in part be accounted for by the fact that during his earthly life and ministry he had no doubt aged considerably, since he was "a man of sorrows and acquainted with grief" (Isa. 53:3). After his resurrection, Jesus would have been restored to full and perfect strength and youthfulness of appearance. Just as we sometimes do not immediately recognize a friend who has aged considerably since the last time we saw him or her, so the disciples may have had initial difficulty in recognizing Christ because the opposite of aging had occurred.[9] On the other hand, significant continuity between Jesus' body before and after the resurrection is seen in the fact that even the nail prints in his hands and feet and the wound in his side remained in his resurrection body (John 20:20, 27).

Another piece of evidence indicating continuity between our earthly and heavenly bodies is the fact that apparently people will recognize and know one another in heaven. Jesus says that people will come from east and west and "sit at the table with Abraham, Isaac, and Jacob in the kingdom of heaven" (Matt. 8:11). Moreover, Elijah, who had been taken up to heaven in his earthly body, was somehow recognizable to the disciples on the Mount of Transfiguration (Luke 9:30, 33)—of course, the disciples had not known Elijah or Moses in the flesh, but somehow these men retained their personal identities in such a way that the disciples believed that they were there and that they were just as real as Jesus was (see Luke 9:33). Finally, Matthew tells us that when Jesus died, "the tombs also were opened, and many *bodies* of the saints who had fallen asleep were raised, and coming out of the tombs after his resurrection they went into the holy city and appeared to many" (Matt. 27:52–53). The fact that these people's actual bodies were raised, and the fact that they appeared to many in Jerusalem, indicates again that there was some continuity between their dead bodies that were in the graves and the bodies that were raised up. Since they came out of the tombs "after his resurrection" we may assume that these also were saints who had received

---

[8]Someone may object that some bodies completely decay, are absorbed into plants, and then eventually into other bodies, so that nothing of the first body can be found. But in response we must simply say that God can keep track of enough of the elements from each body to form a "seed" from which to form a new body (see Gen. 50:25; Job 19:26; Ezek. 37:1–14; Heb. 11:22).

[9]See discussion on the failure of disciples to recognize Christ at once after his resurrection in chapter 28, p. 609.

resurrection bodies as a kind of foretaste of the final day of glorification when Christ returns.[10] The fact that these people "appeared to many" suggests that they were recognizable—that people knew who they were. Again the evidence is suggestive rather than conclusive, yet it points in the direction of continuity between the body that existed before the resurrection and the one that existed after it.

There is today some hesitancy on the part of many evangelicals to affirm clearly that there will be a "resurrection of the body," or at least that the body that is raised will be a material, physical body that is in some way continuous with the body that was placed in the grave. To some measure, this may be due to a sense of inability to understand how God could raise the same bodies from the grave, especially when some of those bodies had been dead for many centuries. Yet some of this hesitancy is probably also due to the continuing skepticism of unbelievers who challenge the Christian view with exactly the kind of problems just presented—does this not seem like a fantastic, unbelievable position? How could God bring about such a thing?

In both cases—whether the hesitancy comes from the honest questioning of the believer or from the hostile skepticism of the unbeliever—we should realize that our inability to understand or explain something should never be a reason for rejecting it if it is clearly taught in Scripture. The many passages cited above indicating that God will raise *our mortal bodies from the grave,* just as he raised Jesus' body from the grave, indicate quite conclusively that there will be a definite continuity between our present bodies and the bodies we have in the resurrection. And if that is what Scripture teaches, then, even though we may not understand exactly *how* God will bring this about in every case, we should still believe it. The God who created the universe and created each one of us, and who sovereignly rules over every bit of this creation at every moment, and who carries along all things by his word of power, can certainly keep track of the parts of our physical bodies that he wishes to preserve and use as the "seed" from which a new body will be made.

It is important to insist on the resurrection of a real, physical body, not only for the reasons above, but also because this provides a clear affirmation of the goodness of God's physical creation. We will live in bodies that have all the excellent qualities God created us to have, and thereby we will forever be living proof of the wisdom of God in making a material creation that from the beginning was "very good" (Gen. 1:31). We will live as resurrected believers in those new bodies, and they will be suitable for inhabiting the "new heavens and a new earth in which righteousness dwells" (2 Peter 3:13).

## D. The Entire Creation Will Be Renewed As Well

When Adam sinned God cursed the ground because of him (Gen. 3:17–19), so that it brought forth thorns and thistles and would only yield food useful for mankind by painful toil. But Paul says that "the creation itself will be set free from its bondage to decay and obtain the glorious liberty of the children of God" (Rom. 8:21). He explains that this will happen when we receive our resurrection

---

[10]See discussion of this passage in D. A. Carson, *Matthew,* in EBC, 8:581–82.

bodies—in fact, he says that the creation is somehow longing for that day: "For the creation waits with eager longing for the revealing of the sons of God. . . . We know that the whole creation has been groaning in travail together until now; and not only the creation, but we ourselves, who have the first fruits of the Spirit, groan inwardly as we wait for adoption as sons, the redemption of our bodies" (Rom. 8:19, 22–23). In this renewed creation, there will be no more thorns or thistles, no more floods or droughts, no more deserts or uninhabitable jungles, no more earthquakes or tornadoes, no more poisonous snakes or bees that sting or mushrooms that kill. There will be a productive earth, an earth that will blossom and produce food abundantly for our enjoyment. (See chapter 57 for further discussion of the renewed earth.)

### E. The Unbelieving Dead Will Be Raised for Judgment on the Day of Final Judgment

Although the emphasis of Scripture is on the fact that believers will experience a bodily resurrection, there are some passages that state that *unbelievers* will also be raised from the dead, but that they will face the final judgment at the time they are raised. Jesus clearly teaches that "those who have done evil" will come forth "to *the resurrection of judgment*" (John 5:29); Paul also said that he believed "that there will be a resurrection of both the just *and the unjust*" (Acts 24:15; cf. Matt. 25:31–46; Dan. 12:2). (See chapter 56 for further discussion of the final judgment of unbelievers.)

### QUESTIONS FOR PERSONAL APPLICATION

1. Paul says that the expectation of a future bodily resurrection is the "hope" in which we were saved (Rom. 8:24). Is the hope of a future resurrection of your body one of the major things you look forward to in the future? If not, why not? What could increase your hope in the future resurrection of the body?

2. So strong was Paul's longing for the future day of resurrection, and so aware was he of the hardships that we still suffer in this life, that he could say, "If for this life only we have hoped in Christ, we are of all men most to be pitied" (1 Cor. 15:19), and, "If the dead are not raised, 'Let us eat and drink, for tomorrow we die'" (1 Cor. 15:32). Do you have a great longing for the future resurrection that gives you this kind of sentiment in your heart as well? If not, why do you not have the same perspective on the resurrection of the body that Paul did?

3. What do you think might occur in your life to give you a greater longing for the resurrection of your body? If you have a grandfather or grandmother or other older friend or relative who has died and gone to be with Christ, what do you think that person will look like on the day of resurrection? Can you imagine what it will be like meeting that person and becoming acquainted again? How will your relationship be different from what it was in this life?

## SPECIAL TERMS

glorification
spiritual body

## BIBLIOGRAPHY

(For an explanation of this bibliography see the note on the bibliography to chapter 1, p. 38. Complete bibliographical data may be found on pp. 1223–29.)

### Sections in Evangelical Systematic Theologies

1. Anglican (Episcopalian)
    1882–92    Litton, 585–91
2. Arminian (Wesleyan or Methodist)
    1875–76    Pope, 3:401–11
    1892–94    Miley, 2:448–58
    1940    Wiley, 3:320–38
    1960    Purkiser, 561–67
    1983    Carter, 2:1116–18
3. Baptist
    1767    Gill, 2:211–30
    1887    Boyce, 454–61
    1907    Strong, 1015–23
    1917    Mullins, 472–78
    1983–85    Erickson, 997–1002, 1194–1200
4. Dispensational
    1947    Chafer, 3:366–69
    1949    Thiessen, 376–83
    1986    Ryrie, 517–18
5. Lutheran
    1917–24    Pieper, 3:534–39
    1934    Mueller, 625–30
6. Reformed (or Presbyterian)
    1559    Calvin, 2:987–1008 (3.25)
    1861    Heppe, 695–712
    1871–73    Hodge, 3:771–89
    1878    Dabney, 829–41
    1889    Shedd, 2b:647–58
    1937–66    Murray, *CW*, 2:403–13; *RAA*, 174–81
    1938    Berkhof, 720–27
    1962    Buswell, 2:324–46
7. Renewal (or charismatic/Pentecostal)
    1988–92    Williams, 3:397–413

## Sections in Representative Roman Catholic Systematic Theologies

1. Roman Catholic: Traditional
   1955     Ott, 488–92
2. Roman Catholic: Post-Vatican II
   1980     McBrien, 2:1147–50

## Other Works

Gaffin, Richard B., Jr. *Resurrection and Redemption: A Study in Paul's Soteriology.* Formerly, *The Centrality of the Resurrection: A Study in Paul's Soteriology.* Phillipsburg, N.J.: Presbyterian and Reformed, 1978.

Grider, J. K. "Glorification." In *EDT*, pp. 442–43.

Gundry, Robert N. *Sōma in Biblical Theology.* Cambridge: Cambridge University Press, 1975.

Harris, Murray J. *From Grave to Glory: Resurrection in the New Testament, Including a Response to Norman L. Geisler.* Grand Rapids: Zondervan, 1990, pp. 185–287.

———. *Raised Immortal: Resurrection and Immortality in the New Testament.* Grand Rapids: Eerdmans, 1983.

———. "Resurrection, General." In *NDT*, pp. 581–82.

Hoekema, Anthony A. "The Resurrection of the Body." In *The Bible and the Future.* Grand Rapids: Eerdmans, 1979, pp. 239–52.

Murray, John. "Glorification." In *Redemption Accomplished and Applied.* Grand Rapids: Eerdmans, 1955, pp. 174–81.

Schep, J. A. *The Nature of the Resurrection Body.* Grand Rapids: Eerdmans, 1964.

White, R. E. O. "Resurrection of the Dead." In *EDT*, pp. 941–44.

## SCRIPTURE MEMORY PASSAGE

**1 Corinthians 15:42–44:** *So is it with the resurrection of the dead. What is sown is perishable, what is raised is imperishable. It is sown in dishonor, it is raised in glory. It is sown in weakness, it is raised in power. It is sown a physical body, it is raised a spiritual body. If there is a physical body, there is also a spiritual body.*

## HYMN

### "Ten Thousand Times Ten Thousand"

This hymn was written by Henry Alford, a New Testament professor at Cambridge University, England, and one of the greatest Greek scholars of the nineteenth century. The hymn pictures thousands of glorified believers streaming through the gates of heaven on the day of Christ's return, and ends with a prayer that Christ would come back quickly.

Ten thousand times ten thousand in sparkling raiment bright,
   The armies of the ransomed saints throng up the steeps of light:
'Tis finished, all is finished, their fight with death and sin:
   Fling open wide the golden gates, and let the victors in.

What rush of alleluias fills all the earth and sky!
    What ringing of a thousand harps bespeaks the triumph nigh!
O day, for which creation and all its tribes were made;
    O joy, for all its former woes a thousand-fold repaid!

O then what raptured greetings on Canaan's happy shore;
    What knitting severed friendships up where partings are no more!
Then eyes with joy shall sparkle, that brimmed with tears of late;
    Orphans no longer fatherless, nor widows desolate.

Bring near thy great salvation, thou Lamb for sinners slain;
    Fill up the roll of thine elect, then take thy pow'r, and reign:
Appear, desire of nations, thine exiles long for home;
    Show in the heav'n thy promised sign; thou Prince and Saviour,
    come.

AUTHOR: HENRY ALFORD, 1867

# Chapter 43

# Union With Christ

*What does it mean to be "in Christ" or "united with Christ"?*

## EXPLANATION AND SCRIPTURAL BASIS[1]

Although we have now completed our study of the steps in the application of redemption, one other subject is so frequently mentioned in Scripture and so wide-ranging in its application to our lives that it deserves a separate treatment here. That is the concept of union with Christ. As we shall see below, *every aspect* of God's relationship to believers is in some way connected to our relationship with Christ. From God's counsels in eternity past before the world was created, to our fellowship with God in heaven in eternity future, and including every aspect of our relationship with God in this life—all has occurred in union with Christ. So in one sense the entire study of the application of redemption could be included in this subject. However, in this chapter we can simply summarize the incredible richness of the scriptural idea of union with Christ. John Murray says:

> Union with Christ has its source in the election of God the Father before the foundation of the world and has its fruition in the glorification of the sons of God. The perspective of God's people is not narrow; it is broad and it is long. It is not confined to space and time; it has the expanse of eternity. Its orbit has two foci, one the electing love of God the Father in the counsels of eternity; the other glorification with Christ in the manifestation of his glory. The former has no beginning, the latter has no end. . . . Why does the believer entertain the thought of God's determinate counsel with such joy? Why can he have patience in the perplexities and adversities of the present? Why can he have confident assurance with reference to the future and rejoice in hope of the glory of God? It is because he cannot think of past, present, or future apart from union with Christ.[2]

We may define *union with Christ* as follows: *Union with Christ is a phrase used to summarize several different relationships between believers and Christ, through which Christians receive every benefit of salvation. These relationships include the fact that we are in Christ, Christ is in us, we are like Christ, and we are with Christ.*

As this definition indicates, four different aspects of our union with Christ may be specified from the biblical material. We will look at each of these four in turn:

---

[1] The material in this chapter is taken from an essay written for Tyndale House Publishers (Wheaton, Ill.). Used by permission.

[2] John Murray, *Redemption Accomplished and Applied*, p. 164.

1. We are in Christ.
2. Christ is in us.
3. We are like Christ.
4. We are with Christ.[3]

## A. We Are in Christ

The phrase "in Christ" does not have one single sense, but refers to a variety of relationships, as indicated below.

**1. In God's Eternal Plan.** Ephesians 1:4 tells us that, God *chose us in Christ* "before the foundation of the world." It was "in Christ" that we were "destined and appointed to live for the praise of his glory" (vv. 1:11–12). Later he "saved us and called us" because of "his own purpose" and because of the grace which he gave us *"in Christ Jesus before the beginning of time"* (2 Tim. 1:9 NIV).

Since we did not exist before the foundation of the world, these verses indicate that God, looking into the future and knowing that we would exist, thought of us being in a special relationship with Christ. He did not first choose us and later decide to relate us to Christ. Rather, while choosing us, he at the same time thought about us as belonging to Christ in a special way, as being "in Christ." Therefore, he thought about us as eventually having the right to share in the blessings of Christ's work.

**2. During Christ's Life on Earth.** Throughout Christ's entire life on earth, from the time of his birth to the time of his ascension into heaven, God thought of us as being "in Christ." That is, whatever Christ did as our representative, God counted it as being something we did, too. Of course, believers were not consciously present in Christ, since most believers did not even exist yet when Christ was on earth. Nor were believers present in Christ in some mysterious, spiritual way (as if, for example, the souls of thousands of believers were somehow present in Christ's body during his earthly life). Rather, believers were present in Christ *only in God's thoughts.* God *thought of us* as going through everything that Christ went through, because he was our representative.

When Jesus perfectly obeyed God for his whole life, God thought of us as having obeyed, too. "By one man's obedience many will be made righteous" (Rom. 5:19). So Christ is our source of righteousness (1 Cor. 1:30; Phil. 3:9).

Because God thought of us as being "in" Christ, he also could think of our sins as belonging to Christ: "God made him who had no sin to be sin for us" (2 Cor. 5:21 NIV), and "the LORD has laid on him the iniquity of us all" (Isa. 53:6). These were sins we had not yet committed, but God knew about them in advance, and thought of them as belonging to Christ. Thus, it was right that Christ should die for our sins. "He himself bore our sins in his body on the tree" (1 Peter 2:24; see also Rom. 4:25; 1 Cor. 15:3; Col. 2:14; Heb. 9:28).

But it was not just our sins that God thought of as belonging to Christ: it was

---

[3]Union with Christ is also sometimes referred to as the "mystical union." This is because we do not fully understand the workings of these relationships with Christ, and because we know about them only through God's revelation in Scripture.

we ourselves. When Christ died, God thought of us as having died. Our old self was *"crucified with him"* (Rom. 6:6). "I have been crucified with Christ" (Gal. 2:20). "One has died for all; therefore all have died" (2 Cor. 5:14; see also Rom. 6:4–5, 8; 7:4; Col. 1:22; 2:12, 20; 3:3; 2 Tim. 2:11).

In the same way, God thought of us as having been *buried* with Christ, *raised* with him, and *taken up to heaven* with him in glory. "God *raised us up with Christ* and *seated us with him* in the heavenly realms in Christ Jesus" (Eph. 2:6 NIV; see also Rom. 6:4–11; 1 Cor. 15:22; Col. 2:12–13).

When Christ returned to heaven, therefore, all the blessings of salvation were earned for us. God thought of these blessings as being rightfully ours, just as if we had earned them ourselves. Nevertheless, they were stored up for us in heaven— in God's mind, actually, and in Christ, our representative—waiting to be applied to us personally (1 Peter 1:3–5; Col. 3:3–4; Eph. 1:3).

**3. During Our Lives Now.** Once we have been born and exist as real people in the world, our union with Christ can no longer be something just in God's mind. We also must be brought into an actual relationship with Christ through which the benefits of salvation can be applied to our lives by the Holy Spirit. The richness of our present life in Christ can be viewed from four slightly different perspectives:

1. We have died and been raised with Christ.
2. We have new life in Christ.
3. All our actions can be done in Christ.
4. All Christians together are one body in Christ.

**a. Dying and Rising With Christ:** The death, burial, and resurrection of Jesus now have real effects in our lives. "You were *buried with him* in baptism, in which you were also *raised with him* through faith in the working of God, who raised him from the dead" (Col. 2:12). Here Paul's references to baptism and faith indicate that our dying and rising with Christ occur in this present life, at the time we become Christians.

Paul sees this present death and resurrection with Christ as a way of describing and explaining the change that the Holy Spirit brings about in our character and personality when we become Christians. It is as if the Holy Spirit reproduces Jesus' death and resurrection in our lives when we believe in Christ. We become so unresponsive to the pressures, demands and attractions of our previous, sinful way of life, that Paul can say we are "dead" to these influences, because we have died with Christ (Rom. 7:6; Gal. 2:20; 5:24; 6:14; Col. 2:20). On the other hand, we find ourselves wanting to serve God much more, and able to serve him with greater power and success, so much so that Paul says we are "alive" to God, because we have been raised up with Christ: "We were buried therefore with him by baptism into death, so that as Christ was raised from the dead by the glory of the Father, we too might *walk in newness of life*" (Rom. 6:4). "So you also must consider yourselves dead to sin and *alive to God* in Christ Jesus" (Rom. 6:11; see also 1 Peter 1:3; 2:24). Because we died and rose with Christ, we have power to overcome personal sin more and more (Rom. 6:12–14, 19); we have come to "fullness of life" in Christ (Col. 2:10–13); in fact, we have become a "new creation" in him (2 Cor. 5:17, with vv. 14–15), and should therefore set our minds on things that are above, where Christ is (Col. 3:1–3).

**b. New Life in Christ:** These last verses suggest a second perspective on our being "in Christ." We can think not only in terms of Christ's past work of redemption, but also in terms of his present life in heaven, and his continuing possession of all the spiritual resources we need to live the Christian life. Since every spiritual blessing was earned by him and belongs to him, the New Testament can say that these blessings are "in him." Thus, they are available only to those who are "in Christ," and if we are in Christ, these blessings are ours.

John writes, "God gave us eternal life, and this life is *in his Son*" (1John 5:11), and Paul speaks of "the promise of the life which is *in Christ Jesus*" (2 Tim. 1:1). We read that *"in Christ"* are "faith and love" (1 Tim. 1:14; 2 Tim. 1:13), "grace" (2 Tim. 2:1), "salvation" (2 Tim. 2:10), "all the treasures of wisdom and knowledge" (Col. 2:3) and God's "riches in glory" (Phil. 4:19). Paul says that it is because of God's work that Christians are "in Christ Jesus, whom God made our wisdom, our righteousness and sanctification and redemption" (1 Cor. 1:30), and that "God . . . has blessed us in the heavenly realms with *every spiritual blessing in Christ*" (Eph. 1:3).

In fact, every stage of the application of redemption is given to us because we are "in Christ." It is "in Christ" that we are *called* to salvation (1 Cor. 7:22), *regenerated* (Eph. 1:3; 2:10), and *justified* (Rom. 8:1; 2 Cor. 5:21; Gal. 2:17; Eph. 1:7; Phil. 3:9; Col. 1:14). "In Christ" we *die* (1 Thess. 4:16; Rev. 14:13) and "in him" our bodies *will be raised* up again (1 Cor. 15:22). These passages suggest that because our lives are inseparably connected to Christ himself, the Holy Spirit gives us all the blessings that Christ has earned.

**c. All Our Actions Can Be Done in Christ:** The foregoing changes within our individual lives are accompanied by a dramatic change in the realm in which we live. To become a Christian is to enter the newness of the age to come, and to experience to some degree the new powers of the kingdom of God affecting every part of our lives. To be "in Christ" is to be in that new realm that Christ controls.

This means that every action in our lives can be done "in Christ," if it is done in the power of his kingdom and in a way that brings honor to him. Paul *speaks* the truth "in Christ" (Rom. 9:1; 2 Cor. 2:17; 12:19), *is proud* of his work "in Christ" (Rom. 15:17; 1 Cor. 15:31), reminds the Corinthians of his *ways* "in Christ" (1 Cor. 4:17), *hopes* "in the Lord Jesus" to send Timothy to Philippi (Phil. 2:19), *rejoices* greatly "in the Lord" (Phil. 4:10), and "in the Lord" *commands, beseeches,* and *exhorts* other Christians (1 Thess. 4:1; 2 Thess. 3:12; Philem. 8). He says, "I can *do all things* in him who strengthens me" (Phil. 4:13).

Paul also writes to believers about their actions "in Christ." He reminds the Corinthians, "in the Lord your *labor* is not in vain" (1 Cor. 15:58). It is "in the Lord" that children are to *obey* their parents (Eph. 6:1), wives are to *submit* to their husbands (Col. 3:18), and all believers are to *be strong* (Eph. 6:10), *be encouraged* (Phil. 2:1), *rejoice* (Phil. 3:10; 4:4), *agree* (Phil. 4:2), *stand firm* (Phil. 4:1; 1 Thess. 3:8), *live a godly life* (2 Tim. 3:12) and have *good behavior* (1 Peter 3:16). "In the Lord" they *work hard* (Rom. 16:12), *are made confident* (Phil. 1:14) and *are approved* (Rom. 16:10). Paul's hope for Christians is that they *live* in Christ: "Just as you received Christ Jesus as Lord, continue to live in him, rooted and built up in him" (Col. 2:6–7 NIV). Then Paul will achieve his life's goal, to "present every man *mature* in Christ" (Col. 1:28). John similarly encourages believers to "*abide* in him" (1 John 2:28; 3:6, 24), echoing Jesus' words, "He who abides in me, and I in him, he it is that bears much fruit" (John 15:5).

**d. One Body in Christ:** We are not simply in Christ as isolated individual persons. Since Christ is the head of the body, which is the church (Eph. 5:23), all who are in union with Christ are also related to one another in his body. This joining together makes us "one body in Christ, and individually *members one of another*" (Rom. 12:5; 1 Cor. 10:17; 12:12–27). Thus, "If one member suffers, all suffer together; if one member is honored, all rejoice together" (1 Cor. 12:26). The ties of fellowship are so strong that Christians may only marry "in the Lord" (1 Cor. 7:39). In this body of Christ old hostilities disappear, sinful divisions among people are broken down, and worldly criteria of status no longer apply, for "There is neither Jew nor Greek, there is neither slave nor free, there is neither male nor female; for you are all one in Christ Jesus" (Gal. 3:28; cf. Eph. 2:13–22).

Because we are one body in Christ, entire churches can be "in Christ" (Gal. 1:22; 1 Thess. 2:14). And the church universal, the church made up of all true believers, is collectively united to Christ as a husband is united to his wife (Eph. 5:31–32; 1 Cor. 6:17). Christ's purpose is to perfect and cleanse and purify the church, so that it might more completely reflect what he is like and thereby bring glory to him (Eph. 5:25–27).

Yet another metaphor is used in 1 Peter 2:4–5, where believers, in coming to Christ, are said to be like living stones, built into a spiritual house (see also Eph. 2:20–22). Thus, they are unified and forever dependent on one another, just as the stones of a building are united to each other and depend upon each other.

But the boldest analogy of all is used by Jesus, who prays for believers "*that they may all be one; even as you, Father, are in me, and I in you, that they also may be in us*" (John 17:21). Here Jesus prays that our unity would be like the perfect unity between the Father and the Son in the Trinity. This is a reminder to us that our unity should be eternal and perfectly harmonious (as God's unity is).

But this analogy with the members of the Trinity is very important for another reason: it warns us against thinking that union with Christ will ever swallow up our individual personalities. Even though the Father, Son, and Holy Spirit have perfect and eternal unity, yet they remain distinct persons. In the same way, even though we shall someday attain *perfect unity* with other believers and with Christ, yet we shall forever remain *distinct persons* as well, with our own individual gifts, abilities, interests, responsibilities, circles of personal relationships, preferences, and desires.

## B. Christ Is in Us

Jesus spoke of a second kind of relationship when he said, "He who abides in me, and *I in him*, he it is that bears much fruit" (John 15:5). It is not only true that we are in Christ; he is also in us, to give us power to live the Christian life. "I have been crucified with Christ; it is no longer I who live, but *Christ who lives in me*" (Gal. 2:20). The factor that determines whether someone is a Christian is whether Christ is in him (Rom. 8:10; 2 Cor. 13:5; Rev. 3:20). God's wise plan, hidden as a mystery for generations, was to save Gentiles as well as Jews. Therefore, Paul can tell his Gentile readers that God's mystery is "*Christ in you*, the hope of glory" (Col. 1:27).

It is important to maintain, on the basis of these verses, that there is a real, personal dwelling of Christ in us, and that this does not mean that we merely agree with Christ or that his ideas are in us. Rather, *he* is in us and remains in us through faith (Eph. 3:17; 2 Cor. 13:5).[4] To overlook this truth would be to neglect the great source of spiritual strength that we have within us (1 John 4:4). To remember it destroys our pride, gives us a constant feeling of deep dependence on Christ, and gives us great confidence, not in self, but in Christ working in us (Gal. 2:20; Rom. 15:18; Phil. 4:13).

This indwelling of Christ affects our response to those in need. Whatever we do to help a Christian brother or sister, we do to Christ (Matt. 25:40). Keeping Jesus' commandments is an indication that he is in us, and the Holy Spirit also bears witness to us that Christ is in us (1 John 3:24).

## C. We Are Like Christ

A third aspect of union with Christ is our *imitation of him*. "Be imitators of me, as I am of Christ," writes Paul (1 Cor. 11:1). John reminds us, "He who says he abides in him ought to walk in the same way in which he walked" (1 John 2:6). So union with Christ implies that we should imitate Christ. Our lives ought so to reflect what his life was like that we bring honor to him in everything we do (Phil. 1:20).

Thus, the New Testament pictures the Christian life as one of striving to imitate Christ in all our actions. "Welcome one another, therefore, *as Christ has welcomed you*" (Rom. 15:7). "Husbands, love your wives, *as Christ loved the church*" (Eph. 5:25). "*As the Lord has forgiven you*, so you also must forgive" (Col. 3:13). "He laid down his life for us; and we ought to lay down our lives for the brethren" (1 John 3:16). Throughout our lives, we are to run the race before us, "looking to Jesus, the pioneer and perfecter of our faith" (Heb. 13:2; see also Eph. 5:2; Phil. 2:5–11; 1 Thess. 1:6; 1 John 3:7; 4:17). By contrast, disobedience to Christ holds him up in contempt (Heb. 6:6).

Our imitation of Christ is especially evident in suffering. Christians are called to take suffering patiently, "because Christ also suffered for you, leaving you an example, that you should *follow in his steps*" (1 Peter 2:21). Paul's goal is to "share his [Christ's] sufferings, becoming *like him in his death*" (Phil. 3:10; see also 2 Cor. 1:5; 4:8–11; Heb. 12:3; 1 Peter 4:13).

Furthermore, our suffering is connected with sharing in Christ's glory when he returns: "we suffer with him in order that we may also be glorified with him" (Rom. 8:17). This is probably because it is through suffering and difficulty that

---

[4]See chapter 26, pp. 548, 558–59, on the way in which Christ's divine nature is omnipresent but his human nature is not.

God makes us more Christ-like and causes us to grow to maturity in Christ (James 1:2–4; Heb. 5:8–9). Also, since Christ perfectly obeyed his Father even in the face of great suffering, so our obedience, trust, and patience in suffering more fully portray what Christ was like, and so bring more honor to him. It gives us great comfort to know that we are only experiencing what he has already experienced, and that he therefore understands what we are going through, and listens sympathetically to our prayers (Heb. 2:18; 4:15–16; 12:11). As the outcome of a life of obedience, we are able to share in Christ's glory: "He who conquers, I will grant him to sit with me on my throne, as I myself conquered and sat down with my Father on his throne" (Rev. 3:21).

Our imitation of Christ should not be thought of as a mere mimicking of Jesus' actions, however. The far deeper purpose is that in imitating him we are becoming more and more like him: *when we act like Christ we become like Christ*. We grow up to maturity in Christ (Eph. 4:13, 15) as we are "being changed into his likeness from one degree of glory to another" (2 Cor. 3:18). The final result is that we shall become perfectly like Christ, for God has predestined us "to be conformed to the image of his Son" (Rom. 8:29; 1 Cor. 15:49), and "when he appears, *we shall be like him*" (1 John 3:2). When this happens, Christ will be fully glorified in us (2 Thess. 1:10–12; John 17:10).

Yet in all of this we never lose our individual personhood. We become perfectly *like* Christ, but *we do not become Christ,* and we are not absorbed into Christ or lost forever as individuals. Rather, it is we as real individuals who shall still know as we are known (1 Cor. 13:12); it is we who shall see him as he is (1 John 3:2); it is we who shall worship him, and see his face, and have his name on our foreheads, and reign with him for ever and ever (Rev. 22:3–5).

Just as the Father, Son, and Holy Spirit are exactly like one another in character (John 14:7, 9), yet remain distinct persons, so we can become more and more like Christ and still be distinct individuals with different gifts and different functions (Eph. 4:15–16; 1 Cor. 12:4–27). In fact, the more like Christ we become, the more truly ourselves we become (Matt. 10:39; John 10:3; Rev. 2:17; Ps. 37:4). If we forget this, we will tend to neglect the diversity of gifts in the church and will want to make everyone like ourselves. We will also tend to deny any ultimate importance for ourselves as individuals. A proper biblical perspective will allow each believer to say not only, "We Christians are important to Christ," but also, "*I* am important to Christ: he knows my name, he calls me by name, he gives me a new name which is mine alone" (John 10:3; Rev. 2:17).

## D. We Are With Christ

**1. Personal Fellowship With Christ.** Another aspect of union with Christ concerns our personal fellowship with him. It makes little difference whether we say that we are with Christ or that Christ is with us, for both phrases represent the same truth. Christ promised, "Where two or three are gathered in my name, there am I in the midst of them" (Matt. 18:20), and, "I am *with you* always, to the close of the age" (Matt. 28:20). Once again, since Jesus' human body ascended to heaven (John 16:7; 17:11; Acts 1:9–11), these verses must speak of his divine nature being present with us. Yet it is still a very personal presence, in which we *work* together with Christ (2 Cor. 6:1), we *know* him (Phil. 3:8, 10), we are *comforted* by him (2 Thess. 2:16–17), we are *taught* by him (Matt. 11:29), and we live our whole lives *in his presence* (2 Cor. 2:10; 1 Tim. 5:21; 6:13–14; 2 Tim. 4:1). To become a Christian is to be "called into the *fellowship* of [God's] Son, Jesus Christ our Lord" (1 Cor. 1:9). Yet this fellowship can vary in intensity, since Paul's benediction on Christians, "The Lord be with you all" (2 Thess. 3:16; cf. 2 Tim. 4:22) can only express a hope for still closer fellowship with Christ and a deeper awareness of his presence.

Furthermore, in some sense yet imperceptible to us, when we come to worship we now come into heaven itself, to "innumerable angels in festal gathering, and to the assembly of the first-born who are enrolled in heaven, and to a judge who is God of all, and to the spirits of just men made perfect, *and to Jesus,* the mediator of a new covenant" (Heb. 12:22–24). This participation in heavenly worship is what the Apostles' Creed calls the "communion of saints," and what a familiar hymn calls "mystic, sweet communion with those whose rest is won."[5] Hebrews 12 does not seem to suggest that we have a conscious awareness of being in the presence of this heavenly assembly, but it may indicate that those now in heaven witness our worship and rejoice in it, and it certainly implies that we can have a joyful awareness that our praise is being heard in God's temple in heaven.

In all our prayers now we are heard by Jesus and have fellowship with him (1 John 1:3), our great high priest, who has entered "into heaven itself, now to appear in the presence of God on our behalf" (Heb. 9:24; 4:16). Our fellowship with him will be greater yet when we die (2 Cor. 5:8; Phil. 1:23; 1 Thess. 5:10), and even greater still once Jesus returns (1 Thess. 4:17; 1 John 3:1). It gives us great joy to know that Christ actually desires to have us with him (John 17:24).

Our fellowship with Christ also brings us into fellowship with each other. John writes, "That which we have seen and heard we proclaim also to you, *so that you may have fellowship with us;* and our fellowship is with the Father and with his Son Jesus Christ" (1 John 1:3).

**2. Union With the Father and With the Holy Spirit.** This last verse suggests a final aspect of union with Christ. Because we are in union with Christ in these several relationships, we also are brought into union with the Father and with the Holy Spirit. We are *in the Father* (John 17:21; 1 Thess. 1:1; 2 Thess. 1:1; 1 John 2:24; 4:15–16; 5:20) and *in the Holy Spirit* (Rom. 8:9; 1 Cor. 3:16; 6:19; 2 Tim. 1:14). *The Father is in us* (John 14:23) and *the Holy Spirit is in us* (Rom. 8:9, 11). We are *like the Father* (Matt. 5:44–45, 48; Eph. 4:32; Col. 3:10; 1 Peter 1:15–16) and *like the Holy Spirit* (Rom. 8:4–6; Gal. 5:22–23; John 16:13). We have fellowship *with the Father* (1 John 1:3; Matt. 6:9; 2 Cor. 6:16–18) and *with the Holy Spirit* (Rom. 8:16; Acts 15:28; 2 Cor. 13:14; Eph. 4:30).

These additional relationships are not blurred into a distinctionless, mystical ecstasy, however. Both now and in eternity we relate to the Father in his distinct role as our heavenly Father, to the Son in his distinct role as our Savior and Lord, and to the Holy Spirit in his distinct role as the Spirit who empowers us and continually applies to us all the benefits of our salvation.

---

[5]This phrase is taken from the hymn, "The Church's One Foundation," written in 1866 by Samuel J. Stone.

## QUESTIONS FOR PERSONAL APPLICATION

1. Before reading this chapter, had you thought of yourself as being united with Christ from the point of God's choosing you before the foundation of the world to the point of going to be with him in heaven forever? How does this idea change the way you think of yourself and your own life? How does it affect the way you think of difficulties that you may be experiencing at this time? In what ways can the ideas of having died with Christ and having been raised with him be an encouragement in your present efforts to overcome sin that remains in your life?

2. Have you previously thought of doing the actions that you do each day "in Christ" (see Phil. 4:13)? If you thought of doing the reading that you are presently doing "in Christ," how would it change your attitude or perspective? What difference would it make to think of doing your daily work "in Christ"? What about carrying on conversations with friends or family members? Or eating, or even sleeping?

3. How can the idea of union with Christ increase your love and fellowship for other Christians, both those in your church and those in other churches?

4. Do you have any awareness in your day-to-day life of Christ living in you (Gal. 2:20)? What would change in your life if you had a stronger awareness of Christ living in you throughout the day?

5. For one or two days, try reading some section of the gospels and asking how you might better imitate Christ in your own life. What effect will the idea of following in Christ's steps (1 Peter 1:21) and walking as he walked (1 John 2:6) have in your life?

6. Can you name some times in your life when you have sensed an especially close personal fellowship with Christ? What have those times been like? Can you think of anything that brought about that close fellowship with Christ? What can we do to increase the intensity of our daily fellowship with Christ?

7. In your personal experience, do you relate differently to God the Father, to Jesus Christ, and to the Holy Spirit? Can you describe those differences, if there are any?

## SPECIAL TERMS

being raised with Christ          one body in Christ
dying with Christ                 communion of saints
in Christ                         union with Christ
mystical union

## BIBLIOGRAPHY

(For an explanation of this bibliography see the note on the bibliography to chapter 1, p. 38. Complete bibliographical data may be found on pp. 1223–29.)

Note: This topic has not received explicit treatment in many systematic theologies, but the subjects mentioned in this chapter have been treated in a variety of ways under different topics.

## Sections in Evangelical Systematic Theologies

1. Anglican (Episcopalian)
    1882–92     Litton, 328–30
2. Arminian (Wesleyan or Methodist)
                (no explicit treatment)
3. Baptist
    1907        Strong, 795–809
    1917        Mullins, 409–16
    1983–85     Erickson, 948–54
4. Dispensational
    1949        Thiessen, 278–82
5. Lutheran
                (no explicit treatment)
6. Reformed (or Presbyterian)
    1878        Dabney, 612–17
    1937–66     Murray, *RAA*, 161–73
    1938        Berkhof, 447–53

## Sections in Representative Roman Catholic Systematic Theologies

(no explicit treatment)

## Other Works

Baker, J. P. "Union With Christ." In *NDT*, pp. 697–99.
Gordon, Adoniram Judson. *In Christ; or the Believer's Union with His Lord.* 1872; reprint, Grand Rapids: Baker, 1964. (first published in 1872.)
Murray, John. "Union with Christ." In *Redemption Accomplished and Applied.* Grand Rapids: Eerdmans, 1955, pp. 161–73.
Poythress, Vern. "Using Multiple Thematic Centers in Theological Synthesis: Holiness as a Test Case in Developing a Pauline Theology." Unpublished manuscript available from the Campus Bookstore, Westminster Theological Seminary, P.O. Box 27009, Philadelphia, PA 19118.
Smedes, Lewis B. *Union With Christ: A Biblical View of the New Life in Jesus Christ.* 2d ed. Grand Rapids: Eerdmans, 1983.
Walvoord, J. F. "Identification With Christ." In *EDT*, p. 542.

## SCRIPTURE MEMORY PASSAGE

**Galatians 2:20:** *I have been crucified with Christ; it is no longer I who live, but Christ who lives in me; and the life I now live in the flesh I live by faith in the Son of God, who loved me and gave himself for me.*

## HYMN

### "Jesus, Thou Joy of Loving Hearts"

This hymn has been attributed to Bernard of Clairvaux (1090–1153), a monk known for his love of God and deep piety. Other hymns attributed to him are "Jesus, the Very Thought of Thee" and "O Sacred Head Now Wounded." Though written eight hundred years ago, this hymn remains one of the most beautiful expressions of love for Christ in the history of the church.

Jesus, thou joy of loving hearts,
    Thou fount of life, thou light of men,
From the best bliss that earth imparts
    We turn unfilled to thee again.

Thy truth unchanged hath ever stood;
    Thou savest those that on thee call;
To them that seek thee thou art good,
    To them that find thee all in all.

We taste thee, O thou living bread,
    And long to feast upon thee still;
We drink of thee, the fountain-head,
    And thirst our souls from thee to fill.

Our restless spirits yearn for thee,
    Where'er our changeful lot is cast;
Glad when thy gracious smile we see,
    Blest when our faith can hold thee fast.

O Jesus, ever with us stay,
    Make all our moments calm and bright;
Chase the dark night of sin away,
    Shed o'er the world thy holy light.

AUTHOR: BERNARD OF CLAIRVAUX, C. 1150

# Part 6

# The Doctrine of the Church

# Chapter 44

# The Church: Its Nature, Its Marks, and Its Purposes

*What is necessary to make a church? How can we recognize a true church? The purposes of the church.*

## EXPLANATION AND SCRIPTURAL BASIS

### A. The Nature of the Church

**1. Definition:** *The church is the community of all true believers for all time.* This definition understands the church to be made of all those who are truly saved. Paul says, "Christ loved *the church* and gave himself up for her" (Eph. 5:25). Here the term "the church" is used to apply to all those whom Christ died to redeem, all those who are saved by the death of Christ. But that must include all true believers for all time, both believers in the New Testament age and believers in the Old Testament age as well.[1] So great is God's plan for the church that he has exalted Christ to a position of highest authority for the sake of the church: "He has put all things under his feet and has made him the head over all things *for the church,* which is his body, the fulness of him who fills all in all" (Eph. 1:22–23).

Jesus Christ himself builds the church by calling his people to himself. He promised, "I will build my church" (Matt. 16:18). And Luke is careful to tell us that the growth of the church came not by human effort alone, but that "*the Lord* added to their number day by day those who were being saved" (Acts 2:47). But this process whereby Christ builds the church is just a continuation of the pattern established by God in the Old Testament whereby he called people to himself to be a worshiping assembly before him. There are several indications *in the Old Testament* that God thought of his people as a "church," a people assembled for the purpose of worshiping God. When Moses tells the people that the Lord said to him, *"Gather the people to me,* that I may let them hear my words, so that they may learn to fear me all the days that they live upon the earth . . ." (Deut. 4:10), the Septuagint translates the word for "gather" (Heb. *qāhal*) with the Greek term *ekklēsiazō,* "to summon an assembly," the verb that is cognate to the New Testament noun *ekklēsia,* "church."[2]

---

[1]See section 5 below for a discussion of the dispensational view that the church and Israel must be thought of as distinct groups. In this book, I have taken a non–dispensational position on that question, though it should be pointed out that many evangelicals who agree with much of the rest of this book will differ with me on this particular question.

[2]In fact, the Greek word *ekklēsia,* the term translated "church" in the New Testament, is the word that the Septuagint most frequently uses to translate the Old Testament term *qāhal,* the word used to speak of the "congregation" or the "assembly" of God's people. *Ekklēsia* translates *qāhal,* "assembly,"

It is not surprising, then, that the New Testament authors can speak of the Old Testament people of Israel as a "church" (*ekklēsia*). For example, Stephen speaks of the people of Israel in the wilderness as "the *church* (*ekklēsia*) in the wilderness" (Acts 7:38, author's translation). And the author of Hebrews quotes Christ as saying that he would sing praise to God in the midst of the great assembly of God's people in heaven: "In the midst of the church (*ekklēsia*) I will sing praise to you" (Heb. 2:12, author's translation, quoting Ps. 22:22).

Therefore the author of Hebrews understands the present-day Christians who constitute the church on earth to be surrounded by a great "cloud of witnesses" (Heb. 12:1) that reaches back into the earliest eras of the Old Testament and includes Abel, Enoch, Noah, Abraham, Sarah, Gideon, Barak, Samson, Jephthah, David, Samuel, and the prophets (Heb. 11:4–32). All these "witnesses" surround the present-day people of God, and it seems only appropriate that they, together with the New Testament people of God, should be thought of as God's great spiritual "assembly" or "church."[3] Moreover, later in chapter 12 the author of Hebrews says that when New Testament Christians worship we come into the presence of "the *assembly* (lit. "church," Gk. *ekklēsia*) of the first-born who are enrolled in heaven." This emphasis is not surprising in light of the fact that the New Testament authors see Jewish believers and Gentile believers alike to be now united in the church. Together they have been made "one" (Eph. 2:14), they are "one new man" (v. 15) and "fellow citizens" (v. 19), and "members of the household of God" (v. 19).

Therefore, even though there are certainly new privileges and new blessings that are given to the people of God in the New Testament, both the usage of the term "church" in Scripture and the fact that throughout Scripture God has always called his people to assemble to worship himself, indicate that it is appropriate to think of the church as constituting all the people of God for all time, both Old Testament believers and New Testament believers.[4]

---

69 times in the Septuagint. The next most frequent translation is *synagōgē*, "synagogue" or "meeting, place of meeting" (37 times).

Chafer objects to this analysis, for he says that the Septuagint use of the word *ekklēsia* does not reflect the New Testament meaning of the word "church" but is a common term for an "assembly." Therefore we should not call the "assembly" in the theater at Ephesus a church (Acts 19:32) even though the word *ekklēsia* is used there to refer to that group of people. Similarly, when Stephen refers to Israel in the wilderness (Acts 7:38) as an *ekklēsia*, it does not imply that he thinks of it as a "church" but only an assembly of people. Chafer sees this usage of the term as different from its distinctive New Testament meaning to refer to the church (*Systematic Theology*, 4:39). However, the extensive use of the word *ekklēsia* in the Septuagint to refer to assemblies not of pagan mobs but specifically of God's people certainly must be taken into account in understanding the meaning of the word when used by New Testament authors. The Septuagint was the Bible that they most commonly used, and they are certainly using the word *ekklēsia* with awareness of its Old Testament content. This would explain why Luke can so easily record Stephen as referring to the "church" in the wilderness with Moses and yet many times in the surrounding chapters in Acts speak of the growth of the "church" after Pentecost with no indication that there is any difference in meaning intended. The New Testament church is an assembly of God's people that simply continues in the pattern of assemblies of God's people found throughout the Old Testament.

[3]The Greek word *ekklēsia*, translated "church" in the New Testament, simply means "assembly."

[4]For a discussion of the question of whether there remains a distinction between "the church" and "Israel" as two separate peoples of God, see section 5 below.

Millard Erickson, *Christian Theology*, p. 1048, argues that the church does not start until Pentecost because Luke does not use the word "church" (*ekklēsia*) in his gospel, but uses it twenty-four times in Acts. If the church existed before Pentecost, he reasons, why did Luke not speak of it before that time?

**2. The Church Is Invisible, Yet Visible.** In its true spiritual reality as the fellowship of all genuine believers, the church is invisible. This is because we cannot see the spiritual condition of people's hearts. We can see those who outwardly attend the church, and we can see outward evidences of inward spiritual change, but we cannot actually see into people's hearts and view their spiritual state—only God can do that. This is why Paul says, *"The Lord knows those who are his"* (2 Tim. 2:19). Even in our own churches and our own neighborhoods, only God knows who are true believers with certainty and without error. In speaking of the church as invisible the author of Hebrews speaks of the "assembly (literally, "church") of the first-born who are enrolled in heaven" (Heb. 12:23), and says that present-day Christians join with that assembly in worship.

We can give the following definition: *The invisible church is the church as God sees it.*

Both Martin Luther and John Calvin were eager to affirm this invisible aspect of the church over against the Roman Catholic teaching that the church was the one visible organization that had descended from the apostles in an unbroken line of succession (through the bishops of the church). The Roman Catholic Church had argued that only in the visible organization of the Roman Church could we find the one true church, the only true church. Even today such a view is held by the Roman Catholic Church. In their "Pastoral Statement for Catholics on Biblical Fundamentalism" issued March 25, 1987, the (United States) National Conference of Catholic Bishops Ad Hoc Committee on Biblical Fundamentalism criticized evangelical Christianity (which it called "biblical fundamentalism") primarily because it took people away from the one true church:

> The basic characteristic of biblical fundamentalism is that it eliminates from Christianity the church as the Lord Jesus founded it. . . . There is no mention of the historic, authoritative church in continuity with Peter and the other apostles. . . . A study of the New Testament . . . demonstrates the importance of belonging to the church started by Jesus Christ. Christ chose Peter and the other apostles as foundations of his church. . . . Peter and the other apostles have been succeeded by

Yet the reason Luke did not use the word "church" to speak of the people of God during Jesus' earthly ministry is probably because there was no clearly defined or visible group to which it could refer during Jesus' earthly ministry. The true church *did* exist in the sense that it consisted of all true believers in Israel during that time, but this was such a small remnant of faithful Jews (such as Joseph and Mary, Zechariah and Elizabeth, Simeon, Anna, and others like them), that it was not an outwardly evident or well-defined group at all. Large segments of the Jewish population had strayed from God and had substituted other kinds of religious activities, such as legalism (the Pharisees), unbelieving "liberalism" (the Sadducees), speculative mysticism (those who wrote or believed apocalyptic literature and followers of sects such as those in the Qumran community), crass materialism (the tax collectors and others for whom wealth was a false god), or political or military activism (the Zealots and others who sought salvation through political or military means). Though there were no doubt genuine believers among many or all of these groups, the nation as a whole did not constitute an assembly of people who worshiped God rightly.

Moreover, the idea of a people of God newly "called out" as an assembly to follow Christ first came to fruition on the day of Pentecost. Therefore, although the "church" in the sense of the group of all who truly believed in God did exist before the day of Pentecost, it came to much clearer visible expression on the day of Pentecost, and it is natural that Luke should begin to use the name "the church" at that point. Before that point the name "church" could not have referred to any clearly established entity apart from the nation of Israel as a whole; after Pentecost, however, it readily could be used to refer to those who willingly and visibly identified themselves with this new people of God.

We should also note that Jesus did use the word "church" (*ekklēsia*) twice in Matthew's gospel (16:18 and 18:17).

the bishop of Rome and the other bishops, and . . . the flock of Christ still has, under Christ, a universal shepherd.[5]

In response to that kind of teaching both Luther and Calvin disagreed. They said that the Roman Catholic Church had the outward form, the organization, but it was just a shell. Calvin argued that just as Caiaphas (the high priest at the time of Christ) was descended from Aaron but was no true priest, so the Roman Catholic bishops had "descended" from the apostles in a line of succession but they were not true bishops in Christ's church. Because they had departed from the true preaching of the gospel, their visible organization was not the true church. Calvin said, "This pretense of succession is vain unless their descendants conserve safe and uncorrupted the truth of Christ which they have received at their fathers' hands, and abide in it. . . . See what value this succession has, unless it also include a true and uninterrupted emulation on the part of the successors!"[6]

On the other hand, the true church of Christ certainly has a visible aspect as well. We may use the following definition: *The visible church is the church as Christians on earth see it.* In this sense the visible church includes all who profess faith in Christ and give evidence of that faith in their lives.[7]

In this definition we do not say that the visible church is the church as any person in the world (such as an unbeliever or someone who held heretical teachings) might see it, but we mean to speak of the church as it is perceived by those who are genuine believers and have an understanding of the difference between believers and unbelievers.

When Paul writes his epistles he writes to the visible church in each community: "To the *church* of God which is at Corinth" (1 Cor. 1:2); "To the *church* of the Thessalonians" (1 Thess. 1:1); "To Philemon . . . and Apphia . . . and Archippus . . . and the *church* in your house" (Philem. 1–2). Paul certainly realized that there were unbelievers in some of those churches, some who had made a profession of faith that was not genuine, who appeared to be Christians but would eventually fall away. Yet neither Paul nor anyone else could tell with certainty who those people were. Paul simply wrote to the entire church that met together in any one place. In this sense, we could say today that the visible church is the group of people who come together each week to worship as a church and profess faith in Christ.

The visible church throughout the world will always include some unbelievers, and individual congregations will usually include some unbelievers, because we cannot see hearts as God sees them. Paul speaks of "Hymenaeus and Philetus, who have swerved from the truth" and who "are upsetting the faith of some" (2 Tim. 2:17–18). But he is confident that "The Lord knows those who are his" (2 Tim. 2:19). Paul says with sorrow, "Demas, in love with this present world, has deserted me and gone to Thessalonica" (2 Tim. 4:10).

---

[5]The full text of the Bishops' statement can be obtained from the National Catholic News Service, 1312 Massachusetts Avenue NW, Washington, D.C. 20005. The text was published in "Pastoral Statement for Catholics on Biblical Fundamentalism," in *Origins* vol. 17:21 (Nov. 5, 1987), pp. 376–77.

[6]John Calvin, *Institutes* 4.2.2–3, pp. 1043, 1045.

[7]Both Calvin and Luther would add the third qualification that those who are considered part of the visible church must partake of the sacraments of baptism and the Lord's Supper. Others might consider this as a subcategory of the requirement that people give evidence of faith in their life.

Similarly, Paul warns the Ephesian elders that after his departure "fierce wolves will come in among you, not sparing the flock; and *from among your own selves* will arise men speaking perverse things, to draw away the disciples after them" (Acts 20:29–30). Jesus himself warned, "Beware of false prophets, *who come to you in sheep's clothing* but inwardly are ravenous wolves. You will know them by their fruits" (Matt. 7:15–16). Realizing this distinction between the church invisible and the church visible, Augustine said of the visible church, "Many sheep are without and many wolves are within."[8]

When we recognize that there are unbelievers in the visible church, there is a danger that we may become overly suspicious. We may begin to doubt the salvation of many true believers and thereby bring great confusion into the church. Calvin warned against this danger by saying that we must make a "charitable judgment" whereby we recognize as members of the church all who "by confession of faith, by example of life, and by partaking of the sacraments, profess the same God and Christ with us."[9] We should not try to exclude people from the fellowship of the church until they by public sin bring discipline upon themselves. On the other hand, of course, the church should not tolerate in its membership "public unbelievers" who by profession or life clearly proclaim themselves to be outside the true church.

**3. The Church Is Local and Universal.** In the New Testament the word "church" may be applied to a group of believers at any level, ranging from a very small group meeting in a private home all the way to the group of all true believers in the universal church. A "house church" is called a "church" in Romans 16:5 ("greet also *the church in their house*"), 1 Corinthians 16:19 ("Aquila and Prisca, together with *the church in their house,* send you hearty greetings in the Lord"). The church in an entire city is also called "a church" (1 Cor. 1:2; 2 Cor. 1:1; and 1 Thess. 1:1). The church in a region is referred to as a "church" in Acts 9:31: "So *the church throughout all Judea and Galilee and Samaria* had peace and was built up."[10] Finally, the church throughout the entire world can be referred to as "the church." Paul says, "Christ loved *the church* and gave himself up for her" (Eph. 5:25) and says, "God has appointed *in the church* first apostles, second prophets, third teachers . . ." (1 Cor. 12:28). In this latter verse the mention of "apostles," who were not given to any individual church, guarantees that the reference is to the church universal.

We may conclude that the group of God's people considered at any level from local to universal may rightly be called "a church." We should not make the mistake of saying that only a church meeting in houses expresses the true nature of the church, or only a church considered at a city-wide level can rightly be called a

---

[8]Quoted in John Calvin, *Institutes* 4.1.8 (p. 1022).
[9]John Calvin, *Institutes,* 4.1.8 (pp. 1022–23).
[10]There is a textual variant among the Greek manuscripts of Acts 9:31, with some manuscripts having "the church" and some having "the churches." The singular reading "the church" is far preferable to the variant that has the plural. The singular reading is given a "B" probability (next to highest degree of probability) in the United Bible Societies' text. The singular is represented by many early and diverse texts while the plural reading is found in the Byzantine text tradition but in no texts before the fifth century A.D. (In order for the grammar to be consistent, six words have to be changed in the Greek text; therefore the variant is an intentional alteration in one direction or the other.)

church, or only the church universal can rightly be called by the name "church." Rather, the community of God's people considered at any level can be rightly called a church.

**4. Metaphors for the Church.**[11] To help us understand the nature of the church, Scripture uses a wide range of metaphors and images to describe to us what the church is like.[12] There are several family images—for example, Paul views the church as a *family* when he tells Timothy to act as if all the church members were members of a larger family: "Do not rebuke an older man but exhort him as you would a father; treat younger men like brothers, older women like mothers, younger women like sisters, in all purity" (1 Tim. 5:1–2). God is our heavenly Father (Eph. 3:14), and we are his sons and daughters, for God says to us, "I will be a father to you, and you shall be my sons and daughters, says the Lord Almighty" (2 Cor. 6:18). We are therefore brothers and sisters with each other in God's family (Matt. 12:49–50; 1 John 3:14–18). A somewhat different family metaphor is seen when Paul refers to the church as the *bride of Christ*. He says that the relationship between a husband and wife "refers to Christ and the church" (Eph. 5:32), and he says that he brought about the engagement between Christ and the church at Corinth and that it resembles an engagement between a bride and her husband-to-be: "I betrothed you to one husband, that to Christ I might present you as a pure virgin" (2 Cor. 11:2 NASB)—here Paul is looking forward to the time of Christ's return as the time when the church will be presented to him as his bride.

In other metaphors Scripture compares the church to *branches on a vine* (John 15:5), *an olive tree* (Rom. 11:17–24), *a field of crops* (1 Cor. 3:6–9), *a building* (1 Cor. 3:9), and *a harvest* (Matt. 13:1–30; John 4:35). The church is also viewed as *a new temple* not built with literal stones but built with Christian people who are "living stones" (1 Peter 2:5) built up on the "cornerstone" who is Christ Jesus (1 Peter 2:4–8). Yet the church is not only a new temple for worship of God; it is also *a new group of priests,* a "holy priesthood" that can offer "spiritual sacrifices acceptable to God" (1 Pet. 2:5). We are also viewed as *God's house:* "And we are his house" (Heb. 3:6), with Jesus Christ himself viewed as the "builder" of the house (Heb. 3:3). The church is also viewed as *"the pillar* and *bulwark of the truth"* (1 Tim. 3:15).

Finally, another familiar metaphor views the church as *the body of Christ* (1 Cor. 12:12–27). We should recognize that Paul in fact uses two different metaphors of the human body when he speaks of the church. In 1 Corinthians 12 *the whole body* is taken as a metaphor for the church, because Paul speaks of the "ear" and the "eye" and the "sense of smell" (1 Cor. 12:16–17). In this metaphor, Christ is not viewed as the head joined to the body, because the individual members are themselves the individual parts of the head. Christ is in this metaphor the Lord who is "outside" of that body that represents the church and is the one whom the church serves and worships.

---

[11]For more discussion of this topic see Edmund P. Clowney, "Interpreting the Biblical Models of the Church," in *Biblical Interpretation and the Church,* ed. by D. A. Carson (Nashville: Thomas Nelson, 1985), pp. 64–109.

[12]The list of metaphors given in this section is not intended to be exhaustive.

But in Ephesians 1:22–23; 4:15–16, and in Colossians 2:19, Paul uses a different body metaphor to refer to the church. In these passages Paul says that Christ is the head and the church is like *the rest of the body, as distinguished from the head:* "We are to grow up in every way into him who is the head, into Christ, from whom the whole body, joined and knit together by every joint with which it is supplied, when each part is working properly, makes bodily growth and upbuilds itself in love" (Eph. 4:15–16).[13] We should not confuse these two metaphors in 1 Corinthians 12 and Ephesians 4, but keep them distinct.

The wide range of metaphors used for the church in the New Testament should remind us not to focus exclusively on any one. For example, while it is true that the church is the body of Christ, we must remember that this is only one metaphor among many. If we focus exclusively on that metaphor we will be likely to forget that Christ is our Lord reigning in heaven as well as the one who dwells among us. Certainly we should not agree to the Roman Catholic view that the church is the "continuing incarnation" of the Son of God on earth today. The church is not the Son of God in the flesh, for Christ rose in his human body, he ascended in his human body into heaven, and he now reigns as the incarnate Christ in heaven, one who is clearly distinct from the church here on earth.

Each of the metaphors used for the church can help us to appreciate more of the richness of privilege that God has given us by incorporating us into the church. The fact that the church is like a family should increase our love and fellowship with one another. The thought that the church is like the bride of Christ should stimulate us to strive for greater purity and holiness, and also greater love for Christ and submission to him. The image of the church as branches in a vine should cause us to rest in him more fully. The idea of an agricultural crop should encourage us to continue growing in the Christian life and obtaining for ourselves and others the proper spiritual nutrients to grow. The picture of the church as God's new temple should increase our awareness of God's very presence dwelling in our midst as we meet. The concept of the church as a priesthood should help us to see more clearly the delight God has in the sacrifices of praise and good deeds that we offer to him (see Heb. 13:15–16). The metaphor of the church as the body of Christ should increase our interdependence on one another and our appreciation of the diversity of gifts within the body. Many other applications could be drawn from these and other metaphors for the church listed in Scripture.

**5. The Church and Israel.** Among evangelical Protestants there has been a difference of viewpoint on the question of the relationship between Israel and the church. This question was brought into prominence by those who hold to a "dispensational" system of theology. The most extensive systematic theology written by a dispensationalist, Lewis Sperry Chafer's *Systematic Theology,*[14] points

---

[13]This second metaphor is not even a complete or "proper" metaphor, for bodily parts do not grow up into the head, but Paul is mixing the idea of Christ's headship (or authority), the idea of the church as a body, and the idea that we grow to maturity in Christ, and he combines them into one complex statement.

[14]Lewis Sperry Chafer, *Systematic Theology.* Although there are several other distinctive doctrines that usually characterize dispensationalists, the distinction between Israel and the church as two groups in God's overall plan is probably the most important. Other doctrines held by dispensationalists usually include a pretribulational rapture of the church into heaven (see chapter 54), a future literal fulfillment

out many distinctions between Israel and the church, and even between believing Israel in the Old Testament and the church in the New Testament.[15] Chafer argues that God has two distinct plans for the two different groups of people that he has redeemed: God's purposes and promises for *Israel* are for *earthly blessings,* and they will yet be fulfilled on this earth at some time in the future. On the other hand, God's purposes and promises for *the church* are for *heavenly blessings,* and those promises will be fulfilled in heaven. This distinction between the two different groups that God saves will especially be seen in the millennium, according to Chafer, for at that time Israel will reign on earth as God's people and enjoy the fulfillment of Old Testament promises, but the church will already have been taken up into heaven at the time of Christ's secret return for his saints ("the rapture"). On this view, the church did not begin until Pentecost (Acts 2). And it is not right to think of Old Testament believers together with New Testament believers as constituting one church.

While Chafer's position continues to have influence in some dispensational circles, and certainly in more popular preaching, a number of leaders among more recent dispensationalists have not followed Chafer in many of these points. Several current dispensational theologians, such as Robert Saucy, Craig Blaising, and Darrell Bock, refer to themselves as "progressive dispensationalists,"[16] and they have gained a wide following. They *would not see the church as a parenthesis* in God's plan but as the first step toward the establishment of the kingdom of God. On a progressive dispensational view, *God does not have two separate purposes for Israel and the church,* but a single purpose—the establishment of the kingdom of God—in which Israel and the church will both share. Progressive dispensationalists would see *no distinction between Israel and the church in the future eternal state,* for all will be part of the one people of God. Moreover, they would hold that the church will reign with Christ in *glorified bodies on earth during the millennium* (see the discussion of the millennium in chapter 55).

However, there is still a difference between progressive dispensationalists and the rest of evangelicalism on one point: they would say that *the Old Testament prophecies concerning Israel will still be fulfilled in the millennium by ethnic Jewish people* who will believe in Christ and live in the land of Israel as a "model nation" for all nations to see and learn from. Therefore they would not say that the church is the "new Israel" or that all the Old Testament prophecies about Israel will be fulfilled in the church, for these prophecies will yet be fulfilled in ethnic Israel.

The position taken in this book differs quite a bit from Chafer's views on this issue and also differs somewhat with progressive dispensationalists. However, it must be said here that questions about the exact way in which biblical prophecies

---

of Old Testament prophecies concerning Israel, the dividing of biblical history into seven periods or "dispensations" of God's ways of relating to his people, and an understanding the church age as a parenthesis in God's plan for the ages, a parenthesis instituted when the Jews largely rejected Jesus as their Messiah. However, many present-day dispensationalists would qualify or reject several of these other distinctives. Dispensationalism as a system began with the writings of J. N. Darby (1800–1882) in Great Britain, but was popularized in the USA through the Scofield Reference Bible.

[15]Chafer, *Systematic Theology,* 4:45–53.

[16]See Robert L. Saucy, *The Case for Progressive Dispensationalism* (Grand Rapids: Zondervan, 1993), and Darrell L. Bock and Craig A. Blaising, eds., *Progressive Dispensationalism* (Wheaton: Victor, 1993). See also John S. Feinberg, ed., *Continuity and Discontinuity: Perspectives on the Relationship Between the Old and New Testaments* (Wheaton: Crossway, 1988).

about the future will be fulfilled are, in the nature of the case, difficult to decide with certainty, and it is wise to have some tentativeness in our conclusions on these matters. With this in mind, the following may be said.

Both Protestant and Catholic theologians outside of the dispensational position have said that the church includes both Old Testament believers and New Testament believers in one church or one body of Christ. Even on the nondispensational view, a person may hold that there will be a future large-scale conversion of the Jewish people (Rom. 11:12, 15, 23–24, 25–26, 28–31),[17] yet that this conversion will only result in Jewish believers becoming part of the one true church of God—they will be "grafted back into their own olive tree" (Rom. 11:24).

With regard to this question, we should notice the many New Testament verses that understand the church as the "new Israel" or new "people of God." The fact that "Christ loved *the church* and gave himself up for her" (Eph. 5:25) would suggest this. Moreover, this present church age, which has brought the salvation of many millions of Christians in the church, is not an interruption or a parenthesis in God's plan,[18] but a continuation of his plan expressed throughout the Old Testament to call a people to himself. Paul says, "For he is not a real Jew who is one outwardly, nor is true circumcision something external and physical. *He is a Jew who is one inwardly,* and real circumcision is a matter of the heart, spiritual and not literal" (Rom. 2:28–29). Paul recognizes that though there is a literal or natural sense in which people who physically descended from Abraham are to be called Jews, there is also a deeper or spiritual sense in which a "true Jew" is one who is inwardly a believer and whose heart has been cleansed by God.

Paul says that Abraham is not only to be considered the father of the Jewish people in a physical sense. He is also in a deeper and more true sense *"the father of all who believe* without being circumcised . . . and likewise the father of the circumcised who are not merely circumcised but also follow the example of the faith which our father Abraham had" (Rom. 4:11–12; cf. vv. 16, 18). Therefore Paul can say, "not all who are descended from Israel belong to Israel, and not all are children of Abraham because they are his descendants . . . it is not the children of the flesh who are the children of God, but the children of the promise are reckoned as descendants" (Rom. 9:6–8). Paul here implies that the true children of Abraham, those who are in the most true sense "Israel," are not the nation of Israel by physical descent from Abraham but those who have believed in Christ. Those who truly believe in Christ are now the ones who have the privilege of being called "my people" by the Lord (Rom. 9:25, quoting Hos. 2:23); therefore, the church is now God's chosen people. This means that when Jewish people according to the flesh are saved in large numbers at some time in the future, they will not constitute a separate people of God or be like a separate olive tree, but they will be "grafted back *into their own olive tree"* (Rom. 11:24). Another passage

---

[17]See chapter 54, pp. 1098 and 1104, where I affirm the conviction that Rom. 9–11 teaches a future large-scale conversion of the Jewish people, even though I am not a dispensationalist in the commonly understood sense of that term.

[18]Chafer's term is "an intercalation," meaning an insertion of a period of time into a previously planned schedule or calendar of events (p. 41). Here Chafer says, "The present age of the church is an intercalation into the revealed calendar or program of God as that program was foreseen by the prophets of old."

indicating this is Galatians 3:29: "And if you are Christ's, then you are Abraham's offspring, heirs according to promise." Similarly, Paul says that Christians are the "true circumcision" (Phil. 3:3).

Far from thinking of the church as a separate group from the Jewish people, Paul writes to Gentile believers at Ephesus telling them that they were formerly "alienated from the commonwealth of Israel, and strangers to the covenants of promise" (Eph. 2:12), but that now they have been "brought near in the blood of Christ" (Eph. 2:13). And when the Gentiles were brought into the church, Jews and Gentiles were united into one new body. Paul says that God *"has made us both one,* and has broken down the dividing wall of hostility . . . that he might create in himself one new man in place of the two, so making peace, and might *reconcile us both to God in one body* through the cross" (Eph. 2:14–16). Therefore Paul can say that Gentiles are *"fellow citizens with the saints* and members of the household of God, built upon the foundation of the apostles and prophets, Christ Jesus himself being the cornerstone" (Eph. 2:19–20). With his extensive awareness of the Old Testament background to the New Testament church, Paul can still say that "the Gentiles are fellow heirs, members of the same body" (Eph. 3:6). The entire passage speaks strongly of the unity of Jewish and Gentile believers in one body in Christ and gives no indication of any distinctive plan for Jewish people ever to be saved apart from inclusion in the one body of Christ, the church. The church incorporates into itself all the true people of God, and almost all of the titles used of God's people in the Old Testament are in one place or another applied to the church in the New Testament.

Hebrews 8 provides another strong argument for seeing the church as the recipient, and the fulfillment, of the Old Testament promises concerning Israel. In the context of speaking about the new covenant to which Christians belong, the author of Hebrews gives an extensive quotation from Jeremiah 31:31–34, in which he says, "The days will come, says the Lord, when I will establish a new *covenant with the house of Israel and with the house of Judah.* . . . This is the covenant that I will make with the house of Israel after those days, says the Lord: I will put my laws into their minds, and write them on their hearts, and I will be their God, and they shall be my people" (Heb. 8:8–10). Here the author quotes the Lord's promise that he will make a new covenant with the house of Israel and *with the house of Judah,* and says that that is the new covenant that has now been made *with the church.* That new covenant is the covenant of which believers in the church are now members. It seems hard to avoid the conclusion that the author views the church as the true Israel of God in which the Old Testament promises to Israel find their fulfillment.

Similarly, James can write a general letter to many early Christian churches and say that he is writing "To the twelve tribes in the Dispersion" (James 1:1). This indicates that he is evidently viewing New Testament Christians as the successors to and fulfillment of the twelve tribes of Israel.

Peter also speaks in the same way. From the first verse in which he calls his readers "exiles of the Dispersion" (1 Peter 1:1)[19] to the next-to-last verse in which he calls the city of Rome "Babylon" (1 Peter 5:13), Peter frequently speaks of

---

[19]The "Dispersion" was a term used to refer to the Jewish people scattered abroad from the land of Israel and living throughout the ancient Mediterranean world.

New Testament Christians in terms of Old Testament imagery and promises given to the Jews. This theme comes to prominence in 1 Peter 2:4–10, where[20] Peter says that God has bestowed on the church almost all the blessings promised to Israel in the Old Testament. The dwelling-place of God is no longer the Jerusalem temple, for Christians are the new "temple" of God (v. 5). The priesthood able to offer acceptable sacrifices to God is no longer descended from Aaron, for Christians are now the true "royal priesthood" with access before God's throne (vv. 4–5, 9). God's chosen people are no longer said to be those physically descended from Abraham, for Christians are now the true "chosen race" (v. 9). The nation blessed by God is no longer said to be the nation of Israel, for Christians are now God's true "holy nation" (v. 9). The people of Israel are no longer said to be the people of God, for Christians—both Jewish Christians and Gentile Christians—are now "God's people" and those who have "received mercy" (v. 10). Moreover, Peter takes these quotations from contexts in the Old Testament that repeatedly warn that God will reject his people who persist in rebellion against him and who reject the precious "cornerstone" (v. 6) that he has established. What further statement could be needed in order for us to say with assurance that the church has now become the true Israel of God and will receive all the blessings promised to Israel in the Old Testament?[21]

**6. The Church and the Kingdom of God.** What is the relationship between the church and the kingdom of God? The differences have been summarized well by George Ladd:

> The Kingdom is primarily the dynamic reign or kingly rule of God, and, derivatively, the sphere in which the rule is experienced. In biblical idiom, the Kingdom is not identified with its subjects. They are the people of God's rule who enter it, live under it, and are governed by it. The church is the community of the Kingdom but never the Kingdom itself. Jesus' disciples belong to the Kingdom as the Kingdom belongs to them; but they are not the Kingdom. The Kingdom is the rule of God; the church is a society of men.[22]

Ladd goes on to summarize five specific aspects of the relationship between the kingdom and the church: (1) The church is not the kingdom (for Jesus and the early Christians preached that the kingdom of God was near, not that the church was near, and preached the good news of the kingdom, not the good news of the church: Acts 8:12; 19:8; 20:25; 28:23, 31). (2) The kingdom creates the church (for as people enter into God's kingdom they become joined to the human fellowship of the church). (3) The church witnesses to the kingdom (for Jesus said, "this gospel of the kingdom will be preached throughout the whole world," Matt. 24:14). (4) The church is the instrument of the kingdom (for the Holy Spirit, manifesting the power of the kingdom, works through the disciples to heal

---

[20]The remainder of this paragraph is largely taken from Wayne Grudem, *The First Epistle of Peter*, p. 113.

[21]A dispensationalist may grant at this point that the church has been the recipient of many *applications* of Old Testament prophecies concerning Israel, but that the true *fulfillment* of these promises will yet come in the future for ethnic Israel. But with all these evident New Testament examples of clear application of these promises to the church, there does not seem to be any strong reason to deny that this really is the only fulfillment that God is going to give for these promises.

[22]George Eldon Ladd, *A Theology of the New Testament*, p. 111.

the sick and cast out demons, as he did in the ministry of Jesus: Matt. 10:8; Luke 10:17). (5) The church is the custodian of the kingdom (for the church has been given the keys of the kingdom of heaven: Matt. 16:19).[23]

Therefore we should not identify the kingdom of God and the church (as in Roman Catholic theology), nor should we see the kingdom of God as entirely future, something distinct from the church age (as in older dispensational theology). Rather, we should recognize that there is a close connection between the kingdom of God and the church. As the church proclaims the good news of the kingdom, people will come into the church and begin to experience the blessings of God's rule in their lives. The kingdom manifests itself through the church, and thereby the future reign of God breaks into the present (it is "already" here: Matt. 12:28; Rom. 14:17; and "not yet" here fully: Matt. 25:34; 1 Cor. 6:9–10). Therefore those who believe in Christ will begin to experience something of what God's final kingdom reign will be like: they will know some measure of victory over sin (Rom. 6:14; 14:17), over demonic opposition (Luke 10:17), and over disease (Luke 10:9). They will live in the power of the Holy Spirit (Matt. 12:28; Rom. 8:4–17; 14:17), who is the dynamic power of the coming kingdom. Eventually Jesus will return and his kingdom reign will extend over all creation (1 Cor. 15:24–28).

## B. The "Marks" of the Church (Distinguishing Characteristics)

**1. There Are True Churches and False Churches.** What makes a church a church? What is necessary to have a church? Might a group of people who claim to be Christians become so unlike what a church should be that they should no longer be called a church?

In the early centuries of the Christian church, there was little controversy about what was a true church. There was only one world-wide church, the "visible" church throughout the world, and that was, of course, the true church. This church had bishops and local clergymen and church buildings which everyone could see. Any heretics who were found to be in serious doctrinal error were simply excluded from the church.

But at the Reformation a crucial question came up: how can we recognize a true church? Is the Roman Catholic Church a true church or not? In order to answer that question people had to decide what were the "marks" of a true church, the distinguishing characteristics that lead us to recognize it as a true church. Scripture certainly speaks of false churches. Paul says of the pagan temples in Corinth, "What pagans sacrifice they offer to demons and not to God" (1 Cor. 10:20). He tells the Corinthians that "when you were heathen, you were led astray to dumb idols" (1 Cor. 12:2). These pagan temples were certainly false churches or false religious assemblies. Moreover, Scripture speaks of a religious assembly that is really a "synagogue of Satan" (Rev. 2:9; 3:9). Here the risen Lord Jesus seems to be referring to Jewish assemblies that claim to be Jews but were not true Jews who had saving faith. Their religious assembly was not an assembly of Christ's people but of those who still belonged to the kingdom of darkness, the kingdom of Satan. This also would certainly be a false church.

---

[23]These five points are summarized from Ladd, *Theology*, pp. 111–19.

In large measure there was agreement between Luther and Calvin on the question of what constituted a true church. The Lutheran statement of faith, which is called the Augsburg Confession (1530), defined the church as "the congregation of saints in which the gospel is rightly taught and the Sacraments rightly administered" (Article 7).[24] Similarly, John Calvin said, "Wherever we see the Word of God purely preached and heard, and the sacraments administered according to Christ's institution, there, it is not to be doubted, a church of God exists."[25] Although Calvin spoke of the pure preaching of the Word (whereas the Lutheran Confession spoke of the right preaching of the gospel) and although Calvin said that the Word must not only be preached but heard (whereas the Augsburg Confession merely mentioned that it had to be rightly taught), their understanding of the distinguishing marks of a true church is quite similar.[26] In contrast to the view of Luther and Calvin regarding the marks of a church, the Roman Catholic position has been that *the visible church* that descended from Peter and the apostles *is the true church*.

It seems appropriate that we take Luther and Calvin's view on the marks of a true church as correct still today. Certainly if the Word of God is not being preached, but simply false doctrines or doctrines of men, then there is no true church. In some cases we might have difficulty determining just how much wrong doctrine can be tolerated before a church can no longer be considered a true church, but there are many clear cases where we can say that a true church does not exist. For example, the Church of Jesus Christ of Latter Day Saints (the Mormon Church) does not hold to any major Christian doctrines concerning salvation or the person of God or the person and work of Christ. It is clearly a false church. Similarly, the Jehovah's Witnesses teach salvation by works, not by trusting in Jesus Christ alone. This is a fundamental doctrinal deviation because if people believe the teachings of the Jehovah's Witnesses, they simply will not be saved. So the Jehovah's Witnesses also must be considered a false church. When the preaching of a church conceals the gospel message of salvation by faith alone from its members, so that the gospel message is not clearly proclaimed, and has not been proclaimed for some time, the group meeting there is not a church.

The second mark of the church, the right administration of the sacraments (baptism and the Lord's Supper) was probably stated in opposition to the Roman Catholic view that saving grace came through the sacraments and thereby the sacraments were made "works" by which we earned merit for salvation. In this way, the Roman Catholic Church was insisting on payment rather than teaching faith as the means of obtaining salvation.

But another reason exists for including the sacraments as a mark of the church. Once an organization begins to practice baptism and the Lord's Supper, it is a continuing organization and is *attempting to function as a church*. (In modern American society, an organization that begins to meet for worship and prayer and Bible teachings on Sunday mornings also would clearly be attempting to function as a church.)

Baptism and the Lord's Supper also serve as "membership controls" for the

[24]Quoted from Philip Schaff, *The Creeds of Christendom*, pp. 11–12.
[25]Calvin, *Institutes* 4.1.9 (p. 1023).
[26]Later confessions sometimes added a third mark of the church (the right exercise of church discipline), but neither Luther nor Calvin themselves listed this mark.

church. Baptism is the means for admitting people into the church, and the Lord's Supper is the means for allowing people to give a sign of continuing in the membership of the church—the church signifies that it considers those who receive baptism and the Lord's Supper to be saved. Therefore these activities indicate what a church thinks about salvation, and they are appropriately listed as a mark of the church today as well. By contrast, groups who do not administer baptism and the Lord's Supper signify that they are not intending to function as a church. Someone may stand on a street corner with a small crowd and have true preaching and hearing of the Word, but the people there would not be a church. Even a neighborhood Bible study meeting in a home can have the true teaching and hearing of the Word without becoming a church. But if a local Bible study began baptizing its own new converts and regularly participating in the Lord's Supper, these things would signify *an intention to function as a church,* and it would be difficult to say why it should not be considered a church in itself.[27]

**2. True and False Churches Today.** In view of the question posed during the Reformation, what about the Roman Catholic Church today? Is it a true church? Here it seems that we cannot simply make a decision regarding the Roman Catholic Church as a whole, because it is far too diverse. To ask whether the Roman Catholic Church is a true church or a false church today is somewhat similar to asking whether Protestant churches are true or false today—there is great variety among them. Some Roman Catholic parishes certainly lack both marks: there is no pure preaching of the Word and the gospel message of salvation by faith in Christ alone is not known or received by people in the parish. Participation in the sacraments is seen as a "work" that can earn merit with God. Such a group of people is not a true Christian church. On the other hand, there are many Roman Catholic parishes in various parts of the world today where the local priest has a genuine saving knowledge of Christ and a vital personal relationship with Christ in prayer and Bible study. His own homilies and private teaching of the Bible place much emphasis on personal faith and the need for individual Bible reading and prayer. His teaching on the sacraments emphasizes their symbolic and commemorative aspects much more than it speaks of them as acts that merit some infusion of saving grace from God. In such a case, although we would have to say that we still have profound differences with Roman Catholic teaching on some doctrines,[28] nonetheless, it would seem that such a church would have a close enough approximation to the two marks of the church that it would be hard to deny that it is in fact a true church. It would seem to be a genuine congregation of believers in which the gospel is taught (though not purely) and the sacraments are administered more rightly than wrongly.

Are there false churches within Protestantism? If we again look at the two

---

[27]The Salvation Army is an unusual case because it does not observe baptism or the Lord's Supper, yet it seems in every other way to be a true church. In this case the organization has substituted other means of signifying membership and continuing participation in the church, and these other means of signifying membership provide a substitute for baptism and the Lord's Supper in terms of "membership controls."

[28]Significant doctrinal differences would still include matters such as the continuing sacrifice of the mass, the authority of the pope and the church councils, the veneration of the Virgin Mary and her role in redemption, the doctrine of purgatory, and the extent of the biblical canon.

distinguishing marks of the church, in the judgment of this present writer it seems appropriate to say that many liberal Protestant churches are in fact false churches today.[29] Is the gospel of works-righteousness and unbelief in Scripture that these churches teach any more likely to save people than did Roman Catholic teaching at the time of the Reformation? And is not their administration of the sacraments without sound teaching to anyone who walks in the door likely to give as much false assurance to unregenerate sinners as did the Roman Catholic use of the sacraments at the time of the Reformation? When there is an assembly of people who take the name "Christian" but consistently teach that people cannot believe their Bibles—indeed a church whose pastor and congregation seldom read their Bibles or pray in any meaningful way, and do not believe or perhaps even understand the gospel of salvation by faith in Christ alone, then how can we say that this is a true church?[30]

## C. The Purposes of the Church

We can understand the purposes of the church in terms of ministry to God, ministry to believers, and ministry to the world.

**1. Ministry to God: Worship.** In relationship to God the church's purpose is to worship him. Paul directs the church at Colossae to "sing psalms and hymns and spiritual songs with thankfulness in your hearts to God" (Col. 3:16). God has destined us and appointed us in Christ "to live for the praise of his glory" (Eph. 1:12). Worship in the church is not merely a preparation for something else: it is in itself fulfilling the major purpose of the church with reference to its Lord. That is why Paul can follow an exhortation that we are to be "making the most of the time" with a command to be filled with the Spirit and then to be "singing and making melody to the Lord with all your heart" (Eph. 5:16–19).

**2. Ministry to Believers: Nurture.** According to Scripture, the church has an obligation to nurture those who are already believers and build them up to maturity in the faith. Paul said that his own goal was not simply to bring people to initial saving faith but to "present every man *mature in Christ*" (Col. 1:28). And he told the church at Ephesus that God gave the church gifted persons "to equip the saints for the work of ministry, *for building up the body of Christ,* until we all attain to the unity of the faith and of the knowledge of the Son of God, to mature manhood, to the measure of the stature of the fullness of Christ" (Eph. 4:12–13). It is clearly contrary to the New Testament pattern to think that our only goal

---

[29]A similar conclusion was expressed by J. Gresham Machen as long ago as 1923: "The Church of Rome may represent a perversion of the Christian religion; but naturalistic liberalism is not Christianity at all" (*Christianity and Liberalism* (Grand Rapids: Eerdmans, 1923), p. 52).

[30]In the next chapter we shall discuss the question of the purity of the church. Although Christians should not voluntarily associate with a false church, we must recognize that among true churches there are more-pure and less-pure churches (see discussion in chapter 45, below). It is also important to note here that some liberal Protestant denominations today can have many false churches within the denomination (churches where the gospel is not preached or heard) and still have some local congregations that preach the gospel clearly and faithfully and are true churches.

with people is to bring them to initial saving faith. Our goal as a church must be to present to God every Christian "mature in Christ" (Col. 1:28).

**3. Ministry to the World: Evangelism and Mercy.** Jesus told his disciples that they should "make disciples of all nations" (Matt. 28:19). This evangelistic work of declaring the gospel is the primary ministry that the church has toward the world.[31] Yet accompanying the work of evangelism is also a ministry of mercy, a ministry that includes caring for the poor and needy in the name of the Lord. Although the emphasis of the New Testament is on giving material help to those who are part of the church (Acts 11:29; 2 Cor. 8:4; 1 John 3:17), there is still an affirmation that it is right to help unbelievers even if they do not respond with gratitude or acceptance of the gospel message. Jesus tells us,

> Love your enemies, and do good, and lend, expecting nothing in return; and your reward will be great, and you will be sons of the Most High; for *he is kind to the ungrateful and the selfish.* Be merciful, even as your Father is merciful. (Luke 6:35–36)

The point of Jesus' explanation is that we are to imitate God in being kind to those who are being ungrateful and selfish as well. Moreover, we have the example of Jesus who did not attempt to heal only those who accepted him as Messiah. Rather, when great crowds came to him, "he laid his hands *on every one of them* and healed them" (Luke 4:40). This should give us encouragement to carry out deeds of kindness, and to pray for healing and other needs, in the lives of unbelievers as well as believers. Such ministries of mercy to the world may also include participation in civic activities or attempting to influence governmental policies to make them more consistent with biblical moral principles. In areas where there is systematic injustice manifested in the treatment of the poor and/or ethnic or religious minorities, the church should also pray and—as it has opportunity—speak against such injustice. All of these are ways in which the church can supplement its evangelistic ministry to the world and indeed adorn the gospel that it professes. But such ministries of mercy to the world should never become a substitute for genuine evangelism or for the other areas of ministry to God and to believers mentioned above.

**4. Keeping These Purposes in Balance.** Once we have listed these three purposes for the church someone might ask, Which is most important? Or someone else might ask, Might we neglect one of these three as less important than the others?

To that we must respond that all three purposes of the church are commanded by the Lord in Scripture; therefore all three are important and none can be neglected. In fact, a strong church will have effective ministries in all three of these areas. We should beware of any attempts to reduce the purpose of the church to only one of these three and to say that it should be our primary focus. In fact, such attempts to make one of these purposes primary will always result in some neglect of the other two. A church that emphasizes only worship will end up with inadequate Bible teaching of believers and its members will remain shallow in their

---

[31]I do not mean to say that evangelism is more important than worship or nurture, but only that it is our primary ministry towards the world.

understanding of Scripture and immature in their Christian lives. If it also begins to neglect evangelism the church will cease to grow and influence others; it will become ingrown and eventually begin to wither.

A church that places the edification of believers as a purpose that takes precedence over the other two will tend to produce Christians who know much Bible doctrine but have spiritual dryness in their lives because they know little of the joy of worshiping God or telling others about Christ.

But a church that makes evangelism such a priority that it causes the other two purposes to be neglected will also end up with immature Christians who emphasize growth in numbers but have less and less genuine love for God expressed in their worship and less and less doctrinal maturity and personal holiness in their lives. All three purposes must be emphasized continually in a healthy church.

However, *individuals* are different from churches in placing a relative priority on one or another of these purposes of the church. Because we are like a body with diverse spiritual gifts and abilities, it is right for us to place most of our emphasis on the fulfillment of that purpose of the church that is most closely related to the gifts and interests God has given to us. There is certainly no obligation for every believer to attempt to give exactly one third of his or her time in the church to worship, one-third to nurturing other believers, and one-third to evangelism or deeds of mercy. Someone with the gift of evangelism should of course spend some time in worship and caring for other believers, but may end up spending the vast majority of his or her time in evangelistic work. Someone who is a gifted worship leader may end up devoting 90 percent of his time in the church toward preparation for and leading of worship. This is only an appropriate response to the diversity of gifts that God has given us.

## QUESTIONS FOR PERSONAL APPLICATION

1. When you think of the church as the invisible fellowship of all true believers throughout all time, how does it affect the way you think of yourself as an individual Christian? In the community in which you live, is there much visible unity among genuine believers (that is, is there much visible evidence of the true nature of the invisible church)? Does the New Testament say anything about the ideal size for an individual church?

2. Would you consider the church that you are now in to be a true church? Have you ever been a member of a church that you would think to be a false church? Do you think there is any harm done when evangelical Christians continue to give the impression that they think liberal Protestant churches are true Christian churches? Viewed from the perspective of the final judgment, what good and what harm might come from our failure to state that we think unbelieving churches are false churches?

3. Did any of the metaphors for the church give you a new appreciation for the church that you currently attend?

4. To which purpose of the church do you think you can most effectively contribute? Which purpose has God placed in your heart a strong desire to fulfill?

## SPECIAL TERMS

| | |
|---|---|
| body of Christ | invisible church |
| church | marks of the church |
| *ekklēsia* | visible church |

## BIBLIOGRAPHY

(For an explanation of this bibliography see the note on the bibliography to chapter 1, p. 38. Complete bibliographical data may be found on pp. 1223–29.)

### Sections in Evangelical Systematic Theologies

1. Anglican (Episcopalian)
    1882–92    Litton, 363–86
    1930       Thomas, 265–80
2. Arminian (Wesleyan or Methodist)
    1875–76    Pope, 3:259–87
    1892–94    Miley, 2:385–94
    1940       Wiley, 3:103–17, 126–27
    1960       Purkiser, 393–408
    1983       Carter, 2:571–613
3. Baptist
    1767       Gill, 2:558–74
    1887       Boyce, 1:418–22
    1907       Strong, 887–94
    1976–83    Henry, 4:524–92
    1983–85    Erickson, 1025–68
4. Dispensational
    1947       Chafer, 4:30–153
    1949       Thiessen, 305–13, 326–32
    1986       Ryrie, 391–404, 435–36
5. Lutheran
    1917–24    Pieper, 3:397–425
    1934       Mueller, 541–56
6. Reformed (or Presbyterian)
    1559       Calvin, 2:1009–52 (4.1–2)
    1861       Heppe, 657–70
    1937–66    Murray, *CW*, 1:231–52; *CW*, 2:321–36
    1938       Berkhof, 555–78
    1962       Buswell, 2:216–26; 1:418–24
7. Renewal (or charismatic/Pentecostal)
    1988–92    Williams, 3:15–157

## Sections in Representative Roman Catholic Systematic Theologies

1. Roman Catholic: Traditional
   - 1955     Ott, 270–324
2. Roman Catholic: Post-Vatican II
   - 1980     McBrien, 2:565–730

## Other Works

Banks, Robert J. *Paul's Idea of Community: The Early House Churches in Their Historical Setting.* Grand Rapids: Eerdmans, 1980.

Bannerman, James. *The Church of Christ.* Cherry Hill, N.J.: Mack Publishing, 1972. (First published in 1869.)

Berkouwer, G. C. *The Church.* Trans. by James E. Davidson. Grand Rapids: Eerdmans, 1976.

Bock, Darrell L., and Craig A. Blaising, eds. *Progressive Dispensationalism.* Wheaton: Victor, 1993.

Carson, D. A., ed. *Biblical Interpretation and the Church: Text and Context.* Exeter: Paternoster, 1984.

————. *The Church in the Bible and the World.* Grand Rapids: Baker, and Exeter: Paternoster, 1987.

Clowney, Edmund. "Church." In *NDT*, pp. 140–43.

————. *The Doctrine of the Church.* Philadelphia: Presbyterian and Reformed, 1969.

Feinberg, John S., ed. *Continuity and Discontinuity: Perspectives on the Relationship Between the Old and New Testaments.* Wheaton: Crossway, 1988.

Gaffin, Richard B. "Kingdom of God." In *NDT*, pp. 367–69.

Ladd, George Eldon. "The Kingdom and the Church." In *A Theology of the New Testament.* Grand Rapids: Eerdmans, 1974, pp. 105–19.

Martin, Ralph P. *The Family and the Fellowship: New Testament Images of the Church.* Grand Rapids: Eerdmans, 1979.

Omanson, R. L. "Church, The." In *EDT*, pp. 231–33.

Poythress, Vern. *Understanding Dispensationalists.* Grand Rapids: Zondervan, 1987.

Saucy, Robert. *The Case for Progressive Dispensationalism.* Grand Rapids: Zondervan, 1993.

————. *The Church in God's Program.* Chicago: Moody, 1972.

Snyder, Howard A. *The Community of the King.* Downers Grove, Ill.: InterVarsity Press, 1977.

VanGemeren, Willem. *The Progress of Redemption.* Grand Rapids: Zondervan, 1988.

Watson, David C. *I Believe in the Church.* Grand Rapids: Eerdmans, 1979.

## SCRIPTURE MEMORY PASSAGE

**Ephesians 4:11–13:** *And his gifts were that some should be apostles, some prophets, some evangelists, some pastors and teachers, to equip the saints for the work of ministry, for building up the body of Christ, until we all attain to the unity of the faith and of the* *knowledge of the Son of God, to mature manhood, to the measure of the stature of the fulness of Christ.*

## HYMN

### "The Church's One Foundation"

The church's one foundation is Jesus Christ her Lord;
    She is his new creation by water and the Word:
From heav'n he came and sought her to be his holy bride;
    With his own blood he bought her, and for her life he died.

Elect from ev'ry nation, yet one o'er all the earth,
    Her charter of salvation one Lord, one faith, one birth;
One holy name she blesses, partakes one holy food,
    And to one hope she presses, with ev'ry grace endued.

Though with a scornful wonder men see her sore oppressed,
    By schisms rent asunder, by heresies distressed,
Yet saints their watch are keeping, their cry goes up, "How long?"
    And soon the night of weeping shall be the morn of song.

The church shall never perish! Her dear Lord to defend,
    To guide, sustain and cherish, is with her to the end;
Though there be those that hate her, and false sons in her pale,
    Against or foe or traitor she ever shall prevail.

'Mid toil and tribulation, and tumult of her war,
    She waits the consummation of peace forevermore;
Til with the vision glorious her longing eyes are blest,
    And the great church victorious shall be the church at rest.

Yet she on earth hath union with God the Three in One,
    And mystic sweet communion with those whose rest is won:
O happy ones and holy! Lord, give us grace that we,
    Like them, the meek and lowly, on high may dwell with thee.

AUTHOR: SAMUEL J. STONE, 1866

# Chapter 45

# The Purity and Unity
# of the Church

*What makes a church more or less pleasing to God?*
*What kinds of churches should we cooperate with*
*or join?*

## EXPLANATION AND SCRIPTURAL BASIS

### A. More-Pure and Less-Pure Churches

In the previous chapter we saw that there are "true churches" and "false churches." In this chapter a further distinction must be made: there are *more-pure* and *less-pure* churches.

This fact is evident from a brief comparison of Paul's epistles. When we look at Philippians or 1 Thessalonians we find evidence of Paul's great joy in these churches and the relative absence of major doctrinal or moral problems (see Phil. 1:3–11; 4:10–16; 1 Thess. 1:2–10; 3:6–10; 2 Thess. 1:3–4; 2:13; cf. 2 Cor. 8:1–5). On the other hand, there were all sorts of serious doctrinal and moral problems in the churches of Galatia (Gal. 1:6–9; 3:1–5) and Corinth (1 Cor. 3:1–4; 4:18–21; 5:1–2, 6; 6:1–8; 11:17–22; 14:20–23; 15:12; 2 Cor. 1:23–2:11; 11:3–5, 12–15; 12:20–13:10). Other examples could be given, but it should be clear that among true churches there are *less pure* and *more pure* churches. This may be represented as in figure 45.1.

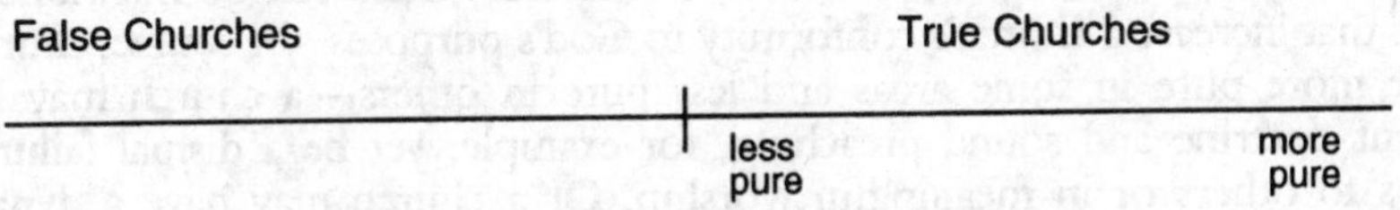

| False Churches | | True Churches | |
|---|---|---|---|
| | less<br>pure | | more<br>pure |

AMONG TRUE CHURCHES, THERE ARE LESS PURE
AND MORE PURE CHURCHES
*Figure 45.1*

### B. Definitions of Purity and Unity

We may define the purity of the church as follows: *The purity of the church is its degree of freedom from wrong doctrine and conduct, and its degree of conformity to God's revealed will for the church.*

As we shall see in the following discussion, it is right to pray and work for the greater purity of the church. But purity cannot be our only concern, or Christians

873

would have a tendency to separate into tiny groups of very "pure" Christians and tend to exclude anyone who showed the slightest deviation in doctrine or conduct of life. Therefore the New Testament also speaks frequently about the need to strive for the *unity* of the visible church. This may be defined in the following way: *The unity of the church is its degree of freedom from divisions among true Christians.*

The definition specifies "true Christians" because, as we saw in the previous chapter, there are those who are Christian in name only, but have had no genuine experience of regeneration by the Holy Spirit. Nonetheless, many of these people take the name "Christian" and many churches that are filled with such unbelievers still call themselves Christian churches. We should not expect or work for organizational or functional unity that includes all of those people, and therefore there will never be unity with all churches that call themselves "Christian." But, as we shall also see in the following discussion, the New Testament certainly encourages us to work for the unity of all true believers.

## C. Signs of a More-Pure Church

Factors that make a church "more pure" include:

1. Biblical doctrine (or right preaching of the Word)
2. Proper use of the sacraments (or ordinances)
3. Right use of church discipline
4. Genuine worship
5. Effective prayer
6. Effective witness
7. Effective fellowship
8. Biblical church government
9. Spiritual power in ministry
10. Personal holiness of life among members
11. Care for the poor
12. Love for Christ

There may be other signs than these, but at least these can be mentioned as factors that increase a church's conformity to God's purposes. Of course, churches can be more pure in some areas and less pure in others—a church may have excellent doctrine and sound preaching, for example, yet be a dismal failure in witness to others or in meaningful worship. Or a church may have a dynamic witness and very God-honoring times of worship but be weak in doctrinal understanding and Bible teaching.

Most churches will tend to think that the areas in which they are strong are the most important areas, and the areas where they are weak are less important. But the New Testament encourages us to work for the purity of the church in all of these areas. Christ's goal for the church is "*that he might sanctify her*, having cleansed her by the washing of water with the word, *that he might present the church to himself* in splendor, *without spot or wrinkle or any such thing*, that she might be holy and without blemish" (Eph. 5:26–27). Paul's ministry was one of "warning every man and teaching every man in all wisdom, that we may present every man mature in Christ" (Col. 1:28). Moreover, Paul told Titus that elders must "be able to give instruction in sound doctrine and also to confute those who contradict it" (Titus 1:9), and he said that false teachers "must be silenced" (Titus 1:11). Jude urged Christians to "contend for the faith which was once for all delivered to the saints" (Jude 3). Proper use of the sacraments is commanded in 1 Corinthians 11:17–34, and right use of church discipline to protect the purity of the church is required in 1 Corinthians 5:6–7, 12–13.

The New Testament also mentions a number of other factors: we are to strive for spiritual worship (Eph. 5:18–20; Col. 3:16–17), effective witness (Matt. 28:19–20; John 13:34–35; Acts 2:44–47; 1 John 4:7), proper government of the church (1 Tim. 3:1–13), spiritual power in ministry (Acts 1:8; Rom. 1:16; 1 Cor. 4:20; 2 Cor. 10:3–4; Gal. 3:3–5; 2 Tim. 3:5; James 5:16), personal holiness (1 Thess. 4:3; Heb. 12:14), care for the poor (Acts 4:32–35; Rom. 15:26; Gal. 2:10), and love for Christ (1 Peter 1:8; Rev. 2:4). In fact, all Christians are to "strive to excel in *building up the church*" (1 Cor. 14:12), an exhortation that applies not only to an increase in the number of church members, but also (and in fact primarily) to the "edification" or growth of the church toward Christian maturity. The force of all of these passages is to remind us that *we are to work for the purity of the visible church.*

Of course, if we are to work for the purity of the church, especially of the local church of which we are a part, we must recognize that this is a process, and that any church of which we are a part will be somewhat impure in various areas. There were no perfect churches at the time of the New Testament and there will be no perfect churches until Christ returns.[1] This means that Christians have no obligation to seek the *purest church* they can find and stay there, and then leave it if an even purer church comes to their attention. Rather, they should find a *true church* in which they can have effective ministry and in which they will experience Christian growth as well, and then should stay there and minister, continually working for the purity of that church. God will often bless their prayers and faithful witness and the church will gradually grow in many areas of purity.

But we must realize that not all churches will respond well to influences that would bring them to greater purity. Sometimes, in spite of a few faithful Christians within a church, its dominant direction will be set by others who are determined to lead it on another course. Unless God graciously intervenes to bring reformation, some of these churches will become cults, and others will just die and close their doors. But more commonly these churches will simply drift into liberal Protestantism.

It is helpful at this point to remember that classical liberal Protestantism is humanistic, and its approaches are *primarily man-centered* rather than God-centered.[2] When a church begins to stray from faithfulness to Christ, this will be evident not only in the shift to impure doctrine (which can sometimes be concealed from church members by the use of evasive language) but also in the daily life of the church: its activities, its preaching, its counseling, and even the casual conversations among members will tend to become more and more man-centered and less and less God-centered. There will tend to be a repeated emphasis on the typical kinds of self-help advice given in popular journals and by secular

---

[1]This is recognized by the Westminster Confession of Faith: "The purest Churches under heaven are subject both to mixture and error" (25.5).

[2]See the remarkably accurate analysis by J. Gresham Machen, *Christianity and Liberalism* (repr. ed., Grand Rapids: Eerdmans, 1968; first published in 1923), esp. pp. 64–68.

psychologists. There will be a horizontal orientation as opposed to a vertical or God-centered orientation, there will be fewer and fewer extended times of prayer and less and less emphasis on the direct application of Scripture to daily situations, but more emphasis on simply being a caring and sensitive person, and on affirming others and acting in love toward them. The conversation and activities of the church will have very little genuine spiritual content—little emphasis on the need for daily prayer for individual concerns and for forgiveness of sins, little emphasis on daily personal reading of Scripture, and little emphasis on moment-by-moment trust in Christ and knowing the reality of his presence in our lives. Where there are admonitions to moral reformation, these will often be viewed as human deficiencies that people can correct by their own discipline and effort, and perhaps encouragement from others, but these moral aspects of life will not primarily be viewed as sin against a holy God, sin which can only effectively be overcome by the power of the Holy Spirit working within. When such humanistic emphases become dominant in a church, it has moved far toward the "less-pure" end of the scale in many of the areas listed above, and it is moving in the direction of becoming a false church.

## D. New Testament Teaching on the Unity of the Church

There is a strong emphasis in the New Testament on the unity of the church. Jesus' goal is that "there shall be *one flock, one shepherd*" (John 10:16), and he prays for all future believers "that they may all be one" (John 17:21). This unity will be a witness to unbelievers, for Jesus prays "that they may become *perfectly one, so that the world may know that you have sent me* and have loved them even as you have loved me" (John 17:23).

Paul reminds the Corinthians that they are "called to be saints *together with all those who in every place call on the name of our Lord Jesus Christ,* both their Lord and ours" (1 Cor. 1:2). Then Paul writes to Corinth, "I appeal to you, brethren, by the name of our Lord Jesus Christ, that *all of you agree* and that there be no dissensions among you, but *that you be united* in the same mind and the same judgment" (1 Cor. 1:10; cf. v. 13).

He encourages the Philippians, "complete my joy by being of the same mind, having the same love, *being in full accord and of one mind*" (Phil. 2:2). He tells the Ephesians that Christians are to be "eager to maintain the *unity* of the Spirit in the bond of peace" (Eph. 4:3), and that the Lord gives gifts to the church "for building up the body of Christ, *until we all attain to the unity of the faith and of the knowledge of the Son of God,* to mature manhood, to the measure of the stature of the fulness of Christ" (Eph. 4:12–13).

Paul can *command* the church to live in unity because there already is an *actual* spiritual unity in Christ which exists among genuine believers. He says, "There is one body and one Spirit, just as you were called to the one hope that belongs to your call, one Lord, one faith, one baptism, one God and Father of us all, who is above all and through all and in all" (Eph. 4:4–6).

And though the body of Christ consists of many members, those members are all "*one body*" (1 Cor. 10:17; 12:12–26).

Because they are jealous to protect this unity of the church, the New Testament writers give strong warnings against those who cause divisions:

I appeal to you, brethren, to take note of those who create dissensions and difficulties, in opposition to the doctrine which you have been taught; avoid them. For such persons do not serve our Lord Christ, but their own appetites. (Rom. 16:17–18)

Paul opposed Peter to his face because he separated from Gentile Christians and began eating only with Jewish Christians (Gal. 2:11–14). Those who promote "strife . . . dissension, party spirit . . . shall not inherit the kingdom of God" (Gal. 5:20–21). And Jude warns that those who "set up divisions" are "worldly people, devoid of the Spirit" (Jude 19).

Consistent with this New Testament emphasis on the unity of believers is the fact that the direct commands to *separate* from other people are always commands to separate *from unbelievers,* not from Christians with whom one disagrees. When Paul says, "Therefore come out from them, and *be separate from them*" (2 Cor. 6:17), it is in support of his opening command of that section, "Do not be mismated *with unbelievers*" (2 Cor. 6:14). And Paul tells Timothy that he is to "avoid such people" (2 Tim. 3:5), referring not to believers but to unbelievers, those who are "lovers of pleasure rather than lovers of God, holding the form of religion but denying the power of it" (2 Tim. 3:4–5). He says that these people are "men of corrupt mind and counterfeit faith" (2 Tim. 3:8). Of course, there is a kind of church discipline that requires separation from an individual who is causing trouble within the church (Matt. 18:17; 1 Cor. 5:11–13), and there may be other reasons for which Christians conclude that separation is required,[3] but it is important to note here, in discussing the unity of the church, that there are no direct New Testament commands to separate from Christians with whom one has doctrinal differences (unless those differences involve such serious heresy that the Christian faith itself is denied).[4]

These passages on church unity tell us that, in addition to working for the purity of the visible church, *we are also to work for the unity of the visible church.* Yet we must realize that such unity does not actually require one worldwide church government over all Christians. In fact, the unity of believers is often demonstrated quite effectively through voluntary cooperation and affiliation among Christian groups. Moreover, different types of ministries and different emphases in ministry may result in different organizations, all under the universal headship of Christ as Lord of the church. Therefore the existence of different denominations, mission boards, Christian educational institutions, college ministries, and so forth is not necessarily a mark of disunity of the church (though in some cases it may be), for there may be a great deal of cooperation and frequent demonstrations of unity among such diverse bodies as these. (I think the modern term *parachurch organization* is unfortunate, because it implies that these organizations are somehow "beside" and therefore "outside of" the church, whereas in reality they are simply different parts of the one universal church.) Moreover, many Christians argue that there *should not* be a worldwide government of the church, because the New Testament pattern of church government never shows elders having authority over any more than their own local congregations (see chapter 47

---

[3]See the discussion on reasons for separation in section F below, pp. 879–83.
[4]2 John 10 forbids Christians to give a greeting to itinerant heretical teachers who were not proclaiming the true gospel at all; see discussion below.

below). In fact, even in the New Testament the apostles agreed that Paul should emphasize missionary work to the Gentiles while Peter would emphasize missionary work to the Jews (Gal. 2:7), and Paul and Barnabas went their separate ways for a time because of a disagreement over whether they should take Mark with them (Acts 15:39–40), though certainly they had unity in every other way.[5]

## E. Brief History of Organizational Separation in the Church

There are sometimes reasons why the outward or visible unity of the church cannot be maintained. A brief survey of the history of organizational separation in the church may highlight some of these reasons,[6] and help explain where present-day denominational divisions came from.

During the first thousand years of the church there was for the most part outward unity. There had been some minor divisions during controversies with groups like the Montanists (second century) and the Donatists (fourth century), and there was a minor separation by some Monophysite churches (fifth and sixth centuries), but the prevailing sentiment was one of strong opposition to division in the body of Christ. For example, Irenaeus, a second century bishop, said about those who cause divisions in the church, "No reformation able to be effected by them will be of great enough importance to compensate for the damage arising from their schism" (*Against Heresies* 4.33.7).

The first major division in the church came in A.D. 1054 when the Eastern (now Orthodox) church separated from the Western (Roman Catholic) church. The reason was that the pope had changed a church creed simply on his own author-ity,[7] and the Eastern church protested that he had no right to do that.

The Reformation in the sixteenth century then separated the Western church into Roman Catholic and Protestant branches, yet there was often a strong reluctance to cause formal division. Martin Luther wanted to reform the church without dividing it, but he was excommunicated in 1521. The Anglican (Episcopalian) church did not separate from Rome, but was excommunicated in 1570; thus it can say, "We suffer schism, we did not cause it." On the other hand, there were many Protestants, especially among the Anabaptists, who wanted to form churches of believers only, and began as early as 1525 to form separate churches in Switzerland and then other parts of Europe.

In the centuries following the Reformation, Protestantism splintered into hundreds of smaller groups. Sometimes leaders of the new groups regretted such divisions: John Wesley, although he was the founder of Methodism, claimed that he lived and died a member of the Anglican church. It was often the case that matters of conscience or religious freedom forced the division, as with the Puritans

---

[5]Scripture hints that Paul was right and Barnabas wrong in this controversy, since it tells us that Paul and Silas left Antioch "being commended by the brethren to the grace of the Lord" (Acts 15:40), whereas nothing similar is said about Barnabas. This incident is simply reported in Acts but is not strong evidence for the appropriateness of diversification of ministry, since the report of a "sharp contention" (v. 39) between Paul and Barnabas indicates that we should not think of them as entirely free from fault.

[6]From this point to the end of the chapter much of the material has been taken from the article, "Separation, Ecclesiastical" by Wayne Grudem, prepared for *The Tyndale Encyclopedia of Christian Knowledge* (Wheaton, Ill.: Tyndale House, copyright 1971, but never published). Used by permission.

[7]See the discussion of the *filioque* clause in chapter 14, pp. 246–47.

and many Pietist groups. On the other hand, sometimes language differences among immigrant groups in America led to the founding of separate churches.

Have the reasons for separation into different organizations and denominations always been proper ones? Although there have almost always been strong theological differences in major church divisions, one fears that too often, especially in more recent history, the real motives for beginning or maintaining separation have been selfish ones, and that John Calvin may have been correct in saying, "Pride or self-glorification is the cause and starting point of all controversies, when each person, claiming for himself more than he is entitled to have, is eager to have others in his power."[8] Moreover, he says, "Ambition has been, and still is, the mother of all errors, of all disturbances and sects."[9]

In the mid-twentieth century the ecumenical movement sought greater organizational unity among denominations, but without noteworthy success. It by no means received wholehearted approval or support from evangelicals. On the other hand, since the 1960s, the growth of the charismatic movement across almost all denominational lines, the rise of neighborhood Bible study and prayer groups, and a greatly diminished doctrinal awareness among lay people, have brought about a remarkable increase in actual unity of fellowship—even between Protestants and Catholics—at the local level.

Although the previous paragraphs spoke of separation in the sense of (1) the formation of *separate organizations,* there are two other, more severe kinds of separation that should be mentioned: (2) *"No cooperation":* in this case a church or Christian organization refuses to cooperate in joint activities with other churches (activities such as evangelistic campaigns or joint worship services or mutual recognition of ordination). (3) *"No personal fellowship":* this involves the extremely strict avoidance of all personal fellowship with members of another church, and prohibits any joint prayer or Bible study, and sometimes even ordinary social contact, with members of another church group. We will discuss the possible reasons for these kinds of separation in the following section.

## F. Reasons for Separation

As we examine the motives people have had for church separation throughout history, and as we compare those motives with the New Testament requirements that we seek both the unity and the purity of the visible church, we can find *both right and wrong reasons for separation.* Wrong reasons would include such things as personal ambition and pride, or differences on minor doctrines or practices (doctrinal or behavioral patterns that would not affect any other doctrine and that would not have a significant effect on the way one lives the Christian life).[10]

On the other hand, there are some reasons for separation that we may consider to be right (or possibly right, depending on the specific circumstances). In most cases these reasons will flow from the need to work for the purity of the church as well as its unity. These reasons for separation can be considered in three categories: (1) doctrinal reasons; (2) reasons of conscience; (3) practical consid-

---

[8]Commentary on 1 Cor. 4:6.
[9]Commentary on Num. 12:1.
[10]See chapter 1, pp. 29–30, on the differences between major and minor doctrines.

erations. In the following section, I have listed some situations where it seems to me that Christians would be *required* to leave a church. Then I have listed some other situations that seem to me less clear, in which some Christians may think it *wise* to leave a church, and others will think it *unwise*. In these less-clear cases, I have generally not drawn any conclusions, but simply listed the kinds of factors that Christians will want to consider.

**1. Doctrinal Reasons.** A need for separation may arise when the doctrinal position of a church deviates from biblical standards in a serious way. This deviation may be in official statements or in actual belief and practice, insofar as that can be determined. But when does doctrinal deviation become so serious that it requires withdrawing from a church or forming a separate church? As we noted above, there are no commands in the New Testament to separate from any true church, so long as it is still a part of the body of Christ. Paul's response even to people in erring churches (even in churches like the one at Corinth, which tolerated serious doctrinal and moral error, and for a time tolerated some who rejected Paul's apostolic authority) is not to tell faithful Christians to separate from those churches, but to admonish the churches, work for their repentance, and pray for them. Of course there are commands to discipline those who cause trouble within the church, sometimes by excluding them from church fellowship (1 Cor. 5:11–13; 2 Thess. 3:14–15; Titus 3:10–11), but there are no instructions to leave the church and cause division if this cannot be done immediately (see Rev. 2:14–16, 20–25; cf. Luke 9:50; 11:23).

Second John 10–11, which forbids the receiving of false teachers, makes perhaps the strongest statement in the entire New Testament: "Do not take him into your house or welcome him. Anyone who welcomes him shares in his wicked work" (NIV). But it should be noted that such a visitor is teaching a serious heresy about the person of Christ, one that prevents people from having saving faith. (John is talking about anyone who "does not abide in the doctrine of Christ" and "does not have God" [v. 9].) Moreover, this verse refers to false teachers, not to all individuals who hold false beliefs, because it speaks of someone who comes to you and "does not bring this doctrine" (v. 10; cf. v. 7, "Many deceivers have gone out into the world, men who will not acknowledge the coming of Jesus Christ in the flesh"). John even uses the word *antichrist* for such teachers. Finally, the greeting John has in mind refers either to an official church greeting or one that would give an appearance of endorsement of this doctrine, because the prohibition talks about someone who "*comes to you* and does not *bring this doctrine*" (v. 10), which suggests that the person in view is a traveling teacher who comes not to an individual home but to address the church as a whole.[11]

On the principle of separation from unbelievers or from fundamental error that would involve the denial of the Christian faith, Christians would seem to be *required* on doctrinal grounds to withdraw from a church and join or form a new organization only when the doctrinal error is so serious and so pervasive that the parent church *has become a false church,* no longer part of the body of Christ. This would be a church which is no longer a fellowship of true believers, no longer a

---

[11]See the discussion in John Stott, *The Epistles of John,* TNTC (London: Tyndale Press, 1964), pp. 212–15.

true part of the body of Christ, or no longer a place where those who believe its teachings will find salvation.[12] In the case of leaving a false church, those who separate will claim that in fact they have not *left* the true church, but that they *are* the true church, and that the parent organization has left by means of its error. In fact, both Luther and Calvin eventually said that the Roman Catholic Church was not a true church.

However, even when withdrawal or separation is not absolutely required, many Christians may find that it is *wise* or *expedient* to withdraw before the church has become a false church, but when serious doctrinal deviation occurs. For instance, some would argue that doctrinal deviation has become intolerable whenever heretical views on major doctrines (such as the Trinity, the person of Christ, the atonement, the resurrection, etc.) can be advocated by a church leader without causing him to be subject to church discipline or to exclusion from the fellowship of the church. In other cases many would say that separation should occur when the church as a body publicly approves of some serious doctrinal or moral error (such as endorsing a doctrinal error in a church creed or statement of faith). However, other Christians would not think separation to be wise or expedient in such cases, but would advocate praying and working for revival and reformation within the church, and giving clear public statements of disagreement with any doctrinal error that has been tolerated. In such cases, those who decide to stay and those who decide they must leave should both recognize that God may call different Christians to different roles and ministries, and therefore to different decisions, and we would do well to give considerable freedom to others to seek God's wisdom in such a case and to obey it as they best understand it for their own lives.

**2. Matters of Conscience.** In the area of conscience, if a Christian had no freedom to preach or teach as his or her conscience, informed by Scripture, would dictate, it might be thought that separation was necessary or at least wise. But caution and great humility are in order here: individual judgment may be distorted, especially if it is not informed by the consensus of faithful believers throughout history, and by the counsel of believers in the present.

Moreover, the command in 2 Corinthians 6:14 not to be yoked together with unbelievers could also require a person to separate if the parent church became so dominated by those who gave no evidence of saving faith that such "yoking together" could not be avoided. In this passage the prohibition against being "yoked together" with unbelievers forbids not mere association or even acceptance of help (cf. Luke 9:50, but also 3 John 7), but rather *the giving up of control over one's activities and the loss of freedom to act in obedience to God,* for these restraints are what is implied in the metaphor of being "yoked" together. Some people might also find it necessary or at least wise to leave a church on the basis of conscience if staying implied approval of some unbiblical doctrine or practice within the church, and thereby encouraged others to follow that wrong doctrine or practice.

---

[12]After saying that "The purist Churches under heaven are subject both to mixture and error," the Westminster Confession of Faith adds, "and some have so degenerated, as to become no Churches of Christ, but synagogues of Satan" (25.5).

But others may think it right to stay in the church and voice clear disapproval of the faulty doctrine.

In other cases, some have argued that it is required to leave a denomination when a higher governing authority in that denomination, which one has promised to obey, commands an action which is clearly sinful (that is, an action which is clearly contrary to Scripture). In such a case some would say that leaving the denomination is the only way to avoid doing either the sinful act which is commanded or the sinful act of disobedience to those in authority. But this does not seem to be a necessary requirement, for many Scripture passages could be cited showing that disobedience to a higher authority is not wrong when one is commanded to sin (see Acts 5:29; Dan. 3:18; 6:10), and that one may disobey but remain in the parent church until forced out.

**3. Practical Considerations.** Christians may decide to separate from a parent church if, after prayerful consideration, it seems that staying in the parent church will very likely result in more harm than good. This could be because their work for the Lord would become frustrated and ineffectual due to opposition to it from within the parent church, or because they would find little or no fellowship with others in that church. Moreover, some may decide that staying in the church would harm the faith of other believers or would hinder unbelievers from coming to true faith because their continued affiliation with the parent church would seem to imply approval of false teachings within that church. Again, Christians might find themselves in situations where they have prayed and worked for change for some time but there seems to be no reasonable hope for change in the parent church, perhaps because the present leadership group is resistant to correction from Scripture, is firmly entrenched, and is self-perpetuating. In all of these situations much prayer and mature judgment will be required, because withdrawing from a church, especially by people who have been there a long time or have established leadership functions in the church, is a serious action.

**4. Are There Times When Cooperation and Personal Fellowship Are Prohibited?** Finally, when should Christians take stronger steps than those mentioned above and engage in the kind of separation that we earlier called "no cooperation" or "no personal fellowship"? The biblical passages we have looked at seem to require that Christians practice "no cooperation" in certain activities with another group only when the other group is an unbelieving one, and then, it seems, only when the unbelieving group shares control of the activity (this is implied in the metaphor of being "yoked together" in 2 Cor. 6:14). Of course, it may be found wise or expedient on other grounds to decide not to cooperate in a particular function, but non-cooperation would not seem to be required except when the other group is an unbelieving one. Certainly *opposition* to activities such as evangelistic campaigns by other true believers would be seen by the New Testament authors as divisiveness and a failure to demonstrate the unity of the body of Christ.[13]

---

[13]The New Testament authors would probably also think it tragic that most divisions among Protestants have come about or been maintained today because of differences over some of the least emphasized and least clearly taught doctrines in the New Testament, such as the form of church

The third and most extreme kind of separation, the avoidance of all personal fellowship with members of another entire church group, is never commanded in the New Testament. Such an extreme measure of "no fellowship" is only implied in serious cases of church discipline of individuals, not in cases of differences with entire churches.

## QUESTIONS FOR PERSONAL APPLICATION

1. In what areas is your own church "more pure"? In what areas do you think it is "less pure"?

2. On a scale of 1 to 10 (1 equals less pure; 10 equals more pure), where would you rank your church in each of the categories that mark a more-pure church?

3. What do you think that you should be doing in order to work for greater purity in your own church? Does the fact that you recognize a specific need in the church mean that God is calling you (rather than someone else) to meet that need?

4. Do you know of other churches in your area that you would consider more pure than your own? What are the reasons that you might think it right to stay in your own church even though it may not be the most pure church you know of?

5. Are there marks of a more-pure church that evangelicals generally in this century have been negligent in emphasizing?

6. Since the first century, do you think that by and large the church has continued to increase in purity over time? Can you give specific reasons to support your answer?

7. In your lifetime, what encouraging signs do you see that the church is increasing in purity? What signs do you see that the church is increasing in unity?

8. In what ways do you think your own local church could grow in unity among its members?

9. In what ways could your church demonstrate greater unity with other true churches in the same geographical area? What do you think are the barriers to that unity (if any)? In what ways could that unity be expressed? What might be the benefits of such expressions of unity?

10. Are you in a church where you have wondered if God would have you leave and join another church? After reading this chapter, do you now think that you should stay in your present church or leave it? Has there been significant change for the better in your church in the last ten years? If you knew that the church were to remain substantially the same for the next ten years, would you decide to stay now or to leave it?

---

government, the exact nature of Christ's presence in the Lord's Supper, and the details of the end times. (Many people would want to add to that list: differences over the proper subjects for baptism.)

11. What are some ways in which the worldwide unity of true believers is already being expressed and demonstrated? What would the church around the world look like if there were much greater demonstration of the unity of the church? What would be the result in the world as a whole?

12. If a community already has several active and effective evangelical churches, is there any justification for another evangelical denomination to attempt to plant its own church in that community?

13. Do you think it hinders evangelism and witness to society generally when the popular culture thinks of unbelieving or false churches and believing churches both as "Christians"? Can anything be done to change that impression?

14. What kinds of unity and cooperation can appropriately be demonstrated with believers within the Roman Catholic Church today? What are the limits to such cooperation?

## SPECIAL TERMS

Eastern church                                    unity of the church
purity of the church                          Western church
separation

## BIBLIOGRAPHY

(For an explanation of this bibliography see the note on the bibliography to chapter 1, p. 38. Complete bibliographical data may be found on pp. 1223–29.)

### Sections in Evangelical Systematic Theologies

1. Anglican (Episcopalian)
    1882–92    Litton, 380–86, 413–18
2. Arminian (Wesleyan or Methodist)
    1875–76    Pope, 3:267–79
    1940    Wiley, 3:112–13
    1983    Carter, 2:594–95
3. Baptist
    1983–85    Erickson, 1129–46
4. Dispensational
(no explicit treatment)
5. Lutheran
    1917–24    Pieper, 3:423–27
    1934    Mueller, 556–62
6. Reformed (or Presbyterian)
    1559    Calvin, 2:1011–53 (4.1–2)
    1861    Heppe, 670–72
    1887–1921    Warfield, SSW, 1:299–307

1937–66        Murray, *CW*, 1:269–91; *CW*, 2:321–36
        1962       Buswell, 1:421–24
7. Renewal (or charismatic/Pentecostal)
        1988–92    Williams, 3:25–35

### Sections in Representative Roman Catholic Systematic Theologies

1. Roman Catholic: Traditional
        1955       Ott, 290–309
2. Roman Catholic: Post-Vatican II
        1980       McBrien, 2:854–58

### Other Works

Bromiley, G. W. "Unity." In *EDT*, pp. 1127–28.
Carson, Donald A. "Evangelicals, Ecumenism and the Church." In *Evangelical Affirmations*. Ed. by Kenneth S. Kantzer and Carl F. H. Henry. Grand Rapids: Zondervan, 1990, pp. 347–85.
Puritan and Reformed Studies Conference. *Approaches to Reformation of the Church*. London: *The Evangelical* magazine, 1965. Contains papers by D. W. Marshall, D. P. Kingdon, J. I. Packer, G. S. R. Cox, S. M. Houghton, and D. M. Lloyd-Jones.

### SCRIPTURE MEMORY PASSAGE

**Ephesians 4:14–16:** *So that we may no longer be children, tossed to and fro and carried about with every wind of doctrine, by the cunning of men, by their craftiness in deceitful wiles. Rather, speaking the truth in love, we are to grow up in every way into him who is the head, into Christ, from whom the whole body, joined and knit together by every joint with which it is supplied, when each part is working properly, makes bodily growth and upbuilds itself in love.*

### HYMN

#### "Blest Be the Tie That Binds"

This hymn speaks of the unity or the "tie" that binds the hearts of Christians together in love. It continues to speak of fellowship as like the fellowship of heaven: it is "like to that above." It also speaks of sharing in prayer and concern for each other and bearing of one another's burdens. The hymn goes on to speak of our hope that we will one day be united in "perfect love and friendship" for eternity in heaven.

> Blest be the tie that binds
> Our hearts in Christian love:
> The fellowship of kindred minds
> Is like to that above.
>
> Before our Father's throne
> We pour our ardent prayers;

Our fears, our hopes, our aims, are one,
   Our comforts and our cares.

We share our mutual woes,
   Our mutual burdens bear,
And often for each other flows
   The sympathizing tear.

When we asunder part,
   It gives us inward pain;
But we shall still be joined in heart,
   And hope to meet again.

This glorious hope revives
   Our courage by the way,
While each in expectation lives,
   And longs to see the day.

From sorrow, toil and pain,
   And sin, we shall be free;
And perfect love and friendship reign
   Through all eternity.

AUTHOR: JOHN FAWCETT, 1782

# Chapter 46

# The Power of the Church

*What kind of authority does the church have?*
*How should church discipline function?*

## EXPLANATION AND SCRIPTURAL BASIS

When we look at the powerful governments of the world and at other business and educational organizations that have great influence, and then consider our local churches, or even our denominational headquarters, the church may seem to us to be weak and ineffective. Moreover, when we recognize the rapid growth of evil that is seen daily in our society, we may wonder if the church has power to make any changes at all.

On the other hand, in some countries the officially recognized church has great influence on the conduct of national affairs. This was certainly true of the influence of the Roman Catholic Church in former times in some southern European and Latin American countries (and is still true today to some extent). It was true of the Church of England in previous centuries, and of John Calvin's church in Geneva, Switzerland, while he was alive, and of the church founded by the pilgrims in the Massachusetts Bay Colony in 1620. Situations like these where the church appears to have great influence cause us to ask whether Scripture places any limitations on the church's power.

We may define the power of the church as follows: *The power of the church is its God-given authority to carry on spiritual warfare, proclaim the gospel, and exercise church discipline.*

Although these three areas overlap and could be treated in any order, since the category of "spiritual warfare" is the broader category it will be treated first. This perspective on the church's power also reminds us that the power of the church, unlike the worldly influence exercised by human armies and governments, directly affects the spiritual realm.

## A. Spiritual Warfare

Paul reminds the Corinthians, "For though we live in the world we are not carrying on a worldly war, for *the weapons of our warfare are not worldly but have divine power to destroy strongholds*" (2 Cor. 10:3–4). These weapons, used against demonic forces that hinder the spread of the gospel and the progress of the church, include such things as prayer, worship, the authority to rebuke demonic forces, the words of Scripture, faith, and righteous conduct on the part of the members of the church. (Paul gives further details about our spiritual conflict and the armor we wear for it in Eph. 6:10–18.)

When we consider this spiritual power in a broad sense, it certainly includes the power of the gospel to break through sin and hardened opposition and awaken faith in the hearts of unbelievers (see Rom. 10:17; James 1:18; 1 Peter 1:23). But this power also includes spiritual power that will render demonic opposition to the gospel ineffective. We see examples of this in Acts 13:8–11, where Paul pronounced judgment on Elymas the magician, who was opposing the preaching of the gospel, and in Acts 16:16–18, where Paul rebuked an evil spirit in the soothsaying girl who was annoying Paul while he proclaimed the gospel.[1] Such spiritual power to defeat evil opposition was seen frequently in the early church, such as in the freeing of Peter from prison (Acts 12:1–17), and perhaps also in the subsequent judgment on King Herod Agrippa I (Acts 12:20–24).[2]

Yet Paul realizes that he can use this spiritual power not only against those outside the church who oppose the gospel, but also against those within the church who are active opponents of his apostolic ministry. He says about some arrogant troublemakers in the church, "I will come to you soon, if the Lord wills, and I will find out not the talk of these arrogant people but their power. For the kingdom of God does not consist in talk but in power" (1 Cor. 4:19–20). Such power was not to be trifled with, for it was the same power of the Holy Spirit that had brought death to Ananias and Sapphira (Acts 5:1–11) and blindness to Elymas (Acts 13:8–11). Paul did not wish to use this power in a judgmental capacity, but he was prepared to do so if necessary. Later he wrote again to the Corinthians that his actions when present would be as powerful as his letters when absent (2 Cor. 10:8–11), and he warned those who opposed his authority and had sinned publicly and not repented, "If I come again I will not spare them— since you desire proof that Christ is speaking in me. . . . For we are weak in him, but in dealing with you we shall live with him by the power of God" (2 Cor. 13:2–4). He then adds a final reminder of his reluctance to use this authority, telling them that he is writing before he comes "in order that when I come I may not have to be severe in my use of the authority which the Lord has given me for building up and not for tearing down" (2 Cor. 13:10).

Now we may question whether the church today has the same degree of spiritual power that the apostles Peter or Paul did. Certainly there is a distinction between the apostles and the other early Christians even in the book of Acts (note that immediately after the death of Ananias and Sapphira "many signs and wonders" were done "by the hands of the apostles," but "None of the rest dared join them, but the people held them in high honor," Acts 5:12–13). Moreover, Paul did not instruct any leaders of the church at Corinth, or even Timothy or Titus, to exercise that spiritual power at Corinth against his opponents. He spoke

---

[1]Jesus often rebuked demonic spirits that created disturbances when he was ministering to people: see Mark 1:23–26; 5:1–13; et al.

[2]The text does not specify that Herod's death was in any way connected to the "earnest prayer" (Acts 12:5) that was made for Peter by the church, but the fact that the narrative about Herod's death follows immediately upon the story of his killing James the brother of John with the sword and his putting Peter in prison certainly hints at the fact that God intended this as a judgment upon one of the primary enemies of the church, showing that no opposition could stand against the progress of the gospel. This understanding is also supported by the fact that the sentence immediately following the narrative of Herod's death is, "But the word of God grew and multiplied" (Acts 12:24).

about the power which the Lord "has given *me*" (2 Cor. 13:10), not about the power which the Lord had given to the church or to Christians generally.

On the other hand, Paul did direct the Corinthian church to exercise church discipline in a case of incest in the church at Corinth, and to do it "when you are assembled, and my spirit is present, with the power of our Lord Jesus" (1 Cor. 5:4). Moreover, the descriptions of spiritual warfare in Ephesians 6:10–18 and 2 Corinthians 10:3–4 seem applicable to Christians generally, and few today would deny that the church has authority to pray against and to speak with authority against demonic opposition to the work of the gospel.[3] So there would seem to be at least some significant degree of spiritual power against evil opposition that God is willing to grant to the church in every age (including the present one). Perhaps it is impossible to define more specifically the degree of spiritual power God will grant to the church in times of conflict against evil, but we do not need to know the details in advance: our calling is simply to be faithful to Scripture in praying and in exercising church discipline, and then to leave the rest in God's hands, knowing that he will grant sufficient power to accomplish his purposes through the church.

## B. The Keys of the Kingdom

The phrase "the keys of the kingdom" occurs only once in the Bible, in Matthew 16:19, where Jesus is speaking to Peter: "I will give you the keys of the kingdom of heaven; and whatever you shall bind on earth shall have been bound in heaven and whatever you shall loose on earth shall have been loosed in heaven" (NASB). What is the meaning of these "keys of the kingdom of heaven"?[4]

Elsewhere in the New Testament a key always implies *authority to open a door and give entrance to a place or realm.* Jesus says, "Woe to you lawyers! for you have taken away the key of knowledge; you did not enter yourselves, and you hindered those who were entering" (Luke 11:52). Moreover, Jesus says in Revelation 1:18, "I have the keys of Death and Hades," implying that he has the authority to grant entrance and exit from those realms. (Cf. also Rev. 3:7; 9:1; 20:1; also the messianic prediction in Isa. 22:22.)

The "keys of the kingdom of heaven" therefore represent at least the authority to preach the gospel of Christ (cf. Matt. 16:16) and thus to open the door of the kingdom of heaven and allow people to enter.

Peter first used this authority by preaching the gospel at Pentecost (Acts 2:14–42). But the other apostles also were given this authority in a primary sense (they wrote the gospel in permanent form in the New Testament). And all believers have this "key" in a secondary sense, for they can all share the gospel with others, and thereby open the kingdom of heaven to those who will enter it.

But is there any other authority, in addition to this, that Jesus implies by the phrase "the keys of the kingdom of heaven"? There are two factors suggesting that the authority of the keys here also includes *the authority to exercise discipline within the church:* (1) The plural "keys" suggests authority over more than one door.

---

[3]See chapter 20, pp. 419–33, on conflict with demonic forces in general, and p. 421 on the question of "strategic level spiritual warfare."

[4]The rest of this section discussing the keys of the kingdom of heaven is adapted from the article, "Keys of the Kingdom" by Wayne Grudem, in *EDT,* pp. 604–5, and is used here by permission.

Thus, more than simply entrance into the kingdom is implied; some authority *within* the kingdom is also suggested. (2) Jesus completes the promise about the keys with a statement about "binding" and "loosing," which closely parallels another saying of his in Matthew 18, in which "binding" and "loosing" mean placing under church discipline and releasing from church discipline:

If he refuses to listen even to the church, let him be to you as a Gentile and a tax-gatherer. Truly I say to you, whatever you shall *bind* on earth shall have been bound in heaven; and whatever you *loose* on earth shall have been loosed in heaven. (Matt. 18:17–18 NASB)

But if "binding" and "loosing" clearly refer to church discipline in Matthew 18, then it seems likely that they would also refer to church discipline in Matthew 16, where Jesus' words are very similar.[5]

This understanding of binding and loosing in terms of church discipline also fits the context of Matthew 16:19, for, on this understanding, after promising to build his church (v. 18), Jesus promises to give not only the authority to open the door of entrance into the kingdom, but also some administrative authority to regulate the conduct of people once they are inside.[6] Therefore it seems that "the keys of the kingdom of heaven" which Jesus promised to Peter in Matthew 16:19 included both (1) ability to admit people to the kingdom through preaching the gospel, and (2) authority to exercise church discipline for those who do enter.

In Matthew 16:16–19, Jesus does not indicate whether the authority of the keys will later be given to others besides Peter. But certainly the authority to preach the gospel is given to others at a later time, and in Matthew 18:18 Jesus does state explicitly that the authority to exercise church discipline is given to the church generally whenever it meets and corporately carries out such discipline ("Tell it to the church," Matt. 18:17). Thus both aspects of the authority of the keys, though first given to Peter, were soon expanded to include the authority given to the church as a whole. In preaching the gospel and in exercising discipline the church now exercises the authority of the keys of the kingdom.

What persons or actions are subject to the kind of church discipline implied by the authority of the keys? In both Matthew 16:19 and 18:18, the term "whatever" is neuter in Greek, and seems to indicate that Jesus is speaking not specifically to *persons* ("whoever," for which a masculine plural would be ordinarily expected), but rather more generally to *situations* and *relationships* that come up within the church. This would not exclude the authority to exercise discipline over

---

[5]The statement in Matt. 16:19 uses singular pronouns for "whatever" and "you" (referring to Peter), while Matt. 18:18 uses plurals (referring to Christians generally), but the same Greek words are used for "bind" (*deō*) and "loose" (*luō*), and the grammatical construction (periphrastic future perfect) is the same.

[6]Some have argued that binding and loosing do not refer to actions of church discipline, but to an authority to make various rules for conduct, because in the rabbinic literature that comes from Jewish teachers around the time of Jesus the words *bind* and *loose* are sometimes used for forbidding and permitting various kinds of conduct. This interpretation does not seem persuasive, however, because these rabbinic statements are a much more distant parallel than the statement of Jesus himself in Matt. 18:18, where church discipline is clearly in view. Moreover, it is difficult to know whether any of the rabbinic parallels pre-date the time of the New Testament, or to show that such words would have functioned as technical terms in the ordinary vocabulary of Jesus and his hearers—in fact, Matt. 18:18 shows that they did not function as technical terms in that way, because they were used rather to refer to church discipline in that verse.

individuals, but the phrase is broader than that, and includes specific actions that are subject to discipline as well.

Yet the authority of the keys with respect to church discipline is not completely unlimited. It will only be effective against true sin (cf. Matt. 18:15), sin as defined by God's Word. The church does not have authority on its own to legislate what is morally right and wrong in an absolute sense, for the authority to define right and wrong belongs to God alone (see Rom. 1:32; 2:16; 3:4–8; 9:20; Ps. 119:89, 142, 160; Matt. 5:18). The church can only declare and teach what God has already commanded in his Word. Nor can the authority of the keys involve authority to forgive sins in any absolute sense, because in Scripture it is clear that that can only be done by God himself (Isa. 43:25; 55:7; Mark 2:7, 10; Ps. 103:3; 1 John 1:9).[7] Therefore the authority to carry out discipline in the church is an authority that must be carried out in accordance with the standards of Scripture.

Is it possible to be any more specific about the kind of spiritual authority that is involved in this use of the keys of the kingdom of heaven? Both Matthew 16:19 and 18:18 use an unusual Greek verbal construction (a periphrastic future perfect). It is best translated by the NASB, "Whatever you shall bind on earth *shall have been bound* in heaven, and whatever you shall loose on earth *shall have been loosed* in heaven."[8] Several other examples of this construction show that it indicates not just a future action ("shall be bound"), for which a common Greek tense was available (future passive), but rather *an action that would be completed before some future point*, with effects that would continue to be felt.[9] Thus, Jesus is teaching that church discipline will have heavenly sanction. But it is not as if the church must wait for God to endorse its actions after the actions have occurred. Rather, whenever the church *enacts discipline* it can be confident that God has already begun the process spiritually. Whenever it *releases from discipline*, forgives the sinner, and restores personal relationships, the church can be confident that God has already begun the restoration spiritually (cf. John 20:23). In this way Jesus promises that the spiritual relationship between God and the person subject to discipline will be immediately affected in ways consistent with the direction of the church's disciplinary action. Legitimate church discipline, therefore, involves the awesome certainty that corresponding heavenly discipline has already begun.

Moreover, this teaching on the power of the keys has a significant application to individual Christians who begin to be subject to the discipline of a true church: Christians should submit to this discipline and not run from it, because God himself has also put them under discipline for that sin.

## C. The Power of the Church and the Power of the State

The previous sections have discussed spiritual power and spiritual warfare to be exercised by the church. But should the church ever use physical force (weapons

---

[7]In John 20:23, the forgiveness of sins by the disciples is best understood as freeing from church discipline and restoring personal relationships in a sense similar to the "loosing" of Matt. 16:19 and 18:18.

[8]See the grammatical discussion in D. A. Carson's commentary on Matthew in *The Expositors' Bible Commentary*, pp. 370–72.

[9]See examples in Luke 12:52; Gen. 43:9; 44:42; Ex. 12:6; Sirach 7:25; Hermas, *Similitudes* 5.4.2; *Letter of Aristeas* 40.

and armies, for example) to carry out its mission? The phrase commonly used to refer to the idea of physical, worldly warfare is "to take up the sword."

There are several indications in Scripture that the church must never take up the sword to carry out its purposes in the new covenant age. This was a dreadful mistake made in the Crusades, when church-sponsored armies marched across Europe and Asia to attempt to reclaim the land of Israel. In these cases the church was trying to use physical force to bring about its triumph over earthly territories. But Jesus said, "*My kingdom is not of this world.* If it were, my servants would fight" (John 18:36 NIV). The church has the power of the keys, which is spiritual power. It is to carry out spiritual battles using spiritual weapons, but is not to use the power of the sword to accomplish its purposes. "The weapons of our warfare are not worldly" (2 Cor. 10:4).

Certainly God does give *to civil government* the right to bear the sword, that is, to use force to punish evil in the world (Rom. 13:1–7). But there is no indication that the power of government is to be used to enforce adherence to Christianity upon any people.[10] Moreover, there are several indications that Jesus refused to use the power of physical force to compel people to accept the gospel. For example, when a Samaritan village would not receive Jesus, James and John asked, "Lord, do you want us to bid fire come down from heaven and consume them?" (Luke 9:54). But Jesus "rebuked them" (v. 55) for even making that suggestion. Jesus came the first time to offer the gospel to all who would receive it, not to execute punishment on those who rejected it. This is why he could say, "For God sent the Son into the world, not to condemn the world, but that the world might be saved through him" (John 3:17). He will one day come again in judgment, at the end of the church age, but during this age it is not the prerogative of the church to use physical force to carry out judgment.

Jesus clearly made a distinction between the authority granted to the government and the authority that God exercises in our personal allegiance to him when he said, "Render therefore to Caesar the things that are Caesar's, and to God the things that are God's" (Matt. 22:21). And though Jesus recognized the authority of civil government, he refused to usurp that authority himself, telling someone, "Man, who made me a judge or divider over you?" with respect to a matter of family inheritance (Luke 12:13–14).

A further reason why the government should not use force to require allegiance to Christianity is that in the new covenant, membership in the church and allegiance to Christ must be voluntary. They cannot be compelled by family or by the state. In fact, faith in Christ, to be truly held and practiced, cannot be compelled by force. If it is compelled, it changes its essential quality and is no longer a voluntary act of the individual, and cannot be true faith.

From this it also follows that *the civil government should not enforce laws requiring or prohibiting kinds of church doctrine, or abridging the people's freedom to worship as they choose.* On the other hand, the church does not and should not rule over the state, as if it were some kind of higher authority over the state; it is not. Rather, the authority of the church and that of the state belong to distinct spheres (Matt.

---

[10]Edmund Clowney rightly observes, "We may not suppose that Christ denied to his apostles the right to bring in his kingdom with the sword, but conceded that right to Pilate" ("The Biblical Theology of the Church," in *The Church in the Bible and the World,* ed. by D. A. Carson [Exeter: Paternoster, and Grand Rapids: Baker, 1987], p. 33).

22:21; John 18:36; 2 Cor. 10:3–4), and each should respect the authority God has given the other in its own sphere of operation.

These limitations on the activities of the church and the state are different from the practice of the Catholic Church through much of the Middle Ages, where it often had more power than the civil government. These principles also differ from the practice of the Church of England, which is subject to the authority of the Queen and Parliament in the appointment of bishops and any change in doctrinal standards. The failure to respect the distinct roles of church and state is seen in many Roman Catholic countries today, where the church still has strong influence on the government, and in the compulsory membership in state-sponsored Protestant churches of Northern Europe after the Reformation, a situation that caused many emigrants to flee to America for religious freedom.

However, it should be said that the degree of state-enforced religion in Protestant or Catholic countries is mild indeed compared to state-sponsored and state-enforced religion in most Muslim countries today, and in many Hindu and Buddhist countries as well. In fact, it is difficult to find genuine freedom of religion apart from the strong influence of healthy evangelical Christianity in any country around the world (except where various religions are so weak or so evenly balanced that no one religion has dominant political power). Whenever Christians are involved in the political realm, they ought clearly to affirm freedom of religion as a political policy that is nonnegotiable, and they should be willing to defend that freedom for religions other than their own as well. The Christian faith can stand on its own two feet and compete very well in the market-place of ideas in any society and in any culture, provided it has the freedom to do so.

Finally, what has been said above should not be misunderstood as a prohibition against Christians attempting to bring positive moral influence on government and attempting to persuade governments to make laws consistent with biblical standards of morality. It is right for Christians to attempt to persuade governments to make laws that protect families and private property and the lives of human beings—laws that both outlaw and punish murder, adultery, theft, and the breaking of contracts (things that violate the Ten Commandments), as well as prohibit homosexual conduct, drunkenness, drug abuse, abortion, and other things that are inconsistent with biblical standards of morality. These things are far different from requiring belief in certain types of church doctrine or theological conviction, and from requiring that people attend certain kinds of church or worship services. The latter are clearly "religious" activities in the narrow sense in that they pertain to our relationship to God and our beliefs about him.[11] Governments should refrain from making laws about these things.

---

[11]The fact that Christians should try to influence government to make laws consistent with biblical standards is indicated by passages such as Matt. 6:10; 14:4; Acts 24:25; and 1 Tim. 2:1–4. We may hope that the moral standards of Scripture will also eventually gain general consent from most of the people of a given society, since those moral standards have also been inscribed on their hearts and therefore they have a witness in their consciences that these standards are correct (see Rom. 2:14–15). It is also the case that God holds all societies and cultures responsible for obeying his moral standards, and often in the Old Testament God's prophets pronounced judgments upon not only the people of Israel but also upon immoral pagan societies, even though they did not have his written laws (see Deut. 9:5; Isa. 13–23; Ezek. 25–32; Dan. 4:27; Amos 1–2; Obadiah [written to Edom]; Jonah [prophesied to Nineveh]; Nahum [prophesied to Nineveh]; Hab. 2; Zeph. 2). In fact, civil

## D. Church Discipline

Since church discipline is one aspect of the use of the power of the church, it is appropriate here to give some discussion of the biblical principles relevant to the practice of church discipline.

## 1. The Purpose of Church Discipline.

**a. Restoration and Reconciliation of the Believer Who Is Going Astray:** Sin hinders fellowship among believers and with God. In order for reconciliation to occur, the sin must be dealt with. Therefore, the primary purpose of church discipline is to pursue the twofold goal of *restoration* (of the offender to right behavior) and *reconciliation* (between believers, and with God).[12] Just as wise parents discipline their children (Prov. 13:24: "He who loves [his son] is diligent to discipline him"), and just as God our Father disciplines those whom he loves (Heb. 12:6; Rev. 3:19), so the church in its discipline is acting in love to bring back a brother or sister who has gone astray, reestablishing that person in right fellowship and rescuing him or her from destructive patterns of life. In Matthew 18:15, the hope is that discipline will stop at the first step, when someone goes alone: "If he listens to you, you have gained your brother." The phrase "you have gained your brother" implies that those carrying out discipline should keep the goal of personal reconciliation among Christians always in mind. Paul reminds us that we are to "restore" the sinning brother or sister "in a spirit of gentleness" (Gal. 6:1), and James encourages us to "bring back a sinner from the error of his way" (James 5:20).

In fact, if church members were actively involved in giving private words of gentle admonition and in praying for one another when the first clear evidence of sinful conduct is seen, very little formal church discipline would have to be carried out, because the process would begin and end with a conversation between two people that never becomes known to anyone else.

Even when the final step of "excommunication" (that is, putting someone out of the fellowship or "communion" of the church) is taken, it is still with the hope that repentance will result. Paul delivered Hymenaeus and Alexander to Satan *"that they may learn not to blaspheme"* (1 Tim. 1:20), and the man living in incest at Corinth was to be delivered to Satan "that his spirit may be saved in the day of the Lord Jesus" (1 Cor. 5:5).[13]

If Christians who must take steps of church discipline will continue to remember this first purpose—the reconciliation of believers who are going astray

---

governments are sent by God "to punish those who do wrong and to praise those who do right" (1 Peter 2:14).

[12]In their excellent book on church discipline, *Church Discipline That Heals* (Downers Grove, Ill.: InterVarsity Press, 1985; originally published as *Healing the Wounded*), John White and Ken Blue note that a failure to keep reconciliation as the primary goal of church discipline has led to many abuses of the process in the history of the church (see esp. pp. 45–56). But they themselves say that "true reconciliation never takes place without change in the parties involved" (p. 46). Therefore I have combined reconciliation and restoration in this first section.

[13]The unusual phrase "deliver to Satan" in these verses seems to mean "put out of the church" since that is clearly what Paul tells the Corinthians to do in 1 Cor. 5:2, 7, 13. Putting someone out of the church puts that person back into the kingdom of this sinful age, which is ruled by Satan.

with each other and with God, and their restoration to right patterns of life—then it will be much easier to continue to act in genuine love for the parties involved, and feelings of anger or desires for revenge on the part of those who have been hurt, which often lie near the surface, will much more easily be avoided.

**b. To Keep the Sin From Spreading to Others:** Although the primary goal of church discipline is restoration and reconciliation for the erring believer, in this present age reconciliation and restoration will not always come about. But whether restoration comes about or not, the church is told to carry out discipline because two other purposes are served as well.

One other purpose is that the sin will be kept from spreading to others. The author of Hebrews tells Christians to see to it that "no 'root of bitterness' spring up and cause trouble, and by it *the many become defiled*" (Heb. 12:15). This means that if conflict between persons is not resolved quickly, the effects may spread to many others—something that sadly seems to be true in many cases of church division. Paul also says, *"A little leaven leavens the whole lump,"* and tells the Corinthians to put out of the church a man living in incest (1 Cor. 5:2, 6–7), lest his sin affect the whole church. If that man were not disciplined, the effects of the sin would spread to many others who were aware of it and saw that the church paid little attention to it. This would cause many to think that perhaps that sin was not as bad as they had thought, and others might be tempted to commit similar or related kinds of sin. Moreover, if discipline against one specific offense is not carried out, then it will be much more difficult for the church to carry out discipline if a similar kind of sin is committed by someone else in the future.

Paul also told Timothy that elders who persist in sin are to be rebuked in the presence of all, *"so that the rest may stand in fear"* (1 Tim. 5:20)—that is, so that many others would realize that the sin will not be tolerated but will receive discipline both from the church and from God himself. In fact, Paul rebuked Peter publicly, in order that others would not follow Peter's bad example of separating himself and eating only with Jewish believers (Gal. 2:11).

**c. To Protect the Purity of the Church and the Honor of Christ:** A third purpose of church discipline is that the purity of the church is to be protected, so that Christ will not be dishonored. Of course, no believer in this age has a completely pure heart, and we all have remaining sin in our lives. But when a church member continues to sin in a way that is outwardly evident to others, especially to unbelievers,[14] this clearly brings dishonor to Christ. It is similar to the situation of Jews who disobeyed God's law and led unbelievers to scoff and blaspheme God's name (Rom. 2:24: "The name of God is blasphemed among the Gentiles because of you").

This is why Paul is shocked that the Corinthians have not disciplined the man who continued in willful sin that was publicly known in the church (1 Cor. 5:1–2: "And you are arrogant! Ought you not rather to mourn?"). He is also greatly distressed to know that "brother goes to law against brother, and that before unbelievers" (1 Cor. 6:6). Rather than allowing such moral blemishes on the character of the church, Peter encourages believers to "be zealous to be found by

---

[14]But also to angels (see Eph. 3:10; 1 Tim. 5:21).

[Christ] without spot or blemish, and at peace" (2 Peter 3:14). And our Lord Jesus wants to present to himself a church "without spot or wrinkle . . . holy and without blemish" (Eph. 5:27), for he is the head of the church, and its character reflects on his reputation. Even angels and demons look at the church and behold the wisdom of God expressed in it (Eph. 3:10); therefore (Eph. 4:1) Paul encourages Christians to be "eager to maintain the unity of the Spirit in the bond of peace" (Eph. 4:3).

This is a very serious matter. Since the Lord Jesus is jealous for his own honor, if the church does not exercise proper discipline, he will do it himself, as he did at Corinth, where the Lord's discipline resulted in sickness and death (1 Cor. 11:27–34), and as he warned he would do both at Pergamum (Rev. 2:14–15) and at Thyatira (Rev. 2:20). In these last two cases the Lord was displeased with the whole church for tolerating outward disobedience and not exercising discipline: "But I have this against you, that *you tolerate the woman Jezebel,* who calls herself a prophetess and is teaching and beguiling my servants to practice immorality and to eat food sacrificed to idols" (Rev. 2:20; cf. vv. 14–16).[15]

**2. For What Sins Should Church Discipline Be Exercised?** On the one hand, Jesus' teaching in Matthew 18:15–20 tells us that if a situation involving personal sin against someone else cannot be resolved in a private or small group meeting, then the matter must be brought to the church:

> If your brother sins against you, go and tell him his fault, between you and him alone. If he listens to you, you have gained your brother. But if he does not listen, take one or two others along with you, that every word may be confirmed by the evidence of two or three witnesses. If he refuses to listen to them, tell it to the church; and if he refuses to listen even to the church, let him be to you as a Gentile and a tax collector. (Matt. 18:15–17)

In this case the matter has progressed from a private and informal situation to a public and much more formal process of discipline by the whole church.

On the other hand, there does not seem to be any explicit limitation specified for the kinds of sin that should be subject to church discipline. The examples of sins subject to church discipline in the New Testament are extremely diverse: divisiveness (Rom. 16:17; Titus 3:10), incest (1 Cor. 5:1), laziness and refusing to work (2 Thess. 3:6–10), disobeying what Paul writes (2 Thess. 3:14–15), blasphemy (1 Tim. 1:20), and teaching heretical doctrine (2 John 10–11).

Nonetheless, a definite principle appears to be at work: all sins that were explicitly disciplined in the New Testament were publicly known or outwardly evident sins,[16] and many of them had continued over a period of time. The fact

---

[15]The purposes of church discipline discussed above are well summarized in the Westminster Confession of Faith, chapter 30, paragraph 3: "Church censures are necessary, for the reclaiming and gaining of offending brethren, for deterring of others from the like offenses, for purging out of that leaven which might infect the whole lump, for vindicating the honor of Christ, and the holy profession of the gospel, and for preventing the wrath of God, which might justly fall upon the church, if they should suffer his covenant, and the seals thereof, to be profaned by notorious and obstinate offenders."

[16]One exception was the secret sin of Ananias and Sapphira in Acts 5:1–11. In this situation the Holy Spirit (vv. 3, 8) was so powerfully present that he brought an intrusion of final judgment, when the secrets of all hearts will be disclosed, into the church age, "and great fear came upon the whole church" (v. 11).

that the sins were publicly known meant that reproach was being brought on the church, Christ was being dishonored, and there was a real possibility that others would be encouraged to follow the wrongful patterns of life that were being publicly tolerated.

There is always the need, however, for mature judgment in the exercise of church discipline, because there is lack of complete sanctification in all our lives. Furthermore, when we realize that someone is already aware of a sin and struggling to overcome it, a word of admonition may in fact do more harm than good. We should also remember that where there are issues of conduct on which Christians legitimately disagree, Paul encourages a wide degree of tolerance (Rom. 14:1–23).

## 3. How Should Church Discipline Be Carried Out?

**a. Knowledge of the Sin Should Be Kept to the Smallest Group Possible:** This seems to be the purpose in Matthew 18:15–17 behind the gradual progression from a private meeting, to a meeting with two or three others, to telling the entire church. The fewer people who know about some sin, the better, because repentance is easier, fewer people are led astray, and less harm is done to the reputation of the person, the reputation of the church, and the reputation of Christ.[17]

**b. Disciplinary Measures Should Increase in Strength Until There Is a Solution:** Once again in Matthew 18 Jesus teaches us that we cannot stop simply with a private conversation if that has not brought satisfactory results. He requires that the wronged person first go alone, and then take one or two others (Matt. 18:15–16). Moreover, if a Christian thinks that he or she has wronged someone else (or even if that other person *thinks* that he or she has been wronged), Jesus requires that the person who has done the wrong (or is thought to have done the wrong) go to the person who considers himself the victim of wrongdoing (Matt. 5:23). This means that whether we have been wronged or others think they have been wronged, *it is always our responsibility* to take the initiative and go to the other person. Jesus does not allow us to wait for the other person to come to us.

After a private meeting and a small group meeting, Jesus does not specify that the elders or officers of the church are next to be consulted as a group, but certainly this intermediate step seems to be appropriate, because Jesus may simply be summarizing the process without necessarily mentioning every possible step in it. In fact, there are several examples of small group admonition in the New Testament which are carried out by elders or other church officers (see 1 Thess. 5:12; 2 Tim. 4:2; Titus 1:13; 2:15; 3:10; James 5:19–20). Moreover, the principle of keeping the knowledge of sin to the smallest group possible would certainly encourage this intermediate step as well.

Finally, if the situation cannot be resolved Jesus says to "tell it to the church" (Matt. 18:17). In this case the church would be assembled to hear the facts of the case and to come to a decision. Since Jesus allows for the possibility that the

---

[17]However, see section c below on the requirement for public disclosure of the serious sins of a church leader.

person "refuses to listen even to the church" (v. 17), the church may have to meet once to decide what to say to the offender, and then meet again to exclude that person from the fellowship of the church.[18]

When Jesus gives these directions about church discipline, he reminds the church that his own presence and his own power are behind the decisions made by the church: "Again I say to you, if two of you agree on earth about anything they ask, it will be done for them by my Father in heaven. For where two or three are gathered in my name, *there am I in the midst of them*" (Matt. 18:19–20). Jesus promises to be present in church gatherings generally, but specifically here with respect to the church being gathered for discipline of an offending member. And Paul similarly tells the Corinthians to discipline the erring member when they are assembled *"with the power of our Lord Jesus"* (1 Cor. 5:4). This is not an activity to be taken lightly, but is carried out in the presence of the Lord, the spiritual component of it actually being carried out by the Lord himself.

If this ever must be done, the whole church will then know that the erring person is no longer considered a member of the church, and that person would not be allowed to take Communion, since partaking in the Lord's Supper is a sign of partaking in the unity of the church (1 Cor. 10:17: "Because there is one bread, we who are many are one body, *for we all partake of the one bread*").

There are other passages in the New Testament that speak of avoiding fellowship with the excommunicated person. Paul tells the Corinthians, "I wrote to you *not to associate* with any one who bears the name of brother if he is guilty of immorality or greed, or is an idolater, reviler, drunkard, or robber—not even to eat with such a one" (1 Cor. 5:11). He tells the Thessalonians, "Now we command you, brethren, in the name of our Lord Jesus Christ, that you keep away from any brother who is living in idleness and not in accord with the tradition that you received from us" (2 Thess. 3:6). Moreover, he says, "If any one refuses to obey what we say in this letter, note that man, and have nothing to do with him, that he may be ashamed. Do not look on him as an enemy, but warn him as a brother" (2 Thess. 3:14–15). Second John 10–11 also prohibits greeting or welcoming into the house anyone who is promoting false teaching. These instructions are apparently given to prevent the church from giving to others the impression that it approves of the disobedience of the erring person.

**c. Discipline of Church Leaders:** In one passage Paul gives special directives concerning the discipline of church elders:

> Never admit any charge *against an elder* except on the evidence of two or three witnesses. As for those who persist in sin, *rebuke them in the presence of all, so that the rest may stand in fear*. In the presence of God and of Christ Jesus and of the elect angels I charge you to keep these rules without favor, doing nothing from partiality. (1 Tim. 5:19–21)

Paul here gives a special caution to protect elders from individual attacks: action regarding wrongdoing in this case should require the evidence of two or three witnesses. "Those who persist in sin"[19] are to be rebuked *"in the presence of all."*

---

[18]1 Cor. 5:4 also requires that the church be assembled for this final step in church discipline.
[19]This is apparently the sense of *tous harmartanontas* in 1 Tim. 5:20, since the present participle gives the sense of continuing in an action over a period of time.

This is because the bad example of wrongful conduct by elders will very likely have a widespread negative effect on others who see their lives. Then Paul reminds Timothy to do "nothing from partiality" in this situation, a very helpful warning, since Timothy was probably a close friend to many of the elders in the church at Ephesus.

Paul's command to rebuke a sinning elder publicly means that some statement of the nature of the offense must be made to the church (*"rebuke them* in the presence of all," v. 20).[20] On the other hand, not every detail of the sin has to be disclosed to the church. A helpful guideline is that the church should be told enough that (1) they will understand how serious the offense was, (2) they will be able to understand and support the discipline process, and (3) they will not subsequently feel the sin was minimized or covered up if more details somehow leak out later.

Such a public disclosure of the sin of a leader will signal to the congregation that the leaders of the church will not hide such matters from them in the future. This will increase the confidence of the church in the integrity of the leadership board. It will also allow the sinning leader to begin the gradual process of rebuilding relationships and trust with the congregation, because he will not have to deal with people who have a hundred different speculations about what his sin was, but with people who know the specific sin, and can see the genuine repentance and change regarding that area of sin in his life.

What about the serious sins of people who are not church leaders? Scripture gives no command to disclose publicly the sins of people who are ordinary members but not recognized leaders in the church. Leaders, however, are treated differently because their lives are to be "above reproach" (1 Tim. 3:2), and their lives should be examples for other Christians to imitate (see 1 Tim. 4:12).[21]

**d. Other Aspects of Church Discipline:** Once discipline has occurred, as soon as there is repentance at any stage of the process, the Christians who have known about the discipline should welcome the repentant person back quickly into the fellowship of the church. Paul says, "You should rather turn to *forgive and comfort him,* or he may be overwhelmed by excessive sorrow. . . . I beg you to reaffirm your love for him" (2 Cor. 2:7–8; cf. 7:8–11). Once again, our purpose in church discipline should never be to punish out of a desire for vengeance, but always to restore and heal.

The attitude with which discipline is carried out at any stage is also very important. It must be done with gentleness and humility, and with a genuine appreciation for our own weakness and with a fear that we might fall into similar

---

[20]When churches have to discipline a church leader, an easy mistake to make is failing to take Paul's command seriously, and thereby failing to give adequate disclosure to the church of the nature of the sin involved. If that happens, the congregation only hears that a leader was removed from office because of some sin (or maybe a general category of sin is mentioned). But this is not really an effective public rebuke. Because it is so vague, it will only result in confusion, speculation, and gossip. Moreover, serious divisions can arise in the church because in the absence of information some people will think the discipline process too harsh and others will think it too lenient, and the church will not be united in supporting the process.

[21]I understand "above reproach" to mean that their lives are such that no charge of serious wrongdoing can be rightfully brought against them.

sins. "If a man is overtaken in any trespass, you who are spiritual should restore him *in a spirit of gentleness. Look to yourself, lest you too be tempted*" (Gal. 6:1).

It is unwise to set any timetable in advance, telling people how long the discipline process is expected to last. This is because it is impossible for us to predict how long it will be until the Holy Spirit brings about deep, genuine repentance and a change in the condition of the person's heart that led to the sin in the first place.

Finally, we should notice that immediately following the passage on church discipline in Matthew 18:15–20, Jesus strongly teaches the need for personal forgiveness of those who sin against us (Matt. 18:21–35). We are to forgive those who harm us "seventy times seven" (v. 22), and Jesus tells us that our heavenly Father will punish us severely if we do not *forgive our brother from the heart* (v. 35). We should see the passage on church discipline and this passage as complementary, not contradictory. As individuals we must always forgive in our hearts and not bear grudges. Yet we can certainly forgive someone in our hearts and still seek church discipline for the good of the person who is committing a sin, for the good of the church, for the honor of Christ, and because God's Word commands it.

## QUESTIONS FOR PERSONAL APPLICATION

1. Have you previously thought of the church as rather weak or rather strong in its influence on the affairs of the world? How has your thinking changed as a result of this chapter? Do you now think there is any hope for transforming society apart from the strong redemptive influence of the church?

2. Have you previously thought of yourself as holding any of the "keys of the kingdom of heaven"? Do you in fact have some of those keys now? What are you doing with them?

3. In what ways could your church exercise its spiritual power against the forces of the enemy more effectively? In what ways could you use this power more effectively yourself?

4. What is the strongest enemy to the effective proclamation of the gospel in your community now? How might the power of the church be used against that enemy?

5. If you accept the principles that the church should not rule the state and the state should not rule over or restrict the freedom of the church, are these principles being played out effectively in your own country or local situation? What could be done to increase conformity to these principles? (Do you agree with these principles?)

6. Are you aware of situations where a gentle word of admonition has resulted in a positive change in your own behavior or the behavior of another Christian? Are you aware of situations where church discipline has gone a step or two further than this and has resulted in restoration of the erring person? If you are aware of situations where the practice of church discipline has not brought a good result, what could have been done differently to bring about a better result?

7. If a church refuses to carry out church discipline at all for a number of years, even though there is an evident need for it, what will be the harmful results in the church? Are you aware of situations where those harmful results have occurred?

8. Have there been times when you wished that someone would have come to you earlier with a word of admonition or counsel concerning an area of sin that you were unaware of or that you were uncertain about? If so, why didn't that happen?

9. Are there now any relationships in your life where Matthew 5:23 and Matthew 18:15 combine to tell you that you have an obligation to go to another person and seek to make the situation right?

## SPECIAL TERMS

binding and loosing
excommunication
keys of the kingdom

power of the church
to take up the sword

## BIBLIOGRAPHY

(For an explanation of this bibliography see the note on the bibliography to chapter 1, p. 38. Complete bibliographical data may be found on pp. 1223–29.)

### Sections in Evangelical Systematic Theologies

1. Anglican (Episcopalian)
    1882–92   Litton, 402–13, 418–27
    1930   Thomas, 281–97, 434–46
2. Arminian (Wesleyan or Methodist)
    1940   Wiley, 3:136–37
3. Baptist
    1767   Gill, 2:607–20
    1907   Strong, 924–26
4. Dispensational
    1986   Ryrie, 433–35
5. Lutheran
    1917–24   Pieper, 1:530–31; 3:178–83, 416–20
6. Reformed (or Presbyterian)
    1559   Calvin, 2:1149–1240 (4.8–12)
    1724–58   Edwards, 2:118–22
    1861   Heppe, 684–94
    1878   Dabney, 873–87
    1937–66   Murray, CW, 1:253–59
    1938   Berkhof, 593–603

7. Renewal (or charismatic/Pentecostal)
   1988–92     Williams, 3:120–23, 265–85

## Sections in Representative Roman Catholic Systematic Theologies

1. Roman Catholic: Traditional
   1955     Ott, 417–25
2. Roman Catholic: Post-Vatican II
   1980     McBrien, 2:817–48

## Other Works

Adams, Jay E. *Handbook of Church Discipline.* Grand Rapids: Ministry Resources
    Library, 1986.
Bauckham, Richard. *The Bible in Politics: How to Read the Bible Politically.*
    Louisville: Westminster/John Knox, 1989.
DeKoster, L. "Church Discipline." In *EDT,* p. 238.
Eidsmoe, John. *God and Caesar: Christian Faith and Political Action.* Westchester,
    Ill.: Crossway, 1984.
Grudem, W. A. "Keys of the Kingdom." In *EDT,* pp. 604–6.
Laney, J. Carl. *A Guide to Church Discipline.* Minneapolis: Bethany, 1985.
Linder, R. D. "Church and State." In *EDT,* pp. 233–38.
Robertson, O. Palmer. "Reflections on New Testament Testimony Concerning
    Civil Disobedience." *JETS.* Vol. 33, No. 3 (Sept., 1990), pp. 331–51.
Schaeffer, Francis. *A Christian Manifesto.* Westchester, Ill.: Crossway, 1981.
Stott, John R. W. *The Preacher's Portrait: Some New Testament Word Studies.*
    Grand Rapids: Eerdmans, 1961.
White, John, and Ken Blue. *Church Discipline That Heals: Putting Costly Love into
    Action.* (First published as *Healing the Wounded.*) Downers Grove, Ill.:
    InterVarsity Press, 1985.

## SCRIPTURE MEMORY PASSAGE

**2 Corinthians 10:3–4:** *For though we live in the world we are not carrying on a worldly war, for the weapons of our warfare are not worldly but have divine power to destroy strongholds.*

## HYMN

### "Onward Christian Soldiers"

This hymn does not talk about earthly warfare with swords and shields, but with the spiritual warfare of prayer and praise, and the enemies are not earthly unbelievers but Satan and his demonic hosts: "Hell's foundations quiver at the shout of praise;/Brothers, lift your voices, loud your anthems raise."

The hymn pictures the church moving as a worldwide army of God against the forces of Satan, and it proclaims the unity of the church as well: "We are not divided, all one body we, /One in hope and doctrine, one in charity." It is a triumphant, joyful song of spiritual warfare by a church that will not be divided and will not be defeated.

Onward, Christian soldiers, marching as to war,
  With the cross of Jesus going on before:
Christ the royal Master leads against the foe;
  Forward into battle, see his banners go.

*Refrain:*
Onward, Christian soldiers, marching as to war,
  With the cross of Jesus going on before.

At the sign of triumph Satan's host doth flee;
  On then, Christian soldiers, on to victory:
Hell's foundations quiver at the shout of praise;
  Brothers, lift your voices, loud your anthems raise.

Like a mighty army moves the church of God;
  Brothers, we are treading where the saints have trod;
We are not divided, all one body we,
  One in hope and doctrine, one in charity.

Crowns and thrones may perish, kingdoms rise and wane,
  But the church of Jesus constant will remain;
Gates of hell can never 'gainst that church prevail;
  We have Christ's own promise, and that cannot fail.

Onward, then ye people, join our happy throng,
  Blend with ours your voices in the triumph song;
Glory, laud, and honor unto Christ the King;
  This through countless ages men and angels sing.

AUTHOR: SABINE BARING-GOULD, 1865

# Chapter 47

# Church Government

*How should a church be governed? How should church officers be chosen? Should women serve as pastors of churches?*

## EXPLANATION AND SCRIPTURAL BASIS

Churches today have many different forms of government. The Roman Catholic Church has a worldwide government under the authority of the Pope. Episcopalian churches have bishops with regional authority, and archbishops over them. Presbyterian churches grant regional authority to presbyteries and national authority to general assemblies. On the other hand, Baptist churches and many other independent churches have no formal governing authority beyond the local congregation, and affiliation with denominations is on a voluntary basis.

Within local churches, Baptists often have a single pastor with a board of deacons, but some have a board of elders as well. Presbyterians have a board of elders and Episcopalians have a vestry. Other churches simply have a church board.

Is there a New Testament pattern for church government? Is any one form of church government to be preferred over another? These are the questions addressed in this chapter.

However, at the outset it must be said that the form of church government is not a major doctrine like the Trinity, the deity of Christ, substitutionary atonement, or the authority of Scripture. Although I believe, after examining the New Testament evidence, that one particular form of church government is preferable to the others, nevertheless, each form has some weaknesses as well as strengths. And church history attests that several different forms of government have worked fairly well for several centuries. Moreover, while some aspects of church government seem to be reasonably clear from the New Testament, other matters (such as the way in which church officers should be chosen) are less clear, mainly because the New Testament evidence on them is not extensive, and thus our inferences from this evidence are less certain. It seems to me, then, that there ought to be room for evangelical Christians to differ amicably over this question, in the hope that further understanding may be gained. And it also seems that individual Christians—while they may have a preference for one system or another, and while they may wish at appropriate times to argue forcefully for one system over another—should nevertheless be willing to live and minister within any of several different Protestant systems of church government in which they may find themselves from time to time.

But I do not mean to say that this is an entirely unimportant matter. In this area as well as others, a church may be more or less pure. If there are clear New Testament patterns regarding some aspects of church government, then there will be negative consequences in our churches if we disregard them, even if we cannot foresee all of those consequences at the present time. Therefore Christians are certainly free to speak and write on this subject in order to work for increased purity in the church.

In this chapter we shall first survey the New Testament data concerning church officers, especially *apostle, elder,* and *deacon.* Then we shall ask how church officers should be chosen. After that we shall look at two controversial questions: Which form of church government—if any—is closest to the New Testament pattern? And, may women serve as officers in the church?

## A. Church Officers

For purposes of this chapter, we will use the following definition: *A church officer is someone who has been publicly recognized as having the right and responsibility to perform certain functions for the benefit of the whole church.*

According to this definition, elders and deacons would be considered officers in a church, as would the pastor (if that is a distinct office). The church treasurer and church moderator would also be officers (these titles may vary from church to church). All of these people have had public recognition, usually at a service in which they are "installed" or "ordained" in an office. In fact, they *need* public recognition in order to fulfill their responsibilities: for example, it would not be appropriate for people to wonder from week to week who was to receive the offering and deposit it in the bank, or for various people to argue that they had been gifted to take that responsibility in any particular week! The orderly functioning of the church requires that one person be recognized as having that responsibility. Similarly, the pastor who is responsible to do Bible teaching each Sunday morning must be recognized as having the right and responsibility to do that (at least, in most forms of church government). If this were not the case, then many people might prepare sermons and all claim the right to preach, or on some Sundays no one might prepare. Similarly, in order for people to follow the elders of the church and look to them for guidance, they must know who the elders are.

By contrast, many other people exercise gifts in the church, but we do not say they have an "office" because they do not need formal public recognition for their gifts to function. Those who have a gift of "helps" (see 1 Cor. 12:28), or who have a gift of especially strong faith, or a gift of "distinguishing between spirits" (1 Cor. 12:10), or a gift of exhorting or contributing (Rom. 12:8) do not need public recognition in order to function effectively in the church.

In the material that follows, we shall see that the New Testament discusses one church office which was limited to the time when the early church was founded (the office of apostle), and two other church offices which continue throughout the church age (the offices of elder and deacon).

**1. Apostle.** Earlier in this book we saw that the New Testament *apostles* had a unique kind of authority in the early church: authority to speak and write words which were "words of God" in an absolute sense. To disbelieve or disobey them was to disbelieve or disobey God. The apostles, therefore, had the authority to write words which became words of Scripture.[1] This fact in itself should suggest to us that there was something unique about the office of apostle, and that we would not expect it to continue today, for no one today can add words to the Bible and have them be counted as God's very words or as part of Scripture.[2]

In addition, the New Testament information on the qualifications of an apostle and the identity of the apostles also leads us to conclude that the office was unique and limited to the first century, and that we are to expect no more apostles today.[3] We shall see this as we ask the following questions: What were the requirements for being an apostle? Who were the apostles? How many apostles were there? And are there apostles today?

At the outset it must be made clear that the answers to these questions depend on what one means by the word *apostle*. Today some people use the word *apostle* in a very broad sense, to refer to an effective church planter, or to a significant missionary pioneer ("William Carey was an apostle to India," for example). If we use the word *apostle* in this broad sense, everyone would agree that there are still apostles today—for there are certainly effective missionaries and church planters today.

The New Testament itself has three verses in which the word *apostle* (Gk. *apostolos*) is used in a broad sense, not to refer to any specific church office, but simply to mean "messenger." In Philippians 2:25, Paul calls Epaphroditus "your *messenger (apostolos)* and minister to my need"; in 2 Corinthians 8:23, Paul refers to those who accompanied the offering that he was taking to Jerusalem as "*messengers [apostoloi]* of the churches"; and in John 13:16, Jesus says, "Nor is *he who is sent [apostolos]* greater than he who sent him."

But there is another sense for the word *apostle*. Much more frequently in the New Testament the word refers to a special office, "*apostle of Jesus Christ*." In this narrow sense of the term, there are no more apostles today, and we are to expect no more. This is because of what the New Testament says about the qualifications for being an apostle and about who the apostles were.

**a. Qualifications of an Apostle:** The two qualifications for being an apostle were (1) having seen Jesus after his resurrection with one's own eyes (thus, being an "eyewitness of the resurrection"), and (2) having been specifically commissioned by Christ as his apostle.[4]

The fact that an apostle had to have seen the risen Lord with his own eyes is indicated by Acts 1:22, where Peter said that person to replace Judas "must become with us *a witness to his resurrection*." Moreover, it was "to the apostles

---

[1]See chapter 3, pp. 60–63, and chapter 4, pp. 76–77, for a discussion of the authority of the apostles.

[2]See chapter 3, pp. 63–68, for a discussion of the closing of the New Testament canon.

[3]The material from this point through p. 911 has been taken from Wayne Grudem, *The Gift of Prophecy in the New Testament and Today* (Eastbourne, U.K.: Kingsway, and Westchester, Ill.: Crossway, 1988), pp. 269–76, and is used by permission.

[4]These two qualifications are discussed in detail in the classic essay by J. B. Lightfoot, "The Name and Office of an Apostle," in his commentary, *The Epistle of St. Paul to the Galatians* (first published 1865; repr. Grand Rapids: Zondervan, 1957), pp. 92–101; see also K. H. Rengstorf, "*apostolos*," *TDNT*, 1:398–447.

whom he had chosen" that "he presented himself alive after his passion by many proofs, appearing to them during forty days" (Acts 1:2–3; cf. 4:33).

Paul makes much of the fact that he did meet this qualification even though it was in an unusual way (Christ appeared to him in a vision on the road to Damascus and appointed him as an apostle: Acts 9:5–6; 26:15–18). When he is defending his apostleship he says, "Am I not an apostle? *Have I not seen Jesus our Lord?*" (1 Cor. 9:1). And when recounting the people to whom Christ appeared after his resurrection, Paul says, "Then *he appeared to James,* then *to all the apostles. Last of all, as to one untimely born, he appeared also to me.* For I am the least of the apostles, unfit to be called an apostle" (1 Cor. 15:7–9).

These verses combine to indicate that unless someone had seen Jesus after the resurrection with his own eyes, he could not be an apostle.

The second qualification, specific appointment by Christ as an apostle, is also evident from several verses. First, though the term *apostle* is not common in the gospels, the twelve disciples are called "apostles" specifically in a context where Jesus is commissioning them, "sending them out" to preach in his name:

> And he called to him his twelve disciples and gave them authority over unclean spirits, to cast them out, and to heal every disease and every infirmity. The names of the twelve *apostles* are these. . . . *These twelve Jesus sent out,* charging them, ". . . preach as you go, saying, 'The kingdom of heaven is at hand.'" (Matt. 10:1–7)

Similarly, Jesus commissions his apostles in a special sense to be his "witnesses . . . to the end of the earth" (Acts 1:8). And in choosing another apostle to replace Judas, the eleven apostles did not take the responsibility on themselves, but prayed and asked the ascended Christ to make the appointment:

> "Lord, who knows the hearts of all men, *show which one of these two you have chosen* to take the place in this ministry and apostleship from which Judas turned aside. . . ." And they cast lots for them, and the lot fell on Matthias; and he was enrolled with the eleven apostles. (Acts 1:24–26)

Paul himself insists that Christ personally appointed him as an apostle. He tells how, on the Damascus Road, Jesus told him that he was appointing him as an apostle to the Gentiles: "I have appeared to you for this purpose, to appoint you to serve and to bear witness . . . delivering you from the people and from the Gentiles—to whom I send you" (Acts 26:16–17). He later affirms that he was specifically appointed by Christ as an apostle (see Rom. 1:1; Gal. 1:1; 1 Tim. 1:12; 2:7; 2 Tim. 1:11).

**b. Who Were Apostles?** The initial group of apostles numbered twelve—the eleven original disciples who remained after Judas died, plus Matthias, who replaced Judas: "And they cast lots for them, and the lot fell on Matthias; and *he was enrolled with the eleven apostles*" (Acts 1:26). So important was this original group of twelve apostles, the "charter members" of the office of apostle, that we read that their names are inscribed on the foundations of the heavenly city, the New Jerusalem: "And the wall of the city had twelve foundations, and on them *the twelve names of the twelve apostles of the Lamb*" (Rev. 21:14).

We might at first think that such a group could never be expanded, that no one could be added to it. But then Paul clearly claims that he, also, is an apostle. And

Acts 14:14 calls both Barnabas and Paul apostles: "when *the apostles Barnabas and Paul* heard of it. . . ." So with Paul and Barnabas there are fourteen "apostles of Jesus Christ."[5]

Then James the brother of Jesus (who was not one of the twelve original disciples) seems to be called an apostle in Galatians 1:19: Paul tells how, when he went to Jerusalem, "I saw none of *the other apostles* except James the Lord's brother."[6] Then in Galatians 2:9 James is classified with Peter and John as "pillars" of the Jerusalem church. And in Acts 15:13–21, James, along with Peter, exercises a significant leadership function in the Jerusalem Council, a function which would be appropriate to the office of apostle. Furthermore, when Paul is listing the resurrection appearances of Jesus he once again readily classifies James with the apostles:

> Then he appeared *to James,* then *to all the apostles.* Last of all, as to one untimely born, he appeared also to me. For I am the least of the apostles, unfit to be called an apostle, because I persecuted the church of God. (1 Cor. 15:7–9)

Finally, the fact that James could write the New Testament epistle which bears his name would also be entirely consistent with his having the authority which belonged to the office of apostle, the authority to write words which were the words of God. All these considerations combine to indicate that James the Lord's brother was also commissioned by Christ as an apostle. That would bring the number to fifteen "apostles of Jesus Christ" (the twelve plus Paul, Barnabas, and James).

Were there more than these fifteen? There may possibly have been a few more, though we know little if anything about them, and it is not certain that there were any more. Others, of course, had seen Jesus after his resurrection ("Then he appeared to more than five hundred brethren at one time," 1 Cor. 15:6). From this large group it is possible that Christ appointed some others as apostles—but it is also very possible that he did not. The evidence is not sufficient to decide the issue.

Romans 16:7 says, "Greet *Andronicus and Junias,* my kinsmen and my fellow prisoners; they are *men of note among the apostles,* and they were in Christ before

---

[5]If the apostles' writings were accepted as Scripture, someone may wonder why the extrabiblical document called *The Epistle of Barnabas* is not included in Scripture. The answer is that nearly unanimous scholarly opinion has concluded that it was not written by Barnabas, but by some unknown Christian who probably lived in Alexandria between A.D. 70 and 100. The epistle claims that much of the Old Testament, including animal sacrifices, much of the Mosaic law, and the construction of a physical temple, were mistakes that were contrary to God's will (see ODCC, p. 134). (Text and translation are found in Kirsopp Lake, translator, *The Apostolic Fathers* [Cambridge, Mass.: Harvard University Press, and London: Heinemann, 1970], 1:335–409).

[6]It is not absolutely necessary to translate the verse this way, including James among the apostles. (The NIV reads, "I saw none of the other apostles—only James, the Lord's brother.") Yet the translation "except James the Lord's brother" seems clearly preferable, because (1) the Greek phrase is *ei mē,* which ordinarily means "except" (BAGD, p. 22, 8a), and in the great majority of New Testament uses designates something that is part of the previous group but is "excepted" from it; and (2) in the context of Gal. 1:18, it would not make much sense for Paul to say that when he went to Jerusalem he saw Peter, and no other people except James—or Peter, and no other church leaders except James—for he stayed there "fifteen days" (Gal. 1:18). So he must mean he saw Peter, and *no other apostles* except James. But this classifies James with the apostles. See discussion in E. D. Burton, *The Epistle to the Galatians,* ICC (Edinburgh: T. & T. Clark, 1920), p. 60. (Burton says, "*ei mē* means here, as always before a noun, 'except'" [ibid.].)

me." Because there are several translation problems in the verse, no clear conclusions can be reached. "Men of note" may be also translated "men noted by" (the apostles). "Junias" (a man's name) may also be translated "Junia" (a woman's name).[7] "Apostles" here may not mean the office "apostles of Jesus Christ," but may simply mean "messengers" (the broader sense which the word takes in Phil. 2:25; 2 Cor. 8:23; John 13:16). The verse has too little clear information to allow us to draw a conclusion.

Others have been suggested as apostles. Silas (Silvanus) and sometimes Timothy are mentioned because of 1 Thessalonians 2:6: "though *we* might have made demands *as apostles of Christ.*" Does Paul include Silas and Timothy here, since the letter begins, "Paul, Silvanus, and Timothy" (1 Thess. 1:1)?

It is not likely that Paul is including Timothy in this statement, for two reasons. (1) He says just four verses earlier, "we had already suffered and been shamefully treated at Philippi, as you know" (1 Thess. 2:2), but this refers to the beating and imprisonment which happened just to Paul and Silas, not to Timothy (Acts 16:19). So the "we" in verse 6 does not seem to include all of the people (Paul, Silvanus, Timothy) mentioned in the first verse. The letter in general is from Paul, Silas and Timothy, but Paul knows that the readers will naturally understand the appropriate members of the "we" statements when he does not mean to include all three of them in certain sections of the letter. He does not specify "we—that is, Silas and I—had already suffered and been shamefully treated at Philippi, as you know," because the Thessalonians will know who the "we" are that he is talking about.

(2) This is also seen in 1 Thessalonians 3:1–2, where the "we" certainly cannot include Timothy:

> Therefore when we could bear it no longer, we were willing to be left behind at Athens alone, and *we sent Timothy,* our brother and God's servant in the gospel of Christ, to establish you in your faith and to exhort you. (1 Thess. 3:1–2)

In this case, the "we" refers either to Paul and Silas, or else just to Paul alone (see Acts 17:14–15; 18:5). Apparently Silas and Timothy had come to Paul in Athens "as soon as possible" (Acts 17:15)—though Luke does not mention their arrival in Athens—and Paul had sent them back to Thessalonica again to help the church there. Then he himself went to Corinth, and they later joined him there (Acts 18:5).

---

[7]For an extensive discussion of whether to translate "Junias" or "Junia" here, see John Piper and Wayne Grudem, eds., *Recovering Biblical Manhood and Womanhood* (Wheaton: Crossway, 1991), pp. 79–81, 214, 221–22. Some have claimed that Junia was a common woman's name in ancient Greece, but this is incorrect, at least in written Greek literature: A computer search of 2,889 ancient Greek authors over thirteen centuries (ninth century B.C.–fifth century A.D.) turned up only two examples of Junia as a woman's name, one in Plutarch (c. A.D. 50—c. 120) and one in the church father Chrysostom (A.D. 347—407), who referred to Junia as a woman in a sermon on Rom. 16:7. It is not common as a man's name either, since this search found only one example of Junia as a man's name, in Epiphanius (A.D. 315—403), bishop of Salimis in Cyprus, who refers to Junias in Rom. 16:7 and says he became bishop of Apameia in Syria (*Index of Disciples* 125.19–20; this quotation is the most significant, since Epiphanius knows more information about Junias). The Latin text of the church father Origen (d. A.D. 252) also refers to Junias in Rom. 16:7 as a man (J. P. Migne, *Patrologia Graeca,* vol. 14, col. 1289). Therefore the available data give some support to the view that Junias was a man, but the information is too sparse to be conclusive.

It is most likely that *"We* were willing to be left behind at Athens alone" (1 Thess. 3:1), refers to Paul alone, both because he picks up the argument again in verse 5 with the singular "I" ("When I could bear it no longer, I sent that I might know your faith," 1 Thess. 3:5), and because the point concerning extreme loneliness in Athens would not be made if Silas had stayed with him.[8] In fact, in the previous paragraph, Paul means "I," for he says, "We wanted to come to you—I, Paul, again and again—but Satan hindered us" (1 Thess. 2:18). Apparently he is using "we" more frequently in this epistle as a courteous way of including Silas and Timothy, who had spent so much time in the Thessalonian church, in the letter to that church. But the Thessalonians would have had little doubt who was really in charge of this great mission to the Gentiles, and on whose apostolic authority the letter primarily (or exclusively) depended.

So it is just possible that Silas was himself an apostle, and that 1 Thessalonians 2:6 hints at that. He was a leading member of the Jerusalem church (Acts 15:22), and could well have seen Jesus after his resurrection, and then been appointed as an apostle. But we cannot be very certain.

The situation with Timothy is different, however. Just as he is excluded from the "we" of 1 Thessalonians 2:2 (and 3:1–2), so he seems to be excluded from the "we" of 1 Thessalonians 2:6. Moreover, as a native of Lystra (Acts 16:1–3) who had learned of Christ from his grandmother and mother (2 Tim. 1:5), it seems impossible that he would have been in Jerusalem before Pentecost and would there have seen the risen Lord and come to believe in him, and then suddenly have been appointed as an apostle. In addition, *Paul's pattern of address in his letters always jealously guards the title "apostle" for himself,* never allowing it to be applied to Timothy or others of his traveling companions (note 2 Cor. 1:1; Col. 1:1: *"Paul, an apostle* of Christ Jesus . . . *and Timothy our brother";* and then Phil. 1:1: *"Paul and Timothy, servants* of Christ Jesus"). So Timothy, as important a role as he had, should not rightly be considered one of the apostles.

This gives us a limited but somewhat imprecisely numbered group who had the office "apostles of Jesus Christ." There seem to have been at least fifteen, and perhaps sixteen or even a few more who are not recorded in the New Testament.

Yet it seems quite certain that there were none appointed after Paul. When Paul lists the resurrection appearances of Christ, he emphasizes the unusual way in which Christ appeared to him, and connects that with the statement that this was the "last" appearance of all, and that he himself is indeed "the least of the apostles, unfit to be called an apostle."

He appeared to Cephas (Peter), then to the twelve. Then he appeared to more than five hundred brethren at one time, most of whom are still alive, though some have fallen asleep. Then he appeared to James, then to all the apostles. *Last of all,* as to one untimely born, *he appeared also to me.* For I am the least of the apostles, unfit to be called an apostle." (1 Cor. 15:5–9)

---

[8]See the discussion in Leon Morris, *The First and Second Epistles to the Thessalonians,* NIC (Grand Rapids: Eerdmans, 1959), pp. 98–99. Morris says, "The practice in this epistle differs somewhat from that in the Pauline epistles generally. The plural is used almost throughout, whereas in most of his letters Paul prefers the singular" (p. 98; cf. pp. 46–47). Morris takes the plurals here to refer only to Paul himself.

**c. Summary:** The word *apostle* can be used in a broad or narrow sense. In a broad sense, it just means "messenger" or "pioneer missionary." But in a narrow sense, the most common sense in the New Testament, it refers to a specific office, "apostle of Jesus Christ." These apostles had unique authority to found and govern the early church, and they could speak and write words of God. Many of their written words became the New Testament Scriptures.

In order to qualify as an apostle, someone (1) had to have seen Christ with his own eyes after he rose from the dead, and (2) had to have been specifically appointed by Christ as an apostle. There was a limited number of apostles, perhaps fifteen or sixteen or a few more—the New Testament is not explicit on the number. The twelve original apostles (the eleven plus Matthias) were joined by Barnabas and Paul, very probably James, perhaps Silas, and maybe even Andronicus and Junias or a few unnamed others. It seems that no apostles were appointed after Paul, and certainly, since no one today can meet the qualification of having seen the risen Christ with his own eyes, there are no apostles today.[9] In place of living apostles present in the church to teach and govern it, we have instead the writings of the apostles in the books of the New Testament. Those New Testament Scriptures fulfill for the church today the absolutely authoritative teaching and governing functions which were fulfilled by the apostles themselves during the early years of the church.

Though some may use the word *apostle* in English today to refer to very effective church planters or evangelists, it seems inappropriate and unhelpful to do so, for it simply confuses people who read the New Testament and see the high authority that is attributed to the office of "apostle" there. It is noteworthy that no major leader in the history of the church—not Athanasius or Augustine, not Luther or Calvin, not Wesley or Whitefield—has taken to himself the title of "apostle" or let himself be called an apostle. If any in modern times want to take the title "apostle" to themselves, they immediately raise the suspicion that they may be motivated by inappropriate pride and desires for self-exaltation, along with excessive ambition and a desire for much more authority in the church than any one person should rightfully have.

---

[9]Someone may object that Christ could appear to someone today and appoint that person as an apostle. But the foundational nature of the office of apostle (Eph. 2:20; Rev. 21:14) and the fact that Paul views himself as the last one whom Christ appeared to and appointed as an apostle ("last of all, as to one untimely born," 1 Cor. 15:8), indicate that this will not happen. Moreover, God's purpose in the history of redemption seems to have been to give apostles only at the beginning of the church age (see Eph. 2:20).

Another objection to the idea that there are no apostles today, one that comes especially from people in the charismatic movement, is the argument that the "fivefold ministry" of Eph. 4:11 should continue today, and we should have (1) apostles, (2) prophets, (3) evangelists, (4) pastors, and (5) teachers, since Paul says that Christ "gave some as apostles, and some as prophets, and some as evangelists, and some as pastors and teachers" (Eph. 4:11 NASB).

However, Eph. 4:11 talks about a one-time event in the past (note the aorist *kai edōken*, "and he gave"), when Christ ascended into heaven (vv. 8–10) and then at Pentecost poured out initial giftings on the church, giving the church apostles, prophets, evangelists, and pastor-teachers (or pastors and teachers). Whether or not Christ would later give more people for each of these offices *cannot be decided from this verse alone*, but must be decided based on other New Testament teachings on the nature of these offices and whether they were expected to continue. In fact, we see that there were many prophets, evangelists, and pastor-teachers established by Christ throughout all of the early churches, but there was only one more apostle given after this initial time (Paul, "last of all," in unusual circumstances on the Damascus Road).

## 2. Elder (Pastor/Overseer/Bishop).

**a. Plural Elders: The Pattern in All New Testament Churches:** The next church office to be considered is that of "elder." Although some have argued that different forms of church government are evident in the New Testament,[10] a survey of the relevant texts shows the opposite to be true: there is quite a consistent pattern of *plural elders* as the main governing group in New Testament churches. For instance, in Acts 14:23 we read, "And when they had appointed elders[11] for them in every church, with prayer and fasting, they committed them to the Lord in whom they believed." This is on Paul's first missionary journey, when he is returning through the cities of Lystra, Iconium, and Antioch. It indicates that Paul's normal procedure from the time of his first missionary journey was to establish a group of elders in each church shortly after the church began. We know that Paul also established elders in the church at Ephesus, for we read, "From Miletus he sent to Ephesus and called to him the *elders* of the church" (Acts 20:17). Moreover, Paul's apostolic assistants apparently were instructed to carry out a similar process, for Paul wrote to Titus, "This is why I left you in Crete, that you might amend what was defective, and *appoint elders in every town* as I directed you" (Titus 1:5). Shortly after a church has been established, once again we see elders being established in office, in "every town" in which there was a church. And Paul reminded Timothy of the time "when the *elders* laid their hands upon you" (1 Tim. 4:14).

James writes, "Is any among you sick? Let him call for the *elders* of the church, and let them pray over him, anointing him with oil in the name of the Lord" (James 5:14). This is a significant statement because the epistle of James is a general letter written to many churches, all the believers scattered abroad, whom James characterizes as "the twelve tribes in the Dispersion" (James 1:1). It indicates that James expected that there would be elders *in every New Testament church to which his general epistle went*—that is, in *all the churches in existence at that time*.

A similar conclusion can be drawn from 1 Peter. Peter writes, "So I exhort the *elders* among you. . . . Tend the flock of God that is your charge . . ." (1 Peter 5:1–2). First Peter is also a general epistle, written to dozens of churches scattered throughout four Roman provinces in Asia Minor (see 1 Peter 1:1; Bithynia and Pontus constituted one Roman province). Far from expecting different kinds of church government when he was writing (around A.D. 62, more than thirty years after Pentecost), Peter assumes that *all* these churches, whether founded by Paul or by others, whether predominantly Gentile or predominantly Jewish or evenly divided in their make-up, would have elders leading them. Moreover, there were elders in the Jerusalem church (Acts 11:30; 15:2), and, though the word *elders* is not used, there is a plurality of leaders in the congregation to which the epistle to the Hebrews is directed, for the author says, "Obey your leaders and submit to them; for they are keeping watch over your souls, as men who will have to give account" (Heb. 13:17).

---

[10]See, for example, Millard Erickson, *Christian Theology,* p. 1084.

[11]The word translated "elder" in the New Testament is the Greek word *presbyteros,* which also was used in other contexts to mean simply an older person.

Two significant conclusions may be drawn from this survey of the New Testament evidence. First, no passage suggests that any church, no matter how small, had only one elder. The consistent New Testament pattern is a plurality of elders "in every church" (Acts 14:23) and "in every town" (Titus 1:5).[12] Second, we do not see a diversity of forms of government in the New Testament church, but a unified and consistent pattern in which every church had elders governing it and keeping watch over it (Acts 20:28; Heb. 13:17; 1 Peter 5:2–3).

**b. Other Names for Elders: Pastors, Overseers, Bishops:** Elders are also called "pastors" or "bishops" or "overseers" in the New Testament. The least commonly used word (at least in the noun form) is *pastor* (Gk. *poimēn*). It may be surprising to us to find that this word, which has become so common in English, only occurs once in the New Testament when speaking about a church officer. In Ephesians 4:11, Paul writes, "And his gifts were that some should be apostles, some prophets, some evangelists, some *pastors* and teachers." The verse is probably better translated "pastor-teachers" (one group) rather than "pastors and teachers" (suggesting two groups) because of the Greek construction (though not every New Testament scholar agrees with that translation).[13] The connection with teaching suggests that these pastors were some (or perhaps all) of the elders who carried on the work of teaching, for one qualification for an elder is that he be "able to teach" (1 Tim. 3:2).

Although the noun *pastor* (*poimēn*) is not used of church officers elsewhere in the New Testament,[14] the related verb which means "to act as a shepherd" or "to act as a pastor" (Gk. *poimainō*) is applied to elders in Paul's address to the Ephesian elders. He tells them "to *shepherd* the church of God" (Acts 20:28, literally translating the verb *poimainō*), and in the same sentence he referred to God's people as "all the *flock*," using another related noun (Gk. *poimnion*) which means "a flock of sheep." So Paul directly charges these Ephesian elders to act as shepherds or "pastors."[15]

The same verb is used in 1 Peter 5:2 where Peter tells the elders to "*shepherd* (*poimainō*) the flock of God that is your charge" (author's translation). Then two verses later Jesus is called the chief pastor or "chief shepherd" (Gk. *archipoimēn*,

---

[12]Some have suggested that perhaps there was one elder in every "house church" in a town, and that all of those elders from the different house churches together constituted the elders that Titus was to appoint in each town. If this was true, perhaps some support could be given for the idea of one pastor ("elder") over every church.

In response to this suggestion, we must note that this is a theory without any evidence to support it, for no verse in the New Testament hints at the idea that there was one elder in each "house church." In terms of supporting evidence, this suggestion stands in the same category as the statement, "Perhaps all the elders in Crete were blind in the left eye." Of course, scholars can say "perhaps" to any event for which there is no evidence, but such statements should carry no weight in our attempts to determine what pattern of church government actually existed in the first century.

[13]The phrase "some pastors and teachers" has one definite article in front of two nouns joined by *kai* ("and"), a construction that always in Greek indicates that the two nouns are viewed by the writer as unified in some way. This construction often is used where two nouns refer to the same person or thing, but it is sometimes used of two different persons or groups viewed as a unity. In either case, the phrase ties together "pastors" and "teachers" more closely than any other titles.

[14]It is used several times to speak of a "shepherd" who cares for his sheep, however.

[15]The English word *pastor* is derived from a Latin term that means "one who cares for sheep," and the English word *pastor* earlier meant "shepherd" in the literal sense of one who took care of sheep (see *Oxford English Dictionary*, Vol. P, p. 542).

1 Peter 5:4), implying quite clearly that Peter also viewed the elders as shepherds or "pastors" in the church. Therefore, although the noun *pastor* is only used once to refer to elders, the related verb is used twice in passages that explicitly identify the task of shepherding with the office of elder.

Another term used for elders in the New Testament is a Greek word *episkopos,* which is variously translated as "overseer" or "bishop," depending on the individual passage and the English translation.[16] But this word also seems quite clearly to be another term for elders in New Testament usage. For example, when Paul has called to him the *elders* of the church at Ephesus (Acts 20:17), he says to them, "Take heed to yourselves and to all the flock, in which the Holy Spirit has made you *overseers* (Gk. *episkopos*)" (Acts 20:28). Paul quite readily refers to these Ephesian elders as "overseers" (or "bishops").

In 1 Timothy 3:1–2, Paul writes, "If any one aspires to the office of *bishop,* he desires a noble task. Now a bishop must be above reproach. . . ." We must remember that Paul is writing to Timothy when Timothy is at Ephesus (see 1 Tim. 1:3, "remain at Ephesus") and we already know from Acts 20 that there are *elders* at Ephesus (Acts 20:17–38). Furthermore, in 1 Timothy 5:17, we see that elders were ruling the church at Ephesus when Timothy was there, because it says, "Let the *elders who rule well* be considered worthy of double honor." Now the "bishops" in 1 Timothy 3:1–2 *also* are to rule over the church at Ephesus because one qualification is that "He must manage his own household well . . . for if a man does not know how to manage his own household, how can he care for God's church?" (1 Tim. 3:4–5). So here it also seems that "bishop" or "overseer" is simply another term for "elder," since these "bishops" fulfill the same function as elders quite clearly do elsewhere in this epistle and in Acts 20.

In Titus 1:5, Paul tells Titus to "appoint *elders* in every town" and gives some qualifications (v. 6). Then in the very next sentence (v. 7), he gives reasons for those qualifications, and he begins by saying, "For a *bishop,* as God's steward, must be blameless." Here again he uses the word "bishop" to refer to the elders whom Titus was to appoint, giving another indication that the terms *elder* and *bishop* were interchangeable.

Finally, in Philippians 1:1, Paul writes "To all the saints in Christ Jesus who are at Philippi, with the *bishops* and deacons." Here it also seems appropriate to think that "bishops" is another name for "elders," because there certainly were elders at Philippi, since it was Paul's practice to establish elders in every church (see Acts 14:23). And if there were elders ruling in the church at Philippi, it is unthinkable that Paul would write to the church and single out bishops and deacons—but not elders—if their offices were both different from that of the elders. Therefore, by "bishops and deacons" Paul must have meant the same thing as "elders and deacons."[17] Although in some parts of the church from the second century A.D. onward, the word *bishop* has been used to refer to a single individual with

---

[16]The NIV regularly uses "overseer" instead of "bishop" to translate *episkopos.*

[17]Even the Anglican scholar J. B. Lightfoot, says, "It is a fact now generally recognised by theologians of all shades of opinion, that in the language of the New Testament the same officer in the Church is called indifferently 'bishop' (*episkopos*) and 'elder' or 'presbyter' (*presbyteros*)" (*St. Paul's Epistle to the Philippians* [Grand Rapids: Zondervan, 1953; first published 1868], p. 95; on pp. 95–99 Lightfoot discusses the data to support this conclusion).

authority over several churches, this was a later development of the term and is not found in the New Testament itself.

**c. The Functions of Elders:** One of the major roles of elders in the New Testament is to govern the New Testament churches. In 1 Timothy 5:17 we read, "Let the elders who *rule* well be considered worthy of double honor." Earlier in the same epistle Paul says that an overseer (or elder) "must manage his own household well, keeping his children submissive and respectful in every way; for if a man does not know how to manage his own household, how can he care for God's church?" (1 Tim. 3:4–5).

Peter also indicates a ruling function for elders when he exhorts them:

> Tend the flock of God that is your charge, not by constraint but willingly, not for shameful gain but eagerly, not as domineering over those in your charge but being examples to the flock. And when the chief Shepherd is manifested you will obtain the unfading crown of glory. Likewise you that are younger be subject to the elders. (1 Peter 5:2–5)

The fact that they are to act as shepherds of the flock of God, and the fact that they are not to domineer (that is, not to rule harshly or oppressively) strongly suggest that elders have ruling or governing functions in the churches to which Peter is writing. This is consistent with his charge that especially those who are younger should "be subject to the elders" (v. 5).[18]

Although Hebrews 13:17 does not name elders, certainly there are some church officers with governing authority over the church, for the author says, *"Obey your leaders and submit to them; for they are keeping watch over your souls, as men who will have to give account."* Since the New Testament gives no indication of any other officers in the church with this kind of authority, it is reasonable to conclude that the congregation is to submit to and obey its elders. (This conclusion is also consistent with the description of responsibilities Paul gives to the Ephesian elders in Acts 20:28.)

In addition to governing responsibility, elders also seem to have had some *teaching responsibilities* in the New Testament churches. In Ephesians 4:11, elders are referred to as "pastor-teachers" (or, on an alternative translation, pastors who are viewed as quite closely united to teachers). And in 1 Timothy 3:2, an overseer (elder) must be "an *apt teacher.*" Then in 1 Timothy 5:17, Paul says, "Let the elders who rule well be considered worthy of double honor, especially those who labor in *preaching and teaching.*" Here Paul seems to imply that there is a special group of elders who "labor in preaching and teaching." This means at least that there are some among the elders who give more time to the activities of preaching and teaching, and may even mean that there are some who "labor" in the sense of earning their living from that preaching and teaching. The same conclusions can be drawn from Titus, where Paul says that an elder "must hold firm to the sure word as taught, so that he may be *able to give instruction* in sound doctrine and also to confute those who contradict it" (Titus 1:9).[19]

---

[18]For a defense of the view that church officers and not just older people are referred to in 1 Peter 5:5, see Wayne Grudem, *The First Epistle of Peter*, pp. 192–93.

[19]Paul never says that all the elders are to be able to teach publicly or to preach sermons to the congregation, and it would be reasonable to think that an "apt teacher" could be someone who is able

Elders, then, had responsibility to rule and to teach in New Testament churches.

**d. Qualifications for Elders:** When Paul lists the qualifications for elders, it is significant that he combines requirements concerning character traits and heart attitudes with requirements that cannot be fulfilled in a short time but will only become evident over a period of several years of faithful Christian living:

> Now a bishop must be above reproach, the husband of one wife, temperate, sensible, dignified, hospitable, an apt teacher, no drunkard, not violent but gentle, not quarrelsome, and no lover of money. He must manage his own household well, keeping his children submissive and respectful in every way; for if a man does not know how to manage his own household, how can he care for God's church? He must not be a recent convert, or he may be puffed up with conceit and fall into the condemnation of the devil; moreover he must be well thought of by outsiders, or he may fall into reproach and the snare of the devil. (1 Tim. 3:2–7)

Similar but differently worded qualifications are found in Titus 1:6–9, where Paul says that Titus is to appoint elders in every town:

> If any man is blameless, the husband of one wife, and his children are believers and not open to the charge of being profligate or insubordinate. For a bishop, as God's steward, must be blameless; he must not be arrogant or quick-tempered or a drunkard or violent or greedy for gain, but hospitable, a lover of goodness, master of himself, upright, holy, and self-controlled; he must hold firm to the sure word as taught, so that he may be able to give instruction in sound doctrine and also to confute those who contradict it. (Titus 1:6–9)

Those who are choosing elders in churches today would do well to look carefully at candidates in the light of these qualifications, and to look for these character traits and patterns of godly living rather than worldly achievement, fame, or success. Especially in churches in western industrial societies, there seems to be a tendency to think that success in the world of business (or law, or medicine, or government) is an indication of suitability for the office of elder, but this is not the teaching of the New Testament. It reminds us that elders are to be "examples to the flock" in their daily lives, and that would certainly include their own personal relationships with God in Bible reading, prayer, and worship. Just as Paul could say, "*Be imitators of me*, as I am of Christ" (1 Cor. 11:1; cf. 2 Tim. 3:10–11), and just as he could command Timothy to "*set the believers an example* in speech and conduct, in love, in faith, in purity" (1 Tim. 4:12), and just as he could tell Titus, "Show yourself in all respects a *model of good deeds*, and in your teaching show integrity, gravity, and sound speech that cannot be censured" (Titus 2:7), so the pattern is to be continued in the lives of all church leaders today. It is not optional that their lives be examples for others to follow; it is a requirement.

**e. What Is the Meaning of "Husband of One Wife"?** The qualification *"the husband of one wife"* (1 Tim. 3:2; Titus 1:6) has been understood in different ways. Some people have thought that it excludes from the office of elder men who have

---

to explain God's Word privately. So perhaps not all elders are called to do public teaching—perhaps not all have gifts for teaching in that specific way. What is clear here is that Paul wants to guarantee that elders have a mature and sound understanding of Scripture and can explain it to others.

been divorced and have then married someone else, since they have then been the husband of two wives. But this does not seem to be a correct understanding of these verses. A better interpretation is that Paul was prohibiting a polygamist (a man who *presently* has more than one wife) from being an elder. Several reasons support this view: (1) All the other qualifications listed by Paul refer to a man's *present status,* not his entire past life. For example, 1 Timothy 3:1–7 does not mean "one who has *never been* violent," but "one who is *not now* violent, but gentle." It does not mean "one who has *never been* a lover of money," but "one who is *not now* a lover of money." It does not mean "one who has been above reproach for his whole life," but "one who is now above reproach." If we made these qualifications apply to one's entire past life, then we would exclude from office almost everyone who became a Christian as an adult, for it is doubtful that any non-Christian could meet these qualifications.

(2) Paul could have said "having been married only once" if he had wanted to, but he did not.[20] (3) We should not prevent remarried widowers from being elders, but that would be necessary if we take the phrase to mean "having been married only once." The qualifications for elders are all based on a man's moral and spiritual character, and there is nothing in Scripture to suggest that a man who remarried after his wife had died has lower moral or spiritual qualifications.[21] (4) Polygamy was possible in the first century. Although it was not common, polygamy was practiced, especially among the Jews. The Jewish historian Josephus says, "For it is an ancestral custom of ours to have several wives at the same time."[22] Rabbinic legislation also regulated inheritance customs and other aspects of polygamy.[23]

Therefore it is best to understand "the husband of one wife" to prohibit a polygamist from holding the office of elder. The verses say nothing about divorce and remarriage with respect to qualifications for church office.

---

[20]The Greek expression for "having been married only once" would be *hapax gegamēmenos,* using the word "once" (*hapax*) plus a perfect participle, giving the sense, "having been married once and continuing in the state resulting from that marriage." (Such a construction is found, for example, in Heb. 10:2, and a similar construction is found in Heb. 9:26. Related expressions with aorist verbs are found in Heb. 6:4; 9:28; and Jude 3.)

Another way Paul could have expressed the idea of having been married only once is using a perfect participle of *ginomai* to say "having been a husband of one wife" (*gegonos mias gunaikos andra*). This is, in fact, the force of the requirement for widows in 1 Tim. 5:9, "having been the wife of one husband" (the force of the perfect participle *gegonuia* carries over from the previous phrase, and all the qualifications for enrolling widows in 1 Tim. 5:9–10 speak of past history in their lives). But in 1 Tim. 3:2 and Titus 1:6 the sense is different, because present tense forms of *eimi* ("to be") are used: (literally) "It is necessary for a bishop *to be* blameless, the husband of one wife. . . ."

[21]Some interpreters in the early church did try to exclude remarried widowers from church office (see, for example, *Apostolic Constitutions* 2.2; 6.17 [third or fourth century A.D.], and *Apostolic Canons* 17 [fourth or fifth century A.D.], but these statements reflect not a biblical perspective but a false asceticism which held that celibacy in general was superior to marriage. (These texts can be found in the *Ante-Nicene Fathers* series, 7:396, 457, and 501.)

However, Chrysostom (d. A.D. 407) understood 1 Tim. 3:2 to prohibit polygamy, not second marriages after death or divorce (see his *Homilies* on 1 Tim. 3:2).

[22]Josephus, *Antiquities* 17.14; in 17.19 he lists the nine women who were married to King Herod at the same time.

[23]See Mishnah, *Yebamoth* 4:11; *Ketuboth* 10:1, 4, 5; *Sanhedrin* 2:4; *Kerithoth* 3:7; *Kiddushin* 2:7; *Bechoroth* 8:4. Other evidence on Jewish polygamy is found in Justin Martyr, *Dialogue with Trypho,* chapter 134. Evidence for polygamy among non-Jews is not as extensive but is indicated in Herodotus (d. 420 B.C.) 1.135; 4.155; 2 Macc. 4:30 (about 170 B.C.); Tertullian, *Apology* 46.

**f. The Public Installation of Elders:** In connection with the discussion of elders Paul says, "Do not be hasty in the laying on of hands" (1 Tim. 5:22). Although the context does not specify a process of selection of elders, the immediately preceding context (1 Tim. 5:17–21) deals entirely with elders, and laying on of hands would be an appropriate ceremony for setting someone apart to the office of elder (note the laying on of hands to ordain or establish people in certain offices or tasks in Acts 6:6; 13:3; 1 Tim. 4:14). Therefore the setting apart of elders seems the most likely possibility for the action Paul has in mind. In this case he would be saying, "Do not be hasty in ordaining people as elders." This would be consistent with a process whereby deacons also are to be "tested first; then if they prove themselves blameless let them serve as deacons" (1 Tim. 3:10). Although Paul did ordain elders quite soon after the establishment of each church (Acts 14:23), here he cautions that such appointment should not be rushed, lest a mistake be made. And in the entire process, the church must be careful not to judge as the world judges, for "man looks on the outward appearance, but the LORD looks on the heart" (1 Sam. 16:7; cf. 2 Cor. 5:16). This necessity for evaluation of spiritual condition was also evident when the apostles encouraged the church at Jerusalem to pick out "seven men of good repute, *full of the Spirit and of wisdom,* whom we may appoint to this duty" (Acts 6:3). Among those chosen was "Stephen, a man full of faith and of the Holy Spirit" (Acts 6:5).

We should also note that the appointment of elders in Paul's early churches was accompanied by "prayer and fasting," perhaps in connection with the process of selection of the elders. (Note the example of Jesus who "went out to the mountain to pray; and all night he continued in prayer to God" before he chose his twelve disciples [Luke 6:12–13].)[24]

**3. Deacon.** The word *deacon* is a translation of the Greek word *diakonos,* which is the ordinary word for "servant" when it is used in contexts not dealing with church officers.

Deacons are mentioned clearly in Philippians 1:1: "To all the saints in Christ Jesus who are at Philippi, with the bishops and *deacons.*" But there is no specification of their function, other than to indicate that they are different from the bishops (elders). Deacons are also mentioned in 1 Timothy 3:8–13 in a more extensive passage:

> Deacons likewise must be serious, not double-tongued, not addicted to much wine, not greedy for gain; they must hold the mystery of the faith with a clear conscience. And let them also be tested first; then if they prove themselves blameless let them serve as deacons. The women [or 'wives'; the Greek can take either meaning] likewise must be serious, no slanderers, but temperate, faithful in all things. Let deacons be the husband of one wife, and let them manage their children and their households well; for those who serve well as deacons gain a good standing for

---

[24]We have not discussed the office held by Timothy and Titus under the category of apostle or under the category of elder. This is because Timothy and Titus, together with some of Paul's other co-workers, are not apostles, but neither are they elders or deacons. They seem to fall in an unusual category that we might call "apostolic assistants," for they had some delegated authority from the apostles to supervise early churches while they were being established. Since there is today no living apostle to whom people like this would be accountable and from whom they would derive their authority, we should not expect to have any apostolic assistants like this in the church today either.

themselves and also great confidence in the faith which is in Christ Jesus. (1 Tim. 3:8–13)

The function of deacons is not spelled out here, but the qualifications for deacons suggest some functions. For instance, they seem to have had some responsibility in caring for the finances of the church, since they had to be people who were "not greedy for gain" (v. 8). They perhaps had some administrative responsibilities in other activities of the church as well, because they were to manage their children and their households well (v. 12). They may also have ministered to the physical needs of those in the church or community who needed help (see discussion of Acts 6 below). Moreover, if verse 11 speaks of their wives (as I think it does), then it would also be likely that they were involved in some house-to-house visitation and counseling, because the wives are to be "no slanderers." It would do no good for deacons if their wives (who would no doubt also be involved in prayer and counseling with the deacons) spread confidential matters around the church. But these are only suggestions of possible areas of responsibility hinted at in this passage.

The noun *deacon* is not itself used in Acts 6:1–6, but a related verb (Gk. *diakoneō*, "to serve") is found in verse 2: "It is not right that we should give up preaching the word of God to *serve* tables." Here the apostles who ruled over the Jerusalem church found it necessary to delegate some administrative responsibilities to others. In this case, the responsibilities included the distribution of food to widows who were in need. It seems appropriate to think of these seven men as "deacons" even though the name *deacon* had perhaps not yet come to be applied to them as they began this responsibility, for they seem to be given tasks which fit well with the responsibilities of deacons hinted at in 1 Timothy 3:8–12.

There are other texts in which it is difficult to know whether the New Testament is speaking about a deacon as a special church officer or is simply using the word to refer to a "servant" in a general sense. This is the difficulty in Romans 16:1, where Phoebe is called a "servant" or a "deaconess" or "deacon" (this type of Greek noun has the same form in both masculine and feminine genders, so it is simply a question of which English word is most appropriate) of the church at Cenchreae. Because Paul's requirement for deacons was that they be "the husband of one wife" (1 Tim. 3:12), the translation "servant" seems preferable in Romans 16:1 (*diakonos* takes this sense in Rom. 13:4; 15:8; and 1 Cor. 3:5).[25] In general,

---

[25]Some have argued that 1 Tim. 3:11 refers to women deacons: "The *women likewise* must be serious, no slanderers, but temperate, faithful in all things." However, if Timothy and the church at Ephesus knew that women could be deacons, it would seem very strange for Paul to have to add a separate verse that talked specifically about women deacons, and then specify nothing more about them than would have been required if the verse had not been there at all. Moreover, it would seem very odd for Paul to sandwich only one verse about women deacons in the middle of five verses (three preceding and two following) about men who are deacons. On the other hand, a verse referring to the wives of deacons in the middle of a list of qualifications for deacons would be very appropriate: Paul elsewhere includes family conduct as one aspect of the requirement for church office (1 Tim. 3:2, 4–5). It is true that Paul simply says "the wives" rather than "their wives," but Greek frequently omits possessive adjectives when the person named (brother, sister, father, mother, etc.) would have an obvious relationship to the person being discussed in the immediate context.

For two views of this verse, and two views on whether women should be deacons today, see Thomas R. Schreiner, "The Valuable Ministries of Women in the Context of Male Leadership: A Survey of Old and New Testament Examples and Teaching," *Recovering Biblical Manhood and Womanhood*, ed. John Piper and Wayne Grudem (Wheaton, Ill.: Crossway, 1991), pp. 213–14, 219–221, and p. 505, n.

the verses on deacons show that they had recognized offices to "serve" the church in various ways. Acts 6:1–6 suggests that they had some administrative responsibilities, but were nevertheless subject to the authority of those who had rule over the entire church.

It is significant that nowhere in the New Testament do deacons have ruling authority over the church as the elders do, nor are deacons ever required to be able to teach Scripture or sound doctrine.

**4. Other Offices?** In many churches today, there are other offices, such as treasurer, moderator (one responsible for chairing church business meetings), or trustees (in some forms of church government, these are people who have legal accountability for the property owned by the church). Moreover, churches with more than one paid staff member may have some staff members (such as music director, education director, youth worker, etc.) who are "publicly recognized as having the right and responsibility to perform certain functions in the church," and who thus fit our definition of church officer, and who may even be paid to perform such functions as a full-time occupation, but who may not be elders or deacons in the church.

There does not seem to be any reason to say that these should not be offices in the church as well, even though all of them could probably be put in the category of either elder or deacon (most of those mentioned above could be deacons with specific responsibilities, or the moderator could also be an elder who simply moderates church business meetings). Nevertheless, if these or other similar offices seem helpful for the functioning of the church, there seems to be no reason why they should not be established. Yet if they are established, it would be necessary to see that they not overshadow the importance of the offices specifically named in Scripture, and that they not have any authority that is not subject to the governing authority of those officers that are clearly named in Scripture. If significant influence or authority is gained by those who have offices not named in Scripture, then it is much less likely that people in the congregation or the office holders themselves will look to Scripture and find detailed descriptions of how they should act or how they should be chosen. This would tend to diminish the effective authority of Scripture to govern the church in the area of church leadership.

## B. How Should Church Officers Be Chosen?

In the history of the church there have been two major types of process for the selection of church officers—selection by a higher authority, or selection by the local congregation. The Roman Catholic Church has its officers appointed by a higher authority: the Pope appoints cardinals and bishops, and the bishops appoint priests in local parishes. This is a "hierarchy" or system of government by a priesthood[26] that is distinct from the lay people in the church. This system claims an unbroken line of descent from Christ and the apostles, and claims that the

---

13; and, in the same volume, George W. Knight III, "The Family and the Church: How Should Biblical Manhood and Womanhood Work Out in Practice?" pp. 353–54.

[26]The word *hierarchy* means "government by priests," and derives from the Greek words for "priest" (*hierus*) and "rule" (*archē*).

present priesthood stands as Christ's representatives in the church. Although the Church of England (the Episcopalian Church in the United States) does not submit to government by the Pope or have cardinals, it does have some similarities to the hierarchical system of the Roman Catholic Church, since it is governed by bishops and archbishops, and its clergy are thought of as priests. It also claims direct succession from the apostles, and priests and bishops are appointed by a higher authority outside the local parish.[27]

In distinction from this system of appointment by higher authority, in most other Protestant groups church officers are chosen by the local church, or by some group within the local church, even though the form of church government may vary in other significant ways (see below). Since this is an area in which there is no absolutely decisive biblical text, we ought to be patient with some diversity among evangelicals on this issue. However, there are several reasons why it seems most appropriate that church officers (such as elder and deacon, and certainly including the "pastor") should be chosen or at least affirmed or recognized in some way by the whole congregation:

(1) In the New Testament, there are several examples where church officers were apparently chosen by the whole congregation. In Acts 6:3, the apostles do not themselves pick out the seven early deacons (if we see them as deacons), but say to the whole church, "*Pick out from among you* seven men of good repute, full of the Spirit and of wisdom, whom we may appoint to this duty." The initial selection of these men was done by the whole congregation. When a replacement was chosen for Judas to be numbered among the apostles, *the whole congregation of 120 persons* (see Acts 1:15) made the initial selection of two, from whom the Lord himself indicated which one he would appoint: "And *they* put forward two, Joseph called Barsabbas, who was surnamed Justus, and Matthias" (Acts 1:23). At the end of the Jerusalem council, the whole church had a part with the apostles and elders in choosing representatives to convey the decisions to the other churches, for the choosing and sending was done by "the apostles and elders, *with the whole church*" (Acts 15:22; cf. "in assembly," v. 25). Moreover, when some of the churches sent an offering with Paul to be taken to the Jerusalem church, the churches also sent a representative to accompany Paul, one who, according to Paul, "has been appointed *by the churches* to travel with us in this gracious work" (2 Cor. 8:19).[28]

It may be objected that Paul and Barnabas "*appointed*" elders in every church (Acts 14:23), and Paul also told Titus to "*appoint* elders in every town" (Titus 1:5). Does this not seem more like the Roman Catholic or Anglican system than a system of congregational choice? Yet even those verses need not imply that the apostles alone made the selection, but could certainly include congregational consultation and even consent before an official appointment or installation was made (as with the appointment in Acts 6:3, 6). The word *appoint* may also mean "install."[29]

---

[27]The Methodist Church in the United States has appointment of local clergy by bishops, and has some similarities to the Episcopal Church, from which it came.

[28]Of course, this church representative *may* have been appointed only by officers within the church, but there is no statement to that effect: Paul just says that he had been "appointed by the churches," and certainly does not mention any higher authority outside the churches.

[29]See BAGD, p. 881.

(2) Another reason for congregational participation in the selection of church officers is that in the New Testament generally, final governing authority seems to rest not with any group outside the church or any group within the church, but with the church as a whole. The final step in church discipline before excommunication is to *"tell it to the church"* (Matt. 18:17). Excommunication, or the act of excluding someone from the fellowship of the church, is done when the *whole congregation* is "assembled" (1 Cor. 5:4), and is therefore apparently done by the entire congregation. One other consideration that is suggestive, but not conclusive, is the fact that the epistles that are written to churches are not sent to the elders or some other group of leaders within the churches, but are all written to entire churches, and the whole congregation is encouraged to read and expected to give heed to these epistles (Rom. 1:7; 1 Cor. 1:2; 2 Cor. 1:1; cf. 2 Cor. 1:13; Col. 4:16; 1 Tim. 4:13). This means that the apostles relate directly to the congregations, not to the congregations through the officers.

There are also some practical reasons that can be mentioned:

(3) If the entire congregation selects the officers of the church, there is more accountability to the congregation. Paul assumed some level of accountability when he provided for the fact that "two or three witnesses" could bring a charge of wrongdoing against an elder (1 Tim. 5:19). This accountability provides an additional safeguard against temptations to sin and excessive lust for power.[30]

(4) Historically, false doctrine often seems to be adopted by the theologians of the church first, by the pastors second, and by the informed laity, who are daily reading their Bibles and walking with the Lord, last. Therefore, if the leadership begins to stray in doctrine or in life, and there is no election by the congregation, then the church as a whole has no practical means of getting hold of the situation and turning it around. But if officers are elected by the church, then there is a system of "checks and balances" whereby even the governing authority of the church has some accountability to the church as a whole.[31]

(5) Government works best when it has the consent of those governed (cf., in the Old Testament, Ex. 4:29–31; 1 Sam. 7:5–6; 10:24; 2 Sam. 2:4; 1 Kings 1:39–40; and note the mistake of Rehoboam in 1 Kings 12:1, 15).

These factors combine to indicate that although Scripture does not explicitly command one specific system of choosing church officers, it would seem most wise to have a system whereby the entire church has a significant role in the selection and recognition of the officers of the church—perhaps through a congregational vote, or through some other process whereby congregational recognition is required before church officers can assume office.[32]

---

[30]However, this situation also has a potential for abuse if a few influential members exert influence to keep the pastor from dealing with issues of sin in their own lives.

[31]I am not using the phrase "checks and balances" to reflect a preference for an American form of civil government at this point, but intend the phrase to be understood in a broader sense to mean safeguards that prevent excessive power from being concentrated in the hands of any one individual or group. (In fact, the system of plural elders which I see represented in the New Testament is very different from the concentration of power found in the office of the President of the United States.)

[32]When I mention a congregational vote I do not mean to suggest the idea of a competitive election such as is found in secular politics. It may simply involve a requirement that the congregation vote to ratify candidates who have been nominated by a mature group within the church (such as the present elders), or, on the other hand, it may involve a church-wide election, or other processes may be used. Scripture is silent regarding the actual process; therefore, God has decided to leave the matter to the wisdom of each congregation in its own setting.

Can anything else be said about the process of selecting officers? Some additional congregational checks against excessive use of authority might be built into the selection process. There is room for wide variation here, but provisions such as election to limited terms of office, a requirement for a mandatory year off (except for full-time pastoral staff members who are elders) every few years, a requirement for periodic reaffirmation of election, and a provision in the nominating process whereby nominations can be made by the members of the congregation (even if most nominations come from the elders themselves), would all provide additional measures of accountability to the congregation without forfeiting any essential aspects of governing authority over the congregation once elders are elected.

These factors would also provide some arguments against a self-perpetuating group of elders which is not subject to election or periodic reconfirmation by the congregation, but once again it must be said that no specific directives are listed in Scripture and there is room for variation at this point.

## C. Forms of Church Government

In discussing forms of church government there is some overlap with the previous section on the method of choosing church officers, for the selection of officers is one very important aspect of authority in the church. Different philosophies of church government will be reflected in different methods used for selecting officers of the church, as explained above.

This is evident in the fact that forms of church government can be broken down into three large categories, which we may term "episcopalian," "presbyterian," and "congregational." The *episcopalian* forms have a government by a distinct category of church officers known as a priesthood, and final authority for decision-making is found outside the local church.[33] The Episcopal Church system is the primary representative among Protestants of this form of government. The *presbyterian* forms have a government by elders, some of whom have authority not only over their local congregation, but also, through the presbytery and the general assembly, over all the churches in a region and then in the denomination as a whole. The *congregational* forms of church government all have final governing authority resting with the local congregation, although various degrees of self-rule are given up through denominational affiliation, and the actual form of local church government may vary considerably. We shall examine each of these forms of government in the following discussion.

## 1. Episcopalian.

In the episcopalian system, an archbishop has authority over many bishops. They in turn have authority over a "diocese," which simply means the churches under the jurisdiction of a bishop. The officer in charge of a local parish is a rector (or sometimes a vicar, who is an "assistant" or one who substitutes for the rector). Archbishops, bishops, and rectors are all priests, since they have all at one time

---

[33]The Roman Catholic Church also has government by a priesthood, and is therefore "episcopalian" in form of government. Sometimes an episcopalian form of government is called a "hierarchical" government, especially when referring to the Roman Catholic Church.

been ordained to the episcopalian priesthood (but in practice the rector is most often called the priest).[34]

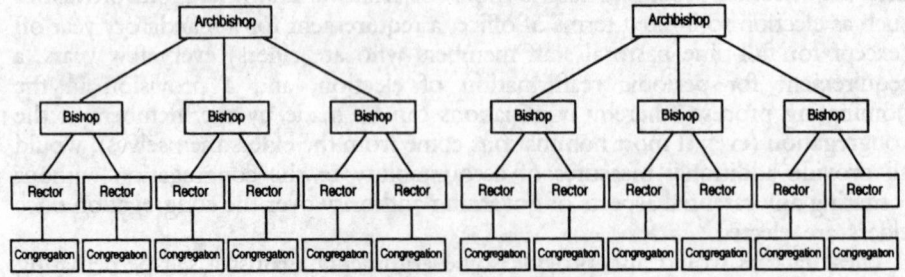

**EPISCOPALIAN GOVERNMENT**
*Figure 47.1*

The argument for the episcopalian system is not that it is found in the New Testament, but that it is a natural outgrowth of the development of the church which began in the New Testament, and it is not forbidden by the New Testament. E. A. Litton writes, "No order of Diocesan Bishops appears in the New Testament," but immediately adds:

> The evidence is in favour of the supposition that Episcopacy sprang from the Church itself, and by a natural process, and that it was sanctioned by Saint John, the last survivor of the Apostles. The Presbytery, when it assembled for consultation, would naturally elect a president to maintain order; first temporarily, but in time with permanent authority. . . . Thus it is probable that at an early period an informal episcopate had sprung up in each church. As the Apostles were one by one removed . . . the office would assume increased importance and become invested with greater powers.[35]

Moreover, since the office of bishop and the corresponding government structure found in the Episcopalian Church is both historical and beneficial, Litton argues that it should be preserved. Finally, the benefit of direct descent from the apostles is regarded as a strong reason in favor of the episcopalian system. Litton says, "The Apostles are the first link in the chain, and there is no reason why a succession, as regards to the external commission, should not proceed from age to age, the existing body of ministers handing down the official authority to their successors, and these latter in turn to theirs."[36]

But there are arguments that may be given on the other side of this question. (1) It is significant that the office of "bishop" is not a distinct office in the New Testament, but is simply a synonym for the name "elder," as Litton himself agrees.[37] There is no *single* bishop in the New Testament, but bishops (or

---

[34]However, Episcopalians understand the English word *priest* to be equivalent to the term *presbyter* (the Greek term for "elder"), while Roman Catholics understand the word *priest* differently, relating it to the Old Testament priesthood in its duty of offering sacrifices and representing the people to God and God to the people.

[35]Edward Arthur Litton, *Introduction to Dogmatic Theology*, ed. by Philip E. Hughes (London: James Clarke, 1960; first published in 2 vols., 1882, 1892), p. 401.

[36]Ibid., p. 390.

[37]Ibid., p. 400.

overseers) are always plural in number. This should not be seen merely as an incidental fact, for even among the apostles Jesus did not leave one with superior authority over the others, but left a group of twelve who were equal in governing authority (and to whom others were later added, such as Paul). Though some apostles, such as Peter, James, and Paul, had prominence among the group, they did not have any greater authority than the others, and even Peter was rebuked by Paul in Antioch (Gal. 2:11).[38] This may well reflect the wisdom of Christ in guarding against the abuse of power that inevitably comes when any one human being has too much power without sufficient checks and balances from others. Just as Jesus left a plurality of apostles to have ultimate (human) authority in the early church, so the apostles always appointed a plurality of elders in every church, never leaving only one person with governing authority.

(2) The theory of a group of bishops established to replace the apostles is not taught in the New Testament, nor is there an implication of a need for *physical* continuity of ordination through the laying on of hands by those who have been ordained in an unbroken chain of succession from the apostles. For example, in Acts 14:3, it was not the Jerusalem apostles who ordained Paul and Barnabas, but people in the church at Antioch who laid hands on them and sent them out. In fact, there is very little evidence that the apostles had any concern for a line of succession. Timothy apparently was ordained not simply by Paul but also by a "council of elders" (1 Tim. 4:14), though this may well have included Paul as well (see 2 Tim. 1:6). More importantly, ordaining is ultimately from the Lord himself (Acts 20:28; 1 Cor. 12:28; Eph. 4:11), and there is nothing in the nature of "ordaining" (when it is simply seen as public recognition of an office) that requires that it be done *only* by those previously ordained in *physical* descent from the apostles. If God has called an elder, he is to be recognized, and no concern about physical descent needs to be raised. In addition, if one is convinced that the local church should elect elders (see discussion above), then it would seem appropriate that the church that elected the elder—not an external bishop— should be the group to confer the outward recognition at election by installing the person in office or ordaining the pastor.[39]

(3) While it may be argued that the development of an episcopalian system with single bishops in authority over several churches was a beneficial development in the early church, one may also argue that it was a deviation from New Testament standards and a result of human dissatisfaction with the system of elected local elders that had been established by the apostles and that had apparently worked very well from A.D. 30 to 100 throughout all of the New Testament church. But one's evaluation of the historical data will of course depend on one's evaluation of earlier arguments for and against an episcopalian system.

**2. Presbyterian.** In this system, each local church elects elders to a session (E in figure 47.2 stands for elder, and the dotted lines indicate that the whole congregation elects the elders). The pastor of the church will be one of the elders

---

[38]Roman Catholics argue that Peter had greater authority than the other apostles from the beginning, but the New Testament evidence does not bear this out. (On the "power of the keys" in Matt. 16:19, see chapter 46, pp. 889–91.)

[39]Episcopalians, who favor appointment of officers by a bishop, would of course not agree with the premise of this last consideration.

in the session, equal in authority to the other elders. This session has governing authority over the local church. However, the members of the session (the elders) are also members of a presbytery, which has authority over several churches in a region. This presbytery consists of some or all of the elders in the local churches over which it has authority. Moreover, some of the members of the presbytery are members of the "general assembly" which usually will have authority over all the presbyterian churches in a nation or region.[40]

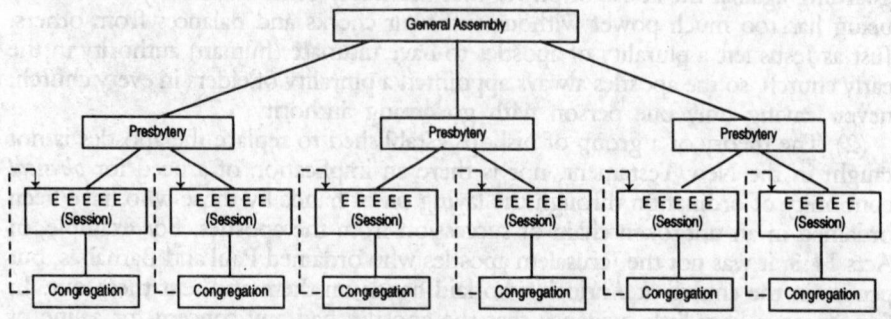

## PRESBYTERIAN GOVERNMENT
### Figure 47.2

The arguments in favor of this presbyterian system are: (1) that those who have wisdom and gifts for eldership should be called on to use their wisdom to govern more than just one local church, and (2) a national (or even worldwide) government of the church shows the unity of the body of Christ. Moreover (3) such a system is able to prevent an individual congregation from falling into doctrinal error much more effectively than any voluntary association of churches.[41]

The presbyterian system outlined above has many adherents among evangelical Christians today, and it certainly works effectively in many cases. However, some objections can be brought against this system: (1) Nowhere in Scripture do *elders* have regularly established authority over more than their own local church. The pattern is rather that elders are appointed in local churches and have authority over local churches. Against this claim the Jerusalem council in Acts 15 is often mentioned, but we should notice that this council was held in Jerusalem because of the presence of the apostles. Apparently the apostles and the elders in Jerusalem, with the representatives from Antioch (Acts 15:2), together sought God's wisdom on this matter. And there seems to have been some consultation with the whole church as well, for we read, at the conclusion of the discussion, "Then it seemed good to the apostles and the elders, *with the whole church,* to choose men from among them and send them to Antioch with Paul and Barnabas" (Acts 15:22). (If this narrative gives support to regional government by elders, it

[40]In the Christian Reformed Church, the form of government is similar to a presbyterian system, but the names of the governing bodies are different: the elders in a local church are called a *consistory* (instead of a session), the regional governing body is called a *classis* (instead of a *presbytery*), and the national governing assembly is called a *synod* (instead of a *general assembly*).

[41]A fuller defense of the presbyterian system of church government is found in Louis Berkhof, *Systematic Theology,* pp. 581–92.

therefore also gives support to regional government by whole congregations!) This situation with the elders in Jerusalem is not a good pattern to defend a system whereby elders have authority over more than their local churches: the Jerusalem church did not send for all the elders in Judea, Samaria, and Galilee, and call a meeting of "the Judean presbytery" or a "general assembly." Although the apostles in Jerusalem certainly had authority over all the churches, there is no indication that elders by themselves, even in the Jerusalem church, had any such authority. And certainly there is no New Testament pattern for elders exercising authority over any other than their own local churches.[42]

(2) This system, in practice, results in much formal litigation, where doctrinal disputes are pursued year after year all the way to the level of the general assembly. One wonders if this should be characteristic of the church of Christ—perhaps so, but it seems to the present author to be a system that encourages such litigation far more than is necessary or edifying for the body of Christ.

(3) The effective power in church government seems, in practice, to be too removed from the final control of the lay people in the church. Although Berkhof, who defends this system of government, affirms quite clearly that "the power of the church resides *primarily* in the governing body of the local church,"[43] he also admits that, "the more general the assembly, the more remote it is from the people."[44] Thus the system is very hard to turn around when it begins to go wrong since the lay persons who are not elders have no vote in the session or the presbytery or the general assembly, and the governing structure of the church is more removed from them than in other church government structures.

(4) Although in some cases it is true that a doctrinally sound denomination with a presbyterian system of government can keep a local church from going astray in its doctrine, in actuality very frequently the opposite has been true: the national leadership of a presbyterian denomination has adopted false doctrine and has put great pressure on local churches to conform to it.

(5) Although the presbyterian system does represent in one form the national or even worldwide unity of Christ's church, such unity can certainly be shown in other ways than through this system of government. The churches with more purely congregational forms of government do have voluntary associations that manifest this unity. In fact, these associations involve *all* the people in the churches, not just the elders or the clergy, as in a presbyterian system. The national meeting of a Baptist denomination, for example, where large numbers of ministers and lay persons (who are not necessarily elders or deacons, but just delegates from their churches) join together in fellowship might be seen as a better demonstration of the unity of Christ's body than a presbyterian general assembly where only elders are present.

---

[42]On the other hand, advocates of a presbyterian system could answer that nowhere in the New Testament do we find an example of an *independent* church—every church in the New Testament is subject to the worldwide governing authority of the apostles. Of course, a defender of independent churches might answer that we have no apostles today to exercise such authority. However, if we are looking to the New Testament for a pattern, the fact still remains that *no independent churches are to be found there,* and we would expect that something rather than nothing would replace a government by the apostles. This seems to me to indicate that some sort of denominational authority over local churches is still appropriate (though that will take different forms in different denominations).

[43]Berkhof, *Systematic Theology,* p. 584.

[44]Ibid., p. 591.

## 3. Congregational.

**a. Single Elder (or Single Pastor):** We can now look at five varieties of congregational government for the church. The first one, which is currently the most common among Baptist churches in the United States, is the "single elder" form of government. In this kind of government the pastor is seen as the only elder in the church, and there is an elected board of deacons who serve under his authority and give support to him (D in figure 47.3 stands for deacon).

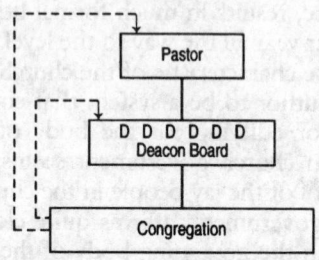

SINGLE-ELDER (SINGLE-PASTOR) GOVERNMENT
*Figure 47.3*

In this system, the congregation elects the pastor and also elects the deacons. The amount of authority the pastor has varies greatly from church to church, and will generally increase the longer a pastor remains in a church. The authority of the deacon board is often thought to be merely an advisory authority. In the way this system ordinarily functions, especially in smaller churches, many decisions must be brought before the congregation as a whole.

The arguments in favor of this system are clearly presented in A. H. Strong's *Systematic Theology,* a text that has been widely used in Baptist circles.[45] Strong gives the following arguments:

(1) The New Testament does not require a plurality of elders, but the pattern of plural elders seen in the New Testament was only due to the size of the churches at that time. He says:

> In certain of the New Testament churches there appears to have been a plurality of elders. . . . There is, however, no evidence that the number of elders was uniform, or that the plurality which frequently existed was due to any other cause than the size of the churches for which these elders cared. The New Testament example, while it permits the multiplication of assistant pastors according to need, does not require a plural eldership in every case.[46]

In this quotation Strong shows that he would regard additional pastors hired by a larger church to be elders as well, so that this system could be expanded beyond a single elder/pastor to include two or more elder/pastors. But the crucial distinction is that *the governing authority of the office of elder is possessed only by the professional*

---

[45]A. H. Strong, *Systematic Theology* (Valley Forge, Pa.: Judson Press, 1907), pp. 914–17. Strong was President of Rochester Theological Seminary from 1872 to 1912.

[46]Ibid., pp. 915–16.

*pastor(s) of the church,* and is not shared by any lay persons in the church. And we must realize that in practice, the vast majority of churches that follow this pattern today are relatively small churches with only one pastor; therefore, in actuality, this usually becomes a single elder form of government.[47]

(2) Strong adds that "James was the pastor or president of the church at Jerusalem," and cites Acts 12:17; 21:18; and Galatians 2:12 to show that this leadership by James was a pattern which could then be imitated by other churches.

(3) Strong notes that some passages have "bishop" in the singular but "deacons" in the plural, hinting at something similar to this common Baptist form of government. A literal translation of the Greek text shows a singular definite article modifying "bishop" in two verses: "*The bishop* therefore must be without reproach" (1 Tim. 3:2, literal translation) and that "*the bishop* must be blameless" (Titus 1:7, literal translation), but by contrast, we read, "*Deacons* likewise must be serious . . ." (1 Tim. 3:8).

(4) Finally, the "angel of the church" in Revelation 2:1, 8, 12, 18; 3:1, 7, 14, according to Strong, "is best interpreted as meaning the pastor of the church; and, if this be correct, it is clear that each church had, not many pastors, but one."[48]

(5) Another argument, not made by Strong, is found in recent literature on church growth. The argument is that churches need a strong single pastor in order to grow rapidly.[49]

Once again it must be said that this single elder form of government has also worked very successfully in many evangelical churches. However, there can be objections to the case presented by Strong and others.

(1) It seems inconsistent to argue that the New Testament falls short of giving a clear *command* that all churches should have a plurality of elders when the passages on qualifications of elders in 1 Timothy 3:1–7 and Titus 1:5–7 are used as scriptural *requirements* for church officers today. How can churches say that the *qualifications for elders* found in these verses are commanded for us today but the *system of plural elders* found in these very same verses is not commanded, but was required only in that time and in that society? Though it could be objected that these are commands written only to individual situations in Ephesus and Crete, much of the New Testament consists of apostolic commands written to individual churches on how they should conduct themselves. Yet we do not therefore say that we are free to disobey these instructions in other parts of the epistles. In fact, 1 Timothy and Titus give us a great deal of material on the conduct of the local church, material which all believing churches seek to follow.

Moreover, it seems to be quite unwise to ignore a clear New Testament pattern

---

[47]Another Baptist theologian, Millard Erickson, supports Strong's claim that the New Testament does not require plural elders in a church. He says that the New Testament examples of elders are "descriptive passages" that tell about a church order that already existed, but that "churches are not commanded to adopt a particular form of church order" (*Christian Theology,* p. 1084). Moreover, Erickson sees no one pattern of church government in the New Testament, but says, "There may well have been rather wide varieties of governmental arrangements. Each church adopted a pattern which fit its individual situation" (ibid.).

[48]Strong, *Systematic Theology,* p. 916.

[49]See, for example, C. Peter Wagner, *Leading Your Church to Growth* (Ventura, Calif.: Regal, 1984). He says, "The principal argument of this book is that if churches are going to maximize their growth potential they need pastors who are strong leaders. . . . Make no mistake about it: it is a rule" (p. 73). The book is filled with anecdotes and pronouncements from church growth experts telling the reader that leadership by a strong single pastor is essential to significant church growth.

which existed throughout all the churches for which we have evidence at the time the New Testament was written. When the New Testament shows us that *no* church was seen to have a single elder ("in *every* church," Acts 14:23; "in every town," Titus 1:5; "let him call for the *elders,*" James 5:14; "I exhort the *elders* among you," 1 Peter 5:1), then it seems unpersuasive to say that smaller churches would have only had one elder. Even when Paul had just founded churches on his first missionary journey, there were *elders* appointed "in every church" (Acts 14:23). And "every town" on the island of Crete was to have elders, no matter how large or small the church was.

In addition, there is an inconsistency in Strong's argument when he says that the large churches were those which had plural elders, for then he claims that "the angel of the church in Ephesus" (Rev. 2:1) was a single pastor, according to this common Baptist pattern. Yet the church at Ephesus at that time was exceptionally large: Paul, in founding that church, had spent three years there (Acts 20:31), during which time "*all the residents of Asia heard the word of the Lord,* both Jews and Greeks" (Acts 19:10). The population of Ephesus at that time was more than 250,000.[50]

We may ask, why should we follow Strong and adopt as the norm a pattern of church government which is *nowhere* found in the New Testament, and reject a pattern *everywhere* found in the New Testament?

(2) James may well have acted as moderator or presiding officer in the church in Jerusalem, for all churches will have some kind of designated leader like this in order to conduct meetings. But this does not imply that he was the "pastor" of the church in Jerusalem in a "single elder" sense. In fact, Acts 15:2 shows that there were *elders* (plural) in the church in Jerusalem, and James himself was probably numbered among the apostles (see Gal. 1:19) rather than the elders.

(3) In 1 Timothy 3:2 and Titus 1:7, the Greek definite article modifying "bishop" simply shows that Paul is speaking of general qualifications as they applied to any one example.[51] In fact, in both cases which Strong cites we know there were *elders* (plural) in the churches involved. 1 Timothy 3:2 is written to Timothy at Ephesus, and Acts 20:17 shows us that there were "elders" in the church at Ephesus. And even in 1 Timothy, Paul writes, "Let the *elders* who rule well be considered worthy of double honor, especially those who labor in preaching and teaching" (1 Tim. 5:17). With regard to Titus 1:7 we need only look to verse 5, where Paul directs Titus explicitly to "appoint *elders* in every town."

(4) The angels of the seven churches in Revelation 2–3 are unusual and rather weak evidence for single elders. "The angel of the church in Ephesus" (Rev. 2:1) can hardly mean that there was only one elder in that church, since we know there were "elders" there in this very large church (Acts 20:17). The word "angel" used in the address to the seven churches in Revelation 2–3 may simply designate a

---

[50]Robert H. Mounce, *The Book of Revelation,* NIC (Grand Rapids: Eerdmans, 1977), p. 85.

[51]In terms of Greek grammar, the use of the definite article here is best understood as a "generic" use, which is defined as a use of the article "to select a normal or representative individual" (MHT 3, p. 180). Paul's use of the singular was natural after he said, "If *any one* aspires to the office of bishop, he desires a noble task" (1 Tim. 3:1), or "if *any man* is blameless . . ." (Titus 1:6).

The rsv gives a more appropriate translation for English readers, reflecting this generic use, at these two verses: "*a* bishop."

special messenger to each church, perhaps even the human messenger who would take what John wrote to each church,[52] or it may represent "the prevailing spirit of the church" rather than the ruling official of the congregation,[53] or may even simply refer to an angel who was given special care over each congregation. Even if it did represent a presiding officer of some sort in each congregation, this "angel" is not shown to have any ruling authority or any functions equivalent to today's single pastor, or any functions equivalent to that of "elder" in the New Testament churches. This passage does not furnish strong enough evidence to dislodge the clear data throughout the New Testament showing plural elders in every church, even in the church in Ephesus.

It is interesting that all of the New Testament passages cited by Strong (Acts 15, Jerusalem; 1 Tim. 3:2, Ephesus; Titus 1:7, Crete; Rev. 2–3, the seven churches, including Ephesus) speak of situations in which the New Testament itself points quite clearly to a plurality of elders in authority in the churches mentioned.

(5) The argument from church growth studies does not really prove that government led by a single pastor is necessary, for at least three reasons: (a) We should not reject a pattern supported in Scripture and adopt a different one just because people tell us that the different pattern seems to work well in producing large churches—our role here, as in all of life, should rather be to obey Scripture as closely as we can and expect God to bring appropriate blessing as he wills. (b) There are many large churches with government by plural elders (both Presbyterian churches and independent churches), so the argument from pragmatic considerations is not conclusive. (c) C. Peter Wagner admits that strong leaders can be found in various forms of church government,[54] and we must agree that a system of plural elders in which all have equal authority does not prevent one elder (such as the pastor) from functioning as a sort of "first among equals" and having a significant leadership role among those elders.

(6) A common practical problem with a "single elder" system is either an excessive concentration of power in one person or excessive demands laid upon him. In either case, the temptations to sin are very great, and a lessened degree of accountability makes yielding to temptation more likely. As was mentioned above, it was never the pattern in the New Testament, even with the apostles, to concentrate ruling power in the hands of any one person.

Here it should be noted that the "single elder" view of church government really has no more New Testament support than the "single bishop" (episcopalian) view. Both seem to be attempts to justify what has already happened in the history of the church, not conclusions that have grown out of an inductive examination of the New Testament itself.

(7) Finally, it should be noted that in actual practice the "single elder" system can change and *function* more like a "plural elders" government, only those who function as elders are instead called "deacons." This would happen if the deacons share the actual governing authority with the pastor, and the pastor and other

---

[52]The word *angelos* ["angel"] in Rev. 2:1 et al. can mean not only "angel" but also just "messenger."
[53]So Robert Mounce, *The Book of Revelation*, p. 85.
[54]Wagner says at one point that a pastor can be a strong leader within a variety of kinds of church government (*Leading Your Church to Growth*, pp. 94–95). Therefore it is not appropriate to take his study as an argument that solely supports a single elder form of government.

deacons see themselves as accountable to the deacon board as a whole. The system then begins to look like figure 47.4.

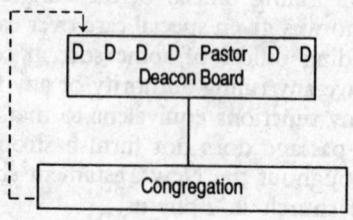

### THE PASTOR AND DEACONS MAY GOVERN TOGETHER AND THUS FUNCTION LIKE A GOVERNMENT OF PLURAL ELDERS
*Figure 47.4*

The problem with this arrangement is that it does not use biblical terminology to apply to the functions that people are carrying out, for "deacons" in the New Testament never had governing or teaching authority in the church. The result in such a situation is that people in the church (both the deacons and the other church members) will fail to read and apply scriptural passages on elders to those who are *in fact functioning as elders* in their church. Therefore these passages lose the direct relevance that they should have in the church. In this case however, the problem could be solved by changing the name "deacon" to "elder," and considering the pastor an elder along with the others.

**b. Plural Local Elders:** Is there any kind of church government that preserves the pattern of plural elders found in the New Testament and that avoids the expansion of elders' authority beyond the local congregation? Although such a system is not distinctive of any denomination today, it is found in many individual congregations. Using the conclusions reached to this point on the New Testament data, I would suggest figure 47.5 as a possible pattern.

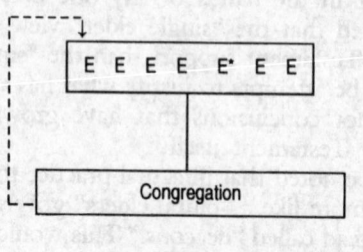

\* Pastor

### PLURAL LOCAL ELDER GOVERNMENT
*Figure 47.5*

Within such a system the elders govern the church and have authority to rule over it, authority which has been conferred by Christ himself, the head of the church, and by the Holy Spirit (Acts 20:28; Heb. 13:17). In this system of government, there is always more than one elder, a fact which distinguishes this form of government from the "single elder system" discussed above. In a contemporary congregation, the "pastor" (or "senior pastor") would be one among the elders in this system. He does not have authority over them, nor does he work for them as an employee. He has a somewhat distinct role in that he is engaged in the full-time work of "preaching and teaching" (1 Tim. 5:17), and derives part or all of his income from that work (1 Tim. 5:18). He also may frequently assume a leadership role (such as chairman) among the elders, which would fit with his leadership role among the congregation, but such a leadership role *among the elders* would not be necessary to the system. In addition, the pastor will ordinarily have considerable authority to make decisions and provide leadership in many areas of responsibility that have been delegated to him by the elder board as a whole. Such a system would allow a pastor to exercise strong leadership in the church while still having equal governing authority with the other elders.

The strength of this system of government is seen in the fact that the pastor does not have authority on his own over the congregation, but that authority belongs collectively to the entire group of elders (what may be called the elder board). Moreover, the pastor himself, like every other elder, is subject to the authority of the elder board as a whole. This can be a great benefit in keeping a pastor from making mistakes, and in supporting him in adversity and protecting him from attacks and opposition.[55]

In such a system, are there limitations that should be placed on the authority of the elders? In the section above on the manner of choosing church officers, several reasons were given to have some "checks and balances" that would put restrictions on the authority of the officers of a church.[56] Those arguments are also helpful here in indicating that, though elders have substantial governing authority over the church, it should not be unlimited authority. Examples of such limitations might be suggested, such as: (1) they may be elected rather than self-perpetuat-

---

[55]If the church has more than one pastor who is paid for his work, these other associate or assistant pastors may or may not be viewed as elders (depending on the qualifications of each staff member and the policies of the church), but in either case, it would be entirely consistent with this form of government to have those associate pastors accountable to the senior pastor alone in their day-to-day work, and he accountable to the elder board with respect to his supervision of their activity.

[56]The arguments given above (pp. 921–22) for restrictions on the authority of church officers may be summarized as follows: (1) Church officers in the New Testament were apparently chosen by the whole congregation. (2) The final governing authority in New Testament churches seemed to rest with the whole church. (3) Accountability to the congregation provides a safeguard against temptations to sin. (4) Some degree of control by the entire congregation provides a safeguard against the leadership falling into doctrinal error. (5) Government works best with the consent of those governed. In addition to those, there is another reason for restricting the authority of church officers: (6) The doctrine of the clarity of Scripture (see chapter 6), and the doctrine of the priesthood of all believers (whereby the New Testament affirms that all Christians have access to God's throne in prayer and all share as members in a "royal priesthood" [1 Peter 2:9; cf. Heb. 10:19–25; 12:22–24]) combine to indicate that all Christians have some ability to interpret Scripture and some responsibility to seek God's wisdom in applying it to situations. All have access directly to God in order to seek to know his will. The New Testament allows for no special class of Christians who have greater access to God than others. Therefore, it is right to include all believers in some of the crucial decision-making processes of the church. "In an abundance of counselors there is safety" (Prov. 11:14).

ing; (2) they may have specific terms with a mandatory year off the board (except for the pastor, whose continuing leadership responsibilities require continuous participation as an elder); (3) some large decisions may be required to be brought to the whole church for approval. Regarding this third point, congregational approval is already a biblical requirement for church discipline in Matthew 18:17 and for excommunication in 1 Corinthians 5:4. The principle of congregational election of elders would imply that the decision to call any pastor would also have to be approved by the congregation as a whole. Major new directions in the ministry of the church, which will require large-scale congregational support, may be brought to the church as a whole for approval. Finally, it would seem wise to require congregational approval on such large financial decisions as an annual budget, the decision to purchase property, or the decision to borrow money for the church (if that is ever done), simply because the church as a whole will be asked to give generously to pay for these commitments.[57]

In fact, the reasons for placing some limitations on the authority of church officers may appear so strong that they would lead us to think that all decisions and all governing authority should rest with the congregation as a whole. (Some churches have adopted a system of almost pure democracy in governing the church, whereby everything must come to the congregation as a whole for approval.) However, this conclusion ignores the abundant New Testament evidence about the clear ruling and governing authority given to elders in New Testament churches. Therefore, while it is important to have *some recognized checks* on the authority of elders, and to rest ultimate governing authority with the congregation as a whole, it still is necessary, if we are to remain faithful to the New Testament pattern, to have a strong level of authority vested in the elders themselves.[58]

I have labeled this system one of "plural *local* elders" in order to distinguish it from a presbyterian system where elders, when gathered on the level of the presbytery or general assembly, have authority over more than their own local congregations. But in such a system of elected local elders, can there be any wider associations with churches beyond the local congregation? Yes, certainly. While

---

[57]It should be noted that a church government system with a self-perpetuating group of elders, rather than one elected by the congregation, would be very similar in function to this system, but would not be as extensive in the checks and balances put on the authority of the elders. Such a church may still wish to have some mechanism whereby the congregation could remove elders who strayed from faithfulness to Scripture in serious ways.

[58]When this kind of system functions in a large church, it is important that a majority of the elder board be persons *who are not associate pastors in the church*. This is because the associate pastors are subject to the senior pastor in all of their church work (he usually hires and fires them and sets their pay, and they report to him). Therefore, if a majority of the elders consists of these associate pastors, the interpersonal dynamics involved will make it impossible for the senior pastor to be subject to the authority of the elders as a group, and the system will in fact function as a (somewhat disguised) form of "single pastor" government, not as a plural elder government.

Someone may object that in a large church only full-time staff members know enough about the life of the church to be effective elders, but this is not a persuasive objection: Government by boards who are not closely involved in the everyday activities of those whom they govern works well in many realms of human activity, such as college and seminary boards, local school boards, boards of directors of corporations, and even state and national governments. All of these governing bodies direct policies and give guidance to full-time administrators, and they are able to obtain detailed information about specific situations when the need arises. (I realize that all these systems *can* work poorly, but my point is simply that they can work very well when the right people are put in leadership positions.)

churches with this system may choose to remain entirely independent, most will enter into voluntary associations with other churches of similar convictions in order to facilitate fellowship, pooling of resources for mission activity (and perhaps for other things such as Christian camps, publications, theological education, etc.). However, the only authority these larger associations would have over the local congregation would be the authority to exclude an individual church from the association, not the authority to govern its individual affairs.

**c. Corporate Board:** The remaining three forms of congregational church government are not commonly used, but are sometimes found in evangelical churches. The first one is patterned after the example of a modern corporation, where the board of directors hires an executive officer who then has authority to run the business as he sees fit. This form of government could also be called the "you-work-for-us" structure. It is depicted in figure 47.6.

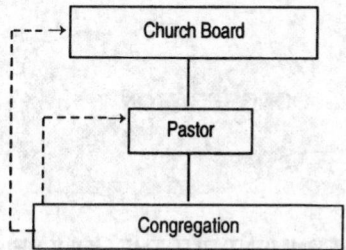

**CORPORATE BOARD MODEL OF CHURCH GOVERNMENT**
*Figure 47.6*

In favor of this structure it might be argued that this system in fact works well in contemporary businesses. However, there is no New Testament precedent or support for such a form of church government. It is simply the result of trying to run the church like a modern business, and it sees the pastor not as a spiritual leader, but merely as a paid employee.

Further objections to this structure are the fact that it deprives the pastor of sharing in the ruling authority that must be his if he is to carry out his eldership responsibilities effectively. Moreover, the members of the board are also members of the congregation over whom the pastor is supposed to have some authority, but that authority is seriously compromised if the leaders of the congregation are in fact his bosses.

**d. Pure Democracy:** This view, which takes congregational church government to its logical extreme, can be represented as in figure 47.7.

In this system *everything* must come to the congregational meeting. The result is that decisions are often argued endlessly, and, as the church grows, decision-making reaches a point of near paralysis. While this structure does attempt to do justice to some of the passages cited above regarding the need for final governing authority to rest with the congregation as a whole, it is unfaithful to the New

Testament pattern of recognized and designated elders who have actual authority
to rule the church in most situations.

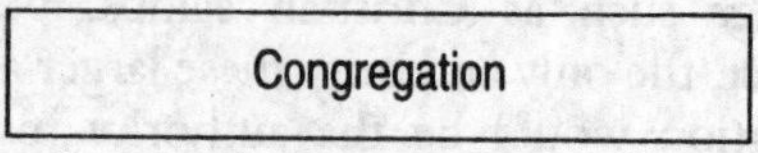

```
┌─────────────────────────────────────┐
│              Congregation             │
└─────────────────────────────────────┘
```

GOVERNMENT BY PURE DEMOCRACY
*Figure 47.7*

e. **"No Government but the Holy Spirit":** Some churches, particularly very new
churches with more mystical or extremely pietistic tendencies, function with a
church government that looks something like figure 47.8.

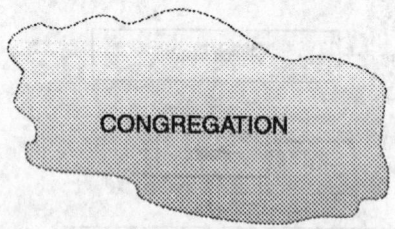

NO GOVERNMENT BUT THE HOLY SPIRIT
*Figure 47.8*

In this case, the church would deny that any form of government is needed, it
would depend on all the members of the congregation being sensitive to the
leading of the Holy Spirit in their own lives, and decisions would generally be
made by consensus. This form of government never lasts very long. Not only is it
unfaithful to the New Testament pattern of designated elders with governing
authority in the church, but·it is also subject to much abuse, because subjective
feelings rather than wisdom and reason prevail in the decision-making process.

**4. Conclusions.** It must be made clear, in concluding this discussion of church
government, that the form of government adopted by a church is not a major
point of doctrine. Christians have lived comfortably and ministered very
effectively within several different kinds of systems, and there are many
evangelicals within each of the systems mentioned. Moreover, a number of
different types of church government systems seem to work *fairly well*. Where
there are weaknesses that appear to be inherent in the governing structure,
individuals within the system generally recognize those weaknesses and attempt to
compensate for them in whatever ways the system will allow.

Nevertheless, a church can be *more pure* or *less pure* on this point, as in other
areas. As we are persuaded by Scripture concerning various aspects of church
government, then we should continue to pray and work for the greater purity of
the visible church in this area as well.

## D. Should Women be Church Officers?

Most systematic theologies have not included a section on the question of whether women can be church officers, because it has been assumed through the history of the church, with very few exceptions, that only men could be pastors or function as elders within a church.[59] But in recent years a major controversy has arisen within the evangelical world: may women as well as men be pastors? May they share in all the offices of the church? I have treated this question much more extensively elsewhere[60] but a brief summary of the question can be given at this point.

We must affirm at the outset that the creation narrative in *Genesis 1:27 views men and women as equally created in the image of God.* Therefore, men and women have equal value to God, and should be seen by us as having absolutely equal value as persons, and equal value to the church. Moreover, Scripture assures men and women of equal access to all the blessings of salvation (see Acts 2:17–18; Gal. 3:28).[61] This is remarkably affirmed in the high dignity and respect which Jesus accorded to women in his earthly ministry.[62]

We must also admit that evangelical churches have often failed to recognize the full equality of men and women, and thereby have failed to count women equal in value to men. The result has been a tragic failure to recognize that God often gives women equal or greater spiritual gifts than men, a failure to encourage women to have full and free participation in the various ministries of the church, and a failure to take full account of the wisdom that God has given to women with respect to important decisions in the life of the church. If the present controversy over women's roles in the church can result in the eradication of some of these past abuses, then the church as a whole will benefit greatly.

Yet the question remains, should women be pastors or elders in churches? (Or should they fill roles equivalent to that of an elder in churches that have alternative forms of government?) My own conclusion on this issue is that the Bible does not permit women to function in the role of pastor or elder within a church. This has also been the conclusion of the vast majority of churches in various societies throughout history. The reasons that seem to me to be most persuasive in answering this question are the following:

**1. 1 Timothy 2:11–14.** The single passage in Scripture that addresses this question most directly is 1 Timothy 2:11–14:

[59]See William Weinrich, "Women in the History of the Church: Learned and Holy, But Not Pastors," in *Recovering Biblical Manhood and Womanhood: A Response to Evangelical Feminism,* ed. John Piper and Wayne Grudem (Wheaton, Ill.: Crossway, 1991), pp. 263–79. See also Ruth A. Tucker and Walter L. Liefeld, *Daughters of the Church: Women and Ministry from New Testament Times to the Present* (Grand Rapids: Zondervan, 1987).
[60]See *Recovering Biblical Manhood and Womanhood,* ed. John Piper and Wayne Grudem. The position I have taken in the following paragraphs is consistent with the "Danvers Statement" issued in 1988 by the Council on Biblical Manhood and Womanhood, P.O. Box 317, Wheaton, IL 60189, USA.
[61]See also Raymond C. Ortlund, Jr., "Male-Female Equality and Male Headship: Gen. 1–3," in *Recovering Biblical Manhood and Womanhood,* pp. 95–112.
[62]See James A. Borland, "Women in the Life and Teachings of Jesus," in *Recovering Biblical Manhood and Womanhood,* pp. 113–23.

Let a woman learn in silence with all submissiveness. *I permit no woman to teach or to have authority over men;* she is to keep silent. For Adam was formed first, then Eve; and Adam was not deceived, but the woman was deceived and became a transgressor.

Here Paul is speaking about the church when it is assembled (see vv. 8–9). In such a setting, Paul says, "I permit no woman to *teach* or to *have authority* over men" (v. 12). These are the functions that are carried out by the elders of the church, and especially by what we know as a pastor in contemporary church situations.[63] It is specifically these functions unique to elders that Paul prohibits for women in the church.[64]

Several objections have been brought against this position:[65]

(a) It has been said that this passage applies only to a specific situation that Paul is addressing, probably one where women were teaching heretical doctrine within the church at Ephesus. But this objection is not persuasive, since there is no clear statement in 1 Timothy that says that women were actually *teaching* false doctrines. (1 Tim. 5:13 talks about women who are gossiping, but does not mention false doctrine.) Moreover, Paul does not simply tell certain women who are teaching false doctrine to be silent, but he says, "I permit *no woman* to teach or to have authority over men." And finally, the *reason* Paul gives for this prohibition is not the one proposed in this objection, but a far different one: the situation of Adam and Eve before the fall, and before there was any sin in the world (see v. 13), and the way in which a reversal in male and female roles occurred at the time of the fall (see v. 14). These reasons are not limited to one situation in the church at Ephesus, but have application to manhood and womanhood generally.

(b) Another objection is to say that Paul gave this prohibition because women were not well educated in the first century, and therefore were not qualified for teaching or governing roles in the church. But Paul does not give lack of education as a reason for saying that women cannot "teach or . . . have authority over men," but rather points back to creation (vv. 13–14). It is precarious to base an argument on a reason Paul did *not* give instead of the reason he *did* give.

In addition, this objection misunderstands the actual facts of the ancient church and the ancient world. Formal training in Scripture was not required for church leadership in the New Testament church, because several of the apostles did not have formal biblical training (see Acts 4:13). On the other hand, the skills of basic literacy and therefore the ability to read and study Scripture were available to men and women alike (note Acts 18:26; Rom. 16:1; 1 Tim. 2:11; Titus 2:3–4). There were many well-educated women in the ancient world, and particularly in a cultural center such as Ephesus.[66]

Finally, those who make such an argument are sometimes inconsistent in that elsewhere they point to women who had leadership positions in the ancient

---

[63]See discussion on pp. 915–16 above regarding the teaching and ruling functions of elders in a church.

[64]For a more extensive treatment of this passage, see Douglas Moo, "What Does It Mean Not to Teach or Have Authority Over Men?: 1 Tim. 2:11–15," in *Recovering Biblical Manhood and Womanhood*, pp. 179–93.

[65]For more extensive statements of these objections see the books marked "Favors women as pastors" in the bibliography at the end of this chapter, especially the books by Mickelsen, Spencer, and Bilezikian.

[66]See Piper and Grudem, *Recovering Biblical Manhood and Womanhood*, p. 82.

church, such as Priscilla. This point is especially relevant to 1 Timothy 2, because Paul was writing to Ephesus (1 Tim. 1:3), which was the home church of Priscilla and Aquila (see Acts 18:18–19, 21). It was in this very church at Ephesus that Priscilla knew Scripture well enough to help instruct Apollos in A.D. 51 (Acts 18:26). Then she had probably learned from Paul himself for another three years while he stayed at Ephesus teaching "the whole counsel of God" (Acts 20:27; cf. v. 31; also 1 Cor. 16:19). No doubt many other women in Ephesus had followed her example and also had learned from Paul. Although they later went to Rome, we find Aquila and Priscilla back in Ephesus at the end of Paul's life (2 Tim. 4:19), about A.D. 67 Therefore, it is likely that they were in Ephesus in A.D. 65, about the time Paul wrote 1 Timothy (about *fourteen years after Priscilla had helped instruct Apollos*). Yet Paul does not allow even well-educated Priscilla or any other well-educated women at Ephesus to teach men in the public assembly of the church. The reason was not lack of education, but the order of creation which God established between men and women.

## 2. 1 Corinthians 14:33b–36. In a similar teaching, Paul says:

> As in all the churches of the saints, the women should keep silence in the churches. For they are not permitted to speak, but should be subordinate, as even the law says. If there is anything they desire to know, let them ask their husbands at home. For it is shameful for a woman to speak in church. What! Did the word of God originate with you, or are you the only ones it has reached? (1 Cor. 14:33b–36)

In this section Paul cannot be prohibiting all public speech by women in the church, for he clearly allows them to pray and prophesy in church in 1 Corinthians 11:5. Therefore, it is best to understand this passage as referring to speech that is in the category being discussed in the immediate context, namely, the spoken evaluation and judging of prophecies in the congregation (see v. 29: "Let two or three prophets speak, and *let the others weigh what is said*"). While Paul allows women to speak and give prophecies in the church meeting, he does not allow them to speak up and give evaluations or critiques of the prophecies that have been given, for this would be a ruling or governing function with respect to the whole church.[67] This understanding of the passage depends on our view of the gift of prophecy in the New Testament age, namely, that prophecy involves not authoritative Bible teaching, and not speaking words of God which are equal to Scripture, but rather reporting something which God spontaneously brings to mind.[68] In this way, Paul's teachings are quite consistent in 1 Corinthians 14 and 1 Timothy 2: in both cases he is concerned to preserve male leadership in the teaching and governing of the church.[69]

---

[67]For a fuller discussion of this question, see D. A. Carson, " 'Silent in the Churches': On the Role of Women in 1 Cor. 14:33b–36," in *Recovering Biblical Manhood and Womanhood*, pp. 140–153. See also Wayne Grudem, *The Gift of Prophecy in the New Testament and Today*, pp. 217–24; also Wayne Grudem, "Prophecy—Yes, but Teaching—No: Paul's Consistent Advocacy of Women's Participation Without Governing Authority," *JETS* 30/1 (March 1987), pp. 11–23.

[68]This view of the gift of prophecy is explained more fully in chapter 53, pp. 1049–61.

[69]One recent evangelical objection to this conclusion on 1 Cor. 14:33–36 is simply to say that these verses were not written by Paul and do not belong in the text of 1 Corinthians, and are therefore not to be considered authoritative Scripture for us today: see Gordon Fee, *The First Epistle to the Corinthians*, pp. 699–708. Fee's basic argument is that it is impossible to reconcile this passage with 1 Cor. 11:5,

**3. 1 Timothy 3:1–7 and Titus 1:5–9.** Both 1 Timothy 3:1–7 and Titus 1:5–9 assume that elders are going to be men. An elder (or bishop/overseer) must be "the husband of one wife" (1 Tim. 3:2; also Titus 1:6), and "must manage his own household well, keeping his children submissive and respectful in every way" (1 Tim. 3:4).

Some may object that these were directions given only for the cultural situation in the ancient world, where women were not well educated, but the same response that was given above concerning 1 Timothy 2 would apply in this case as well.

**4. The Relationship Between the Family and the Church.** The New Testament makes frequent connections between the life of the family and the life of the church. Paul says, "If a man does not know how to manage his own household, how can he care for God's church?" (1 Tim. 3:5). He says to Timothy, "Do not rebuke an older man but exhort him as you would a *father;* treat younger men like *brothers,* older women like *mothers,* younger women like *sisters,* in all purity" (1 Tim. 5:1–2). Several other passages could be cited, but the close relationship between the family and the church should be clear.

Because of this connection, it is inevitable that leadership patterns in the family will reflect leadership patterns in the church, and vice versa. It is very appropriate that, as godly men fulfill their leadership responsibilities in the family, they should also fulfill leadership responsibilities in the church. Conversely, if patterns of female leadership are established in the church, it will inevitably bring pressures toward greater female leadership, and toward abdication of male leadership, within the family.[70]

**5. The Example of the Apostles.** While the apostles are not the same as elders in local churches, it is still important to realize that Jesus established a pattern of male leadership in the church when he appointed twelve men as apostles. It is simply not true that women have equal access to all offices in the church, for Jesus, the head of the church, is a man. And the twelve apostles who will sit on twelve thrones judging the twelve tribes of Israel (see Matt. 19:28), and whose names are written forever on the foundations of the heavenly city (Rev. 21:14), are all men. Therefore, *there will be no eternal modeling of equal roles for men and women at all levels of authority in the church.* Rather, there is a pattern of male leadership in the highest governing roles of the church, a pattern that will be evident to all believers for all eternity.

One objection brought against this argument is the claim that the culture at that time would not have allowed Jesus to choose six men and six women as apostles,

---

where Paul clearly allows women to speak in the church. (He also places much weight on the fact that vv. 34–35 are moved to the end of 1 Cor. 14 in some ancient manuscripts.) But Fee does not give adequate consideration to the view represented here, namely, that Paul is simply prohibiting women from the authoritative task of judging prophecies in the assembled church. Fee's position is surprising in light of the fact that no ancient manuscript of 1 Corinthians omits these verses. (The few manuscripts that place this section at the end of chapter 14 are far less reliable manuscripts that have frequent variations elsewhere in 1 Corinthians as well.)

[70]For further discussion of this point, see Vern Poythress, "The Church as Family: Why Male Leadership in the Family Requires Male Leadership in the Church," in *Recovering Biblical Manhood and Womanhood,* pp. 233–47.

or six husband-wife teams as apostles, and this is the reason he did not do so. But such an objection impugns Jesus' integrity and courage. Jesus was not afraid to break social customs when a moral principle was at stake: he criticized the Pharisees publicly, healed on the Sabbath, cleansed the temple, spoke with a Samaritan woman, ate with tax collectors and sinners, and ate with unwashed hands.[71] If Jesus had wanted to establish a principle of equal access to church leadership by both men and women, he certainly could have done so in the appointment of his apostles, and he would have done so, in spite of cultural opposition, if it had been the pattern he wanted to establish in his church. But he did not.[72]

Another objection to this argument is to say that, if this is true, then only Jews can be leaders in our churches, since all twelve apostles were Jewish as well. But this objection is not persuasive because it fails to recognize that the church was entirely Jewish at its beginning. This was because it was God's plan to bring salvation through the Jews, and this led to twelve Jewish apostles. Yet within the pages of the New Testament, we see that the church soon expanded to include Gentiles (Matt. 28:19; Eph. 2:16) and Gentiles soon became elders and leaders in the New Testament church. A Gentile (Luke) wrote two books of the New Testament (Luke and Acts), and several Gentiles such as Titus and Epaphroditus were Paul's apostolic assistants and co-workers. In fact, God had progressively revealed from the time of Abraham (Gen. 12:3; 17:5) that it was his plan eventually to include countless Gentiles among his people.

So the Jewishness of the early apostles is not like their maleness. The church began as entirely Jewish, but soon became Jewish and Gentile as well. But the church did not begin all male, and only later include females as well. *Christ's followers were male and female from the beginning,* and both men and women were present at the beginning of the church at Pentecost. So this objection is not persuasive either.

**6. The History of Male Teaching and Leadership Through the Whole Bible.** Sometimes opponents of the view presented here have said it is based only on one text, 1 Timothy 2. Several of the foregoing arguments have demonstrated that this is not the case, but there is one further argument that can be made: throughout the history of the entire Bible, from Genesis to Revelation, there is a consistent pattern of male leadership among God's people. Though there are occasional examples of women having leadership in government positions such as queen (Athaliah did reign as sole monarch in 2 Kings 11:1–20, but she is hardly an example to imitate) or judge (note Deborah in Judg. 4–5), and though there were occasionally women such as Deborah and Huldah who were prophetesses (see Judg. 4–5; 2 Kings 22:14–20), we should note that these are rare exceptions in unusual circumstances. They occur in the midst of an overwhelming pattern of male leadership in teaching and governance, and, as such, they hardly serve as patterns for New Testament church office.[73] Moreover, *there is not one*

---

[71]This argument and the following one are taken from James Borland, "Women in the Life and Teachings of Jesus," in *Recovering Biblical Manhood and Womanhood,* pp. 120–22.

[72]Regarding "Junia" or "Junias" in Rom. 16:7, see pp. 908–9.

[73]For further discussion of these narrative examples, see Thomas R. Schreiner, "The Valuable Ministries of Women in the Context of Male Leadership: A Survey of Old and New Testament

*example in the entire Bible of a woman doing the kind of congregational Bible teaching that is expected of pastors/elders in the New Testament church.* In the Old Testament it was the priests who had teaching responsibilities for the people, and the priesthood was exclusively male; moreover, even the women prophets Deborah and Huldah prophesied only privately, not publicly to a congregation of people.[74]

**7. The History of the Church.** As was mentioned above, the overwhelming pattern through the entire history of the church has been that the office of pastor/elder (or its equivalent) has been reserved for men. Although this does not demonstrate conclusively that such a position is correct, it should give us reason to reflect very seriously on the question before we rush ahead and declare that almost the entire church throughout its history has been wrong on this issue.[75]

**8. Objections.** Numerous objections have been brought against the position outlined here, only a few of which can be treated at this point.[76] It is objected that *ministry should be determined by gifts, not by gender.* But in response, it must be said that spiritual gifts have to be used within the guidelines given in Scripture. The Holy Spirit who empowers spiritual gifts is also the Holy Spirit who inspired the Bible, and he does not want us to use his gifts in disobedience to his words.

Another objection is to say that *if God has genuinely called a woman to be a pastor, she should not be prevented from acting as one.* The response to this objection is similar to the one given above: an individual claim to have experienced a call from God must always be tested by subjecting it to the words of God in Scripture. If the Bible teaches that God wills for men alone to bear the primary teaching and governing responsibilities of the pastorate, then by implication the Bible also teaches that God does not call women to be pastors. However, we should add that often what a woman discerns as a divine call to the pastorate may be indeed a call to full-time Christian ministry, but not to be a pastor/elder in a church. In fact, many opportunities for full-time occupational ministry exist within the local church and elsewhere, apart from being a teaching pastor or an elder—for example, church staff positions in counseling, women's ministries, Christian

Examples and Teaching," in *Recovering Biblical Manhood and Womanhood,* pp. 209–24. With reference to Deborah in particular, we must realize that the historical events narrated in the entire book of Judges require great care in interpretation before we can assume that they should be taken as models for us to imitate. And Deborah was different from other (male) prophets in that she did not prophesy in public, only in private (Jud. 4:5; Huldah does the same in 2 Kings 22:14–20); she handed over her leadership role to a man (Judg. 4:6–7); and, although God did bring blessing through her, it is interesting that there is no explicit affirmation of the fact that the LORD raised her up—making her unlike the other major judges such as Othniel (3:9), Ehud (3:15), Gideon (6:14), Jephthah (11:29), and Samson (13:25; 14:6), for whom there is explicit statement of their calling from God.

[74]See the previous footnote. Regarding the fact that women could prophesy in New Testament congregations, see the discussion under section 2 above (pp. 939–40).

[75]See footnote 59 above. A number of recent books have highlighted the neglected contributions that women have made to the church throughout its history: see especially Ruth Tucker and Walter Liefeld, *Daughters of the Church,* a book that is a treasure-house of information and provides extensive additional bibliography. But none of these studies overthrows the clear conclusion that the great majority of the church throughout its history has not accepted women as pastors.

[76]For further discussion, see *Recovering Biblical Manhood and Womanhood,* esp. pp. 60–92. Fuller statements of the objections listed here can be found in the books marked "Favors women as pastors" in the bibliography at the end of this chapter, esp. the volumes by Mickelsen, Spencer, and Bilezikian.

education, and children's ministries, as well as ministries of music and worship, campus student ministries, evangelistic ministries, ministries to the poor, and administrative responsibilities that do not involve functioning in the elder's role of government over the entire church.[77] This list could be expanded, but the point is that we should not make restrictions where Scripture itself does not place restrictions, but should allow and encourage full and free participation by women as well as men in all of these other areas.

Some object that *the New Testament emphasis is on servant leadership,* and therefore that we should not be so concerned about authority, since that is more a pagan than a Christian concern. But this objection makes a false distinction between servanthood and authority. Certainly Jesus himself is the model of a servant leader, but Jesus also has authority—great authority! He is the Lord of our lives and the Lord of the church. By analogy, elders ought to follow Jesus' example of servant leadership (see 1 Peter 5:1–5) but that does not mean that they should neglect to govern with authority when the Bible itself gives them this responsibility (see 1 Tim. 5:17; Heb. 13:17; 1 Peter 5:5).[78]

Sometimes people object that, *just as the church finally realized that slavery was wrong, so the church today should recognize that male leadership is wrong,* and is an outdated cultural tradition that should be discarded. But this objection fails to realize the difference between the temporary cultural institution of slavery, which God certainly did not establish at creation, and the existence of a difference in male-female roles in marriage (and, by implication, in relationships within the church) which God established at creation. The seeds for the destruction of slavery were sown in the New Testament (see Philem. 16; Eph. 6:9; Col. 4:1; 1 Tim. 6:1–2), but no seeds for the destruction of marriage, or the destruction of male-female differences as created, are sown in the Bible. Moreover, the objection can be turned around: it is likely that a closer parallel to the Christian defenders of slavery in the nineteenth century is found in evangelical feminists who today use arguments from the Bible to justify conformity to some extremely strong pressures in contemporary society (in favor of slavery then, and women being pastors now).

It is sometimes objected that *Priscilla and Aquila together spoke to Apollos* and "expounded to him the way of God more accurately" (Acts 18:26). This is true, and it is helpful evidence showing that informal discussion of Scripture by men and women together, in which both men and women play a significant role in helping one another understand Scripture, is approved by the New Testament. Once again, an example such as this cautions us not to prohibit activities which are not prohibited by Scripture, yet it does not overturn the principle that the publicly recognized governing and teaching role within a church is restricted to men. Priscilla was not doing anything contrary to this restriction.

Sometimes it is objected that *it is inconsistent to allow women to vote in churches that have congregational government, but not to serve as elders.* But the authority of the church as a whole is not the same as the authority given to specific individuals within the church. When we say that the congregation as a whole has authority, we do not mean that each man and each woman in the congregation has the authority to speak or act for the congregation. Therefore, gender, as a part of

---

[77]For further discussion, see *Recovering Biblical Manhood and Womanhood,* pp. 54–59.
[78]See also the discussion of the authority of elders on pp. 915–16, above.

individual personhood, is not significantly in view in corporate congregational decisions.

Another way of putting this is to say that the only question we are asking in this section is whether women can be officers within the church, and specifically whether they can be elders within the church. In any congregational system where the elders are elected by the congregation, it is evident to everyone in the church that the elders have a kind of delegated authority which other members of the congregation do not have—even though the other members of the congregation have voted for these people in the first place. It is the same in all systems of government where officials are elected: once the President of the United States or the mayor of a city is elected, that person has a delegated authority over the people who elected him or her and it is an authority that is greater than the authority of any individual person who voted.[79]

At this point it is also appropriate to recognize that God has given much insight and wisdom to women as well as to men, and that any church leaders who neglect to draw on the wisdom that women have are really acting foolishly. Therefore, any group of elders or other male leaders who make decisions affecting the entire church should frequently have procedures within the church whereby the wisdom and insight of other members of the church, especially the wisdom and insight of women as well as men, can be drawn upon as an aid in making decisions.

**9. What About Other Offices Within the Church?** The entire discussion above has focused on the question of whether women should function as pastors or elders within the church. But what about other offices?

The biblical teaching regarding the office of *deacon* is much less extensive than that regarding the office of elder,[80] and what is involved in the office of deacon varies considerably from church to church. If deacons are actually functioning as elders and have the highest governing authority within a local church, then the arguments given above against women being elders would apply directly to this situation, and it would follow that Scripture does not permit women to be deacons in this sense. On the other hand, if deacons simply have delegated administrative responsibility for certain aspects of the ministry of the church, then there seems to be no good reason to prevent women from functioning as deacons. Regarding the question of women as deacons in 1 Timothy 3:8–13, it does not seem to the present author that this passage allows women to be deacons *in the way deacons are understood in that situation*, but there is a significant difference of viewpoint among evangelicals over the understanding of this passage,[81] and it is much less clear to us exactly what deacons did at that time than it is clear what elders did.[82]

With regard to other offices, such as treasurer, for example, or other staff positions such as youth minister or counseling director or children's minister, and so forth, the only question to be asked is whether these offices include the ruling

---

[79]See above, pp. 921–22, for arguments in favor of participation by the entire congregation in some decision-making in the church, and especially in the selection of officers in the church.

[80]See above, pp. 918–20, on the office of deacon.

[81]See footnote 25 above for information. .

[82]Note that Acts 6:3 also requires that only men (Gk. *anēr*) be selected as the first deacons (if we understand that passage to be speaking of the office of deacon).

and teaching functions reserved for elders in the New Testament. If not, then *all of these offices would be open to women as well as to men,* for we must be careful not to prohibit what the New Testament does not prohibit.

## QUESTIONS FOR PERSONAL APPLICATION

1. No matter what kind of church government structure you currently find yourself in, are there ways in which you could be more encouraging and supportive to the current leaders in your church?

2. If you are currently an officer in your church, or if you someday would like to be one, is your pattern of life such that you would like to see it imitated by others in the church? If you have had a part in the process of selecting church leaders, have you tended to emphasize the character traits and spiritual qualifications talked about in Scripture, or have you emphasized other qualifications that the world would look for in selecting its leaders?

3. Do you think that the current governing structure of your church works quite well? How could it be improved, without changing the basic philosophy of church government to which it is committed? Whether or not your church has officers who are called "elders," who are the people who carry out the functions of elders in your church? Do you know if your own pastor would like to see some modifications in the government of your church, to enable him to carry out his task more effectively?

4. Before reading this chapter, what was your view on the question of women serving as teaching pastors or elders in a church? How has this chapter changed your view, if at all? Why do you think people's emotions are often very strong concerning this issue? Can you explain how you personally feel (emotionally) about the teaching presented in this chapter? Does it seem right to you, or not?

## SPECIAL TERMS

| | |
|---|---|
| apostle | local elders |
| bishop | officer |
| classis | overseer |
| congregational government | pastor |
| consistory | presbyterian government |
| deacon | presbytery |
| diocese | priest |
| elder | rector |
| episcopalian government | session |
| general assembly | synod |
| hierarchical government | vicar |

## BIBLIOGRAPHY

(For an explanation of this bibliography see the note on the bibliography to chapter 1, p. 38. Complete bibliographical data may be found on pp. 1223–29.)

## Sections in Evangelical Systematic Theologies

1. Anglican (Episcopalian)
    - 1882–92    Litton, 384–418
    - 1930       Thomas, 313–18, 429–33, 452–58
2. Arminian (Wesleyan or Methodist)
    - 1875–76    Pope, 3:335–59
    - 1892–94    Miley, 2:415–19
    - 1940       Wiley, 3:117–37
    - 1983       Carter, 2:619–20
3. Baptist
    - 1767       Gill, 2:574–607
    - 1907       Strong, 894–929
    - 1983–85    Erickson, 1069–88
4. Dispensational
    - 1947       Chafer, 4:150–53
    - 1949       Thiessen, 314–318
    - 1986       Ryrie, 403–20
5. Lutheran
    - 1917–24    Pieper, 3:427–38, 439–72
    - 1934       Mueller, 563–84
6. Reformed (or Presbyterian)
    - 1559       Calvin, 2:1053–1228 (4.3–11)
    - 1861       Heppe, 672–84
    - 1937–66    Murray, CW, 1:260–68; CW, 2:336–65
    - 1938       Berkhof, 579–92
    - 1962       Buswell, 1:424–28
7. Renewal (or charismatic/Pentecostal)
    - 1988–92    Williams, 3:177–220

## Sections in Representative Roman Catholic Systematic Theologies

1. Roman Catholic: Traditional
    - 1955       Ott, 276–90, 450–60
2. Roman Catholic: Post-Vatican II
    - 1980       McBrien (no explicit treatment)

## Other Works

Babbage, S. B. "Church Officers." In EDT, pp. 243–45. (Contains a list of various titles for church officers used in different denominations today, with definitions.)

Bannerman, James. The Church of Christ. 2 vols. London: Banner of Truth, 1960. (First published in 1869.)

Baxter, Richard. *The Reformed Pastor.* Carlisle, Pa.: Banner of Truth, 1979. [Reprint.]

Bilezikian, Gilbert. *Beyond Sex Roles.* 2d ed. Grand Rapids: Baker, 1985. (Favors women as pastors.)

Burge, G. M. "Deacon, Deaconness." In *EDT,* pp. 295–96.

Carson, D. A. "Church, Authority in." In *EDT,* pp. 228–31.

Clark, Stephen B. *Man and Women in Christ.* Ann Arbor, Mich.: Servant, 1980. (Opposes women as pastors.)

Clowney, Edmund. *Called to the Ministry.* Chicago: InterVarsity Press, 1964.

———. "Presbyterianism." In *EDT,* pp. 530–31.

Evans, Mary J. *Women in the Bible.* Exeter: Paternoster, and Downers Grove: InterVarsity Press, 1983. (Favors women as pastors.)

Foh, Susan. *Women and the Word of God: A Response to Biblical Feminism.* Philadelphia: Presbyterian and Reformed, 1980. (Opposes women as pastors.)

Fung, Ronald Y. K. "Ministry in the New Testament." In *The Church in the Bible and the World.* Ed. by D. A. Carson. Exeter: Paternoster, and Grand Rapids: Baker, 1987.

Gundry, Patricia. *Neither Slave nor Free: Helping Women Answer the Call to Church Leadership.* San Francisco: Harper and Row, 1987. (Favors women as pastors.)

———. *Women Be Free! The Clear Message of Scripture.* Grand Rapids: Zondervan, 1988. (Favors women as pastors.)

Hodge, Charles. *Discussions in Church Polity.* New York: Charles Scribner's Sons, 1878.

Hort, F. J. A. *The Christian Ecclesia.* London: Macmillan, 1898.

House, H. Wayne. *The Role of Women in Ministry Today.* Nashville: Thomas Nelson, 1990. (Opposes women as pastors.)

Hurley, James B. *Man and Woman in Biblical Perspective.* Leicester: Inter-Varsity Press, and Grand Rapids: Zondervan, 1981. (Opposes women as pastors.)

Kirby, G. W. "Congregationalism." In *EDT,* pp. 159–61.

Knight, George W., III. *The Role Relationship of Men and Women.* Revised ed. Chicago: Moody, 1985. (Opposes women as pastors.)

Kroeger, Richard and Catherine. *I Suffer Not a Woman.* Grand Rapids: Baker, 1992. (Favors women as pastors.)

Macleod, D. "Church Government." In *EDT,* pp. 143–46.

Marshall, I. Howard. "Apostle." In *EDT,* p. 40.

Mickelsen, Alvera, ed. *Women, Authority, and the Bible.* Downers Grove, Ill.: InterVarsity Press, 1986. (A collection of essays by several authors, most of whom favor women as pastors.)

Morris, L. "Church Government." In *EDT,* pp. 238–41.

———. *Ministers of God.* London: Inter-Varsity Press, 1964.

Piper, John, and Wayne Grudem, eds. *Recovering Biblical Manhood and Womanhood: A Response to Evangelical Feminism.* Wheaton, Ill.: Crossway, 1991. (A collection of twenty-eight essays by twenty-two authors; opposes women as pastors.)

Richards, Lawrence O. *A Theology of Church Leadership.* Grand Rapids: Zondervan, 1980.

Saucy, Robert L. "Authority in the Church." In *Walvoord: A Tribute*. Ed. by
    Donald K. Campbell. Chicago: Moody, 1982. pp. 219–37. (An extensive
    argument in favor of congregational government.)
_____. *The Church in God's Program*. Chicago: Moody, 1972.
Spencer, Aida Besancon. *Beyond the Curse: Women Called to Ministry*. Nashville:
    Thomas Nelson, 1985. (Favors women as pastors.)
Stott, John R. W. *The Preacher's Portrait*. Grand Rapids: Eerdmans, 1961.
Strauch, Alexander. *Biblical Eldership: An Urgent Call to Restore Biblical Church
    Leadership*. Littleton, Col.: Lewis and Roth, 1986.
Tiller, J. "Ministry." In *EDT*, pp. 430–33.
Toon, Peter. "Bishop." In *EDT*, pp. 157–58.
Tucker, Ruth A., and Walter L. Liefeld. *Daughters of the Church: Women and
    Ministry from New Testament Times to the Present*. Grand Rapids: Zondervan,
    1987. (Favors women as pastors.)
Wallace, R. S. "Elder." In *EDT*, pp. 347–48.

## SCRIPTURE MEMORY PASSAGE

**1 Peter 5:1–4:** *So I exhort the elders among you, as a fellow elder and a witness of the
sufferings of Christ as well as a partaker in the glory that is to be revealed. Tend the flock
of God that is your charge, not by constraint but willingly, not for shameful gain but
eagerly, not as domineering over those in your charge but being examples to the flock.
And when the chief Shepherd is manifested you will obtain the unfading crown of glory.*

## HYMN

### "Glorious Things of Thee Are Spoken"

There are not many hymns—if any—written about church government! I have put here a hymn
which thanks God for the blessings of being a member of God's people in general, and therefore a
citizen of the heavenly Mount Zion, the heavenly city where God's people dwell. But in the hymn the
author also uses Old Testament imagery from the journey of God's people through the wilderness ("see
the cloud and fire appear," v. 3), and the entire hymn can also be seen as one of thanks to God for the
blessing of dwelling (spiritually) within the walls of the church today.

The author, John Newton, is also the author of the well-known hymn "Amazing Grace."

Glorious things of thee are spoken, Zion, city of our God;
    He whose Word cannot be broken formed thee for his own abode:
On the Rock of Ages founded, what can shake thy sure repose?
    With salvation's walls surrounded, thou may'st smile at all thy foes.

See, the streams of living waters, springing from eternal love,
    Well supply thy sons and daughters, and all fear of want remove:
Who can faint, while such a river ever flows their thirst t'assuage?
    Grace which, like the Lord, the giver, never fails from age to age.

Round each habitation hov'ring, see the cloud and fire appear
    For a glory and cov'ring, showing that the Lord is near:
Thus deriving from their banner light by night and shade by day,

Safe they feed upon the manna which he gives them when they
pray.

Savior, if of Zion's city I, through grace, a member am,
Let the world deride or pity, I will glory in thy name:
Fading is the worlding's pleasure, all his boasted pomp and show;
Solid joys and lasting treasure none but Zion's children know.

AUTHOR: JOHN NEWTON, 1779

# Chapter 48

# Means of Grace Within the Church

*What are the different activities within the life of the church that God uses to bring blessing to us? What do we miss if we neglect involvement in a local church?*

## EXPLANATION AND SCRIPTURAL BASIS

### A. How Many Means of Grace Are Available to Us?

All of the blessings we experience in this life are ultimately undeserved—they are all of *grace*. In fact, for Peter, the entire Christian life is lived by grace (1 Peter 5:12).

But are there any special *means* that God uses to give additional grace to us? Specifically, *within the fellowship of the church* are there certain means—that is, certain activities, ceremonies, or functions—that God uses to give more grace to us? Another way of formulating that question is to ask whether there are certain *means* through which the Holy Spirit works to convey blessings into the life of the believer. Of course, personal prayer, worship, and Bible study, and personal faith, are all means through which God works to bring grace to us as individual Christians. But in this chapter we are dealing with the doctrine of the church, and we are asking specifically *within the fellowship of the church* what the means of grace are that God uses to bring blessing to us.

We may define the means of grace as follows: *The means of grace are any activities within the fellowship of the church that God uses to give more grace to Christians.*

In the history of the discussion of "means of grace within the church," some theologians have restricted them to three: the preaching of the Word, and the two sacraments (baptism and the Lord's Supper).[1]

---

[1]This is the position of Louis Berkhof, *Systematic Theology*, pp. 604–6. He calls these three means "objective channels which Christ has instituted in the church" (pp. 604–5), but the significant criterion in Berkhof's thinking appears to be the fact that these three are the special functions administered by the ordained clergy: Berkhof calls these "the *official* means of the church of Jesus Christ" (p. 605), and later says, "As the *official* means of grace placed at the disposal of the Church, both the Word and the sacraments *can only be administered by the lawful and properly qualified officers of the Church*" (p. 610). In this way, he clearly restricts the "means of grace" to those means administered by the ordained clergy.

Although those who follow Berkhof on this point could argue that this procedure is wise and serves the interest of maintaining good order in the church, we may ask whether in fact this restriction carries overtones of "sacerdotalism," the view of the Roman Catholic Church (and, to a lesser degree, the Anglican Church) that there is a special "priesthood" of ordained people within the church who have a special authority or ability to extend God's grace to people in the church.

(See chapter 49, p. 966, for a discussion of the use of the two terms *sacraments* and *ordinances* to refer to baptism and the Lord's Supper.)

But is it wise to make such a short list of "means of grace"? If we wish to list and discuss all the means of receiving the Holy Spirit's blessing that come to believers specifically through the fellowship of the church, then it does not seem wise to limit the "means of grace" to three activities whose administration is restricted to the ordained clergy or officers of the church. There is wisdom, for example, in Charles Hodge's view that prayer is a fourth means of grace.[2]

But should we limit our discussion of the means of grace to these four activities only? It would seem more helpful to list all of the *many varied activities* within the church that God has given as special ways of receiving his "grace" day by day and week by week. Such a list may become quite long, and, depending on how it is organized, may include various numbers of elements. The following list may not be exhaustive, but it does include most of the means of grace that believers have access to within the fellowship of the church:

1. Teaching of the Word
2. Baptism
3. The Lord's Supper
4. Prayer for one another
5. Worship
6. Church discipline
7. Giving
8. Spiritual gifts
9. Fellowship
10. Evangelism
11. Personal ministry to individuals

All these are available to believers *within* the church. The Holy Spirit works through all of them to bring various kinds of blessing to individuals. Therefore, departing from the much shorter lists usually given in systematic theologies, I have decided to call all of these "means of grace" within the church.

The Roman Catholic Church has traditionally believed that God's "grace" comes to people only through the official ministry of the church, particularly through the priests of the church. Therefore, when it specifies the means of grace (what it calls the "sacraments") that are available to people within the church, it has in view activities that are supervised and/or performed by only the priests of the church. The seven "sacraments" in Roman Catholic teaching are the following:

1. Baptism
2. Confirmation
3. Eucharist (the Lord's Supper as experienced in the mass)
4. Penance
5. Extreme unction (popularly known as the "last rites," the anointing with oil that is administered to a dying person)
6. Holy orders (ordination to the priesthood or diaconate)
7. Matrimony

There is not only a difference in the lists given by Catholics and Protestants; there is also a difference in fundamental meaning. Catholics view these as "means of

<hr>

[2]Hodge, *Systematic Theology*, 3:692–709.

salvation" that make people more fit to receive justification from God.[3] But on a Protestant view, the means of grace are simply means of additional blessing within the Christian life, and do not add to our fitness to receive justification from God.[4] Catholics teach that the means of grace impart grace whether or not there is subjective faith on the part of the minister or the recipient,[5] while Protestants hold that God only imparts grace when there is faith on the part of the persons administering or receiving these means. And while the Roman Catholic Church firmly restricts the administration of the sacraments to the clergy, our list of means of grace includes many activities that are carried out by all believers.

## B. Discussion of Specific Means

**1. Teaching of the Word.** Even before people become Christians, the Word of God as preached and taught brings God's grace to them in that it is the instrument God uses to impart spiritual life to them and bring them to salvation. Paul says that the gospel is the "power of God for salvation" (Rom. 1:16) and that the preaching of Christ is "the power of God and the wisdom of God" (1 Cor. 1:24). God caused us to be born again or "brought . . . forth by the word of truth" (James 1:18) and Peter says, "You have been born anew, not of perishable seed but of imperishable, through the living and abiding word of God" (1 Peter 1:23). It is the written Word of God, the Bible, that is "able to instruct you for salvation through faith in Christ Jesus" (2 Tim. 3:15).[6]

Moreover, once we have become Christians, Paul reminds us that it is the Word of God that is "able to build you up" (Acts 20:32). It is necessary for spiritual nourishment and for maintaining spiritual life, because we do not live on bread alone but on "every word that proceeds from the mouth of God" (Matt. 4:4). Moses speaks of the absolute necessity of the written Word of God when he tells the people, "It is no trifle for you, but it is your life, and thereby you shall live long in the land which you are going over the Jordan to possess" (Deut. 32:47).

It is the Word of God that convicts us of sin and turns us to righteousness, for it is profitable "for teaching, for reproof, for correction, and for training in righteousness" (2 Tim. 3:16). It gives direction and guidance as a "lamp" to our feet and a "light" to our path (Ps. 119:105). In the midst of an ungodly culture Scripture gives wisdom and guidance like "a lamp shining in a dark place" (2 Peter 1:19). Moreover, it is active in giving wisdom to all, even "making wise the simple" (Ps. 19:7). It gives hope to those who are in despair, because Paul says that it was written "that by steadfastness and by the encouragement of the scriptures we might have hope" (Rom. 15:4).

The Word of God is not weak or powerless in accomplishing these goals, for it speaks to us with the power of God and accomplishes God's purposes. The Lord says,

> For as the rain and the snow come down from heaven,
> and return not thither but water the earth,

---

[3]See chapter 36, pp. 727–29, on the Roman Catholic view of justification.
[4]However, the Anglican Church teaches that baptism is "generally necessary" for salvation.
[5]See chapter 49, p. 972, on the Roman Catholic view that the sacraments work *ex opere operato*.
[6]See chapter 33 for a fuller discussion of the gospel call.

making it bring forth and sprout,
    giving seed to the sower and bread to the eater,
so shall my word be that goes forth from my mouth;
    it shall not return to me empty,
but it shall accomplish that which I purpose,
    and prosper in the thing for which I sent it. (Isa. 55:10–11)

God's Word is not weak but has his divine power accompanying it: "Is not my word *like fire,* says the LORD, and *like a hammer* which breaks the rock in pieces?" (Jer. 23:29). It is so sharp and powerful that it is the "*sword* of the Spirit" (Eph. 6:17), and it is so effective in speaking to people's needs that the author of Hebrews says, "the word of God is living and active, sharper than any *two-edged sword,* piercing to the division of soul and spirit, of joints and marrow, and discerning the thoughts and intentions of the heart" (Heb. 4:12).

So closely are the growth and strength of the church linked to the reign of the Word of God in people's lives that more than once the book of Acts can describe the growth of the church as the growth of the Word of God: "*And the word of God increased;* and the number of the disciples multiplied greatly in Jerusalem" (Acts 6:7); "But *the word of God grew and multiplied*" (Acts 12:24); "And *the word of the Lord spread* throughout all the region" (Acts 13:49).

So important is the Bible as the primary means of grace that God gives to his people that Charles Hodge reminds us that throughout history true Christianity has flourished "just in proportion to the degree in which the Bible is known, and its truths are diffused among the people." Moreover, he notes that there are no evidences of salvation or sanctification to be found where the Word of God is not known. "The nations where the Bible is unknown sit in darkness."[7]

It is appropriate that we list the teaching of the Word as the first and most important means of grace within the church. But we should add that such teaching includes not only officially recognized teaching by ordained clergy in the church, but also all the teaching that occurs in Bible studies, Sunday School classes, the reading of Christian books on Scripture, and even in personal Bible study.

**2. Baptism.** Since Jesus commanded his church to baptize (Matt. 28:19), we would expect that there would be a measure of blessing connected with baptism, because all obedience to God by Christians brings God's favor with it. This obedience is specifically a public act of confessing Jesus as Savior, an act which in itself brings joy and blessing to a believer. Moreover, it is a sign of the believer's death and resurrection with Christ (see Rom. 6:2–5; Col. 2:12), and it seems fitting that the Holy Spirit would work through such a sign to increase our faith, to increase our experiential realization of death to the power and love of sin in our lives, and to increase our experience of the power of new resurrection life in Christ that we have as believers. Since baptism is a physical symbol of the death and resurrection of Christ and our participation in them, it should also give additional assurance of union with Christ to all believers who are present. Finally, since water baptism is an outward symbol of inward spiritual baptism by the Holy Spirit, we

---

[7]Hodge, *Systematic Theology,* 3:468–69.

may expect that the Holy Spirit will ordinarily work alongside the baptism, giving to believers an increasing realization of the benefits of the spiritual baptism to which it points.

When baptism very closely accompanies someone's initial profession of faith and is in fact the outward form that profession of faith takes, there is certainly a connection between baptism and receiving the gift of the Holy Spirit, for Peter says to his hearers at Pentecost, "Repent, and be baptized every one of you in the name of Jesus Christ for the forgiveness of your sins; and you shall receive the gift of the Holy Spirit" (Acts 2:38). Moreover, Paul says, "You were buried with him in baptism, in which you were also raised with him through faith in the working of God, who raised him from the dead" (Col. 2:12). The statement that it is *through faith* in the working of God" that this happens reminds us that there is no magical property in the act of baptism itself, which causes a spiritual result to come about, yet the verse also indicates that when faith accompanies baptism there is genuine spiritual work in the life of the person being baptized. As we would expect, sometimes great spiritual joy follows upon baptism—a great joy in the Lord and in the salvation that baptism so vividly pictures (see Acts 8:39; 16:34).

Although we must avoid the Roman Catholic teaching that grace is imparted even *apart from* the faith of the person being baptized, we must not react so strongly to this error that we say that there is no spiritual benefit at all that comes from baptism, that the Holy Spirit *does not* work through it and that it is *merely symbolic*. It is better to say that where there is genuine faith on the part of the person being baptized, and where the faith of the church that watches the baptism is stirred up and encouraged by this ceremony, then the Holy Spirit certainly does work through baptism, and it becomes a "means of grace" through which the Holy Spirit brings blessing to the person being baptized and to the church as well. (Baptism will be more fully discussed in the next chapter.)

**3. The Lord's Supper.** In addition to baptism, the other ordinance or ceremony that Jesus commanded the church to carry out is participation in the Lord's Supper. Although this subject will be discussed more thoroughly in chapter 50, it is appropriate to note here that participation in the Lord's Supper is also very clearly a means of grace which the Holy Spirit uses to bring blessing to the church. The Lord's Supper is not simply an ordinary meal among human beings—it is a fellowship with Christ, in his presence and at his table.

Once again, we must avoid the idea that any automatic or magical benefit comes from sharing in the Lord's Supper, whether a person participates in faith or not.[8] But when a person participates in faith, renewing and strengthening his or her own trust in Christ for salvation, and believing that the Holy Spirit will bring spiritual blessing through such participation, then certainly additional blessing may be expected. We must be careful here, as with baptism, to avoid the mistake of overreacting to Roman Catholic teaching and maintaining that the Lord's Supper is *merely symbolic* and not a means of grace. Paul says, "The cup of blessing which we bless, is it not a *participation* (Gk. *koinōnia,* "sharing," "fellowship") in

---

[8]This view that there is blessing that comes automatically from participation in the Lord's Supper is the Roman Catholic doctrine of *ex opere operato* ("by the work performed"), which is discussed in chapter 50, pp. 991–94; see also p. 972.

the blood of Christ? The bread which we break, is it not a *participation* [*koinōnia*] in the body of Christ?" (1 Cor. 10:16). Because there is such a sharing in the body and blood of Christ (apparently meaning a sharing in the benefits of Christ's body and blood given for us), the unity of believers is beautifully exhibited at the time of the Lord's Supper: "Because there is one bread, we who are many are one body, for we all partake of the one bread" (1 Cor. 10:17). And since we are participants at "the table of the Lord" (1 Cor. 10:21), Paul warns the Corinthians that they cannot participate in the Lord's table and also participate in idol worship: "You cannot partake in the table of the Lord and the table of demons" (1 Cor. 10:21). There is a spiritual union among believers and with the Lord that is strengthened and solidified at the Lord's Supper, and it is not to be taken lightly.

This is why the Corinthians were experiencing judgment for their abuse of the Lord's Supper (1 Cor. 11:29–30: "For any one who eats and drinks without discerning the body eats and drinks judgment upon himself. That is why many of you are weak and ill, and some have died"). But if Paul says there will be judgment for *wrong* participation in the Lord's Supper, then certainly we should expect *blessing* for right participation in the Lord's Supper. When we obey Jesus' command, "Take, eat" (Matt. 26:26), and go through the physical activity of eating and drinking at the Lord's table, our physical action *pictures* a corresponding spiritual nourishment, a nourishment of our souls that will occur when we participate in obedience and faith. Jesus says, "For my flesh is food indeed, and my blood is drink indeed. He who eats my flesh and drinks my blood abides in me, and I in him" (John 6:55–56; cf. vv. 52–54, 57–58; also vv. 27, 33–35, 48–51).

As with baptism, therefore, we should expect that the Lord would give spiritual blessing as we participate in the Lord's Supper in faith and in obedience to the directions laid down in Scripture, and in this way it is a "means of grace" which the Holy Spirit uses to convey blessing to us.

**4. Prayer.** We have already studied prayer in chapter 18, so we need only note here that corporate prayer within the church as it assembles, and prayer by church members for one another, are powerful means which the Holy Spirit uses daily to bring blessing to Christians within the church. Certainly we are to *pray together* as well as individually, following the example of the early church. When they heard the threats of the Jewish leaders, "they lifted their voices *together* to God" in prayer (Acts 4:24–30), "And when they had prayed, the place in which they were gathered together was shaken; and they were all filled with the Holy Spirit and spoke the word of God with boldness" (Acts 4:31; cf. 2:42). When Peter was put in prison, "earnest prayer for him was made to God by the church" (Acts 12:5).

If prayer from the church is not simply the mouthing of words without heartfelt intention, but is the genuine expression of our hearts and the reflection of sincere faith, then we should expect that the Holy Spirit will bring a great blessing through it. Certainly when prayer is done "in the Spirit" (Eph. 6:18; cf. Jude 20: "pray in the Holy Spirit"), it involves fellowship with the Holy Spirit and therefore a ministry of the Holy Spirit to the people praying. And the author of Hebrews reminds us that as we "draw near" to God in prayer before the throne of grace, we do so "that we may receive mercy and find grace to help in time of need" (Heb. 4:16).

The more the genuine fellowship of a church increases, the more there ought to be continual prayer for one another within the church, and the more genuine spiritual blessing from the Holy Spirit may be expected to flow through the church.

**5. Worship.** Genuine worship is worship "in spirit" (John 4:23–24; Phil. 3:3), which probably means worship that is in the spiritual realm of activity (not merely the outward physical action of attendance at a worship service or singing of songs).[9] When we enter that spiritual realm of activity and minister to the Lord in worship, God also ministers to us. So, for example, in the church at Antioch, it was *"While they were worshiping the Lord* and fasting" that "the Holy Spirit said, 'Set apart for me Barnabas and Saul for the work to which I have called them'" (Acts 13:2). This parallels the experience of the people of Israel in the Old Testament who knew the presence of God when they engaged in genuine worship:

> *When the song was raised,* with trumpets and cymbals and other musical instruments, *in praise to the Lord,* "For he is good, for his steadfast love endures forever," the house, the house of the Lord was filled with a cloud, so that the priests could not stand to minister because of the cloud; for *the glory of the Lord filled the house of God.* (2 Chron. 5:13–14).

When God's people worshiped, he came in a very visible way to dwell in their midst. Similarly in the New Testament, James promises, "Draw near to God and *he will draw near to you"* (James 4:8).

In fact, as God's people worshiped, he delivered them from their enemies (2 Chron. 20:18–23), or at other times gave them true spiritual insight into the nature of events around them (Ps. 73:17: "Until I went into the sanctuary of God; then I perceived their end").

If worship is genuinely an experience of drawing near to God, coming into his presence, and giving him the praise he deserves, then we certainly ought to count it one of the primary "means of grace" available to the church. Through genuine congregational worship God will very often bring great blessing, both individually and corporately, to his people.

**6. Church Discipline.** Because church discipline is a means by which the purity of the church is advanced and holiness of life is encouraged, we certainly should count it as a "means of grace" as well. However, blessing is not automatically given: when the church disciplines, no spiritual good comes to the wrongdoer unless the Holy Spirit convicts him or her of sin and brings about a "godly grief" that "produces a repentance that leads to salvation and brings no regret" (2 Cor. 7:10), and no spiritual good comes to the church unless the Holy Spirit is active in the other members' lives when they become aware of the process. This is why the church is to carry out discipline with the knowledge that it is done in the

---

[9]See the discussion of worship "in spirit" in chapter 51, p. 1010. (The whole of chapter 51 discusses worship in general.)

presence of the Lord (1 Cor. 5:4; cf. 4:19– 20), and with the assurance that it has heavenly sanction connected with it (Matt. 16:19; 18:18–20).[10]

It would be very healthy for the church to begin to think of church discipline not as an onerous burden placed upon it by the Lord, but as a genuine "means of grace" by which great blessing can come to the church—in reconciling believers to one another and to God, in restoring the erring brother or sister to walk in obedience, in warning all to "stand in fear" (1 Tim. 5:20), in increasing moral purity in the church, and in protecting and advancing Christ's honor. Though sorrow and pain are often connected with church discipline, when it is rightly done, with faith that the Lord is working through it, the sorrow will "bring no regret" (2 Cor. 7:10). When carried out in this way, church discipline should certainly be seen as a means of grace by which the Holy Spirit will bring blessing to his church.[11]

**7. Giving.** Giving is ordinarily done through the church as it receives and distributes gifts to the various ministries and needs cared for by the church. Once again, there is no automatic or mechanical bestowing of benefits on those who give. Simon the sorcerer was strongly rebuked for thinking that he "could obtain the gift of God with money" (Acts 8:20). But if giving is done in faith, out of commitment to Christ and love for his people, then certainly there will be great blessing in it. It is most pleasing to God when gifts of money are accompanied by an intensification of the giver's own personal commitment to God, as was the case among the Macedonians who "first . . . *gave themselves* to the Lord and to us by the will of God" (2 Cor. 8:5), and then gave to help the poor Christians in Jerusalem. When giving is carried out joyfully, "not reluctantly or under compulsion," there is the great reward of God's favor with it, "for God loves a cheerful giver" (2 Cor. 9:7).

Paul views the giving of money to the Lord's work as spiritual sowing that will lead to a harvest: "he who sows sparingly will also reap sparingly, and he who sows bountifully will also reap bountifully" (2 Cor. 9:6). And Paul expects that as the Corinthians give rightly God will bless them: "And God is able to make *all grace abound to you,* that always having all sufficiency in everything, you may have an abundance for every good deed" (2 Cor. 9:8 NASB). He tells them, "*You will be enriched in every way for great generosity,* which through us will produce thanksgiving to God" (2 Cor. 9:11). Therefore giving blesses the *recipient* in that his or her needs are met and faith and thanksgiving for God's provision are increased; it blesses the *giver* because "God loves a cheerful giver" and will grant an abundant spiritual harvest, and brings blessing to *all who know about it* since it produces a harvest of "many thanksgivings to God" (2 Cor. 9:12). Rather than seeing giving as an unpleasant obligation, we would do well to view it as a rich means of grace within the church, and to expect that through it the Holy Spirit will bring blessing.

**8. Spiritual Gifts.** Peter views spiritual gifts as channels through which God's grace comes to the church because he says, "As each has received a gift, employ it

[10]See discussion of the "power of the keys" in chapter 46, pp. 889–91.
[11]See chapter 46, pp. 894–900, for a more full discussion of church discipline.

for one another, *as good stewards of God's varied grace*" (1 Peter 4:10). When gifts are used for one another in the church, God's grace is thereby dispensed to those for whom God intended it. Great blessing will come to the church through proper use of spiritual gifts, as the church follows Paul's command to use the gifts to "strive to excel in building up the church" (1 Cor. 14:12; cf. Eph. 4:11–16).

If we listed all the spiritual gifts as separate means of grace, our list of the means of grace would be much longer than eleven items. But even if we contain them all in this one category, we should recognize that the different spiritual gifts in the church are all means by which the Holy Spirit brings blessing through individual Christians. This should remind us of the abundant favor that God has given us as undeserving sinners, and should also make us realize that many different Christians, with diverse gifts, can be the channels through which grace comes to us. In fact, in Peter's exhortation to use spiritual gifts as stewards of "God's *varied* grace" (1 Peter 4:10), the word translated "varied" (Gk. *poikilos*) means "having many facets or aspects; richly varied; having great diversity." Moreover, we should remember that these gifts are distributed not only to clergy or a limited number of Christians, but to all believers who have the Holy Spirit within them (1 Cor. 12:7, 11; 1 Peter 4:10).[12]

**9. Fellowship.** We should not neglect ordinary Christian fellowship as a valuable means of grace within the church. The early church "devoted themselves to the apostles' teaching *and fellowship*, to the breaking of bread and the prayers" (Acts 2:42). And the author of Hebrews reminds believers, "Let us consider how to stir up one another to love and good works, *not neglecting to meet together*, as is the habit of some, but encouraging one another, and all the more as you see the Day drawing near" (Heb. 10:24–25). In the fellowship of believers, ordinary friendship and affection for one another will grow, and Jesus' injunction that we "love one another" (John 15:12) will be fulfilled. Moreover, as believers care for one another, they will "Bear one another's burdens, and so fulfil the law of Christ" (Gal. 6:2).

An emphasis on the fellowship of believers with one another as a means of grace would also help to overcome an excessive focus on the ordained clergy as the primary dispensers of grace within the church, and particularly when the church as a whole is assembled. It would also be healthy for Christians to recognize that a measure of God's grace is experienced when Christians talk together and eat together, when they have times of work and play together, enjoying one another's fellowship. "And day by day, attending the temple together and breaking bread in their homes, they partook of food with glad and generous hearts, praising God and having favor with all the people" (Acts 2:46–47).

**10. Evangelism.** In Acts, there is a frequent connection between proclaiming the gospel (even in the face of opposition) and being filled with the Holy Spirit (see Acts 2:4 with vv. 14–36; 4:8, 31; 9:17 with v. 20; 13:9, 52). Evangelism is a means of grace, then, not only in the sense that it ministers saving grace to the unsaved, but also because those who evangelize experience more of the Holy Spirit's presence and blessing in their own lives. Sometimes evangelism is carried

---

[12]See chapters 52 and 53 for a discussion of spiritual gifts.

out by individuals, but at other times it is a corporate activity of the church (as in evangelistic campaigns). And even individual evangelism often involves other church members who will welcome an unbelieving visitor and give attention to his or her needs. So evangelism is rightly considered a means of grace in the church.

**11. Personal Ministry to Individuals.** Along with the previous ten "means of grace" within the church, it is appropriate to list one more specific means that the Holy Spirit very frequently uses to bring blessing to individual Christians. This means of grace operates when one or more Christians within the church take time to minister, in various ways, to very specific needs of another individual in the church.

Sometimes this ministry takes the form of *words of encouragement or exhortation or wise counsel.* We are to "teach and admonish one another in all wisdom" (Col. 3:16), and to speak words that "impart grace to those who hear" (Eph. 4:29). We are to attempt to bring back "a sinner from the error of his way" (James 5:20) and to "consider how to stir up one another to love and good works" and to be "encouraging one another" (Heb. 10:24–25). At other times such ministry involves *giving to assist the material needs of a brother or sister:* James rebukes those who merely say, "Go in peace, be warmed and filled," without "giving them the things needed for the body" (James 2:16). John warns us, "If any one has the world's goods and sees his brother in need, yet closes his heart against him, how does God's love abide in him?" (1 John 3:17). Therefore the early church gave readily to the needs of poor Christians, so that "There was not a needy person among them" (Acts 4:34). And Paul said that the leaders of the church in Jerusalem "would have us remember the poor, which very thing I was eager to do" (Gal. 2:10).

Another form this interpersonal ministry may take is the *anointing with oil* in conjunction with prayer for a sick person. Jesus' disciples "anointed with oil many that were sick and healed them" (Mark 6:13). Similarly, James says that a sick person should "call for the elders of the church, and let them pray over him, anointing him with oil in the name of the Lord" (James 5:14). In these cases the oil seems to have been a physical symbol of the healing power of the Holy Spirit coming to the sick person.

Finally, one more means of exercising personal ministry to individuals in the New Testament is the use of physical touch, particularly the *laying on of hands* in connection with prayer for someone in need. A survey of the New Testament may bring surprise to many modern Christians (as it did to the present author) when they see how frequently the laying on of hands and other kinds of physical touch are seen to function as a "means of grace" in the ministry of Jesus and the early church.

It seems that the laying on of hands was by far the most common method that Jesus used to pray for people. When crowds came bringing people "with various diseases" to him, "*he laid his hands on every one of them* and healed them" (Luke 4:40). Other passages specifically describe Jesus' placing his hands on people to heal them (Matt. 8:3; Mark 1:41; 6:5; 8:23–25; Luke 5:13; 13:13). But more significant than these individual passages is the fact that people who came to Jesus for healing would come specifically asking him to lay his hands on a sick person:

"*Come and lay your hand on her,* and she will live" (Matt. 9:18), or "*Come and lay your hands on her,* so that she may be made well, and live" (Mark 5:23; cf. 7:32). The fact that people came with this request suggests that the laying on of hands was commonly recognized as the method Jesus usually used to heal people. In imitation of Jesus' method of healing, when the father of Publius was sick, "Paul visited him and prayed, and *putting his hands on him* healed him" (Acts 28:8).[13]

In other cases people sought more generally to touch Jesus, or asked that he would touch them, in order to be healed. "And some people brought to him a blind man, and begged him to *touch* him" (Mark 8:22). Similarly, people "brought to him all that were sick, and besought him that they might only touch the fringe of his garment; and as many as touched it were made well" (Matt. 14:35–36). This was because the power of the Holy Spirit was conveyed through Jesus' physical touch, and came forth and healed people. "All the crowd sought to *touch* him, for power came forth from him and healed them all" (Luke 6:19; cf. Matt. 9:20–22, 25; 20:34; Mark 1:31; 5:41; 9:27; Luke 7:14; 8:51; 22:51).

However, it was not simply to heal that Jesus and the early church laid on hands or touched people. When children came to Jesus "he took them in his arms and blessed them, laying his hands upon them" (Mark 10:16; cf. Matt. 19:13–15; Luke 18:15).

When Jesus so frequently touched people to bring healing or otherwise to bring blessing to them, it is not surprising that people would mention the miracles done by his hands: "What mighty works (Gk. *dynamis,* "miracle") are wrought *by his hands!*" (Mark 6:2).[14] Similarly, when Paul and Barnabas were on their first missionary journey, the Lord "bore witness to the word of his grace, granting signs and wonders to be done *by their hands*" (Acts 14:3).[15] In the same way, "God did extraordinary miracles by the *hands* of Paul" (Acts 19:11).[16] Since there was, as with the other means of grace, no automatic or magical power inherent in the hands of the early Christians, but healing and other kinds of blessing only came as God himself was pleased to work through the laying on of hands, it is not surprising that the early church prayed specifically that God would stretch forth *his hand* to heal. They prayed, "And now, Lord, look upon their threats, and grant to your servants to speak your word with all boldness, *while you stretch out your hand to heal*" (Acts 4:29–30). They realized that while they stretched forth their hands

[13]Although the longer ending of Mark is doubtful as part of Scripture (see chapter 17, p. 365), Mark 16:18 certainly does represent at least one stream of early tradition within the church as well: it says that those who believe in Jesus "will lay their hands on the sick, and they will recover."

[14]Because the gospels so frequently emphasize the fact that Jesus laid hands on people or touched them with his hands, this expression does not seem to be simply a metaphor meaning "What miracles are done by *him!*" but is better understood to be a reference to the specific way in which Jesus' hands were the means by which his miracles were very frequently brought about. Unfortunately, in this verse and several others mentioning miracles done by people's *hands,* the NIV has decided a literal translation is not important and has given the English reader no mention of hands. For example, it simply translates Mark 6:2, "*He* even does miracles!" But the Greek text specifically says that miracles are done "*through his hands*" (*dia tōn cheirōn autou*). In the following section I have pointed out only some of the places where the NIV fails to translate the Greek word *cheir* ("hand"), but it is present in the Greek text in all the verses I quote, and readers who do not find it in their NIV translations should consult another translation, such as the RSV or NASB, that has a more literal translation policy.

[15]The NIV simply translates, "enabling *them* to do miraculous signs and wonders" (see previous footnote).

[16]The NIV simply says, "God did extraordinary miracles *through Paul*" (see previous two footnotes).

to touch those who were sick it would not be effective at all unless God's own mighty hand of power was working through their hands.

At other times the laying on of hands was done for some other purpose. Apparently it was done in connection with asking God to empower or equip people for some service or ministry. When the first deacons were appointed, the church brought them before the apostles, "and they prayed and *laid their hands upon them*" (Acts 6:6). Similarly, when the church at Antioch sent out Paul and Barnabas, "When they had fasted and prayed and *laid their hands on them,* they sent them away" (Acts 13:3 NASB).

When the gospel came to a new group of people, those who proclaimed the gospel would sometimes lay hands on the new believers in order that they might receive the new covenant power of the Holy Spirit. At Samaria, the apostles "laid their hands on them and they received the Holy Spirit" (Acts 8:17). Ananias laid his hands on Saul in order that he might regain his sight and "be filled with the Holy Spirit" (Acts 9:17). When Paul "laid his hands upon" the disciples at Ephesus who had just come to believe in Jesus, "the Holy Spirit came on them" (Acts 19:6).

In other cases the laying on of hands resulted in the impartation of some spiritual gift. In the incident just mentioned, the disciples at Ephesus also "spoke with tongues and prophesied" (Acts 19:6) after Paul laid his hands on them. Moreover, he reminds Timothy, "Do not neglect the gift you have, which was given you by prophetic utterance (literally, "through prophecy") when the council of elders laid their hands upon you" (1 Tim. 4:14). Paul may have been referring to the same event or a different one when he said later, "I remind you to rekindle the *gift* of God that is within you *through the laying on of my hands*" (2 Tim. 1:6). (In 1 Timothy 5:22, the statement "Do not be hasty in the laying on of hands" refers to the ordination of elders; see chapter 47, p. 918.)

If people in the early church were frequently praying for one another's needs, and if they imitated the example of Jesus and his disciples in the laying on of hands to pray for people for healing, for bringing blessing, for receiving the Holy Spirit at the time of conversion, for receiving spiritual gifts, or for empowering for ministry, then we would expect that instruction given to new Christians would have included the teaching that prayer for individual needs would ordinarily be accompanied by the placing of a hand or hands upon the person who was being prayed for. If this were so, then it would not be surprising that "the laying on of hands" would be classified as an "elementary" doctrine, something that belongs to the "foundation" of Christian instruction—which is in fact what we find in Hebrews 6:1–2. Although some have understood this to refer more narrowly to the laying on of hands that accompanies installation in some specific church office, that is only one small aspect of the pattern of situations in which laying on of hands is found in the New Testament. It seems much better to understand this phrase in Hebrews 6:2 to refer to elementary instruction about how to pray for others in various situations of need so that young Christians would immediately be able to begin ministering to others as well.

It seems appropriate, then, to count the laying on of hands as one other dimension of the rich diversity of "means of grace" that God has placed within the church to bring blessing to his people.

**12. Should Footwashing Be Practiced As a Means of Grace Within the Church?** From time to time some Christian groups have practiced a ceremony of washing one another's feet at a public meeting of the church. They have based this practice on Jesus's command, "If I then, your Lord and Teacher, have washed your feet, *you also ought to wash one another's feet*" (John 13:14). Those who advocate footwashing consider it a ceremony that Jesus commanded, similar to the ceremonies of baptism and the Lord's Supper.

However, there are several reasons why we should not think that in John 13:14 Jesus was establishing another ceremony for the church in addition to baptism and the Lord's Supper. (1) Baptism and the Lord's Supper explicitly symbolize the greatest event in the history of redemption, Christ's death and resurrection for us, but footwashing symbolizes no such redemptive-historical event. (2) Baptism and the Lord's Supper were clearly *symbolic* actions, but when Jesus washed the disciples' feet it was clearly *functional*, not merely symbolic, in that it met an ordinary human need of the day (dirty feet). (3) Baptism and the Lord's Supper are appropriate symbols of beginning and continuing in the Christian life,[17] but no such symbolism attaches to footwashing. (4) To make footwashing an ordinance like baptism and the Lord's Supper reduces it to a symbol—and if it is a symbol, then Jesus' words command us only to perform a symbol, and the real force of Jesus' command (to act in humility and love) is lost. (5) Whereas the epistles give evidence that baptism and the Lord's Supper were continuing ordinances observed by the New Testament churches, there is no evidence that the apostles or the early church observed footwashing as an ordinance. (6) There is a simple and straightforward explanation for Jesus' command: he is telling his disciples to take lowly tasks in serving one another. But if this is what the text means (and the vast majority of the church through history has understood it this way), then we need not look for an additional meaning (that Jesus is also instituting a new ceremony). By contrast, the New Testament texts about baptism and the Lord's Supper cannot be understood to command something *other* than a ceremony. Therefore, while all Christians would profit from pondering the application of Jesus' statement about footwashing to their present patterns of life, none should think that Jesus is encouraging them to practice a ceremony of footwashing.

## C. Conclusions

At the end of this discussion of the means of grace within the church, we should realize first of all that when any of these are carried out in faith and obedience, we should eagerly expect and look for evidence that the Holy Spirit is actually ministering to people at the same time as these actions are being done. We as Christians ought not to neglect to "meet together" (Heb. 10:25), but ought to look forward eagerly to any assembly of believers in which any of these means would occur, expecting that God will bring blessing from each of these means!

On the other hand, we must realize that all of these means of grace occur within the fellowship of the church. Those who neglect the fellowship of the church

---

[17]See chapter 49, pp. 968–69, on the symbolism of baptism, and chapter 50, pp. 989–91, on the symbolism of the Lord's Supper.

willfully cut themselves off from all of these means of grace and thereby cut themselves off from most of the ordinary means that the Holy Spirit uses to bring blessing to his people.

These means of grace ought to give us great appreciation for the amazing privilege of being members of the body of Christ, the church.

## QUESTIONS FOR PERSONAL APPLICATION

1. Before reading this chapter, did you think that it made very much difference if a Christian continued to be active in the fellowship of the church or not? How has this chapter changed your perspective on that question, if at all?

2. Which of the means of grace mentioned in this chapter has been most helpful to you in your own Christian life?

3. Which of the means of grace mentioned in this chapter do you think you appreciated least before reading the chapter? How has your appreciation for that means of grace increased? How do you think this will affect your actions from now on?

4. As you look over the list of means of grace, are there some areas in which people are not actually experiencing "grace" or blessing in your own church? What could be done to increase the effectiveness of these weak areas as means of grace in the life of your church?

5. Which of the means of grace are actually least helpful in your own life? Are there some that have become rather mechanical, and that you are performing only as an outward or physical activity, without any real participation in your heart? What could you do to increase the effectiveness of those means in your life?

6. As you look over the list of the means of grace again, name one or more in which you could begin to help the church be more effective in bringing blessing to its people.

## SPECIAL TERMS

| | |
|---|---|
| Eucharist | laying on of hands |
| extreme unction | means of grace |
| holy orders | sacrament |

## BIBLIOGRAPHY

(For an explanation of this bibliography see the note on the bibliography to chapter 1, p. 38. Complete bibliographical data may be found on pp. 1223–29.)

### Sections in Evangelical Systematic Theologies

1. Anglican (Episcopalian)
    1882–92    Litton, 428–59

                1930        Thomas, 313–38, 343–70, 447–51
2. Arminian (Wesleyan or Methodist)
                1875–76    Pope, 3:294–310, 335–59
                1892–94    Miley, 2:392–94
                1940        Wiley, 3:150–60
                1960        Purkiser, 409–27
                1983        Carter, 2:615
3. Baptist
                1767        Gill, 2:621, 660–82
                1983–85    Erickson, 1003–15
4. Dispensational
                1949        Thiessen, 296–304
                1986        Ryrie, 421, 427
5. Lutheran
                1917–24    Pieper, 3:104–215, 439–72
                1934        Mueller, 441–69
6. Reformed (or Presbyterian)
                1559        Calvin, 2:1276–1302, 1448–84 (4.14, 19)
                1861        Heppe, 590–610
                1871–73    Hodge, 3:466–526
                1878        Dabney, 726–57
                1889        Shedd, 2b:561–87
                1937–66    Murray, *CW,* 2:366–69
                1938        Berkhof, 604–21
                1962        Buswell, 2:226–41
7. Renewal (or charismatic/Pentecostal)
                1988–92    Williams, 2:287–94, 3:159–63


**Sections in Representative Roman Catholic Systematic Theologies**

1. Roman Catholic: Traditional
                1955        Ott, 325–472
2. Roman Catholic: Post-Vatican II
                1980        McBrien, 2:731–49, 775–816


**Other Works**

Hughes, P. E. "Grace, Means of." In *EDT,* pp. 482–83.
Milne, Bruce. *We Belong Together: The Meaning of Fellowship.* Downers Grove, Ill.:
    InterVarsity Press, 1978.

## SCRIPTURE MEMORY PASSAGE

**Acts 2:41–42:** *So those who received his word were baptized, and there were added that day about three thousand souls. And they devoted themselves to the apostles' teaching and fellowship, to the breaking of bread and the prayers.*

## HYMN

### "I Love Thy Kingdom, Lord"

This hymn expresses joy at the privilege of being in the church. In fact, the author exclaims, "Beyond my highest joy I prize her heavenly ways, /Her sweet communion, solemn vows, her hymns of love and praise." Here he is meditating on some of the means of grace within the church ("her heavenly ways"), particularly the fellowship or communion that comes within the church, the vows to God that are made there, and the hymns that are sung within it. Moreover, using the figure of Mount Zion to refer to the church, he says that "to Zion shall be given /The brightest glories earth can yield, and brighter bliss of heaven." When we sing this we can think of all the rich blessings that the Holy Spirit bestows on the church through the many means of grace.

The author of this hymn, Timothy Dwight, was President of Yale University from 1795 to 1817, during which time he reformed the administration and the curriculum and tripled the enrollment. He also was Professor of Divinity, and under his preaching a revival broke out in 1802, in which a third of the students were converted.

I love thy kingdom, Lord, the house of thine abode,
    The church our blest Redeemer saved with his own precious
blood.

I love thy church, O God: her walls before thee stand,
    Dear as the apple of thine eye, and graven on thy hand.

For her my tears shall fall, for her my prayers ascend;
    To her my cares and toils be giv'n, till toils and cares shall end.

Beyond my highest joy I prize her heav'nly ways,
    Her sweet communion, solemn vows, her hymns of love and
praise.

Jesus, thou Friend divine, our Savior and our King,
    Thy hand from ev'ry snare and foe shall great deliv'rance bring.

Sure as thy truth shall last, to Zion shall be giv'n
    The brightest glories earth can yield, and brighter bliss of heav'n.

AUTHOR: TIMOTHY DWIGHT, 1800

# Chapter 49

# Baptism

*Who should be baptized? How should it
be done? What does it mean?*

## EXPLANATION AND SCRIPTURAL BASIS

In this chapter and the next we treat baptism and the Lord's Supper, two
ceremonies that Jesus commanded his church to perform. But before we begin
consideration of either one of them we must note that there is disagreement
among Protestants even over the general term that should be applied to them.
Because the Roman Catholic Church calls these two ceremonies "sacraments," and
because the Catholic Church teaches that these sacraments *in themselves* actually
*convey grace* to people (without requiring faith from the persons participating in
them), some Protestants (especially Baptists) have refused to refer to baptism and
the Lord's Supper as "sacraments." They have preferred the word *ordinances*
instead. This is thought to be an appropriate term because baptism and the Lord's
Supper were "ordained" by Christ.[1] On the other hand, other Protestants such as
those in the Anglican, Lutheran, and Reformed traditions, have been willing to
use the word "sacraments" to refer to baptism and the Lord's Supper, without
thereby endorsing the Roman Catholic position.

It does not seem that any significant point is at issue here in the question of
whether to call baptism and the Lord's Supper "ordinances" or "sacraments."
Since Protestants who use both words explain clearly what they mean by them, the
argument is not really over doctrine but over the meaning of an English word. If
we are willing to explain clearly what we mean, it does not seem to make any
difference whether we use the word *sacrament* or not.[2] In this text, when referring
to baptism and the Lord's Supper in Protestant teaching, I will use both
"ordinances" and "sacraments" interchangeably, and regard them as synonymous
in meaning.

Before beginning our discussion of baptism we must recognize that there has
been historically, and is today, a strong difference of viewpoint among evangelical

---

[1] A. H. Strong, *Systematic Theology,* says, "No ordinance is a sacrament in the Romanist sense of
conferring grace" (p. 930). He also says, "The Romanist regards the ordinances as actually conferring
grace and producing holiness" (ibid.).

[2] The *American Heritage Dictionary* (Boston: Houghton Mifflen, 1981) allows a range of meanings,
defining a sacrament as a rite considered as "a testament to inner grace *or* a channel that mediates grace"
(p. 1141). Even the most conscientious Baptist would not object to calling baptism "a testament to
inner grace" while Catholics would not object to calling baptism "a channel that mediates grace."

Christians regarding this subject. The position advocated in this book is that baptism is not a "major" doctrine that should be the basis of division among genuine Christians,[3] but it is nonetheless a matter of importance for ordinary church life, and it is appropriate that we give it full consideration.

The position advocated in this chapter is "Baptistic"—namely, that *baptism is appropriately administered only to those who give a believable profession of faith in Jesus Christ.* During the discussion, we shall interact particularly with the paedobaptist ("infant baptist") position as advocated by Louis Berkhof in his *Systematic Theology,* since this is a careful and responsible representation of the paedobaptist position, and it is in a widely used systematic theology text.

## A. The Mode and Meaning of Baptism

The practice of baptism in the New Testament was carried out in one way: the person being baptized was *immersed* or put completely under the water and then brought back up again. Baptism *by immersion* is therefore the "mode" of baptism or the way in which baptism was carried out in the New Testament. This is evident for the following reasons:

(1) The Greek word *baptizō* means "to plunge, dip, immerse" something in water. This is the commonly recognized and standard meaning of the term in ancient Greek literature both inside and outside of the Bible.[4]

(2) The sense "immerse" is appropriate and probably required for the word in several New Testament passages. In Mark 1:5, people were baptized by John "*in* the river Jordan" (the Greek text has *en,* "in," and not "beside" or "by" or "near" the river).[5] Mark also tells us that when Jesus had been baptized "he came up *out of the water*" (Mark 1:10). The Greek text specifies that he came "out of" (*ek*) the water, not that he came away from it (this would be expressed by Gk. *apo*). The

---

[3]See chapter 1, pp. 29–30, for a discussion of major and minor doctrines. Not all Christians agree with my view that this is a minor doctrine. Many Christians in previous generations were persecuted and even put to death because they differed with the official state church and its practice of infant baptism. For them, the issue was not merely a ceremony: it was the right to have a believers' church, one that did not automatically include all the people born in a geographical region. Viewed in this light, the controversy over baptism involves a larger difference over the nature of the church: does one become part of the church by birth into a believing family, or by voluntary profession of faith?

[4]So *LSJ,* p. 305: "plunge"; passive, "to be drowned." Similarly, BAGD, p. 131: "dip, immerse," and middle, "dip oneself, wash (in non-Christian literature also 'plunge, sink, drench, overwhelm')." Also Albrecht Oepke, "*baptō, baptizō,* etc.," in *TDNT,* 1:530: "to immerse . . . to sink the ship"; passive, "to sink . . . to suffer shipwreck, to drown (the sense of 'to bathe' or 'to wash' is only occasionally found in Hellenism . . . the idea of going under or perishing is nearer the general usage)" (ibid.). A. H. Strong, *Systematic Theology,* pp. 933–35 gives much additional evidence to this effect.

Berkhof, *Systematic Theology,* p. 630, objects and gives some counter-examples, but his evidence is unconvincing because he indiscriminately mixes examples of *baptizō* with a related but different word, *baptō.* (Passages that speak of "bathing" or washing [in the Septuagint, Judith 12:7, for example, and in the New Testament, Mark 7:4] would most likely involve covering one's body [or hands, in Mark 7:4] completely with water.)

If any New Testament author had wanted to indicate that people were sprinkled with water, a perfectly good Greek word meaning "to sprinkle" was available: *rhantizō* is used in this sense in Heb. 9:13, 19, 21; 10:22; see BAGD, p. 734.

[5]Berkhof asks, "Was John the Baptist capable of the enormous task of immersing the multitudes that flocked unto him at the river Jordan. . . ?" (p. 630). Certainly over a period of several days he would have been capable of immersing many hundreds of people, but it is also possible that his disciples (Matt. 9:14; et al.) assisted him with some of the baptisms.

fact that John and Jesus went into the river and came up out of it strongly suggests immersion, since sprinkling or pouring of water could much more readily have been done standing beside the river, particularly because multitudes of people were coming for baptism. John's gospel tells us, further, that John the Baptist "was baptizing at Aenon near Salim, because there was much water there" (John 3:23). Again, it would not take "much water" to baptize people by sprinkling, but it would take much water to baptize by immersion.

When Philip had shared the gospel with the Ethiopian eunuch, "as they went along the road they came to some water, and the eunuch said, 'See, here is water! What is to prevent my being baptized?'" (Acts 8:36). Apparently neither of them thought that sprinkling or pouring a handful of water from the container of drinking water that would have been carried in the chariot was enough to constitute baptism. Rather, they waited until there was a body of water near the road. Then "he commanded the chariot to stop, and they both went *down into the water,* Philip and the eunuch, and he baptized him. And when they came *up out of the water,* the Spirit of the Lord caught up Philip; and the eunuch saw him no more, and went on his way rejoicing" (Acts 8:38–39). As in the case of Jesus, this baptism occurred when Philip and the eunuch went down into a body of water, and after the baptism they came up out of that body of water. Once again baptism by immersion is the only satisfactory explanation of this narrative.[6]

(3) The symbolism of union with Christ in his death, burial, and resurrection seems to require baptism by immersion. Paul says,

> Do you not know that all of us who have been baptized into Christ Jesus were baptized into his death? We were buried therefore with him by baptism into death, so that as Christ was raised from the dead by the glory of the Father, we too might walk in newness of life. (Rom. 6:3–4)

Similarly, Paul tells the Colossians, "You were *buried with him in baptism,* in which you were also *raised with him* through faith in the working of God, who raised him from the dead" (Col. 2:12).

Now this truth is clearly symbolized in baptism by immersion. When the candidate for baptism goes down into the water it is a picture of going down into the grave and being buried. Coming up out of the water is then a picture of being raised with Christ to walk in newness of life. Baptism thus very clearly pictures death to one's old way of life and rising to a new kind of life in Christ. But baptism by sprinkling or pouring simply misses this symbolism.[7]

---

[6]Berkhof (pp. 630–631) objects that in Acts 8:38 the Greek word *eis* can mean "to" and not necessarily "into." It is true that the word can take either meaning, but we must also note v. 39, where *ek* certainly means "out of," not "away from," which would be expressed by *apo*. And the going down and coming up (*katabainō* and *anabainō*) are not going down from the chariot and going back up into the chariot, but are specifically said to be going down *into the water* and coming up *out of the water*.

[7]In fact, the waters of baptism have an even richer symbolism than simply the symbolism of the grave. The waters also remind us of the waters of God's judgment that came upon unbelievers at the time of the flood (Gen. 7:6–24), or the drowning of the Egyptians in the Exodus (Ex. 14:26–29). Similarly, when Jonah was thrown into the deep (Jonah 1:7–16), he was thrown down to the place of death because of God's judgment on his disobedience—even though he was miraculously rescued and thus became a sign of the resurrection. Therefore those who go down into the waters of baptism really are going down into the waters of judgment and death, death that they deserve from God for their sins. When they come back up out of the waters of baptism it shows that they have come safely through God's judgment only because of the merits of Jesus Christ, with whom they are united in his death and

Sometimes it is objected that the essential thing symbolized in baptism is not death and resurrection with Christ but purification and cleansing from sins. Certainly it is true that water is an evident symbol of washing and cleansing, and the waters of baptism do symbolize washing and purification from sins as well as death and resurrection with Christ. Titus 3:5 speaks of "the washing of regeneration" and, even though the word *baptism* is not used in this text, it is certainly true that there is a cleansing from sin that occurs at the time of conversion. Ananias told Saul, "Rise and be baptized, and *wash away your sins,* calling on his name" (Acts 22:16).

But to say that washing away of sins is the only thing (or even the most essential thing) pictured in baptism does not faithfully represent New Testament teaching. Both washing and death and resurrection with Christ are symbolized in baptism, but Romans 6:1–11 and Colossians 2:11–12 place a clear emphasis on dying and rising with Christ. Even the washing is much more effectively symbolized by immersion than by sprinkling or pouring, and death and resurrection with Christ are symbolized only by immersion, not at all by sprinkling or pouring.

What then is the positive meaning of baptism? In all the discussion over the mode of baptism and the disputes over its meaning, it is easy for Christians to lose sight of the significance and beauty of baptism and to disregard the tremendous blessing that accompanies this ceremony. The amazing truths of passing through the waters of judgment safely, of dying and rising with Christ, and of having our sins washed away, are truths of momentous and eternal proportion and ought to be an occasion for giving great glory and praise to God. If churches would teach these truths more clearly, baptisms would be the occasion of much more blessing in the church.

## B. The Subjects of Baptism

The pattern revealed at several places in the New Testament is that only those who give a believable profession of faith should be baptized. This view is often called "believers' baptism," since it holds that only those who have themselves believed in Christ (or, more precisely, those who have given reasonable evidence of believing in Christ) should be baptized. This is because baptism, which is a

---

resurrection. This is why Peter can say in 1 Peter 3:21 that baptism "corresponds to" the saving of Noah and his family from the waters of judgment in the flood.

Douglas Moo, in Romans 1–8, *Wycliffe Exegetical Commentary* (Chicago: Moody Press, 1991), argues that baptism in Rom. 6 "functions as shorthand for the conversion experience as a whole. . . . It is not, then, that baptism is a symbol of dying and rising with Christ." (p. 371). He says that "there is no evidence in Romans 6, or in the NT, that the actual physical movements, immersion, and emersion, involved in baptism were accorded symbolical significance" (p. 379). While I agree that baptism in Rom. 6 functions as shorthand for the conversion experience as a whole, it does not seem to me that we can exclude the symbolism of dying and rising with Christ, for the following reasons: (1) The physical actions of going *down into* the water (where human beings cannot live for more than a few minutes) and coming *up out of* the water are so closely parallel to the actions of going down into the grave and coming up out of the grave that the connection is evident from the surface appearance of the actions, and no detailed explanation would be necessary. (2) The Old Testament background of being immersed by waters of God's judgment confirms this. (3) When Paul says, "You were buried with him in baptism, in which you were also raised with him through faith in the working of God, who raised him from the dead" (Col. 2:12), it is hard to imagine that any of Paul's readers, even children, would have missed the evident parallel between the actions of baptism and dying and rising with Christ. (This would be true even if, with Moo, we translate Col. 2:12 "*by means of* baptism.")

*symbol of beginning the Christian life,* should only be given to those who have *in fact* begun the Christian life.

**1. The Argument From the New Testament Narrative Passages on Baptism.** The narrative examples of those who were baptized suggest that baptism was administered only to those who gave a believable profession of faith. After Peter's sermon at Pentecost we read, *"Those who received his word* were baptized" (Acts 2:41). The text specifies that baptism was administered to those who "received his word" and therefore trusted in Christ for salvation.[8] Similarly, when Philip preached the gospel in Samaria, we read, *"When they believed* Philip as he preached good news about the kingdom of God and the name of Jesus Christ, *they were baptized,* both men and women" (Acts 8:12). Likewise, when Peter preached to the Gentiles in Cornelius' household, he allowed baptism for those who had *heard* the Word and *received the Holy Spirit*—that is, for those who had given persuasive evidence of an internal work of regeneration. While Peter was preaching, "the Holy Spirit fell on all who heard the word" and Peter and his companions "heard them speaking in tongues and extolling God" (Acts 10:44–46). Peter's response was that baptism is appropriate for those who have received the regenerating work of the Holy Spirit: "Can any one forbid water for baptizing these people *who have received the Holy Spirit* just as we have?" Then Peter "commanded them to be baptized in the name of Jesus Christ" (Acts 10:47–48). The point of these three passages is that baptism is appropriately given to those who have received the gospel and trusted in Christ for salvation. There are other texts that indicate this as well—Acts 16:14–15 (Lydia and her household, after "the Lord opened her heart" to believe); Acts 16:32–33 (the family of the Philippian jailer, after Peter preached "the word of the Lord to him and to all that were in his house"); and 1 Corinthians 1:16 (the household of Stephanas), but these will be discussed more fully below when we look at the question of "household baptisms."

**2. The Argument From the Meaning of Baptism.** In addition to these indications from New Testament narratives that baptism always followed upon saving faith, there is a second consideration that argues for believers' baptism: the outward symbol of *beginning* the Christian life should only be given to those who *show evidence* of having begun the Christian life. The New Testament authors wrote as though they clearly assumed that everyone who was baptized had also personally trusted in Christ and experienced salvation. For example, Paul says, "As many of you as were baptized into Christ have put on Christ" (Gal. 3:27). Paul here assumes that baptism is the outward sign of inward regeneration. This simply would not have been true of infants—Paul could not have said, "As many *infants* as have been baptized into Christ have put on Christ," for infants have not yet come to saving faith or given any evidence of regeneration.[9]

---

[8]Berkhof cautions against making too much of the silence of Scripture regarding infant baptism. Commenting on the fact that in some cases whole households were baptized, he says, "And if there were infants, it is morally certain that they were baptized along with the parents" (p. 634). But this is not what Acts 2:41 says: it specifies that *"those who received his word* were baptized," not those who did not receive his word but were infants belonging to the households of those who received his word.

[9]This is not to argue that *no* infants can be regenerated (see above, chapter 24, pp. 500—501), but

Paul speaks the same way in Romans 6:3–4: "Do you not know that *all of us who have been baptized into Christ Jesus* were baptized into his death? We were buried therefore with him by baptism into death." Could Paul have said this of infants?[10] Could he have said that "all infants who have been baptized into Christ Jesus were baptized into his death" and "were buried therefore with him by baptism into death, so that as Christ was raised from the dead"? But if Paul could not have said those things about infants, then those who advocate infant baptism must say that baptism means something different for infants than what Paul says it means for "all of us who have been baptized into Christ Jesus." Those who argue for infant baptism at this point resort to what seems to the present author to be vague language about infants being adopted "into the covenant" or "into the covenant community," but the New Testament does not speak that way about baptism. Rather, it says that all of those who have been baptized have been buried with Christ, have been raised with him, and have put on Christ.

A similar argument can be made from Colossians 2:12: "You were buried with him in baptism, in which you were also raised with him through faith in the working of God, who raised him from the dead." But it could not be said of infants that they were buried with Christ, or were raised with him through faith, since they were not yet old enough to exercise faith for themselves.

**3. Alternative #1: The Roman Catholic View.** The Roman Catholic Church teaches that baptism should be administered to infants.[11] The reason for this is that the Catholic Church believes that baptism is *necessary* for salvation, and that the act of baptism itself *causes regeneration*. Therefore, in this view, baptism is a *means* whereby the church bestows saving grace on people. And if it is this kind of a channel of saving grace it should be given to all people.

Ludwig Ott, in his *Fundamentals of Catholic Dogma*[12] gives the following explanations:

> Baptism is that Sacrament in which man being washed with water in the name of the Three Divine Persons is spiritually reborn. (p. 350; Ott gives John 3:5; Titus 3:5; and Eph. 5:26 in support of this statement)

> Baptism, provided that the proper dispositions (Faith and sorrow for sin) are present, effects: a) the eradication of sins, both original sin and, in the case of adults, also personal, mortal or venial sins; b) inner sanctification by the infusion of sanctifying grace. (p. 354)

> Even if it be unworthily received, valid Baptism imprints on the soul of the recipient an indelible spiritual mark, the Baptismal Character. . . . The baptized person is incorporated, by the Baptismal Character, into the Mystical Body of Christ. . . . Every validly baptized person, even one baptized outside the Catholic Church, becomes a member of the One Holy Catholic and Apostolic Church. (p. 355)

---

simply that Paul could have no theological basis for saying that *all* infants who have been baptized have begun the Christian life. He is talking in Gal. 3:27 of "as many of you as were baptized into Christ."

[10]See section 3 below for a response to the Roman Catholic view that baptism causes regeneration.

[11]The act of baptizing an infant, including giving a name to the infant at that time, is sometimes called "christening," especially in Roman Catholic and Episcopalian churches.

[12]Trans. by Patrick Lynch, ed. by James Bastible, 4th ed. (Rockford, Ill.: Tan Books, 1960).

Ott goes on to explain that baptism is necessary for salvation and is to be performed only by priests:

> Baptism by water . . . is, since the promulgation of the Gospel, necessary for all men without exception for salvation. (p. 356)[13]

Ott explains that, while baptism is ordinarily to be administered by a priest, in unusual circumstances (such as when a child is in danger of dying soon after birth) it may be performed by a deacon or a layperson. Even baptism performed by unbelievers is thought to be valid, for Ott says:

> Yea, even a pagan or a heretic can baptise, provided he adheres to the form of the Church and has the intention of doing what the Church does. (p. 358)

Though infants cannot exercise saving faith themselves, the Roman Catholic Church teaches that the baptism of infants is valid:

> Faith, as it is not the effective cause of justification . . . need not be present. The faith which infants lack is . . . replaced by the faith of the Church. (p. 359)

Essential to understanding the Roman Catholic view of baptism is the realization that Catholics hold that the sacraments work apart from the faith of the people participating in the sacrament. And if this is so, then it follows that baptism would confer grace even on infants who do not have the ability to exercise faith. Several statements in Ott's book make this clear:

> The Catholic Church teaches that the Sacraments have an objective efficacy, that is, an efficacy independent of the subjective disposition of the recipient or of the minister. . . . The Sacraments confer grace immediately, that is, without the mediation of Fiducial faith. (pp. 328–29)

> The Sacraments of the New Covenant contain the grace which they signify, and bestow it on those who do not hinder it. (p. 328)

> The Sacraments work *ex opere operato*. . . . That is, the Sacraments operate by the power of the completed sacramental rite. (p. 329)[14]

> The formula "*ex opere operato*" asserts, negatively that the sacramental grace is not conferred by reason of the subjective activity of the recipient, and positively, that the sacramental grace is caused by the validly operated sacramental sign. (p. 330)

However, Ott is careful to explain that the Catholic teaching must not be interpreted "in the sense of mechanical or magical efficacy" (p. 330). He says,

> On the contrary, in the case of the adult recipient faith is expressly demanded . . . nevertheless the subjective disposition of the recipient is not the cause of grace; it is merely an indispensable precondition of the communication of grace . . . The measure of the grace effected *ex opere operato* even depends on the grade of the subjective disposition. (p. 330)

---

[13]In extreme cases Ott and the teaching of the Catholic Church allow for baptism of desire (for one who sincerely longs to be baptized but cannot be) or baptism by blood (in martyrdom).

[14]The phrase *ex opere operato* represents an essential part of Roman Catholic teaching on the sacraments. This Latin phrase literally means "by work performed," and it means that the sacraments work in virtue of the actual activity done, and that the power of the sacraments does not depend on any subjective attitude of faith in the people participating in them.

In giving a response to this Roman Catholic teaching, we should remember that the Reformation centered upon this issue. Martin Luther's great concern was to teach that salvation depends on faith alone, not on faith *plus works*. But if baptism and participating in the other sacraments are *necessary for salvation* because they are *necessary* for receiving saving grace, then salvation really is based on faith plus works. In contrast to this, the clear New Testament message is that justification is by faith *alone*. "By grace you have been saved *through faith*; and this is not your own doing, it is the gift of God—*not because of works*, lest any man should boast" (Eph. 2:8–9). Moreover, "the *free gift* of God is eternal life in Christ Jesus our Lord" (Rom. 6:23).

The Roman Catholic argument that baptism is necessary for salvation is very similar to the argument of Paul's opponents in Galatia who said that circumcision was necessary for salvation. Paul's response is that those who require circumcision are preaching "a different gospel" (Gal. 1:6). He says that "all who rely on works of the law are under a curse" (Gal. 3:10), and speaks very severely to those who attempt to add any form of obedience as a requirement for justification: "You are severed from Christ, you who would be justified by the law; you have fallen away from grace" (Gal. 5:4). Therefore, we must conclude that no *work* is necessary for salvation. And therefore *baptism* is not necessary for salvation.

But what about John 3:5, "Unless one is *born of water* and the Spirit, he cannot enter the kingdom of God"? Although some have understood this as a reference to baptism, it is better understood against the background of the promise of the new covenant in Ezekiel 36:

> I will sprinkle clean water upon you, and you shall be clean from all your uncleannesses, and from all your idols I will cleanse you. A new heart I will give you, and a new spirit I will put within you; and I will take out of your flesh the heart of stone and give you a heart of flesh. And I will put my spirit within you, and cause you to walk in my statutes and be careful to observe my ordinances. (Ezek. 36:25–27)

Ezekiel here speaks of a "spiritual" washing that will come in the days of the new covenant when God puts his Spirit within his people. In the light of this, to be born of water and the Spirit is a "spiritual" washing that occurs when we are born again, just as we receive a spiritual, not a physical, "new heart" at that time as well.

Similarly, Titus 3:5 specifies not water baptism but "the washing of regeneration," explicitly stating that it is a *spiritual* giving of new life. Water baptism is simply not mentioned in this passage. A spiritual rather than literal washing is also referred to in Ephesians 5:26, where Paul says that Christ gave himself up for the church "that he might sanctify her, having cleansed her by the washing of water with the word." It is the Word of God that does the washing referred to here, not physical water.

As for the Roman Catholic view that baptism conveys grace apart from the subjective disposition of the recipient or the minister (a position that is consistent with baptizing infants, who do not exercise faith for themselves), we must recognize that no New Testament examples exist to prove this view, nor is there New Testament testimony to indicate this. Rather, the narrative accounts of those who were baptized indicate that they had first come to saving faith (see above).

And when there are doctrinal statements about baptism they also indicate the need of saving faith. When Paul says, "You were buried with him in baptism, in which you were also raised with him," he immediately specifies *"through faith* in the working of God, who raised him from the dead" (Col. 2:12).

Finally, what about 1 Peter 3:21, where Peter says, *"Baptism . . . now saves you"?* Does this not give clear support to the Roman Catholic view that baptism itself brings saving grace to the recipient?[15] No, for when Peter uses this phrase he continues in the same sentence to explain exactly what he means by it. He says that baptism saves you *"not as a removal of dirt from the body"* (that is, not as an outward, physical act which washes dirt from the body—that is not the part which saves you), *"but as an appeal to God for a clear conscience"* (that is, as an inward, spiritual transaction between God and the individual, a transaction symbolized by the outward ceremony of baptism). We could paraphrase Peter's statement by saying, "Baptism now saves you—not the *outward* physical ceremony of baptism but the *inward* spiritual reality which baptism represents." In this way, Peter guards against any view of baptism that would attribute automatic saving power to the physical ceremony itself.

Peter's phrase, "an appeal to God for a clear conscience," is another way of saying "a request for forgiveness of sins and a new heart." When God gives a sinner a "clear conscience," that person has the assurance that every sin has been forgiven and that he or she stands in a right relationship with God (Heb. 9:14 and 10:22 speak this way about the cleansing of one's conscience through Christ). To be baptized rightly is to make such an "appeal" to God: it is to say, in effect, "Please, God, as I enter this baptism which will cleanse my body outwardly I am asking you to cleanse my heart inwardly, forgive my sins, and make me right before you." Understood in this way, baptism is an appropriate symbol for the beginning of the Christian life.[16]

So 1 Peter 3:21 certainly does not teach that baptism saves people automatically or confers grace *ex opere operato.* It does not even teach that the act of baptism itself has saving power, but rather that salvation comes about through the inward exercise of faith that is represented by baptism (cf. Col. 2:12). In fact, Protestants who advocate believers' baptism might well see in 1 Peter 3:21 some support for their position: baptism, it might be argued, is appropriately administered to

---

[15]The next three paragraphs are adapted from Wayne Grudem, *The First Epistle of Peter,* TNTC (Leicester: IVP, and Grand Rapids: Eerdmans, 1988), pp. 163–65, and are used by permission.

[16]Some have argued that "pledge" is a better word than "appeal" in this verse. Thus, the NIV translates, "the *pledge* of a good conscience towards God." The data from other examples of the word is slim with regard to both meanings, and no conclusions can be drawn from an examination of other uses of the word alone (see discussion in W. Grudem, *1 Peter,* p. 164).

But much more significant is the fact that the translation "pledge" introduces a theological problem. If baptism is a "pledge to God" to maintain a good conscience (or a pledge to live an obedient life, which flows from a good conscience), then the emphasis is no longer on dependence on God to give salvation, but is rather on dependence on one's own effort or strength of resolve. And since this phrase in 1 Peter 3:21 is so clearly connected with the beginning of the Christian life and identified as the feature of baptism that "saves you," the translation "pledge" seems to be inconsistent with the New Testament teaching on salvation by faith alone; it would be the only place where a promise to be righteous is said to be the thing that "saves you." And since the lexical data are inconclusive for both senses (while suggesting that both senses are apparently possible), it is better to adopt the translation "appeal" as a sense much more in accord with the doctrinal teaching of the rest of the New Testament.

anyone who is old enough personally to make "an appeal to God for a clear conscience."[17]

In conclusion, the Roman Catholic teachings that baptism is necessary for salvation, that the act of baptism in itself confers saving grace, and that baptism is therefore appropriately administered to infants, are not persuasive in the light of New Testament teachings.

**4. Alternative #2: The Protestant Paedobaptist View.** In contrast both to the Baptist position defended in the earlier part of this chapter and to the Roman Catholic view just discussed, another important view is that baptism is rightly administered to *all infant children of believing parents*. This is a common view in many Protestant groups (especially Lutheran, Episcopalian, Methodist, Presbyterian and Reformed churches). This view is sometimes known as the covenant argument for paedobaptism. It is called a "covenant" argument because it depends on seeing infants born to believers as part of the "covenant community" of God's people. The word "paedobaptism" means the practice of baptizing infants (the prefix *paido-* means "child" and is derived from the Greek word *pais*, "child").[18] I will be interacting primarily with the arguments put forth by Louis Berkhof, who explains clearly and defends well the paedobaptist position.

The argument that infants of believers should be baptized depends primarily on the following three points:

**a. Infants Were Circumcised in the Old Covenant:** In the Old Testament, circumcision was the outward *sign* of entrance into the covenant community or the community of God's people. Circumcision was administered to all Israelite children (that is, male children) when they were eight days old.

**b. Baptism Is Parallel to Circumcision:** In the New Testament, the outward sign of entrance into the "covenant community" is baptism. Therefore baptism is the New Testament counterpart to circumcision. It follows that baptism should be administered to all infant children of believing parents. To deny them this benefit is to deprive them of a privilege and benefit that is rightfully theirs—the *sign* of belonging to the community of God's people, the "covenant community." The parallel between circumcision and baptism is seen quite clearly in Colossians 2:

> In him also *you were circumcised* with a circumcision made without hands, by putting off the body of flesh in the circumcision of Christ; and *you were buried with him in baptism*, in which you were also raised with him through faith in the working of God, who raised him from the dead. (Col. 2:11–12)

---

[17]Col. 2:12 can be used in the same manner: Paul says that in baptism Christians were "raised with [Christ] *through faith* in the working of God, who raised him from the dead." This presupposes that those who were baptized were exercising faith when they were baptized—that is, that they were old enough to believe.

[18]Roman Catholics are also paedobaptists, but their supporting arguments are different, as explained above (they teach that baptism causes regeneration). In the material that follows, I will be comparing a Protestant defense of *paedobaptism* with a Protestant defense of *believers' baptism*. Therefore, I will use the term *paedobaptist* to refer to Protestant paedobaptists who hold to a covenant paedobaptist position.

Here it is said that Paul makes an explicit connection between circumcision and baptism.

**c. Household Baptisms:** Further support for the practice of baptizing infants is found in the "household baptisms" reported in Acts and the epistles, particularly the baptism of the household of Lydia (Acts 16:15), the family of the Philippian jailer (Acts 16:33), and the household of Stephanas (1 Cor. 1:16). It is also claimed that Acts 2:39, which declares that the promised blessing of the gospel is "to you and to your children," supports this practice.

In response to these arguments for paedobaptism, the following points may be made:

(1) It is certainly true that baptism and circumcision are in many ways similar, but we must not forget that what they symbolize is also different in some important ways. The old covenant had a *physical, external means of entrance* into the "covenant community." One became a Jew by being born of Jewish parents. Therefore all Jewish males were circumcised. Circumcision was not restricted to people who had true inward spiritual life, but rather was given to *all who lived among the people of Israel*. God said:

> Every male among you shall be circumcised. . . . He that is eight days old among
> you shall be circumcised; every male throughout your generations, whether born in
> your house, or bought with your money from any foreigner who is not of your
> offspring, both *he that is born in your house and he that is bought with your money*, shall
> be circumcised. (Gen. 17:10–13)

It was not only the physical descendants of the people of Israel who were circumcised, but also those *servants* who were purchased by them and lived among them. The presence or absence of inward spiritual life made no difference whatsoever in the question of whether one was circumcised. So "Abraham took Ishmael his son *and all the slaves born in his house or bought with his money*, every male among the men of Abraham's house, and he circumcised the flesh of their foreskins that very day, as God had said to him" (Gen. 17:23; cf. Josh. 5:4).

We should realize that circumcision was given to every male living among the people of Israel even though *true circumcision* is something inward and spiritual: "Real circumcision is a matter of the heart, spiritual and not literal" (Rom. 2:29). Moreover, Paul in the New Testament explicitly states that "not all who are descended from Israel belong to Israel" (Rom. 9:6). But even though there was at the time of the Old Testament (and more fully in the time of the New Testament) a realization of the inward spiritual reality that circumcision was intended to represent, there was *no attempt* to restrict circumcision only to those whose hearts were *actually circumcised spiritually* and who had genuine saving faith. Even among the adult males, circumcision was applied to everyone, not just those who gave evidence of inward faith.

(2) But under the new covenant the situation is very different. The New Testament does not talk about a "covenant community" made up of believers *and* their unbelieving children and relatives and servants who happen to live among them. (In fact, in the discussion of baptism, the phrase "covenant community" as used by paedobaptists often tends to function as a broad and vague term that blurs the differences between the Old Testament and the New Testament on this

matter.) In the New Testament church, the only question that matters is whether one has saving faith and has been spiritually incorporated into the body of Christ, the true church. The only "covenant community" discussed is *the church,* the fellowship of the redeemed.

But how does one become a member of the church? The means of entrance into the church is *voluntary, spiritual, and internal.* One becomes a member of the true church by being *born again* and by having *saving faith,* not by physical birth. It comes about not by an external act, but by internal faith in one's heart. It is certainly true that baptism is the sign of entrance into the church, but this means that it should only be given to those who *give evidence* of membership in the church, only to those who profess faith in Christ.[19]

We should not be surprised that there was a change from the way the covenant community was entered in the Old Testament (physical birth) to the way the church is entered in the New Testament (spiritual birth). There are many analogous changes between the old and new covenants in other areas as well. While the Israelites fed on physical manna in the wilderness, New Testament believers feed on Jesus Christ, the true bread that comes down from heaven (John 6:48–51). The Israelites drank physical water that gushed from the rock in the wilderness, but those who believe in Christ drink of the living water of eternal life that he gives (John 4:10–14). The old covenant had a physical temple to which Israel came for worship, but in the new covenant believers are built into a spiritual temple (1 Peter 2:5). Old covenant believers offered physical sacrifices of animals and crops upon an altar, but New Testament believers offer "spiritual sacrifices acceptable to God through Jesus Christ" (1 Peter 2:5; cf. Heb. 13:15–16). Old covenant believers received from God the physical land of Israel which he had promised to them, but New Testament believers receive "a better country, that is, a heavenly one" (Heb. 11:16). In the same way, in the old covenant those who were the physical seed or descendants of Abraham were members of the people of Israel, but in the New Testament those who are the spiritual "seed" or descendants of Abraham by faith are members of the church (Gal. 3:29; cf. Rom. 4:11–12).

In all these contrasts we see the truth of the distinction that Paul emphasizes between the old covenant and the new covenant. The physical elements and activities of the old covenant were "only a shadow of what is to come," but the true reality, the "substance," is found in the new covenant relationship which we have in Christ (Col. 2:17). Therefore it is consistent with this change of systems that infant (male) children would automatically be circumcised in the old covenant, since their physical descent and physical presence in the community of Jewish people meant that they were members of that community in which faith was not an entrance requirement. But in the new covenant it is appropriate that infants *not* be baptized, and that baptism only be given to those who give evidence of genuine saving faith, because membership in the church is based on an internal spiritual reality, not on physical descent.

---

[19]At this point an advocate of paedobaptism may ask whether we should not have an idea of a "covenant community" in the New Testament church which is broader than the church and includes unbelieving children who belong to church families. But the New Testament speaks of no such community, nor does it give indication that unbelieving children of believing parents are members of the new covenant. And it certainly does not speak of baptism as a sign of entrance into such a broader group. Baptism symbolizes new birth and entrance into the church.

(3) The examples of household baptisms in the New Testament are really not decisive for one position or another. When we look at the actual examples more closely, we see that in a number of them there are indications of saving faith on the part of all of those baptized. For example, it is true that the family of the Philippian jailer was baptized (Acts 16:33), but it is also true that Paul and Silas "spoke the word of the Lord to him and *to all that were in his house*" (Acts 16:32). If the Word of the Lord was spoken to all in the house, there is an assumption that all were old enough to understand the word and believe it. Moreover, after the family had been baptized, we read that the Philippian jailer "*rejoiced with all his household* that he had believed in God" (Acts 16:34). So we have not only a household baptism but also a household reception of the Word of God and a household rejoicing in faith in God. These facts suggest quite strongly that the entire household had individually come to faith in Christ.

With regard to the fact that Paul baptized "the household of Stephanas" (1 Cor. 1:16), we must also note that Paul says at the end of 1 Corinthians that "the household of Stephanas were the first converts in Achaia, and they have devoted themselves to the service of the saints" (1 Cor. 16:15). So they were not only baptized; they were also converted and had worked at serving other believers. Once again the example of *household baptism* gives indication of *household faith*.

In fact, there are other instances where baptism is not mentioned but where we see explicit testimony to the fact that an entire household had come to faith. After Jesus healed the official's son, we read that the father "himself believed, *and all his household*" (John 4:53). Similarly, when Paul preached at Corinth, "Crispus, the ruler of the synagogue, *believed* in the Lord, *together with all his household*" (Acts 18:8).

This means that of all the examples of "household baptisms" in the New Testament, the only one that does not have some indication of household faith as well is Acts 16:14–15, speaking of Lydia: "The Lord opened her heart to give heed to what was said by Paul. And when she was baptized, with her household." The text simply does not contain any information about whether there were infants in her household or not. It is ambiguous and certainly not weighty evidence for infant baptism. It must be considered inconclusive in itself.

With regard to Peter's statement at Pentecost that "the promise is to you and to your children," we should note that the sentence continues as follows: "For the promise is to you and to your children and to all that are far off, *every one whom the Lord our God calls to him*" (Acts 2:39). Moreover, the same paragraph specifies not that believers and unbelieving children were baptized, but that "*those who received his word* were baptized, and there were added that day about three thousand souls" (Acts 2:41).

(4) A further argument in objection to the paedobaptist position can be made when we ask the simple question, "What does baptism *do?*" In other words, we might ask, "What does it actually accomplish? What benefit does it bring?"

Roman Catholics have a clear answer to this question: Baptism *causes* regeneration. And Baptists have a clear answer: Baptism *symbolizes* the fact that inward regeneration has occurred. But paedobaptists cannot adopt either of these answers. They do not want to say that baptism causes regeneration, nor are they able to say (with respect to infants) that it symbolizes a regeneration that has already occurred.[20] The only alternative seems to be to say that it symbolizes a regeneration that will occur in the future, when the infant is old enough to come to saving faith. But even that is not quite accurate, because it is not certain that the infant will be regenerated in the future—some infants who are baptized never come to saving faith later. So the most accurate paedobaptist explanation of what baptism symbolizes is that it symbolizes *probable future regeneration*.[21] It does not cause regeneration, nor does it symbolize actual regeneration; therefore it must be understood as symbolizing probable regeneration at some time in the future.

But at this point it seems apparent that the paedobaptist understanding of baptism is quite different from that of the New Testament. The New Testament never views baptism as something that symbolizes a probable future regeneration. The New Testament authors do not say, "Can anyone forbid water for baptizing those who will probably someday be saved?" (cf. Acts 10:47), or, "As many of you as were baptized into Christ will probably someday put on Christ" (cf. Gal. 3:27), or "Do you not know that all of us who have been baptized into Christ Jesus will probably someday be baptized into his death?" (cf. Rom. 6:3). This is simply not the way the New Testament speaks of baptism. Baptism in the New Testament is a sign of being born again, being cleansed from sin, and beginning the Christian life. It seems fitting to reserve this sign for those who give evidence that that is actually true in their lives.

One other perspective on the symbolism of baptism is given by Michael Green.[22] He says:

> Infant baptism stresses the objectivity of the gospel. It points to the solid achievement of Christ crucified and risen, whether or not we respond to it. . . . Not that we gain anything from it unless we repent and believe. But it is the standing demonstration that our salvation does not depend on our own very fallible faith; it depends on what God has done for us. (p. 76)

He goes on to say:

> Infant baptism stresses the initiative of God in salvation. . . . Should it be attached primarily to man's response, or to God's initiative? That is the heart of the question. . . . For the Baptist, baptism primarily bears witness to what *we do* in responding to the grace of God. For the paedobaptist, it primarily bears witness to what *God has done* to make it all possible. (pp. 76–77, emphasis his)

But several points can be noted in response to Green. (a) His analysis at this point overlooks the fact that baptism does not *only* symbolize Christ's death and resurrection; as we have seen in the foregoing analysis of New Testament texts, it *also* symbolizes the application of redemption to us, as a result of our response of faith. Baptism pictures the fact that we have been united with Christ in his death

---

[20]However, some Protestant paedobaptists will *presume* that regeneration has occurred (and the evidence will be seen later). Others, including many Episcopalians and Lutherans, would say that regeneration occurs at the time of baptism.

[21]This is not a quotation from any specific paedobaptist writer, but is my own conclusion from the logic of the paedobaptist position, which would seem to require this understanding of what paedobaptism signifies with respect to regeneration.

[22]Michael Green, *Baptism: Its Purpose, Practice, and Power* (London: Hodder and Stoughton, and Downers Grove, Ill.: InterVarsity Press, 1987). This book contains an excellent statement of a paedobaptist position, and also contains much helpful analysis of the biblical teaching about baptism which both sides could endorse.

and resurrection, and the washing with water symbolizes that we have been cleansed from our sins. In saying that the paedobaptist stresses God's initiative and the Baptist stresses man's response, Green has presented the reader with two incorrect alternatives from which to choose, because baptism pictures both of these and more. Baptism pictures (i) Christ's redemptive work, (ii) my response in faith (as I come to be baptized), and (iii) God's application of the benefits of redemption to my life. Believers' baptism pictures all three aspects (not just my faith, as Green suggests), but according to Green's view paedobaptism pictures only the first one. It is not a question of which is "primary"; it is a question of which view of baptism includes all that baptism stands for.

(b) When Green says that our salvation does not depend on our faith but on God's work, the expression "depend on" is capable of various interpretations. If "depend on" means "what we rely on," then of course both sides would agree that we rely on Christ's work, not on our faith. If "depend on" means that faith does not have any merit in itself whereby we can earn favor with God, then also both sides would agree. But if "depend on" means it makes no difference to our salvation whether we believe or not, then neither side would agree: Green himself says in the previous sentence that baptism does us no good unless we repent and believe. Therefore if baptism in any way represents the application of redemption to a person's life, then it is not enough to practice a form of baptism that *only* pictures Christ's death and resurrection; we should also picture our response in faith and the subsequent application of redemption to us. By contrast, on Green's view, there is a real danger of portraying a view (which Green would disagree with) that people will have salvation applied to them by God whether they believe or not.

(5) Finally, those who advocate believers' baptism often express concern about the practical consequences of paedobaptism. They argue that the practice of paedobaptism in actual church life frequently leads persons baptized in infancy to presume that they have been regenerated, and thereby they fail to feel the urgency of their need to come to personal faith in Christ. Over a period of years, this tendency is likely to result in more and more *unconverted* members of the "covenant community"—members who are not truly members of Christ's church. Of course, this would not make a paedobaptist church a false church, but it would make it a less-pure church, and one that will frequently be fighting tendencies toward liberal doctrine or other kinds of unbelief that are brought in by the unregenerate sector of the membership.

## C. The Effect of Baptism

We have argued above that baptism symbolizes regeneration or spiritual rebirth. But does it only symbolize? Or is there some way in which it is also a "means of grace," that is, a means that the Holy Spirit uses to bring blessing to people? We have already discussed this question in the previous chapter,[23] so here it only is necessary to say that when baptism is properly carried out then of course it brings some spiritual benefit to believers as well. There is the blessing of God's favor that comes with all obedience, as well as the joy that comes through public profession

---

[23]See chapter 48, pp. 953-54.

of one's faith, and the reassurance of having a clear physical picture of dying and rising with Christ and of washing away sins. Certainly the Lord gave us baptism to strengthen and encourage our faith—and it should do so for everyone who is baptized and for every believer who witnesses a baptism.

## D. The Necessity of Baptism

While we recognize that Jesus commanded baptism (Matt. 28:19), as did the apostles (Acts 2:38), we should not say that baptism is *necessary* for salvation.[24] This question was discussed to some extent above under the response to the Roman Catholic view of baptism. To say that baptism or any other action is *necessary* for salvation is to say that we are not justified by faith alone, but by faith plus a certain "work," the work of baptism. The apostle Paul would have opposed the idea that baptism is necessary for salvation just as strongly as he opposed the similar idea that circumcision was necessary for salvation (see Gal. 5:1–12).

Those who argue that baptism is necessary for salvation often point to Mark 16:16: "*He who believes and is baptized will be saved;* but he who does not believe will be condemned.*" But the very evident answer to this is simply to say that the verse says nothing about those who *believe* and *are not baptized.* The verse is simply talking about general cases without making a pedantic qualification for the unusual case of someone who believes and is not baptized. But certainly the verse should not be pressed into service and made to speak of something it is not talking about.[25]

More to the point is Jesus' statement to the dying thief on the cross, "Today you will be with me in Paradise" (Luke 23:43). The thief could not be baptized before he died on the cross, but he was certainly saved that day. Moreover, the force of this point cannot be evaded by arguing that the thief was saved under the old covenant (under which baptism was not necessary to salvation), because the new covenant took effect at the death of Jesus (see Heb. 9:17), and Jesus died *before* either of the two thieves who were crucified with him (see John 19:32–33).

Another reason why baptism is not necessary for salvation is that our justification from sins takes place at the point of saving faith, not at the point of water baptism, which usually occurs later.[26] But if a person is already justified and has sins forgiven eternally at the point of saving faith, then baptism is not necessary for forgiveness of sins, or for the bestowal of new spiritual life.[27]

Baptism, then, is not necessary for salvation. But it is necessary if we are to be obedient to Christ, for he commanded baptism for all who believe in him.

---

[24]At this point I am differing not only with Roman Catholic teaching, but also with the teaching of several Protestant denominations that teach that, in some sense, baptism is necessary for salvation. Although there are different nuances in their teaching, such a position is held by many Episcopalians, many Lutherans, and by the Churches of Christ.

[25]Moreover, it is doubtful whether this verse should be used in support of a theological position at all, since there are many ancient manuscripts that do not have this verse (or Mark 16:9–20), and it seems most likely that this verse was not in the gospel as Mark originally wrote it. (See discussion of Mark 16:9–20 in chapter 17, p. 365.)

[26]See discussion of justification in chapter 36, pp. 722–35.

[27]See chapter 34, pp. 699–708, for a discussion of regeneration.

## E. The Age for Baptism

Those who are convinced by the arguments for believers' baptism must then begin to ask, "How old should children be before they are baptized?"

The most direct answer is that they should be old enough to give a *believable* profession of faith. It is impossible to set a precise age that will apply to every child, but when parents see convincing evidence of genuine spiritual life, and also some degree of understanding regarding the meaning of trusting in Christ, then baptism is appropriate. Of course, this will require careful administration by the church, as well as a good explanation by parents in their homes. The exact age for baptism will vary from child to child, and somewhat from church to church as well.[28]

## F. Remaining Questions

**1. Do Churches Need to Be Divided Over Baptism?** In spite of many years of division over this question among Protestants, is there a way in which Christians who differ on baptism can demonstrate greater unity of fellowship? And is there a way that progress can be made in bringing the church closer to unity on this question?

One way forward could be for paedobaptists and advocates of believers' baptism both to come to a common admission that baptism is not a major doctrine of the faith, and that they are willing to live with each other's views on this matter and not allow differences over baptism to be a cause for division within the body of Christ.[29] Specifically, this would mean allowing both views of baptism to be taught and practiced in denominations on both sides of the question.

No doubt this would be a difficult thing to do both for Baptist denominations and for paedobaptist denominations, because they have long traditions of arguing

---

[28]I participated in baptizing my own three children at a time when each was between seven and ten years old and showed a fair degree of understanding of the gospel together with genuine evidence of faith in Christ. In all three cases, I think they could have been baptized somewhat earlier, but we delayed out of deference to the ordinary pattern followed by the churches we were in, whereby children under seven were not usually baptized. (Among Baptists in the United Kingdom it is customary to wait until children are somewhat older than this, however.)

[29]I realize that some readers will object to this sentence and will say that baptism is *very important* because of what the differing positions represent: differing views of the nature of the church. Many Baptists would argue that *practicing* infant baptism is inherently inconsistent with the idea of a church made up of believers only, and many paedobaptists would argue that *not practicing* infant baptism is inherently inconsistent with the idea of a covenant community that includes the children of believers.

I would encourage those who reason this way to consider how much they hold in common with evangelical believers on the other side of this issue—not necessarily with those far from them on other matters as well, but especially with those on the other side who agree with them on most other aspects of the Christian life. Many Baptists *do* encourage and demonstrate a valued place for their children within their churches, and many paedobaptists *do* pray for the salvation of their *baptized* children with the same fervency with which Baptist parents pray for the salvation of their *unbaptized* children. Regarding church membership, evangelical paedobaptists *do* require a believable profession of faith before children can become full members of the church (their term is "communicant members'; that is, those who take Communion). They also require a believable profession of faith before any adults are allowed to join the church.

When these procedures are functioning well, both Baptists and paedobaptists use very similar procedures as they seek to have a church membership consisting of believers only, and both love and teach and pray for their children as most precious members of the larger church family who they hope will someday become true members of the body of Christ.

for one side or the other on this question. Certainly Christians are entitled to make up their own minds regarding baptism, but it does not seem appropriate that denominational divisions should depend on and reinforce these differences, nor does it seem right that churches require one view or another on baptism for those who wish to be ordained or to function as teachers within the church.[30] Specifically, this would mean that Baptist churches would have to be willing to allow into membership those who had been baptized as infants and whose conviction of conscience, after careful consideration, is that their infant baptism was valid and should not be repeated. Of course, Baptist churches could be free to teach and to attempt to persuade prospective church members that they should be baptized as believers, but if some, after careful consideration, are simply not persuaded, it does not seem appropriate to make this a barrier to membership. What good is accomplished by such a barrier? And certainly much harm can be accomplished in failure to demonstrate the unity of the church and in barring from full participation in the church those whom the Lord has in fact brought into that fellowship.

On the other hand, those who believe in paedobaptism would have to agree not to put undue pressure upon parents who do not wish to have their infants baptized and not to count those parents as somehow disobedient to the Lord. There might need to be a willingness to have some kind of brief ceremony of dedication of children to the Lord shortly after they are born, instead of a ceremony of baptism, if the parents so desired. And of course both sides would have to agree not to make one view on baptism a criterion for church office or for ordination.[31]

If such concessions in actual practice were made by both sides on this question, the issue might in fact diminish the level of controversy within a generation, and baptism might eventually cease to be a point of division at all among Christians.

**2. Who Can Baptize?** Finally, we may ask, "Who can perform the ceremony of baptism? Can only ordained clergy perform this ceremony?"

We should recognize here that Scripture simply does not specify any restrictions on who can perform the ceremony of baptism. Those churches that have a special priesthood through which certain actions (and blessings) come (such as Roman Catholics, and to some extent Anglicans) will wish to insist that only properly ordained clergy should baptize in ordinary circumstances (though exceptions could be made in unusual circumstances). But if we truly believe in the priesthood of all believers (see 1 Peter 2:4–10), then there seems to be no need *in principle* to restrict the right to perform baptism only to ordained clergy.

However, another consideration arises: Since baptism is the sign of entrance into the body of Christ, the church (cf. 1 Cor. 12:13 on inward spiritual

[30]In the United States, the Evangelical Free Church denomination has functioned quite well for many decades while allowing both paedobaptists and advocates of believers' baptism to be members of their churches and to be ordained as pastors in their churches.

[31]Note that my proposed first steps toward less divisiveness over this question do not include asking individuals on either side to act in a way that would violate their own personal convictions: I am not suggesting that those who hold a Baptist view personally begin baptizing infants when the parents request it, or that those who hold a paedobaptist view personally begin baptizing those who make a profession of faith and request baptism, even though they had been baptized as infants.

baptism), then it seems appropriate that it be done *within the fellowship of the church* wherever possible, so that the church as a whole can rejoice with the person being baptized and so that the faith of all believers in that church might be built up.[32] Moreover, since baptism is a sign of beginning the Christian life and therefore of beginning life in the true church as well, it is fitting that the local church be assembled to give testimony to this fact and to give visible welcome to the baptized person. Also, in order that the people being baptized have a right understanding of what actually is happening, it is right for the church to safeguard the practice of baptism and keep it from abuse. Finally, if baptism is the sign of entering the fellowship of the visible church, then it seems appropriate that some officially designated representative or representatives of the church be selected to administer it. For these reasons it is usually the ordained clergy who baptize, but there seems to be no reason why the church from time to time, and where it deems it appropriate, might not call on other church officers or mature believers to baptize new converts. For example, someone effective in evangelism in a local church may be an appropriately designated person to baptize people who have come to Christ through the practice of that person's evangelistic ministry. (Note in Acts 8:12 that Philip preached the gospel in Samaria and then apparently baptized those who came to faith in Christ.)

## QUESTIONS FOR PERSONAL APPLICATION

1. Have you been baptized? When? If you were baptized as a believer, what was the effect of the baptism on your Christian life (if any)? If you were baptized as an infant, what effect did the knowledge of your baptism have in your own thinking when you eventually learned that you had been baptized as an infant?

2. What aspects of the meaning of baptism have you come to appreciate more as a result of reading this chapter (if any)? What aspects of the meaning of baptism would you like to see taught more clearly in your church?

3. When baptisms occur in your church, are they a time of rejoicing and praise to God? What do you think is happening to the person being baptized at that moment (if anything)? What do you think should be happening?

4. Have you modified your own view on the question of infant baptism versus believers' baptism as a result of reading this chapter? In what way?

5. What practical suggestions can you make for helping to overcome the differences among Christians on the question of baptism?

6. How can baptism be an effective help to evangelism in your church? Have you seen it function in this way?

---

[32]The fact that baptism is an outward sign of *entrance* into the church, the body of Christ, would also make it appropriate to require baptism before someone is counted as a member of a local church.

## SPECIAL TERMS

believable profession of faith        *ex opere operato*
believers' baptism                    immersion
covenant community                    paedobaptism

## BIBLIOGRAPHY

(For an explanation of this bibliography see the note on the bibliography to
chapter 1, p. 38. Complete bibliographical data may be found on pp. 1223–29.)

### Sections in Evangelical Systematic Theologies

1. Anglican (Episcopalian)
   - 1882–92   Litton, 459–74
   - 1930      Thomas, 371–87, 521–22
2. Arminian (Wesleyan or Methodist)
   - 1875–76   Pope, 3:310–24
   - 1892–94   Miley, 2:395–410
   - 1940      Wiley, 3:161–89
   - 1960      Purkiser, 409–11
   - 1983      Carter, 2:616
3. Baptist
   - 1767      Gill, 4:621–47
   - 1907      Strong, 931–59
   - 1983–85   Erickson, 1089–1106
4. Dispensational
   - 1947      Chafer, 7:32–43
   - 1949      Thiessen, 319–22
   - 1986      Ryrie, 421–25
5. Lutheran
   - 1917–24   Pieper, 7:253–89
   - 1934      Mueller, 486–505
6. Reformed (or Presbyterian)
   - 1559      Calvin, 2:1303–58 (4.15–16)
   - 1861      Heppe, 611–26
   - 1871–73   Hodge, 3:526–611
   - 1878      Dabney, 758–99
   - 1887–1921 Warfield, *SWW*, 1:325–31
   - 1889      Shedd, 2b:574–87
   - 1937–66   Murray, *CW*, 2:370–75
   - 1938      Berkhof, 622–43
   - 1962      Buswell, 2:241–66

7. Renewal (or charismatic/Pentecostal)
   1988–92    Williams, 2:278–87, 3:136–39, 221–41

## Sections in Representative Roman Catholic Systematic Theologies

1. Roman Catholic: Traditional
      1955    Ott, 350–61
2. Roman Catholic: Post-Vatican II
      1980    McBrien, 1:248–52; 2:349–54

## Other Works

Beasley-Murray, G. R. *Baptism in the New Testament*. Grand Rapids: Eerdmans, 1962.

————, and R. F. G. Burnish. "Baptism." In *EDT*, pp. 69–73.

Berkouwer, G. C. *The Sacraments*. Trans. by Hugo Bekker. Grand Rapids: Eerdmans, 1969.

Bridge, Donald, and David Phypers. *The Water That Divides*. Downers Grove, Ill.: InterVarsity Press, 1977.

Bromiley, G. W. "Baptism." In *EDT*, pp. 112–14.

————. *The Baptism of Infants*. London: Vine Books, 1955.

————. *Children of Promise*. Grand Rapids: Eerdmans, 1979.

Brown, R. "Baptist Theology." In *EDT*, pp. 75–76.

Cottrell, Jack. *Baptism: A Biblical Study*. Joplin, Mo.: College Press, 1989. (Written from a Churches of Christ perspective, understanding baptism as necessary for salvation.)

Green, Michael. *Baptism: Its Purpose, Practice, and Power*. London: Hodder and Stoughton, and Downers Grove, Ill.: InterVarsity Press, 1987.

Jewett, Paul K. *Infant Baptism and the Covenant of Grace*. Grand Rapids: Eerdmans, 1978.

Kingdon, David. *Children of Abraham: A Reformed Baptist View of Baptism, the Covenant, and Children*. Haywards Heath, England: Carey Publications, 1973.

Marcel, Pierre Ch. *The Biblical Doctrine of Infant Baptism*. Trans. by Philip E. Hughes. London: J. Clarke, 1953.

Murray, John. *Christian Baptism*. Philadelphia: Presbyterian and Reformed, 1970.

Watson, T. E. *Baptism Not for Infants*. Worthing, England: Henry E. Walter, 1962.

## SCRIPTURE MEMORY PASSAGE

**Romans 6:3–4:** *Do you not know that all of us who have been baptized into Christ Jesus were baptized into his death? We were buried therefore with him by baptism into death, so that as Christ was raised from the dead by the glory of the Father, we too might walk in newness of life.*

# HYMN

## "Up From the Grave He Arose"

There are few familiar hymns written specifically to be used during a baptismal service. It would be helpful for the church if more were written.

This hymn is appropriate for the topic of baptism, because it speaks triumphantly of Christ's resurrection. When we sing it, we should realize that Jesus not only triumphed over death and the grave for himself, but also for all of us who believe in him. This fact is vividly symbolized in the ceremony of baptism.

Alternative hymn: Most paedobaptist hymnals contain hymns to be sung at the baptism of infants, but I did not find any that were widely familiar.

Low in the grave he lay—Jesus, my Savior,
Waiting the coming day—Jesus, my Lord.

*Refrain:*
Up from the grave he arose,
    With a mighty triumph o'er his foes.
He arose a Victor from the dark domain,
    And he lives forever with his saints to reign.
He arose! He arose! Hallelujah! Christ arose!

Vainly they watch his bed—Jesus, my Savior;
Vainly they seal the dead—Jesus, my Lord.

Death cannot keep his prey—Jesus, my Savior;
He tore the bars away—Jesus, my Lord.

AUTHOR: ROBERT LOWREY, 1874.

# Chapter 50

# The Lord's Supper

*What is the meaning of the Lord's Supper?*
*How should it be observed?*

## EXPLANATION AND SCRIPTURAL BASIS

The Lord Jesus instituted two ordinances (or sacraments) to be observed by the church. The previous chapter discussed *baptism,* an ordinance that is only observed once by each person, as a sign of the beginning of his or her Christian life. This chapter discusses *the Lord's Supper,* an ordinance that is to be observed repeatedly throughout our Christian lives, as a sign of continuing in fellowship with Christ.

### A. Background in the History of Redemption

Jesus instituted the Lord's Supper in the following way:

Now as they were eating, Jesus took bread, and blessed, and broke it, and gave it to the disciples and said, "Take, eat; this is my body." And he took a cup, and when he had given thanks he gave it to them, saying, "Drink of it, all of you; for this is my blood of the covenant, which is poured out for many for the forgiveness of sins. I tell you I shall not drink again of this fruit of the vine until that day when I drink it new with you in my Father's kingdom. (Matt. 26:26–29)

Paul adds the following sentences from the tradition he received (1 Cor. 11:23):

This cup is the new covenant in my blood. Do this, as often as you drink it, in remembrance of me. (1 Cor. 11:25)

Is there a background to this ceremony in the Old Testament? It seems that there is, for there were instances of eating and drinking in the presence of God in the old covenant as well. For example, when the people of Israel were camped before Mount Sinai, just after God had given the Ten Commandments, God called the leaders of Israel up to the mountain to meet with him:

Then Moses and Aaron, Nadab, and Abihu, and seventy of the elders of Israel went up, and they saw the God of Israel . . . *they beheld God, and ate and drank.* (Ex. 24:9–11)

Moreover, every year the people of Israel were to tithe (give one-tenth of) all their crops. Then the law of Moses specified,

*Before the LORD your God,* in the place which he will choose, to make his name dwell there, *you shall eat the tithe of your grain, of your wine, and of your oil, and the firstlings of your herd and flock;* that you may learn to fear the LORD your God always. . . . *You shall eat there before the LORD your God and rejoice,* you and your household. (Deut. 14:23, 26)

But even earlier than that, God had put Adam and Eve in the Garden of Eden and given them all of its abundance to eat (except the fruit of the tree of the knowledge of good and evil). Since there was no sin in that situation, and since God had created them for fellowship with himself and to glorify himself, then every meal that Adam and Eve ate would have been a meal of feasting in the presence of the Lord.

When this fellowship in God's presence was later broken by sin, God still allowed some meals (such as the tithe of fruits mentioned above) that the people would eat in his presence. These meals were a partial restoration of the fellowship with God that Adam and Eve enjoyed before the Fall, even though it was marred by sin. But the fellowship of eating in the presence of the Lord that we find in the Lord's Supper is far better. The Old Testament sacrificial meals continually pointed to the fact that sins were not yet paid for, because the sacrifices in them were repeated year after year, and because they looked forward to the Messiah who was to come and take away sin (see Heb. 10:1–4). The Lord's Supper, however, reminds us that Jesus' payment for our sins has already been accomplished, so we now eat in the Lord's presence with great rejoicing.

Yet even the Lord's Supper looks forward to a more wonderful fellowship meal in God's presence in the future, when the fellowship of Eden will be restored and there will be even greater joy, because those who eat in God's presence will be forgiven sinners now confirmed in righteousness, never able to sin again. That future time of great rejoicing and eating in the presence of God is hinted at by Jesus when he says, "I tell you I shall not drink again of this fruit of the vine *until that day when I drink it new with you* in my Father's kingdom" (Matt. 26:29). We are told more explicitly in Revelation about the marriage supper of the Lamb: "And the angel said to me, 'Write this: Blessed are those who are invited to the marriage supper of the Lamb'" (Rev. 19:9). This will be a time of great rejoicing in the presence of the Lord, as well as a time of reverence and awe before him.

From Genesis to Revelation, then, God's aim has been to bring his people into fellowship with himself, and one of the great joys of experiencing that fellowship is the fact that we can eat and drink in the presence of the Lord. It would be healthy for the church today to recapture a more vivid sense of God's presence at the table of the Lord.

## B. The Meaning of the Lord's Supper

The meaning of the Lord's Supper is complex, rich, and full. There are several things symbolized and affirmed in the Lord's Supper.

**1. Christ's Death.** When we participate in the Lord's supper we symbolize the death of Christ because our actions give a picture of his death for us. When the bread is broken it symbolizes the breaking of Christ's body, and when the cup is poured out it symbolizes the pouring out of Christ's blood for us. This is why participating in the Lord's Supper is also a kind of proclamation: "For as often as you eat this bread and drink the cup, *you proclaim the Lord's death* until he comes" (1 Cor. 11:26).

**2. Our Participation in the Benefits of Christ's Death.** Jesus commanded his disciples, "Take, eat; this is my body" (Matt. 26:26). As we individually reach out and take the cup for ourselves, each one of us is by that action proclaiming, "I am taking the benefits of Christ's death to myself." When we do this we give a symbol of the fact that we participate in or share in the benefits earned for us by the death of Jesus.

**3. Spiritual Nourishment.** Just as ordinary food nourishes our physical bodies, so the bread and wine of the Lord's Supper give nourishment to us. But they also picture the fact that there is spiritual nourishment and refreshment that Christ is giving to our souls—indeed, the ceremony that Jesus instituted is in its very nature designed to teach us this. Jesus said,

> Unless you eat the flesh of the Son of man and drink his blood, you have no life in you; he who eats my flesh and drinks my blood has eternal life, and I will raise him up at the last day. For my flesh is food indeed, and my blood is drink indeed. He who eats my flesh and drinks my blood abides in me, and I in him. As the living Father sent me, and I live because of the Father, so he who eats me will live because of me. (John 6:53–57)

Certainly Jesus is not speaking of a literal eating of his flesh and blood. But if he is not speaking of a literal eating and drinking, then he must have in mind a spiritual participation in the benefits of the redemption he earns. This spiritual nourishment, so necessary for our souls, is both symbolized and experienced in our participation in the Lord's Supper.

**4. The Unity of Believers.** When Christians participate in the Lord's Supper together they also give a clear sign of their unity with one another. In fact, Paul says, "Because there is one bread, we who are many are one body, for we all partake of the one bread" (1 Cor. 10:17).

When we put these four things together, we begin to realize some of the rich meaning of the Lord's Supper: when I participate I come into the presence of Christ; I remember that he died for me; I participate in the benefits of his death; I receive spiritual nourishment; and I am united with all other believers who participate in this Supper. What great cause for thanksgiving and joy is to be found in this Supper of the Lord!

But in addition to these truths visibly portrayed by the Lord's Supper, the fact that Christ has instituted this ceremony for us means that by it he is also promising or affirming certain things to us as well. When we participate in the Lord's Supper, we should be reminded again and again of the following affirmations that Christ is making to us:

**5. Christ Affirms His Love for Me.** The fact that I am able to participate in the Lord's Supper—indeed, that Jesus *invites me* to come—is a vivid reminder and visual reassurance that Jesus Christ loves *me*, individually and personally. When I come to take of the Lord's Supper I thereby find reassurance again and again of Christ's personal love for me.

**6. Christ Affirms That All the Blessings of Salvation Are Reserved for Me.** When I come at Christ's invitation to the Lord's Supper, the fact that he has invited me into his presence assures me that he has abundant blessings for me. In this Supper I am actually eating and drinking at a foretaste of the great banquet table of the King. I come to his table as a member of his *eternal* family. When the Lord welcomes me to this table, he assures me that he will welcome me to all the other blessings of earth and heaven as well, and especially to the great marriage supper of the Lamb, at which a place has been reserved for me.

**7. I Affirm My Faith in Christ.** Finally, as I take the bread and cup for myself, by my actions I am proclaiming, "I need you and trust you, Lord Jesus, to forgive my sins and give life and health to my soul, for only by your broken body and shed blood can I be saved." In fact, as I partake in the breaking of the bread when I eat it and the pouring out of the cup when I drink from it, I proclaim again and again that *my sins* were part of the cause of Jesus' suffering and death. In this way sorrow, joy, thanksgiving, and deep love for Christ are richly intermingled in the beauty of the Lord's Supper.

## C. How Is Christ Present in the Lord's Supper?

**1. The Roman Catholic View: Transubstantiation.** According to the teaching of the Roman Catholic Church, the bread and wine *actually become* the body and blood of Christ. This happens at the moment the priest says, "This is my body" during the celebration of the mass. At the same time as the priest says this, the bread is raised up (elevated) and adored. This action of elevating the bread and pronouncing it to be Christ's body can only be performed by a priest.

When this happens, according to Roman Catholic teaching, grace is imparted to those present *ex opere operato*, that is, "by the work performed,"[1] but the amount of grace dispensed is in proportion to the subjective disposition of the recipient of grace.[2] Moreover, every time the mass is celebrated, the sacrifice of Christ is repeated (in some sense), and the Catholic church is careful to affirm that this is a real sacrifice, even though it is not the same as the sacrifice that Christ paid on the cross.

So Ludwig Ott's *Fundamentals of Catholic Dogma* teaches as follows:

---

[1] See discussion of the term *ex opere operato* in relationship to baptism in chapter 49 above, p. 972.
[2] Ludwig Ott, *Fundamentals of Catholic Dogma*, says, "Since the measure of the grace conferred *ex opere operato* is in proportion to the subjective disposition of the recipient, the reception of Holy Communion should be preceded by a good preparation, and an appropriate thanksgiving should follow it. . . . An unworthy Communion is a sacrilege" (p. 399).

Christ becomes present in the Sacrament of the Altar by the transformation of the whole substance of the bread into His Body and of the whole substance of the wine into His Blood. . . . This transformation is called Transubstantiation. (p. 379)

The power of consecration resides in a validly consecrated priest only. (p. 397)

The Worship of Adoration (Latria) must be given to Christ present in the Eucharist. . . . It follows from the wholeness and permanence of the Real Presence that the absolute worship of adoration (Cultus Latriae) is due to Christ present in the Eucharist. (p. 387)[3]

In Catholic teaching, because the elements of bread and wine literally become the body and blood of Christ, the church for many centuries did not allow the lay people to drink from the cup of the Lord's Supper (for fear that the blood of Christ would be spilled) but only to eat the bread.[4] Ott's textbook tells us,

Communion under two forms is not necessary for any individual member of the Faithful, either by reason of Divine precept or as a means of salvation. . . . The reason is that Christ is whole and entire under each species. . . . The abolition of the reception from the chalice in the Middle Ages (12th and 13th centuries) was enjoined for practical reasons, particularly danger of profanation of the Sacrament. (p. 397)

With respect to the actual sacrifice of Christ in the mass, Ott's textbook says,

The Holy Mass is a true and proper Sacrifice. (p. 402)

In the Sacrifice of the Mass and in the Sacrifice of the Cross the Sacrificial Gift and the Primary Sacrificing Priest are identical; only the nature and mode of the offering are different. . . . The Sacrificial Gift is the Body and Blood of Christ. . . . The Primary Sacrificing Priest is Jesus Christ, who utilizes the human priest as His servant and representative and fulfills the consecration through him. According to the Thomistic view, *in every Mass Christ also performs an actual immediate sacrificial activity* which, however, must not be conceived as a totality of many successive acts but as one single uninterrupted sacrificial act of the Transfigured Christ.

The purpose of the Sacrifice is the same in the Sacrifice of the Mass as in the Sacrifice of the Cross; primarily the glorification of God, secondarily atonement, thanksgiving and appeal. (p. 408)

*As a propitiatory sacrifice . . . the Sacrifice of the Mass effects the remission of sins and the punishment for sins;* as a sacrifice of appeal . . . it brings about the conferring of supernatural and natural gifts. The Eucharistic Sacrifice of propitiation can, as the Council of Trent expressly asserted, be offered, not merely for the living, but also for the poor souls in Purgatory. (pp. 412–13)

In response to the Roman Catholic teaching on the Lord's Supper, it must be said that it first fails to recognize the symbolic character of Jesus' statements when he declared, "This is my body," or, "This is my blood." Jesus spoke in symbolic ways many times when speaking of himself. He said, for example, *"I am the true*

---

[3]The word *eucharist* simply means the Lord's Supper. (It is derived from the Greek word *eucharistia*, "giving of thanks." The related verb *eucharisteō*, "to give thanks," is found in the biblical records of the Last Supper in Matt. 26:27; Mark 14:23; Luke 22:19; and 1 Cor. 11:24: "when he had *given thanks*.") The term *eucharist* is often used by Roman Catholics and frequently by Episcopalians as well. Among many Protestant churches the term *Communion* is commonly used to refer to the Lord's Supper.

[4]However, since the Vatican II council (1962–65), administration of both the bread and the wine to laypersons has been allowed, but it is not always practiced.

*vine"* (John 15:1), or *"I am the door;* if any one enters by me, he will be saved" (John 10:9), or "I am the bread which came down from heaven" (John 6:41). In a similar way, when Jesus says, "This is my body," he means it in a symbolic way, not in an actual, literal, physical way. In fact, as he was sitting with his disciples holding the bread, the bread was in his hand but it was distinct from his body, and that was, of course, evident to the disciples. None of the disciples present would have thought that the loaf of bread that Jesus held in his hand was actually his physical body, for they could see his body before their eyes. They would have naturally understood Jesus' statement in a symbolic way. Similarly, when Jesus said, *"This cup* which is poured out for you *is the new covenant* in my blood" (Luke 22:20), he certainly did not mean that the cup was actually the new covenant, but that the cup *represented* the new covenant.

Moreover, the Roman Catholic view fails to recognize the clear New Testament teaching on the *finality* and *completeness* of Christ's sacrifice once for all time for our sins: the book of Hebrews emphasizes this many times, as when it says, *"Nor was it to offer himself repeatedly,* as the high priest enters the Holy Place yearly with blood not his own; for then he would have had to suffer repeatedly since the foundation of the world. But as it is, he has appeared *once* for all at the end of the age to put away sin by the sacrifice of himself . . . Christ, having been offered *once* to bear the sins of many" (Heb. 9:25–28). To say that Christ's sacrifice continues or is repeated in the mass has been, since the Reformation, one of the most objectionable Roman Catholic doctrines from the standpoint of Protestants. When we realize that Christ's sacrifice for our sins is finished and completed (*"It is finished,"* John 19:30; cf. Heb. 1:3), it gives great assurance to us that our sins are all paid for, and there remains no sacrifice yet to be paid. But the idea of a continuation of Christ's sacrifice destroys our assurance that the payment has been made by Christ and accepted by God the Father, and that there is "no condemnation" (Rom. 8:1) now remaining for us.

For Protestants the idea that the mass is in any sense a repetition of the death of Christ seems to mark a return to the repeated sacrifices of the old covenant, which were "a reminder of sin year after year" (Heb. 10:3). Instead of the assurance of complete forgiveness of sins through the once for all sacrifice of Christ (Heb. 10:12), the idea that the mass is a repeated sacrifice gives a constant reminder of sins and remaining guilt to be atoned for week after week.[5]

With regard to the teaching that only priests can officiate at the Lord's Supper, the New Testament gives no instructions at all that place restrictions on the people who can preside at Communion. And since Scripture places no such restrictions on us, it would not seem to be justified to say that only priests can dispense the elements of the Lord's Supper. Moreover, since the New Testament teaches that all believers are priests and members of a "royal priesthood" (1 Peter 2:9; cf. Heb. 4:16; 10:19–22), we should not specify a certain class of people who have the rights of priests, as in the old covenant, but we should emphasize that all believers share the great spiritual privilege of coming near to God.

Finally, any continuation of the restriction that will not allow laypersons to

---

[5]It is for this reason that many Protestants have felt that they could readily partake of the Lord's Supper in any other Protestant church, even in high church Anglican services that in form appear quite similar to Roman Catholic services, but they could not in good conscience participate in a Roman Catholic mass, because of the Roman Catholic teaching on the nature of the mass itself.

drink of the cup of the Lord's Supper would be arguing from caution and tradition to justify disobedience to Jesus' direct commands, not only the command to his disciples where he said, "Drink of it, *all of you*" (Matt. 26:27), but also the direction Paul recorded, in which Jesus said, "Do this, as often as *you drink it*, in remembrance of me" (1 Cor. 11:25).

**2. The Lutheran View: "In, With, and Under."** Martin Luther rejected the Roman Catholic view of the Lord's Supper, yet he insisted that the phrase "This is my body" had to be taken in some sense as a literal statement. His conclusion was not that the bread actually *becomes* the physical body of Christ, but that the physical body of Christ *is present* "in, with, and under" the bread of the Lord's Supper. The example sometimes given is to say that Christ's body is present in the bread as water is present in a sponge—the water is not the sponge, but is present "in, with, and under" a sponge, and is present wherever the sponge is present. Other examples given are that of magnetism in a magnet or a soul in the body.

The Lutheran understanding of the Lord's Supper is found in the textbook of Francis Pieper, *Christian Dogmatics*.[6] He quotes Luther's Small Catechism: "What is the Sacrament of the Altar? It is the true body and blood of our Lord Jesus Christ, under the bread and wine, for us Christians to eat and to drink, instituted by Christ Himself."[7] Similarly, the Augsburg Confession, Article X, says, "Of the Supper of the Lord they teach that the Body and Blood of Christ are truly present, and are distributed to those who eat in the Supper of the Lord."[8]

One passage that may be thought to give support to this position is 1 Corinthians 10:16, "The bread which we break, is it not a participation in the body of Christ?"

However, in order to affirm this doctrine, Luther had to answer an important question: How can Christ's physical body, or more generally Christ's human nature, be everywhere present? Is it not true that Jesus in his human nature ascended into heaven and remains there until his return? Did he not say that he was leaving the earth and would no longer be in the world but was going to the Father (John 16:28; 17:11)? In answer to this problem Luther taught the *ubiquity* of Christ's human nature after his ascension—that is, that Christ's human nature was present everywhere ("ubiquitous"). But theologians ever since Luther's time have suspected that he taught the ubiquity of Christ's human nature, not because it is found anywhere in Scripture, but because he needed it to explain how his view of consubstantiation could be true.

In response to the Lutheran view, it can be said that it too fails to realize that Jesus is speaking of a *spiritual* reality but using *physical* objects to teach us when he says, "This is my body." We should take this no more literally than we take the corresponding sentence, "*This cup* which is poured out for you *is the new covenant* in my blood" (Luke 22:20). In fact, Luther does not really do justice to Jesus' words in a literal sense at all. Berkhof rightly objects that Luther really makes the words of Jesus mean, "This accompanies my body."[9] In this matter it would help

---

[6]4 vols. (St. Louis: Concordia, 195–57); also Mueller, pp. 524–28.

[7]Pieper, p. 296.

[8]Ibid. Mueller, p. 528, says Lutherans reject the term "consubstantiation" to describe their view.

[9]Berkhof, *Systematic Theology*, p. 653.

to read again John 6:27–59, where the context shows that Jesus is talking in literal, physical terms about bread, but he is continually explaining it in terms of spiritual reality.

**3. The Rest of Protestantism: A Symbolic and Spiritual Presence of Christ.** In distinction from Martin Luther, John Calvin and other Reformers argued that the bread and wine of the Lord's Supper did not change into the body and blood of Christ, nor did they somehow contain the body and blood of Christ. Rather, the bread and wine *symbolized* the body and blood of Christ, and they gave a visible sign of the fact that Christ himself was truly present.[10] Calvin said:

> By the showing of the symbol the thing itself is also shown. For unless a man means to call God a deceiver, he would never dare assert that an empty symbol is set forth by him. . . . And the godly ought by all means to keep this rule: whenever they see symbols appointed by the Lord, to think and be persuaded that the truth of the thing signified is surely present there. For why would the Lord put in your hand the symbol of his body, except to assure you of a true participation in it? (*Institutes,* 4.17.10; p. 1371)

Yet Calvin was careful to differ both with Roman Catholic teaching (which said that the bread became Christ's body) and with Lutheran teaching (which said that the bread contained Christ's body).

> But we must establish such a presence of Christ in the Supper as may neither fasten him to the element of bread, nor enclose him in bread, nor circumscribe him in any way (all which things, it is clear, detract from his heavenly glory). (*Institutes,* 4.17.19; p. 1381)

Today most Protestants would say, in addition to the fact that the bread and wine symbolize the body and blood of Christ, that Christ is also *spiritually present* in a special way as we partake of the bread and wine. Indeed, Jesus promised to be present whenever believers worship: "Where two or three are gathered in my name, there am I in the midst of them" (Matt. 18:20).[11] And if he is especially present when Christians gather to worship, then we would expect that he will be present in a special way in the Lord's Supper:[12] We meet him at *his* table, to which he comes to give himself to us. As we receive the elements of bread and wine in the presence of Christ, so we partake of him and all his benefits. We "feed upon

---

[10]There was some difference between Calvin and another Swiss Reformer, Ulrich Zwingli (1484–1531) on the nature of the presence of Christ in the Lord's supper, both agreeing that Christ was present in a symbolic way, but Zwingli being much more hesitant about affirming a real spiritual presence of Christ. However, the actual teaching of Zwingli in this regard is a matter of some difference among historians.

[11]It is true that this sentence is spoken in a context that applies specifically to church discipline (vv. 15–19), but it is a statement of a general truth used here to support a specific application, and there is no good reason to restrict its application to occasions of church discipline. It tells us that Jesus is always present when believers gather in his name.

[12]Sometimes Protestants have become so concerned to deny the Roman Catholic view of the "real presence" of Christ in the elements that they have wrongly denied even any spiritual presence. Millard Erickson notes the humorous situation that results: "Out of a zeal to avoid the conception that Jesus is present in some sort of magical way, certain Baptists among others have sometimes gone to such extremes as to give the impression that the one place where Jesus most assuredly is not to be found is the Lord's supper. This is what one Baptist leader termed 'the doctrine of the real absence' of Jesus Christ" (*Christian Theology,* p. 1123).

him in our hearts" with thanksgiving. Indeed, even a child who knows Christ will understand this without being told and will expect to receive a special blessing from the Lord during this ceremony, because the meaning of it is so inherent in the very actions of eating and drinking. Yet we must not say that Christ is present apart from our personal faith, but only meets and blesses us there in accordance with our faith in him.

In what way is Christ present then? Certainly there is a symbolic presence of Christ, but it is also a genuine spiritual presence and there is genuine spiritual blessing in this ceremony.

## D. Who Should Participate in the Lord's Supper?

Despite differences over some aspects of the Lord's Supper, most Protestants would agree, first, that *only those who believe in Christ* should participate in it, because it is a sign of being a Christian and continuing in the Christian life.[13] Paul warns that those who eat and drink unworthily face serious consequences: "For any one who eats and drinks without discerning the body eats and drinks judgment upon himself. That is why many of you are weak and ill, and some have died" (1 Cor. 11:29–30).

Second, many Protestants would argue from the meaning of baptism and the meaning of the Lord's Supper that, ordinarily, *only those who have been baptized* should participate in the Lord's Supper. This is because baptism is so clearly a symbol of *beginning* the Christian life, while the Lord's Supper is clearly a symbol of *continuing* the Christian life. Therefore if someone is taking the Lord's Supper and thereby giving public proclamation that he or she is continuing in the Christian life, then that person should be asked, "Wouldn't it be good to be baptized now and thereby give a symbol that you are beginning the Christian life?"

But others, including the present author, would object to such a restriction as follows: A different problem arises if someone who is a genuine believer, but not yet baptized, is *not* allowed to participate in the Lord's Supper when Christians get together. In that case the person's nonparticipation symbolizes that he or she is *not* a member of the body of Christ which is coming together to observe the Lord's Supper in a unified fellowship (see 1 Cor. 10:17: "Because there is one bread, we who are many are one body, for we all partake of the one bread"). Therefore churches may think it best to allow non-baptized believers to participate in the Lord's Supper but to urge them to be baptized as soon as possible. For if they are willing to participate in one outward symbol of being a Christian, there seems no reason why they should not be willing to participate in the other, a symbol that appropriately comes first.

Of course, the problems that arise in both situations (when unbaptized believers take Communion and when they do not) can all be avoided if new Christians are regularly baptized shortly after coming to faith. And, whichever position a church takes on the question of whether unbaptized believers should take Communion, in

---

[13]However, some in the Church of England and elsewhere have recently begun to allow young children to participate in the Lord's Supper, reasoning that if they have been given the sign of baptism it is wrong to deny them the sign of the Supper.

the teaching ministry of the church, it would seem wise to teach that the ideal situation is for new believers first to be baptized and then to partake of the Lord's Supper.

The third qualification for participation is that *self-examination:*

> Whoever, therefore, eats the bread or drinks the cup of the Lord in an unworthy manner will be guilty of profaning the body and blood of the Lord. *Let a man examine himself, and so eat of the bread and drink of the cup.* For any one who eats and drinks without discerning the body eats and drinks judgment upon himself. (1 Cor. 11:27–29)

In the context of 1 Corinthians 11 Paul is rebuking the Corinthians for their selfish and inconsiderate conduct when they come together as a church: "When you meet together, it is not the Lord's supper that you eat. For in eating, each one goes ahead with his own meal, and one is hungry and another is drunk" (1 Cor. 11:20–21). This helps us understand what Paul means when he talks about those who eat and drink "without discerning the body" (1 Cor. 11:29). The problem at Corinth was *not* a failure to understand that the bread and cup represented the body and blood of the Lord—they certainly knew that. The problem rather was their selfish, inconsiderate conduct toward each other while they were at the Lord's table. They were not understanding or "discerning" the true nature of the church *as one body.* This interpretation of "without discerning the body" is supported by Paul's mention of the church as the body of Christ just a bit earlier, in 1 Corinthians 10:17: "Because there is one bread, we who are many *are one* body, for we all partake of the one bread."[14] So the phrase "not discerning the *body*" means "not understanding the unity and interdependence of people in the church, which is the body of Christ." It means not taking thought for our brothers and sisters when we come to the *Lord's* Supper, at which we ought to reflect his character.[15]

What does it mean, then, to eat or drink "in an unworthy manner" (1 Cor. 11:27)? We might at first think the words apply rather narrowly and pertain only to the way we conduct ourselves when we actually eat and drink the bread and wine. But when Paul explains that unworthy participation involves "not discerning the body," he indicates that we are to take thought for all of our relationships within the body of Christ: are we acting in ways that vividly portray not the unity of the one bread and one body, but disunity? Are we conducting ourselves in ways that proclaim not the self-giving sacrifice of our Lord, but enmity and selfishness? In a broad sense, then, "Let a man examine himself" means that we ought to ask whether our relationships in the body of Christ are in fact reflecting the character of the Lord whom we meet there and whom we represent.

---

[14]Moreover, from this very brief mention of the idea of one body we may rightly suppose that it was not a new idea, but that Paul had taught them this idea while staying in Corinth for two years when he founded the church there.

[15]Two other reasons for this interpretation are: (1) Paul only says "not discerning the body," and he does not say "not discerning the body and blood of the Lord," which he more likely would have done if he had meant "not understanding that the bread and cup represent the body and blood of the Lord." (2) In addition, Paul says, "Let a man examine *himself*" (and this would no doubt include examining his relationships with others in the church), but Paul does not say, "Let him see if he understands what the bread and wine stand for."

In this connection, Jesus' teaching about coming to worship in general should also be mentioned:

> So if you are offering your gift at the altar, and there remember that your brother has something against you, leave your gift there before the altar and go; first be reconciled to your brother, and then come and offer your gift. (Matt. 5:23–24)

Jesus here tells us that whenever we come to worship we should be sure that our relationships with others are right, and if they are not, we should act quickly to make them right and then come to worship God. This admonition ought to be especially true when we come to the Lord's Supper.

Of course, no pastor or church leader will know whether people are examining themselves or not (except in cases where clearly offensive or sinful conduct becomes evident to others). For the most part, the church must depend on the pastors and teachers to explain clearly the meaning of the Lord's Supper and to warn of the dangers of participating unworthily. Then people will have the responsibility to examine their own lives, in accordance with what Paul says. Indeed, Paul does not say that the pastors should examine everyone else's lives, but encourages individual self-examination instead: "Let a man examine himself" (1 Cor. 11:28).[16]

## E. Other Questions

Who should administer the Lord's Supper? Scripture gives no explicit teaching on this question, so we are left simply to decide what is wise and appropriate for the benefit of the believers in the church. In order to guard against abuse of the Lord's Supper, a responsible leader ought to be in charge administering it, but it does not seem that Scripture requires that only ordained clergy or selected church officers could do this. In ordinary situations, of course, the pastor or other leader who ordinarily officiates at the worship services of the church would appropriately officiate at Communion as well. But beyond this, there would seem to be no reason why only officers or only leaders, or only men, should distribute the elements. Would it not speak much more clearly of our unity and spiritual equality in Christ if both men and women, for example, assisted in distributing the elements of the Lord's Supper?[17]

---

[16]In cases of church discipline or in cases where outward behavior gives clear evidence that a person is straying from Christ, the leaders of the church may wish to give a strong and clear verbal warning against participation in the Lord's Supper, so that the erring brother or sister does not eat and drink judgment upon himself or herself. But these cases should be rare, and we must also avoid the mistake of some churches that have been so strict in administration of the Lord's Supper that many true believers have been kept away and thus the unity of the true body of Christ has not been represented, nor have believers had access to the spiritual blessings that should rightly be theirs in Christ in participating in this ordinance and thereby obeying their Lord.

[17]Of course, where distribution of the Lord's Supper is thought to be a priestly function (as in Anglican churches), churches may decide that another approach to this question is more consistent with their own teachings. Moreover, in a church where only the leading officers of the church have assisted in serving Communion for many years, the church may decide that allowing anyone else to participate in distributing the elements would be symbolizing the participation of those people in the leadership and governing of the church, and they may wish to delay making a change at least until some clear teaching could be given. Other churches may feel that the leadership function of the church is so clearly tied up with the distribution of the elements that they would wish to continue with that restriction on their practice.

How often should the Lord's Supper be celebrated? Scripture does not tell us. Jesus simply said, "As often as you eat this bread and drink the cup . . ." (1 Cor. 11:26). Paul's directive here regarding worship services would also be appropriate to consider: "Let all things be done for edification" (1Cor. 14:26). In actuality it has been the practice of most of the church throughout its history to celebrate the Lord's Supper every week when believers gather. However, in many Protestant groups since the Reformation, there has been a less frequent celebration of the Lord's Supper—sometimes once a month or twice a month, or, in many Reformed churches, only four times a year. If the Lord's Supper is planned and explained and carried out in such a way that it is a time of self-examination, confession, and thanksgiving and praise, then it does not seem that celebrating it once a week would be too often, however, and it certainly could be observed that frequently "for edification."

## QUESTIONS FOR PERSONAL APPLICATION

1. What things symbolized by the Lord's Supper have received new emphasis in your thinking as a result of reading this chapter? Do you feel more eager to participate in the Lord's Supper now than before you read the chapter? Why?

2. In what ways (if any) will you approach the Lord's Supper differently now? Which of the things symbolized in the Lord's Supper is most encouraging to your Christian life right now?

3. What view of the nature of Christ's presence in the Lord's Supper have you been taught in your church previously? What is your own view now?

4. Are there any broken personal relationships that you need to make right before you come to the Lord's Supper again?

5. Are there areas in which your church needs to do more teaching about the nature of the Lord's Supper? What are they?

## SPECIAL TERMS

Communion
consubstantiation
Eucharist
not discerning the body

spiritual presence
symbolic presence
transubstantiation
ubiquity of Christ's human nature

## BIBLIOGRAPHY

(For an explanation of this bibliography see the note on the bibliography to chapter 1, p. 38. Complete bibliographical data may be found on pp. 1223–29.)

### Sections in Evangelical Systematic Theologies

1. Anglican (Episcopalian)
   1882–92     Litton, 472–542
2. Arminian (Wesleyan or Methodist)

1875–76    Pope, 3:325–34
1892–94    Miley, 2:411–14
1940    Wiley, 3:189–208
1960    Purkiser, 411–15
1983    Carter, 2:616–19
3. Baptist
1767    Gill, 2:647–60
1907    Strong, 959–80
1983–85    Erickson, 1107–28
4. Dispensational
1947    Chafer, 7:229
1949    Thiessen, 322–25
1986    Ryrie, 425–26
5. Lutheran
1917–24    Pieper, 3:290–96
1934    Mueller, 506–40
6. Reformed (or Presbyterian)
1559    Calvin, 2:1359–1448 (4.27–28)
1724–58    Edwards, 1:431–532
1861    Heppe, 627–56
1871–73    Hodge, 3:611–92
1878    Dabney, 800–817
1887–1921    Warfield, SSW, 1:332–38
1889    Shedd, 2b:564–74
1937–66    Murray, CW, 2:376–84; CW, 3:275–88
1938    Berkhof, 644–58
1962    Buswell, 2:266–79
7. Renewal (or charismatic/Pentecostal)
1988–92    Williams

## Sections in Representative Roman Catholic Systematic Theologies

1. Roman Catholic: Traditional
1955    Ott, 370–416
2. Roman Catholic: Post-Vatican II
1980    McBrien, 2:757–68; 1:552–56

## Other Works

Beckwith, Roger T. "Eucharist." In EDT, pp. 236–38.
Berkouwer, G. C. The Sacraments. Trans. by Hugo Bekker. Grand Rapids: Eerdmans, 1969.

Bridge, D., and D. Phypers. *Communion: The Meal That Unites?* London: Hodder and Stoughton, 1981.

Marshall, I. Howard. *Last Supper and Lord's Supper.* Grand Rapids: Eerdmans, 1980.

Osterhaven, M. E. "Lord's Supper, Views of." In *EDT,* pp. 653–56.

Wallace, R. S. "Lord's Supper." In *EDT,* pp. 651–53.

## SCRIPTURE MEMORY PASSAGE

**1 Corinthians 11:23–26:** *For I received from the Lord what I also delivered to you, that the Lord Jesus on the night when he was betrayed took bread, and when he had given thanks, he broke it, and said, "This is my body which is for you. Do this in remembrance of me." In the same way also the cup, after supper, saying, "This cup is the new covenant in my blood. Do this, as often as you drink it, in remembrance of me." For as often as you eat this bread and drink the cup, you proclaim the Lord's death until he comes.*

## HYMN

### "Here, O My Lord, I See Thee Face to Face"

This beautiful hymn is not frequently sung, but it speaks so directly to Jesus himself and speaks so clearly of the spiritual reality that we need to remember in the Lord's supper that it is one of the greatest hymns ever written regarding this doctrine. It conveys an attitude of reverence in the Lord's presence, joy in salvation, and genuine repentance for sin as well. The sweet beauty of spirit that Horatius Bonar exemplified in this hymn is matched by very few hymns in the history of the church.

Tune: "Spirit of God, Descend Upon My Heart"

Here, O my Lord, I see thee face to face;
    Here would I touch and handle things unseen,
Here grasp with firmer hand th' eternal grace,
    And all my weariness upon thee lean.

Here would I feed upon the bread of God,
    Here drink with thee the royal wine of heaven;
Here would I lay aside each earthly load,
    Here taste afresh the calm of sin forgiven.

This is the hour of banquet and of song;
    This is the heav'nly table spread for me:
Here let me feast, and, feasting, still prolong
    The brief, bright hour of fellowship with thee.

I have no help but thine, nor do I need
    Another arm save thine to lean upon:
It is enough, my Lord, enough indeed;
    My strength is in thy might, thy might alone.

Mine is the sin, but thine the righteousness;
   Mine is the guilt, but thine the cleansing blood;
Here is my robe, my refuge, and my peace,
   Thy blood, thy righteousness, O Lord my God.

AUTHOR: HORATIUS BONAR, 1855

# Chapter 51

# Worship

*How can our worship fulfill its great purpose in the New Testament age? What does it mean to worship "in spirit and in truth"?*

## EXPLANATION AND SCRIPTURAL BASIS

The term *worship* is sometimes applied to all of a Christian's life, and it is rightly said that everything in our life should be an act of worship, and everything the church does should be considered worship, for everything we do should glorify God. However, in this chapter I am not using the word in that broad sense. Rather, I am using *worship* in a more specific sense to refer to the music and words that Christians direct to God in praise, together with the heart attitudes that accompany that praise, especially when Christians assemble together. Since the chapters in this part of the book deal with the doctrine of the church, it is appropriate in this chapter to focus attention on the worship activities of the assembled church.

## A. Definition and Purpose of Worship

*Worship is the activity of glorifying God in his presence with our voices and hearts.* In this definition we note that worship is an act of glorifying God. Yet all aspects of our lives are supposed to glorify God, so this definition specifies that worship is something we do especially when we come into God's presence, when we are conscious of adoration of him in our hearts, and when we praise him with our voices and speak about him so others may hear. Paul encourages the Christians in Colossae, "Let the word of Christ dwell in you richly, *teach and admonish one another* in all wisdom, and *sing psalms and hymns and spiritual songs with thankfulness in your hearts to God*" (Col. 3:16).

In fact, the primary reason that God called us into the assembly of the church is that as a corporate assembly we might worship him. Edmund Clowney wisely says:

> God had demanded of Pharaoh, "Let my people go, *so that they may worship me* in the desert" (Ex. 7:16b). . . . God brings them out that he might bring them in, into his assembly, to the great company of those who stand before his face. . . . *God's assembly at Sinai is therefore the immediate goal of the exodus. God brings his people into his presence that they might hear his voice and worship him.*

But Clowney explains that the worshiping assembly at Mount Sinai could not remain in session before God forever. Therefore God established other festivals in which the whole nation would assemble before him three times a year. He says that "Israelites are a nation formed for worship, called to assemble in the courts of the Lord, and to praise together the name of the Most High."[1]

Yet Clowney points out that, rather than worshiping God in a unified, holy assembly, the people turned aside to serving idols and, rather than assembling the people to worship before him, "in judgment God scattered the people in exile."[2]

But God promised that his purposes for his people would yet be fulfilled, that there would someday be a great assembly not just of Israel but of all nations before his throne (Isa. 2:2–4; 25:6–8; 49:22; 66:18–21; cf. Jer. 48:47; 49:6, 39). Clowney notes that the fulfillment of that promise began only when Jesus started to build his church:

> Pentecost was the time of the firstfruits, the beginning of the great harvest of redemption. Peter preached the fulfillment of the prophecy of Joel. The Spirit had been poured out, *the worship of the new age had been ushered in. The church, the assembly for worship, was praising God.* . . . Now the ingathering had begun.
>
> The gospel call is a call to worship, to turn from sin and call upon the name of the Lord. . . . The picture of the church as a worshiping assembly is nowhere more powerfully presented than by the author of the Epistle to the Hebrews (12:18–29). . . . In our worship in Christ's church we approach the throne of God the judge of all. *We enter the festival assembly of the saints and the angels.* We gather in spirit with the spirits of just men made perfect. We enter the assembly of glory through Christ our mediator, and the blood of his atoning death. . . .
>
> *Reverent corporate worship,* then, is not optional for the church of God. . . . Rather, it *brings to expression the very being of the church.* It manifests on earth the reality of the heavenly assembly.[3]

Worship is therefore a *direct* expression of our ultimate purpose for living, "to glorify God and fully to enjoy him forever."[4] God speaks of his "sons" and "daughters" as "every one who is called by my name, whom I created *for my glory,* whom I formed and made" (Isa. 43:6–7). And Paul uses similar language when he says that "we who first hoped in Christ have been destined and appointed *to live for the praise of his glory*" (Eph. 1:12). Scripture is clear here and in many other passages that God created us to glorify him.[5]

When we reflect on the purpose of worship it also reminds us that *God is worthy of worship and we are not.* Even the apostle John had to be told that he should not worship any creature, not even a powerful angel in heaven. When he "fell down to worship" at the feet of the angel who showed him marvelous visions in heaven, the angel said to him, "You must not do that! . . . Worship God" (Rev. 22:8–9).

[1]Edmund Clowney, "The Biblical Theology of the Church" in *The Church in the Bible and the World,* ed. D. A. Carson, pp. 17–19.
[2]Ibid.
[3]Ibid., pp. 20–22.
[4]This familiar phrase has been widely used in Christian teachings. It is found in the *Westminster Larger Catechism,* Question One: "*What is the chief and highest end of man? Answer:* Man's chief and highest end is to glorify God, and fully to enjoy him forever."
[5]See the additional discussion in chapter 21, pp. 440–42, on the fact that God created us for his own glory.

This is because God is jealous for his own honor and he rightly seeks his own honor. He says, "I the LORD your God am a jealous God" (Ex. 20:5) and "My glory I will not give to another" (Isa. 48:11). Something within us should tremble and rejoice at this fact. We should tremble with fear lest we rob God's glory from him. And we should rejoice that it is *right* that God seek his own honor and be jealous for his own honor, for he, infinitely more than anything he has made, is *worthy* of honor. The twenty-four elders in heaven feel this reverence and joy, for they fall down before God's throne and cast their crowns before him singing, "You are worthy, our Lord and God, to receive glory and honor and power, for you created all things, and by your will they existed and were created" (Rev. 4:11). When we feel the absolute *rightness* of this deep within ourselves we then have the appropriate heart attitude for genuine worship.

Because God is worthy of worship and seeks to be worshiped, everything in our worship services should be designed and carried out not to call attention to ourselves or bring glory to ourselves, but to call attention to God and to cause people to think about him. It would be appropriate for us frequently to re-evaluate the various elements in our Sunday services—the preaching, public prayer, leading of worship, special music, celebration of the Lord's Supper, and even the announcements and the offering. Are they really bringing glory to God in the way they are done?[6] Peter says that spiritual gifts are to be used in such a way that "in everything God may be glorified through Jesus Christ" (1 Peter 4:11).

## B. The Results of Genuine Worship

When we worship God in the sense described above, truly giving him glory in our hearts and with our voices, several things happen as a result:

**1. We Delight in God.** God created us not only to glorify him but also to enjoy him and delight in his excellence.[7] We probably experience delight in God more fully in worship than in any other activity in this life. David confesses that the "one thing" that he will seek for above all else is "that I may dwell in the house of the LORD all the days of my life, to behold the beauty of the LORD, and to inquire in his temple" (Ps. 27:4). He also says, *"In your presence there is fulness of joy,* in your right hand are pleasures for evermore" (Ps. 16:11). Similarly, Asaph knows that God alone is the fulfillment of all his hopes and desires: *"Whom have I in heaven but you? And there is nothing upon earth that I desire besides you"* (Ps. 73:25). And the sons of Korah say:

> How lovely is your dwelling place,
>      O LORD of hosts!
> My soul longs, yea, faints
>      for the courts of the LORD;

---

[6]Few things destroy an atmosphere of worship more quickly than a soloist or choir who enjoy drawing attention to themselves, or a preacher who parades his own intelligence or skill in speaking. "God opposes the proud, but gives grace to the humble" (1 Peter 5:5).

[7]See the excellent discussion of living all of life by delighting in God in John Piper, *Desiring God* (Portland, Ore.: Multnomah, 1986); also his analysis of God's delight in himself and what reflects his excellence, in John Piper, *The Pleasures of God* (Portland, Ore.: Multnomah, 1991).

My heart and flesh sing for joy
    to the living God . . .
Blessed are those who dwell in your house,
    ever singing your praise! . . .

For a day in your courts is better
    than a thousand elsewhere. (Ps. 84:1–2, 4, 10)

The early church knew such joy in worship, for "day by day, attending the
temple together and breaking bread in their homes, they partook of food with
glad and generous hearts, *praising God* and having favor with all the people" (Acts
2:46). In fact, immediately after Jesus' ascension into heaven, the disciples
"returned to Jerusalem with great joy, *and were continually in the temple blessing
God.*" (Luke 24:52–53)

Of course, such activity of continual praise cannot last forever in this age, for
living in a fallen world requires that we give time to many other responsibilities as
well. But extended praise does give us a foretaste of the atmosphere of heaven,
where the four living creatures "never cease to sing, 'Holy, holy, holy, is the Lord
God Almighty, who was and is and is to come!'" (Rev. 4:8), and the other
heavenly creatures and the redeemed who have died join in that heavenly worship
and extol "the Lamb who was slain" (Rev. 5:12).

**2. God Delights in Us.** What does God do when we worship him? The amazing
truth of Scripture is that as the creation glorifies God, he also takes delight in it.
When God first made the universe, he looked on all of it with delight, and saw
that "it was very good" (Gen. 1:31). God takes special delight in human beings
whom he has created and redeemed. Isaiah reminded the people of the LORD,

You shall be a crown of beauty in the hand of the LORD . . .
you shall be called My delight is in her . . .
for the LORD delights in you . . .
as the bridegroom rejoices over the bride,
    so shall your God rejoice over you. (Isa. 62:3–5)

Zephaniah echoes the same theme when he says,

The LORD, your God, is in your midst,
    a warrior who gives victory;
he will rejoice over you with gladness,
    he will renew you in his love;
he will exult over you with loud singing.

                        (Zeph. 3:17)

This truth should bring great encouragement to us, for as we love God and praise
him we realize that we are bringing joy and delight to his heart. And the deepest
joy of love is the joy of bringing delight to the heart of the one you love.

**3. We Draw Near to God: the Amazing Unseen Reality of New Covenant
Worship.** In the old covenant believers could only draw near to God in a limited
way through the temple ceremonies; indeed, most of the people of Israel could

not enter into the temple itself, but had to remain in the courtyard. Even the priests could only go into the outer court of the temple, the "Holy Place," when it was their appointed duty. But into the inner room of the temple, the "Holy of Holies," no one could go except the high priest, and he only once a year (Heb. 9:1–7).

Now, under the new covenant, believers have the amazing privilege of being able to enter directly into the holy of holies in heaven when they worship. "We have confidence to enter the Most Holy Place by the blood of Jesus" (Heb. 10:19 NIV).[8] Since we have that confidence to enter into the very presence of God, the author of Hebrews encourages us, "*Let us draw near* with a true heart in full assurance of faith" (Heb. 10:22). Worship in the New Testament church is not simply practice for some later heavenly experience of genuine worship, nor is it simply pretending, or going through some outward activities. It is *genuine worship* in the presence of God himself, and when we worship we enter before his throne.

This reality is expressed more fully by the author of Hebrews in chapter 12, when he tells Christians that they have not come to a place like the earthly Mount Sinai where the people of Israel received the Ten Commandments from God, but they have come to something far better, the heavenly Jerusalem:

> For *you have not come* to what may be touched, a blazing fire, and darkness, and gloom, and a tempest, and the sound of a trumpet, and a voice whose words made the hearers entreat that no further messages be spoken to them. . . . *But you have come to Mount Zion and to the city of the living God,* the heavenly Jerusalem, and to innumerable angels in festal gathering, and to the assembly of the first-born who are enrolled in heaven, and to a judge who is God of all, and to the spirits of just men made perfect, and to Jesus, the mediator of a new covenant, and to the sprinkled blood that speaks more graciously than the blood of Abel. (Heb. 12:18–24)

This is the reality of new covenant worship: it actually *is* worship in the presence of God, though we do not now see him with our physical eyes, nor do we see the angels gathered around his throne or the spirits of believers who have gone before and are now worshiping in God's presence. But it is all there, and it is all real, more real and more permanent than the physical creation that we see around us, which will someday be destroyed in the final judgment. And if we believe Scripture to be true, then we must also believe it to be actually true that *we ourselves* come to that place and join *our* voices with those already worshiping in heaven whenever we come to God in worship. Our only appropriate response is this: "Let us offer to God acceptable worship, with reverence and awe; for our God is a consuming fire" (Heb. 12:28–29).

**4. God Draws Near to Us.** James tells us, "Draw near to God and he will draw near to you" (James 4:8). This has been the pattern of God's dealings with his

---

[8]The Greek text literally says that we "have confidence into the entrance of *the holy places,*" because the plural *tōn hagiōn* is used elsewhere in Hebrews to refer to the holy place and the holy of holies together as "the holy places" (Heb. 8:2; 9:8, 25; 13:11). The RSV regularly renders this expression by "the sanctuary," but that translation obscures the fact that it is referring both to the holy place and to the holy of holies (the NASB renders these plurals as singulars, an uncommon departure from its ordinary tendency to translate more literally).

people throughout the Bible, and we should be confident that it will be true also today.

In the Old Testament, when God's people began to praise him at the dedication of the temple, he descended and made himself known in their midst:

> when the song was raised, with trumpets and cymbals and other musical instruments, in praise to the LORD, "For he is good, for his steadfast love endures for ever," the house, the house of the LORD, was filled with a cloud, so that the priests could not stand to minister because of the cloud; for the glory of the LORD filled the house of God. (2 Chron. 5:13–14)

Though this only speaks of one specific incident, it does not seem wrong to suppose that God will also make his presence known at other times among his people, whenever he is pleased with the praise they offer (even if he does not come in the form of a visible cloud). David says, "Yet you are holy, enthroned on the praises of Israel" (Ps. 22:3).

**5. God Ministers to Us.** Although the primary purpose of worship is to glorify God, the Scriptures teach that in worship something also happens to us: we ourselves are built up or edified. To some extent this happens, of course, when we learn from the Bible teachings that are given or the words of encouragement that others speak to us—Paul says, "Let all things be done for edification" (1 Cor. 14:26), and he says that we are to "teach and admonish one another in all wisdom" (Col. 3:16), and to be "addressing one another in psalms and hymns and spiritual songs" (Eph. 5:19; cf. Heb. 10:24–25).

But in addition to the edification that comes from growth in understanding the Bible and hearing words of encouragement from others, there is another kind of edification that occurs in worship: when we worship God he meets with us and directly ministers to us, strengthening our faith, intensifying our awareness of his presence, and granting refreshment to our spirits. Peter says that as Christians are continually coming to Christ (in worship and prayer and faith), they are then "being built up as a spiritual house for a holy priesthood, to offer up spiritual sacrifices acceptable to God through Jesus Christ" (1 Peter 2:5 NASB). When we come to worship we come into God's presence in a special way, and we may expect that he will meet us there and minister to us: as we "draw near to the throne of grace" we will "receive mercy and find grace to help in time of need" (Heb. 4:16).[9] During genuine worship we will often experience an intensification of the sanctifying work of the Holy Spirit, who is at work continually changing us into the likeness of Christ "from one degree of glory to another" (2 Cor. 3:18).[10]

---

[9]See also Ps. 34:4–5, 8; 37:4.

[10]Somehow, the more we see of God the more we become like him. That is evident especially when we enter the age to come, for John says, "When he appears we shall be like him, for we shall see him as he is" (1 John 3:2). But it is also true to some degree in this life, as we run the race that is set before us, "looking to Jesus the pioneer and perfecter of our faith" (Heb. 12:2). At times the presence of the Lord and the accompanying working of the Holy Spirit in our hearts will be so evident that we will recognize that God is doing something within us—as the disciples certainly did when Jesus walked with them on the Emmaus road, for later they said, "Did not our hearts burn within us while he talked to us on the road, while he opened to us the scriptures?" (Luke 24:32).

**6. The Lord's Enemies Flee.** When the people of Israel began to worship, God at times would fight for them against their enemies. For example, when the Moabites, Edomites, and Syrians came against Judah, King Jehoshaphat sent out the choir praising God in front of the army:

> He appointed those who were to sing to the LORD and praise him in holy array, as they went *before the army.* . . . And *when they began to sing and praise,* the LORD set an ambush against the men of Ammon, Moab, and Mount Seir, who had come against Judah, so that they were routed. (2 Chron. 20:21–22)

Similarly, when God's people offer him worship today, we may expect that the Lord will battle against demonic forces that oppose the gospel and cause them to flee.

**7. Unbelievers Know They Are in God's Presence.** Though Scripture does not emphasize evangelism as a primary purpose when the church meets for worship, Paul does tell the Corinthians to take thought for unbelievers and outsiders who come to their services, to be sure that the Christians speak in understandable ways (see 1 Cor. 14:23). He also tells them that if the gift of prophecy is functioning properly, unbelievers will from time to time have the secrets of their heart disclosed, and they will fall on their face and *"worship God and declare that God is really among you"* (1 Cor. 14:25; cf. Acts 2:11). But evangelism is not seen as a primary purpose when the church assembles for worship, and it would therefore not be right to have the only weekly gathering of believers designed primarily with an evangelistic purpose. Paul's concern is rather that visitors understand what is going on (and not think that Christians are "mad," 1 Cor. 14:23), and that they recognize that "God is really among you" (1 Cor. 14:25).

## C. The Eternal Value of Worship

Because worship glorifies God and fulfills the purpose for which God created us, it is an activity of eternal significance and great value. When Paul cautions the Ephesians not to waste their time but to use it well, he puts it in the context of living as those who are wise: "Look carefully then how you walk, not as unwise men but as wise, *making the most of the time,* because the days are evil" (Eph. 5:15–16).

Paul then explains what it is to be wise and to make the most of the time:

> Therefore do not be foolish, but understand what the will of the Lord is. And do not get drunk with wine, for that is debauchery; but be filled with the Spirit, addressing one another in psalms and hymns and spiritual songs, *singing and making melody to the Lord with all your heart,* always and for everything giving thanks in the name of our Lord Jesus Christ to God the Father. (Eph. 5:17–20)

Therefore in the context of using time wisely and making the most of the time, Paul includes both singing of spiritual psalms to one another and singing to the Lord with our hearts.

This means that *worship is doing the will of God!* Worship is the result of understanding "what the will of the Lord is." It is "making the most of the time." Moreover, because God is eternal and omniscient, the praise that we give him will never fade from his consciousness but will continue to bring delight to his heart for all eternity (cf. Jude 25: "To the only God, our Savior through Jesus Christ our Lord, be glory, majesty, dominion, and authority, before all time and now *and for ever*").

The fact that worship is an activity of great significance and eternal value is also evident in the fact that it is the primary activity carried on by those who are already in heaven (cf. Rev. 4:8–11; 5:11–14).

## D. How Can We Enter Into Genuine Worship?

Ultimately, worship is a spiritual activity and it must be empowered by the Holy Spirit working within us. This means that we must pray that the Holy Spirit will enable us to worship rightly.

The fact that genuine worship is to be carried on in the unseen, spiritual realm is evident in Jesus' words:

> The hour is coming, and now is, when the true worshipers will worship the Father *in spirit and truth,* for such the Father seeks to worship him. God is spirit, and those who worship him must worship in spirit and truth. (John 4:23–24)

To worship "in spirit and truth" is best understood to mean not "in the Holy Spirit," but rather *"in the spiritual realm, in the realm of spiritual activity."*[11] This means that true worship involves not only our physical bodies but also our spirits, the immaterial aspect of our existence that primarily acts in the unseen realm. Mary knew she was worshiping in that way, for she exclaimed, *"My soul* magnifies the Lord, and *my spirit* rejoices in God my Savior" (Luke 1:46–47).

We should realize also that God continually "seeks" (John 4:23) those who will worship him in the spiritual realm and therefore those whose spirit as well as body and mind is worshiping God. Such worship is not optional because those who worship God *"must* worship in spirit and truth" (v. 24). Unless our spirits are worshiping God we are not truly worshiping him.

An attitude of worship comes upon us when we begin to see God as he is and then respond to his presence. Even in heaven the seraphim who behold God's glory cry out, "Holy, holy, holy is the LORD of hosts; the whole earth is full of his glory" (Isa. 6:3). When the disciples saw Jesus walking on the water, and then saw the wind cease when he got into the boat, "those in the boat *worshiped him,* saying, 'Truly you are the Son of God'" (Matt. 14:33). The author of Hebrews knows that when we come into the presence of God (Heb. 12:18–24), the proper response is to "offer to God acceptable worship, with reverence and awe; for our God is a consuming fire" (Heb. 12:28–29). Therefore genuine worship is not something that is self-generated or that can be worked up within ourselves. It

---

[11]This is because (1) the discussion that Jesus is having with the woman at the well in this context is a discussion about the *location* of worship (see vv. 20–21)—should it be in Samaria or in Jerusalem? Jesus' answer would fit this inquiry much better if he were speaking about the spiritual realm in which we worship, as opposed to the physical location of Jerusalem or Samaria. (2) In the Greek text the word *en* ("in") of the phrase "in spirit and truth" corresponds to the same word (*en*) used in v. 21 to speak of (literally) "in this mountain" and "in Jerusalem." Once again the contrast is in terms of location "in" which one is to worship. (3) The word *truth* refers to a quality of worship, not to a person. The parallel would be more understandable if "in spirit" likewise referred not to a person but to some quality of the worship, such as the realm in which it is to be done.

must rather be the outpouring of our hearts *in response* to a realization of who God is.

It is appropriate to ask whether there is much genuine, deep, heartfelt worship in our churches. In many evangelical churches people do not truly worship God in their hearts until the last hymn, after the sermon has focused their attention on who God is so that they begin to rejoice in God with a heart full of praise. But then, just when heartfelt worship has begun, the service abruptly ends. It should be just beginning! If genuine worship is lacking in our churches, we should ask how we can bring ourselves to experience much more of the depth and richness of worship, which is the natural response of the believing heart to a clear awareness of God's presence and character.[12]

Is there anything else we can do to make worship more effective? We must remember that worship is a spiritual matter (John 4:21–24), and the primary solutions will therefore be spiritual ones. There will need to be much prayer in preparation for worship, especially on the part of those in leadership, asking that God will bless the worship times and make himself known to us. Also, congregations will need teaching about the spiritual nature of worship and the New Testament understanding of worship in God's presence (see Heb. 12:22–24). In addition, Christians need to be encouraged to make right any broken interpersonal relationships. Paul says that men are to lift holy hands "without anger or quarreling" (1 Tim. 2:8), and Jesus reminds us that we are first to "be reconciled" to our brother, and then come before God's altar and offer a gift (Matt. 5:24). In fact, John says that anyone who says, "I love God" but hates his brother "is a liar" (1 John 4:20). Husbands particularly need to make sure they are living "considerately" with their wives, and honoring them, in order that their prayers "may not be hindered" (1 Peter 3:7). And the entire church is responsible to watch "that no 'root of bitterness' spring up and cause trouble, and by it the many become defiled" (Heb. 12:15)—an indication that sin and broken relationships among a few can spread to many and result in the withholding of God's blessing from the whole congregation.

Moreover, if we are truly to draw near to God in worship, there must be a striving for personal holiness of life. The author of Hebrews reminds believers to strive for "the holiness without which no one will see the Lord" (Heb. 12:14), and Jesus says that it is the "pure in heart" who shall "see God" (Matt. 5:8)—a promise that is fulfilled partially in this life and completely in the age to come. Specifically in connection with prayer, John says, "If our hearts do not condemn us, we have confidence before God" (1 John 3:21), but this principle certainly applies to worship as well, as we have boldness to come into God's presence to offer him praise. James indicates a similar concern when, immediately after saying, "Draw near to God and he will draw near to you," he adds, "*Cleanse* your hands, you sinners, and *purify* your hearts, you men of double mind" (James 4:8).[13]

Yet the physical setting and the structure of worship services do matter, for

---

[12]Of course, God's character can be revealed not only through the preaching of the Word, but also through the words of the hymns that are sung, through prayer, and through the reading of Bible passages even without comment.

[13]Other Scripture passages indicate a connection between personal holiness and worship of God: see Prov. 15:8: "The sacrifice of the wicked is an abomination to the LORD, but the prayer of the upright is his delight." See also Prov. 15:29; 28:9; also Ps. 34:15–18; 66:18.

there are indications that Jesus thought that the atmosphere of worship was very important. He "entered the temple of God and drove out all who sold and bought in the temple, and he overturned the tables of the money-changers and the seats of those who sold pigeons." In explanation of this action, Jesus insisted that the temple was to be a house of prayer, for he said, "It is written, 'My house shall be called a house of prayer'; but you make it a den of robbers" (Matt. 21:12–13). He also told believers, "When you pray, *go into your room and shut the door* and pray to your Father who is in secret" (Matt. 6:6), not only because in our rooms we will not be seen by men, and will not pray so as to receive glory from men, but also because the knowledge that others are watching us in our prayers so easily distracts our attention, so that then we pray in part to be heard by others or at least so as not to offend them. This does not mean that corporate worship and prayer are forbidden (for both are very evident in both the Old Testament and New Testament), but it is to say that we should choose a *setting* for prayer or for worship that avoids distractions as much as possible. This is consistent with the fact that worship is to be done in an orderly way, for "God is not a God of confusion but of peace" (1 Cor. 14:33; cf. v. 40). The atmosphere and mood of worship are important, because we are to "offer to God acceptable worship, with reverence and awe" (Heb. 12:28). This means that it is appropriate to come together as a church in a setting that is conducive to worship, one that is ordinarily private and free from distractions, giving opportunity to focus attention on the Lord.[14]

Singing is especially important to worship in both Old and New Testaments. In our day there has been quite a change in both the standard English that is spoken by people and the musical forms that people are familiar with, and churches need to talk and plan openly and honestly in order to find a mix of songs that can be sung well by the whole congregation, and that people can genuinely identify with as a vehicle for expressing their praise to God. Songs that address God directly in the second person (that is, speaking to God as "you" rather than speaking about him as "he") will often be especially effective as worship songs—though the Psalms show that both kinds of songs are pleasing to God.

In addition, it is important to allow enough time for the various aspects of corporate worship. Genuine prayer can certainly take time (see Luke 6:12; 22:39–46; Acts 12:12; 13:2). Solid Bible teaching can often take a long time as well (Matt. 15:32; Acts 20:7–11). Moreover, genuine, heartfelt worship and praise will also take quite a bit of time if it is to be effective.

This is true in part because different aspects of a worship service require

---

[14]The practical considerations discussed in this section can be applied to many different forms of worship, but I have not discussed the actual forms that worship will take. Those will vary widely, from the extensive structured liturgies of Episcopalian services to the unstructured spontaneity of charismatic services. Since Scripture does not prescribe any one form, the major principle to use is Paul's directive, "Let all things be done for edification" (1 Cor. 14:26). Evangelicals need to be cautious, however, that they do not too quickly dismiss unfamiliar forms of worship: people in liturgical churches should realize that spontaneity can be managed in an orderly way, and people in charismatic groups should realize that edification and genuine worship can occur within a detailed structure. (Regarding the unison reading of a liturgy, if Christians can worship and pray by *singing* words in unison, there is nothing to prevent them from genuinely worshiping and praying by *reading* words aloud in unison!) Yet any one form that is used excessively can become a meaningless routine for most participants.

different attitudes and states of mind. Listening to Bible teaching requires
attentiveness to the text and the teacher. Praise requires joy and a focus on the
Lord and his excellence. Prayers of petition require a focus on needs and a deep
concern for others. Times when offerings are given require a focus on sacrificing
ourselves to the Lord as well as giving to him from our means and trusting him to
provide for our needs. The Lord's Supper requires a time of reflection, self-
examination, and perhaps repentance, along with thanksgiving. But we cannot
have all of these attitudes at once, for we are finite. Different attitudes of mind
require time to attain and dwell in. For that reason it is impossible to fulfill all the
tasks necessary for an assembled congregation simply in one hour on Sunday
morning, and it is harmful even to try. Those who do try to do everything crowd
too much into a brief time and fail to do anything well.[15] If congregations are to
fulfill the various purposes for which God wants them to assemble together, and
especially to have extended times of reverent worship, they will probably need to
find creative solutions that enable them to meet for longer periods of time, and
omit or reschedule some activities that have become habitual or traditional on
Sunday mornings but are really not necessary.

## QUESTIONS FOR PERSONAL APPLICATION

1. Do you experience genuine, fulfilling worship in your church each Sunday?
   How much time is specifically allotted to worship (narrowly defined)—that
   is, to times of praise and thanksgiving to God? Would you like the time
   to be longer? What aspects of the worship time do you find most
   meaningful? Which aspects are least meaningful? How could your church
   take steps to strengthen and deepen its experience of worship (if that is
   needed)?

2. Have you ever felt a strong sense of the presence of God in corporate
   worship? When was this? Can you describe it? Do you know what factors
   contributed to this sense?

3. During times of worship, can you describe the emotions that are most
   prominent in your consciousness? Is this experience similar to other
   experiences in daily life, or are these feelings unique to times of worship?
   Have you ever sensed that God is ministering to you while you are
   worshiping him? What made you aware of that?

4. Do you think there is enough genuine worship in a typical week in your
   life? If not, what are the hindrances to such worship?

---

[15]Unfortunately, pastors who try to officiate at a service into which too many activities are crowded
begin to resemble the master of ceremonies at a three-ring circus who shouts, "Look here! Look
there!" at one act after another. In a similar way the pastor exhorts, "Praise God! Be generous! Think
about Scripture! Pray! Shake hands with your neighbor! Say hello to your friends! Examine yourselves!
Repent of your sins! Sing to the Lord! Amen? Amen!" In a situation like this people's emotions are
jerked back and forth so quickly that they are unable to respond as whole persons, and the result is that
they withdraw emotionally and do not respond from the heart. They will leave the service feeling
frustrated and disappointed because the need of their hearts to experience genuine worship, prayer, and
learning from Scripture has not been satisfied.

For most human beings, focused attention is slowly attained and easily lost. Because of this, I
personally find that a worship leader who talks to the congregation between songs usually distracts my
attention away from the Lord and onto himself, and my attitude of worship is greatly diminished.

5. How do you feel about the fact that God is jealous for his own honor and seeks his honor? Can you think of anything in the universe that would be more right than for God to seek his own honor? Can you think of anything other than worship of God that would make you feel more deeply that you are doing the thing for which you were created?

## SPECIAL TERMS

worship

## BIBLIOGRAPHY

(For an explanation of this bibliography see the note on the bibliography to chapter 1, p. 38. Complete bibliographical data may be found on pp. 1223–29.)

### Sections in Evangelical Systematic Theologies

1. Anglican (Episcopalian)
   1882–92     Litton (no explicit treatment)
2. Arminian (Wesleyan or Methodist)
   1875–76     Pope, 3:287–94
   1940        Wiley, 3:138–50
   1960        Purkiser, 415–20
   1983        Carter, 2:614–15
3. Baptist
   1767        Gill, 2:341–52, 558, 682–729
   1987–94     Lewis/Demarest
4. Dispensational
   1986        Ryrie, 428–30
5. Lutheran
               (no explicit treatment)
6. Reformed (or Presbyterian)
   1724–58     Edwards, 2:913–18
   1937–66     Murray, *CW*, 1:165–68
7. Renewal (or charismatic/Pentecostal)
   1988–92     Williams

### Sections in Representative Roman Catholic Systematic Theologies

(no explicit treatment)

### Other Works

Allen, Ronald, and Borror, Gordon. *Worship: Rediscovering the Missing Jewel.* Portland, Ore.: Multnomah, 1982.

Carson, Herbert M. *Hallelujah! Christian Worship*. Welwyn, Hertfordshire, England: Evangelical Press, 1980.

Engle, Paul E. *Discovering the Fullness of Worship*. Philadelphia: Great Commission, 1978.

Harrison, E. F. "Worship." In *EDT*. pp. 1192–1193.

Kraueter, Tom. *Keys to Becoming an Effective Worship Leader*. Available from Psalmist Resources, 9820 E. Watson Rd., St. Louis, MO 63126. 1991.

Manson, P. D. "Worship." In *EDT*, pp. 730–32.

Martin, Ralph P. *Worship in the Early Church*. Westwood, N.J.: Revell, 1964.
_____. *The Worship of God*. Grand Rapids: Eerdmans, 1982.

Moule, C. F. D. *Worship in the New Testament*. Richmond, Va.: John Knox, 1961.

Peterson, David. *Engaging With God: A Biblical Theology of Worship*. Leicester: Inter-Varsity Press, and Grand Rapids: Eerdmans, 1992.

Rayburn, Robert G. *O Come, Let Us Worship*. Grand Rapids: Baker, 1980.

Taylor, Jack R. *The Hallelujah Factor*. Nashville, Tenn.: Broadman, 1983.

Wainwright, Geoffrey. *Doxology: The Praise of God in Worship, Doctrine, and Life*. New York: Oxford University Press, 1980.

Webber, Robert E. *Worship Old and New*. Grand Rapids: Zondervan, 1982.

## SCRIPTURE MEMORY PASSAGE

**Revelation 4:11:**

> You are worthy, our Lord and God,
> to receive glory and honor and power,
> for you created all things,
> and by your will they existed and were created.

## HYMN

### "Thou Art Worthy"

Thou art worthy, thou art worthy, thou art worthy, O Lord.
To receive glory, glory and honor, glory and honor and power.
For thou hast created, hast all things created, thou hast created all
    things;
And for thy pleasure, they are created, thou art worthy, O Lord.

# Chapter 52

# Gifts of the Holy Spirit (1): General Questions

*What are spiritual gifts? How many are there? Have some gifts ceased? Seeking and using spiritual gifts.*

## EXPLANATION AND SCRIPTURAL BASIS

### A. Questions Regarding Spiritual Gifts in General

In previous generations, systematic theologies did not have chapters on spiritual gifts, for there were few questions regarding the nature and use of spiritual gifts in the church. But the twentieth century has seen a remarkable increase in interest in spiritual gifts, primarily because of the influence of the Pentecostal and charismatic movements within the church. In this chapter we will first look at some general questions regarding spiritual gifts, then examine the specific question of whether some (miraculous) gifts have ceased. In the next chapter we shall analyze the New Testament teaching about particular gifts.

Before beginning the discussion, however, we may define spiritual gifts as follows: *A spiritual gift is any ability that is empowered by the Holy Spirit and used in any ministry of the church.* This broad definition includes both gifts that are related to natural abilities (such as teaching, showing mercy, or administration) and gifts that seem to be more "miraculous" and less related to natural abilities (such as prophecy, healing, or distinguishing between spirits). The reason for this is that when Paul lists spiritual gifts (in Rom. 12:6–8; 1 Cor. 7:7; 12:8–10, 28; and Eph. 4:11) he includes both kinds of gifts. Yet not every natural ability that people have is included here, because Paul is clear that all spiritual gifts must be empowered "by one and the same Spirit" (1 Cor. 12:11), that they are given "for the common good" (1 Cor. 12:7), and that they are all to be used for "edification" (1 Cor. 14:26), or for building up the church.[1]

**1. Spiritual Gifts in the History of Redemption.** Certainly the Holy Spirit was at work in the Old Testament, bringing people to faith and working in remarkable ways in a few individuals such as Moses or Samuel, David or Elijah. But in general

---

[1]When seemingly natural gifts (such as teaching, helps, administration, or musical gifts) are empowered by the Holy Spirit, they will generally show increased effectiveness and power in their use. Paul says the Corinthians were "enriched" in all their speech and knowledge as spiritual gifts came to them (1 Cor. 1:5–7). Any pastor who has preached for a time knows the difference between preaching in his own "natural" ability and preaching the same sermon under the anointing or empowering of the Holy Spirit.

there was *less powerful* activity of the Holy Spirit in the lives of most believers. Effective evangelism of the nations had been diminished, casting out of demons[2] was unknown, miraculous healing was uncommon (though it did happen, especially in the ministries of Elijah and Elisha), prophecy was restricted to a few prophets or small bands of prophets, and "resurrection power" over sin in the sense of Romans 6:1–14 and Philippians 3:10 was rarely experienced.

But at several points the Old Testament looks forward to a time when there would be a greater empowering of the Holy Spirit that would reach to all of God's people. Moses said, "Would that all the LORD's people were prophets, that the LORD would put his spirit upon them!" (Num. 11:29). And the LORD prophesied through Joel:

> And it shall come to pass afterward,
> that I will pour out my spirit on all flesh;
> your sons and your daughters shall prophesy,
> your old men shall dream dreams,
> and your young men shall see visions.
> Even upon the menservants and maidservants
> in those days, I will pour out my spirit. (Joel 2:28–29)

John the Baptist heightens people's expectations of the fulfillment of Joel's prophecy when he announces that someone is coming after him who "will baptize you with the Holy Spirit and with fire" (Matt. 3:11; cf. Mark 1:8; Luke 3:16; John 1:33; Acts 1:5).

When Jesus begins his ministry he comes bringing the fullness and power of the Holy Spirit in his person. Luke writes, "And Jesus returned *in the power of the Spirit* into Galilee" (Luke 4:14). The result is that he teaches with great power (Luke 4:15–22) and he heals and casts out demons from all who are oppressed (Luke 4:31–41). Clearly, Jesus has come in the *greater new covenant power of the Holy Spirit,* and he has come to *conquer* Satan's kingdom.

In fact, he says that the power of the Holy Spirit at work in him enabling him to cast out demons is an indication that the kingdom of God has come in power: "If it is by the Spirit of God that I cast out demons, then the kingdom of God has come upon you" (Matt. 12:28). Looking back on Jesus' life and ministry, John tells us, "The reason the Son of God appeared was to destroy the works of the devil" (1 John 3:8).

But this new covenant power of the Holy Spirit is not limited to the ministry of Jesus alone. He sent his disciples out, saying, "The kingdom of heaven is at hand" and told them, "Heal the sick, raise the dead, cleanse lepers, cast out demons" (Matt. 10:7–8). Nevertheless, this new covenant power of the Holy Spirit is not yet distributed to all who believed in Jesus or followed him, but only to his twelve disciples or to the seventy disciples (Luke 10:1–12).

The pouring out of the Holy Spirit in new covenant fullness and power in the church occurred at Pentecost. Before Jesus ascended into heaven he commanded

---

[2]The only thing that comes close to casting out of demons in the Old Testament is the fact that when David played the lyre for King Saul, "Saul was refreshed, and was well, and the evil spirit departed from him" (1 Sam. 16:23), but David had to do this "whenever the evil spirit from God was upon Saul" (ibid.), indicating that there was no permanent relief from the demonic oppression that Saul experienced.

his apostles "not to depart from Jerusalem, but to wait for the promise of the Father," and the content of that promise was, "Before many days you shall be baptized with the Holy Spirit" (Acts 1:4–5). He promised them, *"You shall receive power when the Holy Spirit has come upon you"* (Acts 1:8). When the Spirit was poured out on the church at Pentecost Peter recognized that Joel's prophecy was being fulfilled, for he said, "this is what was spoken by the prophet Joel" (Acts 2:16), and he then quoted Joel's prophecy (vv. 17–21). Peter recognized that the new covenant empowering of the Holy Spirit had come to God's people and the new covenant age had begun as a direct result of the activity of Jesus in heaven, for Peter said,

> This Jesus God raised up, and of that we are all witnesses. Being therefore exalted at the right hand of God, and *having received from the Father the promise of the Holy Spirit, he has poured out this which you see and hear*. (Acts 2:32–33)

Against the background of Jesus' ministry and the earlier ministry of the disciples with Jesus, the disciples present at Pentecost would rightly have expected that powerful evangelistic preaching, deliverance from demonic oppression, physical healing, and perhaps also prophecy, dreams, and visions would all begin and continue among those who believe in Christ, and that these things would be *characteristic* of the new covenant age that began at Pentecost. A further characteristic of this outpouring of the Holy Spirit was a widespread distribution of spiritual gifts to all people—sons and daughters, young men and old men, menservants and maidservants, in the words of Joel—*all* received a new covenant empowering of the Holy Spirit, and it would also be expected that all would receive gifts of the Holy Spirit then as well.[3] In fact, that is what happened in the early church (see 1 Cor. 12–14; Gal. 3:5; James 5:14–15). As B. B. Warfield said:

> We are justified in considering it characteristic of the Apostolic churches that such miraculous gifts should be displayed in them. The exception would be, not a church with, but a church without, such gifts. . . . *The Apostolic Church was characteristically a miracle-working church*.[4]

(This is true regardless of what view one takes about the continuation of miraculous gifts after the time of the apostles.)

**2. The Purpose of Spiritual Gifts in the New Testament Age.** Spiritual gifts are given *to equip the church to carry out its ministry until Christ returns*. Paul tells the Corinthians, *"You are not lacking in any spiritual gift, as you wait for the revealing of our Lord Jesus Christ"* (1 Cor. 1:7). Here he connects the possession of spiritual gifts and their situation in the history of redemption (waiting for Christ's return), suggesting that gifts are given to the church for the period between Christ's ascension and his return. Similarly, Paul looks forward to the time of Christ's return and says, "When the perfect comes, the imperfect will pass away" (1 Cor. 13:10), indicating also that these "imperfect" gifts (mentioned in vv. 8–9) will be in operation until Christ returns, when they will be superseded by something far

---

[3]See chapter 39, pp. 763–87, on the question of baptism in the Holy Spirit.
[4]Warfield, *Counterfeit Miracles*, p. 5.

greater.[5] Indeed, the pouring out of the Holy Spirit in "power" at Pentecost (Acts 1:8) was to equip the church to preach the gospel (Acts 1:8)—something that will continue until Christ returns. And Paul reminds believers that in their use of spiritual gifts they are to "strive to excel in *building up* the church" (1Cor. 14:12). Finally, in writing to the Ephesians, Paul specifies that when Christ ascended into heaven he gave gifts "to *equip* the saints for the work of ministry, for building up the body of Christ" (Eph. 4:12).

But spiritual gifts not only equip the church for the time until Christ returns, they also *give a foretaste of the age to come*. Paul reminds the Corinthians that they were *"enriched"* in all their speech and all their knowledge, and that the result of this enriching was that they were "not lacking in any spiritual gift" (1 Cor. 1:5, 7). Of course, this *enrichment* in their speech and knowledge did not give them the perfect speech or the perfect knowledge that would be theirs in heaven, but only a foretaste or down payment of that heavenly perfection. Similarly, Paul reminds the Corinthians that spiritual gifts are "imperfect" but when the "perfect" way of knowing comes at the Lord's return, then these gifts will pass away (1 Cor. 13:10). Just as the Holy Spirit himself is in this age a "down payment" (2 Cor. 1:22 NASB mg.; cf. 2 Cor. 5:5; Eph. 1:14) of the fuller work of the Holy Spirit within us in the age to come, so the gifts the Holy Spirit gives us are *partial foretastes* of the fuller working of the Holy Spirit that will be ours in the age to come.

In this way, gifts of insight and discernment prefigure the much greater discernment we will have when Christ returns. Gifts of knowledge and wisdom prefigure the much greater wisdom that will be ours when we "know as we are known" (cf. 1 Cor. 13:12). Gifts of healing give a foretaste of the perfect health that will be ours when Christ grants to us resurrection bodies. Similar parallels could be found with all the New Testament gifts. Even the diversity of gifts should lead to greater unity and interdependence in the church (see 1 Cor. 12:12–13, 24–25; Eph. 4:13), and this diversity in unity will itself be a foretaste of the unity that believers will have in heaven.

**3. How Many Gifts Are There?** The New Testament epistles list specific spiritual gifts in six different passages. Consider the table on the next page.

What is obvious is that these lists are all quite different. No one list has all these gifts, and no gift except prophecy is mentioned on all the lists (prophecy is not mentioned in 1 Cor. 7:7, where only the subject of marriage and celibacy is under discussion, but it is certainly included in the "whoever speaks" of 1 Peter 4:11). In fact, 1 Corinthians 7:7 mentions two gifts that are not on any other list: in the context of speaking of marriage and celibacy, Paul says, "Each has his own special *gifts*[6] from God, one of one kind and one of another."

These facts indicate that Paul was not attempting to construct exhaustive lists of gifts when he specified the ones he did. Although there is sometimes an indication of some order (he puts apostles first, prophets second, and teachers third, but

---

[5]This interpretation of 1 Cor. 13:10 is defended at greater length in section B below.

[6]The Greek term for "gift" here is *charisma*, the same term Paul uses in 1 Cor. 12–14 to talk about spiritual gifts.

**1 Corinthians 12:28**
1. apostle[8]
2. prophet
3. teacher
4. miracles
5. kinds of healings
6. helps
7. administration
8. tongues

**1 Corinthians 12:8–10**
9. word of wisdom
10. word of knowledge
11. faith
(5) gifts of healing
(4) miracles
(2) prophecy
12. distinguishing between spirits
(8) tongues
13. interpretation of tongues

**Ephesians 4:11[7]**
(1) apostle
(2) prophet
14. evangelist
15. pastor-teacher

**Romans 12:6–8**
(2) prophecy
16. serving
(3) teaching
17. encouraging
18. contributing
19. leadership
20. mercy

**1 Corinthians 7:7**
21. marriage
22. celibacy

**1 Peter 4:11**
whoever speaks (covering several gifts)
whoever renders service (covering several gifts)

tongues last in 1 Cor. 12:28), it seems that in general Paul was almost randomly listing a series of different examples of gifts as they came to mind.

Moreover, there is some degree of overlap among the gifts listed at various places. No doubt the gift of administration (*kybernēsis*, 1 Cor. 12:28) is similar to the gift of leadership (*ho proistamenos*, Rom. 12:8), and both terms could probably be applied to many who have the office of pastor-teacher (Eph. 4:11). Moreover, in some cases Paul lists an activity and in other cases lists the related noun that describes the person (such as "prophecy" in Rom. 12:6 and 1 Cor. 12:10, but "prophet" in 1 Cor. 12:28 and Eph. 4:11).[9]

---

[7]This list gives four kinds of persons in terms of offices or functions, not, strictly speaking, four gifts. For three of the functions on the list, the corresponding gifts would be prophecy, evangelism, and teaching.

[8]Strictly speaking, to be an apostle is an office, not a gift (see chapter 47, pp. 905–12, on the office of apostle).

[9]Something can be said at this point about the relationship between gifts and offices in the church As we look at these lists, it is evident that in some cases Paul names the specific gift (such as gifts of healing or administration or tongues), and in other cases he names the *persons* who have those gifts (such as apostles, prophets, or evangelists). Some lists name only the gifts themselves (such as 1 Cor. 12:8–10), while other lists name only the people who possess those gifts (such as Eph. 4:11 or 1 Peter 4:11). And some lists are mixed, naming some gifts and some persons who have the gifts (such as Rom. 12:6–8 and 1 Cor. 12:28).

In addition to that, another distinction should be made: In cases where Paul names *persons*, he sometimes gives a name that refers to an officially recognized *office* in the church (such as "apostles" or "pastor-teachers"). We would expect that such people would begin to function in those offices after they had received formal recognition by the church as a whole (this would be called "ordination" or "installation in office" for the office of pastor [or elder] for example). But in other cases, though the person is named, it is not necessary to think there was any official recognition or establishment in office in front of the entire church. This would be the case, for example, for "he who encourages" and "he who contributes" and "he who does acts of mercy" in Rom. 12:6–8. Similarly, the New Testament does not clearly indicate that prophets or evangelists were established in any formally recognized offices in the early church, and the word "prophet" probably just refers to one who prophesied regularly and with evident blessing in the church. "Evangelist" could similarly refer to those who regularly

Another reason for thinking that Paul could have made much longer lists if he had wanted to is the fact that some of the gifts listed will have many different expressions as they are found in different people. Certainly the gift of serving (Rom. 12:6) or helps (1 Cor. 12:28) will take many different forms in different situations and among different people. Some may serve or help by giving wise counsel, others by cooking meals, others by caring for children or befriending an older person, others by giving specialized legal or medical or financial advice when needed within the church. These gifts differ greatly. Among those who possess the gift of evangelism, some will be good at personal evangelism within a neighborhood, others at evangelism through writing of tracts and Christian literature, and others at evangelism through large campaigns and public meetings. Still others will be good at evangelism through radio and television. Not all of these evangelistic gifts are the same, even though they fall under the broad category of "evangelism." The same could be said about gifts of teaching or administration.[10] All of this simply means that no two people's gifts are exactly alike.

How many different gifts are there then? It simply depends on how specific we wish to be. We can make a very short list of only two gifts as Peter does in 1 Peter 4:11: "whoever *speaks*" and "whoever *renders service*." In this list of only two items Peter includes all the gifts mentioned in any other list because all of them fit in one of these two categories. On the other hand, we could take the Old Testament offices of prophet, priest, and king, and have a list of three kinds of gifts: *prophetic* gifts (in this broad sense) would include anything that involves teaching, encouraging, exhorting, or rebuking others. *Priestly* gifts would include anything that involves showing mercy and care for those in need or involve interceding before God (such as praying in tongues). The *kingly* gifts would involve anything having to do with administration or government or order in the church.

Other classifications of gifts are gifts of *knowledge* (such as distinguishing between spirits, word of wisdom, and word of knowledge), gifts of *power* (such as healing, miracles, and faith), and gifts of *speech* (tongues, interpretation, and prophecy).[11] Then again we could make a much longer list, such as the list of twenty-two gifts enumerated above. But even that list does not include all the possible gifts (no list includes a gift of intercessory prayer, for instance, which may be related to a gift of faith but is not the same as a gift of faith; no musical gifts are included on any list either, and neither is any gift of casting out demons, even though Paul must have known that some Christians were more effective in that

functioned effectively in the work of evangelism, and "teachers" could include both those who had formally recognized teaching functions in the church, perhaps in connection with the office of elder, and those who had teaching functions in less-formal capacities in the church but regularly taught with effectiveness in informal or smaller group settings.

For convenience, we will continue to refer to these lists as lists of "spiritual gifts," although, to be more precise, we should realize that they include both spiritual gifts and persons who exercise those gifts. Since both the gifts and the persons are given to the church by Jesus Christ, it is appropriate that both are named in various parts of these lists.

[10]See the excellent discussion in John R. W. Stott, *Baptism and Fullness: The Work of the Holy Spirit Today* (Downers Grove, Ill. InterVarsity Press, 1964), pp. 88–89.

[11]This classification is from Dennis and Rita Bennett, *The Holy Spirit and You* (Plainfield, N.J.: Logos International, 1971), p. 83. The Bennetts' actual categorization is gifts of revelation, gifts of power, and inspirational or fellowship gifts, and they list them in reverse order to what I have given here.

area than others). And if we wished to divide up *different kinds* of service or administration or evangelism or teaching, then we could quite easily have a list that included fifty or even a hundred items.[12]

The point of all of this is simply to say that God gives the church an amazing variety of spiritual gifts, and they are all tokens of his varied grace. In fact, Peter says as much: "As each has received a gift, employ it for one another, as good stewards of God's *varied grace*" (1 Peter 4:10; the word "varied" here is *poikilos*, which means "having many facets or aspects; having rich diversity").

The practical outcome of this discussion is that we should be willing to recognize and appreciate people who have gifts that differ from ours and whose gifts may differ from our expectations of what certain gifts should look like. Moreover, a healthy church will have a great diversity of gifts, and this diversity should not lead to fragmentation but to greater unity among believers in the church. Paul's whole point in the analogy of the body with many members (1 Cor. 12:12–26) is to say that God has put us in the body with these differences *so that we might depend on each other.* "The eye cannot say to the hand, 'I have no need of you,' nor again the head to the feet, 'I have no need of you.' On the contrary, the parts of the body which seem to be weaker are indispensable" (1 Cor. 12:21–22; cf. vv. 4–6). It runs counter to the world's way of thinking to say that we will enjoy greater unity when we join closely together with those who are different from us, but that is precisely the point that Paul makes in 1 Corinthians 12, demonstrating the glory of God's wisdom in not allowing anyone to have all the necessary gifts for the church, but in requiring us to depend upon each other for the proper functioning of the church.

**4. Gifts May Vary in Strength.** Paul says that if we have the gift of prophecy, we should use it *"in proportion to our faith"* (Rom. 12:6), indicating that the gift can be more or less strongly developed in different individuals, or in the same individual over a period of time. This is why Paul can remind Timothy, "Do not neglect the gift you have" (1 Tim. 4:14), and can say, "I remind you to *rekindle* the gift of God that is within you" (2 Tim. 1:6). It was possible for Timothy to allow his gift to weaken, apparently through infrequent use, and Paul reminds him to stir it up by using it and thereby strengthening it. This should not be surprising, for we realize that many gifts increase in strength and effectiveness as they are used, whether evangelism, teaching, encouraging, administration, or faith. Apollos had a strong gift of preaching and teaching, for we read that he was "mighty (or "powerful," Gk. *dynatos*) in the Scriptures" (Acts 18:24 NASB). And Paul apparently had a frequently used and very effective gift of speaking in tongues because he says, "I thank God that I speak in tongues more than you all" (1 Cor. 14:18).[13]

All of these texts indicate that *spiritual gifts may vary in strength.* If we think of any gift, whether teaching or evangelism on the one hand, or prophecy or healing

---

[12]This variety of ways of classifying gifts allows us to say that many types of classification are possible for teaching purposes, but we should beware of any claim that a certain way of classifying or listing gifts is the only valid one, for Scripture does not limit us to any one scheme of classification.

[13]See also 1 Cor. 13:1–3 where Paul gives examples of some gifts developed to the highest imaginable degree, examples which he uses to show that even such gifts without love would bring no benefit.

on the other, we should realize that within any congregation there will likely be people who are very effective in the use of that gift (perhaps through long use and experience), others who are moderately strong in that gift, and others who probably have the gift but are just beginning to use it. This variation in strength in spiritual gifts depends on a combination of divine and human influence. The divine influence is the sovereign working of the Holy Spirit as he "apportions to each one individually as he wills" (1 Cor. 12:11). The human influence comes from experience, training, wisdom, and natural ability in the use of that gift. It is usually not possible to know in what proportion the divine and human influences combine at any one time, nor is it really necessary to know, for even the abilities we think to be "natural" are from God (1 Cor. 4:7) and under his sovereign control (see chapter 16 on God's providence and human responsibility).

But this leads to an interesting question: how strong does an ability have to be before it can be called a spiritual gift? How much teaching ability does someone need before he or she could be said to have a gift of teaching, for example? Or how effective in evangelism would someone need to be before we would recognize a gift of evangelism? Or how frequently would someone have to see prayers for healing answered before he or she could be said to have a gift of healing?

Scripture does not directly answer this question, but the fact that Paul speaks of these gifts as useful for the building up of the church (1 Cor. 14:12), and the fact that Peter likewise says that each person who has received a gift should remember to employ it "for one another" (1 Peter 4:10), suggest that both Paul and Peter thought of gifts as abilities that were *strong enough to function for the benefit of the church,* whether for the assembled congregation (as in prophecy or teaching), or for individuals at various times in the congregation (as helps or encouragement).

Probably no definite line can be drawn in this matter, but Paul does remind us that *not all have every gift or any one gift.* He is quite clear in this in a set of questions that expect the answer no at each point: "Are all apostles? Are all prophets? Are all teachers? Do all work miracles? Do all possess gifts of healing? Do all speak with tongues? Do all interpret?" (1 Cor. 12:29–30)
The Greek text (with the particle *mē* before each question) clearly expects the answer no to every question. Therefore, not all are teachers, for example, nor do all possess gifts of healing, nor do all speak in tongues.

But even though not all have the gift of teaching, it is true that all people "teach" *in some sense* of the word *teach.* Even people who would never dream of teaching a Sunday school class will read Bible stories to their own children and explain the meaning to them—indeed, Moses commanded the Israelites to do this very thing with their children (Deut. 6:7), explaining God's words to them as they sat in their house or walked on the road. So we must say on the one hand that not everyone has the *gift* of teaching. But on the other hand we must say that there is *some general ability* related to the gift of teaching that all Christians have. Another way of saying this would be to say that there is no spiritual gift that all believers have, yet there is some general ability similar to every gift that all Christians have.

We can see this with a number of gifts. Not all Christians have a gift of evangelism, but all Christians have the ability to share the gospel with their neighbors. Not all Christians have gifts of healing (in fact, as we shall see below, some people say that no one today has genuine gifts of healing), but nevertheless every Christian can and does pray for God to heal friends or relatives who are ill.

Not every Christian has the gift of faith, but every believer has some degree of faith, and we would expect it to be growing in the life of an ordinary Christian.

We can even say that other gifts, such as prophecy and speaking in tongues, not only vary in strength among those who have the gift, but also find a counterpart in some general abilities that are found in the life of every Christian. For example, if we understand prophecy (according to the definition given in chapter 53)[14] to be "reporting something that God spontaneously brings to mind," then it is true that not everyone experiences this as a gift, for not everyone experiences God spontaneously bringing things to mind with such clarity and force that he or she feels free to speak about them among an assembled group of Christians. But probably every believer has at one time or another had a sense that God was bringing to mind the need to pray for a distant friend or to write or phone a word of encouragement to someone distant, and later has found that that was exactly the thing that was needed at the moment. Few would deny that God sovereignly brought that need to mind in a spontaneous way, and, though this would not be called a gift of prophecy, it is a general ability to receive special direction or guidance from God that is similar to what happens in the gift of prophecy, although it is functioning at a weaker level.

We can even consider the gift of speaking in tongues from this perspective. If we think of speaking in tongues as prayer in syllables not understood by the speaker (see 1 Cor. 14:2, 14),[15] then it is true that not every Christian has the gift of speaking in tongues (and once again it must be said that some Christians would argue that no one has that gift today, since the age of the apostles has ended). But on the other hand we must recognize that every Christian has times of prayer in which his or her prayer is expressed not only in intelligible words and syllables, but also in terms of sighs, groans, or weeping that we know is understood and heard by the Lord, and that expresses needs and concerns of our hearts that we cannot fully put into words (cf. Rom. 8:26–27). Once again we should not call this a gift of speaking in tongues, but it does seem to be a general ability in our Christian lives that is somewhat related to the gift of speaking in tongues, in that it gives expression to prayer in syllables that we do not fully understand, but that the Holy Spirit nonetheless makes into effective prayer that is heard by God.

The point of this whole discussion is simply to say that spiritual gifts are not as mysterious and "other worldly" as people sometimes make them out to be. Many of them are only intensifications or highly developed instances of phenomena that most Christians experience in their own lives. The other important point to be drawn from this discussion is that even though we have been given gifts by God, we are still responsible to use them effectively, and to seek to grow in their use that the church may receive more benefit from the gifts of which God has allowed us to be stewards.

Finally, the fact that gifts may vary in strength allows us to recognize that a certain person's gift (such as teaching or administration, for example) may not be strong enough to function for the benefit of the entire church in a large church where many people already have that gift developed to a very high degree. But that same person, moving to a younger, smaller church where few have gifts of

---

[14]See chapter 53, pp. 1049–61, for a definition of the gift of prophecy in the church.
[15]See also the discussion of the gift of speaking in tongues in chapter 53, pp. 1069–80.

teaching or administration, may find that his or her gifts are very much in demand and able to function for the benefit of the entire congregation. (In this sense, something that is only considered a general ability in one setting might rightly be considered a spiritual gift in another setting.)

**5. Do Christians Possess Gifts Temporarily or Permanently?** In most cases, it seems that the New Testament pictures a *permanent* possession of spiritual gifts. The analogy of the parts of the body in 1 Corinthians 12:12–26 fits this, in that the eye does not become a hand, nor does the ear become a foot, but various parts exist in the body permanently.[16] Moreover, Paul says that some people have titles that describe a continuing function. Some people can be called "prophets" or "teachers" (1 Cor. 12:29) or "evangelists" (Eph. 4:11). We would expect that those people have a permanent possession of the gifts of prophecy, teaching, and evangelism, unless some unusual circumstance would come along which would take that gift away. Similarly, Paul talks in terms of possessing spiritual gifts when he says, "If I *have* the gift of prophecy" (1 Cor. 13:2 NIV). And when Paul requires that there be an interpreter present for anyone to speak in tongues (1 Cor. 14:28), he assumes that the church will know whether someone who has the gift of interpretation is present, which implies that that gift would be possessed by someone over time. When he says, "If any one thinks that he is a prophet" (1 Cor. 14:37), he realizes that some at Corinth will have functioned with the gift of prophecy frequently enough to think of themselves as "prophets." All of these verses point in the direction of a permanent, or at least abiding and continuing, possession of spiritual gifts.

Indeed, in Romans 12, Paul begins his sentence, "*Having gifts* that differ according to the grace given to us" (Rom. 12:6). And he tells Timothy, "Do not neglect the gift *that is in you*" (1 Tim. 4:14, literal translation), again indicating that Timothy had had that gift over a period of time. Therefore it seems that in general the New Testament indicates that people have spiritual gifts given to them and, once they have them, they are usually able to continue to use them over the course of their Christian life.

However, some important qualifications must be made, because there are some senses in which gifts are *not permanent*. There are some gifts that are nonpermanent by their very nature, such as the gifts of marriage and celibacy (1 Cor. 7:7). Though Paul calls them gifts, in the lives of most believers there will be times at which they are unmarried, and times at which they are married. Moreover, some gifts, though perhaps exercised fairly frequently, still cannot be exercised at will. Effectiveness in the gift of healing, for example, depends on God's sovereign will in answering prayer for healing. Similarly, prophecy depends on the giving of a spontaneous "revelation" (1 Cor. 14:30) from God, and simply cannot be exercised at will. The same could even be said about the gift of evangelism: It is ultimately the work of the Holy Spirit to bring regeneration and enable someone to believe, so the evangelist may pray and preach, but only God can give the harvest of souls.

---

[16]We should not press the metaphor of the body too far, of course, for people *do* receive other gifts, and Paul even encourages people to seek additional spiritual gifts (1 Cor. 14:1). But the metaphor does suggest *some* degree of stability or permanence in the possession of gifts.

In other cases, some particular gift may be given for a unique need or event. Though it is not, strictly speaking, a spiritual gift in the New Testament sense, the return of Samson's strength one last time at the end of his life (Judg. 16:28) was given temporarily for one final moment in his life. And, in the New Testament, the remarkable revelation of heaven Stephen had when he, "full of the Holy Spirit, gazed into heaven and saw the glory of God, and Jesus standing at the right hand of God" (Acts 7:55) was a manifestation of the Spirit given to him only for that specific moment.

Another sense in which a gift may be non-permanent is if a person neglects his or her gift, and perhaps grieves the Holy Spirit or falls into serious doctrinal or moral error (as Samson did in the Old Testament, for example). In such a case the gift may be withdrawn. Certainly Paul warned Timothy, "Do not neglect the gift you have" (1 Tim. 4:14), and we may perhaps also learn from the parable of the talents, in which Jesus says that "to every one who has will more be given, and he will have abundance; but from him who has not, even what he has will be taken away" (Matt. 25:29).[17]

Moreover, we must remember that *the Holy Spirit is still sovereign in distributing gifts:* he "apportions to each one individually *as he wills*" (1 Cor. 12:11). The word here translated "apportions" is a present participle, which indicates continuing activity over time, and we could paraphrase, "The Holy Spirit *is always continuing to distribute or apportion gifts* to each person individually just as he wills to do." This means that, although it is *ordinarily* the custom of the Holy Spirit to continue to empower the same gift or gifts in people over time, nonetheless, there is a continual willing and deciding of the Holy Spirit to do this or not, and he may for his own reasons withdraw a gift for a time, or cause it to be much stronger or much weaker than it was.

Finally, 1 Corinthians 13:8–13 (to be discussed below) indicates that the present spiritual gifts which we have are only for this age, and will be superseded by something far greater. Therefore in that sense no gift is "permanent" since every gift will be rendered useless at the time of the Lord's return.

Within this discussion of the question of whether spiritual gifts are temporary or permanent, sometimes Romans 11:29 is mentioned: "For the gifts and the call of God are irrevocable." It does not seem to be appropriate to use the verse in the context of this discussion, however, for in this case Paul is talking about the status of the Jewish people, including their calling as God's people and the gifts or blessings bestowed on them as a result of that status. Here Paul is arguing that God still has a purpose for his people Israel, but the question of gifts of the Holy Spirit in the sense of 1 Corinthians 12–14 is not in view at all in Romans 11:29. And certainly in any case this sentence would not be true as a totally unrestricted statement concerning spiritual gifts, for it is evident that through misuse, neglect, or grieving of the Holy Spirit, people can have their gifts diminished or removed by God's sovereign choice.

---

[17]Although the primary point of this parable has to do with rewards at the final judgment, it nonetheless encourages faithfulness in stewardship with what one has been given, and it is not unreasonable to expect that God would act toward us in that way, at least in principle, in this life as well.

**6. Are Gifts Miraculous or Nonmiraculous?** The answer to this question really depends on the definition of the word *miracle*. If we define *miracle* as "a direct activity of God in the world," then all the spiritual gifts are miraculous because they are all empowered by the Holy Spirit (1 Cor. 12:11; cf. vv. 4–6). But in that sense *everything* that happens in the world might be said to be miraculous, because all of it is brought about by God's providential work in creation (see Eph. 1:11; Dan. 4:35; Matt. 5:45).[18] Therefore the word *miracle* loses its usefulness, because it is difficult for us to find something that happens in the world that is *not* miraculous in this sense.

It is better to define *miracle* in a narrower sense, as we did in chapter 17, above: A miracle is a "less common activity of God in which he arouses people's awe and wonder and bears witness to himself."[19] In terms of this definition, only some gifts are "miraculous": namely, those gifts that people think to be miraculous because they are amazed at the activity of God operating in them. Certainly we would include in this category prophecy (note the amazement of the unbeliever in 1 Cor. 14:24–25), healing (similarly, note the response of people in Acts 3:10 et al.), casting out of demons (see Acts 19:11–13, 17), or speaking in tongues when it is an actual foreign language and understood by others (see the description of Pentecost in Acts 2:7). Probably other remarkable phenomena would be included in the gift of miracles (1 Cor. 12:10) as well.

On the other hand, in this definition, some gifts would be thought of as nonmiraculous. Gifts of serving, teaching, encouraging, contributing, and doing acts of mercy (in Rom. 12:7–8) would fall in this category, as would the gifts of those who act as helpers and administrators (1 Cor. 12:28). But it is still the same Holy Spirit who gives them and works through them.

The point of this analysis is to caution us against making a supernatural/natural distinction in our minds whereby we think that some gifts are "supernatural" and some gifts are simply "natural." The Bible makes no such distinction, and the danger of doing this is that we may tend to think that some gifts (which we think to be "supernatural") are more important or more clearly from the Lord, and we may tend to devalue or deemphasize the gifts which we think to be "natural." If we do this we will fail to see God's hand in the working of all the gifts and fail to thank him for all of them.

On the other hand, the misleading supernatural/natural distinction could also cause us to be very suspicious about those which we think to be "supernatural," or could lead us to think that they are very unlikely to happen in our own experience. In that case, we would tend to emphasize the gifts we thought to be "natural" and have a very low degree of expectation or faith regarding anything which we thought to be "supernatural."

In contrast to this perspective, Scripture says that "all" the gifts are worked in us by the same Holy Spirit, the same Lord, and the same God (1 Cor. 12:4–6). The worldview of Scripture is one of continuity and continual interaction between the *visible world* that we can see and touch and the *invisible world* that Scripture tells us is there and is real. God works in both, and we do ourselves and the church a great

---

[18]See the discussion of various definitions for the word *miracle* in chapter 17, pp. 355–56.
[19]See chapter 17, p. 355.

disservice by separating these aspects of creation into "supernatural" and "natural."

Finally, should we seek the more unusual or miraculous gifts, or should we seek the more ordinary gifts? Once again, Scripture does not make this kind of distinction when it tells us what kind of gifts to seek. Paul says to the Corinthians, "Since you are eager for manifestations of the Spirit, *strive to excel in building up the church*" (1 Cor. 14:12). This means that we should learn which gifts are most needed in the church we attend, and then pray that God would give those gifts to ourselves or to others. Whether those gifts are thought to be miraculous or non-miraculous really is not the important point at all.[20]

**7. Discovering and Seeking Spiritual Gifts.** Paul seems to assume that believers will know what their spiritual gifts are. He simply tells those in the church at Rome to use their gifts in various ways: "if prophecy, in proportion to our faith . . . he who contributes, in liberality; he who gives aid, with zeal; he who does acts of mercy, with cheerfulness" (Rom. 12:6–8). Similarly, Peter simply tells his readers how to use their gifts, but does not say anything about discovering what they are: "*As each has received a gift,* employ it for one another, as good stewards of God's varied grace" (1 Peter 4:10).

But what if many members in a church do not know what spiritual gift or gifts God has given to them? In such a case, the leaders of the church need to ask whether they are providing sufficient opportunities for varieties of gifts to be used. Though the lists of gifts given in the New Testament are not exhaustive, they certainly provide a good starting point for churches to ask whether at least there is opportunity for *these gifts* to be used. If God has placed people with certain gifts in a church when these gifts are not encouraged or perhaps not allowed to be used, they will feel frustrated and unfulfilled in their Christian ministries, and will perhaps move to another church where their gifts can function for the benefit of the church.

In the case of individuals who do not know what their gifts are, they can begin by asking what the needs and opportunities for ministry are in their church. Specifically, they can ask what gifts are most needed for the building up of the church at that point. In addition, each individual believer who does not know what his or her gifts are should do some self-examination. What interests and desires and abilities does he or she have? Can others give advice or encouragement pointing in the direction of specific gifts? Moreover, has there been blessing in the past in ministering in a particular kind of service? In all of this, the person seeking to discover his or her gifts should pray and ask God for wisdom, confident that it will be given according to his promise, "If any of you lacks wisdom, let him ask God, who gives to all men generously and without reproaching, and it will be given him. But let him ask in faith, with no doubting" (James 1:5–6). Sometimes God will grant this wisdom in terms of more accurate insight into one's own abilities. At other times it may come through advice from others or through seeing increased blessing in one area of ministry. And Paul indicates that in some cases there may be prophecy that gives indication of a specific gift, for he says to

---

[20]See chapter 17, pp. 369–72, for a discussion of the objection that it is wrong to seek miraculous gifts or miracles today.

Timothy, *"Do not neglect the gift you have, which was given you through prophecy* with the laying on of hands of the council of elders" (1 Tim. 4:14, author's translation).

Finally, the person wondering what his or her spiritual gifts are should simply begin to try ministering in various areas and see where God brings blessing. Teaching a Sunday school class or home Bible study is an excellent way to begin using the gift of teaching. Every community has opportunities for greater use of the gift of evangelism. People who think they may have a gift of healing could ask their elders for opportunities to accompany them when they go to pray for the sick. People who think they may have a gift of faith or a gift of intercessory prayer could begin to ask some Christian friends for specific needs about which to pray. In all of this, churches can give encouragement and opportunities for people to try out using various gifts, and can also give teaching and practical training in the proper methods of using various gifts. In addition, churches should continually be praying that God would allow people to find what their gifts are and then to be able to use them. In all of this the goal is that the body of Christ in each location grow up to maturity, until "the whole body, joined and knit together by every joint with which it is supplied, *when each part is working properly,* makes bodily growth and upbuilds itself in love" (Eph. 4:16).

Beyond the question of discovering what gifts one has is the question of seeking additional spiritual gifts. Paul commands Christians, *"Earnestly desire the higher gifts"* (1 Cor. 12:31), and says later, "Make love your aim, and *earnestly desire the spiritual gifts,* especially that you may prophesy" (1 Cor. 14:1). In this context, Paul defines what he means by "higher gifts" or "greater gifts" because in 1 Corinthians 14:5 he repeats the word he used in 12:31 for "higher" (Gk. *meizōn*) when he says, "He who prophesies is *greater* than he who speaks in tongues, unless someone interprets, *so that the church may be edified"* (1 Cor. 14:5). Here the "greater" gifts are those that most edify the church. This is consistent with Paul's statement a few verses later, when he says, "since you are eager for manifestations of the Spirit, strive to excel in building up the church" (1 Cor. 14:12). The *higher gifts* are *those that build up the church more and bring more benefit to others.*

But how do we seek more spiritual gifts? First, we should *ask God for them.* Paul says directly that "he who speaks in a tongue *should pray for the power to interpret"* (1 Cor. 14:13; cf. James 1:5, where James tells people that they should ask God for wisdom). Next, people who seek additional spiritual gifts should *have right motives.* If spiritual gifts are sought only so that the person may be more prominent or have more influence or power, this certainly is wrong in God's eyes. This was the motivation of Simon the Sorcerer in Acts 8:19, when he said, "Give me also this power, that any one on whom I lay my hands may receive the Holy Spirit" (see Peter's rebuke in vv. 21–22). Similarly, Ananias and Sapphira sought glory for themselves when they purported to be giving the entire proceeds of the sale of their land to the church, but it was not true, and both lost their lives (Acts 5:1–11). It is a fearful thing to want spiritual gifts or prominence in the church only for our own glory, not for the glory of God and for the help of others. Therefore those who seek spiritual gifts must first ask if they are seeking them out of love for others and a concern to be able to minister to their needs, because those who have great spiritual gifts but "have not love" are "nothing" in God's sight (cf.

1 Cor. 13:1–3). This is why Paul says, *"Make love your aim,"* and only after that adds, "and earnestly desire the spiritual gifts" (1 Cor. 14:1). He repeats the same theme again when he says, "since you are eager for manifestations of the Spirit, *strive to excel in building up the church"* (1 Cor. 14:12). Every person asking God for an additional spiritual gift should search his or her own heart frequently, asking why this particular gift is desired. Is it really out of a love for others and a desire to build up the church and to see God glorified?

After that, it is appropriate to *seek opportunities to try the gift,* just as in the case of a person trying to discover his or her gift, as explained above. Small group Bible studies or prayer meetings in homes often provide a good setting in which people can try gifts of teaching or intercessory prayer or encouragement or prophecy or healing, for example.

Finally, those who are seeking additional spiritual gifts should *continue to use the gifts they now have,* and should *be content* if God chooses not to give them more. The master approved of the servant whose pound had "made ten pounds more," but condemned the one who hid his pound in a napkin and did nothing with it (Luke 19:16–17, 20–23)—certainly showing us that we have responsibility to *use* and *attempt to increase* whatever talents or abilities God has given to us as his stewards.

To balance this emphasis on seeking and growing in spiritual gifts we must also remember that Paul clearly says that spiritual gifts are apportioned to each person individually by the Holy Spirit *"as he wills"* (1 Cor. 12:11), and that "God arranged the organs in the body, each one of them, *as he chose"* (1 Cor. 12:18). He says that God has put various gifts in the church and not all are apostles or prophets or teachers (1 Cor. 12:28–30). In this way he reminds the Corinthians that ultimately the distribution of gifts is a matter of God's sovereign will, and it is for the good of the church and for our good that none of us have all of the gifts, and that we will need continually to depend on others who have gifts differing from ours. These considerations should make us content if God chooses not to give us the other gifts that we seek.

**8. Gifts Are Tools for Ministry, and Not Necessarily Related to Christian Maturity.** We must recognize that spiritual gifts are given to *every* believer (1 Cor. 12:7, 11; 1 Peter 4:10). Even immature Christians receive spiritual gifts from the Lord—this was certainly evident in the Corinthian church, which had an abundance of spiritual gifts (1 Cor. 1:7), but was still very immature in many areas of doctrine and conduct. Paul says, "But I, brethren, could not address you as spiritual men, but as men of the flesh, as babes in Christ" (1 Cor. 3:1). So spiritual gifts are not necessarily a sign of spiritual maturity. It is possible to have remarkable spiritual gifts in one area or another but still be quite immature in doctrinal understanding or in Christian conduct, as was the case at Corinth. Indeed, on occasion even *unbelievers* are able to prophesy and cast out demons and do miracles, for Jesus says that at the last day many will say to him, "Lord, Lord, did we not prophesy in your name, and cast out demons in your name, and do many mighty works in your name?" But Jesus will declare to them, "I *never* knew you; depart from me, you evildoers" (Matt. 7:22–23). It is not that Jesus knew them once and later did not know them; he says, "I never knew you." They were never Christians, yet they performed many remarkable works. So *we must not evaluate spiritual maturity on the basis of spiritual gifting.* Maturity comes through a close walk with Jesus, and results in obedience to his commands in everyday life: "He who says he abides in him ought to walk in the same way in which he walked" (1 John 2:6).

Why then does the Holy Spirit give us spiritual gifts? They are given for the work of ministry and are *simply tools* to be used for that end. They should never be a source of personal pride on the part of those who possess them, nor should they be thought of as a mark of maturity. We should strive simply to excel in loving others, caring for their needs, building up the church, and living a life of conformity to the pattern of Christ's life. If we do that, and if God chooses to give us spiritual gifts that equip us for those tasks, then we should thank him for that, and pray that he would keep us from pride over gifts that have been freely and graciously given, and which we did not earn.

## B. Have Some Gifts Ceased? The Cessationist Debate

Within the evangelical world today there are differing positions over the question, "Are all the gifts mentioned in the New Testament valid for use in the church today?" Some would say yes.[21] Others would say no, and would argue that some of the more miraculous gifts (such as prophecy, tongues plus interpretation, and perhaps healing and casting out of demons) were given only during the time of the apostles, as "signs" to authenticate the apostles during the early preaching of the gospel. They state that these gifts are no longer needed as signs today, and that they ceased at the end of the apostolic age, probably at the end of the first century or beginning of the second century A.D.

We should also realize that there is a large "middle" group with respect to this question, a group of "mainstream evangelicals" who are neither charismatics or Pentecostals on the one hand, nor "cessationists"[22] on the other hand, but are simply undecided, and unsure if this question can be decided from Scripture.[23]

Although some aspects of this question were discussed in chapter 17 on miracles, there are some additional considerations that can be addressed here, specifically related to the topic of spiritual gifts.

## 1. Does 1 Corinthians 13:8–13 Tell Us When Miraculous Gifts Will Cease? Paul says:

Love never ends; as for prophecies, they will pass away; as for tongues, they will cease; as for knowledge, it will pass away. For our knowledge is imperfect and our prophecy is imperfect; but *when the perfect comes, the imperfect will pass away.* When I was a child, I spoke like a child, I thought like a child, I reasoned like a child; when

---

[21]Many who say yes, such as the present author, would add the qualification that "apostle" is an office, not a gift, and that the office of apostle does not continue today (see chapter 47, pp. 905–12, for this argument).

[22]*Cessationist* refers to someone who thinks that certain miraculous spiritual gifts *ceased* long ago, when the apostles died and Scripture was complete.

[23]The discussion in the remainder of this section on the cessationist debate is adapted from Wayne Grudem, *The Gift of Prophecy in the New Testament and Today* (Eastbourne: Kingsway, and Westchester, Ill.: Crossway, 1988), pp. 227–52, and is used by permission.

I became a man, I gave up childish ways. For now we see in a mirror dimly, but then face to face. Now I know in part; then I shall understand fully, even as I have been fully understood. So faith, hope, love abide, these three; but the greatest of these is love. (1 Cor. 13:8–13)

This passage is important to the discussion because in it Paul mentions the gift of prophecy as something that is "imperfect," and then says that what is "imperfect" will "pass away" (1 Cor. 13:10). He even says when this will happen: "when the perfect comes." But when is that? And even if we can determine when it is, does that mean that Paul had in mind something that would answer this "cessation" question for the church today? Can the gift of prophecy in this passage be representative of miraculous gifts in general in the church age?

**a. The Purpose of 1 Corinthians 13:8–13:** Paul interrupts his discussion of spiritual gifts with chapter 13 of 1 Corinthians, in which he intends to put the entire discussion of gifts in proper perspective. It is not enough simply to "seek the greater gifts" (12:31a, author's translation). One must also "seek after love" (14:1, author's translation), thus coupling proper goals with proper motives. Without love, the gifts are without value (13:1–3). In fact, Paul argues, love is superior to all the gifts and therefore it is more important to act in love than to have any of the gifts.

In order to show the superiority of love, Paul argues that it lasts forever, whereas the gifts are all temporary (13:8). Verses 9–12 further explain why the gifts are temporary. Our present knowledge and prophesying are partial and imperfect (v. 9), but someday something perfect will come to replace them (v. 10). This is explained by the analogy of a child who gives up childish thought and speech for the thought and speech of an adult (v. 11). Paul then elaborates further on verses 9–10 by explaining that our present perception and knowledge are indirect and imperfect, but that someday they will be direct and perfect (v. 12).

In this argument Paul connects the function of prophecy with the time of its cessation. It fills a certain need now, but does so only imperfectly. When "the perfect" comes, that function will be better fulfilled by something else, and prophecy will cease because it will be made obsolete or useless (this is the probable nuance of the Greek term used here, *katargeō*, "pass away" in vv. 8, 10). So the overall function of 1 Corinthians 13:8–13 is to show that love is superior to gifts like prophecy because those gifts will pass away but love will not pass away.

**b. 1 Corinthians 13:10: The Cessation of Prophecy When Christ Returns:** Paul writes in verse 10, "But *when the perfect comes,* the imperfect will pass away." The phrase "the imperfect" (Gk. *ek merous*, "partial, imperfect") refers most clearly to knowing and prophesying, the two activities that are said to be done "partially, imperfectly" in verse 9 (also using in both cases the same Greek phrase, *ek merous*). To bring out this connection, we could translate,

> Love never fails. Whether there be prophecies, they will *pass away;* whether there be tongues, they will *cease;* whether there be knowledge, it will *pass away.* This is because we know *imperfectly* and we prophesy *imperfectly*—but when the perfect comes, the imperfect will *pass away.*

Thus, the strong links between the statements are made clear by the repetition of two key terms, "pass away" and "imperfect."

No doubt Paul also intended tongues to be included in the sense of verse 9 as among those activities that are "imperfect," but omitted overly pedantic repetition for stylistic reasons. Yet tongues must be understood as part of the sense of verse 9, for verse 9 is the reason for verse 8, as the word "for" (Gk. *gar*) shows. Thus verse 9 must give the reason why tongues, as well as knowledge and prophecy, will cease. In fact, the repeated "if . . . if . . . if" in verse 8 suggests that Paul could have listed more gifts here (wisdom, healing, interpretation?) if he had wished.

So 1 Corinthians 13:10 could be paraphrased, "When the perfect is come, *prophecy and tongues and other imperfect gifts* will pass away." The only remaining problem is to determine what time is meant by the word "when." Several factors in the context argue that the time of the Lord's return is what Paul has in mind.

(1) First, the meaning of verse 12 seems to require that verse 10 is talking about the time of the Lord's return. The word "then" (Gk. *tote*) in verse 12 refers to the time "when the perfect comes" in verse 10. This is evident from looking at verse 12: "For now we see in a mirror dimly, but then face to face. Now I know in part; *then* I shall know even as I have been known" (author's translation).

When shall we see "face to face"? When shall we know "even as we have been known"? These events can only happen when the Lord returns.

The phrase "see face to face" is several times used in the Old Testament to refer to seeing God personally[24]—not fully or exhaustively, for no finite creature can ever do that, but personally and truly nonetheless. So when Paul says, "but then face to face" he clearly means, "but then *we shall see God* face to face." Indeed, that will be the greatest blessing of heaven and our greatest joy for all eternity.(Rev. 22:4: "They shall see his face").

The second half of verse 12 says, "Now I know in part; then I shall know even as I have been known." The second and third word for "know"—the one used for "Then I shall *know* even as I have been *known*"—is a somewhat stronger word for knowing (Gk. *epiginōskō*), but certainly does not imply infinite knowledge or omniscience. Paul does not expect to know all things, and he does not say, "Then I shall know all things," which would have been easy to say in Greek.[25] Rather, he means that when the Lord returns Paul expects to be freed from the misconceptions and inabilities to understand (especially to understand God and his work) which are part of this present life. His knowledge will resemble God's present knowledge of him because it will contain no false impressions and will not be limited to what is able to be perceived in this age. But such knowledge will only occur when the Lord returns.

Now what is the word "then" in verse 12 referring to? Paul says, "For now we see in a mirror dimly, but *then* we shall see face to face. Now I know in part; but *then* I shall know even as I have been known" (author's translation). His word "then" has to refer back to something in the previous verses that he has been explaining. We look first to verse 11, but see that nothing in verse 11 can be a

[24]See, for example, Gen. 32:30 and Judg. 6:22 (exactly the same Greek wording as 1 Cor. 13:12); Deut. 5:4; 34:10; Ezek. 20:35 (very similar wording); Ex. 33:11 (the same concept, and the same wording as some of the preceding passages in Hebrew, but different wording this time in the Greek translation of the Septuagint).
[25]Greek *epignōsomai ta panta* would say, "I shall know all things."

future time Paul refers to as "then": "When I was a child, I spoke like a child, I thought like a child, I reasoned like a child; when I became a man, I gave up childish ways." All of this refers to the past, not the future. It speaks of past events in Paul's life by way of providing a natural human illustration of what he has said in verse 10. But nothing in the verse speaks of a future time when something *will* happen.

So we look back to verse 10: "but when the perfect comes, the imperfect will pass away." Here is a statement about the future. At some point in the future, Paul says that "the perfect" *will* come, and "the imperfect" *will* pass away, *will* be "made useless." When will this happen? This is what is explained by verse 12. *Then,* at the time the perfect comes, we shall see "face to face" and know "even as we are known."

This means that the time when "the perfect" comes must be the time of Christ's return.[26] Therefore, we can paraphrase verse 10: "But *when Christ returns,* the imperfect will pass away."[27] Or, to use our conclusion above that "the imperfect" included prophecy and tongues, we can paraphrase, "But *when Christ returns, prophecy and tongues (and other imperfect gifts) will pass away."* Thus we have in 1 Corinthians 13:10 a definite statement about the time of the cessation of imperfect gifts like prophecy: they will "be made useless" or "pass away" *when Christ returns.* And this would imply that they will continue to exist and be useful for the church, throughout the church age, including today, and right up to the day when Christ returns.

(2) Another reason why the time when "the perfect" comes is the time when Christ returns is also evident from the purpose of the passage: Paul is attempting to emphasize the greatness of love, and in so doing he wants to establish that "Love never ends" (1 Cor. 13:8). To prove his point he argues that it will last beyond the time when the Lord returns, unlike present spiritual gifts. This makes a convincing argument: love is so fundamental to God's plans for the universe that it will last beyond the transition from this age to the age to come at Christ's return—it will continue for eternity.

(3) A third reason why this passage refers to the time of the Lord's return can be found in a more general statement from Paul about the purpose of spiritual gifts in the New Testament age. In 1 Corinthians 1:7 Paul ties the possession of spiritual gifts (Gk. *charismata*) to the activity of waiting for the Lord's return: "you are not lacking in any spiritual gift, as you wait for the revealing of our Lord Jesus Christ."

---

[26]I have stated it this way because, more precisely, "the perfect" in 1 Cor. 13:10 is not Christ himself, but is a method of acquiring knowledge which is so superior to present knowledge and prophecy that it makes these two obsolete. For when this "perfect" comes it renders the imperfect useless. But only the kind of knowledge Paul expected in the final consummation of all things could be so qualitatively different from present knowledge that it could provide this kind of contrast and be called "the perfect" as opposed to "the imperfect."

[27]D. A. Carson, *Showing the Spirit: A Theological Exposition of 1 Corinthians 12–14* (Grand Rapids: Baker, 1987), pp. 70–72, gives several similar reasons why the time "when the perfect comes" must be the time of Christ's return (with references to other views, and to the relevant literature).

Among "cessationists" (those who hold that gifts such as prophecy have "ceased" and are not valid for today), some, but not all, agree that the time "when the perfect comes" must be the time of Christ's return: see John F. MacArthur, Jr., *The Charismatics: A Doctrinal Perspective* (Grand Rapids: Zondervan, 1978), pp. 165–66, and Richard B. Gaffin, *Perspectives on Pentecost* (Phillipsburg, N.J.: Presbyterian and Reformed, 1979), p. 109.

This suggests that Paul saw the gifts as a temporary provision made to equip believers for ministry *until the Lord returned*. So this verse provides a close parallel to the thought of 1 Corinthians 13:8–13, where prophecy and knowledge (and no doubt tongues) are seen, similarly, as useful until Christ's return but unnecessary beyond that time.

1 Corinthians 13:10, therefore, refers to the time of Christ's return and says that these spiritual gifts will last among believers until that time. This means that we have a clear biblical statement that Paul expected these gifts to continue through the entire church age and to function for the benefit of the church until the Lord returns.

**c. Objections:** Various objections to this conclusion have been raised, usually by those who hold that these gifts have ceased in the church and should no longer be used.

**(1) This Passage Does Not Specify When the Gifts Will Cease**

The first objection to our conclusion above comes from Richard Gaffin's thoughtful study, *Perspectives on Pentecost.* While Dr. Gaffin agrees that "when the perfect comes" refers to the time of Christ's return, he does not think that this verse specifies the time of the cessation of certain gifts. He thinks, rather, that Paul is just viewing "the entire period until Christ's return, without regard to whether or not discontinuities may intervene during the course of this period."[28]

In fact, Gaffin argues, Paul's overall purpose is to emphasize the enduring qualities of faith, hope, and love, especially love, and not to specify the time in which certain gifts will cease. He says:

> Paul is not intending to specify the time when any particular mode will cease. What he does affirm is the termination of the believer's present, fragmentary knowledge . . . when "the perfect" comes. The time of the cessation of prophecy and tongues is an open question so far as this passage is concerned and will have to be decided on the basis of other passages and considerations.[29]

He also says that, in addition to prophecy, tongues, and knowledge, Paul might just as well have added "inscripturation," too—and if he had done this, the list would then have included an element that ceased long before Christ's return. (Inscripturation is the process of writing Scripture.) So, Gaffin concludes, it might be true of some of the others in the list as well.

In response to this objection it must be said that it does not do justice to the actual words of the text. Evangelicals have rightly insisted (and I know that Dr. Gaffin agrees with this) that passages of Scripture are true not only in the main point of each passage, but also in the minor details that are affirmed as well. The main point of the passage may well be that love lasts forever, but another point, and certainly an important one as well, is that verse 10 affirms not just that these imperfect gifts will cease sometime, but that they will cease "*when* the perfect comes." Paul specifies a certain time: "*When the perfect comes,* the imperfect will pass away." But Dr. Gaffin seems to claim that Paul is not actually saying this. Yet

---

[28]Richard B. Gaffin, *Perspectives on Pentecost,* pp. 109–10.
[29]Ibid., p. 111.

the force of the words cannot be avoided by affirming that overall theme of the larger context is something else.

In addition, Dr. Gaffin's suggestion does not seem to fit with the logic of the passage. Paul's argument is that it is specifically the coming of "the perfect," which does away with prophecy, tongues, and knowledge, because then there is a new, far-superior way of learning and knowing things "even as I have been known." But *until* that time, the new and superior way of knowing has not come, and therefore these imperfect gifts are still valid and useful. Finally, it is precarious to put much weight on something we think Paul might have said but in fact did not say. To say that Paul might have included "inscripturation" in this list means that Paul might have written, "When Christ returns, inscripturation will cease." But I cannot believe at all that Paul could have written such a statement, for it would have been false—indeed, a "false prophecy" in the words of Scripture. For "inscripturation" ceased long ago, when the book of Revelation was written by the apostle John.

So Dr. Gaffin's objections do not seem to overturn our conclusions on 1 Corinthians 13:10. If "the perfect" refers to the time of Christ's return, then Paul says that gifts such as prophecy and tongues will cease at that time, and implies therefore that they continue through the church age.

### (2) "When the Perfect Comes" in 1 Corinthians 13:10 Refers to a Time Earlier Than the Time of the Lord's Return

Those who make this second objection argue that "when the perfect comes" means one of several different things, such as "when the church is mature" or "when Scripture is complete" or "when the Gentiles are included in the church." Probably the most careful statement of this view is found in the book by Robert L. Reymond, *What About Continuing Revelations and Miracles in the Presbyterian Church Today?*[30] but another clear statement of a similar position is found in Walter Chantry's book, *Signs of the Apostles.*[31]

Chantry's argument depends on the fact that elsewhere in 1 Corinthians the word here translated "perfect" (Gk. *teleios*) is used to refer to human maturity (1 Cor. 14:20, "in thinking be mature") or to maturity in the Christian life (as in 1 Cor. 2:6). Yet here again we must note that a word does not have to be used to refer to the same thing every time it is used in Scripture—in some cases *teleios* may refer to "mature" or "perfect" manhood, in other cases some other kind of "completeness" or "perfection." The word *teleios* is used in Hebrews 9:11, for example, to refer to the "more perfect tent"—yet we would not therefore conclude that "perfect" in 1 Corinthians 13:10 must refer to a perfect tent. The precise referent of the word must be determined by the individual context, and there, as we have seen, the context indicates that "when the perfect comes" refers to the time of Christ's return.

[30]Robert L. Reymond, *What About Continuing Revelations and Miracles in the Presbyterian Church Today?* (Phillipsburg, N.J.: Presbyterian and Reformed, 1977), pp. 32–34. Kenneth L. Gentry, Jr., *The Charismatic Gift of Prophecy: A Reformed Analysis* (Memphis, Tenn.: Whitefield Seminary Press, 1986), pp. 31–33, lists both this view and the view of Dr. Gaffin (see objection 1, above) as acceptable options. See also the entries under Robert Thomas, Victor Budgen, and Thomas Edgar in the bibliography to chapter 53, pp. 1084–87.

[31]Walter J. Chantry, *Signs of the Apostles*, pp. 50–52.

Dr. Reymond's argument is somewhat different. He reasons as follows (p. 34):

(a) "The imperfect" things mentioned in verses 9–10—prophecy, tongues, and knowledge—are incomplete means of revelation, "all relating to God's making his will known to his church."

(b) "The perfect" in this context must refer to something in the same category as the "imperfect" things.

(c) Therefore "the perfect" in this context must refer to a means of revelation, but a completed one. And this completed means of God's making his will known to his church is Scripture.

(d) Conclusion: "When the perfect comes" refers to the time when the canon of Scripture will be complete.

Reymond notes that he is not saying that "the perfect" refers exactly to the canon of Scripture, but rather to "the completed revelatory process" that resulted in Scripture (p. 32). And in response to the objection that "then we shall see face to face" in verse 12 refers to seeing God face to face, he answers that it may not mean this, but may simply mean seeing "plainly" as opposed to "obscurely" (p. 32).

In response, it may be said that this argument, while careful and consistent in itself, still depends on one prior assumption which is really the point at issue in this whole discussion: the authority of New Testament prophecy and related gifts. Once Reymond assumes that prophecy (and tongues and the kind of "knowledge" mentioned here) are Scripture-quality revelation, the whole argument falls into place. The argument could be recast as follows:

(a) Prophecy and tongues are Scripture-quality revelation.

(b) Therefore this whole passage is about Scripture-quality revelation.

(c) Therefore "the perfect" refers to the perfection or completion of Scripture-quality revelation, or the completion of Scripture.

In such an argument the initial assumption determines the conclusion. However, before this assumption can be made, it needs to be demonstrated from an inductive analysis of the New Testament texts on prophecy.[32] Yet, to my knowledge, no such inductive demonstration of the Scripture-quality authority of New Testament congregational prophecy has been made.

Moreover, there are some other factors in the text of 1 Corinthians 13:8–13 that are hard to reconcile with Reymond's position. The regular Old Testament usage of seeing "face to face" as an expression not just for seeing clearly but for *personally* seeing God (see above) remains unexplained. And the fact that Paul includes himself in the expressions "Then *we* shall see face to face" and "Then I shall know even as I have been known" make it difficult to view these as references to the time of the completion of Scripture. Does Paul really think that when the other apostles finally finish their contributions to the New Testament he will suddenly gain such a remarkable change in his knowledge that he will know as he has been known, and will go from seeing in a mirror dimly to seeing face to face?

In addition to the views of Reymond and Chantry, there have been other attempts to see "when the perfect comes" as some time before Christ's return, but we will not treat them in detail here. Such views all break down at verse 12, where

---

[32]See chapter 53, pp. 1049–61, for a fuller discussion of the gift of prophecy; also Wayne Grudem, *The Gift of Prophecy in the New Testament and Today*.

Paul implies that believers will see God "face to face" "when the perfect comes." This cannot be been said about the time suggested in any of these other proposals.

The proposal about the completion of the canon of New Testament Scripture (the group of writings that came to be included in the New Testament) also fails to fit Paul's purpose in the context. If we take A.D. 90 as the approximate date of the writing of Revelation, the last New Testament book written, then the end of the writing of Scripture came about thirty-five years after Paul wrote 1 Corinthians (about A.D. 55). But would it be persuasive to argue as follows: "We can be sure that love will never end, for we know that it will last more than thirty-five years"? This would hardly be a convincing argument. The context requires rather that Paul be contrasting this age with the age to come, and saying that love will endure into eternity.[33] In fact, we see a similar procedure elsewhere in 1 Corinthians. When Paul wants to demonstrate the eternal value of something, he does this by arguing that it will last beyond the day of the Lord's return (cf, 1 Cor. 3:13-15; 15:51-58). By contrast, prophecy and other gifts will not last beyond that day.

Finally, these proposals fail to find any support in the immediate context. Whereas Christ's return is mentioned clearly in verse 12, no verse in this section mentions anything about the completion of Scripture or a collection of the books of the New Testament or the inclusion of the Gentiles in the church or the "maturity" of the church (whatever that means—is the church really mature even today?). All of these suggestions bring in new elements not found in the context to replace the one element—Christ's return—which clearly is right there in the context already. In fact, Richard Gaffin, who himself holds that the gift of prophecy is not valid for today, nevertheless says that the "perfect" in verse 10 and the "then" in verse 12 "no doubt refer to the time of Christ's return. The view that they describe the point at which the New Testament canon is completed cannot be made credible exegetically."[34]

Dr. D. Martyn Lloyd-Jones observes that the view that makes "when the perfect comes" equal the time of the completion of the New Testament encounters another difficulty:

> It means that you and I, who have the Scriptures open before us, know much more than the apostle Paul of God's truth. . . . It means that we are altogether superior . . . even to the apostles themselves, including the apostle Paul! It means that we are now in a position in which . . . "we know, even as also we are known" by God . . . indeed, there is only one word to describe such a view, it is nonsense.[35]

John Calvin, referring to 1 Corinthians 13:8-13, says, "It is stupid of people to make the whole of this discussion apply to the intervening time."[36]

---

[33]Some argue that faith and hope will not endure in heaven, so 1 Cor. 13:13 only means that faith and hope last until, not beyond, Christ's return. However, if faith is dependence on God and trust in him, and if hope is a confident expectation of future blessings to be received from God, then there is no reason to think that we will cease to have faith and hope in heaven. (See Carson's good discussion of faith, hope, and love as "eternally permanent virtues" in *Showing the Spirit*, pp. 74–75.)

[34]Gaffin, *Perspectives*, p. 109; cf. Max Turner, "Spiritual Gifts Then and Now," *Vox Evangelica* 15 (1985), p. 38.

[35]D. Martyn Lloyd-Jones, *Prove All Things*, ed. by Christopher Catherwood (Eastbourne, England: Kingsway, 1985), pp. 32–33.

[36]John Calvin, *The First Epistle of Paul the Apostle to the Corinthians*, trans. by J. W. Fraser, ed. by D. W. Torrance and T. F. Torrance (Grand Rapids: Eerdmans, 1960), p. 281 (on 1 Cor. 13:10).

## 2. Would the Continuation of Prophecy Today Challenge the Sufficiency of Scripture?

**a. The Authority of the Gift of Prophecy:** Those who take a "cessationist" view argue that once the last New Testament book was written (probably the book of Revelation around A.D. 90), there were to be no more "words of God" spoken or written in the church. This is especially relevant for the gift of prophecy, according to the cessationist position, because from that point on *Scripture* was the complete and sufficient source of God's words for his people. To add any more words from continuing prophetic utterances would be, in effect, either to add to Scripture or to compete with Scripture. In both cases, the sufficiency of Scripture itself would be challenged, and, in practice, its unique authority in our lives compromised.

Now *if* New Testament congregational prophecy was like Old Testament prophecy and New Testament apostolic words in its authority, then this cessationist objection would indeed be true. *If* prophets today, for example, spoke words that we knew were the very words of God, then these words *would be* equal to Scripture in authority, and we *would be* obligated to write them down and add them to our Bibles whenever we heard them. But if we are convinced that God stopped causing Scripture to be written when the book of Revelation was completed, then we have to say that *this* kind of speech, uttering the very words of God, cannot happen today. And any claims to have "new" Scripture, "new" words of God, must be rejected as false.

This question is very important, because the claim that New Testament congregational prophecy had authority equal to Scripture is the basis of many cessationist arguments. Yet it must be noted that noncessationists themselves do not seem to view prophecy that way. George Mallone writes, "To my knowledge no noncessationist in the mainstream of Christianity claims that revelation today is equal with Scripture."[37] Perhaps it would be good for those arguing against continuing prophecy today to give a more sympathetic hearing to the most responsible charismatic writers, simply for the purpose of being able to respond to something that charismatics *actually believe* (even if not always expressed in theologically precise form), instead of responding to something that cessationists say that charismatics believe or say that charismatics should believe.

Furthermore, aside from the question of current practice or belief, I have argued extensively elsewhere that ordinary congregational prophecy in New Testament churches did *not* have the authority of Scripture.[38] It was not spoken in words that were the very words of God, but rather in merely human words. And because it has this lesser authority, there is no reason to think that it will not continue in the church until Christ returns. It does not threaten or compete with Scripture in

---

[37]George Mallone, ed., *Those Controversial Gifts* (Downers Grove, Ill.: InterVarsity Press, 1983), p. 21.

[38]For further discussion of the authority of the gift of prophecy, see chapter 53, pp. 1049–61. See also Wayne Grudem, *The Gift of Prophecy in 1 Corinthians*; Wayne Grudem, *The Gift of Prophecy in the New Testament and Today*; D. A. Carson, *Showing the Spirit: A Theological Exposition of 1 Corinthians 12–14*, pp. 91–100; Graham Houston, *Prophecy: A Gift For Today?* (Downers Grove, Ill.: InterVarsity Press, 1989). (Alternative views are noted in the discussion in chapter 53; see esp. the book by Richard Gaffin, *Perspectives on Pentecost*.)

authority but is subject to Scripture, as well as to the mature judgment of the congregation.

**b. The Question of Guidance:** Another objection is sometimes raised at this point. Some will argue that even if those who use the gift of prophecy today *say* that it does not equal Scripture in authority, *in fact* it functions in their lives to compete with or even replace Scripture in giving guidance concerning God's will. Thus, prophecy today, it is said, challenges the doctrine of the sufficiency of Scripture for guidance in our lives.

Here it must be admitted that many mistakes have been made in the history of the church. John MacArthur points to the way in which the idea of further revelations has given rise to many heretical movements in the church.[39]

But here the question must be, Are abuses *necessary* to the functioning of the gift of prophecy? If we are to argue that mistakes and abuses of a gift make the gift itself invalid, then we would have to reject Bible teaching too (for many Bible teachers have taught error and started cults), and church administration as well (for many church leaders have led people astray), and so forth. The *abuse* of a gift does not mean that we must prohibit the *proper use* of the gift, unless it can be shown that there cannot be proper use—that *all* use has to be abuse.[40]

Moreover, specifically with respect to guidance, it is good to note how cautious many in the charismatic movement are about the use of prophecy to give specific guidance. Several quotations will illustrate this point.

Michael Harper (Church of England):

Prophecies which tell other people what they are to do—are to be regarded with great suspicion.[41]

Dennis and Rita Bennett (American Episcopalians):

We should also be careful of personal, directive prophecy, especially outside the ministry of a mature and submitted man of God. Unrestrained "personal prophecy"

---

[39]John F. MacArthur, Jr., *The Charismatics: A Doctrinal Perspective,* chapters 2–6; see esp. pp. 27ff. MacArthur has expanded his criticisms in an updated edition, *Charismatic Chaos* (Grand Rapids: Zondervan, 1992), pp. 47–84. A thoughtful and extensive critique of MacArthur is found in Rich Nathan, *A Response to Charismatic Chaos* (Anaheim, Calif.: Association of Vineyard Churches, 1993).

[40]Some may object that prophecy has more potential for abuse than other gifts because the idea that God can reveal things to people today (in prophecies) inevitably leads to competition with the authority of Scripture. In response, three points can be made: (1) Teaching on the fallible nature of all contemporary prophecies has not been as extensive as needed to prevent abuse, especially at the popular level, among groups that allow prophecy today. Therefore there has been more misuse of prophecy than there should have been. Even where strong cautions have been proclaimed, there has seldom been an explanation of how prophecy can be from God but still not equal to God's words in authority—that is, very few Pentecostal or charismatic writers have explained prophecy as a *human* report of something that God has spontaneously brought to mind (the view which I defend in chapter 53, pp. 1049–61). (However, see the helpful cautions from several charismatic writers in the following paragraphs in the text above.) (2) It is simply not true that teaching a congregation that prophecy must always be *subject* to Scripture inevitably leads people to exalt prophecies *above* Scripture. This will happen where such teaching is neglected, not where it is propagated. (3) If the Bible indeed teaches that prophecy can be expected to continue today in a form that does not challenge scriptural authority, then we are not free to reject it because we recognize a potential for abuse. (Other gifts have potential for abuse in other areas.) Rather, we should encourage the gift and do our best to guard against abuse.

[41]Michael Harper, *Prophecy: A Gift for the Body of Christ* (Plainhill, N.J.: Logos, 1964), p. 26.

did much to undermine the movement of the Holy Spirit which began at the turn of the century. . . . Christians are certainly given words for one another "in the Lord" . . . and such words can be most refreshing and helpful, but there must be a witness of the Spirit on the part of the person receiving the words, and extreme caution should be used in receiving any alleged directive or predictive prophecy. Never undertake any project simply because you were told to by presumed prophetic utterance or interpretation of tongues, or by a presumed word of wisdom, or knowledge. Never do something just because a friend comes to you and says: "The Lord told me to tell you to do thus and thus." If the Lord has instructions for you, He will give you a witness in your own heart, in which case the words coming from a friend . . . will be a confirmation to what God *has already been* showing you. Your guidance must also agree with Scripture. . . .[42]

Donald Gee (Assemblies of God):

[There are] grave problems raised by the habit of giving and receiving personal "messages" of guidance through the gifts of the Spirit. . . . The Bible gives a place for such direction from the Holy Spirit. . . . But it must be kept in proportion. An examination of the Scriptures will show us that as a matter of fact the early Christians did *not* continually receive such voices from heaven. In most cases they made their decisions by the use of what we often call "sanctified common-sense" and lived quite normal lives. Many of our errors where spiritual gifts are concerned arise when we want the extraordinary and exceptional to be made the frequent and habitual. Let all who develop excessive desire for "messages" through the gifts take warning from the wreckage of past generations as well as of contemporaries. . . . The Holy Scriptures are a lamp unto our feet and a light unto our path.[43]

On the other hand, even among very Reformed cessationists, there is a willingness to admit some kind of continuing "illumination" by the Holy Spirit in believers' lives. For example, Westminster Seminary professor Richard Gaffin says,

Often, too, what is seen as prophecy is actually a spontaneous, Spirit-worked application of Scripture, a more or less sudden grasp of the bearing that biblical teaching has on a particular situation or problem. All Christians need to be open to these more spontaneous workings of the Spirit.[44]

And Robert Reymond defines *illumination* as "the Holy Spirit's enabling of Christians generally to understand, to recall to mind, and to apply the Scriptures they have studied."[45]

But if these writers will allow for the present activity of the Holy Spirit enabling Christians to "understand" or "recall to mind" or "apply" or "grasp" the teachings of Scripture, then there does not seem to be such a great difference in principle between what they are *saying* and what many in the charismatic movement are *doing* (even though there will probably be some remaining differences over the precise way guidance functions—yet this is not so much a difference about prophecy as about guidance generally, and particularly the way guidance from Scripture relates to guidance from advice, counsel, conscience, circumstances, sermons, etc.). The larger point is that what Gaffin and Reymond here call

---

[42]Dennis and Rita Bennett, *The Holy Spirit and You,* p. 107.
[43]Donald Gee, *Spiritual Gifts in the Work of Ministry Today* (Springfield, Mo.: Gospel Publishing House, 1963), pp. 51–52.
[44]Gaffin, *Perspectives,* p. 120.
[45]Reymond, *What About . . .?* pp. 28–29.

"illumination," the New Testament seems to call a "revelation," and what they would call a spoken report of such illumination, the New Testament seems to call a "prophecy."

So I wonder if there may be room for more joint theological reflection in this area. Charismatics need to realize that cessationists are skeptical about the scope and frequency of such "illumination," whether it is right to call it New Testament prophecy, whether it really does have value for the church, and whether it should be sought after. And cessationists need to realize that their own highly developed and carefully formulated doctrine of the sufficiency of Scripture in guidance is not usually shared or even understood by much of evangelicalism, including those in the charismatic movement. Nevertheless, perhaps the Reformed idea of "illumination" allows for what is happening in prophecy today, and may provide a way of understanding it that is not seen as challenging the sufficiency of Scripture.

What shall we conclude then about the relationship between the gift of prophecy and the sufficiency of Scripture? We must say that we appreciate the desire of the cessationists to protect the uniqueness of Scripture and not to allow anything to compete with the authority of Scripture in our lives. We also must be thankful for the desire of cessationists that Christians understand and follow sound principles of guidance in their daily lives, and not get off into an area of excessive subjectivism that does not have the controls of Scripture attached to it. On the other hand, there is certainly a danger that comes with the cessationist viewpoint if it is wrong here. It is the very real danger of opposing something that God is doing in the church today and failing to give him glory for that work. God is jealous for his works and seeks glory from them for himself, and we must continually pray not only that he would keep us from endorsing error, but also that he would keep us from opposing something that is genuinely from him.

### 3. Were Miraculous Gifts Limited to the Apostles and Their Companions?

Another cessationist argument is that miraculous gifts were limited to the apostles and their close companions. Since I have discussed this argument at length in chapter 17, I will not repeat the discussion here.[46]

### 4. Did Miraculous Gifts Only Accompany the Giving of New Scripture?

Another objection is to say that miraculous gifts accompanied the giving of Scripture, and since there is no new Scripture given today, we should expect no new miracles today.

But in response to that it must be said that this is not the only purpose for miraculous gifts. As we noted in chapter 17, miracles have several other purposes in Scripture: (1) they authenticate the gospel message throughout the church age; (2) they give help to those in need, and thereby demonstrate God's mercy and love; (3) they equip people for ministry; and (4) they glorify God.[47]

We should also note that not all miracles accompany the giving of additional Scripture. For example, the ministries of Elijah and Elisha were marked by several miracles in the Old Testament, but they wrote no books or sections of the Bible.

---

[46]See chapter 17, pp. 361–68, for a discussion of the question of whether miraculous gifts were limited to the apostles and their close companions.
[47]See chapter 17, pp. 359–61, for a discussion of these purposes for miracles.

In the New Testament, there were many occurrences of miracles that were not accompanied by the giving of Scripture. Both Stephen and Philip in the book of Acts worked miracles but wrote no Scripture. There were prophets who wrote no Scripture in Caesarea (Acts 21:4) and Tyre (Acts 21:9–11) and Rome (Rom. 12:6) and Thessalonica (1 Thess. 5:20–21) and Ephesus (Eph. 4:11) and the communities to which 1 John was written (1 John 4:1–6). There were apparently many miracles in the churches of Galatia (Gal. 3:5). There were many miraculous things occurring at Corinth (1 Cor. 12:8–10), but in 1 Corinthians 14:36 Paul denies that any Scripture has come forth from the Corinthian church.[48] And James expects that healing will occur at the hands of the elders in all the churches to which he writes (see James 5:14–16).

**5. Is It a Historical Fact That Miraculous Gifts Ceased Early in the History of the Church?** Some cessationists have argued that miraculous gifts in fact ceased when the apostles died, because the purpose of miracles was to give authentication to the apostles. For this reason, it is argued, there should be no miraculous gifts today. B. B. Warfield argued this extensively in his book, *Counterfeit Miracles.*[49]

In response, it must be said first that the premise just stated is very doubtful on historical grounds. There is increasing historical evidence[50] that miraculous gifts

[48]See chapter 53, p. 1054, for a discussion of 1 Cor. 14:36.

[49]London: Banner of Truth, 1972 (reprint of 1918 edition). It should be noted that Warfield's argument, though frequently quoted, is really a historical survey, not an analysis of biblical texts. Moreover, Warfield's purpose was not to refute any use of spiritual gifts among Christians like those in much of the charismatic movement today, whose doctrine (on all matters other than spiritual gifts) and whose church affiliation put them in the mainstream of evangelical Protestantism. Warfield rather was refuting the spurious claims to miracles which had come from some branches of Roman Catholicism at various periods in the history of the church, and from various heretical sects (Warfield includes discussion of the followers of Edward Irving [1792–1834], who strayed into eccentric teachings and was excommunicated from the Church of Scotland in 1833). It is open to question whether modern-day cessationists are right to claim Warfield's support when opposing something which is far different in doctrine and life from that which Warfield himself opposed.

[50]Warfield's position has come in for criticism from recent evangelical studies: see Max Turner, "Spiritual Gifts Then and Now," *Vox Evangelica* 15 (1985), pp. 41–43, with notes to other literature; Donald Bridge, *Signs and Wonders Today* (Leicester: Inter-Varsity Press, 1985), pp. 166–77; and Ronald A. Kydd, *Charismatic Gifts in the Early Church* (Peabody, Mass.: Hendriksen, 1984). Significant evidence of miraculous gifts in early church history is found in Eusebius A. Stephanou, "The Charismata in the Early Church Fathers," *The Greek Orthodox Theological Review* 21:2 (Summer, 1976), pp. 125–46.

A broad-ranging but popularly written study of the history of miraculous gifts in the church is found in Paul Thigpen, "Did the Power of the Spirit Ever Leave the Church?" *Charisma* 18:2 (Sept. 1992), pp. 20–28. Most recently, see Jon Ruthven, *On the Cessation of the Charismata: The Protestant Polemic on Post-Biblical Miracles* (Sheffield: Sheffield University Academic Press, 1993); this is a revision and expansion of the author's Ph.D. dissertation responding to the arguments of cessationists from Warfield to the present.

The argument from church history can be turned the other way by an analysis of events from about 1970 to the present. Church growth analysts tell us that Pentecostal and charismatic churches, which encourage miraculous gifts, are experiencing growth unprecedented in the history of the church. Fuller Seminary professor C. Peter Wagner says, "While back in 1945 Pentecostals/charismatics could count only sixteen million members worldwide, by 1975 they had grown to ninety-six million and then ten years later in 1985 they numbered an astounding 247 million. I am not aware of any non-political, non-militaristic voluntary association which has grown at that rate in all of human history" ("Exploring the Supernatural Dimensions of Church Growth," *Global Church Growth* [Oct.-Dec., 1988], p. 3). (By way of comparison, if the world population was 5 billion, the 1985 figure of 247 million constituted 5 percent of the population of the world.)

were occurring throughout the history of the church in greater or lesser degree, even when exaggerated or evidently spurious claims are discounted. Healings and other kinds of miraculous answers to prayer are often recorded. There were also people claiming to be prophets throughout the history of the early church—the problem was that too often they misunderstood their gift, or others misunderstood it, so that their utterances were (mistakenly) treated like actual words of God. Sometimes they would be tolerated, and sometimes they were too much of a threat to the established leadership of the churches and they would begin splinter groups—tragically, no longer under the restraining and evaluating authority of the established churches. Then too, others may have had "revelations" given to them which they then did not express, or simply included without comment in a prayer, or in a sermon or word of exhortation, or in the writing of a hymn or some devotional literature.[51]

It should also be clear that when Paul said, "When the perfect comes, the imperfect will pass away" (1 Cor. 13:10), he was not saying anything about the relative *frequency* of miraculous gifts in the history of the church. That would be subject to much variation depending on the spiritual maturity and vitality of the church in various periods, the degree to which these gifts were sought as a blessing or rejected as a heresy, the frequency with which the meetings of the church normally made provision for the exercise of these gifts, the degree to which the nature of these gifts was correctly understood, and, over all of this, the Holy Spirit's sovereign work in distributing gifts to the church.

What Paul is speaking about, however, is the total and final abolition of these gifts that is to be brought about by divine initiative at the return of Christ. And he is saying that he thinks that until the time of the return of Christ these gifts will at least to some extent remain available for use, and the Holy Spirit will continue to distribute these gifts to people. Calvin notes the abundance of spiritual gifts in Paul's day and then comments (on 1 Cor. 14:32):

> Today we see our own slender resources, our poverty in fact; but this is undoubtedly the punishment we deserve, as the reward for our ingratitude. For God's riches are not exhausted, nor has His liberality grown less; but we are not worthy of His largess, or capable of receiving all that He generously gives.[52]

## 6. Are Miraculous Gifts Today the Same As the Miraculous Gifts in Scripture? Yet another objection to the continuation of miracles today is to say

---

[51]We must realize that unless people understand prophecy as the fallible report of something that God spontaneously brings to mind, it will be very difficult for the church to encourage or even tolerate it. If prophecy is indeed based on something God suddenly brings to mind, it would eventually be very easy for Christian prophets, whether for good or ill motives, to begin to claim not only that they had received a "revelation" from God or Christ, but also that they spoke with a divine authority like that of Scripture. This apparently happened, at least in Montanism (second century A.D.) and probably in many other cases as well. Of course, if these prophets began to promote heretical ideas, the reaction of the rest of the church would eventually be to drive them out altogether: someone who claims absolute divine authority would eventually be accepted or rejected; he could not be merely tolerated.

But along with this rejection of prophets who misunderstood their status there was perhaps also a rejection of the gift of prophecy altogether, so that a failure on the part of the church itself to understand the nature of the gift of prophecy might have been the cause of a fairly complete suppression of at least the public expression of the gift of prophecy in the church.

[52]John Calvin, *The First Epistle of Paul the Apostle to the Corinthians*, p. 305.

that the alleged miracles today are not like the miracles in Scripture because they are far weaker and often are only partially effective. In response to this objection we must ask whether it really matters whether the miracles today are exactly as powerful as those that occurred at the time of the New Testament. For one thing, we have very little information about the kind of miracles done by ordinary Christians in various congregations, such as the Christians at Corinth or in the churches in Galatia. Moreover, although remarkable miracles done by Jesus are recorded in the gospels, when Jesus healed "every disease and every infirmity" (Matt. 9:35) this must have included many with less serious diseases. We must also ask what the expected benefit is for the objection that miracles today are not as powerful as those in Scripture. If today only three hundred are converted at an evangelistic meeting instead of the three thousand converted on the day of Pentecost (Acts 2:41), shall we say that the speaker does not really have the gift of evangelism, since the gift did not operate as powerfully as it did with the apostles? Or if only 30 percent of the people we pray for regarding physical illness are fully healed instead of 100 percent in the life of Jesus or of the apostles, shall we say this is not the New Testament gift of healing?[53] We must remember that gifts can vary in strength and no gift is perfect in this age. But does that mean that we should stop using these gifts altogether, or oppose them where we see them functioning with some degree of effectiveness? Shall we not praise God if 300 are converted rather than three thousand , or if 30 percent are healed rather than 100 percent of those for whom we pray? Is not the work of the Lord being done? If the quantity is not as great as in New Testament times, then we may ask the Lord for more grace or mercy, but it does not seem appropriate to give up on the use of these gifts or to oppose those who do use them.

### 7. Is It Dangerous for a Church to Allow for the Possibility of Miraculous Gifts Today?

A final objection from the cessationist position is to say that a church that emphasizes the use of miraculous gifts is in danger of becoming imbalanced, and will likely neglect other important things such as evangelism, sound doctrine, and moral purity of life.

To say that the use of miraculous gifts is "dangerous" is not by itself an

---

[53]The figure of 30 percent is simply an example for illustrative purposes, but it is close to two recent tabulations concerning people who received prayer for healing. One tabulation is found in David C. Lewis, *Healing: Fiction, Fantasy, or Fact?* (London: Hodder and Stoughton, 1989), an academic investigation of 1,890 people who attended one of John Wimber's conferences in Harrogate, England, in 1986. The author is a social anthropologist who prepared a detailed questionnaire that people filled out during the conference, and then followed up some randomly selected cases several months later. Of 862 cases of prayer for physical healing, 32 percent (or 279) reported a "great deal" of healing or "total healing." Another 26 percent (or 222) reported a "fair amount" of healing. The remaining 42 percent (or 366) reported "little" or "no healing" (pp. 21–22). Many case studies are reported in detail, in several instances with medical reports quoted at length. All the physical problems prayed for are listed in a detailed appendix (pp. 276–83). (These physical problems are distinguished from prayer for spiritual problems such as inner healing and deliverance, which are tabulated separately by Lewis.) The other tabulation is found in John Wimber, *Power Healing*, p. 188, who says that, of people who received extended prayer for healing at his church, "During 1986 thirty-two percent of all people prayed for were completely healed, while overall eighty-six percent showed evidence of some significant healing." (D. A. Carson, *How Long, O Lord?* [Grand Rapids: Baker, 1990], p. 124, says, "Wimber is quite candid: he estimates that his 'success rate' is about 2 percent," but Carson gives no documentation for this statement, and it is apparently incorrect in light of what Wimber has actually written.)

adequate criticism, because some things that are *right* are dangerous, at least in some sense. Missionary work is dangerous. Driving a car is dangerous. If we define *dangerous* to mean "something might go wrong," then we can criticize *anything* that anybody might do as "dangerous," and this just becomes an all-purpose criticism when there is no specific abuse to point to. A better approach with respect to spiritual gifts is to ask, "Are they being used in accordance with Scripture?" and "Are adequate steps being taken to guard against the dangers of abuse?"

Of course it is true that churches can become imbalanced, and some in fact have done so. But not all will, nor do they have to do so. Furthermore, since this argument is one based on actual results in the life of a church, it is also appropriate to ask, "Which churches in the world today have the most effective evangelism? Which have the most sacrificial giving among their members? Which in fact have the most emphasis on purity of life? Which have the deepest love for the Lord and for his Word?" It seems to me that it is difficult to answer these questions clearly, but I do not think that we can fairly say that those churches in the charismatic and Pentecostal movements *by and large* are *weaker* in these areas than other evangelical churches. In fact, in some cases they may be stronger in these areas. The point is simply that any argument that says that churches emphasizing miraculous gifts *will* become imbalanced is simply not proven in actual practice.

**8. A Final Note: Cessationists and Charismatics Need Each Other.** Finally, it can be argued that those in the charismatic and Pentecostal camps, and those in the cessationist camp (primarily Reformed and dispensational Christians) really need each other, and they would do well to appreciate each other more. The former tend to have more practical experience in the use of spiritual gifts and in vitality in worship that cessationists could benefit from, if they were willing to learn. On the other hand, Reformed and dispensational groups have traditionally been very strong in understanding of Christian doctrine and in deep and accurate understanding of the teachings of Scripture. Charismatic and Pentecostal groups could learn much from them if they would be willing to do so. But it certainly is not helpful to the church as a whole for both sides to think they can learn nothing from the other, or that they can gain no benefit from fellowship with each other.

## QUESTIONS FOR PERSONAL APPLICATION

1. Before reading this chapter, what spiritual gift or gifts did you think you had? Has your understanding of your own spiritual gift(s) changed after studying this chapter? In what way?

2. Explain how each of the spiritual gifts that you understand yourself to have is greater than what would have been known to most old covenant believers. Explain how each gift is a foretaste of some knowledge or ability you will have after Christ returns.

3. What can you do to stir up or strengthen those spiritual gifts in you that need strengthening? Are there some gifts that you have been given but have neglected? Why do you think you have neglected them? What could be done to stir up or rekindle them in you?

4. As you think about your own church, which spiritual gifts do you think are most effectively functioning at the present time? Which are most needed in your church? Is there anything you can do to help meet those needs?

5. What do you think could be done to help churches avoid having controversies, and even divisions, over the question of spiritual gifts? Are there tensions in your own church with regard to these questions today? If so, what can you do to help alleviate these tensions?

6. Do you think that some spiritual gifts mentioned in the New Testament ceased early in the history of the church, and are no longer valid for today? Has your opinion on this question changed as a result of reading this chapter?

7. In your viewpoint, would a church be healthier and more unified if it concentrated on a few gifts and used them carefully and well, or if it encouraged a multiplicity of different gifts, and allowed them to be used at many different times by many different people? If you answered with the latter option, what things might your church do to include a greater diversity and distribution in the use of spiritual gifts? What are some of the dangers that might accompany such widespread use, and how can they be guarded against?

## SPECIAL TERMS

See the list at the end of the next chapter.

## BIBLIOGRAPHY

See the list at the end of the next chapter.

## SCRIPTURE MEMORY PASSAGE

**1 Peter 4:10–11:** *As each has received a gift, employ it for one another, as good stewards of God's varied grace: whoever speaks, as one who utters oracles of God; whoever renders service, as one who renders it by the strength which God supplies; in order that in everything God may be glorified through Jesus Christ. To him belong glory and dominion for ever and ever. Amen.*

## HYMN

### "Come, Thou Almighty King"

This is a trinitarian hymn in which the first verse is addressed to God the Father, the second to God the Son, and the third to God the Holy Spirit. The third verse is a request that the Holy Spirit would come and rule in our hearts, be ever-present among us, and dwell among us as the "Spirit of power." The final verse is a hymn of praise to God "the great One in Three." In the midst of a long discussion on spiritual gifts, it is good to refocus our attention on God himself, who is the giver of all good gifts, and whose glory is the goal of the use of every gift.

Come, thou almighty King, Help us thy name to sing,
Help us to praise:
Father, all glorious, O'er all victorious,
Come, and reign over us, Ancient of Days.

Come, thou incarnate Word, Gird on thy mighty sword,
Our prayer attend:
Come, and thy people bless, And give thy Word success;
Spirit of holiness, on us descend.

Come, holy Comforter, Thy sacred witness bear
In this glad hour:
Thou who almighty art, Now rule in every heart,
And ne'er from us depart, Spirit of pow'r.

To the great One in Three, Eternal praises be,
Hence evermore.
His sovereign majesty May we in glory see,
And to eternity love and adore.

AUTHOR: ANON., 1757

# Chapter 53

# Gifts of the Holy Spirit (2): Specific Gifts

*How should we understand and use specific spiritual gifts?*

## EXPLANATION AND SCRIPTURAL BASIS

In this chapter we will build on the general discussion about spiritual gifts in the previous chapter and examine several specific gifts in more detail. We will not consider every gift mentioned in the New Testament, but will focus on several gifts that are not well understood or whose use has aroused some controversy today. Therefore we will not examine gifts whose meaning and use are self-evident from the term involved (such as serving, encouraging, contributing, showing leadership, or showing mercy), but will rather concentrate on those in the following list, primarily taken from 1 Corinthians 12:28 and 12:8–10:

1. prophecy
2. teaching
3. miracles
4. healing
5. tongues and interpretation
6. word of wisdom/ word of knowledge
7. distinguishing between spirits

## A. Prophecy

Although several definitions have been given for the gift of prophecy, a fresh examination of the New Testament teaching on this gift will show that it should be defined not as "predicting the future," nor as "proclaiming a word from the Lord," nor as "powerful preaching"—but rather as *"telling something that God has spontaneously brought to mind."* The first four points in the following material support this conclusion; the remaining points deal with other considerations regarding this gift.[1]

---

[1] For a more extensive development of all of the following points about the gift of prophecy, see Wayne Grudem, *The Gift of Prophecy in 1 Corinthians,* and Wayne Grudem, *The Gift of Prophecy in the New Testament and Today.* (The first book is more technical, with much more interaction with the scholarly literature.)

Much of the following material on prophecy is adapted from my article, "Why Christians Can Still Prophesy," in *CT* (Sept. 16, 1988), pp. 29–35, and is used by permission; see also my articles, "What Should Be the Relationship Between Prophet and Pastor?" in *Equipping the Saints* (Fall 1990), pp. 7–9, 21–22; and "Does God Still Give Revelation Today?" in *Charisma* (Sept. 1992), pp. 38–42.

**1. The New Testament Counterparts to Old Testament. Prophets Are New Testament Apostles.** Old Testament prophets had an amazing responsibility—they were able to speak and write words that had absolute divine authority. They could say, "Thus says the Lord," and the words that followed were the very words of God. The Old Testament prophets wrote their words as God's words in Scripture for all time (see Num. 22:38; Deut. 18:18–20; Jer. 1:9; Ezek. 2:7; et al.). Therefore, to disbelieve or disobey a prophet's words was to disbelieve or disobey God (see Deut. 18:19; 1 Sam. 8:7; 1 Kings 20:36; and many other passages).

In the New Testament there were also people who spoke and wrote God's very words and had them recorded in Scripture, but we may be surprised to find that Jesus no longer calls them "prophets" but uses a new term, "apostles." The apostles are the New Testament counterpart to the Old Testament prophets (see 1 Cor. 2:13; 2 Cor. 13:3; Gal. 1:8–9; 11–12; 1 Thess. 2:13; 4:8,15; 2 Peter 3:2). It is the apostles, not the prophets, who have authority to write the words of New Testament Scripture.

When the apostles want to establish their unique authority they never appeal to the title "prophet" but rather call themselves "apostles" (Rom. 1:1; 1 Cor. 1:1; 9:1–2; 2 Cor. 1:1; 11:12–13; 12:11–12; Gal. 1:1; Eph. 1:1; 1 Peter 1:1; 2 Peter 1:1; 3:2; et al.).

**2. The Meaning of the Word *Prophet* in the Time of the New Testament.** Why did Jesus choose the new term *apostle* to designate those who had the authority to write Scripture? It was probably because the Greek word *prophētēs* ("prophet") at the time of the New Testament had a very broad range of meanings. It generally did not have the sense "one who speaks God's very words" but rather "one who speaks on the basis of some external influence" (often a spiritual influence of some kind). Titus 1:12 uses the word in this sense, where Paul quotes the pagan Greek poet Epimenides: "One of themselves, a *prophet* of their own, said, 'Cretans are always liars, evil beasts, lazy gluttons.' " The soldiers who mock Jesus also seem to use the word *prophesy* in this way, when they blindfold Jesus and cruelly demand, "Prophesy! Who is it that struck you?" (Luke 22:64). They do not mean, "Speak words of absolute divine authority," but, "Tell us something that has been revealed to you" (cf. John 4:19).

Many writings outside the Bible use the word *prophet* (Gk. *prophētēs*) in this way, without signifying any divine authority in the words of one called a "prophet." In fact, by the time of the New Testament the term *prophet* in everyday use often simply meant "one who has supernatural knowledge" or "one who predicts the future"—or even just "spokesman" (without any connotations of

---

Several writers have differed with my understanding of the gift of prophecy. For alternative views to the position presented in this chapter, see Richard Gaffin, *Perspectives on Pentecost:* (Gaffin is primarily responding to an unpublished version of my 1982 book), and the bibliography entries at the end of the chapter under Victor Budgen, F. David Farnell, Kenneth L. Gentry, Jr., Robert Saucy, Robert L. Thomas, and R. Fowler White. On the other hand, the studies listed in the bibliography by D. A. Carson, Roy Clements, Graham Houston, Charles Hummel, and M. M. B. Turner, along with several book reviews, have expressed substantial agreement with the position I advocated in my 1982 and 1988 books.

divine authority). Several examples near the time of the New Testament are given in Helmut Krämer's article in *Theological Dictionary of the New Testament*:[2]

A philosopher is called "a *prophet* of immortal nature" (Dio Chrysostom, A.D. 40–120)

A teacher (Diogenes) wants to be "a *prophet* of truth and candor" (Lucian of Samosata, A.D. 120–180)

Those who advocate Epicurean philosophy are called "*prophets* of Epicurus" (Plutarch, A.D. 50–120)

Written history is called "the *prophetess* of truth" (Diodorus Siculus, wrote c. 60–30 B.C.)

A "specialist" in botany is called a "*prophet*" (Dioscurides of Cilicia, first century A.D.)

A "quack" in medicine is called a "*prophet*" (Galen of Pergamum, A.D. 129–199)

Krämer concludes that the Greek word for "prophet" (*prophētēs*) "simply expresses the formal function of declaring, proclaiming, making known." Yet, because "every prophet declares something which is not his own," the Greek word for "herald" (*kēryx*) "is the closest synonym."[3]

Of course, the words *prophet* and *prophecy* were *sometimes used of the apostles* in contexts that emphasized the external spiritual influence (from the Holy Spirit) under which they spoke (so Rev. 1:3; 22:7; and Eph. 2:20; 3:5),[4] but this was not the ordinary terminology used for the apostles, nor did the terms *prophet* and *prophecy* in themselves imply divine authority for their speech or writing. Much more commonly, the words *prophet* and *prophecy* were used of ordinary Christians who spoke not with absolute divine authority, but simply to report something that God had laid on their hearts or brought to their minds. There are many indications in the New Testament that this ordinary gift of prophecy had authority less than that of the Bible, and even less than that of recognized Bible teaching in the early church, as is evident from the following section.

---

[2]The following examples are taken from *TDNT* 6, p. 794.

[3]Ibid., p. 795.

[4]I have a long discussion of Eph. 2:20 in *The Gift of Prophecy in the New Testament and Today*, pp. 45–63, in which I argue that Paul says that the church is "built up on the foundation of the apostle-prophets" (or "apostles who are also prophets"). This is a grammatically acceptable translation of the phrase *tōn apostolōn kai prophetōn*. As such, the passage refers to the apostles, to whom the mystery of Gentile inclusion in the church was revealed (see Eph. 3:5, which specifies that this mystery "has now been revealed to his holy apostles and prophets [or "apostle-prophets" or, "apostles who are also prophets"] by the Spirit").

I do not think that Eph. 2:20 has much relevance to the entire discussion of the nature of the gift of prophecy. Whether we see one group here as I do (apostle-prophets) or two groups, as Richard Gaffin and several others do (apostles and prophets), we all agree that *these* prophets are ones who provided the foundation of the church, and therefore these are prophets who spoke infallible words of God. Where we disagree is on the question of whether this verse describes the character of *all who had the gift of prophecy* in the New Testament churches. I see no convincing evidence that it describes all who prophesied in the early church. Rather, the context clearly indicates a very limited group of prophets who were (a) part of the very foundation of the church, (b) closely connected with the apostles, and (c) recipients of the revelation from God that the Gentiles were equal members with Jews in the church (Eph. 3:5). Whether we say this group was only the apostles, or was a small group of prophets closely associated with the apostles who spoke Scripture-quality words, we are still left with a picture of a very small and unique group of people who provide this foundation for the church universal.

## 3. Indications That "Prophets" Did Not Speak With Authority Equal to the Words of Scripture.

**a. Acts 21:4:** In Acts 21:4, we read of the disciples at Tyre: "Through the Spirit they told Paul not to go on to Jerusalem." This seems to be a reference to prophecy directed towards Paul, but Paul disobeyed it! He never would have done this if this prophecy contained God's very words and had authority equal to Scripture.

**b. Acts 21:10–11:** Then in Acts 21:10–11, Agabus prophesied that the Jews at Jerusalem would bind Paul and "deliver him into the hands of the Gentiles," a prediction that was nearly correct but not quite: the Romans, not the Jews, bound Paul (v. 33; also 22:29),[5] and the Jews, rather than delivering him voluntarily, tried to kill him and he had to be rescued by force (v. 32).[6] The prediction was not far off, but it had inaccuracies in detail that would have called into question the validity of any Old Testament prophet. On the other hand, this text could be perfectly well explained by supposing that Agabus had had a vision of Paul as a prisoner of the Romans in Jerusalem, surrounded by an angry mob of Jews. His own interpretation of such a "vision" or "revelation" from the Holy Spirit would be that the Jews had bound Paul and handed him over to the Romans, and that is what Agabus would (somewhat erroneously) prophesy. This is exactly the kind of fallible prophecy that would fit the definition of New Testament congregational prophecy proposed above—reporting in one's own words something that God has spontaneously brought to mind.

One objection to this view is to say that Agabus' prophecy was in fact fulfilled, and that Paul even reports that in Acts 28:17: "I was delivered prisoner from Jerusalem into the hands of the Romans."[7]

But the verse itself will not support that interpretation. The Greek text of Acts 28:17 explicitly refers to Paul's transfer *out of* Jerusalem as *a prisoner*.[8] Therefore Paul's statement describes his transfer out of the Jewish judicial system (the Jews were seeking to bring him again to be examined by the Sanhedrin in Acts 23:15, 20) and *into* the Roman judicial system at Caesarea (Acts 23:23–35). Therefore Paul correctly says in Acts 28:18 that the same Romans into whose hands he had been delivered as a prisoner (v. 17) were the ones who (Gk. *hoitines*, v. 18), "When they had examined me . . . wished to set me at liberty, because there was

---

[5]In both verses Luke uses the same Greek verb (*deō*) that Agabus had used to predict that the Jews would bind Paul.

[6]The verb that Agabus used (*paradidōmi,* "to deliver, hand over") requires the sense of voluntarily, consciously, deliberately giving over or handing over something to someone else. That is the sense it has in all 119 other instances of the word in the New Testament. But that sense is not true with respect to the treatment of Paul by the Jews: they did not voluntarily hand Paul over to the Romans!

[7]This is the view of Gaffin, *Perspectives,* pp. 65–66, and F. David Farnell, "The Gift of Prophecy in the Old and New Testaments," *BibSac* 149:596 (Oct.–Dec. 1992), p. 395, both of whom refer to Acts 28:17 for support.

[8]The NIV translation, "I was arrested *in* Jerusalem and handed over to the Romans," completely misses the idea (which the Greek text requires) of being delivered *out of* (*ex*) Jerusalem, and removes the idea that he was delivered as a prisoner (Gk. *desmios*), adding rather the idea that he was arrested in Jerusalem, an event that is not mentioned in the Greek text.

no reason for the death penalty in my case" (Acts 28:18; cf. 23:29; also 25:11, 18–19; 26:31–32). Then Paul adds that when the Jews objected he was compelled "to appeal to Caesar" (Acts 28:19; cf. 25:11). This whole narrative in Acts 28:17–19 refers to Paul's transfer out of Jerusalem to Caesarea in Acts 23:12–35, and explains to the Jews in Rome why Paul is in Roman custody. The narrative does not refer to Acts 21:27–36 and the mob scene near the Jerusalem temple at all. So this objection is not persuasive. The verse does not point to a fulfillment of either half of Agabus' prophecy: it does not mention any binding by the Jews, nor does it mention that the Jews handed Paul over to the Romans. In fact, in the scene it refers to (Acts 23:12–35), once again Paul had just been taken from the Jews "by force" (Acts 23:10), and, far from seeking to hand him over to the Romans, they were waiting in an ambush to kill him (Acts 23:13–15).

Another objection to my understanding of Acts 21:10–11 is to say that the Jews did not really have to bind Paul and deliver him into the hands of the Gentiles for the prophecy of Agabus to be true, because the Jews were *responsible* for these activities even if they did not carry them out. Robert Thomas says, "It is common to speak of the responsible party or parties as performing an act even though he or they may not have been the immediate agent(s)."[9] Thomas cites similar examples from Acts 2:23 (where Peter says that the Jews crucified Christ, whereas the Romans actually did it) and John 19:1 (we read that Pilate scourged Jesus, whereas his soldiers no doubt carried out the action). Thomas concludes, therefore, "the Jews were the ones who put Paul in chains just as Agabus predicted."[10]

In response, I agree that Scripture can speak of someone as doing an act that is carried out by that person's agent. But *in every case* the person who is said to do the action both *wills* the act to be done and *gives directions* to others to do it. Pilate directed his soldiers to scourge Jesus. The Jews actively demanded that the Romans would crucify Christ. By contrast, in the situation of Paul's capture in Jerusalem, there is no such parallel. The Jews did not order him to be bound but the Roman tribune did it: "Then the tribune came up and arrested him, and ordered him to be bound with two chains" (Acts 21:33). And in fact the parallel form of speech is found here, because, although the tribune *ordered* Paul to be bound, later we read that "the tribune also was afraid, for he realized that Paul was a Roman citizen and that *he had bound him*" (Acts 22:29). So this narrative does speak of the binding as done either by the responsible agent or by the people who carried it out, but in both cases these are Romans, not Jews. In summary, this objection says that the Jews put Paul in chains. But Acts says twice that the Romans bound him. This objection says that the Jews turned Paul over to the Gentiles. But Acts says that they violently refused to turn him over, so that he had to be taken from them by force. The objection does not fit the words of the text.[11]

---

[9]Robert L. Thomas, "Prophecy Rediscovered? A Review of The Gift of Prophecy in the New Testament and Today," *BibSac* 149:593 (Jan.–Mar. 1992), p. 91. The same argument is made by Kenneth L. Gentry, Jr. *The Charismatic Gift of Prophecy: A Reformed Response to Wayne Grudem*, 2d ed. (Memphis, Tenn.: Footstool Publications, 1989), p. 43.

[10]Thomas, "Prophecy Rediscovered?," p. 91.

[11]See below, p. 1056, on the question of Agabus' introductory phrase, "Thus says the Holy Spirit."

**c. 1 Thessalonians 5:19–21:** Paul tells the Thessalonians, "do not despise prophesying, but test everything; hold fast what is good" (1 Thess. 5:20–21). If the Thessalonians had thought that prophecy equaled God's Word in authority, he would never have had to tell the Thessalonians not to despise it—they "received" and "accepted" God's Word "with joy from the Holy Spirit" (1 Thess. 1:6; 2:13; cf. 4:15). But when Paul tells them to "test everything" it must include at least the prophecies he mentioned in the previous phrase. He implies that prophecies contain some things that are good and some things that are not good when he encourages them to "hold fast *what is good.*" This is something that could never have been said of the words of an Old Testament prophet, or the authoritative teachings of a New Testament apostle.

**d. 1 Corinthians 14:29–38:** More extensive evidence on New Testament prophecy is found in 1 Corinthians 14. When Paul says, "Let two or three prophets speak, and *let the others weigh what is said*" (1 Cor. 14:29), he suggests that they should listen carefully and sift the good from the bad, accepting some and rejecting the rest (for this is the implication of the Greek word *diakrinō,* here translated "weigh what is said"). We cannot imagine that an Old Testament prophet like Isaiah would have said, "Listen to what I say and weigh what is said—sort the good from the bad, what you accept from what you should not accept"! If prophecy had absolute divine authority, it would be sin to do this. But here Paul commands that it be done, suggesting that New Testament prophecy did not have the authority of God's very words.[12]

In 1 Corinthians 14:30, Paul allows one prophet to interrupt another one: "If a revelation is made to another sitting by, let the first be silent. For you can all prophesy one by one." Again, if prophets had been speaking God's very words, equal in value to Scripture, it is hard to imagine that Paul would say they should be interrupted and not be allowed to finish their message. But that is what Paul commands.

Paul suggests that no one at Corinth, a church that had much prophecy, was able to speak God's very words. He says in 1 Corinthians 14:36, "What! *Did the word of God come forth from you,* or are you the only ones it has reached?" (author's translation).[13]

Then in verses 37 and 38, in he claims authority far greater than any prophet at Corinth: "If any one thinks that he is a prophet, or spiritual, he should acknowledge that what I am writing to you is a command of the Lord. If any one does not recognize this, he is not recognized."

All these passages indicate that the common idea that prophets spoke "words of

---

[12]Paul's instructions are different from those in the early Christian document known as the *Didache,* which tells people, "Do not test or examine any prophet who is speaking in a spirit (or: in the Spirit)" (chapter 11). But the *Didache* says several things that are contrary to New Testament doctrine (see W. Grudem, *The Gift of Prophecy in the New Testament and Today,* pp. 106–8; also p. 67, above).

[13]The RSV translates, "Did the word of God *originate* with you?" but there is no need to make the Greek verb here (the aorist of *exerchomai,* "to go out") speak so specifically of the origin of the gospel message: Paul does not say, "Did the word of God *first* go forth from you?" but simply, "Did the word of God go forth from you?" He realizes they must admit that the Word of God *has not* come forth from them—therefore, their prophets cannot have been speaking words of God equal to Scripture in authority.

the Lord" when the apostles were not present in the early churches is simply incorrect.

**e. Apostolic Preparations for Their Absence:** In addition to the verses we have considered so far, one other type of evidence suggests that New Testament congregational prophets spoke with less authority than New Testament apostles or Scripture: the problem of successors to the apostles is solved not by encouraging Christians to listen to the *prophets* (even though there were prophets around) but by pointing to the *Scriptures*.[14]

So Paul, at the end of his life, emphasizes "rightly handling the word of truth" (2 Tim. 2:15), and the "God-breathed" character of "scripture" for "teaching, for reproof, for correction, and for training in righteousness" (2 Tim. 3:16). Jude urges his readers to "contend for the faith which was once for all delivered to the saints" (Jude 3). Peter, at the end of his life, encourages his readers to "pay attention" to Scripture, which is like "a lamp shining in a dark place" (2 Peter 1:19–20), and reminds them of the teaching of the apostle Paul "in all his letters" (2 Peter 3:16). In no case do we read exhortations to "give heed to the prophets in your churches" or to "obey the words of the Lord through your prophets," etc. Yet there certainly were prophets prophesying in many local congregations after the death of the apostles. It seems that they did not have authority equal to the apostles, and the authors of Scripture knew that. The conclusion is that prophecies today are not "the words of God" either.

**4. How Should We Speak About the Authority of Prophecy Today?** So prophecies in the church today should be considered merely human words, not God's words, and not equal to God's words in authority. But does this conclusion conflict with current charismatic teaching or practice? I think it conflicts with much charismatic practice, but not with most charismatic teaching.

Most charismatic teachers today would agree that contemporary prophecy is not equal to Scripture in authority. Though some will speak of prophecy as being the "word of God" for today, there is almost uniform testimony from all sections of the charismatic movement that prophecy is imperfect and impure, and will contain elements that are not to be obeyed or trusted. For example, Bruce Yocum, the author of a widely used charismatic book on prophecy, writes, "Prophecy can be impure—our own thoughts or ideas can get mixed into the message we receive—whether we receive the words directly or only receive a sense of the message."[15]

But it must be said that in actual practice much confusion results from the habit of prefacing prophecies with the common Old Testament phrase, "Thus says the Lord" (a phrase nowhere spoken in the New Testament by any prophets in New Testament churches). This is unfortunate, because it gives the impression that the words that follow are God's very words, whereas the New Testament does not justify that position and, when pressed, most responsible charismatic spokesmen

---

[14]I have taken this idea from the very helpful booklet by Roy Clements, *Word and Spirit: The Bible and the Gift of Prophecy Today* (Leicester: UCCF Booklets, 1986), p. 24; cf. D. A. Carson, *Showing the Spirit*, p. 96.

[15]See *Prophecy* (Ann Arbor: Word of Life, 1976), p. 79.

would not want to claim it for every part of their prophecies anyway. So there would be much gain and no loss if that introductory phrase were dropped.

Now it is true that Agabus uses a similar phrase ("Thus says the Holy Spirit") in Acts 21:11, but the same words (Gk. *tade legei*) are used by Christian writers just after the time of the New Testament to introduce very general paraphrases or greatly expanded interpretations of what is being reported (so Ignatius, *Epistle to the Philadelphians* 7:1–2 [about A.D. 108] and *Epistle of Barnabas* 6:8; 9:2, 5 [A.D. 70–100]). The phrase can apparently mean, "This is generally (or approximately) what the Holy Spirit is saying to us."

If someone really does think God is bringing something to mind which should be reported in the congregation, there is nothing wrong with saying, "*I think* the Lord is putting on my mind that . . ." or "*It seems to me that* the Lord is showing us . . ." or some similar expression. Of course that does not sound as "forceful" as "Thus says the Lord," but if the message is really from God, the Holy Spirit will cause it to speak with great power to the hearts of those who need to hear.

## 5. A Spontaneous "Revelation" Made Prophecy Different From Other Gifts.

If prophecy does not contain God's very words, then what is it? In what sense is it from God?

Paul indicates that God could bring something spontaneously to mind so that the person prophesying would report it in his or her own words. Paul calls this a "revelation": "If a revelation is made to another sitting by, let the first be silent. For you can all prophesy one by one, so that all may learn and all be encouraged" (1 Cor. 14:30–31). Here he uses the word *revelation* in a broader sense than the technical way theologians have used it to speak of the words of Scripture—but the New Testament elsewhere uses the terms *reveal* and *revelation* in this broader sense of communication from God that does not result in written Scripture or words equal to written Scripture in authority (see Phil. 3:15; Rom. 1:18; Eph. 1:17; Matt. 11:27).

Paul is simply referring to something that God may suddenly bring to mind, or something that God may impress on someone's consciousness in such a way that the person has a sense that it is from God. It may be that the thought brought to mind is surprisingly distinct from the person's own train of thought, or that it is accompanied by a sense of vividness or urgency or persistence, or in some other way gives the person a rather clear sense that it is from the Lord.[16]

Figure 53.1 illustrates the idea of a revelation from God that is reported in the prophet's own (merely human) words.

Thus, if a stranger comes in and all prophesy, "the secrets of his heart are disclosed; and so, falling on his face, he will worship God and declare that God is really among you" (1 Cor. 14:25). I have heard a report of this happening in a clearly noncharismatic Baptist church in America. A missionary speaker paused in the middle of his message and said something like this: "I didn't plan to say this, but it seems the Lord is indicating that someone in this church has just walked out

---

[16]Although we argued above that the *authority* of prophecy in the New Testament church is far different from the authority of Old Testament canonical prophecy, this does not mean that everything about New Testament prophecy has to be different. With respect to *the form in which the revelation comes* to the prophet, there may be not only words or ideas that come to mind, but also mental pictures (or "visions," Acts 2:17) and dreams (Acts 2:17) as well.

on his wife and family. If that is so, let me tell you that God wants you to return to them and learn to follow God's pattern for family life." The missionary did not know it, but in the unlit balcony sat a man who had entered the church moments before for the first time in his life. The description fitted him exactly, and he made himself known, acknowledged his sin, and began to seek after God.

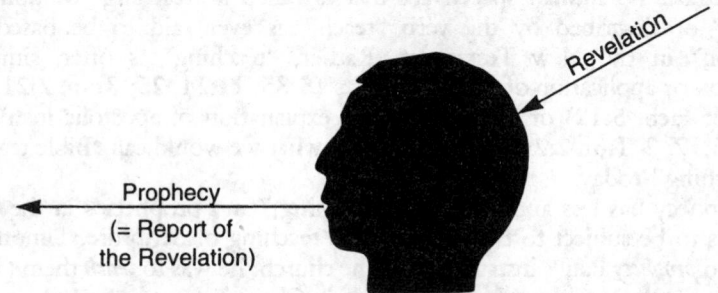

PROPHECY OCCURS WHEN A REVELATION FROM GOD IS REPORTED
IN THE PROPHET'S OWN (MERELY HUMAN) WORDS
*Figure 53.1*

In this way, prophecy serves as a "sign" for believers (1 Cor. 14:22)—it is a clear demonstration that God is definitely at work in their midst, a "sign" of God's hand of blessing on the congregation. And since it will work for the conversion of unbelievers as well, Paul encourages this gift to be used when "unbelievers or outsiders enter" (1 Cor. 14:23).

Many Christians in all periods of the church have experienced or heard of similar events—for example, an unplanned but urgent request may have been given to pray for certain missionaries in Nigeria. Then much later those who prayed discovered that just at that time the missionaries had been in an auto accident or at a point of intense spiritual conflict, and had needed those prayers. Paul would call the sense or intuition of those things a "revelation," and the report to the assembled church of that prompting from God would be called a "prophecy." It may have elements of the speaker's own understanding or interpretation in it and it certainly needs evaluation and testing, yet it has a valuable function in the church nonetheless.[17]

---

[17]We must caution people, however, that the mere fact of a "revelation" that seems supernatural (and that even may contain some surprisingly accurate information) does not guarantee that a message is a true prophecy from God, for false prophets can "prophesy" under demonic influence. (See chap. 20, pp. 415–16, on the fact that demons can know about hidden activities or private conversations in our lives, even though they cannot know the future or read our thoughts.)

John warns that "many false prophets have gone out into the world" (1 John 4:1), and he gives tests of true doctrine to discern them (vv. 1–6), and says "The world listens to them" (v. 5). Other marks of false prophets can be found in 2 John 7–9 (denying the incarnation and not abiding in the doctrine of Christ); Matt. 7:15–20 ("You will know them by their fruits," v. 16); Matt. 24:11 (leading many astray); and Matt. 24:24 (showing signs and wonders for the purpose of leading astray the elect). On the other hand, 1 Cor. 12:3 seems to tell us that we should not think that genuine Christians will be false prophets, speaking by the power of demons (see the discussion of 1 Cor. 12:3 on p. 1077, and 1 John 4:4 reassures Christians that "he who is in you is greater than he who is in the world."

**6. The Difference Between Prophecy and Teaching.** As far as we can tell, all New Testament "prophecy" was based on this kind of spontaneous prompting from the Holy Spirit (cf. Acts 11:28; 21:4, 10–11; and note the ideas of prophecy represented in Luke 7:39; 22:63–64; John 4:19; 11:51). Unless a person receives a spontaneous "revelation" from God, there is no prophecy.

By contrast, no human speech act that is called a "teaching" or done by a "teacher," or described by the verb "teach," is ever said to be based on a "revelation" in the New Testament. Rather, "teaching" is often simply an explanation or application of Scripture (Acts 15:35; 11:11, 25; Rom. 2:21; 15:4; Col. 3:16; Heb. 5:12) or a repetition and explanation of apostolic instructions (Rom. 16:17; 2 Tim. 2:2; 3:10; et al.). It is what we would call "Bible teaching" or "preaching" today.

So prophecy has less authority than "teaching," and prophecies in the church are always to be subject to the authoritative teaching of Scripture. Timothy was not told to *prophesy* Paul's instructions in the church; he was to *teach* them (1 Tim. 4:11; 6:2). Paul did not *prophesy* his lifestyle in Christ in every church; he *taught* it (1 Cor. 4:17). The Thessalonians were not told to hold firm to the traditions that were "prophesied" to them but to the traditions that they were "taught" by Paul (2 Thess. 2:15). Contrary to some views, it was teachers, not prophets, who gave leadership and direction to the early churches.

Among the elders, therefore, were "those who labor in preaching and teaching" (1 Tim. 5:17), and an elder was to be "an apt teacher" (1 Tim. 3:2; cf. Titus 1:9)—but nothing is said about any elders whose work was prophesying, nor is it ever said that an elder has to be "an apt prophet" or that elders should be "holding firm to sound prophecies." In his leadership function Timothy was to take heed to himself and to his "teaching" (1 Tim. 4:16), but he is never told to take heed to his prophesying. James warned that those who teach, not those who prophesy, will be judged with greater strictness (James 3:1).

The task of interpreting and applying Scripture, then, is called "teaching" in the New Testament. Although a few people have claimed that the prophets in New Testament churches gave "charismatically inspired" interpretations of Old Testament Scripture, that claim has hardly been persuasive, primarily because it is hard to find in the New Testament any convincing examples where the "prophet" word group is used to refer to someone engaged in this kind of activity.

So the distinction is quite clear: if a message is the result of conscious reflection on the text of Scripture, containing interpretation of the text and application to life, then it is (in New Testament terms) a teaching. But if a message is the report of something God brings suddenly to mind, then it is a prophecy. And of course, even prepared teachings can be interrupted by unplanned additional material that the Bible teacher suddenly felt God was bringing to his mind—in that case, it would be a "teaching" with an element of prophecy mixed in.

**7. Objection: This Makes Prophecy "Too Subjective."** At this point some have objected that waiting for such "promptings" from God is "just too subjective" a process. But in response, it may be said that, for the health of the church, it is often the people who make this objection who need this subjective process most in their own Christian lives! This gift requires waiting on the Lord, listening for him, hearing his prompting in our hearts. For Christians who are completely evangelical, doctrinally sound, intellectual, and "objective," probably what is needed most is the strong balancing influence of a more vital "subjective" relationship with the Lord in everyday life. And these people are also those who have the least likelihood of being led into error, for they already place great emphasis on solid grounding in the Word of God.

Yet there is an opposite danger of excessive reliance on subjective impressions for guidance, and that must be clearly guarded against. People who continually seek subjective "messages" from God to guide their lives must be cautioned that subjective personal guidance is not a primary function of New Testament prophecy. They need to place much more emphasis on Scripture and seeking God's sure wisdom written there.

Many charismatic writers would agree with this caution, as the following quotations indicate:

Michael Harper (Anglican charismatic pastor):

Prophecies which tell other people what they are to do—are to be regarded with great suspicion.[18]

Donald Gee (Assemblies of God):

Many of our errors where spiritual gifts are concerned arise when we want the extraordinary and exceptional to be made the frequent and habitual. Let all who develop excessive desire for "messages" through the gifts take warning from the wreckage of past generations as well as of contemporaries. . . . The Holy Scriptures are a lamp unto our feet and a light unto our path.[19]

Donald Bridge (British charismatic pastor):

The illuminist constantly finds that "God tells him" to do things. . . . Illuminists are often very sincere, very dedicated, and possessed of a commitment to obey God that shames more cautious Christians. Nevertheless they are treading a dangerous path. Their ancestors have trodden it before, and always with disastrous results in the long run. Inner feelings and special promptings are by their very nature subjective. The Bible provides our objective guide.[20]

**8. Prophecies Could Include Any Edifying Content.** The examples of prophecies in the New Testament mentioned above show that the idea of prophecy as only "predicting the future" is certainly wrong. There were some predictions (Acts 11:28; 21:11), but there was also the disclosure of sins (1 Cor. 14:25). In fact, anything that edified could have been included, for Paul says, "He who prophesies speaks to men *for their upbuilding and encouragement and consolation*" (1 Cor. 14:3). Another indication of the value of prophecy was that it could speak to the needs of people's hearts in a spontaneous, direct way.

**9. Many People in the Congregation Can Prophesy.** Another great benefit of prophecy is that it provides opportunity for participation by everyone in the

---

[18]*Prophecy: A Gift for the Body of Christ* (Plainfield, N.J.: Logos, 1964), p. 26.

[19]*Spiritual Gifts in the Work of Ministry Today* (Springfield, Mo.: Gospel Publishing House, 1963), pp. 51–52.

[20]*Signs and Wonders Today* (Leicester: Inter-Varsity Press, 1985), p. 183.

congregation, not just those who are skilled speakers or who have gifts of teaching. Paul says that he wants "all" the Corinthians to prophesy (1 Cor. 14:5), and he says, "You can all prophesy one by one, so that all may learn and all be encouraged" (1 Cor. 14:31).[21] This does not mean that every believer will actually be able to prophesy, for Paul says, "Not all are prophets, are they?" (1 Cor. 12:29, author's translation). But it does mean that anyone who receives a "revelation" from God has permission to prophesy (within Paul's guidelines), and it suggests that many will.[22] Because of this, greater openness to the gift of prophecy could help overcome the situation where many who attend our churches are merely spectators and not participants. Perhaps we are contributing to the problem of "spectator Christianity" by quenching the work of the spirit in this area.

**10. We Should "Earnestly Desire" Prophecy.** Paul valued this gift so highly that he told the Corinthians, "Make love your aim, and earnestly desire the spiritual gifts *especially that you may prophesy*" (1 Cor. 14:1). Then at the end of his discussion of spiritual gifts he said again, "So, my brethren, *earnestly desire to prophesy*" (1 Cor. 14:39). And he said, "He who prophesies edifies the church" (1 Cor. 14:4).

If Paul was eager for the gift of prophecy to function at Corinth, troubled as the church was by immaturity, selfishness, divisions, and other problems, then should we not also actively seek this valuable gift in our congregations today? We evangelicals who profess to believe and obey all that Scripture says, should we not also believe and obey this? And might a greater openness to the gift of prophecy perhaps help to correct a dangerous imbalance in church life, an imbalance that comes because we are too exclusively intellectual, objective, and narrowly doctrinal?

**11. Encouraging and Regulating Prophecy in the Local Church.** Finally, if a church begins to encourage the use of prophecy where it has not been used before, what should it do? How can it encourage this gift without falling into abuse?

For all Christians, and especially for pastors and others who have teaching responsibilities in the church, several steps would be both appropriate and pastorally wise: (1) Pray seriously for the Lord's wisdom on how and when to approach this subject in the church. (2) There should be teaching on this subject in the regular Bible teaching times the church already provides. (3) The church should be patient and proceed slowly—church leaders should not be "domineering" (or "pushy") (1 Peter 5:3), and a patient approach will avoid frightening people away or alienating them unnecessarily. (4) The church should recognize and encourage the gift of prophecy in ways it has already been functioning in the church—at church prayer meetings, for example, when someone has felt unusually "led" by the Holy Spirit to pray for something, or when it has seemed that the

---

[21]Here Paul's meaning is that all who receive a revelation in the sense just mentioned in v. 29 will be able to take turns and prophesy one at a time. He does not mean that every single Christian at Corinth had the gift of prophecy.

[22]In a large church, only few would be able to speak when the whole church assembled, for Paul says, "Let two or three prophets speak" (1 Cor. 14:29). But many more would find opportunities to prophesy in smaller gatherings in homes.

Holy Spirit was bringing to mind a hymn or Scripture passage, or when giving a common sense of the tone or the specific focus of a time of group worship or prayer. Even Christians in churches not open to the gift of prophecy can at least be sensitive to promptings from the Holy Spirit regarding what to pray for in church prayer meetings, and can then express those promptings in the form of a prayer (what might be called a "prophetic prayer") to the Lord.

(5) If the first four steps have been followed, and if the congregation and its leadership will accept it, some opportunities for the gift of prophecy to be used might be made in the less formal worship services of the church, or in smaller home groups. If this is allowed, those who prophesy should be kept within scriptural guidelines (1 Cor. 14:29–36), should genuinely seek the edification of the church and not their own prestige (1 Cor. 14:12, 26), and should not dominate the meeting or be overly dramatic or emotional in their speech (and thus attract attention to themselves rather than to the Lord). Prophecies should certainly be evaluated according to the teachings of Scripture (1 Cor. 14:29–36; 1 Thess. 5:19–21).

(6) If the gift of prophecy begins to be used in a church, the church should place even more emphasis on the vastly superior value of Scripture as the source to which Christians can always go to hear the voice of the living God. Prophecy is a valuable gift, as are many other gifts, but it is in Scripture that God and only God speaks to us his very words, even today, and throughout our lives. Rather than hoping at every worship service that the highlight would be some word of prophecy, those who use the gift of prophecy need to be reminded that we should find our focus of joy, our expectation, and our delight in God himself as he speaks to us through the Bible. There we have a treasure of infinite worth: the actual words of our Creator speaking to us in language we can understand. And rather than seeking frequent guidance through prophecy, we should emphasize that it is in Scripture that we are to find guidance for our lives. In Scripture is our source of direction, our focus when seeking God's will, our sufficient and completely reliable standard. It is of God's words in Scripture that we can with confidence say, "Your word is a lamp to my feet and a light to my path" (Ps. 119:105).

## B. Teaching

The gift of teaching in the New Testament is *the ability to explain Scripture and apply it to people's lives.* This is evident from a number of passages. In Acts 15:35, Paul and Barnabas and "many others" are in Antioch *"teaching* and preaching the word of the Lord." At Corinth, Paul stayed one and a half years *"teaching* the word of God among them" (Acts 18:11). And the readers of the epistle to the Hebrews, though they ought to have been teachers, needed rather to have someone to teach them again "the first principles of God's word" (Heb. 5:12). Paul tells the Romans that the words of the Old Testament Scriptures "were written for our instruction (or "teaching," Gk. *didaskalia*)" (Rom. 15:4), and writes to Timothy that "all scripture" is "profitable for teaching [*didaskalia*]" (2 Tim. 3:16).

Of course, if "teaching" in the early church was so often based on Old Testament Scripture, it is not surprising that it could also be based on something equal to Scripture in authority, namely, a received body of apostolic instructions.

So Timothy was to take the teaching he had received from Paul and commit it to faithful men who would be able to "teach others also" (2 Tim. 2:2). And the Thessalonians were to "hold firm to the traditions" they were "taught" by Paul (2 Thess. 2:15). Far from being based on a spontaneous revelation that came during the worship service of the church (as prophecy was), this kind of "teaching" was the repetition and explanation of authentic apostolic teaching. To teach contrary to Paul's instructions was to teach different or heretical doctrine (*heterodidaskalō*) and to fail to give heed to "the sound words of our Lord Jesus Christ and the *teaching* that accords with godliness" (1 Tim. 6:3). In fact, Paul said that Timothy was to remind the Corinthians of Paul's ways "as I *teach* them everywhere in every church" (1 Cor. 4:17). Similarly, Timothy was to "command and teach" (1 Tim. 4:11) and to "teach and urge" (1 Tim. 6:2) Paul's instructions to the Ephesian church. Thus it was not prophecy but teaching which in a primary sense (from the apostles) first provided the doctrinal and ethical norms by which the church was regulated. And as those who learned from the apostles also taught, their teaching guided and directed the local churches.[23]

So teaching in terms of the New Testament epistles consisted of repeating and explaining the words of Scripture (or the equally authoritative teachings of Jesus and of the apostles) and applying them to the hearers. In the New Testament epistles, "teaching" is something very much like what is described by our phrase "Bible teaching" today.

## C. Miracles

Just after apostles, prophets and teachers, Paul says "then miracles" (1 Cor. 12:28). Although many of the miracles seen in the New Testament were specifically miracles of healing, Paul here lists healing as a separate gift. Therefore in this context he must have something other than physical healing in view.

We should realize that the English word *miracles* may not give a very close approximation to what Paul intended, since the Greek word is simply the plural form of the word *dynamis,* "power."[24] This means that the term may refer to any kind of activity where God's mighty power is evident. It may include answers to prayer for deliverance from physical danger (as in the deliverance of the apostles from prison in Acts 5:19–20 or 12:6–11), or powerful works of judgment on the enemies of the gospel or those who require discipline within the church (see Acts 5:1–11; 13:9–12), or miraculous deliverance from injury (as with Paul and the viper in Acts 28:3–6). But such acts of spiritual power may also include power to triumph over demonic opposition (as in Acts 16:18; cf. Luke 10:17).

Since Paul does not define "works of miracles" any more specifically than this, we can say that the gift of miracles may include the working of divine power in deliverance from danger, in intervention to meet special needs in the physical world (as in the case of Elijah in 1 Kings 17:1–16), in judgment on those who irrationally and violently oppose the gospel message, in vanquishing the demonic forces that wage war against the church, and in any other way in which God's

---

[23]See also the discussion in section A.6 above, p. 1058, on the differences between prophecy and teaching.

[24]The NIV translates this word "miraculous powers" at 1 Cor. 12:10, and the NASB mg. translates "works of power" in both places.

power is manifested in an evident way to further God's purposes in a situation. All of these would be works of "power" in which the church would be helped and God's glory would be made evident. (See also the discussion of miracles in chapter 17.)

## D. Healing

**1. Introduction: Sickness and Health in the History of Redemption.** We must realize at the outset that physical sickness came as a result of the fall of Adam, and illness and disease are simply part of the outworking of the curse after the fall, and will eventually lead toward physical death. However, Christ redeemed us from that curse when he died on the cross: "Surely *he took up our infirmities* and carried our sorrows . . . *by his wounds we are healed*" (Isa. 53:4–5 NIV). This passage refers to both physical and spiritual healing that Christ purchased for us, for Peter quotes it to refer to our salvation: "He himself *bore our sins* in his body on the tree, that we might die to sin and live to righteousness. *By his wounds you have been healed*" (1 Peter 2:24).

But Matthew quotes the same passage from Isaiah with reference to the physical healings Jesus performed: "and he cast out the spirits with a word, and *healed all who were sick.* This was to fulfill what was spoken by the prophet Isaiah, '*He took our infirmities* and bore our diseases'" (Matt. 8:16–17).

All Christians would probably agree that in the atonement Christ has purchased for us not only complete freedom from sin but also complete freedom from physical weakness and infirmity in his work of redemption (see chapter 42 on glorification). And all Christians would also no doubt agree that our full and complete possession of all the benefits that Christ earned for us will not come until Christ returns: it is only "at his coming" (1 Cor. 15:23) that we receive our perfect resurrection bodies. So it is with physical healing and redemption from the physical sickness that came as a result of the curse in Genesis 3: our complete possession of redemption from physical illness will not be ours until Christ returns and we receive resurrection bodies.[25]

But the question that confronts us with respect to the gift of healing is whether God may from time to time grant us a foretaste or a down payment of the physical healing which he will grant us fully in the future.[26] The healing miracles of Jesus certainly demonstrate that at times God is willing to grant a partial foretaste of the perfect health that will be ours for eternity. And the ministry of healing seen in the lives of the apostles and others in the early church also indicates that this was part of the ministry of the new covenant age. As such, it fits the larger pattern of blessings in the new covenant, many or all of which give partial foretastes of the

---

[25]When people say that complete healing is "in the atonement," the statement is true in an ultimate sense, but it really does not tell us anything about when we will receive "complete healing" (or any part of it).

[26]For two very helpful treatments of this question, and of the gift of healing in general, see John Wimber, with Kevin Springer, *Power Healing,* and Ken Blue, *Authority to Heal* (Downers Grove, Ill.: InterVarsity Press, 1987). See also the excellent discussion in Jack Deere, *Surprised by the Power of the Holy Spirit* (Grand Rapids: Zondervan, 1993). Several scholarly defenses of a ministry of healing today are found in Gary Greig and Kevin Springer, eds., *The Kingdom and the Power* (Ventura, Calif.: Gospel Light, 1993).

blessings that will be ours when Christ returns. We "already" possess some of the blessings of the kingdom, but those blessings are "not yet" fully ours.

**2. The Purposes of Healing.** As with other spiritual gifts, healing has several purposes. Certainly it functions as a "sign" to authenticate the gospel message, and show that the kingdom of God has come. Then also healing brings comfort and health to those who are ill, and thereby demonstrates God's attribute of mercy toward those in distress. Third, healing equips people for service, as physical impediments to ministry are removed. Fourth, healing provides opportunity for God to be glorified as people see physical evidence of his goodness, love, power, wisdom, and presence.

**3. What About the Use of Medicine?** What is the relationship between prayer for healing and the use of medicine and the skill of a physician? Certainly we should use medicine if it is available because God has also created substances in the earth that can be made into medicine with healing properties. Medicines thus should be considered part of the whole creation that God considered "very good" (Gen. 1:31). We should willingly use medicine with thankfulness to the Lord, for "The earth is the LORD's and the fulness thereof" (Ps. 24:1). In fact, when medicine is available and we refuse to use it (in cases where it would put ourselves or others in danger), then it seems that we are wrongly "forcing a test" on the Lord our God (cf. Luke 4:12): this is similar to the case of Satan tempting Jesus to jump from the temple rather than walking down the steps. Where ordinary means of getting down from the temple (the steps) are available, it is "forcing a test" on God to jump and thereby demand that he perform a miracle at that exact moment. To refuse to use effective medicine, insisting that God perform a miracle of healing instead of healing through the medicine, is very similar to this.

Of course, it is wrong to rely on doctors or medicine *instead* of relying on the Lord, a mistake tragically made by King Asa:

> In the thirty-ninth year of his reign Asa was diseased in his feet, and his disease became severe; yet even in his disease he did not seek the LORD, but sought help from physicians. And Asa slept with his fathers, dying in the forty-first year of his reign. (2 Chron. 16:12–13)

But if medicine is used in connection with prayer, then we should expect God to bless and often multiply the effectiveness of the medicine.[27] Even when Isaiah had received from the Lord a promise of healing for King Hezekiah, he told Hezekiah's servants to bring a cake of figs and apply it (as a medical remedy) to a boil that Hezekiah suffered from: "And Isaiah said, 'Bring a cake of figs. And let them take and lay it on the boil, that he may recover'" (2 Kings 20:7).

However, sometimes there is no appropriate medicine available, or the medicine does not work. Certainly we must remember that God can heal where doctors and medicine cannot heal (and it may amaze us to realize how frequently doctors cannot heal, even in the most medically advanced countries). Moreover, there may be many times when an illness is not putting us or others in immediate danger,

---

[27]Note Paul's recommendation of a use of wine for health purposes in 1 Tim. 5:23: "No longer drink only water, but use a little wine for the sake of your stomach and your frequent ailments."

and we decide to ask God to heal our sickness without the use of medicine, simply because we wish for another opportunity to exercise our faith and give him glory, and perhaps because we wish to avoid spending the time or money to use medical means, or we wish to avoid the side-effects that some medicines have. In all of these cases, it is simply a matter of personal choice and would not seem to be "forcing a test" on God. (However, a decision not to use medicine in these cases should be a personal choice and not one that is forced on others.)

We see Jesus healing explicitly where medical means have failed, when "a woman who had had a flow of blood for twelve years and *could not be healed by any one*" then "came up behind him, and touched the fringe of his garment; and immediately her flow of blood ceased" (Luke 8:43–44). There were no doubt many people beyond the help of physicians who came whenever Jesus was teaching and healing, yet we read that "*all* those who had *any* that were sick with various diseases brought them to him; and he laid his hands on *every one of them* and healed them" (Luke 4:40). There was no disease that Jesus was unable to heal.

**4. Does the New Testament Show Common Methods Used in Healing?** The methods used by Jesus and the disciples to bring healing varied from case to case, but most frequently they included laying on of hands.[28] In the verse just quoted, Jesus no doubt could have spoken a powerful word of command and healed everyone in the large crowd instantly, but instead, "*he laid his hands on every one of them* and healed them" (Luke 4:40). Laying on of hands seems to have been the primary means Jesus used to heal, because when people came and asked him for healing they did not simply ask for prayer but said, for example, "come and lay your hand on her, and she will live" (Matt. 9:18).[29]

Another physical symbol of the Holy Spirit's power coming for healing was anointing with oil. Jesus' disciples "*anointed with oil* many that were sick and healed them" (Mark 6:13). And James tells the elders of the church to anoint the sick person with oil when they pray: "Is any among you sick? Let him call for the elders of the church, and let them pray over him, *anointing him with oil* in the name of the Lord; and the prayer of faith will save the sick man, and the Lord will raise him up; and if he has committed sins, he will be forgiven" (James 5:14–15).[30]

The New Testament often emphasizes the role of faith in the healing process— sometimes the faith of the sick person (Luke 8:48; 17:19), but at other times the faith of others who bring the sick person for healing. In James 5:15 it is the elders who pray, and James says it is "the prayer of faith" that saves the sick person—this then must be the faith of the elders praying,[31] not the faith of the one who is sick.

---

[28]See the discussion of laying on of hands in chapter 48, pp. 959–61.

[29]See also Luke 5:13; 13:13; Acts 28:8; also Mark 6:2, and several other verses in the gospels that mention laying on of hands. Jesus did not always heal in this way, however.

[30]The anointing with oil in James 5:14 should be understood as a symbol of the power of the Holy Spirit, not simply as medicinal, because oil would not be appropriate as a medicine for all diseases. Moreover, if its use were just medicinal, it is hard to see why only the elders should apply it. Oil is frequently a symbol of the Holy Spirit in the Old Testament (see Ex. 29:7; 1 Sam. 16:13; cf. Ps. 45:7), and this seems to be the case here as well. (See the thorough discussion in Douglas J. Moo, *The Letter of James*, pp. 177–81.)

[31]We may wonder why it is the elders who are called to come and pray for healing in James 5:14–15. Although James does not give a reason, it may be because they had responsibilities for pastoral

When the four men let down a paralytic through a hole in the roof where Jesus was preaching, we read, "And when Jesus saw *their* faith . . ." (Mark 2:5). At other times Jesus mentions the faith of the Canaanite woman regarding the healing of her daughter (Matt. 15:28), or of the centurion for the healing of his servant (Matt. 8:10, 13).[32]

**5. How Then Should We Pray for Healing?** How then should we pray regarding physical illness? Certainly it is right to ask God for healing, for Jesus tells us to pray, "Deliver us from evil" (Matt. 6:13), and the apostle John writes to Gaius, "I pray that all may go well with you and *that you may be in health*" (3 John 2). Moreover, Jesus frequently healed *all* who were brought to him, and he never sent people away, telling them it would be good for them to remain ill for a longer time! In addition to this, whenever we take any kind of medicine or seek any medical help for an illness, *by those actions we admit that we think it to be God's will that we seek to be well*. If we thought that God wanted us to continue in our illness, we would never seek medical means for healing! So when we pray it seems right that our first assumption, unless we have specific reason to think otherwise, should be that God would be pleased to heal the person we are praying for—as far as we can tell from Scripture, this is God's revealed will.[33]

Ken Blue has a helpful observation here. He argues that if we want to understand God's attitude toward physical healing we should look at Jesus' life and ministry. Blue says, "If Jesus truly reveals the character of God to us, then we may cease speculating about and arguing over God's will in sickness and healing. Jesus healed people because he loved them. Very simply, he had compassion for them; he was on their side; he wanted to solve their problems."[34] This is a strong argument, especially when coupled with the realization that Jesus came to inaugurate the presence of the kingdom of God among us and to show us what the kingdom of God would be like.

How then should we pray? Certainly it is right to ask God for healing, and we should go to him with the simple request that he give physical healing in time of need. James warns us that simple unbelief can lead to prayerlessness and failure to receive answers from God: "You do not have, because you do not ask" (James 4:2). But when we pray for healing we should remember that we must pray for God to be glorified in the situation, whether he chooses to heal or not. And we also ought to pray out of the same compassion of heart that Jesus felt for those whom he healed. When we pray this way, God will sometimes—and perhaps often—grant answers to our prayers.

Someone may object at this point that, from a pastoral standpoint, much harm

---

care, maturity and wisdom in dealing with the possible sin involved (see vv. 15–16), and a measure of spiritual authority that accompanied their office. They would certainly be able to bring others with gifts of healing if they wished. Moreover, James broadens his directions to include all Christians in v. 16: "Therefore confess your sins to one another, and *pray for one another, that you may be healed.*"

[32]By contrast, we can note that when the disciples could not cast out a demon, Jesus says it was "because of your little faith" (Matt. 17:20).

[33]See discussion in chapter 13, pp. 213–16, on the secret and revealed will of God. Of course we realize that God's *secret* will, unknown to us in any specifics, is that not all will be healed, just as it is his secret will that not all will be saved. But in both situations we should pray for what we see in Scripture to be God's revealed will: to save sinners and to heal those who are ill.

[34]*Authority to Heal*, pp. 72, 78.

is done when people are encouraged to believe that a miracle of healing will occur and then nothing happens—disappointment with the church and anger at God may result. Those who pray for people to be healed today need to hear this objection and use wisdom in what they tell people who are ill.

But we also need to realize that there is more than one kind of mistake to make: (1) *Not praying for healing at all* is not a correct solution, for it involves disobedience to James 5. (2) Telling people that *God seldom heals today* and that they should expect nothing to happen is not a correct solution either, for it does not provide an atmosphere conducive to faith and is inconsistent with the pattern we see in the ministry of Jesus and the early church in the New Testament. (3) Telling people that *God always heals today* if we have enough faith is a cruel teaching not supported by Scripture (see section 6 below).

The pastorally wise solution, it seems, lies between (2) and (3) above. We can tell people that God frequently heals today (if we believe that is true), and that it is very possible that they will be healed,[35] but that we are still living in an age when the kingdom of God is "already" here but "not yet" fully here. Therefore Christians in this life will experience healing (and many other answers to prayer), but they will also experience continuing illness and eventual death. In each individual case it is God's sovereign wisdom that decides the outcome, and our role is simply to ask him and wait for him to answer (whether "yes" or "no" or "keep praying and wait"). .

Those with "gifts of healings" (a literal translation of the plurals in 1 Cor. 12:9, 28) will be those people who find that their prayers for healing are answered more frequently and more thoroughly than others. When that becomes evident, a church would be wise to encourage them in this ministry and give them more opportunities to pray for others who are ill. We should also realize that gifts of healing could include ministry not only in terms of physical healing, but also in terms of emotional healing. And it may at times include the ability to set people free from demonic attack, for this is also called "healing" sometimes in Scripture (see Luke 6:18; Acts 10:38). Perhaps the gifts of being able to pray effectively in different kinds of situations and for different kinds of needs are what Paul referred to when he used the plural expression, *"gifts of healings."*

**6. But What if God Does Not Heal?** Nonetheless, we must realize that not all prayers for healing will be answered in this age. Sometimes God will not grant the special "faith" (James 5:15) that healing will occur, and at times God will choose not to heal, because of his own sovereign purposes. In these cases we must remember that Romans 8:28 is still true: though we experience the "sufferings of this present time," and though we "groan inwardly as we wait for . . . the redemption of our bodies" (Rom. 8:18, 23), nonetheless, "we know that in everything God works for good with those who love him, who are called

[35]Sometimes God may grant a strong subjective assurance of faith, something like what James calls "the prayer of faith" (James 5:15), and Heb. 11:1 calls "the assurance of things hoped for," and Mark 11:24 calls believing "that you have received it." In those cases the person praying may feel confidence to say that it is probable or even very likely that someone will be healed. But I do not think that God gives anyone warrant to promise or "guarantee" healing in this age, for his written Word makes no such guarantee, and our subjective sense of his will is always subject to some degree of uncertainty and some measure of error in this life.

according to his purpose" (Rom. 8:28). This includes working in our circumstances of suffering and illness as well.

Whatever Paul's "thorn in the flesh" was (and centuries of work by Bible-believing interpreters have failed to turn up a definitive answer), Paul realized that God allowed it to remain with him "to keep me from being too elated" (2 Cor. 12:7), that is, to keep Paul humble before the Lord.[36] So the Lord told him, "My grace is sufficient for you, for my power is made perfect in weakness" (2 Cor. 12:9). There are indications in the early church that even in the presence of the apostles not all people were healed. Paul recognized that "our outer nature is wasting away" (2 Cor. 4:16), and sometimes disease and illness will not be healed. When Epaphroditus came to visit Paul, he had an illness that brought him "near to death" (Phil. 2:27). Paul indicates in the narrative of Philippians 2 that it appeared as though Epaphroditus were going to die—that God did not heal him immediately when he became ill. But eventually God did heal (Phil. 2:27) in answer to prayer. Paul told Timothy that he should drink a little wine "for the sake of your stomach and your frequent ailments" (1 Tim. 5:23). He said, "Trophimus I left *ill* at Miletus" (2 Tim. 4:20). And both Peter (1 Peter 1:6–7; 4:19) and James (James 1:2–4) have words of encouragement and counsel for those who are suffering trials of various kinds:[37]

> Count it all joy, my brethren, when you meet various trials, for you know that the testing of your faith produces steadfastness. And let steadfastness have its full effect, that you may be perfect and complete, lacking in nothing. (James 1:2–4)

When God chooses not to heal, even though we ask him for it, then it is right that we "give thanks in all circumstances" (1 Thess. 5:18) and realize that God can use sickness to draw us closer to himself and to increase in us obedience to his will. So the psalmist can say, "*It is good for me that I was afflicted,* that I might learn your statutes" (Ps. 119:71), and, "Before I was afflicted I went astray; but now I keep your word" (Ps. 119:67).

Therefore God can bring increased sanctification to us through illness and

---

[36]After some study of 2 Cor. 12:7, my own conclusion at this point is that there is not enough information in the text to decide what Paul's thorn in the flesh was. There are reasons that can be given in support of all three main possibilities: (1) a physical ailment of some kind; (2) a demon that was harassing him; or (3) Jewish persecutors. The fact that we are unable to decide conclusively has some benefits, however: it means that we can apply this text to all of these kinds of situations in our own lives, when the Lord in his sovereign wisdom decides not to remove them from us.

[37]Some have attempted to establish a difference between sickness and other kinds of suffering, and to say that the passages in Scripture tell Christians that they should expect to suffer have to do with *other* kinds of suffering, such as persecution, but do not include physical sickness.

This argument seems unconvincing to me for two reasons: first, Scripture talks about "*various* trials" (James 1:2; also 1 Peter 1:6), and the intention of the authors in both cases seems to be to speak of *all* the kinds of trials that we experience in this life, including physical illness and affliction. Did James and Peter *not* want Christians who were ill to apply those passages to their own situations? This is hardly likely. (These are both general epistles written to thousands of Christians.)

Second, unless the Lord returns, we will all know the progressive aging and deterioration of our physical bodies, and eventually we will die. Paul says, "Our outer nature is wasting away" (2 Cor. 4:16). Almost inevitably this aging process includes various kinds of physical ailments.

It seems best to conclude that the sufferings which God allows us to experience from time to time in this life may at times include physical illness, which God in his sovereign wisdom decides not to heal. There may in fact be many cases when, for various reasons, we do not feel freedom to ask in faith for God to heal. Yet even in these cases the heart of faith will take God's Word as true and believe that this also has come into our lives "for good" (Rom. 8:28), and that God will bring good to us from it.

suffering—just as he can bring sanctification and growth in faith through miraculous healing. But the emphasis of the New Testament, both in Jesus' ministry and in the ministry of the disciples in Acts, seems to be one that encourages us in most cases eagerly and earnestly to seek God for healing, and then to continue to trust him to bring good out of the situation, whether he grants the physical healing or not. The point is that in everything God should receive glory and our joy and trust in him should increase.

## E. Tongues and Interpretation

It should be said at the outset that the Greek word *glōssa*, translated "tongue," is used not only to mean the physical tongue in a person's mouth, but also to mean "language." In the New Testament passages where speaking in tongues is discussed, the meaning "languages" is certainly in view. It is unfortunate, therefore, that English translations have continued to use the phrase "speaking in tongues," which is an expression not otherwise used in ordinary English and which gives the impression of a strange experience, something completely foreign to ordinary human life. But if English translations were to use the expression "speaking in languages," it would not seem nearly as strange, and would give the reader a sense much closer to what first century Greek speaking readers would have heard in the phrase when they read it in Acts or 1 Corinthians.[38] However, because current usage of the phrase "speaking in tongues" is so widely established, we will continue to use it in this discussion.

**1. Tongues in the History of Redemption.** The phenomenon of speaking in tongues is unique to the new covenant age. Before Adam and Eve fell into sin, there was no need to speak in other languages, because they spoke the *same language* and were *united in service of God* and in fellowship with him. After the fall people spoke the *same language* but eventually became *united in opposition to God,* and "the wickedness of man was great in the earth" and "every imagination of the thoughts of his heart was only evil continually" (Gen. 6:5). This unified language used in rebellion against God culminated in the building of the tower of Babel at a time when "the whole earth had one language and few words" (Gen. 11:1). In order to stop this united rebellion against him, God at Babel "confused the language of all the earth" and scattered people abroad over the face of the earth (Gen. 11:9).

When God called Abraham to himself (Gen. 12:1), he promised to make of Abraham a "great nation" (Gen. 12:2), and the nation of Israel that resulted from this call had one language that God wanted them to use in service for him. Yet this language was not spoken by the rest of the nations of the world, and they remained outside the reach of God's plan of redemption. So the situation was improved somewhat, for *one language out of all the languages of the world was used in service of God,* whereas in Genesis 11 God was not praised with any language.

Now if we pass over the age of the New Testament church and look at eternity future, we see that once again unity of language will be restored, but this time

---

[38]The NIV margin does translate "or *languages*" or "*other languages*" in Acts 2:4, 11; 10:46; 19:6, and throughout 1 Cor. 12–14. This is a preferable translation, for reasons mentioned above.

everyone will once again speak the *same language in service of God,* and in praise to him (Rev. 7:9–12; cf. Zeph. 3:9; 1 Cor. 13:8; perhaps Isa. 19:18).

In the New Testament church, there is something of a foretaste of the unity of language that will exist in heaven, but it is given only at some times, and only in a partial way. At Pentecost, which was the point at which the gospel began to go to all nations, it was appropriate that the disciples gathered in Jerusalem "began to speak in other tongues, as the Spirit gave them utterance" (Acts 2:4).[39] The result was that Jewish visitors to Jerusalem from various nations all heard in their own languages a proclamation of "the mighty works of God" (Acts 2:11). This was a remarkable symbol of the fact that the gospel message was about to go forth to all the nations of the world.[40] Such a symbolic action would have been inappropriate in the Old Testament, for there the evangelistic message was one of inviting people from other nations to come and join themselves to the Jewish people and become Jews, and thereby worship God. But here the message is about to go to each nation in its own language, inviting people in every place to turn to Christ and be saved.[41]

Moreover, within the context of the worship service of the church, speaking in tongues plus interpretation gives further indication of a promise that one day the differences in languages that originated at Babel will be overcome. If this gift is operating in a church, no matter what language a word of prayer or praise is given in, once there is an interpretation, everyone can understand it. This is, of course, a two-step process that is "imperfect," as are all gifts in this age (1 Cor. 13:9), but it is still an improvement on the situation from Babel to Pentecost when there was no provision to enable people to understand a message in a language they did not know.

Finally, prayer in tongues in a private setting is another form of prayer to God. Paul says, "If I pray in a tongue, *my spirit prays* but my mind is unfruitful" (1 Cor. 14:14). In the overall context of the history of redemption, this also may be seen as one more partial solution to the results of the fall, whereby we were cut off from fellowship with God. Of course, this does not mean that people's spirits can *only* have fellowship with God when they speak in tongues—for Paul affirms that he prays and sings both in tongues and in his own language (1 Cor. 14:15). However, Paul does see prayer in tongues as an additional means of fellowship directly with God in prayer and worship. Once again, this aspect of the gift of speaking in tongues was not operative, so far as we know, before the new covenant age.

**2. What Is Speaking in Tongues?** We may define this gift as follows: *Speaking in tongues is prayer or praise spoken in syllables not understood by the speaker.*

---

[39]This verse shows that the miracle was one of speaking, not of hearing. The disciples "began to *speak* in other tongues (or languages)."

[40]The speaking in tongues at Pentecost was unusual in that it was accompanied by "tongues as of fire, distributed and resting on each one of them" (Acts 2:3). Since fire in Scripture is often a symbol of God's purifying judgment, the presence of fire here may be a symbol of the fact that God was purifying language for use in his service.

[41]It is true that the first hearers of this message were still only Jews in Jerusalem (Acts 2:5), not Gentiles, but the symbolism of the gospel being proclaimed in many languages did give an indication of the worldwide evangelistic effort that would soon follow.

**a. Words of Prayer or Praise Spoken to God:** This definition indicates that speaking in tongues is primarily speech directed toward God (that is, prayer or praise). Therefore it is unlike the gift of prophecy, which frequently consists of messages directed *from* God toward people in the church. Paul says, "one who speaks in a tongue speaks not to men but *to God*" (1 Cor. 14:2), and if there is no interpreter present at the church service, Paul says that someone who has a gift of speaking in tongues should "keep silence in church and speak to himself and *to God*" (1 Cor. 14:28).

What kind of speech is this that is directed toward God? Paul says, "If I *pray* in a tongue, *my spirit prays* but my mind is unfruitful" (1 Cor. 14:14; cf. vv. 14–17, where Paul categorizes speech in tongues as praying and giving thanks, and v. 28). Therefore speaking in tongues apparently is prayer or praise directed to God, and it comes from the "spirit" of the person who is speaking. This is not inconsistent with the narrative in Acts 2, because the crowd said, "we hear them telling in our own tongues the mighty works of God" (Acts 2:11), a description that certainly could mean that the disciples were all glorifying God and proclaiming his mighty works in worship, and the crowd began to listen to this as it occurred in various languages. In fact, there is no indication that the disciples themselves were speaking to the crowd until Acts 2:14, when Peter then stands and addresses the crowd directly, presumably in Greek.[42]

**b. Not Understood by the Speaker:** Paul says that "one who speaks in a tongue speaks not to men but to God; *for no one understands him*, but he utters mysteries in the Spirit" (1 Cor. 14:2). Similarly, he says that if there is speaking in tongues without interpretation no meaning will be communicated: "I shall be a foreigner to the speaker and the speaker a foreigner to me" (1 Cor. 14:11). Moreover, the entire paragraph of 1 Corinthians 14:13–19 assumes that speech in tongues in the congregation, when it is not accompanied by interpretation, is not understood by those who hear:

> Therefore, he who speaks in a tongue should pray for the power to interpret. For if I pray in a tongue, my spirit prays but my mind is unfruitful. What am I to do? I will pray with the spirit and I will pray with the mind also; I will sing with the spirit and I will sing with the mind also. Otherwise, if you bless with the spirit, how can any one in the position of an outsider say the "Amen" to your thanksgiving when he does not know what you are saying? For you may give thanks well enough, but the other man is not edified. I thank God that I speak in tongues more than you all; nevertheless, in church I would rather speak five words with my mind, *in order to instruct others,* than ten thousand words in a tongue.

---

[42]In Acts 10:46 the people at Cornelius' household began "speaking in tongues and extolling God." Again, this either means that the speech consisted of praise to God or was very closely connected with it—grammatically one cannot tell from the text itself.

I do not want to rule out the possibility that speaking in tongues could sometimes include speech directed to people, not to God, because it is just possible that Paul's statement in 1 Cor. 14:2 is a generalization that is not intended to cover every instance, and, in any case, the main point of the verse is that only God can *understand* uninterpreted tongues, not that God is the only one to whom speech in tongues can be addressed. In fact, speech to men might be what is happening in Acts 2. Nevertheless, the evidence that we do have in 1 Cor. 14 indicates speech directed toward God, and it seems safe to say that that is generally what speaking in tongues will be.

Now at Pentecost speech in tongues was in known languages that were understood by those who heard: "each one heard them speaking *in his own language*" (Acts 2:6). But once again the speech was not understood by the speakers, for what caused the amazement was that Galileans were speaking all these different languages (v. 7). It seems, therefore, that *at times* speaking in tongues may involve speech in actual human languages, sometimes even languages that are understood by some of those who hear. But at other times—and Paul assumes that this will ordinarily be the case—the speech will be in a language that "no one understands" (1 Cor. 14:2).

Some have objected that speaking in tongues must always consist of speech in *known* human languages, since that is what happened at Pentecost. But the fact that speaking in tongues occurred in known human languages *once* in Scripture does not require that it *always* happen with known languages, especially when another description of speaking in tongues (1 Cor. 14) indicates exactly the opposite. Paul does not say that foreign visitors to Corinth will understand the speaker, but he says that when someone speaks in tongues "*no one*" will understand and the outsider will not know what the person is saying (1 Cor. 14:2, 16).[43] In fact, Paul explicitly says that quite the opposite of the phenomenon at Pentecost will happen in the ordinary conduct of church life: if "all speak in tongues" and "outsiders or unbelievers enter," far from understanding the message, they will say "that you are mad" (1 Cor. 14:23). Moreover, we must realize that 1 Corinthians 14 is Paul's general instruction based on a wide experience of tongues-speaking in many different churches, whereas Acts 2 simply describes one unique event at a significant turning point in the history of redemption (Acts 2 is historical narrative while 1 Cor. 14 is doctrinal instruction). Therefore it would seem appropriate to take 1 Corinthians 14 as the passage that most closely describes the ordinary experience of New Testament churches, and to take Paul's instructions there as the standard by which God intends churches to regulate the use of this gift.[44]

Are tongues known human languages then? Sometimes this gift may result in speaking in a human language that the speaker has not learned, but ordinarily it seems that it will involve speech in a language that no one understands, whether that be a human language or not.[45]

---

[43]Robertson and Plummer note that 1 Cor. 14:18, "I thank God that I speak in tongues more than you all," is "strong evidence that Tongues are not foreign languages" (A. Robertson and A. Plummer, *A Critical and Exegetical Commentary on the First Epistle of St. Paul to the Corinthians,* ICC [Edinburgh: T. & T. Clark, 1914], p. 314). If they were known foreign languages that foreigners could understand, as at Pentecost, why would Paul speak more than all the Corinthians in private, where no one would understand, rather than in church where foreign visitors could understand?

[44]Note that at Pentecost this speaking in tongues had another characteristic that was not shared by any later speech in tongues: there were tongues of fire appearing over the heads of those who spoke (Acts 2:3). But this is not a paradigm for all later experiences of speaking in tongues, not even for those found later in Acts.

[45]Paul does say, "If I speak in the tongues of men *and of angels*" (1 Cor. 13:1), suggesting that he sees the possibility that speaking in tongues may include more than merely human speech. Whether he thinks this is only a hypothetical possibility or a real one is difficult to say, but we certainly cannot rule out the idea that angelic languages would be involved with this speech as well.

Some have objected that since *glōssa* elsewhere in Greek (outside the New Testament) refers to *known* human languages, it must refer to known languages in the New Testament as well. But this objection is not convincing, since there was no other word in Greek better suited to refer to this phenomenon, even if it involved talking to God in languages that were not human languages or not

**c. Prayer With the Spirit, Not With the Mind:** Paul says: "If I pray in a tongue, *my spirit prays* but my *mind is unfruitful*. What am I to do? I will pray with the spirit and I will pray with the mind also; I will sing with the spirit and I will sing with the mind also" (1 Cor. 14:14–15).

Paul is not here talking about the Holy Spirit praying through us. The contrast between "my spirit" and "my mind" in verse 14 indicates that it is Paul's own human spirit that he is talking about, the nonmaterial aspect of his being. As he uses this gift, his spirit speaks directly to God, even though his mind does not have to formulate words and sentences and decide what to pray for.[46] Paul sees this kind of prayer as an activity that occurs in the spiritual realm, whereby our spirits speak directly to God but our mind is somehow bypassed and does not understand what we are praying.

We may wonder why God would give the church a gift that operates in the unseen, spiritual realm and that is not understood by our minds. One reason may be to keep us humble, and to help prevent intellectual pride. Another reason may be to remind us that God is greater than our understanding and that he works in ways that transcend our understanding. Finally, it is characteristic of much that God does in the new covenant age that it is done in the unseen, spiritual realm: regeneration, genuine prayer, worship "in spirit and in truth," the spiritual blessings that come through the Lord's Supper, spiritual warfare, laying up treasures in heaven, setting our minds on things above, where Christ is—all these and many more elements of the Christian life involve activities that occur in the unseen, spiritual realm, activities that we do not see or fully understand. In that light, speaking in tongues is simply another activity that occurs in the unseen spiritual realm, an activity we believe is effective because Scripture tells us it is, not because we can comprehend it with our minds (cf. 1 Cor. 14:5).

**d. Not Ecstatic but Self-controlled:** The New English Bible translated the phrase "speaking in tongues" as "ecstatic speech," thus giving further support to the idea that those who speak in tongues lose awareness of their surroundings or lose self-control or are forced to speak against their will. Moreover, some of the extreme elements in the Pentecostal movement have allowed frenzied and

---

fully developed languages of any sort, so long as some content or information was conveyed by the speech.

I am not here arguing that speaking in tongues in Acts 2 was a different phenomenon from the speaking in tongues that Paul discusses in 1 Cor. 14. I am simply saying that the phrase "speaking in tongues" in Acts 2 and 1 Cor. 14 refers to speech in syllables not understood by the speaker but understood by God, to whom this speech is directed. In Acts 2 this happened to be speech in known human languages that had not been learned by the speakers, whereas in 1 Cor. 14 the speech may have been in unknown human languages, or in angelic languages, or in some specialized kind of language given by the Holy Spirit to various speakers individually. The expression is broad enough to include a wide variety of phenomena.

[46]The phrase "pray in the Holy Spirit" in Jude 20 is not the same expression, since it is specifically the "Holy Spirit" who is designated. Jude is simply saying that Christians should pray in conformity to the character and leading of the Holy Spirit, and that may certainly include prayer in tongues, but it would include any other kind of prayer in an understandable language as well. Similarly, "Pray at all times *in the Spirit,* with all prayer and supplication" (Eph. 6:18) is specifically a statement that claims to cover all prayer that is made at all times. It refers to prayer in conformity to the character of the Holy Spirit and sensitive to the leading of the Holy Spirit, but it should not be restricted to speaking in tongues. Once again, it may include speaking in tongues, but should include all other types of prayer as well. (See the discussion of activities done "in the Holy Spirit" in chapter 30, pp. 651–52.)

disorderly conduct at worship services, and this has, in the minds of some, perpetuated the notion that speaking in tongues is a kind of ecstatic speech.

But this is not the picture given in the New Testament. Even when the Holy Spirit came with overwhelming power at Pentecost, the disciples were able to stop speaking in tongues so that Peter could give his sermon to the assembled crowd. More explicitly, Paul says:

> If any speak in a tongue, let there be *only two or at most three, and each in turn;* and let one interpret. But if there is no one to interpret, let each of them keep silence in church and speak to himself and to God. (1 Cor. 14:27–28)

Here Paul requires that those who speak in tongues take turns, and he limits the number to three, indicating clearly that those who spoke in tongues were aware of what was going on around them, and were able to control themselves so as to speak only when it was their turn, and when no one else was speaking. If there was no one to interpret, they were easily able to keep silence and not speak. All of these factors indicate a high degree of self-control and give no support to the idea that Paul thought of tongues as ecstatic speech of some kind.

**e. Tongues Without Interpretation:** If no one known to have the gift of interpretation is present in the assembly, the passage just quoted indicates that speaking in tongues should be in private. No speech in tongues without interpretation should be given in the church service.[47]

Paul speaks of praying in tongues and singing in tongues when he says, "I will *pray with the spirit* and I will pray with the mind also; I will *sing with the spirit* and I will sing with the mind also" (1 Cor. 14:15). This gives further confirmation to the definition given above in which we viewed tongues as something primarily directed toward God in prayer and praise. It also gives legitimacy to the practice of singing in tongues, whether publicly or privately. Yet the same rules apply for singing as for speaking: if there is no interpreter, it should only be done in private.[48]

In 1 Corinthians 14:20–25 Paul says that if believers speak in tongues without

---

[47]It is troubling that, in some churches today where speaking in tongues is allowed, those who do *not* give a message publicly (perhaps because it is not the appropriate time in the service or perhaps because they do not know if someone will interpret) will still sometimes speak in tongues not "silently" but so that four or five people nearby can hear their speech in tongues. This is simply disobedience to Paul's directive, and is not acting in love toward others in the church. Paul says to "keep *silence* in church" if one is not giving a public message in tongues. (Many who have spoken in tongues today say that it can easily be done in an inaudible whisper, so that no one else will hear, and Paul's directions will be obeyed.)

[48]Many churches today, however, practice what is sometimes called "singing in the Spirit," in which many or all the congregation will simultaneously sing in tongues, individually improvising their melodies around a certain dominant musical chord. While many people will testify that there is beauty and spiritual power in such occurrences, once again we must object that it is directly contrary to Paul's instructions in 1 Cor. 14:27–28, where those who speak in tongues are to take turns, and there are to be at most three in a worship service, and interpretation is to follow. Though this practice may sound beautiful to those who are familiar with it, and though God may at times graciously use it as a means of winning an unbeliever, Paul explicitly says that the expected result generally will be that unbelievers will say "that you are mad" (1 Cor. 14:23). An alternative to this practice, and one that would both be consistent with Scripture and follow the path of love toward outsiders, would be for everyone to sing in this way, not in tongues, but in an understandable language (whether English or whatever language is commonly understood in the area where the church assembles).

interpretation in church, they will be acting and thinking like "children" (1 Cor. 14:20). He first quotes a prophecy of judgment from Isaiah 28:11–12: "In the law it is written, 'By men of strange tongues and by the lips of foreigners will I speak to this people, and even then they will not listen to me, says the Lord'" (1 Cor. 14:21).

In the context of Isaiah 28, God is warning the rebellious people of Israel that the next words they heard from him would be words of foreigners that they could not understand—the Assyrian army would come on them as agents of God's judgment. Now Paul is about to take this as a general principle—when God speaks to people in language they cannot understand, it is quite evidently a sign of God's judgment.

Paul rightly applies that to the situation of speaking in tongues without interpretation in the church service. He calls it a sign (that is, a sign of judgment) on unbelievers:

> Thus, *tongues are a sign* not for believers but *for unbelievers, while prophecy is* not for unbelievers but *for believers*. If, therefore, the whole church assembles and all speak in tongues, and outsiders or unbelievers enter, will they not say that you are mad? (1 Cor. 14:22–23)

Here Paul uses the word "sign" to mean *"sign of God's attitude"* (whether positive or negative). Tongues that are not understood by outsiders are certainly a *negative* sign—a sign of judgment. Therefore Paul cautions the Corinthians not to give such a sign to outsiders who come in. He tells them if an outsider comes in and hears only unintelligible speech, he will certainly not be saved but will conclude that the Corinthians are mad, and the uninterpreted tongues will in his case function as a sign of God's judgment.

By contrast, Paul says that prophecy is a sign of God's attitude as well, but here a *positive* sign of God's blessing. This is why he can say that prophecy is a sign "for believers" (v. 22). And this is why he concludes his section by saying, "If all prophesy, and an unbeliever or outsider enters, he is convicted by all, he is called to account by all, the secrets of his heart are disclosed; and so, falling on his face, he will worship God and declare that God is really among you" (vv. 24–25). When this happens, believers will certainly realize that God is active among them to bring blessing, and prophecy will regularly function as a sign *for believers* of God's positive attitude for them.[49]

Nevertheless, however much Paul warns against using tongues without interpretation *in church,* he certainly views it positively and encourages it in *private.* He says, "He who speaks in a tongue *edifies himself,* but he who prophesies edifies the church" (1 Cor. 14:4). What is his conclusion? It is not (as some would argue) that Christians should decide not to use the gift or decide that it has no value when used privately. Rather he says, "What am I to do? I will pray with the spirit and I will pray with the mind also" (v. 15). And he says, "I thank God that I speak in tongues more than you all" (v. 18), and "Now *I want you all to speak in tongues,* but even more to prophesy" (v. 5), and "Earnestly desire to prophesy, and do not forbid speaking in tongues" (v. 39). If our previous

---

[49]For further discussion of this passage, see Wayne Grudem, "1 Corinthians 14:20–25: Prophecy and Tongues as Signs of God's Attitude," *WTJ* 41:2 (Spring 1979), pp. 381–96.

understanding of tongues as prayer or praise to God is correct, then we would certainly expect that edification would follow, even though the speaker's mind does not understand what is being said, but his or her own human spirit is communicating directly with God. Just as prayer and worship in general edify us as we engage in them, so this kind of prayer and worship edifies us too, according to Paul.

**f. Tongues With Interpretation: Edification for the Church:** Paul says, "He who prophesies is greater than he who speaks in tongues, *unless someone interprets, so that the church may be edified*" (1 Cor. 14:5). Once a message in tongues is interpreted, all can understand. In that case, Paul says that the message in tongues is *as valuable* to the church as prophecy. We should note that he does not say they have the same functions (for other passages indicate that prophecy is communication from God toward human beings, while tongues is generally communication from human beings to God). But Paul clearly says they have equal value in edifying the church.

**g. Not All Speak in Tongues:** Just as not all Christians are apostles, and not all are prophets or teachers, and not all possess gifts of healing, so not all speak with tongues. Paul clearly implies this when he asks a series of questions, all of which expect the answer "no," and includes the question "Do all speak with tongues?" (1 Cor. 12:30). The implied answer is no.[50] Some have argued that Paul here only means that not all speak with tongues *publicly*, but that perhaps he would have admitted that all can speak in tongues privately. But this distinction seems foreign to the context and unconvincing. He does not specify that not all speak with tongues *publicly* or *in church*, but simply says that not all speak with tongues. His next question is, "Do all interpret?" (v. 30). His previous two questions were, "Do all work miracles? Do all possess gifts of healing?" (vv. 29–30). Would we wish to make the same arguments about these gifts—that not all interpret tongues *publicly*, but that all Christians are able to do it *privately*? Or that not all work miracles publicly, but that all are able to work miracles privately? Such a distinction seems unwarranted by the context in every case.

In actuality, the desire to say that every Christian can speak in tongues (even though Paul says that not all speak in tongues) is probably motivated in most cases by a prior doctrinal understanding that views baptism in the Holy Spirit as an experience subsequent to conversion,[51] and sees speaking in tongues as an initial "sign" of receiving this baptism in the Holy Spirit.[52] But there are serious questions that remain about this doctrinal position (as explained in chapter 39). It seems better to take 1 Corinthians 12:30 to mean just what it says: not all speak in tongues. The gift of tongues—just like every other gift—is not given by the Holy Spirit to every Christian who seeks it. He "apportions to each one individually as he wills" (1 Cor. 12:11).

However, there is nothing in Scripture that says that only a few will receive the

---

[50]The Greek particle *mē*, which precedes this question, expects the answer "no" from the reader. The NASB captures this sense: "All do not speak with tongues, do they?"

[51]See chapter 39 for a discussion of baptism in the Holy Spirit.

[52]This is still the official doctrinal position of the Assemblies of God, for example.

gift of speaking in tongues, and, since it is a gift Paul views as edifying and useful in prayer and worship (on a personal level even if not in church), it would not be surprising if the Holy Spirit gave a very widespread distribution of this gift and many Christians in fact received it.[53]

**h. What About the Danger of Demonic Counterfeit?** At times Christians have been afraid to speak in tongues, wondering if speaking something they do not understand might involve them in speaking blasphemy against God or speaking something that is prompted by a demon rather than by the Holy Spirit.

First, it must be said that this is not Paul's concern, even in the city of Corinth where many had come from pagan temple worship, and where Paul had clearly said that "what pagans sacrifice they offer to demons and not to God" (1 Cor. 10:20). Nonetheless, Paul says, "I want you all to speak in tongues" (1 Cor. 14:5). He gives no warning that they should beware of demonic counterfeit or even think that this would be a possibility when they use this gift.

The theological reason underlying Paul's encouragement at that point is the fact that the Holy Spirit is working powerfully within the lives of believers. Paul says, "I want you to understand that no one speaking by the Spirit of God ever says 'Jesus be cursed!' and no one can say 'Jesus is Lord' except by the Holy Spirit" (1 Cor. 12:3). Here Paul reassures the Corinthians that if they are speaking by the power of the Holy Spirit working within them, they will not say, "Jesus be cursed!"[54] Coming as it does at the beginning of a discussion of spiritual gifts, 1 Corinthians 12:3 is intended to function as reassurance to the Corinthians who may have suspected some Christians who came from backgrounds of demon worship in the temples at Corinth. Might this demonic influence still affect their use of a spiritual gift? Paul lays down the ground rule that those who genuinely profess faith that "Jesus is Lord" are doing so by the Holy Spirit working within, and that no one speaking by the power of the Holy Spirit will ever speak blasphemy or curses against Jesus.[55] This fear, then, is not one that Paul seemed

---

[53]Mark 16:17 is sometimes used to claim that all Christians can speak in tongues: "And these signs will accompany those who believe: in my name they will cast out demons; they will speak in new tongues." But in response to this verse it must be noted (1) that the verse probably was not originally part of Mark's gospel, since many early and very reliable manuscripts do not include Mark 16:9–20, and its doubtful status means that it is a precarious basis upon which to build doctrine (see chapter 17, p. 365); (2) that even if it is not part of Scripture, it does of course bear witness to a very early tradition in the history of the church, but even in this case, it does not affirm that all believers will speak with tongues: the immediately following phrase says, "They will pick up serpents" (v. 18), something that no responsible interpreter would say should be true of every Christian; and (3) that no connection is made between speaking in tongues and baptism in the Holy Spirit in this passage.

[54]It might be objected at this point that speaking in tongues is not speech empowered by the Holy Spirit, but is speech that comes from the speaker's own human spirit. But Paul clearly views all these spiritual gifts as generally *empowered* by the Holy Spirit, even the ones in which human personality comes fully into play. This would be true of teachers and helpers and administrators, as well as those who speak with tongues. In each of these cases the active agent in performing the activity is the Christian who has the particular gift and uses it, but all these are nonetheless empowered by the Holy Spirit in their functioning, and that would also be true of the gift of tongues as well.

[55]Also relevant at this point is John's reassurance to his readers, in the context of demonic spirits that had gone out into the world: "He who is in you is greater than he who is in the world" (1 John 4:4).

troubled by. He simply encouraged believers to pray in tongues and said that if they did so they would be edifying themselves.[56]

### i. Is Romans 8:26–27 Related to Speaking in Tongues? Paul writes in Romans 8:26–27:

> Likewise the Spirit helps us in our weakness; for we do not know how to pray as we ought, but the Spirit himself intercedes for us with sighs too deep for words. And he who searches the hearts of men knows what is the mind of the Spirit, because the Spirit intercedes for the saints according to the will of God.

Paul does not mention speaking in tongues explicitly here, and the statement is a general one concerning the life of all Christians, so it does not seem correct to say that Paul here is referring to speaking in tongues. He is referring to a more general experience that occurs in the prayer life of every Christian.

But what exactly is he talking about? Some have thought that he is referring to an intercessory activity completely imperceptible to us, in which the Holy Spirit intercedes for us by making sighs and groans to the Father. On this view, such intercessory work of the Spirit goes on continually, but we have no idea that it is happening (except for the fact that Scripture tells us this). In this way it would be

---

[56]Some popular books have given anecdotal accounts of Christians who say they spoke in tongues for a time and then found that there was a demon within them who was empowering this speech, and the demon was cast out. (See, for example, C. Fred Dickason, *Demon Possession and the Christian* [Westchester, Ill.: Crossway, 1987], pp. 126–27; 188–91; 193–97.) But this is just another example of a case where experience is to be subject to Scripture and tested by Scripture, and the teaching of Scripture should not be subject to experience. We must be careful that we not let such reports of experiences cause us to adopt a different position than Scripture itself on this issue. Specifically, if 1 Cor. 12–14 views tongues as a good gift from the Holy Spirit that is valuable for edification and for the good of the church, and if Paul can say, "I want you all to speak in tongues" (1 Cor. 14:5), then interpretations of contemporary experiences that, in effect, say, "I want you all to be afraid of tongues," go contrary to the emphasis of the New Testament. (Note Dickason's quotation of Kurt Koch: "Seeking this gift for ourselves can be a very dangerous experience" [p. 127].) This is just not the perspective Paul has in the New Testament.

I realize that Dickason has a cessationist view with respect to speaking in tongues today (see p. 189: "I told her I doubted that there were any genuine tongues from God today in the New Testament sense"). Therefore, from his perspective, he is not making Scripture subject to experience, but sees these experiences as confirming his understanding of Scripture. (I have discussed the cessationist position in chapter 52, pp. 1031–46.)

There is the possibility of demonic counterfeit of every gift *in the lives of unbelievers* (see Matt. 7:22; also chapter 17, pp. 368–69, on false miracles). Therefore the fact that there is some kind of "speaking in tongues" in pagan religions should not surprise us or cause us to think that all speaking in tongues is false. But *in the lives of believers,* especially when there is positive fruit in their lives and positive fruit from their gifts, 1 Cor. 12:3, 1 John 4:4, and Matt. 7:16–20 tell us that these are not counterfeit gifts but real gifts from God. We must remember that Satan and demons do not do good; they do evil; and they do not bring blessing; they bring destruction.

(Neil T. Anderson, in *The Bondage Breaker* [Eugene, Oreg.: Harvest House, 1990], pp. 159–60, relates a story of a man who was apparently a Christian and who had a counterfeit gift of tongues. But Anderson notes that the gift was conferred on the man "by false teachers" [p. 159] and that this "gift" brought obviously destructive consequences in the man's life. These factors, and not just the words of a demon as the only evidence, gave clear indication of the counterfeit nature of that supposed "gift." Unlike Dickason, Anderson affirms that he is not opposed to speaking in tongues; see p. 160.)

An alternative explanation for the stories given by Dickason is to say that the demons who *said* they were "tongues spirits," and that they came in when some charismatics laid hands on the Christian in question, were lying. Satan "is a liar and the father of lies" (John 8:44), and he would love to have Christians afraid of as many of the Holy Spirit's gifts as possible.

similar to the intercessory work of Christ mentioned in Romans 8:34 and Hebrews 7:25.

But this does not appear to be a satisfactory explanation of the passage, for several reasons: (1) It would not seem probable that Paul would say that the intercessory work of the Holy Spirit, who is the infinite, omnipotent, omniscient God, would be carried out in "wordless *groans*" (literal translation of *stenagmois alalētois* in Rom. 8:26), especially when we realize that "groans" refers to the intense sighs of fatigue that are appropriate to weary, burdened creatures in a fallen world.[57] (2) Within the larger context the groanings in view seem to be those due to the burden of living in this present evil age, particularly the groans associated with our suffering in this age (see vv. 17, 18, 23). (3) The verb "helps" in Romans 8:26 ("The Spirit *helps* us in our weakness") does not refer to something the Holy Spirit does *apart from us and on our behalf*, but rather something the Holy Spirit does *in cooperation with us*. The verb Paul uses here (*sunantilambanomai*) is also used in Luke 10:40, where Martha wants Jesus to tell Mary "to *help* me"—certainly she does not want Mary to do the food preparation *instead* of her, but rather to come and take part *with* her in doing it.[58] Therefore Paul is not talking about something the Holy Spirit does completely apart from our participation, but something the Holy Spirit does in cooperation with our activity.

These reasons combine to indicate that Paul is not talking about a work of the Holy Spirit done apart from us and unknown by us, but about the inarticulate sighs and groans which we ourselves utter in prayer, which the Holy Spirit then makes into effective intercession before the throne of God. We could paraphrase, "The Holy Spirit assists our prayers when he intercedes (for us) by taking our wordless groans and making them into effective prayer."[59]

What is the relationship between this and speaking in tongues? There is some similarity because it is effective prayer which *we pray* even though we do not understand fully what we are praying. But there are some differences in that the sighs or groans that we utter in prayer very often relate to situations or hardships that we are very conscious of in our minds as we pray, so we know what we are praying about. But Paul says that we do not know how to pray for these situations as we ought to pray. Therefore the Holy Spirit helps us and intercedes in these situations "according to the will of God" (Rom. 8:27). There is no explicit mention of our spirit praying (though that may indeed be true as well), nor is

---

[57]The word "groan" (*stenagmos*) is elsewhere used in the New Testament only at Acts 7:34, of the groanings of Israel under oppression in Egypt. But the related verb *stenazō* is used several times, always of finite creatures groaning under the burden of this fallen creation. In the immediately previous context *stenazō* refers to our groaning because our redemption is incomplete (Rom. 8:23; a related compound word is used in v. 22 of the creation itself). The verb is also used of finite creatures groaning under the burden of this creation in Mark 7:34 (Jesus as a man); 2 Cor. 5:2, 4 (believers who have a corruptible, earthly body); Heb. 13:17 (church leaders who may be tempted to groan under the burden of church leadership); and James 5:9 (a warning for Christians not to grumble or groan against one another). Though the verb was once used of Jesus who groaned while under the limitations of this human existence, it does not seem an appropriate term to use of the activity of the Holy Spirit, who would not experience a similar weakness because he never took on human nature.

[58]Though the word is not elsewhere used in the New Testament, its sense is also transparent from the *sun* ("with") prefix that Paul attaches to a very common word for "help."

[59]An alternative view is found in the helpful discussion by Douglas Moo, *Romans 1–8*, pp. 559–63, who (hesitantly) understands the groans to be not ours but the Holy Spirit's.

there mention of our mind being unfruitful or lacking understanding (though that may at times be at least partially true). Nor do these sighs or groans come forth in anything that could be called "other tongues" or "other languages." So there are several differences, even though Romans 8:26–27 talks about intercession that we make in sounds that are not fully understood by us, and therefore it is a phenomenon that has some similarities to speaking in tongues.

## F. Word of Wisdom and Word of Knowledge

Paul writes, "For to one is given the *word of wisdom* through the Spirit, and to another the *word of knowledge* according to the same Spirit. (1 Cor. 12:8 NASB) At the beginning of this discussion it must be understood that these two gifts are mentioned nowhere else in Scripture,[60] and no other early Christian literature outside the Bible has been found to use these phrases of any spiritual gift either. This means that the *only* information we have about these gifts is contained in this verse: we have the words used to describe these two gifts, and we have the context in which the phrases occur. No interpreter anywhere has any more information than this to work with. This warns us that our conclusions will probably be somewhat tentative in any case.

The major alternatives for understanding these gifts are two: (1) These gifts are commonly thought to be the ability to receive a special revelation from the Holy Spirit and on that basis to speak words that give wisdom in a situation or give specific knowledge of a situation in the life of someone present in a congregation. In this interpretation these gifts would be more "miraculous," in that they would call forth wonder and amazement from the people present since they would not be based on information ordinarily available to the person using the gift.

(2) The other interpretation of these gifts would see them as more "non-miraculous" or ordinary: the "word of wisdom" simply means the ability to speak a wise word in various situations, and "word of knowledge" is the ability to speak with knowledge about a situation. In both cases the knowledge and wisdom would not be based on a special revelation spontaneously given by the Holy Spirit, but would be based on wisdom acquired in the ordinary course of life, the knowledge and wisdom that would be characteristic of Bible teachers or elders and other mature Christians in a church, for example. These would be empowered by the Holy Spirit and thereby made effective when they were spoken. Examples of "words of wisdom" in this sense would be found in Acts 6:1–6 (the appointment of the first "deacons" or assistants to the apostles); Acts 6:10 (Stephen's wisdom in proclaiming the gospel); Acts 15:19–29 (the decision of the Jerusalem council); and even in King Solomon's statement, "Divide the living child in two, and give half to the one, and half to the other" (1 Kings 3:25; see also 1 Cor. 6:5–6).

In favor of the first interpretation, it might be argued that all the other seven gifts listed in 1 Corinthians 12:8–10 are in the "miraculous" category, and therefore these two gifts should be understood that way as well.

However, there are some weighty considerations against this view: (1) The

---

[60]At least no other place in Scripture calls something a "word of wisdom" or "word of knowledge" or uses those phrases in any other way.

words Paul uses for "word" (*logos*), "wisdom" (*sophia*), and "knowledge" (*gnōsis*) are not specialized or technical terms, but are extremely common words in the Greek New Testament. They are simply the ordinary words frequently used for "word" and "wisdom" and "knowledge." Moreover, they are not ordinarily used to denote miraculous events (as are the words *revelation* and *prophecy,* for example), but are simply the words used for human knowledge and wisdom. So from the meanings of the words themselves, no indication of a miraculous gift seems to be given.

(2) In the context of 1 Corinthians 12:8, Paul's purpose in the argument seems to weigh against thinking of them as miraculous. Paul's larger purpose in verses 8–10 is to demonstrate that *no matter what kind of gift a person has,* he or she can be assured that that gift has been given by the Holy Spirit. He precedes the section by saying, "To *each* is given the manifestation of the Spirit for the common good," and follows this immediate section by saying, "All these are inspired by one and the same Spirit, who apportions to *each one* individually as he wills" (vv. 7, 11). But if Paul's purpose in this section is to show that *every Christian's gift* is given by the Holy Spirit, then that purpose would not be well served by giving only examples of miraculous gifts. If he did that, those with non-miraculous gifts would feel left out of the argument and would not be persuaded that their gifts are included in Paul's discussion. Even more importantly, those with miraculous gifts might look at this list and conclude that *only* those with miraculous gifts really had the Holy Spirit at work within them to empower those gifts. This would lead to a dangerous kind of elitism in the congregation. Therefore it seems necessary that Paul would include some *nonmiraculous* gifts in his list in 1 Corinthians 12:8–10.

But which are the nonmiraculous gifts in this list?

    Word of wisdom
    Word of knowledge
    Faith
    Gifts of healings
    Miracles
    Prophecy
    Distinguishing between spirits
    Tongues
    Interpretation of tongues

All the other gifts seem to fall in the more "miraculous" category (with the possible exceptions of speaking in tongues and perhaps faith). But that would make it almost necessary that word of wisdom and word of knowledge be nonmiraculous to guarantee that there are *some* nonmiraculous gifts in the list. This would demonstrate Paul's pastoral wisdom in selecting examples of different kinds of gifts being exercised in the actual congregation. So there must be some nonmiraculous gifts on the list—and if there are some, then these are very good candidates.[61]

---

[61]Even if faith and tongues are considered nonmiraculous, then we have a list that is a mixture of miraculous and nonmiraculous gifts, and then there is no reason why word of wisdom and word of knowledge could not be considered non-miraculous as well, especially on the basis of the fact that the words used to describe them do not ordinarily denote miraculous events.

(3) Probably the most decisive consideration is the fact that the New Testament already has a term to describe the action of receiving a special revelation from the Holy Spirit and reporting it in the congregation—this is what Paul calls "prophecy." Since he discusses prophecy at some length, describing it and regulating it, we can know fairly clearly what prophecy was. But to say that these other gifts functioned in exactly the same way (perhaps differing only in content) does not seem justified by anything in the text other than a preconceived notion of what these gifts should be.[62]

Therefore it would seem preferable to understand these in a "nonmiraculous" way, simply as the ability to speak with wisdom or with knowledge in various situations. What many people today call "word of wisdom" and "word of knowledge" in charismatic circles, it would seem better simply to refer to as "prophecy."[63]

## G. Distinguishing Between Spirits and Spiritual Warfare

The gift of distinguishing between spirits is another gift that is mentioned only once in the New Testament (in the list at 1 Cor. 12:10), but the nature of this gift connects it with a number of other passages that describe the spiritual warfare that occurs between Christians and demonic spirits. We may define the gift of distinguishing between spirits as follows: *Distinguishing between spirits is a special ability to recognize the influence of the Holy Spirit or of demonic spirits in a person.*

In the perspective of the history of redemption, this gift also gives a foretaste of the age to come in that it is a foretaste of the ability to recognize Satan and his influence, which ability will be made perfect for us in heaven, when everything that is covered or hidden will be revealed and brought to the light (Matt. 10:26; cf. Rev. 20:11–15). This ability is probably also stronger than that possessed by most or all believers in the old covenant, where mentions of demonic activity are infrequent, and where demonic attacks against God's people most often were embodied in military attacks by unbelieving nations against the people of Israel, or in overt temptations to go and serve pagan deities. Demonic activity was therefore perceived primarily through observation of outward physical events and circumstances in which Satan's purpose was carried out, and which could be clearly seen.

This New Testament gift of distinguishing between spirits involves the ability to distinguish the presence of evil spirits from the presence of the work of the

---

[62]In fact, everything that modern Pentecostal and charismatic Christians call "words of knowledge" and "words of wisdom" would fit exactly into the definition of prophecy as given by Paul, and should in fact be put under the general umbrella of prophecy. This would have the distinct advantage of making the use of this gift subject to Paul's rules for understanding and regulating prophecy in the church.

Will any harm come from continuing the fairly common practice of thinking of words of wisdom and words of knowledge as miraculous gifts that depend on a special revelation from God? One immediate danger might be that, whereas what is actually happening would be called "prophecy" by Paul, in some cases it is now being called something different, and that tends to distance it from the regulations for prophecy that Paul gives in the New Testament. Whether that would lead to misuse of the gift at some point in the future is impossible to predict. But it does seem to be rather anomalous to have a miraculous gift that is quite widely used and that is only mentioned but never discussed or regulated at all in the New Testament.

[63]For further discussion of these gifts, see Wayne Grudem, "What is the Real Meaning of a 'Word of Wisdom' and a 'Word of Knowledge'?" in *Ministries Today* (Jan.–Feb. 1993), pp. 60–65.

Holy Spirit in a person's life. Paul knows that the Corinthians previously were "led astray to dumb idols" (1 Cor. 12:2), and John similarly realizes that there is a need for Christians to "test the spirits to see whether they are of God; for many false prophets have gone out into the world" (1 John 4:1).

Beyond this, it is also possible that the gift would involve distinguishing between various *types* of evil spirits, such as a spirit of infirmity (Luke 13:11), a spirit of divination (Acts 16:16), a dumb and deaf spirit (Mark 9:25, 29), and a spirit of error (1 John 4:6). From a lexical and grammatical standpoint there is nothing that would prevent us from understanding the gift of "distinguishing between spirits" to include this kind of ability as well.[64]

Of course, to some degree the presence of demonic activity is outwardly evident, sometimes from the blurting out of blatantly false doctrinal statements (see 1 Cor. 12:2–3; 1 John 4:1–6), and sometimes from violent and bizarre physical actions, especially in the face of Christian preaching (see Mark 1:24; 9:20; Matt. 8:29; etc.). Satan's influence is characteristically destructive, and the person influenced by a demon will have a destructive influence on the church and others around him or her, and also a self-destructive influence that harms the life of the troubled individual himself or herself.

But in addition to these outward indications of demonic influence, there is probably also a more subjective perception that occurs at the spiritual and emotional level, whereby the presence of demonic activity is distinguished. When this is more highly developed, and is able to function for the benefit of the church as a whole, then Paul would no doubt call it a gift of distinguishing between spirits.[65]

In connection with the gift of distinguishing between spirits, the discussion of spiritual warfare given above in chapter 20 (on Satan and demons) is also relevant.

## QUESTIONS FOR PERSONAL APPLICATION

1. Have you ever experienced a gift of prophecy as defined in this chapter? What have you called it? Has this gift (or something like it) functioned in your church? If so, what have been the benefits—and dangers? If not, do you think this gift might be of help to your church? (Why or why not?)

2. Does the gift of teaching function effectively in your church? Who uses this gift in addition to the pastor or elders? Do you think your church adequately appreciates sound Bible teaching? In what areas (if any) do you think your church needs to grow in its knowledge and love of the teachings of Scripture?

3. Of the other gifts discussed in this chapter, have you ever used any of them yourself? Are there any which you think your church needs but does not have at this time? What do you think would be best for you to do in response to this need?

---

[64]For a very extensive linguistic and grammatical analysis of this phrase, see Wayne Grudem, "A Response to Gerhard Dautzenberg on 1 Cor. 12:10," in *Biblische Zeitschrift*, N.F., 22:2 (1978), pp. 253–70.

[65]Of course, no gift is perfect in any Christian in this age (1 Cor. 13:9–10), and we should not expect that this gift would be perfect, or that those who have it would never make mistakes. See chapter 52, pp. 1022–25, on the fact that spiritual gifts vary in strength.

## SPECIAL TERMS

(This list applies to chapters 52 and 53.)

apostle

cessationist

distinguishing between spirits

gifts of the Holy Spirit

healing

interpretation of tongues

miracles

miraculous gifts

nonmiraculous gifts

office

prophecy

speaking in tongues

teaching

word of wisdom

word of knowledge

## BIBLIOGRAPHY

(For an explanation of this bibliography see the note on the bibliography to chapter 1, p. 38. Complete bibliographical data may be found on pp. 1223–29. Note: Very few systematic theologies have sections on spiritual gifts, but a few that do are listed below. This bibliography applies to chapters 52 and 53.)

### Sections in Evangelical Systematic Theologies

1. Anglican (Episcopalian)

(no explicit treatment)

2. Arminian (Wesleyan or Methodist)

    1983    Carter, 1:449–57

3. Baptist

    1983–85    Erickson, 877–83

4. Dispensational

    1947    Chafer, 7:215–20

    1986    Ryrie, 367–74

5. Lutheran

(no explicit treatment)

6. Reformed (or Presbyterian)

(no explicit treatment)

7. Renewal (or charismatic/Pentecostal)

    1988–92    Williams, 2:209–36, 243–63, 323–409, 3:159–77

### Sections in Representative Roman Catholic Systematic Theologies

1. Roman Catholic: Traditional

(no explicit treatment)

2. Roman Catholic: Post-Vatican II

    1980    McBrien, 2:1086–88

## Other Works

Baker, J. P. "Gifts of the Spirit." In *NDT,* pp. 269–71.

Bennett, Dennis and Rita. *The Holy Spirit and You.* Plainfield, N.J.: Logos, 1971. (Charismatic)

Blue, Ken. *Authority to Heal.* Downers Grove, Ill.: InterVarsity Press, 1987.

Bridge, Donald. *Signs and Wonders Today.* Leicester: Inter-Varsity Press, 1985. (Charismatic)

———, and David Phypers. *Spiritual Gifts and the Church.* Downers Grove, Ill.: InterVarsity Press, 1973. (Charismatic)

Budgen, Victor. *The Charismatics and the Word of God.* Phillipsburg, N.J.: Presbyterian and Reformed, 1985. (Cessationist)

Carson, D. A. *Showing the Spirit: A Theological Exposition of 1 Corinthians 12–14.* Grand Rapids: Baker, 1987.

Chantry, Walter J. *Signs of the Apostles.* 2d ed. Edinburgh and Carlisle, Pa.: Banner of Truth, 1976. (Cessationist)

Clements, Roy. *Word and Spirit: The Bible and the Gift of Prophecy Today.* Leicester: UCCF Booklets, 1986.

Deere, Jack. *Surprised by the Power of the Holy Spirit: A Former Dallas Seminary Professor Discovers That God Still Speaks and Heals Today.* Grand Rapids: Zondervan, 1993. (This is the most balanced and persuasive argument I have ever read against the cessationist position.)

Edgar, Thomas. "The Cessation of the Sign Gifts." In *BibSac* 145:180 (Oct.–Dec. 1988), pp. 371–86. (Cessationist)

Ellis, E. E. "Prophecy, Theology of." In *NDT,* pp. 537–38.

Farnell F. David. "The Current Debate About New Testament Prophecy." In *BibSac* 149:595 (July–Sept. 1992), pp. 277–303.

———. "Does the New Testament Teach Two Prophetic Gifts?" In *BibSac* 150 (Jan.–March, 1993), pp. 62–88.

———. "Fallible New Testament Prophecy/Prophets? A Critique of Wayne Grudem's Hypothesis." In *The Master's Seminary Journal* 2:2 (Fall 1991), pp. 157–80.

———. "The Gift of Prophecy in the Old and New Testaments." In *BibSac* 149:596 (Oct.–Dec., 1992), pp. 387–410.

———. "When Will the Gift of Prophecy Cease?" In *BibSac* 150 (April–June, 1993), pp. 171–202.

Gaffin, Richard B. *Perspectives on Pentecost: Studies in New Testament Teaching on the Gifts of the Holy Spirit.* Phillipsburg, N.J.: Presbyterian and Reformed, 1979. (Cessationist)

Gee, Donald. *Concerning Spiritual Gifts.* Springfield, Mo.: Gospel Publishing House, 1972 (revised edition). (Traditional Pentecostal)

———. *Spiritual Gifts in the Work of Ministry Today.* Springfield, Mo.: Gospel Publishing House, 1963. (Traditional Pentecostal)

Gentry, Kenneth L., Jr. *The Charismatic Gift of Prophecy: A Reformed Response to Wayne Grudem.* 2d ed. Memphis, Tenn.: Footstool Publications, 1989. (Cessationist)

Green, Michael. *I Believe in the Holy Spirit.* London: Hodder and Stoughton, and Grand Rapids: Eerdmans, 1975.

Greig, Gary, and Kevin Springer, eds. *The Kingdom and the Power: Are Healing and the Spiritual Gifts Used by Jesus and the Early Church Meant for the Church Today?* Ventura, Calif.: Regal Books, 1993.

Gromacki, Robert G. *The Modern Tongues Movement.* Rev. ed. Phillipsburg, N.J.: Presbyterian and Reformed, 1972. (Cessationist)

Grudem, Wayne. "Does God Still Give Revelation Today?" In *Charisma,* Sept., 1992, pp. 38–42.

_____. *The Gift of Prophecy in 1 Corinthians.* Lanham, Md.: University Press of America, 1982.

_____. *The Gift of Prophecy in the New Testament and Today.* Westchester, Ill.: Crossway, 1988.

_____. *Power and Truth: A Response to the Critiques of Vineyard Teaching and Practice by D. A. Carson, James Montgomery Boice, and John H. Armstrong in Power Religion.* Anaheim, Calif.: Association of Vineyard Churches, 1993.

_____. "What Is the Real Meaning of a 'Word of Wisdom' and a 'Word of Knowledge'?" In *Ministries Today* (Jan.–Feb. 1993), pp. 60–65.

_____. "What Should Be the Relationship Between Prophet and Pastor?" In *Equipping the Saints* (Fall 1990), pp. 7–9, 21–22.

Hayford, Jack W. *The Beauty of Spiritual Language.* Irvine, Tex.: Waco, 1993.

Horton, Michael Scott, ed. *Power Religion: The Selling Out of the Evangelical Church?* Chicago: Moody Press, 1992.

Houston, Graham. *Prophecy: A Gift For Today?* Leicester and Downers Grove, Ill.: InterVarsity Press, 1989.

Hummel, Charles E. *Fire in the Fireplace: Charismatic Renewal in the Nineties.* Downers Grove, Ill.: InterVarsity Press, 1993.

MacArthur, John F., Jr. *Charismatic Chaos.* Grand Rapids: Zondervan, 1992. (Cessationist)

_____. *The Charismatics: A Doctrinal Perspective.* Grand Rapids: Zondervan, 1978. (Cessationist)

Mallone, George. *Those Controversial Gifts.* Downers Grove, Ill.: InterVarsity Press, 1983.

Moo, Douglas. "Divine Healing in the Health and Wealth Gospel." In *TrinJ,* Vol. 9 N.S., No. 2 (Fall 1988), pp. 191–209.

Nathan, Richard. *A Response to Charismatic Chaos.* Anaheim, Calif.: Association of Vineyard Churches, 1993. (An extensive response to John MacArthur's 1992 book)

Osborne, Grant. "Tongues, Speaking in." In *EDT,* pp. 1100–1103.

Poythress, Vern. "Linguistic and Sociological Analyses of Modern Tongues-Speaking: Their Contributions and Limitations." In *WTJ* 42 (1979): 367–98.

Pytches, David. *Spiritual Gifts in the Local Church.* Originally published as *Come, Holy Spirit.* Minneapolis: Bethany, 1985. (Charismatic)

Reymond, Robert L. *What About Continuing Revelations and Miracles in the Presbyterian Church Today?* Phillipsburg, N.J.: Presbyterian and Reformed, 1977. (Cessationist)

Robertson, O. Palmer. *The Final Word.* Edinburgh and Carlisle, Pa.: Banner of Truth, 1993. (Cessationist)

Ruthven, Jon. *On the Cessation of the Charismata: The Protestant Polemic on Post-*

*Biblical Miracles*. Sheffield: Sheffield University Academic Press, 1993. (Charismatic; a revision and expansion of the author's Ph.D. dissertation, in which he responds to the arguments of cessationists from Warfield to the present)

Saucy, Robert. "Prophecy Today? An Initial Response." In *Sundoulos* (Talbot Seminary; Spring 1990), pp. 1–5. (Cessationist)

Schatzmann, Siegfried. *A Pauline Theology of Charismata*. Peabody, Mass.: Hendrickson, 1987.

Stephanou, Eusebius A. "The Charismata in the Early Church Fathers," *The Greek Orthodox Theological Review* 21:2 (Summer 1976), pp. 125–46.

Storms, C. Samuel. *Healing and Holiness: A Biblical Response to the Faith-Healing Phenomenon*. Phillipsburg, N.J.: Presbyterian and Reformed, 1990.

Thomas, Robert L. "Prophecy Rediscovered? A Review of *The Gift of Prophecy in the New Testament and Today*." In *BibSac* 149:593 (Jan.–Mar. 1992), pp. 83–96. (Cessationist)

Thompson, J. G. S. S. and Walter A. Elwell. "Spiritual Gifts." In *EDT*, pp. 1042–46.

Turner, M. M. B. "Spiritual Gifts Then and Now." In *Vox Evangelica* 15 (1985), pp. 7–64.

Warfield, Benjamin B. *Counterfeit Miracles*. London: Banner of Truth, 1972 (first published in 1918).

White, John. *When the Spirit Comes with Power*. Downers Grove, Ill.: Inter-Varsity Press, 1988.

White, R. Fowler. "Gaffin and Grudem on Ephesians 2:20: In Defense of Gaffin's Cessationist Exegesis." In *WTJ* 54 (Fall 1993), pp. 303–20. (Cessationist)

———. "Richard Gaffin and Wayne Grudem on 1 Corinthians 13:10: A Comparison of Cessationist and Noncessationist Argumentation." In *JETS* 35:2 (June 1992), pp. 173–82. (Cessationist)

Wilkenson, J. "Healing." In *NDT*, pp. 287–88.

Wimber, John. With Kevin Springer. *Power Evangelism*. San Francisco: Harper and Row, 1986.

———. *Power Healing*. San Francisco: Harper and Row, 1987.

## SCRIPTURE MEMORY PASSAGE

**1 Corinthians 12:7–11:** *To each is given the manifestation of the Spirit for the common good. To one is given through the Spirit the utterance of wisdom, and to another the utterance of knowledge according to the same Spirit, to another faith by the same Spirit, to another gifts of healing by the one Spirit, to another the working of miracles, to another prophecy, to another the ability to distinguish between spirits, to another various kinds of tongues, to another the interpretation of tongues. All these are inspired by one and the same Spirit, who apportions to each one individually as he wills.*

## HYMN

### "Come, O Come Thou Quickening Spirit"

(A possible alternative tune is the tune for "Guide Me, O Thou Great Jehovah.")

Come, O come, thou quick'ning Spirit, God from all eternity!
May thy power never fail us; dwell within us constantly.
Then shall truth and life and light banish all the gloom of night.

Grant our hearts in fullest measure wisdom, counsel, purity,
That we ever may be seeking only that which pleaseth thee.
Let thy knowledge spread and grow, working error's overthrow.

Show us, Lord, the path of blessing; when we trespass on our way,
Cast, O Lord, our sins behind thee and be with us day by day.
Should we stray, O Lord, recall; work repentance when we fall.

Holy Spirit, strong and mighty, thou who makest all things new,
Make thy work within us perfect and the evil foe subdue.
Grant us weapons for the strife and with vict'ry crown our life.

AUTHOR: HEINRICH HELD, 1664

# Part 7

# The Doctrine of the Future

# Chapter 54

# The Return of Christ:
# When and How?

*When and how will Christ return? Could he
come back at any hour?*

## EXPLANATION AND SCRIPTURAL BASIS

As we begin the final unit of this book, we turn to consider events that will
happen in the future. The study of future events is often called *"eschatology,"* from
the Greek word *eschatos,* which means "last." The study of eschatology, then, is the
study of "the last things."

Unbelievers can make reasonable predictions about future events based on
patterns of past occurrences, but in the nature of human experience it is clear that
human beings of themselves cannot *know* the future. Therefore unbelievers can
have no certain knowledge of any future event. But Christians who believe the
Bible are in a different situation. Although we cannot know everything about the
future, God knows everything about the future and he has in Scripture told us
about the major events yet to come in the history of the universe. About these
events occurring we can have absolute confidence because God is never wrong and
never lies.

Regarding our own personal future as individuals, we have already discussed
the teaching of Scripture in chapter 41 (on death and the intermediate state) and
chapter 42 (on glorification). The study of these future events that will happen to
individuals is sometimes called *"personal eschatology."* But the Bible also talks about
certain major events that will affect the entire universe. Specifically, it tells us
about the second coming of Christ, the millennium, the final judgment, eternal
punishment for unbelievers and eternal reward for believers, and life with God in
the new heaven and new earth. The study of these events is sometimes called
*"general eschatology."* In this chapter we will study the question of the return of
Christ, or his "second coming." Subsequent chapters will deal with the remaining
topics in a study of the last things.

There have been many debates—often heated ones—in the history of the
church over questions regarding the future. In this chapter we will begin with
aspects of Christ's second coming with which all evangelicals agree, and then at
the end move to one matter of disagreement: whether Christ could return at any
time. Then in the following chapter we will discuss the question of the
millennium, a topic that has long been a source of disagreement among Christians.

## A. There Will Be a Sudden, Personal, Visible, Bodily Return of Christ

Jesus often spoke about his return. "You also must be ready; for the Son of Man is coming at an hour you do not expect" (Matt. 24:44). He said, "*I will come again* and will take you to myself, that where I am you may be also" (John 14:3). Immediately after Jesus had ascended into heaven, two angels said to the disciples, "This Jesus, who was taken up from you into heaven, *will come* in the same way as you saw him go into heaven" (Acts 1:11). Paul taught, "*The Lord himself will descend from heaven* with a cry of command, with the archangel's call, and with the sound of the trumpet of God" (1 Thess. 4:16). The author of Hebrews wrote that Christ "*will appear a second time,* not to deal with sin but to save those who are eagerly waiting for him" (Heb. 9:28). James wrote, "the coming[1] of the Lord is at hand" (James 5:8). Peter said, "The day of the Lord will come like a thief" (2 Peter 3:10). John wrote, "when he appears we shall be like him, for we shall see him as he is" (1 John 3:2). And the book of Revelation has frequent references to Christ's return, ending with Jesus' promise, "Surely *I am coming soon,*" and John's response, "Amen. Come, Lord Jesus!" (Rev. 22:20).

This theme, then, is frequently mentioned throughout the New Testament. It is the dominant hope of the New Testament church. These verses predict a sudden return of Christ that will be dramatic and visible ("He is coming with the clouds, and every eye will see him," Rev. 1:7). The passages are far too explicit to allow the idea (once popular in liberal Protestant circles) that Christ himself will not return, but simply that the spirit of Christ, meaning an acceptance of his teaching and an imitation of his lifestyle of love, would increasingly return to the earth. It is not his teachings or his style of conduct, but "*the Lord himself*" who will descend from heaven (1 Thess. 4:16). It is Jesus himself "who was taken up from you into heaven" who "will come *in the same way* as you saw him go into heaven" (Acts 1:11). His appearing will not be a mere spiritual coming to dwell within people's hearts, but will be a *personal* and *bodily* return "in the same way as you saw him go into heaven."

## B. We Should Eagerly Long for Christ's Return

John's response at the end of Revelation should characterize Christians' hearts in all ages: "Amen. Come, Lord Jesus!" (Rev. 22:20). True Christianity trains us "to live sober, upright, and godly lives in this world, *awaiting our blessed hope, the appearing of the glory of our great God and Savior Jesus Christ*" (Titus 2:12–13).[2] Paul says, "our commonwealth is in heaven, and from it we *await a Savior,* the Lord Jesus Christ" (Phil. 3:20).[3] The term "Maranatha" in 1 Corinthians 16:22 (NASB) similarly means, "Our Lord, come!" (1 Cor. 16:22 RSV).

---

[1]The term *parousia* is used in theology to mean "second coming" (of Christ). This term comes from the Greek word for "coming" (*parousia*) which is used to refer to Christ's second coming in James 5:8 and several other New Testament passages. Because *parousia* is not a commonly used term in ordinary English, I have not used it in this book.

[2]The word translated "awaiting" here (*prosdechomai*) has a nuance of earnest or eager expectation: it is used of Joseph of Arimathea, who was "looking for the kingdom of God" (Mark 15:43; Luke 23:51) and of righteous Simeon who was "looking for the consolation of Israel" (Luke 2:25).

[3]The word here translated "await" is *apekdechomai,* "await eagerly" (note its use in this sense in Rom. 8:19, 23; 1 Cor. 1:7; Gal. 5:5).

Do Christians in fact eagerly long for Christ's return? The more Christians are caught up in enjoying the good things of this life, and the more they neglect genuine Christian fellowship and their personal relationship with Christ, the less they will long for his return. On the other hand, many Christians who are experiencing suffering or persecution, or who are more elderly and infirm, and those whose daily walk with Christ is vital and deep, will have a more intense longing for his return. To some extent, then, the degree to which we actually long for Christ's return is a measure of the spiritual condition of our own lives at the moment. It also gives some measure of the degree to which we see the world as it really is, as God sees it, in bondage to sin and rebellion against God, and in the power of the evil one (1 John 5:19).

But does this mean that we should not undertake long-term projects? If a scientist who is a Christian eagerly longs for Christ's return, then should he or she begin a ten-year research project? Or should a Christian begin a three-year course in a theological seminary or a Bible college? What if Christ were to return the day before graduation from that institution, before there was any chance to give a significant amount of one's time to actual ministry?

Certainly we should commit ourselves to long-term activities. It is precisely for this reason that Jesus does not allow us to know the actual time of his return (see below): he wants us to be engaged in obedience to him, no matter what our walk of life, up until the very moment of his return. To "be ready" for Christ's return (Matt. 24:44) is to be faithfully obeying him in the present, actively engaged in whatever work he has called us to. In the nature of the situation, since we do not know when he will return, on that day there will no doubt be some missionaries just departing for the mission field, who will never reach their destination. There will be some men in their last year of seminary education who will never use their training to pastor a church. There will be some researchers handing in their doctoral dissertations on that day, the fruit of years of research that will never be published and never have an influence on the world. But to all of those people who are Christians, Jesus will say, "Well done, good and faithful servant; you have been faithful over a little, I will set you over much; enter into the joy of your master" (Matt. 25:21).

## C. We Do Not Know When Christ Will Return

Several passages indicate that we do not, and cannot, know the time when Christ will return. "The Son of man is coming *at an hour you do not expect*" (Matt. 24:44). "Watch therefore, for *you know neither the day nor the hour*" (Matt. 25:13). Moreover, Jesus said, "But of that day or that hour no one knows, not even the angels in heaven, nor the Son, but only the Father. Take heed, watch; for *you do not know* when the time will come" (Mark 13:32–33).

It is simply an evasion of the force of those passages to say that we cannot know the day or the hour, but that we can know the month or the year. The fact remains that Jesus is coming "at an hour you do not expect" (Matt. 24:44), and "at an unexpected hour" (Luke 12:40). (In these verses the word "hour" [*hōra*] is best understood in a more general sense, to refer to the time when something will take place, not necessarily a sixty-minute period of time.)[4] The point of these passages is that Jesus is telling us that we *cannot* know when he is coming back. Since he will come at an unexpected time, we should be ready at all times for him to return.

The practical result of this is that anyone who claims to know specifically when Jesus is coming back is automatically to be considered wrong. The Jehovah's Witnesses have made many predictions of specific dates for Christ's return, and all of them have turned out to be wrong.[5] But others in the history of the church have made such predictions as well, sometimes claiming new insight into biblical prophecies, and sometimes claiming to have received personal revelations from Jesus himself indicating the time of his return. It is unfortunate that many people have been deceived by these claims, because if people are convinced that Christ will return (for example) within a month, they will begin to withdraw from all long-term commitments. They will take their children out of school, sell their houses, quit their jobs, and give up work on any long-term projects whether in the church or elsewhere. They may initially have an increased zeal for evangelism and prayer, but the unreasonable nature of their behavior will offset any evangelistic impact they may have. Moreover, they are simply *disobeying* the teaching of Scripture that the date of Christ's return cannot be known, which means that even their prayer and fellowship with God will be hindered as well. Anyone who claims to know the date on which Christ will return—from whatever source—should be rejected as incorrect.[6]

## D. All Evangelicals Agree on the Final Results of Christ's Return

No matter what their differences on the details, all Christians who take the Bible as their final authority agree that the final and ultimate result of Christ's return will be the judgment of unbelievers and the final reward of believers, and that believers will live with Christ in a new heaven and a new earth for all eternity. God the Father, Son, and Holy Spirit will reign and will be worshiped in a never-ending kingdom with no more sin or sorrow or suffering. We will discuss these details more fully in the following chapters.

---

[4]BAGD, p. 896, 3.

[5]Their attempt to save face by claiming that Jesus actually did return on October 1, 1914, in an invisible way, is incorrect because it denies the visible, bodily nature of Christ's return that is so clearly specified in several passages quoted above.

[6]Even in the "enlightened" twentieth century, such alarms can be persuasive to many people. In the summer of 1988 a former rocket scientist with impressive academic credentials circulated a booklet claiming that Jesus would return on September 12, 1988, and tens of thousands of copies of the book found their way around the United States and to various parts of the world. I was surprised to find that some otherwise sober Christian friends had read it and were alarmed, and to hear that some Christians in our community had pulled their children out of school in order to be together as a family when Christ came back. When the prediction failed, the author, Edgar Whisenant, revised his prediction, saying his calculations were one year off and Christ would return instead on September 1, 1989 (or one day earlier or later), or, if not then, on Rosh Hashanah 1990 or 1991 or 1992, or, at the latest, September 15–17, 1993. Of course, those predictions also failed. But many lives were disrupted and many people had false expectations aroused and then dashed by the publication of this booklet and its sequel. See Edgar Whisenant, *88 Reasons Why the Rapture Will Be in 1988* (Nashville, Tenn.: World Bible Society, 1988), and Edgar Whisenant and Greg Brewer, *The Final Shout: Rapture Report 1989* (Nashville, Tenn.: World Bible Society, 1989).

## E. There Is Disagreement Over the Details of Future Events

Nevertheless, Christians differ over specific details leading up to and immediately following Christ's return. Specifically, they differ over the nature of the millennium and the relationship of Christ's return to the millennium, the sequence of Christ's return and the great tribulation period that will come to the earth, and the question of the salvation of the Jewish people (and the relationship between Jews who are saved and the church).

Before we examine some of those questions in more detail, it is important to affirm the genuine evangelical standing of those who have differing positions on these questions. Evangelicals who hold to these various positions all agree that Scripture is inerrant, and they have a commitment to believe *whatever* is taught by Scripture. Their differences concern the interpretation of various passages relating to these events, but their differences on these matters should be seen as matters of secondary importance, not as differences over primary doctrinal matters.

Nevertheless, it is worth our time to study these questions in more detail, both because we may gain further insight into the nature of the events that God has planned and promised for us, and because there is still hope that greater unity will come about in the church when we agree to examine these issues again in more detail and to engage in discussion about them.

## F. Could Christ Come Back at Any Time?

One of the significant areas of disagreement is over the question of whether Christ could return at any time. On the one hand, there are many passages encouraging us to be ready because Christ will return at an hour we do not expect. On the other hand, there are several passages that speak of certain events that will happen before Christ returns. There have been different ways of resolving the apparent tension between these two sets of passages, with some Christians concluding that Christ could still return at any time, and others concluding that he could not return for at least a generation, since it would take that long to fulfill some of the predicted events that must occur before his return.

**1. Verses Predicting a Sudden and Unexpected Coming of Christ.** In order to feel the cumulative force of the passages that predict that Christ could come very soon, it is helpful simply to list them here in order:

*Watch therefore,* for you do not know on what day your Lord is coming. But know this, that if the householder had known in what part of the night the thief was coming, he would have watched and would not have let his house be broken into. Therefore *you also must be ready;* for the Son of man is coming *at an hour you do not expect.* (Matt. 24:42–44; cf. vv. 36–39)

The master of that servant *will come on a day when he does not expect him* and at an hour he does not know. (Matt. 24:50)

*Watch therefore,* for you know neither the day nor the hour. (Matt. 25:13)

But *of that day or that hour no one knows,* not even the angels in heaven, nor the Son, but only the Father. *Take heed, watch;* for you do not know when the time will come. (Mark 13:32–22)

It is like a man going on a journey, when he leaves home and puts his servants in charge, each with his work, and commands the doorkeeper to be on the watch. *Watch therefore*—for *you do not know when the master of the house will come*, in the evening, or at midnight, or at cockcrow, or in the morning—lest he come suddenly and find you asleep. And what I say to you I say to all: *Watch*. (Mark 13:34–37)

*You also must be ready;* for the Son of man is coming at an *unexpected hour*. (Luke 12:40)

*Our Lord, come!* (1 Cor. 16:22)

For our citizenship is in heaven, from which also *we eagerly wait for a Savior,* the Lord Jesus Christ. (Phil. 3:20 NASB)

For you yourselves know well that *the day of the Lord will come like a thief in the night*. (1 Thess. 5:2)

Training us to . . . live sober, upright, and godly lives in this world, *awaiting our blessed hope,* the appearing of the glory of our great God and Savior Jesus Christ. (Titus 2:12–13)

Encouraging one another, and all the more *as you see the Day drawing near*. (Heb. 10:25)

Be patient, therefore, brethren, until the coming of the Lord. . . . Establish your hearts, for *the coming of the Lord is at hand*. . . . *Behold, the Judge is standing at the doors*. (James 5:7–9)

*The end of all things is at hand*. (1 Peter 4:7)

But *the day of the Lord will come like a thief,* and then the heavens will pass away with a loud noise, and the elements will be dissolved with fire, and the earth and all the works that are upon it will be burned up. (2 Peter 3:10)

*The time is near*. (Rev. 1:3)

Behold, *I am coming soon*. (Rev. 22:7)

Behold, *I am coming soon,* bringing my recompense, to repay everyone for what he has done. (Rev. 22:12)

He who testifies to these things says, *"Surely I am coming soon."* Amen. *Come, Lord Jesus!* (Rev. 22:20)

What shall we say to these passages? If there were no passages in the New Testament about signs that would precede Christ's return, we would probably conclude from the passages just quoted that Jesus could come at any moment. In this sense, we can say that Christ's return is *imminent*.[7] It would seem to blunt the force of the commands to *be ready* and to *watch* if there was a reason to think that Christ would not come soon.

Before we look at passages on signs that precede Christ's coming, another problem must be considered at this point. Were Jesus and the New Testament authors wrong in their expectation that he would return soon? Did they not think

---

[7]In this chapter, it must be made clear that I am *not* using *imminent* as a technical term for a pre-tribulational rapture position (explained below), but simply to mean that Christ could return at any day, or even any hour.

Furthermore, I am not using the word *imminent* to mean that Christ *certainly will* come soon (for then the verses teaching imminence would have been untrue when they were written). I am using the word *imminent* to mean that Christ *could* come and *might* come at any time, and that we are to be prepared for him to come at any day. (Others define *imminent* more broadly, taking it to mean that Christ could come in any generation. I am not using the term in that way in this chapter.)

and even teach that the second coming of Christ would be in just a few years? In fact, a very prominent view among liberal New Testament scholars has been that Jesus mistakenly taught that he would return soon.

But none of the texts just quoted require this interpretation. The texts that say to be ready do not say how long we will have to wait, nor do the texts that say that Jesus is coming at a time we do not expect. As for the texts that say Jesus is coming "soon," we must realize that biblical prophets often speak in terms of "prophetic foreshortening," which sees future events but does not see the intervening time before those events occur.

George Ladd says:

> The prophets were little interested in chronology, and the future was always viewed as imminent . . . the Old Testament prophets blended the near and the distant perspectives so as to form a single canvas. Biblical prophecy is not primarily three-dimensional but two; it has height and breadth but is little concerned about depth, i.e., the chronology of future events . . . the distant is viewed through the transparency of the immediate. It is true that the early church lived in expectancy of the return of the Lord, and it is the nature of biblical prophecy to make it possible for every generation to live in expectancy of the end.[8]

Peter also reminds us that the Lord has a different perspective on time than we do, so that "soon" with him may not be what we expect: "But do not ignore this one fact, beloved, that with the Lord one day is as a thousand years, and a thousand years as one day. The Lord is not slow about his promise as some count slowness" (2 Peter 3:8–9).

**2. Signs That Precede Christ's Return.** The other set of texts to be considered tells of several signs that Scripture says will precede the time of Christ's return. In fact, Berkhof says, "According to Scripture several important events must occur before the return of the Lord, and therefore it cannot be called imminent."[9]

Here it will be helpful to list those passages that most directly refer to signs that must occur before Christ's return.

**a. The Preaching of the Gospel to All Nations:**

> And *the gospel must first be preached to all nations.* (Mark 13:10; cf. Matt. 24:14)

**b. The Great Tribulation:**

> And when you hear of wars and rumors of wars, do not be alarmed; this must take place, but the end is not yet. For nation will rise against nation, and kingdom against kingdom; there will be *earthquakes* in various places, there will be *famines; this is but the beginning of the birth-pangs.* (Mark 13:7–8; cf. Matt. 24:15–22; Luke 21:20–24)

---

[8]George Eldon Ladd, *A Commentary on the Revelation of John* (Grand Rapids: Eerdmans, 1972), p. 22.

[9]Berkhof, *Systematic Theology,* p. 696. He lists several events, such as the preaching of the gospel to all nations, the conversion of the fullness of Israel, the great tribulation, the revelation of the antichrist, and a remarkable conjunction of many ominous signs and wonders (wars, famines, earthquakes, false prophets doing miracles, and fearful signs in the sun, moon, and stars), all of which he discusses on pp. 697–703.

For in those days *there will be such tribulation as has not been from the beginning of the creation which God created until now, and never will be.* And *if the Lord had not shortened the days, no human being would be saved;* but for the sake of the elect, whom he chose, he shortened the days. (Mark 13:19–20)

### c. False Prophets Working Signs and Wonders:

*False Christs and false prophets will arise and show signs and wonders, to lead astray, if possible, the elect.* (Mark 13:22; cf. Matt. 24:23–24)

### d. Signs in the Heavens:

But in those days, *after that tribulation, the sun will be darkened, and the moon will not give its light, and the stars will be falling from heaven, and the powers in the heavens will be shaken.* And then they will see the Son of man coming in clouds with great power and glory. (Mark 13:24–25; cf. Matt. 24:29–30; Luke 21:25–27)

### e. The Coming of the Man of Sin and the Rebellion: Paul writes to the Thessalonians that Christ will not come unless the man of sin is first revealed, and then the Lord Jesus will destroy him at his coming. This "man of sin" is sometimes identified with the beast in Revelation 13, and is sometimes called the antichrist, the final and worst of the series of "antichrists" mentioned in 1 John 2:18. Paul writes:

Now concerning the coming of our Lord Jesus Christ . . . *that day will not come, unless the rebellion comes first, and the man of lawlessness is revealed,* the son of perdition, who opposes and exalts himself against every so-called god or object of worship, *so that he takes his seat in the temple of God, proclaiming himself to be God.* . . . And you know what is restraining him now so that he may be revealed in his time. For the mystery of lawlessness is already at work; only he who now restrains it will do so until he is out of the way. *And then the lawless one will be revealed, and the Lord Jesus will slay him with the breath of his mouth and destroy him by his appearing and his coming.* The coming of the lawless one by the activity of Satan will be with *all power and with pretended signs and wonders, and with all wicked deception for those who are to perish,* because they refused to love the truth and so be saved. (2 Thess. 2:1–10)

### f. The Salvation of Israel: Paul talks about the fact that many Jews have not trusted in Christ, but he says that sometime in the future a large number would be saved:

Now if their trespass means riches for the world, and if their failure means riches for the Gentiles, how much more will their *full inclusion* mean! (Rom. 11:12)[10]

For I do not want you, brethren, to be uninformed of this mystery, lest you be wise in your own estimation, that a partial hardening has happened to Israel until the fulness of the Gentiles has come in; *and thus all Israel will be saved.* (Rom. 11:25–26)

---

[10]The Greek word translated "full inclusion" here is *plērōma*, "fullness." This future full inclusion of Israel among God's people is sometimes also called the "fullness" of Israel.

**g. Conclusions From These Signs That Precede Christ's Return:** The impact of these passages seems so clear that, as was mentioned above, many Christians have felt that Christ simply cannot return at any moment.[11] As we look over the list of signs given above, it would not seem to take much argument to demonstrate that most of these events, or perhaps all of them, have not yet occurred. Or at least that is what appears to be the case on a first reading of these passages.[12]

**3. Possible Solutions.** How can we reconcile the passages that seem to warn us to be ready because Christ could suddenly return, with passages that indicate that several important and visible events must take place before Christ can return? Several solutions have been proposed.

One solution is to say that *Christ could not come at any time.* This position is taken by Louis Berkhof, in the sentence quoted above. Just how long it would be before Christ would return depends on each person's estimate of how long it will take some of the signs to be fulfilled, such as the preaching of the gospel to all nations, the coming of the great tribulation, and the ingathering of the full number of the Jews who will be saved.

The difficulty with this view is twofold. First, it really seems to nullify the force of the warnings of Jesus that we should watch, be ready, and that he is returning at an hour we do not expect. What force is there in a warning to be ready for Christ to come at an unexpected time when we know that this coming *cannot* occur for many years? The sense of urgent expectancy of Christ's return is greatly diminished or denied altogether in this position, and that result seems quite contrary to Jesus' intention in giving these warnings.

Second, this position seems to use these signs in a way quite opposite from the way Jesus intended them to be used. The signs are given so that, when we see them, they will *intensify our expectation* of Christ's return. Jesus said, "Now *when these things begin to take place, look up and raise your heads, because your redemption is drawing near*" (Luke 21:28). And the warnings are also given to keep believers from going astray and following false messiahs: "Take heed that no one leads you astray. Many will come in my name, saying, 'I am he!' and they will lead many astray. . . . And then if any one says to you, 'Look, here is the Christ!' or 'Look, there he is!' do not believe it" (Mark 13:5–6, 21). So the signs are given to keep Christians from being surprised by these remarkable events, to assure them that God knows them all in advance, and to keep them from following after alleged messiahs who do not come in the dramatic, visible, world-conquering way in which Jesus himself will come. *But the signs are never given to make us think, "Jesus couldn't come for a few years."* There is no indication that Jesus gave these signs in order to provide Christians with a reason *not to be ready* for his return or in order

---

[11]Louis Berkhof also mentions Matt. 25:19, in which the master returned "after a long time," and Matt. 25:5, which speaks of the delay of the bridegroom's return (*Systematic Theology*, p. 697). But both passages are vague as to the exact length of time, and both would be consistent even with a delay of ten or twenty years after Jesus returned to heaven.

[12]I have not listed "wars and rumors of wars" and "famines and earthquakes in various places" (Matt. 24:6–7) as signs that must precede Christ's return, because they have been present throughout history, and because they are not given by Jesus as signs that immediately precede his return, but as events that come before those signs, as "the beginning of the birth-pangs" (Matt. 24:8). Nevertheless, an intensification of these things may well indicate the beginning of the last days, with other signs soon to follow.

to encourage them *not to expect* that he could come at any time! To use the signs that will precede Christ's return in this way (as Berkhof does, for example), is to use them in a way that Jesus never intended. Therefore it does not seem convincing to say that Christ could not come at any time.

The other major solution to this problem is to say that *Christ indeed could come at any time,* and to reconcile the two sets of passages in various ways. (1) One way to reconcile them is to say that *the New Testament talks about two distinct returns of Christ,* or two second comings of Christ,[13] that is, a *secret* coming at which Christ takes Christians out of the world (a coming "for his saints"), and then, after seven years of tribulation have occurred on the earth, a visible, *public,* triumphant coming (a coming "with his saints") in which Christ comes to reign over the earth. During the seven-year interval all the signs that have not yet been fulfilled (the great tribulation, the false prophets with signs and wonders, the antichrist, the salvation of Israel, and the signs in the heavens) will be fulfilled, so that there is no tension at all between waiting for a coming that could occur "at any moment" and realizing that a later coming will be preceded by many signs.[14]

The problem with this solution is that it is hard to derive two separate comings of Christ from the passages that predict his return. However, we will not discuss this matter here, but will treat it in the next chapter, when considering the pretribulational premillennial view of Christ's return.[15] It should also be noted that this solution is historically quite recent, for it was unknown in the history of the church before it was proposed in the last century by John Nelson Darby (1800–1882). This should alert us to the fact that this solution is not the only possible one to the tension presented by the passages quoted above.

(2) Another solution is to say that *all the signs have been fulfilled, and therefore Christ in fact could return at any moment.* On this view, one could look for possible fulfillments of these signs in the events of the early church, even in the first century. In some sense, it might be said, the gospel was indeed preached to all nations, false prophets arose and opposed the gospel, there was great tribulation in the persecution the church suffered at the hands of some of the Roman emperors, the man of lawlessness was in fact the emperor Nero, and the full number of the Jewish people who are to be saved has gradually come about through the history of the church, since Paul even gives himself as one example of the beginning of this ingathering of the Jewish people (Rom. 11:1). We will discuss in more detail in the following section the view that the signs preceding Christ's return *might* have already been fulfilled,[16] but here we can simply note that many people have not found convincing any view saying that they *have* happened,

---

[13]Those who hold to this view object to the characterizing of it as two second comings and prefer to speak of two aspects of the same second coming, but since these two comings are separated by an interval of at least seven years, it does not seem inaccurate to characterize the view as holding to two second comings.

[14]This view is the pre-tribulational view, often referred to as the pre-tribulational rapture view, since those who hold this view often refer to Christ's first, secret return to take Christians out of the world as the *"rapture"* (from Lat. *rapio,* "to seize, snatch, carry away"). This view is discussed in chapter 55, pp. 1112–14 and 1132–35.

[15]See chapter 55, pp. 1132–35, for an analysis of the pretribulational premillennial view of Christ's return.

[16]See pp. 1101–5 for a discussion of the view that it is unlikely but possible that all the signs preceding Christ's return have already been fulfilled.

because these signs seem to them to point to much larger events than those that occurred in the first century.

(3) There is another possible way of resolving these two sets of passages. It is to say that it is *unlikely but possible that the signs have already been fulfilled*, and therefore we simply cannot know with certainty at any point in history whether all the signs have been fulfilled or not. This position is an attractive one because it takes seriously the primary purpose for the signs, the primary purpose for the warnings, and the fact that we are not to know when Christ will return. With regard to the signs, their primary purpose is to intensify our expectation of Christ's return. Therefore whenever we see indications of things that resemble these signs, our expectation of Christ's return will be aroused and intensified. With regard to the warnings to be ready, advocates of this position would say that Christ *could* return at any time (since we cannot be certain that the signs have not been fulfilled), and so we must be ready, even though it is *unlikely* that Christ will return at once (because it seems that there are several signs yet to be fulfilled). Finally, this position agrees that we cannot know when Christ will return, and that he is coming at an hour we do not expect.

But is it possible that these signs have been fulfilled? We can examine them one at a time. In each case our conclusion will be that it is *unlikely, but possible, that the sign has been fulfilled already*.

**a. The Preaching of the Gospel to All Nations:** Has the gospel been preached to all nations? Probably not, since there are many language groups and tribes that have still never heard the gospel. It is unlikely, therefore, that this sign has been fulfilled. However, Paul does speak in Colossians about the worldwide spread of the gospel. He speaks of "the gospel which has come to you, as indeed *in the whole world* it is bearing fruit and growing" (Col. 1:5–6). He also speaks of "the gospel which you heard, *which has been preached to every creature under heaven*, and of which I, Paul, became a minister" (Col. 1:23). In these verses he certainly does not mean that every creature alive has heard the proclamation of the gospel, but that the proclamation has gone forth to the whole world and that, in a representative sense at least, the gospel has been preached to the whole world or to all nations.[17] Therefore, though, it is unlikely but possible that this sign was initially fulfilled in the first century and has been fulfilled in a greater sense many times since then.

**b. Great Tribulation:** Once again, it seems likely that the language of Scripture indicates a period of suffering coming to the earth that is far greater than anything that has yet been experienced. But it must be realized that many people have

---

[17]R. T. France, *The Gospel According to Matthew*, TNTC (Leicester: Inter-Varsity Press, Grand Rapids: Eerdmans, 1985), p. 339, says of Jesus' statement that "this gospel of the kingdom will be preached throughout the whole world, as a testimony to all nations" (Matt. 24:12), the following: "The *world* is *oikoumenē*, lit. 'the inhabited area', a standard term originally for the Greek world (as opposed to barbarians), then for the Roman Empire, and subsequently for the whole of the then known world; it is thus not so much a geographical term that must include every area and community now known to be on earth, but rather an indication of the universal offer of the gospel *to all nations*, i.e., outside the confines of the Jewish community. . . In one sense Paul could claim long before A.D. 70 to have 'fully preached the gospel' in a large area of Asia and Europe (Rom. 15:19) and at many times since then similar claims could have been made with reference to an area far wider than the *oikoumenē* known in Jesus' time."

understood Jesus' warnings about great tribulation to refer to the Roman siege of Jerusalem in the Jewish War of A.D. 66–70.[18] The suffering during that war was indeed terrible, and could be what was described by Jesus in predicting this tribulation. In fact, since the first century, there have been many periods of violent and intense persecution of Christians, and even in our century much of it has occurred over large portions of the globe, with Christians being horribly persecuted in the former Soviet Union, in communist China, and in Muslim countries. It would be difficult to convince some Christians in this century who have undergone decades of persecution for their faith, and have known that persecution to affect thousands of other Christians throughout large segments of the world, that such a great tribulation has certainly not yet occurred. They have longed and prayed for years for Christ to come and rescue them from the tribulation that they are enduring.

Once again, though we may think that Jesus' words indicate the likelihood of a yet greater persecution coming in the future, it is difficult to be certain of this. It seems appropriate to conclude that it is unlikely but possible that the prediction of a great tribulation has already been fulfilled.

**c. False Christs and False Prophets:** With regard to the false christs and false prophets who will work signs and wonders, any missionary who has worked among people where witchcraft and demonic activity are rampant will readily testify that seemingly miraculous "signs and wonders" have been worked frequently by demonic power in opposition to the spread of the gospel. Certainly demonic miracles and false signs have been done for centuries, at least since the time that the magicians in Pharaoh's court produced false signs in opposition to Moses' miracles (Ex. 7:11; 8:7; cf. the activity of Simon the Sorcerer in Acts 8:9–11). Whatever the specific form it takes, such working of deceptive miracles is almost always accompanied by false religions, leading many people astray (leaders of such groups could be called false messiahs and false prophets). It seems likely that Jesus' words predict a far greater manifestation of this kind of activity in the time just prior to his return, but again, it is difficult to be certain that this will be so. It is best to conclude that it is unlikely but still possible that this sign has been fulfilled already.

**d. Powerful Signs in the Heavens:** The occurrence of powerful signs in the heavens is the one sign that almost certainly has not yet occurred. Of course, there have been eclipses of the sun and moon, and comets have appeared, since the world began. But Jesus speaks of something far greater: *"The sun will be darkened, and the moon will not give its light, and the stars will fall from heaven, and the powers of the heavens will be shaken"* (Matt. 24:29). Although R. T. France attempts to explain this as symbolic language that refers to the destruction of Jerusalem and God's judgment on it,[19] he must base this claim on the assertion that Isaiah 13:10 (from which Jesus' words in Matt. 24:29 seem to be drawn) is also merely symbolic language to refer to the fall of Babylon, whereas it is more likely that

---

[18]See description of these events in France, *Matthew,* pp. 340–41, with reference to Josephus, *Jewish War* 5.512–18.

[19]France, *Matthew,* pp. 343–44.

both Isaiah 13:10 and Matthew 24:29 speak of a yet future literal falling of the stars and blackening of the sun and moon, something that would be a suitable prelude to the shaking of the earth and heaven and the cosmic destruction that will come after the return of Christ (see Heb. 1:10–12; 12:27; 2 Peter 3:10–11). Moreover, it is significant that this description of cosmic events in Matthew 24:29 is followed in the rest of the sentence with the description of "the Son of man *coming on the clouds of heaven* with power and great glory" (v. 30).[20] Given these facts, it seems unlikely that the descriptions of the falling of the stars from heaven and the darkening of the sun and moon are merely symbolic language. It is better to regard them as literal signs that will occur just before Christ's return, and as such, they fall in a different category from the other signs, since it seems certain that they have not yet occurred. Nonetheless, they could occur very quickly— within the space of a few minutes or at most an hour or two—to be followed immediately by Christ's return. These particular signs are not the type that would lead us to deny that Christ could return at any time.

**e. The Appearance of the Man of Lawlessness:** Many attempts have been made throughout history to identify the man of lawlessness (the "antichrist") with historical figures who had great authority and brought havoc and devastation among people on the earth. The ancient Roman emperors Nero and Domitian, both of whom severely persecuted Christians, were thought by many to be the antichrist. (Many Roman emperors, including these two, claimed deity for themselves and demanded to be worshiped.) In more recent times Adolf Hitler was commonly thought to be the antichrist, as was Joseph Stalin. On the other hand, many Protestants since the Reformation, especially those who were persecuted by the Catholic Church, have thought that one or another of the popes was the antichrist.

But all of these identifications have proved false,[21] and it is likely that a yet worse "man of lawlessness" will arise on the world scene and bring unparalleled suffering and persecution, only to be destroyed by Jesus when he comes again. But the evil perpetrated by many of these other rulers has been so great that, at least while they were in power, it would have been difficult to be certain that the "man of lawlessness" mentioned in 2 Thessalonians 2 has not yet appeared.[22] Once again, it is unlikely but possible that this sign has been fulfilled.

---

[20]The difficulty in France's position is seen in the fact that he must take this seemingly very clear prediction of Christ's return to earth as a prediction of the destruction of the Jewish temple in A.D. 70. He says that Matt. 24:30 speaks of "coming to God to receive vindication and authority," and therefore indicates not Christ's return in the flesh, but the vindication of his authority "over the Jewish establishment which has rejected him" when the temple is destroyed in A.D. 70 (ibid., p. 344).

[21]However, John says, "as you have heard that antichrist is coming, so now many antichrists have come" (1 John 2:18), and he speaks of "the spirit of antichrist," which, he says, "is in the world already" (1 John 4:3). Therefore, even if these previous persecutors of the church were not *the* antichrist, many of them may have been precursors of the final antichrist.

[22]It might be argued that Paul did not want the Thessalonian church to expect that Christ could return at any time, since he writes them "not to be quickly shaken in mind or excited, either by spirit or by word, or by letter purporting to be from us, to the effect that the day of the Lord has come" (2 Thess. 2:2). He then goes on to say, "Let no one deceive you in any way; for that day will not come, unless the rebellion comes first, and the man of lawlessness is revealed" (2 Thess. 2:3). Someone might ask whether Paul is not reasoning as follows: you know that the man of lawlessness has not yet

**f. The Salvation of Israel:** With regard to the salvation of the fullness of Israel, again it must be said that Romans 9–11 seems to indicate that there will be a yet future massive ingathering of the Jewish people as they turn to accept Jesus as their Messiah. But it is not certain that Romans 9–11 predicts this, and many have argued that no further ingathering of the Jewish people will occur beyond the kind that we have already seen through the history of the church, since Paul gives himself as a primary example of this ingathering (Rom. 11:1–2). Once again, it is unlikely but possible that this sign has already been fulfilled.

**g. Conclusion:** Except for the spectacular signs in the heavens, it is unlikely but possible that these signs have already been fulfilled. Moreover, the only sign that seems certainly not to have occurred, the darkening of the sun and moon and the falling of the stars, could occur within the space of a few minutes, and therefore it seems appropriate to say that Christ could now return at any hour of the day or night. It is therefore unlikely but certainly possible that Christ could return at any time.

But does this position do justice to the warnings that we should be ready and that Christ is coming at a time we do not expect? Is it possible to *be ready* for something that we think *unlikely* to happen in the near future? Certainly it is. Everyone who wears a seatbelt when driving, or purchases auto insurance, gets ready for an event he or she thinks to be unlikely.[23] In a similar way it seems possible to take seriously the warnings that Jesus could come when we are not expecting him, and nonetheless to say that the signs preceding his coming will probably yet occur in the future.

This position has positive spiritual benefits as we seek to live the Christian life in the midst of a rapidly changing world. In the ebb and flow of world history, we see from time to time events that *could be* the final fulfillment of some of these signs. They happen, and then they fade away. During the blackest days of World War II, it seemed very likely that Hitler was the antichrist. During times of

---

appeared; therefore, you know that Christ has not yet come. And Christ will not come until this man of lawlessness appears on the scene.

But it must be noted that Paul does not tell the Thessalonians that Christ could not come at anytime. He does not tell them that they should fail to be ready or fail to expect Christ's return. He simply tells them that Christ's return *has not already occurred*, which is something far different. And the reason he gives is not only the fact that the man of lawlessness must first appear, but also that when Christ returns he will defeat this man of lawlessness and destroy him: "And then the lawless one will be revealed, *and the Lord Jesus will slay him with the breath of his mouth and destroy him by his appearing and coming*" (2 Thess. 2:8). It is not just that they have not seen the man of lawlessness—they have not seen him appear *and be destroyed by Jesus at his coming*. The conclusion is that Christ has not come, because he has not come destroying this man of lawlessness. Yet he certainly could have come at any time, even in the context of 2 Thessalonians, and immediately destroyed the currently reigning Roman emperor (for Roman emperors regularly claimed to be God and to be worthy of worship, and John himself said that "many antichrists have come," 1 John 2:18).

[23]I thank God that I have driven thirty years without a major auto accident, and I pray and expect that I will not have one, but I still buckle my seatbelt every time I get in the car. I prepare for an event that I think to be unlikely, but nonetheless possible. Similarly, I *think* that many of the signs will have yet greater fulfillment, and that it is unlikely that Jesus will return within the next few days or weeks. In fact, I am writing this book, which will not be published for many more months, on the assumption that Jesus will not have returned by then. Nonetheless, I frequently examine my heart and my life to see if there is anything of which I would be ashamed when Jesus returns, because I want to be ready for him to return at any moment, even at a moment I do not expect.

persecution against the church, it can seem more likely that Christians are in the middle of the great tribulation. When we hear of earthquakes and famines and wars, it makes us wonder if the coming of Christ might not be near. Then these events fade into the background and world leaders pass off the scene, and the tide of events leading to the end of the age seems to have receded for a time. Then once again a new wave of events will break on the world scene, and once again our expectation of Christ's return is increased. With each successive "wave" of events, *we do not know* which one will be the last. And this is good, because God does not intend us to know. He simply wants us to continue to long for Christ's return and to expect that it could occur at any time. It is spiritually unhealthy for us to say that we know that these signs *have not* occurred, and it seems to stretch the bounds of credible interpretation to say that we know that these signs have occurred. But it seems to fit exactly in the middle of the New Testament approach toward Christ's return to say that *we do not know* with certainty if these events have occurred. Responsible exegesis, an expectation of Christ's sudden return, and a measure of humility in our understanding, are all three preserved in this position.

Then if Christ does return suddenly, we will not be tempted to object, saying that one or another sign has not yet occurred. We will simply be ready to welcome him when he appears. And if there is great suffering yet to come, and if we begin to see intense opposition to the gospel, a large revival among the Jewish people, remarkable progress in the preaching of the gospel through the world, and even spectacular signs in the heavens, then we will not be dismayed or lose heart, because we will remember Jesus' words, "When these things begin to take place, look up and raise your heads, because your redemption is drawing near" (Luke 21:28).

## QUESTIONS FOR PERSONAL APPLICATION

1. Before reading this chapter, did you think that Christ could return at any hour? How did that affect your Christian life? Now what do you think? If your viewpoint has changed, what effect do you think it will have on your own life?

2. Why do you think Jesus decided to leave the world for a time and then return, rather than staying on earth after his resurrection and preaching the gospel throughout the world himself?

3. Do you now eagerly long for Christ's return? Have you had a greater longing for it in the past? If you do not have a very strong yearning for Christ's return, what factors in your life do you think contribute to that lack of longing?

4. Have you ever decided not to undertake a long-term project because you thought Christ's return was near? Do you have any hesitancy now about long-term projects because of that reason? If so, do you think that hesitancy has any negative consequences on your life?

5. Are you ready for Christ to return today? If you knew he were going to return within 24 hours, what situations or relationships would you want to straighten out before he returned? Do you think that the command to "be ready" means that you should attempt to straighten out those things now, even if you think it unlikely that he would return today?

## SPECIAL TERMS

eschatology
general eschatology
imminent
Maranatha

parousia
pesonal eschatology
second coming of Christ

## BIBLIOGRAPHY

(For an explanation of this bibliography see the note on the bibliography to chapter 1, p. 38. Complete bibliographical data may be found on pp. 1223–29.)

### Sections in Evangelical Systematic Theologies

1. Anglican (Episcopalian)
   - 1882–92    Litton, 579–81
   - 1930    Thomas, 87–88, 525
2. Arminian (Wesleyan or Methodist)
   - 1875–76    Pope, 3:387–401
   - 1892–94    Miley, 2:440–47
   - 1940    Wiley, 3:243–81
   - 1960    Purkiser, 537–50
   - 1983    Carter, 2:113–16
3. Baptist
   - 1767    Gill, 2:230–43
   - 1887    Boyce, 451–61
   - 1907    Strong, 1003–15
   - 1917    Mullins, 462–66
   - 1983–85    Erickson, 1185–94, 1203–4
4. Dispensational
   - 1947    Chafer, 4:255–63; 5:280–314
   - 1949    Thiessen, 337–50
   - 1986    Ryrie, 273–74, 463
5. Lutheran
   - 1917–24    Pieper, 3:515–34
   - 1934    Mueller, 619–25
6. Reformed (or Presbyterian)
   - 1871–73    Hodge, 3:790–836
   - 1887–1921    Warfield, *SSW*, 1:348–64

1889     Shedd, 2b:641–46; 3:471–528

1937–66     Murray, *CW*, 1: 86–95; *CW*, 2:387–410

1938     Berkhof, 695–707

1962     Buswell, 2:341–423

7. Renewal (or charismatic/Pentecostal)

1988–92     Williams, 3:297–396

## Sections in Representative Roman Catholic Systematic Theologies

1. Roman Catholic: Traditional

    1955     Ott, 485–88

2. Roman Catholic: Post-Vatican II

    1980     McBrien, 2:1101–6

## Other Works

Archer, Gleason, Paul Feinberg, Douglas Moo, and Richard Reiter. *The Rapture: Pre-, Mid-, or Post-tribulational?* Grand Rapids: Zondervan, 1984.

Bauckham, Richard J. "Apocalyptic." In *NDT*, pp. 33–35.

Beechick, Allen. *The Pre-Tribulation Rapture*. Denver: Accent, 1980.

Berkouwer, G. C. *The Return of Christ*. Trans. by James Van Oosterom. Ed. by Marlin J. Van Elderen. Grand Rapids: Eerdmans, 1972.

Clouse, F. G. "Rapture of the Church." In *EDT*, pp. 908–10.

Dumbrell, William J. *The Search for Order: Biblical Eschatology in Focus*. Grand Rapids: Baker, 1992.

Erickson, Millard. *Contemporary Options in Eschatology*. Grand Rapids: Baker, 1977.

Gundry, R. H. *The Church and the Tribulation*. Grand Rapids: Zondervan, 1973.

Hoekema, Anthony A. *The Bible and the Future*. Grand Rapids: Eerdmans, 1979, pp. 109–238.

Ladd, George Eldon. *The Blessed Hope*. Grand Rapids: Eerdmans, 1956.

Lightner, Robert P. *The Last Days Handbook: A Comprehensive Guide to Understanding the Different Views of Prophecy. Who Believes What About Prophecy and Why*. Nashville, Tenn.: Thomas Nelson, 1990.

Rosenthal, Marvin. *The Pre-Wrath Rapture of the Church*. Nashville, Tenn.: Thomas Nelson, 1990.

Travis, S. H. "Eschatology." In *NDT*, pp. 228–31.

Van Gemeren, Willem. *The Progress of Redemption*. Grand Rapids: Zondervan, 1988.

Van Kampen, Robert. *The Sign*. Wheaton, Ill.: Crossway, 1992.

Vos, Geerhardus. *The Pauline Eschatology*. Grand Rapids: Eerdmans, 1961.

Walvoord, John F. *The Blessed Hope and the Tribulation*. Grand Rapids: Zondervan, 1976.

## SCRIPTURE MEMORY PASSAGE

**1 Thessalonians 4:15–18:** *For this we declare to you by the word of the Lord, that we who are alive, who are left until the coming of the Lord, shall not precede those who have fallen asleep. For the Lord himself will descend from heaven with a cry of command, with the archangel's call, and with the sound of the trumpet of God. And the dead in Christ will rise first; then we who are alive, who are left, shall be caught up together with them in the clouds to meet the Lord in the air; and so we shall always be with the Lord. Therefore comfort one another with these words.*

## HYMN

### "Lo! He Comes, With Clouds Descending"

This song vividly pictures the event of Christ's return, with millions of believers coming with him and many more on earth welcoming him as he comes. The "clouds" with which Christ comes, mentioned in the first line of the hymn, are the clouds of God's glory. The hymn does not hesitate (in v. 3) to portray brilliantly the shaking of the heavens and the earth and the fact that unbelievers will be called to judgment. It ends with a dramatic stanza directly addressing Jesus himself, asking him to come quickly and reign. (Use tune known as "Sicilian Mariners.")

Lo! He comes, with clouds descending, once for favored sinners slain;
  Thousand thousand saints attending swell the triumph of his train:
Alleluia! Alleluia! God appears on earth to reign.

Ev'ry eye shall now behold him, robed in dreadful majesty;
  Those who set at naught and sold him, pierced, and nailed him to the
      tree,
Deeply wailing, deeply wailing, shall the true Messiah see.

Ev'ry island, sea, and mountain, heav'n and earth, shall flee away;
  All who hate him must, confounded, hear the trump proclaim the Day;
Come to judgment! Come to judgment! Come to judgment, come away!

Now redemption, long expected, see in solemn pomp appear!
  All his saints, by man rejected, now shall meet him in the air:
Alleluia! Alleluia! See the Day of God appear!

Yea, amen! Let all adore thee, high on thine eternal throne;
  Savior, take the pow'r and glory, claim the kingdom for thine own:
O come quickly; O come quickly; alleluia! Come, Lord, come.

AUTHORS: CHARLES WESLEY, 1758 (STANZAS 1, 2, 5)
AND JOHN CENNICK, 1752 (STANZAS 3, 4)

Alternative hymn: "Rejoice, All Ye Believers"

# Chapter 55

# The Millennium

*What is the millennium? When does it occur? Will Christians go through the Great Tribulation?*

## EXPLANATION AND SCRIPTURAL BASIS

The word *millennium* means "one thousand years" (from Lat. *millennium,* "thousand years"). The term comes from Revelation 20:4–5, where it says that certain people "came to life, and reigned with Christ *a thousand years.* The rest of the dead did not come to life until *the thousand years* were ended." Just prior to this statement, we read that an angel came down from heaven and seized the devil "and bound him for *a thousand years,* and threw him into the pit, and shut it and sealed it over him, that he should deceive the nations no more, till *the thousand years* were ended" (Rev. 20:2–3).

Throughout the history of the church there have been three major views on the time and nature of this "millennium."

### A. Explanation of the Three Major Views

**1. Amillennialism.** The first view to be explained here, amillennialism, is really the simplest. It can be pictured as in figure 55.1:

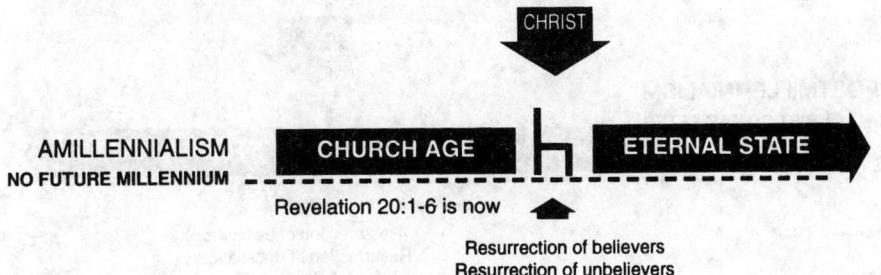

AMILLENNIALISM
*Figure 55.1*

According to this position the passage in Revelation 20:1–10 describes the

*1109*

present church age. This is an age in which Satan's influence over the nations has been greatly reduced so that the gospel can be preached to the whole world. Those who are said to be reigning with Christ for the thousand years are Christians who have died and are already reigning with Christ in heaven. Christ's reign in the millennium, according to this view, is not a bodily reign here on earth but rather the heavenly reign he spoke of when he said, "All authority in heaven and on earth has been given to me" (Matt. 28:18).

This view is called "amillennial" because it maintains that there is no future millennium yet to come. Since amillennialists believe that Revelation 20 is now being fulfilled in the church age, they hold that the "millennium" described there is currently happening. The exact duration of the church age cannot be known, and the expression "thousand years" is simply a figure of speech for a long period of time in which God's perfect purposes will be accomplished.

According to this position, the present church age will continue until the time of Christ's return (see figure 55.1). When Christ returns, there will be a resurrection of both believers and unbelievers. The bodies of believers will rise to be reunited with their spirits and enter into full enjoyment of heaven forever. Unbelievers will be raised to face the final judgment and eternal condemnation. Believers will also stand before the judgment seat of Christ (2 Cor. 5:10), but this judgment will only determine degrees of reward in heaven, for only unbelievers will be condemned eternally. At this time also the new heavens and new earth will begin. Immediately after the final judgment, the eternal state will commence and continue forever.

This scheme is quite simple because all of the end time events happen at once, immediately after Christ's return. Some amillennialists say that Christ could return at any time, while others (such as Berkhof) argue that certain signs have yet to be fulfilled.

**2. Postmillennialism.** The prefix *post-* means "after." According to this view, Christ will return *after* the millennium. The postmillennial view may be represented as in figure 55.2.

POSTMILLENNIALISM
*Figure 55.2*

According to this view, the progress of the gospel and the growth of the church will gradually increase, so that a larger and larger proportion of the world's population will be Christians. As a result, there will be significant Christian influences on society, society will more and more function according to God's standards, and gradually a "millennial age" of peace and righteousness will occur on the earth. This "millennium" will last for a long period of time (not necessarily a literal one thousand years), and finally, *at the end of this period, Christ will return to earth,* believers and unbelievers will be raised, the final judgment will occur, and there will be a new heaven and new earth. We will then enter into the eternal state.

The primary characteristic of postmillennialism is that it is very optimistic about the power of the gospel to change lives and bring about much good in the world. Belief in postmillennialism tends to increase in times when the church is experiencing great revival, when there is an absence of war and international conflict, and when it appears that great progress is being made in overcoming the evil and suffering in the world. But postmillennialism in its most responsible form is not based simply on the observation of events in the world around us, but on arguments from various Scripture passages, which will be examined below.

### 3. Premillennialism.

**a. Classic or Historic Premillennialism:** The prefix "pre-" means "before," and the "premillennial" position says that Christ will come back *before* the millennium.[1] This viewpoint has a long history from the earliest centuries onward. It may be represented as in figure 55.3.

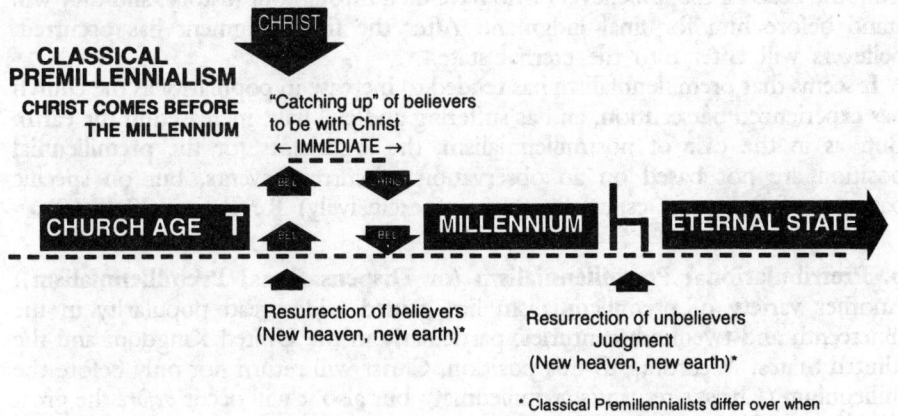

CLASSIC OR HISTORIC PREMILLENNIALISM
*Figure 55.3*

According to this viewpoint, the present church age will continue until, as it nears the end, a time of great tribulation and suffering comes on the earth (T in

---

[1]Another name sometimes used to refer to premillennialism is *chiliasm,* from the Greek word *chilioi,* "a thousand." This term is more often found in older literature and is rarely used today.

the figure above stands for tribulation).[2] After that time of tribulation *at the end of the church age, Christ will return to earth to establish a millennial kingdom.* When he comes back, believers who have died will be raised from the dead, their bodies will be reunited with their spirits, and *these believers will reign with Christ on earth for one thousand years.* (Some premillennialists take this to be a literal one thousand years, and others understand it to be a symbolic expression for a long period of time.) During this time, Christ will be physically present on the earth in his resurrected body, and will reign as King over the entire earth. The believers who have been raised from the dead, and those who were on earth when Christ returns, will receive glorified resurrection bodies that will never die, and in these resurrection bodies they will live on the earth and reign with Christ. Of the unbelievers who remain on earth, many (but not all) will turn to Christ and be saved. Jesus will reign in perfect righteousness and there will be peace throughout the earth. Many premillennialists hold that the earth will be renewed and we will in fact see the new heavens and new earth at this time (but it is not essential to premillennialism to hold to this, for one could be a premillennialist and hold that the new heavens and new earth will not occur until after the final judgment). At the beginning of this time Satan will be bound and cast into the bottomless pit so that he will have no influence on the earth during the millennium (Rev. 20:1–3).

According to the premillennial viewpoint, at the end of the thousand years Satan will be loosed from the bottomless pit and will join forces with many unbelievers who have submitted outwardly to Christ's reign but have inwardly been seething in rebellion against him. Satan will gather these rebellious people for battle against Christ, but they will be decisively defeated. Christ will then raise from the dead all the unbelievers who have died throughout history, and they will stand before him for final judgment. After the final judgment has occurred, believers will enter into the eternal state.

It seems that premillennialism has tended to increase in popularity as the church has experienced persecution, and as suffering and evil have increased in the earth. But, as in the case of postmillennialism, the arguments for the premillennial position are not based on an observation of current events, but on specific passages of Scripture, especially (but not exclusively) Revelation 20:1–10.

**b. Pretribulational Premillennialism (or Dispensational Premillennialism):** Another variety of premillennialism has gained widespread popularity in the nineteenth and twentieth centuries, particularly in the United Kingdom and the United States. According to this position, Christ will return not only before the millennium (Christ's return is *pre*millennial), but also it will occur *before* the great tribulation (Christ's return is *pre*tribulational). This position is similar to the classical premillennial position mentioned above, but with one important difference: it will add another return of Christ before his return to reign on earth in the millennium. This return is thought to be a secret return of Christ to take believers out of the world.[3] The pretribulational premillennial view may be represented as in figure 55.4.

---

[2]An alternative type of premillennialism holds that Christ will come back *before* the period of great tribulation begins on earth. We shall examine that alternative form of premillennialism below.

[3]Sometimes this secret coming of Christ for believers is called the "rapture," from the Latin word *rapio,* meaning "seize, snatch, carry away."

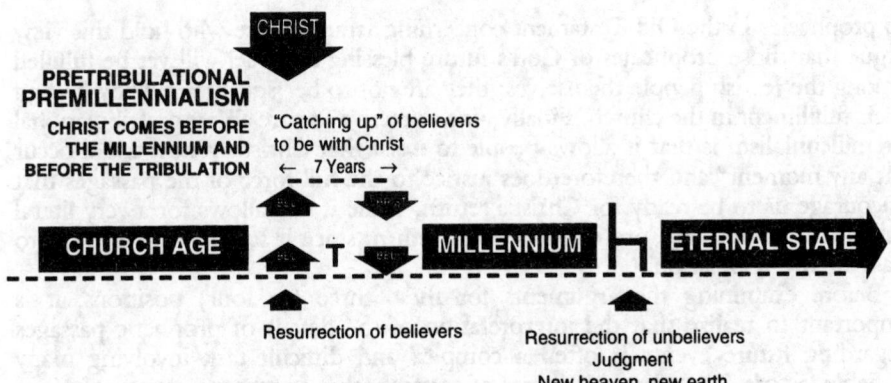

PRETRIBULATIONAL PREMILLENNIALISM
*Figure 55.4*

According to this view, the church age will continue until, *suddenly, unexpectedly, and secretly, Christ will return part way to earth, and then will call believers to himself*: "The dead in Christ will rise first; then we who are alive, who are left, shall be caught up together with them in the clouds to meet the Lord in the air" (1 Thess. 4:16–17). *Christ will then return to heaven with the believers who have been removed from the earth. When that happens, there will be a great tribulation on the earth* for a period of seven years.[4]

During this seven-year period of tribulation, many of the signs that were predicted to precede Christ's return will be fulfilled.[5] The great ingathering of the fullness of the Jewish people will occur, as they trust Christ as their Messiah. In the midst of great suffering there will also be much effective evangelism, especially carried out by the new Jewish Christians. *At the end of the tribulation, Christ will then come back with his saints to reign on the earth for one thousand years*. After this millennial period there will be a rebellion, resulting in the final defeat of Satan and his forces, and then will come the resurrection of unbelievers, the last judgment, and the beginning of the eternal state.

One further characteristic of pretribulational premillennialism should be mentioned: This view is found almost exclusively among dispensationalists who wish to maintain a clear distinction between the church and Israel. This pretribulational viewpoint allows the distinction to be maintained, since the church is taken out of the world before the widespread conversion of the Jewish people. These Jewish people therefore remain a distinct group from the church. Another characteristic of pretribulational premillennialism is its insistence on interpreting biblical prophecies "literally where possible." This especially applies

---

[4]Some interpreters hold to a variation of this view, such that Christ comes back in the middle of the tribulation and rescues believers. After that, there will be three-and-one-half additional years of tribulation on the earth. This is called the "midtribulation rapture" view. For further discussion of this view, see Gleason Archer, "The Case for the Mid-Seventieth-Week Rapture Position" in Gleason Archer, Paul Feinberg, Douglas Moo, and Richard Reiter, *The Rapture: Pre-, Mid-, or Post-Tribulational?* (Grand Rapids: Zondervan, 1984), pp. 113–45.

[5]See chapter 54, pp. 1097–99, for a discussion of the signs that will precede Christ's return.

to prophecies in the Old Testament concerning Israel. Those who hold this view argue that those prophecies of God's future blessing to Israel will yet be fulfilled among the Jewish people themselves; they are not to be "spiritualized" by finding their fulfillment in the church. Finally, one attractive feature about pretribulational premillennialism is that it allows people to insist that Christ's return could occur "at any moment" and therefore does justice to the full force of the passages that encourage us to be ready for Christ's return, while it still allows for a very literal fulfillment of the signs preceding Christ's return, since it says these will come to pass in the tribulation.

Before examining the arguments for these three (or four) positions, it is important to realize that the interpretation of the details of prophetic passages regarding future events is often a complex and difficult task involving many variable factors. Therefore the degree of certainty that attaches to our conclusions in this area will be less than with many other doctrines. Even though I will argue for one position (classical premillennialism), I also think it important for evangelicals to recognize that this area of study is complex and to extend a large measure of grace to others who hold different views regarding the millennium and the tribulation period.

### B. A Consideration of the Arguments for Amillennialism

In favor of the amillennial view, the following arguments are advanced:

1. When we look through the whole of the Bible, amillennialists will say, *only one passage* (Rev. 20:1–6) appears to teach a future earthly millennial rule of Christ, and that passage is itself obscure. It is unwise to base such a major doctrine on one passage of uncertain and widely disputed interpretation.

But how do amillennialists understand Revelation 20:1–6? The amillennial interpretation sees this passage as referring to the present church age. The passage reads as follows:

> Then I saw an angel coming down from heaven, holding in his hand the key of the bottomless pit and a great chain. And he seized the dragon, that ancient serpent, who is the Devil and Satan, and *bound him for a thousand years,* and threw him into the pit, and shut it and sealed it over him, that he should deceive the nations no more, till the thousand years were ended. After that he must be loosed for a little while.
>
> Then I saw thrones, and seated on them were those to whom judgment was committed. Also I saw the souls of those who had been beheaded for their testimony to Jesus and for the word of God, and who had not worshiped the beast or its image and had not received its mark on their foreheads or their hands. *They came to life, and reigned with Christ a thousand years.* The rest of the dead did not *come to life* until the thousand years were ended. This is the first resurrection. Blessed and holy is he who shares in the first resurrection! Over such the second death has no power, but they shall be priests of God and of Christ, and *they shall reign with him a thousand years.*

According to the amillennial interpretation[6] the binding of Satan in verses 1–2 is the binding that occurred during Jesus' earthly ministry. He spoke of binding

---

[6]Here I am largely following the excellent discussion of Anthony A. Hoekema, "Amillennialism," in

the strong man in order that he may plunder his house (Matt. 12:29) and said that
the Spirit of God was at that time present in power to triumph over demonic
forces: "If it is by the Spirit of God that I cast out demons, then the kingdom of
God has come upon you" (Matt. 12:28). Similarly, with respect to the breaking of
Satan's power, Jesus said during his ministry, "I saw Satan fall like lightning from
heaven" (Luke 10:18).

The amillennialist argues that this binding of Satan in Revelation 20:1–3 is for
a specific purpose: "*that he should deceive the nations no more*" (v. 3). This is exactly
what happened when Jesus came and the gospel began to be proclaimed not
simply to Jews but, after Pentecost, to all the nations of the world. In fact, the
worldwide missionary activity of the church, and the presence of the church in
most or all of the nations of the world, shows that the power that Satan had in the
Old Testament, to "deceive the nations" and keep them in darkness, has been
broken.

On the amillennialist view the scene described in verse 4 occurs in heaven: John
said, "I saw the *souls* of those who had been beheaded for their testimony to
Jesus. . . . They came to life, and reigned with Christ a thousand years" (v. 4).
Since John sees "souls" and not physical bodies, it is argued, this scene must be
occurring in heaven. When the text says that "They came to life" it does not mean
that they received a bodily resurrection. It possibly means simply that "they lived,"
since the aorist verb *ezēsan* can readily be interpreted to be a statement of an event
that occurred over a long period of time. (The verb for "they reigned" is also an
aorist indicative and refers to an occurrence over a thousand years, so the verb
"they lived" should have a similar meaning.) On the other hand, some amillennial
interpreters will take the verb *ezēsan* to mean "they came to life" in the sense of
coming into heavenly existence in the presence of Christ and beginning to reign
with him from heaven.

According to this view, the phrase "first resurrection" (v. 5) refers to going to
heaven to be with the Lord. This is not a bodily resurrection but a coming into the
presence of God in heaven. In a similar way, when verse 5 says, "The rest of the
dead did not *come to life* until the thousand years were ended, "this is understood
to mean they did not come into God's presence for judgment until the end of the
thousand years. So in both verses 4 and 5, the phrase "come to life" means "come
into the presence of God." (Another amillennial view of "first resurrection" is that
it refers to the resurrection of Christ, and to believers' participation in Christ's
resurrection through union with Christ.)

2. A second argument often proposed in favor of amillennialism is the fact that
Scripture teaches only *one resurrection,* when both believers and unbelievers will be
raised, not two resurrections (a resurrection of believers before the millennium
begins, and a resurrection of unbelievers to judgment after the end of the
millennium). This is an important argument, because the premillennial view
requires two separate resurrections, separated by a thousand years.

Evidence in favor of only one resurrection is found in at least three passages.
Jesus says, "*The hour is coming when all who are in the tombs will hear his voice and
come forth,* those who have done good, to the resurrection of life, and those who

*The Meaning of the Millennium: Four Views,* ed. Robert G. Clouse (Downers Grove, Ill.: InterVarsity
Press, 1977), pp. 155–87.

have done evil, to the resurrection of judgment" (John 5:28–29). Here Jesus speaks of a single "hour" when both believing and unbelieving dead will come forth from the tombs. Similarly, when Paul is on trial before Felix he explains that he has a hope in God that his Jewish opponents also accept "that *there will be a resurrection of both the just and the unjust*" (Acts 24:15). Once again, he speaks of a single resurrection of both believers and unbelievers. Finally, we read in Daniel: "And many of those who sleep in the dust of the earth shall awake, some to everlasting life, and some to shame and everlasting contempt" (Dan. 12:2).

3. *The idea of glorified believers and sinners living on earth together is too difficult to accept.* Berkhof says, "It is impossible to understand how a part of the old earth and of sinful humanity can exist alongside a part of the new earth and of a humanity that is glorified. How can perfect saints in glorified bodies have communion with sinners in the flesh? How can glorified sinners live in this sin-laden atmosphere and amid scenes of death and decay?"[7]

4. *If Christ comes in glory to reign on the earth, then how could people still persist in sin?* Once Jesus is actually present in his resurrection body and reigning as King over the earth, does it not seem highly unlikely that people would still reject him, and that evil and rebellion would grow on the earth until eventually Satan could gather the nations for battle against Christ?[8]

5. There seems to be no convincing *purpose* for such a millennium. Once the church age has ended and Christ has returned, then what is the reason for delaying the start of the eternal state?

6. In conclusion, amillennialists say that Scripture seems to indicate that *all the major events yet to come* before the eternal state will occur at once. Christ will return, there will be one resurrection of believers and unbelievers, the final judgment will take place, and a new heaven and new earth will be established. Then we will enter immediately into the eternal state, with no future millennium.[9]

At this point we can respond briefly to these amillennialist arguments, though on some points a fuller answer will be developed in the arguments for premillennialism.

1. In response to the objection that only one passage teaches a future earthly millennium, several comments can be made:

a. The Bible only needs to say something once in order for it to be true and something that we must believe. The story of the confusion of languages at the tower of Babel, for example, is only taught in Genesis 11:1–9, yet we believe it to be true because Scripture teaches it. Similarly, even if only one passage taught a future millennial reign of Christ, we still should believe it.

---

[7]Berkhof, *Systematic Theology*, p. 715.

[8]This argument is especially developed in Arthur H. Lewis, *The Dark Side of the Millennium* (Grand Rapids: Baker, 1980).

[9]Since they believe that Rev. 20:1–6 applies to the present age, amillennialists sometimes say, "Premillennialists are *waiting* for the millennium, postmillennialists are *working* for it, but we are *enjoying* it."

It should be noted that some amillennialists dislike the term *amillennial* because it implies they do not believe in any millennium at all, where as it is more accurate to say that they do not believe in a *future* millennium. They prefer a more positive term such as "realized millennialism," which allows them more easily to point out that they do believe in the millennial reign of Christ taught in Rev. 20:1–6; however, they believe the passage speaks of the present church age. (See Jay Adams, *The Time Is at Hand* (Phillipsburg, N.J.: Presbyterian and Reformed, 1970], pp. 7–11.)

Moreover, it is not surprising that this doctrine should be clearly taught in the book of Revelation. There was somewhat of a similar situation at the end of the Old Testament era. The entire Old Testament has no explicit teaching to the effect that the Messiah would come twice, once as a suffering Messiah who would die and rise again, earning our salvation, and then later as a conquering King to rule over the earth. The first and second comings of Christ may be hinted at in the Old Testament prophets, but they are nowhere explicitly taught, because God did not deem it necessary to reveal that amount of detail about his plan of redemption before it happened. Similarly, in several of the Old and New Testament books leading up to the time of the writing of Revelation, there are *hints* of a future earthly millennium prior to the eternal state, but the explicit teaching about it was left until John wrote Revelation. Since Revelation is the New Testament book that most explicitly teaches about things yet future, it is appropriate that this more explicit revelation of the future millennium would be put at this point in the Bible.

b. In response to the allegation that the passage that teaches a millennium is obscure, premillennialists respond that they do not find it obscure at all. They argue that one advantage of the premillennial position is that it understands Revelation 20:1–6 in a straightforward sense: the text says that Satan will be bound and cast into the bottomless pit for a thousand years, and the premillennialist says a time is coming when Satan will be bound and cast into a bottomless pit for a thousand years. The text speaks of a thousand-year reign of Christ, and the premillennialist expects a future thousand-year reign of Christ on earth. It speaks of those raised in the "first resurrection," and the premillennialist says that there will be a first resurrection of believers who are "blessed and holy" (Rev. 20:6) and a second resurrection at the end of the thousand years "for the rest of the dead" (v. 5). According to premillennialists, "obscurity" only enters the passage when an interpreter tries to find in it something other than such a straightforward interpretation.

c. Finally, many premillennialists argue that several other passages, especially in the Old Testament, require us to believe in a future period that is far greater than the present age but that still falls short of the eternal state (see Ps. 72:8–14; Isa. 11:2–9; 65:20; Zech. 14:6–21; 1 Cor. 15:24; Rev. 2:27; 12:5; 19:15).[10] These passages, they say, portray a period that looks very much like the millennium as they understand it.

d. With respect to the interpretation of Revelation 20:1–6 as given by amillennialists, several difficulties arise. Although Matthew 12:28–29 and Luke 10:18 do speak of a "binding" of Satan during Jesus' earthly ministry, the binding of Satan described in Revelation 20 seems to be much more extensive than that. The passage does not simply say that Satan is bound at this time, but speaks of "the bottomless pit" and says that the angel that came down from heaven "*threw him into the pit,* and *shut it* and *sealed it over him,* that he should deceive the nations no more, till the thousand years were ended" (Rev. 20:2–3). More than a mere binding or restriction of activity is in view here. The imagery of throwing Satan into a pit and shutting it and sealing it over him gives a picture of total removal from influence on the earth. To say that Satan is now in a bottomless pit that is shut and sealed over simply does not fit the present world situation during the

---

[10]See below, pp. 1127–30, for a discussion of these passages.

church age, in which Satan's activity is still very strong, in which he "prowls around like a roaring lion, seeking someone to devour" (1 Peter 5:8), in which he can fill someone's heart "to lie to the Holy Spirit" (Acts 5:3), and in which "what pagans sacrifice they offer to demons and not to God" (1 Cor. 10:20).

Moreover, even after the binding of Satan during Jesus' ministry, it remains true that "the god of this world has blinded the minds of the unbelievers, to keep them from seeing the light of the gospel of the glory of Christ" (2 Cor. 4:4). This is why Christians still must contend not "against flesh and blood, but against the principalities, against the powers, against the world rulers of this present darkness, against the spiritual hosts of wickedness in the heavenly places" (Eph. 6:12). This is because even during the church age, though the gospel is able to come with triumph and break down the forces of demonic opposition to the spread of the kingdom of God, nonetheless Satan's influence has not fully been removed from the world: "The spirit of antichrist . . . is in the world already" (1 John 4:3), and, in fact, "We know that we are of God, and *the whole world is in the power of the evil one*" (1 John 5:19). This repeated theme in the New Testament, the theme of Satan's continual activity on earth throughout the church age, makes it extremely difficult to think that Satan has been thrown into the bottomless pit, and it has been shut and sealed over for a thousand years. That imagery can only speak of the total removal of Satan's active influence from the earth.

But what can be said with respect to the fact that amillennialists say that the binding and imprisonment of Satan in Revelation 20 is said to be "that he should *deceive the nations no more*" (v. 3)? Does that not simply mean that the gospel can now be preached effectively among the nations? While the phrase might mean that, it seems more consistent with the use of the word *deceived* (Gk. *planaō*), especially in Revelation, to say that this is a *deception that is now going on during the entire church age* and that ends only when the millennium begins. Satan is called the one "who deceives the whole world" (Rev. 12:9 NASB), and the sorcery of Babylon is said to have "deceived" "all nations" before its judgment comes (Rev. 18:23).[11] Therefore it seems more appropriate to say that Satan is *now* still deceiving the nations, but at the beginning of the millennium this deceptive influence will be removed. There was an even greater deception before Christ came, but there is still significant deception that remains today.

The fact that John saw "souls" in his vision does not require that the scene be set in heaven. Since these souls are persons who then "came to life" in "the first resurrection" we should see these as *people* who obtained resurrection bodies and who began to reign on the earth. Moreover, Revelation 20:1 indicates that the scene is focused on events on the earth, for it says, "Then I saw an angel *coming down from heaven*." But if the angel came down from heaven, then he carries out his activity on the earth, and the entire scene is set on the earth.

Some amillennialists argue that the phrase "came to life" refers to a coming to heavenly existence or coming into the presence of God. But it must be asked, Where does the Greek term *zaō* ("live") ever take that meaning? No other examples of that word in the New Testament take the sense, "come into the presence of God."

---

[11]Both of these passages use the same term *planaō*. The same verb is used in Matthew 24:4, 5, 11, 24 to speak of Jesus' warnings that many will be deceived or led astray by false Christs and false prophets.

Moreover, amillennialist interpretations of the phrase "first resurrection" are unconvincing. The word *resurrection* (Gk. *anastasis*) never elsewhere means "going to heaven" or "going into the presence of God," but rather signifies a bodily resurrection. This is the sense in which first-century readers would have understood the word. The other amillennialist view, which understands "the first resurrection" to be Christ's resurrection (and our union with him) does not seem likely because those who "came to life" are the ones who had been "beheaded for their testimony to Jesus" (v. 4), which suggests a bodily resurrection after death.[12]

2. Does Scripture teach only *one* resurrection, so that believers and unbelievers will be raised at the same time? It is hard to accept this when we realize that Revelation 20 explicitly speaks about "the *first* resurrection," thus implying that there will be a second resurrection as well. Speaking of those who came to life and reigned with Christ a thousand years, we read, "This is the first resurrection. Blessed and holy is he who shares in the first resurrection! Over such the second death has no power" (vv. 5–6). The passage distinguishes those who share in this first resurrection and are blessed from others who do not share in it. They are "the rest of the dead" and the implication is that "the second death" (that is, facing final judgment and being condemned to eternal punishment away from the presence of God) does have power over them, and they will experience it. But if this passage clearly teaches a first resurrection, and the fact that the rest of the dead will come to life at the end of a thousand years, then there is clear teaching on two separate resurrections here in Revelation 20.

As for the other passages that amillennialists claim to support the view that there is only one resurrection, it must be said that those passages do not exclude the idea of two resurrections, but they simply do not specify whether or not the resurrection of believers and unbelievers will be separated in time. In fact, Jesus' statement in John 5 does hint at the possibility of two resurrections. He says that those who are in the tombs will come forth, "those who have done good, *to the resurrection of life*, and those who have done evil, *to the resurrection of judgment*" (John 5:28–29). In this way Jesus in fact speaks of two different resurrections.[13]

---

[12]Other reasons to reject this interpretation are (1) "The rest of the dead" are said to "come to life" after the thousand years are ended (v. 5)—a reference to the bodily resurrection of unbelievers—but this implies that the phrase "came to life" refers to bodily resurrection in both cases, not just to spiritual union with Christ in his resurrection; and (2) when the text says, "This is the first resurrection" (v. 5), the most evident antecedent in context is the coming to life of believers in v. 4, but no mention of Christ's resurrection occurs in the context.

[13]The fact that Jesus says in this context, "*The hour* is coming when all who are in the tombs will hear his voice" does not require that both resurrections happen at the same time, for the word *hour* elsewhere in John's gospel can refer to a long period of time; just three verses previously, Jesus said, "Truly, truly, I say to you, *the hour* is coming, and now is, when the dead will hear the voice of the Son of God, and those who hear will live" (John 5:25). Here the "hour" refers to the entire church age when those who are spiritually dead hear Jesus' voice and come to life. John can also use the word *hour* (Gk. *hōra*) to speak of the time when true worshipers worship the Father in spirit and in truth (John 4:21, 23), or when intense persecution will come on the disciples (John 16:2). These examples also speak of long periods of time, even entire ages.

A similar way of speaking is possible in English: I can tell a class of sixty students, "Don't be discouraged—*graduation day is coming* for every one of you." But I know that some will graduate this year, some will graduate next year, and some will graduate two or three years later. I can still speak of "graduation day" rather than "graduation days" because it is clear that I am speaking about the kind of day it is, not about the time it will occur or whether it will be one day or several that are of the same type.

As for Daniel 12:2, it simply says that those who sleep in the dust of the earth shall awake, "some to everlasting life, and some to shame and everlasting contempt," but it does not specify whether this will happen simultaneously or at different times. It simply says that both types of people will be raised. The same is true of Acts 24:15, where Paul says there will be "a resurrection of both the just and the unjust." This affirms that both types of people will be raised from the dead, but it does not exclude the possibility that this would happen at different times. All of these verses, in the absence of Revelation 20:5–6, might or might not be speaking of a single future time of resurrection. But with the explicit teaching of Revelation 20:5–6 about two resurrections, these verses must be understood to refer to the future certainty of a resurrection for each type of person, without specifying that those resurrections will be separated in time.

3. The idea of glorified believers and sinners living on earth together during the millennium does sound strange to us now, but it is certainly not impossible for God to bring this about. We must realize that Jesus lived on the earth with a glorified body for forty days after his resurrection, and apparently there were many other Old Testament saints who lived with glorified bodies on earth during that time as well (Matt. 27:53).[14] It will indeed be a kind of world situation that is far different and far more God-glorifying than the world is now, but it does not seem that we are justified in asserting that God could not or would not bring about such a state of affairs. Certainly he *could* do it, and several passages seem to indicate that he has a good purpose and intention of doing it as well.

4. It is certainly not impossible that evil and secret rebellion could persist on the earth in spite of the bodily presence of Christ reigning as King. We must remember that Judas lived with Jesus on the closest terms for three years, and still betrayed him. Moreover, many of the Pharisees *saw* Jesus' miracles, and even saw him raising people from the dead, and still did not believe. In fact, even when the disciples were in the presence of the glorified Lord Jesus, we read that "some doubted" (Matt. 28:17). Such persistent unbelief in the very presence of Christ is hard to understand, but we must remember that Satan himself fell from an exalted position in the presence of God in heaven.

When the amillennialists object that people could not persist in sin in the presence of Christ's bodily reign on the earth, their position simply fails to realize the deep-seated and highly irrational nature of sin. It also fails fully to reckon with the fact that even "massive proof" and "undeniable evidence" cannot compel genuine conversion. Genuine repentance and faith is brought about by the enabling and persuasive work of the Holy Spirit in people's hearts. Such is the irrational nature of sin that those who are "dead in trespasses and sins" will often persist in rebellion and unbelief even in the face of overwhelming evidence to the contrary.[15]

This is not to say that no one will be converted to Christ during the millennium. No doubt millions of people will become Christians during that time, and the influence of the reign of Christ will permeate into every aspect of every society in

---

[14]See chapter 42, pp. 834–35, on Matt. 27:52–53.

[15]A somewhat similar example is the fact that many people today refuse to believe that there is a God who created the universe, in spite of the incredible complexity of every living being, and in spite of what is for all practical purposes the mathematical impossibility that the entire universe could have come about by chance.

the world. Yet at the same time it is not at all difficult to understand how evil and rebellion will grow simultaneously.

5. God may have several purposes in mind for a future millennium, not all of which may now be clear to us. But certainly such a millennium would show *the outworking of God's good purposes in the structures of society,* especially the structures of the family and civil government. During the church age, the good purposes of God are primarily seen in individual lives and the blessings that come to those who believe in Christ. To some extent now (and to a greater extent in times of revival) this affects civil government and educational institutions and corporations, and to a larger extent it affects the family. But in none of these structures are God's good purposes manifested to the extent they could be, showing God's great wisdom and goodness not only in his plans for individuals but also for societal structures. In the millennium the beauty of God's wisdom will show forth to his glory from all of these societal structures.

Moreover, the millennium will further vindicate God's righteousness. The fact that some continue in sin and unbelief will show that "sin rebellion against God is not due to an evil society or to a bad environment. It is due to the sinfulness of the hearts of men. Thus the justice of God will be fully vindicated in the day of final judgment."[16] With Satan bound for a thousand years, the fact that sin can persist will also show that the ultimate blame for sin is not demonic influence in people's lives but deep-rooted sinfulness in people's hearts.

Third, the entire scope of the Bible reveals to us that it is God's good pleasure to unfold his purposes and reveal more and more of his glory gradually over time. From the calling of Abraham to the birth of Isaac, the sojourn in Egypt and the exodus, the establishment of the people in the promised land, the Davidic kingdom and the divided monarchy, the exile and return with the rebuilding of the temple, the preservation of a faithful remnant, and finally the coming of Jesus in the flesh, God's purposes were increasingly seen to be glorious and wonderful.Even in Jesus' life the progressive revealing of his glory took thirty-three years, culminating in the last three years of his life. Then in Jesus' death, resurrection, and ascension into heaven, the completion of our redemption was accomplished. Yet the spread of the church throughout all nations has now occupied over 1,900 years, and we do not know how long it is to continue. All this is to say that God's way is not to bring to realization all of his good purposes at once, but to unfold them gradually over time. This is so even in the individual lives of Christians, who grow daily in grace and in fellowship with God and in likeness to Christ. Therefore it would not be surprising if, before the eternal state, God instituted one final step in the progressive unfolding of the history of redemption. It would serve to increase his glory as men and angels look on in amazement at the wonder of God's wisdom and plan.

6. Finally, a major objection to amillennialism must continue to be the fact that it can propose no really satisfying explanation of Revelation 20.[17]

---

[16]George Ladd, "Historic Premillennialism," in *The Meaning of the Millennium: Four Views,* p. 40.

[17]Some other interpretations of Rev. 20 have been proposed by amillennialists, but they all have the disadvantage of having to labor under the burden of explaining away what seems to be a straightforward understanding of the text because they are convinced that the rest of Scripture does not teach a future earthly millennium. But if the rest of Scripture does not deny it (and in some places hints at it), and if this text does teach it, then it would seem much more appropriate to accept it.

## C. A Consideration of Arguments for Postmillennialism

The arguments in favor of postmillennialism are as follows:

1. The Great Commission leads us to expect that the gospel will go forth in power and eventually result in a largely Christian world: Jesus explicitly said, *"All authority in heaven and on earth* has been given to me. Go therefore and make disciples of all nations, baptizing them in the name of the Father and of the Son and of the Holy Spirit, teaching them to observe all that I have commanded you; and lo, I am with you always, to the close of the age" (Matt. 28:18–20). Since Christ has all authority in heaven and on earth, and since he promises to be with us in the fulfillment of this commission, we would expect that it would transpire without hindrance and eventually triumph in the whole world.

2. Parables of the gradual growth of the kingdom indicate that it eventually will fill the earth with its influence. Here postmillennialists point to the following:

> Another parable he put before them, saying, "The kingdom of heaven is like a grain of mustard seed which a man took and sowed in his field; it is the smallest of all seeds, but when it has grown it is the greatest of shrubs and becomes a tree, so that the birds of the air come and make nests in its branches." (Matt. 13:31–32)

We can also note the following verse: "He told them another parable. 'The kingdom of heaven is like leaven which a woman took and hid in three measures of flour, till it was all leavened'" (Matt. 13:33). According to postmillennialists both of these parables indicate that the kingdom will grow in influence until it permeates and in some measure transforms the entire world.

3. Postmillennialists will also argue that the world is becoming more Christian. The church is growing and spreading throughout the world, and even when it is persecuted and oppressed it grows remarkably by the power of God.[18]

At this point we must make a very significant distinction, however. The "millennium" that postmillennialists hold to is *very different* from the "millennium" the premillennialists talk about. In a sense, they are not even discussing the same topic. While *pre*millennialists talk about a renewed earth with Jesus Christ physically present and reigning as King, together with glorified believers in resurrection bodies, *post*millennialists are simply talking about an earth with many, many Christians influencing society. They do not envisage a millennium consisting of a renewed earth or glorified saints or Christ present in bodily form to reign (for they think that these things will only occur after Christ returns to inaugurate the eternal state).[19] Therefore the entire discussion of the millennium is more than simply a discussion of the sequence of events surrounding it. It also involves a significant difference over the nature of this period of time itself.

---

[18]The postmillennialist A. H. Strong argues that Rev. 20:4–10 "does not describe the events commonly called the second advent and resurrection, but rather describes the great spiritual changes in the later history of the church, which are typical of, and preliminary to, the second advent and resurrection." He sees Rev. 20, therefore, simply as a prediction of "the latter days of the church militant" and a time when "under the special influence of the Holy Ghost" the church shall "to an extent unknown before, triumph over the powers of evil, both within and without" (A. H. Strong, *Systematic Theology,* p. 1013).

[19]Similarly, when amillennialists talk about presently "enjoying" the millennium, which they understand on the basis of Rev. 20 to refer to the church age, they are also talking about a very different kind of "millennium" than would be envisaged by either postmillennialists or premillennialists.

In fact, though I am not aware if anyone has done this, it would not be impossible for someone to be a postmillennialist and a premillennialist at the same time, with two different senses of the term *millennium*. Someone could conceivably be a postmillennialist and think that the gospel will grow in influence until the world is largely Christian, and that then Christ will return and set up a literal earthly reign, raising believers from the dead to reign with him in glorified bodies. Or, on the other hand, a very optimistic premillennialist could conceivably adopt many of the postmillennialist teachings about the increasingly Christian nature of this present age.[20]

In response to the postmillennialist arguments, the following points may be made:

1. The Great Commission does indeed speak of the authority that is given into Christ's hand, but that does not necessarily imply that Christ will use that authority to bring about the conversion of the majority of the population of the world. To say that Christ's authority is great is simply another way of saying that God's power is infinite, which no one will deny. But the question is the extent to which Christ will *use* his power to bring about the numerical growth of the church. We may *assume* that he will use it to a very full extent and will bring about worldwide Christianization, but such an assumption is merely that—an assumption. It is not based on any specific evidence in the Great Commission or in other texts that talk about Christ's authority and power in this present age.[21]

2. The parables of the mustard seed and the leaven do tell us that the kingdom of God will gradually grow from something very small to something very large, but they do not tell us the *extent* to which the kingdom will grow. For example, the parable of the mustard seed does not tell us that the tree grew so that it spread throughout the whole earth. And the parable of the leaven simply talks about gradual growth that permeates society (as the church has already done), but it says nothing about the degree or effect that that influence has (it does not tell us, for example, whether in the end 5 percent of the loaf was leaven and 95 percent bread dough, or 20 percent leaven and 80 percent bread, or 60 percent leaven and 40 percent bread, and so forth). It is simply pressing the parable beyond its intended purpose to attempt to make it say more than that the kingdom will grow gradually and eventually have an influence on every society in which it is planted.

3. In response to the argument that the world is becoming more Christian, it must be said that the world is also becoming more evil. No student of history or modern society will argue that mankind has made much progress through the centuries in overcoming the depth of perversity and the extent of immorality that remain in people's hearts. Indeed, modernization in western societies in the twentieth century has often been accompanied not by moral improvement but by an unprecedented level of drug abuse, marital infidelity, pornography, homosexuality, rebellion against authority, superstition (in astrology and the New Age

---

[20]This is not to say that such a position would be free of internal tensions and difficulties (especially the difficulty of explaining how evil could diminish when Christ was absent from the earth but grow into widespread rebellion when he is physically present and reigning), but it is to say that there would be no absolute inconsistency within this position.

[21]1 Cor. 15:25 says, "For he must reign until he has put all his enemies under his feet," but the immediate context (vv. 24, 26) talks about destroying his enemies (including death in v. 26), not about converting people and bringing them into the church.

movement), materialism, greed, theft, and falsehood in speech. Even among professing Christians there is repeated evidence of dismaying imperfection in the Christian life, especially in the realms of personal morality and depth of intimacy with God. In places where Bible-believing Christians comprise large segments of the population, still nothing like an earthly millennial kingdom occurs.[22] It is true that the growth of the church as a percentage of world population has been remarkable in recent decades,[23] and we should be greatly encouraged by this. It is possible that we will someday see a far greater influence of genuine Christianity upon many societies, and if that occurred, it would make the postmillennial position seem more plausible. But such events could also be understood within a premillennial or amillennial framework, so the final decision regarding these competing positions must still be made by interpreting the relevant biblical texts.

4. Finally, we should note that there are several New Testament passages that seem to give explicit denial to the postmillennial position. Jesus said, "Enter by the narrow gate; for the gate is wide and the way is easy, that leads to destruction, and those who enter by it are many. For the gate is narrow and the way is hard, that leads to life, and *those who find it are few*" (Matt. 7:13–14). Rather than teaching that a majority of the world will become Christians, Jesus seems here to be saying that those who are saved will be "few" in contrast to the "many" who travel toward eternal destruction. Similarly, Jesus asks, *"When the Son of man comes, will he find faith on earth?"* (Luke 18:8), a question that suggests that the earth will not be filled with those who believe, but will be dominated rather by those who do not have faith.

Contrary to the view that the world will get better and better as the influence of the church grows, Paul predicts that before Christ returns "the *rebellion*" will come and "the *man of lawlessness*" will be revealed, "the son of perdition" who "takes his seat in the temple of God, proclaiming himself to be God" (2 Thess. 2:3–4).[24]

When writing to Timothy about the last days, Paul says,

---

[22]One interesting example in the United States is the state of Texas. Statistics indicate that over 50 percent of the people of Texas belong to Southern Baptist churches, a denomination that preaches a genuine gospel of salvation by faith alone, and the need for each individual personally to be born again. This in itself is a wonderful fact for which we should be thankful to God, but no one living in Texas today would seriously claim to be living already in the millennium (at least in the way postmillennialists understand it). If we add to the Southern Baptists all the other Bible-believing Christians in the state, far more than half of the state's population consists of born-again Christians. But if a population of 50 percent Christians cannot bring us anywhere near to an earthly millennium, then what percentage of the world would have to become Christian before the postmillennialist's hope would be realized? And where is there evidence throughout history that we are making significant progress toward the realization of such a millennium?

[23]"Between 1950 and 1992, Bible believing Christians went from just 3% of the world population to 10% of the population. This is a jump from 80 million to 540 million" (Rick Wood, "Christianity: Waning or Growing?" in *Mission Frontiers Bulletin* [Pasadena, Calif.; Jan.–Feb., 1993], p. 25). This journal publishes similar statistics from different countries in almost every issue, leading one to conclude that the growth of the church since 1950 is so remarkable as to be without precedent in the history of the world.

[24]Some postmillennialists believe that there will be a final rebellion before Christ's return. These verses would not constitute an objection to their position, but the following verses indicating the dominant non-Christian pattern of world affairs just prior to Christ's return would still weigh against such a postmillennial view, because they picture a world decisively different from the millennium of peace and righteousness brought about by the spread of the gospel in a postmillennial system.

*In the last days* there will come times of stress. For men will be lovers of self, lovers of money, proud, arrogant, abusive, disobedient to their parents, ungrateful, unholy, inhuman, implacable, slanderers, profligates, fierce, haters of good, treacherous, reckless, swollen with conceit, lovers of pleasure rather than lovers of God, holding the form of religion but denying the power of it. (2 Tim. 3:1–5)

He says further:

*All who desire to live a godly life in Christ Jesus will be persecuted, while evil men and impostors will go on from bad to worse, deceivers and deceived* . . . the time is coming when people will not endure sound teaching, but having itching ears they will accumulate for themselves teachers to suit their own likings, and will turn away from listening to the truth and wander into myths. (2 Tim. 3:12–13; 4:3–4)

Finally, and perhaps most conclusively, Matthew 24:15–31 speaks of a great tribulation that will precede the time of Christ's return:

For *then there will be great tribulation, such as has not been from the beginning of the world until now, no, and never will be. And if those days had not been shortened, no human being would be saved;* but for the sake of the elect those days will be shortened. . . . *Immediately after the tribulation of those days the sun will be darkened, and the moon will not give its light, and the stars will fall from heaven, and the powers of the heavens will be shaken; then will appear the sign of the Son of man in heaven, and then all the tribes of the earth will mourn, and they will see the Son of man coming on the clouds of heaven with power and great glory.* (Matt. 24:21–30)

This passage pictures not a Christianized world but a world of great suffering and evil, a great tribulation that exceeds all previous periods of suffering on the earth. It does not say that the great majority of the world will welcome Christ when he comes, but rather that when the sign of the Son of man appears in heaven, "then all the tribes of the earth will mourn" (Matt. 24:30).

Since Matthew 24 is such a difficult passage from the postmillennialist perspective, there have been several attempts to explain it not as a prediction of events that will occur just prior to Christ's second coming, but rather as something that was mainly fulfilled in the destruction of Jerusalem in A.D. 70.

To sustain this interpretation, postmillennialists make most of the elements of Matthew 24:29–31 symbolic:[25] the sun and moon being darkened, the stars falling from heaven, and the powers of the heavens being shaken are not to be understood as literal events, but as imagery for God's coming in judgment. Similar imagery for judgment is said to be found in Ezekiel 32:7; Joel 2:10; and Amos 8:9—but these passages simply speak of judgments of darkness, and do not mention the stars falling from heaven or the powers of the heavens being shaken. R. T. France also mentions Isaiah 13:10 and 34:4, which do talk about the sun and moon being darkened and the host of heaven falling, but it is far from certain that France is correct in claiming that those passages are merely symbolic—they are set in contexts in which they could easily be understood as literal predictions of the cosmic changes preceding the final judgment. So it is far from obvious that these passages are merely apocalyptic imagery for judgment on Jerusalem.[26]

---

[25]Here I am following the interpretation of R. T. France, *The Gospel According to Matthew,* pp. 343–46.

[26]Another argument in favor of the postmillennial view may be taken from the statement "this generation will not pass away till all these things take place" in Matt. 24:34. A postmillennialist can

1126 55 : THE MILLENNIUM

Moreover, the interpretation that sees these as merely symbolic statements grows more difficult as the statement of Jesus continues, for he does not only talk about signs in the sun, moon, and stars, but he says immediately after that, "*then* will appear the sign of the Son of man in heaven . . . and *they will see the Son of man coming on the clouds of heaven with power and great glory*" (Matt. 24:30). Consistent with his previous symbolic interpretation of this passage, France says that "all the tribes of the earth" refers merely to the Jews, that is, "all the tribes (families) of the land,"[27] that is, the land of Israel. And he says that the reference to the Son of man coming on the clouds of heaven with power and great glory does not refer to Christ's return but to his coming *to the Father in heaven* "to receive vindication and authority."[28] France quotes with approval the statement of G. B. Caird, who says that "the coming of the Son of Man in the clouds of heaven was never conceived as a primitive form of space travel, but as a symbol for a mighty reversal of fortunes within history and at the national level."[29] Then the sending out of Christ's angels with a loud trumpet call to gather his elect from one end of heaven to the other is understood to refer to messengers who preach the gospel throughout the earth. The gathering of the elect then is gathering them into the church by the preaching of the gospel.

However, on this interpretation France cannot satisfactorily account for the fact that Jesus says that all the tribes of the earth "*will see* the Son of man coming on the clouds of heaven with power and great glory" (Matt. 24:30). This is not an invisible heavenly transaction in which Christ receives authority from God the Father, but it is his return with power and great glory which is here predicted. Those who preach the gospel are never elsewhere called angels who give a loud trumpet call, and the preaching of the gospel is not elsewhere called the gathering of "his elect from the four winds, from one end of heaven to the other" (Matt. 24:31). Moreover, when Jesus elsewhere speaks of his coming on the clouds, he speaks not of a coming *to God the Father* in heaven, but a coming *to people on earth:* "Behold, he is coming with the clouds, and every eye will see him, every one who pierced him; and all tribes of the earth will wail on account of him" (Rev. 1:7). And when Christ returns, Paul says that we who are alive "shall be caught up together with them *in the clouds* to meet the Lord in the air" (1 Thess. 4:17). When Christ comes on the clouds of glory with great power and authority, he comes to reign over the earth, and this is the sense of Matthew 24:30–31. (France does not comment on the fact that Jesus says the tribes of the earth who mourn "*will see* the Son of man coming on the clouds of heaven" [v. 30]. The fact that these tribes will see Jesus coming makes it difficult to understand any symbolic or

---

take "this generation" in a perfectly natural sense to refer to the people who heard Jesus as he spoke, and thus support is given to the view that all the events of vv. 29–31 (or even vv. 5–31) occurred by A.D. 70. But such an interpretation is not necessary to Matt. 24:34, because "this generation" could be understood to refer to the generation that sees "all these things" (v. 33) take place, whenever that may be. (The "fig tree" in v. 32 should not be understood as a prophetic symbol for a particular time in history—such as the rebirth of Israel as a nation—because Jesus uses it simply as an illustration from nature: when the fig tree puts forth leaves, you know that summer will come soon; similarly, when these signs [vv. 5–31] occur, you know that the Son of man will return soon.)

[27]France, *Matthew,* p. 345.

[28]Ibid., p. 344.

[29]Ibid., p. 344, quoting G. B. Caird, *Jesus and the Jewish Nation* (London: Athlone Press, 1965), p. 20.

invisible heavenly interpretation here.) Moreover, the piling up of factors that we know from other texts to be connected with Christ's return (cosmic signs, Christ's coming with power, the loud trumpet call, the angels gathering the elect) provides a cumulative case for believing that Christ's *second* coming, not just a symbolic representation of his receiving authority, is in view here. And if Matthew 24 talks about Christ's second coming, then it talks about his coming just *after* a period of great tribulation, not after a millennium of peace and righteousness has been established on the earth.[30]

Finally, all of the passages indicating that Christ could return soon and that we must be ready for him to return at any time[31] must be considered a significant argument against postmillennialism as well. For if Christ could return at any time, and we are to be ready for his return, then the long period required for the establishment of the millennium on earth before Christ returns simply cannot be thought a persuasive theory.

## D. A Consideration of the Arguments for Premillennialism

The position advocated in this book is historic premillennialism. The arguments against the premillennial position have essentially been presented in the arguments for amillennialism and postmillennialism, and will therefore not be repeated again herein a separate section, but incidental objections to these arguments will be considered along the way.

1. Several Old Testament passages seem to fit neither in the present age nor in the eternal state. These passages indicate some future stage in the history of redemption which is far greater than the present church age but which still does not see the removal of all sin and rebellion and death from the earth.

Speaking of Jerusalem at some time in the future, Isaiah says:

> No more shall there be in it
>     an infant that lives but a few days,
>     or an old man who does not fill out his days,
> for the child shall die a hundred years old,
>     and the sinner a hundred years old shall be accursed. (Isa. 65:20)

Here we read that there will be no more infants who die in infancy, and no more old men who die prematurely, something far different from this present age. But death and sin will still be present, for the child who is one hundred years old shall die, and the sinner who is one hundred years old "shall be accursed." The larger context of this passage may mingle elements of the millennium and the eternal state (cf. vv. 17, 25), but it is in the nature of Old Testament prophecy not to distinguish among events in the future, just as these prophecies do not distinguish between the first and second comings of Christ. Therefore in the larger context there may be mixed elements, but the point remains that this single

---

[30]It is true that some postmillennialists hold that there will be a time of rebellion at the end of the millennium, just before Christ returns. But a period of rebellion against a dominant millennial kingdom of righteousness and peace is not the same as a tribulation period in which evil is dominant and Christians experience great persecution.

[31]See chapter 54, pp. 1095–97, on the passages teaching Christ's imminent return.

element (the infants and old men who live long, the child dying one hundred years old, and the sinner being accursed) indicates a specific time in the future that is different from the present age.

Isaiah seems to predict a millennial kingdom in another place when he says:

> The wolf shall dwell with the lamb,
>     and the leopard shall lie down with the kid,
> and the calf and the lion and the fatling together,
>     and a little child shall lead them.
> The cow and the bear shall feed;
>     their young shall lie down together;
> and the lion shall eat straw like the ox.
> The sucking child shall play over the hole of the asp,
>     and the weaned child shall put his hand on the adder's den.
> They shall not hurt or destroy
>     in all my holy mountain;
> for the earth shall be full of the knowledge of the LORD
>     as the waters cover the sea. (Isa. 11:6–9)

This passage clearly speaks of a momentous renewal of nature that takes us far beyond the present age, a time in which "the earth shall be full of the knowledge of the LORD as the waters cover the sea" (v. 9). Yet in the very next verse Isaiah says:

> *In that day* the root of Jesse shall stand as an ensign to the peoples; *him shall the nations seek*, and his dwellings shall be glorious.
> *In that day* the Lord will extend his hand yet a second time to recover the remnant which is left of his people, from Assyria, from Egypt, from Pathros, from Ethiopia. (Isa. 11:10–11)

Here some are still seeking the Messiah and apparently coming to salvation, and here also the Lord is still gathering the remnant of his people from various nations of the earth. It does not seem, therefore, that the eternal state has begun, yet the reversal of nature far exceeds anything that will happen in this present age. Does this not indicate a future millennial kingdom?

Psalm 72 seems to go beyond a description of Solomon's reign and to predict the glories of the reign of the Messiah:

> He will rule from sea to sea
>     and from the River to the ends of the earth.
> The desert tribes will bow before him
>     and his enemies will lick the dust.
> The kings of Tarshish and of distant shores
>     will bring tribute to him;
> the kings of Sheba and Seba
>     will present him gifts.
> All kings will bow down to him
>     and all nations will serve him.
> For he will deliver the needy who cry out,
>     the afflicted who have no-one to help.

He will take pity on the weak and the needy
and save the needy from death.
He will rescue them from oppression and violence,
for precious is their blood in his sight. (Ps. 72:8–14 NIV)[32]

This passage certainly speaks of a messianic rule far more extensive than that experienced by David or Solomon, because this Messiah's kingdom extends "to the ends of the earth" and "all nations will serve him" (vv. 8, 11 NIV; note that the psalm also says: "He will endure as long as the sun, as long as the moon, through all generations" in v. 5 NIV). This will be a reign in righteousness in justice—but it certainly will not be the eternal state. There are still "the needy who cry out" and "the afflicted who have no one to help"; there are still people who need to be rescued "from oppression and violence" (vv. 12–14). There will still be enemies who "will lick the dust" under the reign of this righteous King (v. 9). All of this speaks of an age far different from the present age but short of the eternal state in which there is no more sin or suffering.

Zechariah also prophesies a coming age in which there is great transformation in the earth, in which the Lord is King over all the earth, and in which there is still rebellion and sin, suffering, and death:

Then the LORD your God will come, and all the holy ones with him. On that day there shall be neither cold nor frost. And there shall be continuous day (it is known to the LORD), not day and not night, for at evening time there shall be light.

On that day living waters shall flow out from Jerusalem, half of them to the eastern sea and half of them to the western sea; it shall continue in summer as in winter.

And the LORD will become king over all the earth; on that day the LORD will be one and his name one.

And this shall be the plague with which the LORD will smite all the peoples that wage war against Jerusalem: their flesh shall rot while they are still on their feet, their eyes shall rot in their sockets, and their tongues shall rot in their mouths. And the wealth of all the nations round about shall be collected, gold, silver, and garments in great abundance. . . .

Then every one that survives of all the nations that have come against Jerusalem shall go up year after year to worship the King, the LORD of hosts, and to keep the feast of booths. And if any of the families of the earth do not go up to Jerusalem to worship the King, the LORD of hosts, there will be no rain upon them. (Zech. 14:5–17)

Here again the description does not fit the present age, for the Lord is King over all the earth in this situation. But it does not fit the eternal state either, because of the disobedience and rebellion against the Lord that is clearly present. One might object that this is a typical Old Testament prophecy in which distinct future events are conflated and not distinguished in the prophet's vision, though they may be separated by long ages when they actually occur. However, it is difficult to make such a distinction in this passage because it is specifically rebellion against the

[32]The NASB and RSV take these statements not as predictions but as prayers ("May he have dominion. . . . May his foes bow down before him," etc.). But in either case this psalm shows the expectation of a messianic ruler who would someday have dominion "to the ends of the earth."

Lord who is King over all the earth that is punished by these plagues and lack of rain.[33]

2. There are also New Testament passages other than Revelation 20 that suggest a future millennium. When the risen Lord Jesus speaks to the church at Thyatira, he says, "*He who conquers and who keeps my works until the end, I will give him power over the nations,* and *he shall rule them with a rod of iron,* as when earthen pots are broken in pieces, even as I myself have received power from my Father" (Rev. 2:26–27). The imagery used (ruling with a rod of iron; shattering earthen pots) implies a rule of force over rebellious people. But when will believers who conquer over evil participate in this rule? The idea fits well into a future millennial kingdom when glorified saints rule with Christ on the earth, but does not fit well at any time in the present age or in the eternal state. (The idea of ruling the nations "with a rod of iron" is also found in Rev. 12:5–6 and 19:15.)

When Paul talks about the resurrection, he says that each person will receive a resurrection body in his own order: "Christ the first fruits, *then* (*epeita*) at his coming those who belong to Christ. *Then* (*eita*) comes the end, when he delivers the kingdom to God the Father after destroying every rule and every authority and power. For he must reign until he has put all his enemies under his feet" (1 Cor. 15:23–25). The two words translated "then" in this passage (*epeita* and *eita*) both take the sense "after that," not the sense "at that same time." Therefore the passage gives some support to the idea that, just as there is an interval of time between Christ's resurrection and his second coming when we receive a resurrection body (v. 23), so there is an interval of time between Christ's second coming and "the end" (v. 24), when Christ delivers the kingdom to God after having reigned for a time and put all his enemies under his feet.[34]

3. With the background of a number of other passages that hint at or clearly suggest a future time far greater than the present age but short of the eternal state, it is appropriate then to look at Revelation 20 once again. Several statements here are best understood as referring to a future earthly reign of Christ prior to the future judgment.

a. The binding and imprisonment of Satan in the bottomless pit (vv. 2–3) imply a far greater restriction of his activity than anything we know in this present age (see discussion above, under amillennialism).

b. The statement that those who were faithful "came to life" (v.4) is best taken as referring to a bodily resurrection, for the next verse says, "This is the first resurrection." The verb *ezēsan*, "came to life," is the same verb and the same form of the verb used in Revelation 2:8, where Jesus identifies himself as the one "who died and *came to life*," here obviously referring to his resurrection.[35]

---

[33]The passage still describes blessings in terms of old covenant sacrifices and mentions the feast of booths, an old covenant festival. This was the terminology and description available to the people of that day, but the New Testament can allow for greater (spiritual) fulfillment of a number of these items.

[34]The Greek word *eita* does mean "after that" (see Mark 4:17, 28; 1 Cor. 15:5, 7; 1 Tim. 2:13). It does not always indicate temporal sequence, because it can also introduce the next item or argument in a logical progression, but in narrating historical occurrences it indicates something that happens after something else (see BAGD, pp. 233–34; also LSJ, p. 498: "used to denote the sequence of one act or state upon another . . . *then, next*").

[35]I understand the aorist indicative *ezēsan* in both cases as an inceptive aorist, marking the beginning of an action.

c. On a premillennial interpretation, the reigning with Christ (in Rev. 20:4) is something that is still future, not something that is occurring now (as amillennialists claim). This is consistent with the rest of the New Testament, where we are frequently told that believers will reign with Christ and be given authority by him to reign over the earth (see Luke 19:17, 19; 1 Cor. 6:3; Rev. 2:26–27; 3:21). But nowhere does Scripture say that believers in the intermediate state (between their death and Christ's return) are reigning with Christ or sharing in rule with him. In fact, Revelation earlier pictures saints in heaven before Christ's return *waiting* under the altar and crying out to the Lord to begin to judge evildoers on the earth (Rev. 6:9–10). Nowhere is it said that Christians are already reigning with Christ.

Those who come to life and reign with Christ in Revelation 20 include people *"who had not worshiped the beast or its image and had not received its mark on their foreheads or their hands"* (Rev. 20:4). This is a reference to those who did not yield to the persecution by the beast spoken of in Revelation 13:1–18. But if the severity of persecution described in Revelation 13 leads us to conclude that the beast *has not yet come* on the world scene, but is yet future, then the persecution by this beast is still future as well. And *if this persecution is still future, then the scene in Revelation 20* where those "who had not worshiped the beast . . . and had not received its mark on their foreheads or their hands" (Rev. 20:4) *is still future as well*. This means that Revelation 20:1–6 does not describe the present church age but is best understood to refer to a future millennial reign of Christ.

These considerations combine to make a case in favor of premillennialism. If we are convinced of this position, it really is an incidental question whether the thousand-year period is thought to be a literal thousand years or simply a long period of time of indeterminate duration. And though we may not have much clarity on all the details of the nature of the millennium, we can be reasonably certain that there will be a future earthly reign of Christ that will be markedly different from this present age.

## E. The Time of the Great Tribulation

For those who are persuaded by the arguments in favor of premillennialism, one further question must be decided: Will Christ return before or after the "great tribulation"?

The expression "great tribulation" itself comes from Matthew 24:21 (and parallels), where Jesus says, "For then there will be *great tribulation*, such as has not been from the beginning of the world until now, no, and never will be." Historic premillennialism believes that Christ will return after that tribulation, for the passage continues, "Immediately after the tribulation of those days the sun will be darkened . . . then will appear the sign of the Son of man in heaven, and then all the tribes of the earth will mourn, and they will see the Son of man coming on the clouds of heaven with power and great glory" (Matt. 24:29–30). But, as explained above, in the nineteenth and twentieth centuries a variety of premillennialism that holds to a pretribulational coming of Christ became popular. This is often called a "pretribulation rapture" view, because it holds that when Christ first returns the church will be "raptured" or snatched up into heaven to be with him.

The arguments for such a pretribulation rapture are as follows:[36]

1. The entire period of the tribulation will be a time of the outpouring of God's wrath on all the earth. Therefore it would not be appropriate for Christians to be on the earth at that time.

2. Jesus promises in Revelation 3:10, *"I will keep you from the hour of trial which is coming on the whole world,* to try those who dwell upon the earth." This passage indicates that the church will be taken out of the world before that hour of trial comes.

3. If Christ returns *after* the tribulation and defeats all his enemies, then where will the unbelievers come from who are necessary to populate the millennial kingdom? The pretribulation position, however, envisages thousands of Jewish believers who have become Christians during the tribulation and who will go into the millennial kingdom in nonglorified bodies.

4. This view makes it possible to believe that Christ could come at any moment (his coming before the tribulation) and yet that many signs must be fulfilled before he comes (his coming after the tribulation, when the signs will be fulfilled).

Although it is not specifically an argument in favor of a pretribulation position, it must also be noted that pretribulationists then view the teaching about the tribulation in Matthew 24 and the warnings and encouragements given to believers in that situation as applying to Jewish believers during the tribulation, and not to the church generally.[37]

In response to these arguments, the following points may be made:

1. It is inconsistent with the New Testament descriptions of the tribulation to say that *all* the suffering that occurs during that time is specifically the result of the wrath of God. Much of the suffering is due to the fact that "wickedness is multiplied" (Matt. 24:12) and the fact that persecution of the church and opposition from Satan greatly increases during this period. Of course all Christians (whether Gentile or Jewish believers) will avoid the wrath of God at all times, but this does not mean they will avoid all suffering, even in times of intense hardship.

2. The fact that Jesus tells faithful believers in the church in Philadelphia (Rev. 3:10) that he will keep them from the hour of trial that is coming on the whole world is not strong enough evidence to say that the entire church will be taken out of the world before the tribulation. First, this statement is made to one specific church (Philadelphia) and should not be applied to the whole church at some future point in history. Moreover, "the hour of trial which is coming on the whole world" need not refer to the time of the great tribulation, but more likely refers to a time of great suffering and persecution that would come upon the entire Roman Empire or the entire inhabited world. Finally, the promise that the church in Philadelphia will be *guarded* does not imply that they will be taken out of the

---

[36]Much of the argumentation for the pretribulation rapture position is taken from the very thorough essay by Paul D. Feinberg, "The Case for Pretribulation Rapture Position" in *The Rapture: Pre-, Mid-, or Post-Tribulational?* pp. 45–86.

[37]Feinberg gives an additional argument on the differences between the passages he sees as describing the rapture (before the tribulation) and the passages he sees as describing the second coming (after the tribulation). However, most of these differences are not insurmountable contradictions, but only cases where an event is mentioned in one passage and not in another (a point well made by Douglas Moo in his "Response," pp. 99–101).

world, but simply that they will be kept faithful and will be guarded from being harmed by that period of suffering and testing.

3. It is no argument for the pretribulation view to say that there must be some people in nonglorified bodies who will enter the millennium, because (on a posttribulational view) when Christ comes at the end of the tribulation he will *defeat* all the forces arrayed against him, but that does not mean he will kill or annihilate all of them. Many will simply surrender without trusting Christ, and will thus enter the millennium as unbelievers. And during the entire period of the millennium no doubt many will be converted to Christ and become believers as well.

4. The pretribulational view is not the only one consistent with the ideas that Christ could come back at any time that there are signs that precede his return. The position presented in the previous chapter—that is unlikely but possible that the signs have been fulfilled—is also consistent with these ideas.[38]

But it must be said that behind this argument of pretribulationists is probably a more fundamental concern: the desire to preserve a distinction between *the church* (which they think will be taken up into heaven to be with Christ) and *Israel* (which they think will constitute the people of God on earth during the tribulation and then during the millennial kingdom).But, as we noted in an earlier chapter,[39] the New Testament does not support a distinction of this kind between Israel and the church. Hence it does not imply a need to see a distinction between these groups at the time of the tribulation and the millennium.

There is a variation of the pretribulation rapture position that is known as the *midtribulation rapture* view. It is defended by Gleason Archer in his essay, "The Case for the Mid-Seventieth-Week Rapture Position."[40] He sees the tribulation as separated into two halves. The first three and a half years are characterized by the wrath of man, and the church is present at that time. The second three and a half years are characterized by the wrath of God, and during that time the church is absent from the earth. The primary argument from Scripture to support a midtribulational rapture is the fact that in Daniel 7:25, 9:27, and 12:7 and 11, as well as in Revelation 12:14, the seven days or times indicated are cut in half, mentioning the interval of three and a half times or three and a half days in a symbolic week, thus indicating a period of three and a half years, after which God's people will be rescued from tribulation. Another argument in favor of this position is that it gives a heightened sense of expectancy of Christ's return, since three and a half years is a shorter period of time than seven years.

However, though the passages in Daniel do speak of an *interruption* of the seventieth week which Daniel predicts for the future, they do not give any clear indication that mid-way through the week believers will be removed from the earth.[41] It is also hard to see that the expectation of a three-and-a-half-year tribulation provides a much greater sense of imminence than does the expectation of a seven-year tribulation.

Finally, some objections to the *pre*tribulational rapture position can be stated in the form of arguments in favor of the *post*tribulational rapture view (the historic

[38]See chapter 54, pp. 1101–5.
[39]See chapter 44, pp. 859–63, on the question of a distinction between Israel and the church.
[40]In *The Rapture*, pp. 113–45.
[41]See Paul D. Feinberg, "Response," in *The Rapture*, pp. 147–50.

premillennial view that Christ will return after a period of tribulation on the earth):

1. The New Testament nowhere clearly says that the church will be taken out of the world before the tribulation. If this significant event were to happen, we might at least expect that explicit teaching to that effect would be found in the New Testament. Certainly Jesus tells us that he will come again and take us to be with himself (John 14:3), and Paul tells us that we shall be caught up in the clouds to meet the Lord in the air (1 Thess. 4:17), and that we shall be changed in the twinkling of an eye and receive resurrection bodies (1 Cor. 15:51–52), but each of these passages has been understood by believers throughout history as speaking not of a *secret* rapture of the church before the tribulation, but of a very visible *public* rapture (or "taking up") of the church to be with Christ just a few moments prior to his coming to earth *with them* to reign during the millennial kingdom (or, on the amillennial view, during the eternal state).[42]

Moreover, it is very difficult to understand 1 Thessalonians 4:17, the only passage that explicitly speaks of the fact that the church will be "caught up" (or "raptured"), to speak of the idea of a secret coming. It says, "The Lord himself will descend from heaven *with a cry of command, with the archangel's call, and with the sound of the trumpet of God*" (1 Thess. 4:16). Of these words Leon Morris rightly says, "It may be that from this he intends us to understand that the rapture will take place secretly, and that no one except the saints themselves will know what is going on. But one would hardly gather this from his words. It is difficult to see how he could more plainly describe something that is open and public."[43]

The doctrine of a pretribulation rapture is an inference from several passages, all of which are disputed. Moreover, even if one believes this doctrine to be in Scripture, it is taught with such little clarity that it was not discovered until the nineteenth century. This does not make it seem likely.

2. The tribulation is quite clearly linked with the Lord's return in some passages. First, the loud trumpet call to gather the elect in Matthew 24:31, the sound of the trumpet of God in 1 Thessalonians 4:16, and the last trumpet at which our bodies are changed in 1 Corinthians 15:51–52, all seem to be the same trumpet—the last trumpet that is blown just before the millennium. If it is indeed the "last trumpet" (1 Cor. 15:52), then it is hard to see how another loud trumpet call (Matt. 24:31) could follow it seven years later.

In addition, Matthew 24 is very difficult to understand as referring not to the church but to Jewish people who would be saved during the tribulation. Jesus is addressing *his disciples* (Matt. 24:1–4) and warning them of persecution and suffering to come. He tells them of the great tribulation to come, and then says that "immediately after the tribulation of those days" cosmic signs will appear and "then all the tribes of the earth will mourn, and they will see the Son of man

---

[42]When Paul says that "we who are alive, who are left, shall be caught up together with them in the clouds to *meet* the Lord in the air" (1 Thess. 4:17), he uses the Greek word *apantēsis*, for "meet," which is used in Greek literature outside the Bible to speak of citizens going out of a city to meet an arriving magistrate, then to return to the city with him. "The word *apantēsis* is to be understood as a technical term for a civic custom of antiquity whereby a public welcome was accorded by a city to important visitors" (Erik Peterson, *"apantēsis,"* TDNT, 1:380). Moulton and Milligan say, "The word seems to have been a kind of technical term for the official welcome of a newly arrived dignitary—a usage which accords excellently with its New Testament usage" (MM, p. 53).

[43]Leon Morris, *The First and Second Epistles to the Thessalonians,* p. 145.

coming on the clouds of heaven with power and great glory" (Matt. 24:30). But is it likely that Jesus, in saying all these things *to his disciples,* intended his words to apply not to the church but only to a future earthly kingdom of Jewish people who would be converted during the tribulation? How could the disciples have known that he had such a meaning in mind? Nor does it seem likely that the disciples are here as representatives of a future Jewish kingdom and not as representatives of the church, with whose founding they were so integrally connected as to be its foundation (Eph. 2:20).

3. Finally, the New Testament does not seem to justify the idea of two separate returns of Christ (once *for* his church before the tribulation and then seven years later *with* his church to bring judgment on unbelievers). Once again, no such view is explicitly taught in any passage, but it is simply an inference drawn from differences between various passages that describe Christ's return from different perspectives. But it is not at all difficult to see these passages as referring to a single event occurring at one time.[44]

It seems best to conclude, with the great majority of the church throughout history, that the church will go through the time of tribulation predicted by Jesus. We would probably not have chosen this path for ourselves, but the decision was not ours to make. And if God wills that any of us now alive remain on earth until the time of this great tribulation, then we should heed Peter's words, "If you are reproached for the name of Christ, you are blessed, because the spirit of glory and of God rests upon you" (1 Peter 4:14), and, "Christ also suffered for you, leaving you an example, that you should follow in his steps" (1 Peter 2:21). This idea that Christians should be prepared to endure suffering is also seen in Paul's words that we are fellow heirs with Christ, "provided we suffer with him in order that we may also be glorified with him" (Rom. 8:17). And we may remember that from the time of Noah to the time of the martyrdom of the early apostles, it has frequently been God's way to bring his people through suffering to glory, for thus he did even with his own Son. "For it was fitting that he, for whom and by whom all things exist, in bringing many sons to glory, should make the pioneer of their salvation perfect through suffering" (Heb. 2:10). It is from the Savior who himself has suffered more than any of his children will ever suffer that we have the admonition, "Do not fear what you are about to suffer. . . . Be faithful unto death, and I will give you the crown of life" (Rev. 2:10).

## QUESTIONS FOR PERSONAL APPLICATION

1. Before reading this chapter, did you have any conviction about whether Christ's return would be amillennial, postmillennial, or premillennial? And whether it would be posttribulational or pretribulational? If so, how has your view now changed, if at all?

2. Explain how your present view of the millennium affects your Christian life today. Similarly, explain how your view of the tribulation affects your present Christian life.

---

[44]See footnote 37 above; the primary passages are given on p. 1092.

3. What do you think it will feel like to be living on earth with a glorified body, and with Jesus Christ as King over the whole world? Can you describe in any detail some of the attitudes and emotional responses you will have toward various situations in such a kingdom? Do you really look forward to such a kingdom? (Your answers will differ somewhat depending on whether you expect a glorified body during the millennium or not until the eternal state.)

4. What might be both the positive and the negative results of a pretribulation rapture position in the everyday lives and attitudes of Christians? Similarly, what might be the positive and negative results of a posttribulation rapture position?

## SPECIAL TERMS

amillennialism
dispensational premillennialism
great tribulation
historic premillennialism
midtribulation rapture
millennium
postmillennialism

posttribulational premillennialism
posttribulation rapture
premillennialism
pretribulational premillennialism
pretribulation rapture
rapture

## BIBLIOGRAPHY

(For an explanation of this bibliography see the note on the bibliography to chapter 1, p. 38. Complete bibliographical data may be found on pp. 1223–29.)

### Sections in Evangelical Systematic Theologies

1. Anglican (Episcopalian)
       1882–92     Litton, 581–85
2. Arminian (Wesleyan or Methodist)
           1940     Wiley, 3:280–319
           1983     Carter, 2:1118–27
3. Baptist
           1767     Gill, 2:268–302
           1907     Strong, 1010–15
           1917     Mullins, 466–72
       1983–85     Erickson, 1205–24
4. Dispensational
           1947     Chafer, 4:264–78; 5:315–58
           1949     Thiessen, 351–75, 391–95
           1986     Ryrie, 439–52, 461–511
5. Lutheran
           1934     Mueller, 621–25
6. Reformed (or Presbyterian)

```
    1724-58    Edwards, 2:278-313
    1871-73    Hodge, 3:861-68
 1887-1921    Warfield, BD, 643-64
       1938    Berkhof, 695-707
       1962    Buswell, 2:346-538
```
7. Renewal (or charismatic/Pentecostal)
```
    1988-92    Williams, 3:421-44
```

## Sections in Representative Roman Catholic Systematic Theologies

(no explicit treatment)

## Other Works

Adams, Jay. *The Time Is at Hand.* Phillipsburg, N.J.: Presbyterian and Reformed, 1970. (Amillennial.)

Allis, O. T. *Prophecy and the Church.* Philadelphia: Presbyterian and Reformed, 1945. (Amillennial.)

Archer, Gleason, Paul Feinberg, Douglas Moo, and Richard Reiter. *The Rapture: Pre-, Mid-, or Post-tribulational?* Grand Rapids: Zondervan, 1984. (Contains well-argued essays representing the three different positions.)

Bauckham, R. J. "Millennium." In *NDT,* pp. 428-30.

Beechick, Allen. *The Pre-Tribulation Rapture.* Denver: Accent, 1980.

Berkouwer, G. C. *The Return of Christ.* Trans. by James Van Oosterom. Ed. by Marlin J. Van Elderen. Grand Rapids: Eerdmans, 1972.

Boettner, Lorraine. *The Millennium.* Philadelphia: Presbyterian and Reformed, 1957. (Postmillennial.)

Clouse, F. G. "Rapture of the Church." In *EDT,* pp. 908-10.

Clouse, Robert G., ed. *The Meaning of the Millennium: Four Views.* Downers Grove, Ill.: InterVarsity Press, 1977. (The chapters by Ladd and Hoekema are excellent statements of the classical premillennial and amillennial positions.)

Davis, John Jefferson. *Christ's Victorious Kingdom.* Grand Rapids: Baker, 1986. (This is an excellent argument for the postmillennial position.)

Erickson, Millard. *Contemporary Options in Eschatology.* Grand Rapids: Baker, 1977.

Feinberg, Charles L. *Millennialism: The Two Major Views.* Chicago: Moody Press, 1980. (Pretribulational premillennial.)

Grier, W. J. *The Momentous Event.* London: Banner of Truth, 1970.

Gundry, R. H. *The Church and the Tribulation.* Grand Rapids: Zondervan, 1973. (Posttribulational premillennial.)

Hendriksen, William. *More Than Conquerors: An Interpretation of the Book of Revelation.* London: Tyndale Press, 1962. (Amillennial.)

Hoekema, Anthony A. *The Bible and the Future.* Grand Rapids: Eerdmans, 1979, pp. 109-238. (Amillennial.)

Kik, J. Marcellus. *An Eschatology of Victory.* Nutley, N.J.: Presbyterian and Reformed, 1974. (Postmillennial.)

Ladd, George Eldon. *The Blessed Hope*. Grand Rapids: Eerdmans, 1956. (Classic or posttribulational premillennial.)

Lightner, Robert P. *The Last Days Handbook: A Comprehensive Guide to Understanding the Different Views of Prophecy. Who Believes What About Prophecy and Why*. Nashville, Tenn.: Thomas Nelson, 1990.

McClain, Alva J. *The Greatness of the Kingdom*. Grand Rapids: Zondervan, 1959. (Pretribulational premillennial.)

Murray, Iain. *The Puritan Hope*. London: Banner of Truth, 1971. (Postmillennial.)

Pentecost, J. Dwight. *Things to Come*. Findlay, Ohio: Dunham, 1958. (Pretribulational premillennial.)

Poythress, Vern. *Understanding Dispensationalists*. Grand Rapids: Zondervan, 1987. (Amillennial.)

Travis, S. H. "Eschatology." In *NDT*, pp. 228–31.

Vos, Geerhardus. *The Pauline Eschatology*. Grand Rapids: Eerdmans, 1961. (Amillennial.)

Walvoord, John F. *The Blessed Hope and the Tribulation*. Grand Rapids: Zondervan, 1976. (Pretribulational premillennial.)

———. *The Millennial Kingdom*. Findlay, Ohio: Dunham, 1959. (Pretribulational premillennial.)

## SCRIPTURE MEMORY PASSAGE

**Revelation 20:4–6:** *Then I saw thrones, and seated on them were those to whom judgment was committed. Also I saw the souls of those who had been beheaded for their testimony to Jesus and for the word of God, and who had not worshiped the beast or its image and had not received its mark on their foreheads or their hands. They came to life, and reigned with Christ a thousand years. The rest of the dead did not come to life until the thousand years were ended. This is the first resurrection. Blessed and holy is he who shares in the first resurrection! Over such the second death has no power, but they shall be priests of God and of Christ, and they shall reign with him a thousand years.*

## HYMN

### "Jesus Shall Reign Where'er the Sun"

This hymn by Isaac Watts beautifully describes the reign of Christ over the whole earth. Whether our personal convictions on the millennium lead us to understand this hymn as referring to the millennium or to the eternal state, in either case it gives an excellent picture of the kingdom for which our hearts long and the blessings that will come when Jesus is King over the earth.

Jesus shall reign wherever the sun
    Does his successive journeys run;
His kingdom stretch from shore to shore,
    Til moons shall wax and wane no more.

For him shall endless prayer be made,
    And praises throng to crown his head;
His name, like sweet perfume, shall rise
    With every morning sacrifice.

People and realms of every tongue
    Dwell on his love with sweetest song;
And infant voices shall proclaim
    Their early blessings on his name.

Blessings abound where'er he reigns;
    The pris'ner leaps to loose his chains,
The weary find eternal rest,
    And all the sons of want are blest.

Let every creature rise and bring
    Peculiar honors to our King,
Angels descend with songs again,
    And earth repeat the loud amen.

AUTHOR: ISAAC WATTS, 1719

# Chapter 56

# The Final Judgment and Eternal Punishment

*Who will be judged? What is hell?*

## EXPLANATION AND SCRIPTURAL BASIS

### A. The Fact of Final Judgment

**1. Scriptural Evidence for a Final Judgment.** Scripture frequently affirms the fact that there will be a great final judgment of believers and unbelievers. They will stand before the judgment seat of Christ in resurrected bodies and hear his proclamation of their eternal destiny.

The final judgment is vividly portrayed in John's vision in Revelation:

> *Then I saw a great white throne and him who sat upon it;* from his presence earth and sky fled away, and no place was found for them. *And I saw the dead, great and small, standing before the throne, and books were opened.* Also another book was opened, which is the book of life. *And the dead were judged by what was written in the books, by what they had done.* And the sea gave up the dead in it, death and hades gave up the dead in them, and all were judged by what they had done. Then death and hades were thrown into the lake of fire. This is the second death, the lake of fire; and if anyone's name was not found written in the book of life, he was thrown into the lake of fire. (Rev. 20:11–15)

Many other passages teach this final judgment. Paul tells the Greek philosophers in Athens that God "Now . . . commands all men everywhere to repent, because *he has fixed a day on which he will judge the world in righteousness* by a man whom he has appointed, and of this he has given assurance to all men by raising him from the dead" (Acts 17:30–31).[1] Similarly, Paul talks about "the day of wrath when God's righteous judgment will be revealed" (Rom. 2:5). Other passages speak clearly of a coming day of judgment (see Matt. 10:15; 11:22, 24; 12:36; 25:31–46; 1 Cor. 4:5; Heb. 6:2; 2 Peter 2:4; Jude 6; et al.).

This final judgment is the culmination of many precursors in which God rewarded righteousness or punished unrighteousness throughout history. While

---

[1]It is interesting that Paul proclaimed eternal judgment to unbelieving Gentiles who had little if any knowledge of the teachings of the Old Testament. Paul also argued about "future judgment" (Acts 24:25) before another unbeliever, the Roman governor Felix. In both cases Paul apparently realized that the brute fact that a day of accountability before God was coming to all men would give to his hearers a sobering realization that their eternal destiny was at stake as they listened to him preach about Jesus.

he brought blessing and deliverance from danger to those who were faithful to
him, including Abel, Noah, Abraham, Isaac, Jacob, Moses, David, and the faithful
among the people of Israel, he also from time to time brought judgment on those
who persisted in disobedience and unbelief: his judgments included the flood, the
dispersion of the people from the tower of Babel, the judgments on Sodom and
Gomorrah, and continuing judgments throughout history, both on individuals
(Rom. 1:18–32) and on nations (Isa. 13–23; et al.) who persisted in sin.
Moreover, in the unseen spiritual realm he brought judgment on angels who
sinned (2 Peter 2:4). Peter reminds us that God's judgments have been carried
out periodically and with certainty, and this reminds us that a final judgment is yet
coming, for "the Lord knows how to rescue the godly from trial, and to keep the
unrighteousness under punishment until the day of judgment, and especially those
who indulge in the lust of defiling passion and despise authority" (2 Peter 2:9–
10).

**2. Will There Be More Than One Judgment?** According to a dispensational
view, there is more than one judgment to come. For example, dispensationalists
would not see the final judgment in Matthew 25:31–46:

> When the Son of Man comes in his glory, and all the angels with him, then he will
> sit on his glorious throne. *Before him will be gathered all the nations,* and he will
> separate them one from another as a shepherd separates the sheep from the goats,
> and he will place the sheep at his right hand, but the goats at his left. Then the King
> will say to those at his right hand, "Come, O blessed of my father, inherit the
> kingdom prepared for you from the foundation of the world; for I was hungry and
> you gave me food. . . . As you did it to one of the least of these my brothers, you
> did it to me." Then he will say to those at his left hand, "Depart from me, you
> cursed, into the eternal fire prepared for the devil and his angels; for I was hungry
> and you gave me no food. . . . As you did it not to one of the least of these, you did
> it not to me." And they will go away into eternal punishment, but the righteous
> into eternal life.

From a dispensational perspective, this passage does not refer to final judgment
(the "great white throne judgment" spoken of in Rev. 20:11–15), but rather to a
judgment that comes after the tribulation and before the beginning of the
millennium. They say that this will be a *"judgment of the nations"* in which the
nations are judged according to how they have treated the Jewish people during
the tribulation. Those who have treated the Jews well and are willing to submit to
Christ will enter into the millennium, and those who have not will be refused
entrance.

Thus, in a dispensationalist view there are different judgments: (a) a "judgment
of the nations" (Matt. 25:31–46) to determine who enters the millennium; (b) a
"judgment of believers' works" (sometimes called the *bēma* judgment after the
Greek word for "judgment seat" in 2 Cor. 5:10) in which Christians will receive
degrees of reward; and (c) a "great white throne judgment" at the end of the
millennium (Rev. 20:11–15) to declare eternal punishments for unbelievers.[2]
The view taken in this book is that these three passages all speak of the same
final judgment, not of three separate judgments. With regard to Matthew 25:31–

---

[2]Lewis Sperry Chafer, *Systematic Theology*, 7: 213–17, who includes other judgments.

46 in particular, it is unlikely that the dispensational view is correct: There is no mention of entering into the millennium in this passage. Moreover, the judgments pronounced speak not of entrance into the millennial kingdom on earth or exclusion from that kingdom but of eternal destinies of people: "Inherit the kingdom prepared for you from the foundation of the world. . . . Depart from me, you cursed, into the eternal fire prepared for the devil and his angels. . . . And they will go away into *eternal punishment,* but the righteous into *eternal life*" (vv. 34, 41, 46). Finally, it would be inconsistent with God's ways throughout Scripture to deal with people's *eternal* destiny on the basis of what nation they belong to, for unbelieving nations have believers within them, and nations that exhibit more conformity to God's revealed will still have many wicked within them. And "God shows no partiality" (Rom. 2:11). Though indeed "all the nations" are gathered before Christ's throne in this scene (Matt. 25:32), the picture of judgment is one of judgment on individuals (sheep are separated from goats, and those individuals who treated Christ's brothers kindly are welcomed into the kingdom while those who rejected them are rejected, vv. 35–40, 42–45).

## B. The Time of Final Judgment

The final judgment will occur after the millennium and the rebellion that occurs at the end of it. John pictures the millennial kingdom and the removal of Satan from influence on the earth in Revelation 20:1–6 (see the discussion in the previous two chapters) and then says that "when the thousand years are ended, Satan will be loosed from his prison and will come out to deceive the nations . . . to gather them for battle" (Rev. 20:7–8). After God decisively defeats this final rebellion (Rev. 20:9–10), John tells us that judgment will follow: "Then I saw a great white throne and him who sat upon it" (v. 11).

## C. The Nature of the Final Judgment

**1. Jesus Christ Will Be the Judge.** Paul speaks of "Jesus Christ who is to judge the living and the dead" (2 Tim. 4:1). Peter says that Jesus Christ "is the one ordained by God to be the judge of the living and the dead" (Acts 10:42; compare 17:31; Matt. 25:31–33). This right to act as judge over the whole universe is something that the Father has given to the Son: "The Father . . . has given him authority to execute judgment, because he is the Son of Man" (John 5:26–27).

**2. Unbelievers Will Be Judged.** It is clear that all unbelievers will stand before Christ for judgment, for this judgment includes "the dead, great and small" (Rev. 20:12), and Paul says that "on the day of wrath when God's righteous judgment will be revealed," "he will render to every man according to his works . . . for those who are factious and do not obey the truth, but obey wickedness, there will be wrath and fury" (Rom. 2:5–7).

This judgment of unbelievers will include *degrees of punishment,* for we read that the dead were judged "by what they had done" (Rev. 20:12, 13), and this judgment according to what people had done must therefore involve an evaluation of the works that people have done.[3] Similarly, Jesus says:

> And that servant who knew his master's will, but did not make ready or act according to his will, shall receive a severe beating. But he who did not know, and did what deserved a beating, shall receive a light beating" (Luke 12:47–48).

When Jesus says to the cities of Chorazin and Bethsaida, "It shall be *more tolerable* on the day of judgment for Tyre and Sidon than for you" (Matt. 11:22; compare v. 24), or when he says that the scribes "will receive the *greater condemnation*" (Luke 20:47), he implies that there will be degrees of punishment on the last day.

In fact, every wrong deed done will be remembered and taken account of in the punishment that is meted out on that day, because "on the day of judgment men will render account for every careless word they utter" (Matt. 12:36). Every word spoken, every deed done will be brought to light and receive judgment: "For God will bring every deed into judgment, with every secret thing, whether good or evil" (Eccl. 12:14).

As these verses indicate, on the day of judgment the secrets of people's hearts will be revealed and made public. Paul speaks of the day when "God judges the secrets of men by Christ Jesus" (Rom. 2:16; compare Luke 8:17). "Nothing is covered up that will not be revealed, or hidden that will not be known. Therefore *whatever you have said in the dark shall be heard in the light, and what you have whispered in private rooms shall be proclaimed upon the housetops*" (Luke 12:2–3).

**3. Believers Will Be Judged.** In writing to Christians Paul says, *"We shall all stand before the judgment seat of God.* . . . Each of us shall give account of himself to God" (Rom. 14:10, 12). He also tells the Corinthians, "For *we must all appear before the judgment seat of Christ, that each one may receive what is due him for the things done while in the body,* whether good or bad" (2 Cor. 5:10; cf. Rom. 2:6–11; Rev. 20:12, 15). In addition, the picture of the final judgment in Matthew 25:31–46 includes Christ separating the sheep from the goats, and rewarding those who receive his blessing.

It is important to realize that this judgment of believers will be a judgment to evaluate and bestow various degrees of reward (see below), but the fact that they will face such a judgment should never cause believers to fear that they will be eternally condemned. Jesus says, "He who hears my word and believes him who sent me, has eternal life; *he does not come into judgment,* but has passed from death to life" (John 5:24). Here "judgment" must be understood in the sense of eternal condemnation and death, since it is contrasted with passing from death into life. At the day of final judgment more than at any other time, it is of utmost importance that "there is therefore now *no condemnation for those who are in Christ*

---

[3]The fact that there will be degrees of punishment for unbelievers according to their works does not mean that unbelievers can ever do enough good to merit God's approval or earn salvation, for salvation only comes as a free gift to those who trust in Christ: "He who believes in him is not condemned; he who does not believe is condemned already, because he has not believed in the name of the only Son of God" (John 3:18).

For a discussion of the fact that there will be no "second chance" for people to accept Christ after they die, see chapter 41, pp. 822–24.

*Jesus*" (Rom. 8:1). Thus the day of judgment can be portrayed as one in which believers are rewarded and unbelievers are punished:

> The nations raged, but your wrath came, and the time for the dead to be judged, *for rewarding your servants*, the prophets and saints, and those who fear your name, both small and great, and for destroying the destroyers of the earth. (Rev. 11:18)

Will all the secret words and deeds of believers, and all their sins, also be revealed on that last day? It seems that this is so, because in writing to *believers* about the day of judgment he says that when the Lord comes he will "*bring to light the things now hidden in darkness* and will disclose the purposes of the heart. Then every man will receive his commendation from God" (1 Cor. 4:5; compare Col. 3:25). Certainly this fact should provide a motive for godly living, and Paul uses it that way in 2 Corinthians 5:9–10: "*We make it our aim to please him. For* we must all appear before the judgment seat of Christ." But it should not cause terror or alarm on the part of believers, because even sins that are made public on that day will be made public as sins that have been *forgiven*, and thereby they will be the occasion for giving glory to God for the richness of his grace.

Scripture also teaches that there will be *degrees of reward for believers*. Paul encourages the Corinthians to be careful how they build the church on the foundation that has already been laid—Jesus Christ himself.

> Now if anyone builds on the foundation with gold, silver, precious stones, wood, hay, straw—each man's work will become manifest; for the Day will disclose it, because it will be revealed with fire, and the fire will test what sort of work each one has done. *If the work which any man has built on the foundation survives, he will receive a reward*. If any man's work is burned up, he will suffer loss, though he himself will be saved, but only as through fire. (1 Cor. 3:12–15)

Paul similarly says of Christians that "we must all appear before the judgment seat of Christ, that each one may receive *what is due him for the things done while in the body*, whether good or bad" (2 Cor. 5:10), again implying degrees of reward for what we have done in this life. Likewise, in the parable of the pounds, the one who made ten pounds more was told, "You shall have authority over ten cities," and the one whose pound had made five pounds more was told, "And you are to be over five cities" (Luke 19:17, 19). Many other passages likewise teach or imply degrees of reward for believers at the final judgment.[4]

But we must guard against misunderstanding here: Even though there will be degrees of reward in heaven, the joy of each person will be full and complete for eternity. If we ask how this can be when there are different degrees of reward, it simply shows that our perception of happiness is based on the assumption that happiness depends on what we possess or the status or power that we have. In actuality, however, our true happiness consists in delighting in God and rejoicing in the status and recognition that he has given us. The foolishness of thinking that only those who have been highly rewarded and given great status will be fully happy in heaven is seen when we realize that no matter how great a reward we are

---

[4]See also Dan. 12:2; Matt. 6:20–21; 19:21; Luke 6:22–23; 12:18–21, 32, 42–48; 14:13–14; 1 Cor. 3:8; 9:18; 13:3; 15:19, 29–32, 58; Gal. 6:9–10; Eph. 6:7–8; Col. 3:23–24; 1 Tim. 6:18; Heb. 10:34, 35; 11:10, 14–16, 26, 35; 1 Peter 1:4; 2 John 8; Rev. 11:18; 22:12; cf. also Matt. 5:46; 6:2–6, 16–18, 24; Luke 6:35.

given, there will always be those with greater rewards, or who have higher status and authority, including the apostles, the heavenly creatures, and Jesus Christ and God himself. Therefore if highest status were essential for people to be fully happy, no one but God would be fully happy in heaven, which is certainly an incorrect idea. Moreover, those with greater reward and honor in heaven, those nearest the throne of God, delight not in their status but only in the privilege of falling down before God's throne to worship him (see Rev. 4:10–11).

It would be morally and spiritually beneficial for us to have a greater consciousness of this clear New Testament teaching on degrees of heavenly reward. Rather than making us competitive with one another, it would cause us to help and encourage one another that we all may increase our heavenly reward, for God has an infinite capacity to bring blessing to us all, and we are all members of one another (cf. 1 Cor. 12:26–27). We would more eagerly heed the admonition of the author of Hebrews, "*Let us consider how to stir up one another to love and good works,* not neglecting to meet together, as is the habit of some, but *encouraging one another,* and all the more as you see the Day drawing near" (Heb. 10:24–25). Moreover, in our own lives a heartfelt seeking of future heavenly reward would motivate us to work wholeheartedly for the Lord at whatever task he calls us to, whether great or small, paid or unpaid. It would also make us long for his approval rather than for wealth or success. It would motivate us to work at building up the church on the one foundation, Jesus Christ (1 Cor. 3:10–15).

**4. Angels Will Be Judged.** Peter says that the rebellious angels have been committed to pits of nether gloom "to be kept until the judgment" (2 Peter 2:4), and Jude says that rebellious angels have been kept by God "until the judgment of the great day" (Jude 6). This means that at least the *rebellious* angels or demons will be subject to judgment on that last day as well.

Scripture does not clearly indicate whether righteous angels will undergo some kind of evaluation of their service as well, but it is possible that they are included in Paul's statement "Do you not know that *we are to judge angels?*" (1 Cor. 6:3). It is probable that this includes righteous angels because there is no indication in the context that Paul is speaking of demons or fallen angels, and the word "angel" without further qualification in the New Testament would normally be understood to refer to righteous angels. But the text is not explicit enough to give us certainty.

**5. We Will Help in the Work of Judgment.** It is a rather amazing aspect of New Testament teaching that we (believers) will take part in the process of judgment. Paul says:

Do you not know that *the saints will judge the world?* And if the world is to be judged by you, are you incompetent to try trivial cases? Do you not know that *we are to judge angels?* How much more, matters pertaining to this life? (1 Cor. 6:2–3)

It might be argued that this simply means we will be watching the declaration of judgment by Christ and approving it, but this does not seem to fit the context well, for here Paul is encouraging the Corinthians to settle legal disputes among themselves rather than taking them to court before unbelievers. In this very context he says, "Can it be that there is no man among you wise enough to decide between members of the brotherhood, but brother goes to law against brother, and that before unbelievers?" (1 Cor. 6:5–6). This kind of judgment certainly involves careful evaluation and wise discernment. And this implies that such careful evaluation and discernment will be exercised by us in judging angels and in judging the world on the day of final judgment.

This is similar to the teaching of Revelation 20, where John says that he saw thrones, and "seated on them were *those to whom judgment was committed*" (Rev. 20:4). Although the text does not explain the identity of those seated on the thrones, the fact that they are mentioned in the plural indicates that Christ does not reserve every aspect of the process of judging for himself alone. Indeed, he tells his twelve disciples that they will "sit on twelve thrones, *judging* the twelve tribes of Israel" (Matt. 19:28; compare Luke 22:30). This accords with the fact that throughout the history of redemption God has from time to time given the right to exercise judgment into the hands of human authorities, whether Moses and the elders who assisted him, the judges of Israel whom God raised up during the period of the judges, the wise kings such as David and Solomon, the civil government of many nations (see Rom. 13:1–7; 1 Peter 2:13–14), or those who have authority to rule and govern within the church and to oversee the exercise of church discipline.

## D. Necessity of Final Judgment

Since when believers die they pass immediately into the presence of God, and when unbelievers die they pass into a state of separation from God and the endurance of punishment,[5] we may wonder why God has a time of final judgment established at all. Berkhof wisely points out that the final judgment is not for the purpose of letting God find out the condition of our hearts or the pattern of conduct of our lives, for he already knows that in every detail. Berkhof rather says of the final judgment:

> It will serve the purpose rather of displaying before all rational creatures the declarative glory of God in a formal, forensic act, which magnifies on the one hand His holiness and righteousness, and on the other hand, His grace and mercy. Moreover, it should be borne in mind that the judgment at the last day will differ from that of the death of each individual in more than one respect. It will not be secret, but public; it will not pertain to the soul only, but also to the body; it will not have reference to a single individual, but to all men.[6]

## E. Justice of God in the Final Judgment

Scripture clearly affirms that God will be entirely just in his judgment and no one will be able to complain against him on that day. God is the one who "judges each one impartially according to his deeds" (1 Peter 1:17), and "God shows no

---

[5]See chapter 41, pp. 816–24, for evidence supporting the idea that believers go immediately into God's presence when they die, and unbelievers go immediately to a place of punishment separated from God. (See also Luke 16:24–26; Heb. 9:27.)

[6]Berkhof, *Systematic Theology*, p. 731.

partiality" (Rom. 2:11; compare Col. 3:25). For this reason, on the last day "every mouth" will be "stopped," and the whole world will be "held accountable to God" (Rom. 3:19), with no one being able to complain that God has treated him or her unfairly. In fact, one of the great blessings of the final judgment will be that saints and angels will see demonstrated in millions of lives the absolutely pure justice of God, and this will be a source of praise to him for all eternity. At the time of the judgment on wicked Babylon, there will be great praise in heaven, for John says, "I heard what seemed to be the loud voice of a great multitude in heaven, crying, *'Hallelujah! Salvation and glory and power belong to our God, for his judgments are true and just'*" (Rev. 19:1–2).

### F. Moral Application of the Final Judgment

The doctrine of final judgment has several positive moral influences in our lives.

**1. The Doctrine of Final Judgment Satisfies Our Inward Sense of a Need for Justice in the World.** The fact that there will be a final judgment assures us that ultimately God's universe is *fair*, for God is in control, and he keeps accurate records and renders just judgment. When Paul tells slaves to be submissive to their masters, he reassures them, "For the wrongdoer will be paid back for the wrong he has done, and there is no partiality" (Col 3:25). When the picture of a final judgment mentions the fact that "books were opened" (Rev. 20:12; compare Mal. 3:16), it reminds us (whether the books are literal or symbolic) that a permanent and accurate record of all our deeds has been kept by God, and ultimately all accounts will be settled and all will be made right.

**2. The Doctrine of Final Judgment Enables Us to Forgive Others Freely.** We realize that it is not up to us to take revenge on others who have wronged us, or even to want to do so, because God has reserved that right for himself. "Beloved, never avenge yourselves, but leave it to the wrath of God, for it is written, *'Vengeance is mine, I will repay, says the Lord'*" (Rom. 12:19). In this way whenever we have been wronged, we can give into God's hands any desire to harm or pay back the person who has wronged us, knowing that every wrong in the universe will ultimately be paid for—either it will turn out to have been paid for by Christ when he died on the cross (if the wrongdoer becomes a Christian), or it will be paid for at the final judgment (for those who do not trust in Christ for salvation). But in either case we can give the situation into God's hands, and then pray that the wrongdoer will trust Christ for salvation and thereby receive forgiveness of his or her sins. This thought should keep us from harboring bitterness or resentment in our hearts for injustices we have suffered that have not been made right: God is just, and we can leave these situations in his hands, knowing that he will someday right all wrongs and give absolutely fair rewards and punishments. In this way we are following in the example of Christ, who "when he was reviled, he did not revile in return; when he suffered, he did not threaten; but *he trusted to him who judges justly*" (1 Peter 2:22–23). He also prayed, "Father, forgive them, for they know not what they do" (Luke 23:34; compare Acts 7:60, where Stephen followed Jesus' example in praying for those who put him to death).

**3. The Doctrine of the Final Judgment Provides a Motive for Righteous Living.** For believers, the final judgment is an incentive to faithfulness and good works, not as a means of earning forgiveness of sins, but as a means of gaining greater eternal reward.[7] This is a healthy and good motive for us—Jesus tells us, "Lay up for yourselves treasures in heaven" (Matt. 6:20)—though it runs counter to the popular views of our secular culture, a culture that does not really believe in heaven or eternal rewards at all.

For unbelievers, the doctrine of final judgment still provides some moral restraint on their lives. If in a society there is a widespread general acknowledgment that all will someday give account to the Creator of the universe for their lives, some "fear of God" will characterize many people's lives. By contrast, those who have no deep consciousness of final judgment give themselves up to greater and greater evil, demonstrating that "there is *no fear of God* before their eyes" (Rom. 3:18). Those who deny the final judgment, Peter says, will be "scoffers" who "will come in the last days with scoffing, *following their own passions* and saying, 'Where is the promise of his coming?'" (2 Peter 3:3–4). He also declares that evildoers who "are surprised that you do not now join them in the same wild profligacy," and "who abuse you" will nonetheless "give account to him who is ready to judge the living and the dead" (1 Peter 4:4–5). An awareness of final judgment is both a comfort to believers and a warning to unbelievers not to continue in their evil ways.

**4. The Doctrine of Final Judgment Provides a Great Motive for Evangelism.** The decisions made by people in this life will affect their destiny for all eternity, and it is right that our hearts feel and our mouths echo the sentiment of the appeal of God through Ezekiel, *"Turn back, turn back from your evil ways; for why will you die, O house of Israel?"* (Ezek. 33:11). In fact, Peter indicates that the delay of the Lord's return is due to the fact that God "is forbearing toward you, not wishing that any should perish, but that all should reach repentance" (2 Peter 3:9).

## G. Hell

It is appropriate to discuss the doctrine of hell in connection with the doctrine of final judgment. We may define hell as follows: *Hell is a place of eternal conscious punishment for the wicked.* Scripture teaches in several passages that there is such a place. At the end of the parable of the talents, the master says, "Cast the worthless servant into the outer darkness; there men will weep and gnash their teeth" (Matt. 25:30). This is one among several indications that there will be consciousness of punishment after the final judgment. Similarly, at the judgment the king will say to some, "Depart from me, you cursed, into *the eternal fire* prepared for the devil and his angels" (Matt. 25:41), and Jesus says that those thus condemned "will go away into *eternal punishment,* but the righteous into eternal life" (Matt. 25:46).[8]

---

[7]The idea of working for greater heavenly reward is a frequent theme in the New Testament: see the verses listed at footnote 4 above.

[8]The word translated "punishment" here is *kolasis,* which is used elsewhere of great physical suffering or torture that was endured by persecuted Christians (*Martyrdom of Polycarp* 2.4; compare Ignatius, *To the Romans* 5.3). At other times it simply refers to divine punishment in general, without specification of the nature of that punishment (cf. BAGD, pp. 440–41).

In this text, the parallel between "eternal life" and "eternal punishment" indicates that both states will be without end.[9]

Jesus refers to hell as "the unquenchable fire" (Mark 9:43), and says that hell is a place "where their worm does not die, and the fire is not quenched" (Mark 9:48).[10] The story of the rich man and Lazarus also indicates a horrible consciousness of punishment:

> The rich man also died and was buried; and in Hades, being in torment, he lifted up his eyes, and saw Abraham far off and Lazarus in his bosom, and he called out, "Father Abraham, have mercy upon me, and send Lazarus to dip the end of his finger in water and cool my tongue; for I am in anguish in this flame." (Luke 16:22–24)

He then begs Abraham to send Lazarus to his father's house, "for I have five brothers, so that he may warn them, lest they also come into *this place of torment*" (Luke 16:28).

When we turn to Revelation, the descriptions of this eternal punishment are also very explicit:

> If anyone worships the beast and its image, and receives a mark on his forehead or on his hand, he also shall drink the wine of God's wrath, poured unmixed into the cup of his anger, and he shall be tormented with fire and sulphur in the presence of the holy angels and in the presence of the Lamb. *And the smoke of their torment goes up forever and ever; and they have no rest, day or night, these worshipers of the beast and its image,* and whoever receives the mark of its name. (Rev. 14:9–11)

This passage very clearly affirms the idea of eternal conscious punishment of unbelievers.

With respect to the judgment on the wicked city of Babylon, a large multitude in heaven cries, "Hallelujah! *The smoke from her goes up for ever and ever*" (Rev. 19:3). After the final rebellion of Satan is crushed, we read, "The devil who had deceived them was thrown into the lake of fire and sulphur where the beast and the false prophet were, and *they will be tormented day and night for ever and ever*" (Rev. 20:10). This passage is also significant in connection with Matthew 25:41, in which unbelievers are sent "into the eternal fire prepared for the devil and his angels." These verses should make us realize the immensity of the evil that is found in sin and rebellion against God, and the magnitude of the holiness and the justice of God that calls forth this kind of punishment.

The idea that there will be *eternal* conscious punishment of unbelievers has been denied recently even by some evangelical theologians.[11] It has previously been denied by the Seventh Day Adventist Church and by various individuals throughout church history. Those who deny eternal conscious punishment often advocate *"annihilationism,"* a teaching that, after the wicked have suffered the

---

[9]These texts and others which are quoted in the following paragraphs clearly indicate that the Bible does not teach *universalism* (the doctrine that all people will ultimately be saved).

[10]Compare Isa. 66:24, speaking of those who have rebelled against God: "For their worm shall not die, and their fire shall not be quenched."

[11]See Philip E. Hughes, *The True Image: The Origin and Destiny of Man in Christ* (Grand Rapids: Eerdmans, 1989), pp. 405–407; David L. Edwards and John R. W. Stott, *Essentials: A Liberal-Evangelical Dialogue* (London: Hodder and Stoughton, 1988), pp. 275–76; Clark Pinnock, "The Destruction of the Finally Impenitent," *CThRev* 4 (Spring 1990), pp. 243–59.

penalty of God's wrath for a time, God will "annihilate" them so that they no longer exist.[12] Many who believe in annihilationism also hold to the reality of final judgment and punishment for sin, but they argue that after sinners have suffered for a certain period of time, bearing the wrath of God against their sin, they will finally cease to exist. The punishment will therefore be "conscious" but it will not be "eternal."

Arguments advanced in favor of annihilationism are: (1) the biblical references to the *destruction* of the wicked, which, some say, implies that they will no longer exist after they are destroyed (Phil. 3:19; 1 Thess. 5:3; 2 Thess. 1:9; 2 Peter 3:7; et al.); (2) the apparent inconsistency of eternal conscious punishment with the *love of God;* (3) the apparent injustice involved in the *disproportion* between sins committed in time and punishment that is eternal; and (4) the fact that the *continuing presence of evil creatures in God's universe* will eternally mar the perfection of a universe that God created to reflect his glory.

In response, it must be said that the passages which speak of *destruction* (such as Phil. 3:19; 1 Thess. 5:3; 2 Thess. 1:9; and 2 Peter 3:7) do not necessarily imply the cessation of existence, for in these passages the terms used for "destruction" do not necessarily imply a ceasing to exist or some kind of annihilation, but can simply be ways of referring to the harmful and destructive effects of final judgment on unbelievers.[13]

With respect to the argument from the love of God, the same difficulty in reconciling God's love with eternal punishment would seem to be present in reconciling God's love with the idea of divine punishment at all, and, conversely, if (as Scripture abundantly testifies) it is consistent for God to punish the wicked for a certain length of time after the last judgment, then there seems to be no necessary reason why it would be inconsistent of God to inflict the same punishment for an unending period of time.

This kind of reasoning may lead some people to adopt another kind of annihilationism, one in which there is no conscious suffering at all, not even for a brief time, and the only punishment is that unbelievers cease to exist after they die. But, in response, it may be wondered whether this kind of immediate annihilation can really be called a punishment, since there would be no consciousness of pain. In fact, the guarantee that there would be a cessation of existence would seem to many people, especially those who are suffering and in difficulty in this life, to be

---

[12]A variation of the view that God will eventually annihilate unbelievers (annihilationism proper) is the view called *"conditional immortality,"* the idea that God has created people so that they only have immortality (the power to live forever) if they accept Christ as Savior. Those who do not become Christians, then, do not have the gift of immortal life and at death or at the time of final judgment they simply cease to exist. This view is very close to that of annihilationism, and I have not discussed it separately in this chapter. (Some versions of conditional immortality deny conscious punishment altogether, even for a brief time.)

[13]In Phil. 3:19 and 2 Peter 3:7, the term for "destruction" is *apōleia,* which is the same word used by the disciples in Matt. 26:8 to speak of the "waste" (in their view) of the ointment that had just been poured on Jesus' head. Now the ointment did not cease to exist; it was very evident on Jesus' head. But it had been "destroyed" in the sense that it was no longer able to be used on someone else, or sold. In 1 Thess. 5:3 and 2 Thess. 1:9 another word, *olethros,* is used of the destruction of the wicked, but again this word does not imply that something will cease to exist, for it is used in 1 Cor. 5:5 of delivering a man to Satan (putting him out of the church) for the *destruction* of the flesh—but certainly his flesh did not cease to exist when he was put out of the church, even though he may have suffered in his body (this would be true whether we take "flesh" to mean his physical body or his sinful nature).

in some ways a desirable alternative. And if there was no punishment of unbelievers at all, even people like Hitler and Stalin would have nothing coming to them, and there would be no ultimate justice in the universe. Then people would have great incentive to be as wicked as possible in this life.

The argument that *eternal* punishment is unfair (because there is a disproportion between temporary sin and eternal punishment) wrongly assumes that we know the extent of the evil done when sinners rebel against God. David Kingdon observes that "sin against the Creator is heinous to a degree utterly beyond our sin-warped imaginations' [ability] to conceive of. . . . Who would have the temerity to suggest to God what the punishment . . . should be?"[14] He also responds to this objection by suggesting that unbelievers in hell may go on sinning and receiving punishment for their sin, but never repenting, and notes that Revelation 22:11 points in this direction: "Let the evildoer still do evil, and the filthy still be filthy."[15]

At this point, moreover, an argument based on God's justice may be brought against annihilationism. Does the short time of punishment envisaged by the annihilationist actually *pay* for all of the unbeliever's sin and satisfy God's justice? If it does not, then God's justice has not been satisfied and the unbeliever should not be annihilated. But if it does, then the unbeliever should be allowed to go to heaven, and he or she should not be annihilated. In either case, annihilationism is not necessary or right.

Regarding the fourth argument, while evil *that remains unpunished* does detract from God's glory in the universe, we also must realize that when God *punishes* evil and *triumphs* over it, the glory of his justice, righteousness, and power to triumph over all opposition will be seen (see Rom. 9:17, 22–24). The depth of the riches of God's mercy will also then be revealed, for all redeemed sinners will recognize that they too deserve such punishment from God and have avoided it only by God's grace through Jesus Christ (cf. Rom. 9:23–24).

Yet after all this has been said, we have to admit that the ultimate resolution of the depths of this question lies far beyond our ability to understand, and remains hidden in the counsels of God. Were it not for the scriptural passages cited above which so clearly affirm eternal conscious punishment, annihilationism might seem to us to be an attractive option. Though annihilationism can be countered by theological arguments, it is ultimately the clarity and forcefulness of the passages themselves that convince us that annihilationism is incorrect and that Scripture does indeed teach the eternal conscious punishment of the wicked.[16]

What are we to think of this doctrine? It is hard—and it should be hard—for us to think of this doctrine today. If our hearts are never moved with deep sorrow when we contemplate this doctrine, then there is a serious deficiency in our

---

[14]David Kingdon, "Annihilationism: Gain or Loss?" (March, 1992; unpublished paper obtained from the author), p. 9.

[15]Ibid., pp. 9–10.

[16]Because the doctrine of eternal conscious punishment is so foreign to the thought patterns of our culture, and, on a deeper level, to our instinctive and God-given sense of love and desire for redemption for every human being created in God's image, this doctrine is emotionally one of the most difficult doctrines for Christians to affirm today. It also tends to be one of the first doctrines given up by people who are moving away from a commitment to the Bible as absolutely truthful in all that it affirms. Among liberal theologians who do not accept the absolute truthfulness of the Bible, there is probably no one today who believes in the doctrine of eternal conscious punishment.

spiritual and emotional sensibilities. When Paul thinks of the lostness of his kinsmen the Jews, he says, "I have *great sorrow* and *unceasing anguish* in my heart" (Rom. 9:2). This is consistent with what God tells us of his own sorrow at the death of the wicked: "As I live, says the Lord God, *I have no pleasure in the death of the wicked,* but that the wicked turn from his way and live; turn back, turn back from your evil ways; for why will you die, O house of Israel?" (Ezek. 33:11). And Jesus' agony is evident as he cries out, "O Jerusalem, Jerusalem, killing the prophets and stoning those who are sent to you! How often would I have gathered your children together as a hen gathers her brood under her wings, and you would not! Behold, your house is forsaken and desolate" (Matt. 23:37–38; cf. Luke 19:41–42).

The reason it is hard for us to think of the doctrine of hell is because God has put in our hearts a portion of his own love for people created in his image, even his love for sinners who rebel against him. As long as we are in this life, and as long as we see and think about others who need to hear the gospel and trust in Christ for salvation, it should cause us great distress and agony of spirit to think about eternal punishment. Yet we must also realize that whatever God in his wisdom has ordained and taught in Scripture is *right*. Therefore we must be careful that we do not hate this doctrine or rebel against it, but rather we should seek, insofar as we are able, to come to the point where we acknowledge that eternal punishment is good and right, because in God there is no unrighteousness at all.

It may help us to realize that if God were not to execute eternal punishment, then, apparently, his justice would not be satisfied and his glory would not be furthered in the way he deems wise. And it will perhaps also help us to realize that from the perspective of the world to come there is a much greater recognition of the necessity and rightness of eternal punishment. Martyred believers in heaven are heard by John to cry out, "O sovereign Lord, holy and true, how long before you will judge and avenge our blood on those who dwell upon the earth?" (Rev. 6:10). Moreover, at the final destruction of Babylon, the loud voice of a great multitude in heaven cries out with praise to God for the rightness of his judgment as they finally see the heinous nature of evil for what it really is:

> Hallelujah! Salvation and glory and power belong to our God, for his judgments are true and just; he has judged the great harlot who corrupted the earth with her fornication, and he has avenged on her the blood of his servants. . . . Hallelujah! The smoke from her goes up forever and ever." (Rev. 19:1–3)

As soon as this happened, "the 24 elders and the four living creatures fell down and worshiped God who is seated on the throne, saying, 'Amen. Hallelujah!'" (Rev. 19:4). We cannot say that this great multitude of the redeemed and the living creatures in heaven have wrong moral judgment when they praise God for executing justice on evil, for they are all free from sin and their moral judgments are pleasing to God.

In this present age, however, we should only approach such a celebration of the justice of God in the punishment of evil when we meditate on the eternal punishment given to Satan and his demons. When we think of them we do not instinctively love them, though they too were created by God. But now they are fully devoted to evil and beyond the potential of redemption. So we cannot long for their salvation as we long for the redemption of all humanity. We must believe that eternal punishment is true and just, yet we should also long that even those people who most severely persecute the church should come to faith in Christ and thus escape eternal condemnation.

## QUESTIONS FOR PERSONAL APPLICATION

1. Have you thought before that there will be a final judgment for believers? How do you think of it now? How does the awareness of the fact that we will all stand before the judgment seat of Christ affect your life today? What do you think it will feel like to have all your words and deeds made public on that last day? Is there an element of fear as you contemplate that day? If so, meditate on 1 John 4:16–18:

   So we know and believe the love God has for us. God is love, and he who abides in love abides in God, and God abides in him. In this is love perfected with us, *that we may have confidence for the day of judgment,* because as he is so are we in this world. *There is no fear in love, but perfect love casts out fear.* For fear has to do with punishment, and he who fears is not perfected in love.

2. Have you previously thought very much about laying up treasures in heaven, or about earning greater heavenly reward? If you really believe this doctrine, what kind of effect do you think it should have on your life?

3. How do you think it will feel to participate with Christ in the judging of angels, and indeed in the judging of the whole world (see 1 Cor. 6:2–3)? What does the fact that God allows us to participate in this final judgment say about our creation in the image of God and his purposes for us in the universe? How does that make you feel about yourself and your eternal relationship to God?

4. Think of some of your Christian friends in your church. How do you think you will feel when you watch them stand before Christ at the final judgment? How will they feel about you at that time? Does the contemplation of this future judgment affect the way you think of your fellowship with each other as brothers and sisters in Christ today?

5. Are you glad that there will be a final judgment of both believers and unbelievers? Does it make you feel a sense of God's justice, or do you sense some unfairness and injustice in the whole idea?

6. Are you convinced that Scripture teaches that there will be eternal conscious punishment of the wicked? When you think of that idea in relationship to Satan and demons, do you feel that it is right?

7. Is there anyone who has wronged you in the past, and whom you have had difficulty forgiving? Does the doctrine of final judgment help you to be more able to forgive that person?

## SPECIAL TERMS

annihilationism
conditional immortality
eternal conscious punishment
final judgment

great white throne judgment
hell
judgment of the nations
universalism

## BIBLIOGRAPHY

(For explanation of this bibliography see note at bibliography to chapter 1, p. 38.
Complete bibliographical data may be found on pp. 1223–29.)

### Sections in Evangelical Systematic Theologies

1. Anglican (Episcopalian)
    1882–92    Litton, 591–600
    1930    Thomas, 525–26
2. Arminian (Wesleyan or Methodist)
    1875–76    Pope, 3:401–47
    1892–94    Miley, 2:458–71
    1940    Wiley, 3:338–75
    1960    Purkiser, 567–74
    1983    Carter, 2:1105–9, 1127–30, 1133–36
3. Baptist
    1767    Gill, 2:302–29
    1887    Boyce, 461–71, 477–93
    1907    Strong, 1023–29, 1033–56
    1917    Mullins, 478–83, 488–503
    1976–83    Henry, 4:593–614; 6:492–513
    1983–85    Erickson, 1005–22, 1234–41, 1200–1204
4. Dispensational
    1947    Chafer, 4:402–12, 427–33
    1949    Thiessen, 383–90, 396–97
    1986    Ryrie, 512–16, 520–22
5. Lutheran
    1917–24    Pieper, 3:539–50
    1934    Mueller, 630–39
6. Reformed (or Presbyterian)
    1724–58    Edwards, 2:122–30, 190–213, 515–25
    1861    Heppe, 703–6
    1871–73    Hodge, 3:837–54, 868–80
    1878    Dabney, 842–62
    1889    Shedd, 2b:659–63, 667–754

1937-66    Murray, *CW*, 2:413-17
   1938    Berkhof, 728-38
   1962    Buswell, 2:306-8, 508-11
7. Renewal (or charismatic/Pentecostal)
   1988-92    Williams, 3:413-20, 445-77

## Sections in Representative Roman Catholic Systematic Theologies

1. Roman Catholic: Traditional
      1955    Ott, 479-82, 492-96
2. Roman Catholic: Post-Vatican II
      1980    McBrien, 2:1150-55

## Other Works

Beckwith, R. T. "Purgatory." In *NDT*, pp. 549-50.
Blamires, Harry. *Knowing the Truth About Heaven and Hell.* Knowing the Truth Series, eds. J. I. Packer and Peter Kreeft. Ann Arbor: Servant, 1988.
Buis, Harry. *The Doctrine of Eternal Punishment.* Philadelphia: Presbyterian and Reformed, 1957.
Cameron, Nigel M. de S., ed. *Universalism and the Doctrine of Hell.* Carlisle, U.K.: Paternoster, and Grand Rapids: Baker, 1992.
Crockett, William V., Z. J. Hayes, Clark H. Pinnock, and John F. Walvoord. *Four Views on Hell.* Grand Rapids: Zondervan, 1992.
Gerstner, John H. *Repent or Perish.* Ligonier, Pa.: Soli Deo Gloria, 1990.
Helm, Paul. "Universalism and the Threat of Hell." *TrinJ* vol. 4 N.S., No. 1 (Spring 1983): 35-43.
Hoekema, Anthony A. *The Bible and the Future.* Grand Rapids: Eerdmans, 1979, pp. 253-73.
Hubbard, D. A. "Last Judgment, The." In *EDT*, pp. 620-21.
Martin, James P. *The Last Judgment.* Grand Rapids: Eerdmans, 1983.
Morris, L. "Eternal Punishment." In *EDT*, pp. 369-70.
O'Donovan, O. M. T., and R. J. Song. "Punishment." In *NDT*, pp. 547-49.
Packer, J. I. "Evangelicals and the Way of Salvation: New Challenges to the Gospel—Universalism and Justification by Faith." In *Evangelical Affirmations*. Ed. Kenneth S. Kantzer and Carl F. H. Henry. Grand Rapids: Zondervan, 1990, pp. 107-36.
Travis, S. H. "Judgment of God." In *NDT*, p. 358.

## SCRIPTURE MEMORY PASSAGE

**Revelation 20:11-13:** *Then I saw a great white throne and him who sat upon it; from his presence earth and sky fled away, and no place was found for them. And I saw the dead, great and small, standing before the throne, and books were opened. Also another book was opened, which is the book of life. And the dead were judged by what was written in the books, by what they had done. And the sea gave up the dead in it, Death and Hades gave up the dead in them, and all were judged by what they had done.*

## HYMN

### "O Quickly Come, Dread Judge of All"

(The tune is the familiar tune for "Eternal Father, Strong to Save")

O quickly come, dread judge of all; for, awful though thine advent be,
All shadows from the truth will fall, and falsehood die, in sight of thee:
O quickly come; for doubt and fear like clouds dissolve when thou art
     near.

O quickly come, great king of all; reign all around us, and within;
Let sin no more our souls enthrall, let pain and sorrow die with sin:
O quickly come; for thou alone canst make thy scattered people one.

O quickly come, true life of all; for death is mighty all around;
On ev'ry home his shadows fall, on ev'ry heart his mark is found:
O quickly come; for grief and pain can never cloud thy glorious reign.

O quickly come, sure light of all; for gloomy night broods o'er our way;
And weakly souls begin to fall with weary watching for the day:
O quickly come; for round thy throne no eye is blind, no night is
     known.

AUTHOR: LAWRENCE TUTTIETT, 1854

Alternate hymn:
### "Great God, What Do I See and Hear!"

A tone of gloom and judgment pervades both these hymns, yet this alternate also contains a strong
focus on the soul's preparing to meet Christ and a sense of joyful anticipation.

Great God, what do I see and hear! The end of things created!
The Judge of mankind doth appear, on clouds of glory seated!
The trumpet sounds; the graves restore the dead which they contained
     before:
Prepare, my soul, to meet him.

The dead in Christ shall first arise, at the last trumpet's sounding,
Caught up to meet him in the skies, with joy their Lord surrounding;
No gloomy fears their souls dismay; his presence sheds eternal day
On those prepared to meet him.

But sinners, filled with guilty fears, behold his wrath prevailing;
For they shall rise, and find their tears and sighs are unavailing:
The day of grace is past and gone; trembling they stand before the throne,
All unprepared to meet him.

Great God, what do I see and hear! The end of things created!
The Judge of mankind doth appear, on clouds of glory seated!
Beneath his cross I view the day when heav'n and earth shall pass away,
And thus prepare to meet him.

AUTHOR: FIRST STANZA, ANONYMOUS, 1802;
STANZAS 2–4, WILLIAM B. COLLYER, 1812;
ALTERNATE RENDERING, THOMAS COTTERILL, 1820

# Chapter 57

# The New Heavens and New Earth

*What is heaven? Is it a place? How will the earth be renewed? What will it be like to live in the new heavens and new earth?*

## EXPLANATION AND SCRIPTURAL BASIS

### A. We Will Live Eternally With God in New Heavens and a New Earth

After the final judgment, believers will enter into the full enjoyment of life in the presence of God forever. Jesus will say to us, "Come, O blessed of my Father, inherit the kingdom prepared for you from the foundation of the world" (Matt. 25:34). We will enter a kingdom where "there shall no more be anything accursed, but the throne of God and of the Lamb shall be in it, and his servants shall worship him" (Rev. 22:3).

When referring to this place, Christians often talk about living with God "in heaven" forever. But in fact the biblical teaching is richer than that: it tells us that there will be new heavens *and a new earth*—an entirely renewed creation—and we will live with God there.

The Lord promises through Isaiah, "For behold, I create *new heavens and a new earth;* and the former things shall not be remembered" (Isa. 65:17), and speaks of "the new heavens and the new earth which I will make" (Isa. 66:22). Peter says, "according to his promise we wait for *new heavens and a new earth* in which righteousness dwells" (2 Peter 3:13). In John's vision of events to follow the final judgment, he says, "Then I saw a *new heaven and a new earth;* for the first heaven and the first earth had passed away" (Rev. 21:1). He goes on to tell us that there will also be a new kind of unification of heaven and earth, for he sees the holy city, the "new Jerusalem," coming "down out of heaven from God" (Rev. 21:2), and hears a voice proclaiming that "the dwelling of God is with men. He will dwell with them, and they shall be his people, and God himself will be with them" (v. 3). So there will be a joining of heaven and earth in this new creation, and there we will live in the presence of God.

**1. What Is Heaven?** During this present age, the place where God dwells is frequently called "heaven" in Scripture. The Lord says, "Heaven is my throne" (Isa. 66:1), and Jesus teaches us to pray, "Our Father who art in *heaven*" (Matt. 6:9). Jesus now "*has gone into heaven,* and is at the right hand of God" (1 Peter

3:22). In fact, heaven may be defined as follows: *Heaven is the place where God most fully makes known his presence to bless.*

We discussed earlier how God is present everywhere[1] but how he especially manifests his presence to bless in certain places. The greatest manifestation of God's presence to bless is seen in heaven, where he makes his glory known, and where angels, other heavenly creatures, and redeemed saints all worship him.

**2. Heaven Is a Place, Not Just a State of Mind.** But someone may wonder how heaven can be joined together with earth. Clearly the earth is a *place* that exists at a certain location in our space-time universe, but can heaven also be thought of as a *place* that can be joined to the earth?

Outside of the evangelical world the idea of heaven as a place is often denied, chiefly because its existence can only be known from the testimony of Scripture. Recently even some evangelical scholars have been hesitant to affirm the fact that heaven is a place.[2] Should the fact that we *only* know about heaven from the Bible, and cannot give any empirical evidence for it, be a reason not to believe that heaven is a real place?

The New Testament teaches the idea of a location for heaven in several different ways, and quite clearly. When Jesus ascended into heaven, the fact that he went to a *place* seems to be the entire point of the narrative, and the point that Jesus intended his disciples to understand by the way in which he gradually ascended even while speaking to them: "As they were looking on, he was lifted up, and a cloud took him out of their sight" (Acts 1:9; cf. Luke 24:51: "While he blessed them, he parted from them"). The angels exclaimed, "This Jesus, who was taken up from you *into heaven,* will come in the same way as you saw him go into heaven" (Acts 1:11). It is hard to imagine how the fact of Jesus' ascension to a *place* could be taught more clearly.

A similar conclusion can be drawn from the story of Stephen's death. Just before he was stoned, he, "full of the Holy Spirit, *gazed into heaven* and saw the glory of God, and Jesus standing at the right hand of God; and he said, 'Behold, I see the heavens opened, and the Son of Man standing at the right hand of God'" (Acts 7:55–56). He did not see mere symbols of a state of existence. It seems rather that his eyes were opened to see a spiritual dimension of reality which God has hidden from us in this present age, a dimension which nonetheless really does exist in our space/time universe, and within which Jesus now lives in his physical resurrection body, waiting even now for the time when he will return to earth.[3] Moreover, the fact that we will have resurrection bodies like Christ's resurrection body indicates that heaven will be a place, for in such physical bodies (made

---

[1]See chapter 11, pp. 173–77, on the omnipresence of God.

[2]Millard Erickson, *Christian Theology,* says, "While heaven is both a place and a state, it is primarily a state" (p. 1232), a statement that is difficult to understand. Something either is a place or it is not a place; it is not somewhat a place but "primarily a state." Even stronger is Donald Guthrie, who says of the New Testament, "We shall not expect, however, to find a description of a place, so much as the presence of a person," (*New Testament Theology,* p. 875) and "Paul does not think of heaven as a place, but thinks of it in terms of the presence of God" (*New Testament Theology,* p. 880). But does such a distinction make any sense? If a person is *present,* then by definition there is a *place,* because to be "present" means to be "located in this place."

[3]See the discussion of Christ's resurrection body and his ascension in chapter 28, pp. 608–20.

perfect, never to become weak or die again),[4] we will inhabit a specific place at a specific time, just as Jesus now does in his resurrection body.

The idea of heaven as a place is also the easiest sense in which to understand Jesus' promise, "I go to prepare a *place* for you" (John 14:2). He speaks quite clearly of going from his existence in this world back to the Father, and then returning again: "And when I go and prepare a *place* for you, I will come again and will take you to myself, that *where I am* you may be also" (John 14:3).

These texts lead us to conclude that heaven is even now a place—though one whose location is now unknown to us and whose existence is now unable to be perceived by our natural senses. It is this place of God's dwelling that will be somehow made new at the time of the final judgment and will be joined to a renewed earth.

**3. The Physical Creation Will Be Renewed and We Will Continue to Exist and Act in It.** In addition to a renewed heaven, God will make a "new earth" (2 Peter 3:13; Rev. 21:1). Several passages indicate that the physical creation will be renewed in a significant way. "The creation waits with eager longing for the revealing of the sons of God; for the creation was subjected to futility, not of its own will but by the will of him who subjected it in hope; because *the creation itself will be set free from its bondage to decay and obtain the glorious liberty of the children of God*" (Rom. 8:19–21).

But will earth simply be renewed, or will it be completely destroyed and replaced by another earth, newly created by God? Some passages appear to speak of an entire new creation: The author of Hebrews (quoting Ps. 102) tells us of the heavens and earth, "They will perish, but you remain; they will all grow old like a garment, like a mantle you will roll them up, and they will be changed" (Heb. 1:11–12). Later he tells us that God has promised, "Yet once more I will shake not only the earth but also the heaven," a shaking so severe as to involve "the removal of what is shaken . . . in order that what cannot be shaken may remain" (Heb. 12:26–27). Peter says, "The day of the Lord will come like a thief, and then *the heavens will pass away with a loud noise,* and the elements will be dissolved with fire, and *the earth and all the works that are upon it will be burned up*" (2 Peter 3:10). A similar picture is found in Revelation, where John says, "From his presence earth and sky fled away, and no place was found for them" (Rev. 20:11). Moreover, John says, "Then I saw a new heaven and a new earth; for the first heaven and the first earth had passed away, and the sea was no more" (Rev. 21:1).

Within the Protestant world, there has been disagreement as to whether the earth is to be destroyed completely and replaced, or just changed and renewed. Berkhof says that Lutheran scholars have emphasized the fact that it will be an entirely new creation, while Reformed scholars have tended to emphasize those verses that say simply that this present creation will be renewed.[5] The Reformed position seems preferable here, for it is difficult to think that God would entirely annihilate his original creation, thereby seeming to give the devil the last word and scrapping the creation that was originally "very good" (Gen. 1:31). The passages above that speak of shaking and removing the earth and of the first earth passing

---

[4]See chapter 42, pp. 831–35, on the nature of our resurrection bodies.
[5]Berkhof, *Systematic Theology,* p. 737.

away may simply refer to its existence in its present form, not its very existence itself, and even 2 Peter 3:10, which speaks of the elements dissolving and the earth and the works on it being burned up, may not be speaking of the earth as a planet but rather the surface things on the earth (that is, much of the ground and the things on the ground).

**4. Our Resurrection Bodies Will Be Part of the Renewed Creation.** In the new heavens and new earth, there will be a place and activities for our resurrection bodies, which will never grow old or become weak or ill. A strong consideration in favor of this viewpoint is the fact that God made the original physical creation "very good" (Gen. 1:31). There is therefore nothing inherently sinful or evil or "unspiritual" about the physical world that God made or the creatures that he put in it, or about the physical bodies that he gave us at creation. Though all these things have been marred and distorted by sin, God will not completely destroy the physical world (which would be an acknowledgement that sin had frustrated and defeated God's purposes), but rather he will perfect the entire creation and bring it into harmony with the purposes for which he originally created it. Therefore we can expect that in the new heavens and new earth there will be a fully perfect earth that is once again "very good." And we can expect that we will have physical bodies that will once again be "very good" in God's sight, and that will function to fulfill the purposes for which he originally placed man on the earth.

When the author of Hebrews says that we do "not yet" see everything in subjection to man (Heb. 2:8), he implies that eventually all things will eventually be subject to us, under the kingship of the man Christ Jesus (note v. 9: "But we see Jesus . . . crowned with glory and honor"). This will fulfill God's original plan to have everything in the world subject to the human beings that he had made.[6] In this sense, then, we will "inherit the earth" (Matt. 5:5) and reign over it as God originally intended.

For that reason, it should not strike us as surprising to find that some of the descriptions of life in heaven include features that are very much part of the physical or material creation that God has made. We shall *eat and drink* at "the marriage supper of the Lamb" (Rev. 19:9). Jesus will once again *drink wine* with his disciples in the heavenly kingdom (Luke 22:18). The *"river* of the water of life" will flow "from the throne of God and of the Lamb through the middle of the *street of the city*" (Rev. 22:1). The *tree of life* will bear "twelve kinds of fruit, yielding its fruit each month" (Rev. 22:2). There is no strong reason to say these expressions are merely symbolic, without any literal reference. Are symbolic banquets and symbolic wine and symbolic rivers and trees somehow superior to real banquets and real wine and real rivers and trees in God's eternal plan? These things are just some of the excellent features of the perfection and final goodness of the physical creation that God has made.

Of course, there are symbolic descriptions in the book of Revelation, and it is inevitable that at some points we will be unable to decide whether something is to be taken symbolically or literally. But it does not seem difficult to think that the description of the heavenly city with gates and a wall and foundations is a description of something that is literal and real, "the holy city Jerusalem coming

---

[6]See pp. 272–73 and 447–48 on God's original purpose to have man rule over all creation.

down out of heaven from God, having the glory of God, its radiance like a most rare jewel" (Rev. 21:10–11). "And the street of the city is pure gold, transparent as glass. . . . And the kings of the earth shall bring their glory into it, and its gates shall never be shut by day—and there shall be no night there; they shall bring into it the glory and the honor of the nations" (Rev. 21:21–26).

While we may have some uncertainty about the understanding of certain details, it does not seem inconsistent with this picture to say that we will eat and drink in the new heavens and new earth, and carry on other physical activities as well. Music certainly is prominent in the descriptions of heaven in Revelation, and we might imagine that both musical and artistic activities would be done to the glory of God. Perhaps people will work at the whole range of investigation and development of the creation by technological, creative, and inventive means, thus exhibiting the full extent of their excellent creation in the image of God.

Moreover, since God is infinite and we can never exhaust his greatness (Ps. 145:3), and since we are finite creatures who will never equal God's knowledge or be omniscient,[7] we may expect that for all eternity we will be able to go on learning more about God and about his relationship to his creation. In this way we will continue the process of learning that was begun in this life, in which a life "fully pleasing to him" is one that includes continually "increasing in the knowledge of God" (Col. 1:10).

## 5. The New Creation Will Not Be "Timeless" but Will Include an Unending Succession of Moments.

Although a popular hymn speaks of the time "when the trumpet of the Lord shall sound and time shall be no more," Scripture does not give support to that idea. Certainly the heavenly city that receives its light from the glory of God (Rev. 21:23) will never experience darkness or night: "There shall be no night there" (Rev. 21:25). But this does not mean that heaven will be a place where time is unknown, or where things cannot be done one after another. Indeed, all the pictures of heavenly worship in the book of Revelation include words that are spoken one after another in coherent sentences, and actions (such as falling down before God's throne and casting crowns before his throne) that involve a sequence of events. When we read that "the kings of the earth . . . shall bring into it the glory and honor of the nations" (Rev. 21:24–26), we see another activity that involves a sequence of events, one happening after another. And certainly that is the clear implication of the fact that the tree of life has twelve kinds of fruit, "yielding its fruit each month" (Rev. 22:2). (On Rev. 10:6 see chapter 11, p. 173, n. 18.)

Since we are finite creatures, we might also expect that we will always live in a succession of moments. Just as we will never attain to God's omniscience or omnipresence, so we shall never attain to God's eternity in the sense of seeing all time equally vividly and not living in a succession of moments or being limited by time. As finite creatures, we will rather live in a succession of moments that will never end.

---

[7]1 Cor. 13:12 does not say that we will be omniscient or know everything (Paul could have said we will know all things, *ta panta*, if he had wished to do so), but, rightly translated, simply says that we will know in a fuller or more intensive way, "even as we have been known," that is, without any error or misconceptions in our knowledge.

## B. The Doctrine of the New Creation Provides a Great Motivation for Storing Up Treasures in Heaven Rather Than on Earth

When we consider the fact that this present creation is a temporary one and that our life in the new creation will last for eternity, we have a strong motivation for godly living and for living in such a way as to store up treasures in heaven. In reflecting on the fact that heaven and earth will be destroyed, Peter says the following:

> Since all these things are thus to be dissolved, what sort of persons ought you to be in lives of holiness and godliness, waiting for and hastening the coming of the day of God, because of which the heavens will be kindled and dissolved, and the elements will melt with fire! But according to his promise we wait for new heavens and a new earth in which righteousness dwells. (2 Peter 3:11–13)

And Jesus very explicitly tells us:

> Do not lay up for yourselves treasures on earth, where moth and rust consume and where thieves break in and steal, but lay up for yourselves treasures in heaven, where neither moth nor rust consumes and where thieves do not break in and steal. For where your treasure is, there will your heart be also. (Matt. 6:19–21)[8]

## C. The New Creation Will Be a Place of Great Beauty and Abundance and Joy in the Presence of God

Amid all the questions that we naturally have concerning the new heavens and new earth, we must not lose sight of the fact that Scripture consistently portrays this new creation as a place of great beauty and joy. In the description of heaven in Revelation 21 and 22, this theme is repeatedly affirmed. It is a "holy city" (21:2), a place "prepared as a bride adorned for her husband" (21:2). In that place "death shall be no more, neither shall there be mourning nor crying nor pain any more" (21:4). There we can drink "from the fountain of the water of life without payment" (21:6). It is a city that has "the glory of God, its radiance like a most rare jewel, like a jasper, clear as crystal" (21:11). It is a city of immense size, whether the measurements be understood as literal or symbolic. Its length measures "12,000 stadia" (21:16), or about 1,400 miles (2,250 kilometers), and "its length and breadth and height are equal" (21:6). Parts of the city are constructed of immense precious jewels of various colors (21:18–21). It will be free from all evil, for "nothing unclean shall enter it, nor anyone who practices abomination or falsehood, but only those who are written in the Lamb's book of life" (21:7). In that city we shall also have positions of rule over God's entire creation, for "they shall reign for ever and ever" (22:5).

But more important than all the physical beauty of the heavenly city, more important than the fellowship we will enjoy eternally with all God's people from all nations and all periods in history, more important than our freedom from pain and sorrow and physical suffering, and more important than reigning over God's kingdom—more important by far than any of these will be the fact that we will be in the presence of God and enjoying unhindered fellowship with him. "Behold, the dwelling of God is with men. He will dwell with them, and they shall be his

---

[8]See the discussion of degrees of heavenly reward in chapter 56, pp. 1143–45.

people, and *God himself will be with them;* he will wipe away every tear from their eyes" (21:3–4).

In the Old Testament, when the glory of God filled the temple, the priests were unable to stand and minister (2 Chron. 5:14). In the New Testament, when the glory of God surrounded the shepherds in the field outside Bethlehem "they were filled with fear" (Luke 2:9). But here in the heavenly city we will be able to endure the power and holiness of the presence of God's glory, for we will live *continually* in the atmosphere of the glory of God. "And the city has no need of sun or moon to shine upon it, *for the glory of God is its light, and its lamp is the Lamb*" (21:23). This will be the fulfillment of God's purpose to call us "to his own glory and excellence" (2 Peter 1:3): then we shall dwell continually in *"the presence of his glory with rejoicing"* (Jude 1:24; cf. Rom. 3:23; 8:18; 9:23; 1 Cor. 15:43; 2 Cor. 3:18; 4:17; Col. 3:4; 1 Thess. 2:12; Heb. 2:10; 1 Peter 5:1, 4, 10).

In that city we shall live in the presence of God, for "the throne of God and of the Lamb shall be in it, and his servants shall worship him" (22:3). From time to time here on earth we experience the joy of genuine worship of God, and we realize that it is our highest joy to be giving him glory. But in that city this joy will be multiplied many times over and we will know the fulfillment of that for which we were created. Our greatest joy will be in seeing the Lord himself and in being with him forever. When John speaks of the blessings of the heavenly city, the culmination of those blessings comes in the short statement, *"They shall see his face"* (22:4). When we look into the face of our Lord and he looks back at us with infinite love, we will see in him the fulfillment of everything that we know to be good and right and desirable in the universe. In the face of God we will see the fulfillment of all the longing we have ever had to know perfect love, peace, and joy, and to know truth and justice, holiness and wisdom, goodness and power, and glory and beauty. As we gaze into the face of our Lord, we will know more fully than ever before that *"in your presence there is fullness of joy, at your right hand are pleasures for evermore"* (Ps. 16:11). Then will be fulfilled the longing of our hearts with which we have cried out in the past, "One thing I have asked of the Lord, that will I seek after; that I may dwell in the house of the Lord all the days of my life, *to behold the beauty of the Lord,* and to inquire in his temple" (Ps. 27:4).

When we finally see the Lord face to face, our hearts will want nothing else. *"Whom have I in heaven but you?* And there is nothing upon earth that I desire besides you. . . . God is the strength of my heart and my portion forever" (Ps. 73:25–26). Then with joy our hearts and voices will join with the redeemed from all ages and with the mighty armies of heaven singing, "Holy, holy, holy, is the Lord God Almighty, who was and is and is to come!" (Rev. 4:8).

## QUESTIONS FOR PERSONAL APPLICATION

1. In your Christian life to this point, have you spent much time thinking about life in the new heavens and new earth? Do you think there is a very strong longing for this in your heart? If it has not been strong, why do you think this has been the case?

2. In what ways has this chapter made you more excited about entering the heavenly city? What positive effects on your Christian life do you think would come about because of a stronger longing for the life to come?

3. Are you convinced that the new creation is a place where we will exist with physical bodies that are made perfect? If so, are you encouraged or discouraged by this idea? Why? Why do you think it is necessary to insist that heaven is an actual place even today?

4. What are some ways in which you already have stored up treasure in heaven rather than on earth? Are there more ways you could do that in your own life now? Do you think you will?

5. Sometimes people have thought that they would be bored in the life to come. Do you feel that way yourself? What is a good answer to the objection that the eternal state will be boring?

6. Can you describe at all what you think you will feel like when you finally stand in the presence of God and see him face-to-face?

## SPECIAL TERMS

heaven
new heavens and new earth

## BIBLIOGRAPHY

(For explanation of this bibliography see note at bibliography to chapter 1, p. 38. Complete bibliographical data may be found on pp. 1223–29.)

### Sections in Evangelical Systematic Theologies

1. Anglican (Episcopalian)
   - 1882–92      Litton, 600–605
2. Arminian (Wesleyan or Methodist)
   - 1875–76      Pope, 3:447–54
   - 1892–94      Miley, 2:472–75
   - 1940      Wiley, 3:375–93
   - 1960      Purkiser, 574–77
   - 1983      Carter, 2:1130–33, 1136–40
3. Baptist
   - 1767      Gill, 2:258–68, 329–40
   - 1887      Boyce, 471–77
   - 1907      Strong, 1029–33
   - 1917      Mullins, 483–88
   - 1976–83      Henry, 4:593–614
   - 1983–85      Erickson, 1225–34
4. Dispensational
   - 1947      Chafer, 4:433–39; 5:365–76

## Sections in Representative Roman Catholic Systematic Theologies

### Other Works

Blamires, Harry. *Knowing the Truth About Heaven and Hell.* Knowing the Truth series, eds. J. I. Packer and Peter Kreeft. Ann Arbor: Servant, 1988.

Gilmore, John. *Probing Heaven: Key Questions on the Hereafter.* Grand Rapids: Baker, 1989.

Grider, J.K. "Heaven." In *EDT,* pp. 499–500.

Hoekema, Anthony A. "The New Earth." In *The Bible and the Future.* Grand Rapids: Eerdmans, 1979, pp. 274–87.

Lincoln, Andrew T. *Paradise Now and Not Yet: Studies in the Role of the Heavenly Dimension in Paul's Thought With Special Reference to His Eschatology.* Society for New Testament Studies Monograph Series. London; New York: Cambridge, 1981.

Murray, John. "Glorification." In *Redemption Accomplished and Applied.* Grand Rapids: Eerdmans, 1955, pp. 174–81.

Smith, Wilbur M. *The Biblical Doctrine of Heaven.* Chicago: Moody, 1968.

### SCRIPTURE MEMORY PASSAGE

**Revelation 21:3–4:** *And I heard a loud voice from the throne saying, "Behold, the dwelling of God is with men. He will dwell with them, and they shall be his people, and God himself will be with them; he will wipe away every tear from their eyes, and death shall be no more, neither shall there be mourning nor crying nor pain any more, for the former things have passed away."*

## HYMN

### "The Sands of Time Are Sinking"

This is one of the most beautiful hymns ever written in any language. It expresses so clearly the fact that the beauty of heaven is the glory of God, and the great beauty of God's glory is the Lamb who died for us and now reigns.

The sands of time are sinking, the dawn of heaven breaks,
  The summer morn I've sighed for, the fair sweet morn awakes;
Dark, dark hath been the midnight, but dayspring is at hand,
  And glory, glory dwelleth in Emmanuel's land.

The king there in his beauty without a veil is seen;
  It were a well-spent journey though sev'n deaths lay between:
The Lamb with his fair army doth on Mount Zion stand,
  And glory, glory dwelleth in Emmanuel's land.

O Christ, he is the fountain, the deep sweet well of love!
  The streams on earth I've tasted, more deep I'll drink above:
There to an ocean fullness his mercy doth expand,
  And glory, glory dwelleth in Emmanuel's land.

The bride eyes not her garment, but her dear bridegroom's face;
  I will not gaze at glory, but on my King of grace;
Not at the crown he giveth, but on his pierced hand:
  The lamb is all the glory of Emmanuel's land.

AUTHOR: ANNE R. COUSIN, 1857

# Appendix 1:
# Historic Confessions of Faith

This appendix reprints several of the most significant confessions of faith from various periods in the history of the church. From the ancient church I have included the four great ecumenical confessions: the Apostles' Creed (third–fourth centuries A.D.), the Nicene Creed (A.D. 325/381), the Athanasian Creed (late fourth–early fifth century A.D.), and the Chalcedonian Creed (A.D. 451). From the Protestant churches since the Reformation I have included four other confessions: the Thirty-nine Articles (1571) [Church of England; also Methodist]; the Westminster Confession of Faith (1643–1646) [British Reformed and Presbyterian]; the New Hampshire Baptist Confession (1833); and the Baptist Faith and Message (1925/1963) [Southern Baptist]. Finally, I have also included the Chicago Statement on Biblical Inerrancy (1978), because it was the product of a conference representing a broad variety of evangelical traditions, and because it has gained widespread acceptance as a valuable doctrinal standard concerning an issue of recent and current controversy in the church.

Because of space limitations, I was able to include only one of the very long confessions of faith that came out of the Reformation, and I chose the Westminster Confession of Faith, which represents a doctrinal position very close to the position of this book. This meant that I did not have space to include either of the two great Lutheran confessions, the Augsburg Confession (1530) or the Formula of Concord (1576).[1]

Students who take the time to read these creeds thoughtfully will find that they provide excellent summaries of the doctrinal teachings of Scripture.

These creeds begin on the following pages of this appendix:

---

[1]These Lutheran confessions may conveniently be found in Philip Schaff, *The Creeds of Christendom*, 3 vols. (Grand Rapids: Baker, 1983, reprint of 1931 edition), 3:3–73, 93–180.

## THE APOSTLES' CREED
### (third–fourth centuries A.D.)

I believe in God the Father Almighty; Maker of heaven and earth.

And in Jesus Christ his only Son our Lord; who was conceived by the Holy Spirit,[2] born of the virgin Mary; suffered under Pontius Pilate, was crucified, dead and buried;[3] the third day he rose from the dead; he ascended into heaven; and sitteth at the right hand of God the Father Almighty; from thence he shall come to judge the quick and the dead.

I believe in the Holy Spirit; the holy catholic Church; the communion of saints; the forgiveness of sins; the resurrection of the body; and the life everlasting. Amen.

\* \* \*

## THE NICENE CREED
### (A.D. 325; revised at Constantinople A.D. 381)

I believe in one God the Father Almighty; Maker of heaven and earth, and of all things visible and invisible.

And in one Lord Jesus Christ, the only-begotten Son of God, begotten of the Father before all worlds, God of God, Light of Light, very God of very God, begotten, not made, being of one substance with the Father; by whom all things were made; who, for us men and for our salvation, came down from heaven, and was incarnate by the Holy Spirit of the Virgin Mary, and was made man; and was crucified also for us under Pontius Pilate; he suffered and was buried; and the third day he rose again, according to the Scriptures; and ascended into heaven, and sitteth on the right hand of the Father; and he shall come again, with glory, to judge both the quick and the dead; whose kingdom shall have no end.

And in the Holy Spirit, the Lord and Giver of Life; who proceedeth from the Father and the Son;[4] who with the Father and the Son together is worshiped and glorified; who spake by the Prophets. And one Holy Catholic and Apostolic Church. I acknowledge one Baptism for the remission of sins; and I look for the resurrection of the dead, and the life of the world to come. Amen.

\* \* \*

## THE CHALCEDONIAN CREED
### (A.D. 451)

We, then, following the holy Fathers, all with one consent, teach men to confess one and the same Son, our Lord Jesus Christ, the same perfect in Godhead and also perfect in manhood; truly God and truly man, of a reasonable soul and body; consubstantial with the Father according to the Godhead, and consubstantial with us according to the Manhood; in all things like unto us, without sin; begotten before all ages of the Father according to the Godhead, and in these latter days, for us and for our salvation, born of the Virgin Mary, the Mother of God, according to the Manhood; one and the same Christ, Son, Lord, Only-begotten, to be acknowledged in two natures, inconfusedly, unchangeably, indivisibly, inseparably; the distinction of natures being by no means taken away by the union, but

---

[2] I have used the modern translation "Holy Spirit" instead of the archaic name "Holy Ghost" throughout the ancient creeds. (But I have not made such a change in the Westminster Confession, which is still used today in its original wording and which sometimes uses "Holy Ghost.")

[3] I have not included the phrase, "he descended into hell," because it is not attested in the earliest versions of the Apostles' Creed, and because of the doctrinal difficulties associated with it (see further discussion in chapter 27, pp. 586–94).

[4] The phrase "and the Son" was added after the Council of Constantinople in 381 but is commonly included in the text of the Nicene Creed as used by Protestant and Roman Catholic churches today. The phrase is not included in the text used by Orthodox churches. (See discussion in chapter 14, pp. 246–47.) The phrase "God of God" was not in the version of 381 but was in the version of 325 and is commonly included today.

rather the property of each nature being preserved, and concurring in one Person and one Subsistence, not parted or divided into two persons, but one and the same Son, and only begotten, God the Word, the Lord Jesus Christ, as the prophets from the beginning have declared concerning him, and the Lord Jesus Christ himself has taught us, and the Creed of the holy Fathers has handed down to us.

\* \* \*

## THE ATHANASIAN CREED
### (fourth—fifth centuries A.D.)

1. Whosoever will be saved: before all things it is necessary that he hold the Catholic Faith:
2. Which Faith except every one do keep whole and undefiled: without doubt he shall perish everlastingly.
3. And the Catholic Faith is this: That we worship one God in Trinity, and Trinity in Unity;
4. Neither confounding the Persons: nor dividing the Substance.
5. For there is one Person of the Father: another of the Son: and another of the Holy Spirit.
6. But the Godhead of the Father, of the Son, and of the Holy Spirit, is all one: the Glory equal, the Majesty coeternal.
7. Such as the Father is: such is the Son: and such is the Holy Spirit.
8. The Father uncreated: the Son uncreated: and the Holy Spirit uncreated.
9. The Father incomprehensible: the Son incomprehensible: and the Holy Spirit incomprehensible.
10. The Father eternal: the Son eternal: and the Holy Spirit eternal.
11. And yet they are not three eternals: but one eternal.
12. And also there are not three uncreated: nor three incomprehensibles, but one uncreated: and one incomprehensible.
13. So likewise the Father is Almighty: the Son Almighty: and the Holy Spirit Almighty.
14. And yet they are not three Almighties: but one Almighty.
15. So the Father is God: the Son is God: and the Holy Spirit is God.
16. And yet they are not three Gods: but one God.
17. So likewise the Father is Lord: the Son Lord: and the Holy Spirit Lord.
18. And yet not three Lords: but one Lord.
19. For like as we are compelled by the Christian verity: to acknowledge every Person by himself to be God and Lord:
20. So are we forbidden by the Catholic Religion: to say, There be three Gods, or three Lords.
21. The Father is made of none: neither created, nor begotten.
22. The Son is of the Father alone: not made, nor created: but begotten.
23. The Holy Spirit is of the Father and of the Son: neither made, nor created, nor begotten: but proceeding.
24. So there is one Father, not three Fathers: one Son, not three Sons: one Holy Spirit, not three Holy Spirits.
25. And in this Trinity none is afore, or after another: none is greater, or less than another.
26. But the whole three Persons are coeternal, and coequal.
27. So that in all things, as aforesaid: the Unity in Trinity, and the Trinity in Unity, is to be worshipped.
28. He therefore that will be saved, must thus think of the Trinity.

29. Furthermore it is necessary to everlasting salvation: that he also believe rightly the Incarnation of our Lord Jesus Christ.
30. For the right Faith is, that we believe and confess: that our Lord Jesus Christ, the Son of God, is God and Man;
31. God, of the Substance of the Father; begotten before the worlds: and Man, of the Substance of his Mother, born in the world.
32. Perfect God: and perfect Man, of a reasonable soul and human flesh subsisting.
33. Equal to the Father, as touching his Godhead: and inferior to the Father as touching his Manhood.
34. Who although he be God and Man; yet he is not two, but one Christ.
35. One; not by conversion of the Godhead into flesh: but by taking of the Manhood into God.
36. One altogether; not by confusion of Substance: but by unity of Person.
37. For as the reasonable soul and flesh is one man; so God and Man is one Christ;
38. Who suffered for our salvation: descended into hell: rose again the third day from the dead.
39. He ascended into heaven, he sitteth on the right hand of the Father God Almighty.
40. From whence he shall come to judge the quick and the dead.
41. At whose coming all men shall rise again with their bodies;
42. And shall give account for their own works.
43. And they that have done good shall go into life everlasting: and they that have done evil, into everlasting fire.
44. This is the Catholic Faith: which except a man believe faithfully, he can not be saved.

* * *

## ARTICLES OF RELIGION (THIRTY-NINE ARTICLES)
### (1571: Church of England)

### I. OF FAITH IN THE HOLY TRINITY.

There is but one living and true God, everlasting, without body, parts, or passions; of infinite power, wisdom, and goodness; the Maker, and Preserver of all things both visible and invisible. And in unity of this Godhead there be three Persons, of one substance, power, and eternity: the Father, the Son, and the Holy Spirit.

### II. OF THE WORD OR SON OF GOD, WHICH WAS MADE VERY MAN.

The Son, which is the Word of the Father, begotten from everlasting of the Father, the very and eternal God, and of one substance with the Father, took Man's nature in the womb of the blessed Virgin, of her substance: so that two whole and perfect Natures, that is to say, the Godhead and Manhood, were joined together in one Person, never to be divided, whereof is one Christ, very God, and very Man; who truly suffered, was crucified, dead and buried, to reconcile his Father to us, and to be a sacrifice, not only for original guilt, but also for actual sins of men.

### III. OF THE GOING DOWN OF CHRIST INTO HELL.

As Christ died for us, and was buried, so also is it to be believed, that he went down into Hell.

### IV. OF THE RESURRECTION OF CHRIST.

Christ did truly rise again from death, and took again his body, with flesh, bones, and all things appertaining to the perfection of Man's nature; wherewith he ascended into Heaven, and there sitteth, until he return to judge all Men at the last day.

### V. OF THE HOLY SPIRIT.

The Holy Spirit, proceeding from the Father and the Son, is of one substance, majesty, and glory, with the Father and the Son, very and eternal God.

### VI. OF THE SUFFICIENCY OF THE HOLY SCRIPTURES FOR SALVATION.

Holy Scripture containeth all things necessary to salvation: so that whatsoever is not read therein, nor may be proved thereby, is not to be required of any man, that it should be believed as an article of the Faith, or be thought requisite or necessary to salvation. In the name of the Holy Scripture we do understand those canonical Books of the Old and New Testament, of whose authority was never any doubt in the Church.

### OF THE NAMES AND NUMBER OF THE CANONICAL BOOKS.

| | |
|---|---|
| Genesis, | The First Book of Chronicles, |
| Exodus, | The Second Book of Chronicles, |
| Leviticus, | The First Book of Esdras, |
| Numbers, | The Second Book of Esdras, |
| Deuteronomy, | The Book of Esther, |
| Joshua, | The Book of Job, |
| Judges, | The Psalms, |
| Ruth, | The Proverbs, |
| The First Book | Ecclesiastes or Preacher, |
| The Second | Cantica, or Song of Solomon, |
| The First Book | Four Prophets the greater, |
| The Second Book | Twelve Prophets the less. |

And the other Books the Church doth read for example of life and instruction of manners; but yet doth it not apply to them to establish any doctrine: such are these following:

| | |
|---|---|
| The Third Book of Esdras, | Baruch the Prophet, |
| The Fourth Book of Esdras, | The Song of the Three Children, |
| The Book of Tobias, | The Story of Susanna, |
| The Book of Judith, | Of Bel and the Dragon, |
| The rest of the Book of Esther | The Prayer of Manasses, |
| The Book of Wisdom, | The First Book of Maccabees, |
| Jesus the Son of Sirach, | The Second Book of Maccabees. |

All the Books of the New Testament, as they are commonly received, we do receive, and account them Canonical.

### VII. OF THE OLD TESTAMENT.

The Old Testament is not contrary to the New: for both in the Old and New Testament everlasting life is offered to mankind by Christ, who is the only Mediator between God and Man, being both God and Man. Wherefore they are not to be heard, which feign that the old Fathers did look only for transitory promises. Although the Law given from God by Moses, as touching Ceremonies and Rites, do not bind Christian men, nor the Civil precepts thereof ought of necessity to be received in any commonwealth; yet notwithstanding, no Christian man whatsoever is free from the obedience of the Commandments which are called Moral.

### VIII. OF THE CREEDS.

The Nicene Creed, and that which is commonly called the Apostles' Creed, ought thoroughly to be received and believed: for they may be proved by most certain warrants of Holy Scripture.

## IX. OF ORIGINAL OR BIRTH-SIN.

Original Sin standeth not in the following of Adam, (as the Pelagians do vainly talk;) but it is the fault and corruption to the Nature of every man, that naturally is ingendered of the offspring of Adam; whereby man is very far gone from original righteousness, and is of his own nature inclined to evil, so that the flesh lusteth always contrary to the spirit; and therefore in every person born into this world, it deserveth God's wrath and damnation. And this infection of nature doth remain, yea in them that are regenerated; whereby the lust of the flesh, called in the Greek *phronēma sarkos* (which some do expound the wisdom, some sensuality, some of the affection, some of the desire, of the flesh), is not subject to the Law of God. And although there is no condemnation for them that believe and are baptized; yet the Apostle doth confess, that concupiscence and lust hath of itself the nature of sin.

## X. OF FREE-WILL.

The condition of Man after the fall of Adam is such, that he cannot turn and prepare himself, by his own natural strength and good works, to faith, and calling upon God. Wherefore we have no power to do good works pleasant and acceptable to God, without the grace of God by Christ preventing us, that we may have a good will, and working with us, when we have that good will.

## XI. OF THE JUSTIFICATION OF MAN.

We are accounted righteous before God, only for the merit of our Lord and Saviour Jesus Christ by Faith, and not for our own works or deservings. Wherefore, that we are justified by Faith only, is a most wholesome Doctrine, and very full of comfort, as more largely is expressed in the Homily of Justification.

## XII. OF GOOD WORKS.

Albeit that Good Works, which are the fruits of Faith, and follow after Justification, cannot put away our sins, and endure the severity of God's judgment; yet are they pleasing and acceptable to God in Christ, and do spring out necessarily of a true and lively faith; insomuch that by them a lively Faith may be as evidently known as a tree discerned by the fruit.

## XIII. OF WORKS BEFORE JUSTIFICATION.

Works done before the grace of Christ, and the Inspiration of his Spirit, are not pleasant to God, forasmuch as they spring not of faith in Jesus Christ; neither do they make men meet to receive grace, or (as the School-authors say) deserve grace of congruity: yea rather, for that they are not done as God hath willed and commanded them to be done, we doubt not but they have the nature of sin.

## XIV. OF WORKS OF SUPEREROGATION.

Voluntary Works besides, over and above, God's Commandments, which they call Works of Supererogation, cannot be taught without arrogancy and impiety: for by them men do declare, that they do not only render unto God as much as they are bound to do, but that they do more for his sake, than of bounden duty is required: whereas Christ saith plainly, When ye have done all that are commanded to you, say, We are unprofitable servants.

## XV. OF CHRIST ALONE WITHOUT SIN.

Christ in the truth of our nature was made like unto us in all things, sin only except, from which he was clearly void, both in his flesh, and in his spirit. He came to be the Lamb without spot, who, by sacrifice of himself once made, should take away the sins of the world; and sin, (as Saint John saith) was not in him. But all we the rest, although baptized, and born again in Christ, yet offend in many things; and if we say we have no sin, we deceive ourselves, and the truth is not in us.

### XVI. OF SIN AFTER BAPTISM.

Not every deadly sin willingly committed after Baptism is sin against the Holy Spirit, and unpardonable. Wherefore the grant of repentance is not to be denied to such as fall into sin after Baptism. After we have received the Holy Spirit, we may depart from grace given, and fall into sin, and by the grace of God we may arise again, and amend our lives. And therefore they are to be condemned, which say, they can no more sin as long as they live here, or deny the place of forgiveness to such as truly repent.

### XVII. OF PREDESTINATION AND ELECTION.

Predestination to Life is the everlasting purpose of God, whereby (before the foundations of the world were laid) he hath constantly decreed by his counsel secret to us, to deliver from curse and damnation those whom he hath chosen in Christ out of mankind, and to bring them by Christ to everlasting salvation, as vessels made to honour. Wherefore, they which be endued with so excellent a benefit of God, be called according to God's purpose by his Spirit working in due season: they through Grace obey the calling: they be justified freely: they be made sons of God by adoption: they be made like the image of his only-begotten Son Jesus Christ: they walk religiously in good works, and at length, by God's mercy, they attain to everlasting felicity.

As the godly consideration of Predestination, and our Election in Christ, is full of sweet, pleasant, and unspeakable comfort to godly persons, and such as feel in themselves the working of the Spirit of Christ, mortifying the works of the flesh, and their earthly members, and drawing up their mind to high and heavenly things, as well because it doth greatly establish and confirm their faith of eternal Salvation to be enjoyed through Christ, as because it doth fervently kindle their love towards God: So, for curious and carnal persons, lacking the Spirit of Christ, to have continually before their eyes the sentence of God's Predestination, is a most dangerous downfall, whereby the Devil doth thrust them either into desperation, or into wretchlessness of most unclean living, no less perilous than desperation.

Furthermore, we must receive God's promises in such wise, as they be generally set forth to us in Holy Scripture: and, in our doings, that Will of God is to be followed, which we have expressly declared unto us in the Word of God.

### XVIII. OF OBTAINING ETERNAL SALVATION ONLY BY THE NAME OF CHRIST.

They also are to be had accursed that presume to say, That every man shall be saved by the Law or Sect which he professeth, so that he be diligent to frame his life according to that Law, and the light of Nature. For Holy Scripture doth set out unto us only the Name of Jesus Christ, whereby men must be saved.

### XIX. OF THE CHURCH.

The visible Church of Christ is a congregation of faithful men, in the which the pure Word of God is preached, and the Sacraments be duly ministered according to Christ's ordinance, in all those things that of necessity are requisite to the same.

As the Church of Jerusalem, Alexandria, and Antioch, have erred; so also the Church of Rome hath erred, not only their living and manner of Ceremonies, but also in matters of Faith.

### XX. OF THE AUTHORITY OF THE CHURCH.

The Church hath power to decree Rites or Ceremonies, and authority in Controversies of Faith: and yet it is not lawful for the Church to ordain any thing that is contrary to God's

Word written, neither may it so expound one place of Scripture, that it be repugnant to another. Wherefore, although the Church be a witness and a keeper of Holy Writ, yet, as it ought not to decree any thing against the same, so besides the same ought it not to enforce any thing to be believed for necessity of Salvation.

## XXI. OF THE AUTHORITY OF GENERAL COUNCILS.

General Councils may not be gathered together without the commandment and will of Princes. And when they be gathered together (foreasmuch as they be an assembly of men, whereof all be not governed with the Spirit and Word of God) they may err, and sometimes have erred, even in things pertaining unto God. Wherefore, things ordained by them as necessary to salvation have neither strength nor authority, unless it may be declared that they be taken out of holy Scripture.

## XXII. OF PURGATORY.

The Romish Doctrine concerning Purgatory, Pardons, Worshipping and Adoration, as well of Images as of Relics, and also Invocation of Saints, is a fond thing, vainly invented, and grounded upon no warranty of Scripture, but rather repugnant to the Word of God.

## XXIII. OF MINISTERING IN THE CONGREGATION

It is not lawful for any man to take upon him the office of public preaching, or ministering the Sacraments in the Congregation, before he be lawfully called, and sent to execute the same. And those we ought to judge lawfully called and sent, which be chosen and called to this work by men who have public authority given unto them in the Congregation, to call and send Ministers into the Lord's vineyard.

## XXIV. OF SPEAKING IN THE CONGREGATION IN SUCH A TONGUE AS THE PEOPLE UNDERSTANDETH.

It is a thing plainly repugnant to the Word of God, and the custom of the Primitive Church, to have public Prayer in the Church, or to minister the Sacraments in a tongue not understanded of the people.

## XXV. OF THE SACRAMENTS.

Sacraments ordained of Christ be not only badges or tokens of Christian men's profession, but rather they be certain sure witnesses, and effectual signs of grace, and God's good will toward us, by the which he doth work invisibly in us, and doth not only quicken, but also strengthen and confirm our Faith in him.

There are two Sacraments ordained of Christ our Lord in the Gospel, that is to say, Baptism, and the Supper of the Lord.

Those five commonly called Sacraments, that is to say, Confirmation, Penance, Orders, Matrimony, and Extreme Unction, are not to be counted for Sacraments of the Gospel, being such as have grown partly of the corrupt following of the Apostles, partly are states of life allowed in the Scriptures; but yet have not like nature of Sacraments with Baptism, and the Lord's Supper, for that they have not any visible sign or ceremony ordained of God.

The Sacraments were not ordained of Christ to be gazed upon, or to be carried about, but that we should duly use them. And in such only as worthily receive the same, they have a wholesome effect or operation: but they that receive them unworthily, purchase to themselves damnation, as Saint Paul saith.

## XXVI. OF THE UNWORTHINESS OF THE MINISTERS, WHICH HINDERS NOT THE EFFECT OF THE SACRAMENT.

Although in the visible Church the evil be ever mingled with the good, and sometimes the evil have chief authority in the Ministration of the Word and Sacraments, yet forasmuch as they do not the same in their own name, but in Christ's, and do minister by his commission and authority, we may use their Ministry, both in hearing the Word of God, and in receiving the Sacraments. Neither is the effect of Christ's ordinance taken away by their wickedness, nor the grace of God's gifts diminished from such as by faith, and rightly, do receive the Sacraments ministered unto them; which be effectual, because of Christ's institution and promise, although they be ministered by evil men.

Nevertheless, it appertaineth to the discipline of the Church, that inquiry be made of evil Ministers, and that they be accused by those that have knowledge of their offences; and finally, being found guilty, by just judgment be deposed.

### XXVII. OF BAPTISM.

Baptism is not only a sign of profession, and mark of difference, whereby Christian men are discerned from others that be not christened, but it is also a sign of Regeneration or New-Birth, whereby, as by an instrument, they that receive Baptism rightly are grafted into the Church; the promises of forgiveness of sin, and of our adoption to be the sons of God by the Holy Spirit, are visibly signed and sealed; Faith is confirmed, and Grace increased by virtue of prayer unto God. The Baptism of young Children is in any wise to be retained in the Church, as most agreeable with the institution of Christ.

### XXVIII. OF THE LORD'S SUPPER.

The Supper of the Lord is not only a sign of the love that Christians ought to have among themselves one to another; but rather it is a Sacrament of our Redemption by Christ's death: insomuch that to such as rightly, worthily, and with faith, receive the same, the Bread which we break is a partaking of the Body of Christ; and likewise the Cup of Blessing is a partaking of the Blood of Christ.

Transubstantiation (or the change of the substance of Bread and Wine) in the Supper of the Lord, cannot be proved by Holy Writ; but is repugnant to the plain words of Scripture, overthroweth the nature of a Sacrament, and hath given occasion to many superstitions.

The Body of Christ is given, taken, and eaten, in the Supper, only after an heavenly and spiritual manner. And the mean whereby the Body of Christ is received and eaten in the Supper, is Faith.

The Sacrament of the Lord's Supper was not by Christ's ordinance reserved, carried about, lifted up, or worshipped.

### XXIX. OF THE WICKED, WHICH EAT NOT THE BODY OF CHRIST IN THE USE OF THE LORD'S SUPPER.

The Wicked, and such as be void of a lively faith, although they do carnally and visibly press with their teeth (as Saint Augustine saith) the Sacrament of the Body and Blood of Christ; yet in no wise are they partakers of Christ: but rather, to their condemnation, do eat and drink the sign or Sacrament of so great a thing.

### XXX. OF BOTH KINDS.

The Cup of the Lord is not to be denied to the Lay-people: for both the parts of the Lord's Sacrament, by Christ's ordinance and commandment, ought to be ministered to all Christian men alike.

### XXXI. OF THE ONE OBLATION OF CHRIST FINISHED UPON THE CROSS.

The Offering of Christ once made is that perfect redemption, propitiation, and satisfaction, for all the sins of the whole world, both original and actual; and there is none other satisfaction for sin, but that alone. Wherefore the sacrifices of Masses, in the which it was commonly said that the Priest did offer Christ for the quick and the dead, to have remission of pain or guilt, were blasphemous fables, and dangerous deceits.

## XXXII. OF THE MARRIAGE OF PRIESTS.

Bishops, Priests, and Deacons, are not commanded by God's Law, either to vow the estate of single life, or to abstain from marriage: therefore it is lawful for them, as for all other Christian men, to marry at their own discretion, as they shall judge the same to serve better to godliness.

## XXXIII. OF EXCOMMUNICATE PERSONS, HOW THEY ARE TO BE AVOIDED.

That person which by open denunciation of the Church is rightly cut off from the unity of the Church, and excommunicated, ought to be taken of the whole multitude of the faithful, as a Heathen and Publican, until he be openly reconciled by penance, and received into the Church by a judge that hath authority thereunto.

## XXXIV. OF THE TRADITIONS OF THE CHURCH.

It is not necessary that Traditions and Ceremonies be in all places one, or utterly like; for at all times they have been divers, and may be changed according to the diversities of countries, times, and men's manners, so that nothing be ordained against God's Word. Whosoever through his private judgment, willingly and purposely, doth openly break the Traditions and Ceremonies of the Church, which be not repugnant to the Word of God, and be ordained and approved by common authority, ought to be rebuked openly, (that others may fear to do the like) as he that offendeth against the common order of the Church, and hurteth the authority of the Magistrate, and woundeth the consciences of the weak brethren.

Every particular or national Church hath authority to ordain, change, and abolish, Ceremonies or Rites of the Church ordained only by man's authority, so that all things be done to edifying.

## XXXV. OF THE HOMILIES.

The Second Book of Homilies, the several titles whereof we have joined under this Article, doth contain a godly and wholesome Doctrine, and necessary for these times, as doth the former Book of Homilies, which were set forth in the time of Edward the Sixth; and therefore we judge them to be read in Churches by the Ministers, diligently and distinctly, that they may be understanded of the people.

### OF THE NAMES OF THE HOMILIES

1. Of the right Use of the Church.
2. Against Peril of Idolatry.
3. Of the repairing and keeping clean of Churches.
4. Of good Works: first of Fasting.
5. Against Gluttony and Drunkenness.
6. Against Excess of Apparel.
7. Of Prayer.
8. Of the Place and Time of Prayer.
9. That Common Prayers and Sacraments ought to be ministered in a known tongue.
10. Of the reverend Estimation of God's Word.
11. Of Alms-doing.
12. Of the Nativity of Christ.
13. Of the Passion of Christ.
14. Of the Resurrection of Christ.
15. Of the worthy receiving of the Sacrament of the Body and Blood of Christ.
16. Of the Gifts of the Holy Spirit.
17. For the Rogation-days.
18. Of the State of Matrimony.
19. Of Repentance.
20. Against Idleness.
21. Against Rebellion.

### XXXVI. OF CONSECRATION OF BISHOPS AND MINISTERS.

The Book of Consecration of Archbishops and Bishops, and Ordering of Priests and Deacons, lately set forth in the time of Edward the Sixth, and confirmed at the same time by authority of Parliament, doth contain all things necessary to such Consecration and Ordering: neither hath it any thing that of itself is superstitious and ungodly. And therefore whosoever are consecrated or ordered according to the Rites of that Book, since the second year of the forenamed King Edward unto this time, or hereafter shall be consecrated or ordered according to the same Rites; we decree all such to be rightly, orderly, and lawfully consecrated and ordered.

### XXXVII. OF THE CIVIL MAGISTRATES.

The Queen's Majesty hath the chief power in this Realm of England, and other her Dominions, unto whom the chief Government of all Estates of this Realm, whether they be Ecclesiastical or Civil, in all causes doth appertain, and is not, nor ought to be, subject to any foreign Jurisdiction.

Where we attribute to the Queen's Majesty the chief government, by which Titles we understand the minds of some slanderous folks to be offended; we give not to our Princes the ministering either of God's Word, or of the Sacraments, the which thing the Injunctions also lately set forth by Elizabeth our Queen do most plainly testify; but that only prerogative, which we see to have been given always to all godly Princes in holy Scriptures by God himself; that is, that they should rule all estates and degrees committed to their charge by God, whether they be Ecclesiastical or Temporal, and restrain with the civil sword the stubborn and evil-doers.

The Bishop of Rome hath no jurisdiction in this Realm of England.

The Laws of the Realm may punish Christian men with death, for heinous and grievous offences.

It is lawful for Christian men, at the commandment of the Magistrate, to wear weapons, and serve in the wars.

### XXXVIII. OF CHRISTIAN MEN'S GOODS, WHICH ARE NOT COMMON.

The Riches and Goods of Christians are not common, as touching the right, title, and possession of the same; as certain Anabaptists do falsely boast. Notwithstanding, every man ought, of such things as he possesseth, liberally to give alms to the poor, according to his ability.

### XXXIX. OF A CHRISTIAN MAN'S OATH.

As we confess that vain and rash Swearing is forbidden Christian men by our Lord Jesus Christ, and James his Apostle, so we judge, that Christian Religion doth not prohibit, but that a man may swear when the Magistrate requireth, in a cause of faith and charity, so it be done according to the Prophet's teaching, in justice, judgment, and truth.

\* \* \*

## WESTMINSTER CONFESSION OF FAITH
### (1643-46)

### *CHAPTER 1: OF THE HOLY SCRIPTURE*

1. Although the light of nature, and the works of creation and providence do so far manifest the goodness, wisdom, and power of God, as to leave men unexcusable; yet are they not sufficient to give that knowledge of God, and of his will, which is necessary unto salvation. Therefore it pleased the Lord, at sundry times, and in divers manners, to reveal himself, and to declare that his will unto his church; and afterwards, for the better preserving and propagating of the truth, and for the more sure establishment and comfort of the church against the corruption of the flesh, and the malice of Satan and of the world, to commit the same wholly unto writing: which maketh the holy Scripture to be most necessary; those former ways of God's revealing his will unto his people being now ceased.

2. Under the name of holy Scripture, or the Word of God written, are now contained all the books of the Old and New Testaments, which are these:

### OLD TESTAMENT

| | | |
|---|---|---|
| Genesis | Chronicles | Daniel |
| Exodus | Ezra | Hosea |
| Leviticus | Nehemiah | Joel |
| Numbers | Esther | Amos |
| Deuteronomy | Job | Obadiah |
| Joshua | Psalms | Jonah |
| Judges | Proverbs | Micah |
| Ruth | Ecclesiastes | Nahum |
| 1 Samuel | Song of Songs | Habakkuk |
| 2 Samuel | Isaiah | Zephaniah |
| 1 Kings | Jeremiah | Haggai |
| 2 Kings | Lamentations | Zechariah |
| 1 Chronicles | Ezekiel | Malachi |

### NEW TESTAMENT

| | |
|---|---|
| Matthew | 1 Timothy |
| Mark | 2 Timothy |
| Luke | Titus |
| John | Philemon |
| Acts | Hebrews |
| Romans | James |
| 1 Corinthians | 1 Peter |
| 2 Corinthians | 2 Peter |
| Galatians | 1 John |
| Ephesians | 2 John |
| Philippians | 3 John |
| Colossians | Jude |
| 1 Thessalonians | Revelation |
| 2 Thessalonians | |

All which are given by inspiration of God to be the rule of faith and life.

3. The books commonly called Apocrypha, not being of divine inspiration, are no part of the canon of the Scripture, and therefore are of no authority in the church of God, nor to be any otherwise approved, or made use of, than other human writings.

4. The authority of the holy Scripture, for which it ought to be believed, and obeyed, dependeth not upon the testimony of any man, or church; but wholly upon God (who is

truth itself) the author thereof: and therefore it is to be received, because it is the Word of God.

5. We may be moved and induced by the testimony of the church to an high and reverent esteem of the holy Scripture. And the heavenliness of the matter, the efficacy of the doctrine, the majesty of the style, the consent of all the parts, the scope of the whole (which is, to give all glory to God), the full discovery it makes of the only way of man's salvation, the many other incomparable excellencies, and the entire perfection thereof, are arguments whereby it doth abundantly evidence itself to be the Word of God: yet notwithstanding, our full persuasion and assurance of the infallible truth and divine authority thereof, is from the inward work of the Holy Spirit bearing witness by and with the Word in our hearts.

6. The whole counsel of God concerning all things necessary for his own glory, man's salvation, faith and life, is either expressly set down in Scripture, or by good and necessary consequence may be deduced from Scripture: unto which nothing at any time is to be added, whether by new revelations of the Spirit, or traditions of men. Nevertheless, we acknowledge the inward illumination of the Spirit of God to be necessary for the saving understanding of such things as are revealed in the Word: and that there are some circumstances concerning the worship of God, and government of the church, common to human actions and societies, which are to be ordered by the light of nature, and Christian prudence, according to the general rules of the Word, which are always to be observed.

7. All things in Scripture are not alike plain in themselves, nor alike clear unto all: yet those things which are necessary to be known, believed, and observed for salvation, are so clearly propounded, and opened in some place of Scripture or other, that not only the learned, but the unlearned, in a due use of the ordinary means, may attain unto a sufficient understanding of them.

8. The Old Testament in Hebrew (which was the native language of the people of God of old), and the New Testament in Greek (which, at the time of the writing of it, was most generally known to the nations), being immediately inspired by God, and, by his singular care and providence, kept pure in all ages, are therefore authentical; so as, in all controversies of religion, the church is finally to appeal unto them. But, because these original tongues are not known to all the people of God, who have right unto, and interest in the Scriptures, and are commanded, in the fear of God, to read and search them, therefore they are to be translated into the vulgar language of every nation unto which they come, that, the Word of God dwelling plentifully in all, they may worship him in an acceptable manner; and, through patience and comfort of the Scriptures, may have hope.

9. The infallible rule of interpretation of Scripture is the Scripture itself: and therefore, when there is a question about the true and full sense of any Scripture (which is not manifold, but one), it must be searched and known by other places that speak more clearly.

10. The supreme judge by which all controversies of religion are to be determined, and all decrees of councils, opinions of ancient writers, doctrines of men, and private spirits, are to be examined, and in whose sentence we are to rest, can be no other but the Holy Spirit speaking in the Scripture.

## CHAPTER 2: OF GOD, AND OF THE HOLY TRINITY

1. There is but one only, living, and true God, who is infinite in being and perfection, a most pure spirit, invisible, without body, parts, or passions; immutable, immense, eternal, incomprehensible, almighty, most wise, most holy, most free, most absolute; working all things according to the counsel of his own immutable and most righteous will, for his own glory; most loving, gracious, merciful, long-suffering, abundant in goodness and truth, forgiving iniquity, transgression, and sin; the rewarder of them that diligently seek him; and withal, most just, and terrible in his judgments, hating all sin, and who will by no means clear the guilty.

2. God hath all life, glory, goodness, blessedness, in and of himself; and is alone in and

unto himself all-sufficient, not standing in need of any creatures which he hath made, nor deriving any glory from them, but only manifesting his own glory in, by, unto, and upon them. He is the alone fountain of all being, of whom, through whom, and to whom are all things; and hath most sovereign dominion over them, to do by them, for them, or upon them whatsoever himself pleaseth. In his sight all things are open and manifest, his knowledge is infinite, infallible, and independent upon the creature, so as nothing is to him contingent, or uncertain. He is most holy in all his counsels, in all his works, and in all his commands. To him is due from angels and men, and every other creature, whatsoever worship, service, or obedience he is pleased to require of them.

3. In the unity of the Godhead there be three persons, of one substance, power, and eternity: God the Father, God the Son, and God the Holy Ghost: the Father is of none, neither begotten, nor proceeding; the Son is eternally begotten of the Father; the Holy Ghost eternally proceeding from the Father and the Son.

## CHAPTER 3: OF GOD'S ETERNAL DECREE

1. God, from all eternity, did, by the most wise and holy counsel of his own will, freely, and unchangeably ordain whatsoever comes to pass: yet so, as thereby neither is God the author of sin, nor is violence offered to the will of the creatures; nor is the liberty or contingency of second causes taken away, but rather established.

2. Although God knows whatsoever may or can come to pass upon all supposed conditions, yet hath he not decreed anything because he foresaw it as future, or as that which would come to pass upon such conditions.

3. By the decree of God, for the manifestation of his glory, some men and angels are predestinated unto everlasting life; and others foreordained to everlasting death.

4. These angels and men, thus predestinated, and foreordained, are particularly and unchangeably designed, and their number so certain and definite, that it cannot be either increased or diminished.

5. Those of mankind that are predestinated unto life, God, before the foundation of the world was laid, according to his eternal and immutable purpose, and the secret counsel and good pleasure of his will, hath chosen, in Christ, unto everlasting glory, out of his mere free grace and love, without any foresight of faith, or good works, or perseverance in either of them, or any other thing in the creature, as conditions, or causes moving him thereunto; and all to the praise of his glorious grace.

6. As God hath appointed the elect unto glory, so hath he, by the eternal and most free purpose of his will, foreordained all the means thereunto. Wherefore, they who are elected, being fallen in Adam, are redeemed by Christ, are effectually called unto faith in Christ by his Spirit working in due season, are justified, adopted, sanctified, and kept by his power, through faith, unto salvation. Neither are any other redeemed by Christ, effectually called, justified, adopted, sanctified, and saved, but the elect only.

7. The rest of mankind God was pleased, according to the unsearchable counsel of his own will, whereby he extendeth or withholdeth mercy, as he pleaseth, for the glory of his sovereign power over his creatures, to pass by; and to ordain them to dishonor and wrath for their sin, to the praise of his glorious justice.

8. The doctrine of this high mystery of predestination is to be handled with special prudence and care, that men, attending the will of God revealed in his Word, and yielding obedience thereunto, may, from the certainty of their effectual vocation, be assured of their eternal election. So shall this doctrine afford matter of praise, reverence, and admiration of God; and of humility, diligence, and abundant consolation to all that sincerely obey the gospel.

## CHAPTER 4: OF CREATION

1. It pleased God the Father, Son, and Holy Ghost, for the manifestation of the glory of

his eternal power, wisdom, and goodness, in the beginning, to create, or make of nothing, the world, and all things therein whether visible or invisible, in the space of six days; and all very good.

2. After God had made all other creatures, he created man, male and female, with reasonable and immortal souls, endued with knowledge, righteousness, and true holiness, after his own image; having the law of God written in their hearts, and power to fulfil it: and yet under a possibility of transgressing, being left to the liberty of their own will, which was subject unto change. Beside this law written in their hearts, they received a command, not to eat of the tree of the knowledge of good and evil; which while they kept, they were happy in their communion with God, and had dominion over the creatures.

## CHAPTER 5: OF PROVIDENCE

1. God the great Creator of all things doth uphold, direct, dispose, and govern all creatures, actions, and things, from the greatest even to the least, by his most wise and holy providence, according to his infallible foreknowledge, and the free and immutable counsel of his own will, to the praise of the glory of his wisdom, power, justice, goodness, and mercy.

2. Although, in relation to the foreknowledge and decree of God, the first Cause, all things come to pass immutably, and infallibly; yet, by the same providence, he ordereth them to fall out, according to the nature of second causes, either necessarily, freely, or contingently.

3. God, in his ordinary providence, maketh use of means, yet is free to work without, above, and against them, at his pleasure.

4. The almighty power, unsearchable wisdom, and infinite goodness of God so far manifest themselves in his providence, that it extendeth itself even to the first fall, and all other sins of angels and men; and that not by a bare permission, but such as hath joined with it a most wise and powerful bounding, and otherwise ordering, and governing of them, in a manifold dispensation, to his own holy ends; yet so, as the sinfulness thereof proceedeth only from the creature, and not from God, who, being most holy and righteous, neither is nor can be the author or approver of sin.

5. The most wise, righteous, and gracious God doth oftentimes leave, for a season, his own children to manifold temptations, and the corruption of their own hearts, to chastise them for their former sins, or to discover unto them the hidden strength of corruption and deceitfulness of their hearts, that they may be humbled; and, to raise them to a more close and constant dependence for their support upon himself, and to make them more watchful against all future occasions of sin, and for sundry other just and holy ends.

6. As for those wicked and ungodly men whom God, as a righteous Judge, for former sins, doth blind and harden, from them he not only withholdeth his grace whereby they might have been enlightened in their understandings, and wrought upon in their hearts; but sometimes also withdraweth the gifts which they had, and exposeth them to such objects as their corruption makes occasions of sin; and, withal, gives them over to their own lusts, the temptations of the world, and the power of Satan, whereby it comes to pass that they harden themselves, even under those means which God useth for the softening of others.

7. As the providence of God doth, in general, reach to all creatures; so, after a most special manner, it taketh care of his church, and disposeth all things to the good thereof.

## CHAPTER 6: OF THE FALL OF MAN, OF SIN, AND OF THE PUNISHMENT THEREOF

1. Our first parents, being seduced by the subtlety and temptation of Satan, sinned, in eating the forbidden fruit. This their sin, God was pleased, according to his wise and holy counsel, to permit, having purposed to order it to his own glory.

2. By this sin they fell from their original righteousness and communion with God, and so became dead in sin, and wholly defiled in all the parts and faculties of soul and body.

3. They being the root of all mankind, the guilt of this sin was imputed; and the same death in sin, and corrupted nature, conveyed to all their posterity descending from them by ordinary generation.

4. From this original corruption, whereby we are utterly indisposed, disabled, and made opposite to all good, and wholly inclined to all evil, do proceed all actual transgressions.

5. This corruption of nature, during this life, doth remain in those that are regenerated; and although it be, through Christ, pardoned, and mortified; yet both itself, and all the motions thereof, are truly and properly sin.

6. Every sin, both original and actual, being a transgression of the righteous law of God, and contrary thereunto, doth, in its own nature, bring guilt upon the sinner, whereby he is bound over to the wrath of God, and curse of the law, and so made subject to death, with all miseries spiritual, temporal, and eternal.

## CHAPTER 7: OF GOD'S COVENANT WITH MAN

1. The distance between God and the creature is so great, that although reasonable creatures do owe obedience unto him as their Creator, yet they could never have any fruition of him as their blessedness and reward, but by some voluntary condescension on God's part, which he hath been pleased to express by way of covenant.

2. The first covenant made with man was a covenant of works, wherein life was promised to Adam; and in him to his posterity, upon condition of perfect and personal obedience.

3. Man, by his fall, having made himself incapable of life by that covenant, the Lord was pleased to make a second, commonly called the covenant of grace; wherein he freely offereth unto sinners life and salvation by Jesus Christ; requiring of them faith in him, that they may be saved, and promising to give unto all those that are ordained unto eternal life his Holy Spirit, to make them willing, and able to believe.

4. This covenant of grace is frequently set forth in Scripture by the name of a testament, in reference to the death of Jesus Christ the Testator, and to the everlasting inheritance, with all things belonging to it, therein bequeathed.

5. This covenant was differently administered in the time of the law, and in the time of the gospel: under the law, it was administered by promises, prophecies, sacrifices, circumcision, the paschal lamb, and other types and ordinances delivered to the people of the Jews, all foresignifying Christ to come; which were, for that time, sufficient and efficacious, through the operation of the Spirit, to instruct and build up the elect in faith in the promised Messiah, by whom they had full remission of sins, and eternal salvation; and is called the Old Testament.

6. Under the gospel, when Christ, the substance, was exhibited, the ordinances in which this covenant is dispensed are the preaching of the Word, and the administration of the sacraments of Baptism and the Lord's Supper: which, though fewer in number, and administered with more simplicity, and less outward glory, yet, in them, it is held forth in more fullness, evidence and spiritual efficacy, to all nations, both Jews and Gentiles; and is called the New Testament. There are not therefore two covenants of grace, differing in substance, but one and the same, under various dispensations.

## CHAPTER 8: OF CHRIST THE MEDIATOR

1. It pleased God, in his eternal purpose, to choose and ordain the Lord Jesus, his only begotten Son, to be the Mediator between God and man, the Prophet, Priest, and King, the Head and Savior of his church, the Heir of all things, and Judge of the world: unto whom he did from all eternity give a people, to be his seed, and to be by him in time redeemed, called, justified, sanctified, and glorified.

2. The Son of God, the second person in the Trinity, being very and eternal God, of one

substance and equal with the Father, did, when the fullness of time was come, take upon him man's nature, with all the essential properties, and common infirmities thereof, yet without sin; being conceived by the power of the Holy Ghost, in the womb of the virgin Mary, of her substance. So that two whole, perfect, and distinct natures, the Godhead and the manhood, were inseparably joined together in one person, without conversion, composition, or confusion. Which person is very God, and very man, yet one Christ, the only Mediator between God and man.

3. The Lord Jesus, in his human nature thus united to the divine, was sanctified, and anointed with the Holy Spirit, above measure, having in him all the treasures of wisdom and knowledge; in whom it pleased the Father that all fullness should dwell; to the end that, being holy, harmless, undefiled, and full of grace and truth, he might be thoroughly furnished to execute the office of a mediator, and surety. Which office he took not unto himself, but was thereunto called by his Father, who put all power and judgment into his hand, and gave him commandment to execute the same.

4. This office the Lord Jesus did most willingly undertake; which that he might discharge, he was made under the law, and did perfectly fulfil it; endured most grievous torments immediately in his soul, and most painful sufferings in his body; was crucified, and died, was buried, and remained under the power of death, yet saw no corruption. On the third day he arose from the dead, with the same body in which he suffered, with which also he ascended into heaven, and there sitteth at the right hand of his Father, making intercession, and shall return, to judge men and angels, at the end of the world.

5. The Lord Jesus, by his perfect obedience, and sacrifice of himself, which he, through the eternal Spirit, once offered up unto God, hath fully satisfied the justice of his Father; and purchased, not only reconciliation, but an everlasting inheritance in the kingdom of heaven, for all those whom the Father hath given unto him.

6. Although the work of redemption was not actually wrought by Christ till after his incarnation, yet the virtue, efficacy, and benefits thereof were communicated unto the elect, in all ages successively from the beginning of the world, in and by those promises, types, and sacrifices, wherein he was revealed, and signified to be the seed of the woman which should bruise the serpent's head; and the Lamb slain from the beginning of the world; being yesterday and today the same, and forever.

7. Christ, in the work of mediation, acts according to both natures, by each nature doing that which is proper to itself; yet, by reason of the unity of the person, that which is proper to one nature is sometimes in Scripture attributed to the person denominated by the other nature.

8. To all those for whom Christ hath purchased redemption, he doth certainly and effectually apply and communicate the same; making intercession for them, and revealing unto them, in and by the Word, the mysteries of salvation; effectually persuading them by his Spirit to believe and obey, and governing their hearts by his Word and Spirit; overcoming all their enemies by his almighty power and wisdom, in such manner, and ways, as are most consonant to his wonderful and unsearchable dispensation.

### CHAPTER 9: OF FREE WILL

1. God hath endued the will of man with that natural liberty, that it is neither forced, nor, by any absolute necessity of nature, determined to good, or evil.

2. Man, in his state of innocency, had freedom, and power to will and to do that which was good and well pleasing to God; but yet, mutably, so that he might fall from it.

3. Man, by his fall into a state of sin, hath wholly lost all ability of will to any spiritual good accompanying salvation: so as, a natural man, being altogether averse from that good, and dead in sin, is not able, by his own strength, to convert himself, or to prepare himself thereunto.

4. When God converts a sinner, and translates him into the state of grace, he freeth him

from his natural bondage under sin; and, by his grace alone, enables him freely to will and to do that which is spiritually good; yet so, as that by reason of his remaining corruption, he doth not perfectly, nor only, will that which is good, but doth also will that which is evil.

5. The will of man is made perfectly and immutably free to good alone, in the state of glory only.

## CHAPTER 10: OF EFFECTUAL CALLING

1. All those whom God hath predestinated unto life, and those only, he is pleased, in his appointed and accepted time, effectually to call, by his Word and Spirit, out of that state of sin and death, in which they are by nature, to grace and salvation, by Jesus Christ; enlightening their minds spiritually and savingly to understand the things of God, taking away their heart of stone, and giving unto them a heart of flesh; renewing their wills, and, by his almighty power, determining them to that which is good, and effectually drawing them to Jesus Christ: yet so, as they come most freely, being made willing by his grace.

2. This effectual call is of God's free and special grace alone, not from anything at all foreseen in man, who is altogether passive therein, until, being quickened and renewed by the Holy Spirit, he is thereby enabled to answer this call, and to embrace the grace offered and conveyed in it.

3. Elect infants, dying in infancy, are regenerated, and saved by Christ, through the Spirit, who worketh when, and where, and how he pleaseth: so also are all other elect persons who are incapable of being outwardly called by the ministry of the Word.

4. Others, not elected, although they may be called by the ministry of the Word, and may have some common operations of the Spirit, yet they never truly come unto Christ, and therefore cannot be saved: much less can men, not professing the Christian religion, be saved in any other way whatsoever, be they never so diligent to frame their lives according to the light of nature, and the laws of that religion they do profess. And, to assert and maintain that they may, is very pernicious, and to be detested.

## CHAPTER 11: OF JUSTIFICATION

1. Those whom God effectually calleth, he also freely justifieth: not by infusing righteousness into them, but by pardoning their sins, and by accounting and accepting their persons as righteous; not for anything wrought in them, or done by them, but for Christ's sake alone; nor by imputing faith itself, the act of believing, or any other evangelical obedience to them, as their righteousness; but by imputing the obedience and satisfaction of Christ unto them, they receiving and resting on him and his righteousness, by faith; which faith they have not of themselves, it is the gift of God.

2. Faith, thus receiving and resting on Christ and his righteousness, is the alone instrument of justification: yet is it not alone in the person justified, but is ever accompanied with all other saving graces, and is no dead faith, but worketh by love.

3. Christ, by his obedience and death, did fully discharge the debt of all those that are thus justified, and did make a proper, real, and full satisfaction to his Father's justice in their behalf. Yet, inasmuch as he was given by the Father for them; and his obedience and satisfaction accepted in their stead; and both, freely, not for anything in them; their justification is only of free grace; that both the exact justice and rich grace of God might be glorified in the justification of sinners.

4. God did, from all eternity, decree to justify all the elect, and Christ did, in the fullness of time, die for their sins, and rise again for their justification: nevertheless, they are not justified, until the Holy Spirit doth, in due time, actually apply Christ unto them.

5. God doth continue to forgive the sins of those that are justified; and, although they can never fall from the state of justification, yet they may, by their sins, fall under God's fatherly displeasure, and not have the light of his countenance restored unto them, until

they humble themselves, confess their sins, beg pardon, and renew their faith and repentance.

6. The justification of believers under the Old Testament was, in all these respects, one and the same with the justification of believers under the New Testament.

## CHAPTER 12: OF ADOPTION

1. All those that are justified, God vouchsafeth, in and for his only Son Jesus Christ, to make partakers of the grace of adoption, by which they are taken into the number, and enjoy the liberties and privileges of the children of God, have his name put upon them, receive the spirit of adoption, have access to the throne of grace with boldness, are enabled to cry, Abba, Father, are pitied, protected, provided for, and chastened by him, as by a Father: yet never cast off, but sealed to the day of redemption; and inherit the promises, as heirs of everlasting salvation.

## CHAPTER 13: OF SANCTIFICATION

1. They, who are once effectually called, and regenerated, having a new heart, and a new spirit created in them, are further sanctified, really and personally, through the virtue of Christ's death and resurrection, by his Word and Spirit dwelling in them: the dominion of the whole body of sin is destroyed, and the several lusts thereof are more and more weakened and mortified; and they more and more quickened and strengthened in all saving graces, to the practice of true holiness, without which no man shall see the Lord.

2. This sanctification is throughout, in the whole man; yet imperfect in this life, there abiding still some remnants of corruption in every part; whence ariseth a continual and irreconcilable war, the flesh lusting against the Spirit, and the Spirit against the flesh.

3. In which war, although the remaining corruption, for a time, may much prevail; yet, through the continual supply of strength from the sanctifying Spirit of Christ, the regenerate part doth overcome; and so, the saints grow in grace, perfecting holiness in the fear of God.

## CHAPTER 14: OF SAVING FAITH

1. The grace of faith, whereby the elect are enabled to believe to the saving of their souls, is the work of the Spirit of Christ in their hearts, and is ordinarily wrought by the ministry of the Word, by which also, and by the administration of the sacraments, and prayer, it is increased and strengthened.

2. By this faith, a Christian believeth to be true whatsoever is revealed in the Word, for the authority of God himself speaking therein; and acteth differently upon that which each particular passage thereof containeth; yielding obedience to the commands, trembling at the threatenings, and embracing the promises of God for this life, and that which is to come. But the principal acts of saving faith are accepting, receiving, and resting upon Christ alone for justification, sanctification, and eternal life, by virtue of the covenant of grace.

3. This faith is different in degrees, weak or strong; may be often and many ways assailed, and weakened, but gets the victory: growing up in many to the attainment of a full assurance, through Christ, who is both the author and finisher of our faith.

## CHAPTER 15: OF REPENTANCE UNTO LIFE

1. Repentance unto life is an evangelical grace, the doctrine whereof is to be preached by every minister of the gospel, as well as that of faith in Christ.

2. By it, a sinner, out of the sight and sense not only of the danger, but also of the filthiness and odiousness of his sins, as contrary to the holy nature, and righteous law of God; and upon the apprehension of his mercy in Christ to such as are penitent, so grieves for, and hates his sins, as to turn from them all unto God, purposing and endeavoring to walk with him in all the ways of his· commandments.

3. Although repentance be not to be rested in, as any satisfaction for sin, or any cause of

the pardon thereof, which is the act of God's free grace in Christ; yet it is of such necessity to all sinners, that none may expect pardon without it.

4. As there is no sin so small, but it deserves damnation; so there is no sin so great, that it can bring damnation upon those who truly repent.

5. Men ought not to content themselves with a general repentance, but it is every man's duty to endeavor to repent of his particular sins, particularly.

6. As every man is bound to make private confession of his sins to God, praying for the pardon thereof; upon which, and the forsaking of them, he shall find mercy; so, he that scandalizeth his brother, or the church of Christ, ought to be willing, by a private or public confession, and sorrow for his sin, to declare his repentance to those that are offended, who are thereupon to be reconciled to him, and in love to receive him.

## CHAPTER 16: OF GOOD WORKS

1. Good works are only such as God hath commanded in his holy Word, and not such as, without the warrant thereof, are devised by men, out of blind zeal, or upon any pretense of good intention.

2. These good works, done in obedience to God's commandments, are the fruits and evidences of a true and lively faith: and by them believers manifest their thankfulness, strengthen their assurance, edify their brethren, adorn the profession of the gospel, stop the mouths of the adversaries, and glorify God, whose workmanship they are, created in Christ Jesus thereunto, that, having their fruit unto holiness, they may have the end, eternal life.

3. Their ability to do good works is not at all of themselves, but wholly from the Spirit of Christ. And that they may be enabled thereunto, beside the graces they have already received, there is required an actual influence of the same Holy Spirit, to work in them to will, and to do, of his good pleasure: yet are they not hereupon to grow negligent, as if they were not bound to perform any duty unless upon a special motion of the Spirit; but they ought to be diligent in stirring up the grace of God that is in them.

4. They who, in their obedience, attain to the greatest height which is possible in this life, are so far from being able to supererogate, and to do more than God requires, as that they fall short of much which in duty they are bound to do.

5. We cannot by our best works merit pardon of sin, or eternal life at the hand of God, by reason of the great disproportion that is between them and the glory to come; and the infinite distance that is between us and God, whom, by them, we can neither profit, nor satisfy for the debt of our former sins, but when we have done all we can, we have done but our duty, and are unprofitable servants: and because, as they are good, they proceed from his Spirit; and as they are wrought by us, they are defiled, and mixed with so much weakness and imperfection, that they cannot endure the severity of God's judgment.

6. Notwithstanding, the persons of believers being accepted through Christ, their good works also are accepted in him; not as though they were in this life wholly unblamable and unreprovable in God's sight; but that he, looking upon them in his Son, is pleased to accept and reward that which is sincere, although accompanied with many weaknesses and imperfections.

7. Works done by unregenerate men, although for the matter of them they may be things which God commands; and of good use both to themselves and others: yet, because they proceed not from an heart purified by faith; nor are done in a right manner, according to the Word; nor to a right end, the glory of God, they are therefore sinful, and cannot please God, or make a man meet to receive grace from God: and yet, their neglect of them is more sinful and displeasing unto God.

## CHAPTER 17: OF THE PERSEVERANCE OF THE SAINTS

1. They, whom God hath accepted in his Beloved, effectually called, and sanctified by his

Spirit, can neither totally nor finally fall away from the state of grace, but shall certainly persevere therein to the end, and be eternally saved.

2. This perseverance of the saints depends not upon their own free will, but upon the immutability of the decree of election, flowing from the free and unchangeable love of God the Father; upon the efficacy of the merit and intercession of Jesus Christ, the abiding of the Spirit, and of the seed of God within them, and the nature of the covenant of grace: from all which ariseth also the certainty and infallibility thereof.

3. Nevertheless, they may, through the temptations of Satan and of the world, the prevalency of corruption remaining in them, and the neglect of the means of their preservation, fall into grievous sins; and, for a time, continue therein: whereby they incur God's displeasure, and grieve his Holy Spirit, come to be deprived of some measure of their graces and comforts, have their hearts hardened, and their consciences wounded; hurt and scandalize others, and bring temporal judgments upon themselves.

## CHAPTER 18: OF ASSURANCE OF GRACE AND SALVATION

1. Although hypocrites and other unregenerate men may vainly deceive themselves with false hopes and carnal presumptions of being in the favor of God, and estate of salvation (which hope of theirs shall perish): yet such as truly believe in the Lord Jesus, and love him in sincerity, endeavoring to walk in all good conscience before him, may, in this life, be certainly assured that they are in the state of grace, and may rejoice in the hope of the glory of God, which hope shall never make them ashamed.

2. This certainty is not a bare conjectural and probable persuasion grounded upon a fallible hope; but an infallible assurance of faith founded upon the divine truth of the promises of salvation, the inward evidence of those graces unto which these promises are made, the testimony of the Spirit of adoption witnessing with our spirits that we are the children of God, which Spirit is the earnest of our inheritance, whereby we are sealed to the day of redemption.

3. This infallible assurance doth not so belong to the essence of faith, but that a true believer may wait long, and conflict with many difficulties before he be partaker of it: yet, being enabled by the Spirit to know the things which are freely given him of God, he may, without extraordinary revelation, in the right use of ordinary means, attain thereunto. And therefore it is the duty of everyone to give all diligence to make his calling and election sure, that thereby his heart may be enlarged in peace and joy in the Holy Ghost, in love and thankfulness to God, and in strength and cheerfulness in the duties of obedience, the proper fruits of this assurance; so far is it from inclining men to looseness.

4. True believers may have the assurance of their salvation divers ways shaken, diminished, and intermitted; as, by negligence in preserving of it, by falling into some special sin which woundeth the conscience and grieveth the Spirit; by some sudden or vehement temptation, by God's withdrawing the light of his countenance, and suffering even such as fear him to walk in darkness and to have no light: yet are they never utterly destitute of that seed of God, and life of faith, that love of Christ and the brethren, that sincerity of heart, and conscience of duty, out of which, by the operation of the Spirit, this assurance may, in due time, be revived; and by the which, in the meantime, they are supported from utter despair.

## CHAPTER 19: OF THE LAW OF GOD

1. God gave to Adam a law, as a covenant of works, by which he bound him and all his posterity to personal, entire, exact, and perpetual obedience, promised life upon the fulfilling, and threatened death upon the breach of it, and endued him with power and ability to keep it.

2. This law, after his fall, continued to be a perfect rule of righteousness; and, as such, was delivered by God upon Mount Sinai, in ten commandments, and written in two tables:

the four first commandments containing our duty towards God; and the other six, our duty to man.

3. Beside this law, commonly called moral, God was pleased to give to the people of Israel, as a church under age, ceremonial laws, containing several typical ordinances, partly of worship, prefiguring Christ, his graces, actions, sufferings, and benefits; and partly, holding forth divers instructions of moral duties. All which ceremonial laws are now abrogated, under the New Testament.

4. To them also, as a body politic, he gave sundry judicial laws, which expired together with the state of that people; not obliging any other now, further than the general equity thereof may require.

5. The moral law doth forever bind all, as well justified persons as others, to the obedience thereof; and that, not only in regard of the matter contained in it, but also in respect of the authority of God the Creator, who gave it. Neither doth Christ, in the gospel, any way dissolve, but much strengthen this obligation.

6. Although true believers be not under the law, as a covenant of works, to be thereby justified, or condemned; yet is it of great use to them, as well as to others; in that, as a rule of life informing them of the will of God, and their duty, it directs and binds them to walk accordingly; discovering also the sinful pollutions of their nature, hearts, and lives; so as, examining themselves thereby, they may come to further conviction of, humiliation for, and hatred against sin, together with a clearer sight of the need they have of Christ, and the perfection of his obedience. It is likewise of use to the regenerate, to restrain their corruptions, in that it forbids sin: and the threatenings of it serve to show what even their sins deserve; and what afflictions, in this life, they may expect for them, although freed from the curse thereof threatened in the law. The promises of it, in like manner, show them God's approbation of obedience, and what blessings they may expect upon the performance thereof: although not as due to them by the law as a covenant of works. So as, a man's doing good, and refraining from evil, because the law encourageth to the one, and deterreth from the other, is no evidence of his being under the law; and, not under grace.

7. Neither are the forementioned uses of the law contrary to the grace of the gospel, but do sweetly comply with it; the Spirit of Christ subduing and enabling the will of man to do that freely, and cheerfully, which the will of God, revealed in the law, requireth to be done.

## CHAPTER 20: OF CHRISTIAN LIBERTY, AND LIBERTY OF CONSCIENCE

1. The liberty which Christ hath purchased for believers under the gospel consists in their freedom from the guilt of sin, the condemning wrath of God, the curse of the moral law; and, in their being delivered from this present evil world, bondage to Satan, and dominion of sin; from the evil of afflictions, the sting of death, the victory of the grave, and everlasting damnation; as also, in their free access to God, and their yielding obedience unto him, not out of slavish fear, but a childlike love and willing mind. All which were common also to believers under the law. But, under the New Testament, the liberty of Christians is further enlarged, in their freedom from the yoke of the ceremonial law, to which the Jewish church was subjected; and in greater boldness of access to the throne of grace, and in fuller communications of the free Spirit of God, than believers under the law did ordinarily partake of.

2. God alone is Lord of the conscience, and hath left it free from the doctrines and commandments of men, which are, in anything, contrary to his Word; or beside it, if matters of faith, or worship. So that, to believe such doctrines, or to obey such commands, out of conscience, is to betray true liberty of conscience: and the requiring of an implicit faith, and an absolute and blind obedience, is to destroy liberty of conscience, and reason also.

3. They who, upon pretense of Christian liberty, do practice any sin, or cherish any lust, do thereby destroy the end of Christian liberty, which is, that being delivered out of the

hands of our enemies, we might serve the Lord without fear, in holiness and righteousness before him, all the days of our life.

4. And because the powers which God hath ordained, and the liberty which Christ hath purchased, are not intended by God to destroy, but mutually to uphold and preserve one another, they who, upon pretense of Christian liberty, shall oppose any lawful power, or the lawful exercise of it, whether it be civil or ecclesiastical, resist the ordinance of God. And, for their publishing of such opinions, or maintaining of such practices, as are contrary to the light of nature, or to the known principles of Christianity (whether concerning faith, worship, or conversation), or to the power of godliness; or, such erroneous opinions or practices, as either in their own nature, or in the manner of publishing or maintaining them, are destructive to the external peace and order which Christ hath established in the church, they may lawfully be called to account, and proceeded against, by the censures of the church.

## CHAPTER 21: OF RELIGIOUS WORSHIP, AND THE SABBATH-DAY

1. The light of nature showeth that there is a God, who hath lordship and sovereignty over all, is good, and doth good unto all, and is therefore to be feared, loved, praised, called upon, trusted in, and served, with all the heart, and with all the soul, and with all the might. But the acceptable way of worshiping the true God is instituted by himself, and so limited by his own revealed will, that he may not be worshiped according to the imaginations and devices of men, or the suggestions of Satan, under any visible representation, or any other way not prescribed in the holy Scripture.

2. Religious worship is to be given to God, the Father, Son, and Holy Ghost; and to him alone; not to angels, saints, or any other creature: and, since the fall, not without a Mediator; nor in the mediation of any other but of Christ alone.

3. Prayer, with thanksgiving, being one special part of religious worship, is by God required of all men: and, that it may be accepted, it is to be made in the name of the Son, by the help of his Spirit, according to his will, with understanding, reverence, humility, fervency, faith, love, and perseverance; and, if vocal, in a known tongue.

4. Prayer is to be made for things lawful; and for all sorts of men living, or that shall live hereafter: but not for the dead, nor for those of whom it may be known that they have sinned the sin unto death.

5. The reading of the Scriptures with godly fear, the sound preaching and conscionable hearing of the Word, in obedience unto God, with understanding, faith, and reverence, singing of psalms with grace in the heart; as also, the due administration and worthy receiving of the sacraments instituted by Christ, are all parts of the ordinary religious worship of God: beside religious oaths, vows, solemn fastings, and thanksgivings upon special occasions, which are, in their several times and seasons, to be used in an holy and religious manner.

6. Neither prayer, nor any other part of religious worship, is now, under the gospel, either tied unto, or made more acceptable by any place in which it is performed, or towards which it is directed: but God is to be worshiped everywhere, in spirit and truth; as, in private families daily, and in secret, each one by himself; so, more solemnly in the public assemblies, which are not carelessly or wilfully to be neglected, or forsaken, when God, by his Word or providence, calleth thereunto.

7. As it is the law of nature, that, in general, a due proportion of time be set apart for the worship of God; so, in his Word, by a positive, moral, and perpetual commandment binding all men in all ages, he hath particularly appointed one day in seven, for a sabbath, to be kept holy unto him: which, from the beginning of the world to the resurrection of Christ, was the last day of the week; and, from the resurrection of Christ, was changed into the first day of the week, which, in Scripture, is called the Lord's day, and is to be continued to the end of the world, as the Christian sabbath.

8. This sabbath is then kept holy unto the Lord, when men, after a due preparing of their hearts, and ordering of their common affairs beforehand, do not only observe an holy rest, all the day, from their own works, words, and thoughts about their worldly employments and recreations, but also are taken up, the whole time, in the public and private exercises of his worship, and in the duties of necessity and mercy.

## CHAPTER 22: OF LAWFUL OATHS AND VOWS

1. A lawful oath is a part of religious worship, wherein, upon just occasion, the person swearing solemnly calleth God to witness what he asserteth, or promiseth, and to judge him according to the truth or falsehood of what he sweareth.

2. The name of God only is that by which men ought to swear, and therein it is to be used with all holy fear and reverence. Therefore, to swear vainly, or rashly, by that glorious and dreadful Name; or, to swear at all by any other thing, is sinful, and to be abhorred. Yet, as in matters of weight and moment, an oath is warranted by the Word of God, under the New Testament as well as under the Old; so a lawful oath, being imposed by lawful authority, in such matters, ought to be taken.

3. Whosoever taketh an oath ought duly to consider the weightiness of so solemn an act, and therein to avouch nothing but what he is fully persuaded is the truth: neither may any man bind himself by oath to anything but what is good and just, and what he believeth so to be, and what he is able and resolved to perform.

4. An oath is to be taken in the plain and common sense of the words, without equivocation, or mental reservation. It cannot oblige to sin; but in anything not sinful, being taken, it binds to performance, although to a man's own hurt. Nor is it to be violated, although made to heretics, or infidels.

5. A vow is of the like nature with a promissory oath, and ought to be made with the like religious care, and to be performed with the like faithfulness.

6. It is not to be made to any creature, but to God alone: and, that it may be accepted, it is to be made voluntarily, out of faith, and conscience of duty, in way of thankfulness for mercy received, or for the obtaining of what we want, whereby we more strictly bind ourselves to necessary duties; or, to other things, so far and so long as they may fitly conduce thereunto.

7. No man may vow to do anything forbidden in the Word of God, or what would hinder any duty therein commanded, or which is not in his own power, and for the performance whereof he hath no promise of ability from God. In which respects, popish monastical vows of perpetual single life, professed poverty, and regular obedience, are so far from being degrees of higher perfection, that they are superstitious and sinful snares, in which no Christian may entangle himself.

## CHAPTER 23: OF THE CIVIL MAGISTRATE

1. God, the supreme Lord and King of all the world, hath ordained civil magistrates, to be, under him, over the people, for his own glory, and the public good: and, to this end, hath armed them with the power of the sword, for the defense and encouragement of them that are good, and for the punishment of evil doers.

2. It is lawful for Christians to accept and execute the office of a magistrate, when called thereunto: in the managing whereof, as they ought especially to maintain piety, justice, and peace, according to the wholesome laws of each commonwealth; so, for that end, they may lawfully, now under the New Testament, wage war, upon just and necessary occasion.

3. Civil magistrates may not assume to themselves the administration of the Word and sacraments; or the power of the keys of the kingdom of heaven; or, in the least, interfere in matters of faith. Yet, as nursing fathers, it is the duty of civil magistrates to protect the church of our common Lord, without giving the preference to any denomination of Christians above the rest, in such a manner that all ecclesiastical persons whatever shall

enjoy the full, free, and unquestioned liberty of discharging every part of their sacred functions, without violence or danger. And, as Jesus Christ hath appointed a regular government and discipline in his church, no law of any commonwealth should interfere with, let, or hinder, the due exercise thereof, among the voluntary members of any denomination of Christians, according to their own profession and belief. It is the duty of civil magistrates to protect the person and good name of all their people, in such an effectual manner as that no person be suffered, either upon pretense of religion or of infidelity, to offer any indignity, violence, abuse, or injury to any other person whatsoever: and to take order, that all religious and ecclesiastical assemblies be held without molestation or disturbance.

4. It is the duty of people to pray for magistrates, to honor their persons, to pay them tribute or other dues, to obey their lawful commands, and to be subject to their authority, for conscience' sake. Infidelity, or difference in religion, doth not make void the magistrates' just and legal authority, nor free the people from their due obedience to them: from which ecclesiastical persons are not exempted, much less hath the pope any power and jurisdiction over them in their dominions, or over any of their people; and, least of all, to deprive them of their dominions, or lives, if he shall judge them to be heretics, or upon any other pretense whatsoever.

## CHAPTER 24: OF MARRIAGE AND DIVORCE

1. Marriage is to be between one man and one woman: neither is it lawful for any man to have more than one wife, nor for any woman to have more than one husband, at the same time.

2. Marriage was ordained for the mutual help of husband and wife, for the increase of mankind with legitimate issue, and of the church with an holy seed; and for preventing of uncleanness.

3. It is lawful for all sorts of people to marry, who are able with judgment to give their consent. Yet it is the duty of Christians to marry only in the Lord. And therefore such as profess the true reformed religion should not marry with infidels, papists, or other idolaters: neither should such as are godly be unequally yoked, by marrying with such as are notoriously wicked in their life, or maintain damnable heresies.

4. Marriage ought not to be within the degrees of consanguinity or affinity forbidden by the Word. Nor can such incestuous marriages ever be made lawful by any law of man or consent of parties, so as those persons may live together as man and wife.

5. Adultery or fornication committed after a contract, being detected before marriage, giveth just occasion to the innocent party to dissolve that contract. In the case of adultery after marriage, it is lawful for the innocent party to sue out a divorce: and, after the divorce, to marry another, as if the offending party were dead.

6. Although the corruption of man be such as is apt to study arguments unduly to put asunder those whom God hath joined together in marriage: yet, nothing but adultery, or such wilful desertion as can no way be remedied by the church, or civil magistrate, is cause sufficient of dissolving the bond of marriage: wherein, a public and orderly course of proceeding is to be observed; and the persons concerned in it not left to their own wills, and discretion, in their own case.

## CHAPTER 25: OF THE CHURCH

1. The catholic or universal church, which is invisible, consists of the whole number of the elect, that have been, are, or shall be gathered into one, under Christ the head thereof; and is the spouse, the body, the fullness of him that filleth all in all.

2. The visible church, which is also catholic or universal under the gospel (not confined to one nation, as before under the law), consists of all those throughout the world that

profess the true religion; and of their children: and is the kingdom of the Lord Jesus Christ, the house and family of God, out of which there is no ordinary possibility of salvation.

3. Unto this catholic visible church Christ hath given the ministry, oracles, and ordinances of God, for the gathering and perfecting of the saints, in this life, to the end of the world: and doth, by his own presence and Spirit, according to his promise, make them effectual thereunto.

4. This catholic church hath been sometimes more, sometimes less visible. And particular churches, which are members thereof, are more or less pure, according as the doctrine of the gospel is taught and embraced, ordinances administered, and public worship performed more or less purely in them.

5. The purest churches under heaven are subject both to mixture and error; and some have so degenerated, as to become no churches of Christ, but synagogues of Satan. Nevertheless, there shall be always a church on earth, to worship God according to his will.

6. There is no other head of the church but the Lord Jesus Christ. Nor can the pope of Rome, in any sense, be head thereof.

### CHAPTER 26: OF COMMUNION OF SAINTS

1. All saints, that are united to Jesus Christ their head, by his Spirit, and by faith, have fellowship with him in his graces, sufferings, death, resurrection, and glory: and, being united to one another in love, they have communion in each other's gifts and graces, and are obliged to the performance of such duties, public and private, as do conduce to their mutual good, both in the inward and outward man.

2. Saints by profession are bound to maintain an holy fellowship and communion in the worship of God, and in performing such other spiritual services as tend to their mutual edification; as also in relieving each other in outward things, according to their several abilities and necessities. Which communion, as God offereth opportunity, is to be extended unto all those who, in every place, call upon the name of the Lord Jesus.

3. This communion which the saints have with Christ, doth not make them in any wise partakers of the substance of his Godhead; or to be equal with Christ in any respect: either of which to affirm is impious and blasphemous. Nor doth their communion one with another, as saints, take away, or infringe the title or propriety which each man hath in his goods and possessions.

### CHAPTER 27: OF THE SACRAMENTS

1. Sacraments are holy signs and seals of the covenant of grace, immediately instituted by God, to represent Christ, and his benefits; and to confirm our interest in him: as also, to put a visible difference between those that belong unto the church, and the rest of the world; and solemnly to engage them to the service of God in Christ, according to his Word.

2. There is, in every sacrament, a spiritual relation, or sacramental union, between the sign and the thing signified: whence it comes to pass, that the names and effects of the one are attributed to the other.

3. The grace which is exhibited in or by the sacraments rightly used, is not conferred by any power in them; neither doth the efficacy of a sacrament depend upon the piety or intention of him that doth administer it: but upon the work of the Spirit, and the word of institution, which contains, together with a precept authorizing the use thereof, a promise of benefit to worthy receivers.

4. There be only two sacraments ordained by Christ our Lord in the gospel; that is to say, Baptism, and the Supper of the Lord: neither of which may be dispensed by any, but by a minister of the Word lawfully ordained.

5. The sacraments of the Old Testament, in regard of the spiritual things thereby signified and exhibited, were, for substance, the same with those of the New.

## CHAPTER 28: OF BAPTISM

1. Baptism is a sacrament of the New Testament, ordained by Jesus Christ, not only for the solemn admission of the party baptized into the visible church; but also, to be unto him a sign and seal of the covenant of grace, of his ingrafting into Christ, of regeneration, of remission of sins, and of his giving up unto God, through Jesus Christ, to walk in newness of life. Which sacrament is, by Christ's own appointment, to be continued in his church until the end of the world.

2. The outward element to be used in this sacrament is water, wherewith the party is to be baptized, in the name of the Father, and of the Son, and of the Holy Ghost, by a minister of the gospel, lawfully called thereunto.

3. Dipping of the person into the water is not necessary; but Baptism is rightly administered by pouring, or sprinkling water upon the person.

4. Not only those that do actually profess faith in and obedience unto Christ, but also the infants of one, or both, believing parents, are to be baptized.

5. Although it be a great sin to contemn or neglect this ordinance, yet grace and salvation are not so inseparably annexed unto it, as that no person can be regenerated, or saved, without it; or, that all that are baptized are undoubtedly regenerated.

6. The efficacy of Baptism is not tied to that moment of time wherein it is administered; yet, notwithstanding, by the right use of this ordinance, the grace promised is not only offered, but really exhibited, and conferred, by the Holy Ghost, to such (whether of age or infants) as that grace belongeth unto, according to the counsel of God's own will, in his appointed time.

7. The sacrament of Baptism is but once to be administered unto any person.

## CHAPTER 29: OF THE LORD'S SUPPER

1. Our Lord Jesus, in the night wherein he was betrayed, instituted the sacrament of his body and blood, called the Lord's Supper, to be observed in his church, unto the end of the world, for the perpetual remembrance of the sacrifice of himself in his death; the sealing all benefits thereof unto true believers, their spiritual nourishment and growth in him, their further engagement in and to all duties which they owe unto him; and, to be a bond and pledge of their communion with him, and with each other, as members of his mystical body.

2. In this sacrament, Christ is not offered up to his Father; nor any real sacrifice made at all, for remission of sins of the quick or dead; but only a commemoration of that one offering up of himself, by himself, upon the cross, once for all: and a spiritual oblation of all possible praise unto God, for the same: so that the popish sacrifice of the mass (as they call it)is most abominably injurious to Christ's one, only sacrifice, the alone propitiation for all the sins of his elect.

3. The Lord Jesus hath, in this ordinance, appointed his ministers to declare his word of institution to the people; to pray, and bless the elements of bread and wine, and thereby to set them apart from a common to an holy use; and to take and break the bread, to take the cup, and (they communicating also themselves) to give both to the communicants; but to none who are not then present in the congregation.

4. Private masses, or receiving this sacrament by a priest, or any other, alone; as likewise, the denial of the cup to the people, worshiping the elements, the lifting them up, or carrying them about, for adoration, and the reserving them for any pretended religious use; are all contrary to the nature of this sacrament, and to the institution of Christ.

5. The outward elements in this sacrament, duly set apart to the uses ordained by Christ, have such relation to him crucified, as that, truly, yet sacramentally only, they are sometimes called by the name of the things they represent, to wit, the body and blood of Christ; albeit, in substance and nature, they still remain truly and only bread and wine, as they were before.

6. That doctrine which maintains a change of the substance of bread and wine, into the substance of Christ's body and blood (commonly called transubstantiation) by consecration of a priest, or by any other way, is repugnant, not to Scripture alone, but even to common sense, and reason; overthroweth the nature of the sacrament, and hath been, and is, the cause of manifold superstitions; yea, of gross idolatries.

7. Worthy receivers, outwardly partaking of the visible elements, in this sacrament, do then also, inwardly by faith, really and indeed, yet not carnally and corporally but spiritually, receive, and feed upon, Christ crucified, and all benefits of his death: the body and blood of Christ being then, not corporally or carnally, in, with, or under the bread and wine; yet, as really, but spiritually, present to the faith of believers in that ordinance, as the elements themselves are to their outward senses.

8. Although ignorant and wicked men receive the outward elements in this sacrament; yet, they receive not the thing signified thereby; but, by their unworthy coming thereunto, are guilty of the body and blood of the Lord, to their own damnation. Wherefore, all ignorant and ungodly persons, as they are unfit to enjoy communion with him, so are they unworthy of the Lord's table; and cannot, without great sin against Christ, while they remain such, partake of these holy mysteries, or be admitted thereunto.

## CHAPTER 30: OF CHURCH CENSURES

1. The Lord Jesus, as king and head of his church, hath therein appointed a government, in the hand of church officers, distinct from the civil magistrate.

2. To these officers the keys of the kingdom of heaven are committed; by virtue whereof, they have power, respectively, to retain, and remit sins; to shut that kingdom against the impenitent, both by the Word, and censures; and to open it unto penitent sinners, by the ministry of the gospel; and by absolution from censures, as occasion shall require.

3. Church censures are necessary, for the reclaiming and gaining of offending brethren, for deterring of others from the like offenses, for purging out of that leaven which might infect the whole lump, for vindicating the honor of Christ, and the holy profession of the gospel, and for preventing the wrath of God, which might justly fall upon the church, if they should suffer his covenant, and the seals thereof, to be profaned by notorious and obstinate offenders.

4. For the better attaining of these ends, the officers of the church are to proceed by admonition; suspension from the sacrament of the Lord's Supper for a season; and by excommunication from the church; according to the nature of the crime, and demerit of the person.

## CHAPTER 31: OF SYNODS AND COUNCILS

1. For the better government, and further edification of the church, there ought to be such assemblies as are commonly called synods or councils: and it belongeth to the overseers and other rulers of the particular churches, by virtue of their office, and the power which Christ hath given them for edification and not for destruction, to appoint such assemblies; and to convene together in them, as often as they shall judge it expedient for the good of the church.

2. It belongeth to synods and councils, ministerially to determine controversies of faith, and cases of conscience; to set down rules and directions for the better ordering of the public worship of God, and government of his church; to receive complaints in cases of maladministration, and authoritatively to determine the same: which decrees and determinations, if consonant to the Word of God, are to be received with reverence and submission; not only for their agreement with the Word, but also for the power whereby they are made, as being an ordinance of God appointed thereunto in his Word.

3. All synods or councils, since the apostles' times, whether general or particular, may err;

and many have erred. Therefore they are not to be made the rule of faith, or practice; but to be used as a help in both.

4. Synods and councils are to handle, or conclude nothing, but that which is ecclesiastical: and are not to intermeddle with civil affairs which concern the commonwealth, unless by way of humble petition in cases extraordinary; or, by way of advice, for satisfaction of conscience, if they be thereunto required by the civil magistrate.

### CHAPTER 32: OF THE STATE OF MEN AFTER DEATH, AND OF THE RESURRECTION OF THE DEAD

1. The bodies of men, after death, return to dust, and see corruption: but their souls, which neither die nor sleep, having an immortal subsistence, immediately return to God who gave them: the souls of the righteous, being then made perfect in holiness, are received into the highest heavens, where they behold the face of God, in light and glory, waiting for the full redemption of their bodies. And the souls of the wicked are cast into hell, where they remain in torments and utter darkness, reserved to the judgment of the great day. Beside these two places, for souls separated from their bodies, the Scripture acknowledgeth none.

2. At the last day, such as are found alive shall not die, but be changed: and all the dead shall be raised up, with the selfsame bodies, and none other (although with different qualities), which shall be united again to their souls forever.

3. The bodies of the unjust shall, by the power of Christ, be raised to dishonor: the bodies of the just, by his Spirit, unto honor; and be made conformable to his own glorious body.

### CHAPTER 33: OF THE LAST JUDGMENT

1. God hath appointed a day, wherein he will judge the world, in righteousness, by Jesus Christ, to whom all power and judgment is given of the Father. In which day, not only the apostate angels shall be judged, but likewise all persons that have lived upon earth shall appear before the tribunal of Christ, to give an account of their thoughts, words, and deeds; and to receive according to what they have done in the body, whether good or evil.

2. The end of God's appointing this day is for the manifestation of the glory of his mercy, in the eternal salvation of the elect; and of his justice, in the damnation of the reprobate, who are wicked and disobedient.For then shall the righteous go into everlasting life, and receive that fullness of joy and refreshing, which shall come from the presence of the Lord; but the wicked who know not God, and obey not the gospel of Jesus Christ, shall be cast into eternal torments, and be punished with everlasting destruction from the presence of the Lord, and from the glory of his power.

3. As Christ would have us to be certainly persuaded that there shall be a day of judgment, both to deter all men from sin; and for the greater consolation of the godly in their adversity: so will he have that day unknown to men, that they may shake off all carnal security, and be always watchful, because they know not at what hour the Lord will come; and may be ever prepared to say, Come Lord Jesus, come quickly, Amen.

\* \* \*

## THE NEW HAMPSHIRE BAPTIST CONFESSION
### (1833)

### DECLARATION OF FAITH

### I. OF THE SCRIPTURES.

We believe that the Holy Bible was written by men divinely inspired, and is a perfect treasure of heavenly instruction; that it has God for its author, salvation for its end, and truth without any mixture of error for its matter; that it reveals the principles by which God will judge us; and therefore is, and shall remain to the end of the world, the true center of Christian union, and the supreme standard by which all human conduct, creeds, and opinions should be tried.

### II. OF THE TRUE GOD.

We believe that there is one, and only one, living and true God, an infinite, intelligent Spirit, whose name is JEHOVAH, the Maker and Supreme Ruler of heaven and earth; inexpressibly glorious in holiness, and worthy of all possible honor, confidence, and love; that in the unity of the Godhead there are three persons, the Father, the Son and the Holy Spirit; equal in every divine perfection, and executing distinct and harmonious offices in the great work of redemption.

### III. OF THE FALL OF MAN.

We believe that man was created in holiness, under the law of his Maker; but by voluntary transgression fell from that holy and happy state; in consequence of which all mankind are now sinners, not by constraint, but choice; being by nature utterly void of that holiness required by the law of God, positively inclined to evil; and therefore under just condemnation to eternal ruin, without defense or excuse.

### IV. OF THE WAY OF SALVATION.

We believe that the salvation of sinners is wholly of grace, through the mediatorial offices of the Son of God; who by the appointment of the Father, freely took upon him our nature, yet without sin; honored the divine law by his personal obedience, and by his death made a full atonement for our sins; that having risen from the dead, he is now enthroned in heaven; and uniting in his wonderful person the tenderest sympathies with divine perfections, he is every way qualified to be a suitable, a compassionate, and all-sufficient Saviour.

### V. OF JUSTIFICATION.

We believe that the great gospel blessing which Christ secures to such as believe in him is Justification; that Justification includes the pardon of sin, and the promise of eternal life on principles of righteousness; that it is bestowed, not in consideration of any works of righteousness which we have done, but solely through faith in he Redeemer's blood; by virtue of which faith his perfect righteousness is freely imputed to us of God; that it brings us into a state of most blessed peace and favor with God, and secures every other blessing needful for time and eternity.

### VI. OF THE FREENESS OF SALVATION.

We believe that the blessings of salvation are made free to all by the gospel; that it is the immediate duty of all to accept them by a cordial, penitent, and obedient faith; and that nothing prevents the salvation of the greatest sinner on earth but his own inherent depravity and voluntary rejection of the gospel; which rejection involves him in an aggravated condemnation.

### VII. OF GRACE IN REGENERATION.

We believe that, in order to be saved, sinners must be regenerated, or born again; that regeneration consists in giving a holy disposition to the mind; that it is effected in a manner above our comprehension by the power of the Holy Spirit, in connection with divine truth, so as to secure our voluntary obedience to the gospel; and that its proper evidence appears in the holy fruits of repentance, and faith, and newness of life.

### VIII. OF REPENTANCE AND FAITH.

We believe that Repentance and Faith are sacred duties, and also inseparable graces, wrought in our souls by the regenerating Spirit of God; whereby being deeply convinced of our guilt, danger, and helplessness, and of the way of salvation by Christ, we turn to God with unfeigned contrition, confession, and supplication for mercy; at the same time heartily receiving the Lord Jesus Christ as our Prophet, Priest, and King, and relying on him as the only and all-sufficient Saviour.

### IX. OF GOD'S PURPOSE OF GRACE.

We believe that Election is the eternal purpose of God, according to which he graciously regenerates, sanctifies, and saves sinners; that being perfectly consistent with the free agency of man, it comprehends all the means in connection with the end; that it is a most glorious display of God's sovereign goodness, being infinitely free, wise, holy, and unchangeable; that it utterly excludes boasting, and promotes humility, love, prayer, praise, trust in God, and active imitation of his free mercy; that it encourages the use of means in the highest degree; that it may be ascertained by its effects in all who truly believe the gospel; that it is the foundation of Christian assurance; and that to ascertain it with regard to ourselves demands and deserves the utmost diligence.

### X. OF SANCTIFICATION.

We believe that Sanctification is the process by which, according to the will of God, we are made partakers of his holiness; that it is a progressive work; that it is begun in regeneration; and that it is carried on in the hearts of believers by the presence and power of the Holy Spirit, the Sealer and Comforter, in the continual use of the appointed means— especially the Word of God, self-examination, self-denial, watchfulness, and prayer.

### XI. OF THE PRESERVATION OF SAINTS.

We believe that such only are real believers as endure unto the end; that their persevering attachment to Christ is the grand mark which distinguishes them from superficial professors; that a special Providence watches over their welfare; and they are kept by the power of God through faith unto salvation.

### XII. OF THE HARMONY OF THE LAW AND THE GOSPEL.

We believe that the Law of God is the eternal and unchangeable rule of his moral government; that it is holy, just, and good; and that the inability which the Scriptures ascribe to fallen men to fulfill its precepts arises entirely from their love of sin; to deliver them from which, and to restore them through a Mediator to unfeigned obedience to the holy Law, is one great end of the Gospel, and of the means of grace connected with the establishment of the visible Church.

### XIII. OF A GOSPEL CHURCH.

We believe that a visible Church of Christ is a congregation of baptized believers, associated by covenant in the faith and fellowship of the gospel; observing the ordinances of Christ; governed by his laws, and exercising the gifts, rights, and privileges invested in them by his Word; that its only scriptural offices are Bishops, or Pastors, and Deacons, whose qualifications, claims, and duties are defined in the Epistles to Timothy and Titus.

## XIV. OF BAPTISM AND THE LORD'S SUPPER.

We believe that Christian Baptism is the immersion in water of a believer, into the name of the Father, and Son, and Holy Spirit; to show forth, in a solemn and beautiful emblem, our faith in the crucified, buried, and risen Savior, with its effect in our death to sin and resurrection to a new life; that it is prerequisite to the privileges of a Church relation; and to the Lord's Supper, in which the members of the Church, by the sacred use of bread and wine, are to commemorate together the dying love of Christ; preceeded always by solemn self-examination.

## XV. OF THE CHRISTIAN SABBATH.

We believe that the first day of the week is the Lord's Day or Christian Sabbath; and is to be kept sacred to religious purposes, by abstaining from all secular labor and sinful recreations; by the devout observance of all the means of grace, both private and public; and by preparation for that rest that remaineth for the people of God.

## XVI. OF CIVIL GOVERNMENT.

We believe that civil government is of divine appointment, for the interests and good order of human society; and that magistrates are to be prayed for, conscientiously honored and obeyed; except only things opposed to the will of our Lord Jesus Christ, who is the only Lord of the conscience, and the Prince of the kings of the earth.

## XVII. OF THE RIGHTEOUS AND THE WICKED.

We believe that there is a radical and essential difference between the righteous and the wicked; that such only as through faith are justified in the name of the Lord Jesus, and sanctified by the Spirit of our God, are truly righteous in his esteem; while all such as continue in impenitence and unbelief are in his sight wicked, and under the curse; and this distinction holds among men both in and after death.

## XVIII. OF THE WORLD TO COME.

We believe that the end of the world is approaching; that at the last day Christ will descend from heaven and raise the dead from the grave to final retribution; that a solemn separation will then take place; that the wicked will be adjudged to endless punishment, and the righteous to endless joy; and that this judgment will fix forever the final state of men in heaven or hell, on principles of righteousness.

\* \* \*

## BAPTIST FAITH AND MESSAGE
### Southern Baptist Convention
### (1925, revised 1963)

### I. THE SCRIPTURES

The Holy Bible was written by men divinely inspired and is the record of God's revelation of Himself to man. It is a perfect treasure of divine instruction. It has God for its author, salvation for its end, and truth, without any mixture of error, for its matter. It reveals the principles by which God judges us; and therefore is, and will remain to the end of the world, the true center of Christian union, and the supreme standard by which all human conduct, creeds, and religious opinions should be tried. The criterion by which the Bible is to be interpreted is Jesus Christ.

### II. GOD

There is one and only one living and true God. He is an intelligent, spiritual and personal Being, the Creator, Redeemer, Preserver, and Ruler of the universe. God is infinite in holiness and all other perfections. To him we owe the highest love, reverence, and obedience. The eternal God reveals Himself to us as Father, Son, and Holy Spirit, with distinct personal attributes, but without division of nature, essence, or being.

## 1. GOD THE FATHER

God as Father reigns with providential care over His universe, His creatures, and the flow of the stream of human history according to the purposes of His grace. He is all powerful, all loving, and all wise. God is Father in truth to those who become children of God through faith in Jesus Christ. He is fatherly in his attitude toward all men.

## 2. GOD THE SON

Christ is the eternal Son of God. In His incarnation as Jesus Christ He was conceived of the Holy Spirit and born of the virgin Mary. Jesus perfectly revealed and did the will of God, taking upon Himself the demands and necessities of human nature and identifying Himself completely with mankind yet without sin. He honored the divine law by His personal obedience, and in His death on the cross He made provision for the redemption of men from sin. He was raised from the dead with a glorified body and appeared to His disciples as the person who was with them before His crucifixion. He ascended into heaven and is now exalted at the right hand of God where He is the One Mediator, partaking of the nature of God and of man, and in whose Person is effected the reconciliation between God and man. He will return in power and glory to judge the world and to consummate His redemptive mission. He now dwells in all believers as the living and ever present Lord.

## 3. GOD THE HOLY SPIRIT

The Holy Spirit is the Spirit of God. He inspired holy men of old to write the Scriptures. Through illumination He enables men to understand truth. He exalts Christ. He convicts of sin, of righteousness and of judgment. He calls men to the Saviour, and effects regeneration. He cultivates Christian character, comforts believers, and bestows the spiritual gifts by which they serve God through His church. He seals the believer unto the day of final redemption. His presence in the Christian is the assurance of God to bring the believer into the fullness of the stature of Christ. He enlightens and empowers the believer and the church in worship, evangelism, and service.

## III. MAN

Man was created by the special act of God, in His own image, and is the crowning work of His creation. In the beginning man was innocent of sin and was endowed by his Creator with freedom of choice. By his free choice man sinned against God and brought sin into the human race. Through the temptation of Satan man transgressed the command of God, and fell from his original innocence; whereby his posterity inherit a nature and an environment inclined toward sin, and as soon as they are capable of moral action become transgressors and are under condemnation. Only the grace of God can bring man into His holy fellowship and enable man to fulfill the creative purpose of God. The sacredness of human personality is evident in that God created man in His own image, and in that Christ died for man; therefore every man possesses dignity and is worthy of respect and Christian love.

## IV. SALVATION

Salvation involves the redemption of the whole man, and is offered freely to all who accept Jesus Christ as Lord and Saviour, who by His own blood obtained eternal redemption for the believer. In its broadest sense salvation includes regeneration, sanctification, and glorification.

1. Regeneration, or the new birth, is a work of God's grace whereby believers become new creatures in Christ Jesus. It is a change of heart wrought by the Holy Spirit through conviction of sin, to which the sinner responds in repentance toward God and faith in the Lord Jesus Christ.

Repentance and faith are inseparable experiences of grace. Repentance is a genuine turning from sin toward God. Faith is the acceptance of Jesus Christ and commitment of the entire personality to Him as Lord and Saviour. Justification is God's gracious and full acquittal upon principles of His righteousness of all sinners who repent and believe in Christ. Justification brings the believer into a relationship of peace and favor with God.

2. Sanctification is the experience, beginning in regeneration, by which the believer is set apart to God's purposes, and is enabled to progress toward moral and spiritual perfection through the presence and power of the Holy Spirit dwelling in him. Growth in grace should continue throughout the regenerate person's life.

3. Glorification is the culmination of salvation and is the final blessed and abiding state of the redeemed.

## V. GOD'S PURPOSE OF GRACE

Election is the gracious purpose of God, according to which He regenerates, sanctifies, and glorifies sinners. It is consistent with the free agency of man and comprehends all the means in connection with the end. It is a glorious display of God's sovereign goodness, and is infinitely wise, holy, and unchangeable. It excludes boasting and promotes humility.

All true believers endure to the end. Those whom God has accepted in Christ, and sanctified by His Spirit, will never fall away from the state of grace, but shall persevere to the end. Believers may fall into sin through neglect and temptation, whereby they grieve the Spirit, impair their graces and comforts, bring reproach on the cause of Christ, and temporal judgments on themselves, yet they shall be kept by the power of God through faith unto salvation.

## VI. THE CHURCH

A New Testament church of the Lord Jesus Christ is a local body of baptized believers who are associated by covenant in the faith and fellowship of the gospel, observing the two ordinances of Christ, committed to His teachings, exercising the gifts, rights, and privileges invested in them by His Word, and seeking to extend the gospel to the ends of the earth.

This church is an autonomous body, operating through democratic processes under the Lordship of Jesus Christ. In such a congregation, members are equally responsible. Its Scriptural officers are pastors and deacons.

The New Testament speaks also of the church as the body of Christ which includes all of the redeemed of all the ages.

## VII. BAPTISM AND THE LORD'S SUPPER

Christian baptism is the immersion of a believer in water in the name of the Father, the Son, and the Holy Spirit. It is an act of obedience symbolizing the believer's faith in a crucified, buried, and risen Saviour, the believer's death to sin, the burial of the old life, and the resurrection to walk in newness of life in Christ Jesus. It is a testimony to his faith in the final resurrection of the dead. Being a church ordinance, it is prerequisite to the privileges of church membership and to the Lord's Supper.

The Lord's Supper is a symbolic act of obedience whereby members of the church, through partaking of the bread and the fruit of the vine, memorialize the death of the Redeemer and anticipate His second coming.

## VIII. THE LORD'S DAY

The first day of the week is the Lord's Day. It is a Christian institution for regular observance. It commemorates the resurrection of Christ from the dead and should be employed in the exercises of worship and spiritual devotion, both public and private, and by refraining from worldly amusements, and resting from secular employments, work of necessity and mercy only being excepted.

## IX. THE KINGDOM

The kingdom of God includes both His general sovereignty over the universe and His particular kingship over men who willfully acknowledge Him as King. Particularly the kingdom is the realm of salvation into which men enter by trustful, childlike commitment to Jesus Christ. Christians ought to pray and to labor that the kingdom may come and God's will be done on earth. The full consummation of the kingdom awaits the return of Jesus Christ and the end of this age.

## X. LAST THINGS

God in His own time and in His own way, will bring the world to its appropriate end. According to His promise, Jesus Christ will return personally and visibly in glory to the earth; the dead will be raised; and Christ will judge all men in righteousness. The unrighteous will be consigned to hell, the place of everlasting punishment. The righteous in their resurrected and glorified bodies will receive their reward and will dwell forever in heaven with the Lord.

## XI. EVANGELISM AND MISSIONS

It is the duty and privilege of every follower of Christ and of every church of the Lord Jesus Christ to endeavor to make disciples of all nations. The new birth of man's spirit by God's Holy Spirit means the birth of love for others. Missionary effort on the part of all rests thus upon a spiritual necessity of the regenerate life, and is expressly and repeatedly commanded in the teachings of Christ. It is the duty of every child of God to seek constantly to win the lost to Christ by personal effort and by all other methods in harmony with the gospel of Christ.

## XII. EDUCATION

The cause of education in the kingdom of Christ is co-ordinate with the causes of missions and general benevolence and should receive along with these the liberal support of the churches. An adequate system of Christian schools is necessary to a complete spiritual program for Christ's people.

In Christian education there should be a proper balance between academic freedom and academic responsibility. Freedom in any orderly relationship of human life is always limited and never absolute. The freedom of a teacher in a Christian school, college, or seminary is limited by the pre-eminence of Jesus Christ, by the authoritative nature of the Scriptures, and by the distinct purpose for which the school exists.

## XIII. STEWARDSHIP

God is the source of all blessings, temporal and spiritual; all that we have and are we owe to Him. Christians have a spiritual debtorship to the whole world, a holy trusteeship in the gospel, and a binding stewardship in their possessions. They are therefore under obligation to serve Him with their time, talents, and material possessions; and should recognize all these as entrusted to them to use for the glory of God and for helping others. According to the Scriptures, Christians should contribute of their means cheerfully, regularly, systematically, proportionately, and liberally for the advancement of the Redeemer's cause on earth.

## XIV. CO-OPERATION

Christ's people should, as occasion requires, organize such associations and conventions as may best secure co-operation for the great objects of the kingdom of God. Such organizations have no authority over one another or over the churches. They are voluntary and advisory bodies designed to elicit, combine, and direct the energies of our people in the most effective manner. Members of New Testament churches should co-operate with one another in carrying forward the missionary, educational, and benevolent ministries for the extension of Christ's kingdom. Christian unity in the New Testament sense is spiritual harmony and voluntary co-operation for common ends by various groups of Christ's people. Co-operation is desirable between the various Christian denominations, when the end to be attained is itself justified, and when such co-operation involves no violation of conscience or compromise of loyalty to Christ and his Word as revealed in the New Testament.

## XV. THE CHRISTIAN AND THE SOCIAL ORDER

Every Christian is under obligation to seek to make the will of Christ supreme in his own life and in human society. Means and methods used for the improvement of society and the establishment of righteousness among men can be truly and permanently helpful only when they are rooted in the regeneration of the individual by the saving grace of God in Christ Jesus. The Christian should oppose in the spirit of Christ every form of greed, selfishness, and vice. He should work to provide for the orphaned, the needy, the aged, the helpless, and the sick. Every Christian should seek to bring industry, government, and society as a whole under the sway of the principles of righteousness, truth, and brotherly love. In order to promote these ends Christians should be ready to work with all men of good will in any good cause, always being careful to act in the spirit of love without compromising their loyalty to Christ and his truth.

## XVI. PEACE AND WAR

It is the duty of Christians to seek peace with all men on principles of righteousness. In accordance with the spirit and teachings of Christ they should do all in their power to put an end to war.

The true remedy for the war spirit is the gospel of our Lord. The supreme need of the world is the acceptance of His teachings in all the affairs of men and nations, and the practical application of His law of love.

## XVII. RELIGIOUS LIBERTY

God alone is Lord of the conscience, and He has left it free from the doctrines and commandments of men which are contrary to His Word or not contained in it. Church and state should be separate. The state owes to every church protection and full freedom in the pursuit of its spiritual ends. In providing for such freedom no ecclesiastical group or denomination should be favored by the state more than others. Civil government being ordained of God, it is the duty of Christians to render loyal obedience thereto in all things not contrary to the revealed will of God. The church should not resort to the civil power to carry on its work. The gospel of Christ contemplates spiritual means alone for the pursuit of its ends. The state has no right to impose penalties for religious opinions of any kind. The state has no right to impose taxes for the support of any form of religion. A free church in a free state is the Christian ideal, and this implies the right of free and unhindered access to God on the part of all men and the right to form and propagate opinions in the sphere of religion without interference by the civil power.

\* \* \*

# THE CHICAGO STATEMENT ON BIBLICAL INERRANCY
## (1978)

### PREFACE

The authority of Scripture is a key issue for the Christian Church in this and every age. Those who profess faith in Jesus Christ as Lord and Savior are called to show the reality of their discipleship by humbly and faithfully obeying God's written Word. To stray from Scripture in faith or conduct is disloyalty to our Master. Recognition of the total truth and trustworthiness of Holy Scripture is essential to a full grasp and adequate confession of its authority.

The following Statement affirms this inerrancy of Scripture afresh, making clear our understanding of it and warning against its denial. We are persuaded that to deny it is to set aside the witness of Jesus Christ and of Holy Spirit and to refuse that submission to the claims of God's own word which marks true Christian faith. We see it as our timely duty to make this affirmation in the face of current lapses from the truth of inerrancy among our fellow Christians and misunderstanding of this doctrine in the world at large.

This Statement consists of three parts: a Summary Statement, Articles of Affirmation and Denial, and an accompanying Exposition. It has been prepared in the course of a three-day consultation in Chicago. Those who have signed the Summary Statement and the Articles wish to affirm their own conviction as to the inerrancy of Scripture and to encourage and challenge one another and all Christians to growing appreciation and understanding of this doctrine. We acknowledge the limitations of a document prepared in a brief, intensive conference and do not propose that this Statement be given creedal weight. Yet we rejoice in the deepening of our own convictions through our discussions together, and we pray that the Statement we have signed may be used to the glory of our God toward a new reformation of the Church in its faith, life, and mission.

We offer this Statement in a spirit, not of contention, but of humility and love, which we purpose by God's grace to maintain in any future dialogue arising out of what we have said. We gladly acknowledge that many who deny the inerrancy of Scripture do not display the consequences of this denial in the rest of their belief and behavior, and we are conscious that we who confess this doctrine often deny it in life by failing to bring our thoughts and deeds, our traditions and habits, into true subjection to the divine Word.

We invite responses to this statement from any who see reason to amend its affirmations about Scripture by the light of Scripture itself, under whose infallible authority we stand as we speak. We claim no personal infallibility for the witness we bear, and for any help which enables us to strengthen this testimony to God's Word we shall be grateful.

## A SHORT STATEMENT

1. God, who is Himself Truth and speaks truth only, has inspired Holy Scripture in order thereby to reveal Himself to lost mankind through Jesus Christ as Creator and Lord, Redeemer and Judge. Holy Scripture is God's witness to Himself.

2. Holy Scripture, being God's own Word, written by men prepared and superintended by His Spirit, is of infallible divine authority in all matters upon which it touches: it is to be believed, as God's instruction, in all that it affirms; obeyed, as God's command, in all that it requires; embraced, as God's pledge, in all that it promises.

3. The Holy Spirit, Scripture's divine Author, both authenticates it to us by His inward witness and opens our minds to understand its meaning.

4. Being wholly and verbally God-given, Scripture is without error or fault in all its teaching, no less in what it states about God's acts in creation, about the events of world history, and about its own literary origins under God, than in its witness to God's saving grace in individual lives.

5. The authority of Scripture is inescapably impaired if this total divine inerrancy is in any way limited or disregarded, or made relative to a view of truth contrary to the Bible's own; and such lapses bring serious loss to both the individual and the Church.

## ARTICLES OF AFFIRMATION AND DENIAL

### ARTICLE I

We affirm that the Holy Scriptures are to be received as the authoritative Word of God.

We deny that the Scriptures receive their authority from the Church, tradition, or any other human source.

## ARTICLE II

We affirm that the Scriptures are the supreme written norm by which God binds the conscience, and that the authority of the Church is subordinate to that of Scripture.

We deny that Church creeds, councils, or declarations have authority greater than or equal to the authority of the Bible.

## ARTICLE III

We affirm that the written Word in its entirety is revelation given by God.

We deny that the Bible is merely a witness to revelation, or only becomes revelation in encounter, or depends on the responses of men for its validity.

## ARTICLE IV

We affirm that God who made mankind in His image has used language as a means of revelation.

We deny that human language is so limited by our creatureliness that it is rendered inadequate as a vehicle for divine revelation. We further deny that the corruption of human culture and language through sin has thwarted God's work of inspiration.

## ARTICLE V

We affirm that God's revelation in the Holy Scriptures was progressive.

We deny that later revelation, which may fulfill earlier revelation, ever corrects or contradicts it. We further deny that any normative revelation has been given since the completion of the New Testament writings.

## ARTICLE VI

We affirm that the whole of Scripture and all its parts, down to the very words of original, were given by divine inspiration.

We deny that the inspiration of Scripture can rightly be affirmed of the whole without the parts, or of some parts but not the whole.

## ARTICLE VII

We affirm that inspiration was the work in which God by His Spirit, through human writers, gave us His Word. The origin of Scripture is divine. The mode of divine inspiration remains largely a mystery to us.

We deny that inspiration can be reduced to human insight, or to heightened states of consciousness of any kind.

## ARTICLE VIII

We affirm that God in His Work of inspiration utilized the distinctive personalities and literary styles of the writers whom He had chosen and prepared.

We deny that God, in causing these writers to use the very words that He chose, overrode their personalities.

## ARTICLE IX

We affirm that inspiration, though not conferring omniscience, guaranteed true and trustworthy utterance on all matters of which the Bible authors were moved to speak and write.

We deny that the finitude or fallenness of these writers, by necessity or otherwise, introduced distortion or falsehood into God's Word.

## ARTICLE X

We affirm that inspiration, strictly speaking, applies to the autographic text of Scripture, which in the providence of God can be ascertained from available manuscripts with great accuracy. We further affirm that copies and translations of Scripture are the Word of God to the extent that they faithfully represent the original.

We deny that any essential element of the Christian faith is affected by the absence of the autographs. We further deny that this absence renders the assertion of Biblical inerrancy invalid or irrelevant.

## ARTICLE XI

We affirm that Scripture, having been given by divine inspiration, is infallible, so that, far from misleading us, it is true and reliable in all matters it addresses.

We deny that it is possible for the Bible to be at the same time infallible and errant in its assertions. Infallibility and inerrancy may be distinguished, but not separated.

## ARTICLE XII

We affirm that Scripture in its entirety is inerrant, being free from all falsehood, fraud, or deceit.

We deny that Biblical infallibility and inerrancy are limited to spiritual, religious or redemptive themes, exclusive of assertions in the fields of history and science. We further deny that scientific hypotheses about earth history may properly be used to overturn the teaching of Scripture on creation and the flood.

## ARTICLE XIII

We affirm the propriety of using inerrancy as theological term with reference to the complete truthfulness of Scripture.

We deny that it is proper to evaluate Scripture according to standards of truth and error that are alien to its usage or purpose. We further deny that inerrancy is negated by Biblical phenomena such as a lack of modern technical precision, irregularities of grammar or spelling, observational descriptions of nature, the reporting of falsehoods, the use of hyperbole and round numbers, the topical arrangement of material, variant selections of material in parallel accounts, or the use of free citations.

## ARTICLE XIV

We affirm the unity and internal consistency of Scripture.

We deny that alleged errors and discrepancies that have not yet been resolved vitiate the truth of claims of the Bible.

## ARTICLE XV

We affirm that the doctrine of inerrancy is grounded in the teaching of the Bible about inspiration.

We deny that Jesus' teaching about Scripture may be dismissed by appeals to accommodation or to any natural limitation of His humanity.

## ARTICLE XVI

We affirm that the doctrine of inerrancy has been integral to the Church's faith throughout its history.

We deny that inerrancy is a doctrine invented by Scholastic Protestantism, or is a reactionary position postulated in response to negative higher criticism.

## ARTICLE XVII

We affirm that the Holy Spirit bears witness to the Scriptures, assuring believers of the truthfulness of God's written Word.

We deny that this witness of the Holy Spirit operates in isolation from or against Scripture.

## ARTICLE XVIII

We affirm that the text of Scripture is to be interpreted by grammatico-historical exegesis, taking account of its literary forms and devices, and that Scripture is to interpret Scripture.

We deny the legitimacy of any treatment of the text or quest for sources lying behind it that leads to relativizing, dehistoricizing, or discounting its teaching, or rejecting its claims to authorship.

## ARTICLE XIX

We affirm that a confession of the full authority, infallibility, and inerrancy of Scripture is vital to a sound understanding of the whole of the Christian faith. We further affirm that such confession should lead to increasing conformity to the image of Christ.

We deny that such confession is necessary for salvation. However, we further deny that inerrancy can be rejected without grave consequences, both to the individual and to the Church.

# Appendix 2:
# Scripture Memory Passages
# From the NIV and NASB

The Scripture memory passages quoted at the end of each chapter are taken from the *Revised Standard Version*. This appendix includes all the Scripture memory passages from two other common versions, the *New International Version®* (NIV®) and the *New American Standard Bible* (NASB). (NASB passages begin on p. 1213.)

## NIV PASSAGES

### CHAPTER 1: MATT. 28:18–20:

Then Jesus came to them and said, "All authority in heaven and on earth has been given to me. Therefore go and make disciples of all nations, baptizing them in the name of Father and of the Son and of the Holy Spirit, and teaching them to obey everything I have commanded you. And surely I am with you always, to the very end of the age."

### CHAPTER 2: PS. 1:1–2:

Blessed is the man who does not walk in the counsel of the wicked or stand in the way of sinners or sit in the seat of mockers. But his delight is in the law of the Lord, and on his law he meditates day and night.

### CHAPTER 3: HEB. 1:1–2:

In the past God spoke to our forefathers through the prophets at many times and in various ways, but in these last days he has spoken to us by his Son, whom he appointed heir of all things, and through whom he made the universe.

### CHAPTER 4: 2 TIM. 3:16–17:

All Scripture is God-breathed and is useful for teaching, rebuking, correcting and training in righteousness, so that the man of God may be thoroughly equipped for every good work.

### CHAPTER 5: PS. 12:6:

And the words of the Lord are flawless, like silver refined in a furnace of clay, purified seven times.

### CHAPTER 6: DEUT. 6:6–7:

These commandments that I give you today are to be upon your hearts. Impress them on your children. Talk about them when you sit at home and when you walk along the road, when you lie down and when you get up.

### CHAPTER 7: MATT. 4:4:

Jesus answered, "It is written: 'Man does not live on bread alone, but on every word that comes from the mouth of God.'"

### CHAPTER 8: PS. 119:1:

Blessed are they whose ways are blameless, who walk according to the law of the Lord.

### CHAPTER 9: ROM. 1:18–20:

The wrath of God is being revealed from heaven against all the godlessness and wickedness of men who suppress the truth by their wickedness, since what may be known about God is plain to them, because God has made it plain to them. For since the creation of the world God's invisible qualities—his eternal power and divine nature—have been clearly seen, being understood from what has been made, so that men are without excuse.

### CHAPTER 10: PS. 145:1–3:

I will exalt you, my God the King; I will praise your name for ever and ever. Every day I will praise you and extol your name for ever and ever. Great is the Lord and most worthy of praise; his greatness no one can fathom.

### CHAPTER 11: PS. 102:25–27:

In the beginning you laid the foundations of the earth, and the heavens are the work of your hands. They will perish, but you remain; they will all wear out like a garment. Like clothing you will change them and they will be discarded. But you remain the same, and your years will never end.

### CHAPTER 12: EX. 34:6–7:

And he passed in front of Moses, proclaiming, "The Lord, the Lord, the compassionate and gracious God, slow to anger, abounding in love and faithfulness, maintaining love to thousands, and forgiving wickedness, rebellion and sin. Yet he does not leave the guilty unpunished; he punishes the children and their children for the sin of fathers to the third and fourth generation."

### CHAPTER 13: PS. 73:25–26:

Whom have I in heaven but you? And earth has nothing I desire besides you. My flesh and my heart may fail, but God is the strength of my heart and my portion forever.

### CHAPTER 14: MATT. 3:16–17:

As soon as Jesus was baptized, he went up out of the water. At that moment heaven was opened, and he saw the Spirit of God descending like a dove and lighting on him. And a voice from heaven said, "This is my Son, whom I love; with him I am well pleased."

### CHAPTER 15: NEH. 9:6:

You alone are the Lord. You made the heavens, even the highest heavens, and all their starry host, the earth and all that is on it, the seas and all that is in them. You give life to everything, and the multitudes of heaven worship you.

### CHAPTER 16: ROM. 8:28:

And we know that in all things God works for the good of those who love him, who have been called according to his purpose.

### CHAPTER 17: HEB. 2:3–4:

How shall we escape if we ignore such a great salvation? This salvation, which was first announced by the Lord, was confirmed to us by those who heard him. God also testified to it by signs, wonders and various miracles, and gifts of the Holy Spirit distributed according to his will.

### CHAPTER 18: HEB. 4:14–16:

Therefore, since we have a great high priest who has gone through the heavens, Jesus the Son of God, let us hold firmly to the faith we profess. For we do not have a high priest who is unable to sympathize with our weaknesses, but we have one who has been tempted in every way, just as we are—yet was without sin. Let us then approach the throne of grace with confidence, so that we may receive mercy and find grace to help us in our time of need.

### CHAPTER 19: REV. 5:11–12:

Then I looked and heard the voice of many angels, numbering thousands upon thousands, and ten thousand times ten thousand. They encircled the throne and the living creatures and the elders. In a loud voice they sang: "Worthy is the Lamb, who was slain, to receive power and wealth and wisdom and strength and honor and glory and praise!"

### CHAPTER 20: JAMES 4:7–8:

Submit yourselves, then, to God. Resist the devil, and he will flee from you. Come near to God and he will come near to you. Wash your hands, you sinners, and purify your hearts, you double-minded.

### CHAPTER 21: GEN. 1:26–27:

Then God said, "Let us make man in our image, in our likeness, and let them rule over the fish of the sea and the birds of the air, over the livestock, over all the earth, and over all the creatures that move along the ground." So God created man in his own image, in the image of God he created him; male and female he created them.

### CHAPTER 22: COL. 3:18–19:

Wives, submit to your husbands, as is fitting in the Lord. Husbands, love your wives and do not be harsh with them.

### CHAPTER 23: 2 COR. 7:1:

Since we have these promises, dear friends, let us purify ourselves from everything that contaminates body and spirit, perfecting holiness out of reverence for God.

### CHAPTER 24: PS. 51:1–4:

Have mercy on me, O God, according to your unfailing love; according to your great compassion blot out my transgressions. Wash away all my iniquity and cleanse me from my sin. For I know my transgressions, and my sin is always before me. Against you, you only, have I sinned and done what is evil in your sight, so that you are proved right when you speak and justified when you judge.

### CHAPTER 25: HEB. 8:10:

This is the covenant I will make with the house of Israel after that time, declares the Lord. I will put my laws in their minds and write them on their hearts. I will be their God and they will be my people.

### CHAPTER 26: JOHN 1:14:

The Word became flesh and made his dwelling among us. We have seen his glory, the glory of the One and Only Son, who came from the Father, full of grace and truth.

### CHAPTER 27: ROM. 3:23–26:

For all have sinned and fall short of the glory of God, and are justified freely by his grace through the redemption that came by Christ Jesus. God presented him as a sacrifice of atonement, through faith in his blood. He did this to demonstrate his justice, because in his forbearance he had left the sins committed beforehand unpunished—he did it to demonstrate his justice at the present time, so as to be just and the one who justifies those who have faith in Jesus.

### CHAPTER 28: 1 COR. 15:20–23:

But Christ has indeed been raised from the dead, the firstfruits of those who have fallen asleep. For since death came through a man, the resurrection of the dead comes also through a man. For as in Adam all die, so in Christ all will be made alive. But each in his own turn: Christ, the firstfruits; then, when he comes, those who belong to him.

### CHAPTER 29: 1 PETER 2:9–10:

But you are a chosen people, a royal priesthood, a holy nation, a people belonging to God, that you may declare the praises of him who called you out of darkness into his wonderful light. Once you were not a people, but now you are the people of God; once you had not received mercy, but now you have received mercy.

### CHAPTER 30: ROM. 8:12–14:

Therefore, brothers, we have an obligation—but it is not to the sinful nature, to live according to it. For if you live according to the sinful nature, you will die; but if by the Spirit you put to death the misdeeds of the body, you will live, because those who are led by the Spirit of God are sons of God.

### CHAPTER 31: LUKE 6:35–36:

But love your enemies, do good to them, and lend to them without expecting to get anything back. Then your reward will be great, and you will be sons of the Most High, because he is kind to the ungrateful and wicked. Be merciful, just as your Father is merciful.

### CHAPTER 32: EPH. 1:3–6:

Praise be to the God and Father of our Lord Jesus Christ, who has blessed us in the heavenly realms with every spiritual blessing in Christ. For he chose us in him before the creation of the world to be holy and blameless in his sight. In love he predestined us to be adopted as his sons through Jesus Christ, in accordance with his pleasure and will—to the praise of his glorious grace, which he has freely given us in the One he loves.

### CHAPTER 33: MATT. 11:28–30:

"Come to me, all you who are weary and burdened, and I will give you rest. Take my yoke upon you and learn from me, for I am gentle and humble in heart, and you will find rest for your souls. For my yoke is easy and my burden is light."

### CHAPTER 34: JOHN 3:5–8:

Jesus answered, "I tell you the truth, no one can enter the Kingdom of God unless he is born of water and the Spirit. Flesh gives birth to flesh, but the Spirit gives birth to spirit. You should not be surprised at my saying, 'You must be born again.' The wind blows wherever it pleases. You hear its sound, but you cannot tell where it comes from or where it is going. So it is with everyone born of the Spirit."

### CHAPTER 35: JOHN 3:16:

For God so loved the world that he gave his one and only Son, that whoever believes in him shall not perish but have eternal life.

### CHAPTER 36: ROM. 3:27–28:

Where, then, is boasting? It is excluded. On what principle? On that of observing the law? No, but on that of faith. For we maintain that a man is justified by faith apart from observing the law.

### CHAPTER 37: ROM. 8:14–17:

Because those who are led by the Spirit of God are sons of God. For you did not receive a spirit that makes you a slave again to fear, but you received the Spirit of sonship. And by him we cry, "Abba, Father." The Spirit himself testifies with our spirit that we are God's children. Now if we are children, then we are heirs—heirs of God and co-heirs with Christ, if indeed we share in his sufferings in order that we may also share in his glory.

### CHAPTER 38: ROM. 6:11–14:

In the same way, count yourselves dead to sin but alive to God in Christ Jesus. Therefore do not let sin reign in your mortal body so that you obey its evil desires. Do not offer the parts of your body to sin, as instruments of wickedness, but rather offer yourselves to God, as those who have been brought from death to life; and offer the parts of your body to him as instruments of righteousness. For sin shall not be your master, because you are not under law, but under grace.

### CHAPTER 39: 1 COR. 12:12–13:

The body is a unit, though it is made up of many parts; and though all its parts are many, they form one body. So it is with Christ. For we were all baptized by one Spirit into one body—whether Jews or Greeks, slave or free—and we were all given the one Spirit to drink.

### CHAPTER 40: JOHN 10:27–28:

My sheep listen to my voice; I know them, and they follow me. I give them eternal life, and they shall never perish; no one can snatch them out of my hand.

### CHAPTER 41: PHIL. 1:20–24:

I eagerly expect and hope that I will in no way be ashamed, but will have sufficient courage so that now as always Christ will be exalted in my body, whether by life or by death. For to me, to live is Christ and to die is gain. If I am to go on living in the body, this will mean fruitful labor for me. Yet what shall I choose? I do not know! I am torn between the two: I desire to depart and be with Christ, which is better by far; but it is more necessary for you that I remain in the body.

### CHAPTER 42: 1 COR. 15:42–44:

So will it be with the resurrection of the dead. The body that is sown is perishable, it is raised imperishable; it is sown in dishonor, it is raised in glory; it is sown in weakness, it is raised in power; it is sown a natural body, it is raised a spiritual body. If there is a natural body, there is also a spiritual body.

### CHAPTER 43: GAL. 2:20:

I have been crucified with Christ and I no longer live, but Christ lives in me. The life I live in the body, I live by faith in the Son of God, who loved me and gave himself for me.

### CHAPTER 44: EPH. 4:11–13:

It was he who gave some to be apostles, some to be prophets, some to be evangelists, and some to be pastors and teachers, to prepare God's people for works of service, so that the body of Christ may be built up until we all reach unity in the faith and in the knowledge of the Son of God and become mature, attaining to the whole measure of the fullness of Christ.

### *CHAPTER 45: EPH. 4:14–16:*

Then we will no longer be infants, tossed back and forth by the waves, and blown here and there by every wind of teaching and by the cunning and craftiness of men in their deceitful scheming. Instead, speaking the truth in love, we will in all things grow up into him who is the Head, that is, Christ. From him the whole body, joined and held together by every supporting ligament, grows and builds itself up in love, as each part does its work.

### *CHAPTER 46: 2 COR. 10:3–4:*

For though we live in the world, we do not wage war as the world does. The weapons we fight with are not the weapons of the world. On the contrary, they have divine power to demolish strongholds.

### *CHAPTER 47: 1 PETER 5:1–4:*

To the elders among you, I appeal as a fellow elder, a witness of Christ's sufferings and one who also will share in the glory to be revealed: Be shepherds of God's flock that is under your care, serving as overseers—not because you must, but because you are willing, as God wants you to be; not greedy for money, but eager to serve; not lording it over those entrusted to you, but being examples to the flock. And when the Chief Shepherd appears, you will receive the crown of glory that will never fade away.

### *CHAPTER 48: ACTS 2:41–42:*

Those who accepted his message were baptized, and about three thousand were added to their number that day. They devoted themselves to the apostles' teaching and to the fellowship, to the breaking of bread and to prayer.

### *CHAPTER 49: ROM. 6:3–4:*

Or don't you know that all of us who were baptized into Christ Jesus were baptized into his death? We were therefore buried with him through baptism into death in order that, just as Christ was raised from the dead through the glory of the Father, we too may live a new life.

### *CHAPTER 50: 1 COR. 11:23–26:*

For I received from the Lord what I also passed on to you: The Lord Jesus, on the night he was betrayed, took bread, and when he had given thanks, he broke it and said, "This is my body, which is for you; do this in remembrance of me." In the same way, after supper he took the cup, saying, "This cup is the new covenant in my blood; do this, whenever you drink it, in remembrance of me." For whenever you eat this bread and drink this cup, you proclaim the Lord's death until he comes.

### *CHAPTER 51: REV. 4:11:*

You are worthy, our Lord and God, to receive glory and honor and power, for you created all things, and by your will they were created and have their being.

### *CHAPTER 52: 1 PETER 4:10–11:*

Each one should use whatever gift he has received to serve others, faithfully administering God's grace in its various forms. If anyone speaks, he should do it as one speaking the very words of God. If anyone serves, he should do it with the strength God provides, so that in all things God may be praised through Jesus Christ. To him be the glory and the power for ever and ever. Amen.

### *CHAPTER 53: 1 COR. 12:7–11:*

Now to each one the manifestation of the Spirit is given for the common good. To one there is given through the Spirit the message of wisdom, to another the message of knowledge by means of the same Spirit, to another faith by the same Spirit, to another gifts of healing by that one Spirit, to another miraculous powers, to another prophecy, to another distinguishing between spirits, to another speaking in different kinds of tongues, and to still another the interpretation of tongues. All these are the work of one and the same Spirit, and he gives them to each one, just as he determines.

### CHAPTER 54: 1 THESS. 4: 15–18:

According to the Lord's own word, we tell you that we who are still alive, who are left till the coming of the Lord, will certainly not precede those who have fallen asleep. For the Lord himself will come down from heaven, with a loud command, with the voice of the archangel and with the trumpet call of God, and the dead in Christ will rise first. After that, we who are still alive and are left will be caught up together with them in the clouds to meet the Lord in the air. And so we will be with the Lord forever. Therefore encourage each other with these words.

### CHAPTER 55: REV. 20:4–6:

I saw thrones on which were seated those who had been given authority to judge. And I saw the souls of those who had been beheaded because of their testimony for Jesus and because of the word of God. They had not worshiped the beast or his image and had not received his mark on their foreheads or their hands. They came to life and reigned with Christ a thousand years. (The rest of the dead did not come to life until the thousand years were ended.) This is the first resurrection. Blessed and holy are those who have part in the first resurrection. The second death has no power over them, but they will be priests of God and of Christ and will reign with him for a thousand years.

### CHAPTER 56: REV. 20:11–13:

Then I saw a great white throne and him who was seated on it. Earth and sky fled from his presence, and there was no place for them. And I saw the dead, great and small, standing before the throne, and books were opened. Another book was opened, which is the book of life. The dead were judged according to what they had done as recorded in the books. The sea gave up the dead that were in it, and death and Hades gave up the dead that were in them, and each person was judged according to what he had done.

### CHAPTER 57: REV. 21:3–4:

And I heard a loud voice from the throne saying, "Now the dwelling of God is with men, and he will live with them. They will be his people, and God himself will be with them and be their God. He will wipe every tear from their eyes. There will be no more death or mourning or crying or pain, for the old order of things has passed away."

\* \* \*

## NASB PASSAGES

### CHAPTER 1: MATT. 28:18–20:

And Jesus came up and spoke to them, saying, "All authority has been given to Me in heaven and on earth. Go therefore and make disciples of all the nations, baptizing them in the name of the Father and the Son and the Holy Spirit, teaching them to observe all that I commanded you; and lo, I am with you always, even to the end of the age."

### CHAPTER 2: PS. 1:1–2:

How blessed is the man who does not walk in the counsel of the wicked, nor stand in the path of sinners, nor sit in the seat of scoffers! But his delight is in the law of the Lord, and in His law he meditates day and night.

### CHAPTER 3: HEB. 1:1–2:

God, after He spoke long ago to the fathers in the prophets in many portions and in many ways, in these last days has spoken to us in His Son, whom He appointed heir of all things, through whom also He made the world.

### CHAPTER 4: 2 TIM. 3:16–17

All Scripture is inspired by God and profitable for teaching, for reproof, for correction, for training in righteousness; that the man of God may be adequate, equipped for every good work.

### CHAPTER 5: PS. 12:6:

The words of the Lord are pure words; as silver tried in a furnace on the earth, refined seven times.

### CHAPTER 6: DEUT. 6:6–7:

And these words, which I am commanding you today, shall be on your heart; and you shall teach them diligently to your sons and shall talk of them when you sit in your house and when you walk by the way and when you lie down and when you rise up.

### CHAPTER 7: MATT. 4:4:

But He answered and said, "It is written, 'Man shall not live on bread alone, but on every word that proceeds out of the mouth of God.'"

### CHAPTER 8: PS. 119:1:

How blessed are those whose way is blameless, who walk in the law of the Lord.

### CHAPTER 9: ROM. 1:18–20:

For the wrath of God is revealed from heaven against all ungodliness and unrighteousness of men, who suppress the truth in unrighteousness, because that which is known about God is evident within them; for God made it evident to them. For since the creation of the world His invisible attributes, His eternal power and divine nature, have been clearly seen, being understood through what has been made, so that they are without excuse.

### CHAPTER 10: PS. 145:1–3:

I will extol Thee, my God, O King; and I will bless Thy name forever and ever. Every day I will bless Thee, and I will praise Thy name forever and ever. Great is the Lord, and highly to be praised; and His greatness is unsearchable.

### CHAPTER 11: PS. 102:25–27:

Of old Thou didst found the earth; and the heavens are the work of Thy hands. Even they will perish, but Thou dost endure; And all of them will wear out like a garment; like clothing Thou wilt change them, and they will be changed. But Thou art the same, and Thy years will not come to an end.

### CHAPTER 12: EX. 34:6–7:

Then the Lord passed by in front of him and proclaimed, "The Lord, the Lord God, compassionate and gracious, slow to anger, and abounding in lovingkindness and truth; who keeps lovingkindness for thousands, who forgives iniquity, transgression and sin; yet He will by no means leave the guilty unpunished, visiting the iniquity of fathers on the children and on the grandchildren to the third and fourth generations."

### CHAPTER 13: PS. 73:25–26:

Whom have I in heaven but Thee? And besides Thee, I desire nothing on earth. My flesh and my heart may fail, but God is the strength of my heart and my portion forever.

### CHAPTER 14: MATT. 3:16-17:

And after being baptized, Jesus went up immediately from the water; and behold, the heavens were opened, and he saw the Spirit of God descending as a dove, and coming upon Him, and behold, a voice out of the heavens, saying, "This is My beloved Son, in whom I am well-pleased."

### CHAPTER 15: NEH. 9:6:

Thou alone art the Lord. Thou hast made the heavens, the heaven of heavens with all their host, the earth and all that is on it, the seas and all that is in them. Thou dost give life to all of them and the heavenly host bows down before Thee.

### CHAPTER 16: ROM. 8:28:

And we know that God causes all things to work together for good to those who love God, to those who are called according to His purpose.

### CHAPTER 17: HEB. 2:3-4:

How shall we escape if we neglect so great a salvation? After it was at the first spoken through the Lord, it was confirmed to us by those who heard, God also bearing witness with them, both by signs and wonders and by various miracles and by gifts of the Holy Spirit according to His own will.

### CHAPTER 18: HEB. 4:14-16:

Since then we have a great high priest who has passed through the heavens, Jesus the Son of God, let us hold fast our confession. For we do not have a high priest who cannot sympathize with our weaknesses, but one who has been tempted in all things as we are, yet without sin. Let us therefore draw near with confidence to the throne of grace, that we may receive mercy and may find grace to help in time of need.

### CHAPTER 19: REV. 5:11-12:

And I looked, and I heard the voice of many angels around the throne and the living creatures and the elders; and the number of them was myriads of myriads, and thousands of thousands, saying with a loud voice, "Worthy is the Lamb that was slain to receive power and riches and wisdom and might and honor and glory and blessing."

### CHAPTER 20: JAMES 4:7-8:

Submit therefore to God. Resist the devil and he will flee from you. Draw near to God and He will draw near to you. Cleanse your hands, you sinners; and purify your hearts, you double-minded.

### CHAPTER 21: GEN. 1:26-27:

Then God said, "Let Us make man in Our image, according to Our likeness; and let them rule over the fish of the sea and over the birds of the sky and over the cattle and over all the earth, and over every creeping thing that creeps on the earth." And God created man in His own image, in the image of God He created him; male and female He created them.

### CHAPTER 22: COL. 3:18-19:

Wives, be subject to your husbands, as is fitting in the Lord. Husbands, love your wives, and do not be embittered against them.

### CHAPTER 23: 2 COR. 7:1:

Therefore, having these promises, beloved, let us cleanse ourselves from all defilement of flesh and spirit, perfecting holiness in the fear of God.

### CHAPTER 24: PS. 51:1-4:

Be gracious to me, O God, according to Thy lovingkindness; according to the greatness of Thy compassion blot out my transgressions. Wash me thoroughly from my iniquity, and cleanse me from my sin. For I know my transgressions, and my sin is ever before me. Against Thee, Thee only, I have sinned, and done what is evil in Thy sight, so that Thou art justified when Thou dost speak, and blameless when Thou dost judge.

### CHAPTER 25: HEB. 8:10:

For this is the covenant that I will make with the house of Israel after those days, says the Lord: I will put my laws into their minds, and I will write them upon their hearts. And I will be their God, and they shall be My people.

### CHAPTER 26: JOHN 1:14:

And the Word became flesh, and dwelt among us, and we beheld His glory, glory as of the only begotten from the Father, full of grace and truth.

### CHAPTER 27: ROM. 3:23-26:

For all have sinned and fall short of the glory of God, being justified as a gift by His grace through the redemption which is in Christ Jesus; whom God displayed publicly as a propitiation in His blood through faith. This was to demonstrate His righteousness, because in the forbearance of God He passed over the sins previously committed; for the demonstration, I say, of His righteousness at the present time, that He might be just and the justifier of the one who has faith in Jesus.

### CHAPTER 28: 1 COR. 15:20-23:

But now Christ has been raised from the dead, the first fruits of those who are asleep. For since by a man came death, by a man also came the resurrection of the dead. For as in Adam all die, so also in Christ all shall be made alive. But each in his own order: Christ the first fruits, after that those who are Christ's at His coming.

### CHAPTER 29: 1 PETER 2:9-10:

But you are a chosen race, a royal priesthood, a holy nation, a people for God's own possession, that you may proclaim the excellencies of Him who has called you out of darkness into His marvelous light; for you once were not a people, but now you are the people of God; you had not received mercy, but now you have received mercy.

### CHAPTER 30: ROM. 8:12-14:

So then brethren, we are under obligation, not to the flesh, to live according to the flesh—for if you are living according to the flesh, you must die; but if by the Spirit you are putting to death the deeds of the body, you will live. For all who are being led by the Spirit of God, these are sons of God.

### CHAPTER 31: LUKE 6:35-36:

But love your enemies, and do good, and lend, expecting nothing in return; and your reward will be great, and you will be sons of the Most High; for He Himself is kind to ungrateful and evil men. Be merciful, just as your Father is merciful.

### CHAPTER 32: EPH. 1:3-6:

Blessed be the God and Father of our Lord Jesus Christ, who has blessed us with every spiritual blessing in the heavenly places in Christ, just as He chose us in Him before the foundation of the world, that we should be holy and blameless before Him. In love He predestined us to adoption as sons through Jesus Christ to Himself, according to the kind intention of His will, to the praise of the glory of His grace, which He freely bestowed on us in the Beloved.

### CHAPTER 33: MATT. 11:28–30:

Come to Me, all who are weary and heavy-laden, and I will give you rest. Take My yoke upon you, and learn from Me, for I am gentle and humble in heart; and You shall find rest for your souls. For My yoke is easy, and My load is light.

### CHAPTER 34: JOHN 3:5–8:

Jesus answered, "Truly, truly, I say to you, unless one is born of water and the Spirit, he cannot enter into the kingdom of God. That which is born of the flesh is flesh, and that which is born of the Spirit is spirit. Do not marvel that I said to you, 'You must be born again.' The wind blows where it wishes and you hear the sound of it, but do not know where it comes from and where it is going; so is everyone who is born of the Spirit."

### CHAPTER 35: JOHN 3:16:

For God so loved the world, that He gave His only begotten Son, that whoever believes in Him should not perish, but have eternal life.

### CHAPTER 36: ROM. 3:27–28:

Where then is boasting? It is excluded. By what kind of law? Of works? No, but by a law of faith. For we maintain that a man is justified by faith apart from works of the Law.

### CHAPTER 37: ROM. 8:14–17:

For all who are being led by the Spirit of God, these are sons of God. For you have not received a spirit of slavery leading to fear again, but you have received a spirit of adoption as sons by which we cry out, "Abba! Father!" The Spirit Himself bears witness with our spirit that we are children of God, and if children, heirs also, heirs of God and fellow-heirs with Christ, if indeed we suffer with Him in order that we may also be glorified with Him.

### CHAPTER 38: ROM. 6:11–14:

Even so consider yourselves to be dead to sin, but alive to God in Christ Jesus. Therefore do not let sin reign in your mortal body that you should obey its lusts, and do not go on presenting the members of your body to sin as instruments of unrighteousness; but present yourselves to God as those alive from the dead, and your members as instruments of righteousness to God. For sin shall not be master over you, for you are not under law, but under grace.

### CHAPTER 39: 1 COR. 12:12–13:

For even as the body is one and yet has many members, and all the members of the body, though they are many, are one body, so also is Christ. For by one Spirit we were all baptized into one body, whether Jews or Greeks, whether slaves or free, and we were all made to drink of one Spirit.

### CHAPTER 40: JOHN 10:27–28:

My sheep hear My voice, and I know them, and they follow Me; and I give eternal life to them; and they shall never perish, and no one shall snatch them out of My hand.

### CHAPTER 41: PHIL. 1:20–24:

According to my earnest expectation and hope, that I shall not be put to shame in anything, but that with all boldness, Christ shall even now, as always, be exalted in my body, whether by life or by death. For to me, to live is Christ, and to die is gain. But if I am to live on in the flesh, this will mean fruitful labor for me; and I do not know which to choose. But I am hard pressed from both directions, having the desire to depart and be with

Christ, for that is very much better; yet to remain on in the flesh is more necessary for your sake.

### CHAPTER 42: 1 COR. 15:42–44:

So also is the resurrection of the dead. It is sown a perishable body, it is raised an imperishable body; it is sown in dishonor, it is raised in glory; it is sown in weakness, it is raised in power; it is sown a natural body, it is raised a spiritual body. If there is a natural body, there is also a spiritual body.

### CHAPTER 43: GAL. 2:20:

I have been crucified with Christ; and it is no longer I who live, but Christ lives in me; and the life which I now live in the flesh I live by faith in the Son of God, who loved me, and delivered Himself up for me.

### CHAPTER 44: EPH. 4:11–13:

And He gave some as apostles, and some as prophets, and some as evangelists, and some as pastors and teachers, for the equipping of the saints for the work of service, to the building up of the body of Christ; until we all attain to the unity of the faith, and of the knowledge of the Son of God, to a mature man, to the measure of the stature which belongs to the fullness of Christ.

### CHAPTER 45: EPH. 4:14–16:

As a result, we are no longer to be children, tossed here and there by waves, and carried about by every wind of doctrine, by the trickery of men, by craftiness in deceitful scheming; but speaking the truth in love, we are to grow up in all aspects into Him, who is the head, even Christ, from whom the whole body, being fitted and held together by that which every joint supplies, according to the proper working of each individual part, causes the growth of the body for the building up of itself in love.

### CHAPTER 46: 2 COR. 10:3–4:

For though we walk in the flesh, we do not war according to the flesh, for the weapons of our warfare are not of the flesh, but divinely powerful for the destruction of fortresses.

### CHAPTER 47: 1 PETER 5:1–4:

Therefore, I exhort the elders among you, as your fellow-elder and witness of the sufferings of Christ, and a partaker also of the glory that is to be revealed, shepherd the flock of God among you, not under compulsion, but voluntarily, according to the will of God; and not for sordid gain, but with eagerness; nor yet as lording it over those allotted to your charge, but proving to be examples to the flock. And when the Chief Shepherd appears, you will receive the unfading crown of glory.

### CHAPTER 48: ACTS 2:41–42:

So then, those who had received his word were baptized; and there were added that day about three thousand souls. And they were continually devoting themselves to the apostles' teaching and to fellowship, to the breaking of bread and to prayer.

### CHAPTER 49: ROM. 6:3–4:

Or do you not know that all of us who have been baptized into Christ Jesus have been baptized into His death? Therefore we have been buried with Him through baptism into death, in order that as Christ was raised from the dead through the glory of the Father, so we too might walk in newness of life.

### CHAPTER 50: 1 COR. 11:23–26:

For I received from the Lord that which I also delivered to you, that the Lord Jesus in the night in which He was betrayed took bread; and when he had given thanks, He broke it, and said, "This is My body, which is for you; do this in remembrance of Me." In the same way the cup also, after supper, saying, 'This cup is the new covenant in My blood; do this, as often as you drink it, in remembrance of Me." For as often as you eat this bread and drink the cup, you proclaim the Lord's death until He comes.

### CHAPTER 51: REV. 4:11:

Worthy art Thou, our Lord and our God, to receive glory and honor and power; for Thou didst create all things, and because of Thy will they existed, and were created.

### CHAPTER 52: 1 PETER 4:10–11:

As each one has received a special gift, employ it in serving one another, as good stewards of the manifold grace of God. Whoever speaks, let him speak, as it were, the utterances of God; whoever serves, let him do so as by the strength which God supplies; so that in all things God may be glorified through Jesus Christ, to whom belongs the glory and dominion forever and ever. Amen.

### CHAPTER 53: 1 COR. 12:7–11:

But to each one is given the manifestation of the Spirit for the common good. For to one is given the word of wisdom through the Spirit, and to another the word of knowledge according to the same Spirit; to another faith by the same Spirit, and to another gifts of healing by the one Spirit, and to another the effecting of miracles, and to another prophecy, and to another the distinguishing of spirits, to another various kinds of tongues, to another the interpretation of tongues. But one and the same Spirit works all these things, distributing to each one individually just as He wills.

### CHAPTER 54: 1 THESS. 4:15–18:

For this we say to you by the word of the Lord, that we who are alive, and remain until the coming of the Lord, shall not precede those who have fallen asleep. For the Lord Himself will descend from heaven with a shout, with the voice of the archangel, and with the trumpet of God; and the dead in Christ shall rise first. Then we who are alive and remain shall be caught up together with them in the clouds to meet the Lord in the air, and thus we shall always be with the Lord. Therefore comfort one another with these words.

### CHAPTER 55: REV. 20:4–6:

And I saw thrones, and they sat upon them, and judgment was given to them. And I saw the souls of those who had been beheaded because of the testimony of Jesus and because of the word of God, and those who had not worshiped the beast or his image, and had not received the mark upon their forehead and upon their hand; and they came to life and reigned with Christ for a thousand years. The rest of the dead did not come to life until the thousand years were completed. This is the first resurrection. Blessed and holy is the one who has a part in the first resurrection; over these the second death has no power, but they will be priests of God and of Christ and will reign with Him for a thousand years.

### CHAPTER 56: REV. 20:11–13:

And I saw a great white throne and Him who sat upon it, from whose presence earth and heaven fled away, and no place was found for them. And I saw the dead, the great and the small, standing before the throne, and books were opened; and another book was opened, which is the book of life; and the dead were judged from the things which were written in the books, according to their deeds. And the sea gave up the dead which were in it, and death and Hades gave up the dead which were in them; and they were judged, every one of them according to their deeds.

## CHAPTER 57: REV. 21:3–4:

And I heard a loud voice from the throne, saying, "Behold, the tabernacle of God is among men, and He shall dwell among them, and they shall be His people, and God Himself shall be among them, and He shall wipe away every tear from their eyes; and there shall no longer be any death; there shall no longer be any mourning, or crying, or pain; the first things have passed away."

# Appendix 3: Contemporary Worship Songs Classified by Chapter

Each chapter in this book includes a hymn related to the subject treated in the chapter. In addition, I was able to find contemporary worship songs that correspond to the subjects of twenty-six of the fifty-seven chapters in the book. I have listed the songs here according to chapter and have given the first line and the location in the songbook *Praise Chorus Book* (Nashville: Maranatha Music, 1990). (Perhaps this list may serve as an encouragement to song writers to compose contemporary worship songs related to the subjects of the other chapters of the book.)

| Chapter | First Line of Song | Book Location |
|---|---|---|
| 7 | Seek ye first the kingdom of God | 1 |
| 10 | Father, we love you, we worship and adore you | 13 |
| 11 | For Thou, O Lord, art high (I exalt Thee) | 69 |
| 12 or 13 | Great is the Lord, he is holy and just | 47 |
| 12 or 13 | I will sing of the mercies of the Lord forever | 238 |
| 12 or 13 | Lord, the light of Your love is shining | 259 |
| 12 or 13 | O Lord, You're beautiful | 217 |
| 12 or 13 | The steadfast love of the Lord never ceases | 208 |
| 12 or 13 | Thy loving kindness is better than life | 24 |
| 14 | Holy holy; holy holy | 3 |
| 15 | Thou art worthy | 109 |
| 18 | Seek ye first the kingdom of God | 1 |
| 20 | Mighty Warrior, dressed for battle | 276 |
| 21 | For Thou, O Lord, art high (I exalt Thee) | 69 |
| 21 | In my life, Lord, be glorified | 22 |
| 24 | Create in me a clean heart, O God | 195 |
| 24 | Search me, O God, and know my heart today | 92 |
| 26 | All hail, King Jesus | 71 |
| 26 | Isn't he beautiful? | 179 |
| 26 | Jesus, name above all names | 200 |
| 26 | Open our eyes, Lord, we want to see Jesus | 229 |
| 26 | Praise the name of Jesus | 127 |
| 26 | Son of God, this is our praise song | 241 |
| 26 | There is a Redeemer | 136 |
| 27 | There is a Redeemer | 136 |
| 28 | All hail, King Jesus | 71 |
| 28 | All heaven declares the glory of the risen Lord | 258 |
| 28 | He is Lord, He is Lord | 87 |

# Appendix 4: Annotated Bibliography of Evangelical Systematic Theologies

This bibliography lists most of the major evangelical systematic theologies available in English and a few shorter guides to Christian doctrine. With the exception of the two Roman Catholic theologies (by McBrien and Ott) which are included because I have cross-referenced them at the end of each chapter, all of the authors on this list fall generally within a "conservative evangelical" theological position.[1]

In the appendix following this bibliography I have added a master list of the thirty-four Protestant and two Roman Catholic theologies which I cross-referenced at the end of each chapter.

Arminius, James. *The Writings of James Arminius*. 3 vols. Vols. 1 and 2 trans. by James Nichols. Vol. 3 translated by W. R. Bagnell. Grand Rapids: Baker, 1956.

Arminius (1560–1609) was a Reformed pastor in Amsterdam and later professor of theology at the University of Leyden. His disagreement with some of the central tenets of Calvinism led to a great controversy in the Netherlands which continued long after his death. His ideas became the foundation of a system of thought now known as Arminianism, which continues today in conservative Wesleyan and Methodist churches, and in many other Protestant groups. This collection of writings, assembled after his death, is not strictly organized as a systematic theology, but does contain discussions of most important theological topics.

Bavinck, Herman. *The Doctrine of God*. Trans. by William Hendriksen. Grand Rapids: Eerdmans, 1951. Reprint edition: Carlisle, Pa.: Banner of Truth, 1977.

_____. *Our Reasonable Faith*. Trans. by Henry Zylstra. Grand Rapids: Eerdmans, 1956. Reprint edition: Grand Rapids: Baker, 1977.

_____. *The Philosophy of Revelation*. Trans. by Geerhardus Vos, Nikolas Steffens, and Henry Dosker. Reprint edition Grand Rapids: Baker, 1979. First published 1909 by Longmans, Green, and Co.

Bavinck (1854–1921) was a Dutch theologian and one of this century's most brilliant spokesmen for a Reformed theological position. His great four-volume systematic theology, *Gereformeerde Dogmatiek,* still awaits translation into English (only volume 2, *The Doctrine of God,* has been translated).

Berkhof, Louis. *Introduction to Systematic Theology*. Reprint edition: Grand Rapids: Baker, 1979. First published by Eerdmans, 1932.

_____. *Systematic Theology*. Fourth edition, Grand Rapids: Eerdmans, 1939.

---

[1]A very helpful and more broadly-based annotated bibliography, including notes on works from several prominent liberal scholars, may be found in John Jefferson Davis, *Theology Primer* (Grand Rapids: Baker, 1981), pp. 74–79; see also his "Brief Guide to Modern Theologians" on pp. 39–55. In addition, valuable brief notes on dozens of important theologians from all theological traditions may be found in Millard Erickson, *Concise Dictionary of Christian Theology* (Grand Rapids: Baker, 1986).

The standard Reformed textbook for systematic theology by a former president of Calvin Seminary in Grand Rapids, Michigan. This book is a great treasure-house of information and analysis, and is probably the most useful one-volume systematic theology available from any theological perspective. Berkhof lived from 1873 to 1957.

Berkouwer, G. C. *Studies in Dogmatics*. 14 vols. (1952–1976).

_____. *The Church*. Trans. by James E. Davidson. Grand Rapids: Eerdmans, 1976.

_____. *Divine Election*. Trans. by Hugo Bekker. Grand Rapids: Eerdmans, 1960.

_____. *Faith and Justification*. Trans. by Lewis B. Smedes. Grand Rapids: Eerdmans, 1954.

_____. *Faith and Perseverance*. Trans. by Robert D. Knudsen. Grand Rapids: Eerdmans, 1958.

_____. *Faith and Sanctification*. Trans. by John Vriend. Grand Rapids: Eerdmans, 1952.

_____. *General Revelation*. (No translator named.) Grand Rapids: Eerdmans, 1955.

_____. *Man: The Image of God*. Trans. by Dirk W. Jellma. Grand Rapids: Eerdmans, 1962.

_____. *Holy Scripture*. Trans. and edited by Jack B. Rogers. Grand Rapids: Eerdmans, 1975.

_____. *The Person of Christ*. Trans. by John Vriend. Grand Rapids: Eerdmans, 1954.

_____. *The Providence of God*. Trans. by Louis B. Smedes. Grand Rapids: Eerdmans, 1952.

_____. *The Return of Christ*. Trans. by James Van Oosterom. Ed. by Marlin J. Van Elderen. Grand Rapids: Eerdmans, 1972.

_____. *The Sacraments*. Trans. by Hugo Bekker. Grand Rapids: Eerdmans, 1969.

_____. *Sin*. Trans. by Philip C. Holtrop. Grand Rapids: Eerdmans, 1971.

_____. *The Work of Christ*. Trans. by Cornelius Lambregtse. Grand Rapids: Eerdmans, 1965.

Major contemporary studies by a Reformed theologian who was professor of systematic theology at the Free University of Amsterdam.

Bloesch, Donald G. *Essentials of Evangelical Theology*. 2 vols., New York: Harper & Row, 1978–79.

A work by a contemporary theologian who is broadly in the Reformed tradition, but much less clear on the doctrines of election and the authority of Scripture, for example, than other writers classified as "Reformed" in this bibliography. (More recently, Bloesch has begun to publish a multi-volume systematic theology.)

Boice, James Montgomery. *Foundations of the Christian Faith*. Revised one-volume edition. Downers Grove, Ill.: InterVarsity Press, 1986.

A recent Reformed guide to systematic theology written by the theologian-pastor of Tenth Presbyterian Church, Philadelphia. This work is written in a popular, readable style, with helpful application of doctrines to life. It was previously published in four separate volumes: *The Sovereign God* (1978), *God the Redeemer* (1978), *Awakening to God* (1979), and *God and History* (1981).

Boyce, James Pettigru. *Abstract of Systematic Theology*. Reprint edition: Christian Gospel Foundation, n.d. First published 1887.

A Baptist systematic theology that is also Reformed in doctrinal orientation by a former president and professor of systematic theology in the Southern Baptist Seminary, Louisville, Kentucky. Boyce lived from 1827 to 1888.

Buswell, James Oliver, Jr. *A Systematic Theology of the Christian Religion*. 2 vols. Grand Rapids: Zondervan, 1962–63.
    A Reformed systematic theology by the former dean of the graduate faculty at Covenant College and Seminary in St. Louis, Missouri.

Calvin, John. *Institutes of the Christian Religion*. 2 vols. Ed. by John T. McNeill. Trans. and indexed by Ford Lewis Battles. The Library of Christian Classics, Vols. 20–21. Philadelphia: Westminster, 1960. Trans. from the 1559 text and collated with earlier versions.
    This is the best available English translation of Calvin's systematic exposition of the Christian faith. Calvin (1509–64) was a French reformer who became the greatest theologian of the Reformation and, according to many estimates, the greatest theologian in the history of the church. Reformed in doctrinal perspective.

Carter, Charles W., ed. *A Contemporary Wesleyan Theology: Biblical, Systematic, and Practical*. 2 vols. Grand Rapids: Francis Asbury Press (Zondervan), 1983.
    This is a collection of 24 essays on major doctrinal themes by several scholars representing a wide range of conservative Wesleyan denominations and institutions. The set also includes some essays on practical theology and ethics. Charles Carter, who contributed four of the chapters, is Professor of Religion and Missions at Marion College, Marion, Indiana. The advisory committee for the volumes includes representatives of United Methodist, Free Methodist, Church of the Nazarene, Missionary Church, Salvation Army, Wesleyan Church, and other groups.

Chafer, Lewis Sperry. *Systematic Theology*. 7 vols. plus index vol. Dallas: Dallas Seminary Press, 1947–48.

————. *Systematic Theology: Abridged edition*. 2 vols. Ed. by John F. Walvoord, Donald K. Campbell, and Roy B. Zuck. Wheaton: Victor, 1988.
    Chafer (1871–1952) was the first president of Dallas Theological Seminary. The seven-volume edition is the most extensive dispensational systematic theology ever written. The two volume edition is a condensation of the earlier work.

Cottrell, Jack. *What the Bible Says About God the Creator*. Joplin, Mo.: College Press, 1983.

————. *What the Bible Says About God the Ruler*. Joplin, Mo.: College Press, 1984.

————. *What the Bible Says About God the Redeemer*. Joplin, Mo.: College Press, 1987.
    Cottrell is an articulate and thoughtful Arminian theologian who teaches at Cincinnati Bible Seminary (Christian Church/Churches of Christ). I have indexed these volumes as 1 (*God the Creator*), 2 (*God the Ruler*), and 3 (*God the Redeemer*).

Dabney, Robert L. *Discussions: Evangelical and Theological*. London: Banner of Truth, 1967. Reprint of 1890 edition.

————. *Systematic Theology*. Edinburgh: Banner of Truth, 1985. Reprint of 1878 edition.
    A Southern Presbyterian who represented a strongly Reformed position, Dabney (1820–98) was professor of theology at Union Seminary in Virginia. He was also chaplain and later chief of staff for General Stonewall Jackson during the American Civil War.

Edwards, Jonathan. *The Works of Jonathan Edwards*. 2 vols. Revised and corrected by Edward Hickman. Edinburgh: Banner of Truth, 1974. Reprint of 1834 edition.
    Edwards (1703–1758) was a pastor in Northampton, Massachusetts, and, for one month before his death from a smallpox injection, president of Princeton. Some consider him the greatest American philosopher-theologian. He did not write an entire systematic theology, but his works contain writings on most theological topics. He is strongly Reformed in outlook, and combines profound thought with warm-hearted devotion to

Christ. (A new edition of Edwards' works is in process of publication from Yale University Press.)

Erickson, Millard. *Christian Theology*. Grand Rapids: Baker, 1985.

A clear and very thorough recent textbook in systematic theology from a Baptist perspective. Erickson, who was Academic Dean at Bethel Theological Seminary in St. Paul, Minn., now teaches at Southwestern Baptist Seminary in Ft. Worth, Texas. This book includes interaction with all the major trends in contemporary nonevangelical theology, as well as helpful material for personal application.

Finney, Charles G. *Finney's Lectures on Systematic Theology*. Ed. by J. H. Fairchild. Grand Rapids: Eerdmans, 1953. Reprint of 1878 edition.

Finney (1792–1875) was a revivalist and president of Oberlin College 1851–66. Not representative of any one theological position, but articulated some strong Arminian arguments. Emphasis on personal holiness and perfectionism. Not really a complete systematic theology, because many topics are not covered.

Gill, John. *Complete Body of Doctrinal and Practical Divinity*. 2 vols. Grand Rapids: Baker, 1978. First published as *A Body of Doctrinal Divinity* (1767) and *A Body of Practical Divinity* (1770).

Gill (1697–1771) was a highly influential Baptist pastor, a prolific writer, and a respected theologian in 18th century England. He was also Reformed (or Calvinistic) in his view of God's sovereignty. His book, *The Cause of God and Truth* (1735–38; reprinted Grand Rapids: Baker, 1981) is one of the most thorough defenses of Calvinistic theology ever written.

Henry, Carl F. H. *God, Revelation, and Authority*. 6 vols. Waco, Tex.: Word, 1976–83.

A major work containing detailed interaction with hundreds of other scholarly positions. Henry is a leading evangelical theologian with great strengths especially in the areas of apologetics and philosophical theology.

Heppe, Heinrich. *Reformed Dogmatics: Set Out and Illustrated From the Sources*. Rev. and ed. by Ernst Bizer. Trans. by G. T. Thompson. Reprint edition. Grand Rapids: Baker, 1978. First published 1861. English translation first published 1950.

Heppe (1820–79) was a German scholar who collected and quoted extensively from many earlier Reformed theologians. Because the quotations are arranged according to the topics of systematic theology, this book is a valuable sourcebook.

Hodge, Charles. *Systematic Theology*. 3 vols. Reprint edition: Grand Rapids: Eerdmans, 1970. First published 1871–73.

A major Reformed systematic theology which is still widely used today. Hodge (1797–1878) was professor of systematic theology at Princeton Theological Seminary.

Lewis, Gordon R., and Bruce Demarest. *Integrative Theology*. 3 vols. Grand Rapids: Zondervan, 1987–94.

Lewis and Demarest are both professors of systematic theology at Denver Seminary in Colorado (a Conservative Baptist seminary). This is an excellent contemporary work that integrates historical, biblical, apologetic, and practical material with systematic theology.

Litton, Edward Arthur. *Introduction to Dogmatic Theology*. New edition, ed. by Philip E. Hughes. London: James Clarke, 1960. First published 1882–92.

A standard Anglican (or Episcopalian) systematic theology by an evangelical British theologian of the 19th century. Litton lived from 1813 to 1897.

McBrien, Richard P. *Catholicism*. 2 vols. Minneapolis: Winston Press, 1980.

A responsible and extensive explanation of Catholic teachings as they have been affected by the period since Vatican II. Contains bibliographies with each chapter.

Miley, John. *Systematic Theology*. 2 vols. Library of Biblical and Theological Literature,

Vols. 5–6. New York: Eaton and Mains, 1892–94. Reprint: Peabody, Mass.: Hendriksen, 1989.

This is probably the most scholarly and extensive Arminian systematic theology ever written. Miley was a professor at Drew Theological Seminary, Madison, New Jersey.

Milne, Bruce. *Know the Truth*. Leicester: InterVarsity Press, 1982.

A thoughtful, clearly-written evangelical guide to Christian doctrine which has found wide use among students. Milne lectures in biblical and historical theology at Spurgeon's College, London.

Mueller, John Theodore. *Christian Dogmatics*. St. Louis: Concordia, 1934.

A condensation and translation of Francis Pieper's *Christliche Dogmatik* (Christian Dogmatics) by a professor of systematic theology at Concordia Seminary in St. Louis, a Missouri Synod Lutheran seminary. An excellent statement of conservative Lutheran theology.

Mullins, Edgar Young. *The Christian Religion in Its Doctrinal Expression*. Philadelphia: Judson Press, 1917.

An evangelical systematic theology by a former president of the Southern Baptist Seminary in Louisville, Kentucky. Mullins lived from 1860 to 1928.

Murray, John. *Collected Writings of John Murray*. 4 vols. Carlisle, Pa.: Banner of Truth, 1976–82.

————. *The Imputation of Adam's Sin*. Reprint edition: Nutley, N.J.: Presbyterian and Reformed, 1977. First published Grand Rapids: Eerdmans, 1959.

————. *Principles of Conduct*. Grand Rapids: Eerdmans, 1957.

————. *Redemption Accomplished and Applied*. Grand Rapids: Eerdmans, 1955.

Murray (1898–1975) was professor of systematic theology at Westminster Seminary in Philadelphia and one of the most articulate modern defenders of Reformed theology.

Oden, Thomas. *The Living God*. Systematic Theology, Vol. 1. San Francisco: Harper & Row, 1987.

Oden is a Methodist theologian who has moved from his previous liberal theological convictions to a conservative evangelical position. He interacts extensively with theologians from the early history of the church.

Olson, Arnold T. *This We Believe: The Background and Exposition of the Doctrinal Statement of The Evangelical Free Church of America*. Minneapolis, Minn.: Free Church Publications, 1961.

A guide to Christian doctrine based on the widely-used statement of faith of the Evangelical Free Church of America. Olson was the first president of the Evangelical Free Church.

Ott, Ludwig. *Fundamentals of Catholic Dogma*. Ed. by James Canon Bastible. Trans. by Patrick Lynch. St Louis: Herder, 1955. First published in German in 1952.

A standard textbook of traditional Roman Catholic theology.

Packer, J. I. *Concise Theology: A Guide to Historic Christian Beliefs*. Wheaton, Ill.: Tyndale House, 1993.

This readable volume lives up to its name, because Packer, an Anglican with strong Reformed convictions, is a master of saying much in a few words. He is a professor of theology at Regent College in Vancouver, British Columbia, and one of the most widely-respected evangelical theologians today.

Pieper, Francis. *Christian Dogmatics*. 4 vols. Trans. by Theodore Engelder et al. St. Louis: Concordia, 1950–57. First published in German, 1917–24.

This is standard systematic theology of conservative Lutheranism. Pieper (1852–

1931) was a Missouri Synod theologian and professor and president of Concordia Seminary in St. Louis.

Pope, William Burt. *A Compendium of Christian Theology.* 2d ed. 3 vols. New York: Phillips and Hunt, n.d.

This work, first published in 1875–76, is one of the greatest systematic theologies written from a Wesleyan or Arminian perspective.

Purkiser, W. T., ed. *Exploring our Christian Faith.* Kansas City, Mo.: Beacon Hill Press, 1960.

A more popular Arminian systematic theology with contributions from several authors.

Ryrie, Charles. *Basic Theology.* Wheaton, Ill.: Victor, 1986.

A very clearly written introduction to systematic theology from a dispensationalist perspective, by a former professor of systematic theology at Dallas Theological Seminary.

Shedd, William G. T. *Dogmatic Theology.* 3 vols. in 4. Reprint edition: Minneapolis: Klock and Klock, 1979. Originally published by Charles Scribner's Sons, 1889.

A useful Reformed systematic theology by a former professor at Union Theological Seminary in New York. (Note that the entire range of systematic theology is treated in Vols. I and II, and that Vol. III contains supplementary material for every part of Vols. I and II. Vol. III is not well indexed.) Shedd lived from 1820 to 1894.

Strong, Augustus H. *Systematic Theology.* Valley Forge, Pa.: Judson Press, 1907.

Strong (1836–1921) was president and professor of theology at Rochester Theological Seminary, and, from 1905 to 1910, was the first president of the Northern Baptist Convention. This text was widely used in Baptist circles for most of the twentieth century, until it was largely replaced by Millard Erickson's *Christian Theology* (1983–85).

Thiessen, Henry Clarence. *Introductory Lectures in Systematic Theology.* Rev. by Vernon D. Doerksen. Grand Rapids: Eerdmans, 1977. First published 1949.

An evangelical systematic theology textbook by a former chairman of the faculty of the graduate school at Wheaton College. Thiessen is Baptistic and Dispensational in theological perspective.

Thomas, W. H. Griffith. *The Principles of Theology: An Introduction to the Thirty-Nine Articles.* Fifth edition, revised. London: Church Book Room Press, 1956. (First published 1930.)

Although this book is structured around the Anglican Thirty-Nine Articles, it functions well as a thoughtful introductory text in Christian doctrine even for those outside the Anglican tradition. It has been widely used in British evangelical circles for many years. Thomas (1861–1924) was principal of Wycliffe Hall, Oxford, and then professor of Old Testament at Wycliffe College, Toronto. He also played a role in founding Dallas Seminary just before his death.

Thornwell, James Henley. *The Collected Writings of James Henley Thornwell.* 4 vols. Ed. by John B. Adger. New York: Robert Carter and Brothers, 1871–73. Reprint edition: Edinburgh and Carlisle, Pa.: Banner of Truth, 1974.

Thornwell (1812–62) was a Reformed theologian who was professor of theology in the Presbyterian Theological Seminary at Columbia, South Carolina.

Turretin, Francis. *Institutes of Elenctic Theology.* 3 vols. Trans. by George Musgrave Giger. Ed. by James T. Dennison, Jr. Phillipsburg, N.J.: Presbyterian and Reformed, 1992–. (Two volumes published to date.)

Turretin (1623–87) taught theology for over thirty years at the Academy in Geneva. His work, written in Latin, is said to be one of the fullest expressions of Calvinistic theology ever published. It was reprinted (in Latin) in 1847 and widely used as a theological textbook for American Presbyterians, most notably by Charles Hodge at

Princeton. George Giger translated Turretin's *Institutes* in the mid-nineteenth century, but the translation lay unpublished for over a century. James Dennison of Westminster Seminary has done extensive editorial work to make this great theology text finally available to English readers.

Van Til, Cornelius. *In Defense of the Faith,* Vol. 5: *An Introduction to Systematic Theology.* N.p.: Presbyterian and Reformed, 1976.

This volume contains Van Til's discussions of the nature of systematic theology, of revelation, and of the doctrine of God. Van Til was a Reformed theologian and philosopher who taught at Westminster Theological Seminary in Philadelphia and is best known for his "presuppositional" system of apologetics.

Warfield, Benjamin B. *Biblical and Theological Studies.* Philadelphia: Presbyterian and Reformed, 1976.

————. *Christology and Criticism.* London and New York: Oxford University Press, 1929.

————. *The Inspiration and Authority of the Bible.* Ed. by Samuel G. Craig. Introduction by Cornelius Van Til. Philadelphia: Presbyterian and Reformed, 1967.

————. *The Lord of Glory.* New York: American Tract Society, 1907.

————. *Perfectionism.* Philadelphia: Presbyterian and Reformed, 1958.

A condensation of Warfield's earlier 2-vol. work on perfectionism published by OUP, omitting extensive interaction with particular German theologians.

————. *The Person and Work of Christ.* Philadelphia: Presbyterian and Reformed, 1950.

Contains reprints of 2 articles from *ST,* 5 from *BD,* 6 from *CC,* and 1 other article.

————. *The Plan of Salvation.* Rev. ed. Grand Rapids: Eerdmans, 1942.

————. *Selected Shorter Writings of Benjamin B. Warfield.* 2 vols. Nuttley, N.J.: Presbyterian and Reformed, 1970–73.

————. *Studies in Theology.* New York: Oxford University Press, 1932.

Warfield (1851–1921) was a Reformed theologian who taught New Testament and then systematic theology at Princeton Theological Seminary from 1887–1921. In the estimate of many people, he was one of the greatest American theologians.

Watson, Richard. *Theological Institutes.* 2 vols. New York: G. Lane and P. Sandford, 1843. First published 1823.

This is the earliest systematic theology by a Methodist. Watson (1781–1833) was Arminian in theological perspective.

Wiley, H. Orton. *Christian Theology.* Three vols. Kansas City, Mo.: Nazarene Publishing House, 1940–43.

A recent Arminian systematic theology by a respected theologian in the Church of the Nazarene. Probably the best Arminian systematic theology published in the twentieth century, but it does not match Miley in scholarly depth.

Williams, J. Rodman. *Renewal Theology: Systematic Theology From a Charismatic Perspective.* 3 vols. Grand Rapids: Zondervan, 1988–92.

Williams is a charismatic scholar who teaches at Regent University (formerly CBN University). This clearly written theology interacts extensively with the biblical text and with other literature. It is the first published from an explicitly charismatic perspective.

# Appendix 5: Master List of Systematic Theologies Indexed at the End of Each Chapter

Full bibliographical data for these works may be found in the bibliography in Appendix 4. If one of these works is not listed at the end of a chapter, it means that I was unable to find a treatment of that chapter's topic in that specific work.

## SECTIONS IN EVANGELICAL SYSTEMATIC THEOLOGIES

1. Anglican (Episcopalian)
   - 1882–92 Litton
   - 1930 Thomas
2. Arminian (Wesleyan or Methodist)
   - 1847 Finney
   - 1875–76 Pope
   - 1892–94 Miley
   - 1940 Wiley
   - 1960 Purkiser
   - 1983 Carter
   - 1983– Cottrell
   - 1987–90 Oden
3. Baptist
   - 1767 Gill
   - 1887 Boyce
   - 1907 Strong
   - 1917 Mullins
   - 1976–83 Henry
   - 1983–85 Erickson
   - 1987–94 Lewis/Demarest
4. Dispensational
   - 1947 Chafer
   - 1949 Thiessen
   - 1986 Ryrie
5. Lutheran
   - 1917–24 Pieper
   - 1934 Mueller
6. Reformed (or Presbyterian)
   - 1559 Calvin
   - 1724–58 Edwards
   - 1861 Heppe
   - 1871–73 Hodge

| 1878 | Dabney |
|------|--------|
| 1887–1921 | Warfield |
| 1889 | Shedd |
| 1909 | Bavinck |
| 1937–66 | Murray |
| 1938 | Berkhof |
| 1962 | Buswell |

7. Renewal (or charismatic/Pentecostal)

| 1988–92 | Williams |
|---------|----------|

## SECTIONS IN REPRESENTATIVE ROMAN CATHOLIC SYSTEMATIC THEOLOGIES

1. Roman Catholic: Traditional

| 1955 | Ott |
|------|-----|

2. Roman Catholic: Post-Vatican II

| 1980 | McBrien |
|------|---------|

# Author Index

# Hymn Index

# Scripture Index

**Note:** This index does not list all the Scripture quotations or Scripture references in this book, but only those where a passage is discussed in some way; that is, where an argument is made for a particular understanding of a passage or some other interpretative comments are made.

# Subject Index

Bold type indicates more extensive treatment of a subject or the location of a chapter or section dealing with that subject.

not a true church, 865
Jesus Christ, 529–633
  as example, 541
  as king, 628–629
  as mediator, 541
  as priest, 626–628
  as prophet, 624–626
  as representative, 540
  as ruler, 541
  as sacrifice, 540–541
  crucifixion of, 326–327
  exaltation of, 620
  humiliation of, 620
  obedience on our behalf, 570–571
  person of, 529–567
  prays for us, 628
Jesus Christ: ascension. *See* ascension
Jesus Christ: atonement. *See* atonement
Jesus Christ: death of. *See* atonement
Jesus Christ: deity, 233–237, 543–554
  Apollinarianism, 557
  did Jesus give up divine attributes? 549–552
  divine attributes, 547–549
  emptying himself? 549–552
  eternity, 548
  immortality, 548–549
  is the incarnation "unintelligible"? 552–553
  Jehovah's Witnesses: denial of, 234–235
  Kenosis theory, 549–552
  knowing time of his return, 561
  Mark 13:32, 561–562
  monophysitism, 557
  necessity of, 553–554
  Nestorianism, 557
  omnipotence, 547
  omnipresence, 548
  omniscience, 548, 561
  other claims to deity, 545–547
  Phil. 2:7, 549–552
  Scriptural claims, 543–547
  Son of God, 547
  Son of Man, 546–547
  sovereignty, 548
  the word "God" used of Christ, 543–544
  the word "Lord" used of Christ, 544–545
  worthy of worship, 549
Jesus Christ: humanity, 529–543
  birth of, 529–532
  death of father, 537
  docetism, 540
  human body, 532–533
  human emotions, 533–534
  human mind, 533
  human soul, 533–534
  human weaknesses and limitations, 532–535
  necessary for first redeemed body, 542
  necessary to be example, 541–542
  necessary to be high priest, 542
  necessary to be mediator, 541
  necessary to be representative, 540
  necessary to be substitute sacrifice, 540–541
  necessary to fulfill man's purpose, 541
  necessity of human nature, 540–542
  not married, 455

temptations, 536–537, 560, 571–572
ubiquity (Lutheran view), 558–559
view of people near him, 534–535
virgin birth, 529–532
will be a man forever, 542–543
Jesus Christ: offices of, 624–633
  as priest, brings us to God, 626–627
  as priest, offered himself, 626
  as priest, prays for us, 627–628
  king, 628–629
  our roles as prophet, priest, king, 629–630
  priest, 626–628
  prophet, 624–626
Jesus Christ: one person, 554–563
  all actions belong to the person, 561–562
  Apollinarianism, 554–555
  brief summary sentence, 563
  Chalcedonian Definition, 556–558
  communication of attributes, 563
  conclusion, 563
  different views of person of Christ, 554–558
  Eutychianism, 556, 560–561
  how deity and humanity combine, 558–563
  incarnation: definition, 543
  Monophysitism (Eutychianism), 556, 560
  monothelite view, 560
  Nestorianism, 555, 560–561
  some actions unique to each nature, 558–561
  titles and actions intermixed, 562–563
  two centers of consciousness, 560–561
  two wills, 560–561
Jesus Christ: resurrection. *See* resurrection and
  ascension
Jesus Christ: Second Coming. *See* return of Christ
Jesus Christ: sinlessness, 535–539
  biblical evidence, 535–537
  could Jesus have sinned? 537–539
  impeccability, 537–539
Jesus Christ: states of, 620
Jesus Christ: suffering of. *See* atonement
Jesus Christ: temptations. *See* temptations of Christ
Jesus Christ: union with. *See* union with Christ
"Jesus only" Pentecostals, 242–243
Jewish exorcists, 417–418
Jonah, 326
Joseph, 323, 327
Joseph (father of Jesus): death of, 537
joy, 441, 1005–1006, 1162–1163
Judas, 794
judgment. *See* final judgment
judgment of the nations, 1141
Junias (Junia?), 908–909
justice of God. *See* God: attributes
justification, 722–735
  a legal declaration by God, 723
  and Christ's resurrection, 615
  based wholly on grace, not merit, 729
  comes to us through faith, 730–732
  definition, 723
  God declares us to be just, 724–726
  God imputes righteousness to us, 726–729
  not lost when Christians sin, 504
  why by faith? 730